COST ACCOUNTING

TEXT AND PROBLEMS

COST ACCOUNTING

TEXT AND PROBLEMS

For B.Com., BBA, M.Com. and MBA

Also for CA/CS/ICWA–Inter, CFA and other Professional Courses

M.C. SHUKLA
B.A., B.Com. (Birmingham), Bar-at-Law
Retd. Professor of Commerce and
Director of Correspondence Courses
University of Delhi

T.S. GREWAL
M.A. (Com.)
Former Director of Studies,
Coaching Board, Institute of Chartered
Accountants of India, New Delhi

Dr. M.P. GUPTA
M.Com., Ph.D.
Director, Jagran College, Kanpur
Ex. Head, Deptt. of Commerce, VSSD (PG) College, Kanpur
Ex. Dean, Faculty of Commerce, CSJM Kanpur University, Visiting Faculty
Northern India Regional Council of the Institute of Chartered Accountants of India, Kanpur
and Kanpur Chapter of the Institute of Company Secretaries of India

S. Chand And Company Limited
(ISO 9001 Certified Company)

S. Chand And Company Limited

(ISO 9001 Certified Company)

Head Office: D-92, Sector–2, Noida – 201301, U.P. (India), Ph. 91-120-4682700

Registered Office: A-27, 2nd Floor, Mohan Co-operative Industrial Estate, New Delhi – 110 044, Phone: 011-49731800

www.**schandpublishing.com;** e-mail: **info@schandpublishing.com**

Marketing Offices:

Chennai : Ph: 23632120; chennai@schandpublishing.com
Guwahati : Ph: 2738811, 2735640; guwahati@schandpublishing.com
Hyderabad : Ph: 40186018; hyderabad@schandpublishing.com
Jalandhar : Ph: 4645630; jalandhar@schandpublishing.com
Kolkata : Ph: 23357458, 23353914; kolkata@schandpublishing.com
Lucknow : Ph: 4003633; lucknow@schandpublishing.com
Mumbai : Ph: 25000297; mumbai@schandpublishing.com
Patna : Ph: 2260011; patna@schandpublishing.com

First Edition 1955
Subsequent Editions and Reprints 1962, 66, 68, 70, 71, 73, 74 (Twice), 76, 77, 80, 82, 85, 86, 88, 89, 2000, 2006, 2010
Twelfth Thoroughly Revised Edition 2013
Reprints 2014, 2016, 2017, 2018, 2019, 2020 (Twice), 2021, 2022, 2023

Reprint 2024

ISBN: 978-81-219-1963-0 **Product Code:** H8COA48ACCN10ENAL13O

PRINTED IN INDIA

By Vikas Publishing House Private Limited, Plot 20/4, Site-IV, Industrial Area Sahibabad, Ghaziabad – 201 010 and Published by S. Chand And Company Limited, A-27, 2nd Floor, Mohan Co-operative Industrial Estate, New Delhi – 110 044.

PREFACE TO THE TWELFTH EDITION

It gives me great pleasure and satisfaction to present 12th thoroughly revised edition of **Cost Accounting Text and Problems**. The latest syllabus of various professional courses like CS, ICWA, MBA, BBA, CFA and Unified Syllabus of UGC for B.Com. and M.Com. have been taken into consideration. A separate edition for CA course is available which is also published by S.Chand & Company Pvt. Ltd.

A large number of new problems set in latest examinations have been included. At the end of each chapter some typical illustrations have been included. Almost all chapters have been revised, updated and re-arranged. In this edition, a large number of objective questions, short-answer numerical and short-answer theoretical questions have been added in each chapter.

A separate chapter on ***'Joint Product and By Product'*** has been tailored out from the chapter of Process Costing.

Chapter on ***Activity Based Costing (ABC)*** based on new concept on costing of overheads and a topic on ***Just In Time (JIT)*** have been included. Now the book contains about ***545 most representative and examination oriented problems*** and illustrations.

I am deeply grateful to Management and Editorial Team of S. Chand & Company Ltd. for bringing out this book in time.

Any criticism and constructive suggestion in the direction of making the book a better teaching and studying manual will be gratefully acknowledged by the author.

'*Mansarover*'
117-K-82 Sarvodaya Nagar,
Kanpur 208025.
9415538080
E-mail. mpgupta 1943@gmail.com

Dr. M.P. GUPTA

PREFACE TO THE FIRST EDITION

The objective of the textbook is to present a basic treatment of main principles of *Cost Accounting* with an Indian background. Therefore no doubt, some very good books on the subject are available but they are either advanced or deal with a background unfamiliar to Indian students.

The present book aims to meet in full measure the requirements of students preparing for the various Commerce degree and post-degree examinations of the Indian Universities, and the candidates for the Chartered Accountants Examination, as well as the examinations of the Institute of Cost and Works Accountants. Apart from supplying the text matter in a logical and convenient manner, the book is intended to stimulate students to read more advanced works.

The standard set for the book is complete clarity for the beginners and such simplicity of exposition will make the text practically the best one. It is to this purpose that a maximum range of examples and illustrations form part of the text material. To further add to the value of the book, suitable text questions have been appended to each chapter, list of which have been selected from the various examination papers. Following the text material there are 25 specially selected questions and problems with their answers and solutions. An exhaustive index has been added to the contents of the book.

Our thanks are due to many writers of standard works on *Cost Accounting*, more particularly to Biggs and Sarkar, from whom we have drawn materials and inspiration in preparing this small book. Publishers and Printers of this book deserve our thanks for co-operation.

Any criticism, favourable or unfavourable, and any constructive suggestion in the direction of making the book a better teaching instrument will be gratefully received by us.

M.C. SHUKLA
T.S. GREWAL

CONTENTS

[illegible]

[illegible] Theoretical Questions 524 [illegible]
Questions [illegible]

[illegible]

Standard [illegible]

[illegible]

Introduction and Elements of Cost

Costing has been defined as classifying, recording and appropriate allocation of expenditure for the determination of the costs of products or services, and for the presentation of suitably arranged data for the purposes of control and guidance of the management. It includes ascertainment of the cost of every order, job, contract, process, service or such unit of output as may be appropriate. It deals with the cost of production, selling and distribution. Costing means an analysis of information to enable management to know the cost of producing and selling, that is, the total cost of various products and services and also to know how the total cost is constituted.

For example, it is not sufficient to say that the cost of producing a pair of shoes is ₹. 275. The management must know how much out of that sum is due to material, labour and other expenses which have to be incurred to keep a factory going. Only with proper analysis of various elements of cost, this objective can be achieved. Such an analysis is the purpose of cost accounting.

Costing is a branch of accounting which has developed because of limitations of Financial Accounts. It is developed because of the needs of management which financial account could not meet.

Requirement of Management and Limitations of Financial Accounting

(*i*) **Measurement of performance and efficiency:** These days it is necessary that a business concern should conduct its activities with utmost efficiency or with the minimum possible wastages and losses. This may not be necessary sometimes when there is such a great shortage of goods that the consumers have to buy whatever is offered to them and at a price which the sellers demand. This, however, is not the usual case and, normally, the customers have a wide choice. The choice will naturally be dictated by the value which the product or the service gives to the consumer and by the price he has to pay. The concerns which do not try to continuously improve their product and service and bring down costs and prices will sooner or later find themselves out of business because of the simple fact that there are other concerns which are constantly on the look out for a greater share in the existing market. Managements of business houses, therefore, need something by which they can constantly measure their performance objectively.

Financial accounts cannot serve this purpose at all. One may certainly say that if a concern has earned profits over a period of time, it is on the whole efficient. The existence of profits or losses in a particular year or in a particular period cannot be taken as a sure sign of efficiency or inefficiency. During the Second World War and after it, when there was a sellers' market, almost every business house made huge profit. During a depression it is difficult to avoid a loss and, therefore, if a profit and loss account shows loss, it cannot be taken to be a sign of inefficiency. It is only in normal times that the profit and loss account serves as an indicator of overall efficiency or inefficiency.

Even so, the indications given by the profit and loss account are generally inadequate. It is at best like the thermometer which only indicates the temperature of the human body; sure judgement cannot be made only on the basis of such a temperature and a good physician will have a number of other checks made in order to see what the patient is suffering from. In a similar way, in addition to the results shown by the profit and loss account, there has to be good deal of other information before management can decide about the state of health of the undertaking. It must be remembered that the objective of management is not to achieve overall efficiency, but maximum efficiency—efficiency at every point. To take a simple example, suppose the profit and loss account shows a profit of ₹ 2 lakhs. It is possible that this is a result of profit of ₹. 1,50,000 from article A, a profit of ₹. 1,00,000 from article B and a loss of ₹. 50,000 from article C. Surely the management would be well advised to ascertain the profit or loss of each product separately. This is not all; the management must also try to see that in the making of each unit of product there is no unnecessary wastage or loss as regards materials, labour and other expenses. Information regarding wastages and losses is very difficult to get from financial accounts and it is only Cost Accounts which make such information available to management.

Also, it is not possible to know the exact reasons why there are profits or losses. Financial accounts do not provide the necessary analysis. Particularly, the cost of idle facilities or idle plant cannot be gauged. Also, whether an expenditure or loss is avoidable or unavoidable is difficult to ascertain from financial accounts. It is due to all these limitations that there is need of detailed analysis of the expenses incurred by a concern so that the management can put its finger on the various weak spots and know why there are losses and profits. Having known the exact reason, it becomes easy to take steps which will remove losses and consolidate gains. This is the chief reason why Costing has developed as a distinct branch of accounting.

(*ii*) **Pricing:** Good deal of detailed information is needed to fix prices of products or services. Prices cannot be fixed on the basis of information given by financial accounts simply because these accounts deal with total expenditure and not with expenditure incurred on each product or unit of service. A certain garment factory made a variety of men's and children's clothes. Certain lines, because of their low price, became very popular and their sales grew to 75 per cent of total turnover, the remainder being made up of high-priced quality articles. The management decided that profits could be increased by discontinuing the quality production and concentrating on the popular lines. This was done and a grave loss resulted. An analysis showed that all the profit had been made on the quality goods and this had been sufficient to conceal the loss on the quantity output. By this time the quality market had been lost to a competitor and the firm concerned fell into serious difficulties. An adequate departmentalised cost system would have prevented the management from, in the first instance, selling at a loss in the popular market, and, in the second instance, discontinuing the only profitable section of the output. Another firm, in the electric goods trade, sold an article at a wholesale price of ₹. 55. Several thousand units were sold before it was found that the cost of production amounted to ₹. 57.

Financial accounts cannot indicate the exact remunerative price which may be quoted in periods of difficulties. During depression, prices may have to be even below the total cost but certainly at a level which will not increase the loss which would be incurred if production is stopped. Financial accounts can throw no light on this problem of what prices should be charged in such periods.

(*iii*) **Control:** To maximise profits or minimise costs, it is necessary to set up standards, which are really very careful and somewhat idealistic estimates, and then to compare actual costs against the standards. The reasons for the discrepancy are ascertained and then the possible action to rectify the situation is taken. Such action is not possible on the basis of information provided by financial accounts.

(*iv*) **Forecasting:** Firms these days believe in planning and for this purpose budgets have to be provided. Budgets are prepared on the basis of forecasts of future costs and revenue. In this also, financial accounts are totally inadequate in providing the necessary information. Of course, cost accounting also has to take the help of other disciplines, like Economics and Statistics, for providing reliable forecasts but it is much more capable of helping management in this regard than financial accounting.

(*v*) **Day-to-day decisions:** Besides fixing prices to meet short-term situations, various other decisions have to be taken continually, such as:

(*a*) Whether a component should be made in the factory itself or purchased from outside;

(*b*) in case a factor of production is in short supply, for which product should it be used;

(*c*) when to step or begin operations in case of seasonal industries;

(*d*) whether an old machine should be replaced by a new one; and

(*e*) whether an order at a concessional price should be accepted; etc.

Cost accounting is able to provide the necessary information for such decisions but financial accounting is unable to do so.

Following is an example which points out how cost accounting may reveal such facts and information which cannot be obtained from financial accounting. In this example a profit and loss account is shown which reveals that the firm has earned ₹. 17000 as net profit, but when separate costs of different products are calculated under cost accounting system, it has been shown that product A is sold at loss and there was need to take prompt action to overcome the problems relating to production and sale of product A.

Trading and Profit & Loss Account

	₹.		₹.
Materials	15,000.00	Sales	85,000.00
Wages	23,000.00		
Chargeable Exps.	2,000.00		
Factory Exps.	10,000.00		
Gross Profit	35,000.00		
	85,000.00		85,000.00
Administrative Exps.	8,000.00	By Gross Profit	35,000.00
Selling & Distribution Exps.	10,000.00		
Net Profit (20% of Sales)	17,000.00		
	35,000.00		35,000.00

Cost Statement

Particulars	*Total*	*Products*		
		A	B	C
	₹.	₹.	₹.	₹.
Materials	15,000.00	7,000.00	5,000.00	3,000.00
Wages	23,000.00	9,000.00	7,000.00	7,000.00
Chargeable Exps.	2,000.00	—	1,200.00	800.00
Factory Exps.	10,000.00	4,000.00	3,000.00	3,000.00
Administrative Exps.	8,000.00	3,000.00	2,500.00	2,500.00
Selling & Distribution Exps.	10,000.00	8,000.00	1,000.00	1,000.00
Total Cost	68,000.00	31,000.00	19,700.00	17,300.00
Sales	85,000.00	28,000.00	26,000.00	31,000.00
Profit/Loss	17,000.00	(–)3,000.00	6,300.00	13,700.00
Percentage of Profit on Sales	20%	(Loss) –10.7%	24.33%	44.19%

It is revealed that product A is sold at 10.7 per cent loss while product B and C are producing 24.23 per cent and 44.19 per cent profits. Due to product A, the total profit percentage has come down to 20 per cent. This information is of utmost use to the management. The firm may decide to discontinue product A after making an enquiry of the cost structure of this product. The firm may find out whether or not some more efficient manufacturing, selling and distribution system is possible in this respect. The firm may also review its pricing policy and should also investigate as to whether the selling price of product A may be increased to attain a profitable level.

Thus, in the words of *L W. Hawkins* 'the ordinary trading account is a locked store house of most valuable information to which cost system is the key'.

To put it differently and to *sum up*, financial accounting has the following significant *limitations*:

(1) It cannot measure effectively the efficiency of various operations;

(2) It cannot provide sufficiently detailed information to enable the firm to fix prices either in the short period or in the long term;

(3) It does not provide the necessary tools and information for controlling costs effectively;

(4) Budgeting and forecasting, so essential for modern day managements, will suffer badly if reliance is placed only on financial accounting; and

(5) Managements have to make numerous decisions for which financial accounting is unable to provide the necessary data and information. These all decisions relate to choice of one out of the various alternatives, such as make or buy, according priority to products, etc.

This void left by financial accounting has been quite well filled by Cost Accounting. One can say that the need for cost accounting arose because of the requirement of management to know the cost of various activities in various circumstances. This need is felt by managements everywhere—not merely in private business houses seeking to make a project. A hospital, for example, may not want to earn a profit but it will certainly try to utilise its funds in the best possible manner. That means it must ascertain the cost of each activity that it undertakes and then weigh the cost against the expected benefit. Any institution using resources that are scarce will need cost accounting since only then can the limited resources be put to the best use and for the greatest benefit.

Costing has a vital role to play in almost any activity which involves expenditure of money, whether it is a business house or a charitable concern or whether it is a Government department. Costing can throw a good deal of light on unnecessary losses and wastages. In public enterprises, that is to say, enterprises owned by the Government, normally the profit motive is absent and, therefore, whatever indication the usual profit and loss account gives in case of private enterprise, is unavailable in case of public enterprises. The efficiency of public enterprise, therefore, can be maintained only by a systematic collection of costing data and its study. Costing, therefore, has even a more important role to play in public enterprise than in private enterprise.

Definitions

To understand the meaning of Cost Accounting, there is need of explaining certain related terms also.

(1) **Cost:** Cost has been defined in the terminology given by the *Chartered Institute of Management Accountants* (*CIMA*) as 'the amount of expenditure incurred or attributed on a given thing'. More simply, it can be defined as that which is given or sacrified to obtain something. Thus the cost of an article is its purchase or manufacturing price, *i.e.* it would consist of its direct material cost, direct labour cost, direct and indirect expenses allocated or apportioned to it.

(2) **Cost Accountancy:** The *Chartered Institute of Management Accountants in England* (CIMA) has defined Cost Accountancy as 'the application of costing and Cost Accounting

principles, methods and techniques to the science, art and practice of cost and the ascertainment of profitability. It includes the presentation of information derived therefrom for the purpose of management decision-making'. Cost Accountancy is, thus the science, art and the practice of cost accountant.

Cost Accountancy is *science* because it is the systematic knowledge which a cost accountant should possess so that he may properly discharge his responsibility and functions. Cost Accountancy is also an *art* because it includes the ability and skill with which a cost accountant becomes able to apply his knowledge to the various problems like ascertainment of costs, control of costs, ascertainment of profitability, replacement of plants and technology, marginal costing, etc. Cost Accountancy is also practising the practice of a cost accountant. It includes his continuous efforts in presentation of information for the purpose of managerial decision-making.

Cost Accountancy consists of several subjects, such as Cost Accounting, Costing, Cost Control and Cost Audit.

(3) **Cost Accounting:** The *Chartered Institute of Management Accountants* in England (*CIMA*) has defined Cost Accounting as, 'the process of accounting for cost from the point at which expenditure is incurred or committed to establishment of its ultimate relationship with cost centres and cost units. In its widest usage, it embraces the preparations of statistical data, the application of cost control methods and the ascertainment of the profitability of activities carried or planned'. It is a formal mechanism by means of which costs of products or services are ascertained and controlled. It is concerned with accumulation, classification, analysis and interpretation of cost data for three major purposes (*a*) ascertainment of cost, (*b*) operational planning and control, and (*c*) decision-making.

(4) **Costing:** Costing has been defined by the Institute as, 'the technique and process of ascertaining cost'. *Wheldon* defines costing as follows:

"Costing is the classifying, recording, and appropriate allocation of expenditure for the determination of the costs of products or services; and for the presentation of suitably arranged data for the purposes of control and guidance of the management. It includes the ascertainment of the cost of every order, job, contract, process, service or unit as may be appropriate. It deals with the cost of production, selling and distribution."

Thus, costing means such an analysis of information as to enable management to know the cost of producing and selling, that is the total cost of various products and services and also to know how the total cost is constituted.

(5) **Cost Control:** Cost control has been defined as 'the guidance and regulation by executive action of costs of operating on undertaking'. It is primary job of a cost-accountant, besides ascertainment of cost, to furnish different types of statements and information as to enable the management to control the cost of operating their business. Cost control is exercised through a number of techniques such as Standard Costing and Budgetory Control. *Standard Costing* is a system which seeks to control the cost of each unit through determining beforehand what should be the cost and then its comparison with actual cost and also analysis of variances together with their causes. *Budgetory Control* means laying down in monetary and quantitative terms what exactly has to be done and how exactly it has to be done over a coming period and then to ensure that actual results do not diverge from the planned course more than necessary.

(6) **Cost Audit:** Cost Audit has been defined by the Institute as 'the verification of cost accounts and a check on the adherence to the cost accounting plan. It is an independent expert examination of the cost accounts of different outputs of an undertaking and a verification whether such accounts of the different output, serve the purpose intended.'

OBJECTIVES OF COST ACCOUNTING

The definition given by the *CIMA* brings out the vital point that the Cost Accounting has the following objectives:

(*i*) *Ascertainment of cost* and determining the selling price.

(*ii*) *Cost control i.e.* keeping costs under check;

(*iii*) *Ascertaining profitability* and profits earned on each activity including ascertaining causes that lead to a particular figure; and

(*iv*) *Collection and presentation* of such information or statements as are required by management in its task of planning and making decisions. The decisions to be made may be of various types, some examples of which are:

(*a*) fixing prices under normal and special circumstances;

(*b*) determining priorities for products;

(*c*) deciding whether a component will be bought from the market or made within the factory itself; and

(*d*) deciding on the best processes of manufacture etc.

A particular firm may not desire to realise all the aims stated above and may, therefore, design its Cost Accounting system only for a particular purpose. But, in general, Cost Accounting has a wide role to play.

The nature of cost accounting can be summarised as "analysing, recording, standardising, forcasting, comparing, reporting and recommending. It is the business of the cost accountant to fill in turn the role of historian, news agent and prophet. As historian he must be meticulously accurate and sedulously impartial. As news agent he must be up to date, selective and pithy. As prophet he must combine knowledge and experience with foresight and courage".

FUNCTIONS OF COST ACCOUNTING OR COST-ACCOUNTANT

According to *Blocker and Weltemer* 'Cost Accounting is to serve management in the execution of policies and in comparison of actual and estimated results in order that the value of each policy may be appraised and changed to meet the future conditions'.

Following are main functions of cost accounting:

(*i*) To work out cost per unit of the different products manufactured by the organisation;

(*ii*) To provide an accurate analysis of this cost;

(*iii*) To maintain costs to the lowest point consistent with the most efficient operating conditions. It requires the examination of each cost in the light of the service or benefit obtained so that the maximum utilisation of each rupee will be obtained;

(*iv*) To work out the wastage in each process of manufacture and to prepare reports as may be necessary to assist in the control of wastage;

(*v*) To provide necessary data for the fixation of selling price of commodities manufactured;

(*vi*) To compute profits earned on each of the products and to advise management as to how these profits can be improved;

(*vii*) To help management in control of inventory so that there may be minimum locking up of capital in stocks of raw materials, stores, work-in-process and finished goods

(*viii*) To install and implement cost control systems like *Budgetary Control* and *Standard Costing* for the control of expenditure on materials, labour and overheads;

(*ix*) To advise management on future expansion;

(*x*) To advise management on the profitability or otherwise of new lines of products;

(*xi*) To carry out special cost studies and investigations which are invaluable to management in determining policies and formulating plans directed towards profitable operations.

MANAGEMENT ACCOUNTING

Management accounting is a product of necessity for utilising data of Cost Accounting and Financial Accounting for planning, coordination and control rather than for mere record-keeping.

According to *Robert Anthony*, 'Management Accounting is concerned with accounting information which is useful to the management'. The approach is selective in presenting and interpreting accounting data which facilitates the process of decision-making. *J. Batty* signifies this area as a combination of accounting theory and practice on the one hand and special managerial skills on the other. According to him 'Management Accounting is the term used to describe the accounting methods, systems and techniques, which coupled with special knowledge and ability, assists management in its task of maximising profits or minimising losses'. Thus 'Any form of accounting which enables a business to be conducted more efficiently can be regarded as Management Accounting'.

Management Accounting is more concerned with the improvement in the level of managerial competence in taking right decisions. The nature of management accounting is analytical which views every activity or event in wider perspective in analysing the causes and their effects.

The area of Management Accounting is closely related to the principles and preactice of financial accounting on the one hand and the managerial skills on the other hand. The scope includes the following systems of accounting and management (*i*) Financial Planning and Policy (*ii*) Financial Accounting (*iii*) Standard Costing, Budgeting and Budgetary Control (*iv*) Managerial Costing, Profit Planning and Break-even-Analysis (*v*) Capital Budgeting and Project Planning (*vi*) Dividend and Retention Policy Decisions and (*vii*) Performance Appraisal. Such a wide scope of the area involves the use of a number of quantitative and management technique as tools of analysis such as Ratio Analysis, Trend Analysis, Fund-Flow and Cash-Flow Analysis, Comparative and Common size Financial Statements and many other modern techniques of management like Operations Research, Linear Programming and Computer Programming.

Thus **Management Accounting** serves managers by providing information to help them in decision-making, planning and control, while **Cost Accounting** is concerned with the calculation of product costs for use in the financial accounts.

DIFFERNCE BETWEEN COST ACCOUNTING, FINANCIAL ACCOUNTING, MANAGEMENT ACCOUNTING AND FINANCIAL MANAGEMENT

Cost Accounting is a branch of accounting, which has been developed because of the limitations of Financial Accounting from the point of view of management control and internal reporting. Financial accounting performs admirably, the function of portraying a true and fair overall picture of the results of activities carried on by an enterprise during a period and its financial position at the end of the year. Also, on the basis of financial accounting, effective control can be exercised on the property and assets of the enterprise to ensure that they are not misused or misappropriated. To that extent financial accounting helps to assess the overall progress of a concern, its strength and weaknesses by providing the figures relating to several previous years.

Data provided by Cost and Financial Accounting is further used for the management of all processes associated with the efficient acquisition and deployment of short, medium and long term financial resources. Such a process of management is known as *Financial Management*. The objective of Financial Management is to maximise the wealth of shareholders by taking effective investment, financing and dividend decisions. Investment decisions relate to the effective deployment of scarce resources in terms of funds while the financing decisions are concerned with acquiring optimum finance for attaining financial objectives. The last and very important 'Dividend decision' relates to the determination of the amount and frequency of cash which can be paid out of profits to shareholders.

Management Accounting refers to managerial processes and technologies that are focused on adding value to organisations by attaining the effective use of resources, in dynamic and competitive contexts. Hence, Management Accounting is a distinctive form of resource management which facilitates management's 'decision making' by producing information for managers within an organisation.

ADVANTAGES OF COSTING

The following are the important advantages which a concern can derive from Cost Accounting:

1. **Measurement and Improvement of Efficiency:** The chief advantage to be gained is that Cost Accounting will enable a concern to, first of all, measure its efficiency and then to maintain and improve it. This is done by suitable comparisons and analysis of the differences that may be observed. For example, if materials spent upon a pair of shoes in 2001 come to ₹. 100 and for a similar pair of shoe the amount is ₹. 120 in 2002. It is an indication of decline in efficiency. Of course, the increase may only be due to increase in price of materials; it may also be due to greater wastage in use of materials or inefficiency at the time of buying so that unnecessary high prices were paid. Comparisons may also be made with average figures for the whole industry (if such figures are available) and with ideal figures which may have been determined beforehead. In any case it is this sort of comparison which tells management about the going up or coming down of efficiency. The study will certainly indicate the steps to be taken to remove the causes of inefficiency or to consolidate a factor which leads to greater efficiency.

2. **Profitable and Unprofitable Activities:** It will throw light upon those activities which bring profits and those activities which result in losses. This will be done only if the cost of each product or each job is ascertained and compared with the price obtained.

3. **Fixation of Prices:** In many cases a firm is able to fix a price for its products on the basis of the cost of production. In such a case, price cannot be properly fixed if no proper figures of cost are available. In case of big contracts, no quotation can be made unless the cost of completing that contract can be ascertained. If prices are fixed without costing information, it is possible that the price quoted may either be too high, in which case orders cannot be obtained, or it may be too low, in which case an order will result in a loss. It is a mistake on the part of any management to believe that mere increase in sales volume will result in profits; increased sales at prices lower than the cost may well lead the concern to the bankrupt court. Only Cost Accounting will reveal what price will be profitable.

4. **Guide in Reducing Prices:** In certain periods it becomes necessary to reduce the price even below the total cost. This will be so when there is a depression or slump. Costs, properly ascertained, will guide management in this direction.

5. **Information for Proper Planning:** For a proper system of Costing, it is necessary to have detailed information about the facilities available about machine and labour capacity. This helps in proper planning of work so that no section is overworked and no section remains idle.

6. **Control over Materials etc.:** Information about availability of stocks of various materials and stores must be constantly available if there is a good system of Cost Accounting. This helps in two ways. Firstly, production can be planned according to the availability of materials and fresh stocks can be arranged in time when old stocks are exhausted. Secondly, loss due to carelessness or pilferage or any other mischief will be known and, therefore, put down.

7. **Decision Regarding Machine vs. Labour:** Some of the important questions before management can be solved only with the help of information about costs. For example, if there is the problem of replacement of labour by machinery, Cost Accounting will at least guide management in finding out what the cost of production will be if either machinery or labour is used.

8. **Expansion in Production:** Sometimes it is necessary to decide whether production of one product or the other is to be increased. This problem can also be solved only if proper information about costs is available.

9. **Reasons for Losses Detected:** Exact causes of existence of profits or losses will be revealed by a system of Cost Accounting. For example, a concern may suffer not because the cost of production is high or prices are low but because the output is much below the capacity of the concern. It is only Cost Accounting which will reveal this reason for loss. It also helps in distinguishing between expenditure and loss which is necessary and that which is unnecessary, that is to say, between normal and abnormal losses.

10. **Helps in Taking Decisions:** Cost Accounting inculcates the habit of making calculations with pencil and paper before taking a decision. It will certainly check recklessness. Also some of the silly mistakes that sometimes occur can be avoided if there is a good Cost Accounting system. To give an instance, a well-known firm once quoted for supply of mosquito nets to the Government at a very low price. It was only after the order was obtained that the firm found that, by mistake, the price of materials was not included in the quotation.

11. **Check on Accuracy of Financial Accounts:** A good system of Cost Accounting affords an independent and most reliable check on the accuracy of financial accounts. This check operates through reconciliation of profits shown by Cost Accounts and by Financial Accounts.

On the basis of various advantages of Cost Accounting, it can be easily said that '*a good system of costing serves as a means of control over expenditure and helps to secure economy in manufacture*'.

Control over Expenditure

A good system of costing serves as a means of control over expenditure in the following directions:

(*a*) An efficient system of stores and stock accounting is rendered essential and thus wastage may be detected and reduced to a minimum.

(*b*) By adopting the maximum limits for stores, the total capital outlay is controlled and possible financial loss due to overstocking is avoided.

(*c*) The centralisation of purchasing is facilitated by the use of Cost Accounts and the danger of liabilities exceeding the current financial resources is avoided.

(*d*) The maintenance of time and job records for workers discloses the losses incurred from idle time and indicates the directions in which these losses may be minimised.

(*e*) The data made available by Cost Accounting are invaluable for the purpose of comparison, and steps can be taken to reduce the number of unprofitable or more costly operations, processes etc. in favour of those shown to be more efficient or economical.

(*f*) The exact result of all expenditure is brought to the notice of the management by Cost Accounting in a manner which Financial Accounting fail to achieve. As Cost Accounting should always be up to date, expenditure may be controlled thereby as it becomes necessary whereas information from Financial Accounts may be past history before it receives the attention of the management.

Key to Economy

Cost Accounting helps to secure economy in manufacture because they provide such detailed analysis of expenditure that:

(*a*) Wastage of material, labour and time are revealed, and steps may therefore be taken to minimise such losses in the future.

(*b*) A detailed comparison of operations, process etc. is provided and the less efficient thus detected.

(*c*) The relative advantages of remunerating labour on the time, piecework or premium plans may be ascertained.

(*d*) Unprofitable activities are disclosed and steps may be taken to eliminate or reduce them or to change the method of production or incidence of cost.

(*e*) The location of weakness stimulates the new and improved processes.

Thus the main purpose of ascertaining cost is to provide the management with facts to carry on the business in the most efficient manner. Cost Accounts are designed to provide the management with information which if acted upon, will enable efficiency to be enhanced, waste to be eliminated, a proper control to be imposed over stocks and stores and economic prices and tenders to be fixed. Cost Accounts will also reveal profitable and unprofitable activities and will indicate in what directions production may be usually expanded or contracted.

Service Rendered by Cost Accounting to the Management

Cost Accounting provides cost information to the management. Cost data are compiled for use by operating supervisors, reports are prepared and issued periodically to the appropriate managers and operating executives in an analytical form so that they may manage most effectively and economically the activities immediately under their control. The cost department's daily handling of detailed operated figures reveal the strength and weaknesses of the current methods of production, distribution and administration. Their suggestions are an aid in controlling day-to-day activities, effecting reduction in cost and establishing broad policies relating to improvement and enlargement of plant. Information furnished to sales management includes actual or estimated costs of new products for pricing, suggestion for selling those products which are most profitable and advantageous and choosing the most effective and least costly selling methods and channels of distribution. The cost department must cooperate with other departments of the business in offering timely information and helpful suggestions so that their performance may be improved. Prompt and correct cost information fosters cooperation between department and promotes coordination of their efforts.

Service Rendered to Employees

Cost Accounting strengthens a business and enables it to earn more profits through the adoption of improved techniques. Although higher profit goes directly to the benefit of the proprietors, it is indirectly reflected in higher emolument and security of employment of the employees. Moreover, by devising suitable incentive schemes, it gives all classes of workers including supervisors, clerks departmental heads and major executives opportunity to improve their emoluments while enabling the organisation to earn higher profits. It can also be emphasised that cost figures revealing the true state of affairs of the business may be used in settling industrial disputes.

Cost Accounting and Creditors

Cost reports reveal satisfactory trends and future prospects of a business. Banks, lending companies, share and debenture-holders and suppliers of goods granting credit terms can judge the soundness of a company from its cost statistics.

Interest of Public in Cost Accounting

When Cost accounting lowers the cost of production of commodities by eliminating losses due to improper planning and scheduling, wasteful usage of materials, idle time and inadequate management of employees, improper control of overhead costs, lack of good relation between employees and employers, it is in effect rendering a service to the community by providing goods at lower cost and improving the general standard of living.

OBJECTIONS TO COST ACCOUNTING

Two of the principal objections against the installation of costing system in a factory are that (*a*) it is *unnecessary* and (*b*) it is *expensive*.

(*a*) ***It is unnecessary.*** In this age of competition in the business world, a manufacturer must know the exact cost not only of each article made but also of each element of cost, so that his selling price may be reasonably fixed, neither too high price which may reduce business nor to low price which may lead to loss. The main purpose of ascertaining costs is to provide the management with facts and information to carry on the business in the most efficient manner, and to achieve advantages of a costing system:

(*i*) it enables the business to ascertain the exact cost of each specific unit of output and the extent to which each element of expenditure contributes to such cost.

(*ii*) It provides a reliable basis upon which tenders and estimates may be prepared.

(*iii*) It facilitates the detection and prevention of waste, leakage and inefficiency.

(*iv*) It provides invaluable data for purposes of comparison.

(*v*) It provides an independent and collateral check upon the accuracy of financial accounts.

(*vi*) It enables unprofitable activities of the business disclosed, so that steps may be taken to eliminate or reduce them.

In view of these advantages, the objection that a costing system is unnecessary is not quite correct.

(*b*) ***It is expensive.*** When it is desired to introduce a costing system in a manufacturing business, that business must be studied in detail with special reference to its manufacturing technique and the advice of its technical staff must be obtained in framing the system of costing. The system to be adopted to a particular case must be adopted to the requirement and circumstances of that case. A simple costing system will in many case suffice, and unnecessary elaboration must always be avoided Elaborate costing records should only be kept when their maintenance is warranted, since a system of Cost Accounting must be profitable investment and produce a benefit commensurate with the expenditure incurred upon it. It must be simple and it must be elastic and capable of adaptation to changing conditions. Therefore, it cannot be said that a costing system is expensive.

A number of advantages have been detailed earlier and a good management should be able to benefit greatly from the installation of Cost Accounting, but the character of management is of vital importance here. Really speaking, the cost accountant can only prepare information highlighting the points which should be studied, but action is something which is beyond the cost accountant and is a function of management itself. Unless, therefore, the management is, firstly, willing to study the information compiled and presented by the cost accountant, secondly, capable of doing that and, thirdly, willing to take action on the basis of that information, installation of a Cost Accounting system will prove of no avail.

INSTALLATION OF A COST ACCOUNTING SYSTEM

The very first thing to remember about a Cost Accounting system is that it should always be treated as an investment. This means that if, somehow, it is believed that no advantage will be gained by installing such a system, then it should not be installed at all. Cost Accounting as a matter of fashion is entirely useless and may even be harmful. This has a number of implications.

One is that a concern must itself design the system to be adopted. Books can give only general principles and it is no use copying a system followed by another concern. This is because the personality and problems of a business house are quite different from those of another. It is necessary, therefore, to adopt an available system for the peculiar requirements of the undertaking.

Another implication of this is also that *the amount to be spent upon the installation of the system should be strictly proportionate to the benefits likely to be obtained.* This means that if sufficient information about costs can be obtained from financial books then a separate Cost Accounting department is not necessary. For example, in case of a colliery all the necessary information should be available from the financial books because all expenditure relates to production of coal only. The total expenditure will be required to be analysed in greater details but separate Cost Accounting books are not necessary. But, normally, in case of a jobbing factory or a concern which produces a number of products, an elaborate system of Cost Accounting is necessary.

Another implication of this principle is that in *Cost Accounting reasonable accuracy is sufficient.* For example, it does not really matter much whether the cost of a house is ₹. 1,95,119.85 or whether it is put down as ₹. 1,95,120.00. Of course, much greater accuracy will be required, say, in case of a cotton textile mill where a saving of even one-tenth of a paisa per metre will result in a saving of thousands of rupees. What is reasonable accuracy, therefore, depends upon the nature of the concern; but absolute accuracy in Cost Accounting is not desirable (because it will involve too great an expenditure of time and money). Also, it is not possible because if there is a number of products, allocation of some of the expenses to each product accurately will be well nigh impossible.

The cost of maintaining the Cost Accounting system can be curtailed a great deal by devising suitable forms. These forms will cut down clerical labour and will prevent a number of mistakes which otherwise occur.

Factors to be Considered Before Installations

When a Cost Accounting system is to be installed, the following points should be kept in mind:

1. **Objects:** What are the objects which the management wants to achieve and what sort of information does it need for the achievement of its objectives? Information about costs meant for fixing prices would be quite different from that intended to reveal efficiencies or inefficiencies in operations or that required to make decisions on a rational basis.

2. **The Technical Details:** Technical operations of the concern and whether production is more important than selling or *vice versa* should be kept in mind. Obviously more attention must be paid to the more significant factor.

3. **The Product:** The nature of product should be considered to decide type of cost system. For example, if materials used are insignificant, an elaborate system of materials control will not be necessary.

4. **Factors:** Factors that are or are not amenable to control should be considered. Attention has to be paid to controllable factors. For instance, if a particular method of packing is prescribed by law, it is no use trying to think of an alternative.

5. **Type of Materials:** The type of materials available and the timing of their supplies together with the storage problem, should also be taken into consideration.

6. **Type of Labour:** The type of labour which is required and the methods of their remuneration should also be kept in mind.

7. **Management:** The character of management itself and the decision-making process should also be taken into account. Modern managements usually need detailed information. The information flows will have to be designed with reference to the sources and end uses of the information. For example, if decisions are taken by a person who refuses to divulge any information, the system must keep this in view.

8. **Business Peculiarities:** Any peculiarities of the business, that there may be, must be kept in view. For instance, if purchases of particular item are to be made only from one particular source or firm, the costing system need not build an adequate purchase procedure; it should concentrate on the proper use of the concerned item.

9. **Use of Financial Books:** The possibility of using financial books and procedures should also be kept in mind. As stated above, cost accounting is to be treated as an investment and, therefore, all existing useful procedures, books and records should be used. For example financial accounts need adequate record of purchases and wages. With a little change, these can be made to serve the needs of Cost Accounting also. As far as possible, cost records and financial books should be well coordinated, even fully integrated.

10. **Choice of Unit:** The choice of the unit regarding which costs have to be obtained should also be considered. For example, in case of steel, costs are ascertained per tonne of steel and in case of cotton textiles, the unit is kg. of yarn or cloth. In case of motor transport the cost will be

found per bus-kilometre or passenger-kilometre or sometimes tonne-mile. These are known as units of cost and it is necessary to choose a proper unit—neither too big nor too small.

11. **Full Discussion:** Above all, the system should be designed after a full and frank discussion with all those who will be involved.

Difficulties in Installation of a Costing System

When a costing system is newly introduced, it may have to encounter a number of difficulties. These may be the following:

(*i*) **Management Apathy:** If management is not really convinced of the advantages of the costing system or if it has somehow been made to accept the system against its will, it will merely tolerate it and not encourage it properly. This will lead others also to withhold their cooperation and, therefore, the system may never operate effectively. The reports may all be correct and prompt but probably no one will look at them.

(*ii*) **Hostility from Line Staff:** Line staff people often believe that firstly they know how to run their business and, therefore, they do not need anyone to tell them what information they need and, secondly, that they cannot waste their time in "form filling". They may also be afraid that proper information will expose some of their mistakes or that the new system will make them less useful than before in the eyes of the management. There is a tendency to resent anything new unless it is patently to one's advantage.

(*iii*) **Structure of Authority:** The cost accounting system may be based on formal authority structure whereas in reality the structure may be quite different. If, for example, trade union leaders have a great deal of influence on the various decisions, the system may run into difficulties—it is not likely that the organisation chart will show the authority of the union leaders.

(*iv*) **Changed circumstances:** Business often undergoes rapid changes—the market may change and the production process may change; management ideas change also. If the costing system is not adapted to the changed circumstances, it will cease to be effective. For example, if a cotton textile mill is converted into a mill producing man-made fibres, the Cost Accounting system must also be suitably changed.

(*v*) **Indifference:** Often a part of the system breaks down; if it is not quickly set right, it will affect the whole system. For example, if issues of material are not properly watched and kept under control, the whole materials control system may break down. Also there may be delay in the flow of information and report may be delayed. If this is not corrected the whole decision-making and control system may be vitiated. The same will be the result if there are serious errors in report. It is, therefore, necessary that someone should watch the actual operation of the system continuously and carefully.

(*vi*) **Low Status of Cost Accountant:** The cost accountant will often have to collect and furnish information which may not be liked by someone. If the cost accountant occupies a very junior position, he may not be able to do his work without fear or favour and, therefore, the information suplied by him may not lead to the correct decision. It is essential that the cost accountant should be a high ranking official, having direct access to the top management. He must also be assisted by a properly trained and adequate staff.

(*vii*) **Lack of Clarity about Priorities and Objectives:** If the Cost Accounting staff is not clear about the end uses to which costing information will be put, they may not go about their task in the correct manner; they may even send the wrong sort of or inadequate information.

Because of all these difficulties, it is necessary to proceed slowly, taking everyone along. An educative process for all concerned is essential to see that the costing system is accepted and operated sincerely.

Cost Manual

One way to see that the costing system operates in the way it is intended is to write down in book form the entire system in all its aspects. The book is called Cost Manual which has been defined by the Chartered Institute Management Accountants, London as : "A document which sets out the responsibilities of the persons costing in the routine of and the forms and records required for costing and Cost Accounting."

The cost manual will lay down all the constituent parts of the Cost Accounting system, such as: accounting for materials, labour, overheads of various types, in what manner the whole information will be collected, analysed and integrated, what reports will be prepared, when they will be prepared and in what form and to whom shall they be sent.

For each constituent part the entire process will be specified. For example, in the case of materials, the manual will state:

(*i*) how purchase requisitions will originate;

(*ii*) how and by whom they shall be processed and decisions to purchase will be taken;

(*iii*) whether quotation are to be invited and how the quotations will be compared and who will take the decision to place the order;

(*iv*) in which cases no quotations need be invited; if so, who will decide as how the items are to be procured;

(*v*) the form of the purchase order;

(*vi*) the procedure on receipt of materials—for checking the quality and quantity of the materials received;

(*vii*) the way the materials received are to be priced—the items to be included in their cost:

(*viii*) the recording of materials received—the forms of bin cards and stores ledger;

(*ix*) the persons authorised to draw materials from the stores;

(*x*) the method to be followed for pricing the issues;

(*xi*) the manner in which physical checking will be carried out; and

(*xii*) the analysis of materials issued job-wise and the recording thereof; etc.

The cost manual will specify the duty of each person in the costing department and state precisely how he will do the work allotted to him and to whom he is to pass on his work on completion. Also, all the forms to be used are given in the manual. The way all the forms are to be filled and the person who will fill them are all stated; the manual will also note to whom the form is to be sent on completion. The date by which a particular form is to be completed and sent is also specified.

The cost manual, thus, will contain the procedures to be followed by the concerned firm. It is a way of knowing what loose ends there are and then of tying them up; it is also a way of seeing that there is no duplication of work and that the entire work is done in an integrated manner without delay.

Legal Requirement

Normally, whether a firm instals a Cost Accounting system or not is upto it and, therefore, it does so on the basis of the benefits it expects to derive from the system. The Companies Act, 1956, however, empowers the Central Government to order companies engaged in any particular industry to keep books to record specified particulars. Section 209 requires that books must be maintained to give a true and fair view of such particulars regarding utilisation of materials or labour or other items of cost as may be prescribed by the Central Government in case the company belongs to the specified class of companies engaged in manufacturing, processing and mining. This means that if it belongs to an industry for which the Central Government has ordered the keeping of the partciculars indicated above, the company must keep proper costing books. The Central Government has already prescribed the keeping of such books in the case of a number of industries, for example, cement, cotton textiles, tyres, sugar, etc. Thus, in India, the installation of a costing system is compulsory in many cases.

APPROACH FOR ASCERTAINING COSTS

Costs can be ascertained in two ways, *viz.,* (1) Post Costing, and (2) Continuous Costing.

(1) Post Costing

In this case, no attempt is made to find out costs till the year is actually over and financial books are closed. After the books are finally audited, the information contained in the books is analysed and cost sheets for various products, jobs, etc., are prepared. One advantage of such a procedure is that the figures analysed are the actuals and, hence, the cost arrived at is quite correct.

But there are serious drawbacks which make such a procedure unsuitable and not of much advantage. The analysis will be undertaken towards the close of the next year since it takes time to close and audit the financial book. Information regarding costs, therefore, will come too late to be of any use. No corrective action can be taken on the basis of the information. The information is merely of historical interest. `Look before you leap' is the proverb, but under this method, one looks after leaping.

Post Costing is sometimes conducted by the Government when it awards contracts on the basis of fair price—cost plus a reasonable margin for profit. The object is to find out whether the contractor charged a fair price or more than that. Such contracts are known as "*Cost Plus Contracts*".

(2) Continuous Costing

It means finding out the cost of producing an article during the course of production. It enables the management to know what it is costing to do the jobs in hand and helps it to take corrective action in time to check wastages and losses. If a quotation is to be made, the cost sheet must be prepared in advance. Continuous costing involves very often the use of estimates of expenditure instead of actuals. As will be seen later, actual expenditure on a job regarding materials and labour can always be known easily but actual information about other expenses may not be available for sometime. Hence an estimate of such expenses is necessary. A good system of Cost Accounting has, therefore, to concern itself with intelligent estimation of expenses and with their proper allocation or apportionment.

It should be noted, however, that mere ascertainment of expenses is not enough. We should also try to find out where we are efficient and where inefficient and to what extent. This involves comparison of one's actual performance at all points with that in the whole industry, as well as with one's own performance in the past years. A firm can also set up targets for achievements on the basis of past experience and prepare a standard cost sheet. The comparison of actual cost sheet with the standard cost sheet will reveal where the firm has reached its targets and where it has fallen short of them. This process is known as Standard Costing. This will be discussed in a later chapter.

METHODS OF COSTING

The nature of industries differs. Some are very simple and produce only one product, e.g., brick-making. Some industries may produce only one product but it may really be an assembly of numerous components like a bicycle. Again, there may be a homogeneous product but involving many distinct stages and processes such as vegetable oil. In some cases there may be important bye-products or joint products, e.g., petroleum products. Some firms necessarily undertake work against a definite customer's order such as printing of a book while others undertake continuous production and maintain inventories of finished goods. It is, therefore, natural that the exact method employed to ascertain cost per unit should depend on the nature of the industry. The following are the principal methods.

(1) Job Costing

Work may be performed against individual orders from the customer, as in the case of a motor workshop undertaking repairs of cars or in the case of a printing press undertaking printing jobs of different types. A factory may also produce different types of goods against orders. The production may be undertaken against a 'stock' order, i.e., for keeping the goods in stock for ready supply of customers' requirements. In all these cases the best costing results can be obtained by giving a distinct job number to each order on the factory or workshop and by opening an account to which all expenditure on the job is charged. This will enable us to know the cost of undertaking a particular job. Separate Cost Accounting books are necessary.

(2) Batch Costing

Factories which have to produce a large number of parts in order to make a product undertake the production of each part in batches. For example, a bicycle factory may produce 10,000 handles at one time and then take up the manufacture of other parts. When this supply of handles is exhausted, another lot of handles will be made. Thus production is made in batches. The cost of each batch is ascertained separately and the method is known as batch costing. It is similar to job costing.

(3) Contract or Terminal Costing

This term applies to the system of costing which relates to a business concentrating on the completion of big contracts only. Since all the energies of the business are devoted to one or two contracts, the compilation of cost incurred is comparatively simple although the nature of contract costs is not different from job costs. A 'job' is a small contract; a 'contract' is a big job. Costing information can be obtained from financial books themselves, if suitably modelled.

(4) Unit (Single or Output) Costing

This method is applied where there is only one product, as in the case of a brewery or colliery. As in case of contract costs, the financial books themselves can be made to yield details to make up the cost sheet. No separate set of books is generally required and costing information is presented in the form of a statement known as Cost Sheet.

(5) Process Costing

When a product passes through distinct stages or processes, each having a bearing on the total cost of production or each yielding valuable by-products or each causing considerable wastage of materials, finding out the cost of each process will yield good results. For example, in case of oil, there are three distinct processes—crushing, refining and finishing. Allocating expenditure to each process will give valuable information. The method is known as process costing.

(6) Operation Costing

This is used in case of mechanical products. Generally, many operations are necessary to make an article. For example, if cycle mud-guards are to be made, the steel sheets will first be cut into proper strips and then shaped according to the design and then machined and then polished. Each one of these is an operation and it is possible to find out the cost of each operation separately. The cost of the mud-guard can be found out by adding the cost of these operations. If this is done it is known as operation costs. There is really not much difference between process costing and operation costing.

(7) Operating Costing

Where a business does not produce tangible goods but renders some service, the system of costing would be known as operating cost. A transport company does not produce any article but it carries goods or passengers. It should know the cost per tonne-kilo metre—cost of carrying one tonne of goods one kilometre or the cost per passenger-km—the cost of carrying one passenger one km. In an electricity concern cost would be ascertained per kilowatt hour. The system of finding the cost would be similar to that of single or output costing.

Operating cost may also make use of operation cost. For example, a correspondence course may ascertain the cost of (*i*) preparing study material, (*ii*) examining answer papers, and (*iii*) providing counselling service, etc.

(8) Departmental Costing

A factory may be divided into a number of departments and sometimes good results are obtained by allocating expenditure first to different departments and then to the different products manufactured in that department. It will be seen later that departmental costing, as this is known, is generally advantageous for the purpose of estimating and allocating expenses correctly.

(9) Multiple Costing

This method (a combination of two or more methods) is followed where the final product consists of a number of separate parts, e.g., bicycle, radio set, motor car, etc. The cost of each part has to be ascertained (through batch or job costing) and then the cost of assembling the parts will be tabulated. The cost of the assembly department will be more or less on the lines of single or output costing. The total cost of the final product will consist of the cost of all the parts plus the cost of assembling them.

Fundamentally out of the first eight methods discussed above, there are only two basic methods, namely, job costing and process costing. For example, if a book is printed it is possible to find out the total cost by putting down (1) total amount spent by way of materials, i.e., paper, card-board, etc. (2) the total amount spent upon labour in printing the book and (3) the total expenses which can be allocated to that book. If this method is followed, it would be known as job costing. It is also possible to find out the cost by another method. Firstly, the cost of composing the matter may be found out. This will involve the wages of compositors and proof readers only plus a little amount by way of expenses. Secondly, the cost of machining will be ascertained. Here there will be cost of paper, wages of the machineman and expenses to cover depreciation, power and other expenses of the machine department. Lastly, the cost of binding will be put down; this will mean the cost of binding materials, labour of binders and the expenses pertaining to the binding department. Thus the printing of the book has been broadly divided into three stages, namely, composing, machining and binding. The total cost is ascertained by adding up the cost of each stage. This method is known as process costing. A moment's thought will tell the student that the cost of almost every work in an industrial concern can be ascertained in one of these two ways.

ELEMENTS OF COSTS AND CLASSIFICATION OF EXPENDITURE

It is well known that the cost of making and selling a product can be divided into tnree main classes, namely, materials, labour and expenses. For example, when cloth is produced in a mill, money is spent upon cotton, and other chief materials like caustic soda, soda ash, etc., and wages are paid to workers in the carding department, spinning department, weaving department and dyeing and finishing departments. But in addition to these two main items, expenditure must also be incurred by way of rent, depreciation of machinery, power, supervision, stationery, clerical labour, advertisements, etc. These 'classes' of cost are called 'elements of cost'.

The following definition given by the Chartered Institute of Management Accountants of England should be noted.

Elements of Cost: "*The primary classification of costs according to the factors upon which expenditure is incurred, viz., materials cost, wages (labour cost) and expenses.*"

Materials Cost: "*The cost of commodities supplied to an undertaking.*"

Wages (Labour Cost): "*The cost of remuneration (wages, salaries, commissions, bonus, etc.) of the employees of an undertaking.*"

Expenses: "*The cost of services provided to an undertaking and the notional cost of the use of owned assets.*"

Direct and Indirect Expenses

It is usual to distinguish the total expenditure into two categories—direct and indirect. Direct expenditure is that which can be conveniently allocated to a particular job or product or unit of service. For example, when a book is printed it is rather easy to know how much money has been spent on the paper used and also on wages paid to the workers who were engaged in composing the matter, proof reading and machining the book. Making of some blocks can also be put down to that book. Such are the instances of direct expenditure. But in addition to these expenses, there will be a number of other expenses which will be incurred not for the sole purpose of the book but for the benefit of all the work which is going on. For example, the building is used for all the work done. Therefore, it is not easy to say what exact amount out of rent is to be allocated to the book. Similarly, the wages of clerical labour, supervisory staff, etc. cannot be easily allocated. Such expenses are known as indirect expenditure and it can be defined as that expenditure which cannot be conveniently allocated to a particular product or a job or a unit of service and which is incurred for the benefit of output generally.

The distinction between direct and indirect expenses turns largely on convenience. We can find out the share of an article in large number of expenses incurred, but the time and money spent on this may be out of all proportion to the benefits obtained. We may obtain reasonably. correct figure of cost by treating such difficult cases as indirect. Also, the nature of the business will determine what is Direct Cost and what is Indirect Expenses. In case of big contracts, for example, almost one entire expenditure is direct, while in a firm manufacturing a large variety of articles, most of the expenditure, apart from materials and labour, will be indirect.

Direct Expenditure is made up of :

(1) Direct Materials;

(2) Direct labour; and

(3) Direct Expenses or Charges

Indirect Expenditure can be classified into:

(1) Works or Factory Expenses;

(2) Office and Administrative Expenses; and

(3) Selling and Distributive Expenses.

Direct Materials. Materials which directly enter the product and from a part of finished product are direct materials. These can be identified in the product and can be measured and directly charged to the product. Examples of direct materials are timber in furniture making, cloth in dress making and pig-iron in foundry.

Indirect Materials. Materials which are used for maintenance and repair of machinery, the running of service department, spare and components, packing materials etc. are indirect materials. These do not normally form a part of the finished product.

Direct Labour. Labour is treated as direct if it can be conveniently allocated to different jobs or products, etc. If we know how much time a worker spent on each of the various jobs he undertook during a particular period, his wages would be treated as direct. Thus wages of workers put on definite jobs or products will be direct.

Indirect Labour. Wages which cannot be allocated to different jobs or products are treated as indirect labour. Indirect wages are a part of factory expenses. Wages paid to watch and ward staff, repair gangs, supervisor, etc. are indirect.

Other Direct Expenses or Charges. Expenses which can be allocated conveniently to a unit of cost (other than direct materials and direct labour) are called other direct expenses or charges. Carriage on materials bought for particular job (if not included in the cost of materials) will be direct charge. Royalty paid on the basis of quantity of goods produced is another example of direct expenses.

Manufacturing (Works or Factory) Expenses or Overheads. The term manufacturing include all operations and process starting from the receipt of raw materials and ending with storage of finished good. All expenses incurred in these operations and process, other than direct materials, direct labour and other direct expenses are classified as manufacturing or works expenses. Some examples are depreciation on plant and machinery, depreciation on works building, insurance charges and repair of plant machinery and factory building, power consumption coal and other fuel charges.

Thus all expenses incurred inside a factory and for the benefit of manufacture as such will be included in factory expenses. The following are some of the items so included.

1. Wages paid to indirect workers such as watch and ward staff, repair gangs, foremen etc.
2. Works manager's salary and fees paid to directors devoting their attention to production problems.
3. Work's canteen and welfare activities.
4. Contribution to Employees' State Insurance Corporation and Provident Funds.
5. Cost of indirect materials, carriage inward on such materials, materials of small value.
6. Buying and store-keeping expenses including value of normal losses.
7. Factory rent and rates, insurance and repairs of factory premises and plants, etc.
8. Power and fuel (coal, gas, electricity, etc.) factory lighting.
9. Depreciation on plant and machinery, factory premises, etc.

Office and Administrative Overheads. All expenses relating to general administration (not connected with production or sales) will be included in 'Office and Administrative Overheads'. The usual items comprised in these overheads are as following:

1. Salaries of the general manager, finance manager, the accountents, the secretary and their staff, clerks etc.
2. Office rent and rates and repairs and depreciation of office premises and office equipments. Power used by office equipments.
3. Insurance of office premises and equipments.
4. Fees of directors (other than those connected with sales or production)

5. Telephone, telegrams and postage, printing and stationary.
6. Legal charges, Audit fees, Bank charges etc.

Selling and Distribution Overheads. Selling expenses are expenses of seeking to create and stimulate demand and of securing orders. Distribution expenses are expense incurred in moving the goods from the company's godowns to the customers premises. Selling and distribution expenses form no part of the cost of production but a considerable proporton of the price of the product is taken up by them. The usual items included is selling and distribution expenses are as follows:

1. Salaries of the sales manager and his staff including his office staff and his salesmen.
2. Travelling expenses and commission payable to salesmen.
3. Advertising and showroom expenses including rent and lighting.
4. Printing of catalogues and price lists and general stationary.
5. Rent of finished goods godowns and their repairs, etc.
6. Bad debts, legal charges for recovery of debts.
7. Packing and carriage outwards, insurance in transit
8. Fees of sales directors.
9. Depreciation, repairs and running expenses of delivery vans.
10. Telephone and postage, etc. of sales department.
11. Subscriptions to mercantile agencies and trade journals.

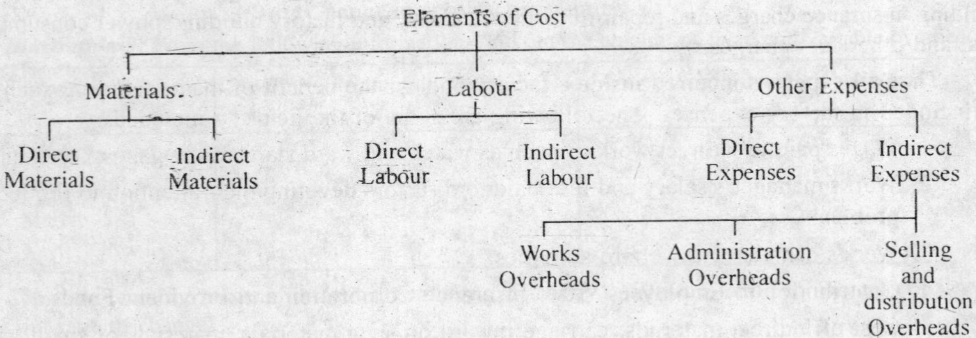

In small concerns office expenses and selling expenses may be grouped together.

The total of the Direct Expenditure—Direct Materials, Direct Labour and Direct Expenses—is known as *Prime cost* or Flat Cost.

Prime cost *plus* Works or Factory Expenses is known as *Works Cost* or Manufacturing Cost or Factory Cost.

Works Cost *plus* Office and Administrative Cost is called Gross or *Office Cost* or *Cost of Production.*

Cost of Production *plus* Selling and Distributive Expenses is *Cost of Sales.* This differs from Selling Price. Selling Price is equal to Cost of Sales *plus* Net Profit (or minus loss).

Conversion Cost : The sum of direct wages, direct expenses and factory expences is known as conversion cost.

These terms should be carefully noted and their misuse avoided. For convenience, the various costs of a manufacturing concern are given ahead:

Chart Showing Classification of Expenses

	Expenses	Cost
(A)	Direct Materials Direct Labour Direct Expenses	Prime Cost
(B)	Works Expenses, such as Indirect Materials Indirect Labour Rent and Taxes of Factory Premises Depreciation Repairs Fuel and Power, etc.	Works or Factory Cost, *i.e.* (A) + (B) (Also, often Production Cost)
(C)	Office Expenses, such as Office Rent and Rates Stationery Directions Fees, etc.	Office Cost. *i.e.* (A) + (B) + (C) or Cost of Production
(D)	Selling Expenses, such as Sales Staff Salaries Show Room Expenses Advertising Carriage Outwards Packing Bad Debts	Cost of Sales, *i.e.*, (A) + (B) + (C) + (D)
(E)	Plus Profit (or minus loss)	Selling Price *i.e.*, (A) + (B) + (C) + (D) + (E)

The undermentioned definitions given by the *CIMA*, London should also be noted.

Prime Cost: "The aggregate of direct materials cost, direct wages (direct labour cost) and valuable direct expenses".

Direct Materials Cost: "Materials cost which can be identified with and allocated to cost centres or cost units".

Direct Expenses: "Expenses which can be identified with and allocated to cost centres or cost units".

Production Cost: "The cost of the sequence of operations which begins with supplying materials, labour and services and ends with primary packing of the product".

Cost of Sales: "The cost which is attributable to the sales made".

Total Cost: "The sum of all costs attributable to the unit under consideration".

Expenses Excluded from Costs: The total cost of a product should include only those items of expenses which form part of cost of production and which are charged against profit. Item of expenses which are appropriation or apportionment of profit should not form a part of the costs. These are (*i*) Income Tax, (*ii*) Dividend to shareholders, (*iii*) Commission to partners, managing agents etc. (*iv*) Capital losses, (*v*) Interest on capital (under certain circumstances), (*vi*) Interest paid on debentures, and (*vii*) Capital expenses, etc.

Treatment of Stock

Stocks are generally of three categories (*i*) Raw Materials, (*ii*) Work-in-Progress, and (*iii*) Finished Goods.

Stocks of Raw Materials: should be adjusted in order to find out cost of comsumption of raw materials:

Value of Raw Materials Consumed = Opening Stock of Raw Materials + Net purchases – Closing Stock of Raw Materials.

Work-in-progress is quantity of semi-finished goods at the time of finding out total cost of production (say preparation of cost-sheet). Work-in-progress usually consists of (*i*) Cost of materials to date, (*ii*) Cost of labour to date and (*iii*) manufacturing expenses to date. The amount of work-in-progress consumed (or in excess) is excess of opening balance of work-in-progress over closing work-in-progress (*i.e.*, opening work-in-progress should be added and closing work-in-progress should be substracted from the works cost).

Opening stock and closing stock of furnished goods should be adjusted in the cost of production to find out cost of goods sold i.e., cost of production + opening stock of finished goods – closing stock of finished goods = cost of goods sold.

Information in a *Statement of cost* is presented in a manner different from that employed in a Trading and P & L Account. In a *Cost Sheet* information about each element of cost per unit should also be given.

Statement of Cost / Cost Sheet		₹	₹
Raw Materials:			
Opening Stock of Raw Materials		✓	
Raw Materials purchases		✓	
Cost of Materials available for use		✓	
Less: Closing Stock of Raw Materials		(✓)	
Cost of Raw Materials used/consumed			✓
Direct Labour/Wages			✓
Other Direct Charges			✓
	Prime Cost		✓
Factory Overheads:			
Indirect Materials		✓	
Indirect Labour		✓	
Depreciation on Factory Building		✓	
Depreciation on Factory Equipments		✓	
Insurance		✓	
Repairs and Maintenance		✓	
Other Factory Overheads		✓	✓
	Gross Factory Cost		✓
Add Work-in-Progress (opening)			✓
Less Work-in-Progress (closing)			(✓)
	Factory Cost		✓
Office and Administration Overheads			
Office Salaries		✓	
Office Rent, Insurance		✓	
Other Ofice Overheads		✓	✓
	Office Cost/Cost of Production		✓
Add Opening Stock of Finished Goods			✓
Goods available for Sale			✓
Less Closing Stock of Furnished Goods			(✓)
	Cost of Goods Sold		✓
Selling and Distribution Expenses			✓
	Cost of Sales		✓
	Profit		✓
	Sales		✓

Illustration 1:

Prepare a Statement of Cost from the following particulars :

	₹
Opening Stock of Raw Materials	10,500.00
Closing Stock of Raw Materials	15,000.00
Purchase of Raw Materials	39,000.00
Direct Expenses	2,600.00
Labour	23,900.00
Fuel and Power	2,500.00
Directors Fees	3,000.00
Carriage Inward	1,750.00
Indirect Wages	5,000.00
Office Salaries	6,600.00
Rent, Rates & Taxes (Factory)	2,000.00
Rent, Rates (Office)	900.00
Depreciation & Repairs of Plant	15,700.00
Insurance (Factory)	900.00
Stationary (Factory)	1,050.00
Sundry Expenses	2,700.00
Stationary (Office)	875.00
Depreciation of Office Furniture	325.00
Travellers Expenses & Salaries	5,000.00
Showroom Expenses	2,000.00
Packing	6,000.00
Carriage Outwards	4,000.00
Stationery (Selling)	500.00
Bad Debts	1,200.00
Sales	1,67,000.00

Solution:

Statement of Cost

	₹	₹
Raw Materials:		
Stock at the beginning	10,500.00	
Add: Purchases	39,000.00	
Raw Materials available for use	49,500.00	
Less: Stock at the end	(15,000.00)	
Materials used		34,500.00
Labour		23,900.00
Direct Expenses		2,600.00
Prime Cost		61,000.00
Factory Overheads:		
Factory Expenses:		
Fuel and Power	2,500.00	
Carriage Inward	1,750.00	
Indirect Wages	5,000.00	
Depreciation & Repairs	15,700.00	
Rates and Taxes	2,000.00	
Insurance	900.00	
Stationery	1,050.00	28,900.00
Works Cost		89,900.00

Office and Admn. Overheads:		
Office Expenses:		
Directors Fees	3,000.00	
Office Salaries	6,600.00	
Rent, Rates etc.	900.00	
Sundry Expenses	2,700.00	
Stationery	875.00	
Depreciation of Office Furniture	325.00	14,400
Office Cost		1,04,300.00
Selling and Dirtribution Expenses:		
Travellers' Expenses & Salaries	5,000.00	
Showroom Expenses	2,000.00	
Packing	6,000.00	
Carriage Outwards	4,000.00	
Stationery	500.00	
Bad Debts	1,200.00	18,700.00
Cost of Sales		1,23,000.00
Profit		44,000.00
Selling Pice		1,67,000.00

Illustration 2:

Prepare the cost sheet to show total cost of production and cost per unit of goods manufactured by a company for the month of July, 2010. Also find out the cost of sales.

	₹		₹
Stock of Raw Materials 1.7.2000	3,000.00	Factory rent and rates	3,000.00
Raw Materials purchased	28,000.00	Office rent	500.00
Stock of Raw Materials 31.7.2000	4500.00	General expenses	400.00
Manufacturing wages	7,000.00	Discount on sales	300.00
Depreciation of plant	1,500.00	Advertisement exp. to be fully charged	600.00
Loss on sale of a part of plant	300.00	Income Tax paid	2,000.00

The number of units produced during the month of July, 2010 was 3,000. The stock of finished goods was 200 and 400 units on 1.7.2000 and 31.7.2000 respectively. The total cost of units on hand on 1.7.2000 was ₹ 2,800. All these have been sold during the month.

Solution:

Cost Sheet

Output 3000 Units

Particulars		*Total Cost*	*Cost per unit*
	₹	₹	₹
Raw Materials Consumed			
Opening stock	3,000.00		
Add: Purchases	28,000.00		
Less: Closing stock	(4,500.00)	26,500.00	8.83
Direct wages		7,000.00	2.33
Prime Cost		33,500.00	11.16

Factory overheads			
Depreciation	1,500.00		
Factory Rent	3,000.00	4,500.00	1.50
Factory Cost		38,000.00	12.66
Office and Administration overheads			
Office Rent	500.00		
General Expenses	400.00	900.00	0.30
Cost of Production		38,900.00	12.96

Statement of Cost of Sales

Cost of production		38,900.00
Add: Opening stock of finished goods		2,800.00
Cost of Goods Available for Sales		41,700.00
Less: Closing stock of finished goods (400 × ₹. 12.96)		5,184.00
Cost of Goods Sold		36,516.00
Add: Selling and Distribution overheads		
Discount on Sales	300.00	
Advertisement Exps.	600.00	900.00
Cost of Sales		37416.00

Illustration 3:

The following extract of costing information relates to commodity 'A' for the half year ending 31st December, 2008.

	₹.
Purchases of Raw Materials	1,20.000
Rent. Rates, Insurance and Works on Cost	40,000
Direct Wages	1,00,000
Carriage Inward	1,440
Stock 1st July 2008	
Raw Materials	20,000
Finished Products–1,000 tons	16,000
Stock 31st December, 2008	
Raw Materials	22,240
Finished Products–2,000 tons	32,000
Works-in-Progress:	
1st July, 2008	4,800
31st Dec., 2008	16,000
Sales of Finished Products	3,00,000
Cost of Factory Supervision	8,000

Advertising, discount allowed and selling exps. cost ₹. 1 per ton sold. 16,000 tons of commodity were produced during the period.

You are to ascertain (*i*) The net profit for the period, (*ii*) The net profit per ton of the commodity, (*iii*) The cost of output for the period, (*iv*) The value of raw materials used and (*v*) The cost of turnover for the period.

Solution:

Statement of Cost
For six months ending 31st Dec. 2008

	₹	₹
Value of Raw Material Used:		
Stock of raw materials on 1st July	20,000	
Add: Purchases of raw material	1,20.000	
Add: Carriage inwards	1,440	
Raw Material Available for use	1,41,440	
Less: Stock of raw materials on 31st Dec.	(22,240)	
		1,19,200
Direct Wages		1,00,000
Prime Cost		2,19,200
Works on Cost:		
Cost of Factory Supervision 8,000		
Rent, Rates, Insurance, work on cost	40,000	48,000
Gross Works Cost		2,67,200
Add: Work-in-progress on 1st July		4,800
		2,72,000
Less: Work-in-progress on 31st Dec.		(16,000)
Work Cost or Cost of Production (16,000 tons)		2,56,000
Add: Opening stock of finished product (1,000 tons)		16,000
Cost of Goods Available for Sales		2,72,000
Less: Closing stock of finished product (2,000 tons)		(32,000)
Cost of Goods Sold (15,000 tons)		2,40,000
Add: Advertising, discount & selling cost @ ₹ 1 per ton sold (15,000 ton)		15,000
Cost of Sales or Turnover		2,55,000
Net Profit		45,000
Selling Price		3,00,000

Illustration 4:

A manufacturer finds that an increase in the cost of production has taken place and that, whereas formerly his goods cost on sales —Raw materials 30%; Wages 20%; Rent, Rates etc. 5%; Fuel 10%; General expenses 15%. Now there has been an increase of 50% in fuel, 30% in materials, 25% in wages and 20% in Rent and Rates, etc. He consults you as to what percentage he must add to the selling price in order to obtain the same ratio profit. What would be the result of your calculation and how would you prove to him that they are correct?

Solution:

Former Elements of Cost

Material	30%
Wages	20%
Rent and Rates	5%
Fuel	10%
Gen exps.	15%
Total	80%
Profit	20%
Selling Price	100%

Here profit is 20% on Sales or 25% on Total Cost.		
Now Increased Cost of Production		
Materials	30% + 30% of it =	39
Wages	20% + 25% of it =	25
Rent & Rates etc.	5% + 20% of it =	06
Fuel	10% + 50% of it =	15
Gen. Exps.	15%	15
Total Cost		100
Profit		25
Selling Price		125

In order to obtain the same profit (i.e. 25% on Total Cost) the Selling Price should be increased by 25%.

Illustration 5:

The Modern Manufacturing Co. submits the following information on 31st March, 2010.

	₹.
Sales for the year	2,75.000
Inventory at the beginning of the year	
Finished Goods	7,000
Work-in-progress	4,000
Purchase of materials for the year	1,10,000
Materials inventory at the beginning of the year	3,000
Materials inventory at the end of the year	4,000
Direct labour	65,000
Factory overheads were 60% of the direct labour cost	
Inventories at the end of the year	
Work-in-Progress	6,000
Finished goods	8,000
Other Expenses for the year	
Selling Expenses 10% of sales	
Administrative Exps. 5% of sales	

Prepare a statement of cost.

Solution:

Statement of Cost of Modern Manufacturing Co.
for The Year Ending 31st March, 2010

		₹.
Materials Consumed		
Inventory at the beginning of the year	3,000	
Add: Purchase	1,10,000	
Materials available for Consumption	1,13,000	
Less: Inventory at end	4000	1,09,000
Direct Labour		65,000
	Prime Cost	1,74,000
Factory overhead @ 60% of Direct Labour		39,000
	Gross Works Cost	2,13,000
Add: Work-in-Progress at the beginning		4,000
Less: Work-in-Progress at end		(– 6000)
	Works Cost	2,11,000
Add: Administrative Expenses		13,750
	Cost of Proauction	2,24,750

Profit or Loss Statement for the Year Ending 31st, March, 2003

		₹.
Cost of Production		2,24,750
Add: Opening inventory of finished goods		7,000
Finished Goods available for sale		2,31,750
Less: Closing inventory of finished goods		8,000
	Cost of Goods Sold	2,23.750
Add: Selling Expenses @ 10% of sales		27,500
	Cost of Sales	2,51,250
Profit (₹. 2,75,000–2,51,250)		23,750
	Sales	2,75,000

Illustration: 6

The books and records of the Anand Manufacturing Co. present the following data for the month of August.

Direct Labour Cost: ₹. 16,000 (160% of factory overhead)

Cost of goods sold ₹. 56,000

Inventory accounts showed these opening and closing balances

	August 1	August, 31
	₹.	₹.
Raw materials	8,000	8,600
Work-in-Progress	8,000	12,000
Finished goods	14,000	18,000
Other data		
Selling Expenses		3,400
General and Administrative Exps.		2,600
Sales for the month		75,000

You are required to prepare and statement showing cost of goods manufactured and sold, and profit earned. **[*CA Inter*]**

Solution:

Anand Manufacturing Co.
Statement of Cost and Profit Earned for the Month of August

		₹.	₹.
Raw Materials consumed			
Opening Stock		8,000	
Add: Purchases		36,000	
		44,000	
Less: Closing Stock		(8,600)	35,400
Direct labour			16,000
	Prime Cost		51,400
Factory Overhead (16000 × 100/160)			10,000
	Gross Factory Cost		61,400
Add: Opening work-in-Progress			8,000
Less: Closing work-in-Progress			(12,000)
	Factory Cost		57,400
Add: General and Administrative Expenses			2,600
	Cost of Production		60,000
Add: Opening Stock of finished goods			14,000
			74,000
Less: Closing Stock of finished goods			(18,000)
	Cost of Goods Sold		56,000

Add: Selling Expenses	3,400
Cost of Sales	59,400
Profit	15,600
Sales	75,000

Illustration 7:

The following figures are extraded from the trial balance of Gogether on 30th September, 2010.

	₹.	₹.
Inventories		
Finished Stock	80,000	
Raw-Materials	1,40,000	
Work-in-Process	2,00,000	
Office Appliances	17,400	
Plant and Machinery	4,60,500	
Building	2,00,000	
Sales		7,68,000
Sales Returns and rebates	14,000	
Materials Purchased	3,20,000	
Frieght incurred on materials	16,000	
Purchase Returns		4,800
Direct Labour	1,60,000	
Indirect Labour	18,000	
Factory Supervision	10,000	
Repairs and Upkeep-factory	14,000	
Heat, Light and Power	65,000	
Rates and Taxes	6,300	
Miscellaneous Factory Expenses	18,700	
Sales Commission	33,600	
Sales Travelling	11,000	
Sales Promotion	22,500	
Distribution Deptt.—Salaries and Expenses	18,000	
Office Salaries and Expenses	8,600	
Interest on Borrowed Funds	2,000	

Further details are available as follows

(*i*) Closing inventories

Finished Goods	1,15,000
Raw Materials	1,80,000
Work-in-Process	1,92,000

(*ii*) Accrued Expenses on

Direct Labour	8000
Indirect Labour	1,200
Interest on Borrowed Funds	2,000

(*iii*) Depreciation to be provided on: Office appliance 5%; Plant 10%; Building 4%.

(*iv*) Distribution of the following: Depreciation on Building; Heat, Light and Power to factory, office and distribution in the ratio of 8 : 1 : 1.

(*v*) Rates and taxes 2/3 to factory and 1/3 to office.

With the help of above information, you are required to prepare a condensed Profit & Loss Statement of Gogether Co. for the year ending 30th September, 2004 along with supporting schedules of (*i*) Cost of Sales, (*ii*) Selling & Distribution Expenses, and (*iii*) Administration Expenses. ***(CA Inter)***

Solution:

Gogether Co.
Profit & Loss Statement for the Year Ended 30th Sept. 2010

	₹.	₹.
Gross Sales	7,68,000	
Less: Sales Return	(14,000)	7,54,000
Less: Cost of Sales [As per Schedule (1)]		7,14,020
Profit		39,980
Less: Interest on Borrowed Funds		4,000
Net Profit		35,980

Schedule 1
Schedule of Cost of Sales

		₹.
Raw Materials Consumed		
Opening Inventory of Raw Materials		1,40,000
Add: Purchase		3,20,000
Add: Frieght on Materials		16,000
Less: Purchase Return		(4,800)
Less: Closing Inventory of Raw Material		(1,80,000)
		2,91,200
Direct Labour		1,68,000
Prime Cost		4,59,200
Factory Overheads		
Indirect Labour	19,200	
Factory Supervision	10,000	
Repairs and factory upkeep	14,000	
Heat, light and power	52,000	
Rates and Taxes	4,200	
Misc. Factory Exps.	18,700	
Depreciation of plant	46,050	
Depreciation of Buildings	6,400	1,70,550
Gross Work Cost		6,29,750
Add: Opening Work-in-Process Inventory	2,00,000	
		8,29,750
Less: Closing Work-in-Process Inventory		(1,92,000)
Works Cost		6,37,750
Add: Administration Expenses [As per Schedule (*iii*)]		18,870
Cost of Production		6,56,620
Add: Opening Finished Goods Inventory		80,000
		7,36,620
Less: Closing Finished Goods Inventory		(1,15,000)
Cost of Goods Sold		6,21,620
Add: Selling and Distribution Expenses [As per Schedule (*II*)]		92,400
Cost of Sales		7,14,020

Schedule II
Schedule of Selling & Distribution Exps.

Sales Commission	33,600
Sales Travelling	11,000
Sales Promotion	22,500
Distribution Deptt.—Salaries & Exps.	18,000
Heat Light & Power	6,500
Depreciation of Building	800
	(₹.) 92,400

Schedule III
Schedule Of Administrative Exps.

Office Salaries and Expenses	8,600
Depreciation of Office Appliances	870
Depreciation of Building	800
Heat Light and Power	6,500
Rate and Taxes	2,100
	(₹.) 18,870

Illustration 8: Popeye Company is a metal and wood cutting manufacturer, selling products to the home construction market. Consider the following data for the month of October, 2004:

	₹.
Sandpaper	5,000
Material-handling Costs	1,75,000
Lubricants and Coolants	12,500
Miscellaneous Indirect Manufacturing Labour	1,00,000
Direct Manufacturing Labour	7,50,000
Direct Materials, October 1, 2004	1,00,000
Direct Materials, October 31, 2004	1,25,000
Finished Goods, October 1, 2004	2,50,000
Finished Goods, October 31, 2004	3,75,000
Work-in-Process, October 1, 2004	25,000
Work-in-Process, October 31, 2004	35,000
Plant-Leasing Costs	1,35,000
Depreciation-Plant Equipment	90,000
Property Taxes on Plant Equipment	10,000
Fire Insurance on Plant Equipment	7,500
Direct Materials Purchased	11,50,000
Sales Revenues	34,00,000
Marketing Promotions	1,50,000
Marketing Salaries	2,50,000
Distribution Costs	1,75,000
Customer-Service Costs	2,50,000

Required:

(*i*) Prepare an income statement with a separate supporting schedule of cost of goods manufactured.

(*ii*) For all manufacturing items, indicate by V or F whether each is basically a variable cost or a fixed cost (where the cost object is a product unit). ***(CAPE II Nov. 2004)***

Solution:

Popeye Co.
Schedule for Cost of Good Manufactured
for the Month of October 2004

	₹.	₹.
Direct Materials		
Beginning Inventory	10,000	
Purchase of Direct Materials	1,15,000	
Cost of Direct Materials available	1,25,000	
Ending Inventory	(12,500)	1,12,500 (V)
Direct Manufacturing Labour	75,000 (V)	
Indirect Manufacturing Cost		
Sand Paper	5,000 (V)	
Material Handling Cost	1,75,000 (V)	
Lubricants and Coolants	12,500 (V)	
Misc. Indirect Mg. Labour	1,00,000 (V)	
Plant Leasing Cost	1,35,000 (F)	
Dep on Plant and Equipment	90,000 (F)	
Property Tax–Plant and Equipment	10,000 (F)	
Fire Insurance–Plant and Equip.	7,500 (F)	5,35,000
Gross Manufacturing Cost		24,10,000
Add Opening Work in Progress		25,000
		24,35,000
Less Closing Work-in-Progress		(35,000)
Cost of Goods Manufactured		24,00,000

Income Statement

	₹.	₹.
Sales Revenues		34,00,000
Cost of Goods Sold		
Beginning Finished good	2,50,000	
Cost of Goods Manufacture	24,00,000	
Cost of Goods Available	26,50,000	
Ending Finished Goods	(3,75,000)	22,75,000
Gross Margin		11,25,000
Marketing distribution and customer Service Costs		
Marketing Promotion	1,50,000	
Marketing Cost	2,50,000	
Distribution Cost	1,75,000	
Customer Service Cost	2,50,000	8,25,000
Operating Income		3,00,000

COST DEPENDS ON CIRCUMSTANCES

The term 'cost' does not have a fixed meaning and, therefore, what items will be added to arrive at the cost will depend on the objective and the circumstances. For example, usually interest on investment is not treated as part of cost but, in case a quotation is to be sent and competition is not stiff, interest may be added to the other costs. For fixing the selling prices in normal times, all costs—labour, material, factory expenses, administrative expenses, and selling expenses are added; but in case there are difficulties in selling or the need is to utilise idle capacity, many expenses (fixed expenses) may be ignored. For valueing inventory, some firms add office and administrative expenses; others do not. Hence, it is not sufficient to say, e.g. that the cost of such and such article is ₹. .... One should really also state what the figure comprises. Cost differs in different circumstances and for different purposes. That is why *Horngren in his book Cost Accounting–A Managerial Approach* talks of "relevant cost".

TYPES OF COSTING

As we proceed with our study we will see that various techniques are applied for ascertaining costs and the word "costs" will itself mean one thing at one time and a different thing at another time. According to the techniques and processes used, the following types of costing may be noted.

(*a*) *Historical Costing:* The ascertainment of costs after they have been incurred is called historical costing. This would indicate, for instance, how much was spent on producing goods in the previous month.

(*b*) *Direct Costing:* The practice of charging all direct costs to operations, processes or products, leaving all indirect costs to be written off against profits in the period in which they arise, is known as direct costing.

(*c*) *Absorption Costing:* The practice of charging variable costs to operations, processes or products is absorption costing. This differs from (*a*) and (*b*) above because in absorption costing fixed costs are excluded.

(*d*) *Uniform Costing:* When a number of enterprises engaged in manufacture of similar or same products or services sometimes form on association and introduced a common method and form of cost accounting to be utilised by all members, it is called uniform costing system. This method of costing provides reliable data for making inter-firm comparison of cost performance. It also measures cost of production for the industry as a whole. It facilitates comparison of the cost of production and the production efficiency between one unit and other. The working of an uniform costing system depends on the cooperation of different units in the industry.

(*e*) *Marginal Costing:* It has also been designated as "Differential Costing" or "Direct Costing". Under this system `fixed costs' is isolated from 'variable cost' Marginal cost is Direct Material, Direct Labour, Direct Expenses plus variable overhead *i.e.* it is total cost less fixed overheads. The system can be followed by any industry where the fixed and variable costs can be separated by analysis. Marginal cost shows the additional amount to be spent if one more unit produced.

(*f*) *Standard Costing:* Standard costing is a system which seeks to control the cost of each unit or batch through determination beforehand of what should be the cost and then its comparison with actual cost. Thus standard costs may be defined as pre-determined or budgeted costs of a unit of a product or a job, Standard costs may be fixed on an idealistic basis assuming that everyone will perform at utmost efficiency or it may be fixed on the basis of past average performance.

Cost Units

The Costing Terminology issued by the Chartered Institute of Management Accountants (*CIMA*) defines, cost-unit as `a unit of quantity of product, service or time (or a combination of these) in relation to which costs may be ascertained or expressed. It is one of the primary objects of Cost Accounting to determines the cost of one unit of product. Choice of cost unit depends upon the nature of the product manufactured, methods of production and trade practices.

Each industry has a unit of its own for measurement of output of finished as well as semi-finished products. The cost of a product unit is the average cost obtained by dividing the total cost of the batch or product or process by the number of product units produced. We may, for instance, determine the cost per ton of coal, per ton kilometer of a transport or cost per machine hour. The forms of measurement used as cost units are normally units of physical measurement like number, length, weight area, time etc. Following are some examples of cost-units.

	Industry/Product	*Cost Unit basis*
1.	Steel	Ton
2.	Sugar	Ton
3.	Cement	Tons 1 Kg.
4.	Chemical	Litre, Kg., Ton
5.	Brick works	1000 bricks
6.	Automobiles	Number
7.	Cosmetics	Grams, Jars or Tubes
8.	Cotton and Jute	Bales
9.	Electricity	Killowatt hours
10.	Gas	1000 Cu. ft.
11.	Mineral waters	Cases or 24 bottles
12.	Printing	1000 impressions
13.	Shoes	Pairs
14.	Timber	Cu. meters, tons
15.	Yarns	Killograms or meters

Cost Centre

Cost centre has been defined as 'a location' persons or item of equipment (or group of these) for which costs may be ascertained and used for the purpose of cost control. Cost centre is a segment of a plant or in some cases an entire plant, which is treated as a functional units for the purpose of applying process overhead. It may be a single work point, such as a machine, a group of work points smaller than a department a processing department or an entire plant.

Cost control is exercised by individuals and groups on the shop floors and in offices. It is, therefore, necessary to define and to delimit the functions, the area of control, and responsibility of such individuals and groups. The concept of cost centre is meant to provide this definition of function and control. The purpose of creating cost centres is to accumulate and control costs by subdivisions of the plant and distribute then to products in the most equitable manner.

So far as plant is concerned, cost centres fall under two categories, namely *productive cost centres and service cost centres*. A *productive cost centre* is directly engaged in productive activity and may consist of similar items of equipment. A cost centre based on similarity of operations is called an operation cost centre. A process consisting of series of operations may constitute a cost centre called *process cost centre*. The costing terminology defines operation cost centre as 'a cost centre which consists of those machines and/or, persons carrying out similar operations. 'A process cost centre is a cost centre which consists of a specific process or a continuous sequence of operations'.

Service cost centres are those cost centres which are not directly engaged in productive work, but provide services to productive cost centres so that production work may be carried out. Steam plant, power plant, repair and maintenance department, etc. are examples of service cost centres.

Costs of service cost-centres (Service departments) are apportioned to productive cost-centres (production departments) on equitable basis. Costs of the productive cost centres together with cost transferred from services cost centres are finally charged to all cost-unit handled by the respective productive cost centres.

Cost centres can also to be defined as Personal Cost Centres and Impersonal Cost Centres. A *personal cost centre* is a cost centre which consists of a person or group of persons'. Inspections, time-study engineers, maintenance engineers etc., may constitute separate personal cost centre which consists of a location or item of equipment (or group of these). Sales territories are examples of Impersonal cost centre.

There is no hard and fast rule as to how many cost centres will be created in a plant. Closer control and greater accuracy of cost absorption are achieved by increasing the number of cost-centre.

Cost Allocation and Cost Apportionment

The process of charging costs either to works orders or to cost centres is called cost allotment. It is made in two ways either by allocation or by apportionment. *Cost Allocation* has been defined as `the allotment of whole items or costs to cost centres or cost units'. *Cost Apportionment* is defined as `the allotment of proportions of items of cost to cost centres or cost units'.

The costs which are allocated to a cost centre are direct costs from the standpoint of the cost-centre. When costs are jointly incurred by more than one cost centres, their costs are apportioned to them either on the basis of actual incurrence of cost or on an equitable basis. These are indirect costs so far as cost centres are concerned.

Cost Estimation and Cost Ascertainment

Cost estimation is the process of computing the probable cost of a job or article under a given set of conditions; while cost ascertainment is the computation of actual cost after the expenditure has been incurred and the job has been executed or the articles made. Cost estimation forms the basis for controlling the costs of production of a business, since the cost incurred should closely approximate to the estimates, and whether or not they do so can only be determined if the actual costs are ascertained.

Both cost estimation and cost ascertainment are important to a manufacturing concern for the following reasons : (*i*) They provide a yard-stick against which current efficiency can be measured, (*ii*) the particular stages at which waste of time and materials occur are revealed, (*iii*) expenditure can be controlled while the work is still in progress and any possible economies made before it is too late, (*iv*) where a new product is being placed on the market, the selling price can be determined by cost estimate and costs controlled by the company, the actual costs of production of the first batch with estimates, thus ensuring that the selling price of the new product is profitable one.

Miscellaneous Costing Terms

Responsibility Centre. Cost centre delineate spheres of responsibility. Some accountants prefer to term cost centre as responsibility centre because the manager incharge of a cost centre is held responsible for the control of costs of that centre. There is controlling function of costs with relation to cost centre which makes it responsibility centre.

As it has been explained earlier, cost centre is a location, person or item of equipment (or group of these) for which cost may be ascertained and used for the purpose of cost control.

Cost centres or responsibility centre are meant to assemble at one recovery area, all costs for which a common base of recovery can be reasonably used. For example, a machine or group of machines performing identical functions may be constituted into an equipment type of cost centre. Such a cost or responsibility centre would form a compact group for the recovery of overhead costs on the basis of machine hours.

Profit Centre. Different cost centres when taken into a group headed by an individual or manager, who will be fully responsible for all cost, revenues and profitabilities of operation, the group is known as profit centre. Profit centres are created to facilitate management control and implementation of responsibility accounting. It is to be noted that cost centres are created for the convenience of accounting the costs and their effective control, while these are combined into profit centres for ascertaining profitability under a separate unit manager.

Opportunity Cost. Opportunity cost is `the opportunities which have been forgone by following one course of action rather than an alternative course; it considers the profit foregone by utilising scarce resources for one particular course of action.' These refer to costs which result from an alternative use of material, labour or other facilities which have been rejected or forgone due to not using the facilities in the mannar originally planned. If men, materials, plant, machinery and finance etc., when utilised in one way, yield a particular return but if used in another way may yield a different return. The original return which is no longer obtainable is the opportunity cost. For example, if fixed deposit in the bank are proposed to be withdrawn for financing a project, the opportunity cost would be the loss of interest on the deposit. The opportunity cost is computed only for comparison purposes in the context of decision-making and it finds no place in the formal accounts.

Imputed Costs or Hypothetical Cost. Imputed costs are hypothetical costs. They do not involve cash outlay and are computed only for the purpose of decision-making. Thus imputed costs are in a way similar to opportunity costs. Interest on capital which is not actually paid but included in the cost is an example of imputed costs. If two projects require equal outlays, their respective profitability would depend upon the respective periods during which capital would be tied up. On the other hand two projects requiring unequal outlays of capital, interest on capital and the cost of raising additional capital would be taken into account.

Sunk Cost and Shut Down Cost. Sunk cost are historical costs which are incurred or are sunk in the past and are not relevant to the particular decision-making problem being considered Sometimes a plant may be closed down permanently, then the total capital invested minus salvaged amount is lost—it is sunk or irrecoverable cost. Sunk cost is not affected by increase or decrease in volume.

Shut down costs are caused by closure of plant, or suspending the work for a short period due to some temporary problem *e.g.*, scarcity of raw materials shortage of labour etc. Although no work is carried out during this period, yet certain costs are incurred. These are for example depreciation, rent, maintenance of plant and building etc.

Replacement Cost. Replacement cost is the cost in the current market of material or asset. In other words the cost which would be incurred if the material or the asset was to be purchased at the current market price and not the cost at which it was actually purchased earlier, is replacement cost:

Incremental Cost or Differential Cost or Marginal Cost. It is that quantity of variable expense which is incurred to produce additional output above the normal capacity of the plant. In other words, if a change is made in the level or method of production, the resulting difference in the total cost is regarded as incremental or differential costs. The incremental costs are matched with incremental revenue (*i.e.* the increased income as result of change) in order to assess the profitability of the change.

Avoidable and Unavoidable Cost. Avoidable cost are those costs which should not have been incurred under stipulated conditions of work performance. For example, wastage of raw material above the normal limit fixed for wastage is avoidable cost. Unavoidable costs are the costs which cannot be avoidded or escaped or minimised. For example, normal wastage of material in the process of production is an unavoidable cost.

Conversion Cost. Conversion cost is the cost of production excluding direct materials, but including wastage in the direct material. It is total of direct labour, direct expenses and works overheads.

Controllable and Uncontrollable Cost. Every undertaking is divided into a number of responsibility centres. Each responsibility centre is in the charge of a manager or person. The manager can control only those costs which relate to items directly under his control and not other matters. Direct costs, comprising direct labour, direct material, direct expenses and some other overhead which are generally controllable by the shop-level management.

Uncontrollable costs are costs which cannot be influenced by the specified person of an undertaking. Costs of a service department which are apportioned to other departments are not controllable by these departments. For example, expenses of Tool Room is controllable by foremen of Tool Room but are uncontrollable by persons of other departments.

Estimated Costs and Standard Costs. Estimated costs are ascertained in advance or before the operations or even before the acceptance of sale orders. Estimated cost are used for the evaluation of performance by comparison with the actuals but are less accurate than the standard costs. Standard cost are predetermined cost based on standards for each element of cost and for each product, process or service. The standard cost is a predetermined cost which determines what each product or service should cost under given circumstances. Standard costs are basic to cost control, which is a essential part of management control. In this method actual costs incurred are compared with standard cost and reasons for difference or variations are found out so that management may take remedial measures to control the costs.

Product Costs and Period Costs. Costs which are assigned to products are Product Costs. Costs which are not assigned to products but are related to period or time are Period Costs. These are charged as expenses against the revenue of the period. All fixed manufacturing, general and administrative, selling and distribution costs are period cost because these are periodically incurred. But variable manufacturing overheads are normally not related to period but to products.

Cost Control. Cost control has been defined as `the guidance and regulation by executive action of the costs of operating an undertaking'. It is exercised by individuals or groups of people responsible for defined functions. Cost control is exercised through numerous techniques some of which are Standard Costing, Budgetary Control, Estimated Costing, Inventory Control, Quality Control and Performance Evaluation, Analysis and Reporting.

The ultimate aim of Cost Accounting is to achieve cost control. In cost control, the first step is to set up the target to be achieved *i.e.* the goal to be reached; the cost control system guides the organisation to reach that goal. If at any stage, it is noticed that the expenses showing a trend away from the goal, resulting thereby in a variation from the target, the cost control system helps to regulate this trend and to eliminate the variations.

The system of cost control, thus, requires certain steps: (*i*) To set up the target, (*ii*) To measure the actuals, (*iii*) To compare actuals with the targets, (*iv*) To localise the causes for the variation between the targets and the actuals, and (*v*) To take such actions as are necessary to eliminate these variations. In the first and last step viz. setting up of the targets, and taking the necessary action, the cost accountant plays only an indirect part inasmuch as he guides in the setting up of targets by giving all the relevant information necessary for the purpose, and keeps a watch on the progress of action taken, by periodically reviewing the extent of variation of the actuals from the targets.

For making cost control a success, the important factors to be taken care of are: (*i*) proper fixation of targets, (*ii*) timely presentation of comparison, and (*iii*) periodical review of results.

Basically there are two systems of cost control, viz. Budgetary Control System and Standard Costing System.[1]

Budgetary Control is the establishment of budgets relating the responsibilities of executives to the requirement of a policy and the continuous comparison of actuals with budgeted results either to secure by individual action the objective of that policy or to provide a basis for its revision.

Standard Cost is the predetermined cost based on technical estimate for material, labour and overhead for a selected period of time and for a prescribed set of working conditions. It also measures the variations from standard costs and analyses the causes for variations with a view to maintain maximum efficiency in production.

Cost Reduction[1] Cost reduction aims at reducing the targets themselves. The necessity for cost reduction arises when the profit margin has to be increased without an increase in the sales turnover *i.e.* for the same volume of sales the cost of sales should be reduced.

Cost reduction can be achieved through certain channels: (*i*) Increased productivity, (*ii*) Improving the method of production, and (*iii*) Altering quality standards for both raw materials and finished goods.

Increased productivity of various elements of cost *viz.* materials, labour and overheads will result in reduction in cost. Quality control techniques, time and motion study, improvement in industrial engineering methods, increased automation are some of the factors which may result in increased productivity. Method of production should also be improved. The cost may be reduced either by increasing the quality standards for raw materials or by reducing the quality standards for the finished goods.

Cost reduction is different to cost control, but both are efficient tools of management. The main points of *difference* between cost control and cost reduction are given below:

(*i*) Cost control represents efforts made towards achieving a target or a goal, but cost reduction represents the achievement in reduction of costs.

(*ii*) In cost control targets are set up, actual performance is ascertained and these are compared with targets and variances are analysed to take remedial measures Cost reduction is not concerned with performance and standards. It is based on savings in the standards.

(*iii*) Cost control is a preventive function while cost reduction is a corrective function. Cost reduction may be operative even when an efficient cost control system is existing. There is always room for reduction in the achieved costs under controlled conditions.

(*iv*) Cost control assumes existence of standards, but cost reduction is a continuous process of analyses, by various methods, of all factors affecting costs, efforts and functions in an organisation.

Activity Based Costing (ABC)[1] – Activity based costing has its genesis in the increasing importance of indirect costs in manufacturing operations. Now a days many organisations have adopted manufacturing technology with a result that indirect costs are increasing enormously and direct costs are becoming a smaller portion of total cost. Traditional costing systems which absorbs indirect costs on direct labour or machine hour basis are, therefore, not relevant in the present set-up. Acitivity based costing is a better approach of cost allocation. ABC is a cost attribution to cost units on the basis of benefit received from different indirect activities *e.g.* order processing, materials handling machine insertion of parts, repairs and maintenance, quality testing etc. An activity based costing systems involves following stages

(*i*) Identify the major activities which take place in an organisation.

(*ii*) Assigning costs to cost pools/cost centres for each activity.

(*iii*) Determine cost-drivers for each major activity.

---

1. These are discussed in detail in separate chapters in this book.

(*iv*) Assign cost activities to products according to each products demand (using cost drivers as a measures of demand) for activities.

Cost Drivers – Cost drivers are used in Activity Based Costing. Cost drivers are underlying factors which causes the incurrence of cost related to the activity. Examples of a few activities and their cost drivers are

Activities Involved	*Cost Drivers*
Issue of purchase orders	No. of purchase orders
Storing the materials	Value of materials stored
Inspection and verification	No. of times inspected
Recruitment of employees	No. of employee recruited
Maintenance of records of attendance and leave	No. of employees
Training of employees	No. of employees trained
Labour turnover	No. of employees replaced
Advertisement	Increase in sales

QUESTIONS

OBJECTIVE QUESTIONS

1. In each of the following only one statement/item is correct. State which.

(*i*) Financial Accounting helps in

(*a*) ascertaining the financial position of the concerned firm,

(*b*) establishing the efficiency of operations,

(*c*) providing data for fixing prices of the products,

(*d*) controlling costs.

(*ii*) Establishment of a costing system in India is essential.

(*a*) in the case of all industrial concerns,

(*b*) for all companies having a paid up capital of ₹ 25 lakhs.

(*c*) in the case of such companies as may be required to maintain costing records by the Central Government under Section 209 of the Companies Act.

(*d*) in case the concerned firm is covered by the Monopolies and Restrictive Trade Practices Act.

(*iii*) Cost Accounting

(*a*) like Financial Accounting is exact and precise,

(*b*) necessarily works on the basis of estimates and, therefore, has to be satisfied with reasonable accuracy.

(*c*) deals only with future costs and ignores historical cost.

(*d*) analyses historical costs.

(*iv*) Cost Accounting is useful for

(*a*) only industrial concerns in the private sector since only they wish to maximise profits.

(*b*) all industrial concerns, whether in the private sector or the public sector, but not for service organisations like banks or insurance companies.

(*c*) all profit seeking concerns provided they are not subject to perfect competition.

(*d*) anyone using scarce resources.

(*v*) A farmer producing only wheat for which price is fixed by government should have a costing system in order to (*a*) ascertain the profit earned by him,

(*b*) establish the cost per quintal of wheat produced by him.

(*c*) control the various costs incurred.

(*d*) ascertain the marginal cost.

[(*i*) (*a*); (*ii*) (*c*); (*iii*) (*b*); (*iv*) (*d*); (*v*) (*c*)]

2. Match the following:

(*i*) Total fixed cost	(*i*) what cost should be
(*ii*) Total variable cost	(*ii*) incurred cost
(*iii*) Unit variable cost	(*iii*) increases in proportion to output
(*iv*) Unit fixed cost	(*iv*) cost of conversion
(*v*) Standard cost	(*v*) what costs are expected to be
(*vi*) Period cost	(*vi*) decreases with rise in output
(*vii*) Actual cost	(*vii*) remains constant in table
(*viii*) Labour and overhead	(*viii*) remains constant per unit
(*ix*) Incremental cost	(*ix*) cost not assigned to products
(*x*) Budgeted cost	(*x*) added value of new product

3. Indicate whether the following statements are true or false:

(*i*) All costs are controllable.

(*ii*) Variable cost per unit varies with the increase or decrease in the volume of output.

(*iii*) Depreciation is an out of pocket cost.

(*iv*) Conversion cost is equal to direct wages plus factory overhead.

(*v*) An item of cost that is direct for one business may be indirect for another.

(*vi*) Fixed cost per unit remain fixed.

4. Explain with reason in brief whether following statements are true or false:

(*i*) Financial Accounts provided information for price determination.

(*ii*) Cost Accounting help in immediate determination of cost.

(*iii*) The scope of cost accounting includes cost determination, cost presentation and cost control.

(*iv*) Cost accounting is a techniques of managerial control.

(*v*) Cost Accounting are not useful to organisation engaged in production and manufacturing.

[Ans. : (*v*) false, others true]

5. *Fill in the blank of following*:

(*i*) Cost accounting is a technique of....................

(*ii*) Cost accounting has been evolved due to..............of financial accounting.

(*iii*) The ordinary trading account is a locked store house of most valuable information, to which cost system is the ....

(*iv*) ....Costing is used in transport enterprises.

[**Ans. :** (*i*) cost determination (*ii*) limitations (*iii*) key (*iv*) Operating

6. *Select correct option from following*:

(*i*) Main objective of Cost Accounting is to:

(*a*) Maximise profit

(*b*) Help in inventory valuation

(*c*) Provide information to management for decision

(*d*) Aid in fixation of selling price.

(*ii*) Unit coting is used in.

(*a*) Oil refunery

(*b*) Car manufacturing company

(*c*) Sugar mill
(*d*) Multi product company.

(*iii*) Contract costing is used in:
(*a*) Ship Building
(*b*) Aeroplane industry
(*c*) Automobile Industry
(*d*) None of these

(*iv*) Which method is used in hospitals for determining cost:
(*a*) Job costing
(*b*) Unit costing
(*c*) Operating costing
(*d*) No method is used

[Ans.: (*i*) *d* (*ii*) *d* (*iii*) *a* (*iv*) *c*]

7. State whether following statements are true or false:
(*i*) Cost Accounting is a branch of financial accounting
(*ii*) Cost Accounting can be used only in manufacturing concern.
(*iii*) A prosperous business does not need costing system.
(*iv*) In hospitals batch costing is used.
(*v*) A firm manufacturing scooters uses multiple costing

[Ans.: (*i*) and (*iv*) True]

8. What is the proper method and unit of cost for the following?

Shipping Company	Water Supply Concern
Cold Storage Plant	Electricity Undertaking
Multiple Shops	Aircraft Factory
Advertising Company	Handloom
Pottery	Aluminium Factory
Oil Refinery	Building Contractor
Oxygen Company	Hospital
Vegetable Ghee Company	Toy Company
Architect	Correspondence Course

9. Describe briefly the various methods of costing. State, giving reasons, which method of costing you would recommend for use in the following:
(*i*) Chemical works;
(*ii*) Road Transport Company;
(*iii*) Painter and Decorator;
(*iv*) Constructional Engineer. **[*B. Com. (Hons.) Delhi*]**

10. Given below is a list of 10 industries, give the method of costing and unit of cost against each industry.

(*i*) Nursing Home	(*ii*) Road Transport
(*iii*) Steel	(*iv*) Bridge construction
(*v*) Coal	(*vi*) Bycycle
(*vii*) Interior Decoration	(*viii*) Advertising
(*ix*) Furniture	(*x*) Sugur industry having its own sugar cane fields

THEORETICAL QUESTIONS

11. What do you understand by Cost Accounts? In what way are they helpful to a manufacturer or a contractor? **[*B. Com., Delhi*]**

12. What is Cost Accounting? What are its advantages as compared to financial accounting? **[*B. Com. Hons., Delhi*]**

13. Cost may be classified in a variety of ways according to their nature and the information needs management'. Explain and discuss this statement giving examples of classifications required for different purposes. **[*B. Com. (H) Delhi*]**
14. Describe briefly the different methods of costing and state the particular industries to which they can be applied. **[*B. Com., Agra*]**
15. "A Cost-keeping System", says a modern writer, "that simply records cost for the purpose of fixing sale prices has accomplished only a small part of its mission." What other functions does costing achieve?
16. List down any eight factors which you will consider before installing a costing system.
17. Distinguish between cost control and cost reduction.
18. Distinguish between (*i*) Variable cost and Direct cost (*ii*) Estimated cost and Standard cost.
19. Distinguish between cost unit and cost centre.
20. Distinguish between cost centre and profit centre.
21. Outline the steps involved in installing a costing system in a manufacturing unit. What are essentials of an effective costing system.
22. Write short notes on chargeable expenses.
23. Distinguish between controllable cost and uncontrollable cost.
24. Distinguish between (*i*) Cost control and Cost reduction (*ii*) Cost allocation and Cost absorption (*iii*) Controllable cost and Uncontrollable Cost.
25. Explain (*i*) Sunk cost (*ii*) Pre-Production cost.
26. Select a suitable unit of cost to be used in (*i*) Hospital (*ii*) City Bus Transport (*iii*) Hotel Providing Lodging facility.

SHORT ANSWER QUESTIONS

1. State whether following statements are true or false. Also give reason in brief.
   (*i*) Prime cost is the total of direct wages and variable overheads.
   (*ii*) Conversion cost is the total of direct labour and factory overhead.
   (*iii*) Rent of factory building is a direct cost.
   (*iv*) Cost of raw material is a direct cost.
   (*v*) There is no difference in works cost and works overhead.
   [Ans.: (*i*) False (*ii*) True (*iii*) False (*iv*) True (*v*) False]
2. (*i*) Prime cost = Direct Material + Direct Labour + ...
   (*ii*) Factory cost = Prime cost + ...
   (*iii*) Cost of production = ... + Office and Administration Overheads.
   (*iv*) Cost of Goods sold = Cost of Production + ...
   (*v*) Cost of Sales = Cost of Goods sold + ...
   [Ans. : (*i*) Direct cost, (*ii*) Factory overheads (*iii*) Works cost (*iv*) Opening stock of finishsed Goods – Closing stock of finished goods (v) Selling and distribution overheads]

SHORT ANSWER NUMERICAL QUESTIONS

1. Calculate Prime Cost from the following

	₹.
Opening Stock of Direct Material	5,000
Purchase of Direct Material	10,000
Direct Materials returned to supplier	2,000
Carriage inward	500
Closing Stock of Direct Material	1,500
Direct Wages	3,000
Indirect Wages	2,500
Other indirect expenses	500

[Ans. : ₹. 15,000]

2. Calculate works cost from the following

	₹.
Prime Cost	30,000
Work-in-Progress (Opening)	2,000
Work-in-Progress (Closing)	1,000
Works overhead	15,000
Sales of scrap	1,000
Other expenses	2,000

[Ans.: ₹. 45,000**]**

3. Calculate the profit on sales

	₹.
Prime Cost	30,000
Work overhead	10,000
Office overhead	10,000
Selling overhead	5,000
Opening stock of finished goods	5,000
Closing stock of finished goods	10,000
Sales	70,000

[Ans.: ₹. 20,000**]**

NUMERICAL QUESTIONS

1. You are required to ascertain from the following figures what percentage: (*a*) The manufacturing cost (*b*) The selling on cost, and (*c*) The management on cost bear to the total cost of the goods sold. You are further required to ascertain by what percentage the average selling price should be raised in order to double the net profit.

	₹.
Opening stock of direct materials	61,700
Work-in-Progress at commencement	1,12,700
Purchase of Direct Material	2,86,500
Direct Wages	3,57,000
Factory on cost	1,99,500
Selling on cost	70,000
Management on cost (applicable to goods sold)	1,10,000
Sales	12,50,000
Closing stock of direct materials	75,400
Closing Works-in-Progress	1,35,600
Sales of Scrap	1,350
Carriage on Direct Materials	5,950

There is no opening or closing stock of finished goods.

[Ans. (*a*) *82%* (*b*) *7%* (*c*) *11%, To double the net profit the selling price should be increased by 20%. Factory Cost ₹ 8,20,000; Total Cost ₹ 10,00,000*]

2. The following is the costing information of production for the half year ended 30th June:

	₹.
Purchases of raw materials	1,32,000
Direct wages	1,10,000
Rent. Taxes. Insurance & Work on cost	44,000
Carriage inwards	1,584
Stocks 1st Jan.	
Raw Materials	22,000
Finished product (1,600 Tones)	17,600

Stock 30th June	
Raw Materials	24,464
Finished product (3,200 Tones)	35,200
Work-in-Progress 1st Jan	5,280
Work-in-Progress 30th June	17,600
Cost of factory supervision	8,800
Sales of Finished Product	3,30,000

Advertising discounts allowed and selling costs 75 paise per ton sold. 25,600 tons of commodity were produced during the period. You are required to prepare cost sheet and ascertain. (*A*) The value of raw materials used. (*B*) The cost of the output for the period. (*C*) The cost of the turnover for the period. (*D*) The net profit for the period (*E*) The net profit per ton of the commodity.

[**Ans.** (*A*) *₹ 1,31,120,* (*B*) *₹ 2,81,600,* (*C*) *₹ 282,000,* (*D*) *₹ 48,000,* (*E*) *₹ 2.*

Hint. *Tons sold = 25600 + 1600 – 3200 = 24,000. Selling Exps. 24000 × .75 = ₹ 18,000*]

3. From the following particulars, obtained from the financial books, prepare a cost statement as would enable an easy comparison of the figures with those used in costing:

	₹.
Stock of direct materials (opening)	20,000
Stock of direct materials (closing)	15,000
Purchase of direct materials	85,000
Carriage inwards	12,000
Direct wages	1,25000
Direct expenses	7,500
Works Expenses:	
Work Salaries	25,000
Factory rent and taxes	5,000
Indirect wages	4,500
Motive power	3,500
Indirect materials	1000
Works, lighting and heating	1,200
Works repairs	1,500
Factory insurance	700
Loose tools consumed	500
Works stationery	200
Plant and works depreciation	1,350
Oiling and cleaning	350
Gas and water	600
Workmen's compensation	1,100
Administrative expenses chargeable to works	2,000
Office Expenses:	
Office salaries and wages	6,000
Office rent and taxes	900
Printing and stationery	650
Office repairs	210
Office lighting and insurance	300
Telephone charges	425
Director's fees-proportionate chargeable to administration.	1,500
Legal expenses	750
Audit fees	1,000
Postage and telegram	325
Selling and Distributive Expenses:	
Advertising	8,500

Printing and stationery	1,750
Travellers' salaries	2,500
Travellers' commission	3,700
Showroom expenses	1,150
Bad debts	700
Postage and sundries	800
Carriage and freight outwards	1,400
Running expenses—delivery vans	2,200
Depreciation—delivery vans	520
Insurance, show room etc.	400
Directors' fees—chargeable to sale expenses	1,000
Total sales	3,70,000

[**Ans.** *Prime cost ₹ 2,34,500; Factory cost ₹ 2,83,000; Cost of production ₹ 2,95,060; Cost of sale ₹ 3,19,680; Net profit ₹ 50,320*]

4. The following particulars relating to the year 2008 have been taken from the books of a chemical works manufacturing and selling a chemical mixture.

	Kg	₹
Stock on, 1 January 2008		
Raw materials	2,000	2,000
Finished Mixture	500	1,750
Factory stores		7,250
Purchases		
Raw Materials	1,60,000	1,80,000
Factory Stores		24,250
Sales Finished Mixture	1,53,050	9,18,000
Factory scrap		8,170
Factory wages		1,78,650
Power		30,400
Depreciation of Machinery		18,000
Salaries		
Factory		72,220
Office		37,220
Selling		41,500
Expenses		
Direct		18,500
Office		18,200
Selling		18,000
Stock on 31st December 2008		
Raw Materials	1,200	
Finished Mixture	450	
Factory Stores		5,550

The stock of finished mixture at the end of the year is to be valued at the Factory Cost of the mixture for that year. The purchase price of raw materials remained unchanged throughout the year. Prepare a statement giving the maximum possible information about cost and its break-up for the year. ***[B.Com.(Hons.) Delhi]***

[**Ans.** *Prime Cost ₹ 3,77,800; Factory Cost ₹ 5,16,200; Cost of Goods sold ₹ 5,71,852; Cost of sales ₹ 6,31,352; Profit ₹ 2,86,648* Factory cost per kg ₹ 3.374; closing stock ₹ 1,518; stores consumed ₹ 25,950; production 1,53,000 kg]

5. The following figures are extracted from the books of Fashions Ltd. for the year ending March 30, 2004. Prepare a cost sheet showing the cost per unit under various elements, direct and indirect cost and also profit/loss per unit.

	₹.
Direct Materials	24,00,000
Direct Labour	5,00,000
Depreciation on Factory Building	15,000
Branch Office Expenses	40,000
Depreciation of Office Building	8,000
Depreciation of Staff Cars	12,000
Insurance of Staff Cars	1,500
Insurance: Office Building	1,200
Insurance: Factory Building	1,500
Delivery vans maintenance & running exps.	10,000
Salaries	
Sales Manager	25,000
Factory Chief Engineer	25,000
Finished goods warehouse expenses	20,000
Electricity (including ₹. 4000 for administration office)	40,000
Advertisement	20,000
Sundry Factory Expenses	3,40,000
Sales Promotion	5,000
Office Administration Exps.	3,00,000
Expenses for participating industrial exhibition	10,000
Sales	42,00,000

Units produced 10,000

[**Ans.** Prime cost: ₹. 29,00,000; Factory cost ₹. 33,17,500; Total cost ₹. 37,74,200; Profit ₹.4,25,800, Factory cost per kg ₹ 3.374, Closing stock ₹ 1518].

6. A fire occurred in the factory premises on October 31, 2003. The accounting records have been destroyed. Certain accounting records were kept in another building. They reveal the following for the period September 1, 2003 to October 31, 2003:

(*i*)	Direct Materials purchased	₹. 2,50,000
(*ii*)	Work in Process inventory, 1.9.2003	₹. 40,000
(*iii*)	Direct Materials inventory, 1..9.2003	₹. 20,000
(*iv*)	Finished goods inventory, 1.9.2003	₹. 37,750
(*v*)	Indirect manufacturing costs	40% of conversion cost
(*vi*)	Sales revenues	₹. 7,50,000
(*vii*)	Direct manufacturing labour	₹. 2,22,250
(*viii*)	Prime costs	₹. 3,97,750
(*ix*)	Gross margin percentage based on revenues	30%
(*x*)	Cost of Goods available for sale	₹. 5,55,775

The loss is fully covered by insurance company. The insurance company wants to know the historical cost of the inventories as a basis for negotiating a settlement, although the settlement is actually to be based on replacement cost, not historical cost.

Required:

(*i*) Finished goods inventory, 31.10.2003

(*ii*) Work-in-Process inventory, 31.10.2003

(*iii*) Direct Materials inventory, 31.10.2003.

[**Ans.** (*i*) ₹ *30,775,* (*ii*) *67,892* (*iii*) *94,500* Conversion cost = Factory cost – Material consumed

Hint. Indirect Manufacturing cost ₹. 1,48,167; Cost of goods available for sale = Cost of Goods Manufactured + Op. inventory of finished Goods, Cost of Goods manufactured ₹. 5,18,025]

Chapter 2 Materials

MATERIALS CONTROL

In calculation of cost of production, raw material is the first element of cost. Materials form a high proportion of the total cost of production usually. In certain cases, like cotton textiles, materials (yarn) may be as much as 60 per cent of total cost. The percentage is rarely less than 25 per cent or 30 per cent in case of most products. It can be rightly said that efficiency as regards materials is a vital factor in total cost of production and in the profit earned. Any saving in materials will be directly reflected in profits. It is, therefore, necessary that utmost care should be devoted to the purchase, storing and use of materials. No system of costing can be said to be complete without a proper system of material control.

Definition of Materials Control

Materials control may be defined as a system which ensures availability of the required quantity of material of proper quality at the proper time and at the same time avoidance of unnecessarily blocking up of capital in stores. The *system of material control* should be so comprehensive that it covers the whole procedure from the point when order is placed with the suppliers up to the stage until the materials are consumed in production.

Objectives of Material Control

The following may be listed as broad objectives of materials control or, in other words, the following steps have to be taken to see that there is no inefficiency as regards materials:

1. *Availability:* The various materials and stores necessary for carrying on production smoothly should always be available. This means not only ensuring supplies of the main raw materials and the chief stores which are required but also of small and inexpensive but necessary materials. For example, in a cotton textile mill supplies of cotton and coal will always be looked after, but it is also necessary that the proper lubricating oil for machines is also always available. Stoppage of production due to any reason is very costly and the person in charge of supply of materials and stores must see to it that production is not interrupted for want of any item of materials and stores.

2. *Proper Quality and Price:* While purchasing the materials and stores, care should be taken to see that the requisite quality of materials is purchased and that the price paid is reasonably low. It is no use purchasing goods of inferior quality or of very superior quality. For every product or job there is a particular quality of materials which is needed and that quality alone should be purchased. For printing text books, for example, neither art paper nor newsprint is to be used; white printing paper of reasonable weightage will be needed. But a book containing art pictures and priced quite high must be printed on good quality art paper; newspapers have to use newsprint as otherwise the cost will be too high. Prices also must be unnecessarily high although in certain cases it may be the company's policy to encourage certain supplies by paying them a price higher than prevailing in the market; but this can be only for a short period and in special cases.

3. *Minimum Wastage:* While various materials are being stored in the godowns, the loss of or damage to the various items must be kept as low as possible. The losses usually are pilferage or damage due to rust dust dirt or water. All these losses must be thoroughly kept under control.

4. *No Overstocking:* Investment in stocks of materials and stores must be kept as low as possible. This means that unnecessarily large stocks must not be maintained.

5. *Information* about availability of stocks. Information must be continuously available regarding stock. This will ensure proper planning of work and also replenishment on time.

6. *Minimum Loss During Process:* While the materials are being used in the factory the wastage must be kept at the minimum possible level. Some wastage is bound to be there, but efficiency demands that the wastage must not be allowed to go above the minimum level.

Important Requirements of Materials Control (Management Expectations)

The important requirements of every system of material control are as follows:

1. Proper coordination of all departments involved in material purchasing, receiving, testing, approving, storage, accounting and distributing of funds.

2. Use of materials, supplies and equipment budgets so that economy in purchasing and use of materials can be realised.

3. Operation of system of internal check so that all transactions involving materials, supplies and equipment purchases are checked and approved by a number of properly authorised persons.

4. Centralisation of purchasing is advisable. Economy in purchasing and use of materials may be achieved through use of materials, supplies and equipment budgets.

5. Standard forms upon which instructions regarding purchases and uses of materials are properly written should be accepted.

6. Storage of all materials and supplies in a designated location, properly safeguarded under effective supervision.

7. A system of perpetual inventory should be adopted so that it is possible to determine at every time the amount and value of each kind of material in stock.

8. Determination of a minimum quantity to each item of material below which point the inventory is not allowed to drop and also a maximum quantity above which stock should not be carried.

9. A proper and effective system of stock control and issue should be adopted so that there will be delivery of materials upon requisition to departments in the right time and right amount at the time they are needed.

10. Development of a system of controlling accounts and subsidiary records which exhibit summary and detailed material cost at each stage of material receipt and consumption from the stock room to finished goods.

11. Regular reports of materials purchased, issued from stock, inventory balances, obsolete stock, goods returned to vendors and spoiled or defective items.

MATERIAL PURCHASE PROCEDURE

The Purchase Department

In order to ensure that various materials and stores are always available, that the price paid is not unnecessarily high and investment in materials and stores is at a reasonably low figure, there must be a separate Purchasing Department if at all the size of the concern permits it. This department will work under an officer designated as the Purchase Manager or the Supply Manager.

Centralised and Decentralised Purchasing: Centralised purchasing means all purchasing of factory requirement under a single head. If purchasing is not centralised, that is to say, if various persons are authorised to make purchases for their requirements, it may mean that some of them indulge in reckless buying. They may buy things or stores which, strictly, are not required. Purchases in small lots will also mean that discounts and economies in transport will not be available. Also, nobody can then become an expert in buying—these days there are many rules and regulations that have to be followed for obtaining supplies of some articles.

The main *advantage of centralised purchasing* is that the purchase officer will automatically develop into an expert and will be able to make purchases at the most opportune time and from the best sources. He can also ensure proper utilisation of trade discounts and use of transport economies.

Advantages of centralised purchasing may be summarised as below:

(*i*) The advantage of undivided responsibility.

(*ii*) Maintenance of consistent buying policy.

(*iii*) Large buying power commanding the largest buying influence.

(*iv*) Economy of records and paper work providing easy reference.

(*v*) Facilitating standardisation of specifications and elimination of varieties.

(*vi*) Reduction of inventories.

(*vii*) Lower selling cost of supplies leading to reduction of buying prices.

It can be said that centralised purchasing will be suitable if (*a*) the company operates a single plant, (*b*) when there are two or more plants not very far away from one another, requiring the same general type raw materials.

There is, however, one question as to whether a company having a large number of factories should centralise all purchasing at the head office or should leave purchasing to individual factories. Centralised purchasing, if requirements are similar, will ensure the economies listed above. In addition, the purchasing department can have an inspectorate of its own to ensure that goods purchased are of suitable quality. There is also economy in negotiating one contract to cover supplies to all the factories. The economy consists of saving in clerical labour and saving in prices because large quantities may be purchased directly at their source of production.

Against this one must put down the disadvantage of delay and, due to this, large stocks will have to be maintained at factories in order to ensure continuous production. On the whole, one can say that if the requirements of the various factories are uniform, there is advantage in centralised purchasing; but if the requirements of various factories, are different then there is no particular economy in making the purchases through the head office. The purchasing department, in that case, will not develop into an expert and since the size of order will not increase price and transport economies will not be available more than when purchasing is decentralised.

Duties/Functions of Purchasing Department: Following are functions of Purchasing Department:

(*a*) Ascertainment and selection of the sources of supply and knowing market conditions as to the demand and supply position and price trends.

(*b*) Knowing in some detail the manufacturing process and requirements of materials.

(*c*) Procuring materials as required and placing orders for their purchases.

(*d*) Following up suppliers so as to avoid delays in procurement of materials.

(*e*) Making sure that the right type of materials have been received in right quantities according to purchase order.

(*f*) Securing adjustment on claims for discrepancies in materials received.

(*g*) Approving of bills of suppliers for payment.

(*h*) Maintaining proper records of materials purchases.

Co-operation between Purchase Manager and Others—Standard List

Since the Purchase Manager has to purchase things to be used by others, there must be full cooperation between the purchasing department and the other departments, specially the production department. This cooperation takes the form of the preparation of standard lists in which all requirements of the factory and other departments are listed. The method to prepare the list is to first of all list the main raw materials and then to take up each department, turn by turn, and list the materials to be used there and the various stores necessary to keep work going on in that department. An examination of machine by machine will give good results. A list of spare parts necessary for each machine must also be drawn up. The Works Manager will also indicate the consumption of each item per unit of time or per given scale of output. If and when the ratio of consumption changes, the purchase manager should be notified of the change so that he may make the necessary alterations in the purchasing schedule.

Code: Having drawn up the standard list, it is desirable to give a code number or symbol to each item. The code or symbol may consist either wholly of numerals or of letters of the alphabet partly and numerals partly. Numerical code is necessary when punched card machines are used. In any case, the fixing of the code or the symbol can save good deal of clerical labour. For example, the symbol for mild steel welding rods 1/16 may be WM 64. The student can see the difference in the effort involved in writing these two things. While drawing up a numerical code, the proper thing to do is to list the various departments and allot the first two digits to indicate the number of the department. 05, for instance, may indicate transport department. Similarly 00 may be used for those materials and stores which are used in all departments, for example, kerosene oil, cotton waste, etc. And then for each department, the list of materials is drawn up. The first digit should indicate whether the material will form part of the product or whether it is used merely to run the machines or whether it is a spare part. I may be designated for materials forming part of the product, 2 for materials for running the machines and 3 for spare parts. The next two or three digits may be allotted to the various materials. Therefore, it may be a six digit code—the first two indicating the department in which the material is required, the third indicating the nature of the material and the last indicating the name of the material. For example, if the code is 042034 it may mean material No. 34 (say, lubricating oil) used in department No. 4 for keeping the machines going.

The code may, of course, be drawn in such a way as to describe the material only but not the purpose for which it is used. The code will then consist of a number to denote its name, another to indicate its size or other particulars such as shade, if necessary. For instance the number allotted to mild steel welding rods may be 43 and that to aluminium welding rods 44. The size may be indicated by 1 for every 1/20 cm. Then the code for aluminium welding rods 3/10 cm. will be 4406 and for mild steel welding rods 1/10 cm will be 4302.

Example: A factory uses rectangular steel and cast iron bars differing in height and breadth by 1/10 cm between ½ and 1½ cm in width and between 1/10 cm and 8/10 cm in height. Two examples of a code are:

Steel	1 cm × 2/5 cm:	211004
Cast Iron	1-1/5 cm. × 1/5 cm:	√221202

What will be the code for steel bars 1½ cm × 7/10 cm and for one iron bars 4/5 cm × 3/10 cm?

It is clear that steel bars are indicated by 21 and cast iron by 22, that width has 1 for 1/10 of cm and height also is indicated by the same digit. Therefore, the code for steel bars 1½ cm × 7/10 cm will be 21 15 07 and for cast iron bars 4/5 × 3/10 cm. will be 22 08 03.

If an item has been entered in the standard list, it is the duty of the Purchase Manager to see to the replenishment of stocks when the old stocks are exhausted. But if the scale of output has been increased, then it is the duty of the Works Manager to inform the Purchase Manager promptly so that additional stocks can be built up in time to see that work does not suffer. If any additional article is required by the Works Manager or anybody else, it would be his duty to send a special purchase requisition to the Purchase Manager. It should be properly ruled. Following is a specimen of a purchase requisition.

Purchase Requisition
(special)

No......... Date.........
Name of Department................. Date by which
Purpose for which materials required Materials are required.........

Serial No.	*Particulars (Exact Specifications)*	*Quantity Required*	*Remarks*

....
INDENTOR

For use in Purchase Office
Quotations invited on.......
From: 1. ... ...
2. ... ...
3. ... ...
4. ... ...
Other Action ... ...
... ...

....
Purchase Officer

Purchase Routine

In case of materials which have been entered on the standard list, the procedure to ensure continuous supply of materials is as follows:

Minimum Quantity and Ordering Level: For each item a minimum quantity is determined on the basis of the time required to get the article from supplier and the average consumption per unit of time. For example, if the consumption of an article is 50 units per week and the experience is that it takes six weeks to actually get the article after placing an order, it is commonsense to know that a new order must go out when the actual stock is more than 300 units, *i.e.* 50 × 6. If this is not so and an order is placed, say, only when the stock is 200 units, the present supply will be exhausted before the new stocks arrive and work will then suffer. Since it is not safe to depend upon the usual period of delivery, a *safety margin* must be added. Therefore, in the above example, the minimum quantity of stocks when a new order is placed will be, say, 300 units plus 100 units for safety stock or 400 units in all. This limit is entered on the stores ledger (which is a collection of accounts both as regards amount and quantity of each item of stores). It is the duty of the stores ledger clerk to inform the Purchase Manager whenever the actual stock approaches the minimum quantity. This is done in the form , which is given below:

Purchase Requisition (or Indent)
(Routine)

No............ Date..........

Serial No.	*Name of the Article Required*	*Symbol or Code*	*Present Stock*	*Minimum Quantity*	*Maximum Quantity*	*Remarks*

....
Stores Ledger Clerk

When this reaches the Purchase Manager, it becomes his duty to initiate the purchase procedure which is outlined a little later.

Some firms use the term "*Ordering Level*" instead of minimum quantity, but some firms use both the terms. In that case, ordering level means what has been written above as regards minimum quantity. Minimum quantity will then mean a lower limit at which the issues of the material concerned may be stopped for ordinary jobs so that only the important jobs are taken up and finished. The authorisation for the issue of such materials may also be from the superintendent and not from the foreman as is usually the case. Some firms still have another level, which is known as "*Danger Level*". This means a limit at which the Purchase Manager must take special steps, say, sending a man personally to bring the required materials and stores.

Maximum Quantity: One of the functions of the Purchase Manager is to see that there is no over-investment in stocks. For this purpose, he has to fix a maximum limit for stocks of various items. This maximum limit will be crossed only in special cases. For example, if an article is in short supply, the maximum limit may be safely ignored, if a lot is available at reasonable prices. But, on the whole, overstocking must be avoided due to the following reasons:

(*a*) It involves investment of very large funds so that there will be loss of interest.

(*b*) Extra large stocks will require more godown space so that extra rent will have to be paid.

(*c*) Large stocks may put a temptation in the minds of some workers leading them to steal small quantities.

(*d*) Since some portion of the stocks will lie for a long period, there may be deterioration in quality.

(*e*) There is the risk of obsolescence. This means that either the product may be given up or the method of making the product may be changed. Old materials will no longer be required as if there are large stocks they may result in heavy losses.

Factors for determining the maximum limit or quantity are following:

(*i*) Finances that can be spared for maintaining stocks.

(*ii*) Godown space or storage capacity that is available.

(*iii*) Firm estimates of the quantity required for consumption in the near future. This involves estimate in respect of sales and production of the finished article concerned and a consideration of any possible changes in the materials required for the production of the article.

(*iv*) Likely movement in prices; if it is certain that prices will rise substantially in the coming period, a comparatively large stock will be kept. In the reverse circumstance, stocks are kept as low as possible.

(*v*) Likely changes in the conditions of supply of the materials. If it is expected that it will be more difficult to obtain supplies in future, large stocks will be built up.

Some firms follow the formula of putting the maximum limit at double the minimum quantity. But this is not proper; the maximum quantity should be determined on a consideration of the factors given above. The basic aim is to avoid loss due to obsolescence and extra expense in the nature of interest on the capital locked up in stocks. For avoiding obsolescence, it is essential to know the firm production plans (rather than those which are being considered); these should cover not only the articles to be produced but also the production processes to be employed—the various quantities of the article and the quantities of each quality that will be produced should also be determined. Materials should be stocked which will be required for the definite production programme; for plans that are not certain, purchases should be made very cautiously.

Apart from this basic consideration, the maximum limits will generally be fixed in consultation with the Finance Manager who generally decides what funds can be spared for inventory purposes. Likely movement in prices and expected conditions of supply will surely have a big influence on this question.

Fixation of Stock Levels

(*i*) *Maximum Level of Stock* = (Reorder Level + Reorder Quantity) – (Minimum rate of consumption × Minimum reorder period)

Maximum Level may be alternatively fixed as Safety Stock + Reorder Quantity or EOQ.

(*ii*) *Minimum level of stock* = Reorder level – (Average rate of consumption × Average reorder period) (*iii*) *Safety Stock* = (Annual Demand/365) × (Maximum Reorder Period – Average Reorder Period)

(*iv*) *Reorder level or Ordering level* = Maximum rate of consumption × Maximum reorder period. Alternatively, it will be = safety stock + lead time consumption

[lead time consumption will be = (Annual consumption ÷ 360) × lead time]

(*v*) *Danger level* = It is slightly below the minimum level. It is a level at which special efforts should be made to obtain supplies of materials. *i.e.*

Minimum rate of consumption × Emergency delivery time

(*vi*) *Average Stock level* = (Maximum stock level + Minimum stock level) × ½

or Minimum Stock level + ½ Reorder Quantity.

Obviously, the Reordering level is bleow the Maximum level, and Minimum level is below the Reordering level and the Danger level is below the Minimum level. Safety Stock is above minimum level. In above calculations, the following elements are important.

(*a*) *Consumption Rate:* It is consumption or use of material per day (or per week) by production department. These rates will be maximum and minimum, the simple average of maximum and minimum rates is average consumption rate per day or per week.

(*b*) *Reorder Period:* It is period between materials ordered and materials received. The average reorder period is simple average of maximum and minimum reorder periods.

(*c*) *Reorder Quantity:* At the time of purchase of material, one of the important problems to be faced is how much quantity of a particular materials to be purchased at a time. If purchases are made frequently in small quantities it will result in loss of trade discounts and economies in purchasing. On the other hand if purchases are made in large quantities it will lead to over stocking and cost of storage will be high. The ordering quantity should be economic and reasonable by all aspects. It should be Economic Order Quantity (*EOQ*). The calculation of *EOQ* has been discussed later on.

Illustration 1: **[Fixation of stock levels]**

Two components A and B are used as follows:

Normal usage 50 units per week each

Minimum usage 25 units per week each

Maximum usage 75 units per week each

Reorder Quantity *A* 300 units; *B* 500 units

Reorder Period *A* 4 to 6 weeks, *B* 2 to 4 weeks

Calculate for each components (*a*) Reorder level, (*b*) Minimum Level, (*c*) Maximum level, (*d*) Average Stock Level.

Solution:

(*a*) Reorder Level = Maximum Rate of Consumption × Maximum Reorder Period.

A = 75 × 6 = 450 units

B = 75 × 4 = 300 units

(*b*) Minimum Level = Reorder Level – (Average Rate of consumption × Average Reorder Period)

A = 450 – (50 – 5) = 200 units

B = 300 – (50 × 3) = 150 units

(*c*) Maximum Stock Level

= (Reorder Level + Reorder Quantity) – (Minimum Consumption Rate × Minimum Reorder Period)

A = (450 + 300) – (25 × 4) = 650 units

B = (300 + 500) – (25 × 2) = 750 units

(*d*) Average Stock Level = (Maximum Stock Level + Minimum Stock Level)/2

$A = (650 + 200)/2 = 425$ units

$B = (750 + 150)/2 = 450$ units

Average Stock Level can also be calculated by the formula.

Minimum Stock Level + ½ of Reorder Quantity

$A = 200 + ½ \times 300 = 350$ units

$B = 150 + ½ \times 500 = 400$ units

Illustration 2: If the minimum stock level and average stock level of raw material A are 4,000 and 9000 units respectively, find out its reorder quantity.

Solution: Average stock level = Minimum stock level + ½ of Reorder Quantity

9000 = 4000 + ½ of Reorder Quantity

½ Reorder Quantity = 9000 – 4000 = 5000

Reorder Quantity = 10,000 units

ECONOMIC ORDER QUANTITY (EOQ)

The quantity to be ordered at one time is known as 'ordering quantity' and should be determined with good care. If it is small, a number of orders will have to be placed in a year involving costs in terms of clerical labour, material handling, etc. Also there will be loss in terms of price and transport costs. Large orders avoid these losses and will lead to economy in transport costs and price concessions. But there will be costs in terms of interest payments for the money locked up and in terms of storing costs. An order should be large enough to enable the firm to earn proper discounts and to take advantage of bulk transport but it should not be too large to involve too heavy payment of interest. If the price to be paid is stable, the optimum quantity to be ordered or economic order quantity (*EOQ*) can be determined by the formula.

$$EOQ = \sqrt{\frac{2AO}{C}}$$

where A = Consumption of the article concerned (in units) during a year;

O = Cost of placing one order including the cost of receiving the goods or ordering cost; and

C = Interest payment per unit per year including other variable cost of storing it (carrying cost per unit per annum)

Suppose a unit of article A cost ₹. 25 and the annual consumption is 2,000 units; the cost of placing an order is ₹. 16 and the interest is 10 per cent p.a. The optimum quantity to order is

$\sqrt{\frac{2 \times 2000 \times 16}{2.5}}$ or 160.

The calculation of EOQ is based upon two elements :

(*i*) Total inventory carrying cost

= Average inventory × Cost of carrying per unit per annum

$= \frac{Q}{2} \times C$ [Here Q is ordering quantity]

(*ii*) Total ordering cost

= Number of orders × Ordering cost per order

$= \frac{A}{Q} \times O$

Thus, annual total cost $= \frac{Q}{2} \times C + \frac{A}{Q} \times O$

Since ordering cost varies inversely as *EOQ* and inventory carrying cost various directly as *EOQ*, the total annual cost will be minimum when above two are equal.

$$\frac{Q}{2} \times C = \frac{A}{Q} \times O$$

or

$$\frac{Q}{2} \times \frac{Q}{A} = \frac{O}{C}$$

$$\frac{Q^2}{2A} = \frac{O}{C} \quad \text{or} \quad Q^2 = \frac{2AO}{C}$$

i.e.

$$Q = \sqrt{\frac{2AO}{C}}$$

[Now *Q* will be *EOQ*]

There is another method of calculating *EOQ i.e. Tabulation Method*. This method is normally used when by increase in the quantity of purchases, there is change in the price also. In this method carrying cost is calculated on average *i.e.* 1/2 of quantity purchased. The least of ordering cost and carrying cost taken together will be the *EOQ*.

Thus, *factors influencing* the size of *EOQ* or standard ordering quantity depends upon the following factors:

(*i*) Purchase price per unit for different ordering quantities.

(*ii*) Cost of purchasing per unit for different ordering quantities.

(*iii*) The size of average inventory in respect of various ordering quantities. This size is again influenced by the Minimum stock level already established (The maximum delivery period and maximum consumption rate decide the reordering level).

(*iv*) Inventory storage charges per unit. The sotrage charges include rent of space, lighting etc.of the store.

(*v*) Inventory carrying charges for different ordering quantities. These include insurance, taxes, depreciation, manual or clerical labour, interest on capital locked up in inventory, risk of spoilage, fall of market price of inventory, obsolescence etc.

It is to be noted that EOQ can be easily calculated when above factors remain stable and not varying. These may be taken as assumptions in the calculation of EOQ.

Illustration 3: [EOQ]: *X* Ltd. bought and consumed during the year 2005, 3,600 units of material Y. The cost of placing an order is ₹. 1,000 and the cost of carrying one unit for a year is ₹. 20. Calculate economic order quantity.

Solution:

$$\text{EOQ} = \sqrt{\frac{2AO}{C}}$$

A = 3,600 units

O = ₹. 1,000

C = ₹. 20

$$= \sqrt{\frac{2 \times 3600 \times 1000}{20}}$$

= 600 units.

Illustration 4: Your factory buys and uses a component for production at ₹. 10 per unit. Annual requirement is 2000 units. Carrying cost of inventory is 10 per cent p.a. and ordering cost is ₹. 40 per order. The purchase manager agrees that as the ordering cost is high, it is advantageous to place a single order for the entire annual requirement. He also says that if we order 2000 units at a time, we can get 3 per cent discount from the supplier. Evaluate his proposal and make your recommendation.

Solution: We should first calculate economic order quantity as per given data.

Annal Requirement (units)	*No. of orders*	*Order size (units)*	*Ordering cost @ ₹. 40 ₹.*	*Average stock (50% of order placed) units*	*Carrying Cost 10% ₹. 10 per unit*	*Total cost (ordering + carrying) ₹.*
2000	10	200	400	100	100	500
2000	5	400	200	200	200	400
2000	4	500	160	250	250	410
2000	2	1000	80	500	500	580
2000 (–3%)	1	2000	40	1000	970	1010

[**Note:** In one order of 2000 units, the carrying cost is average stock × 9.70 × 10% = ₹. 970, while in earlier cases it is average stock × 10 × 10%]

Economic *EOQ* is 400 unit. The cost is minimum at this level. It is therefore, recommended that order be placed for 400 units at a time *i.e.* 5 times in the year.

It can be verified by using formula

$$\text{EOQ} = \sqrt{\frac{2 \times 2000 \times 40}{1}} = 400$$

***Illustration 5:* [*EOQ* Tabulation Method]**

(*a*) *X* Ltd. has received an offer of quantity discounts on its order of material as under

Price per ton (₹)	*Tonnes*
1200	Less than 500
1180	500 and up to 1,000
1160	1000 and up to 2,000
1140	2000 and up to 3000
1120	3000 and above

The annual requirement for the material is 5000 tons. The ordering cost per order is ₹. 1,200 and the stock holding cost is estimated at 20 per cent of materials cost per annum. You are required to compute economic order quantity.

(*b*) What would be your answer to the above if there are no discount offered and the price per tonne is ₹. 1,500?

Solution:

Annal Require-ment	*No. of order*	*Order size (Tons)*	*Ordering cost ₹.*	*Average storage (50% of order placed)*	*Carrying cost*	*Total cost (4) + (6)*	*Cost of purchase ₹.*	*Total Material cost (7) + (8)*
(1)	(2)	(3)	(4)	(5)	(6)	(7)	(8)	(9)
5,000	20	250	24,000	125	30,000	54,000	60,00,000	60,54,000
5,000	10	500	12,000	250	59,000	71,000	59,00,000	59,71,000
5,000	5	1,000	6,000	500	1,16,000	1,22,000	58,00,000	**59,22,000**
5,000	2	2,500	2,400	1,250	2,85,000	2,87,400	57,00,000	59,87,400
5,000	1	5,000	1,200	2,500	5,60,000	5,61,200	56,00,000	61,61,200

[Working Notes (3) order size = Annual requirement/No. of orders; (4) Ordering Cost = No. of order × ₹. 1200; (5) Average Stock = Order size × 50/100 (6) Carrying Cost = Average Order size × Unit Rate × 20%; (8) Cost of Purchase = 5000 × Unit rate according to size of order during the year]

Thus *EOQ* = 1,000 tons per order. (Here total cost is minimum) (*b*) When no discount is offered, the *EOQ* can be calculated by use of formula

$$EOQ = \sqrt{\frac{2AO}{C}}$$

A = 5000 tons

O = ₹. 1200

C = 1500 × 20/100 = ₹. 300

$$= \sqrt{\frac{2 \times 5000 \times 1200}{300}} = \sqrt{40,000} = 200 \text{ tons}$$

Illustration 6: A manufacturing company purchases 24,000 pieces of components from a subcontractor at ₹. 500 per piece and uses them in its assembly department, at a steady rate. The cost of placing an order and following it up is ₹. 2,500. The estimated stock-holding cost is approximately 1% of the value of average stock held. The company is at present placing orders which at present vary between an order placed every two months (*i.e.*, six order p.a.) to one order per annum. **Which policy** would you recommend?

Solution:

Statement showing costs for optimum number of orders placed

No. of orders	*1*	*2*	*3*	*4*	*5*	*6*
1. Order size (pieces)	24,000	12,000	8,000	6,000	4,800	4,000
2. Average stock (order size ÷ 2)	12,000	6,000	4,000	3,000	2,400	2,000
3. Value of average stock @ ₹. 500	60,00,000	30,00,000	20,00,000	15,00,000	12,00,000	10,00,000
4. Stock-holding cost (1% of above value)	60,000	30,000	20,000	15,000	12,000	10,000
5. Order cost @ ₹. 2,500 per order	2,500	5,000	7,500	10,000	12,500	15,000
6. Total cost (stock holding cost + order cost) Optimum order size is 5.	62,500	35,000	27,500	25,000	**24,500**	25,000

Alternative Solution.

$$\text{EOQ} = \sqrt{\frac{2AO}{C}}$$

A = Annual consumption

$$= \sqrt{\frac{2 \times 24,000 \times 2,500}{500 \times 0.01}}$$

O = Ordering cost per order

= 4,899 pieces

S = Storage and other inventory carrying cost per unit per annum

No. of orders = 24,000 ÷ 4,899

= 4.9 or say 5 orders

Total inventory cost	
Ordering cost for 5 orders	₹. 12,500.00
Carrying cost (Average inventory × ₹. 0.50)	12,247.50
	24,747.50

Choosing a Supplier and Inviting Tenders

Before actually placing the order the Supply or Purchase Manager must see that he is buying in the best market. By reading current literature on the subject he should know where and when prices are favourable. For substantial requirements he should ordinarily invite tenders. For regular requirements he can even negotiate a rate running contract whereby the prices are settled, leaving the quantity to be bought for future determination.

Before accepting a tender, the Supply or Purchase Manager should pay attention to price (together with freight, etc.) to be paid, quality, quantity, date of delivery, terms of payment and reliability of the supplier. Lowest tenders should not be accepted mechanically. In highly competitive industries all the above-noted factors are important and have an important bearing on the cost of production of the final product.

Illustration 7: After inviting tenders two quotations are received as follows: (*a*) ₹. 1.20 per unit (*b*) ₹. 1.10 per unit plus ₹. 3000 fixed charge to be added irrespective of the units ordered.

Advise with your arguments with whom orders should be placed and what quantity is to be ordered.

The following additional information may be of interest:

Present Stock	35,000 units
Average Monthly Requirement	10,000 units
Maximum level	80,000 units
Minimum level	30,000 units

Solution: The difference in the two tenders is ₹. 0.10 per unit. To cover up fixed cost of ₹. 3,000, the units to be ordered against second should not be less than 30,000 units. At this point the prices under both quotation will be equal.

If order is less than 30,000 units, it will be profitable to place order against first quotation. If ordered quantity is more than 30,000 units, the second quotation will be more advantageous.

From the additional information, it appears that the present ordering quantity is 45,000 units (*i.e.*) maximum level – present stock), it will therefore, be advantageous to order with second quotation.

(*a*) 45,000 @ ₹. 1.20 = ₹. 54,000

(*b*) 45,000 units @ ₹ 1.10 + ₹. 3,000 = ₹. 52,500

Placing of Order

An order should be made out in quadruplicate. One copy should naturally go to the supplier, one should remain in the Purchase Manager's Office, one copy should go to the Accounts Section and one should go to the Goods Receiving Department or, if there is no such department, to the Storekeeper as an intimation that such and such goods may be expected. This copy should not contain any reference to prices, etc.

Receipt of Goods

In big factories there will be a separate department for receipt of goods. In smaller factories this task may be entrusted to the *Storekeeper*. In either case care has to be exercised at the time of the receipt of goods. Whoever is the person responsible, he should get the cases opened under his supervision. Each case should contain what is known as the packing slip, which states the name of the packer and the contents of the case. The contents should be compared with those named on the packing slip. Any shortage of breakage or leakage should be noted and intimated to the supplier. It is customary to send the packing slip along with the complaint. Total quantity of goods received should then be compared with quanity mentioned in the respective order. Any short supply should be noted. If the supply is in excess, the excess should be kept apart and the Purchase Manager should be contacted to find out whether it is to be kept or returned to the supplier. Goods received should also be tested for quality. The Engineer or the Chemist may be called for inspection purposes, but some goods will have to be tested in the laboratory. In any case, if the quality is found defective, the goods should not be accepted; they should be kept apart and the supplier asked to remove them.

After this a "Stores Received Note" should be prepared. Its form is given below:

STORES (OR GOODS) RECEIVED NOTE

No. .... Date........

Supplier..............

Order No. and Date.........

Serial No.	*Description*	*Symbol*	*Quantity*	*Amount*						*Remarks*
				Due to Supplier		*Charges*		*Total*		
				₹	*P.*	₹	*P.*	₹	*P.*	

Received by .... Inspected by .... Bin Cards posted by........................

Storekeeper..................... Costed by .... Stores Ledger posted by..................

If there is a separate goods receiving department four copies of the note should be prepared. One copy will be kept by the Receiving Department, and three copies along with the goods will be sent to the Storekeeper. He will again check the quantity of goods and compare it with the quantity mentioned on the note. He will keep the goods in the allotted bin, sign all the three copies, keep one for his record and send two of them to the Costing Department. If the goods are received by him in the first instance, only three copies will be prepared by him—one copy to be retained for his record and two copies to be sent to the Costing Department. It should be noted that the amount columns on the Stores Received Note will be left blank both by the Receiving Department and the Storekeeper. It is in the Costing Department that these columns will be filled. The first column under "Amount" will show the amounts of the bill as sent by the supplier. In the second column the various charges which are to be added to the cost of the goods will be entered, and the third column shows the total. It is the amount in the total column which will show the total cost of the goods purchased and it is this amount which will be entered in the Stores Ledger.

COSTING OF INCOMING MATERIALS

From the point of view of proper Cost Accounting, expenses incurred in purchasing, receiving and storing the materials should be treated as cost of the materials purchased. This will ensure that the jobs or products which use a particular material will be charged with the total amount spent upon purchasing, receiving and storing that particular material. But there is another point. It has already been pointed out that the expenses incurred on Costing should not be more than the benefit to be derived. In this regard the effort in trying to allocate some of the expenses, for example, the storekeeper's wages or the rent of the godown may be too big compared with the benefit which will be obtained by such an exact allocation. Therefore, a compromise is generally followed. All cost up to the point when materials and stores are ready for issue should be added to the cost. Expenses incurred after this point should be treated as overheads or indirect expenses. This means that the price charged by the supplier, less any trade discount obtained should be added to transportation expenses, import duty or dock dues (in case of imports) and octroi charges. The purchase office expenses, storekeeper's wages, rent of godowns, etc., and also the expenses of the receiving department should be treated as indirect expenses. It is another matter that in some cases such expenses may be allocated to various jobs on products on the basis of quantities of materials used.

Illustration 8: A sugar factory has a permanent 'cane' staff consisting of one superintendent @ ₹. 1,000 p.m. and two assistants @ ₹. 500 p.m. Two-thirds of the time is devoted to cane development and the rest to cane purchase for crushing during the season, usually of 120 days. During season 150 weighment clerks have to be employed @ ₹. 20 per day. The price paid is ₹. 200 per tonne plus a commission of 2 per cent to the farmers' cooperative society. Average railway freight per tonne works out @ ₹. 10. Average quantity of cane crushed per day is 1,500 tonnes. The annual depreciation and repairs of weighing machines is ₹. 3,600. Ascertain the cost of cane per tonne for costing purposes.

Solution:

Statement showing cost of cane (Per ton)

	₹.
Price paid to farmers per tonne of cane	200.00
Commission @ 2%	4.00
Freight	10.00
Cane purchase staff $\frac{8,000}{120 \times 1,500}$	0.04
Weighment 3000/1500	2.00
Depreciation and Repairs of weighing machines $\frac{3,600}{120 \times 1,500}$	0.02
Cost of one tonne of cane	216.06

Materials Handling Charges: The question of expenses incurred in purchasing, receiving, storing and issuing materials and stores is important. As a rule, such expenses should be charged by way of marking up the price of the materials concerned. For example, in a cotton textile factory, the issue price of cotton can certainly include:

(*a*) the purchase price;

(*b*) the incoming freight and other charges;

(*c*) storing expenses including rent of godown, wages to godown keeper, etc. and

(*d*) expenses to cover movement from godown to the mill.

This is so because, generally, purchase of cotton will be kept separate from other purchases. The same practice can be easily followed in case of sugarcane purchased by a sugar factory except that there will be no storing expenses.

But in most other cases only a few of the expenses can be added conveniently to the cost of the materials. Incoming freight, import or octori duty, dock dues, etc., can be easily added and thus charged directly to the cost of products or jobs using the materials. Other expenses for buying, receiving, storing and issuing will be treated as overheads. If the factory is small, these expenses will be part of the total factory expenses to be recovered by an overall charge. If the factory is big, material handling charges will be treated as a separate item of overheads to be recovered differently from general factory overheads. If a large number of items are handled-no one being of pre-eminent importance—the recovery will be by way of percentage change on the value of materials issued. For instance if the total of material handling expenses comes to ₹. 10,000 for a six-month period and the total value of materials issued to the factory comes to ₹. 2,00,000 for the same period, the charge comes to 5 per cent *i.e.* (10,000/2,00,000 × 100). If a job consumes materials worth ₹. 5,000 then five per cent of this namely, ₹. 250, will be added to the cost of the job for material handling charges.

It is possible that some of the materials may be bulky as will be the case in an engineering concern. Special arrangements, like cranes, may have to be made for handling and storing such bulky materials. The cost of storing materials and for operating these cranes, say for a month, should be ascertained. The cost of operating a crane will consist of the wages of the workers operating it, power consumed, insurance charges, repairs and maintenance, depreciation, etc. The total cost should be divided by the total tonnage handled; this will give the cost of handling one tonne of bulky materials. When such materials are issued for production, the cost of handling will be added to the value of materials. For example, suppose a crane costs ₹. 1,000 to operate and it handles 2,500 tonnes of materials a month. This gives a rate of 40 P. per tonne. If, 20 tonnes of materials are issued for a job, ₹. 20 × 0.40 or 8 will be added to the cost of materials.

It should be noted that to the cost of such bulky materials, a percentage charge by way of recovery of purchasing expenses will have to be added in addition to the charge for handling and storing.

Control over Investment in Stocks or Inventory Control: As has been pointed out already, it is necessary that excessive stocks should not be carried. For this purpose the stores ledger will prove of great benefit. Management can find out whether there is over-investment or not by regularly working out the ratio between the total value of stores carried and the value of stores issued during a particular period, say, a month. If the ratio goes up, it means that investment in stocks is going up. For example, if value of stores issued in January comes to ₹. 15,000 and the total value of all items in stock is ₹. 37,500 the ratio is 37,500/15,000 or 2.50. It means that, taking all items together, stocks are sufficient to last for 2½ months. If the ratio for February worked out similarly is, say, 3.1, it means that more money is locked up in inventory. What is a proper ratio will depend upon the average period of delivery. If goods can be replenished within a period of 8 weeks, the ratio should not be much above 2 (if worked out monthly).

Another way to work out the ratio is to divide the total value of inventory by the value of the materials issued during the delivery period. For example, if (*a*) it takes six weeks to replenish stocks on an average (*b*) the value of issue during a period of six weeks is ₹. 3,00,000 and (*c*) the total of inventory comes to ₹. 9,00,000, the ratio is 9,00,000/3,00,000. This shows investment in stocks at too high a level. This ratio should not be much above 1.

To get better results it would be better to split up the total inventory into its natural categories of (*a*) raw materials (*b*) chief stores, *e.g.*, coal, and (*c*) sundry consumable stores. The ratio should then be worked out separately for each category. This will indicate where exactly overstocking has occurred.

Even this is not enough. The account of each item should be gone through and separate lists should be compiled of items:

(*a*) of which there are large stocks but which were not used at all during the year and are not likely to be used; and

(*b*) of which the stocks are too large compared to the demand likely to arise in the coming months.

Total stocks of items covered by (*a*) and excessive stocks of items covered by (*b*) should be immediately disposed of. Delay will only mean deterioration in quality and a consequent loss in the amount realised.

An exception to the above rule is spares for machinery in use. The fact that a particular part has not been required for a number of years is no guarantee that it will not be required in future also. Thus, as long as a machine is in use, its spares should be kept in stock and not disposed of. Spares of machines no longer in use should certainly be disposed of unless they can be used for other purposes.

Illustration 9: A factory has received one consignment containing two improtant materials X and Y and the invoice pertaining to the same discloses the following information:

	₹.
Materials 'X' 1000 tons @ ₹. 2 per ton	2,000.00
Materials 'Y' 1200 tons @ ₹. 1.60 per ton	1,920.00
Insurance	98.00
Freight etc.	110.00
Sales Tax	196.00

Due to mishandling in the factory store, loss of 20 tons of Materials 'X' and 12 tons of Materials 'Y' was recorded. What rate you would adopt for issuing these materials to jobs. If a provision of 20 per cent is to be made for probable risk of obsolescence, what would be the new rate? Losses of materials were treated as normal loss.

Solution:

Statement of Cost of Materials

	Materials X		Materials Y	
	₹.	Tons	₹.	Tons
Payment to the Supplier	2,000	1,000	1,920	1,200
Add: Insurance	50	—	48	—
Freight	50	—	60	—
Sales Tax	100	—	96	—
Total	2,200	1,000	2,124	1,200
Less: Loss of tons due to mishandling	—	20	—	12
	2,200	980	2,124	1,188
Rate of Issue	$\frac{2,200}{980} = 2.24$		$\frac{2,124}{1,188} = 1.79$	

If a provision of 20% is to be made for probable risk of obsolescence, then new rates will be

	Materials X	*Materials Y*
Rate calculated above	2.24	1.79
Add: 20% for obsolescence	.45	.36
New Rate	2.69	2.15

Note: Insurance, frieght and sales tax have been apportioned as below:

(*a*) Insurance in the ratio of material cost *i.e.* 200:192

(*b*) Frieght in the ratio of weight of material *i.e.* 10:12

(*c*) Sales tax in the ratio of material cost *i.e.* 200:192

Illustration 10: A timber merchant brought 5,000 c.ft. of timber logs on 1st January, 2005 @ ₹. 20 per c.ft. He stored them in his timber yard for six months for seasoning. In the timber yard the following expenses were incurred during the period of seasoning:

(*a*) Rent of the yard (area of the yard 4,000 sq ft) ₹. 125 p.m.

(*b*) Salaries of 5 chowkidars @ ₹. 100 p.m. to each

(*c*) Incidental expenses @ 150 p.m

(*d*) Share of annual general overhead of the business ₹. 2,000

(*e*) Insurance charges @ 1% on the value of logs to be seasoned.

50% of the floor area of the yard has been set apart for seasoning of the timber and the remaining area for stocking seasoned timber. Loss in volume of logs due to seasoning may be taken as 10%. Calculate cost rate of the seasoned logs per cubic-feet as on 30th June, 2005.

Solution:

Statement of Cost

	Qty. C.ft.	Amount ₹.
Cost of timber logs	5,000	1,00,000
Add: Expenses of seasoning:		
(*a*) Rent for six months (½)		375
(*b*) Salaries for six months (½)		1,500
(*c*) Incidental expenses for six months (½)		450
(*d*) Overhead for six month (½)		500
(*e*) Insurance (1% of ₹. 1,00,000)		1,000
	5,000	1,03,825
Less: Loss in volume (10%)	(500)	—
Total cost timber logs seasoned	4,500	1,03,825

Cost per cubic feet 1,03,825/4500 = ₹. 23.07.

Illustration 11: The particulars relating to 1200 kg of a certain raw material purchased by a company during June were as follows:

(*a*) Lot price quoted by supplier and accepted by the company for placing the purchase order

Lot up to 1000 kg @ ₹. 22 per kg
Between 1000 – 1500 kg @ ₹. 20 per kg
Between 1500 – 2000 kg @ ₹. 18 per kg
} For supplies to factory

(*b*) Trade discount 20%

(*c*) Additional charge for containers @ ₹ 10 per drum of 25 kg.

(*d*) Credit allowed on return of containers @ ₹. 8 per drum.

(*e*) Sales tax @ 10% on raw material and 5% on drums.

(*f*) Total freight paid by the purchase ₹. 240.

(*g*) Insurance at 2.5% (on net invoice value) paid by the purchaser.

(*h*) Stores overhead applied at 5% on total purchase cost of materials.

The entire quantity was received and isued to production. The containers were returned in due course. Draw up a suitable statement to show (*a*) Total cost of materials purchased and (*b*) Unit cost of materials issued to production.

Solution:

Statement of Cost of Materials

	₹.	₹.
Raw Materials 1200 kg @ ₹. 20		24,000.00
Less: Trade discount @ 20%		(4.800.00)
		19,200.00
Containers 48 @ ₹. 10		480.00
		19,680.00
Sales Tax: Raw Materials @ 10%	1,920	
Sales Tax: Containers @ 5%	24	1,944.00
Net Invoice value		21,624.00
Freight paid		240.00
Insurance @ 2.5% on ₹. 21,624		540.00
		22,404.60
Less: Credit for containes 48 @ ₹. 8		(384.00)
		22,020.60
Stores overhead @ 5% on ₹. 22,020.60		1,101.03
Total Cost of Materials		23,121.63

Cost per unit ₹. 23,121.63 ÷ 1200 = ₹. 19.27

Payment: The work of costing the materials received will be done either by the Stores Ledger Clerk or by some other person in the Costing Office. After the Stores Received Note is properly costed and entered in the Stores Ledger, one copy will be forwarded to the Accounts Office which must have already received the bill from the supplier. The Accounts Office will then compare the order; the bill and the Stores Received Note and on this basis payment can be safely made.

STORING OF MATERIALS

All manufacturing concerns appoint a person as Storekeeper. His duties include the receipt of goods, their proper storing, issuing when the goods in question are actually required for use, and accounting for the balance. The storekeeper has to see that the damage to goods while they are under his charge is minimum. Certain goods are liable to leakage or evaporation or damage due to moisture, exposure to the sun and rust. The storekeeper must try to check such loss as much as he can. His job, however, cannot be done unless the building to house the stores is properly constructed. Damp floors or walls or leaking roofs, quite obviously, can cause good deal of damage. The godown of the store should also be constructed from the point of view to avoiding pilferage.

The store should be fitted up with racks which should be sub-divided into small spaces. All these spaces should be serially numbered. Each space will be known as **'bin'** and for one article one bin should be allotted; whenever new supplies of that article are received, they should be put in the bin allotted and not anywhere else. The word **'bin'** should not, however, mean only a space on a rack. 'Bin' really means any place where goods are kept. Bales of gunny bags, *e.g.*, will be stacked in a corner. That corner will be a bin and should be numbered like other bins.

All the articles used in a department should, as far as possible, be stored side by side, that is to say, the bins allotted to the requirements of a particular department should be at one place. Also, as far as possible the original packages should be kept intact with the quantity in each package marked clearly. At a time only one package should be broken open.

It would be the duty of the storekeeper to check actual physical stocks now and then and compare the figure with book figures in order to see that no mistakes or thefts have occurred.

Bin card: On receipt of goods, as evident from the Stores Received Note, the storekeeper enters the goods on a bin card, which is an account to record receipt, issue and balance in terms of quantity. The ruling is given below:

BIN CARD

No....................

Name of the article.................... Maximum Quantity....................

Symbol....................Unit.................... Minimum Quantity....................

Bin No. .... Previous year's Consumption....................

Stores Ledger Folio ....

ORDERED			*Date*	*Reference*	*Received*	*Issued*	*Balance*	*Date Checked*	*Remarks*
No. & Date	*Qty.*	*Date Received*							
RESERVED									
Job No.	*Qty.*	*Date Issued*							

How to make entries on the Bin Card: The main columns are those pertaining to Date, Reference, Received, Issued and Balance. The column for Reference is meant to record the number and nature of the document—Store Received Note for receipts and Material Requisition for issues. Naturally when a quantity is entered in the Received column, it will increase the balance and the balance will be reduced when an entry is made in the Issued column. Thus:

BIN CARD

Date	*Reference*	*Received*	*Issued*	*Balanced*
2005				
Jan. 1	Opening Balance			230
15	Requisition Slip No. 68		40	190
20	Stores Received Note No. 212	150		340

The columns under 'ORDERED' are meant to show how much quantity is still on order. When the storekeeper receives a copy of the order placed on a supplier, he should enter the number and date of the order in the first column and the quantity in the second. The third column is not filled until the goods are actually received—until then it will indicate that such and such quantity of goods is still receivable.

The columns under "RESERVED" show the quantity which must be kept aside for a particular job. Reservations will be made for important jobs under the authority of a pre-designated officer, say, the Superintendent of a department. The number of the job is entered in the first column and the quantity concerned in the second. Suppose, 100 units are reserved for job No. 135 and the actual balance is 160 units. The entries in the "Reserved" columns will enable the storekeeper to know that only 60 units can be issued for jobs other than job No. 135. When the material is drawn against the job for which it was reserved, the date will be entered in the third column, showing that the reservation no longer operates.

Stock Control Cards: Bin cards are usually kept in the bin itself along with the materials but if all the cards are kept in one place in the office of the storekeeper, the name usually given is "Stock Control Cards". There is no difference in the form and contents of Bin Cards and Stock Control Cards.

Double Bin System: Some firms divide the bin (the place meant for storing the article physically) in two portion—one, the smaller one, to store the quantity equal to the minimum quantity (or ordering level) and the other to store the remaining quantity. The staff has instructions not to use the quantity in the smaller portion as long as there is stock in the other portion. As soon as it becomes necessary to use the quantity marked as minimum, it is a signal to place a fresh order. When the fresh stock is received, care will be exercised to see that a quantity equal to the minimum quantity is segregated.

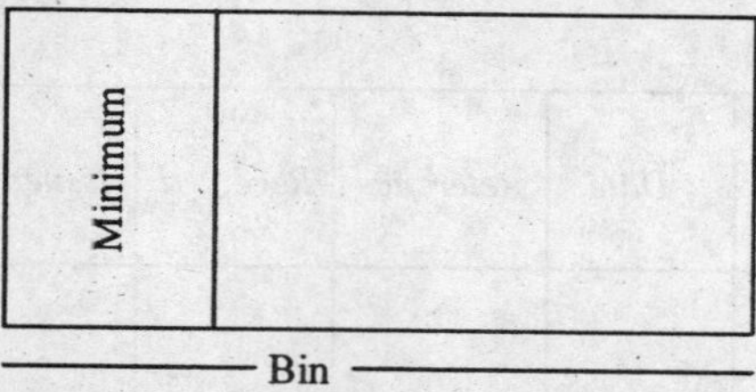

Illustration 12: The following information regarding coal is obtained from the stores records of a factory:

August

1. Opening Balance : 200 tons
2. Issued on Requisition No. 273 : 57 tons

4. Issued on Requisition No. 285 : 83 tons
5. Received from supplier by challan No. 74 of August 5: 120 tons. The supply was expected on this date.
8. Issued on Requisition No. 341 : 92 tons
12. Issued on Requisition No 364 : 30 tons

Examination by the stock Verifier on August 13, revealed shortage of 5 tons. The maximum amount of stock of coal permissible at any time is 200 tons and minimum 50 tons. The ordering level is 100 tons. Draw up the Bin Card for coal with all necessary details.

BIN CARD

Bin No. 23
Department : Coal
Stores Ledger Folio : 51
Symbol : C-25

Description : steam
Max limit : 200 tons
Mini limit : 50 tons
Ordering level : 100 tons

Received			*Issued*			*Balance*		*Remark*
Date	*Ch. No. or Creditslip No.*	*Quantity*	*Date*	*Requisition No.*	*Quantity*	*Quantity*	*Checked*	
Aug.		Tons	Aug.		Tons	Tons		
1	Opening balance	—	—	—	—	200		
—	—	—	2	273	57	143		
—	—	—	4	285	83	60		
5	Challan No. 74	120	—	—	—	180		
—	—	—	8	341	92	88		
—	—	—	12	364	30	58		
—	—	—	13	Shortage	5	53	—	Shortage

ISSUE OF MATERIALS

The storekeeper must not issue stores or materials unless a properly authorised *Requisition Slip* or Material Requisition. (A document which authorises and records the issue of materials for use) is presented below. Generally, it is signed by the foreman but in case of important materials higher authority would probably be necessary.

MATERIALS REQUISITION

No. .... Department................. Date...............
Job No. ....

Quantity	*Description*	*Symbol*	*Bin Card No.*	*Stores Ledger Folio*	*Rate*	*Amount*		*Remarks*
						₹	*P.*	

Authorised by................ Received by ....
Storekeeper's Signature................ Calculations checked by.................
Materials Abstract by......................

Since a large number of people will be authorising the issue of materials, it is not advisable that the number should be already printed. The storekeeper should number the Materials Requisitions as and when he receives them. Quantity, description of materials and the symbols will be already entered and he should issue the materials, if they are available and are not reserved for some other job, against signature of the receiver. To minimise damage, it is essential that issues should be made out of the earliest consignment on hand. If later receipts are issued out first, there is the possibility that earlier receipts may lie for a long time and may get damaged due to rust, dirt or moisture, etc. On issue he should sign the Requisition Slip himself and on the basis of it enter the 'issue' column of the Bin Card. At and end of the day or the next morning, he should send all the requisition slips to the stores ledger section where the columns for amounts will be filled.

Bill of Materials

A complete list of all materials and stores required for a job, complete with quantities, is known as Bill of Materials. When the work is of non-standardised nature is in a jobbing factory, control over use of materials can be exercised only by preparing a Bill of Materials, before the job is undertaken. This will also serve as an indent upon the supply or purchase department, if materials are to be purchased and as a reservation order upon the Storekeeper. Wastage can be easily unearthed if only the exact quantity as laid down by Bill of materials is issued.

Following is the format of Bill of Material.

Bill of Material

Job No. .... No. ....

Deptt. .... Date.................

S.No.	*Code No.*	*Description*	*Qty.*	*Date of Issue and Quantity*		*Rate*	*Amount*
				Date	*Qty.*		

Authorised by .... Received by ....

Storekeeper's Signature Checked by ....

Cost Clerk ....

Four copies of Bill of Materials is prepared which are sent to production, stores, Cost Accounting Deptt. and one is retained by the Planning Department. Bill of Material provides an advance information to all concerned regarding orders to be executed. It enables the stores department to issue purchase requisition. It helps Cost Accounting Deptt. to prepare Material Cost Budget. It provides a controlling technique through comparing actual materials used with the quantity as specified in Bill of Material.

INVENTORY RECORDS AND CONTROL

Perpetual Inventory: The *CIMA* defines perpetual inventory as "A system of records maintained by the controlling department which reflects the physical movement of stock and their current balance."

It means a system of records–a system by which continuous information is available regarding availability of material and stores known as Perpetual Inventory. It involves ascertaining balance after every receipt and issue through bin cards or stores ledgers.

Continuous Stock-taking: It is essential, to prove accuracy of the Perpetual Inventory, that there should be *continuous stock-taking*. Normally physical stock-taking is done once a year or once in six months. The actual quantity of each item is listed and compared with book figures. If no mistake or wastage or theft has taken place, the book figure (as per the Bin Card or the Stores Ledger) should agree with the actual physical stock. If there is any disagreement, it should be capable of an explanation. But since this involves going through the records of the whole year and trying to remember what happened throughout the year, generally the disagreement cannót be explained and the book figures have to be adjusted. The continuous stock-taking removes this drawback. Under this system, fifteen or twenty items of stock are taken up every- day by the Bin Card or the Stores Ledger. If there is a disagreement, the discrepancy is explained there and then. Because the number of receipts or issues would not be large, the cause of the discrepancy would be known and removed. The following day, the next 15 or 20 items are taken up and their physical stock and bóok stock compared. In this way all the items are checked three or four times a year instead of only once under the annual stock-taking. Besides ensuring that the actual stock and book stock agree all the time, the system makes the storekeeper go round his stores and observe any leakage, wastage or pilferage that might be occurring so that all such losses can be, then, promptly checked. The system obviates the need for annual stock-taking and disturbance to the usual work. Stock sheets can be typed out from the stores ledger, knowing that there is no discrepancy between the actual and the book stock. Interim accounts are possible and final accounts can be ready quickly.

To facilitate checking and general storekeeping work, the original packages should be kept intact and should indicate the quantity in each packages. The verifier will then be required to count or weigh only the loose quantity. If the daily check is carried out by somebody other than the storekeeper or his subordinates, it would provide an excellent check on the activities of the storekeeper himself. A few items should be selected at random (in addition to the regular items) to provide an element of surprise. This checking by an "outsider" should not be difficult in view of the fact that the number of the bin is noted on the Bin Card or the Stores Ledger. One can go to the respective bin and count or measure or weigh the article lying there and compare the result with the book figure.

The Record

We have already seen an important piece of record, namely, the Bin Card. We shall now consider other aspects of recording movement of materials and stores.

The Stores Ledger: In any fair sized factory it would be necessary to have continuous information about the values of materials and stores purchased, issued and still in balance. For this purpose, it is necessary to maintain an account for each item both as regards amount and quantity. Accounts of inexpensive materials may not be maintained. The amount spent on their purchases may be charged to Factory Expenses Straightway. The form of the account is given below:

STORES LEDGER

Name of the Article.......................... Minimum Qty. ....
Symbol ....Unit..........................
Maximum Qty. ....
Bin No. .... Previous Year's Consumption........................
Bin Card No. ....
Period of Delivery......................

ORDERED			*Date*	*Reference*	*QUANTITY*			*AMOUNT*						*Rate*	*Remarks*
Qua-ntity	*Order No. & Date*	*Date Received*			*Receipt*	*Issue*	*Balance*	*Receipt*		*Issue*		*Balance*			
								₹.	P.	₹.	P.	₹.	P.		
RESERVED															
Qua-ntity	*Job No.*	*Date Issued*													

Entries in the Stores Ledger are basically made in the same way as in Bin Cards. The only difference is that in the Stores Ledger amounts involved must also be entered. Maintenance of stores ledger so that information about balance in hand and the value of such balance is always available is known as the Perpetual Inventory System. (It cannot be said to be complete without continuous stock taking). This task should be entrusted to a separate clerk and it would not be proper to either entrust the task to the storekeeper himself or to make the clerk a subordinate to him. The Store's Ledger Clerk should work in the Costing Office. It has already been pointed out that the entry in Stores Ledger as regards receipts is made on the basis of the Stores Received Note. As regards issues, the entry will be made on the basis of the Requisition Slip which mentions the quantity issued. It is the Stores Ledger Clerk who will open the ledger at the proper page, find out the rate and make the calculation. The amount thus calculated will be entered on the Requisition Slip and also in the issue column of the Stores Ledger.

Difference between Bin Card and Stores Ledger: The Bin card and stores ledger are the two stock records that are generally kept. The Bin card is purely a quantitative record of receipt, issue and stores in hand. A seperate Bin Card is maintained for each item by the store-keeper. A stores ledger is a stock record showing the receipts, consumption or issues and the balance both in quantity and value. It is maintained by Stores Accounting section. The difference between the two may be summarised as below:

Bin Card	*Stores Ledger*
(*i*) It is mantained by the storekeeper.	(*i*) It is maintained by the Stores Accountant.
(*ii*) It is kept inside the stores.	(*ii*) It is kept outside the stores in stores Accounting Department.
(*iii*) It is purely a quantitative record of receipt, issue and balance of a material-item.	(*iii*) It records both quantity and value of receipts, issues and balance of a material-item.
(*iv*) In Bin card, each transaction is individually posted.	(*iv*) In stores ledger transactions may be posted periodically and in total.
(*v*) Posting are made just before the transaction takes place.	(*v*) Postings are made after the transactions take place.

Forms to be used in Inventory Taking

The most important forms used in inventory taking are the following:

(*i*) *Inventory Tags:* Inventory tags are slips which have two portions showing—Tag number, Material symbol, Quantity after inventory is taken, unit of quantity. The lower portion also shows same information. The upper and lower parts are perforated. The upper portion is attached to the stores bin and the lower portion is torn off and kept for the stock verification.

Inventory Tag

Bin Card No.		No. ....
Stores Code		Stock Verifier ....
Name		Date ....
Quantity		
Bin Card No.		No. ....
Stores Code		Stock Verifier ....
Name		Date ....
Quantity		
Date	Issue After Verification	Receipt After Verification
....	....	....

If any Bin does not contain Tag, it indicates that the item is still to be verified. After proper verification the lower portions of Tags are accounted for the ascertainment of stock. If subsequently it is found that the physical balance and book balance are not in agreement, then these upper portion tags in bins enable the recounting or rechecking.

(2) *Inventory Sheets:* An Inventory Sheet is a list of materials covered by Inventory Tags, with the Inventory balance and the Stores Ledger Balance recorded side by side to show any discrepancy between them. Following is a format of Inventory Sheet.

Inventory Sheet							*S.No.*	
Date of Verification	*Name of Stores*	*Store Code No.*	*Bin. No.*	*Physical*	*Balance Bin Card*	*Stores ledger*	*Surplus or Shortage*	*Remarks*
							.... Signature of Verifier	

After completion of stock verification, this sheet is sent to stores deptt. for making necessary entries. If there are discrepancies necessary investigation is conducted to ascertain causes of discrepancies and also to introduce measures to avoid and control discrepancies.

SELECTIVE INVENTORY MANAGEMENT

A.B.C. System of Selective Inventory Management

The procedure outlined above for fixing minimum quantity (or ordering level) and maximum quantity may not be necessary for every item of material since the effort and the cost of placing an order every now and then may not be worthwhile for items that are very low in value. One should remember that the main aims of the procedure are to avoid interruption of work for want of materials or cost of placing orders repeatedly and to avoid losses arising out of obsolescence and extra interest. The aim can be well realised if

(*i*) for items, that are not at all costly, large orders are placed once, obviating the necessity to review the position again and again and to place orders repeatedly;

(*ii*) for other items that account for a fairly large investment of capital, fresh orders are placed on periodical review basis—say, every month in the beginning the stock position of each such item is compared against liberal estimates of consumption during the next two months, an order being placed if the stock appears to be low; and

(*iii*) for the remaining items (which will be small in number but which will account in the bulk of the investment) the full system of fixing minimum and maximum stocks and placing orders as soon as the stock reach in the ordering level should be operated.

This system of inventory management is called the "*A.B.C. System*". Items covered by (*iii*) above are classed as *A*, those covered by (*ii*) above are classed `*B*' and the remaining items are classed '*C*'.

'*A' category* of items consists of only a small percentage *i.e.,* about 10% of the total items handled by the stores but require heavy investment (cost) about 70% of inventory value, because of their heavy prices.

'*B' Category* of items are relatively less important, these may be around 20% of the total items of materials handled by the stores. the percentage of investment (cost) of such items is around 20% of the total investment in inventories.

'C' category items do not require much investment, it may be about 10% of the total inventory value but they are nearly 70% of the total number of items handled by stores.

For items in class '*A*', the ordering level will be fixed and a fresh order will be placed as soon as actual stock reaches this level. For items in class '*B*', orders are placed on a periodical review and for items in class *C*, large orders are placed once, say, in a year to cover the whole year's consumption. Since the total investment in these items is low (though the number of them will be very large), there will not be much loss by way of obsolescence or interest but the cost of placing many orders will be avoided.

Thus, *ABC Analysis* technique is based on classifying materials into three categories according to their importance. The *A* category items are small in number but high in value and are strictly controlled. Perpetual inventory records are maintained in respect of these materials. *C category* of materials are large in number and of small value. Inventories of such materials are tentatively maintained without having perpetual inventory records. The *B category* of materials are intermediate between the two in importance and are controlled to some extent. Whether or not perpetual inventory records are maintained in respect of these items depend upon their number and values.

Illustration 13: The following information is given about a group of items. Classify the items according to the A.B.C System.

Model No.	*Annual Consumption (Pieces)*	*Unit Price Paise*
501	30,000	10
502	2,80,000	15
503	3,000	10
504	1,10,000	5
505	4,000	5
506	2,20,000	10

507	15,000	5
508	80,000	5
509	60,000	15
510	8,000	10

Solution:

Step 1: Establish the rank consumption-wise of each item

Model No.	*Consumption (Pcs)*	*Unit Price Paise*	*Total Consumption ₹*	*Rank*
501	30,000	10	3,000	6
502	2,80,000	15	42,000	1
503	3,000	10	300	9
504	1,10,000	5	5,500	4
505	4,000	5	200	10
506	2,20,000	10	22,000	2
507	15,000	5	750	8
508	80,000	5	4,000	5
509	60,000	15	9,000	3
510	8,000	10	800	7
Total			87,550	

Step 2: Determine the percentage limits for items to be considered *A*, *B* or *C*. Say, these are:

Items accounting for 80% of consumption are *A*;

Items accounting for the next 15% consumption are *B*: and

The rest are *C*.

Step 3: Listing the item in order to ranks.

Model No.	*Consumption ₹*	*Cumulative Consumption ₹*	*%*	*Cumulative %*	*Category*
502	42,000	42,000	48%	48%	*A*
506	22,000	64,000	25%	73%	
509	9,000	73,000	10%	83%	*B*
504	5,500	78,500	7%	90%	
508	4,000	82,500	4.6%	94.6%	
501	3,000	85,500	3.4%	98.0%	*C*
510	800	86,300	0.9%	98.9	
507	750	87,050	0.8%	99.7	
503	300	87,350	0.2	99.9	
505	200	87,550	0.1	100.0	

Thus items 502 and 506 are *A* items; items 509, 504 and 508 are *B* items and the rest are *C*.

Inventory Turnover Ratios

The Inventory Turnover expresses how many times the average inventory is rotated hrioughout the period. These ratios are useful in identifying unnecessary investments in inventories. If a revision of stores level is called for, appropriate action should be promptly taken to revise ordering quantities.

The inventory turnovers for different classes of materials are ascertained as follows:

Turnover of Raw Materials during the year

$$= \frac{\text{Total cost of Raw Materials issued for production or consumed in production}}{\text{Total cost of Average Inventory of Raw Materials held during the year}}$$

Average inventory may be taken as average of Minimum level and Maximum level of stock or it may be Minimum Level plus 1/2 of ordering quantity.

When the inventory position calls for revision of stock levels and ordering quantities, appropriate action should be promptly taken. In this manner the correct turnover will be maintained and inventories will be properly controlled.

By dividing the number of days in a year by inventory turnover, the number of days for which the average inventory is held, can be calculated. Suppose if the inventory turnover is 5 the average inventory held will be equal to 73 days consumption (365/5 = 73).

Illustration 14: [Stock or Inventory turnover ratio]

Calculate stock turnover ratio from the following particulars

(*a*) For *A Co.*; Opening Stock ₹. 20,000; Closing Stock ₹. 16,000: Purchases 68,000.

(*b*) For *B Co.*; Maximum Stock level ₹. 4,000; Minimum Stock level ₹. 2000: Consumption during the year ₹. 9000.

(*c*) For *C Co.*; Maximum Stock level 1,200 units; Minimum Stock level 600 units; Reorder quantity 800 units; Consumption during the year 6000 units.

Solution:

(*a*) *A* Co.

$$\text{Stock Turnover ratio} = \frac{\text{Consumption during the period}}{\text{Average Stock}}$$

$$= \frac{20,000 + 68,000 - 16,000}{(20,000 + 16,000) \times \frac{1}{2}} = \frac{72,000}{18,000}$$

= 4 (Times during the period)

(b) *B* Co.

$$\text{Average Stock} = \frac{\text{Max. Stock level + Mini. Stock level}}{2}$$

$$= \frac{4000 + 2000}{2} = 3000$$

$$\text{Stock Turnover Ratio} = \frac{\text{Consumption during the period}}{\text{Average Stock}} = \frac{9000}{3000} = 3$$

(*c*) *C* Co.

$$\text{Average Stock} = \text{Mini Stock level} + \frac{1}{2}\ \text{Reorder Quantity}$$

$$= 600 + 800 \times \frac{1}{2} = 1000 \text{ units}$$

$$\text{Stock Turnover Ratio} = \frac{\text{Consumption during the period}}{\text{Average Stock}} = \frac{6000}{1000} = 6$$

Illustration 15: From the following data for the year ended 31st March, 2004, calculate the inventory turnover ratio of the two items, and put forward your comments on them.

	Material A	*Material B*
	₹.	₹.
Opening Stock	10,000	9,000
Purchases	52,000	27,000
Closing Stock	6,000	11,000

Solution:

		Material A	Material B
		₹.	₹.
Opening Stock		10,000	9,000
Add: Purchases		52,000	27,000
		62,000	36,000
Less: Closing Stock		6,000	11,000
Material consumed during		56,000	25,000
Average Stock = $\frac{\text{(Op. Stock + Cl. Stock)}}{2}$	=	$\frac{10,000 + 6,000}{2}$	$\frac{9,000 + 11,000}{2}$
	=	8,000	10,000
Inventory Turnover Ratio = $\frac{\text{Material consumed}}{\text{Average Stock}}$	=	$\frac{56,000}{8,000}$	$\frac{25,000}{10,000}$
	=	7	= 2.5

A high ratio indicates that stock is fast moving whereas a low ratio indicates slow-moving stock. Thus material A is fast-moving item.

PRICING OF ISSUE OF MATERIALS

There are various methods which are in use for pricing issues of materials or stores. Before the methods are discussed, it is worthwhile to point out that, whatever method is followed, *the actual issues of materials will always be on the basis of first in first out*. That is to say, the actual issue of materials will always be from the earliest consignment.

1. At Cost or First in First out or FIFO Method

'It is price paid for the material first taken into the stock from which the material to be priced could have been drawn' (*CIMA*). This method follows the principle of actual issues. The price to be charged is the same which was paid for the particular consignment from which materials are being issued. For example, if on 10th July, 50 units are received at ₹. 5 per unit and on 20th July, another 60 units are received at ₹. 6 per unit and if on 22nd July 70 units are issued, then the cost of the 70 units will be 50 units at ₹. 5 or ₹. 250 and 20 units at ₹. 6 or ₹. 120 or ₹. 370 in all. Under this system the price of materials issued is exactly the same as paid and, hence, the cost of jobs or products will be accurately known, at least as regards materials. But against this there is the disadvantage that clerical labour may be excessive since every time an issue is made, the clerk will have to go through his record to find out what price is to be charged. Also it is possible that if similar jobs are undertaken on the same day or in the same week, the costs may differ simply because the materials have been taken from different lots even though the materials are of the same nature.

This method is *most suitable* when (*i*) materials are subject to deterioration, (*ii*) when inventory items do not move very fast, and (*iii*) when the prices of materials purchased are not subject to violent fluctuations.

Advantages: (*i*) Since materials issued for production are at the original cost, the inventory reflects the current market price, (*ii*) Profit and Loss Account and the Balance Sheet satisfactorily represent the actual conditions, (*iii*) When the price level is declining, the FIFO method shows a lower profit for income tax implications, (*iv*) Next to the Average Cost Method, FIFO is the most commonly accepted basis of valuation of issue, and (*v*) The method simplifies computation of the values of issues.

Demerits: (*i*) When there are price-fluctuations *FIFO* method makes the cost of production fluctuating from period to period. (*ii*) At the time of increasing price-level this method shows profit and inventory at higher figures which have unfavourable income tax implications.

Refund from work order: Materials once issued from stores may be returned by the receiving department. These will be shown as receipts in the stores ledger and may be valued by the rate these were issued but these will be treated as supposed to be received on the date of return of materials to the stores.

Returned to Supplier: When materials are returned to supplier after having been received in the stores and entered in the Stores Ledger, these will be treated in same manner as materials which are issued for regular use. These will be recorded in issue column and will be valued at issue-rate at that date.

Shortage of Stock: Shortage will be deducted from the stock and will be valued at cost price or purchase price.

Illustration 16: The following is a history of the receipts and issue of motives in a factory during February, 2004.

February	1	Opening balance	500 kg @ ₹. 25
"	8	Issue	250 kg
"	13	Receipts	200 kg @ ₹. 24.50
"	14	Refund from a work order	15 kg @ ₹. 24.00
"	16	Issue	180 kg
February	20	Receipts	240 kg @ ₹. 24.37
"	24	Issue	304 kg

Issues are to be priced on the principles of FIFO. Stock verifier of the factory noted on 15th a shortage of 5kgs. Write out the complete Store ledger account in respect of the above motives for February, 2004.

Solution:

Stores Ledger Account for February, 2004

Motive........... Code No............ Maximum quantity..............
Minimum quantity..............

Date	Receipts				Issues				Balance			Remarks
	G.R. No.	*Qnty. kg*	*Price per kg*	*Amount ₹*	*S.R. No.*	*Qnty. kg*	*Price @*	*Amount ₹*	*Qnty. kg*	*Price per kg*	*Amount ₹*	*Rema-rks*
2004 Feb. 1									500	25.00	12,500.00	
8						250	25.00	6250.00	250	25.00	6,250.00	
13	—	200	24.50	4900.00					250 200	25.00 24.50	11,150.00	
14	—	15	24.00	360.00					250 200 15	25.00 24.50 24.00	11,510.00	*Shortage noted
16						180	25.00	4500.00	*65 200 15	25.00 24.50 24.00	6,885.00	on 15th of 5
20	—	240	24.37	5848.80					65 200 15 240	25.00 24.50 24.00 24.37	12,733.80	kg valued on FIFO
24						65 200 15 24	25.00 24.50 24.00 24.37	7469.88	216	24.37	5,263.92	basis

2. Last in First out or LIFO Method

"It is the price paid for the material last taken into the stock from which the material to be priced could have been drawn." (*CIMA*). Under this method the price of the latest consignment is used. In the example given above, 60 units will be costed at ₹ 6 per unit or ₹ 360 and 10 units will be costed at ₹ 5 per unit or ₹ 50, or ₹ 410 in all. This method claims a few *advantages*:

(*a*) The issue will be priced at the market rate prevailing, more or less, near the date of issue. This has the advantage of ascertaining the cost at about the prevailing market price and the cost thus ascertained will enable the prices to be fixed on competitive basis.

(*b*) The principle of costing the goods at cost has not been given up.

(*c*) In case of rising prices the method has the advantage of showing a lower profit which may help in saving tax to some extent. It is not without reason that this method has come into use only when prices have been steadily rising.

The *disadvantages* of this method are the same as those of the *FIFO* method, namely, excessive clerical labour and differing costs of similar jobs using similar materials. Other disadvantages are — (*i*) Under this method the inventory is shown at the oldest market price and so does not reflect the current conditions, (*ii*) Since the inventory value at the end of a period is out of date, large adjustment may be necessary, if the cost or market rule is applied.

Illustration 17: (LIFO/FIFO Methods Compared): The following is the record of the Receipts and Issues of a certain materials in a factory during a week:

January

Opening balance 50 tons @ ₹ 10 per ton.

1. Issued 30 tons
2. Received 60 tons @ ₹ 10.10 per ton
3. Issued 25 tons (Stock verification reveals loss of one ton)
4. Received back from orders 10 tons (previously issued at ₹ 9.90 per ton)
5. Issued 40 tons
6. Received 22 tons at ₹ 10.20 per ton
7. Issued 33 tons

At what price should you issue the materials on January. 1. 3. 5. and 7 respectively. Use two important methods for this purpose and show the comparative result.

Solution: (*A*) According to the FIFO method, the price of the issues will be as follows:

				₹
January	1.	30 tons @ ₹ 10 per ton		300.00
	3.	25 tons :	19 tons @ ₹ 10 per ton	190.00
			6 tons @ ₹ 10.10 per ton	60.60
	5.	40 tons :	40 tons @ 10.10 per ton	404.00
	7.	33 tons :	14 tons @ ₹ 10.10 per ton	141.40
			10 tons @ ₹ 9.90 per ton	99.00
			9 tons @ ₹ 10.20 per ton	91.80
				1,286.80

Note: The price one ton which is found short on stock verification will be included in works overhead at ₹ 10.00.

(*B*) According to LIFO method the price of the issues will be as follows:

			₹.
January	1.	30 tons @ ₹. 10 per ton	300.00
	3.	25 tons : 25 tons @ ₹. 10.10 per ton	252.50
	5.	40 tons : 34 tons @ ₹. 10.10 per ton	343.40
		6 tons @ ₹. 10 per ton	60.00
	7.	33 tons : 22 tons @ ₹. 10.20 per ton	224.40
		11 tons @ ₹. 10 per ton	110.00
			₹. 1,290.30

Note: The price of one ton which is found short on stock verification will be included in works overhead at ₹. 10.10.

Illustration 18: A manufacturing company issues materials to jobs on the `last in first out' (LIFO) basis. At the end of each quarter all materials are valued at the cost of the last delivery. The company made the following purchase of a commodity X:

12th January 2004 — 12 gross at ₹. 40 per gross.
21st January — 12 gross at ₹. 45 per gross
28th February — 12 gross at ₹. 50 per gross
15th March — 12 gross at ₹. 60 per gross

Issues to jobs were made as follows

20th January — 10 gross
17th February — 10 gross
18th March — 10 gross.

Write up the Store ledger Account for the quarter ending 31st March, 2004.

Solution:

STORES LEDGER ACCOUNT
(Last in First Out Method)

Material .... Code No. .... Maximum quantity .... Minimum quantity ....

	Receipts				*Issues*				*Balances*			
Date	*G.R. No.*	*Quantity in Gross*	*Price @ ₹.*	*Amount ₹.*	*S.R. No.*	*Quantity in Gross*	*Price @ ₹.*	*Amount ₹.*	*Quantity in Gross*	*Price ₹.*	*Amount ₹.*	*Remarks*
2004 Jan. 12		12	40	480.00					12	40	480	
Jan. 20						10	40	400	2	40	80	
Jan. 21		12	45	540.00					2 12	40 45	80 540	
Jan. 17						10	45	450	2 2	40 45	80 90	
Jan. 28		12	50	600.00					2 2 12	40 45 50	80 90 600	
Mar. 15		12	60	720.00					2 2 12 12	40 45 50 60	80 90 600 720	
Mar. 18						10	60	600	2 2 12 2	40 45 50 60	80 90 600 120	Closing Stock ₹. 890
Mar. 31									18		890	890

3. Average Cost Method

Average may be of two types—simple arithmetic average and weighted average.

Simple Average Price: "A price which is calculated by dividing the total of the prices of the materials in the stock from which the materials to be priced could be drawn, by the number of prices used in that total."

Weighted Average Price: "A price which is calculated by dividing the total cost of materials in the stock from which the material to be priced could be drawn, by total quantity of materials in that stock." (*CIMA*)

The simple average means only the adding up of the prices and dividing the sum by the number of prices involved. Suppose 50 units have been purchased @ ₹. 5 per unit and 60 units @ ₹. 6 per unit, the simple average would be $\frac{(5+6)}{2}$ or 5.50. The weighted average takes into account the quantity involved. In the above example, the weighted average will be as follows:

50 units at ₹. 5	₹. 250
60 units at ₹. 6	₹. 360
Total of 110 units	₹. 610
The weighted average price is 610 ÷ 110	₹. 5.55

It is better to follow the weighted average. Whatever the average used, the issues will be costed at the average price irrespective of the lot from which the issue is made. The average does not change with issues but it will change with a fresh supply when a new average will be calculated. The method saves clerical labour and adheres to the costing principle. In periods of fluctuating price, the average method will even cut the fluctuations.

Conditions Favouring the Weighted Average Method:

(*i*) When market prices are subject to constant fluctuation, the weighted average method makes the upward or downward trend more gradual. The weighted average is to some extent influenced even by oldest price. If, after a uniform increase in the market price, the latter suddenly falls during a period, the average rate is very little affected by the fall. (*ii*) When materials consist largely of small items issued in small quantities, the Weighted Average Method may be conveniently used.

Advantages of Weighted Average Method: (*i*) This method stabilises costs when prices rapidly fluctuates, (*ii*) This is free from objections by the Income Tax Authorities, (*iii*) It is most acceptable methods of pricing issue.

Disadvantages: (1) This method requires considerable amount of detailed clerical work in computing the average rates, (2) The rate is influenced by the high or low prices in the past and does not reflect current conditions.

***Illustration 19:* (Weighted Average Method):** Following is the record of receipt and issue of a certain materials in a factory during a week:

March	
2nd Opening balance	50 tons @ ₹. 10 a ton.
3rd, Issued	30 tons
4th Received	60 tons @ ₹. 10.125 a ton
5th, Issued	25 tons (Stock verification records normal loss of one ton)
6th Received back from completed word order	10 tons (Previously issued @ 9.94 a ton)
7th, Issued	40 tons

Assume that the issue of material is priced on the Weighted Average Method, calculate the prices of issue on 3rd, 5th and 7th March.

Solution:

Valuation of Issue (Weighted Average Method)

Date of issue	*Quanity of issue*	*Rate at which issues are to be priced*	*Amount ₹*
April 3	30 tons	10.00 per ton	300.00
April 5	25 tons	$\frac{(20\times10)+(60\times10.125)}{80-1}$ = 10.22 approx. per ton.	255.48
April 7	40 tons	$\frac{(54\times10.22)+(10\times9.94)}{54+10}$ = 10.18 per ton	407.20

Periodic Weighted Average Method: In the weighted average method, the issue rate is worked out by taking the quantity and price of each lot of receipt. In the Periodic Weighted Average the rate of issue is not calculated at each lot of receipt but only periodically, usually at interval of one month. The rate worked out in this manner is applicable for issues made in the subsequant month.

The *Advantages* are : (*i*) As with the periodic simple average method, clerical costs are reduced, (*ii*) It is much useful in process costing because intervals at which rates are revised coincide with the process accounting period, (*iii*) The issue rate is not affected by short-term fluctuations in prices.

The *Shortcomings* are (*i*) There will be heavy clerical work at the end of accounting period, (*ii*) In this method, violent fluctuations of purchase prices are ignored.

4. Replacement Cost or Market Price on the Date of Issue

Here cost of the materials in hand is not considered. When an issue is made the market price is ascertained and the issue is priced at that price. It is claimed that where quotations have to be made, this is the best method since it would reflect the latest competitive condition. But this confuses estimating, with costing. We should certainly take into account the ruling prices of materials if we are preparing to make a tender but to find out the cost of doing a job is quite different. For this purpose, the cost of materials and not their prevailing price should be used.

It is also claimed for this method that it would automatically disclose efficiency or inefficiency in buying. The Stores Ledger will use cost for receipts and the market price for issues. Higher rate for issues than for receipts will disclose efficiency in buying (and vice versa). This will leave a proportionately small amount for the quantity in hand. There may even be a negative amount for a positive quantity balance.

It is, however, submitted that this would unnecessarily complicate costing books, and, in any case, costing has nothing to do with profits or losses as such. This method introduces an element of profit or loss in the cost itself because of the use of market price rather than the cost for issue of materials. It is better to avoid the use of the method even though the market price would naturally be taken into consideration at the time of sending tenders or fixing prices.

The method is also called *Replacement Cost Method* since the market price on the date of issue means the price at which present stock could be replaced by new stock. The term "*Replacement Price*" has been defined by the Institute of Cost and Management Accountants of England as:

"The price at which there could be purchase of an asset identical to that which is being replaced or revalued."

5. Fixed Price

Under this method, the issue price is fixed for a whole period. The rate is used for costing the issues irrespective of the purchase price. It is clear that such a method will introduce an element of profit or loss in the value of material used. For example, if the purchase price is ₹. 5 and the issue price has been fixed at ₹. 6 per unit, every time an issue is made a profit of ₹. 1 per unit will be created. Thus, the Store Ledger will be complicated. Even the advantages of the market price method are not available under this method simply because the fixed price will be different from the market price.

6. Standard Price

"Standard Price is predetermined price fixed on the basis of a specification of all the factors affecting that price." Firms which follow standard costing will record all the receipts and issues of materials at the standard price which will be fixed in advance. In this case, both the receipts and issues will be costed at a standard rate. In case the purchase price is more or less than the standard price, the difference is charged to an account which is known as the standard price, the difference is charged to an account which is known as "Price Variance Account". For example, if the standard price is ₹. 5 per unit and the actual price is ₹. 5.50, then the Stores Ledger will be debited at the rate of ₹. 5 and Price Variance Account with 50 paise per unit. Issues are all costed at the standard price. It serves to measure efficiency in use of materials, also it saves clerical labour.

7. Inflated Price

Where materials are subject to natural wastage the cost may be inflated to account for the wastage. Thus, if 100 units of materials are bought for ₹. 150 and if, out of this, only 90 units can be normally used (the other ten going to waste), the issues may be costed not at ₹. 1.50 per unit but at ₹. 1.67 per unti, *i.e.* 150 ÷ 90. With the actual issue of 90 units the amount will be exhausted and so will the actual quantity. Both in the stores ledger a quantity balance of 10 units will remain; it should be written off.

Illustration 20: **(Issue at Standard Price):** Prepare Stores Ledger Account from the following purchases and issue of materials, when issues are priced at standard rate of ₹. 20 per unit:

Purchases	400 units @ ₹. 20 per unit
"	350 units @ ₹. 18 per unit
Issues	300 units
"	400 units
Purchases	400 units @ ₹. 20 per unit
"	250 units @ ₹. 25 per unit
Issues	500 units

Solution:

Stores Ledger Account

Date	*Receipts*			*Issues*			*Balance*		
	Qty.	*Rate* ₹.	*Amt.* ₹.	*Qty.*	*Rate* ₹.	*Amt.* ₹.	*Qty.*	*Rate* ₹.	*Amt.* ₹.
	400	20	8,000	—	—	—	400	—	8,000
	350	18	6,300	—	—	—	750	—	14,300
	—	—	—	300	20	6,000	450	—	8,300
	—	—	—	400	20	8,000	50	—	300
	400	20	8,000	—	—	—	450	—	8,300
	250	25	6,250	—	—	—	700	—	14,550
	—	—	—	500	20	10,000	200	—	4,550

8. Highest in First Out (HIFO) Method

By this method quantities of materials are issued at the highest price of materials on hand. When the quantity having the highest price is exhausted, the next highest price is used in valuing issue. When this method is used in, production becomes highest, so that the profit is reduced. During a period of increasing price level, the method is equivalent to *LIFO* method and in a period of decreasing price level, the method is identical with *FIFO* method. *HIFO* method is of theoretical interest only as it has not received wide acceptance.

9. Next-in-First Out (NIFO) Method

Under the *NIFO* Method, the price of material which is to be next received is used in valuing issued materials. It is based on the assumption that the price of the next consignment is known before it is received. If by the time the materials are received, the production is completed, the production cost of materials shows the value of most current purchases. This method is almost similar to *LIFO* method but is more forward looking and under this method, cost of production reflects the current prices of materials.

10. Moving Average Method

By this method, the issue rate for a certain month is established by taking the average of the periodic weighted average cost prevailing during that month and a number of months preceeding it. It may be moving average on the basis of six months, twelve months etc. For example, if six months moving average is taken for the month of June, the moving average will be simple average of the rates prevailing for six months from January to June and for the month of July, it will be simple average of rates for February to July.

11. Base Stock Method

Under this method, a minimum quantity of stock is always to be held in stores as fixed asset. The minimum stock is known as base stock and it should not be issued unless there is an emergency. The stock in excess of base stock would be issued in accordance with one of the methods of pricing of issue *e.g. LIFO, FIFO, Average*, etc. Thus it is not an independent method in itself.

Illustration 21: **(Base Stock Method):**

During the month of October, 2000 the following receipts and issues of the materials took place in the stock of ABC Ltd.

	Receipts		*Issues*
	Units	*Rate* ₹.	*Units*
Oct. 1 Balance	100	2.00	—
7	80	1.50	—
9	60	2.00	—
11	—	—	140
13	—	—	20
15	40	2.50	—
24	—	—	40
25	—	—	20
28	80	1.50	—

On 31st October a shortage of 10 units was found. Record the above in the Stores Ledger assuming that the Company maintains its ledger on the *LIFO* method with a Base Stock of 80 units.

Stores Ledger Account
(LIFO Method Base Stock 80 units)

Date 2000	Receipts			Issues			Balance		
	Qty.	Rate	Amt.	Qty.	Rate	Amt.	Qty.	Rate	Amt.
Oct. 1	100	2.00	2.00	—	—	—	100	2.00	200
" 7	80	1.50	120	—	—	—	100 80	2.00 1.50	200 120
" 9	60	2.00	120	—	—	—	100 80 60	2.00 1.50 2.00	200 120 120
" 11	—	—	—	60 80	2.00 1.50	120 120	100	2.00	200
" 13	—	—	—	20	2.00	40	80	2.00	160
" 15	40	2.50	100	—	—	—	80 40	2.00 2.50	160 100
" 24	—	—	—	40	2.50	100	80	2.00	160
" 25	—	—	—	—	—	—	80	2.00	160
" 28	80	1.50	120	—	—	—	80 80	2.00 1.50	160 120
" 28	—	—	—	20	1.50	30	80 60	2.00 1.50	160 90
" 31	—	—	—	10 shortage	1.50	15	80 50	2.00 1.50	160 75

Note: On 25th October requisition is received for 20 units. On this date there were 80 units in the stock. If 20 units are issued, then units of base stock will be reduced, therefore 20 units will be issued not on 25th October but on 28th October when 80 units will be received.

Choice of Pricing Method

There are different methods for pricing the material issues. The selection of method depends upon the accounting principles followed in that organisation both for the costing of products and valuation of closing stock. It is the method of pricing of stores that influences the cost of the product and the value of the closing stock. Hence a very careful choice has to be made of the method of pricing the issues.

The method to be selected must satisfy following four basic factors:

(*i*) The total issue price should recover the cost of the material i.e. all issues plus closing stock should not be less than cost of purchase of material.

(*ii*) The issue price should be near to current market price.

(*iii*) There should be no significant variation in issue price from period to period and

(*iv*) Due to issue prices, there should not be heavy adjustments in values of closing stock.

If we consider these factors, we find that *Weighted Average Cost Method* appears to be the one which satisfies all these conditions. But it cannot be the best method for all circumstances and for all industries. The selection of method will largely depend upon (*i*) the frequency of purchases, (*ii*) the fluctuations in market price, (*iii*) the nature and degree of influence which the material cost has on the selling price of the product, and (*iv*) the method of stock valuation.

CONTROL OF ISSUE OF MATERIALS

Materials Abstract or Materials Issue Analysis Sheets.

It is a document which is a classified record of materials issues, returns and transfers." (*CIMA*). In order to ascertain the cost of materials issued for a job conveniently, it is better to analyse the various Requisition slips since usually there will be a number of them for one job. This analysis is known as materials abstract. It is shown in the form given below:

MATERIALS ISSUE ANALYSIS SHEET
(Materials Abstract)

Week ending ....

Requisition slip No.	*Amounts*	*Job Nos.*														*Overheads (Indirect)*	
		105		*106*		*107*		*108*		*109*		*Total for jobs*					
	₹. P.	₹.	P.	₹.	P.	₹.	P.	₹.	P.	₹.	P.	₹.	P.	₹.	P.		
1	10.94			10	94							10	94				
2	11.50	11	50									11	50				
3	12.81							12	81			12	81				
4	9.00					9	00					9	00				
5	21.62			21	62							21	62				
6	16.50							16	50			16	60				
7	8.25					8	25					8	25				
8	13.50									13	50	13	50				
9	15.37	15	37									15	37				
10	6.19													6	19		
11	11.94									11	94	11	94				
12	13.43													13	43		
13	12.19					12	19					12	19				
Etc	Etc.																
Total	163.24	26	87	32	56	29	44	29	31	25	44	143	62	19	62		

The various jobs are debited with the amount shown by the total of their respective columns. Since it is an analysis of Requisition Slips which have been written up for amount on the basis of amounts entered in the issue column of Stores Ledger, it should be remembered that the total amount debited to the various jobs is the same as the total of the value of stores issued in any period.

Return of Stores or Transfer to Other Jobs

It is certainly possible that some materials may not be used on a job although they may have been issued for it. Such materials should be returned to the stores under "*Contra*" Requisition Slip. The word "*Contra*" prominently written across the Requisition Slip would indicate return of stores. The Storekeeper should sign it and enter the quantity in the receipt column of the Bin Card. The "Contra" Requisition slip should then go to the Stores Ledger Section where it would be costed (at the price it was originally issued) and entered in the receipt column of the Store Ledger. Credit would be given to the job for which the materials were originally issued. Sometimes a special form is used to record transfer to stores. The form is known as 'Shop Credit Note' or Materials Return Note.

Sometimes the materials may be used for another job instead of being returned to the stores. In that case, a Material Transfer Note should accompany the materials and later sent to the Stores

Ledger Section where the amount involved would be entered and respective entries in the job accounts made. The following form can be used both for transfer to another job and to Stores.

MATERIALS TRANSFER NOTE

No. .... Date..............

From Job No. .... To..............

Quantity	*Description*	*Symbol*	*Rate*	*Amount*		*Remarks*
				₹	P.	

Transferor........................ Calculations by.....................

Received by .... Store Ledger posted by ....

Job Ledger posted by.....................

The following definition may be noted:

Materials Return Notes: "A document which records the return unused materials."

Materials Transfer Note: "A document which records the return of materials from one store to another, from one cost centre to another, or from one cost unit to another." *(CIMA)*

Purchase Journal

In case accounts are written up by hand it is better to enter all purchases in the Purchase Journal (ruling given below) so that the total amount of stores and material taken into stock and of those directly taken into the factory for production are readily known. This enables the construction of total accounts in respect of stores which, in turn, enables one to check the arithmetic accuracy of entries made in the Stores Ledger. It is not necessary to maintain two Purchase Journals—one for financial accounting and the other for cost accounting. One is enough.

PURCHASE JOURNAL

For the Month of ....

Date	*Stores Received Note No.*	*Order No. & Date*	*Bill No. & Date*	*Name of Supplier and description of Goods*	*Quantity*	*Amount*						*Issued Direct*			*Taken to Stores*	
						Due to Supplier		*Charges*		*Total*		*Amount*		*Job Ledger Folio*		
						₹.	P.	₹.	P.	₹.	P.	₹.	P.		₹.	P.

The Stores Ledger Control Account

A control account to check the arithmetic accuracy of the Stores Ledger is maintained both in the costing books and in the financial books. In both of these books, the account also serves to reveal the total amount of stores on hand. The account is maintained only in totals. Individual receipts are entered in the respective accounts in the Stores Ledger. The total as per the Purchase Journal of these receipts is entered in the control account.

The total of the column "*Taken to Stores*" in the Purchase Journal would naturally correspond with the amounts written in the receipt columns of the Stores Ledger on the basis of the Stores Received Notes. Hence, the total of the column "Taken to Stores" would agree with total of amounts posted as receipt in the Stores Ledger.

Also, as pointed out above, the total of the Materials Abstract equals the total of amounts posted as issued in the Stores Ledger. These are the two main types of entries in the Stores Ledger. If any other entry is made in (say, the writing off of some materials due to wastage, etc.), it should also be made in the Stores Ledger Control Account which may appear as shown below (*figures are assumed*).

STORE LEDGER CONTROL ACCOUNT

Dr. Cr.

Date	*Particular*	*L.F.*	*Amount* ₹	*P.*	*Date*	*Particular*	*L.F.*	*Amount* ₹	*P.*
Jan. 1	To Balance b/d		26.785	53	Jan. 31	By Work in Progress (as per Materials Abstract)		8,990	23
Jan. 31	To Purchases (P. Journal)		10,513	59	"	By Wastage		105	44
Jan. 31	To Retrun of materials of stores (Contra Req. Slip or Materials Transfer Note)		36	62	"	By Theft		53	51
					"	By Balance c/d		28,186	56
			37,335	74				37,335	74

If the Stores Ledger has been correctly posted, the total of the individual balances in it should equal the balance shown by the Stores Ledger Control Account. (The above is only an application of the principle of Self-Balancing Ledgers)

Accounting Entries: From the discussion so far, it should be clear that:

(*i*) On the basis of Stores Received Notes, various stores accounts are debited in the Stores Ledger (each Stores Received Note being posted individually); the total of the Stores Received Notes, as per the Purchase Journal, is debited in the Stores Ledger Control Account; and

(*ii*) On the basis of Material Requisitions, posted individually, various stores accounts in the Stores Ledger are credited through analysis in the Materials Issue Analysis Sheet (Materials Abstract), individual cost units (or jobs) are debited, the total being credited in the Stores ledger Control Account.

In the Chapter Cost Control Accounts, we shall see how cost accounting record can be maintained on Double Entry basis. However, it may be useful to note the entries to be made in the main cost ledger for receipts and issues of materials. These are :

(*a*) For receipts (as per Purchase Journal)—

Debit Stores Ledger Control Account with the total of "Taken to Stores" column.

Debit Work in Progress Account with the total of "Issued Direct" column.

Credit Cost Ledger Control Account with the total amount of purchases made.

(*b*) For issues (as per Materials Issue Analysis Sheet)—

Debit Work in Progress Account with the total amount charged to jobs.

Debit Overheads Account with the value of materials used as indirect expenses.

Credit Stores Ledger Control Account with the total.

MATERIALS LOSSES, WASTAGES AND CONTROL

Normal and Abnormal Losses

It is a principle of costing that expenses and losses which have to be necessarily incurred are treated as part of cost but expenses and losses which are really avoidable and which are, therefore, incurred, so to say, unnecessarily should not be included in costs. Unavoidable expenses and losses are called normal losses or wastages and avoidable losses and wastages are abnormal. In materials also, certain wastages are unavoidable and, therefore, normal; and certain wastages are avoidable and, therefore, abnormal. The former are due to the nature of or issue of materials. Some materials lose their weight while being stored, say, due to evaporation. When a large quantity is purchased but is issued in small lots, there will be a small loss. This is known as loss due to breaking the bulk. Such losses may be reduced slightly but cannot be eliminated. Experience would tell us the percentage of loss thus incurred. There are two methods of dealing with such a loss. Either the price of the materials should be inflated as indicated above (see inflated price method of pricing the issue of stores) or the value of the loss can be included in factory expenses. For example, if 10 tonnes of coal are purchased at ₹. 200 per tonne and if it is expected that only 9.5 tonnes of coal will be actually available for use, either the price may be inflated to ₹. 210.53, i.e. ₹. 2000 ÷ 9.5, or the issues may be made at ₹. 200 per tonne, and the value of ½ tonne of coal, namely, ₹. 100 charged to factory expenses.

Abnormal losses arise due to mischief, bad luck, or inefficiency. Thus, if materials are lost due to theft, fire, or damage through careless handling, it would be a case of abnormal loss. There is only one way of dealing with abnormal losses. The amount of the loss involved is to be charged to Costing Profit and Loss Account and is not to be included in the cost of production of goods either directly or indirectly.

Control over Wastage of Materials in a Workshop: Proper utilisation of materials is of great importance for the purpose of keeping the costs down. Wastage of any type of materials–raw materials or consumable stores—will add to costs and has to be avoided. The following methods are chiefly used:

(*a*) ***Comparison:*** Cost per unit of output as regards materials in one period is compared with that in another. Suppose in 2000 the materials cost per unit comes to ₹. 16.50 and the figure in 2001 is ₹. 15.00. This indicates that there is greater efficiency in use of materials in 2001 as compared to 2000. But the comparison should be on the basis of quantities used. It is likely that ₹. 16.50 may consist of 11 units @ ₹. 1.50 and that the figure of ₹. 15.00 in 2001 consists of 12 units @ ₹. 1.25. This shows that there is greater inefficiency in 2001 than in 2000 because to produce the same article one extra unit of materials is being used. The saving in price is not efficiency unless the Purchase Officer displayed special skill in getting the lower price. However, it is quite clear that consumption of materials per unit of output must be brought back to eleven units.

(*b*) ***Standards:*** The above method indicates only movements in efficiency in the use of materials. Efficiency may go up; yet inefficiency may remain. What if, in the above example, even the use of eleven units of materials is unwarranted? For the purpose of finding out the existence of inefficiency or wastage, it is essential to know beforehand what quantity of raw materials is required to make one unit of finished goods. For example, every tailor can say how much cloth will be required to make a dress, say, a shirt or a pair of trousers. If it should take 3 metres to make one shirt, one can know exactly how much cloth has been wasted. If 100 metres of cloth are issued and if only 30 shirts are made out of it, then clearly 10 metres have been wasted. Most businesses are not fortunate enough to enable such a simple calculation; but the idea can be worked out for almost any business. What is required is study of past experience and experimentation. On this basis, the exact quantity (including normal wastage) of various materials required can be worked out and if the quantity used exceeds the standard quantity, there is inefficiency. An idea, sometimes useful, is to issue only the exact quantity required for the number of units to be produced. If more is demanded, the foreman can enquire into the reason there and then.

It is the job of the Cost Accountant to work out the cost of wastage of materials and present it to management. It should be remembered that the cost of wastage is not merely the cost of materials wasted. To this must be added wastage of labour and expenses. Suppose 99 metres are issued at ₹. 20 per metre, sufficient to make 33 shirts, and the labour comes to ₹. 1000 and expenses to ₹. 980. The total comes to ₹. 3960 as under :

	₹.
Materials (99 × 20)	1980
Labour	1000
Expenses	980
Total	3960

If 33 shirts are produced, the cost per unit is ₹. 120 *i.e.*, 3960 ÷ 33. If a single shirt is not produced due to wastage of materials, the loss is ₹. 120. Thus, if only 30 shirts are produced the loss is ₹. 360 *i.e.*, 3 × 120. It would be a mistake to say that the loss comes to only ₹. 18, the cost of materials wasted.

CONTROL OVER THE USE OF INDIRECT MATERIALS[1] AND SPARES

Estimation of wastage in use of indirect materials, stores and spares presents some difficulty as it is often difficult to determine and allocate exact quantity used per unit of output. The following steps may, however, help in this task:

(1) *Determination of quantity required per unit of time.* For instance the quantity of lubricating oil required for one hour of running of the machine can be worked out and the actual quantity used compared with it.

(2) *Determination of quantity required per unit of service.* For example, petrol consumption for the kilometres covered by trucks can be worked out. Similarly, coal required for steam raised can also be worked out. Comparison with actual quantity used will indicate inefficiency or otherwise.

(3) *Bill of materials for special service jobs* such as repairs.

(4) *Maintenance of record of replacement of important spare parts* or issue of tools. Since the period of time during which a tool or a spare part should work efficiently can be determined, it is proper to enquire into the reasons if replacement is required earlier.

Reclamation of Loss from Defective Mechanical Units: Mechanical parts or products may be found defective and unserviceable but it is often possible to reduce the loss involved substantially. The parts or products are likely to consist of a number of smaller parts; some of them

---

1 "Materials cost which cannot be allocated but can be apportioned to, or absorbed by, cost centres or cost units." – *CIMA*

will be unserviceable but many of them may be quite good. There should be a system to see that the maximum amount is reclaimed from defective parts or products. The following method is suggested:

(*i*) There should be a room set aside for collection and dismantling of all defective parts or products. It should work under the charge of a responsible person. It may be called Reclamation Room.

(*ii*) The inspector who rejects the units should note on a form the number rejected together with causes of rejection.

(*iii*) The rejected units should be sent to the Reclamation Room together with the inspector's report, a copy of which should be signed by the person incharge of the Reclamation Room as acknowledgement.

(*iv*) All units should be dismantled and the various parts categorised into:

(*a*) good and serviceable;

(*b*) defective but which may be serviceable with more work; and

(*c*) completely spoiled.

(*v*) The parts which are good and serviceable should be sent to the store and taken into stock at the current cost.

(*vi*) Parts whose defects can be removed should be sent to the work shop for the purpose and after removal of defects, taken into stock at the current cost of production.

(*vii*) Completely spoiled parts are only so much metal to be either sold as such or used in foundry.

(*viii*) All movements from the Reclamation Room should be accompanied by forms on which quantities are noted and acknowledged by the person receiving them.

Just In Time (*JIT*) Inventory System

As stated earlier firms maintain a minimum stock level of material. This stock has to act as a buffer so that production keep on moving on schedule even if suppliers are late with deliveries. However, it is costly to carry inventories and now it is believed that having excessive inventory levels encourages inefficiency. As a result, Just-in-time (*JIT*) inventory system has come into use.

Under a just in time (*JIT*) inventory system a company strives to purchase only enough inventory to meet daily needs. In other words, raw materials would be received just in time to go into production and goods are completed just-in-time to be dispatched to customers.

Thus under an ideal conditions a company would have no goods still in process at the end of a day and no raw materials left over to store. All goods completed during the day and would be dispatched immediately to customers so that finished goods would not have to be stored in the godown. The focus of the system is on careful planning to increase efficiency and reduce or eliminate inventory levels and thereby reduce costs.

The *JIT* philosophy has resulted in firms giving increasing attention to reducing stock levels to a minimum by implementing *JIT* purchasing technique. The objective of *JIT* purchasing is to purchase goods so that delivery immediately preceeds their use. An arrangement is made with suppliers for more frequent deliveries of smaller quantities of materials, so that each delivery is just sufficient to meet immediate production requirements, stocks can be cut to a minimum, considerable savings in material handling expenses can also be made by requiring suppliers to inspect materials before their delivery and to guarrentee their quality.

Typical Illustrations

Stock Levels

Illustration 22: The following data relate to a particular item in stock:

Normal usage	110 units per day
Minimum usage	50 units per day
Maximum usage	140 units per day
Lead Time	25–30 days
EOQ	5,000 units (calculated earlier)

Using the data, calculate the Re-order, Minimum and Maximum Levels.

Solution:

(*a*) *ROL* = Maximum Usage × Maximum lead time

= 140 × 30 days = 4,200 units.

(*b*) Minimum Level = ROL – (Average Usage × Average lead time)

= 4,200 – (110 × 27.5) = 1,175 Units.

(*c*) Maximum Level = ROL – (Minimum Consumption × Minimum lead time) + *EOQ*

= 4,200 – (50 × 25) + 5,000 = 7,950 Units.

Illustration 23: 'ZEE' is a product manufactured out of three raw materials '*M*' '*N*' and '*Q*'. Each unit of ZEE requires 10 kg, 8 kg and 6 kg of *M, N* and *Q* respectively. The re-order levels of '*M*' and '*N*' are 15,000 kg and 10,000 kg respectively while the minimum level of '*Q*' is 2,500 kgs. The weekly production of ZEE varies from 300 to 500 units, while the weekly average production is 400 units. You are required to compute:

(*i*) The minimum stock level of *M*,

(*ii*) The maximum stock level of *N*, and

(*iii*) The re-order level of *Q*.

The following additional data are given:

	M	*N*	*Q*
Reorder quantity (in kg)	20,000	15,000	20,000
Delivery (in weeks)			
Minimum	2	4	3
Average	3	5	4
Maximum	4	6	5

[*ICWA (Inter)*]

Solution: (*i*) Minimum stock level of *M*:

= Re-order level – (Average consumption × Average lead time)

= 15,000 – (400 units at 10 kg *i.e.* 4,000 × 3 weeks)

= 15,000 – 12,000 = 3.000 kg

(*ii*) Maximum stock level of *N* = Re-order level – (Minimum consumption × Minimum lead time) + Re-order quantity.

= 10,000 – (300 units at 8 kg *i.e.* 2,400 × 4 weeks) + 15,000

= 10,000 – 9,600 + 15,000 = 15,400 kg

(*iii*) Re-order level of *Q* = (Maximum Consumption × Maximum lead time)

= 500 units at 6 kg *i.e.* 3,000 × 5 weeks = 15,000 kg

or Reorder level of *Q* = Minimum level + (Average consumption × Average lead time)

= 2,500 + (400 units at 6 kg *i.e.* 2400 × 4 weeks)

= 2,500 + 9,600 = 12.100 kg

Illustration 24: From the following information you are required to calculate maximum level, minimum level and ordering level for materials *X* and *Y*;

	X	*Y*
Normal usage per week	150	200
Re-ordering quantity	900	1,500
Maximum usage per week	225	250
Minimum usage per week	75	100
Re-ordering period (weeks)	12 to 18	6 to 12

Solution: It is assumed that : (*i*) Ordering level is Re-order level, (*ii*) Reordering period is lead time. (*iii*) Normal usage is Average usage.

(*i*) Ordering Level = Maximum usage × Maximum lead time

Material *X* : 225 × 18 weeks = 4,050 units

Material *Y* : 250 × 12 weeks = 3,000 units

(*ii*) Maximum Level = Re-order level – (Minimum consumption × Minimum lead time) + Re-ordering quantity.

Material *X* : 4,050 – (75 × 12 weeks) + 900 = 4,050 units

Material *Y* : 3,000 – (100 × 6 weeks) + 1,500 = 3,900 units

(*iii*) Minimum Level = Re-order level – (Average usage × Average lead time)

Material *X* : 4,050 – (150 × 15 weeks) = 1,800 units

Material *Y* : 3,000 – (200 × 9 weeks) = 1,200 units

EOQ & Stock Levels

Illustration 25: From the details given below, calculate:

(*i*) Re-ordering level (*iii*) Minimum level

(*ii*) Maximum level (*iv*) Danger level

Re-ordering quantity is to be calculated on the basis of following information :

Cost of placing a purchase order is ₹. 20

Number of units to be purchased during the year is 5,000.

Purchase price per unit inclusive of transportation cost is ₹. 50.

Annual cost of storage per unit is ₹. 5.

Details of lead time: Average 10 days, Maximum 15 days, Minimum 6 days. For emergency purchases 4 days.

Rate of consumption : Average : 15 units per day, Maximum : 20 units per day.

[*CA (Inter)*]

Solution: Re-ordering quantity is *EOQ*.

$$EOQ = \sqrt{\frac{2AO}{C}} = \sqrt{\frac{2 \times 5{,}000 \times 20}{5}}$$

$$= \sqrt{40{,}000} = 200 \text{ units}$$

Note: All purchases have been assumed as consumption of materials

(*i*) Re-ordering level = Maximum consumption × Maximum lead time

= 20 units × 15 days = 300 units

(*ii*) Maximum level = *ROL* – (Minimum Consumption × Minimum Lead Time) + ROQ or *EOQ*

= 300 – (10 units × 6 days) + 200

= 300 – 60 + 200 = 440 units

Note: Since Maximum consumption is 20 units and Average 15 units per day

$$\text{Average} = \frac{\text{Maximum} + \text{Minimum}}{2}$$

$$15 = \frac{20 + \text{Minimum}}{2}; \text{ Hence Minimum} = 10 \text{ units}$$

(*iii*) Minimum level = ROL – (Average Consumption × Average Lead Time)
= 300 – (15 units × 10 days) = 150 units

(*iv*) Danger level = Minimum consumption × Emergency purchase time
= 10 units × 4 days = 40 units

Illustration 26: A materials manager has the following data for procuring a particular item. Annual Demand = 1,000. Ordering cost = ₹. 800. Inventory carrying cost = 40%. Cost per item = ₹. 60. If the order-quantity is more than or equal to 300, a discount of 10% is given. For how much should he place the order in order to minimise total variable cost?

Solution: (*a*) If discount is not availed

Carrying cost = 40% of 60 = ₹. 24.

$$EOQ = \sqrt{\frac{2AO}{C}} = \sqrt{\frac{2 \times 1000 \times 800}{24}} = \sqrt{\frac{16,00,000}{24}} = 258 \text{ units}$$

$$\text{No. of orders} = \frac{1000}{258} = 4 \text{ orders (Approx.)}$$

Variable cost :	₹.
Purchase cost = 1,000 × 60 =	60,000
Ordering cost = 4 orders at the rate of ₹. 800	3,200
Carrying cost = 258/2 or 129 units @ ₹. 24	3,096
	66,296

(*b*) If Discount is availed

Cost per unit = 60 – 10% = ₹. 54

Carrying cost (*C*) = 40% of 54 = ₹. 21.60

$$EOQ = \sqrt{\frac{2AO}{C}} = \sqrt{\frac{2 \times 1000 \times 800}{21.60}} = 272 \textit{ units.}$$

(*c*) If order quantity is 300 units	₹.
Purchase Cost : 900 units at ₹. 54 (3 orders at 300 units each)	48,600
100 units at ₹. 60	6,000
	54,600
Ordering Cost = 4 orders @ ₹. 800	3,200
Carrying Cost = 300/2 or 150 × 21.60	3,240
Variable Cost	61,040
Variable Cost without discount	66,296
Saving, if discount is availed	5,256

(*d*) If the order quantity is 334 units (3 orders):	
Purchase Cost 1,002 × 54 (3 orders at 334 units each)	54,108
Ordering Cost = 3 × 800	2,400
Carrying Cost = 334/2 or 167 × 21.60	3,607
Variable Cost	60,115
Variable Cost without discount	66,296
Saving, if discount is availed	6,181

On the basis of savings, the ordering quantity should be 334 units.

Illustration 27: (*i*) Compute *EOQ* and the total variable cost for the following:

Annual Demand	5,000 units
Unit Price	₹. 20.00
Order Cost	₹. 16.00
Storage Rate	2% per annum
Interest Rate	12% per annum
Obsolescence rate	6% per annum

(*ii*) Determine the total variable cost that would result for the items if an incorrect price of ₹. 12.80 is used.

Solution:

(*i*) Carrying Cost	=	Storage Rate	2%
		Interest Rate	12%
		Obsolescence Rate	6%
		Total	20% per annum

C = 20% of ₹. 20= ₹. 4 per unit per annum.

$$EOQ = \sqrt{\frac{2AO}{C}} = \sqrt{\frac{2 \times 5,000 \times 16}{4}} = \sqrt{40,000} = 200 \text{ Units.}$$

	₹.
Total Variable Cost :	
Ordering Cost = 5,000/200 or 25 orders @ ₹. 16	400
Carrying Cost of average inventory = 200/2 or 100 Units @ ₹. 4	400
Total variable cost	800

(*ii*) If an incorrect price of ₹. 12.80 is used :

C = 20% of 12.80 = ₹. 2.56 per unit per annum.

$$EOQ = \sqrt{\frac{2 \times 5,000 \times 16}{2.56}} = 250 \text{ units}$$

	₹.
Total Variable Cost :	
Ordering Cost = 5,000/250 or 20 orders @ ₹. 16	320
Carrying Cost (of average inventory) 250/2 or 125 units at ₹. 2.56	320
Total Variable Cost	640

Illustration 28: A Company works 50 weeks in a year. For a certain part, included in the assembly of several parts, there is an annual demand of 10,000 units. This part may be obtained from either an outside supplier or a subsidiary company. The following data relating to the part are given:

	From outside supplier ₹.	*From subsidiary company* ₹.
Purchase price/unit	12	13
Cost of placing order	10	10
Cost of receiving an order	20	15
Storage and all carrying costs, including capital cost per unit per annum	2	2

(*i*) What purchase quantity from which source would you recommend?

(*ii*) What would be the minimum total cost?

Solution:

	From outside supplier	*From subsidiary company*
Cost of placing + receiving order:	10 + 20 = ₹. 30	10 + 15 = ₹. 25
EOQ = $\sqrt{\frac{2AO}{C}}$	$\sqrt{\frac{2 \times 10,000 \times 30}{2}}$	$\sqrt{\frac{2 \times 10,000 \times 25}{2}}$
	= $\sqrt{3,00,000}$	= $\sqrt{2,50,000}$
	= 548 Units	= 500 Units
Purchase cost	10,000 × 12 = ₹. 1,20,000	10,000 × 13 = ₹. 1,30,000
Ordering cost	10,000/548 = 19 orders 19 order @ ₹. 30 = ₹. 570	10,000/500 = 20 orders 20 orders @ ₹. 25 = ₹. 500
Carrying cost	548/2 × 2 = ₹. 548	500/2 × 2 = ₹. 500
Minimum Total Cost	₹. 1,21,118	₹. 1,31,000

Purchase cost from Subsidiary Company is higher by about ₹. 10,000, therefore it should be from outside suppliers which will be 548 units at ₹. 1,21,118.

Illustration 29: Assume that the following quantity discount schedule for a particular bearing is available to a retail store:

Order size (units)	*Discount*
0 — 49	0%
50 — 99	5%
100 — 199	10%
200 —	12%

The cost of a single bearing with no discount is ₹. 30. The annual demand is 250 units. Ordering cost is ₹. 20 per order and annual inventory carrying cost is ₹. 4 per unit. Determine the optimal order quantity and the associated minimum total cost of inventory and purchasing costs.

Solution: Working Notes:

1. EOQ without discount.

$$EOQ = \sqrt{\frac{2AO}{C}} = \sqrt{\frac{2 \times 250 \times 20}{4}} = \sqrt{2,500} = 50 \text{ units.}$$

2. Prices with discount :
   5% Discount 30 – 5% = ₹. 28.50
   10% Discount 30 – 10% = ₹. 27.00
   12% Discount 30 – 12% = ₹. 26.40

Statement of Total Cost at Various Order Sizes

Order size (units)	*No. of orders in a year*	*Ordering Cost (₹.)*	*Carrying Cost of average inventory (₹.)*	*Purchase Cost (₹.)*	*Total Cost (₹.) (3 + 4 + 5)*
1	2	3	4	5	6
50	$\frac{250}{50} = 5$	5 × 20 = 100	$\frac{50}{2} \times 4 = 100$	250 × 28.50 = 7,125	7.325
100	$\frac{250}{100} = 2.5$	2.5 × 20 = 50	$\frac{100}{2} \times 4 = 200$	250 × 27 = 6,750	7,000

125	$\frac{250}{125} = 2$	$2 \times 20 = 40$	$\frac{125}{2} \times 4 = 250$	$250 \times 27 = 6,750$	7,040
200	$\frac{250}{200} = 1.25$	$1.25 \times 20 = 25$	$\frac{200}{2} \times 4 = 400$	$250 \times 26.40 = 6,600$	7,025
250	$\frac{250}{250} = 1$	$1 \times 20 = 20$	$\frac{250}{2} \times 4 = 500$	$250 \times 26.40 = 6,600$	7,120

Thus Optimal order quantity (EOQ) is 100 units and minimum total cost of inventory and purchasing cost ₹. 7,000. Theoretically it may be 2.5 orders, but practically 3 orders will be required. Then the ordering cost would be ₹. 60 and total cost ₹. 7,010.

Illustration 30: A Company is considering the possibility of purchasing from a supplier a component it now makes. The supplier will provide the components in the necessary quantities at a unit price of ₹. 9. Transportation and storage costs would be negligible.

The company produces the component from a single raw material in economic lots of 2,000 units at a cost of ₹. 2 per unit. Average annual demand is 20,000 units. The annual holding cost is ₹. 0.25 per unit and the minimum stock level is set at 400 units. Direct labour costs for the component are ₹. 6 per unit, fixed manufacturing overhead is charged at a rate of ₹. 3 per unit based on a normal activity of 20,000 units. The Company also hires the machine on which the components are produced at a rate of ₹. 200 per month.

Should the Company make the component?

Solution: Ordering cost is not given in the question, it should be calculated by EOQ, where O is ordering cost.

$$EOQ = \sqrt{\frac{2AO}{C}}$$

$$2,000 = \sqrt{\frac{2 \times 20,000 \times O}{0.25}}$$

$$2,000 = \sqrt{\frac{40,000\ O}{0.25}} \quad \text{or } 2,000 \times 2,000 \times 0.25 = 40,000\ O$$

$$O = \frac{10,00,000}{40,000} = ₹.\ 25 \text{ Ordering Cost.}$$

$$\text{Average Stock Level} = \text{Minimum stock} + \frac{1}{2}\ EOQ$$

$$= 400 + \left(\frac{1}{2} \times 2,000\right) = 1,400 \text{ Units.}$$

Cost of making the Components (Annual Cost) :	₹.
Ordering Cost 20,000/2000 or 10 Orders @ ₹. 25	250
Carrying Cost 1,400 × 0.25	350
Raw Material 20,000 × 2	40,000
Direct Labour Cost 20,000 × 6	1,20,000
Hire Charges of Machine 200 × 12 months	2,400
Annual Cost	1,63,000
Purchase Cost of Components 20,000 × 9	1,80,000

It may be advised that company should make components because purchase cost is more than cost of making.

Illustration 31: A company manufactures a product from a raw material, which is purchased at ₹. 60 per kg. The company incurs a handlig cost of ₹. 360 plus freight of ₹. 390 per order. The incremental carrying cost of inventory of raw material is Re. 0.50 per kg, per month. In addition, the cost of working capital finance on the investment in inventory of raw material is ₹. 9 per kg. per annum. The annual production of the product is 1,00,000 units and 2.5 units are obtained from one kg of raw material.

Required :

(*i*) Calculate the economic order quantity of raw materials.

(*ii*) Advise, how frequently should orders for procurement be placed.

(*iii*) If the company proposes to rationalise placement of orders on quarterly basis, what percentage of discount in the price of raw materials should be negotiated? **[*CA Inter Nov. 2001*]**

Solution. (*i*) 2.5 unit = 1 kg of raw material

1,00,000 units = (1 kg × 1,00,000)/2.5 or 40,000 kgs.

Annual consumption/requirement – (*A*) = 40,000 kgs.

Handling cost and freight per order – (*O*) = ₹. 360 + ₹. 390 = ₹. 750

Carrying cost per unit p.a. + Cost of investment p.a. = (0.50 × 12) + ₹. 9

C = ₹. 15 per unit

$$\text{Economic Order Quantity} = \sqrt{\frac{2AO}{C}}$$

$$EOQ = \sqrt{\frac{2 \times 40{,}000 \times \text{Rs. } 750}{\text{Rs. } 15}} = 2{,}000 \text{ kgs}$$

(*ii*) **Frequency of orders**

Annual consumption = 40,000 kg.

EOQ = 2,000 kg.

No. of orders for one year or 360 days = (40,000 ÷ 2,000) = 20

Frequency of orders = 360/20 = 18 days

(*iii*) **Percentage of discount to be negotiated in the price of raw material**

It is given that the company proposes to rationalise placement of orders on quarterly basis (*i.e.*, 4 orders in one year). Annual consumption is 40,000 kg.

Quantity per order = 40,000 ÷ 4 = 10,000 kgs.

Total cost when order size is 10,000

Ordering cost (4 orders × ₹. 750)	₹. 3,000	
Carrying cost (5,000 × ₹. 15)		75,000
		78,000 (*a*)

Total cost when order size is equal to EOQ

No. of orders = 20	
Ordering cost (20 orders × ₹. 750)	₹. 15,000
Carrying Cost (1,000 × ₹. 15)	15,000
	30,000 (*b*)
Increase in cost due to quarterly orders = (*a*) – (*b*) =	₹. 48,000
(This increase to be compensated by discount)	
Annual requirement	40,000 units

Reduction per kg in the purchase price of raw material (₹. 48,000 ÷ 40,000) = ₹. 1.20 per unit. % of discount = (₹. 1.20 ÷ ₹. 60) × 100 = 2 %.

Illustration 32: For one of the bought out items the following are the relevant data:

Ordering Cost = ₹. 500 Holding Cost = 40%

Cost per item = ₹. 100 Annual Demand = 1,000 units

The Purchase Manager placed 5 orders of equal quantity in one year, in order to avail the discount of 5% on the cost of the items. Work-out the gain or loss to the organisations due to his ordering policy for this item.

Solution: Total Cost as per Purchase Manager

5 Orders *i.e.* 200 units at a time

Cost = 100 – 5% = ₹. 95 per item

C = 40% of ₹. 95 = ₹. 38

	₹.
Ordering Cost 5 orders @ ₹. 500	2,500
Carrying Cost (200/2) × 38	3,800
Purchase Cost 1,000 @ ₹. 95	95,000
Total Cost	1,01,300

If *EOQ* is allowed the total cost will be

$$EOQ = \sqrt{\frac{2AO}{C}} = \sqrt{\frac{2 \times 1000 \times 500}{40\% \text{ of Rs.} 100}}$$

$$= \sqrt{\frac{2 \times 1000 \times 500}{40}} = 158 \text{ units}$$

	₹.
Ordering Cost 1,000/158 *i.e.* 6.33 orders or 7 orders @ ₹. 500	3,500
Carrying Cost (158/2) × 40	3,160
Purchase Cost 1000 units @ ₹. 100 =	1,00,000
Total Cost if EOQ is followed	1,06,660
Total Cost as per Purchase Manager's ordering policy	1,01,300
Gain due to his ordering policy	5,360

Illustration 33: The Purchase Manager of an organisation has collected the following data for one of the A class items.

Interest of the locked up capital	20%
Order processing cost (₹.) for each order	₹. 100
Inspection cost per lot	₹. 50
Follow up cost for each order	₹. 80
Pilferage while holding inventory	5%
Other holding Cost	15%
Other procurement cost for each order	₹. 170
Annual Demand	1000 units
Cost per item	₹. 10

Discount for a minimum order quantity of 500 items is 10%

What should be the ordering policy of the Purchase Manager?

Solution: C or Inventory Carrying Cost = 20% + 5% + 15% = 40% of ₹. 10 = ₹. 4.00 per item

O or Ordering Cost = 100 + 50 + 80 + 170 = ₹. 400 per order

$$EOQ = \sqrt{\frac{2AO}{C}} = \sqrt{\frac{2 \times 1000 \times 400}{4}} = 447$$

	₹.
Ordering Cost 1000/447 = 2.24 orders say 3 orders @ ₹. 400	1,200

Carrying Cost = (447/2) × 4	894
Purchase Cost 1,000 units @ ₹. 10	10,000
Total Cost	12,094

If discount is availed

Cost per item = 10 – 10% = ₹. 9.00	
C = 40% of 9 = ₹. 3.60	
Ordering Cost (100/500) × 2 orders @ ₹. 40	800
Carrying Cost (500/2) × 3.60 =	900
Purchase cost 1,000 units @ ₹. 9	9,000
Total Cost	10,700

If discount is availed the saving will be ₹. 12,094 – 10,700 = ₹. 1,394. It is, therefore advised that the Purchase Manager should avail the discount and order for a minimum quantity of 500 items.

Illustration 34: JP Limited, manufacturers of a special product, follows the policy of *EOQ* (Economic Order Quantity) for one of its components. The component's values are as follows:

	₹.
Purchase Price per Component	200
Cost of an Order	100
Annual Cost of carrying one unit in Inventory	10% of Purchase Price
Total Cost of inventory and Ordering per annum	4,000

The company has been offered a discount of 2% on the price of the component provided the lot size is 2,000 components at a time.

You are required to:

(*a*) Compute the *EOQ*.

(*b*) Advise whether the quantity discount offer can be accepted. (Assume that the inventory carrying cost does not vary according to discount policy).

(*c*) Would your advise differ if the company is offered 5% discount on a single order?

Solution: (*a*) Carrying cost of one unit per annum is 10% of ₹. 200 *i.e.* ₹. 20. Annual usage of Inventory in units is not known which can be ascertained as below.

Total Cost of Inventory and ordering per annum ₹. 4,000

$$₹.\ 4{,}000 = \sqrt{2A \times O \times C}$$

$$₹.\ 4{,}000 = \sqrt{2A \times 100 \times 20}$$

$$₹.\ 4{,}000 = \sqrt{4{,}000\,A} \quad \text{or} \quad 4{,}000^2 = 4{,}000\,A \quad \text{or} \quad A = 4000 \text{ units}$$

$$EOQ = \sqrt{\frac{2 \times 4{,}000 \times 100}{20}} = 200 \text{ units}$$

We can reconcile the result as below :

Ordering Cost = 4,000/200 = 20 orders @ ₹. 100	₹. 2,000
Carrying Cost (200/2) × 20	2,000
Cost of Inventory and ordering per annum	₹. 4,000

(*b*) Lot size is 2,000 units		
Ordering Cost 4,000/2000 = 2 orders @ ₹. 100		200
Carrying Cost = 1/2 × 2,000 × 20 20,000		
	Total	20,200
Present Cost		4,000
Extra Cost		16,200
Discount : 4000 × 200 *i.e.* ₹. 8,00,000 × 2%		16,000
Net Extra Cost		200

It may be advised that quantity discount offer should not be accepted because it involve net extra cost of ₹. 200. The company should negotiate with the supplier for higher discount.

(*c*) Single order of ₹. 4,000 units : Ordering Cost		100
Carrying Cost = 1/2 × 4,000 × 20		40,000
	Total	₹. 40,100
Present Cost		4,000
Extra Cost		36,100
Discount : ₹. 8,00,000 × 5%		40,000
Gain		3,900

Thus quantity discount offer of 5% can be accepted as it will result into a gain of ₹. 3,900.

Illustration 35: The Purchase Department of your organisation has received an offer of quantity discounts on its orders of materials as under:

Price per ton ₹.	*Tons*
1,400	Less than 500
1,380	500 and less than 1,000
1,360	1,000 and less than 2,000
1,340	2,000 and less than 3,000
1,320	3,000 and above

The annual requirement of the material is 5,000 tons. The delivery cost per order is ₹. 1,200 and the annual stock holding cost is estimated at 20 per cent of the average inventory.

The Purchase Department wants you to consider the following purchase options and advise which among them will be the most economical ordering quantity, presenting the relevant information in a tabular form.

The purchase quantity options to be considered are 400 tons, 500 tons, 1,000 tons, 2,000 tons and 3,000 tons.

Solution: On annual requirement is 5,000 tons, the stock holding cost will be as below:

Order Quantity (Tons)	*Stock Holding Cost (₹.)*
Less than 500	20% of 1,400 = 280
500 and less than 1,000	20% of 1,380 = 276
1,000 and less than 2,000	20% of 1,360 = 272
2,000 and less than 3,000	20% of 1,340 = 268
3,000 and above	20% of 1,320 = 264

Calculation of EOQ

Ordering Qty. (Tons)	*Price per ton (₹)*	*Purchase Cost of 5,000 tons (₹)* I	*Ordering Cost (₹)* II	*Carrying Cost (₹)* III	*Total Cost (₹)* I + II + III
400	1,400	70,00,000	12.5 orders say 13 orders @ ₹. 1,200 = 15,600	$\frac{400}{2} \times 280$ = 56,000	70,71,600
500	1,380	69,00,000	10 order at ₹. 1,200 = 12,000	$\frac{500}{2} \times 276$ = 69,000	69,81,000
1,000	1,360	68,00,000	5 orders at ₹. 1,200 = 6,000	$\frac{1000}{2} \times 272$ = 1,36,000	69,42,000
2,000	1,340	67,00,000	2.5 say 3 orders at ₹. 1,200 = 3,600	$\frac{2000}{2} \times 268$ = 2,68,000	69,71,600
3,000	1,320	66,00,000	2 orders at ₹. 1,200 = 2,400	$\frac{3000}{2} \times 254$ = 3,96,000	69,98,400

Thus *EOQ* is 1000 tons where total cost will be least *i.e.* ₹. 69,42,000.

Illustration 36: The quarterly production of a company's product which has a steady market is 20,000 units. Each unit of a product requires 0.5 kg of raw material. The cost of placing one order for raw material is ₹. 100 and the inventory carrying cost is ₹. 2 per annum. The lead time for procurement of raw material is 36 days and a safety stock of 1,000 kg of raw material is maintained by the company. The company has been able to negotiate the following discount structure with the raw material supplier:

Order quantity Kgs	*Discount* ₹.
Upto 6,000	Nil
6,000–8,000	400
8,000–16,000	2,000
16,000–30,000	3,200
30,000–45,000	4,000

You are required to:

(*i*) Calculate the re-order point taking 30 days in a month.

(*ii*) Prepare a statement showing the total cost of procurement and storage of raw material after considering the discount if the company elects to place one, two, four or six orders in the year.

(*iii*) State the number of orders which the company should place to minimize the costs after taking *EOQ* also into consideration. **[*CA PE II May 2002*]**

Solution:

(*a*) (*i*) Reorder Point = Lead time consumption + Safety stock

= (40,000 kg/360 days) × 36 days + 1,000 kg = 5,000 kg

(*ii*) **Statement showing the total cost of procurement and storage of raw materials (after considering the discount)**

Order Size	*No. of Orders*	*Total Cost of Procurement*	*Average Stock (units)*	*Total Cost of Storage*	*Discount*	*Total Cost*
			$\frac{1}{2}$ × *col. 1*	*(5) = (4) × ₹. 2*		*(3) + (5) − (6)*
Kg.		*₹.*	*Kg.*	*₹.*	*₹.*	*₹.*
(1)	*(2)*	*(3)*	*(4)*	*(5)*	*(6)*	*(7)*
40,000	1	100	20,000	40,000	4;000	36,100
20,000	2	200	10,000	20,000	3,200	17,000
10,000	4	400	5,000	10,000	2,000	8,400
6,666.66	6	600	3,333	6,666	400	6,866

(*iii*) Number of orders which the company should place to minimise the cost after taking *EOQ* also into consideration is 20 orders with order size of 2,000 kg. Total cost of procurement and storage in this case comes to ₹. 4,000, which is minimum (See notes *c* and *d* below)

Working Notes :

(*a*) Annual production (units)
(20,000 units per quarter × 4 quarters) = 80,000

(*b*) Raw material required in kg: 80,000 units × 0.5 kg = 40,000

(*c*) $EOQ = \sqrt{\frac{2 \times 40{,}000 \text{ kg} \times \text{Rs.}100}{2}} = 2{,}000$ kgs.

(*d*) Total cost of procurement and storage when order size is equal to *EOQ* or 2,000 kgs.

No. of orders: (40,000 kgs/2,000 kgs) = 20

Ordering cost (₹.): 20 orders × ₹. 100 — ₹. 2,000

Carrying cost: (Average inventory *i.e.* $\frac{1}{2}$ × 2,000 kgs × ₹. 2) — 2,000

Total Cost — 4,000

Calculation of Cost of Materials

Illustration 37: A manufacturing organisation has imported four types of materials. The invoice reveals the following data:

		Quantity Kg	*Rate US $ per kg.*
Material	*A*	1000	1.50
	B	2000	1.25
	C	1500	2.00
	D	3000	1.00

Import duty	23% of invoice value
Insurance	2% of invoice value
Freight and clearance	₹. 30,000
Exchange Rate US$1	₹. 16.00

50% of the materials imported are issued to production centres. While determining the value of closing stock 5% allowance is provided to cover up storage loss. Determine the value of closing stock of each type of materials.

Solution:

Statement of Value of Closing Stock

Type of Materials	*A*	*B*	*C*	*D*
Quantity in kg. (Total 7,500 kg.)	1,000	2,000	1,500	3,000
Rate per kg. US $	1.50	1.25	2.00	1.00
	₹.	₹.	₹.	₹.
Rate per kg (US$ 1 = ₹. 16)	24	20	32	16
Invoice value	24,000	40,000	48,000	48,000
Import duty: 23% of Invoice value	5,520	9,200	11,040	11,040
Insurance 2% of Invoice value	480	800	960	960
Freight & Clearing Charges 30,000/7,500 *i.e.* ₹. 4 per kg	4,000	8,000	6,000	12,000
Total Cost	34,000	58,000	66,000	72,000
Issued to production 50%	17,000	29,000	33,000	36,000
Value of closing stock	17,000	29,000	33,000	36,000

While determining the value of closing stock, 5% allowance is provided to cover up storage loss as follows:

Material	*Imported (kg)*	*Issued to production (kg)*	*Balance (kg)*	*Storage loss at 5% (kg)*	*Closing Stock (kg)*	*Value ₹.*
A	1,000	500	500	25	475	17,000
B	2,000	1,000	1,000	50	950	29,000
C	1,500	750	750	37.5	712.5	33,000
D	3,000	1,500	1,500	75	1,425	36,000
Total	7,500	3,750	3,750	187.5	3,562.5	1,15,000

If, 5% allowance is made by way of provision for storage loss, the value of stock will be below:

Material	*Value of Closing Stock ₹.*	*5% of Allowance ₹.*	*Net Value*
A	17,000	850	16,150
B	29,000	1,450	27,550
C	33,000	1,650	31,350
D	36,000	1,800	34,200
Total	1,15,000	5,750	1,09,250

Illustration 38: A manufacturer of Surat purchased three Chemicals *A*, *B* and *C* from Bombay. The Invoice gave the following :

	₹.
Chemical *A* : 3,000 kg @ ₹. 4.20 per kg	12,600
Chemical *B* : 5,000 kg @ ₹. 3.80 per kg	19,000
Chemical *C* : 2,000 kg @ ₹. 4.75 per kg	9,500
Sales Tax	2,055
Railway Freight	1,000
Total Cost	44,155

A shortage of 200 kg in Chemical *A*, of 280 kg in Chemical *B* and of 100 kg in Chemical C was noticed due to breakages. At Surat, the manufacturer paid octroi duty @ Re. 0.10 per kg. He also paid cartage ₹. 22 for chemical *A*, ₹. 63.12 for Chemical B and ₹. 31.80 for Chemical *C*. Calculate the stock rate that you would suggest for pricing issue of chemicals assuming a provision of 5% towards further deterioration.

Solution:

Statement of Quantity Available for Issue (kg.)

Chemicals	*A*	*B*	*C*
Quantity Purchased	3,000	5,000	2,000
Less: Shortage (Assumed to be normal)	200	280	100
Quantity received at the store at Surat	2,800	4,720	1,900
Less: Provision for further deterioration 5%	140	236	95
Quantity available for issue	2,660	4,484	1,805

Statement of Rate for Pricing Issue of Chemicals (₹.)

	Basis of Apportionment	*A*	*B*	*C*
Purchase value	As given	12,600	19,000	9,500
Add: Sales Tax ₹. 2,055	At 5% of Purchase value	630	950	475
Railway freight ₹. 1,000	In the ratio of quantity purchased *i.e.* 3 : 5 : 2	300	500	200
Octroi duty	At Re. 0.10 per kg received	280	472	190
Cartage	As given	22	63.12	31.80
Total Cost		13,832	20,985.12	10,396.80
Rate of issue per kg	Total Cost / Qty. available for issue	13,832 / 2,660 = ₹. 5.20	20,985.12 / 4,484 = ₹. 4.68	10,396.80 / 1,805 = ₹. 5.76

Illustration 39: At what price per unit would Part No. A 32 be entered in the Stores Ledger, if the following invoice was received from a supplier:

Invoice	₹.
200 units Part No. A 32 @ ₹. 5	1,000,00
Less: 20% discount	200.00
	800.00
Add: Excise duty @ 15%	120.00
	920.00
Add: Packing charges (5 non-returnable boxes)	50.00
	970.00

Notes:

(*i*) 2% discount will be given for payment in 30 days.

(*ii*) Documents substantiating payment of excise duty is enclosed for claiming MODVAT credit.

Solution:

	₹.
Total Cost	970
Less : MODVAT credit	120
Net Cost	850

Per unit cost = ₹. 850/200 = ₹. 4.25 per unit will be entered in the Stores Ledger.

Note: 2% discount for payment in 30 days is a cash discount. It is not relevant for calculation of cost per unit.

ABC Analysis

Illustration 40: From the following details, draw a plan of ABC selective control:

Item	*Units*	*Unit Cost* ₹. P.
1	7,000	5.00
2	24,000	3.00
3	1,500	10.00
4	600	22.00
5	38,000	1.50
6	40,000	0.50
7	60,000	0.20
8	3,000	3.50
9	300	8.00
10	29,000	0.40
11	11,500	7.10
12	4,100	6.20

Solution:

Statement of Total Cost and Ranking

Item	*Units*	*Unit Cost*	*Total Cost*	*% of Total Cost*	*Ranking*
1	7,000	5.00	35,000	9.84%	4
2	24,000	3.00	72,000	20.24%	2
3	1,500	10.00	15,000	4.22%	7
4	600	22.00	13,200	3.71%	8
5	38,000	1.50	57,000	16.02%	3
6	40,000	0.50	20,000	5.62%	6
7	60,000	0.20	12,000	3.37%	9
8	3,000	3.50	10,500	2.95%	11
9	300	8.00	2,400	0.67%	12
10	29,000	0.40	11,600	3.26%	10
11	11,500	7.10	81,650	22.95%	1
12	4,100	6.20	25,420	7.15%	5
			3,55,770	100.00	

Following basis of selective control may be assumed:

₹. 50,000 and above	—	'*A*' items
₹. 15,000 to 50,000	—	'*B*' items
Below ₹. 15,000	—	'*C*' itmes

Plan of *ABC* Selective Control

Ranking	*Item Nos*	*% of Total Items*	*Cost* ₹	*% of Total Cost*	*Category*
1	11		81,650		
2	2		72,000		
3	5		57,000		
Total	3	25%	2,10,650	59.21%	A
4	1		35,000		
5	12		25,420		
6	6		20,000		
7	3		15,000		
Total	4	33⅓%	95,420	26.82%	B
8	4		13,200		
9	7		12,000		
10	10		11,600		
11	8		10,500		
12	9		2,400		
Total	5	41⅔%	49,700	13.97%	C
Grand Total	12	100	3,55,700	100	

Illustration 41: Draw the ABC curve for the data given below:

Item No.	*Quantity Consumed in a year*	*Cost per unit (₹)*
1	2	40
2	200	5
3	30	1000
4	20	20
5	4	20
6	16	2000
7	24	50
8	5	40
9	100	8
10	250	4
11	120	8
12	140	7
13	10	10
14	20	10
15	200	5

Solution:

Item No.	*Quantity Consumed (Units)*	*Cost per unit* ₹.	*Value* ₹.	*Item No.*	*Quantity Consumed (Units)*	*Cost per unit* ₹.	*Value* ₹.
1	2	40	80	9	100	8	800
2	200	5	1000	10	250	4	1000
3	30	1000	30000	11	120	8	960
4	20	20	400	12	140	7	980
5	4	20	80	13	10	10	100
6	16	2000	32000	14	20	10	200
7	24	50	1200	15	200	5	1000
8	5	40	200				

Arrangement in Descending Order

Item No.	*Value*	*Cum. Value*	*Cum. Value percentage*		*Item No.*	*Value*	*Cum. Value*	*Cum Value percentage*	
6	32000	32,000	45.7	*A*	4	400	69,340	99.1	*C*
3	30000	62,000	88.6		8	200	69,540	99.3	
					14	200	69,740	99.6	
7	1200	63,200	90.3	*B*	13	100	69,740	99.8	
2	1000	64,200	91.7		5	80	69,920	99.9	
10	1000	65,200	93.1		1	80	70,000	100.0	
15	1000	66,200	94.5						
12	980	67,180	96.0						
11	960	68,140	97.3						
9	800	68,940	98.5						

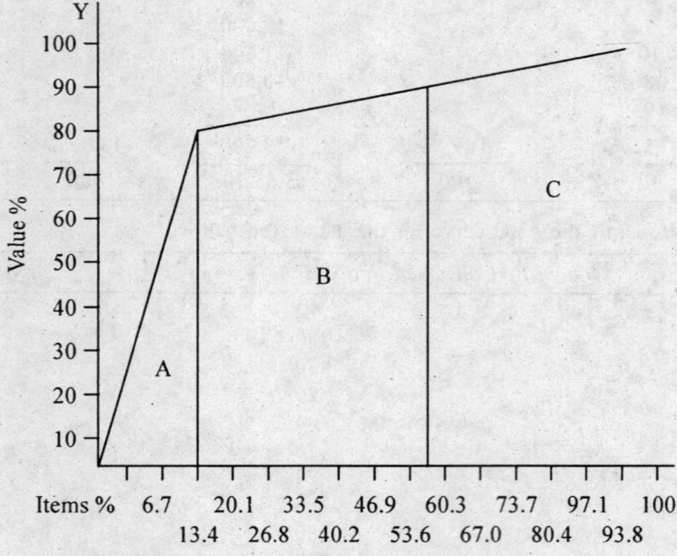

The Item-wise Percentage will be as below (total item 15)

A : 2 items *i.e.* (2/15) × 100	13.4%
B : 7 items *i.e.* (7/15) × 100	46.6%
	60.0%
C : 6 itmes *i.e.* (6/15) × 100	40.0%
Total : 15 items	100%

Pricing of Issue of Material

Illustration 42: The following are the transactions in respect of purchase and issue of components forming part of an assembly of a product manufactured by a firm which requires to update its cost of production, very often for bidding tenders and finalising cost plus contracts.

Date (2000)		*Quantity (in Nos.)*	*Particulars*
January	5	1,000	Purchased at ₹. 1.20 each
	11	2,000	Issued
February	1	1,500	Purchased at ₹. 1.30 each
	18	2,400	Issued
	26	1,000	Issued
March	8	1,000	Purchased at ₹. 1.40 each

17	1,500	Purchased at ₹. 1.30 each
28	2,000	Issued

The stock on January 1, 2000 was 5,000 Nos. valued at ₹. 1.10 each. State the method you would adopt in pricing the issue of components giving reasons. What value would you place on stocks as on March, 31 which happens to be the financial year-end and how would you treat the difference in value if any on the stock account?

Solution: Method of pricing the issue of components should be Weighted Average. There is fluctuation of prices, therefore, it is better to adopt the Weighted Average Method of pricing.

Stores Ledger (Weighted Average Method)

Date	*Receipt*				*ISSUES*				*Balance of Stock*		
	GRN. No.	*Qty No.*	*Rate ₹.*	*Value ₹.*	*SR. No.*	*Qty. No.*	*Rate ₹.*	*Value ₹.*	*Qty No.*	*Rate ₹.*	*Value ₹.*
1–1–2000									5000	1.10	5,500
5–1–2000	—	1000	1.20	1200					6000	1.1167	6,700
11–1–2000					—	2000	1.1167	2233	4000		4,467
1–2–2000	—	1500	1.30	1950					5500	1.1667	6,417
18–2–2000					—	2400	1.1667	2800	3100		3,617
26–2–2000					—	1000	1.1667	1167	2100		2,450
8–3–2000	—	1000	1.40	1400					3100	1.2419	3,850
17–3–2000	—	1500	1.30	1950					4600	1.2609	5,800
28–3–2000					—	2000	1.2609	2522	2600	1.2609	3,278

Closing Stock Value as on 31-3-2000: 2,600 Nos. at ₹. 1.2609 = ₹. 3,278 (at Cost) based on weighted average. But if latest market price is taken it will be 2600 × 1.30 = 3380. The value of closing stock should be shown at cost or market price whichever is lower. In this case, the value of closing stock is lower at cost. ₹. 3,278 should be shown in the Balance Sheet.

Illustration 43: Six units of an item of stores were purchased in the following order:

Lot 1 (3 units) $A1$, $A2$ and $A3$ —at a price of ₹. a each
Lot 2 (2 units) $B1$ and $B2$ —at a price of ₹. b each
Lot 3 (1 unit) C —at a price of ₹. c each

Three issues of 2 units each are made. Show formulae for 5 different methods based on actual prices for pricing the issues when,

(*a*) All issues are made after the receipt of the third lot, and

(*b*) an issue is made after the receipt of each lot.

Solution:

1. FIFO Method	*(a) After third lot* ₹.	*(b) After each lot* ₹.
1st issue	$2 \times a = 2a$	Similar to after third lot
2nd issue	$1 \times a = 1a$ $1 \times b = 1b$	"
3rd issue	$1 \times b = 1b$ $1 \times c = 1c$	" "
2. LIFO Method		
1st issue	$1 \times c = 1c$ $1 \times b = 1b$	$2 \times a = 2a$
2nd issue	$1 \times b = 1b$ $1 \times a = 1a$	$2 \times b = 2b$

3rd issue	$2 \times a = 2a$	$1 \times c = 1c$ $1 \times a = 1a$
3. Simple Average Method		
1st issue	$\frac{a+b+c}{3} \times 2$	$2 \times a = 2a$
2nd issue	”	$\frac{a+b}{2} \times 2$
3rd issue	”	$\frac{b+c}{2} \times 2$
4. Weighted Average Method		
1st issue	$\frac{3a+2b+c}{6} \times 2$	$2 \times a = 2a$
2nd issue	”	$\frac{1a+2b}{3} \times 2$
3rd issue	”	$\frac{1b+1c}{2} \times 2$
5. Standard price method (at ₹. *b* each)		
1st issue	$2 \times b = 2b$	$2 \times b = 2b$
2nd issue	”	”
3rd issue	”	”

Illustration 44: **(Selection of supplier)** After inviting tneders, two quotations are received as under:

Supplier *A*	₹. 2.20 per unit
Supplier *B*	₹. 2.10 per unit + ₹. 2,000 fixed charges irrespective of units ordered.

(*i*) Calculate the order quantity for which the purchase price per unit will be the same.

(*ii*) Select the supplier if the purchase officer wants to place an order for 15,000 units.

[*CS (Intèr)*]

Solution:

Supplier A	= ₹. 2.20 per unit
Supplier B	= ₹. 2.10 per unit + ₹. 2,000 fixed charges
Difference in Tender Price	₹. 0.10 per unit *i.e.* saving equivalent to contribution per unit.

$$BEP = \frac{\text{Fixed cost}}{C \text{ per unit}} = \frac{2{,}000}{0.10} = 20{,}000 \text{ units.}$$

In order to meet the fixed charges of Supplier B, thc ordering quantity should be 20,000 units. At this quantity, the purchase price per unit will be the same in case of both supplier as shown below:

Supplier A	₹. 2.20 per unit × 20,000 = ₹. 44,000
Supplier B	20,000 × 2.10 = 42,000 + 2,000 = ₹. 44,000.

(*ii*) If the order is for less than 20,000 units, Supplier A should be selected. For example for an order of 15,000 units, the cost will be

	₹.
A 15,000 × 2.20 =	33,000
B (15,000 × 2.10) + 2,000	33,500

Hence Supplier A should be selected for placing an order for 15,000 units or less than 20,000 units, if the order is for more than 20,000 units, Supplier B should be selected.

***Illustration 45:* (Use of Alternative Material):**

Raw materials '*X*' costing ₹. 100 per kilogram and 'Y' costing ₹. 60 per kilogram are mixed in equal proportions for making product 'A'. The loss of materials in processing works out to 25% of the output. The production expenses are allocated at 50% of direct material cost. The end product is priced with a margin of $33\frac{1}{3}\%$ over the total cost. Material '*Y*' is not easily available and substitute raw material '*Z*' has been found for '*Y*' costing ₹. 50 per kilogram. It is required to keep the proportion of this substitute material in the mixture as low as possible and at the same time maintain the selling price of the end product at existing levels and ensure the same quantum of profit as at present.

You are required to compute what should be the ratio of mix of the raw materials *X* and *Z*.

Solution:

	Kg.
1. *Output of Product A (assumed)*	1.00
Process loss 25% of output	0.25
Input of raw material *X* and *Y*	1.25

X and *Y* are mixed in equal proportion for making product *A*, therefore 0.625 kg. of *X* and 0.625 kg. of *Y* will be mixed to produce one kg of Product A.

2. *Statement of Cost and Profit for producing one kg. of A;*

	₹.
Raw material *X* (0.625 × ₹. 100)	62.50
Raw material *Y* (0.625 × ₹. 60)	37.50
Material cost	100.00
Add Production Exp. at 50% of material cost	50.00
Total cost	150.00
Add Profit at $33\frac{1}{3}\%$ over total cost	50.00
Selling price	200.00

3. *Ratio of mix of raw material X and Z*

Minimum quantity of Z is to be mixed and maintain the same selling price and same amount of profit. For this purpose, total material cost in one kg of Product *A* should be the same *i.e.* ₹. 100 only. Cost of Z is ₹. 50 per kg. Suppose quantity of *Z* raw material is *Z*.

$Z \times$ ₹. $50 + (1.25 - Z)$ kg $\times$ ₹. $100 =$ ₹. 100

$50Z + 125 - 100Z = 100$

$50Z - 100Z = 100 - 125$

$-50Z = -25$

$Z = .5$

X will be 1.25 – .5 kg *i.e.* 0.75 kg

Ratio will be 3 : 2 between *X* and *Z* (*i.e.* 0.75 kg and .5 kg). It can be proved as below:

Statement of Cost

	₹.
Raw material X 0.75 kg at ₹. 100	75
Raw material Z 0.50 kg at ₹. 50	25
Total material cost	100
Production Exp. 50%	50
Total cost	150
Profit $33\frac{1}{3}\%$ of total cost	50
Selling Price	200

Illustration 46: **(Inventory turnover ratio and average stock holding).**

From the following data for the year ended 31st December 2000. Calculate (*i*) inventory turnover ratio of the two items and (*ii*) their average stock-holding in terms of number of days.

	Material A	*Material B*
Opening Stock 1.1.2000	₹. 20,000	₹. 18,000
Purchases during the year	1,04,000	54,000
Closing stock 31.12.2000	12,000	22,000

[*ICWA Inter June 2001*]

Solution: (*i*) Inventory Turnover Ratio = $\frac{\text{Cost of raw material consumed}}{\text{Average value of raw material in stock}}$

	Material A	*Material B*
Opening Stock	₹. 20,000	₹. 18,000
Add: Purchases	1,04,000	54,000
Total	1,24,000	72,000
Less: Closing stock	12,000	22,000
Cost of raw material consumed	1,12,000	50,000
Average value of stock = (opening balance + closing balance)/2		
	(20,000 + 12,000)/2	(18,000 + 22,000)/2
	= ₹. 16,000	= ₹. 20,000
Inventory Turnover Ratio	₹. 1,12,000 ÷ 16,000	₹. 50,000 ÷ 20,000
	= 7 times	= 2.5 times
(*ii*) Average stock-holding in terms of days	(365 ÷ 7) = 52.14 days	(365 ÷ 2.5) = 146 days

Illustration 48: **(Inventory Turnover Ratio):**

The following data are available in respect of material *X* for the year ended 31st March 2003.

	₹.
Opening Stock	90,000
Purchases during the year	2,70,000
Closing Stock	1,10,000

Calculate (*i*) Inventory Turnover Ratio and (*ii*) Number of days for which average inventory is held.

Solution:

(*i*) Inventory Turnover Ratio $= \frac{\text{Total Raw Material Consumed}}{\text{Average Inventory}}$

$= \frac{2,50,000}{1,00,000} = 2.5$

(*ii*) Number of days for which average inventory is held

$= \frac{\text{Days in a year}}{\text{Inventory Turnover ratio}} = \frac{360}{2.5} = 144$ days.

OBJECTIVE QUESTIONS

I. *True or False Statements*

1. Stores ledger is maintained by the stores department.
2. Purchase Requisition Note is prepared by the purchasing department.
3. The terms 'Materials' and 'Inventory' should not be used synonymously.

4. Prepetual inventory system enables to know stock at any time.
5. Annual stock-taking confirms that perpetual inventory is functioning properly.
6. Bin card show the quantity and value of a Materials at any point of time.
7. Material losses due to careless handling resulting in the breakage should be transferred to Costing Profit and Loss A/c.
8. Bill of Materials is a cash memo sent by the supplier alongwith the Materials.
9. Bin Cards are not a part of accounting records.
10. Re-order level is always higher than minimum stock level.
11. When minimum stock level is 200 kg of a Material and re-order quantity is 1000 kg, then average stock is 600 kg.
12. In A, B, C analysis, 'A' means those Materials which are used in large quantity.
13. Inventory turnover ratios indicates slow moving and fast moving Materials.
14. In seting economic order quantity, ordering cost and carrying cost show inverse relationship.
15. When rate of consumption of a Material is high, its maximum stock level is also set at a relatively higher level.
16. When prices are rising, LIFO Method shows higher profit.
17. Simple average method is considered superior to weighted average method of pricing.
18. Weighted average method of pricing Material issues is recommended when there are wide fluctuations in the purchase price of Materials.
19. Continuous stock taking means comparing bin card and stores ledger on a regular basis through out the year.
20. Perpetual inventory system is a part of continuous stock taking.
21. Storage cost is an important factor in determining economic order quantity.
22. Minimum and maximum stock level once fixed should not be changed at least for one year.
23. The economic order quantity is the re-order quantity.
24. In LIFO method of pricing, the effect of current market prices is refected in the production.
25. In FIFO method, closing stock is valued at oldest prices of Materials.

[Ans. : 1. False ; 2. False; 3. True; 4. True; 5. True; 6. False; 7. True; 8. True; 9. True; 10. True; 11. False; 12. False; 13. True; 14. True; 15.True; 16. False; 17. False; 18. True; 19. True; 20. True; 21. True; 22. True; 23. True; 24. True; 25. False;]

II. Select the correct answer in each of the following cases.

1. Direct Material is a:
   (*a*) Fixed cost (*b*) Variable cost
   (*c*) Semi variable cost
2. Which of the following is an accounting record?
   (*a*) Bill of Materials (*b*) Bin Card
   (*c*) Stores Ledger (*d*) All of these
3. Which of the following note is used in issue of Material to production department:
   (*a*) Purchase Requisition Note (*b*) Stores Requisition Note
   (*c*) Goods Received Note (*d*) Stores Credit Note
4. Which of the following is considered to be a normal loss of Materials?
   (*a*) Loss due to accident (*b*) Pilferage
   (*c*) Loss due to breaking the bulk (*d*) Loss due to careless handling of Materials
   (*e*) None of these
5. According to which of the following methods of pricing, issues are close to current economic values?
   (*a*) Last-in-first-out price (*b*) First-in-first-out price
   (*c*) Replacement price (*d*) Weighted average price
6. Which of the following methods of stock control aims at concentrating efforts on selected items of Materials?

(*a*) Perpetual inventory system (*b*) Material turnover
(*c*) Maximum, minimum and re-order level setting (*d*) A B C analysis

7. In Base stock method of pricing the Materials issues, the term 'Base Stock' represents the
(*a*) Quantity of stock being issued (*b*) Stock in balance
(*c*) Minimum stock (*d*) Maximum stock

8. Continuous stock-taking is a part of
(*a*) Annual stock-taking (*b*) Perpetual inventory system
(*c*) A B C analysis (*d*) Periodic inventory system

9. The classification of items in A B C analysis is made on the basis of
(*a*) Investment value of Materials (*b*) Consumption value of Materials
(*c*) Quantity of Materials consumed (*d*) All of these

10. In which of the following methods, issues of Materials are priced at a predetermined rate?
(*a*) Inflated price method (*b*) Standard price method
(*c*) Replacement price method (*d*) Specific price method

11. The storekeeper should initiate a purchase requisition when stock reaches:
(*a*) Minimum level (*b*) Maximum level
(*c*) Re-order level (*d*) Average level

12. When prices fluctuate widely the method that will smooth out the effect of fluctuations is
(*a*) Simple average (*b*) Weighted average
(*c*) FIFO (*d*) LIFO

13. Expected annual usage of a particular raw Material is 2,00,000 units and the economic order quantity is 10,000 units. The invoice cost of each unit is ₹. 500 and the cost to place an order is ₹. 80. The average inventory is -
(*a*) 1,00,000 units (*b*) 5,000 units
(*c*) 10,000 units (*d*) 7,500 units

14. When Material prices are showing a rising trend, which method of pricing will show lower cost of production.
(*a*) FIFO (*b*) LIFO
(*c*) Weighted average (*d*) Replacement price

15. When prices are showing a falling tendency, which method of pricing of Material issues will show higher closing stock value ?
(*a*) FIFO (*b*) LIFO
(*c*) Weighted average (*d*) Specific price method

[**Ans.** (1) *b* (2) *c* (3) *b* (4) *b* (5) *a* (6) *d* (7) *b* (8) *b* (9) *a* (10) *b* (11) *c* (12) *b* (13) *b* (14) *a* (15) *b*]

III. *Select the correct answer in each of the following cases.*

(*a*) Which of the following is not considered as abnormal loss of materials ?
(*i*) Pilferage (*ii*) Loss due to breaking the bulk
(*iii*) Loss due to accident (iv) Loss arising from careless handling of materials

(*b*) When prices fluctuate widely, which of the following method will be more suitable?
(*i*) Weightage average (*ii*) FIFO
(*ii*) LIFO (*iv*) Simple average.

(*c*) In which of the following methods, material issues are priced at market rate?
(*i*) Replacement price method (*ii*) Specific price method
(*iii*) Inflated price method (*iv*) Standard price method.

(*d*) The storekeeper should initiate a purchase requisition when the stock level reaches :
(*i*) Danger level (*ii*) Average stock level
(*iii*) Maximum level (*iv*) Minimum level.

(*e*) Which of following is an accounting record ?

(i) Bin card (ii) Order for purchase
(iii) Stores ledger (iv) None of these.

(f) Indirect Material is a
(i) Fixed cost (ii) Semi-fixed cost
(iii) Semi-variable cost (iv) Varaible cost

(g) Which of the following does not normally appear on a material requisition form ?
(i) Job number (ii) Unit cost
(iii) Supplier's name (iv) Quantity requisitioned

(h) If lead time is 4 weeks and average weekly consumption is 25 units, what should be the reordering level ?
(i) 100 units (ii) 110 units
(iii) 120 units (iv) 150 units

(i) If price per unit is ₹. 100, annual consumption is 8,000 unit, cost of placing an order and receiving the goods in ₹. 200 and interest and other charges are 20% of cost, what should be the quantity of each order ?
(i) 200 units (ii) 400 units
(iii) 600 units (iv) 800 units

[Ans. (a) (i) ; (b) (iv) ; (e) (i) (d) (i) ; (e) (iii) ; (f) (iii) ; (g) (iii) ; (h) (i) ; (i) (ii)**]**

THEORETICAL QUESTIONS

1. Outline a system of stores control for any manufacturing business which you are familiar.

2. What are the function of a store-keeper and how should be organise the store?

3. Define a 'Bin Card' and give its specimen. What is the difference between a Bin Card and Stores Ledger?

4. 'Stores Ledger are essential to an efficient costing system.' Give your views on this statement and on the uses and values of store ledger.

5. Write short notes on:

(a) Bill of Materials; (b) Purchase Requisition; (c) Bin Card; (d) Maximum level; (e) Minimum level; (f) Ordering Level. ***[B Com (H) Delhi 1994]***

6. Explain main methods of pricing of materials and state which of these methods is, in your opinion the most accurate?

7. Explain 'Perpetual Inventory System' and mention its advantages with examples.

8. Explain with suitable examples the following methods of pricing issues of materials:

(a) *FIFO*

(b) *LIFO*. Which of these methods would you recommend under conditions of rising prices and why?

9. (a) What is meant by 'Perpetual inventory' and 'periodic inventory' system? Describe their advantages.

(b) Bring out clearly and explain as to how perpetual inventory and periodic inventory system affect the operation of *LIFO* and *FIFO* during a period of rising prices.

[B. Com. Delhi & C.A. Inter]

10. (a) What do you understand by 'Inventory Control' state its objects.

(b) Between LIFO and FIFO methods of pricing the issue of materials, which one do you think is better and why?

11. Define: (i) Replacement price and (ii) Standard price. Discuss the objectives of these methods of pricing of materials and state the circumstances in which these are used.

12. Explain the terms Minimum level, Maximum level and Ordering level with regard to maintenance of stock. What are the factors to be taken into account in fixing these levels. Discuss the relevance of these concept in a manufacturing organisation.

13. What is Economic order Quantity. How it is fixed? ***[B. Com. (H) Delhi 1993]***

14. What do you understand by ABC Analysis? What are its advantages?

15. When and why would you recommend the LIFO method of pricing material issue.

SHORT ANSWER QUESTIONS

1. Write short note on ABC Analysis.
2. What is Economic Order Quantity.
3. How does a Bill of Material differ from a Material Requisition Note? Explain the purpose of each.
4. 'To be able to calculate basic EOQ, certain assumptions are necessary. List down these assumption.
5. Draw as speciman draft of 'Purchase Order'.
6. What are the essential ingredients of material control.
7. Write short note on 'Perpetual Inventory System'.
8. Explain the concept of ABC analysis as a technique of inventory control.
9. Write short note on 'Inventory Carrying Cost'.
10. Write short note on 'Periodic Inventory System'.
11. Distinguish between (*i*) Scrap and Wastage and (*ii*) Spoilage and defectives.
12. Write short note on 'Weighted Average Price Method".
13. How would you determine EOQ?

NUMERICAL QUESTIONS

Stock Levels & EOQ

1. The following information is available in respect of a particular material.

   Reorder Quantity 3600 units
   Maximum usage 900 units per week
   Minimum usage 300 units per week
   Normal usage 600 units per week
   Reorder period 3 to 5 weeks

   Calculate the following:
   (*a*) Reorder level (*b*) Minimum level (*c*) Maximum level
   [Ans. *(a) 4500 units (b) 2100 units (c) 7200 units*]

2. Two Components A and B are used as follows:
   Normal usage — 300 units per week each:
   Maximum usage — 450 units per week each
   Minimum usage — 150 units per week each
   Reorder Quantity — *A* 2400 units B 3600 units
   Reorder period — *A* 4 to 6 weeks
   B 2 to 4 weeks
   Calculate for each component:
   (*a*) Reorder level (*b*) Minimum level (*c*) Maximum level (*d*) Average Stock level.
   [Ans. *Reorder level A 2,700 units, B 1800 units; Maximum level A 4,500 units and B 5,100 units; Minimum level A 1,200 units B 900 units; Average stock level A 2,850 units B 3,000 units*]

3. In manufacturing its product, a company uses three raw materials *A*, *B* and *C* in respect of which following facts apply.

Raw material	*Usage per units product (kg)*	*Re-order Quantity (kg.)*	*Price per kg (Paise)*	*Delivery period (weeks)*	*Order level (kg)*	*Minimum level (kg)*
A	10	10,000	10	1 to 3	8,000	—
B	4	5,000	30	3 to 5	4,750	—
C	6	10,000	15	2 to 4	—	2,000

   Weekly production varies from 175 to 225 units averaging 200. What would you expect the quantity of the following to be:
   (*a*) Minimum Stock of *A* (*b*) Maximum Stock of *B* (*c*) Re-order level of *C* (*d*) Average level of *A*.
   [Ans. *(a) 4,000 units (b) 7,650 units (c) 5,400 units (d) 9,000 units*]

4. Following information relating to a type of raw material is available.

Annual Demand	2,400 units
Unit Price	₹. 2.40
Ordering Cost per order	₹. 4
Storage Cost	2% per annum
Interest Rate	10% per annum
Lead time	Half month

Calculate Economic Order Quantity and total annual inventory cost in respect of above raw material.

[**Ans.** *EOQ 258 units. Annual Inventory Cost ₹. 5837.15 (i.e., ₹. 5760 + Ordering Cost for 10 orders ₹. 40 + Carrying Cost 12% of average inventory ₹. 37.15*]

5. From the following particulars find out the Economic Order Quantity.

(*i*) Annual demand 12000 units
(*ii*) Ordering Cost ₹. 90 per order
(*iii*) Inventory Carrying cost per unit per annum ₹.15

[**Ans.** *379 units approx.*]

6. Harsha Ltd. produces a product which has a monthly demand of 4000 units. The product requires a component *X* which is purchased at ₹. 20. For every finished product, one unit of component *X* is required. The ordering cost is ₹. 120 per order and the holding cost is 10% per annum. You are required to calculate (*i*) *EOQ* and (*ii*) if the minimum lot size to be supplied is 4000 units, what is extra cost the company has to incur?

[**Ans.** *(i) 2400 units (ii) Extra cost ₹. 640*]

7. A firm requires 50 items every day for a machine. A fixed cost of ₹. 50 per order is incurred for placing an order. The inventory carrying cost per item amounts to ₹ 0.02 per day. The lead period is 32 days. You are required to compute (*i*) Economic Order Quantity and (*ii*) Reorder level

[**Ans:** *(i) 500 units (ii) 1600 units*

Hint. Carrying cost per unit p.a. ₹. 7.20. Days in a year 360]

8. ABC Co. buys in lots of 125 boxes which is a three months supply. The cost per box is 125 and the ordering cost is ₹. 250 per order. The inventory carrying cost is 20% of unit value per annum. You are required to ascertain : (*i*) What is total cost of the existing inventory policy (*ii*) How much money would be saved by employing the *EOQ* 1.

[**Ans.** *(i) ₹. 65062.50; (ii) EOQ 100 units* saving *₹ 62.50*]

[**Hint.** Total cost include Buying cost, ordering cost and average inventory carrying cost *i.e.* ₹. 62500 + 1000 + 1562.50 = 65062.50. If EOQ is used, total cost will be ₹. 65,000.]

9. A company manufacture 5000 units of a product per month. The cost of placing an order is ₹. 100. The purchase price of raw material is ₹. 10 per kg. The reorder period is 4 to 8 weeks. The consumption of raw materials varies from 100 kg to 450 kg per week, the average consumption being 275 kg. The carrying cost of inventory is 20% p.a. You are required to calculate (*i*) Reorder Quantity (*ii*) Reorder Level (*iii*) Maximum Level (*iv*) Minimum Level (*v*) Average Stock Level.

[**Ans.** *(i) 1,196 kg (ii) 3600 kg (iii) 4396 kg (iv) 1950 kg (v) 2548 kg or 3173 kg*]

10. RST Ltd. has received an offer of quantity discount on its order of materials as under

Price per ton	*Tons number*
₹. 9600	Less than 50
₹. 9360	50 and Less than 100
₹. 9120	100 and less than 200
₹. 8880	200 and less than 300
₹. 8648	300 and above

The annual requirement for the material is 500 tons. The ordering cost per order is ₹. 12500 and the stock holding cost is estimated at 25% of the material cost p.a.. Required: (*i*) Compute the most economical purchase level (*ii*) Compute *EOQ* if there are no quantity discount and the price per ton is ₹. 10,500. **[*CA PE II Nov. 2004*]**

[**Ans.** *(i) 300 tons (ii) 69 tons.*]

[**Hint.** On 300 tons the total cost of material ₹. 46,64,875.]

Calculation of Cost of Material etc.

11. The following details are available in respect of consignment of 1,250 kgs. of material *X*.

(*i*) Invoice price—₹. 20 per kg.

(*ii*) Excise Duty—25% of invoice price.

(*iii*) Sales Tax—8% of invoice price including excise duty.

(*iv*) Trade Discount—10% on invoice price.

(*v*) Insurance—1% of aggregate invoice price.

(*vi*) Delivery charges ₹. 250

(*vii*) Cost of container @ ₹. 60 per container for 50 kg of materials. Rebate is allowed @ ₹. 40 per container if returned within six weeks, which is a normal features.

(*viii*) One container load of material was rejected on inspection and not accepted.

(*ix*) Cost of unloading and handling @ 0.25% of the cost of materials ultimately accepted.

On the basis of above you are required to find out the landed cost per kg of materials *X*

[Ans. *Landed Cost ₹. 31,099.95; per unit ₹. 25.917*]

12. One parcel containing two important materials was received by a factory and the invoice discloses the following information.

	₹.
Materials I 1000 kg @ ₹. 3.00 per kg	3,000
Materials II 600 kg @ 2.50 per kg	1500
Insurance	90
Sales Tax	180
Freight etc.	225

Due to mishandling in the factory's store a loss of 10 kg of material 1 and 9 kg of material II is to be allowed. What rate would you adopt for issue of these vital materials to jobs? And also calculate the rate, if provision of 10% is made towards probable risk of obsolescence.

[Ans. *₹. 3.35 and ₹. 2.83 per kg. Revised rate after provision ₹. 3.73 and ₹. 3.15 per kg*]

Bin Card

13. The following information regarding coal is obtained from the store records of factory :

Aug.

1 Opening balance : 200 tons.

2 Issued on requisition No. 273 : 57 tons.

4 Issued on requisition No. 285 : 83 tons.

5 Received from supplier by challan No. 74 August 5, 120 tons. The supply was expected on this date.

8 Issued on requisition No. 341 : 92 tons.

12 Issued on requisition No. 364 : 30 tons.

17 Received from supplier by challan No. 98 of August 17, 100 tons. The supply was expected on this date.

24 Issued on requisition No. 428 : 69 tons.

28 Issued on requisition No. 447 : 29 tons.

30 Received from supplier by challan no. 171 of August 30, 125 tons. The supply was expected on this date. Received back by credit slip No. 37 : 10 tons.

31 Issued on requisition No. 483 : 85 tons.

Examination by the stock verifier on August 26, revealed a shortage of 5 tons.

The maximum amount of stock of coal permissible at any time is 200 tons, and the minimum 50 tons. The ordering level is 100 tons.

Draw up the Bin Card (No. 23) for coal with all the necessary details showing the transactions in August.

[Ans. *The balance on 31st Aug. 105 Tons.*]

Pricing of Issues

14. *X* Limited has purchased and issued the material in the following order:

			Units	Unit Cost
				₹.
Jan.	1.	Purchase	300	3
"	4.	Purchase	600	4
Jan.	6.	Issue	500	—
	10.	Purchase	700	4
"	15.	Issue	800	—
"	20.	Purchase	300	5
"	23.	Issue	100	—

Ascertain the quantity of closing stock as on 31st Jan. and state what will be its value (in each case) if issues are made under the following methods :

(*A*) Average Cost; (*B*) First-in-First-out (*C*) Last-in, First out.

[**Ans.** *(A) 500 units ₹. 2,220; (B) 500 units ₹. 2,300 (C) 500 units ₹. 1900*]

15. Modern Office Equipment Co. Ltd. are importers of Typewriters and Calculating Machines. No Perpetual Inventory System is in force. Physical inventories taken as on 30th June, 2002 and 31st Dec. 2002 indicate :

	Typewriters	₹.	Calculators	₹.
30th June	400	1,20,000	100	1,50,000
31st Dec.	420	......	180	......

The following purchases were made during the six monthly period July/Dec. 2002.

July	200	Typewriters	@ ₹. 320
August	40	Calculators	@ ₹. 1650
September	100	Typewriters	@ ₹. 340
October	60	Calculators	@ ₹. 1750
November	300	Typewriters	@ ₹. 350
December	100	Calculators	@ ₹. 1800

Sales during the period amounted to : Typewriters 580 for ₹. 2,90,000 and Calculators 120 for ₹. 4,50,000.

Compute the inventory values as at 31st December, 2200 under following methods.

(*a*) *F.I.F.O.* Method (*b*) *L.I.F.O.* Method (*c*) Simple Average Method.

[**Ans.** *Typewriters : (a) ₹. 1,45,400 (b) ₹. 1,26,400 (c) 1,37,550; Calculators : (a) ₹. 3,18,000 (b) ₹. 2,86,000 (c) ₹. 3,01,500*]

16. The stores ledger of a manufacturing company recorded for material item No. P–18 for June 2003, the following information:

		Receipts			*Balance*		
Date		*Qty.*	*Rate*	*Amt.*	*Qty.*	*Rate*	*Value*
June	1	—	—	—	100	2	200
"	10	200	2	400	300	2	600
"	15	300	4	1200	300	2	
					300	4	1800
"	16	—	—	—	100	2	
					300	4	1400
"	20	—	—	—	100	4	400
"	25	400	5	200	100	4	
					400	5	2400
"	28	—	—	—	200	5	1000
"	29	—	—	—	50	5	250

(*i*) State the method of pricing that was employed in the ledger.

(*ii*) Complete the stores ledger as per method followed. **[*B.Com. Pass Delhi*]**

[Ans. *FIFO Method*]

17. The Stock Ledger Account for material *x* in a manufacturing concern reveals the following data for the quarter ended September 30, 2004:

			Receipts		*Issues*	
			Quantity (units)	*Price per unit*	*Quantity (units)*	*Amt. (₹.)*
July	1	Balance	1600	2.00		
July	9		3000	2.20		
July	13		—	—	1200	2,556
Aug.	5		—	—	900	1,917
Aug.	17		3600	2.40		
Aug.	24		—	—	1,800	4,122
Sep.	11		2500	2.50	—	—
Sep.	27		—	—	2,100	4,971
Sept.	29		—	—	700	1,656

Physical verification on September 30, revealed an actual stock of 3800 units. You are required to (*a*) indicate the method of pricing employed in the above (*b*) Complete the above account.

[Ans. *(a) Weighted Average Method (b) Closing stock 3,800 units ₹. 8994*]

18. From the records of a company distributing petrol, the following information is available for the month of March, 2002:

Sales for the month	:	₹. 79,10,000
Opening stock as on 1.3.2002	:	1,25,000 litres @ ₹. 30.00 per litre
Purchases:		
March 5	:	1,50,000 litres @ ₹. 31.10 per litre
March 27	:	1,00,000 litres @ ₹. 31.20 per litre
Closing stock as on 31 March, 2002	:	1,30,000 litres
General Administration expenses for the month of March, 2002	:	₹. 1,72,000

From the information given above, **work out** the following, using *FIFO* and *LIFO* methods of inventory valuation, assuming pricing of issues being done at the end of month, after all receipts during the month:

(*a*) Value of closing stock as on 31.3.2002.

(*b*) Cost of sales for March, 2002.

(*c*) Profit or loss for March, 2002.

[Ans. *(a) under Fifo ₹. 40,53,000, under Lifo ₹. 39,05,500*
(b) under Fifo ₹. 76,54,000, under Lifo ₹. 78,01,500
(c) under Fifo ₹. 2,56,000, under Lifo ₹. 1,08,500]

Employees Cost (Labour)

DIRECT AND INDIRECT LABOUR

Labour is treated as direct if it can be conveniently allocated to different jobs or products, etc. If we know how much time a worker spent on each of the various jobs he undertook during, say, the previous week, then for the past week his wages would be treated as direct; but if, for the same worker, we cannot identify the time spent by him with particular jobs or products, his wages will have to be treated as indirect. Indirect wages are a part of factory expenses. For example, wages paid to watch and ward staff, repair gangs, supervisors, etc., are indirect. Wages of workers put on definite jobs or products will be direct and will be the second element of cost, the first being materials.

The following definitions should be noted:

Direct Wages (Direct labour cost): "Wages (labour cost) which can be identified with, and allocated to cost centres and cost units.

Indirect Wages (Indirect labour cost): "Wages (labour cost) which cannot be allocated but which can be apportioned to, or absorbed by cost centres or cost units. —*CIMA*

Labour constitutes often fifty per cent of the cost to produce an article. It is subject to wastage like any other factor of production. Therefore it requires no argument to show that records should account for every paisa paid out for labour. Without an accurate record, it would be impossible for the manager to trace excessive labour costs for a job. The wastage in labour might then be remedied by a re-arrangement of plant, etc., or the elimination of certain unnecessary operations on the part of the worker. It should always be remembered that labour is the only factor of production which is capable of increasing its productivity; in other cases physical limitations set a limit to the output that can be obtained from given quantity of input. In case of labour also obviously there is a limit but it is much farther away than is commonly believed. Good production management, and therefore cost control, demands that there should be a constant study of labour efficiency and the ways and means to improve it. The one point that will be worth remembering always is that it is the will to work that is the most important single factor in this respect.

This involves (*i*) careful selection so that the worker's aptitudes and skills and the job suit one another; (*ii*) proper training; (*iii*) careful planning of the work; (*iv*) provision of necessary tools and facilities; (*v*) proper treatment and supervision, etc. Thus, management's role is very important to see that labour productivity is at the highest level.

Full records must be kept for every employee. The *employee's record card* should be kept on file and ought to include at least the following details: (1) Name and address, (2) Department and number, (3) Former employer. (4) Date of engagement, (5) Occupation, (6) Rating, and (7) Reasons for leaving. This last item may be most important as regards the future usefulness of the employee card to the firm, and should be as comprehensive as possible but it should not contain any reference which could be construed as libellous in the event of entry being made public. Following is a specimen of Employee's Record Card:

EMPLOYEE CARD

Form No. ....

Name..........................	No..............................	Engaged on.....................
Department...................		As...................................
Category......................		Grade................................
		Starting Pay ₹................

Previous Employer ....

Reasons for leaving him...

Present Address...

Married/Unmarried....................... No. of Children...................... Education....................

Reasons for leaving...

PROGRESS

Promotions	New Grade
1.....................................	1 ....
2.....................................	2 ....
3.....................................	3 ....

Ratings			Increments		
Date	Remarks	Signatures	Date	Amount	Signature
...	... ...	... ...	....	₹.............	....
...	... ...	... ...	....	₹.............	....
...	... ...	... ...	....	₹.............	....
...	... ...	... ...	....	₹.............	....

LABOUR COST CONTROL

Proper control of labour cost is one of the major functions of modern management and costing system. The control should be systematic based on a proper production planning, use of labour budgets and labour standards. To achieve success, it would be necessary that the management should take active interest and take labour cost to be a major factor of production cost. Excess labour cost may be due to idle tune, unusual over time, high rate of labour turnover etc. The control over labour cost can be achieved if there is proper coordination between different departments or sections related to labour. Generally following departments are involved in the control of labour cost.

(1) *Personnel Department:* This department in a large organisation is responsible for recruitment, training discharge, transfer etc and maintaining their records. The main functions are: (*i*) Receiving requisition for labour from various departments (*ii*) Selection and Recruitment (*iii*) Information to the concerned departments like requisioning department and pay roll department.

(2) *Engineering and Work Study Department:* This department helps in labour cost control through following functions: (*i*) Preparing production plans and specifications for each job, (*ii*) Initiating and supervising research and experimental work (*iii*) Maintaining efficient and safe working conditions (*iv*) Performing work-studies *e.g.*, Time study, Motion study etc. (*v*) Analysing jobs and job evaluation and studies (*vi*) Performance appraisals and labour Productivity (*vi*) Fixing Piece rate.

(3) *Time Keeping Department:* Its functions are maintenance of attendance records of employees and job time booking.

(4) *Payroll Department:* This department has to perform following functions: (*i*) To maintain record of job classification and wage rate of each and every employee, (*ii*) To verify and to

summarize the time of each worker as shown on daily time cards, (*iii*) To calculate wages earned by each and every worker (*iv*) To prepare payroll of every department, (*v*) To calculate total amount of wages and deductions for each employee (*vi*) To disburse wages (*vii*) To devise a suitable internal check preparing and paying out wages.

(5) *Cost Accounting Department:* This department is concerned with (*i*) Documentation of Wages Accounting (*ii*) Analysis of total labour cost and (*iii*) Treatment of idle time, Overtime, Leave Pay etc.

IMPORTANT FACTORS FOR THE CONTROL OF LABOUR COST

On the basis of various functions of various departments related to labour, we can outline certain important factors which need consideration for controlling labour cost.

(1) Assessment of Manpower Requirements
(2) Control Over Time-keeping and Time Booking
(3) Time and Motion Study
(4) Control Over Idle Time
(5) Control Over Overtime
(6) Methods of Wages
(7) Incentive Plans
(8) Wage and Cost of Production
(9) Control Over Casual, Contract and Other Workers
(10) Control Over Labour Turnover
(11) Job Evaluation and Merit Rating.

(1) Assessment of Manpower Requirement

It is the personnel department which receives requisitions from each section or department regarding workers. Accordingly personnel department selects and recruits persons by advertising approaching the local employment exchange, putting the demand on the notice board at factory gate etc., when the recruited employee reports for work, information about him is also sent to the concerned department. There is need of proper assessment of total requirements of manpower at various levels of the organisation. A proper forecasting of manpower requirements must be undertaken before recruitment on the basis of workload. The total workload should be break up into specified jobs and then the number of men required should be worked out.

(2) Control Over Time keeping and Time Booking

Time Recording: It is essential that workers including those who are paid on piece basis should be punctual. Its workers come late they cause disturbance even as regards the work of others. It is necessary, therefore, to have a good system of recording the arrival and departure of workers, whether they are direct, indirect, paid on time basis or piece basis.

Timekeeper: All factories generally employ a person known as timekeeper. His office is just near the factory gate and it is his duty to maintain proper records about the time spent by the employers in the factory. If the factory is small he will also be entrusted with the task of maintaining the employee cards and registers under the various Acts, for example, the Factories Act. He will also be responsible for preparation of wages sheets. In big factories, however, such work is done by a section in the Personnel Department.

Methods of Recording Attendance and Time

The following are the methods commonly in use for recording the attendance of workers:

1. *Registers:* If the number of workers is very small the attendance of each worker is recorded in a register as he enters the factory gate. In such a case probably there will be no need for a separate timekeeper and the work will be done by the forman concerned.

2. *Metal Disc Method:* Each worker is allotted a number and that number is put on a round metal disc (or a token) with a hole. All discs are hung on a board which is kept near the gate. As workers enter the gate, they pick up their respective discs and put them in the box which is kept nearby. After the appointed time, say, 8 o'clock the box is taken inside the office and late comers will have to hand over their dics to the timekeeper personally so that the exact time of arrival can be noted. Later the attendance is marked in a register. This method is useful when the number is not large, but it has the following main disadvantages:

(*a*) A worker may try to get his friends marked present by dropping their token also in the box.

(*b*) If the workers go out for lunch, the work of hanging the token back on the board will have to be done again and again each day.

(*c*) There may be disputes regarding the exact time of arrival of a worker.

3. *Time Recording Clocks:* To obviate some of the difficulties, mentioned above, time recording clocks are installed. These clocks are useful when the number is fairly large. Each worker is allotted a card. Cards are kept neatly arranged in a tray. As the worker enters the gates, he picks up his card, inserts it in the clock which will then print the exact time on the card in the proper space against the particular day. This can be repeated for recording time of departure for lunch, return from lunch and the time of leaving the factory in the evening. A specimen of the card is given below:

TIME CARD

Name of the Worker ... ...
No. of the Worker ... ...
Department ... ...
Week Ending ... ...

Day	Regular		Overtime		Total Time	
	In	Out	In	Out	Ordy.	Over
M						
T						
W						
Th						
F						
S						

Total Time:

Ordinary......hrs.
Over.............hrs.

....
Timekeeper

....
Pay Roll Clerk

(The card can be made out for a week or a fortnight.)

The main advantage of this system is that the time of arrival and departure is recorded exactly and there can be no dispute later. But the danger of absent workers being marked present cannot be eliminated here.

Another type of clock is one which is operated by a key which has a distinctive number corresponding to the number of the worker concerned. The worker inserts the key, turns it and the clock will then print the number of the key (that is, the number of the worker) and the exact time of arrival on a roll of paper inside. After the appointed time, the clock will begin to print in red so that the late comers can be easily marked off.

4. *Dial Time Records:* These machines are useful only in very big concerns. They provide on a sheet a record of arrival and departure and therefore, time worked for every worker for the whole week. The machines can themselves transcribe the number of hours to the wages sheets and can also calculate the wages due to the workers. The machines are arranged for 50, 100 or 150 workers.

5. *Use of Computers:* Now a days time is recorded through a computer having separate record of each employee.

Departmental Record: It is, however, necessary that if the number of workers is fairly large there should also be an attendance record kept in the various departments themselves. This will ensure that (1) the workers do not loiter on the way from the factory gate to the factory itself, (2) wages for time not worked are not paid, and (3) no payment is made to bogus workers. The last two are common methods for committing frauds in relation to labour. The activities of the timekeeper can be easily checked by an independent comparison of the record kept by him and the record kept in the factory itself. In fact, no wages should be paid unless the two records have been properly and regularly compared.

Analysis of time of direct workers

Since the purpose of costing is to find out the cost of each product or job, it is necessary to know how much time various workers have spent upon various jobs. This is also necessary from the point of view of checking the wastage of time. The cards on which an analysis is made are known as labour time records. Labour Time Record is defined as: "A document which records the amount of time spent by an employee, showing the analysis between a number of activities during a payment period. It may record the wages (labour cost) of the time spent." (*CIMA*) For workers paid on time basis, these cards are also known as time sheets. Four types of job cards are common in use:—

(*a*) *Combined Time and Job Cards:* This is useful where the worker engages himself for the whole day on the same job and where the number of workers is small enough to obviate the necessity of recording the arrival and departure of a worker and the time spent by him on jobs undertaken by him separately. (See next page)

(*b*) *Simple Job Card:* This is maintained in the department and is independent of time record kept by the timekeeper. Later at the time of preparation of the wages sheet, the time record kept by the timekeeper is compared with the time record in the job card.

(*c*) *Job Card issued for each job:* The job cards mentioned above are issued to each worker and an analysis of his time is maintained therein. But if it is desirable to know at a glance the total wages spent on a job, a job card should be issued for each job and as the work progresses from one worker to another, the job card should travel along with it, each worker recording time spent by him on it. (See next page).

(*d*) *Piece Work Card:* If workers are paid on piece basis, quantity of work done by them is important rather than the time spent by them. Quantity of work done has to be checked for quality as there is a tendency among such workers to hurry and ignore quality.

The job cards are ultimately sent to the costing office where they are costed and analysed so that each job or product may receive its proper debit. They are also utilised to vertify time records. The rulings of the job cards are as given on the following page.

(a) COMBINED TIME AND JOB CARD

Worker's Name.............................. Week Ending....................

Worker's No.............................. Rate per hour....................

Day	Job No.	Time		Time		Amount	
		On	Off	Ordinary	Over	₹.	P.
Monday							
Tuesday							
Wednesday							
Thursday							
Friday							
Saturday							

Total Hours.......... Gross Wages ₹..........

Foreman....................

Timekeeper...............

Entered in Wages Sheet

Wages Abstract written by............

Deductions:

Fine.......................

Insurance..........

etc.

Net Amount Payable ₹............

(b) JOB CARD

Worker's Name..................... Week Ending..................

Worker's No........................ Rate.............................

Day	Job No.	Brief Description	Time		Time (Hours)	Amount	
			On	Off		₹.	P.
Monday							
Tuesday							
Wednesday							
Thursday							
Friday							
Saturday							
				TOTAL			

Foreman................ Cost Clerk.............. Wages Abstract written by...........

(3) Time and Motion Study

'Motion study is a process of analysing a job to find the easiest, most effective and most economical method of doing it or portions thereof.'

'The time study is primarily the art of observing and recording time required to do each detailed element of an individual operations.'

Time and motion study is really two different things, namely, time study and motion study rolled into one. Time study is concerned with the effort to find out how much time is needed for completing a particular operation. Motion study is concerned with an effort to find out the best method of completing an operation. The two are obviously inter-concerned, and have to be carried on simultaneously. Therefore, one can say that the purpose of time and motion study is to find out the most efficient method of doing a job and also to determine the time in which the job should be completed.

In order to conduct time and motion study, a large number of workers is studied while doing a particular job. The movements made by each worker are noted. Incidentally, a movement is known as a *Therblig* (Gilbreth spelt backwards). Even a tiny movement is noted. By means of a stop-watch the time required to complete a movement is also noted. These days cine cameras, time clocks and computers can do the work almost automatically. But it is most essential to win the cooperation of the workers, otherwise the movements made by them will not be the normal ones and the time taken by them will not be the time usually taken by them; and the results, therefore, will not be reliable.

After noting the various movements made by workers a proper method of work is constructed by eliminating the unnecessary movements and by improving other movements so that the body does not get unnecessarily tired. It should be remembered that a movement which does not require the human body to work in an unnatural position alone will mean avoidance of wastage of energy.

The next step is to find out the proper time allowed for completing an operation. In this case what is done is that the time taken by various workers is noted. But from this the time taken by an extraordinary good worker and by a lazy worker are eliminated, so that the time spent by various workers represents the time which is taken by ordinary workers. Further, the readings have to be adjusted for the rating factor so that the probable time which the worker will take while working under an incentive plan is ascertained. The average then is found out. Suppose the following are the times (in seconds) taken for completing an operation: 55, 58, 54, 40, 57, and 70. Then from this 40 and 70 will be struck off and the average of the rest will be found. The average comes to 56 seconds.

To the average thus determined is added a margin for rest. How much is to be added for rest and contingency will depend upon the nature of the work. If a worker has to be under heavy load or has to pay minute attention to the operation, the rest pauses will be of longer duration. Suppose 11 seconds are added to the above for rest and contingency. This makes 67 seconds. It is also necessary to leave a margin for a worker who requires a special incentive to work. This will be so if the work is to be done by a specially qualified worker who is not willing to work for the wages paid to an ordinary worker and if it is undesirable to fix different rates of pay. This problem can be solved by adding a margin of, let us say, 13 seconds to the above noted time so that the time allowed now becomes 80 seconds for completing that operation. An efficient worker will complete the operation in less than 80 seconds and thus will become entitled to a bonus for having saved time or having produced a larger quantity than was laid down.

It is necessary to study tools, materials, and surroundings of work in order to bring about the most efficient methods of work and to see that energy is not unnecessarily wasted. Therefore, along with time and motion study, it is necessary to suggest any changes in the surroundings of work itself in order to see that the work is completed most expeditiously. Time and motion study is of extreme importance in control of labour, and in determining the proper piece rate. By means of time and motion study the standard time allowed for a job can be determined and then the workers may be required to complete the job in that standard time and thus avoid wastage of time. Having once conducted time and motion study, it may not be necessary to conduct it always when a new job is to be undertaken. Time and motion study can lay down the time required for basic movements made by a human body and hence for a new job the standard time may be fixed by simply noting down the various movements which are required for that job.

Procedure in Time Study

The following successive steps are followed in the time study:

(*i*) *Analysis and Standardisation:* The work is analysed, a through study is made improving the operations and quickest and best method of doing the work is establishes by means of motion study the operations are standardised and are more efficiently combined to establish standard methods.

(*ii*) *Recording Operation Time:* Operation times are recorded in respect of a selected average worker. The observed times are recorded on a time study sheet.

(*iii*) *Levelling the Observations:* Although in making time study an average worker is selected, yet in minor details there may be variations from what is expected from an average worker. The observations are therefore convected to bring the results closer to those expected from the average worker. Considering the 'skill', 'effort', 'conditions' and 'consistency' of the worker, a levelling factor is determined the time taken by the experimental worker is multiplied by the levelling factor to deduce the time that should be taken by an average worker.

(*iv*) *Allowance for Delays:* 'The Standard Time': In order to arrive at the time to be allowed for doing the job, allowance are made for fatigue, personal needs, moving the work, unavoidable delays etc. In a general way about 25% of the operating time may be allowed for these delays. But this allowance varies under different circumstances. The allowance should permit the average employee to work on the job regularly without exceptional fatigue and without impairing health and to perform the task set in the allowed or standard time without hurrying up.

Importance of Time and Motion Study to the Management

1. By time and motion study the management may assess the labour requirement correctly.
2. Time and motion studies help the management in standardisation of jobs, equipments and methods by providing guidance for the best method of operating in the set time.
3. With the help of these studies, management may fix wage rates and introduce effective labour incentive schemes.
4. Time and motion studies help the management to achieve improvement in the work-methods on the basis of comparison of time taken to complete the same type of work under different methods.
5. Planning and cost control are also based upon time and motion studies.

(4) Control over Idle Time

Workers are bound to waste some time. In the morning, at lunch time, and in the evening workers will spend some time between the factory gate and the department where they work. Picking up the actual work for the day costs some time. There are other reasons also for wastage which are quite normal. Thus, out of the nine hours that a worker is supposed to put in, the worker's job card may account for, say, only 8.30 hours. 30 minutes will be the normal idle time in such a case. We can deal with this in two ways. We may debit the jobs concerned with the wages for 8.30 hours and debit wages for 30 minutes to the factory expenses. Or, we may inflate the hourly wage rate suitably for purposes of costing only so that the wages for all the nine hours are debited proportionately to the various jobs undertaken by the worker.

The above applies only to normal idle time, but in case of abnormal idle time such as is caused by failure of power or non-supply of materials, the wages of the idle time should be debited to the Costing Profit and Loss Account. Abnormal idle time should not form part of the cost of production.

It will be recognised that the question of normal idle time arises only in case of direct workers paid on time basis. Wages of indirect workers are entirely added to the factory expenses whereas workers paid on piece basis will be paid only on the basis of quantity of goods produced by them, without considering whatever the time spent or wasted by them. Abnormal idle time may arise in case of all types of workers.

Idle time cost is the amount of wages paid to the worker for the hours during which he was idle. This does not include, however, wages paid for to workers for festival holidays, annual leave etc.

Idle time has to be analysed by *functional causes*, which are:

(*i*) *Production Causes:* Production causes are those which arise out of waiting for materials, machinery, breakdown, un-utilised manpower, previous operations etc.

(*ii*) *Administration Causes:* These arises out of poor planning, delayed instructions on the work to be carried out etc.

(*iii*) *Economic Causes:* Economic causes are those arising out of lack of demand for the product necessitating partial loading on machines, stoppage of work on account of strikes and lock-outs etc.

The idle time cost arising out of economic causes are not treated as a part of cost of production and are straightly written off by debiting Profit and Loss Account. The cost of idle time due to administrative causes are recovered as a part of general works overheads, while those due to production causes are charged as an item of departmental overheads. If the idle time due to administrative and production causes have been due to circumstance beyond the control of management, these are also then excluded from the cost of production.

For purpose of cost control the idle time hours would require a more detailed analysis by the specific factors contributing to idle time. The idle time causes for purposes of recovery in costs is one thing and analysing it for purposes of control is another. The latter would require a detailed break-up or analysis under following head:

1. *Machine Break-down:* (*a*) power failure, (*b*) improper maintenance, (*c*) lack of spares and (*d*) normal causes.
2. *Waiting for Workers:* (*a*) absenteeism (*b*) staying away from the job, (*c*) bad planning of work load.
3. *Lack of Materials:* (*a*) delays in procurement, (*b*) imbalancing of production, (*c*) heavy rejections.
4. *Lack of Instructions:* (*a*) From foreman (*b*) From planning, (*c*) From management.

To record the duration and reason of idle time a `Labour Utilisation Statement' is prepared, the format is given ahead :

Labour Utilisation Statement

Department.................................... Week ending..........................

S.N.	*Category of worker*	*No. of hours paid for*	*Standard Time*				*Causes*							
			Output in units	*Time per unit*	*Standard time*	*Idle Time (3-6)*	*Break down*	*Power failure*	*Lack of Materials*	*Lack of Planning*	*Setup Time*	*Inefficency*	*Others*
1	2	3	4	5	6	7	8	9	10	11	12	13	14

Treatment of Normal Idle Time Cost: There are two methods of treating normal and unavoidable idle time cost. (*a*) *Inflated wage rate method.* Under this method normal or unavoidable hours are ascertained and the direct labour cost per hour is accordingly increased (*b*) *Overhead method*: Under this method the cost of normal idle time is charged to Works Overhead Account. But this method is less scientific since an element of direct cost is treated as indirect.

Treatment of Abnormal Idle Time Costs: Abnormal or avoidable idle time should be determined and thereafter treated under any of the two methods (*a*) *Overhead Method:* under this method, cost of abnormal idle time is considered as a part of the works overhead. It will be better to apportion the idle time costs to different departments so that a clear picture may be available to the management so that it may take necessary remedial action (*b*) *Costing Profit and Loss Method:* Under this method, such costs are transferred to Costing Profit and Loss Account and thus these are treated as a loss.

Control Over Abnormal Idle Time

Abnormal idle time arises due to power failure, breakdown of machinery, non supply of raw material in time, delay in previous process, strikes and accidents etc. To eliminate abnormal idle time, these causes should be prevented and following points should be considered:

(*i*) There should be an even flow of raw material from the stores to the machines and workers according to the schedule of production.

(*ii*) The production should be planned in such a way that every machine and man linked in a process or job should be so occupied that there is a perfect balance.

(*iii*) There should be careful production planning so that breakdowns and bottle necks do not occur. There should be proper maintenance of machines and tools.

(*iv*) There should be effective supervision so that wastage of time may be reduced. Workers should be made more alert. Breakdown of machines and power should be attended promptly.

(*v*) There should be prompt reporting about the abnormal wastage of time so that corrective steps may be initiated shortly.

(5) Payment for Overtime

In India, under Factories Act a worker working for more than *nine hours on any day or for more than 48 hours in a week gets wages at double the hourly rate for the extra or overtime put in by him.* This, coupled with the fact that overtime comes at the end of the day when fatigue has set in, should make it clear that jobs done in overtime are rather costly. It should also be remembered that, in addition to double the wages and low productivity, additional expenses like lighting, extra wear and tear of machinery, etc., are incurred. Therefore, overtime should, as a policy, be avoided. There is the danger that the workers may adopt it as a habit, not doing their proper work during the day and thus creating the need for overtime. The Works Manager or some other high officer should personally authorise overtime. Occasional overtime is, however, a healthy sign because it indicates that the labour force and plant and equipment are of the right size and capacity and are not idle.

In case of a rush job, where overtime is necessiated, one should charge the entire wages for the time spent to the cost of the job. Suppose a rush job is done in the morning thus causing some other job to be done in overtime. In this case also the extra wages for overtime should form part of the cost of the emergency. If a number of jobs has to be finished within a short period of time, thus causing overtime, the extra wages should be added not to the cost of any single job, but should be proportionately spread over all the jobs. It would even be better if the extra wages were added to the factory expenses because then the cost of the jobs would not show any abnormality. If overtime arises due to any abnormal reason (such as failure of power), it should be debited to the Costing Profit and Loss Account.

It should be noted that wages for the purpose of computing overtime, will consist of the basic wage, the dearness allowance and the cash value of foodgrains, etc., supplied at a concessional rate.

Illustration 1: In a factory one worker is paid the basic wage of ₹. 100 per month plus a dearness allowance of ₹. 400. The average number of days worked in a month is 25 of 8 hours each. The attendance record of the worker for a week showed the following:

Monday 11 hours, Tuesday 9 hours, Wednesday 8 hours, Thursday 8 hours, Friday 11 hours, Saturday 8 hours. State the overtime wages due to the worker.

Solution:

Wages per hour :	Total payment per month (Basic wage + D.A.)	₹. 500	
	Average no. of hours (25 × 8)	200	
	Wages per hour 500 ÷ 200	₹. 2.50	
Overtime hours :	Total no. of hours in the week	55	
	Excess over 48	7	
	Overtime per hour 2.50 × 2	₹. 5	
Overtime wages :	(7 × 5)		₹. 35

Illustration 2: A worker is paid the basic wage of Re. 1 per hour; in addition there is D.A. of ₹. 500 per month (reckoned for the purpose at 200 hours). The factory works 8 hours per day Monday to Friday and 4 hours on Saturday. In a particular week, the worker's attendance was as follows:

Monday 9 hours, Tuesday 8 hours, Wednesday 11 hours, Thursday 8 hours, Friday 8 hours, Saturday 5 hours.

Compute the wages payable to the worker in total.

Solution:

			₹.
Wage rate per hour :	Basic		1.00
	D.A. per hour 500 ÷ 200		2.50
			3.50
	Number of hours of attendance	49	
	Excess over normal hours of work (49 – 44)	5	
	Overtime as per Factories Act (in excess of 9 on Wednesday)	2	
	Wages: Normal for 44 hours @ 3.50		154.00
	Normal for 3 extra-hours @ 3.50		10.50
	Overtime for 2 hours @ 7.00		14.00
	Total		178.50

Control over Overtime

The overtime should be controlled on following reasons which may also be considered as disadvantages of overtime:

(*i*) Extra payment does not necessarily mean extra work. Workers fatigue curve rise sharply as their work-hours get longer.

(*ii*) Workers usually become used to receive higher wages due to overtime and when overtime work is cut down, they become hostile and their resentment may be very strong.

(*iii*) Overtime means extra cost, both that of wages and other variables like lighting etc., which result in reduction of profit.

(*iv*) If overtime is avoided, same work may be done by additional employees. Thus from the point of view of nations employment potential, it is beneficial to control overtime.

(*v*) Overtime fells upon the health of the workers, it leads to fatigue.

(*vi*) Due to overtime there is unusual strain and work-load on plant and machinery,

(*vii*) If overtime is allowed, there is a tendency to keep work pending to be done during overtime period or to intentionally slow down inorder to compel the management to sanction overtime.

On the other hand it may be said in favour of overtime that it increases the productive capacity of the concern as more work is done with the existing resources. Overtime work is particularly useful in pulling up back-log in production arising due to shut down, breakdown, power failure and such other contingencies.

Though overtime work cannot be completely eliminated, it is essential that proper control should be exercised to keep it to the minimum. The following steps may be suggested to control overtime:

(*i*) All overtime work should be duly authorised either by departmental head or work manager, There should be sanction of overtime after investigating its necessity.

(*ii*) Overtime cost should be separately recorded in respect of each department. This will enable proper investigation and planning of production in future.

(*iii*) There should be effective supervision of overtime work so that there may be no misuse of overtime allotted to workers.

(*iv*) If overtime tends to become a permanent feature the management should consider of recruiting more workers or shifts may be increased.

(*v*) If overtime is due to lack of sufficient equipment, plant and resources, steps should be taken to arrange necessary resources and equipments. The management may opt for giving sub contracts to others.

(*vi*) Weekly overtime reports must be made out to the management or work manager, which will enable him to initiate necessary action to cut down overtime.

Treatment of Overtime Premium

There are different methods of treatment of overtime. Extra costs are in use in different circumstances.

(*i*) When overtime is undertaken on the request of a customer to complete the job within specific period, the overtime cost may be added to the cost of that job.

(*ii*) When overtime work is undertaken to increase production in general and it has become a normal feature, then overtime extra wages may be regarded as works overhead cost.

(*iii*) When overtime work is undertaken in an emergency, such as after a strike, to cope with the current demand, then the overtime extra wages should be transferred to the Profit & Loss Account as abnormal loss.

(6) Methods of Wages

Various systems of wage payment are in use today, and the following are pretty general: the time wage system, piece work, the premium plans, bonus and profit-sharing schemes. Whichever scheme reduces the cost of a labour per unit while increasing output (provided, of course, that the worker receives a fair return for the work) is the one to have. This is the logical principle of business, because excessive labour costs are bound to cause either increase in prices or a loss to the business. It is the function of management to formulate, initiate, and operate a system of wage payment or plan which will stimulate production and sales, encourage efficiency and economy, and promote goodwill and satisfaction among workers. After studying the various conditions, it is often possible to install a system, without prejudicing the loyal employee, which can cut down expenses by a large percentage, possibly increasing output and giving a better return for the conscientious. Obviously, the first step is to eliminate "slackers" and dismiss those who are not pulling their weight and who, by so doing, penalize others. Bearing in mind the human factor which causes variation in the amount of work done by several workers, attempt may be made to equalise them and put them on the same footing by offering incentives, both financial and non-financial. Workers are more responsive and productive when some form of incentive, especially financial, is offered to them for surpassing specified standards of perfection and performance. One should note that efficiency as regards labour consists only in reducing labour costs *per unit of output*. This is not generally obtained by paying low wages. High wages almost always lead to low wages per unit of output because of greater production.

Criteria for Judging a Wage System

A wage system will be treated as fair if it satisfies the following criteria:

(*a*) The worker should have guarantee of a minimum payment for the time spent by him. This should be sufficient for a reasonable standard of living.

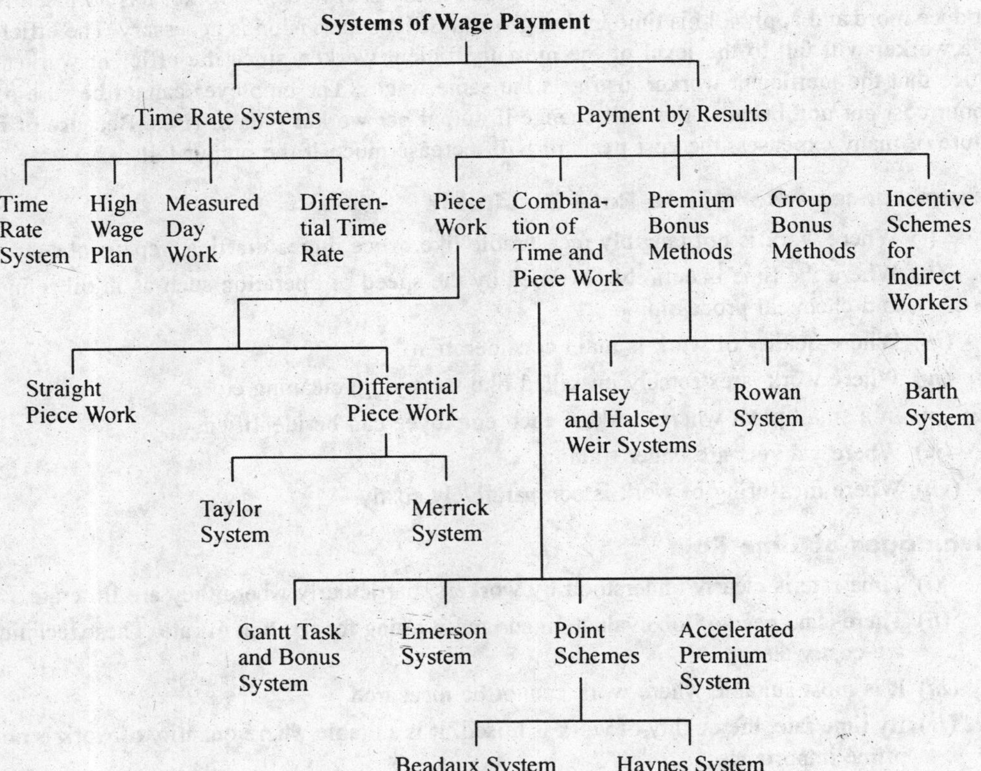

(*b*) Efficient workers should be distinguished from inefficient ones by means of linking wages to output.

(*c*) If extra output is obtained or if time is saved by the worker by his own effort, he should have the full benefit in terms of wages; but if efficiency is obtained due to co-operation between management and the worker, the benefit of extra output or time saved should be shared by management and the worker.

(*d*) Skilled workers should be remunerated for the effort put in by them to acquire the skill

(*e*) There should be equal pay for equal work.

(*f*) There should be uniformity of wage rates in the same area or industry.

Some of the more important systems of wage payment are described below:

(*i*) WAGES ON TIME BASIS

Although, various wage incentive plans are gradually replacing time wages, the straight time wage persists as the most common form of payment. Wages under this method are determined per unit of time that a worker spends in the factory. The unit can be hour, day, week or month. If a worker's wages are ₹. 25.00 per day, his total wages will be the number of days he is present multiplied by ₹. 25.00. If he is paid ₹. 6 per hour and on a day he works for 9 hours, his wage for the day shall be ₹. 54.00. Calculation is very simple and, in addition, the worker is in no hurry (because his wages are independent of the quantity he produces) and, therefore, can turn out better quality work. In fact, if quality is of utmost importance, as in artistic goods, wages should be paid on time basis.

But in case of ordinary work, this system has many *drawback*. A worker has no incentive to produce more and apply all his time in doing work. Strict supervision is necessary. The efficiency of a worker will fall to the level of the most inefficient worker, since the efficient worker will notice that the inefficient worker also gets the same wages. The employer cannot be sure of the labour cost per unit because this will change if output per worker falls or rises. Because of fixed nature of many expenses, the cost per unit will increase much if the output falls.

Circumstances where Time Rate is suitable

(*i*) Where work is not tangibly measurable like office duties drafting, repair jobs etc.

(*ii*) Where the time is entirely governed by the speed of operation such as in oil refineries and chemical processing.

(*iii*) Where quality of work is main consideration.

(*iv*) Where work is extremely unskilled like surveying, cleaning etc.

(*v*) In a small plant where work of each employee can be identified.

(*vi*) Where workers are under training

(*vii*) Where measuring of work is comparatively costly.

Advantages of Time Rate

(*i*) Time rate is clearly understood by workers, particularly where they are illiterate.

(*ii*) There is no need of job evaluation and merit rating for fixation of rate. These techniques are costly also

(*iii*) It is most suitable where work cannot be measured

(*iv*) By time rate, the quality of work is raised. It is suitable where quantity of work is not of prime importance.

Limitations of Time Rate

(*i*) Time rate prevents the workers from doing more work and earning more through higher output.

(*ii*) It deprives the employer of the opportunity of lowering the cost of production by means of higher productivity.

(*iii*) Time rate method provides no impetus to increase individually efficiency and makes the labour force generally efficient.

If this method is adopted, it is desirable from the costing point of view to have separate wage sheets for direct workers, department by department, and indirect workers. From the financial point of view one wage sheet for all workers may suffice, showing total wages earned by the workers and the various deductions to be made from the wages.

(*ii*) WAGES ON PIECE BASIS

In this method, the time spent by the worker is immaterial and payment is made according to the quantity of work done. Rate of wages is per unit of work. A worker may be paid ₹. 5.00 per unit; if his output in a month is 300 units, his wages for the month will be ₹. 1500 *i.e.*, 300 × 5.00. The wage rate may be expressed even as so much per hour; in that case for computing the wages, the output will have to be expressed in terms of standard hours. Suppose a worker is paid ₹. 2 per hour. On a day of 9 hours, he produces 36 units, the standard time for each unit being 20 minutes. The output of the worker may be stated also as 12 hours, *i.e.*, 36 × 20/60. His wages on piece basis will be ₹. 24, *i.e.*, 12 × 2—on time basis it would have been only ₹. 18, *i.e.*, 9 × 2.

The system should mean a good deal of incentive to do the best. Output will thus be maximised and the cost per unit of output will be lowered. The employer will also exactly know the labour cost per unit. This helps in making quotations confidently.

Precaution in Piece Rate Method

Care should be taken to fix proper and scientific rates from the very beginning. Any future cutting of rates will be disastrous for relations between management and workers. The need for proper rates is obvious when we consider that, generally, piece rates are fixed according to the performance of the worker under time basis. Suppose a worker paid at ₹. 25.00 per day usually produced 50 units. The management might be tempted to fix a piece rate of 50 paise. We should remember that 50 units per day was probably a low figure because the worker might have been wasting a lot of his time. On piece basis, his performance might be much better and management might be tempted to reduce the piece rate. From the very beginning, piece rates should be fixed on the basis of time and motion study, if possible.

Circumustances Favouring Piece Rate Method

The following are the circumstance favouring this method of wage payment:

(*i*) Operations should be independent and capable of being steadily continued by a single operator,

(*ii*) There should be steady supply of work so that no time is lost in waiting for next-work.

(*iii*) There should be proper maintenance of tools and equipment so that there may be no interference in the working speed.

(*iv*) The method is suited where increase in the quantity is more important and quality being insured by a proper supervision and inspection.

(*v*) Where job time has been standardised by means of time and motion study.

Advantages of Piece Rate Method

To summarise, following points of advantages can be noted:

(*i*) Plan is simple and easy to understand by the workers.

(*ii*) The method provides direct incentives to increase output and quality is maintained by a good inspection system.

(iii) In this method wages is easy to calculate.

(*iv*) When this method is adopted, fixed manufacturing overheads are lowered per unit.

(*v*) It is favoured by efficient workers because it provides opportunity to earn more by increasing efficiency.

(*vi*) This method discourages inefficiency and increases efficiency of workers in general.

(*vii*) The benefit of increased efficiency is wholly received by the worker. In certain incentive plans, benefit is shared by the management also.

Limitations of Piece Rate Method

Following points may be noted as limitations of this method:

(*i*) The method is not suitable to beginners whose production is naturally low.

(*ii*) The plan is suitable on group basis, but not on individual basis.

(*iii*) It is not suitable to tasks where standard time cannot be fixed on the basis of time and motion study.

(*iv*) It is also not suitable where supply of work is not guaranted.

Under this method the worker pays no attention to quality and hence inspectors have to be there to see that goods of poor quality are not produced.[1] Bad quality goods means a wastage of materials and wages of other workers on the same goods. The worker is also likely to be reckless in the use of materials, machines and tools. He may ignore his own health and insist upon working even when he is ill. Other workers may work at a furious pace for a few days, earn good wages and then have a holiday, upsetting the work in the factory. For this reason, attendance and punctuality are insisted upon even in case of piece workers. Moreover, under this method workers have the fear of losing wages if, some-how, they are not able to work. Workers like to feel that there is a minimum wage available irrespective of the quantity of work done by them. Workers in the habit of turning out quality work will suffer.

It is also necessary to foresee the market conditions. If demand is likely to be steady, the piece rate system will ensure steady production. Otherwise, the time basis will be more useful.

A point of importance is the likely effect on the mind of such workers as cannot be put on piece basis and yet possess good skills. It may be possible that workers possessing lower skills but put on piece basis earn more than higher skilled workers and supervisors. If this is so, the piece rate system will not produce good results. A way must be found to see that unnecessary dissatisfaction is not caused among highly skilled personnel.

Another point to be kept in mind is that management must see to it that work and the required facilities are supplied without interruption. If this is not so, the worker will sit idle and that may cause some dissatisfaction. Generally when such is the case, the workers are paid on time basis for the idle time.

From the point of view of the employer, no reduction in the labour cost of a product is possible since the same rate must be paid for all units. Moreover, slow workers cannot be penalised

1. However, this is not much of a disadvantage because inspectors have to be appointed in any case. Workers, even if paid on time basis, cannot be relied upon to check the quality themselves.

and yet they will cause a loss to the employer. But the employer gains if the output rises because fixed expenses will be spread over larger output.

Two workers *A* and *B* are paid ₹. 2.00 per unit. In 10 hours they produce respectively 15 and 25 units. The cost of materials is ₹. 4.00 per unit and overheads are ₹. 2.50 per hour. The cost per unit will be as follows:

	Worker A	*Worker B*
	₹.	₹.
Materials	60.00	100.00
Wages	30.00	50.00
Overheads	25.00	25.00
Total	115.00	175.00
Units produced	15	25
Cost per unit	₹. 7.67	₹. 7.00

The slow worker causes the cost per unit to be high and this will be very serious if the amount of overheads is large.

Choice Between Time and Piece Rate System

Usually the following principles are observed:

(*a*) If quality is of extreme importance and if quantity of output cannot be adequately measured, wages should be paid on time basis. Also, if the material used is costly.

(*b*) If quantity can be measured and quality controlled, wages should be according to the piece rate system.

(*c*) In case the output is beyond the control of the worker (for example in case of automation and chain assembly method), wages should be paid on the time basis.

(*iii*) BALANCE OF DEBT SYSTEM

In this case, the worker is really paid on piece basis. If his wages according to the piece rate fall below the wages on time basis, he would be paid on time basis. But the difference will be recovered out of his future wages whenever the piece wages exceed the time wage.

(7) Incentive Plans

The time rate method of wage-payment is associated with a disadvantage arising out of slowness or inefficiency of workers, which is borne by the employer alone. Similarly any gain due to efficiency of workers is also taken over by the employer. In piece rate system, the benefit due to efficient work goes to worker and the employer gains only in reduction in overhead rate per unit. There are some incentive or premium plans which differ from the time and piece rate methods in respect of benefits. Under incentive plans the financial advantage on account of efficiency of the worker is shared between the employer and the employee in an agreed proportion. Under premium or incentive plans, speed of work is regular or moderate and worker does not tend to slow down as in the case of time rate system nor does he attempt to speed up causing breakdown of machine and wastage as in the case of piece rate.

In various incentive plans, standard time is fixed for doing a task. The worker is guarranted his daily wages and so long his output is below and upto standard he is paid his daily wage. If work is completed in less than standard time, the benefit of time saved is shared between employer and employee.

Following are some important incentive plans:

(1) Halsey Premium Plan

(2) Rowan Plan
(3) Barth Premium Plan
(4) Taylor's Differential Piece rate system
(5) Merrick Plan
(6) Emerson's Efficiency Plan
(7) Gantt's Task and Bonus Plan
(8) Hayene's Plan
(9) Bedeax Plan
(10) Priestman's Production Bonus
(11) Group Bonus
(12) Profit Sharing Plan

(1) Halsey Premium Plan

Under this method standard time for doing a job is determined and workers are encouraged to do the job in less than the standard time. They are given wages for the actual time they take to do the job, but if they save time they are also paid a bonus equal to one-half (sometimes one-third) of the wages of the time saved. Thus if S is the standard time, T the actual time taken and R the rate of wages per hour, total earnings will be

$$\text{Total Earnings} = (T \times R) + \frac{S - T}{2} \times R$$
$$\text{or} = (T \times R) + (S - T) \times R \times 50\%$$

Illustration 3: Time rate of wages is ₹. 1 per hour, Standard output 50 units per hour; Actual hours worked 8 hours; Actual output 500 units. Calculate wages according to Halsey Plan.

Solution: Time Taken (T) = 8 hours

Wage Rate per hour (R) = ₹. 1

$$\text{Standard Times } (S) = \frac{500}{50} = 10 \text{ hours.}$$

$$\text{Total wages} = (T \times R) + \frac{S - T}{2} \times R$$

$$= (8 \times 1) + \frac{(10 - 8) \times 1}{2} = 8 + 1 = ₹.\ 9.$$

The rate per hour is 9 ÷ 8 = ₹. 1.125.

The main difficulty in this system is about the fixation of standard time. Employers may fix it on the basis of past performance of the workers. If, however, proper time and motion studies are conducted, this difficulty can be resolved. Workers object to this method on the ground that they do not get the whole benefit of the time saved by them. But the objection is not valid if the saving in time is obtained with the cooperation of management or if the standard is inexact. Also, if in expeditious completion of the job, active co-operation of the management is necessary. The system is rather easy to enforce because hourly wages for the actual time spent by the workers are guaranteed.

Conditions favourable for Halsey Premium System: (*i*) where tasks are roughly timed, (*ii*) where accomplishment of task is uncertain due to uncontrolled factors, (*iii*) where workers have been formarily on ordinary time wages, (*iv*) where efficiency of workers are, in general, low.

Merits of Halsey Plan: (*i*) It can be applied when jobs are not accurately time studies. (*ii*) It provides a safe and generous incentive through intermediate range of efficiencies. (*iii*) It is a simple method.

Limitations of Halsey Plan: (*i*) It is an incentive plan favoured by workers whose efficiency is usually less than 100 per cent. It is not favoured by highly efficient workers (*ii*) It is less effective than plans strong at high task. (*iii*) In a plant where high piece rate method has already been experienced, the Halsey Plans normally does not increase the efficiency above 90%. (*iv*) Employees often object because a part of benefit is shared by the employer.

Halsey-Weir Plan: It is similar to Halsey Plan. But the bonus is 30% instead of 50%.

Illustration 4: (Halsey Weir Plan)

Time Rate ₹. 2 per hour;

Standard Time 10 hours;

Time Taken 8 hours;

Calculate wages according to Halsey Weir-Scheme from above data.

Solution: Total wages $= (T \times R) + R \times 30\% \times (S - T)$

$$= (8 \times 2) + \frac{2 \times 30 \times (10-8)}{100} = 16 + 1.20 = ₹.\ 17.20$$

Rate per hour ₹. 17.20 ÷ 8 = ₹. 2.15

(2) Rowan Plan

In its essence, the plan is similar to the Halsey Plan. Wages at the ordinary rate for actual time put in by a worker are guaranteed and a bonus given, if the worker saves time out of the standard time set for him. The difference in the two plans lies only in the calculation of the bonus. Under this plan, the bonus is that proportion of wages of actual time taken which time saved bears to the standard time, whereas in the Halsey Plan the bonus is merely one-half of wages of the time saved. Thus in the Rowan Plan, if standard time is denoted by S, actual time by T and hourly rate by R, the bonus will be

$$\text{Bonus} = T \times R \times \frac{S-T}{S}$$

and the earning will be $T \times R + \left(\frac{S-T}{S} \times T \times R\right)$

In the example given above, the worker will earn—

$$6 \times 3.75 + \frac{4}{10} \times 6 \times 3.75 \text{ or } ₹.\ 31.50$$

The rate per hour comes to ₹. 5.25 *i.e.*, 31.50 ÷ 6.

The system is subject to the same *objections* as the Halsey Plan with the added objection that two workers, one very efficient and the other not quite so efficient, may earn the same bonus under certain circumstances. In the above example, where a worker saves 4 hours, his bonus is ₹. 9.00. If a worker saves 6 hours, spending only 4 hours to do the job, his bonus will also be $\frac{6}{10} \times 4 \times 3.75$ or ₹. 9.00.

Comparison of the Two Plans. Since under the Halsey Plan 50% of the wages of the time saved are to be paid to the worker as bonus, the two systems will yield equal wages if a worker saves exactly half the time set for him. (The student is advised to work out the above example with actual time as five hours). If a worker saves less than half the time as in the above example, he will be better off under the Rowan Plan. But if he saves more than half the time, he will earn more under the Halsey Plan. Thus, if in the above illustration the actual time taken is only 3 hours, the earnings of the worker under the Halsey Plan will be:

$$3 \times 2.00 + 7 \times 2.00 \times \frac{50}{100} \text{ or ₹. } 13.00$$

and the earnings under the Rowan Plan will be

$$3 \times 2.00 + \frac{7}{10} \times 3 \times 2.00 \text{ or ₹. } 10.20$$

To take an impossible case, if actual time is zero hours, the worker will get no wages under the Rowan Plan but will get wages for time saved in the above example, under the Halsey Plan. It is impossible for a worker to double his wages under the Rowan Plan.

An improvement on Rowan Plan is to calculate the bonus as that proportion of the time saved which time saved bears to the standard time. The earnings will then be:

$$T \times R + \frac{\textit{Time Saved}}{\textit{Standard Time}} \times \textit{Time Saved} \times R$$

Illustration 5: Standard time allowed for a job is 50 hours. The hourly rate of wage is ₹.2.00 per hour plus a dearness allowance @ ₹. 2.50 per hour worked.

The actual time taken by the worker was 40 hours. Calculate total wages on :

(1) Time basis; (2) Piece basis; (3) Halsey Plan; and (4) Rowan's Plan.

Solution :

		₹.
(*a*)	*Time Basis:*	
	Basic wages for 40 hours @ ₹. 2.00	80.00
	Dearness Allowance for 40 hours @ ₹. 2.50	100.00
		180.00
(*b*)	*Piece Basis:*	
	Basic wages for 50 hours @ ₹. 2.00	100.00
	Dearness Allowance for 40 hours @ 2.50	100.00
		200.00
(*c*)	*Halsey Plan:*	
	Basic wages for 40 hours @ ₹. 2.00	80.00
	Bonus @ 50% of basic wages for time saved (50 – 40 hours, viz., 10 hours)	10.00
	D.A. for 40 hours	100.00
		190.00
(*d*)	*Rowan's Plan:*	
	Basic wage for 40 hours	80.00
	Bonus for $\frac{10}{50} \times 40$ hours, viz., 8 hours	16.00
	D.A. for 40 hours	100.00
		196.00

Earnings per hour worked:		₹.
Time Basis	$\frac{180}{40}$	4.50
Piece Basis	$\frac{200}{40}$	5.00
Halsey Plan	$\frac{190}{40}$	4.75
Rowan's Plan	$\frac{196}{40}$	4.90

Illustration 6: The following information relates to the week ending 25th November, 2004 for two workers *A* and *B*:

	A	*B*
Work issued (units)	1,800	3,168
Standard time allowed	30 min. per dozen	3 hours per gross
Output rejected	444	758
Basic hourly rate	₹. 4	₹. 6
Hours worked	48	54

Bonus is paid @ 2/3 of basic rate for all time saved and for all output without any deduction for rejected output. The basic week is 42 hours, the first 6 hours of overtime being paid at time plus 1/3 and the next six hours at time plus one-half.

Using the information given above, present in tabulated summary form for each employee:

(*a*) Number of bonus hours earned and amount of hours earned;

(*b*) Basic wages including overtime premium and gross wages; and

(*c*) Direct wages cost per dozen of the finished output (nearest paise) when overtime is worked: (*i*) regularly throughout the year as company policy due to labour shortage, and (*ii*) specifically at the customer's request to expedite delivery.

Solution:

Statement showing Wages and Bonus to Each Employee

		A	*B*
Hours worked		48 hours	54 hours
Overtime		6 "	12 "
Standard time allowed			
$A:\frac{1800}{12}\times\frac{1}{2}, B:\frac{3168}{144}\times 3$		75 "	66 "
Time saved		27 "	12 "
Bonus		₹.	₹.
$27\times\frac{2}{3}\times 4$		72.00	
$12\times\frac{2}{3}\times 6$			48.00
Wages earned:			
A : 42 hours @ ₹. 4	168.00		
6 hours @ $4\times\frac{4}{3}$	32.00	200.00	
B : 42 hours @ ₹. 6	252.00		
6 hours @ $6\times\frac{4}{3}$	48.00		
6 hours × $6\times\frac{3}{2}$	54.00		354.00
Total		272.00	402.00
Output		1800 units	3168 units
Rejection		444 "	756 "
Accepted production		1356 "	2412 "
or		113 Doz.	201 Doz.

Cost per unit (if overtime is paid on regular basis):

			₹.	₹.
Wages earned by:	A	Bonus	72.00	
		Basic wages for time actual worked @ ₹. 4	192.00	264.00
	B	Bonus	48.00	
		Basic wages for time worked @ ₹. 6	324.00	372.00
				636.00
Output :		314 Doz.		
Cost per Doz.		636 ÷ 314		₹. 2.02

The overtime premium will be included in overheads.

Cost per Unit (If overtime is at the request of the customer):

Total wages for the two workers (₹. 272 + 402)	₹. 674
Cost per Doz. (674 ÷ 314)	₹. 2.15

(3) Barth Variable Sharing Plan

The Barth Premium system is defined as follows. Earning = $\sqrt{S \times T} \times R$, where S = Time allowed for low task *i.e.*, for 82.5 % efficiency i.e., standard time; T = Hours actual, that is, the time actually taken to perform the job and R = Hourly rate of workers. For any specific job the time allowed S is determined by time and motion study and it remains constant. T, the actual time taken is variable and varies inversely as efficiency. That is, if efficiency increases, H decreases and *vice-versa*.

It is to be noted that $\sqrt{S \times T}$ is the geometric mean of S and T.

Total wages = $\sqrt{S \times T} \times R$; S = Standard Time; R = Rate per hour.

***Illustration** 7:* The following information is available in respect of a job. Rate per hour ₹. 0.50; Standard Time 12 hours; Actual time taken by: Ram 16 hours; Shyam 12 hours, Sitaram 8 hours; Calculate the wages of the workers under Barth Plan.

Solution:

Total wages of Ram = $\sqrt{12 \times 16} \times 0.50$ = 13.86 × 0.50 or ₹. 6.93

Total wages of Shyam = $\sqrt{12 \times 12} \times 0.50$ = 12 × 0.50 or ₹. 6

Total wages of Sitaram = $\sqrt{12 \times 8} \times 0.50$ = 9.8 × 0.50 or ₹. 4.90

(4) Taylor's Differential Piece Rate System

Taylor, the father of Scientific Management, was all for maximising output. As pointed out above in the discussion about Piece Rate System, slow output causes total cost of production to rise and rapid output causes cost of production to fall. Taylor wanted to make output as rapid as possible. He fixed a standard of output per unit of time on the basis of time and motion studies. A worker achieving the standard or more was paid a certain rate per unit of output. Those who failed to reach the standard were paid at a lower rate. For example, the rate might be 15 paise per piece if the output was 30 pieces or more and only 10 paise if output was less than 30 pieces. Those who reach the standard have a double advantage of large output and higher rate. Those who do not achieve the standard earn less wages because of lower output and lower rate.

Some authorities say that wages below the standard would be 80 to 85% of the day wage and 120 to 125% when the standard is attained.

No minimum wage are guaranteed under the method. This is a disadvantage from the point of view of the workers. Another drawback is that a worker falling just short of the standard would lose very heavily. Moreover, the workers would fear that their failure to reach the standard would some day lead to dismissal since it was an integral part of Taylor's philosophy that work ought to be done by the most efficient worker (for that work) and not by others. The advantage of the system is that the workers have double incentive for increasing the output. But the system is not much in use nowadays.

Illustration 8: Using Taylor's differential piece rate system, find out the earnings of workers *X* and *Y* from the following particulars:

Standard Time per piece = 20 minute; Normal Rate per hour = ₹. 0.90; In a 9 hour day, *X* produces 25 units and *Y* produces 30 units. Lower rate is 80% of normal rate and higher rate is 120% of normal rate.

Solution: Piece Rate $= \frac{0.90 \times 20 \text{ minutes}}{60 \text{ mintues}}$

$= ₹$ 0.30 per unit

Low piece Rate $= \frac{0.30 \times 80}{100}$

$= ₹$ 0.24 per unit

High piece Rate $= \frac{0.30 \times 120}{100}$

$= ₹$ 0.36 per unit

Standard production per day $= 9 \times \frac{60}{20} = 27$ units

X produces 25 units in a day, thus his efficiency is $\frac{25}{27} \times 100$, *i.e.*, below 100%

X's earning = 25 × .24 = ₹. 6.00

Y produces 30 units in a day, his efficiency is $\frac{30}{27} \times 100$, *i.e.*, more than 100%

Y's earnings = 30 × .36 = ₹. 10.80

Illustration 9: The standard production in Presight Co., is 20 units per hour. For the first week in April, a worker's record was as follows:

Monday 140 units; Tuesday 160 units;
Wednesday 175 units; Thursday 180 units;
Friday 200 units.

There was a 8 hours work each day. You are required to draw up a schedule showing the worker's daily earnings, the effective hourly rate and the labour cost per unit, if the company uses:

(*a*) Halsey Premium Plan with a guaranteed rate of ₹. 4.50 per hour and a premium of 60% of the time saved; and

(*b*) Taylor Differential Piece Rate System with rates of 20 paise per unit below standard, 24 paise at standard and upto 20% above standard and 30 paise per unit for all production in excess of 120% standard.

Solution: Statement Showing Wages Earned and Labour Cost Per Unit

(a) Halsey Premium Plan

Day	*Production Units*	*Standard Time Allowed (2 ÷ 20)*	*Actual time*	*Time Saved (3 – 4)*	*Wage for Actual Time @ ₹. 4.50 per hour*	*Bonus 60% of time Saved @ ₹. 4.50 per hour*	*Wages Earned (6 + 7)*	*Labour Cost per unit (8 ÷ 2)*
1	2	3	4	5	6 ₹.	7 ₹.	8 ₹.	9 ₹.
Monday	140	7 hrs.	8 hrs.	—	36.00	—	36.00	0.257
Tuesday	160	8 "	8 "	—	36.00	—	36.00	0.225
Wednesday	175	8.75 "	8 "	0.75 hrs.	36.00	2.03	38.03	0.217
Thurday	180	9.00 "	8 "	1.00 "	36.00	2.70	38.70	0.215
Friday	200	10.00 "	8 "	2.00 "	36.00	5.40	41.40	0.207
Total	855							

(b) Taylor's Differential Piece Rate

	Production units	*% of Standard*	*Rate per unit*	*Wages* ₹.	*Wages per hour* ₹.	*Labour Cost per unit*
Monday	140	87.5%	20 P	28.00	3.50	0.20
Tuesday	160	100%	24 P	38.40	4.80	0.24
Wednesday	175	109.4%	24 P	42.00	5.25	0.24
Thursday	180	112.5%	24 P	43.20	5.40	0.24
Friday	200	125%	30 P	60.00	7.50	0.30
Total	855			211.60		

(5) Merrick Differential Plan

It is also called Multiple Piece Wage Plan. In this plan there are three graded piece-rates, one for the beginners; second for the developing; and third for the highly skilled workers. Normally three piece rates are

Efficiency	*Rate*
(1) Upto 83%	Normal Piece Rate
(2) From 83% to 100%	110% of Normal Piece Rate
(3) Above 100%	120% of Normal Piece Rate

This plan has almost the same advantages as the Taylor's Plan. Besides, the marginal in efficiency is not heavily penalised. However, it retains negative points of the Taylor's Plan.

Illustration 10: Standard production per hour 6 units. Normal rate per hour ₹. 1.20.

In a day of 8 hours, Mohan produces 32 units, Sohan produces 42 units and Jokhan produces 50 units. Calculate the wages of these workers according to Merrick System.

Solution:

$$\text{Piece Rate} = \frac{\text{Normal Rate per hour}}{\text{Units produced per hour}} = \frac{1.20}{6} = ₹\ .20 \text{ per unit}$$

Merrick's differential rates will be:

Efficiency	*Rate*
Upto 83%	₹ 0.20 per unit
From 83% to 100%	110% of 0.20 = ₹ 0.22 per unit *i.e.*,
Above 100%	120% of 0.20 = ₹ 0.24 per unit
Standard production per day	= 6 × 8 or 48 units

$$\text{Mohan's efficiency} = \frac{32 \times 100}{48} = 66.7\% \text{ i.e., below } 83\%$$

$$\text{Sohan's efficiency} = \frac{42 \times 100}{48} = 87.5\%, \text{ i.e., between 83 to } 100\%$$

$$\text{Jokhan's efficiency} = \frac{50 \times 100}{48} = 104.17\%, \text{ i.e., above } 100\%$$

Mohan's wages = 32 × .20 = ₹. 6.40;

Sohan's wages = 42 × 0.22 = ₹. 9.24;

Jokhan's wages = 50 × .24 = ₹. 12.00

(6) Emerson's Efficiency Plans

Emerson was one of Taylor's associates. He guaranteed time wages but wanted to reward efficiency. For the determination of a worker's level of efficiency, it was necessary to see the time for a job or set a task for a unit of time. On that basis efficiency could be determined. If a worker does a job in 10 hours and if the standard time is also 10 hours, his efficiency is 100%. If he does the same job in 20 hours, his efficiency is 50% and if he does the job in 8 hours, his efficiency is 125%. Bonus become payable only when efficiency reaches 66-2/3%. For an efficiency below 66-2/3%, he gets only the time wage. The bonus at 66-2/3% is very small but it becomes 20% when efficiency reaches 100%. A worker showing 100% efficiency will get wages at the hourly rate for the time spent by him plus 20% of the wages. If the worker does a job in less than the standard time, that is, if his efficiency is greater than 100%, he will get the wages for the actual time spent by him plus 20% of the wages earned plus one per cent for every one increase in the efficiency percentage.

The rate of bonus at various levels of efficiency will be as under:

Efficiency %	*Bonus as % of Wages earned on time basis*	*Efficiency %*	*Bonus as % of Wages earned on time basis*
67	0.01	89	9.11
68	0.04	90	9.91
69	0.11	91	10.74
70	0.22	92	11.62
71	0.37	93	12.56
72	0.55	94	13.52
73	0.76	95	14.53
74	1.02	96	15.57
75	1.31	97	16.62
76	1.64	98	17.70
77	1.99	99	18.81
78	2.38	100	20.00
79	2.80	101	21.00

80	3.27	102	22.00
81	3.78	103	23.00
82	4.33	104	24.00
83	4.92	105	25.00
84	5.53	110	30.00
85	6.17	120	40.00
86	6.84	130	50.00
87	7.56	140	60.00
88	8.32	150	70.00

On 100% efficiency bonus is 20%. It will increase by one percentage on every one percentage increase in efficiency.

Illustration 11: Calculate total wages of worker under Emerson Efficiency Bonus Plan from the following information :

Standard output in 12 hours : 192 units,

Actual output in 12 hours: 168 units

Time Rate ₹. 0.75 per hour.

As per Emerson Bonus percentage table, bonus percentages at 87% and 88% efficiency are 7.56 and 8.32 respectively.

What will be the total earnings, if the output of the worker is 240 units?

Solution:

$$\text{Efficiency} = \frac{\text{Actual Output} \times 100}{\text{Standard Output}} = \frac{168 \times 100}{192} = 87.5\%$$

$$\text{Bonus percentage at 87.5 efficiency} = \frac{p \text{ at } 87\% + p \text{ at } 88\%}{2}$$

$$= \frac{7.56 + 8.32}{2} = 7.94$$

Total wages = (12 × .75) + 7.94/100 × 12 × .75 = 9 + .7146 = ₹. 9.7146

$$\text{Efficiency at 240 units} = \frac{240 + 100}{192} = 125\%$$

Bonus percentage = 20 + (125 – 100) × 1% = 45%

$$\text{Total wages} = 12 \times .75 + \frac{45 \times 12 \times .75}{100} = 9 + 4.05 = ₹.\ 13.05$$

Illustration 12: In a manufacturing concern the daily wages guaranteed for workers is ₹. 5. The standard output for the month is 2000 articles representing 100% efficiency. The rate of wages is paid without bonus to those workers who show up to $66\frac{2}{3}\%$ efficiency. Beyond this bonus is payable on a graded scale:

Efficiency	*Bonus*
90%	10%
100%	20%

Further increase of 1% on bonus for every 1% further rise in efficiency.

Calculate the total earning of A, B, C, and D who have worked 26 days in a month. A's output 1000 articles, B's output 1800 articles and C's output 2000 articles and D's output 2400 articles.

Solution: Standard output 2,000 articles per month representing 100% efficiency.

Name	*Output articles*	*Efficiency*	*Percentage of Bonus on Wages*	*Wages for 26 days @ ₹. 5*	*Bonus*	*Total Earning*
A	1000	50%	Nil	130	Nil	130
B	1800	90%	10%	130	13	143
C	2000	100%	20%	130	26	156
D	2400	120%	40%	130	52	182

(7) Gantt's Task and Bonus Plan

This system, like the Emerson's system, involves measurement of efficiency. A standard has to be set on the basis of careful time and motion study. The worker's actual performance is compared with the standard and his efficiency determined. Only time wages are paid if the efficiency is below 100%. At 100% efficiency, a bonus of 20% is paid on the wages earned. For efficiency greater than 100%, or where the worker does the job in less than the standard time, he is paid wages (under piece rate) plus the bonus of $33\frac{1}{3}\%$.

The above two plans are not so harsh as the Taylor's Differential Piece System and they are easy to introduce. But the workers are divided into those who earn bonuses and those who do not.

Illustration 13: The following particulars relate to a factory:

Guaranteed Normal Rate ₹. 2 per hour; Piece Rate ₹. 1.20 per unit; High Task (Standard) 60 units per week; Output of three workers in a 40 hours week:

A—48 units; B—60 units; C—65 units

Total wages of the workers are calculated according to Gantt Premium Scheme, where guaranted time wages will be paid if the worker is below standard; a bonus of 20% on the piece rate will be paid if the worker is at standard and for above standard a bonus of $33\frac{1}{3}\%$ will be paid. Calculate the wages of all the three workers.

Solution: Total wages of *A* (below standard) = 40 Hours × 2 = ₹. 80

Total wages of *B* (at standard) = $(60 \times 1.20) + \frac{20}{100}(60 \times 1.20)$ = 72 + 14.40 = ₹. 86.40

Total wages of *C* (above standard) = (65 × 1.20) + 1/3 (65 × 1.20) = 78 + 26 = ₹. 104

(8) Hayne's Plan

The standard in this plan is set by minutes and is expressed in MANITS, a manit being a standard man minute of work. The standard time for all jobs is expressed in these standard units. The value of the time saved by a worker is shared by him, the foreman and the management if work is non-standardised. If work is standardised the value of time saved is divided, 5/6 to the worker and 1/6 to the foreman. If work is not standardised, the value of the time saved is divided, 5/10 to the worker, 1/10 to the foreman and 4/10 to the management. Time wages for the worker are guaranteed. The foreman loses his bonus to the extent time is lost due to his mistakes.

The plan has the attractive feature of rewarding the supervisory staff without whose cooperation there may not be much efficiency.

(9) The Bedeax Plan

Under this method also, the time wages are assured and like the Hayne's Plan it involves setting the standard task in terms of "*B*'s" or "*points*" which mean standard work to be done in one minute. The standard is naturally set after careful time and motion study. Work expected to be done is always expressed as 60 × B × number of hours. Standard time (in hours) is also determined by dividing the earned points by 60. Bad quality work is automatically eliminated since no points would be awarded for it. Both standard time and actual time are expressed in terms of points or "B's".

The saving (difference between standard time and actual time, or difference between earned B's and actual B's divided by 60) are apportioned, 3/4 to the worker and 1/4 to management. The number of points of `B's' produced by a worker and the premium earned by him are posted daily so that he can know what he earned the previous day.

Illustration 14: A factory remunerates its workers according to Bedaux Scheme. The following particulars are available:

Time allowed 600 B's; Time taken 480 B's (minutes); Rate ₹. 1.20 per hour, Calculate total wage.

Solution: (*a*) When 75% Scheme is adopted.

$$\text{Total Wages} = 8 \text{ hours} \times 1.20 + \frac{75}{100}(2 \text{ hours} \times 1.20) = 9.60 + 1.80 = ₹.\ 11.40$$

$$\text{Time Taken} = \frac{480}{60} = 8 \text{ hours.}$$

$$\text{Time saved} = 600 - 480 = \frac{120}{60} \text{ hours} = 2 \text{ hours}$$

(b) If 100% Scheme is followed:

$$\text{Total wage} = 8 \text{ hours} \times 1.20 + 100\% \text{ of } 2 \text{ hours} \times 1.20 = 9.60 + 2.40 = ₹.\ 12.00$$

(10) Priestman's Production Bonus

This system is designed to benefit every worker in a department whether he is direct or indirect. When the output rises above the standard output (determined before hand), the wages of all workers go up by the percentage of increase in output. Of course, for determining the standard output, the number of workers at work is taken into account. Standard output is fixed in terms of points unless there is only one product (like iron) which can be easily measured.

(11) Group Bonus

It is a good rule that as far as possible tasks should be allotted to individual workers so that each worker can be remunerated according to his performance. This means that, as far as possible, work should not be entrusted to a group of workers—there is the danger then that some of the workers will not contribute their proper share; the performance of the group will be rather poor and the workers who have worked conscientiously will feel disappointed.

However, in many cases work cannot be done unless workers of different types and skill cooperate and if any incentive is to be offered, it must be offered to the group as a whole. Usually, a rate is set for the task as a whole and wages on time basis are guaranteed. If work is completed expeditiously, the workers share in the excess of the set rate over wages on time basis. While dividing the bonus amongst workers care must be taken to keep into view the different skills of the workers. The method to do so is to divide the bonus in the ratio of wages on time basis. Suppose a task is allotted to the following workers jointly for ₹. 150 and the work is completed as stated below.

Workers	*Time spent*	*Wage rate per hour*	*Total wages on time basis*
		₹.	₹.
A	50	1.00	50.00
B	50	0.60	30.00
C	50	0.80	40.00
			120.00

The bonus is ₹. 30, *i.e.*, ₹. 150 less ₹. 120; it will be divided among the three workers in the ratio of A 5/12, B 3/12 and C 4/12.

Illustration 15: Both direct and indirect labour of a department in a factory are entitled to production bonus with a Group Incentive Scheme, the outlines of which are as follows:

(*a*) For any production in excess of the standard rate fixed at 10,000 tonnes per month (of 25 days) a general incentive of ₹. 10 per tonne is paid in aggregate. The total amount payable to each separate group is determined on the basis of an assured percentage of such excess production being contributed by it, namely @ 70% by direct labour, @ 10% by inspection staff, 12% by maintenance staff and @ 8%, by supervisory staff.

(*b*) Moreover, if the excess production is more than 20% above the standard, direct labour also gets a special bonus of ₹. 5 per tonne for all production in excess of 120% of standard.

(*c*) Inspection Staff are penalised at ₹. 20 per tonne for customer rejections in excess of 1% of production.

(*d*) Maintenance Staff are also penalised @ ₹. 20 per hour of machine breakdown.

From the following particulars for a month work out the production bonus earned by each group:

(*a*)	Actual working	20 days
(*b*)	Production	11.000 tonnes
(*c*)	Rejection by customer	200 tonnes
(*d*)	Machine Breakdown	40 hours

Solutions:

		Tonnes
(*i*)	Production	11,000
	Standard for 20 days (10,000 × 20/25)	8,000
	Excess	3,000
	Excess over 120% of standard $11{,}000 - \left(\frac{120}{100} \times 8000\right)$	1,400
(*ii*)	General Group Incentive	₹.
	₹. 10 × 3,000	30,000
	Share of : Direct Labour (70%)	21,000
	Inspection Staff (10%)	3,000
	Maintenance Staff (12%)	3,600
	Supervisory Staff (8%)	2,400

(*iii*) *Final Payments*

			₹.
(*a*)	Direct Labour :	Share out of Group Incentive	21,000
		"extra" excess production, ₹. 5 per tonne on 1,400 tonnes	7,000
			28,000
(*b*)	Inspection Staff :	Share out of Group Incentive	3,000
		Less ₹. 20 per tonne on excess rejection (200 – 1% of 11,000) × 20	1,800
			1,200
(*c*)	Maintenance Staff:	Share out of group Incentive	3,600
		Less ₹. 20 per hour for 40 hours of machine breakdown	800
			2,800
(*d*)	Supervisory Staff :	Share out of Group Incentive	2,400
		Total (a + b + c + d)	34,400

(12) Profit Sharing

Profit sharing is quite fashionable these days. It is thought that by giving a portion of the yearly profits to the workers, better co-operation will be forthcoming and more work will be done. Generally, after the profits are ascertained, interest on the capital employed is set aside. Of the remainder a part may be credited to the reserves as to be available for future contingencies. Of what remains the workers get a share by way of bonus—as addition to their wages already earned.

There are certain difficulties which, sometimes, may not permit the introduction of such schemes. What is a reasonable rate of interest? What is the capital employed at any time? What is a reasonable figure for putting into reserve? And what is a reasonable share for workers to get out of the profit? Even if all the questions are answered to the satisfaction of both the parties—employers and workers—the basic mistrust of figures prepared by employers may still prevent the workers from being enthusiastic about the whole scheme.

From the point of view of increasing the efficiency of workers, profit sharing may be quite useless. The bonus is paid at the end of the year and by that time workers will lose sight of any connection between efficiency and bonus. Moreover, the bonus is paid to all workers, efficient and inefficient alike. The bonus, therefore, cannot make one more efficient than others. All it may do is to make workers slightly less irresponsible in the matter of declaring strikes. But if bonus itself becomes a bone of contention, as is the case in India at present, even this beneficial effect will be lost. The trade unionists in western countries look down upon profit sharing as something which undermines trade unionism.

Profit sharing is supposed to be *ex gratia*, a privilege which may be withdrawn at any time. But in India it has been laid down by the Supreme Court that so long as the actual wages are below the living wage level, workers have a right to get a share of profts earned by the employer. Under the Payment of Bonus Act, it is now compulsory to pay a bonus to workers up to a maximum of 20% of wages earned, the minimum being ₹. 100 or 8.33% of wages whichever is higher. Thus, in India, payment of bonus depending upon profits is compulsory. This means that bonus should be included in the cost of production. Wages to direct workers can be inflated. For example, if a worker gets ₹. 600 a month and is paid (or expected to be paid) two month's wages as bonus or ₹. 1,200, he will get ₹. 8,400 in all. If he works 300 days in a year the effective wage rate is ₹. 28 per day, i.e., 8,400 ÷ 300. For indirect workers this is not necessary. The bonus is charged to factory expenses. Some concerns follow the practice of charging the minimum bonus (8.33% of wages or ₹. 100 whichever is more) as part of wages, charged directly, and the remaining portion of bonus as part of overheads. However, if the bonus is paid over and above the legal limits, because the employer wants to share his prosperity with the worker, it should be debited to the Costing Profit and Loss Account because then it will be an appropriation of profits.

Wages and Cost of Production

Cheap labour may be costly and *vice-versa*. This is due to the fact that the total cost of production of an article is made up among other things by its proportionate share of overheads, a good part of which is fixed or constant. If output is large, each unit's share of fixed expenses will be lower thus leading to reduction in cost of production. It follows, therefore, that if workers produce more they help to reduce the cost of production even if they are paid the same amount per unit. Saving in the cost of production will be larger if workers are paid on time basis. Then the larger output will mean lower labour cost per unit as well as lower overheads per unit. An inefficient worker may raise the cost of production appreciably by lower output. It follows that it is not the wages of the worker that alone determine what the cost of production will be. A very important question is the expected output. Workers paid high wages but producing large quantities may be cheaper than workers getting low wages but producing small quantities. Efficiency lies in aiming at reducing the labour cost per unit plus the overheads per unit. This may mean raising the wages of the worker rather than reducing the wage rates.

Payment of Wages

As frauds in connection with wages are quite common, strict care should be exercised to see that bogus names are not included in the roll of workers and that wages are paid in accordance with the policy laid down by the company in respect of leave, etc.

Time record kept by the timekeeper are generally the basis for writing up the wages sheet. An independent person should compare the time records with the job cards and initial both the cards, noting any serious discrepancy in the two. As a rule, as many persons as possible should be associated with the task of the preparation of the wages sheet and the actual payment. The timekeeper should write down the names and numbers of the workers and the time put in by each worker (if payment is by time). In case of piece workers, a separate sheet should be used and the quantity of work done should be noted. An independent man should check this with job cards. The Accounts Section will fill the rates of pay and make calculations of gross wages and also enter the deduction. All calculations should be rechecked. One cheque should be drawn for the total amount due to be paid (gross wages minus deduction). Actual payment should be made in the presence of the foreman concerned and the timekeeper. The cashier and these two should sign the wages sheet as evidence of the fact that payment was made to the right person. Payment for those who cannot be present should be made only if they send an authorisation to the satisfaction of the Works Manager. Wages remaining unpaid should be credited to an "Unpaid Wages" Account and payment should be made when claimed by the worker.

It should be remembered that under the Payment of Wages Act, 1936, wages must be paid within seven days of the close of the period for which wages are due if the number of workers does not exceed 1,000. For a labour force exceeding this limit, a period of ten days is allowed. The Act also regulates the deduction to be made out of the workers' wages. The permissible deductions are (1) fines; (2) for absence from duty; (3) for damages or loss; (4) for house accommodation; (5) for amenities and services; (6) on account of advances; which the employer is compelled to make, and (7) on account of payments to certain provident funds, cooperative societies and schemes of insurance.

Fines can be imposed for such acts or omissions as are specified in notices and approved by appropriate authorities. A person below the age of 15 years cannot be fined. The total amount of the fine imposed in any wage period must not exceed an amount equal to three paise in the rupee of the wages payable to the worker concerned in respect of that wage period. All the fines are to be credited to a fine fund which can be utilised only for such purposes beneficial to the workers of the factory or the establishment as are approved by appropriate authorities.

Contravention of the provisions of the Payment of Wages Act, 1936 makes a person liable to punishment by fine. It should be noted that in case of workers, the term wages includes dearness allowance for all purposes.

Wages (Labour Cost) Analysis Sheet or Wages Abstract. "It is a document which is a classified record of time and/or wages compiled from labour time records." —*CIMA*

A form of wages sheet is given below:

WAGES SHEET
For the month/Week..............

Serial No.	Worker's Name and Classification	Worker's No.	No. of days attended*	Rate	Wages						Deductions						Net Amount Payable	
					Gross Wages		Allowances		Total		Provident Fund		Employees State Insurance		Fines etc.			
					₹.	P.	₹.	P.	₹.	P.	₹.	P.	₹.	P.	₹.	P.	₹.	P.

* In case of piece workers, the column will show quantity of work done.

As pointed out above, there will be job cards for all direct workers. An analysis of the job cards will tell us the labour cost of all the jobs undertaken in a particular period. Such an analysis is known as Wages Abstract. It is like the Materials Abstract; as given below (figures are imaginary):

WAGES ANALYSIS SHEET
(Wages Abstract)

Week Ending...............................

Job Card No.	Amount		Job. Nos.												Overheads	
			105		106		107		108		109		Total for jobs.			
	₹.	P.	₹.	P.	₹.	P.	₹.	P.	₹.	P.	₹.	P.	₹.	P.	₹.	P.
501	30	50	16	25			14	25					30	50		
502	40	25			21	50	18	75					40	25		
503	35	43	7	00					28	43			35	43		
504	20	25									20	25	20	25		
506	34	56	13	25			21	31					34	56		
507	35	00							20	00	13	00	35	00		
508	67	00			32	00					35	00	67	00		
509	31	25									7	25	7	25	24	00
510	52	00							24	00	10	00	34	00	18	00
Etc.																
Total	346	24	36	50	53	50	54	31	72	43	85	50	304	24	42	00

Prepared by.................................. Job Ledger posted by..

Accounting Entries. Individual job accounts are debited from the Wages Analysis Sheet. For instance job No. 105 will be debited by ₹. 36.50 and job No. 106 by ₹. 53.50 and so on. The total of the amounts charged to Jobs, ₹. 304.24 as shown in the above-given example, will be dibited to Work in Progress Account and ₹. 42.00 to Overheads. Wages Account will be credited by ₹. 346.24. Thus the entry in the Cost Ledger is :

Work-in-Progress Account	...	Dr.	304.24
Overheads, etc.	...	Dr.	42.00
To Wages Account			346.24

On payment of wages, the entry is:

Wages Account	...	Dr.	346.24
To Cost Ledger Control Account			346.24

The Wages Account, after these entries, will normally reveal a debit balance, showing the cost of idle time—the cost of normal idle time will be transferred to Overheads and that of abnormal idle time to Costing Profit and Loss Account. (See Chapter Cost Control and Integral Costing).

Wage Rate for Costing Purposes

In addition to wages paid to workers, a number of the expenses have to be incurred by the employer.

Examples are:

(*i*) Provident Fund Contribution by the employee
(*ii*) Employees State Insurance Corporation premium paid by the employee
(*iii*) Cash value of food concession contribution by the employer.
(*iv*) Canteen Expenses.

Such payments may be included in overheads or indirect expenses. But it will be better to charge direct as many expenses as possible. The method to do this is to put down the wages paid and the other expenses incurred and then divide the total by the effective hours worked. The resulting figure will be the cost incurred when a worker works for one hour. For charging labour to jobs, the time worked should be multiplied by such a figure.

Illustration 16: A worker is paid ₹. 100 per month, as basic wage and D.A. @ ₹. 400 p.m. In addition, a bonus of 10% on wages is common and may be taken as a necessary payment. A contributory provident fund @ 8-1/3% is maintained. The employer has to contribute $1\frac{1}{2}$% of wages as premium to the Employee. State Insurance Corporation, the employee contributing $\frac{1}{3}$% in addition. The premium covers sickness and accident benefit which on the average cause 3 days absence. The employee is entitled to 1/20th of days worked (which average 300 days per annum) as leave on full pay. The employer maintains a fair price shop, there being an annual subsidy of ₹. 10,000 to the shop. The total number of employees is 250. Ascertain the wages cost per hour, the daily hours being 8. Normal idle time is 5%.

Solution:

	₹.
Total expenses incurred per annum:	
Wages paid for 12 months	6,000
Bonus @ 10%	600
Subsidy to Fair Price Shop $\frac{10,000}{250}$	40
Provident Fund contribution @ $8\frac{1}{3}$% on ₹. 6,000	500
Premium to Employees State Insurance Corporation, $1\frac{1}{2}$% of ₹. 6,000	90
	7,230

Number of hours worked:	
Working days 300	
Total working hours @ 8 per day	2,400
Less $\frac{1}{20}$ for leave	120
	2,280
Less 5% for idle time	114
Effective hours	2,166

Wages cost per hour $\frac{7,230}{2,166}$ ₹. 3.34

Continuing the above example, if the worker spends 40 hours on a job, it should be debited with ₹. 133.60, *i.e.*, 40 × 3.34. If due to, say, failure of power, the worker has to sit idle for 5 hours, the amount chargeable to the Costing Profit and Loss Account will be ₹. 16.70, *i.e.*, 5 × 3.34.

Control Over Casual, Contract and Other Workers

In certain businesses, *e.g.*, sanitary engineers, workers have to work at the customers premises. The danger in case of such workers is that they may misuse or waste time. Strict supervision is, therefore, necessary. These workers will also be issued the necessary job cards so that an account of the time spent by the workers is kept and the labour cost of jobs determined.

Outworkers: The term '*outworkers*' also includes those who work at home. Such workers take materials from the stores and make finished articles at home with or without their own tools. Actual time spent by these workers is of no concern because payment is made on piece basis. But careful check should be maintained to see that (1) all the materials issued are accounted for, (2) tools issued from the factory are returned without undue wear and tear, and (3) the quantity and quality of finished articles are correct.

Casual workers: Business houses naturally keep a labour force to suit their purposes, but sometimes, due to extra work, a few more workers may have to be employed for a few days. Such workers are known as casual workers and they are generally paid off every day for the work done by them or as soon as the work is complete. From the point of view of costing, these workers do not present any difficulty. Wages paid to them are treated as factory expenses, if the time spent by them cannot be identified with particular jobs. If such an identification is possible and convenient, the wages are debited direct to the jobs undertaken by them. Casual workers, however, are a source of one of the commonest frauds. If management is lax or careless, time-keepers or foreman may show bogus names as those of casual workers and misappropriate the wages. it is essential that the employment of casual workers should be sanctioned by a high officer in the factory. Care should also be taken to minimise such employment and to see that no misappropriation takes place. The danger of fraud is greater if a foreman is allowed to engage casual workers at work sites away from the factory and himself to make payment of wages. Surprise checks to see that the number of workers actually employed corresponds with wage records and also payment of wages by some one from the head office rather than by the foreman himself will go a long way to eliminate such frauds.

LABOUR TURNOVER

Labour turnover may be defined as the number of workers replaced during a given period relative to the average labour force during the period. It is the number of workers who left the job during a period relative to the average labour force during the period.

It is a factor which affects the efficiency of labour and, therefore, labour costs. It means rate of change in the composition of the labour force. There are three ways to measure it:

(1) Replacement Method $= \dfrac{\text{No. of workers replaced in a year} \times 100}{\text{Average number of workers on rolls}}$

or (2) Separation Method $= \dfrac{\text{No. of workers separated during the year} \times 100}{\text{Average number of workers on rolls}}$

or (3) Flux Method $= \dfrac{(\text{No. of replacement} + \text{No. of separation}) \times 100}{\text{Average number of workers on rolls}}$

or $= \dfrac{\frac{1}{2}[\text{No. of replacement} + \text{No. of separation}) \times 100}{\text{Average number of workers on rolls}}$

Labour turnover due to new recruitment: Workers who join a business concern on account of its expansion do not create labour turnover. Some cost accountant believe that newly recruited worker's are responsible for a change in the composition of labour force. Labour turnover due to new recruitment will be:

$$= \frac{\text{No. of new workers joining in a period (excluding replacement)} \times 100}{\text{Average number of workers on rolls}}$$

New recruitments plus replacements are called accession. Labour turnover of accession is:

$$= \frac{\text{No. of accession in a period} \times 100}{\text{Average number of workers in a period}}$$

Flux method of Labour Turnover considering accession:

$$= \frac{(\text{No. of separtions} + \text{No. of accession}) \times 100}{\text{Average number of workers in a period}}$$

$$\text{Equivalent annual labour turnover rate} = \frac{\text{Turnover rate for the period} \times 365}{\text{No. of days in the period}}$$

A high rate of labour turnover is bad since it indicates that workers do not stay for long. When they go, they take with them their experience. New workers must be engaged and trained. Apart from the cost of recruiting and training a new worker, there will be a fall in output in its quality. Labour turnover is, therefore, quite costly to the employer, although the worker also loses if he remains out of job or if he gets a job not suitable to him.

Both separations and replacements of workers are costly but the major portion of the cost of labour turnover is usually incurred at the time of replacement. Separation is the cause of turnover and is followed by replacement. There is usually a time lag between separation and replacement.

Due to sickness, death, retirement or marriage of women workers, there is a certain amount of irreducible rate of labour turnover. But studies have shown that the actual rate of turnover in most industries is unnecessarily high.

Causes of Labour Turnover

Among the causes that contribute to high labour turnover are that the job and the worker do not suit one another, low wages, bad working conditions, bad treatment on the part of the employer or just the roving nature of the worker.

Thus causes may be avoidable and unavoidable. The *avoidable causes* of labour turnover may be (1) Redundancy *i.e.*, due to seasonal fluctuations, shortage of materials, completion of projects etc. Efficiency and foresight on the part of higher management may eliminate turnover on account of these causes. (2) Boring jobs (3) Bad working conditions (3) Low pay (4) Insecure employment (5) Poor opportunity for promotion (6) Unfair treatment (7) Labour disputes.

The causes which are *unavoidable* may be briefed as below (1) Housing difficulties (2) Personal betterment (3) Domestic responsibilities (4) Illness and accident (5) Leaving the district (6) Discharged for being found unsuitable (7) Discharged for disciplinary reasons (8) Retirement (9) Death.

The employer can appreciably reduce the rate of labour turnover and thus save labour costs.

Cost of Labour Turnover

It would be better if the cost of labour turnover is calculated separately. It would consist of:

(*a*) Recruitment costs in respect of extra men engaged due to excessive turnover;

(b) Training costs of the extra men engaged; and

(c) Loss due to fall in quantity and quality of output because of turnover represented by non-recovery of time wages and fixed expenses.

(d) Costs of lost time, wastage, scrap, defective work and tools and machine breakage on account of inefficiency of new employers.

(e) Cost of lost output on account of delay in obtaining new labour.

(f) Accident frequency due to lack of experience of new employer.

How Labour Turnover can be Reduced

For making remedial measures, the causes of turnover should be studied in detail. Avoidable causes should receive immediate attention. It should be noted that complete elimination is not possible but following steps may be effective in reducing labour turnover:

(i) The worker should be employed and posted on jobs for which he is best suited.

(ii) Every effort should be made to reduce redundancy (shortage of material etc.)

(iii) Working conditions should be improved because bad working conditions reduce productivity and increase irritability

(iv) Suitable incentive schemes should be provided to give the labours opportunity to increase earnings

(v) All insecurities of employment should be removed

(vi) Deserving employees should have opportunities for promotion

(vii) When dealing with individual cases, just and fair treatment is desirable

(viii) Supervisors and foremen should treat workers sympathetically

(ix) Every efforts should be made to reduce labour desputes to the minimum.

The personnel department should prepare periodical labour turnover report to be submitted to the management with its recommendations, so that corrective measures may be timely taken to keep it to the lowest possible level.

Illustration 17: [Labour Turnover Ratio] From the following data given by the personnel department, calculate the labour turnover rate by applying— (a) Separation Method (b) Replacement Method and (c) Flux Method.

Number of workers on the pay-roll :

At the beginning of the month	900
At the end of the month	1100

During the month 10 workers left, 40 person were discharged and 150 workers were recruited. Of these 25 workers are recruited in the vacancies of those leaving, while the rest were engaged for an expansion scheme.

Solution: *(a) Labour Turnover Rate by Separation Method*

$$= \frac{\text{No. of Separation in the month}}{\text{Average No. of workers on roll}} \times 100$$

$$= \frac{10 + 40}{1000} \times 100 = 5\%$$

$$\text{For the year} = \frac{\text{Turnover rate for the month} \times 365}{\text{No. of days in month}}$$

$$= \frac{5 \times 365}{30} = 60.83\%$$

(*b*) *Labour turnover rate by Replacement Method*

$$\text{For the month} = \frac{\text{No. of Replacement in the month} \times 100}{\text{Average no. of workers on roll}}$$

$$= \frac{25 \times 100}{1000} = 2.5$$

$$\text{For the year} = \frac{2.5 \times 365}{30} = 30.42\%$$

(*c*) *Labour Turnover Rate by Flux Method*

$$= \frac{(\text{No. of separation in the month} + \text{No. of replacement in the month}) \times 100}{\text{Average No. of workers on roll}}$$

$$= \frac{(50 + 25) \times 100}{1000} = 7.5\%$$

$$\text{For the year} = \frac{\text{Turnover rate for the month} \times 365}{\text{Average no. of workers on roll}}$$

$$= \frac{7.5 \times 365}{30} = 91.25\%$$

Illustration 18: From the following information, calculate Labour turnover rate and Labour flux rate:

No. of workers as on 01-01.2000 = 7,600

No. of workers as on 31.12.2000 = 8,400

During the year, 80 workers left while 320 workers were discharged, 1,500 workers were recruited during the year. Of these, 300 workers were recruited because of exits and the rest were recruited in accordance with expansion plans.

Solution: *Labour Turnover Rates:*

(*i*) *Separation Method:*

$$= \frac{\text{Number of separations during the period}}{\text{Average number of workers during the same period}} \times 100$$

$$= \frac{80 + 320}{(7{,}600 + 8{,}400) \div 2} \times 100 = \frac{400 \times 100}{8{,}000} = 5\%$$

(*ii*) *Replacement Method:*

$$= \frac{\text{Number of persons replaced}}{\text{Average number of workers}} \times 100$$

$$= \frac{300}{(7{,}600 + 8{,}400) \div 2} \times 100 = \frac{300 \times 100}{8{,}000} = 3.75\%$$

(*iii*) *New Recruitment:*

$$= \frac{\text{Number of persons newly recruited}}{\text{Average number of works}} \times 100$$

$$= \frac{1{,}200}{(7{,}600 + 8{,}400) \div 2} \times 100 = 15\%$$

(*iv*) *Flux Method:*

$$= \frac{\text{Number of separations} + \text{Number of replacements}}{\text{Average number of workers}} \times 100$$

$$= \frac{(400 + 300)}{(7{,}600 + 8{,}400) \div 2} \times 100$$

$$= \frac{700}{8{,}000} \times 100 = 8.75\%$$

Illustration 19: The management of a company are worried about their increasing labour turnover in the factory and before analyzing the causes and taking remedial steps, they want to have an idea of the profit foregone as a result of labour turnover in the last year.

Last year sales amounted to ₹. 83,03,300 and the profit-volume ratio was 20 per cent. The total number of actual hours worked by the direct labour force was 4.45 lakhs. As a result of the delays by the Personnel Department in filling vacanices due to labour turnover, 1,00,000 potential productive hours were lost. The actual direct labour hours included 30,000 hours attributable to training new recruits, out of which half of the hours were unproductive.

The costs incurred consequent on labour turnover revealed on analysis the following:

Settlement costs due to leaving	₹. 43,820
Recruitment costs	26,740
Selection costs	12,750
Training costs	30,490

Assuming that the potential production lost, as a consequence of labour turnover, could have been sold at prevailing prices, find the profit foregone last year on account of labour turnover.

Solution:

Contribution Foregone

Actual hours worked (given)	4,45,000
Less unproductive training	15,000
Actual productive hours	4,30,000

Hours losts are 1,00,000. Sales lost for 1,00,000 hours

$$= \frac{83,03,300}{4,30,000} \times 1,00,000 = ₹.\ 19,31,000$$

Contribution lost for 1,00,000 hours (P/V Ratio 20%)

$$= \frac{19,31,000 \times 20}{100} = ₹.\ 3,86,200$$

Statement Showing Profit Foregone on Account of Labour Turnover

Contribution foregone	₹. 3,86,200
Settlement cost due to leaving	43,820
Recruitment cost	26,740
Selection cost	12,750
Training cost	30,490
Profit foregone	₹. 5,00,000

JOB EVALUATION

Job evaluation is a systematic and orderly process of determining the worth of a job in relation to other jobs. Every job has its own characteristics. Depending upon these characteristics job demand is of varying degrees of the various qualifications, skill, experience etc., on the part of operators performing the jobs. For example, some jobs require physical ability, others may need a high degree of mental ability, while a third category may need skill, experience and high education. *Job evaluation is the process of review, analysis and systematic classification of a job in accordance with its characteristics i.e.*, varying factors it demands from the employees. In other words job evaluation grades all jobs with reference to their main characteristics so that the relative merit of each job in terms of work value may be determined. Proper job evaluation helps in divising a wage structure which is acceptable to the workers as well as the organisation.

Purposes: Job evaluation helps following purposes :

(1) It helps in devising an acceptable wage,

(2) It helps in proper placement of workers in job.

(3) It helps the personnel department to recruit the right person for a job since requirement of each job are clearly indicated.

(4) It helps in formulating the internal training plan

(5) It helps to avoid wage and other discrimination for similar jobs in same organisation or a group of organisations under the same management.

Advantages to the Employer:

(1) By bringing uniformity in wage rates, it brings about simplification of wage administration.

(2) Wage rates can be reviewed easily if a job evaluation machinery exists in the organisation.

(3) Disputes and grievances regarding wage rates are settled which result in uninterrupted going on of work.

(4) By job evaluation proper and rational wage structure can be formulated and implemented. With the result, better workers join the firm more willingly.

(5) Supervisors are trained in the essential function of judging, controlling and helping the workers.

Advantages to Employees:

(1) Workers are rewarded on the basis of their performances. It provides effective motivation to workers.

(2) By Job evaluation, right worker is put in the right place, with the result there is reduction in the labour turnover.

Limitations of Job Evaluation

There are certain limitations. It cannot be applied easily to scientific and research pursuits. Some times, it is seen that workers are not available at the wage suggested by the job evaluation.

Steps of Job Evaluation:

In job evaluation there are some major steps to be carried out in sequence : (1) Invention and construction, (2) Job Standardisation, (3) Job review and analysis, comprising determination of relative values of jobs and grouping of jobs into classes for which minimum and maximum remuneration are established.

Invention and Construction involve the timely development, design and production of the right type of jigs, tools, gauges and auxiliaries required for performing the jobs. Job standardisation is the development and standardisation of the most suitable arrangements, motions and times for production based on time and motion study. *Job Review and Analysis includes* job review, job analysis and job classification. Job review is to identify person needed to fill the job and conditions which affect the rate of pay of the person needed to fill it. Job analysis is analysis and synthesis of the data obtained by job review in order to determine degree of duties, skills, exertion, responsibilities, conditions etc. needed in relation to a job. Job classification is the procedure of sorting the standard job-description specifications into a small number of groups.

Methods of Job Evaluation

There are mainly three methods of job classification: (1) Ranking Methods, (2) Grading Method, (3) The Point System and (4) The Factor Comparison Method.

(1) *Ranking Method:* Under this system different jobs are graded from the highest to the lowest ranks on some basis. The hierarchy for each job group is thus outlined and pay scales are determined. Its greatest merit is simplicity, which is also its great limitation that is the measurement is quite crude. Besides there is no pre-determined scale of values for the rates to be used. This method is useful in a small unit where jobs are a few and are known to raters.

(2) *Grading or Job Classification Method:* In this method individual jobs are classified into a number of grades or classes, for example: skilled, semi-skilled, unskilled, assistant foreman, foreman executives and work manager etc. For each class or grade a general specification is prepared, indicating the types of responsibility and work that may be included. Salary or wage ranges are thereafter fixed for each class or sub-class. Each job is reviewed to place the job in its appropriate grade. The chief merit of the method is its simplicity but this is useful only in small units, since in large organisation job-specifications are quite complicated.

(3) *The Point-rating Method:* Under this method of job evaluation jobs are analysed into its various characteristics or factors and then evaluated in terms of points. Points are allocated to each of the factor or characteristics. The factors may be: (*i*) Education or mental application, (*ii*) Physical application of effort, (*iii*) Experience, expertise or skill, (*iv*) Responsibility for achievement and failures etc. (*v*) Job-hazards or complex nature of job and (*vi*) Working conditions. These factors are outlined in a manual which also prescribes the weightage to be applied to each such factor. Wages scales or ranges are fixed for each of these grades.

(4) *The Factor Comparison Method:* Under this method, certain key jobs are selected and each selected job is further analysed into (i) Mental application (ii) Physical application, (iii) Skill required (iv) Responsibility and (v) Working conditions. (These are also factors in point rating method). Each factor is, thereafter, valued and aggregate values are compared to determine relative worth of each job.

It is to be noted that first two methods are simple and suitable for application in small factories. The last two methods are analytical in approach. But jobs involving high degree of mental applications or hazards cannot be accurately evaluated in fixed factor points.

MERIT RATING (PERFORMANCE APPRAISAL)

Merit rating or performance appraisal is a device for evaluating work performance in a systematic manner. It is a tool for appraising the relative qualities of the employees or workers. Merit rating can be defined as all the formal procedures used in working organisations to evaluate the personalities and contributions and potential of group members.'

It is different to job-evaluation. While job evaluation is the process of analysis and classification of jobs according to their characteristics, Merit Rating refers to the evaluation of the merits of persons and their classification into groups on that basis. The method of merit rating lies, broadly, in keeping an individual's records of performance and assessing these performances through some norms or standards. The intention is to suitably reward an employee on the basis of his merit. Merit rating provides a system of incentive without applying the detailed procedure of work study and is particularly useful for rememberating, on relative merits, indirect workers whose performance is difficult to measure.

In rating the merit *i.e.*, qualities of the individual employee concerned, certain factors are taken into consideration. Following are the examples of factors in common use

(1) Quality of work done
(2) Quantity of work done
(3) Sense of responsibility
(4) Initiative
(5) Reliability and integrity
(6) Knowledges, skill, experience and apptitute of work
(7) Cooperation and discapture
(8) Sense of judgement
(9) Attendance and punctuality
(10) Extra-ordinary personal characteristics

Each factor is assigned a point value or point rating and each employee is rated according to the extent or degree of factors he possesses.

Advantages of Merit Rating

Merit rating develops better undertaking of work and men. Following are main objectives and merits of Merit Rating or Performance Appraisal.

(1) It increases better productivity of workers, as the very fact that a merit rating is in existence, encourages workers to more exertion.

(2) It encourages employee in his growth and development by appraising all phases of his performance and then by following constructive discussion and guidance.

(3) It uncovers special abilities of the employees.

(4) It promotes the employee's job satisfaction and morale by letting him know that his supervisors are interested in his progress and development.

(5) Merit rating eliminates guesswork and prejuidice in evaluating relative qualities of the employees.

(6) It serves as a systematic guide to the supervisors in planning the employee's further training.

(7) It helps in planning personal moves and placement that will utilise capability of each employee.

(8) It provides employees an opportunity to talk to supervisor about job-problem, interest, future etc.

(9) It helps in fixation of fair and equitable pay rates.

(10) It cultivates a spirit of competition among workers and this results in better performance.

Thus merit rating improves labour relations, reduces labour turnover and stimulates competition among the workers resulting in increased production.

Shortcomings and Limitations of Merit Rating

(1) Merit rating is mostly based on opinions, it may tends to be erroneous, which may lead to dissatisfaction and unrest.

(2) Labour-incentives offered on the basis of merit rating may not be regarded enough.

(3) It is quite possible that some irrelevant factors may be given importance or there may be biased rating by supervisors.

(4) Raters may depend upon past rating record which may influence present rating.

MISCELLANEOUS ILLUSTRATIONS

Illustration 20: The standard output of a Product X has been fixed as 12 units per day of 8 hours. The normal wages is ₹. 12 per day. Determine the total wages payable (including bonus) under: (*a*) Time Rate (*b*) Piece Rate (*c*) Halsey Plan and (*d*) Rowan Plan, when the total production is 10, 16, 24 and 30 units per day. Also compute the labour cost per unit in each of the above cases:

Solution: (*a*) Time Rate

Production in units	*Time wages per day ₹.*	*Bonus ₹.*	*Total ₹.*	*Labour cost per unit ₹.*
(*i*) 10	12.00	—	12.00	1.20
(*ii*) 16	12.00	—	12.00	0.75
(*iii*) 24	12.00	—	12.00	0.50
(*iv*) 30	12.00	—	12.00	0.40

(*b*) Piece Rate

Production in units	*Wages per day @ ₹. 1/- per unit*	*Bonus ₹.*	*Total ₹.*	*Labour cost per unit ₹.*
(*i*) 10	10.00	—	10.00	1.00
(*ii*) 16	16.00	—	16.00	1.00
(*iii*) 24	24.00	—	24.00	1.00
(*iv*) 30	30.00	—	30.00	1.00

(*c*) Halsey Plan. (assuming 50% bonus)

Production in units	*Actual Production in terms of Standard Hours*	*Actual Hours taken*	*Time wages ₹.*	*Bonus ₹.*	*Total ₹.*	*Cost per unit ₹.*
(*i*) 10	$\frac{8}{12} \times 10$ = 6.67 hrs.	8 hrs.	12.00	—	12.00	1.20
(*ii*) 16	$\frac{8}{12} \times 16$ = 10.67 hrs.	8 "	12.00	2.00	14.00	0.875
(*iii*) 24	$\frac{8}{12} \times 24$ = 16.00 hrs.	8 "	12.00	6.00	18.00	0.75
(*iv*) 30	$\frac{8}{12} \times 30$ = 20.00 hrs.	8 "	12.00	9.00	21.00	0.70

Note: Bonus has been calculated at 50% of (Rate × Time Saved)

$$\text{Rate per hour} = \frac{₹.12}{8} = ₹.\ 1.50$$

$$\text{Time saved} = \begin{pmatrix}\text{Actual Production} \\ \text{in terms of} \\ \text{Standard Hours}\end{pmatrix} - \begin{pmatrix}\text{Actual} \\ \text{Time} \\ \text{Taken}\end{pmatrix}$$

$$\left.\begin{matrix}\text{Actual Production} \\ \text{in terms of Standard} \\ \text{Hours}\end{matrix}\right] = \frac{\text{Actual Production}}{\text{Standard rate of Production}}$$

(*b*) **Rowan Plan:**

Production in units	*Actual Production in terms of Standard Hours*	*Actual Hours taken*	*Time wages ₹.*	*Bonus ₹.*	*Total ₹.*	*Cost per unit ₹.*
(*i*) 10	6.67 hrs.	8 hrs.	12.00	—	12.00	1.20
(*ii*) 16	10.67 hrs.	8 "	12.00	3.00	15.00	0.94
(*iii*) 24	16.00 hrs.	8 "	12.00	6.00	18.00	0.75
(*iv*) 30	20.00 hrs.	8 "	12.00	7.20	19.20	0.64

Note: $\text{Bonus} = \frac{\text{Time Saved}}{\text{Standard Time}} \times (\text{Actual Time} \times \text{Rate})$

Illustration 21: In a factory bonus to workman is paid according to the *Rowan Plan*. The allotted time for a job is 40 hours and the normal rate of wages is ₹. 1.25 per hour. The factory overhead charges are 50 paise per hour for the hours taken.

The factory cost of a workorder executed by one worker is ₹. 161.875. The cost of material is ₹. 100. Calculate the time taken by the worker.

Solution: Suppose x be the number of hours worked by the worker.

$$1.25\,x + \left(\frac{40-x}{40} \times 1.25\,x\right) + .50\,x + 100 = 161.875$$

or $$1.75\,x + \frac{40-x}{40} \times 1.25\,x = 61.875$$

or $70\,x + 50\,x - 1.25\,x^2 = 2475$

or $120\,x - 1.25\,x^2 - 2475 = 0$

or $96\,x - x^2 - 1980 = 0$

or $x^2 - 96\,x + 1980 = 0$

or $(x - 30)(x - 66) = 0$

or $x = 30$ or 66

Since standard time is 40 hours therefore time taken will be 30 hrs.

Illustration 22: From the following data calculate total monthly remuneration of 3 workers *X, Y* and *Z*:

(*i*) Standard production per month per worker is 1,000 units

(*ii*) Actual production during a month—X 800 units, Y 700 units, Z 900 units.

(*iii*) Piece-work rate per unit of actual production : 15 paise

(*iv*) D.A. ₹. 40 per month (fixed)

(*v*) House rent allowance ₹. 20 per month (fixed)

(*vi*) Additional production bonus at the rate of ₹. 5 for each percentage of actual production exceeding 75% of actual production over standard.

Solution:

Workers	*Production in units*	*Piece wages @ 15 paise* ₹.	*D.A. @ 40.00 p.m.* ₹.	*H. Rent @ 20.00 p.m.* ₹.	*% of actual production to standard*	*Over 75% of standard*	*Bonus @ ₹. 5 for each percentage* ₹.	*Total wages* ₹.
X	800	120.00	40.00	20.00	80%	5%	25.00	205
Y	700	105.00	40.00	20.00	70%	Nil	—	165
Z	900	135.00	40.00	20.00	90%	15%	75.00	270

Illustration 23: A worker under the Halsey method of remuneration has a day rate of ₹. 12 per week of 48 hours, plus a cost of living bonus of 10 P. per hour worked. He is given an 8 hours task to perform, which he accomplishes in 6 hours. He is allowed 30% of the time saved as premium bonus. What would be his total hourly rate of earnings, and what difference would it make if he was paid under the Rowan method?

Solution: Standard Time: 8 hours; Time Taken; 6 hours; Time Saved; 2 hours; Standard wages: ₹. 12 per week (48 hours) or 25 p. per hour; Cost of Living Bonus, 10 p. per hour. Premium Bonus: 30% of time saved.

Under Halsey Method:

	₹.
Wages for 6 hours @ 25 p. per hour	1.50
Bonus for 6 hours @ 10 p. per hour	0.60
Premium : 30% of Time Saved (.25 × 2 × 30%)	0.15
	₹.2.25

Hourly Rate 2.25 ÷ 6 = ₹. 0.375

Under Rowan Method:

Wages for 6 hours @ 25 p. per hour	1.50
Bonus for 6 hour @ 10 p. per hour	0.60
Premium : (Time Saved/Standard Time) × Wages of time worked or 2/8 × 1.50	0.37
Hourly Rate 2.47 ÷ 6 = ₹. 0.4125	₹.2.47

Difference

	For 6 hours	Hourly Rate
Wages under Halsey Method	₹. 2.25	Re. 0.3750
Wages under Rowan Method	₹. 2.475	Re. 0.4125
Difference in earning	₹. 0.225	Re. 0.0375

TYPICAL ILLUSTRATIONS

Illustration 24: [Earning under different plans]

From the following particulars, you are required to work out the earning of worker for a week under (*a*) Straight piece rate, (*b*) Differential piece rate, (*c*) Halsey Premium Scheme (50% sharing) and (*d*) Rowan Premium Scheme.

Weekly Working Hours	48
Hourly wage rate	₹. 7.50
Piece rate per unit	₹. 3.00
Normal time taken per piece	24 minutes
Normal output per week	120 pieces
Actual output for the week	150 pieces
Differential piece rate	80% of piece rate when output is below normal and 120% of piece rate when output above normal.

[*ICWA*]

Solution: (*a*) Earning per week of a worker under piece rate = output per week × Piece rate
=150 × ₹. 3 = ₹. 450

(*b*) Earning per week under differential piece rate
Efficiency level (150/120) × 100 = 125%
Hence rate will be 120% of normal rate *i.e.*, ₹. 3 × 120/100 = ₹. 3.60
Earning = Output × Piece rate = 150 × 3.60 = ₹. 540

(*c*) Earning per week under Halsey Plan
Standard Hours (48 × 150)/120 = 60 hours
Time Saved: 60 – 48 = 12 Hours
Earning = (Time Taken × Rate) + Rate × 50% × (Standard Time – Time Taken)

$$= (48 \times ₹.\ 7.50) + 7.50 \times \frac{50}{100} \times (60 - 48) = ₹.\ 405$$

(*d*) Earning per week under Rowan Method
Earning = (Time Taken × Rate)

$$+ \left(\text{Time Taken} \times \text{Rate} \times \frac{\text{Standard Time} - \text{Time Taken}}{\text{Standard Time}} \right) \pm$$

$$= (48 \times ₹.\ 7.50) + \left(48 \times \text{Rs. } 7.50 \times \frac{60 - 48}{60} \right) = ₹.\ 432$$

Ilustration 25: (*a*) [Rowan Premiun Plan]

A worker whose day work wages is ₹. 2.50 an hour, received production bonus under the Rowan Scheme. He carried out the following work in a 48 hours week.

Job 1	1500	items at 4 hours per 1000 items
Job 2	1800	items at 3 hours per 1000 items
Job 3	9000	items at 6 hours per 1000 items
Job 4	1500	items for which no standard time was fixed and it was arranged that the worker would be paid a bonus of 25%. Actual time taken is 4 hours.
Job 5	2000	items at 8 hours per 1000 items, each item was estimated to be half finished.

Job no. 2 was carried out on a machine running 90% efficiency and an extra allowance of 1/9th of actual time was given to compensate the worker. 4 hours were lost due to power cut. Calculate earning of the worker, clearly stating your assumptions for the treatment given by you for the hours lost due to power cut.

Solution:

Calculation of Standard Time Allowed

Job	Output (units)	Standard Time ₹. 1000 units (hrs)	Standard time allowed for actual output (hrs)	
1	1500	4	4 × 1500/1000	= 6.0
2	1800	3	3 × 1800/1000	= 5.4
			Allowance for machine efficiency 1/9	= 0.6
3	900	6	6 × 9000/1000	= 54.0
4	1500	not fixed	Actual time + 25%	= 5.0
5	2000 (Half-finished)	8	8 × 2000/1000 × 1/2	= 8.0
			Total	79.00

Note: Allowance for machine breakdown in Job 2. been taken as 1/9 of standard time, because actual time is not known.

Calculation of Earnings

1. Basic wages = (Time worked × rate per hour) = 48 × 2.50 = ₹. 120.00
2. Actual time taken on jobs.
   (Time worked – Time lost due to power cut) = 48 – 4 = 44 hrs.
3. Time saved = Time worked – Time taken = 79 – 44 = 35 hrs.
4. Bonus under Rowan Plan = $\frac{\text{Time Saved}}{\text{Time Allowed}}$ × Time Taken × Rate per hour
   $\frac{35}{79}$ × 44 × ₹. 2.50 = ₹. 48.73
5. Total earning = Basic wages + Bonus = 120 + 48.73 = ₹. 168.73.

Note: For time lost on account of power cut, the worker will be entitled for guaranteed wages.

Illustration 26: [Halsey & Rowan Plans]

Three workers Govind, Ram and Shyam produced 80, 100 and 120 pieces of product X on a particular day in May 2004 in a factory. The time allowed for 10 units of product X is one hour and their hourly rate is ₹. 4. Calculate for each of these three workers the following:

(*i*) Earning for the day and

(*ii*) Effective rate of earning per hour under

(*a*) Straight piece rate (*b*) Halsey Premium Bonus (50% sharing) and (*c*) Rowan Premium Bonus Method.

Solution: It has been assumed that there are 8 working hours in a day.

(*a*) **Under Straight Piece Rate**

Workers	*Hours worked*	*Output (units)*	*Piece Rate (₹.)*	*Earning for the day (₹.)*	*Effective rate of earning per hour (₹.)*
Govind	8	80	0.40	32.00	4.00
Ram	8	100	0.40	40.00	5.00
Shyam	8	120	0.40	48.00	6.00

Note: (*i*) Piece rate is hourly rate of standard output per hour *i.e.*, ₹. 4/10 = ₹. 0.40.

(*ii*) Earning for a day = Output × Piece rate.

(*iii*) Effective rate of earning per hour is earning per day ÷ no. of hour in a day.

(*b*) **Under Halsey Premium Plan (50% Sharing)**

Workers	*Hours Worked*	*Time Allowed*	*Time Saved*	*Time Rate*	*Basic wages (₹.)*	*Bonus (₹.)*	*Earning for the day (₹.)*	*Effective earning per hour (₹.)*
Govind	8	8	—	4	32	—	32	4.00
Ram	8	10	2	4	32	4	36	4.00
Shyam	8	12	4	4	32	8	40	5.00

Notes: (*i*) Time allowed is output × time for one unit *i.e.*, 1/10 hrs.

(*ii*) Bonus is 50% of Time Saved × Time Rate

(*iii*) Effective rate per hour is earning for a day/hours worked, *i.e.*, 8

(c) **Under Rowan Premium Bonus**

Workers	*Hours Worked*	*Time Allowed*	*Time Saved*	*Time Rate*	*Basic wages*	*Bonus*	*Earning for the day*	*Effective earning per hour*
Govind	8	8	—	4	32	—	32.00	4.00
Ram	8	10	2	4	32	6.40	38.40	4.80
Shyam	8	12	4	4	32	10.67	42.67	5.33

Note: Bonus under Rowan Plan is $\dfrac{\text{Time saved}}{\text{Time allowed}}$ × Basic wages.

Illustration 27: [Efficiency Premium Plan]. An employee working under a bonus scheme completes a job in 50 hours for which the standard time is 60 hours. Calculate the rate per hour worked and wages payable to the worker, if incentive bonus of 10% on hourly rate is payable when standard time (namely 100% efficiency) is achieved and a further incentive bonus of 1% on hourly rate for each 1% in excess of that 100% efficiency is payable. Assume that the normal wage rate is ₹. 5 per hour.

Solution: When standard time is 60 hours and actual time taken is 50 hours, the efficiency achieved will be:

$$\frac{\text{Standard Time}}{\text{Actual Time}} \times 100 = \frac{60 \times 100}{50} = 120\%$$

Normal Rate	₹. 5.00
Add 10% hourly rate for 100% efficiency	0.50
1% increase for every additional increase *i.e.*, 20% of ₹. 5	1.00
Rate per hour	6.50

Wages Payable 50 hours × 6.50 = ₹. 325

Illustration 28: [Rowan & Halsey]. Two workmen Vishnu and Shiva, produce the same product using the same material. Their normal wage rate is also the same. Vishnu is paid bonus according to Rowan system while Shiva is paid bonus according to the Halsey System. The time allowed to complete the product is 100 hours. Vishnu takes 60 hours while Shiva takes 80 hours to complete the product. The factory overhead rate is ₹. 10 per man hour actually worked.

The factory cost for the product for Vishnu is ₹. 7,280 and for Shiva is ₹. 7,600. You are required (*a*) to find out normal rate of wages; (*b*) to find the cost of materials and (*c*) to prepare a statement comparing the factory cost of products made by the two workmen.

Solution: Let us presume that material cost is M and normal rate of wages is *Y*.

(*a*) **Earning of Vishnu:**

(*i*) Basic wages = $60 \times Y = 60\,Y$

(*ii*) Bonus under Rowan Plan

$$\frac{\text{Time Saved}}{\text{Time Allowed}} \times \text{Hours worked} \times \text{Rate} = \frac{100 - 60}{100} \times 60 \times Y = 24Y$$

(*iii*) Total earning = $60Y + 24Y = 84Y$

(*b*) **Earning of Shiva**

(*i*) Basic wages = $80 \times Y = 80Y$

(*ii*) Bonus under Halsey Plan

50% of Hours Saved × Rate = $1/2\,(100 - 80) \times Y = 10Y$

(*iii*) Total earning = $80Y + 10Y = 90Y$

(*c*) **Factory Cost**

Material cost + Labour cost + Overhead = Factory cost

Of Vishnu : $M + 84\,Y + 60 \times 10 = M + 84\,Y + 600 = 7280$

$= M + 84\,Y = 6680$ ...(1)

Of Shiva : $M + 90\,Y + 80 \times 10 = M + 90\,Y + 800 = 7600$

$= M + 90\,Y = 6800$ ...(2)

Thus we find two equations:

$M + 84Y = 6{,}680$ ...(1)

$M + 90Y = 6{,}800$ ...(2)

Deducting equation 2 from 1

$-6\,Y = -120$

$Y = 120/6 = 20$

Substituting value of Y in equation number (1)

$M + 1680 = 6680$

$M = 6680 - 1680 = 5000$

Thus (*a*) Normal rate of wages is ₹. 20 per hour and (*b*) Cost of Materials is ₹. 5000

Statement Comparing Factory Cost of the Products

	Vishnu	Shiva
Material	5,000	5,000
Labour cost	1,680	1,800
Overhead	600	800
Total	7,280	7,600

Illustration 29 : [Rowan and Halsey-Wier]. The standard time for a job is 60 hours. The hourly rate of guaranteed wages is ₹ 0.75. Because of savings in time, a worker A gets an hourly wage of ₹ 0.90 under Rowan Premium Bonus Plan. For the same savings in time, calculate the hourly rate of wages a worker B will get under Halsey – Weir Premium Bonus Plan assuring 40% to worker.

Solution: It may be presumed that the worker A has taken T hrs and thus he has saved (60 – T) hours.

His total earning under Rowan Plan will be

$$[\text{Time Taken} \times \text{Rate}] + \left[\frac{\text{Time Saved}}{\text{Time Allowed}} \times \text{Time Taken} \times \text{Rate}\right]$$

$$[T \times 0.75] + \left[\frac{60 - T}{60} \times T \times 0.75\right] = 0.90 \times T$$

or $0.75 + \dfrac{60 - T}{60} \times 0.75 = .90$ (dividing both sides by T)

or $\dfrac{45 + 45 - 0.75\,T}{60} = 90$ or $90 - 0.75\,T = 54$

or $-0.75T = -36$ or $T = \dfrac{-36}{-0.75} = 48$

Thus time taken is 48 hrs. *i.e.*, time saved will be = 12 hrs.

If Halsey Weir Plan is applied at 40% premium, the bonus will be:

40/100 × Time saved × Rate = .40 × 12 × .75 = ₹. 3.60.

and total earning will be Basic wages + Bonus *i.e.*, 48 × .75 + ₹. 3.60 = ₹. 39.60

Rate of earning per hour will be earning/actual hours *i.e.*, ₹. 39.60/48 = ₹. 0.825

Illustration 30: [Normal and overtime wages] Calculate the normal and overtime wages payable to a workman from the following data:

Days	Hours Worked	Day	Hours Worked
Monday	8	Thursday	11
Tuesday	10	Friday	9
Wednesday	9	Saturday	4

Normal working hours : 8 hours per day from Monday to Friday and 4 hours on Saturday

Normal Rate : ₹. 5 per hour

Overtime Rate : Upto 9 hours in a day from Monday to Friday and upto 5 hours on Saturday at single rate and over 9 hours in a day from Monday to Friday and over 5 hours on Saturday at double rate.

or

Upto 48 hours a week at a single rate and over 48 hours at double rate whichever is more beneficial to the workers.

Solution:

Calculation of Normal Wages and Overtime Wages

Days	*Hours Worked*	*Normal Hours*	*Normal wages (₹.)*	*Overtime Hrs. Single Rate @ 5*	*Overtime Hrs. at Double Rate @ 10*	*Overtime wages (₹.)*
Monday	8	8	40	—	—	—
Tuesday	10	8	40	1	1	15
Wednesday	9	8	40	1	—	05
Thursday	11	8	40	1	2	25
Friday	9	8	40	1	—	05
Saturday	4	4	20	—	—	—
	51	44	220	4	3	50

Total wages = Normal ₹. 220 + O.T. ₹. 50 = 270

Total wages when alternative scheme of overtime is adopted

Normal wages	48 hours @ 5	₹. 240
Over time	3 hours @ 10	30
		₹. 270

Illustration 31: [Total wage cost]. In a factory's bonus system, bonus hours are credited to the employee in proportion to time which time saved bears to time allowed. Jobs are carried forward from one week to another. No overtime is worked and payment is made in full for all units worked on, including those subsequently rejected. From the following information you are required to calculate for each employee:

(*a*) bonus hours and amount of bonus earned,

(*b*) the total wage cost and,

(*c*) the wage cost of each 100 good units produced.

Employees	A	B	C
Basic Wage rate per hour (₹.)	3.00	4.80	3.60
Units Produced	2,500	2,200	3,600
Time Allowed per 100 units	2 hrs. 36 mts.	3 hrs	1 hr. 30 mts.
Time Taken (hours)	52	75	48
Rejects (units)	100	40	400

Solution:

Calculation of Time Allowed for Units Produced

		A	B	C
		$\frac{\text{2 hrs. 36 mts.} \times 2500}{100} = 65$	$\frac{3 \times 2200}{100} = 66$	$\frac{1.5 \times 3600}{100} = 54$
	Time Allowed (hrs.)	65	66	54
	Time Taken (hrs.)	52	75	48
	Time Saved (hrs.)	13	—	6
	Ratio of time saved to time allowed	1/5	—	1/9
(*a*)	Bonus hours (Time Taken × Ratio)	10.4	—	5.33
	Amt. of Bonus (Bonus hrs. × Rate)	₹. 31.20	—	₹. 19.20
(*b*)	Total wages (₹.)			
	Basic wages (Time Taken × Rate)	156.00	360.00	172.80
	Bonus	31.20	—	19.20
		187.20	360.00	192.00
(*c*)	No. of good units produced	2,400	2,160	3,200
	Wages cost per hundred unit (Total wages cost × 100/good units) ₹.	7.80	16.67	6.00

Illustration 32: **(Wages under guaranteed hourly rate piece work and premium bonus scheme).** A company is undecided as to what kind of wage scheme should be introduced. The following particulars have been compiled in respect of three systems, which are under consideration of the management.

	Workers		
	A	*B*	*C*
Actual hours worked in a week	38	40	34
Hourly rate of wages	₹. 6	₹. 5	₹. 7.20

Production in units:

Product P	21	—	60
Product Q	36	—	135
Product R	46	25	—

Standard time allowed per unit of each product is:

	P	Q	R
Minutes	12	18	30

For the purpose of piece rate, each minutes is valued at ₹. 0.10.

You are required to calculate the wages of each worker under:

(*i*) Guaranteed hourly rates basis.

(*ii*) Piece work earnings basis, but guaranteed at 75% of basic pay (guaranteed hourly rate), if his earnings are less than 50% of basic pay.

(*iii*) Premium bonus basis where the worker receives bonus based on Rowan scheme.

Working Notes:

1. Piece rate per unit:

Product	*Std. time per unit (in minutes)*	*Piece rate each minute*	*Piece rate per unit*
P	12	₹. 0.10	₹. 1.20
Q	18	0.10	1.80
R	30	0.10	3.00

2. Time allowed to each worker:

Worker A : 21 units × 12 minutes + 36 units × 18 + 46 units × 30 = 2,280 minutes or 38 hrs.

Worker B : 25 units × 30 minutes = 750 minutes or 12.5 hrs

Worker C : 60 units × 12 minutes + 135 units × 18 minutes = 3,150 minutes or 52.50 hrs.

Solution: (*i*) **Computation of wages of each grade of worker**

Grade of workers	*Actual hours worked in a week*	*Hourly wage rate*	*Wages*
A	38	₹. 6.00	₹. 228.00
B	40	5.00	200.00
C	34	7.20	244.00

(*ii*) **Statement showing the wages of each worker under piece work earning basis**

Product	*Piece rate*	*Worker A*		*Worker B*		*Worker C*	
		Units	*Wages*	*Units*	*Wages*	*Units*	*Wges*
P	₹. 1.20	21	₹. 25.20	—	—	60	72
Q	1.80	36	64.80	—	—	135	243
R	3.00	46	138.00	25	75	—	—
Total			228.00		75		315

Note: It is given in the question that each worker has been guaranteed at 75% of the basic pay if his earnings are less than 50% of the basic pay. Therefore, workers *A* and *C* will be paid the wages computed above viz. ₹. 228 and ₹. 315 respectively. It is noted that computed wages of worker B is ₹. 75, which is less than 50% of basic pay viz. ₹. 100. Therefore, he would be paid 75% of ₹. 200 or ₹. 150.

(*iii*) **Statement showing the wages of each worker under Premium Bonus basis, where each worker gets bonus based on Rowan Scheme**

Workers	*Time allowed (hrs)*	*Time taken (hrs)*	*Time saved (hrs)*	*Wage rate/hr* ₹.	*Earnings* ₹.	*Bonus* ₹.	*Total* ₹.
A	38.00	38	—	6.00	228.00	—	228.00
B	12.50	40	—	5.00	200.00	—	200.00
C	52.50	34	18.50	7.20	244.80	86.26	331.06

Illustration 33: [Total Labour Cost etc.]. Following are the particulars for April 2003 relating to four employees working in Department M of a factory, exclusively for job no. 120.

Name	Designation	Wages
A	Foreman	800 per month
B	Mechanic	15 per day
C	Machine operator	12 per day
D	Workman	10 per day

The normal working hours per week of six days are 48, at 8 hours per day. Sundays are paid holiday. (and was no other holiday during the month). Provident Fund contribution was 8% of monthly wages by employee, same was the contribution by the employer. Employee State Insurance Contribution was 3% of monthly wages by employee and 5% of monthly wages by employer.

From the foregoing data, calculate:

(*a*) Net wages payable for the month (*b*) The total amount of Provident Fund Contribution to be deposited by employer (*c*) Total labour cost to the employer for the month of April, chargeable to the job and (*d*) The total cost of the job requiring materials valued ₹. 6000 and overheads at 50% of the prime cost.

Solution:

(*a*) **Net wages payable by the employer for the month**

	₹.	₹.
Gross Wages		
A	800.00	
B	450.00	
C	360.00	
D	300.00	1,910.00
Less: Deductions		
Provident Fund 8% of ₹. 1910	152.80	
ESI Contribution 3% of ₹. 1910	57.30	210.10
Net wages		1,699.90

(*b*) Total amount of P.E. Contribution	
PE Contribution deducted from employees wages	152.80
Empolyer's contribution 8% of ₹. 1911	152.80
	305.60
(*c*) ESI Contribution	
ESI Contribution deducted from employees wages	57.30
Employer's contribution 5% of ₹. 1910	95.50
	152.80

(*d*) Total Labour Cost

Gross Wages		1,910.00
Add: Employer's Contribution to Provident Fund	152.80	
Employer's Contribution to ESI	95.50	
		248.30
		2,158.30

(*e*) Total Cost of the job

Materials	6,000.00
Labour	2,158.30
Prime Cost	8,158.30
Overheads (50% of prime cost)	4,079.15
Total Cost	12,237.45

Illustration 34: Calculate the total remuneration of three workers *P*, *Q* and *R* who are working in a factory, based on the following data:

(*i*) Standard production per month per worker: 2000 units.

(*ii*) Piece work rate ₹. 0.50 per unit.

(*iii*) Production bonus to be given as follows:

Up to 85% efficiency	: Nil
Between 85% and 100% efficiency	: Incentive bonus at ₹. 40 for every 5% increase above 85%.
Above 100% efficiency	: Incentive bonus at ₹. 40 for every 5% increase above 85% plus 20% additional bonus on the incentive earned.

(*iv*) *P*, *Q* and *R* had a production of 1600 units, 2000 units and 2200 units respectively during January, 2001.

Solution:

Statement showing total earnings during January 2001

Name of the worker	*Standard production*	*Actual production*	*Efficiency*	*Piece work rate @ Re 0.50/unit*	*Incentive*	*Total earning*
P	2,000	1,600	80%	₹. 800	—	₹. 800
Q	2,000	2,000	100%	1,000	120	1,120
R	2,000	2,200	110%	1,100	240	1,340

Note: (1) Efficiency above 85% is 15% or for every 5% increase, *Q* will get 3 units of incentive @ ₹. 40.

(2) Efficiency above 85% is 25% or for every 5% increase, *R* will get 5 units of incentive @ ₹. 40.

5 units × ₹. 40	=	₹. 200
Add: 20% additional bonus	=	40
		240

Illustration 35: (*a*) Calculate the labour rate of a worker P from the following data :

Basic pay	₹. 200 p.m.
D.A.	₹. 150 p.m.
Fringe Benefits	₹. 100 p.m.

No. of working days in a year 300. 30 days full pay and 20 days half pay leave in a year is available and allowed. Assume 8 hours day.

(*b*) What would be the effect on hourly rate if only 30 days full pay leave is allowed.

[*C.S. (Inter)*]

Solution: (*a*) **Calculation of Labour Rate**

	₹. per month
Basic pay	200
DA	150
Fringe	100
Total wages per month	450
Leave Salary (30 days full pay)	₹. 450
20 days half pay $\frac{450}{30} \times \frac{1}{2} \times 20$ days	150
	600
Working days salary :	
10 months 10 days (4500 + 150)	4,650
Total earnings	5,250
No. of working days in a year (Days)	300
Less: Leave days (30 + 20)	50
Net working days	250

Working hours = 250 × 8 = 2,000 hours

$$\text{Labour Hour Rate} = \frac{₹.5,250}{2000 \text{ hours}} = ₹.\ 2.625 \text{ per hour}$$

(*b*) **If only 30 days full pay leave is allowed**

	₹.
Leave Salary : 30 days	450
Working days salary :	
11 months @ ₹. 450 p.m.	4,950
Total	5,400
No. of working days in a year	300
Less: Leave days	30
Net working days	270

Working hours 270 × 8 = 2160

$$\text{Labour Hour Rate} = \frac{₹.5,400}{\text{Hours } 2.160} = ₹.\ 2.50 \text{ per hour}$$

Effect on Hourly Rate = 2.625 – 2.50 = ₹. 0.125 or 12.5 paise per hour.

Illustration 36: Calculate the earnings of *A* and *B* from the following particulars for a month and allocate the labour cost to each job *X*, *Y* and *Z*:

	A	*B*
(*i*) Basic Wages	₹. 100	160
(*ii*) Dearness Allowance	50%	50%
(*iii*) Contribution to Provident Fund (on basic wages)	8%	8%
(*iv*) Contribution to Employee's State Insurance (on basic wages)	2%	2%
(*v*) Overtime Hours	10	

The normal working hours for the month are 200. Overtime is paid at double the total of normal wages and dearness allowance. Employer's contribution to State Insurance and Provident Fund are at equal rates with employee's contributions. The two workers were employed on jobs *X*, *Y* and *Z* in the following proportions:

	Jobs		
	X	*Y*	*Z*
Worker *A*	40%	30%	30%
Worker *B*	50%	20%	30%

Overtime was done on job *Y*.

Solution:

Statement Showing Earnings of A and B

	A	*B*
	₹.	₹.
Basic Wages	100	160
Dearness Allowance (50% of Basic Wages)	50	80
Overtime Wages	15	—
Gross Wages earned	165	240
Less: Provident Fund 8% of Basic wages and ESI – 2% of Basic wages Total 10% of basic wages.	10	16
Net amt. of wages paid	155	224

Statement of Labour Cost

	₹.	₹.
Gross Wages (excluding overtime)	150	240
Employer's Contribution to P.F. and E.S.I.	10	16
	160	256
Labour Rate per hour of ordinary wages ₹. (160/200) and ₹. 256/200)	0.80	1.28

Statement Showing Allocation of Labour Cost

	Total	Job X	Job Y	Job Z
Total Wages:	₹.	₹.	₹.	₹.
Worker A:				
Ordinary Wages (4 : 3 : 3)	160	64	48	48
Overtime	15		15	
Worker B:				
Ordinary Wages (5 : 2 : 3)	256	128	51.20	76.8
	4.31	192	114.2	124.8

Working Notes:

1. Normal Wages are considered as basic wages

2. Overtime

$$= \frac{2 \times (\text{Basic wage} + \text{D.A}) \times \text{Overtime hours}}{\text{Total Hours}}$$

$$= 2 \times \left(\frac{₹.150}{200}\right) \times 10 \text{ hours} = ₹.\ 15.$$

Illustration 37: From the following information available you are required to calculate the net wage bill as well as total wages cost: and journal entries in Financial and Cost Accounts.

(*i*) As per the time cards the gross earnings of the workmen is ₹. 30,000.

(*ii*) The various deductions from the gross earnings are as under:

	₹.
Employee's contribution to Provident Fund	2,500
ESI-Employee's contribution	400
Advances against wages	800
Cooperative dues	600
Income Tax	500
Canteen charges	100

(*iii*) Company's contributions to Provident Fund and ESI are ₹. 2,500 and ₹. 800 respectively.

(*iv*) Analysis of times cards reveals that 85% of time utilised is on manufacturing operations and the balance is to be treated as indirect.

Solution:

Calculation of Net Wages Bill

	₹.	₹.
Gross Earnings of Workmen		30,000
Deductions:		
Employee's contribution to P.F.	2,500	
Employee's contribution to E.S.I.	400	
Advance against wages	800	
Co-operatives dues	600	
Canteen Charges	100	
Income Tax	500	4,900
Net Wages Payable		25,100

Calculation of Total Wages Cost

Gross	Earnings of Workmen		30,000
Add:	Employer's contribution to P.F.	2,500	
	Employer's contribution to E.S.I.	800	3,300
	Total Wages Cost		33,300

Illustration 38: The standard hours of Job X is 100 hours. The job has been completed by Amar in 60 hours, Akbar in 70 hours and Anthony in 95 hours.

The bonus system applicable to the job is as follows :

Percentage of time saved to time allowed	Bonus
Saving upto 10%	10% of time saved
From 11% to 20%	15% of time saved
From 21% to 40%	20% of time saved
From 41% to 100%	25% of time saved

The rate of pay is ₹. 1 per hour. Calculate the total earnings of each worker and also the rate of earnings per hour.

From 41% to 100% 25% of time saved

The rate of pay is ₹. 1 per hour. Calculate the total earnings of each worker and also the rate of earnings per hour.

Statement of Earnings and Rate of Earnings

	Amar	*Akbar*	*Anthony*
Standard Hours	100	100	100
Time Taken (Hours)	60	70	95
Time Saved (Hours.)	40	30	5
Percentage of time saved to Time Allowed	40%	30%	5%
Percentage of time saved	20%	20%	10%
Bonus Hours	20% of 40 = 8	20% of 30 = 6	10% of 5 = 0.5
	₹.	₹.	₹.
Bonus @ ₹ 1 of Bonus Hours	8.00	6.00	0.50
Wages @ ₹ 1 of Time Taken	60.00	70.00	95.00
Total Earnings	68.00	76.00	95.50
Rate of Earnings per hour	$\frac{68}{60} = 1.13$	$\frac{76}{70} = 1.09$	$\frac{95.50}{95} = 1.01$

Illustration 39: The finishing shop of a company employs 60 direct workers. Each worker is paid ₹. 400 as wages per week of 40 hours. When neccessary, overtime is worked upto a maximum of 15 hours per week per worker at time rate plus one half as premium. The current output on an average is 6 units per man hour which may be regarded as standard output. If bonus scheme is introduced, it is expected that the output will increase to 8 units per man hour. The workers will, if necessary, continue to work overtime upto the specified limit although no premium on incentives will be paid.

The company is considering introduction of *either* Halsey Scheme or Rowan Scheme of Wage Incentive system. The budgeted weekly output is 19,200 units. The selling price is ₹ 11 per unit and the direct material cost is ₹ 8 per unit. The variable overheads amount to ₹ 0.50 per direct labour hour and the fixed overhead is ₹ 9,000 per week.

Prepare a statement to show the effect on the Company's weekly profit of the proposal to introduce (*a*) Halsey Scheme, and (*b*) Rowan Scheme.

Solution: (*b*) **Working Notes:**

1. Total available hours per week (60 workers × 40 hrs.) 2,400
2. Total hours required to produce 19,200 units (19,200/6 units) 3,200
3. Total labour hours required after new bonus scheme to produce 19,200 units (19,200/8 units per manhour) 2,400
4. Time saved in hours (3,200 – 2,400) 800
5. Wage rate per hour (₹ 400/40 hours) ₹ 10
6. Bonus:

(*i*) Halsey Scheme $= \frac{1}{2} \times$ Time saved × Wage rate per hr.

$= \frac{1}{2} \times$ 800 hrs. × ₹ 10 = ₹ 4,000

(*ii*) Rowan Scheme $= \frac{\text{Time saved}}{\text{Time allowed}} \times$ Time taken × Wages rate per hr.

$= \frac{800}{3,200} \times 2,400$ × ₹. 10 = ₹. 6,000

Statement showing the effect on the Company's weekly present profit by the introduction of Halsey and Rowan schemes

	Present	*Halsey*	*Rowan*
	₹.	₹.	₹.
Sales revenue (19,200 × ₹. 11) ...(*A*)	2,11,200	2,11,200	2,11,200
Direct material cost (19,200 × ₹. 8)	1,53,600	1,53,600	1,53,600
Direct wages	32,000	24,000	24,000
Overtime premium (800 hrs × ₹. 5)	4,000	—	—
Bonus	—	4,000	6,000
Variable overheads (3,200 × 0.50); (2,400 × 0.5)	1,600	1,200	1,200
Fixed overheads	9,000	9,000	9,000
Total costs ... (*B*)	2,00,200	1,91,800	1,93,800
Profit (*A*) – (*B*)	11,000	19,400	17,400

Illustration 40: Mr. A is working by employing 10 skilled workers. He is considering the introduction of some incentive scheme—either Halsey Scheme (with 50% bonus) or Rowan Scheme-of wage payment for increasing the labour productivity to cope with the increased demand for the product by 25%. He feels that if the proposed incentive scheme could bring about an average 20% increase over the present earnings of the workers, it could act as sufficient incentive for them to produce more and he has accordingly given this assurance to the workers.

As a result of this assurance, the increase in productivity has been observed as revealed by the following figures for the current month:

Hourly rate of wages (guaranteed)	₹. 2.00
Average time for producing 1 piece by one worker at the previous performance (This may be taken as time allowed)	2 hours
No. of working days in the month	25
No. of working hours per day for each worker	8
Actual production during the month	1,250 unit

Required:

1. Calculate effective rate of earnings per hour under Halsey Scheme and Rowan Scheme.
2. Calculate the saving to Mr. A in terms of direct labour cost per piece under the above scheme.
3. Advise Mr. A about the selection of the scheme to fulfil his assurance.

Solution: Time Allowed = 1250 units × 2 hours = 2,500 hours

Time Taken = 25 × 8 × 10 = 2,000 hours

Time Saved 500 hours

1. Effective Rate: Halsey Scheme:

Earning = T × R + (50% × T.S. × R)

= 2000 × 2 + (50% × 500 × 2)

= 4000 + 500 = ₹. 4,500

$$\text{Rate of earning per hour} = \frac{₹.\,4500}{2000\text{ hours}} = ₹.\,2.25$$

Effective Rate under Rowan Scheme:

Earning = T × R + (TS/TA × T × R)

= 2000 × 2 + (500/2500 × 2000 × 2)

= 4000 + 800 = ₹. 4,800

$$\text{Rate of earnings per hour} = \frac{₹.\,4,800}{2,000\text{ hours}} = ₹.\,2.40$$

2. **Calculation of Savings**

(*a*) Direct labour cost per piece = ₹. 2.00 × 2 hours	₹. 4.00
Under Halsey Scheme = ₹. 4500/1250 units	3.60
Saving under Halsey	0.40
(*b*) Direct labour cost per piece	₹. 4.00
Under Rowan Scheme = ₹. 4800/1250 units	3.84
Saving under *Rowan*	0.16

3. Normal production = $\frac{25 \times 8 \times 10}{2 \text{ hours}}$ = 1000 units

Actual Production	1250 units
Increase in Production	250 units
Increase in labour productivity	25%

(25% increase in production as compared to normal production)

Increase over present earnings of the workers

	₹.
Present earnings per hour	2.00
Under Halsey scheme per hour	2.25
Increase per hour	0.25

Percentage of increase = $\frac{0.25}{2.00} \times 100 = 12.5\%$

Increase of earnings under Rowan Scheme = 2.40 – 2.00 = ₹. 0.40 per hour.

Percentage of increase = $\frac{0.40}{2.00} \times 100 = 20\%$

Rowan Scheme should be selected as it provides 20% increase over the present earnings of the workers. This will also increase productivity by 25%.

Illustration 41: A worker produced 200 units in a week's time. The guaranteed weekly wage payment for 45 hours is ₹. 81. The expected time to produce one unit is 15 minutes which is raised further by 20% under the incentive scheme. What will be the earnings per hour of that worker under Halsey (50% sharing) and Rowan bonus schemes?

Solution:

Wage rate per hour ₹ 81/45	₹. 1.80
Expected time to produce one unit	15 minutes
Add: 20% under incentive scheme	3 minutes
Time allowed for one unit	18 minutes
Time allowed for 200 units (200 × 18/60)	60 hours
Time taken	45 hours
Time saved	15 hours

(*a*) **Earning per hour under Halsey Scheme**

$$E = TT \times R + (50\% \text{ of TS} \times R)$$
$$= 45 \times 1.80 + (50\% \text{ of } 15 \times 1.80)$$
$$= 81 + 13.50 = ₹.\ 94.50$$

Earnings per hour $\frac{94.50}{45}$ = ₹. 2.10 per hour

(*b*) **Earning per hour under Rowan Scheme**

$$E = TT \times R + \left(\frac{TS}{TA} \times TT \times R\right)$$

$$= 45 \times 1.80 + \left(\frac{15}{60} \times 45 \times 1.80\right)$$

$$= 81 + 20.25 = ₹.\ 101.25$$

Earnings per hour $\frac{101.25}{45}$ = ₹. 2.25 per hour.

Illustration 42: In a manufacturing concern 20 workmen work in a group. The concern follows a group incentive bonus system whereby each workman belonging to the group is paid a bonus on the excess output over the hourly production standard of 250 pieces, in addition to his normal wages at hourly rate. The excess of production over the standard is expressed as a percentage and two-thirds of this percentage is considered to be the share of the workman and is applied on the national hourly rate of ₹. 6.00 (considered only for purpose of computation of bonus). The output data for a week are stated below :

Days	*Manhours worked*	*Output (In pieces)*
Monday	160	48.000
Tuesday	172	53,000
Wednesday	164	40,000
Thursday	168	52,000
Friday	160	46,000
Saturday	160	42,000
	984	2,81,000

You are required to :

(*i*) Work out the amount of bonus for the week and the average rate at which each workman is to be paid the same.

(*ii*) Compute the total wages including bonus payable to Ram Jadav who worked for 48 hours at an hourly rate of ₹. 2.50 and to Francis Williams who worked for 52 hours at an hourly rate of ₹. 3.00.

Solution:

(*i*) **Bonus for the week**

	Output (in pieces)
Standard Production (984 × 250)	2,46,000
Actual production	2,81,000
Excess production over standard	35,000

Percentage of excess over standard = $\frac{35,000}{2,46,000} \times 100$ = 14.2276%

Rate of Incentive = 14.2276% × $\frac{2}{3}$ = 9.485% of ₹. 6.00 = ₹. 0.57 per hour.

Amount of the Bonus for the week = 984 × 0.57 = ₹. 560.88

(*ii*) **Earnings of workers:**

		Ram Jadav ₹.		*Francis Williams* ₹.
Wages	(48 × 2.50)	120.00	(52 × 3)	156.00
Bonus	(48 × 0.57)	27.36	(52 × 0.57)	29.64
Earnings		147.36		185.64

Illustration 43: From the following data provided to you find out the Labour Turnover Rate by applying:

(*a*) Flux Method

(*b*) Replacement Method

(*c*) Separation Method

No. of workers on the payroll

At the beginnings of the month	500
At the end of the month	600

During the month, 5 workers left, 20 persons were discharged and 75 worker were recruited. Of these, 10 workers were recruited in the vacancies of those leaving while the rest were engaged for an expansion scheme.

Solution: 1. Average no. of workers during the month : (500 + 600)/2 = 550

2. Out of 75 workers recruited, 10 workers were recruited in the place of those left.

3. 65 workers engaged for an expansion scheme are not taken into labour turnover.

Labour Turnover Ratio

(*a*) Flux Method

$$= \frac{\frac{1}{2}(\text{No. of separations} + \text{No. of replacements}) \times 100}{\text{Average No. of workers}}$$

$$= \frac{\frac{1}{2}(25+10)}{550} \times 100 = 3.18\%$$

(*b*) Replacement Method

$$= \frac{\text{No. of replacements}}{\text{Average No. of workers}} \times 100$$

$$= \frac{10}{550} \times 100 = 1.82\ \%$$

(*c*) Separation Method

$$= \frac{\text{No. of separations}}{\text{Average No. of workers}} \times 100$$

$$= \frac{(5+20)}{550} \times 100 = 4.54\%$$

Illustration 44: Your organisation is experiencing a high labour turnover in recent years and management would like you to sumbit a report on the loss suffered by the Company due to such labour turnover. Following figures are available for your considerations :

Sales	₹. 600 lakhs
Direct Materials	₹. 150 lakhs
Direct Labour	₹. 48 lakhs on 4,80,000 man hours
Other Variable Expenses	₹. 60 lakhs
Fixed Overheads	₹. 80 lakhs

The direct manhours include 9,000 manhours spent on trainees and replacements, only 50% of which were productive. Further, during the year 12,000 manhours of potential works could not be availed of because of delayed replacement. The cost incurred due to separations and replacements amounted to ₹. one lakh.

On the basis of above data, prepare a comparative statement showing actual profit vis-á-vis the profit which would have been realised had there been no labour turnover.

Solution: Basic calculations

1. Hours lost because of delayed replacement	12,000
Unproductive hours 50% of 9,000	4,500
Total hours lost	16,500

2. Productive hours :

Actual manhours	4,80,000
Less : Unproductive hours	4,500
Productive hours	4,75,500

3. Sales on 16500 hours lost i.e., sales lost on account of labour turnover.

$\frac{16,500}{4,75,500} \times 600$ lakhs = ₹. 20.82 lakhs. It is 3.47% of 600 lakh i.e., actual sales.

Comparative Statement of Profit (₹. in lakhs)

	Actual	*Additions*	*If there had been no labour turnover*
Sales	600.00	20.82	620.82
Direct Materials	150.00	3.47% of 150 lakh = 5.21	155.21
Direct Labour	48.00	12000 hours at ₹. 10 = 1.20	49.20
Other Variable Exp.	60.00	3.47% of 60 lakhs = 2.08	62.08
Fixed Overheads	80.00	—	80.00
Cost due to separations and replacement	1.00	—	—
Total Cost	339.00		346.49
Profit	261.00		274.33

Thus, Loss suffered by the company due to labour turnover

= 274.33 – 261.00 = ₹. 13.33 lakhs

Illustration 45: ZED Limited is working by employing 50 skilled workers. It is considered the introduction of incentive scheme-either Halsey scheme (with 50% bonus) or Rowan scheme of wage payment for increasing the labour productivity to cope up the increasing demand for the product by 40%. It is believed that proposed incentive scheme could bring about an average 20% increase over the present earnings of the workers; it could act as sufficient incentive for them to produce more.

Because of assurance, the increase in productivity has been observed as revealed by the figures for the month of April, 2004.

Hourly rate of wages (guaranteed)	₹. 30
Average time for producing one unit by one worker at the previous performance (This may be taken as time allowed)	1.975 hours
Number of working days in the month	24
Number of working hours per day of each worker	8
Actual production during the month	6,120 units

Required:

(*i*) Calculate the effective rate of earnings under the Halsey scheme and the Rowan scheme.

(*ii*) Calculate the savings to the ZED Limited in terms of direct labour cost per piece.

(*iii*) Advise ZED Limited about the selection of the scheme to fulfil their assurance.

[CA PE II May 2004]

Solution:

Working notes:

1. **Computation of time saved (in hours) per month:**

   = (Standard production time of 6,120 units – Actual time taken by the workers)
   = (6,120 units × 1.975 hours – 24 days × 8 hrs per day × 50 skilled workers)
   = (12,087 hours – 9,600 hours)
   = 2,487 hours

2. **Computation of bonus for time saved hours under Halsey and Rowan schemes:**

   Time saved hours = 2,487 hours
   Wage rate per hour = ₹. 30
   Bonus under Halsey Scheme (with 50% bonus) = 1/2 × 2,487 hours × ₹. 30
   = ₹. 37,305

   Bonus under Rowan Scheme $= \dfrac{\text{Time saved}}{\text{Time allowed}} \times \text{Time taken} \times \text{Rate per hour}$

   $= \dfrac{2{,}487 \text{ hours}}{12{,}087 \text{ hours}} \times 9{,}600 \text{ hours} \times ₹.\ 30$

   = ₹. 59,258.38 P

(*i*) **Computation of effective rate of earnings under the Halsey and Rowan schemes:**

Total earnings (under Halsey scheme) = Time wages + Bonus
= 24 days × 8 hours × 50 skilled workers × 30 + ₹. 37,305
= ₹. 2,88,000 + ₹. 37,305 = ₹. 3,25,305

Total earnings (under Rowan scheme) = Time wages + Bonus
= ₹. 2,88,000 + ₹. 59,258.38
= ₹. 3,47,258.38

Effective rate of earnings per hour (under Halsey Plan) (₹. 3,25,305/9,600 hrs)	₹. 33.89
Effective rate of earnings per hour (under Rowan Plan) (₹. 3,47,258.38/9,600 hr)	₹. 36.17

(*ii*) **Savings to the ZED Ltd. in terms of direct labour cost per piece:**

	₹.
Direct labour cost (per unit) under time wages system (1.975 hours per unit × ₹. 30)	59.25
Direct labour cost (per unit) under Halsey Plan (₹. 3,25,305/6,120 units)	53.15
Direct labour cost (per unit) under Rowan Plan (₹. 3,47,258.38/6,120 units)	56.74

Savings of direct labour cost per unit:

- Under Halsey Plan (₹. 59.25 – 53.15) ₹. 6.10
- Under Rowan Plan (₹. 59.25 – 56.74) ₹. 2.51

(*iii*) **Advice to ZED Ltd:** (about the selection of the scheme to fulfil assurance)

Halsey scheme brings more savings to the management of ZED Ltd., over the present earnings of ₹. 2,88,000 but the Rowan fulfils the promise of 20% increase over the present earnings of ₹. 2,88,000 by paying 20.58% in the form of bonus. Hence Rowan Plan may be adopted.

Illustration 46: The capacity usage ratio and the capacity utilisation ratio in respect of a machine for a particular month is 80% and 90% respectively. The available working-hours in a month is 200 hours.

The break-up of idle time is as follows :

Waiting for job	5 hours
Breakdown	4 hours
Waiting for tools	3 hours

Calculate the idle cost time and present the same in a tabular form when the hourly fixed cost of running the machine is ₹. 8.00.

Solution:

Calculations

Available working hours in a month	200
Standard capacity expected (80% of 200)	160
Unavoidable idle time (hours)	40
Capacity utilisation Ratio = 90%	
Actual Hours worked = 90% of 160144	
Unutilised capacity on idle facilities (160 – 144)	16 hours
Avoidable Idle time facilities (16 – 12)	4 hours

Idle Time Report

	Time (Hours)	*Amount (₹.) (at ₹. 8 per hour)*
A. Unavoidable idle time facilities	40	320
B. Avoidable Idle time facilities		
Waiting for job	5	40
Breakdown	4	32
Waiting for tools	3	24
	12	96
Idle facilities	4	32
Total	16	128
C. Total Idle Time (200 – 144)	56	448

Illustration 47: An article passes through five hand operations as follows :

Operation No.	*Time per article*	*Grade of worker*	*Wage rate per hour*
1	15 minutes	A	₹. 0.65
2	25 minutes	B	₹. 0.50
3	10 minutes	C	₹. 0.40
4	30 minutes	D	₹. 0.35
5	20 minutes	E	₹. 0.30

The factory works 40 hours a week and the production target is 600 dozens per week. Prepare a statement showing for each operation and in total the number of operators required, the labour cost per dozen and the total labour cost per week to produce the total target output.

Solution:

Statement showing total number of operators

	Operation No.					*Total*
	1	2	3	4	5	
Time per article (minutes)	15	25	10	30	20	
Total time in hours for prodn. of 600 dozen $\frac{600 \times 12 \times 15}{60}$ (hours)	1800	3000	1200	3600	2400	
No. of operators 1800/40 hours	45	75	30	90	60	300
Labour cost per dozen (15 × 12)/60 = 3 hrs 3 hours × Rate (₹.)	1.95	2.50	0.80	2.10	1.20	8.55
Labour cost per week 1.95 × dozens (₹.)	1170	1500	480	1260	720	5130

OBJECTIVE QUESTIONS

I. *True or False Statements.*

Indicate whether each of the following statements is True or False. Give also reasons in brief.

1. Wages of a machine operator is direct wages.
2. High labour turnover is good for a business.
3. Job tickets or job cards record the time spent by workers on each job.
4. Idle time arises in case of worker paid on time basis.
5. Cost of abnormal idle time is transferred to Costing Profit and Loss Account.
6. Normal Idle time is charged to factory overhead.
7. Overtime wages are transferred to Costing Profit and Loss Account.
8. In Taylor's Differential Piece Rate Plan, time wages are guaranteed to each worker.
9. Overtime wages are to be paid at double the normal wage rate.
10. Rowan incentive plan distributes the benefit of time saved equally between employer and employee.
11. Cost of idle time due to labour strike should be treated as factory overhead.
12. Direct wages is a fixed cost.
13. In Halsey Premium plan, time wages are guaranteed.
14. In Emerson's Efficiency System, bonus is paid only when efficiency is 100%.
15. Under Rowan plan, bonus is a fixed percentage.

[***Ans.*** *(1) T; (2) F : (3) T; (4) T; (5) T; (6) T; (7) F; (8) T; (9) T; (10) F; (11) F; (12) F; (13) T; (14) T; (15) T*]

II. *Point out the statements, which are not true.*

(*a*) Time and motion study is conducted by the pay-roll department.

(*b*) Labour once lost cannot be recouped.

(*c*) A copy of the appointment letter should be sent to the time and motion study department.

(*d*) In merit rating system, a number of traits are measured to know an employer's work.

(*e*) Job evaluation and job analysis are the same.

(*f*) Metal-disc method is a manual method of recording time of workers.

(g) Time keeping is the rcording of time spent by a worker on the different jobs or work orders carried out by him during his period of attendance in the factory.

[***Ans.:*** *(a), (c), (e), and (g) false*]

III. Select correct answer from following alternative:

1. In which of the following incentive plans of wages payment, wages on time basis are not guaranteed?
(*a*) Halsey Plan (*b*) Rowan Plan
(*c*) Taylor's differential piece rate system (*d*) Gantt's task and bonus system.

2. Which of the following incentive methods of wage payment should be used for indirect workers?
(*a*) Rowan Plan (*b*) Taylor's differential piece rate system
(c) Halsey plam (*d*) None of the above

3. Which of the following methods of wage payment is most suitable where quality and accuracy of work is primary importance?
(*a*) Piece rate system (*b*) Time rate system
(*c*) Differential piece work system (*d*) Halsey premium system

4. Cost of Idle time arising due to non-availability of raw material is:
(*a*) Charged to Costing Profit and Loss A/c. (*b*) Charged to factory overhead.
(*c*) Recovered by inflating the wage rate. (*d*) None of these.

5. When overtime is required for meeting orders, overtime premium should be:
(*a*) Charged to Costing. Profit and Loss A/c. (*b*) Charged to overhead costs.
(*c*) Charged to respective jobs. (*d*) None of these

6. Labour turnover is measured by:
(a) No. of workers replaced/average number of workers.
(*b*) No. of workers left/number in the beginning plus number at the end.
(*c*) No. of workers joining/number in the beginning of the period
(*d*) All of these
(*e*) None of these.

7. Under Emerson's Efficiency System, no bonus is payable when efficiency is upto:
(*a*) 50% (*b*) $66\frac{2}{3}$%
(*c*) $83\frac{1}{3}$% (*d*) 100%

8. When standard output is 10 units per hour and actual output is 12 units per hour, the efficiency is:
(*a*) 80% (*b*) 100%
(*c*) 120% (*d*) None of these

9. Given that for a job, standard time is 8 hours, actual time taken is 6 hours and the time rate is ₹. 2 per hour. What is the total wages under Halsey Premium Plan:
(*a*) ₹. 18 (*b*) ₹. 16
(*c*) ₹. 14 (*d*) ₹. 12

10. Using data as given in the above question, what will be the amount of bonus under Rowan plan:
(*a*) ₹. 2 (*b*) ₹. 3
(*c*) ₹. 3 (*d*) None of the above

11. Standard output is 100 units per day of 8 hours and the piece rates are 20 paise per unit and 15 paise per unit under Taylor's differential piece rate system, what will be the amount wages if a workers produces 95 units in a day:
(*a*) ₹. 14.00 (*b*) ₹. 14.25
(*c*) ₹. 18.50 (*d*) ₹. 19.00

12. Comparing the Rowan and Halsey Premium plans, it is seen that when the time saved is less than 50% of the time taken:
(*a*) Rowan Plan allows more wages to a worker than Halsey Plan.
(*b*) Rowan Plan allows less wages to a worker than Halsey Plan.
(*c*) Rowan and Halsey Plan allow equal wages to a worker.

13. Wages under Rowan and Halsey Plans are exactly equal when time saved is:

(*a*) Nil (*b*) 50% of the standard time

(*c*) Both (*a*) and (*b*)

[Ans. : 1 (*c*) ; 2(*d*); 3(*b*) ; 4 (*a*); 5 (*c*); 6 (*a*); 7(*b*); 8 (*c*); 9 (*c*); 10(*b*); 11(*b*) ; 12 (*a*); 13 (*b*);]

IV. *Tick the correct answer* :

(*i*) In which of the following incentive plans of wage payment, time rates are guaranteed?

(*a*) Rowan system ; (*b*) Halsey system ; (*c*) Gantt's task and bonus system ; (*d*) All these methods

(*ii*) Which of the following methods of wage payment will be most appropriate to maintain quality of work ?

(*a*) Time rate system

(*b*) Taylor's differential piece work system

(*c*) Straight piece work system;

(*d*) Halsay system

(*iii*) When standard output is 10 units per hour and actual output is 14 units per hour, the efficiency level will be :

(*a*) 60% (*b*) 120% (*c*) 140% (*d*) None of these

(*iv*) Given that standard time for a job is 10 hours, actual time taken is 6 hours and the time rate is ₹. 3 per hour, what is the total wages under Halsey scheme?

(*a*) ₹. 28 (*b*) ₹. 20 (*c*) ₹. 24 (*d*) ₹. 10

(*v*) What will be the wages if Halsey-weir scheme (30% to workers) is applied on the data in (iv) above ?

(*a*) ₹. 18.00 (*b*) ₹. 21.60 (*c*) ₹. 21.00 (*d*) ₹. 15.20

(*vi*) Using data as given in (*iv*) above, what will be the bonus under Rowan scheme?

(*a*) ₹. 8.0 (*b*) ₹. 7.2 (*c*) ₹. 5.8 (*d*) ₹. 4.5

(*vii*) Using data as given in (*iv*) above, what will be the amount of wages under time rate system?

(*a*) ₹. 18 (*b*) ₹. 15 (*c*) ₹. 12 (*d*) ₹. 16

(*viii*) Using data as given in (*iv*) above, what will be the bonus under Halsey scheme?

(*a*) ₹. 6 (*b*) ₹. 8 (*c*) ₹. 4 (*d*) ₹. 10

(*ix*) Time and motion study is required for :

(*a*) determining the standard time and correct method of performing a job

(*b*) an effective promotion policy

(*c*) ascertaining product prices ;

(*d*) finishing a job in time.

(*x*) By direct labour we mean :

(*a*) Labour which is directly recruited and not supplied by contractors

(*b*) labour completing the job manually

(*c*) labour which can be conveniently associated with a specific cost unit

(*d*) permanent worker of the production department.

(*xi*) Job specification means ;

(*a*) the list of qualifications and qualities which employees should possess to perform the job well

(*b*) the list of operations to be done to finish the job

(*c*) the name of the employees who will be assigned to a job

(*d*) the requirement in terms of articles to be produced or work to be performed.

(*xii*) When time saved exceeds 50% of the standard time, Halsey scheme allows :

(*a*) more wages than Rowan scheme

(*b*) less wages than Rowan scheme

(*c*) equal wages to Rowan scheme.

[Ans. (*i*) *d*; (*ii*) *a*; (*iii*) *c* ; (*iv*) *c* ; (*v*) *b* ; (*vi*) *b* ; (*vii*) *a* ; (*viii*) *a* ; (*ix*) *a* ; (*x*) *c* ; (*xi*) *a* ; (*xii*) *a*]

THEORETICAL QUESTIONS

1. Describe the methods of recording attendence of workers in a manufacturing concern.

2. Explain the functions of the wages department in a big factory.

3. Explain the procedure of recording worker's time spent on various jobs.

4. What are various methods of remunerating labour? Explain any four of them.

5. State briefly, with examples, the difference between the Halsey Premium Plan and the Rowan Premium Plan. What are the main advantages claimed for each system?

6. Write short notes on Idle time, Labour turnover, Profit sharing and Co-partnership, Good wage system.

7. Define Labour Turnover. State its causes and effects.

8. Explain the meanings of idle time and suggest its treatment in costing.

9. What do you understand by time and motion study. Explain how standard time is set under time study? State how time and motion study is useful to the management.

10. Write short notes on : (*i*) Group Bonus Scheme, (*ii*) Methods of recording attendance time (*iii*) Labour Turnover (*iv*) Idle time.

SHORT ANSWER QUESTIONS

11. List down factors to be considered before introducing a scheme of incentive to workers.

12. Distinguish between Job Evaluation and Merit rating.

13. Define idle time. Bring out clearly the treatment of idle time in Cost Accounts.

14. Discuss the objectives of time keeping and time booking.

15. Write short note on Labour Turnover.

16. What is overtime premium ?

17. Distinguish between 'casual worker and outworker'.

18. Discuss two types of cost which are associated with 'Labour Turnover'.

19. Write short note on 'Labour Turnover Cost'.

20. Write short notes on Idle time.

SHORT ANSWER NUMERICAL QUESTIONS

1. Calculate wages under Halsey Premium Plan from following particulars.

Time Rate ₹. 2 per hour

Standard output 50 units per hour

Actual hours worked 8 hours

Actual output 500 units.

[Ans. : 18]

2. From particulars of above question, calculate wages under Rowan Plan.

[Ans. : ₹. 19.20]

3. In a factory standard time for a job is 20 hours and rate of wages is ₹. 1.30 per hour. If a worker completes the job in 15 hours what will be his wages under Halsey and Rowan Plan.

[Ans.: ₹. 22.75 and ₹. 24.38]

4. For a certain work order, the standard time is 20 hours and wages ₹. 5 per hour. A worker took actual time of 13 hours. What will be wages of the worker under Halsey Plan and Rowan Plan.

[Ans. : ₹. 82.50 and ₹. 87.75]

5. A firm carried on a work measurement study for 10 hours and the following information was generated. What will be standard time for that ?

Units produced	350
Idle time	15%

Performance 12%

Allowance time 10% of standard time

[Ans. : 14.11]

6. From the following, calculate Labour Turnover Ratio from Flux Method.

No. of workers at the begining of the month : 900 and at the end of the month : 1100

No. of workers left 50 and 25 workers were replaced.

[Ans. 7.5% per month]

7. In factory standard time alloted to a job is 20 hours and the rate per hour is ₹. 1 *plus* a D.A. @ 30 paise per hour worked. The actual time taken by a worker is 15 hours. Calculate the earning under - (*i*) Time wages system (*ii*) Piece wages system, (*iii*) Halsey system and (*iv*) Rowan plan.

[Ans. : (*i*) ₹. 19.50 (*ii*) ₹. 26 (*iii*) ₹. 22.75 (Bonus for 50% of time saved)]

8. For a certain work order, the standard time is 20 hours and wages ₹. 5 per hour. The actual time taken is 13 hours. The factory overhead charges are 80% of standard time. Set our a comparative statement showing the effect on paying under - (i) Halsey Plan (ii) Rowan Bonus Plan.

[Ans. : (*i*) ₹. 82.50 (*ii*) ₹. 87.75]

9. During one week, the workman X manufactured 200 articles. He received wages for a guranteed 44 hour week at the rate of ₹. 1.50 per hour. The estimated time to produce one article is 15 minute and under incentive scheme the time allowed is increased by 20% . Calculate his gross wages under each of the following methods of remuneration:

(*a*) Time rate.

(*b*) Piece work rate with a guaranteed weekly wages.

(*c*) Rowan Premium Bonus

(*d*) Halsey Premium Bonus, 50% to the workman.

[Ans. : (*a*) ₹. 66 (*b*) ₹. 90 (*c*) ₹. 83.60 (*d*) ₹. 78]

NUMERICAL QUESTIONS

1. During one week the workman X manufactured 200 articles. He received wages for a guaranteed 44 hour week at the rate of ₹. 1.50 per hour. The estimated time to produce one article is 15 minutes and under incentive scheme the time allowed is increased by 20%. Calculate his gross wages under each of the following methods of remuneration:

(*a*) Time rate

(*b*) Piece work rate with a guaranteed weekly wages.

(*c*) Rowan Premium Bonus

(*d*) Halsey Premium bonus, 50% to the workman.

[Ans.: *(a) ₹. 66, (b) ₹. 90, (c) ₹. 83.60, (d) ₹. 78*]

2. Two workers A and B were given an identical Job. The labour cost was estimated at ₹. 1.5 per hour for 32 hours. The overhead recovery rate came to ₹. 4.50 per labour hour. Materials used by both the workers valued at ₹. 120 each.

The works cost of production came to ₹. 270 and ₹. 291 respectively for two jobs with Halsey Plan (50%). Find the time taken by A and B.

[Ans. *A 24 hours and B 28 hours*]

3. In a factory standard time alloted to a job is 20 hours and the rate per hour is ₹. 1 plus a D.A. @ 30 paise per hour worked.

The actual time taken by a worker is 15 hours. Calculate the earning under — (*i*) Time wages system, (*ii*) Piece wages system, (*iii*) Halsey system and (*iv*) Rowan plan.

[Ans.: *(i) ₹. 19.50, (ii) ₹. 24.50, (iii) ₹ 22, (iv) 23.25*]

4. For a certain work order, the standard time is 20 hours and wages ₹. 5 per hour. The actual time taken is 13 hours. The factory overheads charges are 80% of standard time. Set out a comparative statement showing the effect on paying under — (*i*) Halsey plan (*ii*) Rowan Bonus plan.

[Ans.: *(i) ₹. 82.50, (ii) ₹. 87.75*]

5. In a factory the standard time fixed is 8 hours a day and the standard output is 10 units per hour. The daily wages rate is ₹. 6 per worker. There were five workers A, B, C, D and E and output are 50 units, 65 units, 45 units, 75 units and 100 units respectively. The following is the scheme of giving bonus to the workers on the basis of efficiency.

Upto 67% efficiency the amount of bonus is nil. Above 67% efficiency upto 80% efficiency it is 5%. Above 80% efficiency to 90% the rate is 10%. Above 90% efficiency to 100% the rate is 20%. Above 100% efficiency the bonus rate rises by one present for every one percent rise in the efficiency.

Calculate the total earnings of each of the workers.

[**Ans.:** *A ₹. 6, B ₹. 6.60, C ₹. 6, D ₹. 7.20 and E ₹. 8.70*]

6. A worker is allowed 60 hours to complete the job on a guarranted wages of ₹. 10 per hour. Under the Rowan Plans, he gets an hourly wage of ₹. 12 per hour. For the same savings in time how much he will get under the Halsey Plan? ***[CS Inter June 2001]***

[Ans.: *₹. 11.25*]

[Hint.: per hour rate is ₹. 2 above on account of ratio between time saved and time allowed. = 2

Thus time saved is 12 hours]

7. Using Taylor's differential piece rate system, find the earning of Sita, Gita and Nita from the following particulars :

Standard time per piece	20 minutes
Normal rate per hour	₹. 4.50
In an 8 hours day :	
Sita produced	23 units
Nita produced	24 units
Gita produced	30 units

[**Ans.** *Sita ₹. 27.60; Gita ₹. 43.20 and Nita ₹. 54*]

8. The following particulars are available in respect of a work shop.

Standard Production per hour	12 units
Normal rate per hour	₹. 6
In an 8 hours day :	
A produces	64 units
B produces	84 units
C produces	100 units

Calculate the earning of the above workers under Merrick's differential piece rate system.

[**Ans.** *A ₹. 32; B ₹. 46.20; C ₹. 60*]

9. The standard hours of job X is 100 hours. The job has been completed by Amar in 60 hours. Akbar in 70 hours and Anthony in 95 hours. The bonus system applicable to the job is as follows:

Percentage of time saved to time allowed	Bonus
Saving upto 10%	10% of time saved
From 11% to 20%	15% of time saved
From 21% to 40%	20% of time saved
From 41% to 100%	25% of time saved

The rate of pay is ₹. 10 per hour. Calculate the total earning of each worker and also the rate of earning per hour.

[**Ans.** *Amar Total ₹. 680 per hour R.s 11.33; Akbar ₹. 760 and ₹. 10.86; Anthony ₹. 955 and ₹. 10.05*]

10. Production section of a factory working on a job order system pay their workers under the Rowan Bonus Scheme. Workers are also entitled to a dearness allowance of ₹. 240 per week of 48 hours.

A worker's basic wage is ₹. 40 per day of 8 hours and his time sheet for a week is summarised below :

Job No.12	Time Allowed	Time Taken
1	25 hours	20 hours
2	30 hours	24 hours
Idle time (waiting)		4 hours

You are required to calculate the gross wages of the worker for the week.

[Ans.: *₹. 524***]**

11. From the following data, prepare statement showing the cost per day of 8 hours of engaging a particular type of labour.

(*a*)	Monthly Salary (basic plus dearness allowance)	₹. 2,000
(*b*)	Leave Salary—payable to the workmen 5% of salary	
(*c*)	Employer's contribution to Employees State Insurance	2½% of Salary (Items *a* + *b*)
(*d*)	Employer's contribution to Provident Fund	8% of Salary (Items *a* + *b*)
(*e*)	Pro-rata expenditures on amenities to workers	₹. 179.50 per worker per month
(*f*)	No. of working hours in a month.	200 hours

[Ans.: *Wages per month ₹. 2,500; wages per day of 8 hours ₹. 100***]**

12. An analysis of the time card of a worker on a machine shows that of the total 48 hours, he worked 45 hours (including 4 hours overtime due to general increase in work) on production and 3 hours was abnormal idle time due to machine breakdown. The wage rate of the worker is ₹. 5 per hour, but overtime is 100% extra.

You are required to allocate the total wages paid to the worker between direct and indirect labour and the amount chargeable to the Costing Profit and Loss Account if any.

[Ans.: *Total wages ₹. 205, Direct ₹. 225, Indirect ₹. 40 Costing P/L A/c ₹. 15***]**

13. From the following data calculate the labour turnover rate by applying (*i*) Separation Method, (*ii*) Accession Method, (*iii*) Flux Method.

Number of workers on the payroll

At the beginning of the month	₹. 1800
At the end of the month	2200

During the months 20 workers left 80 workers were discharged and 500 workers were recruited. Of these 50 workers were recruited in the vacancies of those separated, while rest were engaged due to expansion.

[Ans. *(i) 5%, (ii) 2.5%, (iii) 3.5%***]**

14. The cost accountant of Adarsh Ltd. has computed labour turnover rates for the quarter anded 31st March 2000 as 20%, 10% and 6% respectively under 'Flux Method' 'Replacement Method' and Separation Method.

If the number of workers replaced during the quarter is 80, find out the number of (*i*) workers left and discharged (*ii*) workers recruited and joined including replacements.

[Ans. *(i) 48 (ii) 112***]**

[Hint. Average number of workers on roll = $80 \times \frac{100}{10} = 800$**]**

15. Using Taylor's differential piece rate system, find the earning of A from the following particulars.

Standard time per piece : 12 minutes

Normal rate per hour in 8 hours day : ₹. 20

A produced 37 units

[Ans. : *₹. 122.84***]**

[Hint: Efficiency 92.5% i.e. 83% of normal rate ₹. 3.32 per unit.

Earning 37 × 3.32 = 122.84**]**

Direct Expenses or Chargeable Expenses

"Expenses which can be identified with and allocated to cost centres or cost units."
(*CIMA*)

It has already been pointed out that the expenditure which can be allocated conveniently to a unit of cost is known as Direct Expenses. Expenses which cannot be so allocated or expenses which are incurred for output generally are known as indirect expenses. Ordinarily most of the expenses are indirect but sometimes there will be a few direct expenses. Following are examples of such charges:

(1) Carriage and freight on materials bought for particular jobs, if such carriage has not been included in the cost of the materials.

(2) Costs incurred in carrying out experiments before undertaking the job concerned.

(3) Cost of defective work, if the nature of work to be done is such that it cannot be completed without turning out a certain number of defective units in the initial stages.

(4) The cost of making designs, patterns or drawings, if such expenses are substantial.

(5) Hire of special machinery or plant for a particular job.

(6) Travelling expenses incurred in connection with the job.

(7) Royalty if paid on the basis of quantity of goods produced.

An example of direct charges would be the cost of laying special railway track to manufacture locomotives of a gauge other than the usual one, *e.g.*, when the Perambur Coach Factory builds coaches for a foreign country.

Characteristics of Direct Expenses

(*i*) These are other than the cost of Direct Materials and Direct Labour.

(*ii*) These are variable in character *i.e.*, increase or decrease as per volume of production.

(*iii*) These are allocated or charged in total amount to cost centres or work orders. These are identified with work order

(*iv*) These are included in the Prime Cost of the product.

It is to be noted that costs which are allocated to a cost centre may be direct with reference to the cost centre but when these costs are charged to works orders as departmental cost, there are indirect or overhead with reference to work orders.

It is also be understood that it is convenience and not principle which determines whether a particular expense is to be classified as direct or indirect expenditure. One organisation may find it convenient to treat as direct expense an expenditure which another organisation may regard as 'indirect'.

Control of Direct Expenses

Control of direct expenses should follow the same pattern as the control of direct materials or direct labour. For this purpose budgets of direct expenses should be prepared with reference to the budgeted volume of output as laid down in the Production Volume Budget. The budget should indicate the physical volume of direct expenses required, item by item when standards are fixed for these costs, comparison of actual costs incurred with the standards set-up, also serves as basis for controlling such cost.

QUESTIONS

1. What is a direct or chargeable expense? Give three examples.
2. Write short note on 'Chargeable Expense'.

Overheads

Amounts spent by a concern in carrying on day-to-day work, except those on prime cost, may be treated as overheads. It comprises indirect materials, indirect labour and indirect expenses. Overheads must not be ignored while ascertaining the cost of anything. In actual life many business houses commit the mistake of quoting a price only on the basis of direct materials, direct labour and direct expenses. Such business houses run the risk of a heavy loss because the margin of profit determined by them may or may not be sufficient to meet the various expenses incurred besides the prime cost.

The following definitions should be noted :

Indirect Material Cost : "Materials which cannot be allocated but which can be apportioned to, or absorbed by, cost centers or cost units."

Indirect Wages (Indirect Labour Cost) : "Wages (labour cost) which cannot be allocated but which can be apportioned to, or absorbed by, cost centres or cost units."

Indirect Expenses : "Expenses which cannot be allocated but which can be apportioned to, or absorbed by, cost centres, or cost units." – *CIMA*

CLASSIFICATION OF OVERHEADS

Overheads are conveniently divided under three heads which are:

(*a*) Works or Factory Expenses;

(*b*) Office and Administrative Expenses; and

(*c*) Selling and Distributive Expenses.

The division is made according to the service obtained from the expenses. If selling benefits from the money spent, it is a selling expense; and if the money is spent in the workshop itself for producing the goods, it is a factory expense. For example, stationery used in the factory office will be a factory expense, stationery used in the sales office will be a selling expense and stationery used in the general office will be office and administrative expense.

In small factories no distinction may be made between office and administrative expenses and selling and distributive expenses. A big factory, on the other hand, may, however, further sub-divide the main types of overheads. For example, the works or factory expenses may be sub-divided into materials handling charges, labour overheads and general factory administration expenses etc. Office and administrative expenses may be separated-administrative expenses comprising the salaries paid to the executive officers and the expenses incurred to enable them to work, for example, air conditioning expenses of the General Manager's office. Office expenses will then mean the expenses incurred in enabling the clerical establishment to work. Selling expenses are those which are incurred in order to obtain an order from the customer, for example advertisement and showroom expenses. Distributive expenses will mean the expenses incurred to move the goods from the company's go downs to the customer's premises, for instance godown expenses, packing, and carriage outwards.

Other Classifications

Overheads may be classified as to *nature*:

(*i*) Indirect Materials (*e.g.* consumable stores, loose tools cotton waste, lubricating oil etc.)

(*ii*) Indirect Labour (*e.g.* wages of stores keeper, foreman, time keepers, director's Fees, salaries of salesman etc.)

(*iii*) Indirect expenses (*e.g.* canteen expenses, repairs, depreciation, insurance, taxes and maintenance)

These three have been defined earlier. Overheads may also be classified on the basis of *controllability*.

(*i*) *Controllable overheads* : These are overheads which can be controlled by the management, for example cost of power is controllable by the department manager.

(*ii*) *Uncontrollable overheads* : These are overheads which are not controllable. Overheads which are of fixed nature (like rent of factory and office), are normally uncontrollable.

Overheads may also be classified as to *variability* :

(*i*) Fixed overheads

(*ii*) Variable overheads

(*iii*) Semi-variable overheads

This classification is of much importance. We shall discuss it in detail.

(*i*) Fixed Overheads

There are certain expenses which are not affected by a change in the level of output. For instance, if the output goes up or come down, there will be no change in the rent or in salaries. Such expenses are known as *fixed* or *constant expenses*. It should be noted that such expenses will certainly change, say, due to increments given to staff, but the changes will not depend upon output.

(*ii*) Variable Overheads

There are expenses which change almost in the same ratio in which the output changes. For instance, if output goes up it is expected that the consumption of electricity or power will also go up because of the longer running of machines. Similarly, the consumption of certain stores will also go up. If the output falls such expenses will come down almost proportionately. Such expenses are known as variable expenses.

Fixed expenses remain constant per unit of time. Variable expenses remain constant per unit of output. Fixed expenses are said to be uncontrollable because the money must be spent irrespective of output. Variable expenses are said to be controllable.

(*iii*) Semi-Variable Overheads

These expenses change in the same direction in which output changes, *i.e.*, they go up when the output rises and they come down when the output declines, but they do not change in the same proportion as the change in output. To take an example, depreciation is not doubled if output is doubled even if two shifts are required whereas previously one was sufficient. Probably in this case depreciation will go up only by 50 per cent. Expenses are semi-variable because they combine themselves in two parts—one fixed and the other variable. Depreciation, to continue the example, depends upon efflux or passage of time and upon wear and tear. That portion which is due to passage of time is fixed whereas the portion due to wear and tear is variable. This is the reason why depreciation is semi-variable. This means that the semi-variable expenses can be split again into two portions—fixed and variable. Therefore, ultimately all the expenses can be split into two main categories of fixed and variable.

The nature of the expenses is illustrated by the diagram given below.

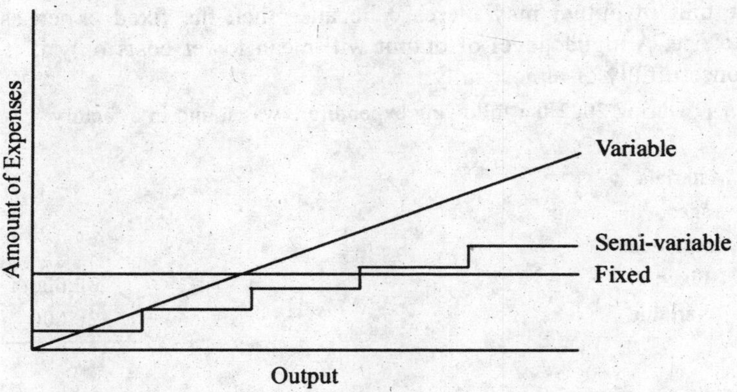

The distinction helps one in making an estimate of indirect expenses for a coming period. Suppose the following figures are given for August, 2005.

Output	1,000 units
Fixed expenses	₹. 6,000
Variable expenses	₹. 8,000

If the output in August, 2005, is expected to be 1,200 units, the indirect expenses would be as under :

Fixed	₹. 6,000
Variable $\left(\frac{8,000 \times 1,200}{1,000}\right)$	₹. 9,600
Total	₹. 15,600

Of course, if it is known that since August, 2005 certain changes have taken place in fixed expenses, say, the employment of two more foremen, such changes should be taken into account while estimating the fixed expenses. It will thus be clearly advantageous to have a list of expenses actually incurred in a recent period and examine each one of them to know whether the amount will change, and if so by how much.

It must be remembered that expenses remain fixed and variable only if the change in output is not big. For a big change the fixed expenses will also change and the variable expenses will also not change in the same proportion in which the output changes. In other words for a big change in output almost all expenses will become semi-variable. Suppose a factory runs one shift and produces 8,000 units in a month against the capacity of 10,000 units, there will be no increase in fixed expenses if the output goes up to 10,000 units, *i.e.*, if idle capacity is utilised. (This is the reason why greater output will bring down the cost per unit). But the fixed expenses cannot be expected to be the same if the factory begins to run two shift. There may even be a saving in variable expenses, because of greater activity and because of the possibility of employment of machines in place of workers. The cost of materials per unit may also go down because the larger purchase of materials may mean availability of greater trade discounts and greater economy in transport.

Fixed expenses will move up by jumps. If the output goes above present level of capacity the fixed expenses may record a big increase. But then they will remain at the same level until the output again exceeds the (new) capacity. If a concern has idle capacity, the cost of production per unit can come down if the idle capacity is utilized, *i.e*, if the output goes up. This is because of there being less fixed expenses per unit of output at the higher level of production. But if the output exceeds per unit of output at the higher level of production. But if the output exceeds the capacity, the cost of one unit of output may increase because then the fixed expenses may record a disproportionate rise. A higher level of output will mean lower costs only if it can utilize the capacity of a concern fully or almost fully.

Illustration 1: During 2002 the following expenditure was found in a factory:

		₹.
Direct Materials		1,00,000
Direct Wages		60,000
Factory expenses:		
Fixed	30,000	
Variable	20,000	50,000
		2,10,000

It was expected that in 2003 the following changes will take place:

(*a*) Output will be raised by employing 50 per cent more workers;

(*b*) Efficiency will decline by 10 per cent because of new workers;

(*c*) Fixed expenses will increase by 20 per cent; and

(*d*) Direct materials will be purchased at a price 5 per cent lower than 2002 prices.

Variable expenses vary with number of men employed.

Draw up the budget for 2003.

Solution:

BUDGET FOR 2003

		₹.	₹.
Direct Materials			
Add: 35% due to increased output*		1,00,000	
		35,000	
		1,35,000	
Less: 5% decline in price		6,750	1,28,250
Direct Wages		60,000	
Add: 50% increase		30,000	90,000
Factory Expenses:			
Fixed	₹. 30,000		
Add: 20% increase	6,000	36,000	
Variable	20,000		
Add: 50% increase	10,000	30,000	66,000
		Total	2,84,250

**Note:* Total output will increase by 35 per cent as shown below:

Output in 2002	100%
Increased labour	50%
	150%
Less: 10% decline in efficiency	15%
	135%

Advantages of Making the Distinction between Fixed and Variable Expenses

Besides the advantage of estimating indirect expenses there are certain other advantages of dividing expenses into fixed and variable categories.

(*i*) *Better control* can be exercised over expenses if the estimate of expenses is properly made.

(*ii*) It enables the *ascertainment of marginal cost i.e.*, that cost which can be avoided if a unit of output is given up, or additional cost which will have to be incurred if another unit is produced.

(*iii*) This helps in determining the *level of output* where all the expenses can be met.

(*iv*) It also helps in determining the *price during a slump* or a depression or in special markets.

(*v*) Another advantage is that one can decide whether to make a part or to buy that from outside sources. This decision will be made only on the basis of comparing the price demanded by outsiders with marginal cost.

(*vi*) The decision to give up a product or to increase the capacity of another product is also made on the basis of difference between the price obtained and the marginal cost.

(*vii*) One can realise the advantages of making a distinction between variable and fixed expenses later when one has studied *Marginal Costing* and *Budgetary Control.*

The Process of Distinguishing Variable and Fixed Costs

For making a really effective distinction between the variable portion and fixed portion of expenses, it is necessary to study the behaviour of each expense at various levels of output. The change in the amount spent is noted as capacity utilisation (or the level of activity) changes. For example, see the following data :

	Capacity Utilisation								
	80%	85%	90%	95%	100%	105%	110%	115%	120%
	₹.	₹.	₹.	₹.	₹.	₹.	₹.	₹.	₹.
Salaries	5,000	5,000	5,000	5,000	5,000	5,000	5,000	5,000	6,000
Consumable stores	1,000	1,100	1,200	1,300	1,400	1,500	1,600	1,700	1,800
Indirect Labour	800	800	800	1,000	1,000	1,000	1,000	1,000	1,100

The figures show that up to 115 per cent of capacity utilisation salaries remain ₹. 5,000 but increase in output beyond that level means that salaries increase by ₹. 1,000. Consumable stores increase by ₹. 100 for each 5 per cent increase in capacity utilisation. Indirect labour is constant at ₹. 800 upto 90 per cent of capacity utilisation; then it increases by ₹. 200 for capacity utilisation up to 115 per cent and increase beyond that level means another increase but only of ₹. 100. Such is the nature of study that has to be made of the various expenses in various situations—ideally, each expense or item of cost should be studied separately.

One may, however, be content with studying the behaviour of total costs and thus establishing the total of fixed expenses and of variable expenses. The method is to compare the total costs at different levels of output and note the change in total cost for the change in output. The relationship between the two will establish the variable cost per unit of output since only variable costs change when the output changes. See the following figures:

	April 2005	May 2005
Number of units produced	15,000	16,500
Total of Factory Overheads	₹. 2,00,000	₹. 2,12,000

The output has increased by 1,500 units whereas the amount of factory overheads has increased by ₹. 12,000. It is apparent, therefore, that the variable factory expenses are ₹. 8 per unit, *i.e.*, 12,000 ÷ 1,500. The fixed expenses come to ₹. 80,000, as shown below:

	₹.
Total factory overheads (for 15,000 units)	2,00,000
Variable factory overheads for 15,000 units @ ₹. 8 per unit	1,20,000
Fixed Factory Overheads	80,000

To compare figures for two periods only is surely limited in usefulness. It would be much better if total expenses at various levels of output were studied. There is an algebraical method—the sum of least squares—that can give the amount of fixed expenses on a study of a number of figures. But if output in various periods and the accompanying total expenses are plotted on a graph paper and then a line as close to the various points as possible is drawn, the point where it meets the *Y*-axis (showing total costs), will indicate the amount of fixed expenses or costs. This is illustrated below:

Illustration 2: The following are the figures of output and the total factory expenses, taken from the books of a factory:

Output (units)	*Total Factory Expenses* ₹.	*Output (units)*	*Total Factory Expenses* ₹.
10.000	1,50,000	25,000	2,20,000
12,500	1,65,000	22,500	2,15,000
14,000	1,75,000	21,000	2,06,000
17,500	1,90,000	19,000	1,97,000
15,000	1,80,000	18,000	1,92,000
20,000	2,00,000	15,000	1,85,000

Solution:

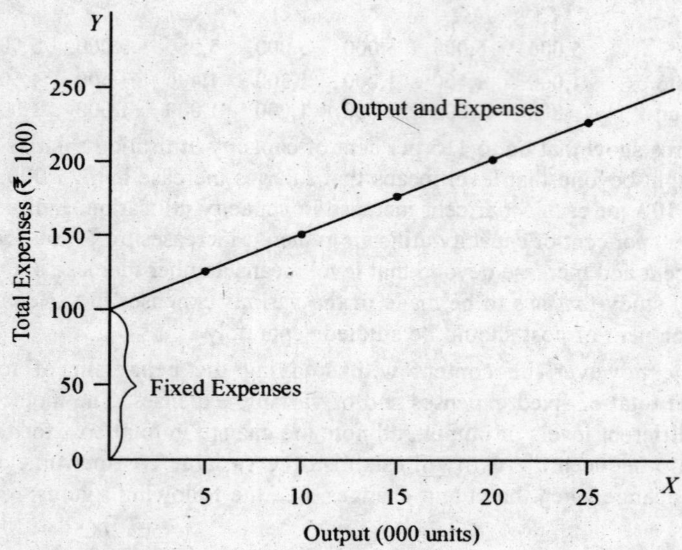

The graph shows that the fixed expenses are ₹. 1,07,500. The variable expenses can now be worked out. At 15,000 units, total expenses are ₹. 1,80,000. Deducting the fixed expenses, the remaining amount is ₹. 72,500. The amount per unit is ₹. 4.80 (*i.e.*, 72500 ÷ 15000)

Collection and Absorption of Overheads

Because of the need to ascertain the cost of a job as soon as it is completed and since overheads must be included, it is necessary to

(*i*) make an estimate of the overheads before a month begins, and

(*ii*) then spread the amount of overheads over the various cost units.

The former process is called "Collection of Overheads" and the latter "Absorption" or "Recovery" of overheads. These process will be discussed in detail under the three classifications of overheads.

The Functional classification (Factory Overheads, Administration Overheads and selling and Distribution Overheads) is conventional method of dividing overheads. We shall first deal with Works or Factory Expenses.

FACTORY OR WORKS OVERHEADS

Items constituting Works or Factory Expenses

All expenses incurred inside a factory and for the benefit of manufacture as such will be included in factory expenses. The following are some of the items so included:

1. Wages paid to indirect workers such as watch and ward staff, repair gangs, foremen, etc.
2. Works Manager's salary and fees paid to directors devoting their attention to production problems.
3. Works' canteen and welfare expenses.
4. Contribution to any social security schemes such as the Employees' State Insurance Corporation.
5. Provident fund contributions by the employer.
6. Carriage inward on materials purchased, if such carriage has not been included in the cost of materials.
7. Materials of small value whose accounts are not kept.
8. Buying and storekeeping expenses including value of normal losses.
9. Normal idle time wages of direct workers if this has not been charged out to jobs through inflation of wage rates.
10. Factory rent and rates.
11. Insurance of factory premises, plant, etc.
12. Factory lighting and heating.
13. Power and fuel (coal, gas, electricity, etc.), Motive power.
14. Depreciation on plant and machinery, tools, factory premises and repair of these.
15. Works stationery and cost of works telephone.
16. Cost of training of new workers.
17. Internal transportation (Haulage)
18. Drawing office expenses.
19. Stores expenses including salaries of store keeper.
20. Works telephone expenses.

Collection of Factory Overheads

The process of ascertaining the amount of overheads for a period is called "*collection of overheads*". The process may involve dealing with actual figures as already passed through accounts or recorded on documents or with estimates. Essentially, it means ascertaining the amount for the various items listed above department by department and then consolidating them suitably. It helps in the task if the various accounts are suitably coded—the code should be such as to permit both analysis and consolidation.

Coding: The proper way for coding is to allot one digit for the main classification, another one or two digits for subclassification and another one or two digits for the account head proper. Suppose factory overheads are allotted the digit 1 and the following sub-classifications and account heads are allotted digits as under :

Sub-classification		*Account heads*	
Stores Overheads	01	Salaries	11
Labour Overheads	02	Provident Fund	12
Machine Overheads	03	Employees' State Insurance Premium	13
General Administration (Factory)	04	Rent	14
		Lighting	15
		Insurance	16
		Power	17
		Stores	18

The code for salaries in respect of general factory administration will be 10411 and for salaries paid in stores department 10111; similarly rent paid for factory canteen will be 10214. Such a code enables one to ascertain the total of any expense (by its type) or the total of expenses under any sub-classification. For instance, the total of all accounts begining with the figure 1 will give the total of factory overheads and if the total of general factory administration overheads is desired, all accounts whose second and third figures are 04 should be listed and totalled.

Standing Orders: These indicate the general authority to incur expenses of a regular nature (rent, salaries, etc.) so that management action is necessary only when an additional amount is to be spent. Standing Order numbers is the same as the code meant for accounts representing regular expenses.

Estimation: It has already been pointed out that the proper system of ascertaining cost is that of continuous costing, *i.e.*, ascertaining the cost of production as and when the work is proceeding. This necessitates the estimation of indirect expenses even before a period of time begins. For example, the indirect expenses for the month of August must be estimated before this month begins. An estimate can be prepared either on the basis of actual figures of, say, August of the previous year or on the basis of the preceding June. However, the estimate must not be prepared blindly. If the actual indirect expenses for the month of August, 1996 were ₹. 14,000, it cannot be said that the expenses for August 1997 also will be ₹. 14,000. This is because of the fact that expenses differ in their nature.

Departmentalisation of Factory Overheads

Usually a big factory is divided into a number of departments in order to facilitate work and supervision. Departmentalisation also helps in the estimation of indirect expenses. We may, if we like, try to estimate the expenses for the whole factory first and then apportion them among the departments and then among products. But if we have departments, the better plan would be to try to estimate expenses department-wise as far as possible. Even if a factory is not officially divided into departments, the Cost Accountant may divide it into imaginary departments for his own purpose. For example, he may try to estimate expenses connected with every big machine or a group of machines or men that there may be. Such imaginary departments are known as "*cost centres*"[1]. Cost centres are homogeneous and are adopted if a department is too big and contains heterogeneous factors.

One big *advantage of departmentalisation*, in addition to easier estimation, is that a different but proper method of cost may be followed for each department. In a foundry, for instance, the melting of metal demands single or output cost whereas other operations may demand multiple costs. Another main advantage is control. If expenses are ascertained department-wise, separately for those that are incurred directly and for those that are allocated, individual responsibility for expenses may be fixed.

Some of the factory or works expenses are confined to a department and are independent of other departments. We can, therefore, arrive at the figure for each department separately and this will be more accurate than if we estimate all the expenses of the factory together and then apportion them to various departments. Examples of such expenses as can be separately and directly estimated for each department are :

(1) *Wages paid to indirect workers:* Each department is likely to have its separate complement of indirect workers and hence estimates department-wise will be more accurate.

(2) *Normal idle time wages:* Each department will know separately its own proportion of normal idle time to total time. This will differ from department to department.

(3) *Contributions to provident fund or any social security schemes.*

(4) *Depreciation and repairs of plant and machinery:* Estimate for each department individually in respect of depreciation and repairs and maintenance will be better because, as will be pointed out later, these expenses will be estimated machine by machine.

(5) *Insurance of plant and machinery.*

Quite a few expenses, however, will not be incurred by the departments separately but will be incurred by the *factory as a whole*. There is no option but to estimate such expenses for the whole factory and then to allocate them to departments. Such expenses are 'allocated' in the following manner: (The word 'allocate' should be used when the basis is exact, if it is only an estimate, the word used should be appropriate.

(1) *Works canteen and welfare expenses* should be allocated according to the number of workers benefited.

(2) *Works manager's salary and fees paid to technical directors* should be allocated according to estimated time devoted to each department.

---

1 *Cost Centre* : "A location, person, or item of equipment (or group of these) for which costs may be ascertained and used for the purposes of cost control."

Impersonal Cost Centre : "A cost centre which consists of a location of items of equipment or group of these."

Personal Cost Centre : "A cost centre which consists of a person or group of persons."

Operation Cost Centre : "A cost centre which consists of machines and/or persons carrying out similar operations."

Process Cost Centre : "A cost centre which consists of a specific process or a continuous sequence of operations." [*CIMA*]

Note : Cost centre has been discussed in the first chapter.

(3) *Factory rent and rates, depreciation and repairs and insurance of factory premises* should be allocated according to floor space occupied by each department taking into account any specially advantageous area occupied by a department.

(4) *Fuel and power* should be allocated according to the metered consumption or according to the horse power of machinery installed in the various departments. Steam is best allocated according to horse power. This is because enough steam will generally be generated to run, if necessary, all the machines and if a machine does not run, a corresponding quantity of steam goes waste.

(5) *Factory lighting* is allocated according to number of points in each department or, if possible, according to separated meter readings.

(6) *Carriage inward on materials purchased, storekeeping expenses, buying expenses and normal losses of materials* are best allocated according to the value of materials used in each department.

(7) *Materials of small value, stationery or other sundries* will have to be allocated as best can be according to the judgment of the Works Manager.

The basis of allocation has been summarised in the following table:

Overhead Cost	*Basis of Apportionment*
1. Depreciation and insurance on plant, machinery and building.	Capital value or Floor area occupied.
2. Rent, rates, lighting and maintenace of building.	Floor area occupied.
3. Canteen exps. Time keeping Exps. labour welfare exps.	Number of employees.
4. Electricity Lighting.	Light Point or Floor area or hours of use or separate meter reading or number of workers.
5. Electric Power.	Horse power of machine or machine hours or Horse Power X machine hours.
6. Steam.	Consumption of steam.
7. Material handling, storekeeping.	Weight of materials of each department.
8. Factory Management and supervision expenses, research and development etc.	Labour Hours or Machine Hours.
9. Supervision.	Number of workmen or Amount of wages.
10. Delivery Exps.	Weight, volume, Distance.
11. Others	Direct wage/Labour Hours or Miscellaneous.

Illustration 3: Ashok Ltd. is having four departments, Departments *X*, *Y* and *Z* are producing departments and '*S*' is service department. The expenditures for the whole concern during a period are :

	₹.
Rent	4,000
Depreciation	1,800
Repairs	2,400
Light	400
Insurance (Stock)	2,000
Supervision	6,000
Employees State Insurance	600
Power	3,600

The following particulars are available in respect of four departments :

	X	Y	Z	S
Area (Sqr.ft)	150	110	90	50
No. of workers	24	16	12	8
Total wages	8,000	6,000	4,000	2,000
Value of Plant	48,000	36,000	24,000	12,000
Value of Stock	30,000	18,000	12,000	—

Apportion the above expenditures to the various departments on the most suitable method.

Solution:

Apportionment of Expenditure

Expenditures	*Basis*	*Departments*			
		X	Y	Z	S
Rent	Area	1500	1100	900	500
Depreciation	Value of plant	720	540	360	180
Repairs	Value of plant	960	720	480	240
Light	Area	150	110	90	50
Insurance	Value of stock	1000	600	400	—
Supervision	No. of workers	2400	1600	1200	800
E.S.I.	Wages	240	180	120	60
Power	Value of plant	1440	1080	720	360
	Total	8,410	5,930	4,270	2,190

[Note: Power is apportioned on the basis of value of plant.]

Production and Service Departments

Departments can be divided into two broad categories namely, production departments and service departments. Service departments are those which enable other departments to work. Production departments are concerned directly with the production of goods. For example, in a cotton textile mill carding, spinning, weaving and finishing departments will be known as production departments. But the boiler room, the transport department and repair and maintenance departments will be known as service departments. For ascertaining the expenses of each department, first of all no distinction is made between the production and service departments. But after finding out the cost of service departments, the total of each service department is apportioned to the production departments. For example, the cost of running the boiler room will be apportioned to production departments in the ratio of the horse power of machinery installed in each production department. The cost of repairs and maintenance department may be apportioned in two ways—either the cost of each repair job undertaken may be found out and the total cost of the repairs and maintenance departments apportioned on the basis of actual service rendered or the cost is charged to different departments on the basis of running hours of various machines. The cost of transport department will be apportioned on the basis of quantity of goods handled on behalf of each department.

Apportioning of Service Department Costs to Production Departments

It has been pointed out above that, though at first expenses of running the two types of departments are tabulated separately, ultimately the service department costs have to be spread over the various production departments. It is only then that the overheads can be charged to production.

One must remember that service is often rendered by one service department to another; the process of apportionment really demands that expenses of a particular service department should be ascertained including the proper share of other service department expenses. It is called secondary distribution of overhead cost.

Basis for Apportioning Service Department Expenses

It is commonly thought that service department expenses should be apportioned to production departments on the basis of *benefit derived by the latter*. This may be capable of being measured exactly, for example, recording the number of units of electricity consumed by each department. However, often it is not capable of exact measurement; it is not easy, for instance, to know exactly the time devoted by the works manager and his staff to the various departments. In such a case, the expenses concerned are apportioned on the basis of an estimate of the benefit derived by the production departments. This method may be called "*survey basis*" as against the method which involves exact measurement.

There is the possibility of apportioning service department expenses not on the basis of service rendered but on the basis of *ability to pay*. This means that first the difference between the market value of the goods produced by a department and the expenses incurred in the department should be ascertained; the "difference" may be termed "*contribution*". Service department expenses may then be apportioned according to the contribution of each department.

Yet another basis can be what *Blocker* calls the incentive basis. Under this method in the beginning of period and amount by way of overheads is charged to a department (on the basis of past experience and estimates). The department is then encouraged to lessen the burden of overheads per unit of output by increasing the output.

It is considered that the proper basis for apportioning service department expenses is service (measured exactly or estimated) rendered to the production departments—that seems to be the implication of ascertaining the cost of running a production department.

The various basis commonly used for this purpose are summarised below:

Service Department Cost	*Basis of Apportionment*
1. Storekeeping Department.	No. of requisitions received from each department or value or quantity of materials issued to each department.
2. Maintenance Department.	Hours worked for each department or actual services utilised if records are maintained by each department.
3. Payroll or Time Keeping Department.	No. of employees or labour hours of each department.
4. Personnel Department.	No. employees or Rate of Labour Turnover of each department.
5. Purchase Department.	Value of materials purchased or number of purchase orders of each department.
6. Welfare canteen etc.	Number of employees of each departments.
7. Internal Transport Services etc.	Weight or value of products of each department or distance covered in each department.
8. Building Service Department.	Area of each department.
9. Fire Protection Department.	Capital value.
10. Inspection Department.	Inspection hours spent.

Direct Material and Direct Labour Cost of Service Department

Service departments have only indirect costs which are to be absorbed by production departments. Direct Material and Direct Labour related to service department will also become indirect because total expenses of service departments are apportioned to production department.

Methods of Apportionment of Service Department Overheads

(*a*) **Step-ladder Method:** Under this method, expenses of one service department (generally the one which received the least service and gives the maximum service from and to other service departments) are apportioned to all other departments in the proportion of benefit derived by them; then expenses of the next service department are apportioned to the remaining departments and so on till expenses of all service departments are dealt with.

Illustration 4: For a period, the expenses in the various departments of a factory were as follows:

	₹.		₹.
Service Departments:		Production Departments:	
Canteen	1,000	Cutting and Shaping	6,000
Repairs and Maintenance	2,500	Machining	4,000
Power House	3,000	Assembly	2,000

The expenses are to be apportioned as follows:

	Repairs and Maintenance	*Power House*	*Cutting and Shopping*	*Machining*	*Assembly*
Canteen	10%	20%	20%	25%	25%
Repairs and Maintenance		20%	30%	30%	20%
Power House			40%	45%	15%

Ascertain the expenses of the production departments.

Solution:

	Service Deptts.			*Production Deptt.*		
	Canteen ₹	*Repairs and Maintenance* ₹	*Power House* ₹	*Cutting and Shaping* ₹.	*Machining* ₹	*Assembly* ₹
Expenses as given	1,000	2,500	3,000	6,000	4,000	2,000
Canteen Expenses		100	200	200	250	250
Repairs and Maintenance		2,600	520	780	780	520
Power House			3,720	1,488	1,674	558
Total				8,468	6,704	3,328

Illustration 5: There are three production departments in a factory viz. Turning, Milling and Grinding. The factory also keeps four service departments *viz.* Stores, Planning, Canteen and Time Office. Departmental overheads for the month of November 2003 are as under :

Production Depts.		*Service Depts.*	
Turning	₹. 48,000	Stores	₹. 18,000
Milling	₹. 52,000	Planning	₹. 24,000
Grinding	₹. 72,000	Canteen	₹. 30,000
		Time Office	₹. 12,000

The overheads of stores are to be apportioned on a percentage basis that is 20 per cent and 40 per cent and 40 per cent to Turning. Milling and Grinding respectively. The expenses of planning are to be apportioned on the basis of machine hours worked *viz.* Turning 5,000 hours, Milling 8,000 hours and Grinding 11,000 hours. The expenses of Canteen and Time office are to be apportioned according to number of workers employed in each production department *i.e.* 22 : 32 : 46.

Prepare a statement showing the apportionment of overheads of service departments to the production departments.

Solution:

Apportionment of Overheads of Service Departments

Service departments overheads	*Basis*	*Total*	*Production Departments*		
			Turning	*Milling*	*Grinding*
		₹.	₹.	₹.	₹.
Departmental Overheads	—	1,72,000	48,000	52,000	72,000
Stores	Agreed Percentage	18,000	3,600	7,200	7,200
Planning	Machine Hours	24,000	5,000	8,000	11,000
Canteen	No. of workers	30,000	6,600	9,600	13,800
Time office	No. of workers	12,000	2,640	3,840	5,520
		2,56,000	65,840	80,640	1,09,520

Illustration 6: Company's costing books for the year ended 30th June, 2004 furnish the following information:

Item	*Production Departments*			*Office*	*Stores*	*Workshop*
	P_1	P_2	P_3			
	₹.	₹.	₹.	₹.	₹.	₹.
Wages	20,000	25,000	30,000	10,000	10,000	5,000
Material	30,000	35,000	45,000	—	—	5,000
Indirect Wages	3,000	3,000	4,000	—	—	—
Indirect Material	2,000	3,000	3,000	—	—	—
Other Information :						
Area in Sq. metres	200	250	300	150	100	250
Book Value of Machinery	₹. 30,000	35,000	25,000			15,000
H.P. of machines	15	20	25			5
Machine Hours worked	10,000	20,000	15,000			5,000

General Expenses:	₹.	
Rent	12,500	
Insurance	1,050	
Depreciation	15%	of the value of machinery
Power	3,800	
Light	1,250	
Stationery	3,000	(to be apportioned between Office & Stores in the ratio of 2:1)

The total of office expenses are to be apportioned equally over the other departments. Afterwards the stores expenses are to be apportioned on the basis of total materials consumed and workshop expenses on the basis of direct wages, using the step-ladder system. Prepare a statement to show the overhead expenses of each production department and ascertain the relationship between direct wages and total overheads in each case.

Solution:

Statement showing Total Overheads For Each Department

Item	*Basis*	*Overheads Total* ₹	*Production Departments* P_1 ₹	P_2 ₹	P_3 ₹	*Service Departments* *Office* ₹	*Stores* ₹	*Workshop* ₹
Direct Wages	Actual					10,000	10,000	5,000
Direct Material	,,					—	—	5,000
Indirect Wages	,,	10,000	3,000	3,000	4,000	—	—	—
Indirect Material	,,	8,000	2,000	3,000	3,000	—	—	—
Rent	Space	12,500	2,000	2,500	3,000	1,500	1,000	2,500
Insurance	Book value of Machine	1,050	300	350	250	—		150
Depreciation	,,	15,750	4,500	5,250	3,750	—		2,250
Power	HP × Hrs worked	3,800	600	1,600	1,500			100
Light	Space	1,250	200	250	300	150	100	250
Stationary	Office 2 Stores 1	3,000	—	—	—	2,000	1,000	—
Total		85,350	12,600	15,950	15,800	13,650	12,100	15,250
Office	Equally		2,730	2,730	2,730	(13,650)	2,730	2,730
Stores	Total Materials		3,858	4,581	5,788		(14,830)	603
Workshop	Direct Wages		4,955	6,194	7,434			(18,583)
Total			24,143	29,455	31,752			
Percentage on Direct Wages			120.72%	117.82%	105.84%			

Note: Direct wages and Direct materials of service departments are treated as overheads.

(*b*) **Inter-service departmental mutual allocation system (Simultaneous Equation Method):** The method given above assumes that service is rendered by say, Repairs and Maintenance department to the Power House but not by the latter to the former. This assumption is not valid since service departments not only render service to production departments but also mutually. This fact should be considered while apportioning expenses. An algebraical equation will be needed to ascertain the true expenses of a service department in such cases. Suppose a factory has two production departments. *A* and *B*, and two service departments *X* and *Y*; the expenses of departments *X* and *Y* are respectively ₹. 3,000 and 2,000 and are to be apportioned as:

	A	*B*	*X*	*Y*
X	40%	50%	...	10%
Y	50%	30%	20%	...

In this case the expenses of department *X* (say *X*) are ₹. 3,000 plus 20% or 1/5 of expenses of department *Y* (say *Y*) and expenses of department *Y* are ₹. 2,000 + 10% of *X*. The two equations are :

$$X = 3{,}000 + \frac{1}{5}Y$$

$$Y = 2{,}000 + \frac{1}{10}X$$

$$Y = 2{,}000 + \frac{1}{10}\left(3{,}000 + \frac{1}{5}Y\right) \text{ (substituting the value of } X)$$

$$= 2{,}000 + 300 + \frac{1}{50}Y$$

$$= 2{,}300 \times \frac{1}{50}Y$$

$50Y = 1{,}15{,}000 + Y$ (multiplying both sides by 50)

$49Y = 1{,}15{,}000$

$Y = 2{,}347$

$X = 3{,}000 + \frac{1}{5} \times 2{,}347 = 3{,}000 + 469 = 3{,}469$

Expenses of departments X and Y can now be apportioned to production departments, as follows:

			A		*B*	
Department	X (₹. 3,469)	₹.	1,388	(40%)	1,735	(50%)
"	Y (₹. 2,347)		1,173	(50%)	704	(30%)
	Total		2,561		2,439	

The total for the two departments comes to ₹. 5,000 which is also the total of the expenses of the two service departments as originally given.

***Illustration** 7:* You are supplied with the following information and required to work out the production hour rate recovery of overhead in departments *A, B* and *C* reapportioning service department expenses by simultaneous equation method as well as by repeated distribution method.

		Production Deptt.			*Service Deptt.*	
Particulars	*Total* ₹	*A* ₹	*B* ₹	*C* ₹	*P* ₹	*Q* ₹
Rent	12,000	2,400	4,800	2,000	2,000	800
Electricity	4,000	800	2,000	500	400	300
Indirect Labour	6,000	1,200	2,000	1,000	800	1,000
Depreciation	5,000	2,500	1,600	200	500	200
Sundries	4,500	910	2,143	847	300	300
Estimated	31,500	7,810	12,543	4,547	4,000	2,600
Working Hours		1,000	2,500	1,400		

Expenses of service departments *P* and *Q* are apportioned as under :

	A	*B*	*C*	*P*	*Q*
P	30%	40%	20%	—	10%
Q	10%	20%	50%	20%	—

Solution: Total overheads of various departments :

Total	*A*	*B*	*C*	*P*	*Q*
31,500	7,810	12,543	4,547	4,000	2,600

True overheads of service departments *P* and *Q* can be computed by simultaneous equation method. We should presume that X is the total overheads of *P* deptt. and Y is the total overheads of *Q* deptt. then

$$X = ₹.\ 4000 + 20/100\ Y \text{ or } ₹.\ 4000 + .20Y$$

$$Y = ₹.\ 2600 + 10/100\ X \text{ or } ₹.\ 2600 + .10X$$

After rearranging the equation, and multiplying by 10.

$$10X - 2Y = 40{,}000 \quad ...(1)$$

$$-X + 10Y = 26{,}000 \quad ...(2)$$

Multiplying equation (1) by 5 and adding it to (2)

$$50X - 10Y = 2{,}00{,}000$$

$$-X + 10Y = 26{,}000$$

$$49X = 2{,}26{,}000$$

$$X = ₹.\ 4{,}612.25$$

By substituting this value in equation (1) we have

$$10 \times 4{,}612.25 - 2Y = 40{,}000$$

$$-2Y = -6{,}122.50 \text{ or } Y = 3{,}061.25$$

Distribution of Overheads of Service Deptts.

Particulars	*Total* ₹	*A* ₹	*B* ₹	*C* ₹	*P* ₹	*Q* ₹
Overheads:	31,500	7,810	12,543	4,547	4,000	2,600
Apportionment of true overheads of P ₹. 4612 in given proportion *i.e.* 30 : 40 : 20 : Nil : 10		1,384	1,845	922	–4,612	461
Apportionment of true overheads of *Q* ₹. 3061 in given proportion *i.e.* 10: 20 : 50 : 20 : Nil		306	612	1531	612	–3061
Total	31,500	9500	15000	7000	—	—
Estimated working Hours		1000	2500	1400		
Rate per Hour (₹.)		9.50	6.00	5.00		

(*c*) **"Cycles" Methods or Repeated Distribution Method:** Instead of having an algebraic equation, the expenses of one service department may be apportioned to all other departments (production as well as service) and then the expenses of other service departments may be similarly treated until the amount apportioned to a service department becomes insignificant. Then the service departments may be ignored for apportioning the expenses. The figures in the illustration given in the begining under simultaneous equation method may be treated as below:

	Departments			
	A ₹	*B* ₹	*X* ₹	*Y* ₹
Total amount	?	?	3,000	2,000
Expenses of Deptt. *X*	1,200	1,500	(3000)	300
Expenses of Deptt. *Y* (₹. 2,300)	1,150	690	460	(2300)
Expenses of Deptt. *X*	184	230	(460)	46
Expenses of Deptt. Y (Ratio 5 : 3)	29	17		(46)
	2,563	2,437		

It may be noted that in the last step expenses of department *Y* have been apportioned between *A* and *B* in the ratio of 5:3 and nothing is apportioned to *X* since this would not have substantially increased the accuracy of the work. It will be seen that in all there are four steps or cycles in the working given above.

Illustration 8: Solve previous illustration according to 'Repeated Distribution Method'.

Distribution under Repeated Distribution Method and Computation of Rate per Hour

Particulars		*Production Deptt.*			*Service Deptt.*	
	Total ₹	*A* ₹	*B* ₹	*C* ₹	*P* ₹	*Q* ₹
Overheads	31,500	7,810	12,543	4,547	4,000	2,600
Apportionment of true overheads of *P* in given ratio		1,200	1,600	800	(4,000)	400
					Nil	3,000
Apportionment of overheads of *Q* in given ratio		300	600	1500	600	(3000)
					600	Nil

Overheads of *P* further apportioned		180	240	120	(600)	60
					Nil	60
Overheads of *Q* further					12	(60)
apportioned		6	12	30	12	Nil
Overheads of *P* further apportioned	—	4	5	3	(12)	—
					Nil	Nil
Total	31,500	9,500	15,000	7,000		
Estimated working hours		1,000	2,500	1,400		
Rate per Hour (₹.)		9.50	6.00	5.00		

Illustration 9: You are given the following information in respect of overheads in a factory:

Production Deptts		*Service Deptts.*	
A's overheads	₹. 7,810	*X*'s overheads	₹. 4,000
B's ,,	₹. 12,543	*Y*'s "	₹. 2,600
C's ,,	₹. 4,547		

Expenses of Service Departments *X* and *Y* are apportioned as under :

	A	*B*	*C*	*X*	*Y*
X	30%	40%	20%	—	10%
Y	10%	20%	50%	20%	—

Apportion the overheads of Service Depts. to Production Depts.

Solution:

Apportionment of Overheads of Service Depts.

	Total	*Production Depts.* *A*	*B*	*C*	*X*	*Y*
Total overheads.	31,500	7,810	12,543	4,547	4,000	2,600
Apportionment of overheads of *X* Dept.	—	1,200	1,600	800	– 4,000	400
Apportionment of overheads of	31,500	9,010	14,143	5,347	—	3,000
Y Dept.	—	300	600	1,500	600	(3,000)
Apportionment of overheads of	31,500	9,310	14,743	6,847	600	—
X Dept.	—	180	240	120	(600)	60
Apportionment of overheads of	31,500	9,490	14,983	6,967	—	60
Y Dept.	—	6	12	30	12	(60)
Apportionment of overheads of	31,500	9,496	14,995	6,997	12	—
X Dept.	—	4	5	3	(12)	—
	31,500	9,500	15,000	7,000	—	—

(*d*) *Trial and Error Method:* In this method the overheads of each service department is allocated only to other service department in the given basis or ratio. Thus true overhead cost of each service department is ascertained. Thereafter these are distributed to production department.

Some Important Factory Overheads

(1) Depreciation

Depreciation[1] means the diminution in value due to age and other contributory cases, viz. wear and tear. This term should be distinguished from upkeep which means carrying out the repairs necessary to keep the machine in working order. In order that correct cost of production be ascertained and that the value of an asset be stated in the balance sheet at its proper figure, it is necessary to write off a reasonable amount of depreciation of plant and machinery and all other assets which are liable to wear and tear. An adequate provision for depreciation is important from financial point of view, too, inasmuch as this makes available sufficient funds for replacing the machinery when it is no longer serviceable.

The proper determination or depreciation is most important as any error in calculation may render both factory cost and profit inexact. Naturally, the conditions prevailing in any particular business must bear on the proper determination of its depreciation figure, and no hard and fast rule can be laid down. The principles underlying depreciation are, however, well marked out and agreed upon.

Methods of Calculating Depreciation

(*a*) **Straight Line Method:** "The method providing for depreciation by means of equal periodic charges over the assumed life of the assets." In costing, depreciation is best dealt with on the system of fixed instalment which is determined by taking into consideration the estimated life of the machinery and its scrap value at the end of its life. Due to risks of obsolescence,[2] a piece of machinery may become useless, or may have to be sold at much loss, much earlier than its natural life. A machine may run 15 years if we are adamant on using it, but if we expect that at the end of 10 years a new and better machine will be available, the machine should be depreciated over a period of 10 years and not 15 years. If the purchase price of the machine is, save ₹. 10,000 and its scrap value at the end of 10 years is ₹. 500, the annual depreciation will be ₹. 950, *i.e.*, ₹. (10,000–500)/10.

(*b*) **Production Hour Method:** "The method of providing for depreciation by means of a fixed rate per hour of production calculated. by dividing the value of the asset by the estimated number of working hours of its life." This method is only a variation of the straight line method. In this case the life of the machine is estimated in terms of hours for which it is expected to be used. Dividing the cost (minus scrap value) by the total number of hours, depreciation per running hour will be ascertained. If, in the above example, the total number of hours for all ten years is expected to be 18,000, the depreciation per hour will be 9,500/18,000 or 53 paise per hours.

The advantage of the above two methods is that from year to year the charge for depreciation will be the same and not different. This is so because in terms of output the service of the machine is uniform over its entire life. But we should remember that the total charge in respect of machinery is depreciation plus repairs without which machinery will not remain serviceable. In order to maintain uniformity of charge in respect of machinery, we shall have to estimate the total amount to be spent on repairs of machine in question during its life and divide it by the number of years

1 "The diminution in the value of a fixed asset due to the use and/or lapse of time." (*CIMA*)

2 *Obsolescence:* "The loss in the value of an asset due to its becoming out of date at an earlier date than was foreseen." (*I.C.M.A.*)

of its estimated life. This is because in the earlier years repairs are negligible and in later years they are very heavy. Thus, if we expect that the total amount to be spent by way of repairs will be ₹. 1,000 in all the ten years, the annual charge in respect of the machine will be ₹. 1,050 (₹. 950 for depreciation plus ₹. 100 annually for repairs).

(*c*) **Repair Provision Method:** "The method of providing for an aggregate of depreciation and maintenance cost by means of periodic charges each of which is a constant proportion of the aggregate of the cost of the asset depreciated and the expected maintenance cost during its life."

Under this method the cost of the repairs to be effected throughout the life of the asset is estimated and is added to the cost of the asset. The total amount (as reduced by the estimated scrap value) is divided by the estimated life to give a comprehensive charge both in respect of depreciation and repairs and maintenance. The method makes for uniformity of charge year by year—this is the proper thing to do if the service rendered by the asset is also uniform over the life of the asset.

(*d*) **Reducing Balance Method:** "The method of providing for depreciation by means of periodic charges calculated as a constant proportion of the balance of the value of the asset after deducting the amounts previously provided."

In this method, depreciation is calculated by applying a fixed percentage to the value of the asset in the books as it diminishes year by year. Suppose, an asset is acquired for ₹. 50,000 and depreciation is to be provided at 20 per cent. The amount will be ₹. 10,000 in the first year and ₹. 8,000 in the second year, *i.e.*, 20 per cent of ₹. 50,000 less ₹. 10,000 written off already. The amount of depreciation will go on diminishing and the asset value cannot be completely exhausted under this method.

The amount written off will be the heaviest in the first year which recognises the fact that an asset loses much of its value as soon as it is put to use—it becomes second hand. Also, repairs will be light in the beginning but will go on increasing yearly—the total of the amount spent on repairs and that written off as depreciation will be more or less uniform over the life of the asset, which is as it should be since the cost of using an asset consists really of the two.

It should be noted that the percentage of the asset to be written off under this method will be nearly three times the percentage in case of the Straight Line Method, if the asset is to be written off within the same period.

(*e*) **Sum of the Digits Method:** "The method providing for depreciation by means of differing periodic rates computed according to the following formula;

If '*n*' is the estimated life of the asset, the rate is calculated each period as a fraction in which the denominator is always the sum of the series 1, 2, 3... *n* and the numerator for the first period is *n*, for the second *n* – 1, and so on."

The total amount to be written off in respect of any asset is, of course, the cost less its estimated scrap value. Under this method the amount to be written off each year is calculated as follows:

$$\text{Amount to be written off} \times \frac{\text{The number of years of the remaining life of the asset (including the current year)}}{\text{The total of all the degits representing the life of the asset (in years)}}$$

Suppose the life of an asset is estimated at 10 years. The total of all the digits 1 to 10 is 55. The depreciation to be written off in the first year will be 10/55 of the cost of the asset less its scrap value and, in the second year, 9/55 of this figure will be written off and so on.

The method has the same advantages and disadvantages as the Reducing Balance Method.

(*f*) **Production Unit Method or Depletion Method:** "The method of providing for depreciation by means of a fixed rate per unit of production calculated by dividing the value of the asset by the estimated number of units to be produced during its life".

Under this method, depreciation is calculated by the formula :

$$\frac{\text{Cost of the asset less its estimated scarp value}}{\text{Number of units expected to be produced during the whole life of the asset}}$$

Suppose a machine whose cost is ₹. 50,000 will produce a total of 1,50,000 units of goods, the scrap value being estimated at ₹. 2,000. The depreciation per unit of output will be 32P, *i.e.*, (50,000 – 2,000)/150000. If in the first year, 20,000 units are produced, the depreciation to be written off will be ₹. 6,400, *i.e.*, 20,000 × 32P; the amount will be ₹. 4,800 in the second year if output that year is 15,000 units. This method is useful if passage of time does not affect the useful life of the asset or if it is to be worked so intensively that it will be fully depreciated much before any danger of obsolescence.

When this method is applied to assets like mines, quarries, etc., it is known as the *Depletion Method*. In the case of a mine, the amount to be written off is with reference to the quantity mined and to the total quantity that is estimated to be available. Per unit of output, the depreciation will be : $\frac{\text{Cost of the mine}}{\text{Total estimated available quantity of minerals}}$. For a particular year, the depreciation will be : quantity mined × the rate per unit (as calculated above).

(*g*) **Revaluation Method:** "The method of providing for depreciation by means of periodic charges each of which is equivalent to the difference between the values assigned to the asset at the beginning and at the end of the period."

This method is useful for calculating depreciation of assets like loose tool, livestock, etc., which are not subject to regular rates of depreciation. At the end of each year, the asset concerned is valued and if the value is less than the book value, the difference is written off as depreciation. Appreciation in value is unlikely. If it is there it is likely to be because of a rise in prices; it is better ignored.

(*h*) **Annuity Method:** "The method of providing for depreciation by means of periodic charges, each of which is a constant proportion of the aggregate of the cost of the asset depreciated and interest at a given rate per period on the written down values of the asset at the beginning of each period."

This method takes into consideration the interest lost by acquiring the asset; the depreciation to be written off totals not only the cost of the asset but also the interest. Each year, interest is added to the book value of the asset as in the beginning of the year at the rate which the firm consider proper. The amount to be written off is the same every year and is ascertained from Annuity Tables. The interest added to the value of the asset is a notional charge only and is credited to the Profit and Loss Account. Most cost accountants do not include interest in overheads (see page 126 below for a discussion on the subject) and hence this method of providing depreciation may not be suitable for costing purposes.

(*i*) **Sinking Fund Method:** "The method of providing for depreciation by means of fixed periodic charges which, aggregated with compound interest over the life of the asset, would equal the cost of that asset. Simultaneously with each periodic charge, an investment of the same amount would be made in fixed interest securities which would accumulate at compound interest to provide, at the end of the life of the asset, a sum equal to its cost."

This method is used to ensure that at the time the useful life of the asset is over, ready funds will be available to replace it. The process is:

(*i*) each year an amount is provided by debit to Depreciation Account and credit to Depreciation Fund Account;

(*ii*) an amount equal to that mentioned in (*i*) above and (*iii*) below is invested in readily saleable securities, the account being named as Depreciation Fund Investment Account;

(*iii*) interest, received each year on the investments made, is credited to the Depreciation Fund Account—the amount is reinvested along with the annual depreciation;

(*iv*) at the end of the life of the asset, investments are sold to provide the funds for replacement of the asset; and

(*v*) the old asset is written off against the credit balance in the Depreciation Fund Account.

The amount to be provided each year will be ascertained from Sinking Fund Tables on the basis of the expected rate of interest and the period over which the fund is to be built up. This method is suitable in financial accounting since building up funds is a function with which a cost accountant is not really concerned.

(*j*) **Endowment Policy Method:** "The method of providing for depreciation by means of fixed periodic charges equivalent to the premiums on an endowment policy for the amount required to provide, at the end of the life of the asset, a sum equal to its cost."

This method is roughly the same as the Sinking Fund method. The differences are that arrangements are made with an insurance company which agrees to pay a fixed sum of money at the end of stated period in return for an annual premium. The annual premium then becomes the amount to be provided for as depreciation each year. This method also concerns the financial accountant and not the cost accountant.

Continued use of asset after it is written off. It may happen sometimes that a machine which has been completely written off is still in use, *i.e.*, the estimated life of the machine may be over but due to good repairs and maintenance or non-availability of new machines, the machine is still being used. As far as financial accounts are concerned there will be no need to write off any depreciation after the estimated life is over, but that cannot be the case in costing. Any use of machine after their estimated life is over is an abnormality and we should always separate the effect of abnormal factors just as we do in case of abnormal loss of materials or abnormal idle time. The normal feature of business is that for manufacture of goods machines are used and their depreciation charged to the cost of production. We should continue to charge normal depreciation to the cost of production even if no value stands in books against the particular machine used, otherwise the results will not be comparable with those of past years or future years (when new machinery will be bought and used) or those of similar other concerns and we shall have an exaggerated idea of our efficiency. The credit in respect of the 'depreciation' will go to the Costing Profit and Loss Account. It is a notional charge.

Obsolescence: It can also happen that a machine may have to be discarded before its estimated life is over. This may be due to heavy damage or obsolescence. In such a case, it is desirable that the difference between the book value of the machine in question and what it can realise on sale should be treated as a special loss and written off to the Costing Profit and Loss Account.

Plant Ledger: As has been pointed out, we should keep a record of depreciation and repairs machine by machine. There is a necessity, therefore, for maintaining a 'Plant Ledger' so that particulars of each piece of machinery may be separately available. The form of the Ledger is given below:

PLANT LEDGER

Name of Machine..............................	Data Installed..............................
No. .... Drawing No.	Cost ₹. ....
Department..............................	Estimated
Makers..............................	Scrap Value ₹. ....
Estimated Life .... years	Remarks..............................
Depreciation per year ₹.	....
Repairs per year. (estimated) ₹.	....

Overhauls			*Additions*		
Date	*Amount Spent ₹.*	*Remarks*	*Date*	*Particulars ₹.*	*Amount*

Year Ending.................. Year Ending..................

Date	*Particulars*	*Repairs ₹.*	*Depreciation written off ₹.*	*Date*	*Particulars*	*Repairs ₹.*	*Depreciation written off ₹.*
					Total b/f		
	Total carried forward				Total carried forward		
	Total for the year				Total for the year		

The idea is to have the record for as many years as possible on one card and, therefore, similar ruling for the amount columns will be made on the back also. The total expenditure for each year is carried forward to the next year so that the total expenditure incurred to date in respect of repairs, renewals and maintenance and depreciation may be readily ascertained.

Loose Tools of considerable value should be revalued each year and thus the amount of depreciation ascertained. An average of the amounts written off in the past few years may be taken to be the estimated depreciation on loose tools for the years for which factory expenses are being estimated. Where the tools possess a very short life they may be written off straight way on purchase and included in the factory expenses. Care will have to be taken against pilferage whose chances will increase if no records of the tools bought and in use are kept. A register should be kept to record the issues of tools to various workmen. Costly tools may be issued to workmen like library books.

Pattern, Dies, Moulds, etc., are generally of considerable value and they should be depreciated like a piece of machinery. Generally, there will be no repairs and no scrap value.

(2) Interest

There is a controversy with regard to the inclusion or otherwise of interest in the indirect expenses.

Arguments in favour of inclusion of interest in expenses :

(*a*) Just as for the use of labour wages are paid, so for the use of capital interest is paid. There is no difference between the remuneration of these two factors of production, and while determining the total cost, both wages and interest should be included in the cost of production.

(*b*) Comparison of cost is rendered difficult if no account of interest is taken in businesses where raw materials in different states of readiness can be used. For example, a timber merchant may buy standing trees and season the timber himself, waiting a number of years before he can use or sell it. Another merchant may buy his timber already seasoned and, therefore, ready for use or sale. This merchant will pay a much higher price per unit than in the former case, but in reality both have bought different articles. For the purpose of comparison costs, the former merchant must add interest to his outlay for the period he has to wait.

(*c*) Without inclusion of interest profits on different jobs requiring different amounts of capital or requiring different periods for completion are not comparable. Suppose (1) a job is completed in three months with ₹. 1,000 capital and yields ₹. 150 as profit; (2) another job requiring ₹. 2,500 capital is completed in four months and yields ₹. 200 profit. If interest is charged at 12 per cent, the profit on the first job is reduced to ₹. 120 and on the second job to ₹. 125. Better comparison is possible now.

(*d*) The question whether human labour should be replaced by machinery or whether an existing machine be replaced by a new one cannot be decided without adequate consideration of interest. If it is ignored wrong decision may follow. Suppose 20 workers getting ₹. 500 per month are proposed to be replaced by a machinery costing ₹. 5 lakhs. Suppose the expenses on the machine are :

2 workers @ ₹. 500 p.m.	₹. 1,000
Fuel and Power	500
Insurance	200
Depreciation and repairs	5,000

Total expenses including these items will be ₹. 6,700 which is appreciably lower than ₹. 10,000 (wages of 20 workers at ₹. 500 p.m.). But actually the machinery is costlier because if we allow 9 per cent interest on the money spent on buying the machinery, the monthly interest will be ₹. 3,750 raising the total expenses on machinery to ₹. 10,450 p.m. Some years ago a sugar factory was considering whether lorries should be bought for transport of cane or whether carts should be used for the job. Due to heavy depreciation and interest on money required to buy lorries, carts were found to be cheaper.

(*e*) Cost of articles of considerably different values and, therefore, requiring different amounts of capital cannot be compared without taking interest into account.

(*f*) Heavy and fluctuating stocks require different amounts of capital to maintain and, hence, interest is again required to be considered in determining the cost of maintenance of such stocks.

(*g*) While submitting tenders interest on money required to undertake the job should be taken into account as otherwise a price may be quoted which may leave such a small margin as will be sufficient to pay interest only, leaving no profit.

(*h*) A person having money can invest it in government or other safe securities and get an income without much effort. If he engages in business with that money his gains should normally be higher than the interest he can earn without exerting himself. He should, therefore, include interest in his costs and thus arrive at the true profit which may be considered as his reward for his exertions.

Arguments against the inclusion of interest in expenses are :

(*a*) Payment of interest by a firm depends purely on its financial policies. A firm may work mostly with proprietor's capital in which case the amount of interest paid will be small. Another firm may work mostly with borrowed capital in which case the amount of interest will be heavy. The inclusion of interest will, therefore, mean that the cost of production in the first firm will be lower than in the second firm. Such a comparison will lead to erroneous conclusions in respect of efficiency; cost of production should really reflect the level of efficiency which will not be the case when interest is included. To take another case, suppose a firm in one year works mostly with borrowed money, thus making heavy interest payments, and in the next year repays all the loans and works with its own capital, making no payments for interest. If interest is included, cost of production in the second year will be lower than in the first, leading one to believe that higher efficiency was achieved in the second year. Actually this would be a wrong conclusion; in order to make the results of the two years strictly comparable, interest should be excluded.

This argument can be answered by stating that it is not necessary to include only that amount of interest which is actually paid. We may allow interest on the entire capital—whether it is borrowed or not. In that case there will be difficulty in comparing the cost of production in one year with that of another year or in one firm with that in another.

(*b*) Difficulty arises as regards the amount of capital on which interest should be calculated. Some people advocate that interest should be allowed only on the fixed capital, but there is no reason to exclude working capital. But working capital fluctuates from day-to-day. The difficulty is accentuated if interest has to be allocated to the various departments. Accurate records will have to be kept as regards the capital invested—both fixed and working—in each department from month to month.

(*c*) Difficulty also arises in determining a proper rate of interest. In the market there is a bewildering variety of interest rates which depend on a host of factors such as risk, period of maturity, bank rate, etc. Rates of interest will vary from industry to industry (due to risk being different) and from firm to firm. Then, should we take long-term, medium-term or short-term rates? It will be difficult for a firm to determine a proper rate for itself and for each of its departments.

(*d*) If we allow interest on capital which is not borrowed, we inflate the cost of production to that extent and thus anticipate profits. There will be no difficulty if there is no closing stock. But there is generally a closing stock which will be valued at a figure higher than the cost, if interest is included. This is clearly undesirable. However, reserves can be maintained against the unrealised profit.

Conclusion: It appears that at least on the ground of practical difficulty in calculating the amount of interest, we have to exclude this item from costing records. But we should remember that if we exclude interest we shall have to exclude it altogether—even the amount actually paid. This is because if we include the actual amount paid, the results will not be comparable either with those of other firms or with those of past or future years. On the other hand, if we decide to include interest, we must include interest on the entire capital whether it is borrowed or contributed by the proprietors of the firm. The weight of the argument appears to be in favour of exclusion of interest from Cost Accounts. However, if it is easy to calculate the amount of capital and the rate of interest and if it is general practice in the industry, there would be no objection to the inclusion of interest in expenses.

This is not to say that interest should be excluded from all our calculations. When we have to decide, for example, replacement of human labour by machinery, or quoting for some big contract, we must take into consideration the interest which will have to be paid (if the required funds are to be borrowed) or lost (if funds belonging to the firm are available); otherwise we might find that our decision was wrong.

(3) Rent

Rent, like interest, is payable in certain cases and not so in cases where the premises are owned by the firm. In order to preserve uniformity it is desirable that rent should always be included in expenses even if the premises are the property of the firm. There will be no difficulty to find out the amount in towns where there is a property tax; the municipal authorities will make a survey and fix the annual rental value which can safely be taken as the correct figure for rent.

(4) Royalties

There is no doubt that royalties have to be included in expenses. Royalties based on quantity of output will be part of manufacturing cost as a direct charge and royalties based on sales will form part of selling expenses. This also applies to excise duty.

(5) Repairs

If repairs are carried out by outside firms there will be no difficulty is knowing the amount.

But quite often big manufacturers maintain their own repair staff. In this case, there is need for knowing correctly the amount spent on repairs. For ascertaining the amount, an account for each repair job undertaken will be separately opened under distinctive numbers. The series is known as "Service Orders". The sanction for repairs to be undertaken is given by the Works Manager and then costing is done just as if it were undertaken for some customers. Besides material and labour, a proportionate charge for factory expenses will have to be added and the total will then be included in the factory expenses. An alternative is to charge out to various departments the cost of maintaining repairs and maintenance facilities according to machine hours run. This has better logic behind it because the repairs and maintenance department is meant to keep all machines in good working order. If this department does its job well, the department will often be quite idle. Nevertheless the department must be maintained—it is in the nature of insurance.

(6) Fuel and Power

If electricity is bought from some outside authority, the total charges for the power consumed can be easily ascertained. But many concerns have their own generating stations; and, if steam is used, there will be a boiler house. The amount to be included in factory overheads in such cases as "fuel and power" will comprise materials used, wages of working in the power house and other expenses direct to it, and an equitable share of other overheads such as for general factory administration, stores etc. In short, the power house should be treated as a separate department and the cost of running it compiled as such; the cost should be included in total factory overheads and apportioned to production departments according to the horse power of machinery installed.

ABSORPTION OF FACTORY OVERHEADS

The absorption is allotment of overhead to cost units.

Overheads absorption is usually achieved by the use of one or a combination of overhead 'recovery' rates. The use of this term is somewhat confusing since it may be understood to imply ultimate recovery in selling price which is not necessarily achieved, and for this reason 'absorption' is recommended. (*CIMA*)

A very important task for the purpose of proper costing is the determination of the amount which should be charged to each unit of cost—each product for each job. For example, it is not sufficient to say that the total overheads for a factory for a month are ₹. 10,000. It is also necessary to apportion these ₹. 10,000 over the various products or over the various jobs that are produced or done in the factory during that particular month. It was usual at one time to term the amount thus apportioned to a cost unit as 'oncost', but this term is now not popular. This task is of importance because it is necessary that the amount per unit should be such as to enable the total overheads to be recovered. If, for example, the total of overheads is ₹. 5,000 and the total of the amounts apportioned to individual jobs comes to ₹. 4,000 only, it means that ₹. 1,000 of overheads will not be recovered and the various jobs would be then undercosted. Similarly, it is wrong to apportion such amounts as will lead to very large over-recovery. it must, however, be understood that there will always be a small difference between the actual overheads and the amount recovered (or apportioned to various cost units). This is necessarily due to estimation. It may be noted that the terms recovery and absorption of overheads mean the same thing—the apportionment of overheads to the various cost units, *i.e.*, jobs, products etc.

The task of allocating indirect expenses is easy if there is only one product. What is needed in this case is that the estimated overheads should be divided by the estimated number of units likely to be produced. We shall then get the overheads per unit of output. This approach obviously cannot work when there is a large number of products or different types of jobs. In that case suitable methods have to be followed for the purpose of allotting overheads. Before we discuss the methods, it would be better to know the criteria for judging the suitability of various methods.

Criteria: It goes without saying that the total amount of factory overheads recovered by inclusion in the cost of various jobs of products should be more or less equal to the actual factory expenses for the period concerned. In addition to this, there are *three other points* which must be kept in mind while selecting the system for allotting factory overheads. These points are as follows:

(*a*) *The time taken by various jobs* must be kept in mind. Obviously if a job takes two weeks to complete and another job takes six weeks to complete, the amount of works expenses charged to the second job should be three times the amount charged to the first job, that is if other factors are ignored.

(b) Distinction must be made between *work done by skilled workers and that by unskilled workers*. Normally unskilled workers cause a greater wastage of materials and more wear and tear of machinery and they need greater supervision. Hence work done by unskilled workers should have correspondingly higher proportion of works expenses. What is of importance is that each category of workers requires different sorts of expenses to enable them to work. For example, welders need oxygen gas, acetylene gas, welding rods, fluxes, etc., for their work. But fitters do not require these materials; they work only with simple tools. Therefore, when a welder works there will be larger expense than when a fitter works. Proper absorption of factory expenses demands a consideration of this factor.

(*c*) Work done by manual labour only should obviously not be charged for anything in respect of machine expenses, like depreciation, power, repairs, etc. On the other hand, *work done with the help of machines* should certainly be charged with their full quota of such expenses. It is, therefore, necessary that while allotting factory expenses, a distinction is made between work done by *manual labour and work done on machines*.

Method of Absorption of Factory Overheads

1. **The "Percentage on Materials" or Direct Materials cost basis:** On the basis of estimates or past experience, the percentage of factory overheads to the total value of materials used is determined. On the assumption that for various jobs the relationship between materials and overheads will not change, a charge for these is made to the cost of production of each unit of cost

as such and such proportion of materials used. Suppose total value of materials likely to be used is ₹. 10,00,000 and total factory overheads are ₹. 2,00,000. This shows that factory expenses are 20 per cent of materials Works Overheads/Direct Materials × 100. When we want to find out the cost of any job we add 20 per cent of materials used on that job for factory overheads.

The method is naturally very simple. But unless only one simple product is turned out and unless there is stability in the prices of the materials used, the system *is not a suitable one because* of the following reasons :

(*a*) A perusal of the items that make up factory overheads shows that *only a small part of the factory expenses is connected with materials*. Normal wastage of materials or coal or other sundry small stores used naturally would vary with the value of materials used (in the sense that if prices go up, the amounts for such items would also go up). But for the great bulk of factory overheads, there is no reason to assume any connection between the value of materials used and the factory expenses. Value of materials used will always fluctuate due to price changes. Such changes will not affect such items as wages of indirect workers, rent of factory premises, depreciation and repairs of machinery, etc. We must conlcude, therefore, that there being little logical connection between materials and factory expenses, the system of "percentage on materials" is fundamentally wrong and may lead to seriously wrong results. Suppose, to continue the example given above, in the current year prices go up by 20 per cent so that materials used may amount to ₹. 12,00,000. The total of charge made to various jobs, *etc.*, will then equal to ₹. 2,40,000 (20 per cent on ₹. 12,00,000). As actually factory overheads are likely to remain in the neighbourhood of ₹. 2,00,000; the result of following this method would be to grossly overestimate the cost of each unit.

(*b*) Under this method, *the charge made to a job requiring expensive materials will be heavier than to a job requiring cheap materials*. Since the value of materials used is no indication of the labour and effort involved in making the product or finishing the job (sometimes jobs requiring cheap and inexpensive materials require much greater effort and skill and supervision than job done with expensive materials), the method will over-estimate the cost in some cases and under-estimate the costs in others, (giving a wrong idea of the profitability of each. Consider the two examples given below:

	Job No. 1	*Job No. 2*
	₹	₹
Materials	1,000	200
Labour (one week)	50	50
Prime Cost	1,050	250
Factory Overheads (20% on materials)	200	40
Works Cost	1,250	290
Office Overheads (say 10% on works cost)	125	29
Cost of Production	1,375	319
Net Profit	125	181
Selling Price	1,500	500

At first sight Job No. 2 appears to be more profitable, especially if one considers that smaller capital would be necessary to do it. But it would be a mistake to concentrate on the second type of jobs and give up the first. Both the jobs take one week to complete and hence it is reasonable to suppose that the charge in respect of factory overheads should also be the same for both the jobs. If we debit ₹. 200 to the second job (same as that debited to the first job) the cost of Job No. 2 will go up to ₹. 495, leaving a profit by ₹. 5 only.

(*c*) The system makes no *distinction between jobs done by unskilled workers and those by skilled workers*. Materials do not indicate which type of workers have done the job and hence, under this system, this distinction is ignored.

(*d*) The system also does not distinguish between *jobs done by machine and jobs done by manual labour*. This is so because it is impossible to say on the basis of materials as to which job has been done by manual labour and which by machines.

Illustration 10: The following information relates to the production department of a factory :

Materials used	₹. 40,000
Direct wages	₹. 30,000
Overheads	₹. 20,000

On one order carried out in the department, materials consumed amounted to ₹. 8,000. Find out the overheads chargeable to this order on the basis of Direct Materials.

Solution: Ratio of Overheads to direct Materials

$$= \frac{\text{Overheads} \times 100}{\text{Direct Materials}} = \frac{20{,}000 \times 100}{40{,}000} = 50\%$$

Overheads chargeable to the order $= 8000 \times \dfrac{50}{100} =$ ₹. 4,000

2. **The "Percentage on Direct Wages" or Direct Labour Cost Basis:** This method is also quite simple. From past experience or on the basis of estimates it can be determined as to what per cent are factory overheads of direct wages. Suppose last year total direct wages were ₹. 4,00,000 and the factory overheads amounted to ₹. 3,00,000. We may say, therefore, that factory overheads are 75 per cent of direct wages and assume that in the current year also this percentage will hold good (Factory overheads/Direct Wages × 100). A percentage calculated on the basis of current estimates will even be better. The method is far better than the "percentag on materials" basis. There is a *logical connection between direct wages and factory expenses*. Factory expenses certainly depend to a large extent on the number of workers employed and their rates of wages. If more direct workers are employed, thereis bound to be some increase in the number of indirect workers also and if wage rates of direct workers are increased, wage rates of indirect workers have to be increased. To this extent, factory expenses will vary with direct wages but since other items also constitute factory overheads, these cannot be said to vary in direct proportion to direct wages.

Since direct wages are not expected to fluctuate much, the system of calculating works expenses on the basis of direct wages is likely to give stable results. Over-costing and under-costing will be avoided and the difference between the actual overheads and the amount recovered (by inclusion in the cost of various jobs) is not likely to be big.

Another advantage of this method is that automatic consideration is given to the time factor, since a reasonable persumption can be made that if more direct wages are shown against a job, then more time was spent and fittingly, therefore, more should be charged to that job for factory expenses.

However, there are a *few drawbacks* of the system. These are the following:

(1) As already pointed out *unskilled workers give rise to more factory expenses* than skilled workers; and jobs done by unskilled workers should bear a higher charge for factory expenses than job done by skilled workers but the reverse is likely to happen under this system. Skilled workers get much higher rates of pay. If two jobs show the same amount for direct wages, time spent on

one may be much less than the other due to one job being done by skilled workers and the other by unskilled workers. Under the system, however, both the jobs will be charged with the same amount for factory overheads.

(2) If workers are remunerated on piece *basis, direct wages will not be connected with time* and this system will ignore the question of time taken by different jobs for completion.

(3) No distinction is made between *jobs done on machines and those done by hand only*. There is a need to distinguish not only between such jobs but also between jobs done by different machines. Each type of machine costs differently to buy and run and hence we must charge only an appropriate amount for depreciation, repairs, fuel and power supervision, etc., to each job.

From the above, it is clear that the system is appropriate only if the labour employed and work done is of uniform type. Even if a factory as a whole does not satisfy these conditions, some of the departments of the factory may and, therefore, such departments can legitimately adopt this system for work done there.

An improvement on this is to *correlate total man hours and factory overhead*. Suppose last year total number of man hours were 80,000 and total factory expenses ₹. 2,00,000, giving a rate of ₹. 2.50 per man hour. The current production may be charged with factory expenses at the rate of ₹. 2.50 for every hour of work done. The system still would not distinguish between machine work and hand work and between jobs done by skilled labour and those by unskilled workers. It may be called Productive Labour Hour Rate.

Illustration 11: The following information relates to the production deptt. of a factory:

Materials used	₹. 60,000
Direct Wages	₹. 40,000
Overheads	₹. 10,000

On one order carried out in the department, direct wages amounted to ₹. 6,000. Find out the overhead chargeable to this order on the basis of Direct Wages.

Solution:

$$\text{Ratio of Overheads to Direct Wages} = \frac{\text{Overheads} \times 100}{\text{Direct Wages}} = \frac{10{,}000 \times 100}{40{,}000} = 25\%$$

Overheads chargeable to the order = 6000 × 25% = 1,500

(3) **The "Percentage on Prime Cost" basis:** It is argued that since both materials and labour give rise to factory overheads, both should be taken into consideration for determining the amount to be debited to various jobs in respect of factory overheads $\frac{\text{Factory overheads} \times 100}{\text{Prime cost}}$. It is claimed that "Percentage on Prime Cost" basis provides for this. It is argued that the system would combine the advantages of both the systems on materials and on direct wages—at the same time avoiding the disadvantages. There is no reason why this should necessarily be so.

The system is likely to degenerate into either the one based on materials or the one based on direct wages as the following examples will show :

	Job A ₹.	*Job B* ₹.
Direct Materials	2,000	200
Labour	100	2,000
Prime Cost	2,100	2,200
Works Overheads (say 40% on Prime Cost)	840	880
Works Cost	2,940	3,086

In Job *A* works expenses are mostly based on materials and in Job *B* mostly on direct wages.

If two jobs use the same value of materials but consume more or less time, the effect of this system will be to water down the charge which should have been legitimately put down to a job requiring more time to complete. If such a job does not consume so much materials, the watering down will be still more as the following example shows:

	Job. No. 1	*Job. No.2*
	₹	₹
Materials	1,000	200
Wages	200	1,000
Prime Cost	1,200	1,200
Works Overheads (40% of Prime Cost)	480	480
	1,680	1,680

Although the second job presumably takes much more time than the first job, the amount of overheads allotted is the same for both the jobs.

In common with the previous two systems, this system does not distinguish between jobs done by skilled labour and unskilled labour and between machine production and hand production.

Illustration 12: The following particulars relate to a production department of a factory:

Materials used	₹. 40,000
Direct wages	₹. 20,000
Overheads	₹. 15,000

On an order carried out in the department, materials consumed was ₹. 8,000 and direct wages paid amounted to ₹. 4,000. What would be the amount of overheads chargeable to this order on the basis of prime cost?

Solution:

Prime Cost of Deptt. = 40,000 + 20,000 = ₹. 60,000

$$\text{Ratio of Overheads to Prime Cost} = \frac{\text{Overheads} \times 100}{\text{Prime cost}} = \frac{15{,}000 \times 100}{60{,}000} = 25$$

Prime Cost of this order = 8,000 + 4,000 = ₹. 12,000

Overheads chargeable to this order = 12,000 × 25% or ₹. 3,000

Illustration 13: M/s. Rajpal and sons manufacture three types of toys viz. Doll, Electric Train and Musical Van. Total factory overheads for the month of October were ₹. 30,000. You are required to find out the amount of overheads chargeable to each product assuming that one Doll is equivalent to two Musical Vans and one Electric Train is equivalent to five Musical Vans.

The production for the month of October was :

Doll	100 units
Electric Train	20 units
Musical Van	200 units

Solution:

100 Dolls = 200 Musical Vans

20 Electric Trains = 100 Musical Vans

200 Musical Vans = 200 Musical Vans

The ratio is 2 : 1 : 2

Overheads chargeable to each product :

$$\text{Doll} : \frac{30{,}000 \times 2}{5} = ₹.\ 12{,}000 \text{ or } \frac{12{,}000}{100} = ₹.\ 120 \text{ per Doll}$$

Electric Train = $\frac{30,000 \times 1}{5}$ = ₹. 6,000 or $\frac{6,000}{20}$ = ₹. 300 per Electric Train

Musical Van = $\frac{30,000 \times 2}{5}$ = ₹. 12,000 or $\frac{12,000}{200}$ = ₹. 60 per Musical Van

A *Combination of the Percentage on Materials and on Wages:* A point made above that some factory expenses are connected with materials and some others are connected with labour is of some interest. It is possible to have a system which will use both systems—percentage on materials and that on direct wages. Suppose, the estimated materials for the month of September are ₹. 50,000 and direct wages come to ₹. 40,000. Suppose, further, that the factory overheads connected with materials are ₹. 5,000 and those connected with labour are ₹. 20,000. In that case one can say that the method of apportioning factory expenses should be 10 per cent on materials (the ratio of ₹. 5,000 to ₹. 50,000) and 50 per cent on labour (the ratio of ₹. 20,000 to ₹. 40,000). Below is an example of cost determined on this basis :

	Job No. 1	*Job No. 2*
Materials	1,000	200
Wages	200	1,000
Prime cost	1,200	1,200
Works overheads :		
10% of materials	100	20
and		
50% of labour	100	500
Works cost	1,400	1,720

This system can prove really useful provided the allocation between the two categories of factory overheads is made properly. What is required is, firstly, a list of expenses which will change if the quantity of materials or price of materials used changes, and, secondly, a list of expenses which will change in proportion to changes in labour. Value of indirect materials used will come in the first list but the wages of the storekeeper and his assistants will come in the second list.

Hourly Rate Basis

Of the system discussed above, the system on direct wages is quite good for ordinary use. If, however, the work is of a very complicated nature then this system will not give good result. For this purpose two more systems have been developed which are :

1. *The Machine Hour Rate; and*
2. *The Direct Labour Hour Rate*

The purpose of both these systems, it must be remembered, is to apportion factory expenses over various jobs or over various products.

(4) **The Machine Hour Rate:** This method seeks to determine the expenses incurred when a machine is run for one hour and to then determine the amount chargeable to a job on the basis of the number of hours for which the machine is used on that job. Suppose, it is found that if machine A runs for one hour it costs ₹. 5 then the charge to a job using this machine for 30 hours will be ₹. 150.

The method of finding out the machine hour rate is to treat the machine as a small department and to apportion the various expenses to the machine just as the expenses are charged to bigger departments.

Some of the expenses connected with a machine are peculiar to that machine in the sense that such expenses will be different for each machine. Examples of such expenses are depreciation, repairs and electricity or oil, etc. Certain other expenses are common to the whole department and will have to be apportioned to each machine suitably. Example are rent and supervisor's salary. The basis for such expenses are indicated below:

Expenses	*Basis*
1. Rent and Rates and other expenses connected with premises.	— Effective area occupied by each machine including the surrounding space.
2. Lighting and heating	— The number of points used. or Floor area occupied by each machine.
3. Supervision	— Estimated time devoted by the supervisory staff to each machine. Suppose a foreman devotes one-fourth of his time to machine, then one-quarter of his salary should be allocated to that machine.
4. Oil, waste and sundries	— As best past experience indicates or Equally.
5. Insurance	— Actual value of machine being known and rate of premium being also known, insurance charges can be calculated for each machine individually.
6. Steam	— Horse power of the machines.
7. Labour welfare	No. of workers engaged on each machine.

If the degree of accuracy desired is great all the factory expenses will have to be dealt with. But the above expenses together with depreciation repairs and electricity will give a fair measure of accuracy; the remaining expenses can be taken care of by following the "percentage on direct wages" method. In fact, some people include only the direct machine expenses—depreciation, repairs, power, insurance, etc., in the machine hour rate, all the other expenses being recovered by a suitable percentage on the direct wages.

The expenses should be estimated for a short period as then the changes occurring from period to period can be taken into account. Where payment of wages and expenses is made weekly, the best period is a four-week period but where wages are paid on monthly basis, expenses can be estimated per month. The hours, however, must be estimated for a year (to eliminate the effect of holidays or heavy rush of work in a certain period). The annual estimate of hours should be divided by 12, if monthly estimate of expenses is made, or by 13 if the expenses are estimated for a four-week period, or by 52 if a weekly estimate of expenses is desired. It should be remembered that the machinist's wages are not included in the machine hour rate because the wages will form part of direct wages for the job concerned. Some people, however, include the machinist's wages also to give a comprehensive rate indicating the cost of doing work with the help of a machine.

The total of expenses is divided by the number of hours of which the machine is expected to run. The result will be the machine hour rate. It is used to first list the fixed or constant expenses for running the machine, i.e., those expenses which will not be affected if the machine is idle. The total of such expenses is divided by the total number of hours for the period. This gives the fixed expenses per hour. To this are added depreciation per hour, repairs per hour, power per hour, etc., and thus the total machine hour rate will be found out.

Machine Setting Time and Idle Time: In estimating total machine hours for computation of the machine hour rate, it is general practice to adopt the total potential hours available including the possible idle hours. The advantage in this is that, the cost of idle time can be separately worked out, based upon the number of hours the machine is lying idle, and this can serve as a guidance to control the idle expenses. Alternatively, in assessing machine hours, an allowance can be made for idle time and only net hours are considered for working out the machine hour rate. The effect will be that idle time cost will be spread over all productive jobs.

Similar to idle time certain machine hours are also lost in tool setting or machine setting. If this is considered as productive, it should be added to machine hours and in case it is found unproductive it may be excluded. The trial run hours may be considered productive and should added to machine hours.

Fixed (Standing) and Variable (Machine) Expenses: All factory overheads related to machine may be grouped as fixed and variable. Fixed overheads are those which are incurred for whole department and remain unaffected by the operation of machine. The total fixed overhead as apportioned to the machine are divided by the number of effective machine hours. Variable or Machine expenses should be divided individually by machine hours.

This grouping helps in calculating the cost of idle time lost because such cost will be on account of fixed or standing overheads.

Illustration 14: A Machine costing ₹. 10,000 is expected to run for 10 years at the end of which period its scrap value is likely to be ₹. 900. Repairs during the whole life of the machine are expected to be ₹. 1,800 and the machine is expected to run 4,380 hours per year on the average. Its electricity consumption is 15 units per hour, the rate per unit being 5 paise. The machine occupies one-fourth of the area of the department and has two points out of a total of ten for lighting. The foreman has to devote about one-third of his time to the machine. The monthly rent of the department is ₹. 300 and the lighting charges amount to ₹. 80 per month. The foreman is paid a monthly salary of ₹. 480. Ascertain the machine hour rate, assuming insurance is @ 1 per cent p.a. and the expenses on oil, etc., are ₹. 9 per month.

Solution:

Statement Showing Machine Hour Rate

		₹.
Constant (or Standing) expenses per month		₹.
Rent (one-fourth of the total)		75.00
Lighting (one-fifth of the total)		16.00
Foreman's Salary (one-third of the total)		160.00
Sundry expenses—oil, waste, etc.		9.00
Insurance (1% on the value of machine per year)		8.33
Total constant expenses per month		268.33
Total number of hours per year 4,380		
Total number of hours per month 365		
Constant expenses per hour (₹. 268.33 ÷ 365)		0.735
Variable (or Machine) expenses per hour:		
Depreciation:	₹.	
Original value of the machine	10,000	
Less	900	
	9,100	
Depreciation per year	910	
Depreciation per hour (910 ÷ 4,380)		0.208
Repairs for one hour (1800 ÷ 43800)		0.041
Electricity for one hour: 15 units @ 0.05		0.750
Machine Hour Rate		1.734

Comprehensive Machine Hour Rate: If the wages of the machine operators are also included, it will be the *comprehensive amount* which it costs to use that machine including the worker. The usual practice is, however, *not to include the wages of the machine operator if the wages are direct*. But if the operator attends a number of machines at the same time then his wages cannot be direct and a proportion of his wages will have to be included in the expenses of the machine.

Illustration 15: Calculate the Machine Hour Rate in respect of Machine No. 179 from the following particulars :

Cost of machine	₹.	20,000	Cost of repairs and maintenance (estimated) per annum	₹.	1,500
Estimated life	Hrs.	15,000	Number of operators (looking after also 3 other machines)		2
Estimated scrap value	₹.	500	Wages per operator p.m.	₹.	450
Estimated working hours per annum		2,200	Chemicals required for operating the machine p.m.	₹.	100
Estimated hours required for maintenance, etc. (included in above)	Hrs.	100	Overheads chargeable to the machine p.m.		200
Setting up time (included in above)	Hrs.	100	Insurance premium 1% p.a.		
Power 20 units @ 0.07 per hour					

Solution:

Machine No. 179
Machine Hours Rate

	₹.
Fixed Expenses per annum:	
Overheads (200 × 12)	2,400
Insurance	200
Wages of operators $\left(\frac{2 \times 450 \times 12}{4}\right)$	2,700
Total	5,300
Working hours per annum (2,200 – 200) = 2000	
Fixed Expenses per hour 5,300 ÷ 2,000	2.65
Variable Expenses per hour:	
Depreciation $\frac{20,000 - 500}{15,000}$	1.30
Repairs and Maintenance $\frac{1,500}{2,000}$	0.75
Chemicals $\frac{100 \times 12}{2,000}$	0.60
Power 20 units @ 0.07	1.40
Machine Hour Rate	6.70

Illustration 16: Work out in the appropriate form the machine hour rate of a factory machine, with reference to the following items:

(*a*) Purchase price of machine ₹. 45,000.

(*b*) Railway freight, other incidental charges and installation charges incurred for the equipment ₹. 5,000.

(*c*) Life of machine : 10 years @ 2,000 hours per year.

(*d*) Repair charges : 50% of depreciation.

(*e*) Consumption of power : 10 units per hour @ 10 paise per unit.

(*f*) Lubricating oil : ₹. 2 per day of 8 hours.

(*g*) Consumable stores : ₹. 10 per day of 8 hours.

(*h*) Wages of machine operator ₹. 4 per day of 8 hours.

(*i*) The residual scrap value of machine is nil.

Solution:

Computation of Machine Hour Rate

		Per day of 8 hours ₹	*Per hour* ₹
Standing Charges:			
Lubricating oil		2.00	
Consumable stores		10.00	
Wages of machine operator		4.00	
		16.00	
Hourly Rate for standing charge (16 ÷ 8)			2.00
Machine Expenses:			
Depreciation:	₹.		
Cost of purchase price	45,000		
Add: Installation charges	5,000		
	50,000		
Less: Scrap value	Nil		
	50,000		
Hourly rate of depreciation: (50,000 ÷ 20,000)			2.50
Repairs and maintenance—50% of depreciation			1.25
Power (10 units per hour @ 10 paise per unit)			1.00
Machine Hour Rate			6.75

Illustration 17: The following yearly charges are incurred in respect of machines in a shop, where manual labour is almost, nil, and where work is done by means of 5 machines of exactly similar type and specification :

		₹.
1.	Rent and rates of the shop	4,800
2.	Depreciation on each machine	500
3.	Repairs and maintenance for 5 machines	1,000
4.	Power consumed (as per meter @ 5 p. per unit)	3,000
5.	Electric charges for the shop	450
6.	Attendants : 2 attendants, looking after 5 machines paid ₹. 60 p.m. each	
7.	Superviser: looking after 5 machines and is paid ₹. 250 p.m.	
8.	Sundry supplies for the shop	450
9.	Hire-Purchase instalment for the machine (including ₹. 300 for interest)	1,200

The machine uses 10 units of power per hour. Calculate the machine hour-rate.

Solution:

Computation of Machine Hour-Rate

(1200 hrs. in a year)

Standing Charges:	*Per year* ₹.	*Per hour* ₹.
1. Rent etc. 1/5th of ₹. 4,800	960	
2. Sundry supplies 1/5th of ₹. 450	90	
3. Electric charges 1/5th of ₹. 450	90	
4. Attendants 60 × 2 × 12 = 1440/5	288	
5. Supervision 250 × 12 = 3000/5	600	
Yearly Standing Charges	2,028	
Machine Expenses:		
Depreciation	500	
Repairs ₹. 1000/5	200	
	2,728	
Hourly rate 2728 ÷ 1200		2.27
Power 10 units @ 5 paise per unit		0.50
Machine Hour Rate		2.77

Note: 1. Total power bill ₹. 3,000 (Rate 5 paise per unit).
60,000 units were consumed (3000 × 100 ÷ 5 = 60,000) for 5 machines.

2. For one machine 12,000 units. As 10 units consumed in an hour, there will be, therefore, 1200 hours in a year.

3. Interest ₹. 300 included in the instalment is not considered as an item of cost, hence excluded.

Illustration 18: A factory works on an average 168 hours in a month. There are four machines in the factory for which necessary particulars are given as under :

	I ₹.	*II* ₹.	*III* ₹.	*IV* ₹.
Annual Depreciation	660	2,400	360	6,600
Annual Interest on Capital	240	900	210	1,350
Annual repairs	120	1,110	90	180
Monthly Exps. for power	28	150	22	480
Monthly Misc. Exps.	19.60	60	9.70	78
Portion of the floor area	12%	10%	15%	8%

The monthly charges for rent and taxes for the entire factory are ₹. 3,300. One foreman supervises all these 4 machines, his salary is ₹. 2,520 per month. An attendant getting ₹. 192 p.m. looks after all these machines.

In the execution of a certain work, the I machine is used for 84 hours, the II for 72 hours, the III for 100 hours and the IV for 120 hours. The cost of materials is ₹. 35,930, and that of direct labour ₹. 670.

Calculate the factory cost of the work order.

Solution:

Calculate of Machine Hour Rate

	Machine Nos.			
	I	*II*	*III*	*IV*
	₹.	₹.	₹.	₹.
Standing Charges:				
Rent etc. p.m. (12%, 10%, 15%, 8%)	396.00	330.00	495.00	264.00
Interest on capital outlay p.m.	20.00	75.00	17.50	112.50
Misc. charges p.m.	19.60	60.00	9.70	78.00
Supervisor's salary (equally)	630.00	630.00	630.00	630.00
Attendant's (equally)	48.00	48.00	48.00	48.00
Monthly standing charges	1,113.60	1,143.00	1,200.20	1,132.50
Monthly Machine Exp.				
Depreciation	55.00	200.00	30.00	550.00
Repairs	10.00	92.50	7.50	15.00
Power	28.00	150.00	22.00	480.00
Total Monthly Charges	1,206.60	1,585.50	1,259.70	2,177.50
Machine Hour Rate (168 hours)	7.182	9.438	7.50	12.96

Caclculation of Factory Cost

		₹.
Materials		35,930
Wages		670
	Prime Cost	36,600
Works overheads		
(*i*) 84 hours @ 7.182	603.288	
(*ii*) 72 hours @ 9.438	679.536	
(*iii*) 100 hours @ 7.50	750.000	
(*iv*) 120 hours @ 12.96	1555.200	3,588.024
Factory Cost of the work order		40,188.024

Illustration 19: The following is the schedule of expenses incurred on three machines *X*, *Y* and *Z*.

	X	*Y*	*Z*
	₹.	₹.	₹.
Rent etc.	75	59	120
Insurance	2	1	4
Power	128	146	273
Supervision	40	30	60
Organisation	10	7	15
Store Services	20	29	46
Tool setters	93	78	129
Tool makers	194	145	214
Repairs	29	63	15
Oil and Sundries	8	12	7
Depreciation	40	37	68
	639	607	951

Besides these expenses, there was the expense of operating an overhead crane, which was necessary to bring heavy materials to machines. The expenses of crane are as follows:

	₹.		₹.
Power consumed by crane	227	Depreciaiton	49
Wages of crane drive	216	Oil and sundries	5
Repairs	28	Miscellaneous	45

The machine were in use as follows (hours) :

	X	Y	Z
With the use of crane	160	130	480
Without the use of crane	428	577	—
	588	707	480

Calculate the machine hour rate applicable to each machine, distinguishing the hours in which the crane was used and the hours in which it was not.

Solution:

Computation of Machine Hour Rate

	X ₹	X ₹	X ₹
(*i*) Without the use of Crane Expenses of machine	639	607	951
Divided by hours worked	$\left(\frac{639}{588}\right)$	$\left(\frac{607}{707}\right)$	$\left(\frac{951}{480}\right)$
Mach. Hour Rate	1.09	0.86	1.98
(*ii*) Hourly Rate of Crane Exp.	₹.	₹.	₹.
Expenses of crane ₹. 570 divided in the ratio of hours worked with crane (160 : 130 : 480)	118.44	96.23	355.33
Hourly rate	$\left(\frac{118.44}{160}\right)$	$\left(\frac{96.23}{130}\right)$	$\left(\frac{355.33}{480}\right)$
	0.74	0.74	0.74

	X ₹.	Y ₹.	Z ₹.
Hourly rate without the use of crane	1.09	0.86	1.98
Hourly rate of expenses of crane	0.74	0.74	0.74
Machine hour rate with the use of crane	1.83	1.60	2.72

Note: The machines will work in all for 588, 707 and 480 hours even without the use of crane.

Illustration 20: The new products Ltd. has three departments. Department *B* covers the operations of two large machines, No. 1 and No. 2 each operated by several employees.

It is estimated that during the year ending 31st March 2003, No. 1 machine will operate for 40 hours per week for 50 weeks and No. 2 machine for 30 hours per week for 40 weeks. No. 2 machine is used for special process and is normally not worked to capacity.

Estimates of costs and expenses for Department *B* for the year are as follows:

	Machine No. 1	Machine No. 2	Total
	₹.	₹.	₹.
Wages	40,000	24,000	64,000
Repairs and Maintenance	5,500	6,000	11,500
Power			3,200
Rent			12,180
Insurance of Machine			4,860
Proportion of General factory overhead			3,200

The following additional facts are supplied :

(*i*) The area occupied by each machine is—No.1 : 1,000 sq. meters and No. 2 : 2,750 sq. meters.

(*ii*) The cost of machines No. 1. ₹. 2,00,000 and No. 2 ₹. 1,00,000.

(*iii*) The depreciation rates used per annum and calculated on cost are No. 1, 10 per cent and No. 2, 7.5 per cent.

(*iv*) Wages which are estimated to represent payment for holiday and sickness will be 5 per cent for Machine No. 1, and 8 per cent for Machine No. 2.

(*v*) No. 1 Machine uses 25 units of power per hour and No. 2 Machine also uses 25 units of power.

Calculated the Machine Hour Rate for each machine for the year ending 31st March 2003.

Solution:

Computation of Machine Hour Rate
for the year ending on 31st March 2003

Items of overheads	*Total Amount*	*Basis of allocation*	*Machine No. 1*	*Machine No. 2*
Standing Charges:	₹.		₹.	₹.
Rent	12,180	Area (4 : 11)	3,248	8,932
Wages for sick and holiday etc.	3,920	5% and 8% of wages	2,000	1,920
Insurance	4,860	Value of machine (2 : 1)	3,240	1,620
Factory overhead	3,200	Direct wages (5 : 3)	2,000	1,200
Machine Expenses				
Repairs and Maintenance	11,500	Units consumed	5,500	6,000
Power	3,200	Hours worked (equal)	1,600	1,600
Depreciation	27,500	10% and 7-1/2%	20,000	7,500
Total overhead	66,360		37,588	28,772
Production Hours			2,000	1,200
Machine Hour Rate			18.794	23.976

Illustration 21: A.T. Ltd, an engineering company having 25 different types of automatic machines, furnishes you the following data for a year in respect of Machine *B*:

	₹.
1. Cost of Machine Life 10 years, Scrap value : Nil	2,00,000
2. Overhead expenses are	
Factory Rent	2,00,000 p.a.
Lighting and heating	1,60,000 p.a.
Supervision	6,00,000 p.a.
Reserve equipment of machine B	20,000 p.a.

Area of the factory 80,000 sq. ft.

Area occupied by the machine B 3,000 sq. ft.

Power Cost ₹. 2 per hour while in operation

3. Wages of operator are ₹. 96 per day of 8 hours including fringe-benefits. He attends to one machine when it is being set-up and two machines while under operation.

4. Estimated production hours 3,600 hrs. p.a.

Estimated set up time 400 hrs. p.a.

Prepare a Schedule of Comprehensive Machine hour rate and find the cost of the following jobs.

	Job 1102	*Job 1308*
Set up (hours)	80	40
Operation time (hours)	130	160

Solution:

Computation of Comprehensive Machine Hour Rate of Machine B.

Standing Charges (Fixed Exps.) p.a.	Basis	₹.	₹.
Rent	Area	7,500	
Lighting & Heating	Area	6,000	
Supervision	No. of Machines	24,000	
Reserve Equipment	Actual	20,000	
		57,500	
Per Hour [₹. 57500 ÷ 4000]			14.375

	Set up cost per Machine ₹.	*Operation Cost per Machine* ₹.
Fixed Exps (Standing Charges)	14.375	14.375
Machine Exps:		
Depreciation (₹. 2,00,000/40,000)	5.000	5.000
Power	—	2.000
Machine Hour Rate	19.375	21.375
Labour	12.000	6.000
Comprehensive MHR	31.375	27.375

Charging of Machine Overheads to jobs

	Rate	*Job 1102*		*Job 1308*	
	₹	*Hours*	₹	*Hours*	₹
Set up	31.375	80	2,510.00	40	1,255.00
Operation	27.375	130	3,558.75	160	4,380.00
			6,068.75		5,635.00

Illustration 22: From the following data work out the pre-determined machine hour rates for departments *A* and *B* of a factory:

Preliminary Estimates of Expenses

	Total	Dept. A ₹	Dept. B ₹
Power	1,50,000	—	—
Spare parts	80,000	30,000	50,000
Consumable Stores	50,000	20,000	30,000
Depreciation of Machinery	3,00,000	1,00,000	2,00,000
Insurance of Machinery	30,000		
Indirect Labour	4,00,000		
Building maintenance	70,000		

The final estimates are to be prepared on the basis of above figures after considering the following factors: (*i*) An increases of 10 per cent in the price of spare-parts (*ii*) an increase of 20 per cent in the consumption of spare parts in department B only; (*iii*) Increase in the straight line rate of depreciation from 10 per cent on the original value of machinery to 12 per cent; and (*iv*) 15 per cent general increase in wages rates.

The following other information is available

	Dept. A	Dept. B
Estimated direct labour hours	80,000	1,20,000
Ratio of KW rating	3	2
Estimated machine hours	25,000	30,000
Floor space (sq.ft)	15,000	20,000

Solution:

Statement showing adjustment of Preliminary Estimates

	Total ₹	Dept. A ₹	Dept. B ₹
1. Spare Parts—Preliminary estimates	80,000	30,000	50,000
Add increase 10%	800	3000	5000
	88,000	33,000	55,000
Add increase 20% in Dept. *B*	11,000	—	11,000
	99,000	33,000	66,000
2. Depreciation—Preliminary (10% of original estimates cost)	3,00,000	1,00,000	2,00,000
Add increase 2% of original cost	60,000	20,000	40,000
	3,60,000	1,20,000	2,40,000
3. Indirect Labour	4,00,000		
Add increase 15%	60,000		
	4,60,000		

Computation of Machine Hour Rate

	Department A		Department B	
	Total ₹	Per Hour ₹	Total ₹	Per Hour ₹
Standing Charges:				
(*a*) Spare parts	33,000		66,000	
(*b*) Consumable stores	20,000		30,000	
(*c*) Insurance (In the ratio of depreciation *i.e.* 1 : 2)	10,000		2,000	
(*d*) Indirect Labour (in the ratio of labour hours *i.e.* 2 : 3)	1,84,000		2,76,000	
(*e*) Building maintenance (in the ratio of floor *i.e.* 3 : 4)	30,000		40,000	
Total	2,77,000		4,32,000	
Standing charges as per machine hours (*i.e.* divided by 25,000 hours and 30,000 hours)		11.08		14.40
Machine Expenses:				
Depreciation		4.80		8.00
Power (KW ratio)	(₹. 90,000/25,000)	3.60	(60,000/30,000)	2.00
	—		—	
	—		—	
Machine Hour Rate	—	19.48	—	24.40

Illustration 23: P.H. Ltd. is a manufacturing Co. having three production departments *A, B* and *C* and two service departments *X* and *Y*. The following is the budget for December.

	Total ₹	A ₹	B ₹	C ₹	X ₹	Y ₹
Direct material		1,000	2,000	4,000	2,000	1,000
Direct wages		5,000	2,000	8,000	1,000	2,000
Factory Rent	4,000					
Power	2,500					
Depreciation	10,000					
Other overheads	9,000					
Additional information:						
Area (sq.feet)		500	250	500	250	500
Capital value of assets (₹.)		20,000	40,000	20,000	10,000	10,000
Machine Hours		1,000	2,000	4,000	1,000	1,000
Horse-power of machines		50	40	20	15	25

(The column group A–E is headed "Departments".)

A technical assessment of the apportionment of expenses of service departments is as under.

	A %	B %	C %	X %	Y %
Service Deptt. *X*	45	15	30	—	10
Service Deptt. *Y*	60	35	—	5	—

Required (*i*) A statement showing distribution of overheads to various departments; (*ii*) A statement showing re-distribution of service departments expenses to production deptts. (*iii*) Comprehensive machine hour rates of production departments.

Solution:

(*i*) Statement showing Distribution of Overheads to Various Departments

Particulars	*Basis of*	*Total*	*Production Deptts.*			*Service Deptts.*	
(Overheads)	*Distribution*		*A*	*B*	*C*	*X*	*Y*
		₹	₹	₹	₹	₹	₹
Direct Materials	Given	3,000	—	—	—	2,000	1,000
Direct wages	Given	3,000				1,000	2,000
Factory Rent	Area	4,000	1,000	500	1,000	500	1,000
Power	HP × MH	2,500	500	800	800	150	250
Depreciation	Assets Value	10,000	2,000	4,000	2,000	1,000	1,000
Other Overheads	MH	9,000	1,000	2,000	4,000	1,000	1,000
	Total	31,500	4,500	7,300	7,800	5,650	6,250

(*ii*) Statement Showing Redistribution of Expenses of Service Deptts. to Production Departments

	Production Deptt.			*Service Deptt.*	
	A	*B*	*C*	*X*	*Y*
Total overheads	4,500	7,300	7,800	5,650	6,250
Overheads of Dept. *X* ₹. 5650 apportioned in the ratio of 45 : 15 : 30 : 10	2,543	847	1,695	–5,650	565
Overheads of Dept *Y* ₹. 6815 in the ratio of 60 : 35 : Nil : 5	4,089	2,385		341	–6,815
Overheads of Dept × ₹. 341 in the ratio of 45 : 15 : 30 : 10	154	51	102	341	34
Overheads of dept *Y* ₹. 34 in the ratio of 60 : 35 : Nil : 5	20	12	—	2	–34
Overheads of Dept. *X* ₹. 2 in the ratio of 45 : 15 : 30 : 10	1	—	1	–2	
Total	11,307	10,595	9,598	Nil	Nil

(*iii*) Computation of Machine Hour Rate

	A	*B*	*C*
Total Overheads	(₹.) 11,307	10,595	9,598
Machine Hours	1000	2000	4000
Machine Hour Rate (OH ÷ MH)	(₹.) 11.31	5.30	2.40

(5) Direct Labour Hour Rate

The principle for finding out direct labour rate is same as that for the machine hour rate. Attempt is made to allocate the various factory expenses to the various categories of workers. Each category of workers needs more or less supervision, causes different measures of wastage of materials or wear and tear of tools. Careful observation over a period of time is likely to reveal valuable information on the above point and we can then find out what amount of factory expenses works for an hour. Suitable rates for each category of workers have to be found out and then only we can really distinguish between work done by a skilled worker as against that done by an unskilled one.

Suppose in a factory there are 25 welders and suppose the following expenses are incurred for keeping them at work:

	₹.
Rent	200
Lighting	40
Supervision	400
Sundry Materials	1,000
Depreciation of tools	200
Miscellaneous	160
Total	2,000

The total number of hours put in by welders is 5,000 (assuming a welder works for 8 hours a day and 25 days in a month). It means that ₹. 2,000 is being spent for 5,000 hours of welders. The rate per hour comes to 40 P. It means that if a welder works then, in addition to his wages, another sum of ₹. 0.40 has to be spent for doing the work. Hence, if a job is done by 5 welders in six days, taking, therefore, 240 hours (5 × 6 × 8), the factory overheads chargeable to that job will be ₹. 240 × 40 P. or ₹. 96.

It should be remembered that the *two systems described above are not competitive*, in the sense that if we use one we cannot use the other. Both are complementary. The "Machine Hour Rate" is meant for use in those departments where work is done mainly by machines and the direct labour hour rate is meant for use in those departments where work is done mostly by hand. The two methods will be simultaneously in use in a factory having both the types of departments. The two methods together distinguish between jobs completed by hand and jobs done by machine. The "Direct Labour Hour Rate" method makes a thorough distinction between skills of various workers. Both the systems take the time spent on a job fully into account.

While computing the machine hour rate or the direct labour hour rate, some of the expenses are not included due to inconvenience. For example, labour welfare expenses or the salary paid to superintendents or works manager, or storekeeping expenses, are not included. Thus, if works expenses are charged only on the basis of machine hour rate or direct labour hour rate, a good proportion of the factory expenses will remain unrecovered. Due to this, along with machine hour rate and direct hour rate the percentage on direct wages will also be used for recovering the unallocated expenses. Therefore, for good results it is desirable to have a battery of the three systems—machine hour rate, direct labour hour rate and a percentage on direct wages.

Illustration 24: You are required to compute Direct Labour Hour Rate from the following information:

(*i*) Total number of workers working in the department : 400.

(*ii*) Working days in a year : 300 and the number of hours worked in a day : 8.

(*iii*) Total department overheads are ₹. 45,600.

(*iv*) Idle time @ 5% of day's hours to be deducted from total number of day's hour.

Solution:

Total working hours	300 × 8 = 2,400
Less : Idle time @ 5%	120
Net Working Hours	2,280

Total labour hours = 2,280 × 400 = 9,12,000 Hours.

$$\text{Direct Labour Hour Rate} = \frac{\text{Total Overheads}}{\text{Total Labour hours}} = \frac{45,600}{9,12,000} = ₹.\ 0.05$$

Illustration 25: In a factory the factory overheads are charged on a fixed percentage of wages and office overheads are calculated on the basis of percentage of works cost.

Following information is available :

	First order	*Second order*
Materials	₹. 25,000	₹. 36,000
Wages	₹. 20,000	₹. 28,000
Sales Value	₹. 85,800	₹. 1,23,760
Percentage of Profit on Cost	10%	12%

Find out the percentage of factory overhead to wages and percentage of office overheads to works cost.

Solution:

	First order	*Second order*
	₹.	₹
Sales	85,800	1,23,760
Less profit	7,800	13,260
Total Cost	78,000	1,10,500
Less Prime cost	45,000	64,000
Works overheads + Office overheads	33,000	46,500

Let x be the percentage of Factory Overheads to Wages and y be the percentage of Office Overheads to Factory cost:

Factory overheads will be

First order : $20,000 \times \frac{x}{100} = 200x$

Second order : $28,000 \times \frac{x}{100} = 280x$

Office overheads will be:

First order : $(45,000 + 200x) \times \frac{y}{100}$

Second order : $(64,000 + 280x) \times \frac{y}{100}$

Now two equations are:

$$33,000 = 200x + (45,000 + 200x) \times \frac{y}{100}$$

$$46,500 = 280x + (64,000 + 280x) \times \frac{y}{100}$$

or $33,000 = 200x + 450y + 2xy$ ...(1)

$46,500 = 280x + 640y + 2.8xy$ ...(2)

By multiplying (1) by 7 and (2) by 5 we have

$$2,31,000 = 1400x + 3150y + 14xy$$

$$2,32,500 = 1400y + 3200y + 14xy$$

$$-1500 = -50y$$

or $y = 1500/50 = 30$

Substituting the value of y in equation (1)

$$33,000 = 200x + 450 \times 30 + 2x \times 30 = 200x + 13,500 + 60x$$

$$33,000 - 13,500 = 260x \text{ or } x = 19600/260 = 75$$

Thus percentage of factory overhead to wages is 75 per cent and percentage of office overhead to works cost is 30 per cent.

Illustration 26: An Engineering firm has two departments, the estimated expenses for which are as under.

	Dept. A	*Dept. B*
Materials	₹. 1,00,000	₹. 1,00,000
Direct wages	₹. 1,38,400	₹. 90,120
Works expenses	₹ 97,600	₹. 65,880
Office expenses	₹. 26,880	₹. 25,600
Direct labour hours	39,040 hrs.	21,960 hrs.

Works expenses are charged to output on the basis of direct labour hour rate and office expenses are charged as a percentage of works cost.

What would be the total cost of Job No. 14 on which following expenses are incurred :

	Dept. A	*Dept. B*
Materials	₹. 2,100	₹. 1,500
Direct wages	₹. 2,300	₹. 1,750
Labour hours	1,200 hrs.	1,500 hrs.

Solution:

Workings

	Dept. A	*Dept. B*
Direct Labour Rate:		
Works expenses	₹. 97,600	₹. 65,880
Direct labour hours	39,040	21,960
Direct labour rate (Works Exps ÷ Labour Hours)	₹. 2.50	₹. 3.00
Works Cost:		
Materials	1,00,000	1,00,000
Wages	1,38,400	90,120
Works expenses	97,600	65,880
Works cost	3,36,000	2,56,000
Office expenses	26,880	25,600
% of Office Exp. on Works Cost	8%	10%

Calculation of Total Cost

	Dept. A ₹.	*Dept. B* ₹.
Materials	2,100	1,500
Wages	2,300	1,750
Works Expenses:		
1,200 hrs, @ 2.50 per hour.	3,000	
1,500 hrs. @ 3.00 per hour.		4,500
Works Cost	7,400	7,750
Office Expenses:		
8% of 7,400	592	
10% of 7,750		775
Total Cost	7,992	8,525
Total Cost of Job 14 = 7,992 + 8,525 = ₹. 16,517		

Illustration 27: The monthly budget of a department is as under :

	₹.
Direct material	45,000
Direct wages	60,000
Overheads	90,000
Direct Labour Hour	15,000
Machine hour	30,000

Find out the overhead recovery rate based on atleast five different possible methods of absorption of overheads.

Solution:

1. Direct Labour Hour (DLH) Rate Method :
   Overhead rate = Overheads/DLH = 90,000/15,000 = ₹. 6 per DLH.
2. Direct Labour Cost (DLC) Method :
   $$\text{Overhead rate} = \frac{\text{Overheads}}{\text{DLC}} \times 100 = \frac{90{,}000}{60{,}000} \times 100 = 150\% \text{ on DLC}$$
3. Machine Hour (MH) rate method :
   Overhead rate = Overheads/MH = 90,000/30,000 = ₹. 3 per MH.
4. Direct Material Cost (DMC) Method :
   $$\text{Overhead rate} = \frac{\text{Overheads}}{\text{DMC}} \times 100 = \frac{90{,}000}{45{,}000} \times 100 = 200\% \text{ on DMC}$$
5. Prime Cost (PC) Method :
   $$\text{Overhead rate} = \frac{\text{Overheads}}{\text{PC}} \times 100 = \frac{90{,}000}{45{,}000 + 60{,}000} \times 100 = 85.71\% \text{ on Prime Cost.}$$

Illustration 28: The following are some of the expenses incurred in a factory:

(*i*) Work Manager's Salary ₹. 75,000
(*ii*) Factory Rent ₹. 54000 (The total area is 67,500 sq feet out of which shop is in 60,000 sq. ft.)
(*iii*) Peons and Sweepers Wages ₹. 10,500
(*iv*) Other Factory Overheads ₹. 80,000

Annual wages bill for direct labour amount to ₹. 7,20,000. A work order is executed in a part of the shop occupying an area of 10,000 sq.ft and cost ₹. 16,000 in wages. If the total wages for all work orders executed in the shop amount is ₹. 2,40,000. Calculate the amount of factory overhead charges to be allocated to this order.

Solution:

$$\text{Total rent for the shop} = \frac{54{,}000 \times 60{,}000}{67{,}500} = ₹.\ 48{,}000$$

Rent for the rest area = 54,000 – 48,000 = ₹. 6,000

Overheads to be allocated :

(*i*) Rent of that part of the shop's area in which work order is excuted.

$$= \frac{48{,}000 \times 10{,}000}{60{,}000} = ₹.\ 8{,}000$$

(*ii*) Other Factory Overheads :

(*a*) Work Manager Salary	₹. 75,000
(*b*) Other Factory Rent.	₹. 6,000
(*c*) Wages of Peons etc.	₹. 10,500
(*d*) Other	₹. 80,000
	₹. 1,71,500

Factory overheads chargeable to work order :

(*i*) Rent = $\frac{8{,}000 \times 16{,}000}{2{,}40{,}000}$ = 533.33

(*ii*) Others = $\frac{1{,}71{,}500 \times 16{,}000}{7{,}20{,}000}$ = 3811.11 ₹. 4344.44

OVER AND UNDER-ABSORPTION OF OVERHEADS

Absorbed Overheads: "The overheads which, by means of rates of overhead absorption, is allotted to cost units."

Under- or Over-Absorbed Overheads: "The difference between the amount of overhead absorbed and the amount of overhead incurred." — *CIMA*

Overheads are apportioned or allotted to cost units, jobs or products on an estimated basis, It is quite natural that there may be a difference between the two. If the total amount `recovered' or allotted to cost units is less than the actual, there is an under-absorption (also called under-recovery) and if the amount recovered exceeds the actual there is an over-absorption (also termed over-recovery) of overheads.

Reasons for Over or Under Absorption

Apart from the fact that estimated amounts will differ from the actuals, the reasons for over- or under-allocation of expenses may be the following:

(*a*) *Error in estimating work done:* The amount of work done may be substantially less or more than anticipated. For example, if only 80,000 hours of work are put in whereas the rate of absorption was fixed on the basis of 1,00,000 hours, the amount of expenses charged to jobs will be 20 per cent less.

(*b*) *Error in estimating overhead expenses:* The amount actually spent as expenses may greatly exceed the estimated amount. For instance, a number of supervisory posts may be created after the estimates have been prepared. Supervisory salaries (and thus the total of expenses) will then be much more than the figure included in estimates.

(*c*) *Error in using method of absorption:* The method of absorption or allotment of expenses may be unsuitable. If `a percentage on materials' is used, fluctuations in prices of materials will lead to over- or under-recovery of expenses.

(*d*) *Change in proportion of work by machine and labour:* The proportion of different types of work may change. For example, if there is more machine work and less manual work than was formerly the case, there will be under-recovery of expenses, if the recovery is on the basis of a percentage on direct wages.

(*e*) *Seasonal fluctuation in overhead:* Due to seasonal nature of work, overhead may fluctuate from one period to another.

(*f*) *Under or over utilisation of capacity:* There may be over or under absorption of overhead due to over- or under utilisation of productive capacity.

Treatment of Over or Under Absorption of Overheads

The question of dealing with the over-recovery or under-recovery of expenses can be dealt with only with reference to the cause leading to over- or under-absorption.

(*i*) *Writing off to Costing Profit and Loss Account:* At the outset one should say that a small difference between the actual and absorbed amounts should simply be transferred to the Costing Profit and Loss Account. If, however, the difference is large, the cause should be investigated. Should the cause be abnormal (if the output has fallen, for instance) the amount of over- or under-recovery should be treated as an abnormal loss and transferred to the Costing Profit and Loss Account.

(*ii*) *Use of Supplementary Rate:* Under this method, the balance of over and under absorbed overheads may be charged to cost of work-in-progress, and finished stock and cost of sales proportionately. This is done with the help of supplementary rate of overhead. If there has been a mistake in either working out the proper rate or selecting the proper method, it should be permissible to amend the cost and arrive at new (but correct) figures of cost. To the extent goods have already been sold, the difference in the two figures of cost (as already arrived at and the new correct one) should be debited or credited to the Cost of Sales Account or even to the Costing Profit and Loss Account. The goods remaining unsold should be costed at the correct rate. The corrective rate should be applied also to work-in-progress.

(*iii*) *Carry Forward to Subsequent Year:* Some people, however, recommend that the difference should be carried forward in the expectation that next year the position will be automatically corrected. This would really mean that costing data of two years would be wrong.

Illustration 29: In a manufacturing unit, overhead was recovered at a predetermined rate of ₹. 25 per man-day. The total factory overhead expenses incurred and the man days actually worked were ₹. 41.50 lakhs and 1.50 lakhs days respectively.

Out of 40,000 units produced during a period 30,000 were sold.

On analysing the reasons it was found that 60% of the unabsorbed overheads were due to defective planning and the rest were attributable to increase in overhead costs.

How would unabsorbed overheads be treated in cost-accounts. **[*B.Com.(H) Delhi*]**

Solution:

Overheads actually incurred	₹. 41,50,000
Overheads absorbed @ ₹. 25 per man days (1,50,000 × ₹. 25)	₹. 37,50,000
	₹. 4,00,000
Under Recovery of Overheads	
Reasons for Under Recovery:	
Defective Planning (60%)	₹. 2,40,000
Increase in Overhead Cost (40%)	₹. 1,60,000
	₹. 4,00,000

Treatment of Unabsorbed Overheads:

(*a*) Under recovery (₹. 2,40,000) due to defective planning is abnormal, therefore, it should be charged to Costing Profit and Loss Account.

(*b*) Under recovery of ₹. 1,60,000 due to increase in overhead cost should be recovered from Cost of Sales Account and Finished Stock in the ratio of 30,000 and 10,000 (being units of sales and closing stock) *i.e.* 3 : 1.

1,60,000 × 3/4 = ₹. 1,20,000 to be charged to Cost of Sales.

1,60,000 × 1/4 = ₹. 40,000 to be charged to finished stock.

Normal unabsorbed overheads *i.e.* ₹. 1,60,000 may be charged through supplementary overhead absorption rate which will be ₹. 1,60,000/40,000 = ₹. 4 per units.

Illustration 30: In a factory, overheads of a particular department are recovered on the basis of ₹. 5 per machine hour. The total expenses incurred and the actual machine hours for the department for the month of August were ₹. 80,000 and 10,000 hours respectively. Of the amount of ₹. 80,000 ₹. 15,000 became payable due to an award of the labour court and ₹. 5000 was in respect of expenses of the previous year booked in the current month (August) Actual production was 40,000 units, of which 30,000 units were sold. On analysing the reasons, it was found that 60% of the under-absorbed overhead was due to defective planning and the rest was attributed to normal cost increase. How would you treat the under- absorbed overhead in the cost account. **[*CA Inter*]**

Solution:

Under Absorbed Overheads During the Month of August

		₹.	₹.
(A)	**Total Expenditure**		80,000
	Less: Non-Recurring expenses		
	Amount paid due to the award	15,000	
	Exps. of Previous year	5,000	20,000
	Acutal Expenditure for the Month		60,000
	Overhead Recovered		
	Actual Machine Hour × Hourly Rate *i.e.*, 10,000 × 5		50,000
	Under-absorbed Overhead		10,000
(B)	**Causes of Under Absorption:**		
	Due to defective planning 60% of ₹. 10,000		6,000
	Normal cost-increase (balancing)		4,000
			10,000

(C) Treatment of Under Absorbed Overhead in the Cost Accounts

(*i*) Abnormal to be written off to Costing Profit & Loss Account: ₹. 6000 of under absorption due to defective planning.

(*ii*) Normal to be adjusted in cost of production: Normal cost increase ₹. 4000 is to be apportioned between cost of sales and finished goods in the ratio of units sold and finished stock i.e. 3 : 1.

Cost of Sale	₹. 4000 × 3/4 = ₹. 3,000
Finished Goods	₹. 4000 × 1/4 = ₹. 1,000

Note: Usually supplementary rates should be used. It will be (₹. 4000/50,000) × 100 *i.e.* 8% of absorbed overhead. Alternatively it can be rate per unit i.e. ₹. 4000/40,000 or 0.10 per unit.

Illustration 31: In a factory the cost sheet of a product, the only one produced in the factory, was prepared as shown below:

		₹.
Materials		5,50,000
Labour @ ₹. 3 per hour (91,000 × 3)		2,73,000
Factory Overheads—	Variable @ ₹. 1.50 per hour	1,35,000
	Fixed @ ₹. 2.00 " "	1,80,000
		11,38,000

The production was 1,00,000 units out of which 85,000 were sold at ₹. 13.00 per unit.

The overheads were found to be actually ₹. 4,35,000—₹. 1,50,000 variable and the rest fixed. It was ascertained that the increase in variable overheads was due to increase in the relevant rates. Also, there was a power cut of 20% throughout the year. The actual fixed overheads included *ex gratia* of 15 days' wages paid to the workers on the occasion of the wedding of the proprietor's son, the amount being ₹. 25,000. Machine breakdowns beyond those taken into account while computing capacity were responsible for loss of 10%, of the budgeted hours available.

State in what respect you would like to amend the cost per unit as already computed and set up the journal entries that may be required.

Solution:

	₹.
Under recovery of Overheads:	
Actual	4,35,000
Recovered as per cost sheet	3,15,000
	1,20,000

Causes: Increase in rates relevant to variable overheads	15,000
Loss of time: Breakdown 13,000 hrs. @ 2.00 (10%) (Abnormal)	26,000
Power cut 26,000 hrs. (20%) (Normal)	52,000
Ex-gratia Payment	25,000
Increase in fixed expenses (balancing figure)	2,000
	1,20,000

Actual time: 91,000 hours

Loss 30%

Budgeted: $91{,}000 \times \frac{100}{70}$ or 1,30,000 hours

The amount in respect of *ex gratia* payment and breakdown of machines are abnormal and controllable, hence these amounts should be charged to the Costing Profit and Loss Account. There should be supplementary charge in respect of the remaining amounts. These are ₹. 15,000 for variable overheads coming to 1/9 of already charged and ₹. 54,000 for fixed overhead working out at 30% of the amount already charged.

The amounts chargeable are as follows :

	Total	*Cost of Sales (85,000 units)* ₹.	*Stock (15,000 units)* ₹.
Variable Overheads (1,50,000 – 1,35,000)	15,000	12,750	2,250
Fixed Overheads (52,000 + 2000)	54,000	45,900	8,100
	69,000	58,650	10,350

Journal Entry

		Dr. ₹.	Cr. ₹.
Overheads Under-Absorbed A/c		1,20,000	
To Overheads Account			1,20,000
(To record the amount of overheads under absorbed during the period pending disposal)			
Costing Profit & Loss Account (26000 + 25000)	Dr.	51,000	
Cost of Sales Account	Dr.	58,650	
Stock Account	Dr.	10,350	
To Overheads Under-Absorbed Account (Abnormal amounts charged to Costing P. & L. A/c and the balance to Cost of Sales A/c and Stock A/c respectively for units sold and in stock)			1,20,000

OTHER OVERHEADS

Importance of Other Overheads

In recent times, overheads other than factory overheads have assumed great importance; there are some industries like the drugs industry, where *selling overheads* are more important than the manufacturing expenses. Even in other cases, the proportion of administrative and selling expenses to total costs has a tendency to rise. The *reasons* for this seem to be the following :

(*i*) The great increase in the *size* of industrial concerns so that, for controlling the concern and doing the routine office work, a number of managers are required;

(*ii*) The increasing *complexity in modern life* because of legislation, trade union, public relations, relations with government and other concerns.

(*iii*) The need to *study labour* and employees so that they become willing workers.

(*iv*) Modern *management* techniques like the employment of staff or experts at various levels, planning department, etc.

(*v*) *Stiff competition* necessitating heavy expenditure on advertising and sales promotion.

(*vi*) The tendency to *reach the retailer or consumer* directly so that expenses previously incurred by wholesalers are incurred by the producer himself.

Control over other overheads

These overheads must also be recovered like factory overheads—ignoring administrative and selling overheads may be quite dangerous. It should, however, be remembered that the bulk of such overheads is fixed and, like all fixed expenses, control in this respect implies :

(*i*) that care should be exercised before commitment to incur the expenses is made—later it may be too late to stop incurring it. For example, if a decision to open own retail shops is taken, it will involve spending good deal of money on retail shop rents, salaries, etc, and no saving in these will be possible without dislocation of sales; and

(*ii*) full utilisation of the facilities represented by these overheads—in other words, sales should be maximised.

OFFICE AND ADMINISTRATIVE OVERHEADS

An expenses relating to general administration (not connected will production or sales) will be included in "Office and Administrative Overheads". The usual items comprised in these overheads are the following :

1. Salaries of the General Manager, Finance Manager, the Accountant, the Secretary and their staff etc.
2. Office rent and rates, and repairs and depreciation of office premises.
3. Depreciation and repairs of and power required for office equipment.
4. Insurance of office premises and equipment.
5. Fees of directors (other than those connected with sales or production).
6. Telephone, telegrams and postage.
7. Printing and Stationery.
8. Audit Fees.
9. Legal charges.
10. Bank charges.
11. Counting or Accounting house salaries
12. Computer Exps.

Office and administrative expenses are usually fixed or constant and, hence, there is not much difficulty in making an estimate of these, but it will be better if each item is considered separately. The profit and loss account of the period recently completed will be a good basis for the purpose of making an estimate.

Administrative Costs: It has been defined by the *CIMA* as:

"The cost of formulating the policy, directing the organisation, and controlling the operations of an undertaking, which is not related directly to a production, selling, distribution, research or development activity or function."

In other words it means the salaries paid to management personnel (like Directors, Managing Director, Finance Manager, etc.) and their personal staffs and expenses incurred on facilities meant for them, e.g., air-conditioning of their offices.

Office Expenses: Properly speaking, expenses incurred on carrying on the day-to-day office routine are called office expenses. These will comprise salaries paid to clerks and supervising staff, postage, stationery, office rent, etc.

Expenses of the Costing Department: The Costing Department exists for the benefit of the whole firm. Its costs may strictly be apportioned among the three types of overheads—factory, administrative and selling. But for the sake of convenience, the cost of maintaining the Costing Department should be included in the administrative overheads. In any case this department helps general management much more than production or selling departments.

Absorption of Office and Administrative Overheads

The more popular view regarding office and administrative expenses is that, since these are period costs or costs connected with time and not the volume of production, these should not be treated as part of the cost of production and should be debited to the Cost of Sales Account wholly. Suppose costs in 2005 for X Ltd. (newly started) were as follows:

		₹.
Materials Used		6,00,000
Wages		3,50,000
Factory Overheads		2,00,000
Office and Administrative Overheads	1,70,000	
Selling Expenses		1,20,000

90% of the output was sold for ₹. 15,00,000. The cost sheet and the statement of profit or loss will be as shown below:

	Cost Sheet for 2005	₹.
Materials Used		6,00,000
Wages		3,50,000
	Prime Cost	9,50,000
Factory Overheads		2,00,000
Cost of Production		11,50,000

	Statement of Profit or Loss for 2005	
Cost of goods produced		11,50,000
Less: Value of stock, 10%		1,15,000
	Cost of Goods Sold	10,35,000
Add : Office and Adm. Overheads		1,70,000
Selling Expenses		1,20,000
Cost of Sales		13,25,000
Profit		1,75,000
Sales		15,00,000

This view is not accepted by all. Another view is that administrative expenses are incurred for the benefit of production like other fixed factory overheads and should be considered as part of production cost.

If office and administrative expenses are to be treated as part of the cost of production, in the above case, it will become ₹. 13,20,000, *i.e.*, ₹. 11,50,000 plus ₹. 1,70,000 for administrative expenses. Then the *Statement of Profit or Loss* will be as given below:

	₹.
Cost of goods produced	13,20,000
Less: Value of stock, 10%	1,32,000
Cost of Goods Sold	11,88,000
Add: Selling Expenses	1,20,000
Cost of Sales	13,08,000
Profit	1,92,000
Sales	15,00,000

The student will see that in this case a part of the office and administrative expenses has been added to the value of the closing stock or has been inventorised.

If this view is accepted, then another suggestion is made. It is argued that administration is concerned with both production and sales. Hence the administrative expenses should be apportioned between the Production and Sales Departments and then the share falling to the Production Department should be considered a part of Factory Overheads and that relating to the Sales Department as Selling Overheads and treated accordingly.

The view is sound if a suitable basis for apportionment is available. This, however, is not often the case. There is the added complexity that administration is often concerned more with matters other than production and sales, such as strategic planning, financial management, negotiations with government, etc. Therefore either:

(*i*) office and administrative expenses are wholly charged off to the Cost of Sales Accounts; or

(*ii*) these are added to the cost of production on the basis of wages or works cost—the works cost method is traditional in this respect.

An analysis of the past Trading and Profit and Loss Accounts will reveal what percentage office and administrative expenses bear to works cost of work done, in the respective year. An average of such percentages will then be quite suitable for adoption in the current year. After the factory cost of a job is ascertained, office expenses would be added at the ascertained percentages based on works cost.

SELLING AND DISTRIBUTION OVERHEADS

Selling expenses form no part of the cost of production. The line between making and selling is clearly drawn. Nor is it possible to set down any comparable figures for production and selling costs. The demand for the product may be such that the cost of selling is merely concerned with loading the article on the lorries, in which case the ratio between production cost and selling expense may be as much as 100 : 1. On the other hand, very high expense may be entailed in marketing a product—out of all proportion to its production cost; consequently, the ratio may be the other way round. This is particularly the case with articles like cosmetics that are easy to produce and which require extensive advertising and sales campaigns. Generally, selling expenses, these days, are so large that a considerable proportion of the price is taken up by them. These should, therefore, be compiled separately and not lumped with the office expenses, as is the practice in some business houses. Selling expenses should also be included in Cost Accounts and not merely taken into account when the price is being fixed. Very often the fixation of the price may be affected by factors which can be considered only if the selling expenses are included in cost accounts. But all through, the line between Prime Cost, Production Overhead Expenses and Selling Expenses should be kept sharply in mind. The usual items to be included in selling expenses are as follows:

1. Salaries of the sales manager and his staff including his office staff and his salesmen.
2. Travelling expenses and commission payable to salesmen.
3. Advertising and showroom expenses.
4. Printing of catalogues and price lists and general stationery.
5. Rent of finished goods godowns and their repairs, etc.
6. Showroom expenses including rent and lighting, etc.
7. Bad debts.
8. Packing and carriage outwards.
9. Insurance of finished goods godowns, show-rooms and goods in transit.
10. Fees of directors who pay attention to sales.
11. Depreciation of delivery vans, etc., and their running expenses.
12. Telephone and postage.
13. Legal charges for recovery of debts.
14. Entertainment expenses.
15. Subscription to mercantile agencies and trade journals.

It will be seen that some of the above expenses will not be affected by the volume of sales, such as salaries of the various people employed by the Sales Department, rent, stationery, catalogues, etc. Such expenses are naturally fixed or constant. Other expenses will vary with the volume of sales and will be variable. Examples of variable expenses are : packing, freight outwards, insurance of goods in transit, commission to salesmen, bad debts, etc. Advertising is really neither fixed nor variable, because the amount to be spent on advertising is decided rather arbitrarily by the sales manager in consultation with the finance manager. It does not depend on the volume of sales and it is included in fixed sales expenses. The above is naturally important from the point of view of making a correct estimate of the selling and distribution expenses.

Items like bad debts and rebates may present certain amount of difficulty as regards correct determination of the amount to be included in the expenses. The only safe way would be to find out the actuals in the past few years and strike a percentage to the actual sales. In this way the amount to be included can be determined with regard to estimated sales.

Discounts: Discounts are of two types, namely, trade discounts and cash discounts. Trade discounts are deducted from purchases or sales as the case may be. Trade discounts are allowed in order to attract big orders. Cash discounts are allowed for prompt payment. This, therefore, is treated in the same way as interest and, therefore, there are a number of people who exclude cash discounts from costing just as interest is excluded. Both discount allowed and discount received would be ignored for costing purposes. On the other hand, it can be said that the selling price is fixed after taking the cash discount into account. Suppose, the selling price otherwise comes to ₹. 98, but then it is declared to be ₹. 100 with the provision that if payment is made within a certain period, a cash discount of ₹. 2 would be allowed. The net price obtained, therefore, in any case is ₹. 98. But if the credit to sales is at the rate of ₹. 100 it is fair that the cash discount allowed should be either deducted from sales or treated as a selling expense. There is, therefore, conflicting opinion on the question of treating cash discount. Each concern has to decide for itself.

Distinction between Selling and Distribution Expenses: Selling expenses consist of those expenses which are incurred for the purpose of convincing a customer of the desirability of placing an order with the firm. These expenses, therefore, consist of the following :

(*a*) Advertising.

(*b*) Major portion of the Sales Manager's salary and the salaries paid to the sales staff (according to the attention devoted to creation of markets).

(*c*) Cost of maintaining show rooms.

(*d*) The salaries and travelling expenses and commission paid to salesmen.

(*e*) Commission paid to agents.

Distribution Expenses are expenses incurred in moving the goods from the company's godowns to the customer's premises. These expenses would comprise the following:

(*a*) All finished goods godown expenses.

(*b*) Packing.

(*c*) Carriage outward including freight on goods sent for central storage or local godowns.

(*d*) Insurance in transit.

(*e*) Bad debts.

(*f*) Costs incurred on reconditioning empties or containers.

The following definition given by *CIMA* may be now:

Selling Cost: "The cost of seeking to create and stimulate demand (sometimes termed marketing) and of securing orders."

Distribution Cost: "The cost of the sequence of operations which begins with making the packed product available for despatch and ends with making the reconditioned returned empty package, if any, available for re-used.

Note : As well as including expenditure incurred in transporting articles to central or local storage, distribution cost includes expenditure incurred in moving articles to and from prospective customers as in the case of goods on sales or return basis. In the gas, electricity and water industries, 'distribution' means pipes, mains and services which may be regarded as the equivalent of packing and transportation."

ABSORPTION OF SELLING OVERHEADS

The following are the methods usually followed for determining the amount to be added to the cost of production as selling oncost :

1. *A Percentage on the Selling Price:* From an analysis of past accounts one can determine the percentage which normal selling and distribution expenses bear to the normal turnover.

$$\frac{\text{Selling overheads} \times 100}{\text{Sales}}$$

On this basis, selling expenses may be charged to the cost of each article. Suppose, on the basis of the previous year's accounts it is ascertained that selling expenses are 5 per cent of the turnover, we may add 5 per cent of the selling price of each product to its cost of production. The method assumes that selling price would be known. The method can be followed properly in those cases where the products are sold at fixed prices and, if there are more than one product, the proportion of each product in the total turnover remains constant. If prices fluctuate or if in one year a high priced article sells more and in another year it sells less, the method will not give good results. The amount recovered as selling expenses will then fluctuate because it is based on a fixed percentage of the total turnover. One may also note that the selling price of an article does not always indicate the selling effort involved. The method however is a simple one if it can be adopted.

2. *A Percentage on Works Cost or Cost of Products.* In this case, on the basis of past Trading and Profit and Loss Accounts, the percentage of selling expenses to works cost of all work done is ascertained and used for finding out the selling expenses to be charged to each product or job.

$$\frac{\text{Selling overheads} \times 100}{\text{Works cost}}$$

The method can be followed successfully only if one product is marketed. But then, if only one commodity is produced, a simpler method would be to divide the total estimated amount of selling overheads by the number of units to be sold. Works cost is likely to fluctuate and if selling expenses are recovered as a percentage on works cost, the total amount recovered may be considerably different from actual selling expenses. In case of there being a number of products, the method will not take into consideration different effort involved in selling each product. It cannot be said that selling effort will be in the same proportion as the manufacturing cost.

3. *An Estimated Rate Per Unit.* If there is only one product, the total estimated selling expenses can be divided by the total estimated number of units to be sold to give the selling expenses per unit.

$$\frac{\text{Selling overheads}}{\text{No. of units sold}}$$

It would be better, for control purposes, if the constant expenses are separated from the variable expenses. The separate treatment of constant and variable expenses is essential if there are more than one product.

The constant selling expenses, as already pointed out in the previous pages, are salaries of the sales manager and people working in the sales department, travelling expenses and salaries of travelling salesmen, rent of show rooms and expenses connected with them, rent, etc., of finished goods godowns and advertising. Advertising really is not constant, being dependent on the financial position of the firm as well as on the persuasive powers of the sales manager. The amount to be spent for advertising is arbitrarily fixed without strict reference to the volume of sales, etc. However, it is better to include advertising among constant selling expenses.

Apportionment Over Various Products : These expenses have to be apportioned over various products. The volume of sales cannot be the proper basis. One product may be popular and may, therefore, contribute the major share of turnover but not much will be spent on trying to sell that product. Another product may not be so popular and hence its sales may be low but, all the same, the firm may be devoting the major share of its energies and efforts towards making it popular. It follows that, if in such a case constant selling expenses are charged on the basis of sales, the results may be wrong. Good results would be obtained only on the basis of apportioning the various expenses individually on the basis of the service rendered to each product. Following may be the broad rules for this purpose:

(*a*) *Sales Office Expenses:* On the basis of the proportion of time devoted to each line of products.

(*b*) *Salesmen and Travelling Expenses:* If different salesmen are kept for individual products, the exact amount paid would be allocated to the product concerned. But if the salesmen handle all the products then again the 'allocation' will be on the basis of the proportion of time which the salesmen devote to each product.

(*c*) *Advertising:* In this case an analysis of the advertising effort will have to be made. Sometimes advertisment are inserted only for individual products but often an advertisement will be for all the products. In the first case there is no difficulty because the amount spent will be known for each product separately. In the second case, the apportioning may be made on the basis of sales obtained or turnover.

(*d*) *Show Rooms:* In this case the space occupied for each product will be the basis for allocating the expenses. The show room expenses will include not only the rent paid but also the wages of the persons attending.

(*e*) *Godowns:* Average quantities stored will be the basis.

(*f*) *Transport Charges:* If the company maintains its own vans, *etc.*, the expenses will be allocated on the basis of the average quantities delivered. If the arrangement is with a contractor and so much per case is paid, the allocation becomes easy.

If, however, information regarding the various items is not available separately, the total of fixed expenses can be apportioned on the basis of turnover.

Variable Selling Expenses: Variable expenses will be determined per unit of sale for each product. By definition the variable expenses depend upon the sales. Following are some of the variable selling expenses commonly found :

(*a*) *Bad debts are unavoidable to a point:* The amount to be written off as bad debt varies with turnover and, therefore, on the basis of past experience the percentage of bad debts to total sales should be determined. The amount so ascertained should be added to the selling overheads for each individual product.

(*b*) *Packing charges* for each product should be found out by costing the materials and labour used for the purpose. The main purpose of packing is to safeguard the articles against damage in transit or while in storage. Delicate articles require better packing. Another purpose which packing serves is to make the article attractive in appearance to the customer and to advertise the other products of the firm to the buyer. Properly speaking, expenses on this part of packing should be included in advertisement expenses.

(*c*) *Carriage outwards* should be determined on the basis of average distance travelled by the product concerned. Suppose last year 100 units were sold locally involving no rail transportation, 200 units were sold at a distance of 100 km and another 300 were sold at a distance of 500 km. The average distance for one unit comes to 283 km and, therefore, freight for 283 km for the product concerned (weight or cubic measurements being known) can be easily determined. This expense like packing, will naturally differ from product to product.

(*d*) *Insurance in transit* is easy to determine because the value of the article per unit is known and the rate at which the insurers charge premium for insurance in transit is also known. Even if the rate for all articles as the same (which is not), the value of products being different, the amount to be included in the selling overheads for each product for insurance in transit will be different.

(*e*) *Rebate to customers* is allowed if customers buy more than a certain quantity of an article or place orders for more than a certain value in a particular period. For example, a firm may allow a rebate of 5 per cent on the total value of orders placed by a customer if the orders in all amount to ₹. 10,000 or more in 6 months. Not all customers will be entitled to this refund because only some will place orders for ₹. 10,000 or more during a period of six months. Previous year's figures should tell us the total turnover and the total rebate allowed and we can find out the percentage on selling price expected to be allowed as rebate; and an amount thus calculated on the selling price of an article should be included in the selling overheads.

(*f*) *Commission to salesmen* presents no difficulty as the rate of commission to be allowed as well as the price on which the commission is allowed is known.

The total amount to be included by way of selling overheads in the cost of production of an article will, thus, consist of (1) constant selling expenses and (2) variable selling and distributive expenses. The latter should be listed separately.

Illustration 32: A company has three products, *P*, *Q* and *R*. You are given the undermentioned information about the products :

		P	*Q*	*R*
Sales	₹.	10,00,000	15,00,000	5,00,000
Quantity	Tonnes	20,000	25,000	5,000
No. of invoices		1,000	2,000	1,000
Average distance per consignment	Kms.	300	400	200
Average quantity stored	Tonnes	1,000	2,000	500

The undermentioned expenses were incurred :

	₹.
Commission to salesmen	30,000
Salaries of salesmen and sales staff	1,50,000
Bad Debts	3,000
Packing	25,000
Freight	51,000
Rent for godown and insurance	21,000
Clerical Expenses	10,000

Establish the overheads rate for recovery of selling expenses for each product.

Solution:

Statement Showing Apportionment of Expenses

	Basics	*Total* ₹.	*P* ₹.	*Q* ₹.	*R* ₹.
Sales		30,00,000	10,00,000	15,00,000	5,00,000
Expenses:					
Commission	Sales	30,000	10,000	15,000	5,000
Salaries, etc.,	"	1,50,000	50,000	75,000	25,000
Bad Debts,	"	3,000	1,000	1,500	500
Packing	Quantities Sold	25,000	10,000	12,500	2,500
Freight	Qty. × distance	51,000	18,000	30,000	3,000
Rent	Average Qty. stored	21,000	6,000	12,000	3,000
Clerical Expenses	No. of Invoices	10,000	2,500	5,000	2,500
Total		2,90,000	97,500	1,51,000	41,500
Percentage on Sales		9.67	9.75	10.06	8.30

***Freight will be apportioned among the different products in the ratio of quantities sold × average distance per consignment. The figures for the three products are :**

P	20,000 × 300	or	60,00,000
Q	25,000 × 400	or	100,00,000
R	5,000 × 200	or	10,00,000

The ratio is 6 : 10 : 1 for *P*, *Q*, and *R* respectively.

The percentage of expenses to sales is the overhead recovery rate for selling expenses.

OVERHEADS APPORTIONMENT BOOK

When work on a job or product is completed, amounts allotted to the job or product for factory and administrative overheads are added to the prime cost. In case a job is still incomplete at the time the books are due to be closed, the amounts in respect of these overheads will be calculated but not added to the cost of the job. The total of such amounts is kept in suspense and carried forward to the next period. The overheads allotted to each job for a period are entered in the Overheads Apportionment Book. Its ruling is quite simple as shown below:

Overheads Apportionment Book

Department..................... Period.................................

Job Nos.	*Overheads Apportioned*		
Completed Jobs	*Factory* ₹.	*Office & Administrative* ₹.	*Total* ₹.
Charged to Work-in-Progress Account			
Incomplete Jobs.			
Debit Suspense Account			

Date.....................

Prepared by .... Checked by ....

The totals of overheads allotted to completed job or work orders are recorded in the Cost Ledger by the entry:

Work-in-Progress Account ... Dr.
To Factory Overheads Account
To Administrative Overheads Account

The amounts in respect of incomplete jobs are recorded as:

(*i*) Factory Overheads Suspense Account ... Dr.
To Factory Overheads Account

(*ii*) Administrative Overheads Suspense Account ... Dr.
To Administrative Overheads Account

When the overheads are incurred, the entry is :

Factory Overheads Account ... Dr.
Administrative Overheads Account ... Dr.
Selling Distribution Overheads Account ... Dr.
To Cost Ledger Control Account

(For explaination see Chapter of 'Cost Control Accounts')

RESEARCH AND DEVELOPMENT COSTS

Modern industrial concerns maintain research departments for developing new products and processes. Once these new products or processes are developed, further expenses have to be incurred for taking the necessary steps for using the new process or producing the new product. The former type of expenses is called research cost and the latter is development cost. Both should be treated as *capital expenditure* and not as part of goods being currently produced. If research has not been fruitful, the expenditure incurred becomes an abnormal loss. The following definitions may be noted :

Research Cost: "The cost of searching for new or improved products, new applications of materials, or new or improved methods."

Development Cost: "The cost of the process which begins with the implementation of the decision to produce a new or improved product or to employ a new or improved method and ends with the commencement of formal production of that product or by that method." *[CIMA]*

ABSORPTION OF FIXED OVERHEADS OVER OUTPUT–ACTUAL OR AT NORMAL CAPACITY

We have seen that recovery of overheads—factory, office, and selling—is very important. The question is whether these overheads should be included in the cost sheet on the basis of actual or estimated output of the year concerned or on the basis of normal output of the firm with regard to the capacity of the firm. At first it seems obviously fair that the recovery should be on the basis of actual or estimated output since expenses incurred during a year are supposed to be for the output of that year. But let us have a look at the following imaginary cost sheet (*a*)showing the cost sheet on the basis of actual output of 40,000 units and (*b*) showing cost sheet on the basis of normal capacity output of 50,000 units.

	(*a*) *On the basis of actual output* (40,000 units)	(*b*) *On the basis of normal output (capacity)* (50,000 units)
Materials	5.00	5.00
Direct Labour	4.50	4.50
Prime Cost	9.50	9.50
Factory overtheads:		
Constant (say, ₹. 2,00,000 in all)	5.00	4.00
Variable	1.50	1.50
Works Cost	16.00	15.00
Office overheads:		
(assumed to be ₹. 1,00,000 in all)	2.50	2.00
Cost of Production	18.50	17.00
Selling overhedads:		
Constant (₹. 1,00,000 in all)	2.50	2.00
Variable	1.00	1.00
Cost of Sales	22.00	20.00

If we suppose further that the selling price obtainable in the market is only ₹. 23.00 per unit, the margin of net profit in the first case is ₹. 1,00 yielding a total of ₹. 40,000 on the production and sale of 40,000 units. But if we consider the cost sheet (*b*), the profit per unit is ₹. 3.00 and the profit for 50,000 units should have been ₹. 1,50,000.

However, if actually 40,000 units are produced and sold, the profit will only be ₹. 40,000 as the following figures show :

Trading and Profit and Loss Account

	₹.		₹.
To Materials	2,00,000	By Sales	9,20,000
To Labour	1,80,000		
To Factory Expenses	2,60,000		
To Office Expenses	1,00,000		
To Selling Expenses	1,40,000		
To Net Profit	40,000		
	9,20,000		9,20,000

The point is, however, that had 50,000 units been produced and sold there would have been a profit of ₹. 1,50,000 and hence the diminution of the profit by ₹. 1,10,000 must be laid at the door of reduction in output by 10,000 units. It is the measure of the loss due to idleness. Having ascertained the cost (which we would not have known if we had prepared the cost sheet only on the basis of actual output), it only remains to find out why the idleness arose. It may have been due to the sales manager's slackness in getting orders or it may have been due to some bottlenecks in the factory or some other mismanagement, say, non-availability of raw materials.

The difference in the profit shown by the above two cases can be explained as follows:

	₹.
Constant factory expenses unrecovered (10,000 × ₹. 4)	40,000
Constant office expenses unrecovered (10,000 × ₹. 2)	20,000
Constant selling expenses unrecovered (10,000 × ₹. 2)	20,000
Profit of ₹. 3 per unit lost on 10,000 units 30,000	
Total cost of idleness	1,10,000

For the output of 40,000 units, in this case, the cost sheet should be made as under :

	Total Cost ₹.	*Cost per Unit* ₹.	*Amount unrecovered* ₹.
Materials	2,00,000	5.00	
Direct labour	1,80,000	4.50	
Prime cost	3,80,000	9.50	
Factory Expenses:			
Fixed	1,60,000	4.00	40,000
Variable	60,000	1.50	
Factory Cost	6,00,000	15.00	
Office Expenses	80,000	2.00	20,000
Cost of Production	6,80,000	17.00	
Sellint Expenses:			
Fixed	80,000	2.00	20.000
Variable	40,000	1.00	
Cost of Sales	8,00,000	20.00	
Profit	1,20,000	3.00	
Sales	9,20,000	23.00	80.000
Actual Profit : Profits as per Cost Sheet			1,20,000
Less: Expenses unrecovered			80,000
Actual Profit			40,000

₹. 80,000, fixed overheads not recovered, is cost of idleness. It may also be computed as fixed expenses percentage of idle capacity.

Advantages of Ascertaining Cost on the Basis of Normal Capacity: The following are the advantages of preparing cost sheets, etc., on the basis of normal capacity rather than on the basis of actual output :

(*a*) The object of costing is to reflect changes in manufacturing methods or efficiency. If expenses are apportioned on actual output basis, the cost per unit will fluctuate but in no way will it be connected with change in efficiency in manufacturing processes. The cost of a job should be the same irrespective of the amount of work done in the factory; and profit or loss resulting from changes in the level of output itself should be separated from the profit or loss connected with manufacturing efficiency or inefficiency. As pointed out above, the cost of idleness or windfall profit due to unduly heavy rush of orders can be found out only if cost is ascertained on the basis of normal capacity. Such cost or windfall profits have their proper place in the profit and loss account and not as part of cost of production.

(*b*) If selling prices are based on cost and if costs are determined on actual output basis, it is obvious that high prices will be fixed when output is low, the costs being high. Such is likely to be the case in depression periods when prices have to be lowered. During boom periods, when there is rush of orders, costs on actual output basis will be low and hence prices will be kept unnecessarily low.

(*c*) It cannot be said that if, say, a factory works only half of its capacity, the output gives rise to all the expenses. At best, in addition to variable expenses, it can be said to cause only half of the constant expenses (the other half being incurred in order to keep the factory alive for work when normal output can be attained). Cost of an article should truly reflect this and if we charge off all the constant expenses to the actual output, the cost per unit will be inflated. To the extent stocks lie unsold, the value of inventory will be inflated. In the illustration given above the cost per unit on the basis of 40,000 units is ₹. 18.50 and on the basis of 50,000 units it is ₹. 17.00. If the former is adopted, unsold stocks will be valued at ₹. 18.50 per unit. It cannot be said or maintained that as production declines, the value of unsold stocks rises. This will be the case if ₹. 18.50 instead of ₹. 17.00 is adopted for valuation of closing stocks.

What is normal capacity? Normal capacity depends on management's decision about plant capacity having regard to the estimate of demand—it is lower of the two. Suppose the estimate of demand for a product is 50,000 whereas plant is available with capacity of either 55,000 units or 45,000 units. If the large size plant is installed, the capacity will be reckoned to be 50,000 units: if the smaller size plant is installed, the capacity will be 45,000 units.

The decision obviously is a one-time decision and, therefore, normal capacity does not change from time to time but if a factory beyond one's control comes to operate, the capacity may be temporarily treated as having been reduced. Suppose in the above example, the larger size plant is installed but there is a 40 per cent power cut throughout one year. The capacity for that year should be considered to be 33,000 units *i.e.*, 60 per cent of 55,000.

ITEMS EXCLUDED FROM COST ACCOUNTS

The following items may figure in the financial accounts (in addition to those items which are included in cost accounts and which have been discussed above):

(*a*) *Matters of pure finance* including interest paid and received, dividend received on investments, rents received, loss or profit on sale of company's property or investments, transfer fees or transfer office expenses.

(*b*) *Appropriation of profits* including income tax, dividends paid, transfers to sinking funds or reserve funds, excessive depreciation with a view to create secret reserves, goodwill or other fictitious assets written off, *etc.*

(*c*) *Arbitrary or abnormal items*, *e.g.*, excessive salary to some one (because he happens to be in control of the concern).

But normal expenses should be included even if it is not incurred. For example, if partners of a manufacturing firm do not draw any salary, reasonable salary should be included. Such "expenses" are called *notional expenses*.

ACTIVITY BASED COSTING (*ABC*)[1]

Cooper and Kaplan, during 1988–90 draw attention to the limitations of tradtional product costing system based on allocation of overheads to products (as described in this chapter). Traditional costing methods of overhead allocation use volume-related measures, such as direct labour hours or machine hours. But there are many expenses or overheads which are not related to physical volume. These are related to support activities such as material handling, material procurement, performing set-ups, production scheduling and inspection activities. These activities and their cost should not be allocated to products on the basis of production volumes.

It is important to note that trading overhead allocation system were designed decades ago when most companies manufactured a limited range of products. Then direct material and labour were main elements of factory cost and overhead costs were relatively small. To day production is carried on of a wide range of products, direct labour represent a small part of total cost and overhead costs are of considerable importance.

Activity Based Costing System emphasises the need to obtain better understanding of the behaviour of overhead costs and thus ascertains what causes overheads and how they relate to products. *ABC* system involves the following stages.

1. Identify the *major activities* which take place in an organisation.
2. Assigning costs to *cost pools/cost centres* for each major activity.
3. Determine the *cost drivers* for each major activity. Cost drives are activities which determine cost, for example number of receiving orders for receiving departments, number of production runs, number of set-ups etc.
4. Assign the cost of activities to products according to each product's demand (using cost drivers as a measure of demand) for activities.

Thus in activity-based costing cost are not initially traced to departments. These are first allocated to activites and then to products. Activities, known as cost drivers, causing overheads to occur are identified. These activites or cost drivers are later used as a basis for allocating overhead costs to products.

TYPICAL ILLUSTRATIONS

Overhead Absorption

Illustration 33: Superclass Co. Ltd. has three production departments *X, Y* and *Z* and two service departments *A* and *B*.

The following estimated figures for a certain period have been made available:

	₹.
Rent and Rates	10,000
Lighting and Electricity	1,200
Indirect Wages	3,000
Power	3,000
Depreciation of machinery	20,000
Other expenses and Sundries	20,000

Following are further details which are also available :

	Total	*X*	*Y*	*Z*	*A*	*B*
Floor space (sq. mtr.)	10,000	2,000	2,500	3,000	2,000	500
Light points (Nos.)	120	20	30	40	20	10

1 See separate chapter on *ABC*.

	Total	X	Y	Z	A	B
Direct wages ₹.	20,000	6,000	4,000	6,000	3,000	1,000
Horse power of machines.	300	120	60	100	20	—
Cost of machinery	₹. 100,000	24,000	32,000	40,000	2,000	2,000
Working hours		4,670	3,020	3,050		

The expenses of service departments *A* and *B* are to be allocated as follows:

		X	*Y*	*Z*	*A*	*B*
A	%	20	30	40	—	10
B	%	40	20	30	10	—

(*a*) You are required to calculate overhead absorption rates per hour in respect of the three production departments.

(*b*) What will be the total cost of an article with material cost of ₹. 80 and labour cost of ₹. 40 which passes through *X, Y* and *Z* for 2, 3 and 4 hours respectively.

Solution:

Particulars	*Basis of Apportionment*	*Total*	*Production Deptt.* *X*	*Y*	*Z*	*Service Deptt.* *A*	*B*
		₹.	₹.	₹.	₹.	₹.	₹.
Rent & Rages	Floor Space	10,000	2000	2500	3000	2000	500
Lighting & Electricity.	Light Points	1,200	200	300	400	200	100
Indirect Wages.	Direct Wages	3,000	900	600	900	450	150
Power	H.P × Working Hours.	3,000				—	—
	120 × 4670 :		1606				
	60 × 3020 :			520			
	100 × 3050				874		
Depreciation of Machinery	Cost of Machinery.	20,000	4800	6400	8000	400	400
Other Exp. & Sundries.	Direct wages.	20,000	6000	4000	6000	3000	1000
Total		57,200	15,506	14,320	19,174	6,050	2,150
Expenses of *A* Deptt.	As percentage in the questions		1,210	1,815	2420	(6,050)	605
Expenses of *B* Deptt.	" "		1,102	551	827	275	(2,755)
Expenses of *A* Deptt.	" "		55	83	110	(275)	27
Expenses of B Deptt.	" "		11	5	8	3	(27)
Expenses of *A* Deptt.	" "		1	1	1	(3)	—
Total Overheads Overheads		57,200	17,885	16,775	22,540	—	—

	X	Y	Z
Overhead absorption rate per hour =	17,885,	16,775	22,540
Overhead incurred ÷ Working hours.	4,670	3020	3,050
	= 3.83	= 5.55	= 7.39

(b) **Statement Showing Cost per Article**

		₹.
Material Cost		80.00
Labour Cost		40.00
Direct Expenses		—
Prime Cost		120.00
Dept. X (2 × 3.83)	7.66	
Dept. Y (3 × 5.55)	16.65	
Dept. Z (4 × 7.39)	29.56	53.87
Total Cost of an Article.		173.87

Illustration 34: The Company is having three production departments A, B and C and two service departments boiler-house and pump-room. The boiler-house has to depend upon the pump-room for supply of water and pump-room in its turn is dependent on the boiler-house for the supply of steam power for driving the pump. The expenses incurred by the production departments are :

A : ₹. 4,00,000; B : ₹. 3,50,000; and C : ₹. 2,50,000

The expenses for boiler-house is ₹. 1,17,000 and the pump-room is ₹. 1,50,000.

The expenses of the boiler-house and pump-room are apportioned to the production departments on the following basis :

	A	*B*	*C*	*Boiler House*	*Pump Room*
Expenses of boiler-house	20%	40%	30%	—	10%
Expenses of pump-room	40%	20%	20%	20%	—

Show clearly as to how the expenses of boiler-house and pump-room would be apportioned to A, B and C departments?

Solution:

Statement Showing Apportionment of Overheads (Repeated Distribution Method)

Particulars	*Production Deptts.*			*Service*	*Deptts.*
	A	*B*	*C*	*Boiler House*	*Pump Room*
	₹.	₹.	₹.	₹.	₹.
Expenses incurred	4,00,000	3,50,000	2,50,000	1,17,000	1,50,000
Boiler-house	23,400	46,800	35,100	(1,17,000)	11,700
Pump-room	64,680	32,340	32,340	32,340	(1,61,700)
Boiler-house	6,468	12,936	9,702	(32,340)	3,234
Pump-room	1,293	647	647	647	(3234)
Boiler-house	129	259	194	(647)	65
Pump-room	26	13	13	13	(65)
Boiler-house	4	5	4	(13)	—
Total	4,96,000	4,43,000	3,28,000	Nil	Nil

Illustration 35: Deccan Manufacturing Ltd. have three departments which are regarded as production departments. Service Departments' costs are distributed to these production departments using the "*Step Ladder Method*" of distribution. Estimates of factory overhead costs to be incurred by each department in the forthcoming year are as follows: Data required for distribution is also shown against each department:

Departments	*Factory Overhead* ₹.	*Direct Labour Hours*	*No. of Employees.*	*Area in Sq. M.*
Production:				
X	1,93,000	4,000	100	3,000
Y	64,000	3,000	125	1,500
Z	83,000	4,000	85	1,500
Service :				
P	45,000	1,000	10	500
Q	75,000	5,000	50	1,500
R	1,05,000	6,000	40	1,000
S	30,000	3,000	50	1,000

The overhead costs of the four service departments are distributed in the same order, *viz.*, *P, Q, R* and *S* respectively on the following basis:

Department		*Basis*
P	...	Number of Employees
Q	...	Direct Labour Hours
R	...	Area in square metres
S	...	Direct Labour Hours.

You are required to :

(*a*) Prepare a schedule showing the distribution of overhead costs of the four service departments to the three production departments; and

(*b*) Calculate the overhead recovery rate per direct labour hour for each of the three production departments.

Solution:

(*a*) **Statement Showing the Distribution of Overhead Cost**

Particulars	*Basis of Approtionment*	*Production Departments*			*Service Departments*			
		X ₹.	*Y* ₹.	*Z* ₹.	*P* ₹.	*Q* ₹.	*R* ₹.	*S* ₹.
Factory overheads	As given	193,000	64,000	83,000	45,000	75,000	1,05,000	30,000
P Deptt.	No. of employees	10,000	12,500	8,500	(45,000)	5,000	4,000	5,000
Q "	Direct Labour Hours	16,000	12,000	16,000	—	(80,000)	24,000	12,000
R "	Area in Sq. M.	57,000	28,500	28,500	—	—	(1,33,000)	19,000
S "	Direct Labour Hour	24,000	18,000	24,000	—	—	—	(66,000)
Total Factory Overhead		3,00,000	1,35,000	1,60,000	—	—	—	—

(*b*) Calculation of overhead recovery rate per Direct Labour Hour

$$= \frac{\text{Overhead incurred}}{\text{Direct Labour Hour}}$$

X Deptt. $= \frac{3,00,000}{4,000}$ = ₹. 75 per Direct Labour Hour

Y " $= \frac{1,35,000}{3,000}$ = ₹. 45 per Direct Labour Hour

Z " $= \frac{1,60,000}{4,000}$ = ₹. 40 per Direct Labour Hour

Illustration 36: A company has three production cost centres A, B and C and two service cost centres X and Y. Costs allocated to service centres are required to be apportioned to the production centres to find out cost of production of different products.

It is found that benefit of service cost centres is also received by each other along with the production cost centres.

Overhead costs as allocated to the five cost centres and estimates of benefit of service cost centres received by each of them are as under :

Cost Centres	*Overheads Costs as Allocated (Rupees)*	*Estimates of Benefits Received From Service* Centres %	
		X	Y
A	80,000	20	20
B	40,000	30	25
C	20,000	40	50
X	20,000	—	5
Y	10,000	10	—

Required:

Work out final overhead costs of each of the production departments including reapportioned cost of service centres using (*a*) Continuous distribution method and (*b*) Simultaneous equation method.

Solution:

Statement of Final Overhead Cost of Production Departments (Continuous Distribution Method)

Particulars	*Basis of apportionment*	*Prodn. Dept.*			*Service Dept.*	
		A	*B*	*C*	*X*	*Y*
Overhead costs	As allocated	80,000	40,000	20,000	20,000	10,000
Overheads of X	% given in question	4,000	6,000	8,000	(–)20,000	2,000
Overheads of Y	" " " "	2,400	3,000	6,000	600	(–)12,000
Overheads of X	" " " "	120	180	240	(–)600	
Overheads of Y	" " " "	12	15	30	3	60
Overheads of X	" " " "	1	1	1	(–)3	(–)60
Final Overhead Cost of Prodn. Dept.		86,533	49,196	34,271	—	—

(*b*) **Simultaneous equation method :** Suppose overheads of X service centre is x and of Y is y.

Overhead of $X = 20{,}000 + 5\%\ y$ ... (*i*)

Overhead of $Y = 10{,}000 + 10\%\ x$ ...(*ii*)

or

$x = 20{,}000 + 0.05\ y$

$y = 10{,}000 + 0.10\ x$

Multiply both above equations by 20.

$20x = 4{,}00{,}000 + y$ ... (*iii*)

$20y = 2{,}00{,}000 + 2x$ ... (*iv*)

Multiply the equaltion (*iii*) by 20

$400x = 80{,}00{,}000 + 20y$

or $400x - 20y = 80{,}00{,}000$

$-2x + 20y = 2{,}00{,}000$ ... (*v*)

$398x = 82{,}00{,}000$

$$x = \frac{82,00,000}{398}$$

= ₹. 20,603 overheads of X

y = 10,000 + (0.10 × 20,603)

= ₹. 12,060 Overheads of Y

(c) Statement of Final Overhead Cost of Production Departments
(Simultaneous Equation Method)

Particulars	*Basis of Apportionment*	*Prodn. Dept.*			*Service Dept.*	
		A	B	C	X	Y
Overhead costs	As allocated	80,000	40,000	20,000	20,000	10,000
Overheads of X	% given	4,121	6,181	8,241	(–)20,603	2,060
Overheads of Y	% given	2,412	3,015	6,030	603	(–)12,060
Final Overhead cost of prodn. Dept.		86,533	49,196	34,271	—	—

Illustration 37: Following particulars have been extracted from the books of Reliable Company.

	₹.	₹.
Indirect Materials		
Shop No. 1	12,000	
Shop No. 2	18,000	
Shop No. 3	6,000	
Tool Room	3,600	
Stores	4,600	
Factory Office	1,800	46,200
Indirect Wages		
Shop No. 1	12,600	
Shop No. 2	17,600	
Shop No. 3	16,000	
Tool Room	11,100	
Stores	4,500	
Factory Office	6,600	68,400
Factory Rent		30,000
Insurance		6,000
Depreciation 10%		30,000
Power		27,000
Light and heat		12,000
Total		2,19,600

Further information regarding the operations are given below:

Department	*Area (Sq. meter)*	*Book value of machinery* ₹.	*Effective H.P.*	*Direct labour*		*Machinery Hours*
				Hours	*Cost* ₹.	
Production						
Shop No. 1	1,000	75,000	90	3,00,000	90,000	1,60,000
Shop No. 2	750	1,35,000	90	3,00,000	60,000	2,40,000
Shop No. 3	1,500	30,000	—	2,00,000	50,000	—
Service						
Tool Room	500	45,000	20	—	50,000	—
Stores	750	7,500	—	—	—	—
Factory Office	500	7,500	—	—	—	—
	5,000	3,00,000	200	8,00,000	2,50,000	4,00,000

You are required to prepare an "Overhead Analysis Sheet" for the departments of Reliable Co. for the year showing the basis of apportionment. **[*ICWA, Inter*]**

Solution:

Overhead Analysis Sheet (₹.)

Overheads	*Basis of apportionment*	*Total*	*Production Shops No.*			*Service Deptts.*		
			No. 1	*No. 2*	*No. 3*	*Tool Room*	*Stores*	*Factory Office*
Ind. Material	As given	46,200	12,000	18,000	6,000	3,600	4,800	1,800
Ind. Wages	As given	68,400	12,600	17,600	16,000	11,100	4,500	6,600
Factory Rent	Area	30,000	6,000	4,500	9,000	3,000	4,500	3,000
Insurance	Book value of Machinery	6000	1,500	2,700	600	900	150	150
Depreciation	Book value of Machinery	30,000	7,500	13,500	3,000	4,500	750	750
Power	HP × MH	27,000	10,800	16,200	—	—	—	—
Light & Heat	Area	12,000	2,400	1,800	3,600	1,200	1,800	1,200
Total Overheads		2,19,600	52,800	74,300	38,200	24,300	16,500	13,500

Note 1.	Shop No.	Effective HP		Machine Hours	Total
	1	90	×	1,60,000	= 1,44,00,000
	2	90	×	2,40,000	= 2,16,00,000

Ratio = 144:216 or 2:3 will be ratio for power

Shop No. 1. 27,000 × 2/5 = ₹ 10,800

Shop No. 2. 27,000 × 3/5 = ₹. 16,200

2. In the Tool Room, Effective HP is 20 but Machine hours is nil. The machine has not worked. Hence, power charges have not been apportioned to Tool Room.

Illustration 38: A textile mill has two production departments, "spinning" and "weaving" and two service departments, S_1 and S_2. Variable costs of operating the two service departments, their outputs and quantum of service rendered to other departments are as follows

		From service departments	
		S_1	S_2
To	Spinning	30%	25%
	Weaving	20%	35%
	S_1	—	40%
	S_2	50%	—

	S_1	S_2
Variable cost of service departments	₹. 1,20,000	₹. 2,60,000
Output of service departments (units)	10,000	20,000

Calculate:

(*i*) Cost per unit of service produced by S_1 and S_2.

(*ii*) Cost of service received by spinning and weaving departments.

Solution: (*i*) Let x_1 and x_2 be the total cost of service departments S_1 and S_2 respectively. From the data given in question, the following equation can be formed:

$$x_1 = 1{,}20{,}000 + 0.4x_2$$

$$x_2 = 2{,}60{,}000 + 0.5x_1$$

Equation can be rewritten as under:

$$x_1 + 0.4x_2 = 1{,}20{,}000 \quad \ldots (i)$$

$$-0.5x_1 + x_2 = 2{,}60{,}000 \quad \ldots (ii)$$

By multiplying equation (*ii*) by 2, we get

$$-x_1 + 2x_2 = 5{,}20{,}000 \quad \ldots (iii)$$

By adding equations (*i*) and (*iii*), we get

$$1.6\ x_2 = 6{,}40{,}000$$

$$x_2 = 4{,}00{,}000$$

Substituting the value of x_2 in equation (*i*)

$$x_1 = 2{,}80{,}000$$

Cost per unit of service department S_1 = 2,80,000 ÷ 10,000 = ₹. 28

Cost per unit of service department S_2 = 4,00,000 ÷ 20,000 = ₹. 20

(*ii*) ***Service rendered to spinnijng department:***

30% of service department S_1 = 0.3 × 2,80,000	=	₹. 84,000
25% of service department S_2 = 0.25 × 4,00,000	=	1,00,000
		1,84,000 (*a*)

Service rendered to weaving department:

20% of service department S_1 = 0.2 × 2,80,000	=	₹. 56,000
35% of service department S_2 = 0.35 × 4,00,000	=	1,40,000
		1,96,000 (*b*)
Total Cost (*a*) + (*b*)		3,80,000

Machine Hour Rate

Illustration 39: Work out the predetermined machine hour rates for departments *A* and *B* of a factory from the following data :

Preliminary Estimate of Expenses

	Total ₹.	*Dept. A* ₹.	*Dept. B* ₹.
Power	15,000		
Spare parts	8,000	3,000	5,000
Consumable Stores	5,000	2,000	3,000
Depreciation (Machinery)	30,000	10,000	20,000
Insurance (Machinery)	3,000		
Indirect Labour	40,000		
Building Maintenance	7,000		

The final estimates are to be prepared on the basis of the above figures after taking into consideration the following factors :

(*a*) An increase of 10 per cent in the price of spare parts.

(*b*) An increase of 20 per cent in the consumption of spare parts in Dept. B only.

(*c*) Increase in the straight line rate of depreciation from 10 per cent of the original value to 12 per cent.

(*d*) 15 per cent general increase in wage rates.

The following further information is available:

	Dept. A	Dept. B
Estimated Direct Labour Hours	80,000	1,20,000
Ratio of Kw rating	3	2
Estimated Machine Hours	25,000	30,000
Floor space (sq.ft.)	15,000	20,000

Solution:

Statement Showing Predetermined Machine Hour Rates

	Basis of apportionment	*Total ₹.*	*Dept. A ₹.*	*Dept. B ₹.*
Power	Ratio of KW rating *i.e.*, 3 : 2	15,000	9,000	6,000
Spare Parts	Allocation plus price increase and quantity increase in Deptt *B*.	9,900	3,300	6,600
Consumable Stores	Given Allocation	5,000	2,000	3,000
Depreciation	12% of Original Value *i.e.*, ₹. 3,00,000.	36,000	12,000	24,000
Insurance of Machinery	Value of Machinery	3,000	1,000	2,000
Indirect Labour	40,000 + 15% in proportion to DLH *i.e.*, 8 : 12	46,000	18,400	27,600
Building Maintenance	Floor area *i.e.*, 15 : 20	7,000	3,000	4,000
Total Overheads		1,21,900	48,700	73,200
Estimated Machine hours			25,000	30,000
Predetermined Machine hour rate (Overhead ÷ Machine Hours)			₹. 1.948	₹. 2.44

Illustration 40: In a manufacturing concern *ABC* Ltd., the machine shop has 8 identical machines manned by 6 operators. The machines cannot be worked without an operator wholly engaged on them. The total cost of the machines are ₹. 8,00,000.

Following information relates to a six monthly period ended 30th June, 2000 :

Normal available hours per month	208
Absenteeism (without pay) hours per month	18
Leave (with pay) hours per month	20
Normal idle time (Unavoidable) hours per month	10
Average rate of wages per day of 8 hours	₹. 20
Production Bonus	15% on wages
Power and Fuel consumption	₹. 9,000
Supervision & Indirect labour	₹. 3,300
Electricity	₹. 1,200
The following particulars are on a yearly basis :	
Repairs and Maintenance	3% of value of machines
Insurance	₹. 42,000

Depreciation	10% of original cost
Other factory expenses	₹. 12,000
Allocated General Management Expenses	₹. 63,670

You are required to work out a comprehensive machine hour rate for the machine shop.

Solution:

Working Notes:

Normal available hours per month			208
Less :	Absenteeism without pay	18	
	Leave with pay	20	
	Normal idle time unavoidable	10	48
	Hours per month		160

Total hours for 6 month for 6 operators

= 160 × 6 × 6 = 5,760

The labour hours have been taken as machine hours because machines cannot work without an operator.

Computation of Machine Hour Rate

Particulars	*Basis of apportionment*	*Amount (₹)*
6 Operators wages	See working Note	17,100
Production Bonus	15% of wages	2,565
Power & Fuel		9,000
Supervision and Indirect Labour		3,300
Electricity		1,200
Repairs & Maintenance	3% of 8,00,000 for 6 months	12,000
Insurance	42,000 × 6/12 =	21,000
Depreciation	10% on 8,00,000 for 6 months	40,000
Other factory expenses	12,000 × 6/12 =	6,000
General Management expensese	63,670 × 6/12 =	31,835
Total		1,44,000
Machine Hour Rate	1,44,000/5,760 =	25

Working Note

(1) Average rate of wages per hour = ₹. 20/8 hours = ₹. 2.50

Actual Hours paid = 208 − 18 = 190

Total wages = 190 × 6 × 6 = 6,840 hours at ₹. 2.50 = ₹. 17,100

Illustration 41: A machine was purchased on January 1, 2000, for ₹. 5 lakhs. The total cost of all machinery inclusive of the new machine was ₹. 75 lakhs. The following further particulars are available:

Expected life of the machine 10 years.

Scrap value at the end of ten year ₹. 5,000.

Repairs and maintenance for the machine during the year ₹. 2,000

Expected number of working hours of the machine per year 4,000 hours.

Insurance premium annually for all the machines ₹. 4,500.

Electricity consumption for the machine per hour @ 75 paise per unit 25 units.

Area occupied by the machine 100 sq. ft.

Area occupied by other machines 1,500 sq. ft.

Rent per month of the department ₹. 800.

Lighting charges for 20 points for the whole department, out of which three points are for the machine. ₹. 120 per month.

Compute the machine hour rate for the new machine on the basis of the data given above.

[*C.A. Inter*]

Solution:

Computation of Machine Hour Rate

	Basis of apportionment	*per year* ₹.	*per hour* ₹.
A. Fixed Costs:			
Depreciation	$\frac{5,00,000 - 5,000}{10 \text{ years}}$	49,500	
Repairs & Maintenance.		2,000	
Insurance premium	$4,500 \times \frac{5}{75}$	300	
Rent (800 × 12)	$9,600 \times \frac{100 \text{ Sft.}}{1,600}$	600	
Lighting (120 × 12)	$1,440 \times \frac{3 \text{ points}}{20}$	216	
Total		52,616	
Per hour	$\frac{52,616}{4000}$		13.15
B. Variable Cost :			
Electricity	25 units @ 75 paise		18.75
Machine Hour Rate			31.90

Illustration 42: A manufacturing unit has added a new machine to its fleet of five existing machines. The total cost of purchase and installation of the machine is ₹. 7,50,000. The machine has an estimated life of 15 years and is expected to realise ₹. 30,000 as scrap at the end of its working-life.

Other relevant data are as follows:

(*i*) Budgeted working-hours is 2,400 based on 8 hours per day for 300 days. This includes 400 hours for plant maintenance.

(*ii*) Electricity used by the machine is 15 units per hour at a cost of ₹. 2.00 per unit. No current is drawn during maintenance.

(*iii*) The machine requires special oil for heating which is replaced once in every month at a cost of ₹. 2,500 on each occasion.

(*iv*) Estimated cost of maintenance of the machine is ₹. 500 per week of 6 working-days.

(*v*) 3 operators control the operations of the entire battery of six machines and the average wages per person amounts to ₹. 450 per week plus 40 per cent fringe benefits.

(*vi*) Departmental and general works overheads allocated to the operation during the last year was ₹. 60,000. During the current year it is estimated that there will be an increase of 12.5 per cent of this amount. No incremental overhead is envisaged for the installation of the new machine.

You are required to compute the machine-hour rate for recovery of the running cost of the machine.

Solution:

Effective Machine Running Hours:

No. of working days for the year—300	
Total Working Hours @ 8 hours per day	2400 hours
Less : Machine maintenance time	400 hours
Effective machine hours	2000 hours

Computation of Machine Hour Rate

			Per Annum ₹.	Per Hour ₹.
Cost of Electricity				
2000 hours × 15 units × ₹. 2.00 per unit			60,000	30.00
Cost of Heating				
Change of special oil—₹. 2500 × 12 months			30,000	15.00
Maintenance Cost				
₹. 500 per week of 6 working days (500/6) × 300			25,000	12.50
Operators Cost				
Wages @ ₹. 450 per week each worker				
for 3 Operators 3 × 450 × 50	67,500			
Add: 40% fringe benefits	27,000			
	94,500			
Cost of operating one machine 94,500/6			15,750	7.875
Departmental and General Overheads				
Allocation for last year	60,000			
Add: for inflation 12.5%	7,500			
Total for this year	67,500			
Cost per machine 67,500/6 =			11,250	5.625
Depreciation				
Cost of machine—Purchase & Installation		7,50,000		
Less: Scrap (realisable after 15 years)		30,000		
Net cost		7,20,000		
Depreciation per annum 7,20,000/15			48,000	24.000
Total Expenses			₹. 1,90,000	95.000

Illustration 43: In a factory, a machine is considered to work for 208 hours in a month. It includes maintenance time of 8 hours and set up time of 20 hours.

The expense data relating to the machine are as under:

— Cost of the machine is ₹. 5,00,000. Life is 10 years. Estimated scrap value at the end of life is ₹. 20,000.	
— Repairs and maintenance per annum	₹. 60,480
— Consumable stores per annum 47,520	
— Rent of building per annum (The machine under reference occupies 1/6 of the area)	72,000
— Supervisor's salary per month (Common to three machines)	6,000
— Wages of operator per month per machine	2,500
— General lighting charges per month allocated to the machine	1,000
— Power 25 units per hour at ₹. 2 per unit.	

Power is required for productive purposes only. Set up time, though productive, does not require power. The Supervisor and Operator are permanent. Repairs and maintenance and consumable stores vary with the running of the Machine.

Required:

Calculate a two-tier machine hour rate for (*a*) set-up time, and (*b*) running time.

Solution:

Working Notes:

1. (*a*) Effective hours for standing charges : (208 – 8) = 200 hrs.

(*b*) Effective hours for variable costs : (208 – 28) = 180 hrs.

2. Standing charges per hour

	Per month	*Per hour*
Supervisor's salary (₹. 6,000 ÷ 3)	₹. 2,000	
General lighting	1,000	
Rent (₹. 72,000 × 1/6) ÷ 12	1,000	
Total standing charges	4,000	
Standing charges per hour (₹. 4,000 ÷ 200)		₹. 20

3. Machine expenses per hour

	Calculations			
	Per month	*Per hour*	*Per month*	*Per hour*
Depreciation	*(See note)*		₹. 4,000	₹. 20.00
Repairs and maintenance	60,480/12	5,040/180	5.040	28.00
Consumable stores	47,520/12	3,960/180	3,960	22.00
Power	25 × ₹. 2 × 180 hrs.	9,000/180	9,000	50.00
Wages—	2,500/200	2,500	12.50	
			24,500	132.50

Statement Showing Computations of Two-tier Machine Hour Rate

	Machine hour rate based on set-up time	*Machine hour rate based on running time*
Standing charges	₹. 20.00	₹. 20.00
Machine expenses:		
Depreciation	20.00	20.00
Repairs and maintenance	—	28.00
Consumable stores	—	22.00
Power	—	50.00
Machine hour rate	40.00	140.00
Wages	12.50	12.50
Comprehensive Machine Hour Rate	52.50	152.50

Note: Dep. per month and per hour.

$$\frac{\text{Rs. }5,00,000 - \text{Rs. }20,000}{10 \times 12} = ₹.\ 4,000$$

Per hour ₹. 4,000 ÷ 200 hrs = ₹. 20

Other Overheads Absorption

Illustration 44: A Company is producing three types of products *A, B, C*. The sales territory of the Company is divided into three areas *X, Y & Z*.

The estimated sales and advertising cost for the next year are as under :

Sales

Products	*Territories*		
	X ₹.	*Y* ₹.	*Z* ₹.
A	25,000	10,000	—
B	15,000	—	40,000
C	—	35,000	20,000

Advertising Cost

	Territories			*Total*
	X ₹.	*Y* ₹.	*Z* ₹.	
Local Direct Cost	3,200	4,500	4,200	11,900
Common Cost	—	—	—	5,800
				17,700

You are required to prepare a statement showing territory-wise advertising cost expressed as a percentage of sales. The allocation of advertising cost should be based on sales as given above.

Solution:

Allocations:

1. **Local Direct Cost :** Apportioned to products in the ratio of productwise sales.
2. **Common Cost :** Apportioned to territories in the ratio of territory-wise sales and then to products in the ratio or product-wise sales as shown below:

$$X = \frac{40,000}{1,45,000} \times 5,800 = 1,600$$

$$Y = \frac{45,000}{1,45,000} \times 5,800 = 1,800$$

$$Z = \frac{60,000}{1,45,000} \times 5,800 = 2,400$$

3. **Productwise Territory Cost:**

Territory *X*	*Local Direct Cost (₹)*	*Common Cost (₹)*	*Total*
Product *A*	$\frac{25,000}{40,000} \times 3,200 = 2,000$	$\frac{25,000}{40,000} \times 1,600 = 1,000$	3,000
Product *B*	$\frac{15,000}{40,000} \times 3,200 = 1,200$	$\frac{15,000}{40,000} \times 1,600 = 600$	1,800
Territory *Y*			
Product *A*	$\frac{10,000}{45,000} \times 4,500 = 1,000$	$\frac{10,000}{45,000} \times 1,800 = 400$	1,400
Product *C*	$\frac{35,000}{45,000} \times 4,500 = 3,500$	$\frac{35,000}{45,000} \times 1,800 = 1,400$	4,900

Territory *Z*

Product *B*	$\frac{40,000}{60,000} \times 4,200 = 2,800$	$\frac{40,000}{60,000} \times 2,400 = 1,600$	4,400
Product *C*	$\frac{20,000}{60,000} \times 4,200 = 1,400$	$\frac{20,000}{60,000} \times 2,400 = 800$	2,200

Statement Showing Territory-wise Advertising Cost

Products	*Territories*			*Total*
	X ₹	*Y* ₹	*Z* ₹	₹
A	3,000	1,400	—	4,400
B	1,800	—	4,400	6,200
C	—	4,900	2,200	6,200
Total Cost (₹.)	4,800	6,300	6,600	17,700
Sales (₹.)	40,000	45,000	60,000	1,45,000
Percentage of Advtising Cost to Sales	12.00%	14.00%	11.00%	12.21%

Illustration 45: *E*-books is an online book retailer. The Company has four departments. The two sales departments are Corporate Sales and Consumer Sales. The two support-departments are Administrative (Human resources, Accounting), and Information Systems. Each of the sales departments conducts merchandising and marketing operations independently.

The following data are available for October, 2003:

Departments	*Revenues*	*Number of Employees*	*Processing Time used (in minutes)*
Corporate Sales	₹. 16,67,750	42	2,400
Consumer Sales	₹. 8,33,875	28	2,000
Administrative	—	14	400
Information Systems	—	21	1,400

Cost incurred in each of four departments for October, 2003 are as follows:

Corporate sales	₹. 12,97,751
Consumers sales	₹. 6,36,818
Administrative	₹. 94,510
Information systems	₹. 3,04,720

The company uses number of employees as a basis to allocate Administrative costs and Processing time as a basis to allocate Information systems costs.

Required:

(*i*) Allocate the support department costs to the sales departments using the direct method.

(*ii*) Rank the support departments based on percentage of their services rendered to other support departments. Use this ranking to allocate support costs based on the step-down allocation method.

(*iii*) How could you have ranked the support departments differently?

(*iv*) Allocate the support department costs to two sales departments using the reciprocal allocation method. **[*CAPE II Nov. 2003*]**

Solution:

Statement showing the allocation of support department costs to the sales departments (Using the direct method)

Particulars	*Basis of allocation*	*Sales department*		*Support department*	
		Corporate sales ₹	*Consumer sales* ₹	*Administrative* ₹	*Information systems* ₹
Cost incurred		12,97,751	6,36,818	94,510	3,04,720
Re-allocation of cost of administrative department	Number of employees (6 : 4)	56,706	37,804	(94,510)	
Re-allocation of costs of information systems department	Processing time (6 : 5)	1,66,211	1,38,509		(3,04,720)
Total		15,20,668	8,13,131	—	—

Ranking of support departments based on percentage of their services rendered to other support departments

- Administration support department provides 23.077% $\left(\frac{21 \times 100}{42 + 28 + 21}\right)$ of its services to Information systems support department. Thus 23.077% of ₹. 94,510 = ₹. 21,810.
- Information system support department provids 8.33% $\left(\frac{400}{2,400 + 2,000 + 400} \times 100\right)$ of its services to Administration support department. Thus 8.33% of ₹. 3,04,720 = ₹. 25,383.

Statement Showing Allocation of Support Costs (By using step-down allocation method)

Particulars	*Basis of allocation*	*Sales department*		*Support department*	
		Corporate sales ₹	*Consumer sales* ₹	*Administrative* ₹	*Information systems* ₹
Cost incurred		12,97,751	6,36,818	94,510	3,04,720
Re-allocation of cost of administrative department	Number of employees (6 : 4 :–: 3)	43,620	29,080	(94,510)	21,810
Re-allocation of costs of information systems department	Processing time (6 : 5 :–: –)	1,78,107	1,48,423		(3,26,530)
Total		15,19,478	8,14,321	—	—

(*iii*) An alternative ranking is based on the rupee amount of services rendered to other service departments, using the rupee figures obtained under requirement (*ii*) This approach would use the following sequence of ranking:

(*a*) Allocation of information systems overheads as first (₹. 25,383 provided to administrative).

(*b*) Allocated administrative overheads as second (₹. 21,810 provided to information systems).

(*iv*) **Working notes:**

(1) *Percentage of services provided by each service department to other service department and sales departments*

Particulars	*Service departments*		*Sale departments*	
	Administrative	*Information system*	*Corporate Sales*	*Consumer Sales*
Administrative	—	23.07%	46.16%	30.77%
Information systems	8.33%	—	50%	41.67%

(2) **Total cost of the support department:** (*By using simultaneous equation method*)

Let AD and IS be the total costs of support departments Administrative and Information systems respectively. These costs can be determined by using the following simultaneous equations:

$$AD = 94{,}510 + 0.0833\ IS$$
$$IS = 3{,}04{,}720 + 0.2307\ AD$$
or $$AD = 94{,}510 + 0.0833\ \{3{,}04{,}720 + 0.2307\ AD\}$$
or $$AD = 94{,}150 + 25{,}383 + 0.01922\ AD$$
or $$0.98078AD = 1{,}19{,}893$$
or $$AD = ₹.\ 1{,}22{,}243$$
and $$IS = ₹.\ 3{,}32{,}922$$

Statement showing the allocation of support department costs to the sales departments
(*Using reciprocal allocation method*)

Particulars	*Sales department*	
	Corporate sales ₹.	*Consumer sales* ₹.
Costs incurred	12,97,751	6,36,818
Re-allocation of cost administrative department (46.16% and 30.77% of ₹. 1,22,243)	56,427	37,614
Re-allocation of cost of information systems department (50% and 41.67% of ₹. 3,32,922)	1,66,461	1,38,729
Total	15,20,639	8,13,161

Over and Under Absorption of Overheads

Illustration 46: The budgeted working conditions for a Cost Centre are as follows:

Normal working per week	42 hours
No. of machines	14
Normal weekly loss of hours on maintenance etc.	5 hours per machine
No. of weeks worked per year	48
Estimated annual overheads	₹. 1,24,320
Estimated direct wage rate	₹. 4 per hour

Actual results in respect of a week period are :

Wages incurred	₹. 9,000
Overheads incurred	₹. 10,200
Machine hours produced	2,000 hours

You are required to calculate :

(*a*) The overhead rate per machine hour; and

(*b*) The amount of under or over absorption of wages and overheads.

Solution:

(*a*) **Calculation of overhead rate per machine hour :**

	₹.
Estimated annual overhead	1,24,320
Normal working hours of machine per year (42 × 48 × 14)	28,224
Less: Loss of hours on maintenance (5 × 48 × 14)	3,360
Net annual working hours	24,864
Overhead rate per machine hour (1,24,320/24,864)	₹. 5.00

(*b*) **Calculation of the Amount of Under or Over Absorption of Overhead and Wages**

	₹.
Overheads incurred	10,200
Overheads absorbed (2,000 hours @ ₹. 5)	10,000
Under-absorption of overheads	200
Wages incurred	₹. 9,000
Wages absorbed (2,000 × 4)	8,000
Under-absorption of wages	1,000

Illustration 47: *XYZ* Company uses a historical cost system and applies overheads on the basis of 'predetermined rates'. The following data are available from the records of the Company for the year ended March, 31, 2010.

	₹.
Manufacturing overheads	8,50,000
Manufacturing overheads applied	7,50,000
Work-in-Progress	2,40,000
Finished Goods Stock	4,80,000
Cost of Goods Sold	16,80,000

Apply two methods for disposal of under-absorbed overheads showing the implications of each method on the profits of the Company.

Solution:

	₹.
Manufacturing overheads Incurred	8,50,000
Manufacturing Overhead Applied	7,50,000
Under-absorbed overheads	1,00,000

First Method: Carrying to next period—Under-absorbed overheads may be carried over to next year's account. In such case, the profit of the year will be more by ₹. 1,00,000.

Second Method : Use of Supplementary Rate—Under-absorbed overheads may be disposed off by applying the supplementary overhead rate to Work-in-progress, Finished goods stock and Cost of goods sold proportionately :

	₹.
Work-in-Progress	2,40,000
Finished goods stock	4,80,000
Cost of goods sold	16,80,000
Total	24,00,000

Proportion of Under-absorbed overheads (1,00,000/24,00,000) 1/24. If supplimentary rate is used the cost will be increased by 1/24 of the cost.

	Existing Amount	*Supplementary Overheads at 1/24*	*Total* ₹.
Work-in-progress	2,40,000	10,000	2,50,000
Finished goods stock	4,80,000	20,000	5,00,000
Cost of goods sold	16,80,000	70,000	17,50,000
	24,00,000	1,00,000	25,00,000

If supplementary rate is used the cost will increase and the profit will be lower by ₹. 1,00,000 as compared to First Method.

There is a *Third Method* where amount of under-absorbed is *transferred to Costing P & L A/c* of the same year. Under this method the net profit will be the same as in case of second method.

Illustration 48: In a manufacturing concern, the predetermined rate of overhead recovery is ₹. 40 per machine hour. During the year, total factory overhead amounted to ₹. 88,96,000 and machine hours actually worked were 1,86,500 only.

Actual production and sales during the year were 1,20,000 units and 1,05,000 units respectively. The production shop had 36,000 unfinished units and based on technical estimates these were considered as 50 per cent complete.

Analysis of the data revealed that 37.5 per cent of the unabsorbed overheads were attributable to initial inaccuracies in the planning and the balance was due to rising price levels.

Show the treatment of unabsorbed overheads in cost accounts.

Solution: (1) **Total Production in units.**

Actual production	1,20,000	Units
Sales	1,05,000	"
Closing stock of finished goods	15,000	"
Actual production	1,20,000	"
Add: Unfinished units 36,000 units equivalent to 50% complete	18,000	"
Total production	1,38,000	

	₹.
(2) **Overheads incurred**	88,96,000
Less : Absorbed (1,86,500 hours @ ₹. 40)	74,60,000
Unabsorbed overheads	14,36,000

(3) Treatment of unabsorbed overheads in cost accounts:

Reason	₹.	*Treatment*
1. Due to initial inaccuracies in planning (37.5% of ₹. 14,36,000)	5,38,500	It is abnormal in nature and therefore it should be debited to Costing P & L A/c.
2. Balance due to rising price levels (14,36,000 – 5,38,500)	8,97,500	To be distributed over cost of sales, closing stock of finished goods, and closing WIP by supplementary rate of overhead as calculated below.

$$\text{Supplementary Rate} = \frac{₹.\ 8,97,500}{1,38,000 \text{ units}} = ₹.\ 6.5036 \text{ per unit}$$

Absorption :

Cost of sales = 1,05,000 units × 6.5036	₹. 6,82,880
Closing stock of finished goods 15000 × 6.5036	₹. 97,555
Closing WIP 36,000 units × 50% × 6.5036	₹. 1,17,065
Unabsorbed overheads	₹. 8,97,500

Illustration 49: In a manufacturing unit overhead was recovered at a pre-determined rate of ₹. 20 per labour-hour. The total factory overhead incurred and the labour-hours actually worked were ₹. 45,00,000 and 2,00,000 labour-hours respectively. During this period 30,000 units were sold. At the end of the period 5,000 units were held in stock while there was no opening stock of finished goods. Similarly though there was no stock of uncompleted units at the beginning of the period, at the end of the period there were 10,000 uncompleted units which may be reckoned at 50% complete.

On analysing the reasons, it was found that 60% of the unabsorbed overheads were due to defective planning and rest were attributable to increase in overheads costs.

How would unabsorbed overheads be treated in cost accounts?

Solution:

Workings

		₹.
1.	Factory overhead incurred	45,00,000
	Factory overhead absorbed	
	2,00,000 labour hours worked @ ₹. 20	40,00,000
	Unabsorbed overheads	₹. 5,00,000
2.	60% of unabsorbed overheads due to defective planning	
	(500,000 × 60%)	3,00,000
	Balance due to increase in overhead cost	2,00,000
3.	Units sold	30,000 units
	Closing stock	5,000 units
	Closing incomplete units equivalent to 10,000 × 50%	5,000 units
	Equivalent Production	40,000 units

Treatment of Unabsorbed Overheads in Cost Accounts

Reason	*Amt. ₹*	*Treatment*
Due to defective planning 60% of 5 lakhs	3,00,000	Defective planning is abnormal feature therefore it should be debited to Costing P & L A/c.
Balance due to increase in overhead cost	2,00,000	Increase in overhead cost may be treated as normal increase, it should be debited to Cost of sales, Closing stock of finished goods and Closing WIP by means of a supplementary rate as calculated below:

Absorption :

Supplementary rate = ₹. 2,00,000/40,000 units *i.e.* ₹. 5 per unit

Absorption in Cost of Sales (30,000 units @ ₹. 5)	₹. 1,50,000
Absorption in Closing Stock of finished goods (5,000 × 5)	25,000
Absorption in Closing uncompleted equivalent to 5,000 units @ ₹. 5	25,000
Total	2,00,000

Illustration 50: A departmental store has several departments. What basis would you recommend for apportioning the following items of expense to its departments :

1. Fire Insurance of Building
2. Rent
3. Delivery Expenses
4. Purchase Department Expenses
5. Credit Department Expenses
6. General Administration Expenses
7. Advertisement
8. Sales Assistants Salaries
9. Personal Department Expenses
10. Sales Commission

Solution :

Items of Expenses	*Basis for Apportionment*
1. Fire Insurance of Building	Floor area of each department.
2. Rent	Floor area of each department.
3. Delivery expenses	Distance or volume or weight of goods sold by each department.
4. Purchase department expenses	No. of purchase orders or value of purchases.
5. Credit department expenses	Value of credit Sales of each department.
6. General Administration expenses	Works cost.
7. Advertisement	Sales volume of each department.
8. Sales Assistants Salaries	Actual salary paid or sales value of each department.
9. Personnel department expenses	No. of employees in each department.
10. Sales commission	Sales value of each department.

Illustration 51: A manufacturing unit produces electronic circuits at the rate of 6 pieces an hour. The unit works in single shift of 8 hours during a six-day week and remains closed for 18 days a year, on account of holidays. Average idle hours per month is 20 for cleaning and maintenance of equipments. Against an average annual output of 12,000 pieces during last ten years, the actual output achieved during the year was 10,800 pieces. The fixed overheads for the year amounted to ₹. 5,40,000.

Your are required to calculate the ***idle capacity costs*** on the assumption that overhead recovery rates are based on maximum capacity, practical capacity, normal capacity and actual capacity utilisation respectively.

Solution :

Calculation of Capacities

		No. of pieces
Maximum capacity (6 pieces × 8 hours × 6 days × 52 weeks)		14,976
Less: 18 days closed (18 × 8 × 6 pieces)	864	
Idle hours (20 × 12 × 6 pieces)	1440	2,304
Practical capacity		12,672
Normal capacity		12,000
Actual capacity utilisation		10,800

Calculation of Idle Capacity Cost

1. *Overhead recovery rate* based on *maximum capacity:*

₹. 5,40,000/14,976 pieces	₹. 36.058 per piece
Fixed overheads incurred	₹. 5,40,000
Less : Absorbed Overheads (10,800 × 36.058)	₹. 3,89,426
Idle Capacity Cost	₹. 1,50,574

2. Overhead recovery rate based on *practical capacity :*

₹. 5,40,000 / 12,672 Pieces ₹. 42.614 per piece	
Fixed overheads incurred	5,40,000
Less : Absorbed Overheads (10,800 × 42.614)	4,60,231
Idle Capacity Cost	₹. 79,769

3. Overhead recovery rate based on *normal capacity :*

₹. 5,40,000/12,000 pieces ₹. 45 per piece	
Fixed overheads incurred	5,40,000
Less : Absorbed Overheads (10,800 × 45)	4,86,000
Idle Capacity Cost	₹. 54,000

4. Overheads recovery rate based on *actual capacity utilisation.*

₹. 5,40,000/10,800 pieces ₹. 50 per piece	
Fixed overheads incurred	5,40,000
Less : Absorbed Overheads (10,800 × 50)	5,40,000
Idle capacity cost	nil

Illustration 52: A Ltd., manufactures two products *A* and *B*. The manufacturing division consists of two production departments P_1 and P_2 and two service departments S_1 and S_2.

Budgeted overhead rates are used in the production departments to absorb factory overheads to the products. The rate of Department P_1 is based on direct machine hours, while the rate of Department P_2 is based on direct labour hours. In applying overheads, the pre-determined rates are multiplied by actual hours.

For allocating the service department costs to production departments, the basis adopted is as follows:

(*i*) Cost of Department S_1 to Department P_1 and P_2 equal and

(*ii*) Cost of Department S_2 to Department P_1 and P_2 in the ratio of 2 : 1 respectively.

The following budgeted and actual data are available.

Annual profit plan data

Factory Overheads budgeted for the year:

		₹.		₹.
Departments	P_1	25,50,000	S_1	6,00,000
	P_2	21,75,000	S_2	4,50,000

Budgeted output in units: Product *A*—50,000; *B*—30,000

Budgeted raw-material cost per unit: Product *A*—₹. 120; Product *B*—₹. 150.

Budgeted time required for production per unit

Department P_1 :	Product *A* : 1.5 machine hours
	Product *B* : 1.0 machine hour
Department P_2 :	Product *A*: 2 Direct labour hours
	Product *B*: 2.5 Direct labour hours.

Average wage rates budgeted in department P_2 are Product *A*—₹. 72 per hour and Product *B*—₹. 75 per hour.

All materials are used in Department P_1 only.

Actual data: (for the month of July, 2003)

Units actually produced :	Product *A* 4,000 units	
	Product *B* 3,000 units	

Actual direct machine hours worked in Department P_1:

On Product *A*—6,100 hours, Product *B*—4,150 hours.

Actual direct labour hours worked in Department P_2 :

On Product *A*—8,200 hours, Product *B*—7,400 hours.

Cost actually incurred:

	Product A		*Product B*
Raw materials:	₹. 4,89,000		₹. 4,56,000
Wages	₹. 5,91,900		₹. 5,52,000
	₹.		₹.
Overheads : Department	P_1 2,31,000	S_1	60,000
	P_2 2,04,000	S_2	48,000

You are required to :

(*i*) Compute the predetermined overhead rate for each production department.

(*ii*) Prepare a performance report for July, 2003 that will reflect the budgeted costs and actual costs.

Solution:

Statement Showing Pre-determined Overhead

Particulars	*Basis of Apportionmen*	*Production Dept.* P_1 ₹.	P_2 ₹.	*Service Dept.* S_1 ₹.	S_2 ₹.
Factory overheads	As given	25,50,000	21,75,000	6,00,000	4,50,000
S_1 Overheads	Equally to P_1 & P_2	3,00,000	3,00,000	(–)6,00,000	
S_2 Overheads	P_1 & P_2 In 2:1 ratio	3,00,000	1,50,000		(–) 4,50,000
Total overheads		31,50,000	26,25,000	—	—

Machine hours of P_1 :	*A* 50,000 × 1.5	75,000
	B 30,000 × 1.0	30,000
Budgeted Machine Hours of P_1 1,05,000		
Labour Hours of P_2 : DLH : *A* 50,000 × 2.0 =		1,00,000
	B 30,000 × 2.5 =	75,000
	Budgeted DLH	1,75,000

Overhead Rates :

Deptt. P_1 = (Total/Machine hours) ₹. 31,50,000/1,05,000 = ₹. 30.00

Deptt. P_2 = (Total/Labour Hour) ₹. 26,25000/1,75,000 = ₹. 15.00

(*ii*) Performance Report for July 2003
Output: Product *A*: 4,000 Units; Product *B*: 3,000 Units

Particulars	*Budgeted Costs*			*Actual Costs*		
	A ₹	*B* ₹	*Total* ₹	*A* ₹	*B* ₹	*Total* ₹
Raw Materials cost	4,000 × 120 = 4,80,000	3,000 × 150 = 4,50,000	9,30,000	4,89,000	4,56,000	9,45,000
Wages	5,76,000	5,62,500	11,38,500	5,91,900	5,52,000	11,43,900
Prime cost	10,56,000	10,12,500	20,68,500	10,80,900	10,08,000	20,88,900
Fy. Overheads						
P1	1,80,000	90,000	2,70,000	1,74,371	1,18,629	2,93,000
P2	1,20,000	1,12,500	2,32,500	1,31,410	1,18,590	2,50,000
Total overheads	3,00,000	2,02,500	5,02,500	3,05,781	2,37,219	5,43,000
Total Cost	13,56,000	12,15,000	25,71,000	13,86,681	12,45,219	26,31,900

Apportionment of Actual Overheads

Particulars	*Basis of apportionment*	*Prodn. Dept.*		*Service Dept.*	
		P_1	P_2	S_1	S_2
Actual overheads	As given	231000	204000	60000	48000
S_1	Equally	30000	30000	(–) 60000	
S_2	In 2:1 ratio	32000	16000		(–) 48000
Total Overhead		293000	250000		
Total Machine Hour		10250			
Total Labour Hours			15600		
Overhead Rate		₹. 28.59	₹. 16.03		

P_1 Overheads : Product $A = 2{,}93{,}000 \times \dfrac{6{,}100}{10{,}250}$ ₹. 1,74,371

Product $B = 2{,}93{,}000 \times \dfrac{4{,}150}{10{,}250} =$ ₹. 1,18,629

P_2 Overheads : Product $A = 2{,}50{,}000 \times \dfrac{8{,}200}{15{,}600} =$ ₹. 1,31,410

Product $B = 2{,}50{,}000 \times \dfrac{7{,}400}{15{,}600} =$ ₹. 1,18,590

Illustration 53: PQR Ltd. has its own power plant, which has two users. Cutting Department and Welding Department. When the plans were prepared for the power plant, top management decided that its practical capacity should be 1,50,000 machine hours. Annual budgeted practical capacity fixed costs are ₹. 9,00,000 and budgeted variable costs are ₹. 4 per machine-hour.

The following data are available :

	Cutting Department	*Welding Department*	*Total*
Actual Usage in 2002-03 (machine hours)	60,000	40,000	1,00,000
Practical capacity for each department (machine hours)	90,000	60,000	1,50,000

Required :

(*i*) Allocate the power plant's cost to the cutting and the welding department using a single rate method in which the budgeted rate is calculated using practical capacity and costs are allocated based on actual usage.

(*ii*) Allocate the power plant's cost to the cutting and welding department, using the dual-rate method in which fixed costs are allocated based on practical capacity and variable costs are allocated based on actual usage.

(*iii*) Allocate the power plant's cost to the cutting and welding departments using the dual-rate method in which the fixed-cost rate is calculated using practical capacity, but fixed costs are allocated to the cutting and welding department based on actual usage. Variable costs are allocated based on actual usage.

(*iv*) Comment on your resúltes in requirements (*i*), (*ii*) and (*iii*). *[CA PEII – May 2003]*

Solution :

(*i*) **Statement showing Power Plant's Cost allocation to the Cutting and Welding Departments by using single rate method on actual usage of machin hours**

	Cutting Department	*Welding Department*	*Total*
Power Plant Cost allocation by using actual usage (machine hours)	₹. 6,00,000 (60,000 × ₹. 10)	₹. 4,00,000 (40,000 × ₹. 10)	₹. 10,00,000

(*ii*) **Statement showing Power Plant's Cost allocation to the Cutting and Welding Departments by using dual rate method**

	Cutting Department	*Welding Department*	*Total*
Fixed Cost (Allocation in the ratio of 90,000 hrs : 60,000 hrs)	₹. 5,40,000	₹. 3,60,000	₹. 9,00,000
Variable Cost	2,40,000 (60,000 × ₹. 4)	1,60,000 (40,000 × ₹. 4)	4,00,000
Total Cost	7,80,000	5,20,000	13,00,000

(*iii*) **Statement showing Power Plant's Cost allocation to the Cutting and Welding Departments using dual rate method**

	Cutting Department	*Welding Department*	*Total*
Fixed Cost (Allocation of fixed cost on actual usage basis)	₹. 3,60,000 (60,000 × ₹. 6)	₹. 2,40,000 (40,000 × ₹. 6)	₹. 6,00,000
Variable Cost (Based on actual usage)	2,40,000 (60,000 × ₹. 4)	1,60,000 (40,000 × ₹. 4)	4,00,000
Total Cost	6,00,000	4,00,000	10,00,000

Comments:

It should be noted that under dual rate method (*iii*) and single rate method, the allocation of fixed cost of practical capacity of plant over each department are based on single ratio. The major advantage of this method is simplicity. The cost of unused ₹. 3,00,000 (*i.e.* ₹. 9,00,000 – ₹. 6,00,000) will not be allocated to the user departments. This highlights the cost of unused capacity. Under (*ii*), fixed cost of capacity are allocated to operating departments on the basis of practical capacity. All the fixed cost is allocated and there is no cost of unused capacity identified with the power plant.

Working Notes:

1. *Fixed practical capacity per machine hour:*

   Practical machine hours = 1,50,000 hrs

   Practical capacity fixed cost = ₹. 9,00,000

Fixed practical capacity cost per machine hour = ₹. 9,00,000 ÷ 1,50,000 = ₹. 6

2. *Budgeted rate per machine hour (using practical capacity)*

= Fixed practical capacity cost per machine hour + Budgeted variable cost per machine hour

= ₹. 6 + ₹. 4 = ₹. 10.

QUESTIONS

OBJECTIVE QUESTIONS

1. *True or False Statements*

Indicate whether each of the following statement is 'True' or 'False'. Give reason in brief.

1. Overhead is the aggregate of all indirect expenditure.
2. Overhead has three elements-indirect materials, indirect wages and indirect expenses.
3. Allocation of overhead means apportionment of overhead to various departments.
4. Re-apportionment of service departments overhead is called secondary distribution of overheads.
5. Material cost percentage method of overhead absorption is considered better than labour cost percentage rate method.
6. Administration overheads are normally absorbed as a percentage of direct wages.
7. Bad debts is a financial loss and thus may be excluded from cost.
8. Factory overheads includes all production costs other than direct material and salaries.
9. Variable overheads vary with time.
10. Overhead are also known as chargeable expenses.
11. When actual overhead are more than absorbed overhead, it is known as over absorption.
12. Carriage inwards is not really an overhead at all, but is a direct.
13. Cash discount are generally excluded completely from the cost.
14. Cost of direct material is apportioned to production departments.
15. When the amount of over or under absorption is quite large, it is transferred to Costing Profit and Loss Account.
16. Wages of delivery van drivers is a selling overhead.
17. Under absorbation of overheads means that actual overheads are more than absorbed overheads.
18. Rent is not included in cost when premises is owned by the company.
19. Examples of factory overhead are salary of plant manager and departmental head, depreciation and wages of foreman.
20. Under or over absorption of overhead arises because of use of predetermined overhead rates.
21. Direct labour cost method of absorption of factory overhead is suitable in those departments where work is done by manual labour.

[*Ans.* : *False are 5, 6, 9, 10, 13, 15, 17, 18 Rest are True*]

II. *State which of following statement is true or false*:

1. Cost of after sales service is a distribution costing.
2. Machine Hour Rate is separately computed from each machine.
3. All the percentage methods of absorption of works overhead normally make no distinction between fixed and variable overheads.

4. Labour hour rate method of absorbing overhead should be adopted only for those departments in which work is mainly done by manual workers.
5. In comprehensive Machine Hour Rate, wages of direct workers are included.
6. Under absorption of overhead results in under statement of cost.
7. When the amount of under or over-absorbed overheads is significant, it is equitably apportioned to work-in-progress, finished stock and cost of sales.
8. Cost of setting up time of the machine is transferred to Costing Profit and Loss.

[**Ans.** : Only 3 and 8 are False]

III. ***Multiple Choice Questions*:**

Select the correct answer in each of the following:

1. Packing cost is a:
   (*a*) Production cost (*c*) Distribution Cost
   (*b*) Selling cost (*d*) It may be any of the above
2. Director's remuneration and expenses form a part of:
   (*a*) Production overhead (*c*) Selling overhead
   (*b*) Administration overhead (*d*) Distribution overhead
3. Administration overheads are recovered as a percentage of:
   (*a*) Direct materials (*c*) Prime cost
   (*b*) Direct wages. (*d*) Work cost
4. Which of the following is a service department?
   (*a*) Refining department (*c*) Receiving department
   (*b*) Machine department (*d*) Finishing department
5. Which of the following is not selling overhead?
   (*a*) Insurance to cover sold goods while in transit.
   (*b*) Royalty on sales
   (*c*) Legal cost for debt realisation.
   (*d*) Distribution of samples.
6. Which method of absorption of factory overheads do you suggest in a concern which produce only uniform type of product?
   (*a*) Percentage of direct wages basis (*b*) Direct labour hour rate
   (*b*) Machine Hour Rate (*d*) A rate per unit of output
   (*e*) None of the above.
7. When the amount of under or over absorption is significant, it should be disposed off by
   (*a*) Transferring to Costing Profit and Loss A/c
   (*b*) The use of supplementary rates.
   (*c*) Carrying over as deferred charge to the next accounting year.
   (*d*) Any one of above.
8. Idle capacity of a plant refers to the difference between:
   (*a*) Maximum capacity and practical capacity
   (*b*) Practical capacity and normal capacity
   (*c*) Practical capacity and capacity based on sales expectancy
   (*d*) Maximum capacity and actual capacity

9. Factory overhead should be absorbed on the basis of :
   (*a*) Direct labour hours
   (*b*) Direct labour cost
   (*c*) Machine hours
   (*d*) Any of these.
10. Which of the following is a scientific and accurate method of absorption of factory overheads.
    (*a*) Percentage on prime cost (*b*) Machine Hour Rate
    (*c*) Percentage on direct labour cost (*d*) Any of these
11. Selling and distribution overheads are absorbed on the basis of:
    (*a*) Rate per unit (*b*) Percentage on direct labour cost
    (*c*) Percentage on selling price of each unit (*d*) Any of these.
12. Pre-determined overhead recovery rate is ₹. 3 per hour and predetermined hours are 50,000 actual hours were 50,500. What is the amount of under or over absorption:
    (*a*) ₹. 20,000 over-absorption (*b*) ₹. 20,000 under-absorption
    (*c*) ₹. 1, 500 over-absorption (*d*) ₹. 5,000 under-absorption

    [***Ans.*** 1 (*d*), 2. (*b*), 3. (*d*), 4. (*c*), 5. (*c*), 6. (*d*), 7 (*b*), 8 (*d*), 9 (*d*), 10 (*d*), 11 (*d*), 12 (*c*)]

IV. *Fill in the blanks* :

(1) Cost are broadly classified into two groups (a)...............(b)...............
(2) Any expenses incurred after Prime Cost is generally known as..........
(3) Overhead costs are total of indirect material, indirect labour and ....
(4) Basis of apportionment of stores service department exps. is.................
(5) Expenses of labour welfare department are apportioned on the basis of ....
(6) Attractive packing in an example of................expenses.
(7) Semi variable expenses are...............fixed.

[**Ans.** : (1) Direct, Indirect (2) Overhead (3) Indirect expenses (4) Consumed material (5) Number of workers (6) Selling (7) Partly]

V. *Fill in the blanks* :

(*i*) ....means allotment of proportions of items of cost to cost centres.
(*ii*) Idle capacity is the..............capacity less capacity utilisation based on expected sales.
(iii) ....means the allotment of whole items of cost to cost centres.
(*iv*) Overhead is the sum of indirect.............., indirect............and indirect............. .
(*v*) Charging of overheads to cost units is called............. .
(*vi*) Actual factory overheads less recovered factory overheads is the...........or.................
(vii) Under or over-absorption of overheads arises when overheads are recovered by...............overhead rates.
(*viii*) Administration overheads are generally absorbed as a percentage of.............. .
(*ix*) Most of the general factory overhead items are apportioned to different departments on the basis of .... or ....
(*x*) Service department expenses are..................... over the..................department.
(*xi*) Cost of personnel department is apportioned to different departments on the basis of number of............ .

(*xii*) Salary of a supervisor is an example of...............overheads.

[**Ans.** (i) Apportionment ; (ii) Practical ; (iii) Allocation ; (*iv*) materials , labour, expenses ; (v) absorption ; (*vi*) under, over-absorbed, overheads ; (*vii*) pre-determined ; (*viii*) Works, cost ; (*ix*) Direct labour hours ; machine hours; (*x*) apportioned, production ; (*xi*) employees ; (*xii*) manufacturing.]

THEORETICAL QUESTIONS

1. Discuss the various methods of calculating 'On Cost'. Explain their respective advantages and disadvantages.

2. What are factory indirect expenses? Discuss the relative merits and demerits of any two methods commonly used for allocating them in Cost Accounts.

3. What are the principal factors to be considered when fixing a machine hour rate? Give a specimen computation.

4. 'Some of the major problems of cost accounting are associated with the allocation of indirect expenditure.' Why is this so? Give a brief indication of the several methods of allocation known to you and indicate the circumstances which would lead you to regard each of them as most appropriate.

5. Give a comparative study of Labour hour rate and Machine hour rate methods of allocating on cost.

6. What do you understand by overhead absorption? Describes briefly the various methods of absorbing factory overheads.

7. What do you mean by the term under/over absorption of production overhead? How does it arise? How it is treated in Cost Accounts? **[*Delhi B.Com. (H)*]**

8. What factors would you consider before formulation of overheads recovery rates?

9. Define and distinguish between selling cost and distribution cost. Describe a system control of selling and distribution cost.

10. Distinguish between allocation, apportionment and absorption of overheads.

11. Write short note on 'Treatment of interest on capital in Cost Accounts.

12. Distinguish between 'Allocation and Apportionment of Overheads'.

13. What is 'Idle Capacity'? How would this be treated in Cost Accounts?

SHORT ANSWER QUESTIONS

1. What do you understand by collection and departmentalisation of indirect expenses?

2. What is meant by departmentalisation of overheads and reapportionment of overheads of service departments.

3. Give names of methods of reapportionment of indirect expenses or overheads of service department and explain in brief any one of these.

4. What do you understand by absorption of indirect expenses or overheads. Give names of three methods of absorption of factory overheads.

5. Write the names of the main methods of absorption of factory overheads and explain any one of these methods.

6. Write two merits and two demerits of absorption of factory overheads on the basis of direct wages.

7. What do you understand by Machine Hour Rate Method of absorption of factory overheads?

8. Write in brief the method of calculating Machine Hour Rate ?

9. What is difference between Labour Hour Rate and Machine Hour Rate ?

10. Name the methods used in the absorption of office and administrative overheads and explain one of these.

11. Name the methods of absorption of selling and distribution overheads and explain any one of these?

SHORT ANSWER NUMERICAL QUESTIONS:

1. A manufacturer has four departments X, Y, Z and S.S is service department. Total overheads were ₹. 25,000; 1/5 of which was apportioned on the basis of number of workers and 4/5 was apportioned on the ratio of area occupied by each departments. Overheads of service departments are apportioned among production department equally. Number of workers of four department were 20, 20, 5 and 5 and the area of four departments is equal.

   [Ans. : *X ₹. 8,833 ; Y ₹. 8,833; Z ₹. 7, 334***]**

2. The overheads of three production departments (*X*, *Y* and *Z*) and two service departments (A and B) of a factory were ₹. 10,000, ₹. 8,000, ₹. 6,000 ₹. 2,000 and ₹. 1,000 respectively. The apportionment of overheads of service department was as below; of department A among X, Y, Z in the ratio 2 : 2 : 1 and that of dept. B in the ratio 1 : 1 : 2. Find out total overheads of the three production departments.

   [Ans. : *₹. 11,050 ; 9,050; 6,900***]**

3. During apportionment overheads it was found that overheads of two service departments X and Y were ₹. 4,000 and ₹. 2,600 respectively but the apportionment of 20% Y to X and 10% of X to Y is still to be done. Calculate total overheads of two service departments.

   [Ans. : *X ₹. 4,612 ; Y 3,061***]**

4. Following information is available regarding a factory:

	₹.
Materials	40,000
Direct wages	25,000
Overheads	20,000

   The factory has to manufacture a commodity where overheads are to be absorbed on the basis of direct labour or direct material. Find out absorption rates.

   [Ans. *80% of wages or 50% of material***]**

5. On the basis of above question, if commodity to be manufactured has material cost ₹. 1,000 and direct labour ₹. 800, what will be cost of production if overheads are absorbed on the basis of direct labour.

   [Ans. *₹. 2440***]**

6. The following information relates to the production dept of a factory:

Direct materials	₹. 60,000
Direct wages	₹. 50,000
Overheads	₹. 10,000

   If overheads are charged on the basis of wages, what will be cost of an order whose wages is ₹. 6,000 and material ₹. 9,000.

   [Ans. : *₹. 16,200***]**

7. On the basis of above questions, what will be total cost of the order if overheaus are absorbed on the basis of direct material?

   [Ans. : *₹. 16,500***]**

8. If a machine runs for 2000 hours in a year, find out Machine Hour Rate of overheads from following particulars.

		₹.
Electric power	(Per hour)	0.55
Steam	(Per hour)	0.44
Water	(Per hour)	0.44
Repair	(Per annum)	180
Rent	(Per annum)	300

[Ans. : *₹. 1.67*]

9. From the following details, calculate Machine Hour Rate:

Depreciation	(Per hour)	0.67
Standing charges	(Per month)	100
Repairs	(Per month)	200
Power	(Per hour)	0.5

Machine runs 150 hours during a month

[Ans. : *₹. 3.17*]

10. Calculate Machine Hour Rate of the machine from following particulars:

Cost of Machine ₹. 21,000

Estimated scrap value ₹ 1,000

Effective working hours during life of machine 20,000 hours Machine worked during the period of four weeks : 150 hours.

Maintenance (per week) ₹. 50

Standing charges (Per week) ₹. 25

Power used per hour : 10 units @ ₹. 1 per unit

[Ans. : *₹. 11.50*]

11. From the following particulars, calculate Direct Labour hour rate of absorption of overheads

Total overheads of the department during the year ₹. 45,600

Number of workers in the department : 400

Working days in the year : 300

Working hours in a day : 8

Idle time @ 5% of days hours.

[Ans. : *₹. 0.50*]

NUMERICAL QUESTIONS

1. A factory has three production departments and two service departments. The following information relates to overheads :

Production Deptt.	₹.	Service Deptt.	₹.
X	690	*A*	315
Y	1,095	*B*	255
Z	645		

Expenses of service departments are apportioned as under :

	X	*Y*	*Z*	*A*	*B*
A	30%	40%	20%	—	10%
B	10%	20%	50%	20%	—

[**Ans.** *Total Overheads of Depts. X, Y and Z ₹. 831, 1,303 and 866 respectively.*]

2. The Space Production Company manufactures components for radio and television satellities using two service departments and two production departments. The inter-departmental relationship and estimated overhead costs are given below:

Percentage of Service Provided to

	Service		Production	
	Maintenance	*Scheduling*	*Moulding*	*Assembly*
From : Maintenance		10%	40%	50%
: Scheduling	20%	—	50%	30%
Total Overhead Cost (₹.)	7,50,000	4,00,000	3,78,000	2,76,000

Required : (*i*) Using the direct method, show the amount of scheduling department costs to be allocated to assembly department; (*ii*) repeat (*i*) using step method and allocating maintenance first; (*iii*) repeat (*i*) Using the reciprocal method (method of simultaneous equation).

[**Ans.** *(i) 30% of ₹. 4,00,000 i.e. ₹. 1,20,000; (ii) Total overheads of Production deptts. Moulding ₹. 9,59,122 and Assembly ₹. 8,44,878; (iii) Total overheads of Maintenance ₹. 8,46,939 and Scheduling ₹. 4,84,694 total overheads after absorption of service deptts. as above no. (ii)*]

3. Modern Manufactures Ltd. have three production departments P_1, P_2 and P_3 and two service department S_1 and S_2, the details pertaining to which are as under.

	P_1	P_2	P_3	S_1	S_2
Direct Wages (₹.)	3,000	2,000	3,000	1,500	195
Working hours	3,070	4,475	2,419	—	—
Value of Machine (₹.)	60,000	80,000	1,00,000	5,000	5,000
H.P. of Machines	60	30	50	10	—
Light Points	10	15	20	10	5
Floor space (sq.ft)	2,000	2,500	3,000	2,000	500

The following figures extracted from the accounting record are relevant.

	₹.		₹.
Rent and Rates	5,000	General Lighting	600
Indirect wages	1,939	Power	1,500
Depreciation of Machines	10,000	Sundries	9,695

The expenses of the service departments are allocated as under :

	P_1	P_2	P_3	S_1	S_2
S_1	20%	30%	40%	—	10%
S_2	40%	20%	30%	10%	—

Find the total cost of Product *X* which is processed for manufacture in departments P_1, P_2 and P_3 for 4, 5 and 3 hours respectively given that its direct materials cost is ₹. 50 and direct labour cost ₹. 30.

[**Ans.** *Distribution of overheads P_1 7,700; P_2 7,300; P_3 9,800; S_1 3200; S_2 734; After redistribution of service deptt. overhead P_1 ₹. 8,787.16; P_2 ₹. 8,504.87; P_3 ₹. 11,441.79; Working Hour Rate P_1 ₹. 2.86; P_2 ₹. 1.90; P_3 ₹. 4.72. Cost of X ₹. 115.13.*]

4. Deccan Manufacturing Ltd. have three departments which are regarded as production departments. Service departments costs are distributed to three production departments using the 'Step Ladder Method' of distribution. Estimates of factory overhead costs to be incurred by each department in the forthcoming year are as follows: Data required for distribution is also shown against each department.

Department		Factory Overheads ₹.	Direct Labour Hours	No. of Employees	Area in Sq. meter
Production	X	1,93,000	4,000	100	3,000
	Y	64,000	3,000	125	1,500
	Z	83,000	4,000	85	1,500
Service	P	45,000	1,000	10	500
	Q	75,000	5,000	50	1,500
	R	1,05,000	6,000	40	100
	S	30,000	3,000	50	1,000

The overhead costs of the four service departments are re-distributed in the same order *viz. P, Q, R* and *S* respectively on the following basis:

Department	Basis	Department	Basis
P	No. of employees	R	Area in square meters
Q	Direct labour hours	S	Direct labour hours

You are required to (*a*) Prepare a schedule showing the distribution of overhead costs of four service departments to the three production departments; (*b*) Calculate the overhead recovery rate per direct labour hour of each of the three production departments.

[Ans. *(a) Total overheads of Production departments X ₹. 3,00,000; Y ₹. 1,35,000; Z ₹. 1,60,000 (b) Overhead recovery rate X ₹. 75 Y ₹. 45 and Z ₹. 40.*]

5. In a factory the factory overheads are charged as a percentage of wages and office overheads are calculated on the basis of works cost.

The following information in available :

	First Order	Second Order
Materials	₹. 30,000	₹. 40,000
Wages	₹. 20,000	₹. 25,000
Sales Value	₹. 75,020	₹. 97,680
Percentage of Profit on cost	10%	11%

Find out :

(*a*) Percentage of factory overheads to wages and

(*b*) Percentage of office overheads to works cost.

[Ans. *(a) 60% (b) 10%*]

6. The production department of a factory has provided the following information for the month of October.

Materials used	₹. 1,08,000
Direct wages	₹. 90,000
Labour hours worked	36,000 hrs.
Machine hours worked	30,000 hrs.
Overheads chargeable to department	₹. 72,000

For an order executed by the department during the period, the relevant information was as under:

Materials used	₹. 12,000
Direct wages	₹. 6,400
Labour hours worked	3,200 hrs.
Machine hours	2,400 hrs.

Calculate the overhead chargeable to this order, by using the following methods:

(*a*) Direct materials cost basis

(*b*) Direct wages basis

(*c*) Labour hour rate basis

(*d*) Machine hour rate basis

[Ans. *(a) ₹. 8,000, (b) ₹. 5,120, (c) ₹. 6,400, (d) ₹. 5.760*]

Machine Hour Rate

7. (*a*) Explain the importance and scope of Machine Hour Rate.

(*b*) The following particular have been obtained for a machine installed in a factory. The number of effective working hours is 1,740. The machine was purchased on the hire-purchase system and the work of the factory has been mostly carried on with the help of this machine.

Year of running		Second
Cash Down Price	₹.	22,259
Scarp Value	₹.	9,259
Number of instalments		6
Amount of Instlment	₹.	5000
Annual rate of interest		4%
Life of Machine (in effective working hours)		30,000 hrs.
Other overhead charges	₹.	913.50

Calculate Machine hour rate.

[Ans. *MHR ₹. 1.37*]

[Hint : *Interest paid with the second instalment has been included as an overhead*]

8. The following annual charges are incurred in respect of a machine in a shop where manual labour is almost nil, where work is done by means of five machines of exactly similar type and specification.

		₹.
(*i*)	Rent and rates (productional to the floor space occupied) for the shop	4,809
(*ii*)	Depreciation on each machine	500
(*iii*)	Repairs and maintenance for the five machines	1,000
(*iv*)	Power consumed (as per meter @ 6.25 paise per unit for the shop)	3,750
(*v*)	Electric charges for light in shop	540
(*vi*)	There are two attendants for the five machines and they are each paid ₹. 60 per month.	
(*vii*)	Supervision: For the five machines in the shop there is one supervisor whose emoluments are ₹. 250 per month.	
(*viii*)	Sundry supplies, such as lubricants, jute and cotton waste, etc., for the shop.	494
(*ix*)	Hire purchase instalment payable for the machines (including ₹. 300 as interest)	1,200
(*x*)	The machine uses 10 units of power per hour.	

Calculate the machine hour rate for the machine for the year.

[Ans. *Machine Hour Rate ₹. 2.92*]

9. A machine shop has 8 identical drilling machines manned by 6 operators. The machine cannot be worked without an operator engaged on it. The original cost of all these 8 machines works out to ₹. 8 lakhs.

These particulars are furnished for a 6 month period:

Normal available hours per month	208
Absenteeism (without pay) hours	18
Leave (with pay) hours	20
Normal idle time unavoidable hours	10
Average rate of wages per day of 8 hours	₹. 20
Production bonus estimated	15% of wages
Value of power consumed	₹. 8050
Supervision and indirect labour	₹. 3,300
Lighting and electricity	₹. 1,200

These particulars are for the year:

Repairs and maintenance including consumable 3% on the value of machines.

Insurance	₹. 40,000
Depreciation	10% on original cost
Other sundry works expenses	₹. 12,000
General management expenses allocated	₹. 54,530

You are required to work out a comprehensive machine hour rate of the machine shop.

[**Ans.** *MHR ₹. 23.87*]

[**Hints :** Total useable hours for 6 operators for 6 month are 5,760, Operators wages ₹. 17,100; Total overheads of the machine shop ₹. 1,37,480. As machines cannot work without an operator, hence 5,760 hours also represent total machine hours]

10. A machine was purchased on January 1, 2000 for ₹. 5,00,000. The total cost of all machinery inclusive of the new machine was ₹. 75 lakhs. The following further particulars are available.

Estimated life of the machine	: 10 years
Scrap value at the end of 10 years	: ₹. 5,000
Repairs and maintenance for the machine	: ₹. 2,000 p.a.
Expected working hours of the machine	: 4,000 p.a.
Insurance premium of all machines	: ₹. 4,500 p.a.
Electricity consumption for the machine per hour @ 75 paise per units	: 25 units.
Area occupied by the machine	: 100 sq.ft.
Area occupied by the other machines	: 1500 sq.ft.
Rent of the department	: ₹. 800 p.m.
Lighting charges (20 points in the dept. 3 points for the machines)	: ₹. 120 p.m.

Compute the machine hour rate for the new machine on the basis of data given above.

[**Ans.** *MHR ₹. 31.90*]

11. Compute a comprehensive machine hour rate for a machine in Production department 'A' of a factory from the following details :

Machine :	Cost including installation charges	: ₹. 20,00,000
	Estimated useful life	: 10 years
	Estimated salvage value	: 10%
Working hours :	Number of working days	: 300
	Number of shifts per day	: 2
	Effective working hrs per shift	: 7
	Stoppages for repairs and maintenance etc.	: 200 hrs

Operating & Other Costs :

(*i*) Wages of two operators (one for each shift) @ ₹. 5,000 p.m.

(*ii*) Salary of supervisor (one for each shift) @ ₹. 7,500. Only one-fifth of the supervisor's time is devoted to this machine

(*iii*)	Electric Power	: 20 units per hour, each unit costing ₹. 3.20
(*iv*)	Insurance Charges	: ₹. 5,000 per annum
(*v*)	Repairs and Maintenance (estimated)	: ₹. 12,500 p.m.
(*vi*)	Rent, rates & taxes (allocated)	: ₹. 10,000 p.a.
(*vii*)	General lighting etc. (allocated)	: ₹. 750 p.m.
(*viii*)	Other factory overheads (allocated)	: ₹. 1,40,000 p.a.

[Ans. *MHR ₹ 226.50; Hints (1) Estimated working hours (300 × 2 × 7) – 200 = 4000 hours*]

12. A manufacturing company uses two identical large and four identical small machines. Each large machine occupies one quarter of the workshop and fully employs three workers, each small machine occupies half the space of a large machine and fully employs two workers. The workers are paid by piece work.

Each of the six machines is estimated to work, 1,440 hours per year, while the effective working life is taken as 12,000 working hours for each large machine and 9000 working hours for each small machine. Large machines cost ₹. 20,000 each and small machines ₹. 4,000 each. Scrap values are ₹. 4,000 and ₹. 100 respectively.

Repairs, maintenance and oil are estimated to cost for each large machine ₹. 6,000 and each small machine ₹. 1,800 during its effective life.

Power consumption costs 5 paise per unit and amounts for a large machine to 20 units per hour and for a small machine to 2 units per hour.

The manager is paid ₹. 4,800 a year and workshop supervision occupies half of his time, which is divided equally among the six machines.

Detail of other expenses are :

Rent and rates of workshop ₹. 3,200 a year.

Lighting (total apportioned in the ratio of workers employed) ₹. 1,820 a year.

Taking a period of the three months as a basis, calculate the machine hour rate for a large machine and small machine.

[Ans. *Machine Hours Rate Large Machine ₹ 3.93; Small Machine ₹ 1.47*]

13. A Machine Cost ₹. 4,50,000 and is deemed to have a scrap value of 5 per cent at the end of its effective life (19 years) ordinarily the machine is expected to run for 2,400 hours per annum but it is estimated that 150 hours will be lost for normal repairs and maintenance and further 750 hours will be lost due to staggering. The other details in respect of the machine shop are.

(*a*) Wages, bonus and provident fund contribution of each of two operators (each operator is in charge of two machines) ₹ 24,000 per year
(*b*) Rent and Rates of the shop ₹. 15,000 per year
(*c*) General lighting of the shop ₹. 1,250 per month
(*d*) Insurance Premium for the machine ₹. 1,000 per quarter
(*e*) Cost of repairs and maintenance per machine ₹. 1,250 per month
(*f*) Shop supervision's salary ₹. 2,500 per month
(*g*) Power consumption of machine per hour 20 units, rate of power per 100 units ₹. 50
(*h*) Other factory overheads attributable to the shop ₹. 20,000 per year

There are four identical machines in the shop. The Supervisor is expected to devote 1/5th of his time for supervision of the machine. Compute comprehensive machine hour rate from the above details.

[**Ans.** *Annual Effective Hour 1500; Comprehensive Machine Hour Rate ₹. 60.00*]

Overhead Recovery

14. The following particulars were extracted from the records of Epsilon Ltd. on 31st December.

	Dept. A	*Dept B*	*Dept. C*
Overhead incurred	₹. 2,000	₹. 1,500	₹. 2,500
Machine hour worked	₹. 440	350	758
Machine hour rate	₹. 5	₹. 4	₹. 3

The departmental loads during the three month to 31st December averaged.

Dept. *A*	100% of Normal Capacity
Dept. *B*	75% of Normal Capacity
Dept. *C*	50% of Normal Capacity

You are required to calculate the amount of overhead under/over absorbed in each department.

[**Ans.** *A ₹. 200 over absorbed; B ₹. 100 under absorbed; C ₹. 226 under absorbed*].

Single or Output or Unit Costing

In those businesses where only one product is turned out, the maintenance of costing records is made under *single (or output or unit) costing*. The system is very easy. In fact, the financial account themselves can be modelled in such a way as to furnish all necessary information for finding out the cost of production. The financial books should be made to disclose information regarding materials used, direct labour, indirect expenses or overheads regarding factory, office and selling departments.

Unit or single output costing is a simple method of ascertaining cost per unit where there is one or uniform product. In other words '*single or output cost system is used in the business where a standard product is turned out and it is desired to find out the cost of a basic unit of production*'. It is applied where the manufacturing process is a simple one and the product also is generally single (may be a few but of same kind not varying in grades or quality). The industries where this method of costing is used are collieries, quarries, brick-making, breweries, etc. The unit of cost is the unit in which ultimate production is measured e.g. per ton of coal, per 1000 bricks or per article of the single product.

STATEMENT OF COST

For calculating cost per unit, a statement of cost is prepared. The technique of preparing this statement has been explained in the First Chapter. This statement shows prime cost, works cost, cost of production, cost of goods sold and cost of sales. Profits may be ascertained if selling price is known or estimated. It is a periodical statement which is prepared weekly, fortnightly, monthly, quarterly or annually.

Various componenets of cost are arranged to ascertain above costs. The total of Direct Material, Direct Wages and other Direct Expenses is called *Prime Cost.* When Factory expenses or overheads are added to the Prime Cost, the total becomes *Factory Cost*. Thereafter Office and Administration overheads are added to Factory Cost. The total at this level is known as Cost of Production or Office Cost. Selling and distribution overheads are added to office cost, the total become *Total Cost* or *Final Cost*. The difference between Total Cost and Sales is Profit. In order to calculate profit, the opening and closing stocks of finished goods are adjusted so that cost of goods sold may be arrived at. The Statement of Profit will be as below:

Cost of Production or Office Cost	–
Add: Opening stock of Finished goods	–
Less: Closing stock of Finished goods	(–)
Cost of Goods sold	–
Add: Selling and distribution overheads	–
Cost of Sales	–
Profit	–
Sales	–

COST SHEET

It is similar to Statement of Cost but it includes and show certain other information, relating to cost. It shows cost per unit of each item of cost and also their percentage to total cost.

According to *CIMA London* Cost Sheet is 'A statement which provides for the assembly of the detailed cost of a centre or a cost unit'. It is also a periodical statement.

'The expenditure which has been incurred upon product for a period is extracted from the financial books and the store records and set out in a memorandum statement. If this statement is confined to the disclosure of the costs of units produced dividing the period, it is termed as *Cost-Sheet*, but where the statement records both total cost, profit and sales, it is usually known as Statement of Cost or Production Account'.

If information derived from the books is set out usually in the form of a statement, it is cost sheet but where it is set out in the form of an account recording the cost incurred, there being separate accounts to show also sales and profit, it would be known as Production or Manufacturing Account.

It is desirable that besides total expenditure incurred, cost per unit of output in case of each elements of cost should be calculated and also the percentage contribution of each item to the cost of production should be indicated. Further, the cost sheet should give *`cost-per unit'* in the previous period also, if available, for the purpose of comparison. Opening and closing block of finished goods may be put in a subsidiary statement, which together with the total cost of production and sales will reveal profit. The opening stock, purchases and the closing stock of raw material should not be shown separately but suitably adjusted to give one figure of raw materials consumed or used. Financial items like interest, discount etc. should be ignored.

Elements of Cost : Although elements of cost have been discussed in detail in previous chapters these are again briefed for convenience and recapitulation.

(*i*) **Direct Materials:** Since there will be only one product and process of manufacture is also simple, the raw material if any is directly charged to the production of the period in total.

Materials consumed :

Opening stock of Raw Materials
Add: Purchases
Add: Carriage inward and other incidental charges
Less: Closing stock of direct material
Less: Scrap of raw material (abnormal)
Less: Materials returned or transferred to other departments.

(2) **Direct Labour :** The labour costs are collected periodically through pay rolls which are prepared separately for each section of work. The cost of abnormal idle time should be deducted.

(3) **Other Direct or Chargeable Expenses:** Expenses other than direct material and direct labour are chargeable expenses e.g. excise duty, royalty, expenses on designs, patterns and models etc.

(4) **Prime Cost :** The total of Direct Materials Consumed, Direct Labour and Other Direct or Chargeabls Expenses is known as Prime Cost

1. Cost of Direct Materials Consumed	—
2. Direct Labour or Wages	—
3. Other Chargeable Exps.	—
PRIME COST	—

(5) **Works Expenses or Overheads :** Factory expenses or manufacturing expenses have been discussed in detail in a separate chapter. In unit costing, these expenses related to the product are added to Prime Cost. These are (*i*) Indirect materials like oil, dusters, lubricants etc., (*ii*) Indirect labour like wages to foremen, storekeeper, watchman, factory clerks etc., (*iii*) Steam, fuel or electric power, (*iii*) Lighting heating and water in the factory (*iv*) Rent, insurance and rates of factory, (*v*) Repairs and depreciation of machines plant, factory building and loose tools, (*vi*) Factory stationery, (*vii*) Factory research expenses, (*viii*) Expenses related to factory establishment, (*ix*) Drawing office salary, (*x*) Welfare expenses and workman's compensation, Insurance, etc.

(6) **Scrap or Wastage:** In the production of anything some wastage or scrap materials is obtained. Sometimes some of the units produced may be defective and such units or scrap or wastage is sold. The amount thus obtained should be deducted from factory expenses or from works cost. If, however, the materials (when about to be used) are found to be defective and then sold, the value of materials used should be reduced by the cost of such materials. The loss on sale of such defective materials should be debited to the Costing Profit and Loss Account.

(7) **Work in Progress:** In any factory or workshop there are always some units which are not yet complete, but on which some work has been done. Such work is known as work-in-progress or work-in-process. The valuation of such work-in-progress is made on the basis of the value of material already used, the amount of wages paid for the work concerned and a proper share of factory expenses. Since various units will be at different stages of production the value of work-in-progress will have to be estimated for each stage separately.

The work-in-progress in the beginning is to be added to the current costs of production and that at the end of the period has to be deducted from the manufacturing cost. This may be done when factory expenses have been added to the prime cost. It may look as follows:

	₹.
Prime Cost	1,20,000
Factory Expenses (Works Overheads)	80,000
Gross Works Cost	2,00,000
Add: Work-in-progress in the beginning	15,000
	2,15,000
Less: Work-in-progress at the end	20,000
Works Cost	1,95,000

After this office expenses will be added as usual and the total cost of production of the finished units is ascertained.

There is an alternate method also. This will be if the analysis of the value of work-in-progress is known. Suppose the figures are available as under :

	Work-in-Progress in the beginning	*Work-in-Progress at the end*
	₹.	₹.
Materials	3,000	4,000
Labour	2,000	2,500
Factory Expenses	1,500	2,000
Total	6,500	8,500

In this case when we ascertain the value of materials used we add ₹. 3,000 for materials included in work-in-progress in the beginning and deduct ₹. 4,000 for materials included in work-in-progress at the end. This will give cost of materials used on finished units produced. The figure for materials used may then be as follows (figures assumed) :

			₹.
Opening Stock			25,000
Materials in work-in-progress in the beginning			3,000
Add: Purchases			1,20,000
			1,48,000
Less :	Closing stock of materials	28,000	
	Materials included in work-in-progress at the end	4,000	32,000
Materials used			1,16,000

Similar treatment will be given to labour and factory expenses, that is to say, in each case the amount included in work-in-progress in the beginning will be added and that included in work-in-progress at the end deducted. Needless to say there will be no necessity then to do anything further about work-in-progress.

(8) Office and Administrative Expenses : Works cost or Manufacturing cost is increased by office and administrative expenses. These are, for example, (*i*) Staff and Management salaries, (*ii*) Directors Fees, (*iii*) Stationery, Printing, Postage, Telephone, Fax and miscellaneous office expenses, (*iv*) Office rent, tax, insurance, light and water etc., (*v*) Counting house or computer and accounting expenses, (*vi*) Repairs, depreciation and insurance of office building, furniture and equipments.

(9) Cost of Production or Office Cost : When office and administration overheads are added to works cost, the total shows cost of production.

(10) Cost of Goods Sold : If all goods produced are not sold, the cost of goods sold should be ascertained

Cost of Production	—
Add: Opening Stock of Finished goods	—
Less: Closing Stock of Finished goods	—
Cost of Goods sold	

(11) Selling and Distribution Expenses : These are added to Cost of Goods sold. The total is known as 'Cost of Sales'.

(12) **Profit:** Profit is difference between sales and cost of sales.

Cost of Goods Sold :	—
Add: Selling and Distribution Exps.	—
Cost of Sales	—
Profit	—
Sales	—

Treatment of Defective or Rejected Production : The production that is not as perfect as the saleable product but is capable of being rectified and brought to required degree of perfection provided some additional expenditure overheads. The cost of rectification is treated to be additional works overheads. On the other hand, the production that has been totally rejected and cannot be rectified, the amount so realised by sale of these goods is used to reduce the cost of factory cost.

Specimen 1 : Cost Sheet (Simple)

For the month ending ... 20 ....

(Output in Tons) (Unit = one ton)

Particulars	*Cost Per ton* ₹.	*Total Cost* ₹.
Direct Materials	—	—
Direct Wages or Direct Labour	—	—
Direct or Chargeable Expenses	—	—
(A) Prime Cost	—	—
Works on cost or Factory on cost or Works overheads (may be a percentage of Direct Labour)	—	—
(B) Works Cost		
Office on cost or office overheads (may be a percentage of works cost or work on cost)	—	—
(C) Cost of Production or Office Cost		
Selling and distribution expenses	—	—
(D) Total Cost		
Profit : Profit (may be a percentage on total cost or selling price		
(E) Selling Price	—	—

Specimen 2 : Comparative Cost Sheet

Three months ending 31–3–20.......			Three months ending 31–6–20.....	
Output (... Units)		*Particulars*	*Output (... Units)*	
Total	*Cost per Unit*		*Total*	*Cost per Unit*
₹.	₹.		₹.	₹.
		Raw Materials		
		Direct Wages		
		Direct Charges		
		(A) **Prime Cost**		
		Works on Cost or		
		Works Expenses :		
		Fuel		
		Electric power		
		Repairs		
		Depreciation ec.		
		(B) **Works Cost**		
		Office on Cost or		
		Office Expenses		
		Office Rent etc.		
		(C) **Total Cost or Production**		
		Profit (% on Cost Price or Selling Price)		
		(D) **Selling Price**		

Specimen 3 : Cost Sheet (detailed)

Particulars	*Cost Per ton*	*Total Cost*
	₹.	₹.
Material Consumed		
Raw Materials on Ist April (opening)		
Add: Purchases during the period		
Add: Carriage Inward		
Less: Raw Materials on 31st March (closing)		
Direct Wages		
Direct or Chargeable Expenses		
(A) Prime Cost		
Works or Factory on cost :		
Indirect wages		
Depreciation on Machines etc.		
Depreciation of Factory Buildings.		
Repairs to Machines, Building etc.		
Fuel Electric Power etc.		
(B) Gross Works Cost		
Add: Work-in-progress (opening)		
Less: Work-in-progress (closing)		
Less: Sale of Scrap etc.		
(C) Works or Factory Cost		
Office on cost:		
Office Salaries		
Office rent		
Depreciation of Office Building and Furniture etc.		
Repairs to Office Building, Furniture etc.		
General Expenses etc.		
(D) Total Cost of Production		
Add: Stock of Finished Goods on Ist April (Opening)		
Less: Stock of Finished Goods on 31st March (Closing)		
(E) Cost of Goods Sold		
Selling and Distribution Expenses		
(F) Cost of Sales		
Profit		
Selling Price		

(*a*) *Calculation of Relative Percentage of Various Expenses*

(*i*) Percentage of Works On Cost with Direct Materials

$$\frac{\text{Works overheads or Works on cost}}{\text{Direct Materials}} \times 100$$

(*ii*) Percentage of Works on Cost with Direct Wages.

$$\frac{\text{Works overheads or Works on cost}}{\text{Direct Wages}} \times 100$$

(*iii*) Percentage of Works on cost with Prime Cost.

$$\frac{\text{Works overheads or Works on cost}}{\text{Prime cost}} \times 100$$

(*iv*) Percentage of Office on cost with Works Cost

$$\frac{\text{Office on cost or office overheads}}{\text{Works Cost}} \times 100$$

(*v*) Percentage of office on cost with works on Cost :

$$\frac{\text{Office on cost or office overheads}}{\text{Works on cost}} \times 100$$

(*b*) *Calculation of percentage of each expense with Total Cost*

(*i*) Percentage of Direct Materials Consumed with Total Cost

$$\frac{\text{Materials Consumed}}{\text{Total Cost}} \times 100$$

(*ii*) Percentage of Direct Wages with Total Cost.

$$\frac{\text{Direct Wages}}{\text{Total Cost}} \times 100$$

(*iii*) Percentage of Works on Cost with Total Cost

$$\frac{\text{Works on Cost}}{\text{Total Cost}} \times 100$$

(*iv*) Percentage of Office on Cost with Total Cost

$$\frac{\text{Office on Cost}}{\text{Total Cost}} \times 100$$

(*c*) *Calculation of Profit by given percentage of profit*

(*i*) $\text{Profit} = \frac{\text{Total Cost} \times \text{Percentage}}{100}$ when percentage of profit is given on total cost.

(*ii*) $\text{Profit} = \frac{\text{Total Cost} \times \text{Percentage}}{100 - \text{Percentage}}$ when percentage of profit is given on sales.

Illustration 1 : Below is the enumerated expending in the manufacture of X.

Raw Materials	56,000
Fuel	13,800
Electric Power	2,680
Process and general wages	1,27,000
Repairs	4,800
Haulage	2,120
Light and water	800
Rent	4,000
Rates and Insurance	600
Office Salaries and General Expenses	14,000
Administration (office)	10,000
Depreciation on Machinery	5,000
Total ₹.	2,40,800

Tons manufactured 34,400

Prepare a cost sheet showing the cost per ton of each expenses and the total cost per ton for the period of three months ending 31.3.2010. ***[Kanpur, B.Com.]***

Solution:

Cost-Sheet
For the three months ending 31st March 2010
(Output 34,400 tons)

		Total Cost	Cost per ton
		₹.	₹.
Raw Materials		56,000	1.63
Process and General Wages		1,27,000	3.69
	Prime Cost	1,83,000	5.32
Works Exps:			
Fuel		13,800	0.40
Electric power		2,680	0.08
Repairs		4,800	0.14
Haulage		2,120	0.06
Light and Power		800	0.02
Rent		4,000	0.12
Rate & Insurance		600	0.02
Depreciation		5,000	0.14
	Works Cost	2,16,800	6.30
Office salaries and general expenses		14,000	0.41
Administration (office)		10,000	0.29
	Total Cost	2,40,800	7.00

Illustration 2: From the following particulars prepare a Cost Sheet showing the cost per item and total cost per ton for the period ended 31st March 2010.

	₹.		₹.
Raw materials	33,000	Rent and Taxes—Office	500
Productive Wages	35,000	Water Supply	1,200
Unproductive Wages	10,500	Factory Insurance	1,100
Factory Rent and Taxes	7,500	Office Insurance	500
Factory Lighting	2,200	Legal Expenses	400
Factory Heating	1,500	Direct Expenses	3,000
Motor Power	4,400	Rent of Warehouse	300
Haulage	3,000	Depreciation of Plant and Machinery	2,000
Directors Fees—Works	1,000	Depreciation on Office Building	1,000
Director Fees—Office	2,000	Depreciation on Delivery vans	200
Factory Cleaning	500	Bad debts	100
Sundry Office Exps.	200	Advertising	300
Factory Stationery	750	Sales Deptt. Salary	1,500
Office Stationery	900	Upkeep of Delivery Van	700
Loose Tools Written off	600	Bank charges	50
		Commission on Sales	1,500

Note : The total output for the period has been 15,000 tons.

Solution:

Cost Sheet for the period ended 31st March 2010
(Output–15,000 tons)

	Cost per ton		*Total cost*	
	₹.	₹.	₹.	₹.
Raw Materials	2.200		33,000	
Productive Wages	2.333		35,000	
Direct Expenses	0.200		3,000	
Prime Cost		4.733		71,000
Works Expenses:				
Unproductive wages	0.700		10,500	
Factory rent and taxes	0.500		7,500	
Factory lighting	0.147		2,200	
Factory heating	0.100		1,500	
Motor power	0.294		4,400	
Haulage	0.200		3,000	
Director's Fees (Works)	0.067		1,000	
Factory cleaning	0.033		500	
Factory stationery	0.050		750	
Loose tools written off	0.040		600	
Water Supply	0.080		1,200	
Factory Insurance	0.073		1,100	
Depreciation of Plant and Machinery	0.133	2.417	2,000	36,250
Works Cost		7.150		1,07,250
Office Expenses:				
Directors Fees (office)	0.133		2,000	
Sundry Expenses	0.013		200	
Office Stationery	0.060		900	
Rent and Taxes	0.033		500	
Office Expenses	0.033		500	
Legal Expenses	0.027		400	
Bank Charges	0.004		50	
Depreciation of office building	0.067	0.370	1,000	5,550
Cost of Production		7.520		1,12,800
Selling and Dist. Exps:				
Rent of Warehouse	0.020		300	
Depreciation of Del. Vans.	0.013		200	
Bad debts	0.007		100	
Advertising	0.020		300	
Sales Deptt. Salaries	0.100		1,500	
Upkeep of Delivery Vans	0.047		700	
Commission on Sales	0.100	0.100	1,500	4,600
Total Cost		7.827		1,17,400

Illustration 3: Prepare a Cost sheet showing cost per cabinet and profit per cabinet from the following particulars.

The cabinets manufactured are classed 'No. 1' and 'No. 2'. There is no opening or closing stock of cabinets.

	No. 1	No. 2
Materials	₹. 12,400	13,232
Labour	₹. 22,540	25,358
No. Sold	520	780
Selling Price (per unit)	₹. 150	110

Works Overhead comes to 100 per cent on labour and Office Overheads to 25 per cent on Works cost. What is the total profit for the year as per above particulars.

Solution :

Cost Sheet

Particulars	*Cabinet No. 1 (Output–520)*		*Cabinet No. 2 (Output–780)*	
	Total Cost of No. I	*Cost per Cabinet No. I*	*Total Cost of No. II*	*Cost per Cabinet No. II*
Materials	12.400	23.85	13.232	16.96
Labour	22.540	43.35	25,358	32.51
Prime Cost	34,940	67.20	38,590	49.47
Works On cost (100% on Labour)	22,540	43.35	25,358	32.51
Works Cost	57,480	110.55	63,948	81.98
Office On cost (25% on Works Cost)	14,370	27.63	15,987	20.50
Cost of Production	71,850	138.18	79,935	102.48
Profit	6,150	11.82	5,865	7.52
Sales	78,000	150.00	85,800	110.00

Illustration 4: The Bihar Musical Products Ltd. are the manufactures of two types of grmophones-08-. From the following particulars, prepare a statement showing cost per gramophone and total profit disclosed by the costing records. There is no opening or closing stock

	Type One ₹.	Type Two ₹.
Materials	90,000	1,50,000
Labour	2,15,000	4,75,000
Number sold	500	750
Selling price per gramophone	1,200	1,500

Overhead expenses are : (*i*) Factory ₹. 5,52,000 and (*ii*) Office ₹. 1,48,200. Allocate factory overheads on the basis of labour and office overheads on the basis of works cost.

Solution :

Cost-Sheet : For Musical Products

	Type I (Output 500)		*Type II (Output 750)*	
	Total Cost	*Cost per Gramophone*	*Total Cost*	*Cost per Gramophone*
	₹.	₹.	₹.	₹.
Materials	90.000	180.00	1,50,000	200.00
Labour	2,15,000	430.00	4,75,000	633.33
Prime Cost	3,05,000	610.00	6,25,000	833.33
Works on Cost (215:475) (on the basis of Labour)	1,72,000	344.00	3,80,000	506.67
Works Cost	4,77,000	954.00	10,05,000	1,340.00
Office on cost (477:1005) (on the basis of works cost)	47,700	95.40	1,00,500	134.00
Total Cost	5,24,700	1,049.40	11,05,500	1,474.00
Profit	75,300	150.60	19,500	26.00
Selling Price	6,00,000	12,00.00	11,25,000	1,500.00

Illustration 5: Mr. Ram manufactures stools, chairs and tables. The materials and wages costs are separated as follows:

	Stool	*Chair*	*Table*
	₹.	₹.	₹.
Materials	36	60	440
Wages	48	40	120

The total factory on cost in the month of January 2003 was ₹. 60,000. You are asked to determine the factory cost of each type of furniture after assuming that one table is equivalent to 4 stools and two chairs are equivalent to one table for the purpose of allocation of factory on cost. The production in the month was stools 600, chairs 300, table 60.

Cost Sheet

Particulars	*Stools (Output 600)*		*Chairs (Output 300)*		*Tables (Output 60)*	
	Cost per Stool	*Total*	*Cost per Chair*	*Total*	*Cost per Table*	*Total*
	₹.	₹.	₹.	₹.	₹.	₹.
Materials	36.00	21,600	60.00	18,000	440.00	26,400
Wages	48.00	28,800	40.00	12,000	120.00	7,200
Prime Cost	84.00	50,400	100.00	30,000	560.00	33,600
Factory On Cost (5 : 5 : 2)	41.67	25,000	83.33	25,000	166.67	10,000
Factory Cost	125.67	75,400	183.33	55,000	726.67	43,600

Working—Absorption of works overhead :

(*a*) One table = 4 Stools, therefore 60 Tables = 240 Stools

(*b*) 2 Chairs = 1 Table = 4 Stools, therefore one Chair = 2 Stools. 300 Chairs = 600 Stools The Ratio will be 600 : 600 : 240 i.e. 5 : 5 : 2

Illustration 6: Asha Ltd. makes different types of vehicles '*ESSEX*' and *WETEX*. The total expenses during a period are shown by the books for assembly of 600 of *ESSEX* and 800 of *WETEX* as under :

	₹.	
Materials	198,000	
Wages	12,000	
Stores Overhead	19,800	
Running expenses of machine	4,400	
Depreciation	2,200	
Labour welfare exp.	1,500	
Works Expenses	30,000	
Administrative exp.	26,790	
Additional information:	*ESSEX*	*WETEX*
Materials Cost ratio per unit	1 :	2
Wages Cost ratio per unit	2 :	3
Machine utilisation per unit	1 :	2

Prepare Cost Sheet for each vechile.

Solution: Working Notes: Different types of expenses have been allocated as below.

1. Material : On the basis of per unit material × Number of units

$$\left.\begin{array}{l}\text{ESSEX} = 600 \times 1 = 600\\ \text{WETEX} = 800 \times 2 = 1600\end{array}\right\} 3:8$$

2. Labour : On the basis of per unit labour × Number of units

$$\left.\begin{array}{l}\text{ESSEX} = 600 \times 2 = 1200\\ \text{WETEX} = 800 \times 3 = 2400\end{array}\right\} 1:2$$

3. Stores overhead on the basis of percentage on Material *i.e.*

$$= \frac{19{,}800 \times 100}{1{,}98{,}000} = 10\%\text{“}$$

4. Running Exps. of Machinery by the ratio of materials
5. Works Exps. and Labour Welfare Exps. on the basis of wages *i.e.*

$$\text{Works Exps. } \frac{30{,}000 \times 100}{12{,}000} = 250\%$$

$$\text{Labour Welfare Exp. } \frac{1500 \times 100}{12{,}000} = 12.5\%$$

6. Administrative Exps. on the basis of Works Cost *i.e.*,

$$\frac{26{,}790 \times 100}{2{,}67{,}900} = 10\%$$

Cost Sheet : Two Vehicles
Output—ESSEX 600, WETEX 800

(In ₹.)

	ESSEX		*WETEX*	
	Total	*Cost per Vehicle*	*Total*	*Cost per Vehicle*
Materials 54,000	90.00	1,44,000	180.00	
Wages	4,000	6.67	8,000	10.00
Prime Cost	58,000	96.67	1,52,000	190.00

Factory Overheads:				
Store overhead	5,400	9.00	14,400	18.00
Machine Expenses	1,200	2.00	3,200	4.00
Depreciation	600	1.00	1,600	2.00
Labour welfare Exp.	500	0.83	1,000	1.25
Works expenses	10,000	16.67	20,000	25.00
Works Cost	75,700	126.17	1,92,200	240.25
Administrative Exp.	7,570	12.61	19,220	24.03
Total Cost	83,270	138.78	2,11,420	264.28

Illustration 7: The following data relate to the manufacturing of an article during the month of Dec., 2010.

Raw Materials Consumed	₹. 52,000
Direct Wages	₹. 15,600
Machine Hours Worked	1,100 Hours
Machine Hour Rate	₹. 4 per Hour
Office Overhead 15% of Works Cost	
Selling Overhead 25 Paise per unit sold	
Unit produced	15,000 units
Units sold	13,500 units; Selling Price ₹. 7 per unit

Compile a cost sheet showing (*a*) Cost per unit (*b*) Profit for the period.

Solution:

Cost Sheet
For the month Dec. 2010 (Output 15,000 units)

	Total ₹.	*Cost per unit* ₹.
Raw Materials Consumed	52,000	3.47
Direct Wages	15,600	1.04
Prime Cost	67,600	4.51
Works Overheads:		
1,100 Machine Hours @ ₹. 4	4,400	0.29
Works Cost	72,000	4.80
Office Overheads 15% of Works Cost	10,800	0.72
Total Cost	82,800	5.52

Profit for the Period

	Total ₹.	*Cost per unit* ₹.
Total Cost of 13,500 units @ ₹. 5.52	74,520	5.52
Add: Selling Overhead 25 Paise per unit.	3,375	0.25
Cost of Sales	77,895	5.77
Profit	16,605	1.23
Sales 13,500 units @ ₹. 7 per unit	94,500	7.00

Illustration 8: The works cost of a certain article is ₹. 4,000 and selling price is ₹. 8,000. The following direct selling and distribution expenses were incurred :

	₹.
Freight	400
Insurance	100
Commission	600
Packing	100

The estimated fixed selling and distribution expenses for the year were ₹. 3,00,000 and the estimated value of sales for the year was ₹. 15,00,000.

You are required to set out the final cost of the article using the method of percentage on sales to recover fixed selling and distribution expenses.

Solution:

$$\text{Ratio of Fixed Selling Exps to Sales} = \frac{3,00,000 \times 100}{15,00,000} = 20\%$$

Calculation of Final Cost

		₹.	₹.
Works Cost			4,000
Selling & Distribution Expenses:			
Variable :	Freight	400	
	Insurance	100	
	Commission	600	
	Packing	100	
		1200	
Fixed : 20% of sales		1600	2,800
Final Cost			6,800

Illustration 9: The following particulars are obtained from the books of an iron foundary at the end of the year 2009-10.

1.	Materials:	
	Opening stock	₹. 7,000
	Purchases	₹. 50,000
	Closing stock	₹. 5,000
2.	Direct Labour	₹. 10,000
3.	Works overheads 50% of Direct Labour	
4.	Stores overheads 10% of Cost of Materials used	

10% of castings were rejected being not up to the specification and a sum of ₹. 400 realised from the sale of scrap.

10% of the finished castings were found to be defective in manufacture and were rectified by expenditure of additional works overhead to the extent of 20 per cent on the proportionate direct wages.

The gross output during the year was 1,000 tons.

Find out the manufacturing cost of the saleable casting per ton.

Solution :

Cost Sheet for the year 2009-10 (Saleable Output 900 Tons)

		Total ₹.	Cost per Ton ₹.
Opening stock of Raw Materials	7,000		
Add: Purchases	50,000		
	57,000		
Less: Closing stock of Raw Material	5,000		
Cost of Materials used		52,000	57.78
Direct Wages		10,000	11.11
Prime Cost		62,000	68.89
Works overhead (50% of Direct Wages)		5,000	5.56
Stores overhead (10% of Cost of Material)		5,200	5.77
		72,200	80.22
Less: Sale of Rejected Casting		400	00.44
		71,800	79.78
Additional Works Overhead (For Rectification)		180	.20
Manufacturing Cost		71,980	79.98

Working :

Calculation of additional works cost for rectification of 90 units

$$10{,}000 \times \frac{90}{1000} \times \frac{20}{100} = ₹.\ 180$$

Illustration 10: From the undermentioned particulars, prepare a Cost Sheet of a brick works showing cost and profit per 1,000 bricks.

Wages (Clay getting machines, drying, setting, burning, drawing, sorting, loading) ₹. 1,50,000
Coal: 5,000 tons at ₹. 15 per ton
Royalties : ₹. 1.50 per 1,000 bricks made
Depreciation of Plant and Machinery at 10% (Capital Outlay ₹. 3,00,000)
Removal of overburnt at one rupee per 1,000 bricks
Works Overhead : 10% of wages and coal
Office Overhead 2.5% of wages and coal
Bricks made : 1,01,52,284 (allows for waste at 1.5% of output)
Bricks sold : 80,00,000 at ₹. 40 per 1,000
Stock of Bricks on 1st January : 20,00,000 at ₹. 30 per 1,000
Stock of Bricks on 31st December : 40,00,000 at ₹. 30 per 1,000

Solution:

Cost-Sheet
For the year ended 31st Dec....

Gross Output 1,01,52,284 Less 1.5% waste = 1,00,00,000 Bricks Effective Output	*Total Cost*	*Cost per 1,000 bricks*
	₹.	₹.
Wages (clay-getting machines, drying setting etc.)	1,50,000	15.00
Coal (5000, tons at ₹. 15 per ton)	75,000	7.50
Royalties (₹. 1.50 per 1,000 bricks)	15,000	1.50
Prime Cost	2,40,000	24.00

Works Expenses :		
Removal of Overburnt at ₹ 1 per 1,000 bricks	10,000	1.00
Depreciation on Plant and Machinery at 10% on ₹. 3,00,000	30,000	3.00
Works Overhead (10% of Wages and Coal *i.e.* 1,50,000 + 75,000 × 10/100)	22,500	2.25
Works Cost	3,02,500	30.25
Office Overhead (2.5% of Wages and Coal *i.e.* 1,50,000 + 75,000 × 2.5/100)	5,625	.56
Cost of Production	3,08,125	30.81

Statement of Profit

	Qty. of Bricks	Total ₹.	Per 1,000 Bricks (₹.)
Stock on 1st Jan. @ ₹. 30 per 1,000	20,00,000	60,000	30.00
Add: Cost of Production	1,00,00,000	3,08,125	30.81
	1,20,00,000	3,68,125	30.68
Less: Closing Stock on 31st Dec. @ ₹. 30 per 1,000	40,00,000	1,20,000	30.00
Cost of Sales	80,00,000	2,48,125	31.02
Profit		71,875	8.98
Sales @ ₹. 40 per 1,000 bricks		3,20,000	40.00

Illustration 11: The following particulars relate to special paper manufactured by Bharat Paper Mills in December 2003. Work out in a cost sheet form the unit cost of production per ton:

Direct Material

Paper pulp 100 tons @ ₹. 250 per ton.

Other Materials 20 tons @ 200 per ton.

Direct Labour

80 Skilled workers @ ₹. 3 per day for 30 days.

40 Unskilled workers @ Re. 1 per day for 30 days.

Direct Expenses

Special equipment ₹. 3,000

Special dyes. ₹. 1,000

Works Overhead : 60% of Direct wages.

Administrative Overheads : 10% of works cost.

Selling & Distribution Overheads : 20% of works cost.

80 ton of special paper was manufactured and ₹. 1,000 was realised from the sale of waste material during course of manufacture.

Solution :

Cost Sheet
For the month of December 2003
(Output — 80 Tons)

		Total cost	*Cost per ton*
	₹.	₹.	₹.
Direct Materials:			
Paper pulp	100 tons @ ₹. 250 per ton = 25,000		
Other Materials	20 tons @ ₹. 200 per ton = 4,000		
	29,000		
Less: Sale of waste materials	1,000	28,000	350.00
Direct Labour :			
Skilled	80 × 3 × 30 = 7,200		
Unskilled	40 × 1 × 30 = 1,200	8,400	105.00
Direct Expenses :			
Special Equipment	3,000		
Special dyes	1,000	4,000	50.00
	Prime Cost	40,400	505.00
Works Overhead (60% of Direct wages)		5,040	63.00
	Works Cost	45,440	568.00
Administrative Overheads : (10% of works cost)		4,544	56.80
	Office Cost	49,984	624.80
Selling & Distribution Overheads : (20% of works cost)		9,088	113.60
	Total Cost of Production	59,072	738.40

Illustration 12: Work out in the cost sheet from the unit cost of producing per meter of Khaki Jeen in a textile factory from the following data for the month of June 2003:

Khaki cotton thread : 2,000 kgs. @ ₹. 7 per kg

Direct Labour : 200 men @ ₹. 4.50 per day for 20 days

Stores Overheads : @ 10% of Direct Materials

Shop Overheads : Variable 50% } on Direct
Fixed 100% } Labour

Sale of cotton thread waste 200 kgs @ ₹. 2 per kg

Office overhead : 10% of Factory Cost

Total output for the month : 33,000 meters

There is no work-in-progress at the beginning of the month or at the end of month.

Solution:

Cost Sheet for the month of June, 2003
(Output 33,000 meters)

	Total Cost	*Cost per meter*
	₹.	₹.
Direct Materials : 2000 kilograms		
Cotton thread at ₹. 7 per kg	14,000	0.424
Direct Labour : 200 men at ₹. 4.50 per day for 20 days	18,000	0.545
Prime Cost	32,000	0.969

Works overheads :		
Stores overheads at 10% of Direct Materials	1,400	0.042
Shop Overheads :		
Variable at 50% on Direct Materials	9,000	0.273
Fixed at 100% on Direct Labour	18,000	0.545
	60,400	1.829
Less: Credit for sale of cotton thread		
Waste : 200 kilograms at ₹. 2 per kilogram	400	0.012
Factory Cost	60,000	1.817
Office Overheads : 10% of factory cost.	6,000	0.182
Total Cost	66,000	1.999
		or say ₹. 2.00

Illustration 13: The Directors of a manufacturing company require a statement showing the production results of the business for the month of April 2010. The cost accounts give the following information:

	₹.
Stock in hand (1.4.2010)	
Raw Materials	25,500
Finished goods	17,300
Stock in hand (30.4.2010)	
Raw Materials	26,200
Finished goods	15,000
Purchases of Raw Materials	22,000
Work-in-progress (1.4.2010)	8,200
Work-in-progress (30.4.2010)	9,000
Sale of Finished goods	72,000
Direct wages	17,100
Non-productive wages	800
Stores	100
Office Expenses	3,000
Works Expenses	3,000
Selling and Distribution Exps.	4,200

The following information is required : (*a*) The value of materials consumed, (*b*) Works Cost, (*c*) Total cost of production, (*d*) Cost of goods sold, (*e*) The profit on goods sold, (*f*) Percentage of works overhead to productive wages, (*g*) Percentage of office on cost to works cost, (*h*) Percentage of selling and distribution expenses to sales.

Solution:

Statement of Cost

	₹.
Stock of Raw materials (1-4-10)	25,500
Add: Purchases of Raw Materials	22,000
	47,500
Less: Stock of Raw Materials (30-4-10)	26,200
Value of Materials Consumed (*a*)	21,300
Direct Wages	17,100
Prime Cost	38,400

	₹.	
Work Overheads:		
Non-Productive wages	800	
Stores	100	
Works Exps.	3,000	
		3,900
Gross Work Cost		42,300
Add: Work-in-Progress (1-4-04)		8,200
		50,500
Less: Work-in-Progress (30-4-04)		9,000
Work Cost (*b*)		41,500
Office Exps.		3,000
Cost of Production (Office Cost) (*c*)		44,500
Add: Stock of Finished goods (1-4-04)		17,300
		61,800
Less: Stock of Finished goods (30-4-04)		15,000
Cost of Goods Sold (*d*)		46,800
Selling and Distribution Expenses		4,200
Cost of Sales		51,000
Profit on Goods Sold (*e*)		21,000
Selling Price		72,000

Calculation of Percentages :

(*f*) Percentage of Works Overhead to Productive Wages

$$\frac{\text{Works Overhead} \times 100}{\text{Productive Wages}} \text{ or } \frac{3,900 \times 100}{17,100} = 22.807\%$$

(*g*) Percentage of Office on Cost to Works Cost

$$\frac{\text{Office on cost} \times 100}{\text{Works Cost}} \text{ or } \frac{3,000 \times 100}{41,500} = 7.228\%$$

(*h*) Percentage of Selling and Distribution Expenses to Sales

$$\frac{\text{Selling \& Dist. Exps.} \times 100}{\text{Sales}} \text{ or } \frac{4,200 \times 100}{72,000} = 5.833\%$$

Illustration 14: The modern manufacturing company submits the following information on 31st March 2010.

	₹.
Sales for the year	2,75,000
Inventories of the beginning of the year were	
Finished goods	7,000
Work-in-Progress	4,000
Purchase of materials for the year were	1,10,000
Material inventory—at the beginning of the year	3,000
—at the end of the year	4,000
Direct Labour	65,000
Factory Overhead was 60% of the Direct Labour Cost	

Inventories at the end of the year were :

Work-in-Progress	6,000
Finished goods	8,000

Other expenses for the year were

Selling expenses 10% of sales

Administrative expenses 5% of sales

Prepare a Statement of Cost

Solution:

Statement of Cost of the Modern Manufacturing Co.
For the year ending 31st March 2010

	₹.	₹.
Material consumed		
Inventory at the beginning	3,000	
Add: Purchases	1,10,000	
	1,13,000	
Less: Inventory at end	4,000	1,09,000
Direct Labour		65,000
	Prime Cost	1,74,000
Factory overheads @ 60% of Labour		39,000
	Gross Works Cost	2,13,000
Add: Work-in-progress at the beginning		4,000
		2,17,000
Less: Work-in-progress at the end		6,000
	Works Cost	2,11,000
Administrative exps. 5% of sales		13,750
	Cost of Production	2,24,750
Add: Opening inventory of finished goods		7,000
		2,31,750
Less: Closing inventory of finished goods		8,000
	Cost of Goods Sold	2,23,750
Add: Selling exps. 10% of sales		27,500
	Cost of Sales	2,51,250
	Profit	23,750
	Sales	2,75,000

Illustration 15: A factory produces a standard product. The following information is given to you from which you are required to prepare cost sheet for the period ending 31st March 2010.

	₹.
Consumable Materials	
Opening stock	10,000
Purchases	85,000
Closing stock	4,000
Direct Wages	20,000
Other Direct Charges	10,000
Factory Overheads	100% of Direct Labour
Office Overheads	10% of Works Cost
Selling and Distribution expenses	₹. 2 per unit sold.

Units of Finished Product	
In hand at the beginning of the period	1000 (Value ₹. 16,000)
Produced during the period	10,000
In hand at the end of the period	2,000

Also find out the selling price per unit on the basis that profit margin is uniformly made to yield a profit of 20 per cent of the selling price. There was no work-in-progress either at the beginning or at the end of the period.

Solution :

Cost Sheet for the Period ended March 31, 2010
(Output 10,000 units)

		Total ₹	Per Unit ₹
Consumable Materials			
Opening Stock	10,000		
Add: Purchases	85,000		
	95,000		
Less: Closing Stock	4,000	91,000	9.10
Direct Wages		20,000	2.00
Other Direct Expenses		10,000	1.00
Prime Cost		1,21,000	12.10
Factory Overheads : 100% of Direct Wages		20,000	2.00
Works Cost		1,41,000	14.10
Office Overheads : 10% of Works Cost		14,100	1.41
Cost of Production (10,000 Units)		1,55,100	15.51
Add: Opening Stock of Finished Goods (1000 units)		16,000	
		1,71,100	
Less: Closing Stock of Finished Goods (2000 units @ ₹. 15.51 per unit *i.e.* Cost of Production per unit)	31,020		
Cost of Goods Sold (9000 units)		1,40,080	
Add: Selling and Distribution Overheads @ ₹. 2 per unit (₹. 2 × 9000 units)		18,000	
Cost of Sales		1,58,080	
Profit (20% of Selling Price *i.e.* 25% of Cost)		39,520	
Selling Price		1,97,600	
(Per Unit Selling Price ₹. $\frac{1,97,600}{9,000}$ units *i.e.* ₹. 21.96)			

Illustration 16: A manufactures two kinds of electric pumps *XA* and *XB*. The following particulars relate to these pumps for the year ended 31st March, 2010.

	XA	*XB*
Pump Manufactured	250	120
Direct Costs	₹.	₹.
Materials	6,280	5,300
Wages	18,800	11,400
Power etc.	4,200	2820
Total	29,280	19,520

Other Costs	₹.
Factory Supervision	7,200
Packing, Wages, etc.	800
Selling Exp.	8,800

You are required to prepare a statement showing the cost of each kind of pump when ready for despatch taking the following into consideration :

(*i*) Factory supervision to be charged in proportion to direct costs.

(*ii*) Packing expenses to be apportioned in the ratio that direct costs plus factory supervision costs of XA bears to similar costs of XB.

(*iii*) Selling exp. to be charged in proportion to the number of pumps manufactured.

Solution:

Statement of Cost
(For the year ended 31st March, 2010)

Particulars	*XA Pumps Output 250 Pumps*	*XB Pumps Output 120 Pumps*
	₹.	₹.
Materials	6,280	5,300
Add: Wages	18,800	11,400
Add: Power etc.	4,200	2,820
Direct Cost	29,280	19,520
Add: Factory Supervision (Apportioned in the ratio of Direct Cost *i.e.* 3 : 2)	4,320	2,880
Factory Cost	33,600	22,400
Add: General on cost;		
Packing Wages etc. (Apportioned in the ratio of direct costs plus factory supervision costs *i.e.* 3:2)	480	320
Selling Exp.(Apportioned in the ratio of pumps manufactured *i.e.* 25:12)	6,000	2,880
Total Cost	40,080	25,600
Cost of Production per Pump	160.32	213.33

PRODUCTION ACCOUNT

Production Account is a statement of cost or cost-sheet in a ledger account form, showing output during a given period, total cost and per unit cost incurred during the period and their components, as also the profit or loss for that period.

According to *Glover and Williams*, 'The term Production Account is used to denote a particular form of Manufacturing Account, prepared in conjunction with the financial accounts in order to show the actual cost of producing the goods manufactured during the period under review. These accounts may be drawn up at short intervals *e.g.* monthly'.

It should be noted that Production Account is prepared in the form in which Trading Account is prepared. It has normally two parts. The first part gives total cost as well as cost per unit. The second part gives the cost of goods sold and sales.

Specimens of Production A/c

Specimen 1
Production Account
(for 3 months ended ....)

Output ...tons

Particulars	*Quantity*	*Amount per ton*	*Total*	*Particulars*	*Quantity*	*Amount per ton*	*Total*
	Tons	₹.	₹.		Tons	₹.	₹.
To Materials Consumed				By Work-in-progress at end			
To Wages				By Cost of Production c/d			
To Indirect Charges							
To Factory Overheads							
To Office Overheads							
To Gen-Exp. etc.							
To Work-in-progress at the beginning							
To Cost of Production b/d				By Sales			
To Stock of Finished Goods (opening)				By Stock of Finished Goods			
To Profit							

Specimen 2
Production or Manufacturing and Profit & Loss Account for the year ending 31st March 20...

Particulars	₹.	*Particulars*	₹.
To Opening Stock of Raw Materials		**By Prime Cost c/d**	
To Purchases of Raw Materials			
To Carriage on Purchases			
Less: Closing Stock of Raw Materials			
= Cost of Materials Consumed			
To Direct Wages			
	₹.		₹.
To Prime Cost b/d		**By Works Cost c/d**	
To Indirect Wages			
To Manufacturing Expenses			
To Rent, Rates and Insurance			
To Light & Power			
To Repairs to Premises			
To Repairs to Plant and Machinery			
To Depreciation of Plant & Machinery			
To Work-in-progress at beginning			
Less: Work-in-progress at end			

To Works Cost b/d		**By Cost of Production c/d**	
To Salaries			
To Rent, Rates and Insurance (office)			
To Light & Power (office)			
To Repairs to Premises (office)			
To Office Expenses			
To Opening Stock of Finished Goods		**By Cost of Goods**	
To Cost of Production b/d		**Sold c/d**	
Less: Closing Stock of Finished Goods			
To Cost of Goods Sold b/d		**By Sales of Finished Goods**	
To Carriage on Sales			
To Profit c/d			

Illustration 17: From the following particulars make out a monthly cost sheet or production account of the Coke and By Products Company showing cost per ton and percentage of coal used in each item of output.

	Tons	January, 2010
Coal used	5000 @	₹. 12.50 per ton
Coke produced	3500 @	₹. 25.00 per ton
Tar produced	210 @	₹. 50.00 per ton
Sulphate of Amonia produced	49 @	₹. 150.00 per ton
Benzol produced	48 @	₹. 65.00 per ton
Raw Materials used		₹. 8.750
Wages paid		₹. 3,585
Repairs and Renewals		₹. 2,815
General Charges		₹. 4,050

Solution :

Cost Sheet or Production Account of Coke and By-Products Company
(For the month ended 31st January 2010)

Particulars	*Cost per ton (₹.)*	*Qty. (Tons)*	*Amount (₹.)*	*% to coal used*	*Particulars*	*Cost per ton (₹.)*	*Qty. (Ton)*	*Amount (₹.)*	*% to Coal used*
To Coal used	12.50	5,000	62,500	100.00	By Coke Produced	25.00	3,500	87,500	70.00
To Raw Materials			8,750		By Tar Produced	50.00	210	10,500	4.20
To Wages			3,585		By Sulphate of Amonia Produced	150.00	49	7,350	0.98
To Repairs and			2,815						
To Renewals					By Benzol Produced	65.00	48	3,120	0.96
To General Charges			4,050		By Loss in Weight	—	1,193	—	23.86
Total Cost			81,700						
To Profit & Loss A/c (profit transferred)			26,770						
	—	5,000	1,08,470	100.00		—	5,000	1,08,470	100.00

Illustration 18: From the following balances of a manufacturing company, you are required to prepare Production Account, number of articles produced is 4,000.

	₹.
Stock of Materials of beginning	35,000
Stock of Materials at end	4,900
Purchase of Materials	52,500
Factory Wages	95,000
Factory Expenses	17,500
Establishment expenses	10,000
Completed Stock at start	Nil
Completed Stock at end	35,000
Sales	1,89,000

Solution:

Production Account
(Output — 4,000 articles)

Particulars		*Cost per article* ₹	*Total* ₹	*Particulars*	*Cost per article* ₹	*Total* ₹
To Materials consumed				By Cost of Production c/d	51.275	2,05,100
Opening stock of						
Raw Materials	35,000					
Add: Purchases	52,500					
	87,500					
Less: Stock at end	4,900	20.650	82.600			
To Factory Wages		23.750	95.000			
Prime Cost		44.400	1,77,600			
To Factory Expenses		4.375	17,500			
Factory Cost		48.775	1,95,100			
To Establishment Expenses		2.500	10,000			
	₹.	51.275	2,05,100	₹.	51.275	2,05,100
To Cost of Production b/d		51.275	2,05,100	By Closing stock of finished articles		35,000
To Profit			18,900	By Sales		1,89,000
		₹.	2,24,000		₹.	2,24,000

Illustration 19: From the following information prepare Pig Iron Production Account showing cost per ton of each item of expenditure and of the Pig Iron produced. (Fig. in ₹)

	Stock 1-1-04	*Purchases During the year*	*Stock on 31-12-04*
Coal	47,000	21,000	3,600
Coke	3,500	29,500	2,000
Lime Stone	1,500	5,000	1,550
Iron Stone	3,600	18,500	3,420
Sundries	2,100	7,850	2,600
Pig Iron	15,500	Nil	21,200
Sales of Slag during the year			₹. 10,500
Sales of Pig Iron during the year			₹. 1,20,000
Wages Paid			₹. 16,000
General Works Charges			₹. 4,000

The total production of Pig Iron amounted to the 30,000 tons.

Solution:

Calculation of Materials Consumed

	Coal ₹.	Coke ₹.	Lime Stone ₹.	Iron Stone ₹.	Sundries ₹.
Opening Stock	47,000	3,500	1,500	3,600	2,100
Add: Purchases	21,000	29,500	5,000	18,500	7,850
	68,000	33,000	6,500	22,100	9,950
Less: Closing Stock	3,600	2,000	1,550	3,420	2,600
Materials Consumed	64,400	31,000	4,950	18,680	7,350

Pig Iron Production Account for the year ended 31-12-04

	Cost per Ton ₹.	Total (30,000 Tons) ₹.		Cost per Ton ₹.	Total (30,000 Tons) ₹.
To Coal Consumed	2.15	64,400	By Sales of Slag	0.35	10,500
To Coke Consumed	1.03	31,000	By Cost of Pig Iron	4.53	1,35,880
To Lime Stone Consumed	0.17	4,950			
To Iron Stone Consumed	0.62	18,680			
To Sundries	0.25	7,350			
To Wages	0.53	16,000			
To Works Expenses	0.13	4,000			
	4.88	1,46,380		4.88	1,46,380

	₹.
Cost of Production of 30,000 tons	1,35,880
Add: Stock on 1-1-04	15,500
	1,51,380
Less: Stock on 31-12-04	21,200
	1,30,180
Sale of Pig Iron	1,20,000
Loss	10.180

Illustration 20: Given below is the Cloth and Yarn Manufacturing Accounts of Arvind Mills for the year ended 31st March 2010.

		₹.			₹.
To	Opening stock :		By	Sales of 2,24,000 kg	
	Yarn 44,800 kg	33,600		of waste being, that portion	
	Cloth 88,200 kg	88,200		of 11,53,600 kg of cotton as	
		1,21,800		per contra which could not be	
To	Cotton consumed			utilized in yarn manufacture	28,000
	11,53,600 kg	9,01,250	By	Yarn Sales 1,68,000 kg	1,89,000
To	Spinning wages	57,050	By	Cloth Sales 7,56,000 kg	8.97.750
To	Weaving wages	91,700			

		₹.		₹.
To	Stores consumed in spinning which increased yarn by 5,600 kg in weight	41,300	By Closing Stock:	
			Yarn 1,40,000 kg	1,48,750
			Cloth 1,90,400 kg	2,14,200
To	Stores and sizing materials consumed in weaving which increased cloth by 1,86,200 kg in weight	1,48,400		
To	Spinning fuel	36,050		
To	Weaving fuel	22,400		
To	Gross Profit	57,750		
		14,77,700		14,77,700

In the above Manufacturing Account (where the closing stock of yarn and cloth is taken at actual cost), it is contended by the Income Tax Authorities that the closing stock is valued below cost price, in order to suppress the gross profit actually made.

For the satisfaction of the authorities you are required to prepare from the above Manufacturing Account a separate Yarn Production Account and separate Cloth Production Account showing the following details :

(*a*) Gross Profit of the department.

(*b*) Total Quantity produced (including the Opening Balance).

(*c*) Total Cost of Production (including the value of Opening Stock which was at cost)

(*d*) Cost of production per kg (including the quantity of the opening stock in total quantity, and the cost of opening stock in the total cost).

In manufacturing cloth 6,72,000 kg of Yarn was consumed which is to be adjusted at the actual cost arrived at in the manner.

Solution :

Yarn Production Account

Particulars	*Quantity kg*	*Amount ₹*	*Particulars*	*Quantity kg.*	*Amount ₹*
To Opening stock	44,800	33,600	By Sales of Waste	2,24,000	28,000
To Cotton consumed	11,53,600	9,01,250	By Cost of Production including Opening Stock (₹. 1.0625 per kgs.)	9,80,000	10,41,250
To Stores consumed in spinning	5,600	41,300			
To Spinning Wages		57,050			
To Spinning Fuel		36,050			
	12,04,000	10,69,250		12,04,000	10,69,250
To Cost of Production including opening stock @ ₹. 1.0625 per kg.	9,80,000	10,41,250	By Sales of Yarn	1,68,000	1,89,000
To Gross Profit		10,500	By Cloth A/c (at cost) (@ 1.0625)	6,72,000	7,14,000
			By Closing Stock on 31st December at cost	1,40,000	1,48,750
	9,80,000	10,51,750		9,80,000	10,51,750

Cloth Production Account

Particulars	Quantity kg	Amount ₹.	Particulars	Quantity kg.	Amount ₹
To Opening stock	88,200	88,200	By Cost of Production		
To Yarn used	6,72,000	7,14,000	including opening stock		
To Stores consumed	1,86,200	1,48,400	₹. 1.1250 per kg	9,46,400	10,64,700
To Weaving Wages		91,700			
To Weaving Fuel		22,400			
	9,46,400	10,64,700		9,46,400	10,64,700
To Cost of Production	9,46,400	10,64,700	By Sales	7,56,000	8,97,750
To Gross Profit		47,250	By Closing Stock on		
			31st December at cost	1,90,400	2,14,200
	9,46,400	11,11,950		9,46,400	11,11,950

(*a*) Gross Profit

Yarn	₹. 10,500
Cloth	₹. 47,250

(*b*) Total quantity produced including opening stock

Yarn	9,80,000 kg
Cloth	9,46,400 kg

(*c*) Total cost of production including opening stock

Yarn	₹. 10,41,250
Cloth	₹. 10,64,700

(*d*) Cost per kg including cost of op. stock.

Yarn	₹. 1.0625
Cloth	₹. 1.1250

Illustration 21: A firm manufactures a standard article in the qualities, of which they produced during 2009:

500	Articles of Quality *X*
1,000	Articles of Quality *Y*
1,200	Articles of Quality *Z*

The stock of Finished Goods at 1st January, 2003 were :

Quality *X* 60 articles; Quality *Y* 40 articles : Quality *Z* 76 articles.

Sales during the year were :

Quality X	510 articles at	₹. 60.	each
Quality Y	960 articles at	₹. 67.50	each
Quality Z	1,248 articles at	₹. 75	each

The following figures, in respect of the year, were extracted from the books of accounts:

	₹.
Work-in-Progress on Jan. 1	15,000
Work-in-Progress on Dec. 31	18,000
Cost of raw materials used in manufacture	43,500
Stores	6,000
Manufacturing wages	78,000
Depreciation (works)	9,000
Works on cost	16,500

From the above prepare Manufacturing and Trading Account for the year showing the amount of Gross Profit carried to P. and L. A/c assume that the rate per cent of Gross Profit is the same for all the three kinds of articles.

Solution:

Manufacturing and Trading Account for the year ended 31st December, 2009

	Amount ₹.			*Amount* ₹.
To Work-in-Progress 1st Jan.	15,000	By Works-in-Progress 31st Dec.,		18,000
To Cost of materials used in manufacture	43,500	By Cost of Production:		
To Cost of store used	6,000	X Quality 500 articles @ ₹. 48		24,000
To Manufacturing wages	78,000	Y Quality 1000 articles @ ₹. 54		54,000
To Depreciation (works)	9,000	Z Quality 1200 articles @ ₹. 60		72,000
To Works on cost	16,500			
	1,68,000			1,68,000
To Opening Stock of Finished Goods		By Sales		
X 60 @ ₹. 48	2,880	X 510 @ ₹. 60	30,600	
Y 40 @ ₹. 54	2,160	Y 960 @ ₹. 67.50	64,800	
Z 76 @ ₹. 60	4,560	Z 1,248 @ ₹. 75	93,600	1,89,000
To Cost of Production				
X 500 @ ₹. 48	24,000	By Stock on 31st Dec.		
Y 1,000 @ ₹. 54	54,000	X 50 @ ₹. 48	2,400	
Z 1,200 @ ₹. 60	72,000	Y 80 @ ₹. 54	4,320	
To Gross Profit @ 20% on Sales	37,800	Z 28 @ ₹. 60	1,680	8,400
	1,97,400			1,97,400

Working Note: GP Rates of the three products are same, therefore, their cost of production will be in proportion to sales.

X	500	@ ₹.60	₹. 30,000
Y	1000	@ ₹.67.5	67,500
Z	1200	@ ₹.75	90,000
		Total SP	1,87,500
		Less: Total Cost	1,50,000
		GP	37,500

Percentage of GP on SP

$$= 37500 \times 100/1{,}87{,}500 = 20\%$$

The cost of the three products will be

X	₹. 60 – 20%	=	₹. 48 per unit
Y	₹. 67.50 – 20%	=	₹. 54 " "
Z	₹. 75 – 20%	=	₹. 60 " "

MISCELLANEOUS ILLUSTRATIONS

Illustration 22: A factory is engaged in making standard which pass through 3 departments. The cost figures of the factory for the month of November, 2004 are furnished below:

		Total ₹.	*Deptt. A* ₹.	*Deptt. B* ₹.	*Deptt. C* ₹.
Direct Materials used		18,600	7,500	6,400	4,700
Labour Cost		15,000	6,000	5,000	4,000
Total Overhead Exps.		7,500	3,000	2,500	2,000
	₹.	41,100	16,500	13,900	10,700

Prepare a Simple Cost Sheet for products X and Y on the basis of data furnished below:

		Deptt. A	*Deptt. B*	*Deptt. C*
Product X :	Material	100	200	300
	Labour	50	60	70
Product Y :	Material	50	90	140
	Labour	70	60	80

Solution:

Cost Sheet of Product X and Y
For the month of November 2004

	Product X ₹.	*Product Y* ₹.
Deptt. A		
Direct Material	100	50
Direct Labour	50	70
Overhead (50% of Labour)	25	35
Cost of Deptt. A	175	155
Deptt. B		
Direct Materials	200	90
Direct Labour	60	60
Overhead (50% Labour)	30	30
Cost of Deptt. B	465	335
Deptt. C		
Direct Materials	300	140
Labour	70	80
Overhead (50% of Labour)	35	40
	870	595

Note: Overhead exps. is taken as 50% of labour.

Illustration 23: **A factory has undertaken a contract for the manufacture of 8,000 units and the following information has been obtained.**

For each article:	₹.
Material Cost	24
Direct Wages	20
Selling Price	70

The overhead charges consist of (*a*) Fixed ₹. 24,000, (*b*) Variable ₹. 14,400, (*c*) Semi-variable (of which 60% is fixed) ₹. 9,600. Calculate the cost per article. What would be the profit per article, if the number of articles manufactured were 10,000 and the total fixed overhead charges remain unchanged.

Solution:

Cost Sheet

	8,000 Units		10,000 Units	
	Total Cost	*Per Unit*	*Total Cost*	*Per Unit*
	₹.	₹.	₹.	₹.
Materials	1,92,000	24.00	2,40,000	24.00
Direct wages	1,60,000	20.00	2,00,000	20.00
Prime Cost	3,52,000	44.00	4,40,000	44.00
Variable Overhead	14,400	1.80	18,000	1.80
Semi-variable Overhead				
40% Variable	3,840	0.48	4,800	0.48
60% Fixed	5,760	0.72	5,760	0.58
Fixed Overhead	24,000	3.00	24,000	2.40
Total Cost	4,00,000	50.00	4,92,560	49.26
Profit	1,60,000	20.00	2,07,440	20.74
Sales	5,60,000	70.00	7,00,000	70.00

Illustration 24: The cost of manufacturing 40 Pianos of which 20 are of Grade A and 20 are of Garde B is ₹. 80,000; Pianos of Grade B cost 55 per cent and Pianos of Grade A costs 45 per cent of the total.

Ascertain the cost of each grade and add thereto 10 per cent for indirect expenses. Transport to and space in the show-room cost ₹. 60 per piano, selling expenses and advertising are 10 per cent on selling price, which is ₹. 3,150 per piano in the case of Grade A and ₹. 3,885 in the case of Grade B.

What is the percentage of profit on total cost and selling price respectively on each grade?

Solution:

Statement of Cost and Profit

	Grade A	*Grade B*
	₹.	₹.
Cost of Manufacture	36,000	44,000
Indirect Expenses 10%	3,600	4,400
Transport and Show Room Charges	1,200	1,200
Selling and Advertising	6,300	7,770
Total Cost	47,100	57,370
Profit	15,900	20,330
Sales (3150 × 20) and (3,885 × 20)	63,000	77,700
Percentage of Profit on Cost	33.76%	35.44%
Percentage of Selling Price	25.24%	26.16%

Illustration 25: A manufacturer, after a period of experimental work, commences as from 1st January 2004 the production of a standard article of which he makes two grades A and B. Both are produced from the same kind of raw material and are sold to wholesalers at uniform prices—Grade A at ₹. 150 per dozen and Grade B at ₹. 240 per dozen, in each case it being the practice to give 13 articles to a dozen. He bases his sale price on the following costings prepared by himself at the beginning of the year at estimated figures:

	Grade A	Grade B
	₹.	₹.
Raw materials	1.50	3.00
Labour	5.00	7.00
Works Overheads	2.50	3.75
Total Works Cost	9.00	13.75
General Overheads	.89	1.37
	9.89	15.12

On making up his accounts for the year ended 31st Dec. 2004 his total costs are found to be as following :

		Grade A	Grade B
		₹.	₹.
Cost of Materials Used		14,350	14,200
Productive Wages		36,900	56,800
Works Expenses	₹. 56,220		
General Expenses	₹. 26,770		

During the same period his sales amounted to ₹. 2,10,000 (Grade *A* ₹. 90,000 and Grade *B* ₹. 1,20,000) and his stocks on hand on 31st December, 2004 valued at works cost as per his costings were: Grade *A* ₹. 3,600 and Grade *B* ₹. 8,250. From the information given above you are required to prepare revised costings showing the cost per article sold during 2004.

Solution:

Revised Cost Statement for 2004

Output : Grade A 8,200 articles Grade B 7,100 articles	Grade A		Grade B	
	Total	per article	Total	per article
	₹.	₹.	₹.	₹.
Raw Materials	14,350	1.75	14,200	2.00
Wages	36,900	4.50	56,800	8.00
Prime Cost	51,250	6.25	71,000	10.00
Works overhead in proportion of wages	22,140	2.70	34,080	4.80
Works Cost	73,390	8.95	1,05,080	14.80
Office Overhead in proportion of Works Cost	11,008	1.34	15,762	2.22
Total Cost	84,398	10.29	1,20,842	17.02

Note: The production of each grade :

	Grade A	Grade B
Sales	₹. 90,000	₹. 1,20,000
Selling price per dozen	₹. 150	₹. 240
Number of dozen sold	600	500
No. of articles sold at 13 per dozen	7,800	6,500
Stock on 31st December, valued at works cost	₹. 3,600	₹. 8,250
Works cost per article according to his own costings	₹. 9	₹. 13.75
Number of articles in stock	400	600
Therefore, the output of the year (being articles sold and those in stock)	8,200	7,100

Illustration 26: *ABC* is manufacturing refrigrators and the following details are furnished in respect of its factory operations for the year ended 31st March, 2003.

	₹.	₹.
Work-in-Progress in the beginning		
At Prime Cost	51,000	
Manufacturing Exps.	15,000	66,000
Work-in-Progress at the end		
At Prime Cost	45,000	
Manufacturing Exps.	9,000	54,000
Stock of Raw Materials in the beginning		2,25,000
Purchases of raw materials		4,77,000
Direct Labour		1,71,000
Manufacturing expenses		84,000
Closing stock of raw materials		2,04,000

On the basis of above data, prepare a statement showing the cost of production.

Solution:

Statement Showing Cost of Production of Refrigerators for the year ending 31st March 2003

	₹.	₹.
Raw Materials : Opening Stock	2,25,000	
Purchases	4,77,000	
	7,02,000	
Less: Closing Stock of Raw Materials	2,04,000	
Cost of Raw Materials Consumed		4,98,000
Direct Labour		1,71,000
		6,69,000
Add: Work-in-progress in the beginning		51,000
		7,20,000
Less: Work-in-progress at end		45,000
Prime Cost		6,75,000
Manufacturing exps.	84,000	
Add: Work-in-progress in beginning	15,000	
	99,000	
Less: Work-in-progress at end	9,000	90,000
Cost of Production		7,65,000

Illustration 27: Smart Shoe-Polish Company manufactures black and brown polish in one standard size of tin retailing at ₹. 1.08 and ₹. 1.20 respectively. Following is supplied to you.

	₹.
Direct Materials	
Polish	7,38,000
Tins	2,88,000
Direct Wages,	2,44,800
Production Overhead	3,67,200
Admn. and Selling Overhead	1,22,400

	Tins
Sales	
Black Polish	14,40,000
Brown Polish	6,00,000
Opening stock	
Black Polish	48,000
Brown Polish	1,60,000
Closing Stock	
Black Polish	1,08,000
Brown Polish	60,000

The opening stock of black and brown polish was valued at its production cost of paise 80.4 per tin and paise 86.4 per tin respectively. The cost of raw materials for brown polish is 10 per cent higher than that for black but there is no difference in the cost of tins. Direct wages for brown are 8 per cent higher than those for black polish and production overheads are considered to vary with direct wages. Administrative and selling overhead is absorbed at a uniform rate per tin of polish sold. Prepare a statement to show the cost and profit per tin of polish.

Solution:

Statement of Cost of Shoe-polishes

	Black (15,00,000 tins)		*Brown (5,00,000 tins)*	
	Total ₹.	*Per Tin Paise*	*Total* ₹.	*Per Tin Paise*
Direct Materials				
Polish	5,40,000	36.00	1,98,000	39.60
Tins	2,16,000	14.40	72,000	14.40
Direct Wages	1,80,000	12.00	64,800	12.96
Prime Cost	9,36,000	62.40	3,34,800	66.96
Production Overhead	2,70,000	18.00	97,200	19.44
Cost of Production	12,06,000	80.40	4,32,000	86.40
Add: Opening Stock	38,592	80.40	1,38,240	86.40
	12,44,592	80.40	5,70,240	86.40
Less: Closing Stock	86,832	80.40	51,840	86.40
	11,57,760	80.40	5,18,400	86.40
Admn. and Selling Overhead	86,400	6.00	36,000	6.00
Cost of Sales	12,44,160	86.40	5,54,400	92.40
Profit	3,11,040	21.60	1,65,600	27.60
Sales	15,55,200	108.00	7,20,000	120.00

Working Note:

1. Total Production — Black Polish: 14,40,000 + 1,08,000 – 48,000 = 15,00,000 Tins

   Total Production — Brown Polish : 6,00,000 + 60,000 – 1,60,000 = 5,00,000 Tins.

2. Direct Material in both polishes :

   Suppose Direct Materials in black polish = ₹. x per tin

$$\text{In Brown Polish Direct Material} = \frac{11x}{10} \text{ per tin}$$

$$15{,}00{,}000x + 5{,}00{,}000\left(\frac{11x}{10}\right) = 7{,}38{,}000$$

$$x = ₹.\ 0.36$$

∵ Brown Polish $1.1x = ₹.\ 0.396$

3. Direct Labour in both polishes:

Suppose wages in Black Polish = y per tin

Therefore, in Brown Polish = $\frac{108}{100}y = \frac{27}{25}y$ per tin

$$15,00,000y + 5,00,000\ \frac{27}{25}y = 2,44,800$$

$$15,00,000y + 5,40,000y = 2,44,800$$

$$20,40,000y = 2,44,800$$

$$y = \frac{2,44,800}{20,40,000} = ₹.\ 0.12$$

4. Production overheads is based on Direct wages

$$\text{Black} = \frac{3,67,200 \times 1,80,000}{2,44,800} = ₹.\ 2,70,000$$

$$\text{Brown} = \frac{3,67,200 \times 64,800}{2,44,800} = ₹.\ 97,200$$

5. Adm. and Selling Exp. $= \frac{1,22,400}{20,40,000} = ₹.\ 0.06$ per tin of polish sold.

Illustration 28: In a Pottery Works, four types of article *A, B, C* and *D* are manufactured for sale. The same raw materials are used for manufacturing all these articles. The manufactured articles that pass inspection and tests are called "finished articles" and sold to the public. The articles which are found defective on inspection are called "defective articles" and are sold only to the employees of the works at concessional rates. The ratio of defective articles is 10 per cent of the finished article. In other words, for every 100 finished articles there are 10 defective articles. The following data are collected from the Manufacturing Account of the pottery works for the month of March 2010.

Type	*Finished Articles*	*Labour*	*Amount realised from sale of defective articles*
			₹
A	1,000	25 P. each	100
B	2,000	37.5 P. each	500
C	3,000	50 P. each	600
D	4,000	75 P. each	1,000

One type of article requires one kg of raw materials at ₹. 2 per kg.

Factory Overhead :

Fixed 200% }
Variable 100% } On Direct Labour

Find out the Factory Cost of an article of each type in an appropriate cost sheet form.

Solution:

Cost Sheet for the Month of March 2010

	A	*B*	*C*	*D*
Number of total articles produced	1,100	2,200	3,300	4,400
Number of finished articles produced	1,000	2,000	3,000	4,000
	₹.	₹.	₹.	₹.
Materials at ₹. 2 per article produced	2,200	4,400	6,600	8,800
Labour:				
At 25 P. per article produced	275	—	—	—
At 37.5 P. per article produced	—	825	—	—
At 50 P. per article produced	—	—	1,650	—
At 75 P. per article produced	—	—	—	3,300
Prime Cost or	2,475	5,225	8,250	12,100
Factory Overhead :				
Fixed at 200% on Direct Labour	550	1,650	3,300	6,600
Variable at 100% on Direct Labour	275	825	1,650	3,300
Factory Cost of total output	3,300	7,700	13,200	22,000
Less: Amount realised from the sale of defective articles	100	500	600	1,000
Factory Cost of finished articles	3,200	7,200	12,600	21,000
Factory Cost of each finished article	3.2	3.6	4.2	5.25

Illustration 29: **Find out in the appropriate cost sheet form, the unit cost of a completed motor in a works with the following data extracted from the books of the factory for the month of May, 2004.**

(*a*) Opening Balance on 1st May, 2004

Semi-manufactured Materials : 100 tons at ₹. 50 per ton

Direct Labour incurred : at ₹. 55 per ton

Overhead : Fixed 50%, Variable 100% } on Direct Labour

Miscellaneous Components : Value ₹. 2,000

(*b*) Expenditure incurred during the month of May, 2004

Materials drawn : 200 tons at ₹. 60 per ton, components drawn : ₹. 10,000

Direct Labour :

1,000 men at ₹. 2 per day for 30 days

2,000 men at ₹. 1 per day for 30 days

Overhead Charges:

Fixed 100%, Variable 150% } on Direct Labour

(*c*) Value on 31st May 2004

Balance of Materials drawn : Nil

Components not utilised : ₹. 2,000

Value of scrap materials returned to stock was 50 tons at ₹. 10 per ton, there were no semi-manufactured materials in hand, and the number of motors completed was 25 on 31st May 2004.

Solution:

Cost Sheet of a Motor
(Output : 25 Motors)

Particulars	₹.	*Total* ₹.	*Per Unit* ₹.
Work-in-progress on Ist May			
Semi-manufactured materials			
100 tons at ₹. 50 per ton	5,000		
Direct Labour incurred ₹. 55 per ton (100 × 55)	5,500		
Overheads: Fixed 50% on Direct labours	2,750		
Variable 60% on Direct Labour	5,500	18,750	750
Materials Consumed	₹.		
200 tons at ₹. 60 per ton	12,000		
Less: Scrap materials returned			
to stores: 50 ton at ₹. 10 per ton	500	11,500	460
Components utilized			
Opening Balance on 31st May	2,000		
Components drawn	10,000		
	12,000		
Less: Value of Components not utilized on 31st May	2,000	10,000	400
Direct Labour:			
1000 men at ₹. 2 per day for 30 days	60,000		
2,000 men at Re. 1 per day for 30 days	60,000	1,20,000	4,800
Prime Cost		1,60,250	6,410
Overhead charges:			
Fixed 100% on Direct Labour	1,20,000		
Variable 150% on Direct Labour	1,80,000	3,00,000	12,000
Total Cost		4,60,250	18,410

Illustration 30: A small manufacturing unit sold its output in 2003-04 for ₹. 12,000 at ₹. 12 per unit. The total fixed charges of establishment amounted to ₹. 1,500 per annum and the variable cost per unit of production was ₹. 8.50. The management wants to reduce the selling price to ₹. 10.50 per unit and to maintain the same amount of profit as before. How many more units should be produced and sold to give effect to this decision.

Solution:

1. Number of units produced ₹. 12,000/12 = 1,000 units.
2. Cost of production = Fixed charges + Variable charges
   i.e. 1,500 + (1,000 × 8.5) = ₹. 10,000
3. Profit 12,000 – 10,000 = ₹. 2,000.

Now, suppose desired output is x; the cost of producing x units will be (₹. 1,500 + $8.5x$) while sale proceeds of x units @ ₹. 10.50 will be ($10.5x$). The manufactures want to earn same amount of profits as before, therefore Sale price—Cost = Profit.

$$(10.5x) - (1{,}500 + 8.5x) = 2{,}000$$

or $10.5x - 8.5x = 2{,}000 + 1{,}500 = 3{,}500$

or $2x = 3{,}500$; $x = 1{,}750$

Thus the increased output should be 1,750 units. He should produce 750 more units.

Illustration 31: A factory's normal capacity is 1,20,000 units per annum. The estimated costs of production are as under.

Direct Material	:	₹. 3 per unit
Direct Labour	:	₹. 2 per unit (subject to minimum of ₹. 12,000 per month)
Indirect Exps.		
Fixed	:	₹. 1,60,000 per annum
Variable	:	₹. 2 per unit
Semi-variable	:	₹. 60,000 per annum up to 50% capacity and an extra ₹. 20,000 for every 20% increase in capacity or part thereof.

Each unit of raw material yields scrap which is sold at 20 paise. In this year the factory worked at 50% capacity for the first 3 months but it was expected to work at 80% capacity for the remaining 9 months. During the first 3 months the selling price per unit was ₹. 12. What should be the per unit selling price price in the remaining 9 months to earn a total profit of ₹. 2,18,000.

Solution:

Cost Sheet for 87,000 units

	3 months 15,000 *units*		*9 months* 72,000 *units*		*Total*
	Per unit ₹	*Total* ₹	*Per unit* ₹	*Total* ₹	87,000 *units* ₹
Direct Material	3.00	45,000	3.00	2,16,000	2,61,000
Less: Sale of Scrap	0.20	3,000	0.20	14,400	17,400
	2.80	42,000	2.80	2,01,600	2,43,600
Direct Labour	2.40	36,000	2.00	1,44,000	1,80,000
Prime Cost	5.20	78,000	4.80	3,45,600	4,23,600
Indirect Exp:					
Fixed					
1,60,000 × 3/12	2.67	40,000			
1,60,000 × 9/12			1.67	1,20,000	1,60,000
Variable	2.00	30,000	2.00	1,44,000	1,74,000
Semi-variable					
60,000 × 3/12	1.00	15,000			
1,00,000 × 9/12			1.04	75,000	90,000
Total Cost	10.87	1,63,000	9.51	6,84,600	8,47,600
Profit	1.13	17,000	2.79	2,01,000	2,18,000
Sales	12.00	1,80,000	12.30	8,85,600	10,65,600

Notes : (1) Semi-variable for 9 months

For 50% capacity	₹. 60,000
For extra 20%	20,000
For next 10%	20,000
For 9 months 1,00,000 × 9/12 = 75,000	₹. 1,00,000

(2) Selling price per unit

Desired profit for 9 months is

2,18,000 – 17,000 = 2,01,000

Total S.P. = 6,84,600 + 2,01,000 = 8,85,600

Per unit S.P. = 885,600/72,000 = ₹. 12.30

Illustration 32: A Company produces a fan and sells it for ₹. 300. An increase of 15 per cent in cost of material and 10 per cent in cost of labour is anticipated. If the only figures available are those given below, what must be the selling price to give the same percentage of gross profit as before:

(*a*) Material cost have been 45 per cent of cost of sales, (*b*) Labour cost has been 40 per cent of cost of sales, (*c*) Overhead costs have been 15 per cent of cost of sales, (*d*) The anticipated increased costs in relation to the present sales price would cause a 35 per cent decrease in the amount of the present gross profit. **(*B. Com. Delhi*)**

Solution:

	Present Cost of Sale (i.e. assumed) to be ₹. 100)	*Increase*	*Anticipated Cost of Sales*
Materials	45	15%	51.75
Labour	40	10%	44.00
Overheads	15		15.00
	100		110.75

Selling price for anticipated cost of sale of ₹. 110.75 which was ₹. 300 at ₹. 100 cost of sales: (300/100) × 110.75 = 332.25 Due to increased cost (*i.e.*, 110.75 – 100 = 10.75) there is 35 per cent decrease in the amount of gross profit.

Gross profit 10.75 × 100/35 = ₹. 30.72

Percentage of G.P. on Sales: 30.72 × 100/300 = 10.24%

Present Cost of Sales: 300 – 30.72 = 269.28

Break-up of present Cost and anticipated Cost:

Material 45% of 269.28	*i.e.*	121.18	+ 15%	=	139.36
Labour 40% of 269.28	*i.e.*	107.72	+ 10%	=	118.50
Overhead 15% of 269.28	*i.e.*	40.38		=	40.38
	₹.	269.28		₹.	298.24
Thus anticipated Cost of Sales				₹.	298.24
Add: Gross profit 10.24%					34.01
				S.P.	332.25

TYPICAL ILLUSTRATIONS

Illustration 33: A firm has purchased a plant to manufacture a new product, the cost data for which is given below.

Estimated Annual Sales	24,000 units
Estimated Costs	₹.
Materials	4.00 per unit
Direct Labour	0.60 per unit
Overheads	24,000.00 per year
Administrative Exps.	28,800.00 per year
Selling expenses	15% of Sales

Calculate selling price if profit per unit is ₹. 1.02.

Solution:

	Per Units ₹.
Materials	4.00
Direct Labour	0.60
Overheads (₹. 24,000/24,000 units)	1.00
Adm. Exps. (₹. 28,800/24,000 units)	1.20
Cost of Production	6.80

Selling Expenses (15% of Sales)			$15x/100$
(Assume Selling Price ₹. x Per Unit)			
		Total Cost	$6.80 + .15x$
		Profit	1.02
		Selling Price	$7.82 + .15x = x$

Hence $7.82 + .15x = x$ or $.15x - x = -7.82$

or $-.85x = -7.82$ or $x = \frac{7.82}{.85} =$ ₹. 9.20

Illustration 34: Find out the selling price of an article whose cost of production and sale of 1,00,000 units are :

	₹.
Materials	50,000
Labour	40,000
Overheads	1,60,000

The fixed portion of capital employed is ₹. 50,000 and the varying portion is 40 per cent of sales turnover. A profit of 8 per cent net on capital employed after payment of tax at 40 per cent of the earning is desired.

Solution:

It is assumed that Sales Turnover = S

(*i*) Capital Employed = ₹. 50,000 + 40/100 S

(*ii*) Profit is 8% after tax *i.e.* 8% of 100/60 on capital employed *i.e.* $13\frac{1}{3}$% before tax.

Profit = $13\frac{1}{3}$% of ₹. 50,000 + .4S

Sales = Total Cost + $13\frac{1}{3}$% (50,000 + .4S)

= 2,50,000 + 40/3 (50,000 + .4S) = S

S = 2,50,000 + 6,667 + 0.0533 S

S – 0.0533 S = 2,56,667

0.9467 S = 2,56,667

S = 2,56,667/.9467 = ₹. 2,71,118

Thus S.P per article = ₹. 2,71,118/1,00,000 = ₹. 2.71

Capital employed = 50,000 + 40% of ₹. 2,71,118 = ₹. 1,58,448

Profit = 8% of 1,58,448 = ₹. 12,675

Sales	₹. 2,71,118
Less: Total Cost	2,50,000
	21,118
Less: Tax @ 40%	8,443
Profit after tax	12,675

Illustration 35: The standard production for a particular work order is 20 units per day and piece-rate wage is 60 paise per unit if daily production is 20 units or more. The rate is 50 paise per unit if production is less than 20 units. Cost of materials is 30 paise per unit. It is proposed to charge factory overheads under one of the following methods.

(*i*) 100% on Labour Cost (*ii*) 80% on Prime Cost.

Tabulate the above data in the form of a suitable statement and indicate the factory cost per unit under each of the above methods if the daily production is (*a*) 15 units, (*b*) 20 units, (*c*) 25 units.

Solution :

Statement Showing Works Cost

(*i*) By Charging Overhead at 100% Labour Cost

	Production 15 Units		*Production 20 Units*		*Production 25 Units*	
	Total ₹	*Per Unit* ₹	*Total* ₹	*Per Unit* ₹	*Total* ₹	*Per Unit* ₹
Material	4.50	0.30	6.00	0.30	7.50	0.30
Labour	7.50	0.50	12.00	0.60	15.00	0.60
Prime Cost	12.00	0.80	18.00	0.90	22.50	0.90
Factory Overhead @ 100% on Labour Cost	7.50	0.50	12.00	0.60	15.00	0.60
Works Cost	19.50	1.30	30.00	1.50	37.50	1.50

(*ii*) By Charging Overheads at 80% Prime Cost

Prime Cost (as above)	12.00	0.80	18.00	0.90	22.50	0.90
Factory overhead @ 80% of Prime Cost	9.60	0.64	14.40	0.72	18.00	0.72
Works Cost	21.60	1.44	32.40	1.62	40.50	1.62

Illustration 36: In a Company manufacturing ball and roller bearing four operations are carried on simultaneously in the manufacture of components. The input, output data and wages cost relating to a year for one component are as follows:

Operation	Gross Input (MT)	Scrap (MT)	Direct Wages (₹.)
A	48,000	8,000	1,24,000
B	50,000	10,000	1,25,000
C	72,000	12,000	2,36,000
D	55,000	5,000	3,27,000

Material is introduced at the start of operation A at a cost of ₹. 600 per MT. Scrap can be sold at ₹. 450 per MT. Overheads are absorbed at 150 per cent on direct wages.

You are appoined as Cost Auditor of the Company. The Company has not maintained cost records so far and seeks your advice in the matter. Show your computation of the total cost per MT of finished product so that the company can adopt the same in future.

Solution:

Statement Showing of Input/Output Ratio

(₹. 000)

Operation	*(In 000 MT)*			*% of Input to Output*	*Direct Wages*	*Overheads*	*Conversion Cost*
	Input	*Scrap.*	*Output*				
A	48	8	40	120	124	186.0	310.0
B	50	10	40	125	125	187.5	312.5
C	72	12	60	120	236	354.0	590.0
D	55	5	50	110	327	490.5	817.5

Statement Showing Conversion Cost per M.T.

Operation	Conversion Cost per MT MT		(₹)	Cumulative Conversion Cost per MT (₹)
A	$\frac{310}{40}$	=	7.75	7.75
B	$\frac{312.5}{40}$	=	7.8125	7.8125 + 125% of 7.75 = 17.50
C	$\frac{590}{60}$	=	9.8333	9.8333 + 120% of 17.50 = 30.8333
D	$\frac{817.5}{60}$	=	16.35	16.35 + 110% of 30.8333 = 50.2666 say ₹. 50.27

Material is introduced at the start of Operation A at a Cost of ₹. 600 per MT. The input to subsequent operations is the output of preceding operation. Hence, the raw material required for 1 tonne of final output is

1.20 × 1.25 × 1.20 × 1.10	=	1.98 tonnes
Output ...	=	1.00 tonnes
Scrap ..		0.98 tonnes

Statement Showing Computation of Total Cost per M.T.

	₹.
Material Cost 1.98 M.T. at ₹. 600	1,188.00
Less : Scrap sale 0.98 M.T. at ₹. 450	441.00
Net Material Cost	747.00
Add : Conversion Cost per M.T.	50.27
Total Cost per M.T.	797.27

Illustration 37: Component 'Pee' is made entirely in Cost Centre 100. Material cost is 6 paise per component and each component takes 10 minutes to produce. The machine operator is paid 72 paise per hour, and the machine hour rate is ₹. 1.50. The setting up of the machine to produce the component 'Pee' takes 2 hours 20 minutes.

On the basis of this information prepare a cost-sheet showing the production and setting up cost, both in total and per component, assuming that a batch of:

(*a*) 10 components, (*b*) 100 components, and (*c*) 1,000 components is produced.

[*C.A. (Inter)*]

Solution :

Cost Sheet of Component 'PEE'

Batch Size	10 Comp.		100 Comp		1000 Comp	
Cost	Total ₹	Per Comp. ₹	Total ₹	Per Comp. ₹	Total ₹	Per Comp. ₹
Setting up Cost: (A)						
Machine Operators Wages						
(2 hours 20 minutes @ 72 P.p.h.)	1.68	0.168	1.68	0.0168	1.68	0.00168
Overheads						
(2 hours 20 minutes @ 1.50 p.h.)	3.50	0.350	3.50	0.035	3.50	0.0035

Production Cost: (B)						
Material Cost						
@ 6 P per component	0.60	0.06	6.00	0.06	60.00	0.06
Machine Operators Wages						
(Working Note (*i*)	1.20	0.12	12.00	0.12	120.00	0.12
Overheads						
(Working Note (*ii*)	2.50	0.25	25.00	0.25	250.00	0.25
Total Cost : (*A* + *B*)	9.48	0.948	48.18	0.4818	435.18	0.43518

Working Notes:

(*i*) *Components*	10	100	1000
Operators Wages Time taken in minutes by machine operators @ 10 minutes per component	100	1000	10,000
Operators Wages @ 72P per hour (₹.)	1.20	12.00	120.00
	$\left(\frac{100}{60} \times 0.72 \text{ P}\right)$	$\left(\frac{1000}{60} \times 0.72 \text{ P}\right)$	$\left(\frac{10,000}{60} \times 0.72 \text{ P}\right)$
(*ii*) *Overhead Expenses*			
Total Overhead Expenses in (₹.) @ ₹. 1.50 per machine hour	2.50	25.00	250.00
	$\left(\frac{100}{60} \times 1.50\right)$	$\left(\frac{1000}{60} \times 1.50\right)$	$\left(\frac{10,000}{60} \times 1.50\right)$

Illustration 38: RST Ltd. manufactures plastic moulded chairs. Three models of moulded chairs, all variation of the same design are Standard, Deluxe and Executive. The company uses an operation costing system.

RST Ltd. has Extrusion, Form Trim and Finish operations. Plastic sheets produced by the Extrusion Operation. During the Forming Operation, the plastic sheets are moulded into chair seats and the legs are added. The standard model is sold after this operation. During the Trim Operation, the arms are added to the Deluxe and Executive models and chair edges are smmothed. Only the Executive model enters the Finish Operation, in which padding is added. All of the units produced receive the same steps within each operation. In April, 2003 units of production and direct material cost incurred are as follows:

	Units Produced	*Extrusion Materials (₹.)*	*Forming Materials (₹.)*	*Triming Materials (₹.)*	*Finishing Materials (₹.)*
Standard Model	10,500	1,26,000	42,000	0	0
Deluxe Model	5,250	63,000	21,000	15,750	0
Executive Model	3,500	42,000	14,000	10,500	21,000
	19,250	2,31,000	77,000	26,250	21,000

The total conversion costs for the month of April, 2003 are :

	Extruction Operaiton	*Forming Operation*	*Triming Operation*	*Finishing Operations*
Total Conversion Costs	₹. 6,06,375	₹. 2,97,000	₹. 1,55,250	₹. 94,500

Required :

(*i*) For each product produced by RST Ltd. during April, 2003, determine the unit cost and the total cost.

(*ii*) Now consider the following information for May. All unit costs in May are identical to the April unit costs calculated as above in (*i*). At the end of May, 1,500 units of the Deluxe model remain in work-in-progress. These units are 100% complete as to materials and 65% complete in the trim operation. Determine the cost of the Deluxe model work-in-process inventory at the end of May.

[*CA PE II – 2003*]

Solution:

(*i*) Statement Showing Unit Cost and Total Cost Model-wise

	Standard Model cost	*Deluxe Model cost*	*Executive Model cost*
Extrusion Material	₹. 12.00	₹. 12.00	₹. 12.00
Form Material	4.00	4.00	4.00
Triming	—	3.00	3.00
Finishing	—	—	6.00
Extrusion Conversion	31.50	31.50	31.50
Form Conversion*	15.43	15.43	15.43
Trim Conversion*	—	17.74	17.74
Finish Conversion*	—	—	27.00
	62.93	83.67	116.67
Total Cost	₹. 6,60,765 (10,500 × ₹. 62.93)	₹. 4,39,267.50 (5,250 × ₹. 83.67)	₹. 4,08,345 (3,500 × ₹. 116.67)

(*ii*) Statement showing cost of 1500 units of Deluxe model of chairs lying in work-in-progress inventory at the end of May, 2003

	Equivalent units	*Units cost (Note 2)*	*Total cost*
	(1)	*(2)*	*(3) = (1) × (2)*
Extrusion Material	1,500	₹. 12.00	₹. 18,000.00
Form Material	1,500	4.00	6,000.00
Trim Material	1,500	3.00	4,500.00
Extrusion Material Convesion	1,500	31.50	47,250.00
Form Material Conversion	1,500	15.43	23,145.00
Trim Mat.Conversion (1,500 units × 65%)	975	17.74	17,296.50
Total cost of 1,500 units of Deluxe Model of chairs lying in WIP			1,16,191.50

Working Notes :

1. Statement showing the number of units produced for three brands (*i.e.* Standard, Deluxe, Executive) by use of Material of Extrusion, Form, Trim and Finish

	Extrusion Material (Units)	*Form Material (Units)*	*Trim Material (Units)*	*Finish Material (Units)*
Output (in units)	19,250	19,250	8,750	3,500

2. Statement showing the number of units produced for three brands (*i.e.* Standard, Deluxe, Executive) by use of material of Extrusion, Form, Trim and Finish

	Extrusion	*Form*	*Trim*	*Finish*
Output in terms of equivalent units (*i*)	19,250	19,250	8,750	3,500
Material Cost (*ii*)	₹. 2,31,000	₹. 77,000	₹. 26,250	₹. 21.000
Conversion Cost (*iii*)	₹. 6,06,375	₹. 2,97,000	₹. 1,55,250	₹. 94,500
Material Cost per equivalen unit (*ii*) ÷ (*i*)	₹. 12.00	₹. 4.00	₹. 3.00	₹. 6.00
Conversion Cost per unit (*iii*) ÷ (*i*)	₹. 31.50	₹. 15.43	₹. 17.74	₹. 27.00

QUESTIONS

OBJECTIVE QUESTIONS

State whether following statements are True or False.

1. Unit costing is useful in such enterprises which manufacture standard product.
2. Cost of production is also called office cost.
3. 'General Overhead is total of office overhead and selling overhead.
4. There is no difference between cost sheet and statement of cost.
5. Cost of work-in-progress is normally adjusted before calculating cost of production.
6. There is no difference between cost of goods sold and cost of sales.
7. Any profit which is 20% of sales, will be 25% of the cost.
8. There is no difference between production account and manufacturing account.
9. In production accounts, details to be shown in cost sheet are presented in an account from.
10. There is difference between cost sheet and cost account.

[**Ans.** : False are 4, 5, 6, 8 rest are true]

THEORITICAL QUESTIONS

1. What is Cost sheet? How does it differ from Cost Accounts?
2. What is meant by Cost-Sheet and why it is prepared? Take a commodity which is of general public use and give particulars regarding materials used and wages and other expenses incurred in its production. Give a Cost-sheet which may explain the toal cost of production.
3. Define unit costing. Mention enterprises which use single or output costing.
4. Distinguish between a Cost Sheet and a Production Account. What advantages are derived from the preparation of Cost Sheet.
5. What is the difference between a Cost Sheet and a Cost Account? Give your views as to their respective merits.
6. Write a short note on `Unit Costing Method' for ascertaining production cost.
7. Draw a proforma of Cost sheet.
8. A manufacturing concern values the work-in-progress at material cost. Do you consider it adequate? Give reasons. Also discuss at least three alternative ways of dealing with the problem of valuation of work-in-progress, stating the elements of costs to be included.

SHORT ANSWER QUESTIONS

1. What do you understand by Cost Sheet?
2. What are main information received from Cost Sheet?
3. What is difference between Cost Sheet and Statement of Cost?
4. What is the difference between Cost Sheet and Cost Account?
5. Give a brief proforma of Cost Sheet.
6. How materials consumed in production is calculated ?

7. How Work-in-progress is shown in the Cost Sheet?
8. How Cost of Goods Sold and Cost of Sales are calculated in the Cost Sheet?
9. Give formula for calculating following percentage.
   (*i*) Percentage of Work on cost on Direct Wages.
   (*ii*) Percentage of Work on cost on Wages.
   (*iii*) Percentage of Office on cost on Works on cost.
   (*iv*) Percentage of Materials consumed to Total cost.
10. Calculate Prime cost and works cost from following

Purchase of Raw Materials	₹. 1320
Direct wages	₹. 1100
Rent rates insurance of Factory	₹. 440
Carriage inward	₹. 10
Opening stock of Raw material	₹. 220
Closing stock of Raw material	₹. 240
Other factory overheads	₹. 560

[**Ans.** : *Prime Cost 2,410 Work Cost ₹. 3,410*]

11. Find out works cost and cost of production from following figures.

	₹.
Prime cost	15,000
Work in progress (opening)	5,000
Work in progress (Closing)	8,000
Other factory overheads	3,000
Indirect Material	1,000
Indirect wages	1,500
Office salaries	3,000
General office overheads	5,000

[**Ans.**: *Works cost ₹. 17,500 : Office Cost ₹. 25,500*]

12. From the following prepare a cost sheet :

	Article A	Article B
		₹.
Material	12,000	10,000
Labour	20,000	8,000

Work overheads are 100% of labour and office overheads are 25% of works cost. Profit is 10% of cost.

[**Ans.** : *Selling Price A ₹. 71,500, B ₹. 35,750*]

13. At the end of the year, following particulars are available in respect of a product of a factory.

	₹.
1. Material Consumed	52,000
2. Direct labour	10,000

Works Overhead 50% of Direct labour

10% of products were found defective in manufacture and were rectified by expenditure of additional works overhead to the extent of 20% of proportionate direct wages. The output was 100 units. Prepare cost sheet.

[**Ans.** : *Total Cost ₹. 67,200 per unit ₹. 672*]

14. From the following particulars of a slate manufacturing company Prepare Cost Sheet.

Wages	₹. 10,000
Coal	₹. 5000
Work overheads	20% direct charges
Cost of removal of overhburnt	₹. 1,000
Office overhead	10% of works cost.

[**Ans.** : *Cost of prod. ₹. 20,900*]

NUMERICAL QUESTIONS

Cost Sheet

1. Below is the enumerated expenditure of the manufacture of X :

	Three months ended 31-12-2003 ₹.
Raw Materials	28,000
Fuel	6,900
Electric Power	1,340
Process and General Wages	63,500
Repairs	2,400
Haulage	1,060
Light and Water	400
Rent	2,000
Rates and Insurance	300
Office Salaries and General Expenses	7,000
Administration (office)	5,000
Depreciation of Machinery	2,500
Tons manufactured 17,200	Total ₹. 1,20,400

Prepare a cost sheet showing the cost per ton of item of expenses and the total cost for the period.

[**Ans.** *Prime cost ₹. 91,500 per ton ₹. 5.32; Works costs ₹. 1,08,400 per ton ₹. 6.30 and Total cost ₹. 1,20,400 per ton ₹. 7.*]

2. The account of X Co. show the following expenditure for the year 2003-04.

Material used ₹. 15,50,000 Manual and machine labour (directly chargeable) ₹. 12,50,000. Works overhead expenditure ₹. 3,00,000. Establishment and general charges ₹. 2,00,000.

Show : (*a*) the works cost and total cost; (*b*) the percentage that the works overhead expenditure bears to the manual and machine labour and the percentage that the establishment and general expenses bear to the works cost.

[**Ans.** *(a) Works cost ₹. 31,00,000. Total cost ₹. 33,00,000 (b) 24% and 6.45%*]

3. The following data relate to the manufacture of a standard product during the month of March 2003.

Raw Materials	₹.	1,60,000
Direct wages	₹.	96,000
Machine hours worked		8,000 hrs.
Machine hour rate	₹.	8 per hour
Office on cost		10% of works cost
Selling on cost	₹.	3 per unit
Units produced		4,000
Units sold		3,600 @ ₹. 100 each

You are required to prepare a Cost Sheet in respect of above showing—(*i*) Cost per unit and (*ii*) Profit for the period.

[**Ans.** *(i) ₹. 88 (ii) ₹. 32,400; Prime cost ₹. 2,56,000, Works cost ₹. 3,20,000; Total cost 3,52,000. Closing stock 35,200*]

4. The following data relate to the manufacture of a standard product during the month of December 2002 and January 2003.

	Dec. 2002	*Jan. 2003*
Raw Materials	₹. 80,000	8,80,000
Wages	₹. 48,000	4,00,000
Machine hour worked	8,000	80,000
Machine hour rate	₹. 4	4
Selling on cost	₹. 1.50 per unit	₹. 2.00 per unit
Office on cost	10% of works cost	10% of works cost
Units produced	4,000	40,000

You are required to prepare a comparative cost sheet in respect of the above.

[**Ans.** *Cost per unit Dec. 2002 ₹. 45.50; Total cost ₹. 1,82,000 Jan. 2003 Cost per unit ₹. 46.00; Total cost 18,40,000*]

5. A factory produces 100 units of each of the commodities : A and B. The cost of production are:

	A	*B*
	₹.	₹.
Direct materials	12,000	10,000
Direct wages	8,000	5,000
Chargeable expenses	1,000	1,000

The overhead expenses are : (*i*) Factory ₹. 6,500 and (*ii*) Office ₹. 3,480. If a profit of 25 per cent on sales is to be realised, what would be the selling price of each article? Prepare a Cost Sheet.

[**Ans.** *Selling price per unit of commodity (A) ₹. 360, (B) ₹. 266.40, Factory on cost has been allocated on the basis of Direct Labour : (A) ₹. 4,000, (B) ₹. 2,500, Office on cost has been allocated on the basis of Factory Cost. A ₹. 2,000 and B ₹. 1,480*]

6. Ram Parkash manufactures three types of toy-fans : table fan, ceiling and man cooler. The materials and wages cost are separated as follows :

	Materials	Wages
	(₹.)	(₹.)
Table fan	12	16
Ceiling fan	20	20
Man cooler	180	40

His total factory overheads in the month of August 2003 was ₹. 20,000. You are asked to determine the factory cost of each type of toy-fan after assuming that one ceiling fan is equivalent to two table fans and one man cooler is equivalent to five table fans for the purpose of overhead allocation. The production in the month of August : Table fan 200; Ceiling fan 100; Man Cooler 20.

[**Ans.** *Allocation of Factory overhead : Table fans ₹. 8,000, Ceiling fans ₹. 8,000 and Man cooler ₹. 4,000 i.e. 2 : 2 : 1. Factory cost : Table fans ₹. 13,600 @ ₹. 68; Ceiling fans ₹. 12,000 @ ₹. 120; Man coolers ₹. 8,400 @ ₹. 420*]

7. From the following particulars of product X, prepare a cost sheet for the month of August.

	₹.
Raw Materials :	
Opening Stock	20,000
Purchases	1,50,000
Closing stock	10,000
Direct Labour	60,000
Factory Overheads	22,500
Office & Administrative Overheads	27,500
Finished Goods	
Opening Stock 500 units @ ₹. 11.20 per unit	
Closing Stock 1,500 units @ current cost price	

Sales ₹. 3,49,250

Selling and Distribution Exps. ₹. 20,000

Units produced during August.: 25,000 units.

[**Ans.** *Cost of Production of 25,000 units ₹ 2,70,000 per unit cost ₹ 10.80; Cost of sales of 24,000. units ₹ 2,79,400. Profit ₹ 69,850*]

8. Master Electronics is manufactures of transistors sets and the following details are furnished in respect of its factory operation in the year ending 31st Dec., 2009.

	Beginning	Closing
Work-in-Progress:	₹.	₹.
Materials	10,000	15,000
Labour	12,000	14,000
Factory Exps.	6,000	7,000
	28,000	36,000

	₹.
Stock or Raw Material in the beginning	80,000
Purchases of Raw Materials	4,00,000
Direct Labour	2,80,000
Stock of Raw Materials at the end	60,000
Manufacturing Exps.	85,000
Office and Administrative Exps.	1,53,000

Prepare a Cost Sheet, Sets produced during the year being 6,000.

[**Ans.** *Total Cost of Production ₹ 9,30,000, per unit ₹ 155.*]

[**Hints :** Raw Materials used ₹. 4,15,000, Labour ₹. 2,78,000, Manufacturing Exps. ₹. 84,000, Prime Cost ₹. 6,93,000, Works Cost ₹. 7,77,000]

Statement of Cost

9. The books of Adarsh Manufacturing Company present the following data for the month of April 2010.

Direct labour cost ₹. 17,500 being 175% of works overheads. Cost of goods sold excluding administrative expenses ₹. 56,000 Inventory accounts showed the followign balances.

	April 1	*April 30*
	₹	₹
Raw Materials	8,000	10,600
Work-in-Progress	10,500	14,500
Finished Goods	17,600	19,000

Other data are

Selling Expenses	₹. 3,500
General and administration exps.	2,500
Sales for the month	75,000

Your are required to (*i*) Compute the value of materials purchased (*ii*) Prepare a Cost-Statement showing the various elements of cost and also the profit earned. **[*CA Inter*]**

[**Ans.** *(i) ₹ 36,500 (ii) Prime Cost ₹ 51,400; Works Cost ₹ 61,400; Cost of Goods Sold; ₹ 58,500; Cost of Sales ₹ 62,000 Profit ₹ 13,000*]

10. The following figures are extracted from the trial balance of Gogetter Co. on 30th September 2010.

	₹.	₹.
Opening Inventories		
Finished Materials	80,000	
Raw Materials	1,40,000	
Work-in-Progress	2,00,000	
Office Appliances	17,400	
Plant and Machinery	4,60,500	
Buildings	2,00,000	
Sales		7,68,000
Sales return and rebates	14,000	
Materials purchased	3,20,000	
Freight incurred on material	16,000	
Purchase returns		4,800
Direct Labour	1,60,000	
Indirect Labour	18,000	
Factory Supervision	10,000	
Repairs and upkeep—factory	14,000	
Heat Light and Power	65,000	
Rates and Taxes	6,300	
Miscellaneous Factory Exps.	18,700	
Sales Commission	33,600	
Sales Travelling	11,000	
Sales Promotion	22,500	
Distribution Deptt. Salaries and Exps.	18,000	
Interest on borrowed funds	2,000	
Office Salaries and Exps.	8,600	

Further details are available as follows

(*a*) Closing Inventories :

Finished Goods	1,15,000
Raw Materials	1,80,000
Work-in-Process	1,92,000

(*b*) Accured expenses on :

Direct Labour	8,000
Indirect Labour	1,200
Interest on borrowed funds	2,000

(*c*) Depreciaiton to be provided on Office Appliances 5 per cent, Plant and Machinery 10 per cent, Buildings 4 per cent.

(*d*) Distribution of the following costs :

(*i*) Heat, light and Power to factory, office and distribution in the ratio 8 : 1 : 1 (*ii*) Rates and taxes two-thrid to factory and one-third to office (*iii*) Depreciation on building to factory, office and selling in the ratio 8 : 1 : 1.

With the help of the above informations, you are required to prepare a Cost Statement.

[**Ans.** *Prime Cost ₹. 4,59,200 Works Cost ₹. 6,37,700; Cost of Production ₹. 6,56,620 Cost of Goods Sold ₹. 6,21,620; Cost of Sales ₹. 7,14,020. Net Profit ₹. 35,980 after charging interest on borrowed capital*]

Production Accounts

11. From the following information, prepare Pig Iron Production Account showing cost per ton of each class of expenditure and of the Pig Iron Produced.

	Coal ₹	*Coke* ₹	*Limestone* ₹	*Iron ore* ₹	*Sundries* ₹
Stock on 1st Jan.	4,720	3,580	1,450	3,930	2,700
Purchases during the year	21,880	29,470	5,080	18,690	7,810
Stock on 31st December	3,600	2,050	1,530	3,620	3,010

The total production of Pig Iron amounted to 32,000 tons; Sales of slag. ₹. 10,500: General Works Charges, ₹. 4,500; Wages ₹. 17,000.

[**Ans.** *Cost of Production per ton ₹. 3.0156 or ₹. 3.02 : Total Cost ₹. 96,500*]

12. The following are the balances of the impersonal ledger of a colliery relating to revenue at the end of the year :

	₹.
Wages paid for coal production	5,80,000
Coal for colliery consumption	45,000
Timber used in coal production	64,000
Ropes used in coal production	12,000
Stores used in coal production	76,000
Royalties paid	42,000
General charges	70,000
Salaries	36,000
Coal sold (including colliery) 1,12,000 tons	8,84,000
Wages paid for coke making	50,000
Stores used for coke making	37,000
Salaries for coke making	8,000
Coke sold (43,500 tons)	5,40,000

The stock of coal at the beginning of the year amounted to 7,000 tons valued at ₹. 5 per ton and at the end of the year 15,000 tons valued at the same rate. The stock of coke at the beginning of the year amounted to 2,000 tons valued at ₹. 10 per ton and at the end of the year 500 tons valued at the same rate.

The total production of the colliery was 1,85,000 tons of coal 42,000 tons of coke, 65,000 tons of coal being used for coke-making.

Prepare separate Production Accounts for coal and coke showing the cost of each item of expenses per ton of coal and coke respectively, taking coal used for coke making at cost price.

[**Ans.** *Cost of Production of Coal : Total ₹. 9,25,000, per ton ₹. 5.00, Profit ₹. 3,24,000. Cost of Production of Coke : Total ₹. 4,20,000, per ton ₹. 10.00, Profit ₹. 1,05,000*]

13. From the following particulars, make out a monthly Cost Sheet and Production Account of the Coke and By-products of the Company :

Coal used 5,000 tons @ ₹. 25 per ton.

Coke produced 3,500 tons @ ₹. 50 per ton.

Tar produced 210 tons @ ₹. 100 per ton.

Sulphate of Ammonia produced 49 tons @ ₹. 300 per ton.

Benzol produced 48 tons @ ₹. 130 per ton.

Raw materials used to the value of ₹. 17,500, Wages paid ₹. 7,170.

Repairs and renewals ₹. 5,630.Salaries and General Charges ₹. 8.100.Show the percentage of each product to the weight of coal used.

[**Ans.** *Total Profit ₹. 53,540. Total Cost ₹. 1,63,400; Percentages; Coke 70%. Tar. 4.2% Sulphate of Ammonia 0.98%, Benzol 0.96%, Loss-in-Weight 23.86%*]

14. A Ltd. manufactures standard articles in three varieties. From the following particulars prepare Manufacturing and Trading Account for the year ending 30st March, 2010 assuming the uniform rate of gross profit on all the three kinds :

	Articles of Quality		
	A	B	C
Production during the year (units)	500	1,000	1,200
Stock of articles on opening (units)	60	40	76
Sales during the year (units)	510	960	1,248
Selling price per article (₹.)	120	135	150

Details of combined cost during the year :	₹.
Work-in-Progress (opening)	30,000
Work-in-Progress (closing)	36,000
Cost of Raw Materials used	87,000
Cost of stores used	12,000
Wages (direct)	1,56,000
Depreciation (works)	18,000
Works on cost	33,000

[**Ans.** *Cost of Production ₹. 3,00,000 (A 500 × 96 = 48,000; B 1,000 × 108 = 10,800; C 1200 × 120 = 1,44,000); Gross Profit ₹. 75,600*]

MISCELLANEOUS QUESTIONS

15. Find out the amount of materials consumed from the following information. Total cost of production ₹. 500, Works Cost is 80% of Cost of Production; Works on cost is 150% of Office on cost, Materials consumed is 25% of wages.

[**Hints :** (*i*) Suppose Materials Consumed = x

It is 25% of wages, therefore wages = $4x$

Prime Cost = Materials consumed + wages

$= x + 4x = 5x$

(*ii*) Cost of Production = ₹. 500

Works Cost is 80% of above = 500 × 80% = 400

Office on cost = Cost of production – Works cost

= 500 – 400 = 100

Works on cost = 150% of office on cost = ₹. 150

(*iii*) Prime cost = Works Cost – Works on cost

= 400 – 150 = 250

Prime cost = $5x = 250$ $\quad x = 50$

Materials Consumed = 50

Wages = 4 × ₹. 50 = ₹. 200]

16. A business has three distinct manufacturing departments using materials in the proportions of *A* 5½. *B* 3 and *C* 1½. From the following information you are required to find the total cost of production of each department for the year 2004 and to ascertain the on cost charge per hour per machine working on a basis of a 40 hour's week throughout the year.

	₹.
Stock on 1st January, (Raw materials)	30,000
Stock on 1st January, (Finished Goods)	43,700
Stock on 31st December, (Raw materials)	35,000
Stock on 31st December, (Finished Goods)	54,000
Purchases of Raw materials for the year	1,20,000

Productive wages	90,000
Unproductive wages	9,720
Sales	3,25,000
Rent, Rate etc.	7,830
Repairs	3,420
Lighting, Heating and Power	7,380
Depreciation on Plant	8,360
Salaries	15,030
General Expenses	13,500
Discount allowed	7,650

The wages of each Department are :

A : ₹. 50,000 in connection with 6 machines

B : ₹. 30,000 in connection with 4 machines

C : ₹. 10,000 in connection with 1 machine

In the absence of any further information all expenses with the exception of depreciation, are to be charged to the Departments in the same proportion as the wages paid; depreciation being approtioned in the same ratio as the number of machines in each department.

[Ans. *Total Cost of Production : A ₹. 1,53,660, B ₹. 89,050, C ₹. 35,180, On cost charge per machine per hour : A ₹. 3.24, B, ₹. 2.95, C ₹. 3.81*]

17. Work out in a cost sheet form the unit cost of production per ton of special paper, manufactured by a paper mill in December, 2003 from the following data

Direct Materials

Paper Pulp — 500 tons @ ₹. 50 per ton.

Other Materials — 100 tons @ ₹. 30 per ton.

Direct Labour

80 skilled men @ 3 per day for 25 days

40 unskilled men @ ₹. 2 per day for 25 days.

Direct expenses

Special Equipment ₹. 3,000

Special dyes ₹. 1,000

Overheads

Work Ove0rheads: Variable @ 100% and Fixed @60% on Direct wages. Administration overhead @10% and Selling and distribution overhead @ 15% on works cost.

400 tons of special paper was manufactured and ₹. 800 was realised by the sale of waste materials during the course of manufacture. The scrap value of the special equipment after utilisation in manufacture is nil.

[Ans. *Prime Cost Total ₹. 39,200; per unit ₹. 98; Works cost total ₹. 52,000 per unit ₹. 130; Total Cost ₹. 65,000; per unit ₹. 162.50*]

18. The following particulars are obtained from the records of a factory :Materials issued ₹. 64,000; Wages paid ₹. 56,000; Factory Overhead 60% of Wages.Out of the materials issued, ₹. 800 worth of goods have been returned to store and ₹. 400 transferred to other jobs.

10% of the production has been scrapped as bad and a further 20% has been brought up to the specification by increasing the factory overhead to 80% of the wages.

If the scrapped production fetched only ₹. 470, find the production cost per unit of the finished product if the total product (including the quantity scrapped) is 100 units.

[Ans. *Prime Cost ₹. 1,18,800 Factory on cost (for 80 units ₹. 26,880 and for 20 unit ₹. 8,960) ₹. 35,840; Factory Cost of 90 units ₹. 1,54,170, cost per unit ₹. 1,713*]

19. The following details are available in respect of factory operations of Jhankar Radios Ltd. for the period ending 31st Dec. 2009.

Work-in-Progress:	1-1-2009	31-12-2009
Raw Materials	8,000	12,000
Labour	10,000	16,000
Factory Overhead	5,000	7,000
	23,000	35,000

	₹.
Opening Stock of Raw Materials	75,000
Purchases made during the year	3,25,000
Closing Stock of Raw Materials	50,000
Production Labour	2,50,000
Indirect Labour	5,000
Factory Overheads	75,000
Office Overheads	50,000
Selling and Distribution Overheads	22,000

There were no opening or closing stock of finished goods. 8,000 Radio sets were sold during the year @ ₹. 100 per set. Prepare Statement of Cost.

[Ans. *Prime Cost ₹. 5,90,000; Factory Cost ₹. 6,68,000 Cost of Production ₹. 7,18,000; Cost of sales ₹. 7,40,000; Profit ₹. 60,000*]

[Hint : Each element of works-in-progress will be dealth with related item of expenses]

20. From the following information obtained from the books of a casting factory for the year 2003-04, find out cost of casting per quintal :

Opening Stock of Works-in-Progress :

Direct Materials ₹. 5,000

Direct Labour ₹. 3,000

Stock overheads 10% of Direct Materials

Factory and General Overheads : 50% of Direct Labour.

Expenses incurred during the year :

Pig Iron used—100 quintal @ ₹. 2 per quintal.

Other direct materials — 10 quintal @ ₹. 1 per quintal.

Stock overheads—5% of other direct materials

Direct Labour—200 workers for 10 days @ ₹. 1.50 per day per worker.

Factory overheads—40% of Direct Labour.

General overheads—20% of Direct Labour.

Sales proceeds from residue—15 quintal @ paise 50 per quintal.

Casting done—100 quintal.

[Ans. *Cost per quintal ₹. 150.03*]

21. A pencil manufacturer makes two types of pencils : 'Circular' and 'Oval'. The following data relate to cost and production for the month August 2010:

	No. of Pencils Manufactured	
	Circular	*Oval*
	12,000	*2,400*
	₹.	₹.
Direct Factory Costs :		
Materials	10,110	2,140
Wages	36,690	9,814
Rent, Power etc.	9,000	2,912
Total	55,800	14,866

Indirect Costs :

Factory Supervision	₹.	14,000
Wages of Packing Dept.	₹.	1,940
Rent etc. of Packing Dept.	₹.	900
Selling Expenses	₹.	1,890

Factory supervision has to be allocated in the ratio of direct factory cost. Selling expenses are allocated equally. Both types of pencils are being packed in packets of one dozen. Find out the cost per dozen of each type of pencil.

[Ans. *Cost per dozen-Circular ₹. 70.15; Oval ₹. 96.21*]

(**Note :** Expenses relating to packing deptt. will be allocated in the ratio of number of pencils manufactured.)

Chapter 7

Unit Costing-2 Calculation of Tender Price or Estimates/Quotations

Very often a manufacturer or producer is asked to submit a tender or cost-estimate for the supply of the product in future. The price quoted for future production is called Quotation Price or Tender Price. This price is ascertained on the basis of previous cost sheet or production account.

In ascertaining expected cost in the future, the items of previous elements of cost are considered with due regard to expected changes in the future. Estimated cost is increased by desired profit to ascertain tender price or quotation.

Tenders of Simillar Type Commodity

When cost of same type and quality of commodity is to be calculated, normally cost per unit of each element of cost will be taken up. If there is any expected change in these elements, the change will be adjusted accordingly. Following examples will explain the technique.

Illustration 1: On 15th August, 2005 the Standard Cycle Co. was required to quote for a contract for the supply of 500 bicycles. From the following details, prepare a statement showing the price to be quoted to give the same percentage of net profit on turnover as was realised during the six months to 30th June 2005.

	₹.
Stock of materials on 1st January, 2005	50,000
Stock of materials on 30th June, 2005	7,000
Purchase of materials during 6 month to 30th June, 2005	75,000
Factory wages	1,50,000
Indirect charges	25,000
Sales	2,70,000
Completed stock-in-hand on 1st January, 2005	Nil
Completed stock-in-hand on 30th June 2005	50,000

The number of bicycles manufactured during the six months was 2,000, including those sold and those in stock at the end of the period. The bicycles to be quoted for are to be of uniform size and quality and similar to those manufactured during the six months to 30th June 2005. As from 1st August, the cost of factory labour has increased by 10 per cent and that of materials by 15 per cent.

Solution:

STATEMENT OF COST/COST SHEET
(For the half-year ending 30th June, 2005)

		Total (2,000 Bicycle)	Cost per unit or per Bicycle
		₹.	₹.
Raw Materials consumed:			
Stock of Materials as on Jan. 1	50,000		
Materials Purchased	75,000		
	1,25,000		
Less: Stock of Materials as on June 30	7,000	1,18,000	59.00
Direct Wages		1,50,000	75.00
Prime Cost		2,68,000	134.00
Indirect Charges		25,000	12.50
Cost of Production		2,93,000	146.50
Less: Completed Stock on 30th June		50,000	
Cost of Sales		2,43,000	
Profit		27,000	
Selling Price		2,70,000	

$$\text{Percentage of Profit on Selling Price} = \frac{\text{Profit}}{\text{Selling Price}} \times 100 = \frac{27,000}{2,70,000} \times 100 = 10\%$$

Statement of Cost for Tender
(For 500 Bicycles)

	Total (500 Bicycle)	Per Bicycle
	₹.	₹.
Materials		
1,18,000 × 500/2000 and Add 15% of it	33,925	67.85
Direct Wages		
1,50,000 × 500/2000 and Add 10% of it	41,250	82.50
Prime Cost	75,175	150.35
Indirect Charges (25,000 × 500/2000)	6,250	12.50
Cost of Production	81,425	162.85
Profit (10% on selling price or 81,425 × 10/90)	9,047	18.09
Selling Price	90,472	180.94

Tenders for Different Product

When the tender or quotation price is to be ascertained for a different product, the cost of direct material, direct labour and other direct expenses will be estimated. The total of these will be prime cost Works overheads, office overheads and selling overheads will be added there to on the basis of absorption rates.

Normally works overhead is charged or absorped on the basis of percentage of works overhead on wages. Thus percentage is calculated on the basis of past records.

$$\text{Works Overhead Rate} = \frac{\text{Works Overhead}}{\text{Wages}} \times 100$$

It may be alternatively charged on the basis of Machine Hour Rate or Labour Hour Rate.

Office overheads may be absorbed on the basis of percentage of office overheads on works cost or works overheads

$$\text{Office Overheads Rate} = \frac{\text{Office Overhead} \times 100}{\text{Works Cost or Works Overheads}}$$

The total of Prime Cost plus absorbed works overheads and office overheads will be Cost of Production. Selling overheads, if any, may be added there to on the basis of its absorption rate. It may be a percentage on cost of production or sales or at selling overheads per unit. By adding desired profit, Tender Price or Quotation Price will be known.

Following examples will explain the technique.

Illustration 2: The accounts of X Ltd. show for three months ending 30th June 2010.

	₹.
Materials used	10,00,000
Direct Manual and Machine Labour Wages	15,00,000
Works Overhead Expenditure	3,00,000
Establishment and General Expenses	2,24,000

Show the Works Cost, the Total cost of manufacturer, the percentage that the Works overhead cost bears to the Manual and machine labour wages and the percentage that the Establishment and General Expenses bear to the Works Costs.

What price should the company quote on the basis of the above to the manufacture of an Electric washing machine, which it is estimated, will require an expenditure of ₹. 800 in Materials and ₹. 600 in Wages, so that it will yield a profit of 15 per cent of the total cost.

Solution:

Statement of Cost

(For the three months ending June 30, 2010)

	₹.
Materials	10,00,000
Direct Manual and Machine Labour Wages	15,00,000
Prime Cost	25,00,000
Works Overhead Expenditure	3,00,000
Works Cost	28,00,000
Establishment and General Expenses	2,24,000
Total Cost	30,24,000

(*a*) The percentage that the works overhead cost bears to the manual and machine labour wages:

$$\frac{\text{Works overhead}}{\text{Wages}} \times 100 \text{ or } \frac{3,00,000 \times 100}{15,00,000} = 20\%$$

(*b*) The percentage that the establishment and general expenses bear to the works cost:

$$\frac{\text{Establishment and General Exps.}}{\text{Works Cost}} \times 100 \text{ or } \frac{2,24,000}{28,00,000} \times 100 = 8\%$$

Quotation for Electric Washing Machine

		₹.
Materials		800.00
Wages		600.00
	Prime Cost	1,400.00
Works Overhead Expenditure (20% of Wages *i.e.* 600 × 20/100)		120.00
	Works Cost	1,520.00
Establishment and General Expenses (8% of Works Cost *i.e.* 1520 × 8/100)		121.60
	Total Cost	1,641.60
Profit (15% of the Total Cost *i.e.* 1641.60 × 15/100)		246.24
	Selling Price	1,887.84

Illustration 3: The accounts of a manufacturer, of a uniform type of product, supply you the following information about the expenditure incurred during the year ended December 31.2009.

	₹.
Materials Consumed	4,50,000
Wages Paid and Outstanding	3,60,000
Rent, Rates and Taxes:	
Office	7,000
Factory	25,000
General Manager's Salary and allowances	35,000
Works Manager's Salary and allowances	20,000
Other Establishment Expenses:	
Office	9,132
Factory	3,000
Power used in the factory	65,000
Electric Charges for fans, light etc.	
Office	800
Factory	200
Advertisement	12,000
Depreciation on Furniture:	
Office	400
Factory	100
Oils and Lubricants used	2,000
Machinery and spare parts consumed	13,000
Printing and Stationery:	
Office	2,500
Factory	500
Postage and Telegrams	3,000
Sundry Charges:	
Office	15,000
Factory	10,000
Depreciation of Plant and Machinery	16,000

Assuming that the rates of Factory and Office overhead charges for the year 2010 are normal, calculate what should be selling price of a commodity for which the cost of Raw Materials is ₹. 5,000 and that of Labour is ₹. 4,000, if a profit of 10 per cent on the total cost is earned, (assume that the factory overhead charges bear a fixed percentage to Direct Wages and Office overhead charges bear another fixed percentage to Factory Cost).

Solution:

Statement of Cost
For the year ended December 31, 2009

		₹.
Materials consumed		4,50,000
Wages paid and Taxes		3,60,000
Prime Cost		**8,10,000**
Factory Overheads:		
Rent, Rates and Taxes	25,000	
Works, Manager's Salary and Allowances	20,000	
Other Establishment Exps.	3,000	
Power used	65,000	
Electric Charges	200	
Depreciation of Plant and Machinery	16,000	
Depreciation of Furniture	100	
Oils and Lubricants used	2,000	
Machinery and spare parts	13,000	
Printing and Stationery	500	
Sundry Charges	10,000	
	1,54,800	1,54,800
Factory Cost		**9,64,800**
Office Overheads:		
Rent, Rates and Taxes	7,000	
General Manager's Salary	35,000	
Other Establishment Expenses	9,132	
Electric charges	800	
Advertisement	12,000	
Depreciation on Furnitrue	400	
Printing and Stationery	2,500	
Postage and Telegrams	3,000	
Sundry Charges	15,000	
	84,832	84,832
Total Cost	₹.	10,49,632

(*a*) Percentage of Factory Overheads to Direct Wages:

$$\frac{\text{Factory Overhead}}{\text{Direct Wages}} \times 100 \text{ or } \frac{1,54,800}{3,60,000} \times 100 = 43\%$$

(*b*) Percentage of Office Overhead Charges to Factory Cost:

$$\frac{\text{Office Overhead}}{\text{Factory Cost}} \times 100 \text{ or } \frac{84,832 \times 100}{9,64,800} = 8.7927\%$$

Statement Showing Selling Price of a Commodity (2010)

		₹.
Materials		5,0000
Wages		4,000
	Prime Cost	9,000
Factory Overheads (43% of Wages)		1,720
	Factory Cost	10,720
Office Overheads (8.79% of Factory Cost)		942
	Total Cost	11,662
Profit (10% on Total Cost)		1,166
	Selling Price	12,828

Illustration 4: In respect of a factory the following figures have been obtained for the year 2009.

	₹.
Cost of Materials	6,00,000
Wages for Labour	5,00,000
Factory Overheads	3,00,000
Administration Charges	3,36,000
Selling Charges	2,24,000
Distribution Charges	1,40,000
Profit	4,20,000

A work order has been executed in 2010 and the following expenses have been incurred.

	₹.
Materials	8,000
Wages of labour	5,000

Assuming that in 2010 the rate of Factory Overheads have gone up by 20 per cent; Distribution charges have gone down by 10 per cent and Selling and Administration Charges have each gone up by 12 percent. Show at what price should the product be sold, so as to earn the same rate of profit on the selling price as in 2003.

Factory Overheads are based on Direct Labour and Administration, Selling and Distribution Overheads on Factory Cost.

Solution:

Statement of Cost
(For the year 2009)

		₹.
Materials Consumed		6,00,000
Direct Labour		5,00,000
	Prime Cost	11,00,00
Factory Overhead		3,00,000
	Factory Cost	14,00,000
Administration Charges		3,36,000
Selling Charges		2,24,000
Distribution Charges		1,40,000
	Total Cost	21,00,000
Profit (20% on cost or $16\frac{2}{3}$% of S.P.)		4,20,000
	Selling Price	25,20,000

Percentages:

(1) Percentage of Factory Overheads on Direct Labour : $\frac{\text{Factory Overhead}}{\text{Direct Labour}} \times 100 = 60\%$

(2) Percentage of Administration Charges on Factory Cost : $\frac{\text{Administration Exps.} \times 100}{\text{Factory Cost}} = 24\%$

(3) Percentage of Selling Charges on Factory Cost : $\frac{\text{Selling Charges} \times 100}{\text{Factory Cost}} = 16\%$

(4) Percentage of Distribution Charges on Factory Cost : $\frac{\text{Distribution Exp.} \times 100}{\text{Factory Cost}} = 10\%$

Statement of Cost of Work Order (2010)

		₹.
Materials		8,000
Wages		5,000
	Prime Cost	13,000
Factory Overheads (60% on wages *Add* 20% of it = 72% of Wages)		3,600
	Factory Cost	16,600
Administration Overheads: (24% on Factory Cost *Add* 12½% of it = 27% on Factory Cost)		4,482
Selling Overheads: (16% on Factory Cost *Add* 12½ of it = 18% on Factory Cost)		2,988
Distribution Overheads: (10% on Factory Cost *Less* 10% of it = 9% on Factory Cost)		1,494
	Total Cost	25,564
	Profit (20% on Cost)	5,113
	Selling Price	30,677

Illustration 5: The All-India Waterproof Manufacturers Ltd., manufactured and sold 850 waterproofs in the year ending 31st March 2009. The summarised Trading and Profit and Loss Account is given below:

	₹.		₹.
To Cost of Materials	64,000	By Sales	3,20,000
To Direct wages	96,000		
To Manufacturing expenses	40.000		
To Gross Profit	1,20.000		
	3,20,000		3,20,000
To Office Salaries	48,000	By Gross Profit b/d	1,20,000
To Rent, Rates and Taxes	8,000		
To Selling expenses	16,000		
To General Expenses	24,000		
To Net Profit	24,000		
	1,20,000		1,20,000

For the year ending 31 March, 2010 it has been estimated that :

(*a*) Output and Sales will be 1,000 waterproofs.

(*b*) Price of materials will rise by 25% on the previous year's level.

(*c*) Wages will rise by 12.5%

(*d*) Manufacturing expenses will rise in proportion to the combined cost of materials and wages.

(*e*) Selling expenses per unit will remain unaffected by the rise in the output.

(*f*) Other expenses will remain unaffected by the rise in the output.

Prepare a Cost-Statement, showing the price at which the waterproofs would be marketed so as to show a profit at 12% on the selling price.

Solution :

Cost Sheet for the year ending 31st March 2009
(Output 850 Waterproofs)

		Total Cost	*Cost per Unit*
		₹.	₹.
Cost of Materials		64,000	75.2941
Direct wages		96,000	112.9412
	Prime Cost	1,60,000	188.2353
Manufacturing Expenses (25% of Materials and Labour)		40,000	47.0588
	Works Cost	2,00,000	235.2941
Office and General Expenses:			
Office Salaries		48,000	56.4706
Rent, Rates and Taxes		8,000	9.4118
General Expenses		24,000	28.2353
	Cost of Production	2,80,000	329.4118
Selling expenses		16,000	18.8235
	Total Cost	2,96,000	348.2353
Net Profit		24,000	28.2353
	Sales	3,20,000	376.4706

Statement of Cost
(Estimate for the year ending 31st Dec. 2010)

Estimated Output 1,000 Waterproofs		₹.	*Total Amount* ₹.	*Per unit* ₹.
Material $\frac{64,000}{850} \times 1,000 =$		75,294		
	Add increase 25%	18,824	94,118	94.118
Wages $\frac{96,000}{850} \times 1,000 =$		1,12,941		
	Add increase 12½%	14,118	1,27,059	127.059
	Prime Cost		2,21,177	221.177
Manufacturing Exps. (in proportion to the combined cost of Materials & wages) *i.e.*, 25% of Prime Cost			55,294	55.294
	Manufacturing Cost		2,76,471	276.471

Estimated Output 1,000 Waterproofs ₹	*Total Amount* ₹	*Per unit* ₹
Other expenses (Office and General): (unaffected by the rise in output)		
Office Salaries	48,000	48,000
Rent, Rates and Taxes	8,000	8.000
General Expenses	24,000	24.000
Office Cost	3,56,471	356.471
Selling expenses (per unit remain uncharged)	18,824	18.824
Total Cost	3,75,295	375.295
Profit (12% on the Selling Price *i.e.* ₹. 3,75,295 × 12/88)	51,177	51.177
Selling Price	4,26,472	426.472

Illustration 6: The summarized Trading and Profit and Profit & Loss Account of Swift Cycles Ltd, for the year ended 30th September, 2009 is as under :

	₹		₹
To Cost of Materials	1,00,000	By Sales	5,80,000
To Direct Wages	1,50,000		
To Manufacturing Exps.	80,000		
To Gross Profit c/d	2,50,000		
	5,80,000		5,80,000
To Staff Salaries	60,000	By Gross Profit b/f	2,50,000
To Rent and Rates	10,000		
To Selling Expenses	50,000		
To General Expenses	40,000		
To Net Profit	90,000		
	2,50,000		2,50,000

During the year the Company manufactured 2,000 cycles. For the year ending 30th September, 2010 it is estimated that :

(*a*) Output and sales will be of 2,100 cycles.

(*b*) Price of materials will rise by 30% on the previous year's level.

(*c*) Wages rates will rise by $33\frac{1}{3}\%$.

(*d*) Manufacturing cost will rise by 25%

(*e*) A bonus of 1/6th of salary is expected to be paid to office staff.

(*f*) Selling cost and other expenses will rise in proportion to the cost of materials.

You are required to submit a statement for the directors showing the price at which cycles should be marketed so as to show a profit of 10% on the selling price.

Solution:

Statement Showing the Selling Price of Cycles for the year ending 30th September, 2010

	Amount	Output 2,100 cycles	
		Amount	*Per cycle*
	₹.	₹.	₹.
Cost of Materials	1,05,000		
Add 30% rise	31,500	1,36,500	65.00
Direct Wages	1,57,500		
Add 33 ⅓% rise	52,500	2,10,000	100.00
Prime Cost		3,46,500	165.00
Manufacturing Cost	84,000		
Add 25% increase	21,000	1,05,000	50.00
Works Cost		4,51,500	215.00
Staff Salaries	60,000		
Add 1/6th bonus	10,000	70,000	33.33
Rent & Rates	10,000		
Add 36.5% increase	3,650	13,650	6.50
General Expenses	40,000		
Add 36.5 increases	14,600	54,600	26.00
Selling Expenses	50,000		
Add 36.5% increase	18,250	68,250	32.50
Total Cost		6,58,000	313.33
Add Profit at 10% on the Selling Price (or 1/9th of Cost)		73,111,11	34.81
Sales		7,31,111.11	348.14

Illustration 7: The Managing Director of a small manufacturing concern consults you as to the minimum price at which he can sell the output of one of the departments of the company which is intended for mass production in future. The company's records show the following particulars for this department for the past year:

	₹.
Production and Sales 100 units	
Materials	13,000
Direct labour	7,000
Direct charges	1,000
Works on cost	7,000
Office on cost	2,800
Selling on cost	3,200
Profit	5,000
Selling Price	39,000

You ascertain that 40% of the Works on cost fluctuates directly with production and 70% of the selling on cost fluctuates with sales. It is anticipated that the department would produce 500 units per annum and that labour charges per unit will be reduced by 20%, while fixed works on cost charges will increase by ₹. 3,000. Office on cost and fixed selling on cost charges are expected to show an increase of 25%, but otherwise no changes are anticipated.

Solution:

Statement of Cost for 500 Units

		₹.	₹.
Direct materials (13,000 × 5)		65,000	
Direct labour (7,000 × 5 *Less* 20% of it)		28,000	
Direct charges (1,000 × 5)		5,000	
	Prime Cost		98,000
Works on cost:			
Fixed (60% of 7,000 + 3,000)		7,200	
Variable (40% of 7,000 × 5)		14,000	21,200
	Works Cost		1,19,200
Office on cost (2,800 + 25% of it)			3,500
	Office Cost		1,22,700
Selling on cost:			
Fixed (30% of 3,200 + 25% of it)		1,200	
Variable (70% of 3,200 × 5)		11,200	12,400
	Total Cost		1,35,100
Profit (14.706% on cost)			19,867.81
	Selling Price		1,54,967.81

Illustration 8: The cost of manufacturing 5,000 units of a commodity comprises:

	₹.
(*a*) Materials	20,000
(*b*) Wages	25,000
(*c*) Chargeable Expenses	400
(*d*) Fixed Overheads	16,000
(*e*) Variable Overheads	4,000

For manufacturing every 1,000 extra units of the commodity, the cost of production increases as follows:

(*a*) Materials : Proportionately,
(*b*) Wages : 10% less than proportionately,
(*c*) Chargeable Expenses : Nil.
(*d*) Fixed Overheads : ₹. 200 extra
(*e*) Variable Overheads : 25% less than proportionately.

You are required to: (*a*) Calculate the estimated cost of producing 8,000 units of the commodity, and (b) Show by how much it would differ if a flat rate of factory overheads on wages were charged.

Solution:

(*a*) Statement of Estimated Cost of 8,000 units

		5000 Units	*3000 Units*	*8000 Units*
		₹.	₹.	₹.
Materials		20,000	12,000	32,000
Wages		25,000	13,500	38,500
Chargeable Exp.		400	—	400
Factory overheads				
Fixed		16,000	600	16,600
Variable		4,000	1,800	5,800
	Factory Cost	65,400	27,900	93,300

(*b*) For 5,000 units, the wages amount to ₹. 25,000 and factory overheads to ₹. 20,000 so the percentage of factory overhead to wages comes to 80%.

If a flat rate of 80% for factory overhead on wages is charged, the cost of producing 8,000 units would be as under :

	₹.
Materials	32,000
Wages	38,500
Chargeable Exp.	400
Factory Overhead (80% of wages)	30,800
Factory Cost **Factory Cost**	1,01,700

The amount by which it differs from the correct cost is 1,01,700 – 93,300 = 8400.

Illustration 9: A certain factory produces uniform type of articles and has a capacity of producing 1,000 units per week. The following information shows the different elements of cost for three consecutive weeks of 48 hours each, when the output has changed from week to week.

Units Produced in 48 hours	*Direct Materials*	*Direct Labour*	*Factory Overhead Partly Fixed and Partly Variable*
	₹.	₹.	₹.
200	400	800	3,400
250	500	1,000	3,500
400	800	1,600	3,800

You are asked to find out the selling price per unit when weekly production will be 1,000 units and a profit of 10% on cost price will be made.

Solution:

Calculation of Fixed and Variable Factory Overhead

	Units	*FOH*
	250	3500
	400	3800
Increase	150	300

Variable @ ₹. 2 per unit

Fixed = 3500 – Variable for 250 units
= 3500 – (250 × 2) = 3000

Statement Showing Selling Price Per Unit
(When the weekly output is 1,000 units)

		Total 1,000 units	*Per unit*
		₹.	₹.
Materials @ ₹. 2 per unit		2,000	2.00
Labour @ ₹. 4 per unit		4,000	4.00
Prime Cost		6,000	6.00
Overheads:	₹.		
Fixed	3,000		
Variable @ ₹. 2 per units	2,000	5,000	5.00
Total Cost		11,000	11.00
Profit 10% on Cost Price		1,100	1.10
Selling Price		12,100	12.10

Illustration 10: The elements comprising the cost of a factory output for the years 2001, 2002, and 2003 were as under.

	2001 ₹	2002 ₹	2003 ₹
Materials	1,50,000	1,12,500	1,87,500
Labour	67,000	65,000	69,000
Work on cost	30,000	22,500	37,500
Administrative Cost	18,000	18,000	18,000
Selling and Distribution costs	9,000	7,000	5,000
	Tons	*Tons*	*Tons*
Output	10,000	7,500	12,500

After examinating the figures, you are required to state on what basis would you allocate oncost in quoting for a contract to supply 17,500 tons of commodity representing the whole of the anticipated output for the year 2004. What price would you quote assuming there was no change in the organisation and that a profit of 15% on Works Cost is considered adequate.

Solution:

Working Note 1: From the figures of 3 years, it is clear that material cost is ₹. 15 per ton.

	2001	2002	2003
Materials/output	1,50,000/10,000 = ₹. 15	1,12,500/7,500 = ₹. 15	1,87,500/12,500 = ₹. 15

2. From figures of labour of 3 years it is clear that for every increase or decrease of 250u tons, the cost of labour vary by ₹. 2,000.

2001 Output	10,000	tons	Labour ₹.	67,000
2002 Output	7,500	tons	Labour ₹	65,000
	–2,500	tons		–2000
2003 Output	12,500	tons	Labour ₹	69,000
2001 Output	10,000	tons	Labour ₹	67,000
	–2,500	tons		–2,000

3. Works Oncost is 20% of Materials in all the three years.

4. Administration Oncost has remained fixed. Selling and distribution expenses have tendency of decreasing by ₹. 2,000 p.a., therefore for 2004 these will be ₹. 3,000.

Quotation for a Contract to Supply 17,500 tons in 2004

		₹.
Materials 17,500 tons @ ₹. 15 per ton		2,62,500
Labour ₹. 69,000 for 12,500 tons + ₹. 4,000 for 5,000 tons extra		73,000
	Prime Cost	3,35,500
Works on cost (20% of materials consumed)		52,500
	Works Cost	3,88,000
Administration on cost (Fixed)		18,000
	Cost of Production	4,06,000
Selling & Distribution on cost		3,000
	Total Cost	4,09,000
Profit (15% of Works Cost)		58,200
	Quotation Price	4,67,200

Illustration 11: The following particulars relate to Jain Motor Engineering Co. Ltd. for a particular period:

	₹.
Opening Stock of Raw Materials	40,000
Purchase of Raw Materials	11,95,000
Carriage of Raw Materials	35,000
Wages	7,00,000
Facory Overheads	1,96,000
Establishment and General Charges	1,49,170
Closing stock of Raw Materials	35,000

Work out what price the Company should quote for a Motor Car, which, it is estimated, will require an expenditure of ₹. 16,500 on raw materials and ₹. 12,000 on wages, so that it would yield a profit of 25% on Total Cost and 15% on Selling Cost (Cost of Sales).

Solution:

Statement of Cost

	₹.	₹.
Opening Stock of Materials	40,000	
Add: Purchases	11,95,000	
Add: Carriage	35,000	
	12,70,000	
Less: Closing Stock of Materials	35,000	
Cost of Materials used		12,35,000
Wages		7,00,000
Prime Cost		19,35,000
Add: Factory Overheads		1,96,000
Factory Cost		21,31,000
Add: Establishment & General Charges		1,49,170
Total Cost		22,80,170

Percentage of Factory Overheads to Wages. = $\frac{1,96,000 \times 100}{7,00,000} = 28\%$

Percentage of Establishment etc. to Factory Cost: = $\frac{1,49,170 \times 100}{21,31,000} = 7\%$

Quotation for One Motor Car

	₹.
Materials	16,500
Wages	12,000
Prime Cost	28,500
Factory Overhead (28% of Wages)	3,360
Factory Cost	31,860
Establihsment etc. (7% of Factory Cost)	2,230
Total Cost	34,090
Selling Expenses (See Note)	22,730
Cost of Sales	56,820
Profit (25% of Total Cost & 15% of Cost of Sales)	8,523
Selling Price	65,343

Profit should be 25% of total cost and 15% of cost of sales. In other words 25% of total cost (*i.e.*, 34090 × 25/100 = 8523) should be 15% of cost of sales. Therefore cost of sales should be 8523 × 100/15 = 56,820

$$\text{Selling Exps.} = \text{Cost of Sales} - \text{Total Cost} = 56{,}820 - 34{,}090 = 22{,}730$$

Illustration 12: The cost structure of an article, the selling price of which is ₹. 500 is as follows:

Direct Materials : 50% of total cost; Direct Labour 30% of total cost, Overhead : Balance of total cost.

Due to anticipated increase in existing materials price by 20% and 10% in the existing labour, the existing profit would come down by 30%, if the selling price remains unchanged.

Prepare a comparative statement showing the cost, profit and sale price under the present conditions and with the increase expected for future, assuming the same percentage of profit on cost as at present had to be earned.

Solution : Working Note: In the question Total Cost of Production is not given. Let it be ₹. x per unit.

Total Cost in future (with increased costs):

Materials	$.5x$ + 20% of it =	$.6x$
Labour	$.3x$ + 10% of it =	$.33x$
Overhead	$.2x$	$.2x$
		₹. $1.13x$

Former profit = Selling price – Cost of production = $500 - x$

Future profit = $500 - 1.13x$

The difference of the two will be 30% of the former profit

$$(500 - x) - (500 - 1.13x) = 30\%\,(500 - x)$$

$$-x + 1.13x = 150 - .3x$$

$$.43x = 150 \quad \text{or} \quad x = 348.84$$

i.e., former Cost of Production was ₹. 348.84

Comparative Cost Statement

	Present Condition	Future Conditions: When Selling Price is not Changed	Future Conditions: When Selling Price is Changed
	₹.	₹.	₹.
Direct Material	174.42	209.30	209.30
Direct Labour	104.65	115.12	115.12
Overheads (20% of ₹. 348.84)	69.77	69.77	69.77
Total Cost	348.84	394.19	394.19
Profit	151.16	105.81	170.81
Selling Price	500.00	500.00	565.00

Note : Formerly under present condition, profit is 30.232% of S.P.

(*i.e.* $\frac{151.16}{500} \times 100 = 30.232\%$), when it is applied under future conditions taking selling price to change, the profit (being 30.232% of S.P.) is ₹. 170.81.

TYPICAL ILLUSTRATIONS

Illustration 13: Electronics Ltd. furnish the following information for a 10,000 T.V. equipment manufactured during the year 2009.

	₹.
Materials	90,000
Direct wages	60,000
Power and consumable stores	12,000
Factory indirect wages	15,000
Lighting of factory	5,500
Defective work (Cost of rectification)	3,000
Clerical salaries and management expenses 33,500	
Selling expenses	5,500
Sale proceeds of scrap	2,000
Plant repairs, maintenance and depreciation	11,500

The net selling price was ₹. 31.60 per unit and all units were sold. As from January 1, 2010, the selling price was reduced to ₹. 31 per unit. It was estimated that production could increase in 2010 by 50% due to spare capacity. Rate for materials and direct labour will increase by 10%.

You are required to prepare (*a*) A Cost sheet for the year 2009 showing various elements of Cost per unit and (*b*) Estimated Cost and profit for the year 2010 assuming that 15,000 units will be produced and sold during the year and factory overheads will be recovered as percentage of direct wages and office and selling expenses as a percentage of works cost.

Solution:

Cost Sheet of Electronics Ltd.
(For the year ending 31st Dec. 2009)

(Output 10,000 units)

		Total ₹.	*Cost per unit* ₹.
Materials		90,000	9.00
Wages		60,000	6.00
	Prime Cost	1,50,000	15.00
Factory Overheads:	₹.		
Power and Consumable stores	12,000		
Factory and Consumbale stores	15,000		
Lighting of factory	5,500		
Defective works (rectification)	3,000		
Plant repairs etc.	11,500		
	47,000		
Less: Sale of scrap	2,000	45,000	4.50
	Works Cost	1,95,000	19.50
Office Overheads			
Clerical salaries and Management Exps.		33,500	3.35
	Cost of Productions	2,28,500	22.85
Selling Overheads		5,500	0.55
	Cost of Goods Sold	2,34,000	23.40
	Profit	82,000	8.20
	Sales	3,16,000	31.60

Estimated Cost Sheet for 2010

(Output 15,000 units)

		Total Cost ₹.	Cost per unit ₹.
Materials @ ₹. 9.00 per unit for 15,000 uints	1,35,000		
Add 10% increase in the cost	13,500	1,48,500	9.90
Direct wages @ ₹. 6 per unit	90,000		
Add 10% increase	9000	99,000	6.60
Prime Cost		2,47,500	16.50
Factory Overheads : 75% of wages		74,250	4.95
Works Cost		3,21,750	21.45
Office and Selling exps : 20% of works cost		64,350	4.29
Cost of Goods Sold		3,86,100	25.74
Profit		79,900	5.26
Sales		4,65,000	31.00

Working notes: (*i*) Percentage of Factory Overhead to Wages 45,000 × 100/60,000 = 75%

(*ii*) Percentage of Office and Selling expenses to Works Cost.

39,000 × 100/1,95,000 = 20%

Illustration 14: A factory can produce 60,000 units per annum at its optimum capacity (100%). The estimated costs of production are as under :

Direct materal	₹. 3 per unit
Direct labour	₹. 2 per unit
Overheads: Fixed	₹. 1,50,000 per annum
Overheads: Variable	₹. 5 per unit
Overheads: Semi-variable	₹. 50,000 per annum up to 50% capacity and an extra expenses of ₹. 10,000 per annum for every 25% increase in capacity or part thereof.

The factory produces only against orders and not for own stock. If production programme of the factory is as indicated below and the management desires to ensure a profit of ₹. 1,00,000 for the year, work out the average Selling Price at which units should be quoted :

First 3 months of the year at 50% of capacity.

Remaining 9 months of the year 80% of capacity.

Solution:

Statement of Estimated Cost
(100% of Capacity : 60,000 units per annum)

Particulars	*50% Capacity First 3 months 7500 units*	*80% Capacity Remaining 9 months 36,000 units*	*Total Cost of 43,500 units*
	₹.	₹.	₹.
Direct materials @ ₹. 3	22,500	1,08,000	1,30,500
Direct labour @ ₹. 2	15,000	72,000	87,000
Prime Cost	37,500	1,80,000	2,17,500

Indirect Expenses:			
Fixed 1,50,000 per annum 37,500	1,12,500	1,50,000	
Variable @ ₹. 5	37,500	1,80,000	2,17,500
Semi-variable @ ₹. 50,000 per annum for 50% capacity plus ₹. 10,000 p.a. for every 25% increase in capacity or part thereof.	12,500	52,500	65,000
Cost of Production	1,25,000	5,25,000	6,50,000

Working Note:

Calculation of Selling Price :	₹.
Cost of Production of 43,500 units	6,50,000
Add: Desired profit	1,00,000
Estimated Selling price of 43,500 units	7,50,000

∴ Selling Price for each unit (7,50,000/43,500) = ₹. 17.24

Notes: Semi-variable expenses in case of 80% capacity of production has been ascertained as under:

₹. 50,000 p.a. for 9 months (on 50% capacity)	37,500
Add: 10,000 p.a. for 9 months for additional 25% capacity	7,500
Add: 10,000 p.a. for 9 months for additional 25% capacity at 50% capacity	7,500
Total Semi-variable Exps.	₹. 52,500

Illustration 15: A firm manufactures metal containers of several types. A simple costing system is in operation under which accurate records are kept of the materials consumed in the manufacture of each type of container and of the number of containers of each type completed during the accounting year. Wages and on cost are allocated in proportion to the cost of raw materials. Accounts are made up to 30th June every year.

During the year to June 30th, 2003, the output of type 'A' was 2,00,000. The cost of raw materials used was ₹. 75,000. The following is the summarised statement of the Manufacturing and Profit and Loss Account for the year.

	₹.		₹.
To Raw Material	3,75,000	By Sales	8,55,000
To Factory Wages	1,50,000	By Stock of finished goods	80,000
To Factory Expenses	1,12,500		
To Stock of Finished	50,000		
To Goods (30.6.2002)	2,47,500		
To Gross Profit	9,35,000		9,35,000
To Office and Administration Expenses	1,05,000	By Gross Profit	2,47,500
To Net Profit	1,42,500		
	2,47,500		2,47,500

In Aug. 2003, the business was offered a Government Contract to manufacture and supply of 50,000 'A' type containers at a price to allow a net profit equal to 10% of the cost. It was agreed that all expenses charged in the above account are admissible elements of cost with exception of the following items included under 'Administration expenses.'

Advertisement ₹. 8,500 : Bad debts ₹. 1,000;

Directors fees ₹. 20,000 to be restricted to ₹. 15,000

It was ascertained that in August, 2003 the cost of Raw Materials is 4% above of last year and the wages per man-hour have increased by 6%. Factory Expenses per unit of output are estimated not to have changed but the proportion of office and administrative expenses (owing to increase in output) have been reduced by 10 per cent. You are required to calculate on the basis of these estimates, total contract price for 50,000 containers.

Solution:

Statement Showing the Estimated Selling Price of 50,000 'A' type Containers

Particulars	₹	Amount ₹
Raw Materials : $\frac{75,000 \times 50,000}{2,00,000}$	18,750	
Add: Anticipated increase in the value of raw materials by 4%	750	19,500.00
Wages : $1,50,000 \times \frac{75,000}{3,75,000} \times \frac{50,000}{2,00,000} =$	7,500	
Add: Increase in wages rate by 6%	450	7,950.00
	Prime Cost	27,450.00
Factory Expenses : $1,12,500 \times \frac{75,000}{3,75,000} \times \frac{50,000}{2,00,000}$		5,625.00
	Factory Cost	33,075.00
Office and Administrative Expenses : 1,05,000 – 14,500 (inadmissible) = 90,500		
$90,500 \times \frac{75,000}{3,75,000} \times \frac{50,000}{2,00,000}$	4,525.00	
Less: 10% reduction	452.50	4,072.50
	Total Cost	37,147.50
Desired Profit 10% on Cost		3,714.75
	Selling Price	40,862.25

Working Note : Proportion of Raw Materials of 2,00,000 'A' Containers is $75,000/3,75,000$ and therefore for 50,000 container this proportion shall further be reduced to $1/4$ of it *i.e.*, $50,000/2,00,000$ of $75,000/3,75,000$.

Illustration 16: In an engineering company, the factory overheads are recovered on a fixed percentage basis on direct wages and the administrative overheads are absorbed on a fixed percentage basis on factory cost.

The company has furnished the following data relating to two jobs undertaken by it in a period:

	Job 101 ₹	*Job 102* ₹
Direct Materials	54,000	37,500
Direct Wages	42,000	30,000
Selling Price	1,66,650	1,28,250
Profit Percentage on Total Cost	10%	20%

Required:

(*i*) Computation of percentage recovery rates of factory and administrative overheads.

(*ii*) Calculation of the amount of factory overheads, administrative overheads and profit for each of the two jobs.

(*iii*) Using the above recovery rates fix the selling price of Job 103.

The additional data being :

Direct Materials	₹. 24,000
Direct Wages	₹. 20,000
Profit Percentage on Selling Price	12 1/2%

Solution : There are two unknown percentages which are calculated below:

(*i*) Let x be % on Direct Wages

Let y be % on Factory Cost.

	Job 101 (₹.)	*Job 102 (₹.)*
Selling Price	1,66,650	1,28,250
Less: Profit 10% on Total cost *i.e.* 1/11 of selling price	(–) 15,150	
Profit 20% on total cost *i.e.* 1/6 of selling price		(–) 21,375
Total Cost	1,51,500	1,06,875
Direct Materials	54,000	37,500
Direct Wages	42,000	30,000
Prime cost	96,000	67,500
Add: Factory overhead	x% on direct wages	x% on direct wages
Factory cost	—	—
Add: Administration overheads	y% on factory cost	y% on factory cost
Total Cost	1,51,500	1,06,875

Factory Cost of Jobs:

Job 101 = 96,000 + 42,000 x

Job 102 = 67,500 + 30,000 x

Total Cost of Jobs :

Job 101 = $(96{,}000 + 42{,}000x) + (96{,}000 + 42{,}000x)y = 1{,}51{,}500$ (1)

Job 102 = $(67{,}500 + 30{,}000x) + (67{,}500 + 30{,}000x)y = 1{,}06{,}875$ (2)

$42{,}000x + 96{,}000y + 42{,}000xy = 1{,}51{,}500 - 96{,}000 = 55{,}500$ (3)

$30{,}000x + 67{,}600y + 30{,}000xy = 1{,}06{,}875 - 67{,}500 = 39{,}375$ (4)

Divide by 1,000

$42x + 96y + 42xy = 55.5$ (5)

$30x + 67.5y + 30xy = 39.375$ (6)

Multiply Equation (5) by 30 and multiply equation (6) by 42.

$1{,}260x + 2{,}880y + 1{,}260xy = 1{,}665$ (7)

$1{,}260x + 2{,}835y + 1{,}260xy = 1{,}653.75$ (8)

$0 + 45y + 0 = 11.25$

$$y = \frac{11.25}{45} = 0.25$$

Substitute y into equation (5)

$$42x + 24 + 10.5x = 55.5$$

$$52.5x = 55.5 - 24 = 31.5$$

$$x = \frac{31.5}{52.5} = 0.6 \text{ i.e. } 60\% \text{ of wages is factory overheads}$$

$y = 0.25$ *i.e.* 25% of factory cost is administrative overheads.

(*ii*) Statement of Costs

	Job 101 (₹)	*Job 102* (₹)
Direct Materials	54,000	37,500
Direct Wages	42,000	30,000
Price Cost	96,000	67,500
Add: Factory overheads at 60% of wages	25,200	18,000
Factory Cost	1,21,200	85,500
Add: Administrative overheads at 25% of factory cost	30,300	21,375
Total Cost	1,51,500	1,06,875
Profit (10% and 20% on total cost)	15,150	21,375
Selling Price	1,66,650	1,28,250

(*iii*) Statement Showing Selling Price of job 103

	₹.
Direct Materials	24,000
Direct wages	20,000
Factory overheads at 60% of direct wages	12,000
Factory Cost	56,000
Add: Administrative overheads at 25% of factory cost	14,000
Total Cost	70,000
Profit (@ 12.5% of selling price *i.e.* 1/7 of total cost)	10,000
Selling Price	80,000

NUMERICAL QUESTIONS

1. The following figures relate to the costing of a trapaulin sheet manufactured for a period of three months:

	₹.
Stock of Materials, 1st January	5,500
Stock of Materials, 31st March	3,500
Factory wages	83,000
Materials purchased	61,500
Sales	1,41,000
Indirect expenses	13,000
Completed stock, 1st January	Nil
Completed stock, 31st March	29,000

The number of sheets manufactured during three months was 2,200 and the price is to be quoted for 648 sheets in order to realize the same percentage of profit as for the period under review, assuming no alternation in rates of wages and cost of materials.

Prepare a statement of cost for the manufacture of 2,200 sheets and quotation for 648 sheets.

[**Ans.** *Cost of production of 2,200 sheets ₹. 1,59,500 and Cost per sheet ₹. 72.50. Quotation Price for 648 sheets ₹. 50,760 and per sheets ₹. 78.33*]

2. On the 30th April 2003 a manufacturer was required to quote for a contract for the supply of 1,000 electric stoves. From the following data, prepare a statement showing the price to be quoted to give the same percentage of net profit on turnover as was realised during the six months to 31st March 2010.

	₹.
Stock of Raw materials 1st October	35,000
Stock of Raw materials 31st March	4,900
Purchase of Raw Materials	52,500
Factory Wages	95,000
Factory Expenses	17,500
Establishment Expenses	10,000
Completed Stock in hand 1st October	Nil
Completed Stock in hand 31st March	35,000
Sales	1,89,000

The number of stoves manufactured during the six months was 4,000 including those sold and those in stock at the close of the period. The stoves to be quoted for are of uniform quality and make and similar to those manufactured during the six months to 31st March. As from 1st April, the cost of factory labour had increased by 10 per cent and material cost by 15 per cent.

[**Ans.** *Total cost ₹. 2,05,100, Profit 10% on sales. Tender price for 1,000 stoves ₹. 63052.78, Cost of tender ₹. 56,747.50*]

3. From the following particulars you are required to prepare a statement showing (*a*) the cost of materials used (*b*) the works cost (*c*) total cost (*d*) the percentage of works on cost to productive wages and (*e*) the percentage of general on cost to works cost:

	₹.
Stock of Finished goods 31st December, 2002	56,000
Stock of Raw Materials 31st December, 2002	25,600
Purchases	5,84,000
Productive Wages	3,97,600
Sales of Finished Goods	11,84,000
Stock of Finished Goods 31st December, 2003	60,000
Stock of Raw Materials 31st December, 2003	27,200
Works Overhead Charges	87,472
Office and General Expenses	71,048

The company is about to send a tender for a large plant. The costing department estimates that the materials required would cost ₹. 40,000 and the wages to workmen for making the plant would cost ₹. 24,000. The tender is to be made at a profit of 20 per cent on the selling price. Show what the amount of tender would be if based on the above percentage.

[**Ans.** *(a) ₹. 5,82,400 (b) ₹. 10,67,472 (c) ₹. 11,38,520 (d) 22%, 6.656%. Tender Price ₹. 92,364.10. Total Cost of Tender ₹. 73891.28*]

4. A manufacturer of scooters finds that in 2003. It costs him ₹. 6,16,000 to manufacturer 200 Baby Scooters which he sold at ₹. 4,000 each. The cost was made up of:

Materials ₹. 2,00,000; Direct wages ₹. 3,00,000; Factory overhead expenses ₹. 60,000; Office overhead expenses ₹. 56,000.

For 2004 season he estimates that each scooter will require material to the value of ₹. 1,000 and wages of ₹. 1,500; that the factory overhead expenses will bear the same relation to direct wages as in the previous year. The percentage of office overhead expenses of factory cost will be the same as in the previous year. Prepare a statement showing the profit he should make per unit if he enhances the price of the baby scooter by ₹. 80.

[Ans. *Percentage of works overhead to wages 20%, Office overhead to works cost 10%, of total cost of Tender ₹. 3,080 Profit ₹. 1,000***]**

5. The trading results for the year 2009 of a manufacturing company (making one model Table) were as follows:

	₹.		₹.
To Opening stock of Raw Material	30,000	By Sales	1,20,000
To Purchase (Raw materials)	51,000	By Closing stock of	
To Productive wages	24,000	Raw materials	27,000
To Rent and rates			
Workshop	3,300		
Office	300		
To Lighting:			
Workshop	600		
Office	240		
To Drawing Office Expenses	2,700		
To Management Salaries:			
Workshop	1,200		
Office	1,860		
To Office Expenses:			
Workshop	300		
Office	2,670		
To Travelling Expenses	3,600		
To Audit fee	600		
To Discounts	2,400		
To Repairs:			
Workshop	3,900		
Office	330		
To Director's Fees	6,000		
To Net Profit	12,000		
	1,47,000		1,47,000

The directors being of the opinion that the 2009 results were normal, decided to adopt them as a basis for the costing of a new 2004 model, which costs ₹. 45 in materials and ₹. 30 in wages. Summarise the above accounts to show the successive elements of costing for the 2009 sales and calculate from the summary the minimum selling price of the new model, if the net profit are to be maintained for 2010 on the assumption that turnover and expenses remain normal for the year.

[Ans. *2003 : Prime Cost ₹. 78,000; Works Cost 90,000, Total Cost ₹. 1,08,000, Work on cost ₹. 12,000 being 50% of wages, General on cost ₹, 18,000 being 20% of works cost, Profit ₹. 12,000 being 10% of the sales.*

*Tender (2004) Total cost ₹. 108, Selling Price ₹. 120***]**

6. Pleasant Cold Limited manufactured and sold 1,000 boxes in the year ended 31st March 2009. The summarised Trading and Profit & Loss Account is set out below:

	₹		₹
To Cost of materials	80,000	By Sales	4,00,000
To Direct wages	1,20,000		
To Manufacturing Exps.	50,000		
To Gross Profit c/d	1,50,000		
	4,00,000		4,00,000
To Management & Staff salaries	60,000	By Gross profit b/d	1,50,000
To Rent, Rates & Insurance	10,000		
To Selling Expenses	30,000		
To General Expenses	20,000		
To Net Profit	30,000		
	1,50,000		1,50,000

For the year ended 31st March 2010 it is estimated that:

(1) Output and sales will be 1,200 boxes.

(2) Prices of raw materials will rise by 20% on previous year's level.

(3) Wages rates will rise by 5%.

(4) Manufacturing exps. will rise in proportion to the combined costs of materials and wages.

(5) Selling expenses per unit will remain unchanged.

(6) Other expenses will remain unaffected by the rise in the output.

You are required to submit a statement for the Board of Directors showing the price at which the boxes should be marketed so as to show a profit of 10% on selling price.

[**Ans.** *Total Selling Price of 1200 Boxes, ₹5,10,000, per unit ₹425, Prime Cost ₹2,66,400, Works Cost ₹3,33,000, Total Cost ₹4,59,000*]

7. The Managing Director of a small manufacturing concern consults you as to the minimum price at which he can sell the output of one of the departments of the company which is intended for mass production in future. The company's records show the following particulars for this department for the past year:

Production and Sales	200 units
	₹
Materials	26,000
Direct Labour	14,000
Direct Charges	2,000
Works on cost	14,000
Office on cost	5,600
Selling on cost	6,400
Profit	10,000
Sales	78,000

You ascertain that 40% of the works on cost fluctuate directly with production and 70% of the selling on cost fluctuates with sales. It is anticipated that the department would produce 500 units per annum and that direct labour charges per unit will be reduced by 20%, while fixed works on cost charges will increase by ₹ 3,000. Office on cost and fixed selling on cost charges are expected to show an increase of 25%, but otherwise no changes are anticipated.

[**Ans.** *Total Cost for 500 units ₹1,44,000. Selling Price ₹1,65,176.50; Prime cost 98,000, Works on cost 11,400 + 14,000 = 25,400, Office on cost ₹7,000, Selling on cost ₹2400 + 11,200 = 13,600, Profit 14.706% on total cost i.e., ₹21,176.50*]

8. A certain factory produces a uniform type of article and has a capacity of producing 1,500 units per week of 48 hours. The following information shows the different elements of cost for three consecutive weeks of 48 hours each when the output has changed week to week:

Units produced in 48 hours	*Direct Materials*	*Direct Labour*	*Factory Overhead (Partly fixed and partly variable)*
	₹.	₹.	₹.
400	800	1,600	3,800
500	1,000	2,000	4,000
800	1,600	3,200	4,600

You are asked to find out the selling price per unit when the weekly output will be 1,000, units and profit of $8\frac{1}{3}\%$ on sale price will be made.

[Ans. *Prime cost ₹ 6,000, Total Cost ₹ 11,000, Selling Price ₹ 12,000, per unit ₹ 12.*]

9. The estimated materials cost of a job is ₹. 5,000 and direct labour cost is likely to be ₹. 1,000. In Machine shop it will require machining by Machine No. 8 for 20 hours and Machine No. 12 for 6 hours. Machine Hour Rates for Machine No. 8 and Machine No. 12 are respectively ₹. 10 and ₹. 15.

The direct wages in all other shops last year amounted to ₹. 80,000 as against ₹. 48,000. of factory overhead. This factory overhead was other than Machine Shop Overheads. Last year Factory Cost of all Jobs amounted to ₹. 2,50,000 as against ₹. 37,500 Office Expenses.

Prepare a statement making out a quotation which guarantees 20% profit on selling price.

[Ans. *Last year percentage of Factory overheads on direct wages 60% and percentage of office overheads to factory cost is 15%; Quotation cost-Prime cost 6,000; Factory cost ₹ 6,890, Cost of Prod. ₹ 7,923.50 Profit ₹ 1,980.88 and Quotation price ₹ 9,904.38*].

[Hint: (1) Last year's percentage of Factory Overheads (other than machine shop overhead) on Direct Wages was $48{,}000 \times 100/80{,}000 = 60\%$

(2) Last year's percentage of Office Overheads on Factory Cost was $37{,}500 \times 100/2{,}50{,}000 = 15\%$]

10. A firm manufactures metal containers of several types. A simple costing system is in operation under which accurate records are kept of the raw materials used in the manufacture of each type of container and of the number of containers of each type completed during the accounting year. Wages and overheads are allocated in proportion to the cost of raw materials. Accounts are made up to 31st December.

During the year ended 31st December, 2003, the output of containers of type "A" was 2,00,000. The cost of raw materials used was ₹. 75,000.

The following is a summarised statement of the Manufacturing and Profit and Loss Account for the year 2003:

	₹.		₹.
To Raw Materials	3,75,000	By Sales	8,85,000
To Factory Wages	1,50,000	By Finished Goods on 31-12-03	50,000
To Factory Expenses	1,12,500		
	6,37,500		
To Finished Goods on 1-1-03	50,000		
To Gross Profit	2,47,500		
	9,35,000		9,35,000
To Office and Administrative Exps.	1,05,000	By Gross Profit	2,47,500
To Net Profit	1,42,500		
	2,47,500		2,47,500

In February, 2004, the firm was offered a government contract to manufacture and supply 'A' type containers, the price to allow a net profit equal to 10% of cost. It was agreed that all expenses charged in the above account are admissible elements of cost with the exception of the following items included under Administrative Expenses: Advertising ₹. 11,500 disallowed; Bad Debts ₹. 1,000 disallowed; Directors' Fees ₹. 20,000 to be restricted to ₹. 10,000.

It was ascertained that in February, 2004 the cost of raw materials was 4% above the average for 2003 and that wages per man hour have increased by 6% Factory expenses per unit of output are estimated not to have changed but the proportion of office and administrative expenses (owing to increase of output) has been reduced by 10%.

You are required, on the basis of these estimates, what the total contract price should be for 50,000 containers.

[**Ans.** *For 50,000 containers : Raw Materials ₹. 19,500, Wages ₹. 7,950, Factory Exps. ₹. 5,625; Works Cost ₹. 33,075 Office Exps. ₹. 3,712.50. Cost of Production 36,787.50. Contract price 40,466.25.*]

11. A company manufactures radios, which are sold at ₹. 1,600 per unit. The total cost is composed of 30% for direct materials, 40% for direct wages and 30% for overheads. An increase in material price by 30% and in wage rates by 10% is expected in the forthcoming year, as a result of which the profit at current selling price may decrease by 40% of the present profit per unit. You are required to prepare a statement showing current and future profit at present Selling Price.

How much Selling Price should be increased to maintain the present rate of profit?

[**Ans.** *Present Cost ₹ 1207.55, Current Cost ₹ 1365.04, Revised S.P. ₹. 1,808*]

12. A manufacturer finds that an advance in the cost of production has taken place and that whereas formely his goods cost raw materials 30%; wages 20% rent rates etc. 5% fuel 10%; general expenses 15%; now there has been an advance of 50% in fuel, 30% in materials, 25% in wages and 20% in rent rates etc.

He consults you as to what percentage he must add to the selling price in order to obtain the same profit. What would be the result of your calculations and how would you prove to him that they were correct.

[**Ans.** *Increase of 25% in SP is needed*]

13. In the current quarter, a company has undertaken two jobs. The data relating to these jobs are as under:

	Job 1102	*Job 1108*
Selling price	₹. 1,07,325	₹. 1,57,920
Profit as percentage on cost	8%	12%
Direct materials	₹. 37,500	₹. 54,000
Direct wages	₹. 30,000	₹. 42,000

It is the policy of the company to charge factory overheads as percentage on direct wages and selling and administration overheads as percentage on factory cost.

The company has received a new order for manufacturing of a similar job. The estimate of direct materials and direct wages relating to the new order are ₹. 64,000 and ₹. 50,000 respectively. A profit of 20% on sale is required.

You are required to compute:

(*i*) The rate of factory overheads and selling and administration overheads to be charged;

(*ii*) The selling price of the new order. [*CA PE II – Nov. 2002*]

[**Ans.** *(i) Factory overhead rate 40% of wages. Selling and administration overhead 25% of factory cost (b) Selling price of new order ₹. 2,09,375*].

Job, Batch and Contract Costing

JOB COSTING

Job costing is a method of costing applied in industries where production is measured in terms of completed jobs. Industries where job costing is generally applied are Printing Press, Automobile Garage, Repair workshops, Ship Building, Foundry and other similar manufacturing units which manufacture to customers' specific requirements.

Job costing is a method of costing whereby cost is compiled for a job or work order. The production is against customer's orders and not for stock. The cost is not related to the unit of production but is a cost for the job, *e.g.* printing of 5000 ledger sheets, repairs of 50 equipments, instead of printing one sheet or repair of one equipment. The elements of cost comprising Prime Cost *viz.* direct materials, direct labour and direct expenses are charged directly to the jobs concerned, the overhead charged to a job is an opportioned portion of the departmental overhead.

Documents used in a Job Order Cost System

The following are the important documents used in a Job Order Cost System.

(*i*) *Production Order or Manufacturing Order:* This is a works order authorising the production department to produce a specified quantity of a product which constitutes the job.

(*ii*) *Cost Sheet:* For recording costs, very often a separate record called a cost sheet is used. The cost sheet and the works order may also be combined, when costs are recorded on the production order itself.

(*iii*) *Other Documents:* The other documents which are used as control mechanism by the despatching function are : Material Requisitions, Tool Orders, Time Tickets, Inspection Order, etc.

Job Cost Accounting Procedure

Cost of direct materials in respect of a job is obtained from copies of Material Requisitions costed by the Stores Accounting Section. Cost of direct wages is obtained from various Time Tickets costed by the Payroll Department. Direct Expenses, if any, are also taken up.

Manufacturing overheads are then applied at predetermined departmental obsorption rates and recorded in the cost-sheet. Various overheads may be recorded in the separate columns meant for these in the cost sheet which are totalled to obtain the total cost of direct material, direct labour, direct expenses and apportioned manufacturing overheads. These are the four elements of cost which together give the production cost or manufacturing cost of the job.

Following is a specimen of a job cost sheet meant for publishing of a book.

JOB COST SHEET

Customer :	Description :	Production Order No.:
Customer's Order No. :	Quantity :	To Start on:
Our Quotation No.:	Bill of Materials No.:	To Finish on:

Week Ended	*Composing*			*Printing*			*Knifing*			*Varnishing*			*Binding*			*Total*			
	Matl.	Lab	O'H.	Matl.	Lab	O'H.	Matl.	Lab	O'H.	Matl.	Lab	O'H.	Matl.	Lab	O'H.	Matl.	Lab	O'H.	Total
Total																			
Estimate																			
Difference																			

Comments on Variations:	Comments:
Production Manager	Bill No. .....for ₹. .... Sent on...... Cost Acct.

Advantages of Job Order Costing

(*i*) Profitability of each job can be individually determined.

(*ii*) It provides a basis for estimating the cost of similar jobs which are to be taken in future.

(*iii*) It provides, the detailed analysis of the cost of material, labour and overheads for each job as and when required.

(*iv*) Plant efficiency can be controlled by confining attention to costs relating to individual jobs.

(*v*) Spoilage and defective work can be identified with a specific job and responsibility for the same may be fixed on individuals.

(*vi*) By adopting pre-determined overhead rates in job costing, we can get all advantages of budgetary control.

(*vii*) Job costing is essential for cost-plus contract where contract price is determined directly on the basis of cost.

Limitations of Job Order Costing

(1) It is expensive to operate as it requires considerable detailed clerical work.

(2) With the increase in the clerical work the chances of errors are increased.

(3) Job order costing cannot be efficiently operated without highly developed production control system. The job costing requires intricate factory organisation system.

(4) The costs as ascertained are historical as they compiled after incidence and therefore does not provide control of cost unless it is used with standard costing system.

Illustration 1: (*Job Cost Sheet*). A has undertaken a job No. DT/07. As per cost ledger, the following expenses have been debited to this job. You are required to prepare a job cost sheet and calculate the total amount to be charged to the customer in order to secure 20 per cent profit on Sales.

Following are additional information based on normal capacity.

	Dept. A	*Dep. B*	*Total for factory as a whole*
Budgeted Production in terms of Direct Labour Hours	9000	13,500	30,000
Budgeted Variable Overhead (₹.)	13,500	16,200	—
Budgeted Fixed Overhead (₹.)	—	—	30,000

Job Cost Details :

Direct Materials

(*i*) Cast Iron 15 kg @ ₹. 2 per kg

(*ii*) Gun Metal 5 kg @ ₹. 10 per kg

Direct Labour

Deptt. A 20 hrs @ ₹. 1 per hour

Deptt. B 15 hrs @ ₹. 0.6 per hour

Direct Exps – Special Tools ₹. 31 (To be paid by the customer)

Solution:

... Co.

Job Cost Sheet

Particulars .... Job No. DT/07

Customers ....

Ref ....

	Qty.	*Rate* ₹.	*Details* ₹.	*Total Cost* ₹.
Direct Material				
Cost Iron	15 kg	2.00	30.00	
Gun Metal	5 kg	10.00	50.00	80.00
Direct Labour				
Dept. *A*	20 hrs.	1.00	20.00	
Dept. *B*	15 hrs.	0.60	9.00	29.00
Direct Expenses				31.00
Prime Cost				140.00
Add: Variable Overheads				
Dept. *A* (13,500/9000) × 20 hrs.	20 hrs.	1.50	30.00	
Dept. *B* (16,200/13500) × 15 hrs.	15 hrs.	1.20	18.00	
Fixed Overheads				
(30,000/30,000) × 35 hrs.	35 hrs.	1.00	35.00	83.00
Total Cost				223.00
Add: Profit (20% on sales or 25% on cost)				55.75
Total Amount to be charged				278.75

Illustration 2: **From the following data given below, procured from the books of a factory, for the year ended on 31st March 2005, prepare (*i*) Consolidated Completed Job Account showing the profit or loss and (*ii*) Consolidated Work-in-Progress Account.**

	Completed Job ₹	*Work-in-Progress* ₹
Raw Material supplied from the stores	18,000	6,000
Chargeable Expenses	2,000	800
Wages	20,000	8,000
Materials transferred to work-in-progress	400	400
Materials returned to store	200	—

Factory overhead is 80% of wages and office overhead 25% of factory cost.

The value of executed job during the year ended 31st March 2005 was ₹. 82,000.

Solution:

Consolidated Completed Job Account

	₹	₹		₹
To Material	18,000		By Contractee A/c (Amount of Job Finished)	82,000
Less: Transfer to WIP	– 400			
Less: Returns	– 200	17,400		
To Wages		20,000		
To Chargeable Exps.		2,000		
To Factory Overheads (80% of Wages)		16,000		
Factory Cost		55,400		
To Office Overhead (25% of Factory cost)		13,850		
To Net Profit		12,750		
		82,000		82,000

Consolidated Work-in-Progress Account

	₹	₹		₹
To Raw Material	6,000		By Balance c/d	27,000
Add: Transferred from completed Job.	400	6,400		
To Wages		8,000		
To Chargeable Exps.		800		
To Factory Overhead (80% of wages)		6,400		
Factory Cost		21,600		
To Office Overhead (25% of Factory cost)		5,400		
		27,000		27,000

Illustration 3: A shop floor supervisor of a factory presented the following cost for Job. No. 421 to determine selling price excluding selling exps.

	₹.
Material	5,600
Direct wages (180 hours @ ₹. 20 per hour) (Deptt *X* 80 hrs: Deptt. *Y* 60 hrs, Deptt. Z 40 hrs.)	3,600
Chargeable Expenses (Special Stores Items)	400
	9,600
Add: 33–1/3% for expenses	3,200
Total Cost	12,800

Analysis of the Profit and Loss Account for the previous year shows the following:

		₹.		₹.
To Materials used		12,00,000	By Sales *Less* returns	20,00,000
To Direct wages :				
Deptt. *X*	80,000			
Y	96,000			
Z	64,000	2,40,000		
To Special Stores Items		32,000		
To Overheads :				
Dep. *X*	40,000			
Y	72,000			
Z	16,000	1,28,000		
To Gross Profit c/d		4,00,000		
		20,00,000		20,00,000
To Selling Exps.		1,60,000	By Gross Profit b/d	4,00,000
To Net Profit		2,40,000		
		4,00,000		4,00,000

It is also noted that average hourly rates for the 3 departments *X*, *Y* and *Z* are similar.

You are required to calculate and enter revised cost of Job No. 421 using the actual figures for the previous year as the basis. Add 20% to the total cost to determine the selling price.

Solution:

Job Cost-Sheet

Job No. 421 — Date of commencement.........

Particulars — Date of completion.................

			Detail	₹.
Materials:				5,600
Direct Wages –	Deptt	*X* 80 hrs @ ₹. 20	1,600	
	Deptt	*Y* 60 hrs @ ₹. 20	1,200	
	Deptt.	*Z* 40 hrs @ ₹. 20	800	3,600
Chargeable Exps.:				400
Overheads	Deptt	*X* 80 hrs @ ₹. 10	800	
	Deptt.	*Y* 60 hrs @ ₹. 15	900	
	Deptt.	*Z* 40 hrs @ ₹. 5	200	1,900
		Total Cost		11,500
		Profit (20% on Total Cost)		2,300
		Selling Price		13,800

Working Notes:

1. Hours of department : Departmental wages ÷ Labour hour rate: Deptt. *X* ₹. 80,000/20 = 4,000 hrs.; Deptt. *Y* ₹. 96,000/20 = 4,800 hrs.; Deptt. *Z* ₹. 64,000/20 = 3,200 hrs.
2. Departmental overheads on the basis of previous year's figures : Deptt. *X* ₹. 40,000/4,000 = ₹. 10; Deptt. *Y* ₹. 72000/4,800 = ₹. 15; Deptt. *Z* ₹. 16,000/3,200 = ₹. 5.

Illustration 4: A company has manufacturing shops. The shop-floor supervisor presented the following cost for Job No. *A* to determine the selling price.

	Per unit ₹.
Materials	70
Direct wages (14 hrs. @ ₹. 2.50 per hour (Deptt. *X*: 8 hrs.; Deptt *Y* : 6 hrs.)	35
Chargeable Exps. (stores)	5
	110
Add: 33-1/3% for overheads	37
	147

Analysis of the Profit & Loss Account

		₹.	₹.
Materials used		1,50,000	
Sales less returns			2,50,000
Direct Wages	*X* 10,000		
	Y 12,000	22,000	
Stores Exps		4,000	
Overheads	*X* 5,000		
	Y 9,000	14,000	
		1,90,000	
Gross Profit c/d		60,000	
	₹.	2,50,000	2,50,000

It is noted that average hourly rates for the two departments *X* and *Y* are similar.

You are required to (*i*) draw up a Job Cost Sheet (*ii*) Calculate the revised cost using overheads figures as shown in the Profit & Loss Account as the basis for charging overheads to *X* and *Y* and (*iii*) Add 20% of total costs to determine the selling price.

Solution: Calculation of overhead rates of different rates

(1) Hourly rate of direct wages

X	₹. 10,000/2.5	= 4,000 hrs.
Y	₹. 12,000/2.5	= 4,800 hrs.

(2) Overheads rate per hour

X	₹. 5000/4000 hrs.	= ₹. 1.25 per hour
Y	₹. 9,000/4,800 hrs.	= ₹. 1.875

(3) Percentage of overhead on Direct wages

X	(5,000/10,000) × 100	= 50%
Y	(9,000 × 12,000) × 100	= 75%

Job Cost Sheet

	Rate ₹.	Quantity (hrs)	₹.
Materials			70.00
Direct wages :			
X	2.5	8 hrs.	20.00
Y	2.5	6 hrs.	15.00
Chargeable Exps.			5.00
Prime Cost			110.00
Overheads:			
X (50% of Direct wages)	1.25	8 hrs.	10.00
Y (75% of Direct wages)	1.875	6 hrs.	11.25
Total Cost			131.25
Profit (20% of total cost)		26.25	
Selling Price			157.50

Illustration 5: The equipments division of M/s Centurion Engineering Works Limited have completed manufactured of a rubber solution mixing equipment as per order received from one of its customers at an agreed price of ₹. 2,55,000. From the following details available, you are required to prepare a Job Order Cost Sheet for consideration by the management.

(A) *Details of the Job*

Customer	*RSA Enterprises*
Order No. of the customer	RS 1691 dated Dec. 21, 2000
Job Order No. allotted	30631
Date of starting the job at works	January 27, 2001
Date of completion at works	March 15, 2001
Date of delivery at site	March 28, 2001
Date of commissioning	March 30, 2001

(B) *Details of Expenditure*		*January*	*February*	*March*
Materials:				
Machining section		₹. 22,350	₹. 1,875	₹. 675
Assembly section		₹. 4,683	₹. 517	₹. 6,100
Direct Labour Hours:	*Rate per hr.*			
Machining	₹. 12.00	160 hrs.	2,000 hrs.	1,650 hrs.
Assembly	₹. 15.00	40 hrs.	800 hrs.	1,260 hrs.
Total machining hours spent in machine section		60 hrs	1,440 hrs.	500 hrs.
Cost of Drawings	₹. 6,500			

The company had to procure some dies and tools worth ₹. 15,000 specifically required for use in executing the above order. However, on completion the value of such used dies and tools was estimated at 30% of the original cost and the company envisages to use them up in executing a future order already in the pipeline.

The company has a system of absorbing production overheads at predetermined rates on machine hours utilised for machining section and direct labour spent for assembly section. The current rates are ₹. 18 per machine hour and ₹. 6 per labour hour for machining and assembly sections respectively.

The company also incurred an expenditure of ₹. 6,150 towards installing and carrying out trial runs at the customer's premises. As per the company's policy these expenses are to be charged as direct production cost.

Selling and distribution costs are to be charged to individual jobs at 16.67% of production cost.

[*ICWA – Inter June 2001*]

Solution:

Job Order Cost Sheet

Job Order No. 30631

Date of commencement	27.01.01	Date of commissioning	30.3.01
Date of completion	15.03.01	Price quoted	₹. 2,55,000

Details			*Jan.*	*Feb.*	*March*	*Total*
Materials:						
Jan.	Machining		₹. 22,350			
	Assembly		4,683			27,033
Feb.	Machining			₹. 1,875		
	Assembly			517		2,392
March	Machining				₹. 675	
	Assembly				6,100	6,775
(*a*) Total material cost						36,200
Labour:						
Jan.	Machining	160 hrs. @ ₹. 12	1,920			
	Assembly	40 hrs. @ ₹. 15	600			2,520
Feb.	Machining	2,000 hrs. @ ₹. 12		24,000		
	Assembly	800 hrs. @ ₹. 15		12,000		36,000
March	Machining	1,650 hrs. @ ₹. 12		19,800		
	Assembly	1,260 hrs. @ ₹. 15		18,900		38,700
(*b*) Total labour cost						77,220
Production Overheads:						
Jan.	Machining	60 hrs. @ ₹. 18	1,080			
	Assembly	40 hrs. @ ₹. 6	240			1,320
Feb.	Machining	1,440 hrs. @ ₹. 18		25,920		
	Assembly	800 hrs. @ ₹. 6		4,800		30,720
March	Machining	500 hrs. @ ₹. 18			9,000	
	Assembly	1,260 hrs. @ ₹. 6			7,560	16,560
(*c*) Total Production Overheads						48,600
Other Direct Costs:						
Cost of drawings						6,500
Dies and tools			₹. 15,000			
Less: ₹idual value (30%)			4,500			10,500
Installation & trial runs						6,150
(*d*) Total direct costs						23,150
Total Cost of Production (*a*) + (*b*) + (*c*) + (*d*)						1,85,170
Selling and Distribution Overheads (16.67% of cost)						30,868
Total Cost of Sales						2,16,038
Profit (balancing figure)						38,962
Selling price						2,55,000

BATCH COSTING

It is a kind of job costing. In this method, the cost of a group of products is ascertained. The unit of cost is a batch or group of identical products, instead of a single job, order or contract. The method is applicable to general engineering factories which produce components in convenient economical batches for subsequent assembly or manufacture on mass scale, comparatively small items of products. Except for the difference that in batch costing, a batch instead of a job constitute the cost unit for which costs are compiled, the procedure for batch costing is similar to that of Job Costing. Separate Job Cost Sheets are maintained for each batch of components manufactured and for the assembly of finished products. When products are stocked for sale, a greater degree of control is required.

Essentials of Batch Costing

(1) Entire production is divided into economic groups or batches and usual and appropriate costing methods are applied to each group or batch.

(2) This method is used where small parts of considerable number are produced, such as factories producing machinery parts, machine tools, etc.

(3) The advantages of the method are that the unit cost of each group is determined so that the total production cost is broken down into its constituent parts and profit and loss of each batch is known separately.

(4) As production cost and volume of sales vary considerably from batch to batch, it sometimes becomes difficult to allocate overhead charges equitably. It is main drawback of the method.

(5) No special costing principles are involved, each batch constituting a separate unit divided into subunits of each piece produced.

Economic Batch Quantity

In Batch Costing Method production is carried on in batches. In each batch, there are a number of units. The ascertainment of economic batch quantity is very useful. Economic batch quantity may be calculated by using the formula meant for calculating Economic Order Quantity (EOQ) in case of material contorl.

$$\text{Economic Batch Quantity} = \sqrt{\frac{2AO}{C}}$$

where A = Demand of components in a year

O = Setting up cost per batch

C = Cost of capital and storage (carrying cost) per unit per annum

Set up cost : Set up cost of tools and machines is a fixed amount which is incurred for a batch of production irrespective of the size of that particular batch. Set up cost varies directly with the number of batches or with batch frequency; as batches become more frequent, the total set up cost increases. In other words, for a given production during a period, the total set up costs increase with a reduction in the number of units manufactured in a batch. Following certain other costs also increase the total set up cost : (*a*) Time cost during change over from one batch to another, (*b*) Loss of skill and speed of worker due to too frequent changes, (*c*) closer supervision of each set up, (*d*) Wastage of material due to change in the machine feeding, (*e*) Other cost related to short runs.

Cost of Capital and Storage (Carrying Cost): Carrying cost depends upon several variable factors such as storage and obsolescence of inventory, interest on locked up capital, depreciation, machine break downs and sub-standard and defective work. This cost varies directly with the size of a batch *i.e.* with the batch quantity. With the increase in the number of units produced in a batch, or in other words, with the decrease in batch frequency, the cost of carrying the inventory rises:

Illustration 6. [*Economic Batch Quantity*] Calculate Economic Batch Quantity:

Total Number of Units to be produced in a year : 10,000

Unit set-up cost per batch : ₹. 200.

Carrying cost per unit of production : ₹ 0.10 per unit

Solution:

$$\text{Economic Batch Quantity} = \sqrt{\frac{2AO}{C}}$$

A = Total number of units or demand of components in a year.

O = Setting up cost per batch

C = Carrying cost per unit.

$$EBQ = \sqrt{\frac{2 \times 10{,}000 \times 200}{0.10}} = 6{,}324 \text{ units}$$

Illustration 7: [*Economic Batch Quantity*]. M/s Kobo Bearings Ltd is committed to supply 24,000 bearings for fans p.a on a steady daily basis. It is estimated that it cost 10 paise as inventory holding cost per bearing per month and that the set up cost per run of bearing manufacturing is ₹. 324.

(*i*) What should be the optimum run size for bearing manufacturing?

(*ii*) What should be the interval between two consecutive optimum runs?

(*iii*) Find out the minimum inventory holding cost.

Solution:

(*i*) Economic Batch Quantity = $\sqrt{\frac{2AO}{C}}$ where

A = Units supplied

O = Setting up cost

C = Cost of inventory handling

$$= \sqrt{\frac{2 \times 24{,}000 \times 324}{0.10 \times 12}} = 3{,}600 \text{ units}$$

(*ii*) Interval between two consecutive optimum runs

= 24,000/3600 = 20/3

= 360 ÷ 20/3 = 54 days

(*iii*) Minimum inventory cost per annum

= (Annual Production/EBQ) × Setting up cost + Average Inventory per annum × holding cost per unit

= (24,000/3600) × 324 + (3,600/2) × (0.10 × 12) = ₹. 4,320

Illustration 8: (*Batch Costing*). Following information relate to the manufacturing of a component – 101 in a cost centre:

Cost of Materials	6 paise per component
Operator's Wages	72 paise an hour
Machine Hour Rate	₹. 1.50
Setting up time of the machine	2 hours 20 minutes
Manufacturing time	10 minutes per component

Prepare cost sheets showing both production and setting up cost, total and per unit when batch consists of (*i*) 10 components (*ii*) 100 components and (*iii*) 1000 components.

Solution.

Cost Statement for a Batch of 10 Components

	Total ₹.	Per Unit ₹.
Setting up costs:		
(*a*) Operations wages : 2hrs. 20 mts @ 72 paise per hour	1.68	
(*b*) Overheads of the machine for 2 hrs. and 20 mts @ ₹ 1.50 per hrs.	3.50	
Total Setting up Cost (A)	5.18	0.52
Production Cost		
(*a*) Material : 10 units @ 6 paise	0.60	0.06
(*b*) Wages 10mts × 10 component @ 72 paise per hrs.	1.20	0.12
(*c*) Overheads 10 × 10 minutes @ 1.50 per hour	2.50	0.25
Total Production Cost (B)	4.30	0.43
Total Production Setting Cost (A + B)	9.48	0.95

Cost Statement for a Batch of 100 Components

	Total ₹.	Per Unit ₹.
Setting up Cost (as calculated above)	5.18	0.05
Production Cost:		
(*a*) Material : 100 unit @ 6 paise per unit	6.00	0.06
(*b*) Wages : 1000 minutes @ 72 paise per hours	12.00	0.12
(*c*) Overhead : 1000 minutes @ 1.50 per hour	25.00	0.25
Total	48.18	0.48

Cost Statement for a Batch of 1000 Components

	Total ₹.	Per Unit ₹.
Setting up Cost (as calculated above)	5.18	0.005
Production Cost:		
(*a*) Material : 1000 unit @ 6 paise per unit	60.00	0.060
(*b*) Wages : 10,000 minutes @ 72 paise per hours	120.00	0.120
(*c*) Overhead : 10,000 minutes @ 1.50 per hour	250.00	0.250
Total	435.18	0.435

Illustration 9: **Leo Ltd. undertakes to supply 1000 units of a component per month for the month of January, February and March. Every month a batch order is opened against which materials and labour costs are booked at actuals. Overheads are levied on the basis of labour hours. The selling price is contracted at ₹. 15 per unit.**

From the following data, present the cost and profit per unit of each batch order and the overall position of the order for 3000 units. Ignore set up costs.

Months	*Batch output (Numbers)*	*Material Cost* ₹.	*Labour Cost* ₹.
January	1250	6250	5000
February	1500	9000	6000
March	1000	5000	4000

Labour is paid at the rate of ₹. 4 per hour. The other details are :

Month	*Overhead (₹.)*	*Total labour hours.*
January	12000	4000
February	9000	4500
March	15000	5000

[CA Inter]

Solution:

LEO Limited
Statement of Cost and Profit per unit

	Batches			
	January 1250 units	*February 1500 units*	*March 1000 units*	*Total 3750 units*
Materials	6250	9000	5000	20250
Wages	5000	6000	4000	15000
Overheads	3750	3000	3000	9750
Total cost	15000	18000	12000	45000
Sales @ ₹. 15 per unit	18750	22500	15000	56250
Profit	3750	4500	3000	11250
Cost per unit (Total cost/units)	12.00	12.00	12.00	12.00
Profit per unit (Profit/units)	3.00	3.00	3.00	3.00

CONTRACT COSTING

Contract costing is a variant of job costing system, which is applied in business engaged in building or other construction work. The jobs are usually the contracts entered into with the customers. The basic principles applied in contract costing are the same as those used in job costing but these are modified to suit the particular requirements of the contracts.

Difference Between Job Costing and Contract Costing

It is considered that contract costing is comparatively simpler in operation than job costing system. The accumulation, analysis, apportionment, allocation and control of cost is simplified in contract costing. Most of the expenses are chargeable direct to Contract Account but direct allocation to such an extent is not possible in Job Costing. Normally the number of jobs in hand at any time in a concern may be large, only a few contracts may be undertaken at a time. As contracts may run for long periods, there arise the problem of assessment and crediting of profits on incomplete contracts at the end of accounting period.

A 'contract' differs from a job only in size. We generally reserve the word `contract' for those jobs which require all the attention or most of it to be devoted to it. Work is done for a customer who agrees to pay a fixed sum of money at the completion of the work. Usually, however, the contractee pays a portion of the work done progressively. A contract may be for the construction of a building, a road, a ship or a complicated piece of machinery, etc. Since the number of contracts in hand is never likely to be large, it is not necessary to maintain separate books of account for costing purposes. Financial books are sufficient but they will have to be remodelled to give the required information. For example, if two contracts are being undertaken simultaneously, wages or materials will have to be separately recorded for each, otherwise it will be difficult to know the total cost of completing a particular contract. It will even be better if, in the account opened to record the cost of a contract, columns are provided to classify the expenditure.

CONTRACT LEDGER

Contract No. .... Contract Price ....

Date of Completion................. Terms of Payment...

Site.............................. Work Certified : ....

Remark.. Date..............................₹. ....

.... Date..............................₹. ....

Date	*Particulars*	*Materials ₹.*		*Wages ₹.*		*Direct Charges ₹.*		*Plant ₹.*		*Indirect Exp. Total*		*Total ₹.*
	Total ₹.											

ELEMENTS OF CONTRACT COST

(1) Materials

There is no special principle involved in the issue of materials to contracts. For materials issued out of stores, requisition slips in the usual form will be made out and they will be costed by the stores ledger clerk, again in the usual manner. On analysis, the amount to be debited to each contract will be found out and, of course, the total of all the requisition slips will be credited to the Stores Control Account maintained in the general ledger, But since each contract is likely to be different in nature and since large quantities of main raw materials will be required, stocks are not maintained of such materials. On the signing up of each contract, arrangements will be made to buy the main materials required. The concerned contract account will then be debited and the suppliers credited.

The return of materials also involves no departure from the principles already discussed. If materials are returned from any contract, a Store Returned Note or Contra Requisition Slip should be made out. The amount involved will be debited to the Stores Control Account and credited to the contract account concerned.

Transfer of materials from one contract to another should, in the usual manner, be accompained by Materials Transfer Note so that the contract receivinig the materials is debited and the contract giving up the materials is credited.

Sometimes surplus materials are sold. In that case the sale proceeds will have to be credited to the respective contract accounts. Sometimes it so happens that the contractee, under the terms of the contract, supplies some materials which do not affect the contract price. The value of such materials should not be brought into books but a note will have to be kept to account for the quantity received and issued. Any balance will naturally belong to the contractee. Should any purchased material be found unsuitable, the cost of such material should not be debited to the cost of the contract concerned. The profit or loss on sale of such materials should be credited or debited to the Profit and Loss Account. This applies not only to materials but also to plant, machinery, tools, etc., that may be found unsuitable for the contract.

2. Labour

The wages of everybody working at the site of the contract will be treated as direct. Normally, in other business, supervisory staff or watch and ward staff are treated as indirect workers but, in case of contracts, everybody is a direct worker if he is present at the site throughout the time it takes to complete the contract. Those, of course, who supervise the completion of two or more contracts are not included in the category of direct workers. Their salaries and the salaries, etc., of the office staff are treated as indirect.

A contract can be divided into different stages. For instance, in the case of construction of a building, firstly foundation have to be dug, then construction is brought up to the plinth level. Construction up to roof level is another stage. The next stage is roofing. Plastering the roofs and walls and laying floors are different stages. It is desirable that the cost of doing work at each stage should be known. Job cards should, therefore, be issued to workers so that they can record their time for the purpose of analysis. But in the contract account itself wages may be recorded as a lump sum for finding out the cost of each section the contract ledger can be used with minor changes.

For facilitating determination of wages spent on each contract, separate wages sheets should be prepared for each contract. Otherwise, wages will have to be analysed as has been explained earlier.

3. Plant

There are two possibilities with regard to plant. Plant may be specially bought for a contract and it may be expected to be exhausted there. In such a case the value of the plant should be debited to the contract account concerned and when the contract is completed or at the end of accounting period, it may be credited with the value that might be placed on the plant. The other possibility is that plant is already in stock and it is expected to be used only for a short while on the contract and not exhausted there. In that case the usual depreciation of the plant should be debited to the contract account concerned.

4. Indirect Expenses

All the expenses at site are treated as direct, but sometimes when two or more contracts are being undertaken at the same time, some of the executive officers of the contractor firm and the office will be paying attention to all the contracts. The total indirect expenses, arising out of such common services, will have to be apportioned equitably among all the contracts. Or, the expenses may be spread according to the ratio of total cost incurred on a contract. Thus, if two contracts have cost ₹. 5 crore and ₹. 3 crore in materials, labour and plant, etc., the indirect expenses may be apportioned between the two contracts in the ratio of 5:3.

5. Cost of Extra Work Done

Sometimes the contractee desires to get some additions or alterations made which may not have been included in the original contract. This extra work will have to be charged for in addition to the contract price. It is essential, therefore, to ascertain the exact cost of doing the extra work. Needless to say, besides materials and labour, an equitable amount for supervision and other indirect expenses (these expenses may be really direct as far as the main contract is concerned) will have to be included. If the extra work is not substantial, the cost of doing it can be included in the cost of the contract. But a separate account should be maintained if the extra work is substantial.

6. Cost of Sub-contract

In contrast with the above, some portion of the contract may be entrusted to another contractor. For example, in the construction of a building, the main contractor may entrust the task of digging foundations to another contractor for a fixed price. If this is done, the price so paid should be included in the cost of the main contract as a separate item. It is of course a direct charge.

7. Cost of Maintenance Periods

Sometimes contractors are required to maintain the work during a specified period after completion, the cost of maintenance is also debited to the Contract Account.

Illustration 10: The following is summarised record relating to Contract No. 103, commenced from 1st January, 20...

	₹.
Materials issued from stores	60,000
Materials from Contract No. 106	6,000
Materials purchased	54,000
Wages	48,000
Outstanding wages	12,000
Plant purchased for this contract	50,000
Indirect Charges	10,000
Outstanding Indirect Charges	2,000

Materials worth ₹. 2,000 and plant costing ₹. 2,500 were returned to sotres at the end of the year. Materials costing ₹. 4,000 and plant costing ₹. 1,500 were stolen. Materials worth ₹. 500 and plant costing ₹. 500 were destroyed by fire. Materials and plant transferred to Contract No. 96 were ₹. 5,250 and ₹. 4,000 respectively. Materials costing ₹. 4,200 were sold for ₹. 6,000 and plant costing ₹. 1,000 were sold for ₹. 1,250. Materials at site were ₹. 2,600. Providing depreciation on plant @ 10%, open Contract Account and found out the cost of work done on the contract. The contract is not completed.

Solution:

Contract No. 103 Account

	₹		₹.
To Materials issued:		By Materials returned to stores	2,000
Purchases	54,000	By Plant returned less dep.	2,500
From Contract 106	6,000	By Materials stolen	4,000
From stores	60,000	By Plant stolen	1,500
To Wages	48,000	By Materials destroyed	500
To Outstanding wages	12,000	By Plant destroyed	500
To Plant issued	50,000	By Materials transferred to	
To Indirect charges	10,000	Contract 96	5,250
To Outstanding Indirect Charges	2,000	By Plant transferred to Contract 96	4,000
		By Materials sold (Cost)	4,200
		By Plant sold (Cost)	1,000
		By Materials at site	2,600
		By Plant at site	36,450
		By Balance being cost of contract done	1,77,500
₹.	2,42,000	₹.	2,42,000

Working Note:

(1) Plant at site has been calculated as below:

	₹.	
Cost of Plant		50,000
Less: Plant returned to stores	2,500	
Plant stolen	1,500	
Plant destroyed	500	
Plant transferred to Contract No. 96	4,000	
Plant sold	1,000	9,500
Cost of Plant at site		40,500
Less: Depreciation 10% of 40,500		4,050
		36,450

Illustration 11: The following is the summarised record as on December 31, 2009 of all transactions relating to Contract No. 80 which was commenced on January 1, 2009 and completed during the year:

	₹.
Material purchased directly	12,700
Materials supplied from stores	5,200
Wages	21,440
Expenses directly chargeable	2,940
Indirect expenses	3,000
Plant installed	18,000
Total contract price	60,000
Value of plant at site on Dec. 31, 2009	10,000
Materials at site in Dec. 31, 2009	900

Prepare Contract Account.

Solution:

Contract No. 80 Account

	₹		₹
To Direct Materials	12,700	By Value of Plant at site	10,000
To Materials supplied from stores	5,200	By Materials at site	900
To Wages	21,440	By Contractee's A/c	60,000
To Expenses directly chargeable	2,940		
To Indirect expenses	3,000		
To Plant	18,000		
To P/L A/c	7,620		
	70,900		70,900

Certificate of Work Completed and Payment Received from the Contractees

It is usual for the contractee to pay a certain percentage (say 80%, 75% or 90%) of the value of a definite stage of work completed. The payment is made after the contractee is satisfied that such stage has been completed. Surveyors or architects issue certificates for this purpose. Suppose the architect certifies that work of the value of ₹. 2,00,000 (out of the total contract price of ₹, 5,00,000) has been completed. Then if the contractee has agreed to pay 80%, he will pay ₹, 1,60,000. The balance of ₹, 40,000, known as *Retention Money*, will be paid when the whole contract is complete. Retention money is a sort of guarantee that the contractor will not run away in the middle of the job, as he might have the temptation to do if he sees nothing but loss in the completion of the contract.

Payment received can be dealt with in two ways. The value of the work done can be debited to the Contractee's Account and credited to the Contract Account. Cash received will, of course, stand to the credit of the Contractee's Account. Thus in the above example the following entries may be passed:

		₹.	₹.
Contractee's Account	Dr.	2,00,000	
To Contract Account			2,00,000
(Being the value of work certified as per architect's certificate)			
Bank Account	Dr.	1,60,000	
To Contractee's Account			1,60,000
(Being cash received being 80% of value of work certified)			

In the Balance Sheet the Contractee's Account will be shown at ₹.40,000 on the assets side. Care will have to be exercised to see that in the following year the value of work certified for the purpose of passing entries does not include ₹, 2,00,000 in respect of which entry has already been passed.

The *second and more popular method* to deal with the payment received is to credit the amount to the account of the contractee. The value of the work completed is debited to the Work-in-Progress Account and credited to the Contract Account. Or, it may be carried down as a balance in the Contract Account itself. In the Balance Sheet, the credit to the contractee is deducted from the value of the work completed, the balance being shown as an asset. In the following year, the Work-in-Progress Account will be transferred to the debit of the Contract Account and the entries to be passed in respect of work done at the end of the next year will be for the amount of total work done, including the amount already certified at the end of the previous year.

Cost of Work Uncertified

Work-in-Progress uncertified shall have to be costed for materials used and labour spent. Uncertified Work-in-Progress arises from the fact that at the end of the financial year certain work may not have reached a stipulated stage and in respect of such work there will be no certificate by the architect and there will be no payment from the contractee. The amount for such work is debited to Work-in-Progress Account and credited to the Contract Account and is transferred to the debit of Contract Account at the beginning of next year. Alternatively, the amount is carried down as a balance in the Contract Account.

Materials and other stores at site are dealt with similarly. Materials at Site Account is debited and Contract Account is credited. Next year the Materials at Site Account will be transferred to the Contract Account. Alternatively, materials and plant site may be treated as a part of work-in-progress and debited to that account.

Work-in-Progress uncertified (as well as Work-in-Progress certified and materials and plant at site) will appear on the asset side of the Balance Sheet at the close of the financial year after deducting the amount received from the contractee and after deducting the *provision* as discussed in the next paragraph.

Calculation of work uncertified : Usually any cost incurred after the date of work certified by the architect or engineer is included in the work uncertified. It may also be equal to proportionate cost. Suppose total cost incurred is ₹, 60,000 which is estimated to be the cost of 2/3 contract, but the architect has certified only 1/2 of the contract price as work completed. The cost of work uncertified will be proportionate cost as calculated below :

		₹.
Cost of 2/3 contract		60,000
Less: Cost of 1/2 contract	60,000 × 3/2 × 1/2	45,000
Cost of work uncertified		15,000

Profit on Incomplete Contracts

In contract accounts there would be no difficulty in dealing with profits if the contracts were completed in the course of the financial year. Then the profit would be credited to the Profit and Loss Account. But difficulty arises when we have to deal with profits arising on contracts which are not complete at the end of the year. We cannot afford to credit the entire profit shown to the Profit and Loss Account. There is the possibility that next year due to rise in prices or wages or due to fines, there may be a loss. A *provision* has to be kept against such a contingency. Nor is it desirable that profit on a contract should be taken into account only when the contract is complete. In that case, the year in which the contract is completed, will show an abnormally high figure for profit. The following rules may be followed for taking credit for profits earned on unfinished contracts :

(*a*) If a contract has not advanced to a sufficiently high stage, no credit for profit should be taken. Generally, no credit is taken unless the contract is at least one-fourth complete.

(*b*) In case the contract is 1/4 but less than 1/2 complete, one-third of the profit disclosed as reduced to the percentage of cash paid by the contractee should be transferred to the Profit and Loss Account, the balance being treated as a *provision*.

(*c*) In case the contract is one-half or more complete, two-thirds of profit (disclosed by the Contract Account) as reduced to the percentages of cash paid by contractee should be transferred to the P&L A/c, the remaining profit being treated as a *provision*.

(*d*) The whole of the loss, if any, should be transferred to the P&L A/c.

Suppose, a contract, not yet complete (*i*) discloses a profit of ₹. 54,000, (*ii*) work-in-progress certified is ₹. 2,00,000 (*iii*) total value of contract is ₹. 5,00,000 and (*iv*) the contractee pays 90% of work certified. Then, according to above rules, the transfer to P & L A/c should be

$$\text{Total Profit} \times \frac{1}{3} \times \frac{\text{Cash}}{\text{Value of work certified}}$$

$$54{,}000 \times \frac{1}{3} \times \frac{90}{100} \text{ or ₹. } 16{,}200$$

Supposing in the above case, the total value of the contract (Contract Price) was only ₹. 4,00,000, the transfer to P&L A/c would have been

$$\text{Total Profit} \times \frac{2}{3} \times \frac{\text{Cash received}}{\text{Value of work certified}} = 54{,}000 \times \frac{2}{3} \times \frac{90}{100} \text{ or ₹. } 32{,}400.$$

However, one should note that the rules are not hard and fast. Different proportions of profit may be transferred to the P&L A/c by different people.

Of course, the actual profit will be ascertained by debiting the Contract Account with all the relevant expenditure and crediting it with the value of work-in-progress—certified and uncertified—and materials and plant etc., at site. No abnormal loss should be debited and no abnormal gain should be credited to the Contract Account.

Profit on Cash Basis: The rules discussed above show that in each case the profit to be transferred to the P&L A/c has to be reduced by the margin retained by the contractee. This is what is meant by calculating profits on cash basis.

Estimated Profit: Some people, however, prefer to take credit for profit on the basis of total estimated profit likely to arise when the contract will be complete. Suppose, for a contract of ₹, 4,00,000, it is estimated that the total cost of completing the contract will be ₹., 3,20,000, thus giving a profit of ₹. 80,000. The value of work done already is ₹. 2,50,000 and therefore, the credit to Profit and Loss Account in respect of work done so far would be ₹. 80,000 × 2,50,000/4,00,000 or ₹. 50,000. If profit on realised basis is desired, ₹. 50,000 will be multiplied by proportion of cash received (say 80%) and thus ₹. 40,000 will be transferred to *P* and *L* A/c. It is desirable that, to be on the safe side, if two-thirds of the realised profit shown by the Contract Account is less than the profit on work done as proportion of total estimated profit (on cash basis), the lower figure should be taken to the Profit and Loss Account. This technique has been explained with example later on in this chapter.

Illustration 12: [*Work Certified Less than 1/4*]. Following expenses were incurred by a contractor on a contract which he started on 1st January 2004.

Materials ₹. 40,000; Wages ₹. 50,000; Other expenses ₹. 15,000; Plant at cost ₹. 50,000; Work certified ₹. 1,20,000; Work not certified ₹. 60,000; Materials in hand on 31st Dec. 2004 ₹. 11,000; Plant at close ₹. 43,000; Cash received from contractees ₹. 1,00,000. Materials returned to stores ₹. 2,000. Prepare Contract Account assuming contract price to be ₹. 6,50,000 and showing profit to be taken to P/L a/c.

Solution:

Contract Account

	₹		₹
To Materials	40,000	By Work Certified	1,20,000
To Wages	50,000	By Work Uncertified	60,000
To Other expenses	15,000	By Materials returned to stores	2,000
To Plant at Cost	50,000	By Materials at site	11,000
To Balance	81,000	By Plant at site	43,000
	2,36,000		2,36,000

Note: Value of work certified is less than 1/4 of the contract price, hence no profit is carried to Profit and Loss Account and entire balance ₹. 81,000 is provision.

Illustration 13: [*Work Certified Less than 1/2*] The contractor accepted a contract for the construction of a building for ₹, 10,00,000 the contractee agreeing to pay 90% of the work certified as completed by the architect. During the first year the amounts spent were :

Materials ₹. 1,20,000, Labour ₹, 1,50,000
Machinery ₹. 30,000, Other Exps. ₹. 90,000.

At the end of the year, the machinery was considered to be of ₹. 20,000, and materials at site of the value of ₹. 5000. Work certified during the year totalled ₹. 4,00,000. In addition work-in-progress, but not certified at the end of the year had cost ₹. 15,000. Prepare Contract Account in the books of the contractor. Also show amount of profit that can reasonably be transferred to the Profit & Loss Account.

Solution:

Contract Account

	₹		₹
To Materials	1,20,000	By Work Certified	4,00,000
To Labour	1,50,000	By Work Uncertified	15,000
To Machinery	30,000	By Plant at site	20,000
To Other Exps.	90,000	By Materials at site	5,000
To Total Profit c/d	50,000		
	4,40,000		4,40,000
To Profit & Loss A/c	15,000	By Total Profit b/d	50,000
To Balance (Reserve or Provision)	35,000		
	50,000		50,000

Note : Profit to P/L A/c = Total profit $\times \frac{\text{Cash received}}{\text{Work certified}} \times 1/3 = 50{,}000 \times \frac{90}{100} \times \frac{1}{3} =$ ₹. 15,000.

Work-in-Progress Account

When work is not complete at the end of the accounting period, this account is opened. Work-in-Progress Account shows value of work certified and cost of work uncertified. The entry will be

Work-in-Progress A/c .... Dr
[(*i*) Value of work certified
(*ii*) Cost of work uncertified]
To Contract Account

Work-in-Progress Account

To Contract Account (*i*) Value of work certified (*ii*) Cost of work uncertified		By Balance c/d	

Work-in-Progress is shown in the asset side of the Balance Sheet. Cash received from the contractee is deducted therefrom. Plant at side and materials at site will also appear as assets in the B/S.

Balance Sheet

		Assets	
		Work-in-Progress *Less :* Cash received Plant at site Materials at site	

Work in progress along with material and plant at site are carried to the next year's Contract Account as opening balance.

Note : Some Cost Accountants are of opinion that Work-in-Progress should also include Plant at site and Material at site at end as shown below:

Work-in-Progress Account

To Contract A/c Value of work certified Cost of work uncertified Plant at site Materials at site		By Contract A/c (Profit not tfd. to P& L A/c) By Balance c/d	

Now plant at site and materials at site will not appear in the Balance Sheet separately.

Contractee's Account

The contractor opens a personal account of the contractee and credits cash received from him

Cash/Bank A/c .... *Dr.*
To Contractee's Account

Contractee's Account

To Balance c/d		By Cash/Bank	

Illustration 14: From the information given below, relating to an incomplete contract, prepare Contract Account and Work-in-Progress Account contract price was ₹ 500,000

	₹
Materials sent to site	86,000
Labour engaged at site	65,000
Plant issued at cost	80,000
Direct expenses	8,000
Establishment charges	4,000
Materials returned to stores	600
Work certified	1,90,000
Work uncertified	7,700
Materials in hand	2,000
Cash Received	1,61,500
Wages Accrued	300
Depreciation on plant	7,000

Solution:

Contract Account

			₹
To Materials issued	86,000	By Materials returned to stores	600
To Wages	65,000	By Work-in-Progress a/c	
To Outstanding wages	300	Certified work	1,90,000
To Plant at cost	80,000	Uncertified work	7,700
To Direct expenses	8,000	By Plant at site	73,000
To Establishment charges	4,000	By Materials at site	2,000
To Balance c/d	30,000		
	2,73,300		2,73,300
To P/L A/c	17,000	By Balance b/d	30,000
To Work-in-Progress A/c	13,000		
	30,000		30,000

Note. 1. Profit to P/L A/c $= 30{,}000 \times \frac{2}{3} \times \frac{1{,}61{,}500}{1{,}90{,}000} = 17{,}000$

2. It has been presumed that work certified is more than half of the contract price.

Work-in-Progress Account

		₹		₹
To Contract A/c:			By Contract A/c	13,000
Certified work	1,90,000		By Balance c/d	1,84,700
Uncertified work	7,700	1,97,700		
		1,97,700		1,97,700

Balance Sheet (Extract only)

Liabilities	₹	*Assets*		₹
P/L A/c	17,000	Work-in-Progress		1,84,700
Wages accrued	300	*Less:* Cash received		1,61,500
				23,200
		Materials at site		2,000
		Plant at site		73,000

Illustration 15: [*Conractee's Account*]. Thakur Dass & Sons took a contract of constructing library building of Rohil Khand University Bareilly. The Contract Price was ₹. 6 lakhs. It was agreed that 75% of the value of work certified shall be paid in advance at the end of each year.

The value of work certified separately for the first two years was:

First year ₹. 2,50,000 Second year ₹. 3,00,000

The entire work was finished by the end of third year and contractee paid the balance of amount through cheque, Open Contractee's A/c in books of the contractor.

Solution:

Contractee's Account

To Balance c/d		1,87,500	I yr. By Bank A/c	1,87,500
	₹.	1,87,500	₹.	1,87,500
To Balance c/d		4,12,500	II yr. By Balance b/d	1,87,500
			By Bank A/c	2,25,000
	₹.	4,12,500	₹.	4,12,500
To Contract A/c		6,00,000	III yr. By Balance b/d	4,12,500
			By Bank A/c	1,87,500
	₹.	6,00,000	₹.	6,00,000

Illustration 16: You are required to prepare a Contract Account showing the profit on contract to 31st March, 2010 from the following particulars. Also show how the values would appear in the next year's Contract Account.

	₹.
Contract Price	1,00,000
Materials sent to site	32,250
Labour engaged on site	27,400
Plant installed at site	5,650
Work certified	71,500
Cash received from contractee	65,000

Value of plant as on 31st March	4,100
Cost of work done but not certified	1,700
Direct expenditure	1,200
Cost of establishment	1,625
Wages outstanding on 31st March	900
Materials in hand on 31st March	700
Direct Exps. outstanding on 31st March	100
Materials returned to stores	200

Solution:

Contract Account

	₹		₹
To Materials	32,250	By Plant at site	4,100
To Labour	27,400	By Materials in hand	700
To Plant	5,650	By Materials returned	200
To Exp. for Establishment	1,625	By Work certified	71,500
To Direct Exps.	1,200	By Cost of work uncertified	1,700
To Outstanding Wages	900		
To Outstanding Direct Exps.	100		
To Total Profit c/d	9,075		
	78,200		78,200
To Profit & Loss A/c	5,500	By Total Profit b/d	9,075
To Balance c/f	3,575		
	9,075		9,075

Balances to be carried over to next year's Contract A/c

	₹		₹
To Plant	4,100	By Outstanding Wages	900
To Materials	700	By Outstanding Direct Expenditure	100
To Work certified	71,500	Bt Balance of Profit	3,575
To Work uncertified	1,700		

Escalation Clause

Escalation clause is often provided in long term contracts under which the settled contract price is subject to enhancement on any likely increase in price or utilisation of materials and labour etc. Following are circumstances when this safeguard is provided to the contractor that the contract price would be suitably enhanced:

(*i*) When the market price of materials used for the contract work are anticipated higher beyond a limit in the future.

(*ii*) When quantity of materials used for the contract are anticipated more than estimated quantity due to the nature of the contract, the correct estimate was not possible unless the work has been sufficiently progressed. It may also due to availability of inferior grades of raw materials resulting in more scraps and spoilage. But normally escalation clause in related to rise in prices.

(*iii*) When labour rates are anticipated to increase or where labour usages cannot be correctly estimated on account of the nature of the contract.

Thus an escalation clause is meant to safeguard the interest of the contractor against unforeseen rise in cost. There may be a De-escalation Clause or Reserve Clause to provide for any future decrease in price etc., so that benefit may be passed on to the contractee.

Illustration 7: (*Escalation clause*). Deluxe Limited under took a contract for ₹. 5,00,000 on 1st April 2009. On 31st March 2010 when the accounts were closed, the following details about the contract were gathered.

	₹.
Materials Purchased	1,00,000
Wages paid	45,000
General Expenses	10,000
Plant purchased	50,000
Materials in hand 31-3-10	25,000
Wages accrued 31-3-10	5,000
Works certified	2,00,000
Cash received	1,50,000
Works uncertified	15,000
Depreciation of plant	5,000

The contract contained an escalation clause which read as follows:

'In the event of increase(*s*) of prices of materials and rates of wages by more than 5%, the contract price would be increased accordingly by 25% of the rise of the cost of materials and wages beyond 5% in each case'.

It was found that since the date of signing the agreement, the prices of materials and wages rates increased by 25%. The value of the work certified does not take into account the effect of the above clause.

Prepare the Contract Account. ***[CS Inter]***

Solution:

Deluxe Limited

Contract Account for the year ended 31st March 2010

		₹.		₹.	₹.
To Materials Purchased		1,00,000	By Work certified	2,00,000	
To Wages paid	45,000		Work uncertified	15,000	
Add: Accrued	5,000	50,000	Effect of escalation		
To General expenses		10,000	caluse	5,000	2,20,000
To Depreciation of plant		5,000	By Materials in hand		25,000
To Total Profit c/d		80,000			
		2,45,000			2,45,000
To Profit & Loss A/c		20,000	By Total Profit b/d		80,000
To Balance (Reserved Profit)		60,000			
		80,000			80,000

Working Notes:

1. Calculation of Escalation

		Total Increase ₹.	*Up to 5%* ₹.	*Beyond 5%* ₹.
(*a*)	Materials (increase in price) (₹. 1,00,000 – 25,000) × 25/125	15,000	3,000	12,000
(*b*)	Wages (increase in rate) (₹. 50,000 × 25/125)	10,000	2,000	8,000
	Total increase	25,000	5,000	20,000

Increase in contract price = 25% of increase in materials and wages beyond 5%
= 25% of ₹. 20,000 = ₹. 5,000

2. Profit to be transferred to Profit & Loss Account (Contract is complete between 1/4 to 1/2, hence 1/3 profit received)

= Total Profit × 1/3 × Cash received/work certified
= 80,000 × 1/3 × 1,50,000/2,00,000
= ₹. 20,000

Cost-plus Contract

Cost-plus contracts provide for the payment by the contractee of the actual cost of the contract plus a stipulated or agreed profit. Thus under cost-plus contract the contract price is determined by adding to the actual cost of direct material, direct labour and direct expenses, a certain amount to cover the overhead costs of the contractor and an agreed profit.

Cost-plus contracts are entered into (*i*) when it is not possible to estimate its cost with reasonable accuracy due to unstable prices at the time the contract is undertaken or when the work is spread over a long period of time and prices of materials, rates of labour etc. are likely to fluctuate, (*ii*) when there is an emergency and no time to negotiate a contract price and the work is more important than its cost, (*iii*) where contract is with a government department. In such cases cost-plus contracts are advantageous both to the contractor and contractee as neither party stands to lose; a fair price is offered by the contractee and a reasonable profit accrues to the contractor.

Advantages of cost-plus contract to the contractor: (*i*) There is no risk of loss arising from changing prices, wrong estimates and underestimated quotation. All agreed costs are recovered; (*ii*) It provides an automatic or ready escalation clause, so that increase in cost are automatically adjusted and recovered; (*iii*) There is no bargaining problem. The work of offering quotation is simplified.

Advantages to contractee: (*i*) The contract is settled at reasonable price; (*ii*) There is no problem of bargaining. Time is saved; (*iii*) Contractee is also benefitted by the fall in prices of material and labour.

Disadvantages to the contractor: (*i*) Advantage on account of favourable market price is denied; (*ii*) The profit earned is usually low; (*iii*) The books and records are confidentially maintained; (*iv*) Profit usually based as a percentage of cost, an efficient working which reduces cost shall not accrue any benefit.

Disadvantages to the contractee: (*i*) The final contract price is uncertain, with the result, the budget of cost cannot be set; (*ii*) Contractor may deliberately incur higher prime cost in order to increase profit.

Moreover in cost-plus contract, no clear-cut line can be laid down regarding the items of cost to be included or excluded from the cost-plus calculations. The other difficulty is to decide the rate of reasonable profit to be added in the cost.

Illustration 18: The following information relate to Contract No. 123. You are required to prepare the Contract Account and Contractee Account assuming the balance of the contract was duly received

		₹.
Direct Materials		20,250
Direct Wages		15,500
Stores Issued		10,500
Loose Tools		2,400
Tractor Expenses		
Running Material	2,300	
Wages of Driver	3,000	5,300
Other Direct Charges		2,650

The contract took 13 weeks in its completion. The values of loose tools and stores returned at the end of the period were ₹. 200 and 3,000 respectively. The plant was also returned at a value of ₹. 16,000 after charging depreciation at 20%. The value of tractor was ₹. 20,000 and the depreciation was to be charged to the tractor @ 15% per annum. The administration and office expenses are to be provided at 10% on works cost. Profit to be charged at 20% of the total cost.

Solution:

Dr. **Contract No. 123 Account**

Particulars		*Amount*	*Particulars*	*Amount*
		₹.		₹.
To Direct Material		20,250	By Stores returned	3,000
To Direct Wages		15,500	By Loose tools returned	200
To Stores Issued		10,500	By Plant returned	16,000
To Plant (original cost)		20,000	By Balance being Works Cost c/d	58,150
To Loose tools		2,400		
To Tractor expenses:				
Running materials	2,300			
Wages to driver	3,000	5,300		
To Depreciation on Tractor @ 15% on ₹. 20,000 for 13 weeks		750		
To Other Direct Charges		2,650		
	₹.	77,350	₹.	77,350
To Balance being Work Cost b/d		58,150	By Contractee's A/c	76,758
To Administration and office expenses @ 10% on works cost		5,815		
To Profit & Loss A/c [20% of (58.150 + 5815)		12,793		
	₹.	76,758	₹.	76,758

Contractee's Account

	₹.		₹.
To Contract A/c	76,758	By Bank	76,758
₹.	76,758	₹.	76,758

Note : The plant was depreciated @ 20% (not @ 20% per annum). The depreciated value is 16,000. So the original cost of the plant comes to ₹. 20,000.

Illustration 19: From the following particulars, write up the Contract Account No. 57 and find out the tender price :

	₹.
Materials used	3,000
Productive wages	2,300
Direct expenses	250

Provide 60% on productive wages for works overheads and 12-1/2% on Works Cost for office overheads. Profit to be realised is 15% on the tender price.

Solution:

Contract No. 57 Account

	₹.		₹.
To Materials used	3,000.00	By Contractee's Account	9,172.06
To Productive Wages	2,300.00		
To Direct Expenses	250.00		
Prime Cost	5,550.00		
To Works Overhead (60% on Productive Wages)	1,380.00		
Works Cost	6,930.00		
To Office Overhead (12-1/2% on Works Cost)	866.25		
Total Cost	7,796.25		
To Profit and Loss Account (15% on tender price or 7796.25 × 15/85)	1,375.81		
	9,172.06		9,172.06

Illustration 20: A firm of contractors undertook a contract on 1st April, 2003. The following was the expenditure on the contract which was for ₹. 4,00,000.

	₹.
Materials issued to contract	60,000
Plant used for contract	20,000
Wages incurred	80,000
Other Expenses	5,000

Cash received on account up to 31st March, 2004 amounted to ₹. 1,60,000 being 80% of work certified.

Of the plant and materials charged to the contract, plant which costs ₹. 4,000 and materials which cost ₹. 3,000 were lost.

On 31st March, 2004 plant which costs ₹. 5,000 was returned to stores; the cost of work done but uncertified was ₹. 2,000 and materials costing ₹. 3,000 were in hand on site.

Charge 10% depreciation on plant and prepare Contract Account, Work-in-Progress Account and Contractee's Account from the above particulars. Show how Work-in-Progress would appear in the Balance Sheet.

Contract Account
(For the year ended 31st March, 2004)

	₹.			₹.
To Materials issued	60,000	By P & L A/c: Plant Lost	4,000	
To Plant	20,000	Materials Lost	3,000	7,000
To Wages	80,000	By Plant returned	5,000	
To Other Expenses	5,000	*Less:* 10% depreciation	500	4,500
To Balance being Profit c/d	61,400	By Materials in hand		3,000
		By Plant at site (20,000 – 4,000 – 5,000)	11,000	
		Less: 10% depreciation	1,100	9,900
		By Work-in-Progress		
		Work certified (1,60,000 × 100/80)		2,00,000
		Work uncertified		2,000
	2,26,400			2,26,400

	₹.		₹.
To Profit transferred to P & L A/c	32,747	By Balance b/d	61,400
To Works-in-progress A/c	28,653		
	61,400		61,400

Work-in Progress Account

	₹.		₹.
To Contract A/c		By Contract A/c	
Work certified	2,00,000	Balance of Profit	
Work uncertified	2,000	to P & L A/c	28,653
		By Balance	1,73,347
	2,02,000		2,02,000

Balance Sheet
(As at 31st March, 2004)

	Assets		₹.
	Materials in hand		3000
	Plant at site		9900
	Work-in-Progress	₹. 1,73,347	
	Less: Advance	1,60,000	13,347

Contractee's Account

	₹.		₹.
To Balance c/d	1,60,000	By Bank	1,60,000
	1,60,000		1,60,000

Illustration 21: The following is a summary of the entires in a Contract Ledger as on 31st Dec., 2003 in respect of Contract No. 27.

	₹.
Materials (direct)	30,000
Materials (from stores)	6,500
Wages	17,210
Direct Expenses	6,710
Establishment charges	8,000
Plant	34,200
Sale of Scrap	1,820
Sub-contract costs	7,210

You obtain following information:

(*a*) Accruals on 31st December, 2003 are : Wages ₹. 800; Direct Exps. ₹. 1,120.

(*b*) Depreciation of Plant up to 31st December, 2003 is ₹. 8,550.

(*c*) Included in the above summary of entries are wages ₹. 1,000 and other expenses ₹. 1,500 since certification. The value of materials used since certification is ₹. 2,080.

(*d*) Materials on site on 31st December 2003 cost ₹. 10,000.

(*e*) ₹. 62,500 had been certified up to 31st December 2003 when three-eighths of the contract remained incomplete.

(*f*) The total contract price is ₹. 1,00,000.

You are required to show what profit or loss would be taken into the accounts for the year ended 31st December 2003 in respect of this contract.

Solution:

Contract No. 27 Account

		₹.			₹.
To Materials (direct)		30,000	By Sales of Scrap.		1,820
To Material (from stores)		6,500	By Work certified		62,500
To Wages	17,210		By Work uncertified:		
Add: Accrued	800	18,010	Wages	1,000	
To Direct Expenses	6,710		Exps.	1,500	
Add: Accrued	1,120	7,830	Materials	2,080	4,580
To Establishment charges		8,000	By Value of Plant		
To Plant		34,200	(34,200–8,550)		25,650
To Sub-contract cost		7,210	By Materials on site		10,000
			By P/L A/c—Loss to date		7,200
	₹.	1,11,750		₹.	1,11,750

Note: Cost of work uncertified is expenses incurred after the date of work certified.

Illustration 22: A contractor who prepares his accounts on 31st December each year, commenced a Contract No. 51 on 1st April, 2003. The costing records concerning the said contract yield the following information at 31st December, 2003.

	₹.
Materials charges out to site	21,500
Labour	50,110
Foremen	6,310

A machine costing ₹. 15,000 has been on the site for 73 days. Its working life is estimated at 5 years and its final scrap value at ₹. 1,000.

A supervisor, who is paid ₹. 1,000 per mensum, has devoted approximately one-half of his time to this contract.

All other expenses and administration amount to ₹. 12,610.

Materials in hand at site on 31st Dec., 2003 cost ₹. 2,480.

The contract price is ₹. 2,00,000. On 31st December, 2003 two-thirds of the contract was completed; architect's certificates had been issued covering ₹. 1,00,000; ₹. 80,000 has so far been paid on account. Prepare Contract Account.

Solution:

Contract No. 21 Account

	₹.			₹.
To Materials	21,500	By Plant in hand	(15000–560)	14,440
To Labour	50,110	By Materials in hand		2,480
To Foremen	6,310	By Work certified		1,00,000
To Supervision	4,500	By Work uncertified		
To Plant	15,000	(see note below)		23,278
To Sundry and Administration Exps.	12,610			
To Balance c/d	30,168			
₹.	1,40,198		₹.	1,40,198
To P/L A/c	16,090	By Balance b/d		30,168
To Bal. c/d	14,078			
	30,168			30,168

Notes: (1) Depreciation on Plant = $\frac{(15,000 - 1,000) \times 73 \text{ days}}{5 \times 365}$ = ₹. 560

Plant at site = 15,000 – 560 = 14,400

(2) Calculation of cost of work uncertified

(*a*) *First method*

(*i*) Contract Completed = 2/3

(*ii*) Total Cost of 2/3 Contract = 1,10,030 – 16,920 = 93,110

(*iii*) Total estimated cost of whole contract = 93,110 × 3/2 = 1,39,665

(*iv*) Ratio of value of work certified to Contract Price 1,00,000/2,00,000 = 1/2

(*v*) Cost of work certified 1,39,665 × 1/2 = 69,832

(*vi*) Cost of work uncertified:

	₹.
Cost of work done	93,110
Less: Cost of work certified	69,832
	23,278

(*b*) *Second Method*

Work done = 2/3

Work certified = 1/2

Work uncertified = 2/3 – 1/3 = 1/6

Cost of 2/3 contract = ₹. 93,110

Therefore cost of 1/6 work = 93,110 × 3/2 × 1/6 = 23,278

Illustration 23: The following figures are disclosed by the books of a contractor for the year ending 31st December 2009.

	₹.	₹.
Work-in-progress as on 31st Dec., 2008	3,40,000	
Less: Advances from contractees as on 31-12-2008	2,20,000	1,20,000
Transactions during the year :		
Materials supplied to contract directly by merchant		20,000
Materials issued from stores		40,000
Wages		40,000
Working Expenses		6,000
Administration Expenses (of which ₹. 2,000 are chargeable to General Profit and Loss Account)		6,000
Plant issued		10,000
Materials returned from contracts directly to merchant		2,000
Materials returned to stores		2,000
Contract finished		90,000
Work certified		60,000
Profit taken upon contracts		46,000
Advances from contractees		1,60,000

Prepare the Contract Ledger Account and the Total Contractee's Account and show how the Work-in-Progress would appear in the Balance Sheet.

Solution:

Contract Ledger Account
(For the year ending 31st Dec., 2009)

	₹		₹
To Work-in-Progress	3,40,000	By Materials returned to suppliers	2,000
To Materials direct	20,000	By Materials returned to store	2,000
To Materials from store	40,000	By Contractee's A/c	
To Wages	40,000	(For contract finished)	90,000
To Working Expenses	6,000	By Work certified	60,000
To Administration Exps.	4,000	By Work uncertified	
To Plant	10,000	(balancing figure)	3,52,000
To Profit & Loss A/c (Profit taken upon contract)	46,000		
	5,06,000		5,06,000

Total Contractee's Account

	₹		₹
To Contract A/c		By Balance b/d	2,20,000
(For contract finished)	90,000	By Bank	1,60,000
To Balance c/d	2,90,000		
	3,80,000		3,80,000

Balance Sheet
(As at 31st Dec., 2009)

Assets		₹
Work-in-Progress:		
Work certified	60,000	
Work uncertified	3,52,000	
	4,12,000	
Less: Advances (balance of contractee's A/c)	2,90,000	1,22,000

Note: Since profit carried to Profit and Loss Account has been given, the balance in the account will be cost of work uncertified.

Illustration 24: The Enterprising Contractors Ltd. having an authorised capital of ₹. 90,000 divided into 400; 6% Cumulative Pref. Shares of ₹. 100 each and 5,000 Equity Shares of ₹. 10 each, commenced operations on 1st January 2003 and during 2004 were engaged on one contract of ₹. 4,00,000. The trial balance extracted from their books on 31st Dec., 2004 stood as follows:

		₹.	₹.
Share Capital :	Preference fully paid		40,000
	Equity ₹. 8 paid		40,000
Sundry Creditors			8,000
Land and Buildings		34,000	
Cash at Bank		9,000	
Contract Account:	Materials	75,000	
	Plant	20,000	
	Wages	1,05,000	
	Expenses	5,000	
Cash Received, being 80% of Work certified			1,60,000
		2,48,000	2,48,000

Of the plant and materials charged to contract, plant costing ₹. 3,000 and materials costing ₹. 2,400 were destroyed by an accident. On 31st December, plant which cost ₹. 4,000 was returned to store, the value of materials on site was ₹. 3,000 and the cost of work done but not certified was ₹. 2,000 Charge 10% depreciation on plant. Prepare Contract Account and the Balance Sheet.

Solution:

Contract A/c

	₹.			₹.
To Materials	75,000	By P&L A/c:		
To Wages	1,05,000	Plant lost	3,000	
To Plant	20,000	Materials lost	2,400	5,400
To Expenses	5,000	By Work Certified		
To Balance of Profit c/d	20,700	(1,60,000 × 100/80)		2,00,000
		By Work Uncertified		2,000
		By Plant Returned to Store	4,000	
		Less: Depreciation 10%	400	3,600
		By Plant at site	13,000	
		Less: Depreciation 10%	1,300	11,700
		By Materials at site		3,000
	2,25,700			2,25,700
To P/L A/c	11,040	By Balance of profit b/d		20,700
To Balance c/d	9,660			
	20,700			20,700

(*i*) Work certified = Cash received × 100/80 = 2,00,000

(*ii*) Plant at site = Plant debited – Plant lost – Plant returned
= 20,000 – 3,000 – 4,000 = 13,000

(*iii*) Profit to Profit & Loss Account

$$= \text{Total Profit} \times 2/3 \times \frac{\text{Cash received}}{\text{Work certified}} = ₹.\ 11,040$$

Enterprises Contractors Ltd.
Balance Sheet as at 31st Dec., 2003

Liabilities		₹.	*Assets*		₹.
Share Capital			**Fixed Assets**		
400; 6% Cum. Pref. Shares		40,000	Land and Building		34,000
5,000 Equity shares ₹. 8 paid		40,000	Plant in stores		3,600
Reserve & Surplus			Plant at site		11,700
Profit & Loss A/c	11,040		**Current Assets**		
Less: Loss on Plant			Cash at Bank		9,000
& Materials	5,400	5,640	Materials at site		3,000
Current Liabilities			Work-in-progress	1,92,340	
Sundry Creditors		8,000	*Less:* Advances	1,60,000	32,340
		93,640			93,640

Note: Work-in-progress has been calculated as below:

	₹.
Work certified	2,00,000
Work uncertified	2,000
	2,02,000
Less: Profit not taken to P & L A/c	9,660
Work-in-progress	1,92,340

Contracts to Run for More than One Year

Usually when contract-work is to complete in two years, the first years contract account will be prepared as incomplete contract and the work-in-progress (value of work certified and cost of work uncertifies less profit not transferred to P&L A/c) and materials and plant at site at end will be carried as opening balance in the second year's contract account. In the second year work will be complete, therefore, total contract price will be credited to find out profit. If contract is to run for 3 years or more normally no profit is ascertained in the first year if work done is less than 1/4 of the contract price. Second year's contract account will be of incomplete work. The work-in-progress at end will be carried to next year as opening balance. The last year's Contract Account will be credited by total contract price.

Illustration 25: A firm of contractors undertook a contract for ₹. 6,00,000 on 1st July, 2003. The following expenses were incurred up to December 31, 2003.

	₹.
Materials charged directly	7,500
Materials issued from stores	52,500
Wages	30,000
Direct charges	3,000

The amount of work certified was ₹. 1,20,000 of which the contractors received 3/4th in cash. The transactions for the year 2004 were as under.

Materials issued from stores	1,35,000
Direct charges	6,000
Wages	60,000

The cost of special plant issued on January 1, 2004 for the contract was ₹. 1,20,000. Further work certified during the year amounted to ₹. 3,30,000, 75% of which was received. Work done and not certified as on 31-12-04 was valued at ₹. 22,500. Special Plant is to be depreciated at 25% per annum on the original cost. Materials on site were valued at ₹. 15,000. The general overhead is to be taken at 5% of the materials consumed and wages paid during the year. Prepare Contract Accounts for 2003 and 2004.

Solution:

Contract Account for 2003

	₹.		₹.
To Materials — Direct	7,500	By Balance c/d	97,500
— Stores	52,500	(Work-in-Progress)	
To Wages	30,000		
To Direct Charges	3,000		
To General overheads			
(5% of 7,500 + 52,500 + 30,000)	4,500		
	97,500		97,500

Note: Since work done is less than 1/4 of the contract-price, no profit is transferred to P/L A/c. Balance of the account is work-in-progress.

Contract Account for 2004

	₹.		₹.
To Balance b/d (For 2003)	97,500	By Plant less depreciation	90,000
To Plant (special)	1,20,000	By Material at sites	15,000
To Materials	1,35,000	By Work uncertified	22,500
To Wages	60,000	By Work certified (Total)	
To Direct charges	6,000	(1,20,000 + 3,30,000)	4,50,000
To General overheads			
5% of (1,35,000 + 60,000 – 15,000)	9,000		
To Total Profit c/d	1,50,000		
	5,77,500		5,77,500
To Profit to P & L A/c		By Total Profit b/d	1,50,000
(1,50,000 × 2/3 × 75/100)	75,000		
To Balance c/d	75,000		
	1,50,000		1,50,000

Illustration 26: Shastri & Co. undertook a contract on 1st january 2000 for ₹. 3,00,000 and completed the same on 30th April 2002. The contract books showed the following at 31st December of each year.

The amount of work certified at the end of the year 2000 was ₹. 75,000 and at the end of 2001 ₹. 2,25,000, 80% of the certified work was received in cash.

Prepare accounts in respect of the contract at the end of each year showing the proportion of profit the company would be justified to take to the credit of Profit & Loss Account. Show also how the Work-in-progress will appear in the Balance Sheet from year to year. Depreciate plant at 10% on the original cost annually.

On 31st December 2000: Materials issued were valued at ₹. 35,000; Wages ₹. 25.000; Other direct charges ₹. 2,000 Materials on site ₹. 5,000.

On 31st December, 2001: Materials issued were valued at ₹. 75,000; Wages ₹. 4,500; Other direct charges ₹. 4,000; Special plant ₹. 90,000; Materials on site ₹. 15,200 and Work completed but not certified was estimated at ₹. 25,000.

On 30th April 2002: Materials issued were valued at ₹. 5,000; Wages ₹. 12,250; Direct charges ₹. 1,270.

Solution

Contract Account

	₹.			₹.
2000		2000		
To Materials issued	35,000	By Materials on site c/d		5,000
To Wages	25,000	By Balance c/d		57,000
To Other direct charges	2,000			
	62,000			62,000
2001		2001		
To Balance b/d	57,000	By Work certified c/d		2,25,000
To Materials on site b/d	5,000	By Work uncertified c/d		25,000
To Materials issued	75,000	By Materials on site c/d		15,200
To Wages	4,500	By Special Plant c/d	90,000	
To Other Direct charges	4,000	*Less:* Depr.	9,000	81,000
To Special Plant	90,000			
To Total Profit c/d	1,10,700			
	3,46,200			3,46,200

	₹.		₹.
2000		2000	
To P/L A/c		By Total b/d	1,10,700
(1,10,700 × 2/3 × 80/100)	59,040		
To Balance of Profit c/d (w/q)	51,660		
	1,10,700		1,10,700
2002		2002	
To Work certified b/d	2,25,000	By Balance of Profit b/d	51,660
To Work uncertified b/d	25,000	By Special Plant	
To Material on site b/d	15,200	(depreciated value)	78,000
To Special Plant b/d	81,000	By Contractee's Account	3,00,000
To Mateial issued	5,000		
To Wages	12,250		
To Direct charges	1,270		
To P/L A/c	64,940		
₹.	4,29,660	₹.	4,29,660

Balance Sheet

Assets Side		₹.
2000		
Work-in-Progress:		
Materials on site	5,000	
Balance of Contract A/c	57,000	
	62,000	
Less: Cash Received (80% of 75,000)	60,000	2,000
2001		
Work-in-Progress:		
Work certified	2,25,000	
Work uncertified	25,000	
Materials on site	15,200	
Special Plant	81,000	
	3,46,200	
Less: Profit not trfd. to P/L A/c	51,660	
	2,94,540	
Less: Cash Received (80% of 2,25,000)	1,80,000	1,14,540

Contractee's Account

	₹.		₹.
2000 To Balance c/d	60,000	2000 By Bank	60,000
2001 To Balance c/d	1,80,000	2001 By Balance b/d	60,000
		By Bank	1,20,000
	1,80,000		1,80,000
2002 To Contract A/c	3,00,000	2002 By Balance b/d	1,80,000
		By Bank	1,20,000
	3,00,000		3,00,000

Contracts Near Completion

If by the end of the year contract is very near to completion, the further expenses to complete it are estimated and added to cost. The excess of contract price over this total estimated cost will be expected profit on completion. The profit to be transferred to Profit and Loss Account on incomplete contract may be calculated on the basis of estimated profit.

$$\text{Profit to P\&L A/c} = \text{Total Estimated Profit} \times \frac{\text{Value of work certified}}{\text{Contract price}}$$

$$\text{or Total estimated profit} \times \frac{\text{Value of WC}}{\text{Contract Price}} \times \frac{\text{Cash Received}}{\text{Value of WC}}$$

Illustration 27: Suggest the profit to be taken to P/L A/c on a contract which is about 95% complete :

	₹
Total cost up to date	3,80,000
Estimated additional expenses	20,000
Contract Price	5,00,000
Value of work certified	4,50,000
Cost of work not certified	25,000
Cash received	4,20,000

Solution:

Total Cost up to date	3,80,000
Add: Estimated Expenses	20,000
(*i*) Total Estimated Cost	4,00,000
Contract Price	5,00,000
Less: Total Estimated Cost	4,00,000
(*ii*) Total Estimated Profit	1,00,000

$$\text{Resonable Profit to P/L A/c} = \frac{1{,}00{,}000 \times 4{,}50{,}000}{5{,}00{,}000} = 90{,}000$$

Actual Total Profit:

Value of work certified	4,50,000
Cost of work certified (3,80,000 – 25,000)	3,55,000
Actual Total Profit	95,000

Illustration 28: On 31st December 2000 ₹. 1,13,000 has been expended upon a contract and certificates have been received to date to the value of ₹. 1,50,000. The cost of work performed but not yet certified is ₹. 3,000. It is estimated that the contract will take a further three months to complete and that it will necessitate the additional expenditure of ₹. 20,000. The total estimated expenditure upon the contract is to include a provision of 5 per cent of the total cost of the contract for contingencies. The contract price is ₹. 1,75,000 and ₹. 1,20,000 has been received in cash to date.

You are required to calculate profit earned to date, estimated total profit and the proportion of profit to be taken to the cerdit of Profit & Loss Account for the period ended 31st December 2000.

Solution:

	₹.
(1) Total expenditure to date	1,13,000
Less: Cost of work uncertified	3,000
Cost of work certified	1,10,000
Value of work certified	1,50,000
Profit (1,50,000 – 1,10,000)	40,000

(2) Total Expenditure	1,13,000
Estimated Additional Exps.	20,000
	1,33,000
Provision for contingencies 5% of total estimated expenditure (*i.e.* 1,33,000 × 5/95)	7000
Total Cost	1,40,000
Total Contract Price	1,75,000
Total Estimated Profit	35,000

(3) Profit to be transferred to P/L A/c

$$= \text{Total Estimated Profit} \times \frac{\text{Work certified}}{\text{Contract price}}$$

$$= 35{,}000 \times \frac{1{,}50{,}000}{1{,}75{,}000} = 30{,}000$$

Contract Account

	₹.		₹.
To Total Exps.	1,13,000	By Work certified	1,50,000
To Total Profit c/d	40,000	By Cost of uncertified	3,000
	1,53,000		1,53,000
To PL A/c	30,000	By Total Profit b/d	40,000
To Balance of profit	10,000		
	40,000		40,000

Illustration 29: Brock Construction Ltd. commenced a contract on November 1, 2003. The total contract was for ₹. 39,37,500. It was decided to estimate the total profit on the contract and to take to the credit of P/L A/c that proportion of estimated profit on cash basis, which work completed bore to the total contract. Actual expenditure for the period of November 1, 2003 to October 31, 2004 and estimated expenditure for November 1, 2004 to March 31, 2005 are given below:

		November 1, 2003 to October 31, 2004 (Actuals) ₹.	*November 1, 2004 to March 31, 2005 (Estimated)* ₹.
Materials issued		6,75,000	12,37,500
Labour :	Paid	4,50,000	5,62,500
	Prepaid	25,000	—
	Outstanding	—	2,500
Plant purchased		3,75,000	—
Expenses :	Paid	2,00,000	4,50,000
	Outstanding	50,000	25,000
Plant returns to store		75,000	3,00,000
(historical cost)		(on March 31, 2004)	(on March 31, 2005)
Work Certified		20,00,000	Full
Work Uncertified		75,000	
Cash received		17,50,000	
Material at site		75,000	37,500

The plant is subject to annual depreciation @ $33\frac{1}{3}\%$ on written down value method. The contract is likely to be completed on March 31, 2005.

Required :

(*i*) Prepare the Contract A/c. Determine the profit on the contract for the year November, 2003 to October, 2004 on prudent basis, which has to be credited to P/L A/c.

[*CA PE II Nov. 2004*]

Solution:

Block Construction Ltd.
Contract Account
(Nov., 2003 to Oct. 31, 2004)

		₹			₹
To Materials issued		6,75,000	By Plant returned on		
To Labour paid	4,50,000		31-3-04 cost	75,000	
Less prepaid	25,000	4,25,000	*Less* Dep. for 5 month	10,417	64,583
To Plant purchased		3,75,000	By Plant at site	3,00,000	
To Exps. paid	2,00,000		Less Depreciation	1,00,000	2,00,000
Add outstanding	50,000	2,50,000	By Materials at site		75,000
To National Profit c/d		6,89,583	By Work-in-progress		
			Value of work certified		20,00,000
			Cost of work uncertified		75,000
		24,14,583			24,14,583
To Profit & Loss A/c		1,04,135.6	By National Profit b/d		6,89,583
To Work-in-progress					
(Reserved profit)		5,85,447.4			
		6,89,583			6,89,583

Comsputation of Estimated Profit
Contract Account
(Ist Nov. 2003 to March 31, 2005)

	₹			₹
To Materials		By Materials at site		37,500
[6,75,000 + 12,37,500]	19,12,500	By Plant returned on		
To Labour [4,25,000 + 25000		31-3-04		64,583
+ 5,62,500 + 2,500]	10,15,000	By Plant at site (cost)	3,00,000	
To Plant	3,75,000	Less Dep. (12 months)	1,00,000	
			2,00,000	
To Exps. [2,50,000 + 4,25000]	6,75,000	Less Dep. (5 months)	27,778	1,72,222
To Estimated Profit	2,34,305	By Contractee's A/c		39,37500
	42,11,805			42,11,805

Profit transferred to P/L A/c on Oct. 31, 2004

$$\text{Total Estimated Profit} \times \frac{\text{Cash Received}}{\text{Contract Price}}$$

$$234{,}305 \times \frac{17{,}50{,}000}{39{,}37{,}500} = 1{,}04{,}135.6$$

Illustration 30: A contractor secured a contract to supply and erect machinery for the sum of ₹. 7,50,000. He was to receive payments on account from time to time equal to 90% of the certified value of work done.

He commenced work on 1st Jan., 2003 and incurred the following expenditure during the year—Plant and tools ₹. 70,000; Machinery and Stores ₹. 2,00,000; Wages ₹. 1,50,000; Sundry Exps. ₹. 30,000; and Establishment charges ₹. 40,000.

A part of the machinery costing ₹. 20,000 was unsuited to the contract and was immediately sold at a profit of ₹. 5,000.

The value of Plant and Tools on 31st December, 2003 was ₹. 40,000 and the value of Machinery and Stores then on had was ₹. 30,000.

By 31st January 2004, he had received payments on account amounted to ₹. 4,38,750 being 90 per cent of the certified value of work done up to the previous year 31st December.

In order to calculate the profit made on the contract to 31st December, 2003, the contractor estimated the further expenditure that would be incurred in completing the contract, and took to the credit of Profit and Loss Account for the year that proportion of the estimated net profit to be realised on the contract, which the certified value of work done bore to the contract price. He estimated:

(1) That the contract would be completed in a further six months.

(2) That plant and tools would have a residual value of ₹. 10,000 upon the completion of the contract.

(3) That the cost of machinery and stores required in addition to those in stock on 31st December, 2003 would be ₹. 1,00,000 and that further sundry expenses of ₹. 20,000 would be incurred.

(4) That the wages on the contract for the six months to 30th June, 2004 would amount to ₹. 80,000.

(5) That establishment expenses would cost the same sum per month as in the previous year.

(6) That 2-1/2% of the total cost of contract (excluding this percentage) should be provided for contingencies.

Prepare the Contract Account for the year ended 31st December, 2003. Show your calculations of the profit to be credited to Profit and Loss Account for the year.

Solution:

Contract Account

(For the year ending on 31st Dec., 2003)

	₹.		₹.
To Plant and Tools	70,000	By Bank (Sales of Plant)	25,000
To Machinery and Stores	2,00,000	By Work Certified $(4,38,750 \times 100/90)$	4,87,500
To Wages	1,50,000	By Plant and tools in hand	40,000
To Sundry Expenses	30,000	By Machinery and stores in hand	30,000
To Establishment Charges	40,000		
To P&L A/c—Profit on plant sold	5,000		
To Balance being Profit c/d	87,500		
	5,82,500		5,82,500
To Profit transferred to Profit & Loss A/c (see note)	34,450	By Balance b/d	87,500
To Balance c/d	53,050		
	87,500		87,500

Note: Calculation of Profit to be credited to Profit and Loss A/c

(A) *Cost to date* (gross : including the Plant and Materials and Stores in hand):

	₹.
Plant and Tools	70,000
Machinery and stores	2,00,000
Wages	1,50,000
Sundry Exps.	30,000
Establishment Charges	40,000
	4,90,000
Less: Cost of Plánt Sold	20,000
	4,70,000

(B) *Estimated further Expenditure:*

Machinery and stores	1,00,000
Sundry Expenses	20,000
Wages	80,000
Establishment Charges for 6 months	20,000
	2,20,000

Total Cost (Estimated):

(A) Cost to date	4,70,000
(B) Estimated further exps.	2,20,000
	6,90,000
Less: Residual value of plant	10,000
	6,80,000
Add: Reserved for Contingencies 2-1/2%	17,000
	6,97,000

Estimated Total Profit on Contract :

Contract Price	7,50,000
Less: Estimated Total Cost	6,97,000
	53,000

Profit to be transferred to P&L A/c

$$\text{Estimated Total Profit} \times \frac{\text{Work Certified}}{\text{Total Contract Price}} = 53{,}000 \times \frac{4{,}87{,}500}{7{,}50{,}000} = ₹.\ 34{,}450$$

Illustration 31: Kapoor Engineering Company undertakes a long term contract which involves the fabrication of pre-stressed concrete blocks and erection of the same at the customer's site.

The following information is supplied regarding the contract which is incomplete on 31st March 2001.

Cost incurred:	₹.
Fabrication cost to date	
Direct Materials	28,00,000
Direct Labour	9,00,000
Overheads	7,50,000
	44,50,000
Erection cost to date	1,50,000
Total	46,00,000
Contract-price	81,90,000
Cash received on account (80% of work certified)	60,00,000
Technical estimated of work completed to date:	

Fabrication: Direct Material 80%

Direct Labour and Overheads 75%

Erection 25%

You are required to prepare a statement for submission to the management indicating the estimated profit to date and on completion of the contract. **[*CA Inter*]**

Solution:

Statement Showing the Estimated Profit to date and on completion on of contract

	Cost of date		Further cost		Total
	% of completion	*Amount ₹*	*% of Completion to be done*	*Amount ₹*	*Cost*
Fabrication					
Direct Materials	80%	28,00,000	20%	7,00,000	35,00,000
Direct Labour	75%	9,00,000	25%	3,00,000	12,00,000
Overheads	75%	7,50,000	25%	2,50,000	10,00,000
Total		44,50,000		12,50,000	57,00,000
Erection cost	25%	1,50,000	75%	4,50,000	6,00,000
Estimated cost		46,00,000		17,00,000	63,00,000
Profit		13,80,000		5,00,000	18,90,000
		58,80,000		22,10,000	81,90,000

Profit on the contract to date is based on estimated total profit on completion *i.e.* total contract price–total cost (₹. 81,90,000—63,00,000) ₹. 18,90,000

Profit to date will be

$$\frac{\text{Estimated Total Profit} \times \text{Cost to date}}{\text{Total cost}} = \frac{18,90,000 \times 46,00,000}{63,00,000} = ₹.\ 13,80,000$$

Alternatively, it can be calculated as below

$$\frac{\text{Estimated Total Profit} \times \text{Cash Received}}{\text{Contract Price}} = \frac{18,90,000 \times 60,00,000}{81,90,000} = ₹.\ 13,84,615$$

TYPICAL ILLUSTRATIONS

Illustration 32: The following information is ascertained from the costing department of a firm of contractors for the month of June.

		₹.	₹.
(1)	Materials Abstract:		
	Balance on 31st May,	61,890	
	Purchases	16,250	
	From Job 36	1,075	79,215
	To Job 42		10,685
	Balance on 30th June		68,530
(2)	Wages Abstract :		
	Job 36	1,100	
	Job 42	11,590	12,690
	Administrative and General Charges		1,160
			13,850

The following balances were shown in the Contract Ledger on 31st May,

Job 36 ₹. 3,62,105

Job 42 ₹. 1,65,930

Job 36 was certified as completed; the balance on 31st May, included ₹. 67,600 in respect of cost of Plant and Machinery, the rest consisted of Wages and Materials, One apparatus, which had been specially purchased for this Contract at ₹. 7,600 was sold during the month of June for ₹. 2,550. Of the remainder, ₹. 47,800 worth had been on the job for eight months and the balance for six months. Depreciation is to be charged at the rate of 15% per annum. Half of the Machinery which had been on the Job for eight months was transferred to Job 42 and the balance was returned to store.

You are required to write up the Contract Account and to ascertain the profit of Job 36, the Contract Price being ₹. 4,60,000; 10% on cost of wages and materials consumed being taken as Administrative and General Charges.

Solution:

Contract No. 36 Account

		₹.				₹.
Ju. 1			Ju. 30	By Contractee's		
" 30	To Balance b/d	3,62,105		Account		4,60,000
	To Wages	1,100		By Materials returned		1,075
	To Administrative and General Charges (10% of ₹. 2,94,530)	29,453		By Proceeds of sale of Machine		2,550
	To P&L Account (Profit on the contract)	1,30,322		By P&L Account (Loss on the sale of machine)		5,050
				By Machinery used for 8 months:		
				Cost	47,800	
				Less: Depreciation	4,780	
					43,020	
				To Job 42	21,510	
				To Store	21,510	43,020
				By Machinery used for 6 months:		
				Cost	12,200	
				Less: depreciation	915	11,285
		5,22,980				5,22,980

Contract No. 42 Account

		₹.	Ju. 30		₹.
Ju. 1	To Balance b/d	1,65,930		By Balance b/d	2,09,715
	To Materials	10,685			
	To Wages	11,590			
	To Machinery from Contract No. 36	21,510			
		2,09,715			2,09,715

[**Note.** (1) Administrative and General Charges in respect of Contract No. 36 have been calculated as under:

	₹.
Opening Balance on 1st June	3,62,105
Less: Cost of plant and machinery included in the above balance	67,600
Wages and Materials on 1st June	2,94,505
Add: Further wages expended as per Wages Abstract	1,100
	2,95,605
Less: Materials returned as per Materials Abstract	1,075
Cost of Wages and Materials consumed	2,94,530

10% of the above = *₹. 29,453*

(2) Depreciation of Machinery and how it has been dealt with is shown below:

Cost of Plant and Machinery on 1st July67,600	
Less: Cost of apparatus sold	7,600
Balance of machinery used on the Contract	60,000

Depreciation on ₹. 47,800 for 8 months @ 15% = ₹. 4,780. Depreciation on the balance of ₹. 12,200 (₹. 60,000 – ₹. 47,800) for 6 months @ 15% = ₹. 915.

The depreciated value of machinery used for eight months is ₹. 43,020 (₹. 47,800 – 4,780) of which ₹. 21,510 is transferred to Contract No. 42 and ₹. 21,510 is transferred to the store.

(3) Profit or loss in respect of work completed on Contract 42 cannot be ascertained as the certified value of work done etc., have not been given in the question.

(4) Loss on the sale of machine has been charged to the General Profit and Loss Account.

Illustration 33: The following relate to contract No. 200 undertaken by R.V. Ltd. in the beginning of 2001

	Work Certified ₹.	*Work Uncertified* ₹.
Materials	1,80,000	20,000
Wages	3,70,000	30,000

Special plant was purchased for the contract ₹. 1,60,000. At the end of the year, it was estimated to be worth ₹. 1,30,000. Overheads other than depreciation amount to 20% of wages. The value of the work certified was ₹. 8,40,000 against which the contractee paid ₹. 7,56,000. The total value of the contract was ₹. 16,00,000. Prepare Contract Account.

Solution:

Contract Account

(For the year ended 31st Dec. 2001)

		₹.			₹.
To Materials:			By Plnat at site		1,30,000
Work Certified	1,80,000		By Work-in-Progress A/c:		
Work Uncertified	20,000	2,00,000	Work Certified		8,40,000
To Labour:			Cost of Work uncertified		
Work Certified	3,70,000		Materials	20,000	
Work Uncertified	30,000	4,00,000	Labour	30,000	
To Special Plant		1,60,000	Overheads		
To Overheads (@ 20% on wages)		80,000	(@ 20% on wages)	6,000	56,000
To Balance		1,86,000			
		10,26,000			10,26,000
To P&L A/c		1,11,600	By Balance		1,86,000
To Work-in-Progress A/c		74,400			
		1,86,000			1,86,000

Illustration 34: The data given below are procured from the books of a factory for the year ended 31st Dec.,

The value of executed jobs during the year was ₹. 20,500.

Prepare : 1. Consolidated Completed Jobs Account showing the profit or loss; and
2. Consolidated Work-in-Progress Account.

	Completed Jobs	*Work-in-Progress*
	₹.	₹.
Raw materials supplied from stores	4,500	1,500
Chargeable expenses	500	200
Wages	5,000	2,000
Materials transferred to work-in-progress	100	100
Materials returned to stores	50	

Factory overhead is 80% of wages and office overhead 25% of factory cost.

Solution:

Consolidated Completed Jobs Account

	₹.	₹.		₹.
To Materials	4,500		By Contractees A/c	
Less: transferred			(Job finished)	20,500
to work-in-Progress	–100			
Less: Retd. to Stores	–50	4,350		
To Wages		5,000		
To Chargeable exp.		500		
To Factory overheads				
80% of wages		4,000		
Factory Cost		13,850		
To Office Overheads				
25% of factory cost (13,850)		3,462.50		
To Net profit transferred				
to Profit and Loss A/c		3,187.50		
		20,500		20,500

Consolidated Work-in-Progress A/c

	₹.		₹.
To Raw material	1,500	By Balance c/d	6,750
To Transferred from completed jobs	100		
To Wages	2,000		
To Chargeable Expenses	200		
To Factory Overheads 80% of wages	1600		
Factory Cost	5,400		
To Office Overheads 20% of factory cost *i.e.* ₹. 5,400	1,350		
	6,750		6,750

Illustration 35: A Contractional Engineering Company undertakes long-term contracts which involve the fabrication of the steel work in the Company's Workshops and the erection of the fabricated steel on consumer's sites. The following information is supplied regarding two of their uncompleted contracts as on 30th April 2003;

	Contract A	Contract B
Costs incurred:		
Fabrication Costs to date:	₹.	₹.
Direct Materials	2,00,000	60,000
Direct Labour	75,000	20,000
Overheads	1,05,000	27,500
	3,80,000	1,07,500
Erection Cost to date	15,000	7,500
Total	3,95,000	1,15,000
Contracts Value	7,00,000	2,00,000
Cash received on account	4,00,000	65,000
Technical estimate of work completed to date:	A	B
Fabrication:	%	%
Direct Materials	80	60
Direct Labour and Overheads	75	50
Erection	25	25

Solution:

Contract A

	Cost to date		Further Cost		Total
	% Completion	*Amount*	*%*	*Amount*	*Cost* ₹
Fabrication		₹.		₹.	₹.
Direct	80	2,00,000	20	50,000	2,50,000
Materials	75	75,000	25	25,000	1,00,000
Direct Labour	75	1,05,000	25	35,000	1,40,000
Overheads		3,80,000		1,10,000	4,90,000
Erection	25	15,000	75	45,000	60,000
		3,95,000		1,55,000	5,50,000

Contract Value	7,00,000
Total Cost	5,50,000
Estimated profit at the completion of contract	1,50,000

$$\text{Estimated profit to date} = \frac{3,95,000}{5,50,000} \times 1,50,000 = ₹.\ 1,07,500$$

Contract B

	Cost to date		Further Cost		Total
	% Completion	*Amount*	*%*	*Amount*	*Cost* ₹
Fabrication		₹.		₹.	₹.
Direct Mateials	60	60,000	40	40,000	1,00,000
Direct Labour	50	20,000	50	20,000	40,000
Overheads	50	27,500	50	27,500	55,000
		1,07,500		87,500	1,95,000
Erection	25	7,500	75	22,500	30,000
		1,15,000		1,10,000	2,25,000

	₹.
Contract Value	2,00,000
Total cost	2,25,000
Estimated loss at the completion of the Contract (as far as can be seen)	25,000

In case of Contract B there can be no estimated profit to date. Instead, the Company should make provision for the whole amount of the loss estimated. Further provision against probable loss should also the made.

Illustration 36: Compute a conservative estimate of profit on a contract (which has been 80% complete) from the following particulars. Illustrate at least 4 methods of computing the profit:

	₹.
Total expenditure to date	85,000
Estimated further expenditure to complete the contract (including contingencies)	17,000
Contract Price	1,53,000
Works certified	1,00,000
Works not certified	8,500
Cash received	81,600

Solution:

		₹.
Value of works certified		1,00,000
Less: Total Expenditure to-date	85,000	
Works not Certified	8,500	76,500
Notional Profit		23,500
Contract price		1,53,000
Less: Total Expenditure to-date	85,000	
Estimated further expenditure	17,000	1,02,000
Estimated Total Profit on completion		51,000

Methods of Computing Profit

1. Notional Profit $\times \frac{2}{3} \times \frac{\text{Cash received}}{\text{Value of work certified}}$

$$= 23,500 \times \frac{81600}{1,00,000} \times \frac{2}{3} = ₹.\ 12,784$$

2. Notional profit $\times \frac{\text{Value of work certified}}{\text{Contract Price}}$

$$= 23,500 \times \frac{1,00,000}{1,53,000} = ₹.\ 15,359$$

3. Estimated Total Profit $\times \frac{\text{Value of work certified}}{\text{Contract Price}} \times \frac{\text{Cash received}}{\text{Value of work Certified}}$

$$= 51,000 \times \frac{1,00,000}{1,53,000} \times \frac{81,600}{1,00,000} = ₹.\ 27,200$$

4. Estimated Total Profit $\times \frac{\text{Cost of work to-date}}{\text{Estimated total cost}} \times \frac{\text{Cash received}}{\text{Value of work certified}}$

$$= 51,000 \times \frac{85,000}{1,02,000} \times \frac{81,600}{1,00,000} = ₹.\ 34,680$$

Illustration 37: A contract for construction of building is governed by *an escalation clause* in respect of prices of steel, cement and stone aggregate. The prices ruling on the date of tender for the building and the actual prices paid by the contractor were as follows :

	On the date of tender (₹.)	Actual ₹.
Steel per ton	610	675
Cement per ton	100	105
Stone aggregate per 100 c.f.t.	40	38

3,00,000 c. ft. of reinforced cement concrete was laid in the building. If 100 lbs. of steel 2,400 lbs of cement and 90 c. ft. of stone are the net quantities required to cast 100 c. ft. of R.CC and the wastages are 5, 3 and 10 per cent respectively. Calculate the difference in contract price according to the escalation clause (1 ton = 2,240 lbs) (Assume the wastage percentages based on the net quantity of material).

Solution:

Statement of difference in contract price according to escalation clause

Particulars	*Steel*	*Cement*	*Stone Aggregate*
Net quantities required to cast 100 c.ft. of RCC	lbs 100	lbs 2,400	C.ft. 90
Net quantities for 3,00,000 c.ft. of RCC	3,00,000	72,00,000	2,70,000
Wastage on net qty.	5% of 3,00,000 = 15,000	3% of 72,00,000 = 2,16,000	10% of 2,70,000 = 27,000
Gross qty. required	3,15,000	74,16,000	2,97,000
Gross quantity required Lbs ÷ 2240 (tons)	140.625 Tons	3310.7142 Tons	2,970 units of 100 c.ft.
Rate difference (₹.)	675 – 610 = 65	105 – 100 = 5	38 – 40 = (–) 2
Amount Escalation for the gross quantity	140.625 × 65 = ₹. 9,141	3310.7142 × 5 = ₹. 16,553	2,970 × (–) 2 = ₹. (–) 5940

According to escalation clause, the difference in contract price is calculated below :

	₹.
Steel	9,141
Cement	16,553
Stone Aggregate	(–) 5,940
Total	19,754

According to Escalation clause the price should be increased by ₹. 19,754.

Illustration 38: A contractor, who prepares his account on 31st December each year, commenced a contract on 1st April, 2000. The costing records concerning the said contract reveal the following information on 31st December, 2000.

	₹.
Materials charged to site	2,58,100
Labour engaged	5,60,500
Foremen's salary	79,300

Plants costing ₹. 2,60,000 had been on site for 146 days. Their working life is estimaed at 7 years and their final scrap value at ₹. 15,000. A supervisor, who is paid ₹. 4,000 p.m., has devoted approximately three-fourths of his time to this contract, The administrative and other expenses amount to ₹. 1,40,000. Materials in hand at site on 31st December, 2000 cost ₹. 25,400. Some of the material costing ₹. 4,500 was found unsuitable and was sold for ₹. 4,000 and a part of the plant costing ₹. 5,500 (on 31-12-2000) unsuited to the contract was sold at a profit of ₹. 1,000.

The contract price was ₹. 22,00,000 but it was accepted by the contractor for ₹. 20,00,000. On 31st December 2000 two-third of the contract was completed. Architect's certificate had been issued covering 50% of the contract price and ₹. 7,50,000 had so far been paid on account. Prepare contract account and state how much profit or loss should be included in the financial accounts to 31st December, 2000. Working should be clearly given. Depreciation is charged on time basis.

Also prepare the Contractee's Account and show how these accounts would appear in the Balance Sheet as on 31st December, 2000.

Solution:

Contract Account

(for the period of 9 months from 1-4-2000 to 31-12-2000)

	₹.		₹.
To Materials	2,58,100	By Materials at site	25,400
To Labour	5,60,500	By Materials sold	4,000
To Foremen's salary	79,300	By P & L A/c (loss on sale of materials)	500
To Supervisor's salary (9 × 4,000 × 3/4)	27,000	By Value of Work certified (50% of 20 lakhs)	10,00,000
To Depreciation $\frac{2,60,000-15,000}{7} \times \frac{146}{365}$	14,000	By Cost of work not certified	2,62,250
To Admn. & Other Exp.	1,40,000		
To Total Profit c/d	2,13,250		
	12,92,150	Total	12,92,150
To P & L A/c (profit taken)	1,06,625	By Total Profit b/d	2,13,250
To Reserved Profit	1,06,625		
	2,13,250		2,13,250

Note : (1) Two-thirds contract was completed. Architect's certificate had been issued covering 50% of the Contract Price. That is 2/3—1/2 = 1/6 of the Contract was not certified.

Cost of 2/3 contract — 10,49,000

Cost of 1/6 contract — 1/6 × 3/2 × 10,49,000

= ₹. 2,62,250 Cost of work not certified

(2) 50% of the work has been certified. Hence the following formula has been applied for including the profit in the financial accounts to 31-12-2000.

$$\text{Total National Profit} \times \frac{2}{3} \times \frac{\text{Cash received}}{\text{Work certified}}$$

$$2,13,250 \times \frac{2}{3} \times \frac{7,50,000}{10,00,000} = ₹.\ 1,06,625$$

Contractee's A/c

	₹.		₹.
To Balance c/d	7,50,000	By Bank	7,50,000
	7,50,000		7,50,000

Balance Sheet

			₹	₹
P/L A/c (1,06,125 + 1000 – 500)		*Work-in-Progress:*		
		Value of work certified	10,00,000	
		Cost of work uncertified	2,62,250	
	1,06,625		12,62,250	
		Less: Reserved Profit	1,06,625	
			11,55,625	
		Less: Cash Received	7,50,000	4,05,625
		Materials at site		25,400
		Plant at site (2,60,000 – 14,000 – 5500)		2,40,500

Illustration 39: Paramount Engineers are engaged in construction and erection of a bridge under a long-term contract. The cost incurred upto 31.03.2001 was as under:

	₹ in lakhs
Fabrication	
Direct Materials	280
Direct Labour	100
Overheads	60
	440
Erection costs to date	110
	550

The contract price is ₹ 11 crores and the cash received on account till 31.03.2001 was ₹ 6 crores. A technical estimate of the contract indicates the following degree of completion of work:

Farbication: Direct Material—70%, Direct Labour and Overheads 60%, Erection: 40%.

You are required to estimate the profit that could be taken to Profit and Loss Account against this partly completed contract as at 31.03.2001. **[*CA (Inter)*]**

Solution:

Statement showing estimated profit to-date and future profit on the completion of the project.

[*₹ Lakhs*]

Particulars	*Cost to date*		*Further cost*		*Total cost*
	% completion to-date	*Amount (a)*	*% completion to be done*	*Amount (b)*	*(a) + (b)*
Farbication cost:					
Direct Material	70%	280.00	30%	120.00	400.00
Labour	60%	100.00	40%	66.67	166.67
Overhead	60%	60.00	40%	40.00	100.00
Total fabrication cost (A)		440.00		226.67	666.67
Erection cost (B)	40%	110.00	60%	165.00	275.00
Total cost (A + B)		550.00		391.67	941.67
Profit		92.48			158.33
Work certified		642.48	Total contract price		1,100.00

(*i*) *Profit to date and future profit*

Profit to-date (National Profit)

$$= \frac{\text{Estimated profit on whole project} \times \text{Cost to date}}{\text{Total cost}}$$

$$= \frac{158.33 \times 550}{941.67} = ₹. 92.48 \text{ lakhs}$$

$$\text{Future profit} = ₹. 158.33 - 92.48 = ₹. 65.85$$

(*ii*) Degree of completion of contract to-date:

$$= \frac{\text{Work certified}}{\text{Contract price}} \times 100$$

$$= \frac{₹. 642.48 \text{ lakhs}}{₹. 1{,}100 \text{ lakhs}} \times 100$$

$$= 58.40\%$$

(*iii*) When work certified is more than ½ of the contract price, but it is still not in the final stage, following formula is used to determine the figure of profit to be credited to profit and loss account:

$$2/3 \times \text{Notional profit} \times \frac{\text{Cash received}}{\text{Work certified}}$$

Estimation of profit to be taken to profit and loss account in a partly completed contract:

Profit to be taken to profit and loss account

$$= \frac{2}{3} \times \text{Notional Profit} \times \frac{\text{Cash received}}{\text{Work certified}}$$

$$= \frac{2}{3} \times ₹. 92.48 \text{ lakhs} \times \frac{₹. 600 \text{ lakhs}}{₹. 642.48 \text{ lakhs}} = ₹. 57.576 \text{ lakhs}$$

Illustration 40: *AB* contractors obtained a contract to build houses, the contract price being ₹. 4,00,000. Work commenced on 1st January, 1999 and the expenditure incurred during the year was—plant and tools, ₹. 20,000; stores and materials, ₹. 72,000; wages, ₹. 65,000; sundry expenses, ₹. 5,300; and establishment charges, ₹. 11,700.

Certain material costing ₹. 12,000 were unsuited to the contract and were sold for ₹. 14,500. A portion of the plant was scrapped and sold for ₹. 2,300.

The value of the plant and tools on the site on 31st December, 1999 was ₹. 6,200 and the value of stores and materials on hand ₹. 3,400. Cash received on account was ₹. 1,40,000 representing 80% of the work certified. The cost of the work done but not certified was ₹. 21,900 and this was certified for ₹. 25,000.

AB decided (*i*) to estimate what further expenditure would be incurred in completing the contract, (*ii*) to compute from this estimate and expenditure already incurred, the total profit that would be made on the contract, and (*iii*) to take to the credit of the profit and loss account for the year 1999 that proportion of the total profit which correspond to the work certified by 31st December. The estimate was as follows:

(*a*) That the contract would be completed by 30th September, 2000.

(*b*) That the wages on the contract in 2000 would amount to ₹. 71,500.

(*c*) That the cost of stores and materials required in addition to those in stock on 31st December 1999 would be ₹. 68,600 and that further expenses relating to contract would amount to ₹. 6,000.

(*d*) That a further ₹. 25,000 would have to be laid out on plant and tools and that residual value of the plant and tools on 30th September, 1999 would be ₹. 3,000.

(*e*) That the establishment charges would cost the same per month as in 1999.

(*f*) That 2.5% of the total cost of the contract would be due to defects, temporary maintenance and contingencies.

Prepare Contract Account for the year ended 31st December, 1999 and show your calculations of the amount credited to the profit and loss account for the year. **[*C.S. Inter*]**

Solution:

Contract A/c for the year ended 31.12.1999

	₹.		₹.
To Plant & Tools	20,000	By Cash (Materials sold at cost)	12,000
To Stores & Materials	72,000	By Cash (Plant sold)	2,300
To Wages	65,000	By Plant & tools on hand	6,200
To Sundry exp.	5,300	By Materials on hand	3,400
To Establishment charges	11,700	By Cost of Contract c/d	1,50,100
	1,74,000		1,74,000
To Cost of Contract b/d	1,50,100	By Value of work certified	
To Total profit c/d	46,800	(1,40,000 × 100/80)	1,75,000
		By Cost of work not certified	21,900
	1,96,900		1,96,900
To P&L A/c.	24,067	By Total profit b/d	46,800
To Reserved Profit	22,733		
	46,800		46,800

Note: Calculation of Profit

		₹.
Cost of contract during 1999		1,50,100
Add: Further expenditure to be incurred in 2000:		
Wages	71,500	
Stores & Materials on hand	3,400	
Further materials	68,600	
Plant & tools on hand	6,200	
Further Plant & tools 25,000 – 3,000	22,000	
Establishment 11,700 × 9/12	8,775	
Further expenses	6,000	1,86,475
		3,36,575
Add: Provision for temporary maintenance and contingencies 2.5% of 3,36,575		8,415
Total cost (estimated)		3,44,990
Contract price		4,00,000
Total estimated profit		55,010

$$\text{Profit transferred to P/L A/c} = \text{Total estimated profit} \times \frac{\text{Work certified}}{\text{Contract price}}$$

$$= 55{,}010 \times \frac{1{,}75{,}000}{4{,}00{,}000} = ₹.\ 24{,}067$$

ACCOUNTING STANDARD (AS - 7) (REVISED)
Accounting for Construction Contracts

Methods of Accounting

Percentage of Completion Method: Under this method, revenue is recognised by reference to the stage of completion of the contract activity at the end of each accounting period. The stage of completion may be measured in proportion the cost incurred to date bear to the estimated total costs of the contract. The costs incurred in reaching the stage of completion are matched with this revenue. Although as per principle of prudence, revenue is recognised only when realised, under this method, the revenue is recognised as the activity progresses even though in certain circumstances it may not be realised. Progress payments and advances received from customers will not be treated as revenue earned.

Normally, the profit is not recognised in fixed price contracts unless the work on a contract has progressed to a reasonable extent. This extent, ordinarily, is 20% to 25% of the work.

While recognizing profit under this method, an appropriate allowance for future unforeseeable factors, which may affect the ultimate quantum of profit, is generally made on either a specific or a percentage basis.

Provisions for Foreseeable Losses: When current estimates of total contract costs and revenues indicate a loss, provision is made for the entire loss on the contract irrespective of the amount of work done and method of accounting followed. Such provision will be made even if work has not commenced on the contract.

Claims under Construction Contracts: Amounts due in respect of claims made by the contractor and of variations in contract work approved by the customer are recognised as revenue only when the contractor has evidence of the final acceptability of the amount **of the claim or variation.**

Claims or penalties payable by the contractor arising out of delays in completion or from other causes are provided in full. Claims in the nature of contingency are treated in accordance with *AS-4*.

Disclosures: Following disclosures should be made in the financial statements:

(*i*) The amount of construction work-in-progress.

(*ii*) Progress payments received and advances and retention on account of contracts included in construction work-in-progress.

(*iii*) Amount receivable in respect of income accrued under cost-plus contracts not included in construction work-in-progress.

(*iv*) Changes in accounting policy giving the effect of change and its amount.

Illustration 41: A firm of contractors obtained a contract for construction of roads. The following details are available in the records kept for the year ended 31st March, 2000:

	(₹ in lakhs)
Total Contract Price	2,000
Work Certified (Cost)	1,000
Work not Certified	210
Estimated further Cost to Completion	990
Progress Payment Received	1,080

The firm seeks your advice and assistance in the presentation of account keeping in view the requirement of *AS-7 "Accounting for Construction Contracts"*.

Solution:

(*a*) *Amount of foreseeable loss*	*(₹ in lakhs)*
Total costs of construction (1,000 + 210 + 990)	2,200
Less: Total contract price	2,000
Total foreseeable loss	200

(*b*) *Contract work-in-progress i.e., costs incurred to date are ₹ 1,210 lakhs.*

Work certified	1,000
Work not certified	210
	1,210

This is 55% of total costs of construction (1210 × 100/2200) (*c*) *Proportion of total contract value recognised as revenue as per AS-7*

55% of ₹. 2,000 lakhs = ₹. 1,100.

Therefore, in the Profit and Loss Account for the year ended 31st March, 2000, a loss of ₹. 110 lakhs will be recognised, being the difference between the costs incurred and the revenue *i.e.*, (in lakhs) 1210 – 1100. AS-7 states that *a forseeable loss on the entire contract should be provided for in the financial statements irrespective of the amount of work done and the method of accounting followed.* Since the total forseeable loss is ₹. 200 lakhs, a provision of ₹. 90 lakhs (200 – 110) is required to be made.

(*d*) *Disclosure requirements* (*₹. in lakhs*)

(*i*) Work-in-Progress:	
Cost incurred till date	1,210
Less: Transfer to Profit and Loss Account as cost of sales	1,210
	Nil
(*ii*) Profit and Loss Account (Extract):	
Revenue	1,100
Less: Cost of Sales	1,210
Loss	110
Provision for loss on contract	90
Net loss including foreseeable loss	200
(*iii*) Balance Sheet (Extract):	
Debtors (*i.e.*, revenue recognised)	1,100
Less: Progress Payment received	1,080
	20

Illustration 42: From the following information in respect of a contract to construct a building for the year 2003-04, calculate the amount of foreseeable loss to be provided for in the financial statement and also show the disclosure requirements as per *Accounting Standard-7* on '*Accounting for Construction Contracts*':

	₹. ('000)
Total Contract Price	558
Cost incurred to date	404
Prudent estimate of costs to completion	293
Progressive payments received	374

Solution:

(*a*) Calculation of amount of foreseeable loss:

	₹. ('000)
Total costs of construction (404 + 293)	697
Less: Total Contract Price	558
Total Foreseeable Loss	139

(*b*) Contract Work-in-Progress *i.e.*, costs incurred to date are ₹. (000) 404, which is 58% of total costs of construction.

(*c*) Proportion of total contract value recognised as turnover as per AS-7 = 58% of ₹. (000) 558 = ₹. 324.

Therefore, a loss of ₹. ('000) 80 will be recognised in the profit and loss account for the year ended 31st March, 2004. This is the difference between cost of sales and turnover *i.e.*, (404-324).

Since total foreseeable loss is ₹. ('000) 139, an additional provision of ₹. ('000) 59 is required to be made in accordance with *AS-7*.

(*d*) Disclosure requirements:

(*i*) Profit and Loss Account (Extract)

Turnover	324
Cost of Sales (58% of total cost)	404
Loss	(80)
Additional Provision for loss	(59)
	(139)

(*ii*) Balance Sheet (Extract)

Debtors (included as turnover)	324
Less: Payments received	374
Excess payment to be shown as liability.	(50)

(*iii*) Work-in-Progress:

Cost incurred till dates.	404
Less: Transfer to Profit and Loss A/c as cost of sales	404
	NIL

Illustration 43: *ABC* Ltd. has undertaken bridge construction as per detail given below. The bridge will be constructed in 3 years:

(*a*) Initial contract revenue ₹. 900 crores

(*b*) Initial contract cost ₹. 800 crores.

	Years		
	Ist	*IInd*	*IIIrd*
Estimated contract cost	805		
Increase in contract revenue	—	20	
Estimated additional increase in cost	—	15	
Contract cost incurred up to	161	584	820

At the end of IInd year cost incurred includes ₹. 10 crores for material stored at the sites to be used in IIIrd year to complete the project.

Solution:

(₹. in crores)

	Year I	*Year II*	*Year III*
(*a*) Initial revenue agreed	900	900	900
(*b*) Variations	—	20	20
(*c*) Total Contract Value	900	920	920
(*d*) Contract cost incurred up to the date of reporting	161	584 (incl. 10 crores of Material)	820
(*e*) Estimated cost to complete (*f* – *d*)	644	236	—
(*f*) Total estimated contract cost	805	820	820
(*g*) Estimated Profit	95	100	100
(*h*) Stage of Completion (d/f × 100)	20% (161/805 × 100)	70% (584 – 10)/820 × 100)	100% (820/820 × 100)

Amount of revenue, expenses and profit recognized in statement of Profit and Loss Account in three years.

	Up to reporting date (A)	*Recognized in prior year (B)*	*Recognized in current yr. (A – B)*
Year I			
Revenue (900 × 20/100)	180	–	180
Expenses	161	–	161
Profit	19	–	19
Year II			
Revenue (920 × 70/100)	644	180	464
Expenses (820 × 70/100)	574	161	413
Profit	70	19	51
Year III			
Revenue	920	644	276
Expenses	820	574	246
Profit	100	70	30

QUESTIONS

OBJECTIVE QUESTIONS

1. *Examine the correctness of following statements*

1. Contractor has more probability of going into loss in cost plus contract.
2. Under cost pius contract, it is certain that final contract price will be paid.
3. In case of incomplete contract under contract costing, only a part of profit is credited to Profit & Loss Account.
4. Escalation clause in the contract provides that contract price is fixed.

[**Ans.** : True 3, Others are incorrect statement]

II. *Fill in blanks*:

1. In contract costing unit of cost is................. .
2. .... of the contract provides that under certain specific condition the cost price will be increased appropriately.
3. Loss of incomplete contract is transferred to ....
4. When contract is complete more than half, the formula of profit to be transferred to profit and loss account is ....

[**Ans.**: (1) Contract (2) Escalation clause (3) Profit and Loss Account (4) National Profit × 2/3; Cash Received/Value of work certified].

III. *State whether following statments are true or false, also give reason in brief.*

1. In cost-plus contracts, contractor runs a risk of incurring a loss.
2. Escalation clause in a contract provides that contract price is fixed.
3. In contract costing the contract which is complete one half of the total contract, one fourth of the profit should be trnasferred to Profit and Loss Account.
4. In contract costing, profit on each contract is computed when the contract is completed.
5. Cost of sub contract work is credited to contract account.
6. Work-in-progress certified and uncertified in a contract is valued at cost.
7. When work-in-progress certified is less than 25% of the contract price, it is a common practice to transfer 25% of the national profit to Profit and Loss Account.
8. The object of inserting escalation clause in contract is to safeguard the interest of contractor against unfavourable changes in cost over the period of the contract.
9. Cost plus contract protects the contractor from the risk of market fluctuations in the prices of material, labour and other.

[**Ans.** : (1) F, (2) F, (3) F, (4) F, (5) F, (6) F, (7) F, (8) T, (9) T]

IV. ***Fill in the blank spaces.***

1. In contract costing, work in progress certified is valued on the basis of ....and uncertified work is valued at ....
2. When cash ratio is 85% the retention money is ....
3. When 60% of the contract price is certified as work-in-progress, the profit to be credited to Profit and Loss Account will be equal to ....
4. The estimated profit is ₹. 60,000 and the contract is almost two third completed. If the case ratio is 90%, the profit to be transferred to Profit and Loss Account is ₹................. .
5. Progress payments in contract is based as a percentage of ....
6. Work-in-progress certified of a contract is 45% of contract price. Profit to be transferred to P & L A/c is.......................... portion of the profit.

[**Ans.** : (1) Contract price, Cost (2) 15% (3) 2/3 (4) ₹. 36,000 (5) Value of work certified (6) 1/3]

V. ***Multiple Choice Questions***

5. Select the correct answer in each of the following:

1. When a contract is not completed at the end of the accounting year, profit on incomplete contract is?
   (*a*) Transferred to Profit and Loss A/c
   (*b*) Transferred to reserve
   (*c*) Transferred partly to Profit and Loss Account and partly to work-in-progress.
2. For contracts which are very near to completion, amount of profit to be credited to Profit and Loss Account is ascertained by the following formula.
   (*a*) Estimated profit × work certified/contract price
   (*b*) Estimated profit × W.C. × Cash Received/contract price
   (*c*) Estimated profit × W.C. × Cost of work done/Contract price × Total Cost do date
3. When contract is 40%, complete, amount of profit to be credited will be:
   (*a*) The amount of profit estimated.
   (*b*) 40% of the estimated profit
   (*c*) 1/3 of the estimated profit multiplied by cash ratio.
4. In contract accounts, the account of work-in-progress consists of:
   (*a*) Cost of work certified
   (*b*) Cost of work uncertified
   (*c*) The amount of profit transferred to Profit and Loss Account.
   (*d*) (a) + (b) above
   (*e*) (a) + (b) and (c)
5. Cost-plus contract is usually entered into in those cases where:
   (*a*) Cost can be easily estimated
   (*b*) It is not possible to compute the cost in advance with a reasonable degree of accuracy.
   (*c*) Contractor wants to earn a higher amount of profit.
   (*d*) None of these
6. Contract price is not fixed in case of:
   (*a*) Cost-plus contracts
   (*b*) Escalation clause
   (*c*) De-escalation clause
   (*d*) All of the above.
7. Cost-plus contract is useful from the point of view of
   (*a*) Contractor
   (*b*) Contractee
   (*c*) both contractor and contractee.
   (*d*) None of these
8. In a building contract of ₹. 2,40,000, at the end of the year work certified is ₹. 1,60,000 and estimated profit is ₹. 15,000. What is the amount of profit to be credited to Profit and Loss Account assuming cash ratio is 80%.

(a) ₹. 15,000 (b) ₹. 12,000 (c) ₹. 8,000

9. In contract costing, valuation of which of the following does not include an element of profit:
(a) Work-in-progress certified (b) Work in progress uncertified
(c) Both (a) and (b) (d) Neither (a) nor (b)

10. A contract of ₹. 5,00,000 is 55% complete as certified. It shows a notional loss of ₹. 20,000. Accounting treatment of this loss is:
(a) Transfer 2/3 of this loss to P & L A/c
(b) Transfer 2/3 × cash ratio of this loss to P & L A/c
(c) Transfer 55% of this loss to P & L A/c.
(d) Transfer entire amount of loss to P & L A/c.

11. Which of the following items is not written in the credit side of the contract account:
(a) Work in progress - certified and uncertified
(b) Materials returned
(c) Cash received from contractee
(d) Plant at site

[Ans. : 1 (c), 2 (a), 3 (c), 4 (e), 5. (b), 6 (d), 7 (c), 8(c), 9 (a), 10 (d), 11 (c) **]**

THEORETICAL QUESTIONS

1. What is the Contract Account? What important points should be borne in mind in its preparation?
2. Explain the purposes which are served by Work-in-Progress Account. How will this account appear in the Balance Sheet?
3. Do you think it desirable to calculate profit on uncompleted contract? If so, to what extent and why? Explain the procedure to ascertain this profit.
4. What do you understand by cost-plus method of contracts? In what cases this method usually employed? **[*B. Com. (H) Delhi*]**
5. Describe the methods used for treatment of plant used on contract or Job in contract account.
6. Is it desirable to take into account the profit on uncompleted contracts in the Balance Sheet? If so, why and to what extent? **[*B. Com. (H) Delhi*]**
7. What items are included in the valuation of Work-in-Progress? How it would appear in the Balance Sheet?

SHORT ANSWER QUESTIONS

1. What is Job Costing ?
2. What is difference between Job and Contract ?
3. What do you understand by Contract Costing ?
4. What is meant by Cost-plus contract ?
5. What do you understand by Escalation Clause in contract costing ?
6. How profit is calculated on incomplete contract ?
7. How work-in-progress is calculated in the contract costing ?
8. How Contractee's account is prepared ?
9. Explain Work certified and work uncertified.
10. How profit is calculated for a contract which is nearly completion ?
11. How work-in-progress of a contract is shown in the Balance Sheet ?

SHORT ANSWER NUMERICAL QUESTIONS

1. Prepare a Contract Account from following:

	₹.
Direct Materials	20,000
Direct Wages	10,000
Depreciation on plant	2,000
Other overheads	8,000
Contract price	50,000

[Ans. : Profit ₹. 10,000**]**

2. Prepare Contract Account from the following:

	₹.
Materials consumed	30,000
Wages paid	40,000
Overheads	10,000
Value of work certified	1,00,000
Cash received from contractee	75,000
Total contract price	1,80,000

[**Ans.** : Total Profit 20,000 Profit tfd. to P & L A/c 10,000]

3. Calculate profit of the contract from following particulars

	₹.
Cost of work certified	80,000
Value of work certified	1,20,000
Cash received from contractee	90,000
Contract Price	2,00,000

[**Ans.** : Total Profit ₹. 40,000, Profit tfd. to P & L A/c ₹. 20,000]

4. Calculate contract profit from the following :

	₹.
Total Contract Price	1,80,000
Cash received from contractee (75% of value of work certified)	75,000
Cost of work certified	75,000
Cost of work uncertified	5,000

[**Ans.** : Total profit ₹. 25,000, Profit to P & L A/c ₹. 12,500]

5. From the following calculate profit to be transferred to P & L Account.
Total profit on contract ₹. 1,02,000, Value of work certified: 40% of the contract price.
Cash received: 75% of Value of work certified.
[**Ans.** : ₹. 25,500]

6. From the following calculate profit to be transferred to P & L Account.
Total profit on contract ₹. 1,02,000, Value of work certified : 60% of the contract price cash received : 75% of Value of work certified.
[**Ans.** : ₹. 51,000]

7. From the following, calculate value of work-in-progress:

	₹.
Value of work certified	50,000
Cost of work uncertified	20,000
Total Profit as per Contract Account	30,000
Cash Received 80% of work certified	

[**Ans.** : ₹. 56,000]

8. As per previous question, how work-in-progress will appear in the Balance Sheet.
[**Ans.** : Work-in-progress ₹. 56,000 Less Cash Received ₹. 40,000 = ₹. 16,000]

9. The contract price of a contract was ₹. 6,00,000. According to agreement, the contractor had to receive 75% of the value of work certified. The contract was completed in two years. The value of work certified at the end of first year was ₹. 3,50,000. Prepare Contractees Account in the books of the contractor.
[**Ans.** : Cash received 1 year ₹. 2,62,500 II year ₹. 3,37,500 which will be credited in the contractees A/c]

10. On the basis of above question, give journal entries in the books of the contractor.
[Ans. : I year Bank A/c Dr. To Contractee's A/c ₹. 2,62.500: II year Contractee's A/c Dr. To Contract A/c ₹. 6,00,000 and Bank A/c Dr. To Contractee's A/c ₹. 3,37,500]

11. From the following particulars, calculate contract-price:

	₹.
Direct Materials	30,000
Direct wages	20,000
Other Exps. on site	10,000
Office & Administration Exps	10% of works cost
Profit 20% of Total Cost	10,000

[**Ans.** ₹. 79,200]

12. From the following particulars prepare Contract Account for the year 2000, when the contract work was completed.

	₹.
Work-in-progress at the end of 1999	40,000
Cost incurred in the years 2000	
Materials	50,000
Wages	50,000
Special plant (Depreciation @ 10%)	1,00,000
Others Exps.	10,000
Contract Price	2,00,000

[**Ans. :** Profit ₹. 40,000]

13. Value of work certified by the architect of a contract was ₹. 1,00,000, While the total contract price was ₹. 2,00,000. As per the contractor 2/3 contract was completed at a cost of ₹. 1,20,000. Calculate cost of work uncertified.

[**Ans. :** ₹. 30,000]

14. From the following particulars of a contract which was 95% complete, calculate profit to be taken to P & L Account from the Contract Account.

	₹.
Total cost upto date	1,90,000
Estimated additional expenses to complete the contract	10,000
Contract Price	2,50,000
Cost of work uncertified	12,500
Value of work certified	2,25,000

[**Ans.:** ₹. 45,000]

NUMERICAL QUESTIONS

1. The following was the expenditure, on a contract, of ₹. 3,00,000 commenced in January, 2000.

	₹.
Materials	60,000
Wages	82,000
Plant	10,000
General Expenses	4,300

Cash received on account to 31st December amounted to ₹. 1,20,000 being 80% of the works certified, the value of materials on hand at 31st December was ₹. 5,000.

Prepare an account, showing position at the end of the year and the position of the profit which might reasonably be taken to Profit and Loss Account after allowing 15% for depreciation on plant.

[**Ans.** *Total Profit ₹. 7,200; Profit to P&L A/c ₹. 3,840.*]

2. Building Contractors Ltd. undertake contracts. On 31st October, 2009 when the actual accounts were prepared, the position of Contract No. 101, which was commenced on 1st January, 2009 was as under :

	₹.
Materials purchased	37,500
Materials in hand	1,500
Wages paid	43,750
Wages outstanding	625
Propotionate share of indirect expenses	1,875
Cost of Plant	6,250

The value of work certified was ₹. 90,000, of which ₹. 67,500 had been received work completed but uncertified was valued at ₹. 2,500. The contract price was ₹. 1,50,000. The plant on the site was valued at ₹. 5,000 on 31st October, 2009. Prepare Contract Account No. 101, after taking credit for profit which you think resonable.

[**Ans.** *Total Profit ₹. 9,000 Profit to P&L A/c ₹. 4,500.*]

3. A contractor undertook a contract for constructing a building. The contract price was ₹. 14,00,000 and the contract commenced on 1st January, 2000. During the year the following expenses were incurred over the contract:

	₹.
Materials issued from stores	10,000
Materials purchased	3,00,000
Labour	2,50,000
Indirect expenses	90,000
Plant	3,50,000
Materials returned to stores	20,000
Materials lost by fire	5,000
Materials at site 31-12-2000	15,000
Plant at site 31-12-2000	3,00,000
Work certified	7,00,000
Cash received from the contractee (80% of the work certified)	5,60,000

Prepare the Contract Account and Work-in-Progress Account and show how will Work-in-Progress appear in the Balance Sheet on 31-12-2000?

[**Ans.** *Total Profit ₹. 40,000; Profit to P/L A/c. ₹. 21,333 Work-in-Progress ₹. 9,96,333; B/S Work-in-Progress less Cash received ₹. 4,36,333.*]

4. Bharat Constructions Ltd. obtained a contract for the construction of arts faculty of a University at 10% less of the estimated cost amounting to ₹. 20,00,000. The work was taken up on 1st April, 2002. On 31st March, 2003 the expenses on the contract were as follows:

	₹.
Materials issued to the contract	3,60,000
Material at site	15,000
Wages	4,93,200
Plant & Machinery specially for contract (subject to depreciation at 10%)	60,000
Direct Expenses incurred	25,800
General overheads (share of the contract)	15,200
Cost of uncertified work	30,000

Up to the close of the year, total sum of ₹. 7,20,000 was received by contractors, being 80% of the amount payable on Architect's-certificate. Prepare the Contract Account showing the profit on the contract.

[**Ans.** *Total Profit ₹. 44,800; Profit to P/L A/c ₹. 11,947 being 1/3 of profit received*].

5. The following information is available in respect of a contract undertaken by a building contractor in 2003, the contract was for ₹. 4,00,000.

	₹.
Materials issued	75,000
Wages paid	1,10,000
General charges	4,000
Plant installed at site on 1st July, 2003	20,000
Materials at hand on close	4,000
Wages accrued and due	4,000
Work certified	2,00,000
Work completed but not certified	6,000
Cash received	1,50,000
Materials transferred to other contracts	4,000
Materials received from other contracts	1,000

Depreciation on plant is to be provided at 10% per annum. Prepare Contract Account and show what part of the profit on contract should be taken credit to P/L Account of 2003.

[**Ans.** *Total Profit ₹. 19,000; Profit to P/L A/c ₹. 9,500.*]

6. A Building Contractor took a contract for the construction of a certain building on 1st Oct., 2002. The contract price was agreed at ₹. 3,00,000. The contractor had made the following transactions during the year:

	₹.
Direct Materials purchased	20,000
Materials issued from stores	30,000
Direct Labour	30,000
Plant	80,000
Direct Expenses	20,000
	1,80,000

From the following further information, prepare a Contract Account for the year ending on 30th November 2003. Also show the amount of Work-in-Progress which will be shown in the Balance Sheet of the Contractor.

	₹.
Value of plant on 30–9–03	60,000
Stock of materials on site on 30–9–03	10,000
Materials returned to stores	2,000
Work certified by the architects	1,50,000
Cash received from the contractee	1,40,000
Cost of work not yet certified	8,000

[**Ans.** *Total Profit ₹. 50,000. Profit Transferred to P&L A/c ₹. 31,111. Work-in-Progress ₹. 1,39,111.*]

7. The following information relates to a contract work done by a firm of Engineers during the year ended 31st December, 2003.

	₹.
Work certified by the Architects	1,10,000
Materials issued	55,000
Wages	51,400
Plant installed at site	9,500
Value of plant at 31st Dec., 2003	7,200
Cash received from the contractee	1,00,000
Establishment charges	2,900

Cost of work not certified	2,200
Direct expenditure	2,100
Wages accrued due at 31st December, 2003	1,600
Materials in hand 31st December, 2003	1,300
Materials returned to store	500
Direct expenditure accrued due at 31st Dec., 2003	150
Contract Price	1,50,000

You are required to show the working of the Contract Account up to 31st December, 2003 in order to ascertain the profit or loss made thereon.

[Ans. *Loss transferred to P&L A/c ₹. 1,450***]**

8. Write up a Contract Account from the following particulars:

	₹.
Direct material	18,000
Wages	12,000
Special Plant	8,000
Stores issued	3,200
Loose Tools	1,500
Cost of Tractor:	
Running Material	1,000
Wages of Driver, etc.	1,600
Workmen's Welfare Expenses	1,200

The contract was completed in 20 weeks at the end of which period plant was returned subject to depreciation of 20% on the original cost. The values of loose tools and stores returned were ₹. 1,000 and ₹. 400 respectively. The value of the tractor was ₹. 19,500 and depreciation was to be charged to this contract at the rate of 20% per annum. You are required to provide Office on cost at the rate of 15% on Works Cost. The contract was executed at a profit of 20% on Total Cost.

[Ans. *Office on cost ₹. 6,030. Profit on Contract ₹. 9,246. Contract price ₹. 55,476***]**

9. A Firm of building contractors began to trade on 1st April, 2000, the following was the expenditure on a contract for ₹. 2,50,000:

	₹.
Materials issued to contract	45,000
Plant used for contract	20,000
Wages incurred	81,000
Other expenses incurred	5,000

Cash received on account to 31st March, 2001 amounted ₹. 1,28,000, being 80% of the work certified. Of the plant and materials charged to the contract, plant which cost ₹. 3,000 and materials which cost ₹. 2,500 were lost. On 31st March, 2001, plant which cost ₹. 2,000 was returned to stores, the cost of work done but uncertified was ₹. 1,000 and materials costing ₹. 2,300 were in hand on site.

Charge 15% depreciation on plant, reserve 1/3 of profit received as Reserve for Contingencies and prepare a Contract Account from the above particulars.

[Ans. *Total Profit ₹. 32,250, Profit transferred to P&L A/c ₹. 17,200 Reserve for Contingencies ₹. 8,600***]**

10. The following figures relate to two jobs of a contractor. You are required to prepare Contract Accounts for both the contracts and state what profit or loss (if any) should be brought to the Profit & Loss Account for the year 2003.

	Contract A ₹.	*Contract B* ₹.
Total Expenditure up to 31-12-2002	9,00,000	6,75,000
Wages (2003)	1,05,000	21,500
Materials and Haulage Hire 2003	1,57,500	7,500
Indirect Expenses	5,250	600

Plant which were originally charged at cost were valued at the close of the year at ₹. 2,50,000 and ₹. 3,75,000 respectively for Contracts A and B. The contract price for A was ₹. 12,00,000 and for B ₹. 3,00,000. The work in each case was actually finished on 30th November, 2003 but the contracts could not be considered as completed until the maintenance period of six months, as stipulated in contract, has expired on 31st May, 2004. The cost of maintenance is estimated at ₹. 5,000 for Contracts A and ₹. 3,500 for Contract B.

[**Ans.** *Contract A profit ₹ 2,77,250. Contract B Loss ₹ 33,100 after debiting maintenance charges*]

11. The following particulars relate to two house which a firm of builders had in course of construction under contract.

	House A ₹.	*House B* ₹.
Work-in-Progress on 1st Jan. (excluding ₹. 800 estimated profit which was taken to Profit and Loss Account of 2002)	14,000	—
Materials Purchased	23,000	16,600
Wages	20,000	14,000
Electrical Service and Fitting	1,400	300
Road Making Charges	8,000	—
Contract Price (including Road Making)	60,000	40,000
Cash Received to 31st Dec. 2003	60,000	24,000
Percentage of Cash Received to Work Certi.	100%	66⅔%
Value of Materials on hand on 31st Dec., 2003	400	540
Completed work not certified	—	2,500
Value of Plant used on sites	12,000	6,000
Period of Plant remained on site during the year	10 months	8 months

The total establishment exp. incurred during the year 2003 amounted to ₹. 12,240. These are to be charged to the two Contracts in proportion to wages. Depreciation of plant is to be taken into account at the rate of 10% per annum. Prepare the two Contract Accounts (in columnar form) showing the profit or loss on each house for the year 2003.

[**Ans.** *House A Loss ₹ 15,000; House B total profit 2,700 and Profit to P&L A/c ₹ 1,200*]

12. Three contracts beginning on 1st February, 1st June and 1st September respectively were undertaken by the Engineers Ltd., in 2003. Their accounts on 31st December, 2003 showed the following position :

	Contract No. 1 ₹	*Contract No.2* ₹	*Contract No. 3* ₹
Contract price	1,60,000	1,08,000	1,20,000
Work certified	80,000	64,000	14,400
Work uncertified	2,400	3,200	800
Materials	28,800	23,200	8,000
Wages	44,000	45,000	5,600
General Expenses	1,600	1,100	400
Cash received in respect of work certified	60,000	48,000	10,000
Wages Accrued	1,400	1,500	700
General Expenses Accured	300	200	100
Materials on hand	1,600	1,600	800
Plant	8,000	6,400	4,800

On the respective dates of the contracts, the plant was installed, depreciation thereon being taken at 15 per cent per annum. You are required to prepare (*a*) Accounts in the contract ledger, and (*b*) A statement showing the estimated profit on Contract No. 1, 2 and 3.

[**Ans.** *Total Profit Contract No. 1 ₹ 6,800, ₹ 3,400 of Profit of Contract No. 1 may be tfd. to P/L A/c; Contract No. 3 Profit ₹ 960; Loss in Contract No. 2. ₹ 2,760 Profit of Contract 3 need not be transferred to P/L A/c.*]

13. The following is a summary of the entries in the Contract Ledger as on 31st December, 2004 in respect of Contract No. 147 :

	₹
Materials (direct)	31,500
Materials (from stores)	6,825
Wages	18,250
Direct expenses	7,035
Establishment charges	8,400
Plant	35,800
Sale of scrap	1,975
Sub-contract costs	7,680

You obtain the following further informations:

(1) Expenses outstanding and not brought into account were : Wages ₹ 850; Direct expenses ₹ 1,175.

(2) Depreciation of Plant up to 31st December 2004 is ₹ 8,980.

(3) Included in the above summary of entries are : Wages ₹ 1,150; Other expenses ₹ 1,475 incurred since certification. The value of materials used since certificationi ₹ 2,180.

(4) Materials on site at 31st December, are valued at ₹ 10,500.

(5) . 65,600 had been certified up to 20th December, when three eight of the contract remained incompleted.

(6) The total contract price is ₹ 1,10,000.

You are required to show what profit or loss should be taken into accounts for the period ended 31st December, in respect of Contract No. 147.

[**Ans.** *Loss on Contract No. 147 ₹ 7,815*]

14. The following is a summary of the expenditure on Job No. 31 up to 31st December, 2005

	₹
Direct Wages	6,900
Direct Materials	34,000
Stores issued	3,800
Stores returned	550
Sub-contract cost	6,300
Plant	12,000

You obtain the following further information:

(1) The job was begun during 2005 and the total contract price is ₹ 60,000.

(2) The architects has certified that four-fifths of the contract had been completed at December 15th.

(3) Depreciation of plant up to December 15th, is ₹ 4,800.

(4) The summary set out above includes items relating to the period since December 15th, follows: Wages ₹ 700, Materials used ₹ 1,620.

(5) Materials on site at December 31st had cost ₹ 5,000 and stores on site had cost ₹ 400.

(6) Establishment charges are 40% on direct wages.

(7) A fine of ₹1,000 is likely to be imposed for late completion.

You are required in respect of Job No. 31 : (*a*) to prepare a Job Cost Ledger Account : (*b*) to show what profit or loss has arisen on the work certified; and (*c*) to suggest what figures should be taken to the Profit and Loss Account for the year to December 31st, 2005.

[**Ans.** *Cost of work uncertified ₹ 2600 Loss tfd. to P/L A/c ₹ 2,010 without debiting probable fine ₹ 1,000*]

15. A contractor who prepares his accounts at 31st December each year, commenced a contract No. 51 on 1st April, 2001. The costing records concerning the said contract yield the following information at 31st December, 2001.

	₹.
Materials charges out to site	25,100
Labour	56,560
Foremen	8,130

A machine costing ₹. 26,000 has been on the site for 146 days. Its working life is estimated at 7 years and its final scrap value at ₹. 1,500.

A supervisor, who is paid ₹. 800 per mensum, has devoted approximately one-half of his time to this contract. All other expenses and administration exps. amount to ₹. 13,650. Materials in hand at site on 31st Dec., cost ₹. 3,540.

The contract price is ₹. 2,00,000. On 31st December, two-thirds of the contract was completed; architect's certificates had been issued covering 50% of the contract price; ₹. 75,000 has so far been paid on account.

Prepare the Contract Account and state how much profit or loss should be included in the financial account to 31st Dec., 2001. **[*Kanpur B. Com*]**

[**Ans.** *Cost of work uncertified ₹. 26,225. Profit to Profit and Loss A/c ₹. 10,662.50.*]

16. The following figures are disclosed by the books of a contractor for the year ending 31st December, 2000.

	₹.	₹.
Work-in-Progress as on 31st Dec., 1999	1,70,000	
Less: Advances from contractee's as on 31–12–1999	1,10,000	60,000
Transaction during the year were:		
Materials supplied to contract directly by merchants		12,000
Materials issued from stores		21,000
Wages		17,000
Working expenses		3,000
Administration expenses (of which ₹. 500 are chargeable to general Profit and Loss Account)		2,500
Plant issued		5,000
Materials returned from contracts directly to merchants		900
Materials returned to store		1,100
Contracts finished		45,000
Work certified		30,000
Profit taken upon contracts		23,000
Advances from contractees'		80,000

Prepare the Contract Ledger Account and the Total Contractees' Account, and show how the Work-in-Progress would appear in the Balance Sheet as on 31st Dec., 2000.

[**Ans.** *Work uncertified ₹. 1,76,000; Work-in-Progress ₹. 2,06,000, Balance of Contractee A/c ₹. 1,45,000*].

Contract Account and Balance Sheet from Trial Balance

17. The following Trial Balance was extracted on 31st December, 2004 from the Books of Swastik Co. Ltd. the contractor:

	₹.
Share Capital : Shares of ₹. 100 each	3,51,800
Profit and Loss A/c on 1st Jan. 2004	25,000
Provision for Depreciation on Machinery	63,000
Cash received on account: Contract No. 7	12,80,000
Creditors	81,200

Land and Buildings (Cost)	74,000	
Machinery (Cost)	52,000	
Bank	45,000	
Contract No. 7		
Materials	6,00,000	
Direct Labour	8,30,000	
Expenses	40,000	
Machinery on site (cost)	1,60,000	
	18,01,000	18,01,000

Contract No. 7 was begun on 1st Jan. 2004, the contract price is ₹. 24,00,000 and the customer has so far paid ₹. 12,80, 000 being 80% of the work certified. The cost of work done since certification is estimated at ₹. 16,000.

On 31st Dec., 2005 after the above trial balance was extracted, machinery costing ₹. 32,000 was returned to stores, and materials then on site were valued at ₹. 27,000.

Provision is to be made for direct labour accrued and due ₹. 6,000 and for depreciation of all machinery at 12.5% on cost.

You are required to prepare (*a*) the Contract Account (*b*) A Statement of profit, if any, to be properly credited to Profit and Loss A/c for and (*c*) the Balance Sheet of Swastik Co., Ltd., as at 31st December 2004.

[**Ans.** *Profit tfd. to P&L A/c ₹. 78,400. Total of Balance Sheet ₹. 6,25,400*]

Contract Accounts of Several Years

18. Excellant Erections Ltd. took up a contract for the construction of a Building at a contract price of ₹. 15,00,000. During the first year, the following amounts spent as against which a sum of ₹. 5,62,500 which represented 90% of the work certified and received by the contractor.

	₹.
Materials	2,62,500
Wages paid to worker	1,50,000
Overhead expenses	37,500

During the second year, the firm spent the following amounts:

Materials	3,75,000
Labour Cost	3,00,00
Overhead Exps.	75,000

In the second year the contract was completed and a sum of ₹. 8,75,000 was received by the contractor. You are required to prepare the Contract Accounts and Contractees' Accounts for both the years and calculate profit.

[**Note:** Consider only 2/5th or 40% of the national profit to be taken to the credit of P&L Account in the first year as the work done is less than 50%]

[**Ans.** *Profit Ist yeat Total ₹. 1,75,000 Tr. to P/L ₹. 63,000 II year total profit 2,37,000.*]

19. The Contractors Ltd., undertook a contract for ₹. 4,00,000 on 1st July, 2002. The following expenses were incurred up to 31st Dec., 2002:

	₹.
Materials issued from stores	35,000
Materials charged direct	5,000
Direct charges	2,000
Wages	20,000

The amount of work certified was ₹. 80,000 of which the contractors received 75 per cent in cash. The transactions for the year 2003 were as under:

Materials issued from stores	90,000
Wages	40,000
Direct charges	4,000

The cost of special Plant and Machinery issued on 1st Jan., 2003 for the contract was ₹. 80,000. Further work certified during the year amounted to ₹. 2,20,000, 75 per cent of which was received. Work done and not certified as on 31st December, 2003, was valued at ₹. 15,000. Special Plant is to be depreciated at 25 per cent per annum on the original cost. Materials on site were valued at ₹. 10,000.

The contract was completed on 30th April, 2004, up to which date the following further expenses were incurred:

Materials issued from stores	40,000
Wages	15,000
Direct charges	1,350

General on cost each year is to be taken at 5 per cent of the amount of materials consumed and wages paid during the year. On 30th April, 2004, the plant was valued at ₹. 50,000; the materials at site were sold for ₹. 7,000 and those, returned to stores amounted to ₹. 13,000.

Prepare Contract Account and Contractee's Account showing the results of the transactions, assuming that the balance due from the contractee was duly received.

[**Ans.** *2002 Profit not taken; 2003 Profit transferred to P/L ₹ 50,000, 2004 Profit to P/L ₹ 76,400*]

Contract Near Completion

20. From the following particulars of a contract which has been completed 95% find profit and compare it with profit which might have been earned on the completion of the contract.

Total cost to date	₹. 1,90,000
Estimated additional cost	10,000
Contract Price	2,50,000
Value of work certified	2,30,000
Cost of uncertified work	5,000
Cash received	2,15,000

[**Ans.** *Total estimated profit on completion of the contract ₹ 50,000; Profit to P/L A/c this year 43,000 i.e. Total Profit × WC/CP × CR/WC.*]

21. Standard Ltd. contractors, commenced work on 1st January, 2003 on a contract of which the agreed price was ₹. 5,00,000. The following expenditure was incurred during the year to 31st Dec., 2003; Wages ₹. 1,40,000; Plant ₹. 35,000; Materials ₹. 1,05,000; Sundry Expenses ₹. 6,500; Head Office charges ₹. 12,500.

Certain of the materials, costing ₹. 10,000 proved unsuitable and were sold for ₹. 11,500 and a part of the plant was scrapped and sold for ₹. 1,700.

Of the Contract Price ₹. 2,40,000 representing 80% of the work certified had been received by 31st December. 2003 and on that date the value of the plant on the job was ₹. 8,000 and the value of the materials ₹. 3,000. The cost of work done but not certified was ₹. 25,000.

It was decided to estimated what further expenditure would be incurred in completing the contract, to computer from this estimate and the expenditure already incurred the total profit that would be made on the contract and to take to the credit of the Profit and Loss Account for the year 2003 that proportion of the total profit which corresponded with the work certified. The estimates were as follows:

(*i*) That the contract would be finished by 30th June, 2004.

(*ii*) That wages to complete would amount to ₹. 84,950.

(*iii*) That materials in addition to those in stock on 31st December, 2003 would cost ₹. 50,000 and further Sundry Expenses on the contract ₹. 3,500.

(*iv*) That a further ₹. 15,000 would have to be spent on plant and that the residual value of the plant on 30th June, 2004 would be ₹. 6,000.

(*v*) The head office charges to the contract would be at the same annual rate as in 2003.

(*vi*) That claims, temporary maintenance and contingencies would require ₹. 9,000.

Prepare Contract Account for the year ended 31st December; 2003 and show your calculation of the sum of credited to Profit and Loss Account for the year.

[**Ans.** *Total Profit ₹. 48,700 (up to 31st December, 03). Total estimated profit on completion of contract ₹. 50,000. Profit and Loss A/c ₹. 30,000.*]

22. A construction company undertook a contract at an estimated price of ₹. 108 lacs, which includes a budgeted profit of ₹. 18 lakhs. The relevant data for the year ended 31.3.2002 are as under:

	(₹. 000's)
Materials issued to site	5,000
Direct wages paid	3,800
Plant hired	700
Site office costs	270
Materials returned from site	100
Direct expenses	500
Work certified	10,000
Progress payments received	7,200

A special plant was purchased specifically for this contract at ₹. 8,00,000 and after use on this contract till the end of 31.2.2002, it was valued at ₹. 5,00,000. The cost of materials at site at the end of the year was estimated at ₹. 18,00,000. Direct wages accrued as on 31.3.2002 were ₹. 1,10,000.

Required:

Prepare the Contract Account for the year ended 31st March, 2002 and compute the profit to be taken to the Profit and Loss Account.

[**Ans.** *Percentage of contract completion is 92.53% profit to be taken to P/L A/c ₹. 12,00,000.*]

[**Hint.** Budgeted profit $\times \dfrac{\text{Cash paid}}{\text{Work certified}} \times \dfrac{\text{Work certified}}{\text{Contract price}}$

$= 1800 \times (7200/10,000) \times (10,000/10,800) = 1200$]

23. Rex Limited commenced a contract on 1.7.2000. The total contract price was ₹. 5,00,000 but Rex Limited accepted the same for ₹. 4,50,000. It was decided to estimate the total profit and to take to the credit of Profit and Loss Account that proportion of estimated profit on cash basis which the work completed bore to the total contract. Actual expenditure till 31-12-2000 and estimated expenditure in 2001 are given below.

Expenses	*Actuals Till 31-12-2000*	*Estimate For 2001*
Materials	75,000	1,30,000
Labour	55,000	60,000
Plant purchased (original cost)	40,000	—
Miscellaneous Expenses	20,000	35,500
Plant returned to stores on 31.12.2000 at original cost	10,000	25,000 (as on 30.9.01)
Materials at site	5,000	Nil
Work certified	2,00,000	Full
Work uncertified	7,500	Nil
Cash received	1,80,000	Full

The plant is subject to annual depreciation @ 20% of original cost. The contract is likely to be completed on 30.9.01. You are required to prepare the contract account for the year ended 31-12-2000.

[**Ans.** *Estimated Profit up to 30.9.01 ₹. 66,000. Total Profit up to 31.12.00 ₹. 58,500. Profit to be transferred to P/L A/c on 31.12.2000 ₹. 26,400*]

Process Costing

'Process costing is a method of costing used to ascertain the cost of production of each process, operation or stage of manufacture where processes are carried on having one or more of the following features (*i*) where the product of one process becomes the material of another process or operation, (*ii*) where there is simultaneous production at one or more process of different products, with or without by product, (*iii*) where, during one or more processes or operations of a series, the products or materials are not distinguishable from one another, as for instance, when finished products differ finally only in shape or form'.

There are a number of industries where:

(*i*) the final product emerges only after two or more process such as paper—the raw material, bamboo or sabai grass or any other, is made into pulp; pulp is made into paper and then it is finished, glazed etc. for sale;

(*ii*) the product of one process becomes the 'raw material' of another process or operation (for example, refined groundnut oil is the material for making vegetable '*ghee*') and

(*iii*) different products may have a common prior process (for example, brass goods will require melting of brass commonly for all goods). Another example is petroleum products produced by the same refinery.

A common feature is that production goes on without interruption and, normally, special production is not arranged for meeting any particular order. In a steel mill, for example, when a customer orders a certain quantity, no special arrangements will be made for him—his order will be executed out of the quantity produced in general. Thus, 100 tonnes of steel sheets of a certain size cannot be distinguished from the remaining quantity of steel sheets of that size.

Further, often important by-products are produced automatically at the end of each process. These by-products may have an importance almost equal to that of the main product. Consider kerosene oil, diesel oil, naptha and petrol which all are produced from the same crude oil, in addition to a host of smaller products.

In such industries the method of cost accounting used is known as Process Accounts. It may be possible to find out the total cost without distinguishing the cost of each process but it is not desirable to do so. Wastage and by-products of different nature may arise out of each operation or process. Each process is likely to entail different types of expenses. It would thus be advisable to find out the cost of each process or operation separately. Sometimes, it is possible to either process the materials ourselves or buy them ready for use in the next process. For instance, if one wants to market perfumed castor oil, one can buy castor seed and carry out all the processes—crushing, refining and finishing—or one can buy refined castor oil and add the necessary perfume and colour and bottle it and market it. The decision will depend upon the cost and the price prevailing in the market. This is another reason why cost of each process should be ascertained.

Definition

In his "A Dictionary for Accounts", *Eric L. Kohler* defines process as:

1. Any unbroken series of acts, steps, or events or any unchanging persisting condition.
2. Hence, the sequence of operations.
3. making up a plan of production, as on an assembly line; and continuous system involving an unbroken chain of activities
4. and a more or less continuous operation on constant output, as distinguished from a job order system of production".

Process costing has been defined by *Kohler* as:

"A method of accounting whereby costs are charged to processes or operations and averaged over units produced; it is employed principally where a finished product is the result of a more or less continuous operation, as in paper mills, refineries, canneries and chemical plants; distinguished from job costing, where costs are assigned to specific orders, lots or units."

Accounts can be kept, if desired, to show the cost of each job or order. It is possible, if it is insisted upon, to find out the cost of producing, say, 100 tonnes of oil ordered by somebody, rather than the cost of the bulk of the oil produced in a period. This involves the issue of requisition slips when the materials for the particular order are drawn, allocating the time of the direct workers for the particular order and allocating a proper share of the indirect expenses. However, since the oil produced against one order is not likely to be different from the bulk, it is unnecessary to ascertain the cost of each order. Accounts are maintained only to show the cost of the output as a whole.

The method is useful in the case of (*i*) metallurgical industries (like steel and aluminium); (*ii*) chemical industries (like plastics and drugs); (*iii*) food processing industries (like cheese, chocolates, etc.) and (*iv*) any other industry where there is continuous output involving two or more processes.

Difference between Process Costing and Job Costings

Job Costing	*Process Costing*
1. In job costing production is carried on by specific order.	1. In process costing production is a continuous flow and the products are homogeneous.
2. Costs are determined by Jobs or batches of products.	2. Costs are compiled on time basis *i.e.* for production for a given accounting period for each process.
3. Various jobs are separate and independent.	3. Processes are related to each other. Products also lose their individual entity.
4. In job costing unit cost of a job is calculated by dividing the total cost by units produced in the lot or batch.	4. The unit cost of a process, which is computed by dividing the total cost for the period into the output of the process during that period is an average cost (after adjusting opening and closing WIP) for the period.
5. In job costing, costs are calculated when a job is completed.	5. In process costing, costs are calculated at the end of period under each process.
6. In job costing there may not be opening or closing WIP in an accounting period.	6. Production in Process costing is continuous and therefore there is normally WIP at beginning and closing.
7. In job costing there is normally no transfer from one job to another. It will be only when there is surplus or excess production.	7. In process costing, transfer from one process to another is an usual feature.
8. In job costing each product unit is different and therefore more managerial attention is needed for proper control.	8. In process costing, production is standardised and stable the control is, therefore, easier.

PROCESS ACCOUNTING

Direct and Indirect Expenses

There is no departure from the principles regarding direct and indirect expenditure. Materials issued for a particular process are debited direct to it and so also labour engaged only on that process. If two or more processes are carried on in the same department, the department expenses will be Apportioned among the processes carried on there.

Apart from direct expenses, some indirect expenses—common to all process—are bound to be incurred. The salary of the works manager, for example, will have to be allocated to all the process. The normal practice is to do that on the basis of direct wages but that naturally would depend on the circumstances of each case. It is quite possible that a complicated process should absorb more indirect expenses.

The total of each process account less any work in progress is transferred to the next Process Account. The balance in the final process is transferred to the Finished Stock Account.

Illustration 1: Product X requires three distinct processes and after the third process, the product is transferrd to Finished Stock. You are required to prepare various Process Accounts from the following information:

	Total	*P1*	*P2*	*P3*
	₹.	₹.	₹.	₹.
Direct Materials	5,000	4,000	600	400
Direct Labour	4,000	1,500	1,600	900
Direct Expenses	800	500	300	–
Production Overhead	6,000	–	–	–

Production overhead is to be allocated to different processes on the basis of 150% of direct wages, Production during the period was 200 units. Assume there is no opening and closing stock.

Solution:

Process I Account
[Production 200 units]

Particulars	*Cost Per unit*	*Total*	*Particulars*	*Cost Per unit*	*Total*
	₹.	₹.		₹.	₹.
To Direct Materials	20.00	4,000.00	By Output Transferred		
" Direct Labour	7.50	1,500.00	to Process II	41.25	8,250.00
" Direct Expenses	2.50	500.00			
" Production Overheads	11.25	2,250.00			
	41.25	8,250.00		41.25	8,250.00

Process II Account

Particulars	*Cost Per unit*	*Total*	*Particulars*	*Cost Per unit*	*Total*
	₹.	₹.		₹.	₹.
To Output Transferred			By Output Transferred to		
from I	41.25	8,250	Process II	65.75	13,150
" Direct Materials	3.00	600			
" Direct labour	8.00	1,600			
" Direct expenses	1.50	300			
" Production Overhead	12.00	2,400			
	65.75	13,150		65.75	13,150

Process III Account

Particulars	Cost Per unit	Total	Particulars	Cost Per unit	Total
	₹.	₹.		₹.	₹.
To Output Transferred from Process II	65.75	13,150	By Output Transferred to Finished Shock A/c	79.00	15,800
" Direct Materials	2.00	400			
" Direct Wages	4.50	900			
" Production Overhead	6.75	1,350			
	79.00	15,800		79.00	15,800

WASTAGE AND BY-PRODUCTS

Normally in each process there is a residue left after transfer of the partially completed product to the next process. For example, in case of crushing of oil seeds, oil produced will be passed on to the refining process and oil cakes will be left. This is strictly speaking not wastage as it can be sold in the market. It is useful as a manure or as cattle feed. But the quantity of oil produced plus the quantity of cake left will not equal the quantity of oil seeds. It will be slightly less. The quantity not accounted for is a loss and effort should be to keep it as low as possible. The residue, if it can be sold in the market and if it can be used as a raw material for another finished article, is known as a *by-product*. In the process of converting coal into coke, useful by-products such as coal tar, sulphate of ammonia and benzol are obtained.

The treatment in accounts is as follows:

(*a*) If the wastage or by-products are sold in the market, the price realised should be credited to the process account in which the wastage or by-products arose. For instance, sale proceeds of oil cakes should be credited to the Crushing Process Account.

(*b*) If the wastage of each process is individually of insignificant value, wastage of all processes should be sold together and the sale proceeds credited to indirect expenses so that all processes reap the benefit.

(*c*) In some cases the residue or wastage is of such a nature that it can be reprocessed in the same process and then passed on to the next process. In that case the value of wastage should be the same as that of the materials introduced into the process. It will be shown as a balance to be carried forward in the same process.

(*d*) In some cases, the wastage is of such a nature that it has to be reprocessed in a previous process. In that case, the value to be put on the wastage will be that of the materials introduced in the previous process. Suppose, the 'wastage' to be credited to process *B* has to be put through process *A* instead of Process B and suppose the price of raw materials introduced into Process *A* was ₹. 2.00 per unit, the value of wastage to be credited to Process B would then be ₹. 2.00. This amount will have to be transferred to Process *A* Account for the next period or to Stores Account, if kept in stores.

Illustration 2: A particular brand of phenyle passed through three important processes. During the week ended 15th January, 2005, 600 gross of bottles are produced. The cost books show the following information:

	Process 1	Process 2	Process 3
	₹.	₹.	₹.
Materials	4,000	2,000	1,500
Labour	3,000	2,500	2,300
Dorect Expenses	600	200	500
Cost of bottles	Nil	2,030	Nil
Cost of corks	Nil	Nil	325

The indirect expenses for the period were ₹. 1,600.
The by-products were sold for ₹. 240 (Process 2).
The residue sold for ₹. 125.50 (Process 3).

Prepare the account in respect of each of the process showing its cost and cost of production of the finished product per gross of bottles.

Solution:

Process I Account
(Output 600 Gross Bottles)

Particulars	*Cost per Gross*	*Total Cost*	*Particulars*	*Cost per Gross*	*Total Cost*
		₹. P.			₹. P.
To Materials	6.6667	4,000.00			
To Labour	5.0000	3,000.00	By Transfer to		
To Direct Expenses	1.0000	600.00	Process No. II	13.6923	8,215.38
To Indirect Expenses	1.0256	615.38			
	13.6923	8,215.38		13.6923	8,215.38

Process II Account
(Output 600 Gross Bottles)

Particulars	*Cost per Gross*	*Total Cost*	*Particulars*	*Cost per Gross*	*Total Cost*
		₹. P.			₹. P.
To Transfer from			By Sales of		
Process I	13.6923	8,215.38	By-Products	0.4000	240.00
To Materials	3.3333	2,000.00	By Transfer to		
To Labour	4.1667	2,500.00	process No. III	25.3636	15,218.20
To Direct Expenses	0.3333	200.00			
To Indirect Expenses	0.8547	512.82			
To Cost of bottles	3.3833	2,030.00			
	25.7636	15,458.20		25.7636	15,458.20

Process III Account
(Output 600 Gross Bottles)

Particulars	*Cost per Gross*	*Total Cost*	*Particulars*	*Cost per Gross*	*Total Cost*
		₹. P.			₹. P.
To Transfer from			By Sales of Residue	0.2092	125.50
Process II	25.3636	15,218.20	By Finished Stock a/c	33.6492	20,189.50
To Materials	2.5000	1,500.00			
To Labour	3.8334	2,300.00			
To Direct Expenses	0.8334	500.00			
To Indirect Expenses	0.7863	471.80			
To Cost of Corks	0.5417	325.00			
	33.8584	20,315.00		33.8584	20,315.00

Illustration 3: The finished goods of a factory pass through three process known as *A*, *B* and *C*. The production of each process being passed on the next process. From the following figures show the cost of each process.

	Process A	*Process B*	*Process C*
	₹.	₹.	₹.
Materials	10,000	20,000	60,000
Wages	9,200	16,000	27,750
Works on cost	16,000	15,000	18,000
General on cost	9,800	10,750	12,000
	Units	Units	Units
Production for the month of July	36,000	37,500	48,000
Stock at beginning (1st July)	–	4,000	16,500
Stock at close (31st July)	–	1,000	5,500

Solution:

Process A Account

Particulars	*Units*	₹.	*Particulars*	*Units*	₹.
To Materials	36,000	10,000	By Transfer to Process		
" Wages		9,200	B Account		
" Works on Cost		16,000	(per unit ₹. 1.25)	36,000	45,000
" General on Cost		9,800			
	36,000	45,000		36,000	45,000

Process B Account

Particulars	*Units*	₹.	*Particulars*	*Units*	₹.
To Stock (1st July			By Stock (31st July		
@ ₹. 1.25 per unit)	4,000	5,000	₹. 1.25 unit)	1,000	1,250
" Process A			" Wastage	1,500	–
Account (Transfer)	36,000	45,000	" Transfer to Process		
" Materials		20,000	C Account (Cost per		
" Wages		16,000	unit ₹. 2.9467)	37,500	1,10,500
" Works on Cost		15,000			
" General on Cost		10,750			
	40,000	1,11,750		40,000	1,11,750

Process C Account

Particulars	*Units*	₹.	*Particulars*	*Units*	₹.
To Stock (1st July @			By Stock (31st July		
₹. 2.9467 per unit)	16,500	48,621	@ ₹. 2.9467 per unit)	5,500	16,207
" Process B			" Wastage	500	–
Account (Transfer)	37,500	1,10,500	" Finished Stock (Cost		
" Materials		60,000	Per unit ₹. 5.4305)	48,000	2,60,664
" Wages		27,750			
" Works on Cost		18,000			
" General on Cost		12,000			
	54,000	2,76,871		54,000	2,76,871

Note: Opening and closing units of Process *B* have been valued at cost per unit of output of Process *A*. Similarly opening and closing units of Process *C* have been valued at cost per unit of output of Process *B*.

Illustration 4: Mody Ltd. produces a patent materials used in building, in the manufacture of which three processes are involved. The materials is produced in three consecutive grades, namely, soft, medium and hard. Figures relating to production for the first six months of 2010 are as follows :

	Process 1	*Process 2*	*Process 3*
Raw materials used (Tons)	1,000	–	–
Cost of materials per ton (₹.)	200	–	–
Manufacturing Wages & Exps. (₹.)	72,500	40,800	10,710
Weight Lost	5%	10%	20%
Scrap (sold at ₹. 50 per ton)	50 Tons	30 Tons	51 Tons
The product is dealt with as follows:			
Transferred to Next Process	66-2/3%	50%	–
Transferred to Warehouse for Sale	33-1/3%	50%	100%

You are required to prepare an account for each process, showing the cost per ton of each process.

Solution:

Process I Account

Particulars	*Tons*	₹.	*Particulars*	*Tons*	₹.
To Raw Materials	1,000	2,00,000	By Loss in weight (5% of 1,000 tons)	50	–
To Mfg. Wages and Expenses		72,500	" Sale of Scrap (50 tons @ ₹. 50 a ton)	50	2,500
			" Transfer to Process 2 (66-2/3% of 900 tons)	600	1,80,000
			" Transfer to Warehouse 33-1/3% of 900 tons (Cost per ton ₹. 300)	300	90,000
	1,000	2,72,500		1,000	2,72,500

Process II Account

Particulars	*Tons*	₹.	*Particulars*	*Tons*	₹.
To Transfer from Process I	600	1,80,000	By Loss-in-weight (10% of 600 tons)	60	–
" Mfg. Wages and Expenses		40,800	" Sale of scrap (30 tons @ ₹. 50 per ton)	30	1,500
			" Transfer to Process III (50% of 510 tons)	255	1,09,650
			" Transfer to warehouse (50% of 510 tons) (cost per tons ₹. 430)	255	1,09,650
	600	2,20,800		600	2,20,800

Process III Account

Particulars	*Tons*	₹.	*Particulars*	*Tons*	₹.
To Transfer from Process 2	255	1,09,650	By Loss-in-weight (20% of 255 tons)	51	–
" Mfg. Wages and and Expenses		10,710	" Sale of Scrap (51 tons @ 50 per ton)	51	2,550
			" Cost of Production transferred to Warehouse (Cost per ton ₹. 770)	153	1,17,810
	255	1,20,360		255	1,20,360

llustration 5: From the following particulars, prepare a Statement of Cost per gross of "Black" and "Coloured" pencils:

Output during the year was "Black" 24,000 gross and "Coloured" 8400 gross.

	₹.		₹.
Raw Materials Factory:		Finishing Wages:	
Opening Stock	38,150	Black	20,000
Purchases during the years	1,07,100	Coloured	5,600
Closing Stock	49,400	Raw Materials Finishing:	
Factory Wages:		Opening Stock	7,200
Black	42,000	Purchases during the year	33,700
Coloured	13,650	Closing Stock	8,900
Factory Charges	37,100	Finishing Charges	19,200
		General Expenses	36,450

Raw materials in the factory and general expenses are to be apportioned in the ratio of output: Factory charges in the ratio of factory wages: Finishing raw materials and finishing charges in the ratio of finishing wages.

Also state what profit per gross is made if 'Black' is sold at ₹. 10 per gross 'Coloured' at ₹. 9.50 per gross.

Solution:

Statement of Process Cost

	Total	*Black Pencils (Output—24,000 Gross)*			*ColouredPencils (Output—8,400 Gross)*		
		Amt.	*Amt.*	*Per Gross*	*Amt.*	*Amt.*	*Per Gross*
	₹.	₹.	₹.	₹.	₹.	₹.	₹.
Factory Process;							
Raw Materials Consumed (20 : 7)	95,850	71,000		2.958	24,850		2.958
Wages	55,650	42,000		1.750	13,650		1.625
Factory Charges (40:13)	37,100	28,000		1.167	9,100		1.084
	1,88,600		1,41,000	5.875		47,600	5.667
Finishing Process :							
Raw Materials consumed (25:7)	32,000	25,000			7,000		
Wages	25,600	20,000			5,600		
Finishing Charges (25:7)	19,200	15,000			4,200		
	76,800		60,000	2.500		16,800	2.000
General Expenses (20:7)	36,450		27,000	1.125		9,450	1,125
Total Cost			2,28,000	9.500		73,850	8.792
Profit				0.500			0.708
Selling Price				10.000			9.500

NORMAL AND ABNORMAL WASTAGE

Elimination of wastage is important anywhere. In industries which are particularly fit for process accounts, each process causes some wastage and in order to see that, as a whole, it is not excessive, wastage in each process will have to be controlled. The figure for reasonable wastage for each process will be determined on the basis of past experience and by experiments in the laboratory and in the factory. This will be treated as '*normal*' *wastage* and anything over this figure will be treated as *abnormal' wastage*, anything below it will be treated as '*abnormal' effective or abnormal gain*. As pointed out in case of labour and materials, normal wastage is a part of cost of production but the value of the abnormal wastage or effective does not affect cost of production but will be transferred to the Costing Profit and Loss Account.

Abnormal Wastage: Suppose 100 units of an article are introduced in Process No. 1 and the total costs incurred in that process amount to ₹. 4,500. If normal wastage is taken to be 10 per cent, then 90 units ought to have been produced and the cost per unit would have been ₹. 50 (₹. 4,500/90). Now, if the output, actually, is only 85 units, we cannot take the cost per unit to be ₹. 4,500/85 or ₹. 53. We must calculate the value of 5 units wasted unnecessarily. That will be at the rate of ₹. 50 per unit. ₹. 250 will be debited to the "Abnormal Wastage" Account and credited to Process I Account and the amount to be transferred to the next Process Account will be only ₹. 4,500–250 or ₹. 4,250 and credited to process I Account for 85 units. In this way, the effect of abnormality will be separated from the normal cost of production which alone can reflect the change in efficiency.

Abnormal Gain : Sometimes it may happen that the actual loss in a process is less than the estimated normal loss or output is more than expected normal output. The difference is regarded as abnormal gain. It is debited to Process Account and credited to Abnormal Gain Account.

If in the above example 93 units were produced, the value of 3 units produced by extra efficiency will be similarly calculated, *i.e.*, at the rate of ₹. 50. ₹. 150 will be put to the credit of the Abnormal Effective Account and debit of Process Account. To the next process 93 units will be transferred and the amount will be ₹. 4,500 + ₹. 150 or ₹. 4,650.

Illustration 6: A product passes through two distinct Processes *A* and *B* and thereafter it is transferred to finished stock. From the following information, you are required to prepare Process Accounts.

	Process A ₹.	*Process B* ₹.
Materials consumed	12,000	6,000
Direct labour	14,000	8,000
Manufacturing exps.	4,000	4,000
Input in Process A (units)	10,000	
Input in Process A (value)	10,000	
Output (units)	9,400	8,300
Normal wastates percentage of input	5%	10%
Value of normal wastage (per 100 units)	8	10

Solution:

Process I Account

Particulars	*Units*	*Amount* ₹.	*Particulars*	*Units*	*Amount* ₹.
To Input value	10,000	10,000	By Normal loss		
" Materials		12,000	" (5% of 10,000		
" Wages		14,000	" @ ₹. 8 per		
" Manufactuing Exps.		4,000	" hundred units)	500	40
			" Abnormal loss	100	421
			" Transfer to Process *B*	9,400	39,539
	10,000	40,000		10,000	40,000

Process II Account

Particulars	Units	Amount ₹	Particulars	Units	Amount ₹
To Transfer value			By Normal loss		
Process A	9,400	39,539	(10% of 9,400		
" Materials		6,000	@ ₹. 10 per		
" Wages		8,000	hundred units?	940	94
" Manufacturing Exps.		4,000	" Abnormal loss	160	1,086
			" Transfer to		
			Finished Stock	8,300	56,359
	9,400	57,539		9,400	57,539

Working Notes:

(1) Cost of Abnormal Loss of *Process I*

$$= \frac{\text{Total Normal Cost}}{\text{Normal Output}} \times \text{AW units}$$

$$= \frac{(40,000-40)}{(10,000-500)} \times 100 = 421$$

(2) Cost of Abnormal Loss in *Process II*

$$= \frac{(57539-94)}{(9400-940)} \times 160 = \frac{57445}{8460} \times 160 = 1086$$

Illustration 7: (Abnormal Gain) The following particulars for process II are given

	Units	₹
Transfer to Process *II* and Cost	4,000	
Direct Wages		2,000
Direct Materials		3,000
Factory Overheads		4,000
Transfer to Finished Stock	3,240	
Direct Wages		2,000
Direct Materials used		3,000

Factory Overhead in Process is absorbed at a rate of 400% of Direct Materials. Allowance for Normal Loss is 20% of units worked. Scrap value is ₹. 5 per unit. Evaluate the cost of transfer to Finished Stock. Using the information supplied above, show the amount of loss or gain in the Process to be taken to Costing and Loss Account.

Solution:

Process II Account

Particulars	Units	Amount ₹	Particulars	Units	Amount ₹
To Transfer from					
Process I	4,000	9,000	By Normal Loss	800	4,000
" Direct Materials		3,000	" Transfer to next		
" Direct Wages		2,000	Process (@		
" Factory Overheads			(₹. 6.88 per unit)	3,240	22,275
(400% of Direct					
Material)		12,000			
" Abnormal Gain A/c	40	275			
	4,040	26,275		4,040	26,275

Alternative Method

Process II Account

Particulars	Units	Amount ₹.	Particulars	Units	Amount ₹.
To Transfer from Process I	4,000	9,000	By Normal Loss	800	4,000
" Direct Materials		3,000	" Transfer to Finished		
" Direct Wages		2,000	stock (@		
" Factory Overheads (400% of Direct Material)		12,000	(₹. 6.88 per unit)	3,200	22,000
	4,000	26,000		4,000	26,000
" Balance b/d	3,200	22,000	By Transfer to		
" Abnormal Gain A/c	40	275	Next process	3,240	22,275
	3,240	22,275		3,240	22,275

Working Note: In the Process *II* 4000 units have been introduced. The normal loss is 20% *i.e.* 800 units. The normal production should be 4000 – 800 = 3200 units. But actual production is 3240 units. Hence these 40 units abnormal gain will be valued at normal cost per unit and will be debited to Process II Account.

$$\text{Cost of Abnormal Gain} = \frac{\text{Nomal cost}}{\text{Normal output units}} \times \text{units of Ab.gain}$$

$$= \frac{26,000 - 4,000}{(4,000 - 800)} \times 40$$

$$= \frac{22,000}{3,200} \times 40 = 275$$

Normal Wastage Account

Particulars	Units	₹.	Particulars	Units	₹.
To Process II A/c	800	4,000	By Sales	760	3,800
			" Abnormal Gain A/c	40	200
	800	4,000		800	4,000

Normal Gain Account

Particulars	Units	₹.	Particulars	Units	₹.
To Normal Wastage A/c	40	200	By Process II A/c	40	275
To Costing Profit and Loss A/c	–	75		–	–
	40	275		40	275

Illustration 8: A product is obtained after it passes through three distinct processes. The following information is obtained from the accounts for the month ending January, 2004.

	Process I ₹.	*Process II* ₹.	*Process III* ₹.
Direct Materials	2,600	1,980	2,962
Direct Wages	2,000	3,000	4,000
Produciton Overhead	2,000	3,000	4,000

1,000 units at ₹. 3 each were introduced to Process I. There was no stock of materials or work-in-progress at the beginning or end of the period. The following additional data are obtained

	Output during the month (units)	*Percentage of Normal wastage in input*	*Value of Scrap Per unit*
	₹.	₹.	₹.
Process *I*	950	5%	2
Process *II*	840	10%	4
Process *III*	750	15%	5

Prepare Process Cost Accounts and Abnormal Loss or Gain Accounts. **[*Delhi B.Com. (H)*]**

Solution :

Process I Account

Particulars	*Units*	₹	*Particulars*	*Units*	₹
To Units introduced @ ₹. 3 per unit.	1,000	3,000	By Nomal Wastage (5% of 1,000 units: value ₹. 2 per unit)	50	100
" Direct Materials		2,600	" Transfer to Process II (Cost per unit ₹. 10)	950	9,500
" Direct Wages		2,000			
" Production Overheads		2,000			
	1,000	9,600		1,000	9,600

Process II Account

Particulars	*Units*	₹	*Particulars*	*Units*	₹
To Transfer from Process I	950	9,500	By Normal Wastage (10% of 950 units: Value: ₹. 4 per unit)	95	380
" Direct Materials		1,980	" Abnormal Wastage	15	300
" Direct Wages		3,000	" Transfer to Process III (Cost per unit ₹. 20)	840	16,800
" Production Overheads		3,000			
	950	17,480		950	17,480

Process III Account

Particulars	*Units*	₹	*Particulars*	*Units*	₹
To Transfer from Process II	840	16,800	By Normal Wastage (15% of 840 units: Value: ₹. 5 per unit)	126	630
" Direct Materials		2,962	" Transfer to Finished Stock (Cost per unit ₹. 38)	750	28,500
" Direct Wages		4,000			
" Production Overheads		4,000			
" Abnormal Gain or Effective	36	1,368			
	876	29,130		876	29,130

Abnormal Wastage or Loss Account (Process II)

Particulars	*Units*	₹	*Particulars*	*Units*	₹
To Process II Account	15	300	By Sale of Scrap @ ₹. 4	15	60
			" Costing Profit and Loss Account		240
	15	300		15	300

Abnormal Gain Account (Process III)

Particulars	Units	₹.	Particulars	Units	₹.
To Normal Wastage A/c @ ₹. 5	36	180	By Process III A/c	36	1,368
" Costing Profit and Loss Account		1,188			
	36	1,368		36	1,368

OIL REFINERY PROCESSES

Oil refineries have normally three processes: 1. Crushing Process, 2. Refining Process, and 3. Finishing Process.

Crushing Process

In this process raw material *i.e.* oil seeds or coconut or copra or kernels etc. are used. Other expenses of the process are debited. Sale of bags or sacks is credited. Oil cakes or oil residue are sold as a by-product. The output is crude oil transferred as input in the next process. There may be loss in weight in the process.

Refining Process

Crude oil from Crushing Process is debited. Other materials, wages and overheads of the process are debited. Loss-in-weight if any, is credited. The output is refined oil. Fats and residual oil may be obtained as by-products which are credited. The output being refined oil is transferred to the next process *i.e.* Finishing Process.

Finishing Process

Refined oil obtained from Refining Process is debited. Other materials wages and overheads of the process are debited. Sale of by-product and loss-in-weight are credited. Sundry sales of finished oil are also credited. The balance of this process is credited as cost of production of refined oil. Cost of drums or barrels or tins for storage of refined oil is also debited to find out cost of stored finished oil.

Illustration 9: In a factory the output passes through three processes to completion *i.e.*, Crushing Refining and Finishing. The details are given below for the month of May,

	Crushing ₹.	*Refining* ₹.	*Finsihing* ₹.
Wages	15,000	12,000	10,000
Power	6,000	5,000	3,000
Steam	2,000	1,000	500
Other Expenses	3,000	2,000	500

Copra purchased 3,000 kgs. costing ₹. 3,00,000. Crude oil produced 2,500 kg Refined oil 1,800 kg and finishing oil 1,760 kg.

500 kg crude oil was sold at cost plus 20% in Crushing Process. Copra residue 300 kg sold for ₹. 10,000 and sacks sold for ₹. 1,000. Wastage of 100 kg of Refining Process sold for ₹. 800. Casks cost ₹. 3,000. Oil stored in casks sold for ₹. 200 per kg. Prepare necessary accounts.

Solution:

Crushing Process Account

Particulars	Kg	₹.	*Particulars*	Kg	₹.
To Copra purchased	3,000	3,00,000	By Loss in Weight	200	–
To Wages		15,000	" Copra residue sold	300	10,000
To Power		6,000	" Sacks sold		1,000
To Steam		2,000	" Crude oil sold		
To Other exps.		3,000	Cost ₹. 63,000		
To Profit and Loss A/c			Plus 20%		
(Profit on			Profit ₹. 12,600	500	75,600
crude oil sold)		12,600	" Refining Process A/c		
			(Cost per kg ₹. 126)	2,000	2,52,000
	3,000	3,38,600		3,000	3,38,600

Refining Process Account

Particulars	Kg	₹.	*Particulars*	Kg	₹.
To Crushing Process A/c			By Loss in Weight	100	–
(output recd)			" Wastage sold	100	800
@ ₹. 126	2,000	2,52,000	" Finishing process A/c		
" Wages		12,000	(ouput transferred)		
" Power		5,000	Cost per kg		
" Steam		1,000	₹. 150.07)	1,800	2,71,200
" Other. Exps.		2,000			
	2,000	2,72,000		2,000	2,72,000

Finishing Process Account

Particulars	Kg	₹.	*Particulars*	Kg	₹.
To Refining Process			By Loss in Weight	40	–
A/c (Refined oil)	1,800	2,71,200	" Finished Stock A/c		
To Wages		10,000	(cost per kg		
To Power		3,000	₹. 162.67)	1,760	2,85,200
To Stream		500			
To Other Exps.		500			
	1,800	2,85,200		1,800	2,85,200

Finishing Stock Account

Particulars	Kg	₹.	*Particulars*	Kg	₹.
To Finishing Process	1,760	2,85,200	By Total Cost of casked		
(Refined oil)			finished oil c/d (cost		
To Cost of casks		3,000	per kg ₹. 163.75)	1,760	2,88,200
	1,760	2,88,200		1,760	2,88,200
To Cost of casked			By Sales @ ₹. 200		
finished oil (per			per kg	1,760	3,52,000
kg ₹. 163.75)	1,760	2,88,200			
To Profit and Loss A/c					
(Profit per kg					
₹. 36.25)		63,800			
	1,760	3,52,000		1,760	3,52,000

Note. 1. Loss in weight is balancing weight in each process.

2. Sale of 500 kg crude oil will have cost = (3,15,000 ÷ 2,500) × 500 = ₹. 63,000. The profit will be added @ 20%. The profit is debited to the Crushing Process.

Illustration 10: An oil company gives the following cost data. You are required to prepare various process accounts. Purchases: 1,000 quintals of copra @ ₹. 500 per quintal.

	Crushing ₹.	*Refining* ₹.	*Finsihing* ₹.
Cost of Labour	6,600	3,000	3,000
Electric Power	1,000	500	400
Sundry Material	700	200	–
Repair to Machinery and Plant	500	400	400
Steam	250	150	100
Cost of casks			580

Other Factory Exp. ₹. 9,450 to be charged at 75% of wages. Normal loss in 1st Process was 30% of input, actual output 690 quintals.

Process II, By-Product 90 quintals value ₹. 6,200.

Porcess III, Normal loss 5% actual output 580 quintals.

Scrap of 1st Process realised ₹. 10 per quintal.

Solution:

Crushing Process Account

Particulars	*Quint.*	*Amount*	*Particulars*	*Quint.*	*Amount*
To Copra used	1,000	5,00,000	By Normal loss (30% of 1,000)	300	3,000
" Cost of labour		6,600	" Abnormal Loss	10	7.300
" Electric power		1,000	" Crude oil transferred to next process (@ ₹. 730 per quint.)	690	5,03,700
" Sundry Material		700			
" Repairs to Mech. and Plant		500			
" Steam		250			
" Other factory exps. 75% of wages		4,950			
	1,000	5,14,000		1,000	5,14,000

Refining Process Account

Particulars	*Quint.*	*Amount*	*Particulars*	*Quint.*	*Amount*
To Transfer from Crushing Process	690	5,03,700	By By-products	90	6,200
" Cost of labour		3,000	" Refined oil transferred to finishing process (@ ₹. 840 per quintal)	600	5,04,000
" Electric power		500			
" Sundry Material		200			
" Repair to Mach. and Plant		400			
" Steam		150			
" Other Factory Exps. (75% of wages)		2,250			
	690	5,10,200		690	5,10,200

Finishing Process Account

Particulars	*Quint.*	*Amount*	*Particulars*	*Quint.*	*Amount*
To Transfer from Refining Process	600	5,04,000	By Normal Loss	30	–
" Labour		3,000	" Transfer to Finished Stock @ ₹. 895 per quintal	580	5,19,100
" Electric power		400			
" Repairs to Mach. and Plant		400			
" Steam		100			
" Factory Expenses (75% of wages)		2,250			
" Abnormal Gain	10	8,950			
	610	5,19,100		610	5,19,100

Finished Stock Account

Particulars	*Quint.*	*Amount*	*Particulars*	*Quint.*	*Amount*
To Finsihing Process	580	5,19,100	By Cost of Stored oil @ ₹. 896 per quintal	580	5,19,680
" Cost of Casks		580			
	580	5,19,680		580	5,19,680

Working Note:

1. Cost of abnormal loss in Crushing Process

$$= \frac{(5,14,000 - 3,000)}{(1,000 - 300)} \times 10 = 7,300$$

2. There is no wastage in the Refining Process.
3. In the Finishing Process, the input is 600 Qtls. and normal loss is 5% i.e. 30 Qtls, therefore normal production should be 570 Qtls. But actual production is 580 units. Hence there is abnormal gain of 10 units to be valued at normal cost per Qtl.

$$= \frac{5,10,150}{570} \times 10$$

$$= ₹. 8,950.$$

Illustration 11: (*Sales of By-Product*). In a Chemical Industry one product has to pass through two-process. The finishd product of the first process becomes the raw material of the last process. Find out the unit cost of the finished product of the last process per kg on the basis of the following data :

	First Process	*Last Process*
Raw Material	1,000 kg @ ₹. 1.50 per kg	
Direct Labour	200 men @ ₹. 2.50 per man	300 men @ ₹. 1.50 man
Works Overhead	50% of Direct Labour	50% of Direct Labour
Finished Product	600 kg	500 kg
Sales value of By-products	400 kg @ ₹. 1 per kg	100 kg @ 25 paise per kg

Solution :

First Process Account

Particulars	*kg.*	*₹.*	*Particulars*	*kg.*	*₹.*
To Raw Materials	1,000	1,500	By Sales of By-Product	400	400
" Direct Labour		500	" Transfer to Last Process (@ ₹. 3,083 per kg)	600	1,850
" Works Overhead		250			
	1,000	2,250		1,000	2,250

Last Process Account

Particulars	*kg.*	₹.	*Particulars*	*kg.*	₹.
To Transfer from First Process	600	1,850	By Sales of By-products	100	25
" Direct Labour		450	" Cost of Finished Product @ ₹. 5 per kg	500	2,500
" Works Overhead		225			
	600	2,525		600	2,525

Illustration 12: (*Salecs of By-Product at profit*). The following details are available from the books of a factory in which two processes are employed.

	Process A	*Process B*
Materials	2,000 tons at ₹. 50 per ton	—
Wages	₹. 60,000	40,000
Factory Overhead	50% Wages	30% of wages
Wastages	100 tons	200 tons
By-product	200 tons sold at cost plus 20%	200 tons sold at cost plus 25%

Solution :

Process A Account

Particulars	*Tons*	₹	*Particulars*		*Tons*	₹
To Materials	2,000	1,00,000	By Wastage		100	–
" Wages		60,000	" Sale of By Product			
" Factory Overhead		30,000	Cost	20,000		
" Profit on Sale or By-product		4,000	*Add*: 20%	4,000	200	24,000
			" Transfer to Process B A/c (@ ₹. 100 per ton)		1,700	1,70,000
	2,000	1,94,000			2,000	1,94,000

Calculations

1. Cost per ton = [1,00,000 + 60,000 + 30,000] / [2,000 – 100] = ₹. 100 (*i.e.* Total Cost/Total tons produced)
2. Cost of By-product [200 tons] = 200 × 100 = ₹. 20,000
3. Profit on By-product 20% on ₹. 20,000 = ₹. 4,000.

Process B Account

Particulars	*Tons*	₹	*Particulars*		*Tons*	₹
To Process *A* A/c	1,700	1,70,000	By Wastage		200	–
" Wages		40,000	" Sale of By-product			
" Factory Overhead		12,000	Cost	29,600		
" Profit on Sale Sale of By-product		7,400	*Add*: 25%	7,400	200	37,000
			" Transfer to Finished Stock A/c (@ ₹. 148 per ton)		1,300	1,92,400
	1,700	2,29,400			1,700	2,29,400

Calculations

1. Cost per ton = (1,70,000 + 40,000 + 12,000)/(1,700 – 200) = ₹. 148
2. Cost of By-Product 200 Tons = 200 × ₹. 148 = ₹. 29,600
3. Profit on By-Product 25% on ₹. 29,600 = ₹. 7,400.

Illustration 13: A certain chemical process yields 75% of the materials introduced as main product, 20% as a by-product, 5% being lost. The percentage of materials consumed by main product and By-product is 80 : 20. Time taken to product one unit of by-product is half the time taken by main product. Overheads have been allocated at 200% of wages of each product.

During the period, 2,000 units of raw materials at a cost of ₹. 10,000 were introduced, labour totalled ₹. 8,500 overheads came to ₹. 17,000. Ascertain the cost of two products.

Solution :

Total number of units produced:

2,000 × 75% = 1,500 units of Main Product

2,000 × 20% = 400 units of By-product

2000 × 5% = 100 units Wastage

Statement of Apportionment of Cost

	Ratio	Total Cast	*Main Product (1,500)*		*By Product (400)*	
			Amount	*Cost per Units ₹.*	*Amount ₹.*	*₹. Per Unit ₹.*
Material	80 : 20	10,000	8,000	5.33	2,000	5.00
Labour	15 : 2	8,500	7,500	5.00	1,000	2.50
Overheads	200% of wages	17,000	15,000	10.00	2,000	5.00
		35,500	30,500	20.33	5,000	12.50

Working Notes:

1. Materials should be divided as to 20% to By-product and rest to the Main Product *i.e.* 80%. But production units will be Main Product 75% of 2,000 *i.e.* 1,500 and By-product 20% of 2,000 *i.e.*, 400 units.
2. Labour will be allocated in the ratio 1,500 × 1 : 400 × 1/2 *i.e.*, 1,500 : 200 or 15 : 2.

WORK-IN-PROGRESS AND EQUIVALENT PRODUCTION

It would be rare to find that there are no partly finished units in a process of manufacture. There is always some quantity of partly finished units or work-in-process or work-in-progress. The valuation of work-in-progress presents good deal of difficulty because there are units in various stages of completion—from those on which work has just begun to those which are only a step short of completion. Work-in-process can be valued on actual basis, i.e., an attempt may be made to find out how much materials have been used on the unfinished units and how much actual amount of labour and expenses has been spent on them. But the degree of accuracy cannot be always satisfactorily ascertained. An alternative method is to *convert partly finished units into equivalent finished units*. For instance if 25% work has been done on the average on units still in process then 120 such units will be equal to 30 completed units. The cost of the work-in-progress will be equal to the cost of 30 finished units. This is known as the concept of equivalent production or equivalent units.

The technique of calculating *equivalent production* is below:

1. Firstly the opening incomplete or work-in-progress units should be converted into equivalent units as complete. For example opening. WIP is 600 units which are 60% complete, therefore only 40% work is to be done on these units in the process. Thus on these units a cost of 600 × 40% = 240 units will be incurred in the process to complete these.

2. To above units, add units started and finished during the period or units completed in the process. These will be new units introduced less closing units and units scrapped.

3. Thereafter, add equivalent units of closing units.

4. The total of all these will be equivalent production. Following illustrations explain this technique.

Valuation of Work-in-Progress under FIFO Method

Under this method it is assumed that new units issued to the work-in-progress pass through the finished goods on the *FIFO* basis which means that unfinished work in the opening stock is completed first and thereafter new units introduced in the process are taken up. This method is suitable when prices of raw materials and rates of direct labour and overheads are relatively stated. The cost-added in each process during the period is pro-rated to the production necessary to complete the opening work-in-process, to complete the units introduced and completed during the period and to partially completed units in the closing work-in-Progress. Thus closing stock is valued at current cost.

Illustration 14: (*Valuation of Equivalent Product*): From the following find out (*a*) Equivalent Production (*b*) Cost per unit of Equivalent Production and (*c*) Prepare Process A Account. Assume there is no opening work-in-progress and process loss.

Input	1,900 units
Output	1,500 units
Closing work-in-progress	400 units

	Degree of Completion of Closing WIP	*Process Costs of the Current Period*
		₹
Materials	80%	3,640
Labour	70%	5,340
Overheads	70%	3,560

Solution :

(*a*) Statement of Equivalent Production

Input		*Output*		*Equivalent Production*					
				Material		*Labour*		*Overhead*	
Items	*Units*	*Items*	*Units*	*%*	*Units*	*%*	*Units*	*%*	*Units*
Units Introduced	1,900	Units Completed	1,500	100	1,500	100	1,500	100	1,500
		Work-in-Progress	400	80	320	70	280	70	280
	1,900		1,900		1,820		1,780		1,780

(*b*) Statement of Cost

Element of Cost	*Cost*	*Equivalent Production units*	*Cost per unit*
Materials	3,640	1,820	2.00
Labour	5,340	1,780	3.00
Overheads	3,560	1,780	2.00

(c) Statement of Evaluation (Cost per unit)

Production	*Element of Cost*	*Equivalent Production units*	*Cost per unit*	*Cost*	*Total Cost*
Finished	Material	1,500	2	3,000	
	Labour	1,500	3	4,500	
	Overheads	1,500	2	3,000	10,500
Work-in-Progress	Material	320	2	640	
	Labour	280	3	840	
	Overheads	280	2	560	2,040

Process Account

	Units	*Amount*		*Units*	*Amount*
To Materials	1,900	3,640	By Finished Stock A/c	1,500	10,500
To Labour		5,340	By Work-in-progress	400	2,040
To Overheads		3,560			
	1,900	12,540		1,900	12,540

Illustration 15 : [*Valuation of Equivalent Product*] Compute the equivalent production for the month of May, from the following data relating to the manufacture of a product.

Opening inventory of work-in-progress 300 units	Materials	30%
Stage of Completion:	Labour	40%
	Overheads	50%
Number of units put into the process		10,000 units
Transferred to next process		9,600 units
Closing inventory of work-in-progress		700 units
Stage of Completion:	Materials	80%
	Labour	75%
	Overheads	60%

Solution:

Statement of Equivalent Production

Input		*Output*		*Equivalent Production*					
				Material		*Labour*		*Overhead*	
Items	*Units*	*Items*	*Units*	*%*	*Units*	*%*	*Units*	*%*	*Units*
Opening Stock	300	Opening stock (completed)	300	70	210	60	180	50	150
Units put into Process	10,000	Completely Processed during the period	9,300	100	9,300	100	9,300	100	9,300
		Work-in-Progress at the end	700	80	560	75	525	60	420
	10,300		10,300		10,070		10,005		9,870

Working Note:

1. Opening stock 300 incomplete units are complete 30% as to material 40% as to labour and 60% as to overheads. These units are to be completed by incuring material equal to 300 × 70% *i.e.*

units, wages equal to 300 × 60% *i.e.* ,180 units and overheads equal to 40% of 300 *i.e.* 120 units.

2. In case of closing incomplete units, there will be considered equal to work done *i.e.* Materials 700 × 80% = 560 units, wages 700 × 75% = 525 units and overheads 700 × 60% = 420 units.
3. Units transferred to next process are 9,600 units which include 300 opening incomplete units. It means 9,300, new units will be completed.

Normal Losses, Abnormal Losses and Abnormal gain

Normal losses are considered as a part of cost of good prduction, it is not charged to closing WIP. Only the scrap realised from such units will be deducted from the cost of Raw Material. Thus while computing equivalent units, normal losses are ignored and the cost of the normal loss will be automatically apportioned to the units produced when it is deducted form cost of Raw Materials.

When there is abnormal loss, these units should be valued at their cost at stage of completion *i.e.*, at their equivalent units (If stage of competion is not given, these may be taken at 100% complete). The abnormal loss is charged to a seperate account and written off as a period cost to the Profit and Loss Account after deducting scrap value of such units.

Abnormal Gain. If there is abnormal gain, it will always be valued at 100% cost

Illustration 16: From the following data calculate: (*a*) Equivalent Production and (*b*) Cost per unit of finished production.

Units introduced in the process	4,000
Units completed and transferred to next process	3,000
Units in process at the end	800
(Stage of completion: Materials 80%; Labour and Overheads 70%)	
Normal process loss (units)	200
Value of scrap per unit	₹. 10
Cost of Raw Materials	₹. 74,800
Wages	₹. 1,06,800
Overheads	₹. 71,200

Solution :

(*a*) Statement of Equivalent Production

Input		*Output*		*Equivalent Production*			
Particulars	*Units*	*Particulars*	*Total Units*	*As regards materials*		*As regards labour and overheads*	
				Stage of completion	*No. of units*	*Stage of completion*	*No.of units*
Units Introduced in the process	4,000	Completed and transferred to next process	3,000	100%	3,000	100%	3,000
		Closing Stock	800	80%	640	70%	560
		Normal Loss	200	—	—	—	—
Total	4,000	Total	4,000				
		Total equivalent completed units			3,640		3,560

(b) Statement of Cost

Elements of Cast	*Cost* ₹.	*Equivalent Production Units*	*Cost per Units* ₹.
Materials	74,800		
Less: Value of scrap 200 units @ ₹. 10	2,000		
(Normal Loss)	72,800	3,640	20
Wages	1,06,800	3,560	30
Overheads	71,200	3,560	20
Total	2,50,800	–	70

Illustration 17: In a process costing system, the following details relate to the month of January, 2004.

Opening stock	1,500 units valued at ₹. 2,325
Degree of their completion:	
Materials	80%
Labour	60%
Overheads	60%
Transfer from pervious process	12,500 units:
Value ₹.	₹. 12,080
Transfer to next process	12,000 units;
Materials added in process	Nil
Labour "	₹. 6,030
Overheads "	₹. 9,045
Units scrapped	800 units;
Value realised	₹. 200
Closing stock	1,200 units
Degree of their completion:	
Materials	90%
Labour	80%
Overhead	80%

You are required to work out: (1) Equivalent Production; (2) Cost Statement showing cost per unit; (3) Process Evaluation Statement showing the value of opening stock and closing stock; and (4) Process Cost Account.

Solution:

Process Cost Account

Particulars	*Units*	₹.	*Particulars*	*Units*	₹.
To Opening stock	1,500	2,325	By Units scrapped	800	200
" Transferred from earlier process	12,500	12,080	" Transferred to next process @ ₹. 2.25 per unit	12,000	27,000
" Labour		6,030	" Closing stock	1,200	2,280
" Overheads		9,045			
	14,000	29,480		14,000	29,480

Note: Various costs have been calculated as below:

(1) Statement Showing Equivalent Production

Input		Output		Material		Labour		Overheads	
Items	*Units*	*Items*	*Units*	*%*	*Units*	*%*	*Units*	*%*	*Units*
Opening stock	1,500	Opening stock	1,500	20	300	40	600	40	600
From Previous Process	12,500	Units Scrapped (Normal Loss)	800		–		–		–
		Units Completed (1200 – 1500)	10,500	100	10,500	100	10,500	100	10,500
		Closing Stock	1,200	90	1,080	80	960	80	960
	14,000	Equivalent Production	14,000		11,880		12,060		12,060

(2) Cost Statement Showing Cost per unit

Cost	₹	₹	*Equivalent Production* Units	*Cost per Units* ₹
Materials transferred from previous process	12,080			
Less: Value of scrap (NL)	200	11,880	11,880	1.00
Labour		6,030	12,060	0.50
Overheads		9,045	12,060	0.75
		26,955		2.25

(3) Process Evaluation Statement

Cost	*Equivalent Production* ₹	*Cost per Unit* ₹	*Cost* ₹	*Total Cost* ₹
Opening Stock:				
Materials	300	1.00	300	
Labour	600	0.50	300	
Overheads	600	0.75	450	1,050
Units completed during the month:				
Materials	10,500	1.00	10,500	
Labour	10,500	0.50	5,250	
Overheads	10,500	0.75	7,875	23,625
Closing Stock:				
Materials	1,080	1.00	1,080	
Labour	960	0.50	480	
Overheads	960	0.75	720	2,280
				26,955

Illustration 18: During a particular month 2,000 units at a cost of ₹ 60,000 were introduced into Process 1. The normal loss was estimated at 5% of input. At the end of the month, 1,400 units had been produced and transferred to the next process, 460 units were partially completed and 140 units had been scrapped.

It was estimated that in respect of various factors of production, the partially complete units had reached the following stage of production.

Materials	100% Complete
Labour	50% Complete
Overheads	50% Complete
Additional costs incurred during the month were:	₹.
Materials	17,000
Direct Wages	33,400
Production Overheads	16,700

The units scrapped realised ₹. 10 each. You are required to prepare Process Accounts and the statements which you consider necessary for the preparation of the Process Account.

Solution:

Statement of Equivalent Production

Input units	*Particulars*	*Output units*	*Equivalent Production*					
			Materials		*Labour*		*Overheads*	
			Units	*%*	*Units*	*%*	*Units*	*%*
2,000	Normal Loss	100	–	–	–	–	–	–
	Abnormal Loss	40	40	100	40	100	40	100
	Finished Units	1,400	1,400	100	1,400	100	1,400	100
	Work-in-Progress	460	460	100	230	50	230	50
2,000	Equivalent Production		1,900		1,670		1,670	

Statement of Cost

Elements of Cost	*Cost* ₹.	*Equivalent Production Units*	*Cost per equivalent Units* ₹.
1. Direct Materials	60,000		
Add: Additional Materials	17,000		
	77,000		
Less: Scrap value realised from normal loss (₹. 10 × 100 units)	1,000		
	76,000	1,900	40.00
2. Labour	33,400	1,670	20.00
3. Overhead	16,700	1,670	10.00
	1,26,100		70.00

Statement of Equivalent Cost

Production	*Elements of cost*	*Equivalent Production Units*	*Cost Per Unit (₹.)*	*Cost* ₹.	*Total (₹.)*
Abnormal Loss	Material	40	40	1600	
	Labour	40	20	800	
	Overhead	40	10	400	2,800
Finished Production	Material	1400	40	56,000	
	Labour	1400	20	28,000	
	Overhead	1400	10	14,000	98,000
Work-in-Progress	Materials	460	40	18,400	
	Labour	230	20	4,600	
	Overhead	230	10	2,300	25,300

Process I Account

	Units	₹.		Units	₹.
To Units introduced	2,000	60,000	By Normal Loss (5%)100	1,000	
To Material		17,000	By Abnormal Loss	40	2,800
To Labour		33,400	By Process 2 A/c	1,400	98,000
To Overhead		16,700	By Balance (W-in-P)460	25,300	
	2,000	1,27,100		2,000	1,27,100

Normal Loss Account

To Process 1 A/c	100	1,000	By Bank	100	1,000

Abnormal Loss Account

To Process 1 A/c	40	2,800	By Bank @ ₹. 10	40	400
			By Costing P & L A/c—	2,400	
	40	2,800		40	2,800

Material I and Material II

Cost of units transferred from previous process is considered as Material I. Material II is further materials used in the process. Opening WIP will not be charged by Material I (since already included in the previous period). Completed units, closing WIP and Abnormal Loss units will be charged 100% by Material I, Material II, Labour and overheads will be charged by given Level of completion.

Abnormal Gain

If actual loss is less than normal loss, the difference will be abnormal gain. These units will be always valued as 100% complete.

Illustration 19: The following information is obtained in respect of Process *B* for the month January.

Opening stock 1,200 units ₹.. 2,100.

Degree of completion : Materials 80%; Labour 60% and Overheads 60%

Transfer from Process *A* 22,000 units ₹. 11,000

Transfer to Process *C* 17,600 units.

Direct Materials added in process ₹. 4,820.

Direct Labour ₹. 14,310.

Production overheads ₹. 19,080.

Units scrapped : 2,400 units.

Degree of completion; Materials 100%; Labour 70%, Overheads 70%

Closing Stock 3,200 units.

Degree of completion; Materials 70%; Labour 60%; Overheads 60%.

Normal Loss – 10% of production.

Units scrapped realised 50 paise per unit.

Solution:

(*a*) Process *B* Statement of Equivalent Production

Input		*Output*		*Equivalent Production Units*							
Particulars	*Units*	*Particulars*	*Units*	*Materials I*		*Materials II*		*Labour*		*Overheads*	
				%	*Units*	%	*Units*	%	*Units*	%	*Units*
Opening stock	1,200	Opening stock (now completed)	1,200	–	–	20	240	40	480	40	480
Process A	22,000	Units processed completely during the period	16,400	100	16,400	100	16,400	100	16,400	100	16,400
		Normal Loss	2,000	–	–	–	–	–	–	–	–
		Abnormal Loss	400	100	400	100	400	70	280	70	280
		Closing stock	3,200	100	3,200	70	2,240	60	1,920	60	1,920
	23,200		23,200								
		Equivalent Production			20,000		19,280		19,080		19,080

(*b*) Statement of Cost Per Unit

Elements of Cast	*Cost*	*Equivalent Production (units)*	*Cost Per cent*
Materials :			
I Transferred from previous process	11,000		
Less: Scrap value of normal loss 2,000 units @ 50 paise per unit	1,000		
	10,000	20,000	0.50
II Materials added in process	4,820	19,280	0.25
Labour	14,310	19,080	0.75
Overheads	19,080	19,080	1.00

(*c*) *Statement of Cost Evaluation*

Opening Stock	*Elements of Cost*	*Equivalent Production (units)*	*Cost Per Unit ₹*	*Cost ₹*	*Total Cost ₹*
Opening Stock	Material I	—	0.50	—	
	Material II	240	0.25	60	
	Labour	480	0.75	360	
	Overheads	480	1.00	480	900
Abnormal Loss	Material I	400	0.50	200	
	Material II	400	0.25	100	
	Labour	280	0.75	210	
	Overhead	280	1.00	280	790
Completely processed during the period	Material I	16,400	0.50	8,200	
	Material II	16,400	0.25	4,100	
	Labour	16,400	0.75	12,300	
	Overhead	16,400	1.00	16,400	41,000
Closing Stock	Material I	3,200	0.50	1,600	
	Material II	2,240	0.25	560	
	Labour	1,920	0.75	1,440	
	Overheads	1,920	1.00	1,920	5,520

Process B Account

	Units	Amount ₹		Units	Amount ₹
To Balance b/d	1,200	2,100	By Normal Loss		
To Process A	22,000	11,000	@ ₹. 0.50 per unit	2,000	1,000
To Material		4,820	By Abnormal Loss	400	790
To Labour		14,310	By Process *C* (Transfer)	17,600	44,000
To Overheads		19,080	By Balance c/d (W/P)	3,200	5,520
	23,200	51,310		23,200	51,310

Process C Account

	Units	Amount		Units	Amount
To Process *B* A/c	17,600	44,000			

Abnormal Loss Account

To Process *B* A/c	400	790	By Cash A/c	400	200
			By Costing Profit and Loss A/c		590
	400	790		400	790

Values of Unit Transferred to Process C

	Units	Amount
Opening Work-in-Progress (old cost)	1,200	2,100
Opening Work-in-Progress (new cost)		900
Units introduced and completed	16,400	41,000
	17,600	44,000

Illustration 20: From the following details prepare Process *B* Account for the month of March, ...

Opening stock	400 units at ₹. 5,150	
Transfer from Process *A*	10,600 units at ₹. 82,300	
Transfer to Process *C*	9,600 units	
Closing Stock	1,000 unit	
Units Scrapped	400 units	
Normal loss in process	5% of production	
Sale of scrap	₹. 3 per unit	
Degree of completion as regards :	Materials %	Labour and Overheads %
Opening stock	80	60
Closing	70	50
Scrap	100	70
Direct Materials added in Process *B*	₹. 39,520	
Direct Wages	₹. 19,520	
Production Overhead	₹. 9,760	

Solution:

(a) Statement Equivalent Production

Input		*Output*		*Material (1)*		*Material (2)*		*Labour & Overheads*	
Particulars	*Units*	*Item*	*Units*	*%*	*Units*	*%*	*Units*	*%*	*Units*
Opening Stock	400	Transfer to							
Transfer from		Process *C*:							
Process *A*	10,600	Fully Processed	9,200	100	9,200	100	9,200	100	9,200
		Opening Stock	400	—	—	20	80	40	160
			9,600	—	9,200	—	9,280	—	9,360
		Normal Loss	500	—	—	—	—	—	—
		Closing Stock	1,000	100	1000	70	700	50	500
			11,100	—	10,200	—	9,980	—	9,860
		Less: Abnormal gain	100	100	100	100	100	100	100
Total	11,000	Total Equivalent Production	11,000	—	10,100	—	9,880	—	9,760

(*b*) Statement of Cost

Element of Cost	₹	*Total Cost* ₹	*Equivalent Production (units)*	*Cost per unit* ₹
Materials (1):				
From Process A	82,300			
Less: Sales of Scrap (Normal) Loss	1,500	80,800	10,100	8
Materials (2)				
(added in Process *B*)		39,520	9,880	4
Direct Wages		19,520	9,760	2
Production Overheads		9,760	9,760	1
	80,000	1,49,600	—	15

(c) Statement of Apportionment of Cost

Particulars	*Elements of Cost*	*Equivalent units*	*Cost per unit*	*Cost*	*Total Cost*
Opening W.I.P.	Material I	—	8	—	
(now completed)	Material II	80	4	320	
	Labour	160	2	320	
	Overheads	160	1	160	800
Introduced & completed	Material I	9,200	8	73,600	
during the period	Material II	9,200	4	36,800	
	Labour	9,200	2	18,400	
	Overheads	9,200	1	9,200	1,38,000
Closing Work-in-Progress	Material I	1,000	8	8,000	
	Material II	700	4	2,800	
	Labour	500	2	1,000	
	Overheads	500	1	500	12,300
Abnormal gain	Material I	100	8	800	
	Material II	100	4	400	
	Labour	100	2	200	
	Overheads	100	1	100	1,500

Process B Account

Particulars	*Units*	₹	*Particulars*	*Units*	₹
To Balance b/d	400	5,150	By Normal Loss	500	1,500
To Process A	10,600	82,300	By Process C	9,600	1,43,950
To Material	—	39,520	By Balance c/d	1,000	12,300
To Wages	—	19,520			
To Overhead	—	9,760			
To Abnormal gain	100	1,500			
	11,100	1,57,750		11,100	1,57,750

[**Notes** : (*i*) Work-in-Progress at the end of March has been valued as under :

Materials (1)	1,000 × 8.00 = 8,000
Materials (2)	700 × 4.00 = 2,800
Wages	500 × 2.00 = 1,000
Overhead	500 × 1.00 = 500
	₹. 12,300

(*ii*) Abnormal gain has been valued @ ₹. 15 per unit *i.e.* (100 × 15) ₹. 1,500.

(*iii*) Normal Loss is 5% of production *i.e.* (opening stock + units introduced – closing stock or (400 + 10,600 – 1,000) = 10,000 units and 5 per cent thereon is 500 units. Actual units lost is 400. Hence there is an extra production of 100 units.

(*iv*) Cost of units transferred to next process:

	₹.
Opening Work-in-Progress (old cost)	5,150
Work on Work-in-Progress (new cost)	800
Introduced completed (cost)	1,38,000
	1,43,950

Valuation of Work-in-Progress under Average Method:

Under FIFO Method opening WIP are completed by adding cost of completing incomplete units and thereafter newly introduced units are completed. When average method of valuation of WIP is followed no distribution is made between partly completed units of preceeding period (opening WIP) and those units which we introduced and completed during the period. Cost of opening inventory is added to cost incurred during inventory current period element wise.

Thus under average method the average process cost is obtained by adding the cost of opening WIP and current cost and dividing the total by total equivalent units. It is not presumed that opening units will be completed first.

$$\text{Unit cost} = \frac{\text{Cost Brought Forword from Previous Period + Cost of Current Period}}{\text{Total Equivalent Units}}$$

Illustration 21: (*Average Cost Method*) The following information is available in respect of Process 2 for the month of March.

Opening Stock 1,000 units
Value : Direct Materials (1) ₹. 4,000; Direct Material (2) ₹. 2,000.
Direct Labour ₹. 350, Production Overhead ₹. 800
Transfer from Process 1: 16,000 units of ₹. 81,000
Transfer to Process 3 : 14,500 units

	₹.
Direct Materials added to Process 2	43,750
Direct Labour amounted to	14,300
Production Overhead absorbed	28,500

Units Scrapped : 500

Degree of Completion : Direct Materials 100%
Direct Labour 60%
Production Overhead 20%

Normal Loss was estimated at 5% of production units, realised ₹. 5 per unit

Closing Stock : 2,000 units

Degree of Completion : Direct Materials 50%
Direct Labour 20%
Production Overhead 20%

Prepare the process and other accounts using *weighted average cost method.*

Solution:

Statement of Equivalent Units

Particulars	*Units*	*Material 1*		*Material 2*		*Direct Labour*		*Production Overheads*	
		Units	*%*	*Units*	*%*	*Units*	*%*	*Units*	*%*
Normal Loss	750	–	–	–	–	–	–	–	–
Completed Units	14,500	14,500	100	14,500	100	14,500	100	14,500	100
Closing Stock	2,000	2,000	100	1,000	50	400	20	400	20
	17,250	16,500		15,500		14,900		14,900	
Abnormal Gain	(250)	(250)	100	(250)	100	(250)	100	(250)	100
Total	17,000	16,250		15,250		14,650		14,650	

Statement of Equivalent Units Cost

	₹.	*Cost (₹.)*	*Equivalent Units*	*Cost per Equivalent unit (₹.)*
Materials (1)				
Opening WIP	4,000			
Process 1	81,000			
Less: Scrap of Normal Loss	85,000			
@ ₹. 5 × 750 units	3,750	81,250	16,250	5.00
Materials (2)				
Opening WIP	2,000			
Add: Materials	43,750	45,750	15,250	3.00
Direct Labour				
Opening WIP	350			
Add: Current Cost	14,300	14,650	14,650	1.00
Production Overhead				
Opening WIP	800			
Add: Current Period	28,500	29,300	14,650	2.00
		1,70,950		

Statement of Cost

Production	*Elements of Cost*	*Equivalent Units*	*Cost Per units*	*Cost (₹.)*	*Total Cost*
Completed Units	Material (1)	14,500	5	72,500	
	Material (2)	14,500	3	43,500	
	Direct. Labour	14,500	1	14,500	
	Prod. Overhead	14,500	2	29,000	1,59,500

Closing Stock	Material (1)	2,000	5	10,000	
	Material (2)	1,000	3	3,000	
	Direct Labour	400	1	400	
	Prod. Overhead	400	2	800	14,200
Abnormal Gain	Material (1)	250	5	1,250	
	Material (2)	250	3	750	
	Direct Labour	250	1	250	
	Prod. Overhead	250	2	500	2,750

Process 2 Account

Particulars	*Units*	₹	*Particulars*	*Units*	₹
To Balance b/d	1,000	7,150	By Normal Loss A/c	750	3,750
" Process 1 A/c	16,000	81,000	" Process 3 A/c	14,500	1,59,500
" Direct Materials		43,750	" Balance c/d	2,000	14,200
" Direct Labour		14,300			
" Prod. Overhead		28,500			
" Abnormal Gain	250	2,750			
	17,250	1,77,450		17,250	1,77,450

Normal Loss Account

To Process 2 A/c	750	3,750	By Bank	500	2,500
			" Abnormal Gain A/c	250	1,250
	750	3,750		750	3,750

Abnormal Gain Account

To Normal Loss A/c	250	1,250	By Process 2 A/c	250	2,750
" Costing P and L A/c		1,500			
	250	2,750		250	2,750

Note : 1. Normal Loss 5% of units processed i.e. 5% of 15,000 = 750 units

2. Units processed = Opening stock + Transfer from Process 1 – Closing stock
= 1,000 + 16,000 – 2,000 = 15,000 units

3. Normal outout = Opening WIP + Transfer from Process 1 – Closing WIP – Normal Loss
= 1,000 + 16,000 – 2,000 – 750 = 14,250 units

4. Abnormal gain = Completed units – Normal output
= 14,500 – 14,250 = 250 units.

Valuation of Work-in-Progress Under Last-in-First Out Method

According to this method, units entering in the process at last are first to be completed. The completed units will be shown at the current cost and closing inventory of work-in progress will be valued at the cost of opening inventory of work in progress because units representing opening inventory are to be completed at last. The closing inventory will be, thus, divided into two categories when number of units of closing inventory are more than opening inventory (*i*) units of opening WIP lying as closing WIP (*ii*) Newly introduced units lying in closing WIP.

Illustration 21A: From the following information relating to the month of April 06, calculate the equivalent production units and the value of finished production and work-in-progress, using the LIFO method.

Opening work-in-progress on 1st April: 5,000 units; 50% complete.

Cost	₹.
Materials	6,000
Labour	8,000
Overheads	8,000
	22,000

Units introduced into the process : 10,000

Cost	₹.
Materials	30,000
Labour	52,500
Overheads	70,000
	1,52,000

During the period 7,500 units were completed and trasnferred to the next proces. Closing work-in-progress on 30th April, 7,500 units, 50% complete.

Solution:

(i) Computation of Equivalent Production Units
(LIFO method)

Units	*Particulars*	*Equivalent production* *Units out*	*% of completion*	*Equivalent units*
5,000	Opening Work-in-Process			
10,000	Units introduced into the process			
	Units completed and transferred			
	Of the units introduced during the period	7,500	100	7,500
	Of the units introduced during the period	2,500	50	1,250
	Of the opening work-in-process	5,000	-	
15,000		15,000		8,750

Note

(*i*) Since the units in the opening work-in-process were already 50% complete, no work has been done on these units during the period.

(ii) Cost per unit of equivalent production = $\frac{₹.1,52,000}{8,750}$ = ₹.17.43

(*iii*) Valuation of finished production and WIP

1. Finished production : 7,500 × ₹. 17.43 = ₹. 1,30,725
2. Closing WIP : 22,000 + (1,250 × ₹. 17.43) = ₹. 43,787.50

INTER-PROCESS PROFIT

The usual practice is to transfer the materials to the next process at cost and from the last process to the finished stock account also at cost. But sometimes the transfer is made at market price. The main advantage of such a method is that each process will then reveal profit or loss and hence the efficiency or inefficiency at each stage will be immediately known and underlined. It will also be demonstrated whether it is advantageous to process the materials within the factory or to get them from the market already processed.

It should be noted that merely to add a margin of profit to the cost while transferring the materials to the next process cannot serve any useful purpose. The transfer should be made at the current market price.

Should the market price be higher than cost, a process account will reveal profit. Then the stock in the next process will not be valued at cost. The value of stock will include a margin of profit which is not proper for balance sheet purposes. Therefore, it is necessary to find out how much profit is included in the stock of each process and then to create a proper reserve for it by debiting the Profit and Loss Account. The calculation is rather involved. The following is a very simple example.

Illustration 22: A product passes through two processes–No. 1 and No. 2. Output of Process No. 1 is passed to Process No. 2 at cost plus 25 per cent profit and finished output is similarly transferred to Finished Stock Account at cost plus 25 per cent profit. There was no partly finished work in either process on 31st December, on which date the following further information was available:

	Process No. 1	*Process No. 2*
	₹.	₹.
Materials consumed	4,000	12,000
Labour	6,000	8,000
Closing Stock (31st Dec.)	2,000	6,000

Out of the finished stocks, a portion remained at hand valued at ₹. 9,000 and the balance was sold for ₹. 29,000. Ignoring the question of overheads and assuming there were no opening stocks, prepare the Process and Finished Stock Accounts.

Solution:

Process No. 1 Account

	₹.		₹.
To Materials	4,000	By Transfer to Process	
To Labour	6,000	No. 2 A/c	10,000
To Profit & Loss Account		By Stock at Hand	2,000
(25% on ₹. 8,000)	2,000		
	12,000		12,000

Process No. 2 Account

	₹.		₹.
To Transfer from Process			
No. 1 A/c	10,000	By Transfer to Finished	
To Materials	12,000	Stock Account	30,000
To Labour	8,000	By Stock at Hand	6,000
To Profit (25% on ₹. 24,000)	6,000		
	36,000		36,000

Finished Stock Account

	₹.		₹.
To Transfer from Process		By Sales	29,000
No. 2 A/c	30,000	By Closing Stock	9,000
To Profit & Loss Account	8,000		
	38,000		38,000

The total profit shown is ₹. 16,000, but a reserve is required for the profit included in the closing stocks of Process No. 2 and in the Finished Stock Account. There is no profit included in the closing stock in Process No. 1 A/c. Taking the closing stock of Process No. 2 first, we consider that there are two elements in it which make up its value, *viz*., (*a*) transferred amount from Process No. 1 and (*b*) costs incurred in Process No. 2 itself. Looking at the debit side we find that (*a*) is ₹. 10,000 and (*b*) is ₹. 20,000. The closing stock of ₹. 6,000 may be considered as made up in the ratio of (*a*) : (*b*) or 1 : 2, *i.e.*, we may consider that out of ₹. 6,000, ₹. 2,000 is for the transferred amount (in which there has been included 25 per cent profit on cost) and ₹. 4,000 for costs incurred in Process No. 2 itself (in which there is nothing by way of profit). On ₹. 2,000, profit is ₹. 400 (20 per cent on transfer price which is the same as 25 per cent on cost). Therefore, for the stock of Process No. 2, a reserve of ₹. 400 is required.

Now taking the stock of finished goods, the stock represents entirely transfer from Process No. 2; 20 per cent profit was included in the transfer price and, therefore, ₹. 1,800 is required as reserve for this stock. The cost, as far as Process No. 2 is concerned, of the stock comes to ₹. 7,200, *i.e.* 9,000 – 1,800. But this includes something by way of transfer from Process No. 1 also. The ratio of transfer from Process No. 1 and cost incurred in Process No. 2 is 1 : 2 as discussed in the above paragraph. Therefore, out of ₹. 7,200, ₹. 2,400 is for transfer from Process No. 1 A/c. A reserve of 20 per cent is required on this sum. This would be ₹. 480. Total reserve required on finished goods stock is ₹. 2,280 and total reserve required on all stocks is ₹. 2,680.

In the Balance Sheet, stocks will be valued as follows:

	₹.
Process No. 1	2,000
Process No. 2 (6,000 – 400)	5,600
Finished Stock (9,000 – 2,280)	6,720
	14,320

Alternative Method of Solution: In each Process Account three columns will be drawn on both sides – Total, Cost and Profit. Only profit included is shown in the profit column.

Illustration 23: From the following information given by a manufacturing company which manufactures a product, you are required to prepare Process Accounts.

	Process I ₹	*Process II* ₹	*Process III* ₹
Direct Materials	30,000	7,500	7,500
Direct Wages	22,500	15,000	15,000
Closing Stock	7,500	8,750	21,300

Finished goods is sold for ₹. 1,30,000, value of closing finished stock is ₹. 5,112. It is the policy of the company to charge 20% on transfer price or 25% on cost price while transferring the goods from Process I to II and 20% on cost price from II to III and from III to the Finished Stock.

Solution:

Process I Account

	Total ₹	*Cost* ₹	*Profit* ₹		*Total* ₹	*Cost* ₹	*Profit* ₹
To Direct Materials	30,000	30,000	—	By Closing Stock	7,500	7,500	—
To Direct Wages	22,500	22,500		By Transfer			
	52,500	52,500	—	to Process II	56,250	45,000	11,250
To Profit 25% on cost price	11,250	—	11,250				
	63,750	52,500	11,250		63,750	52,500	11,250

Process II Account

	Total ₹	Cost ₹	Profit ₹		Total ₹	Cost ₹	Profit ₹
To Transferred from Process I	56,250	45,000	11,250	By Closing Stock	8,750	7,500	1,250
To Materials	7,500	7,500		By Transfer to Process III	84,000	60,000	24,000
	15,000	15,000					
	78,750	67,500	11,250				
To Profit 25% on cost price	14,000		14,000				
	92,750	67,500	25,250		92,750	67,500	25,250

Process III Account

	Total ₹	Cost ₹	Profit ₹		Total ₹	Cost ₹	Profit ₹
To Transferred from Process II	84,000	60,000	24,000	By Closing Stock	21,300	16,500	4,800
To Material	7,500	7,500		By Transfer to finished stock	1,02,240	66,000	36,240
To Wages	15,000	15,000					
	1,06,500	82,500	24,000				
To Profit 20% on cost price	17,040		17,040				
	1,23,540	82,500	41,040		1,23,540	82,500	41,040

Finished Stock Account

	Total ₹	Cost ₹	Profit ₹		Total ₹	Cost ₹	Profit ₹
To Transferred from Process III	1,02,240	66,000	36,240	By Closing Stock	5,112	3,300	1,812
To Profit	32,872		32,872	By Sales	1,30,000	62,700	67,300
	1,35,112	66,000	69,112		1,35,112	66,000	69,112

Working Notes:

1. In Second and Third Processes and in Finished Stock A/c closing stocks include some unrealised profit because outputs transferred from previous processes have been at cost plus profit.
2. The unrealised profit in the closing stock of the second process has been calculated as below:

$$\text{Cost of closing stock} = \frac{\text{Cost}}{\text{Total}} \times \text{Closing stock} = \frac{67,500}{78,750} \times 8750 = 7,500$$

Unrealised Profit = 8750 – 7500 = 1250

3. Similarly in the third process

$$\text{Cost of closing stock} = \frac{\text{Cost}}{\text{Total}} \times \text{Closing stock} = \frac{82,500}{1,06,500} \times 21,300 = 16,500$$

Unrealised Profit = 21,300 – 16,500 = ₹. 4,800

4. In the Finished Stock Account

$$\text{Cost of Closing Stock} = \frac{\text{Cost}}{\text{Total}} \times \text{Closing Stock} = \frac{66,000}{1,02,240} \times 5,112 = 3,300$$

Unrealised Profit = 5,112 – 3,300 = 1,812

5. Total unrealised profit will be

Process II ₹. 1,250 + Process III ₹. 4,800 + Finished Stock ₹. 1,812
= ₹. 7,862

Illustration 24: A certain product passes through three processes before it is transferred to finished stock. The following information is obtained for the month of January.

	I ₹.	*II* ₹.	*III* ₹.	*Finished stock* ₹.
Opening Stock	20,000	24,000	16,000	60,000
Direct Material	40,000	42,000	60,000	—
Direct Wages	30,000	30,000	32,000	—
Production overheads	28,000	12,000	80,000	—
Closing Stock	10,000	12,000	8,000	30,000
Profit on cost of each process	33-1/3%	25%	25%	—
Inter-process profit for opening stock		4,000	4,000	22,000

Stock in processes are valued at prime cost and finished stock has been valued at price at which it is received from Process III. Sales during the period were ₹. 7,00,000.

Solution :

Notes : Calculation of Unrealised Profit on Stock

Process II : $\frac{\text{Cost}}{\text{Total}}$ × Closing Stock or $\frac{20,000}{24,000}$ × 12,000 = ₹. 10,000

∴ Unrealised Profit = 12,000 – 10,000 = ₹. 2,000

Process III :

$\frac{3,06,000}{4,08,000}$ × 8,000 = ₹. 6,000

Unrealised Profit 8,000 – 6,000 = ₹. 2,000

Finished Stock $\frac{3,80,000}{6,00,000}$ × 30,000 = ₹. 19,000

∴ Unrealised Profit 30,000 – 19,000 = ₹. 11,000

Process I Account

	Total ₹.	*Cost* ₹.	*Profit* ₹.		*Total* ₹.	*Cost* ₹.	*Profit* ₹.
To Opening Stock	20,000	20,000	—	By Transfer			
To Materials	40,000	40,000		to Process II	1,44,000	1,08,000	36,000
To Direct Wages	30,000	30,000					
	90,000	90,000	—				
Less: Closing Stock	10,000	10,000					
Prime Cost	80,000	80,000	—				
To Overheads	28,000	28,000	—				
	1,08,000	1,08,000					
To Profit							
($33\frac{1}{3}$ on cost)	36,000		36,000				
	1,44,000	1,08,000	36,000		1,44,000	1,08,000	36,000

Process II Account

	Total ₹	Cost ₹	Profit ₹		Total ₹	Cost ₹	Profit ₹
To Opening Stock	24,000	20,000	4,000	By Transfer			
To Transferred				to III	3,00,000	2,02,000	98,000
from Process I	1,44,000	1,08,000	36,000				
To Materials	42,000	42,000	—				
To Wages	30,000	30,000	—				
	2,40,000	2,00,000	40,000				
Less: Closing Stock	12,000	10,000	2,000				
	2,28,000	1,90,000	38,000				
To Overheads	12,000	12,000	—				
	2,40,000	2,02,000	38,000				
To Profit 25% on cost	60,000		60,000				
	3,00,000	2,02,000	98,000		3,00,000	2,02,000	98,000

Process III Account

	Total ₹	Cost ₹	Profit ₹		Total ₹	Cost ₹	Profit ₹
To Opening Stock	16,000	12,000	4,000	By Transfer			
To Transferred from				to Finished			
Process II	3,00,000	2,02,000	98,000	Stock A/c	6,00,000	3,80,000	2,20,000
To Raw Material	60,000	60,000					
To Wages	32,000	32,000					
	4,08,000	3,06,000	1,02,000				
Less: Closing Stock	8,000	6,000	2,000				
	4,00,000	3,00,000	1,00,000				
To Production overheads	80,000	80,000					
	4,80,000	3,80,000	1,00,000				
To Profit 25% on cost	1,20,000		1,20,000				
	6,00,000	3,80,000	2,20,000		6,00,000	3,80,000	2,20,000

Finished Stock Account

	Total ₹	Cost ₹	Profit ₹		Total ₹	Cost ₹	Profit ₹
To Opening Stock	60,000	38,000	22,000	By Sale	7,00,000	3,99,000	3,01,000
To Process III	6,00,000	3,80,000	2,20,000				
	6,60,000	4,18,000	2,42,000				
Less: Closing Stock	30,000	19,000	11,000				
	6,30,000	3,99,000	2,31,000				
To Profit	70,000		70,000				
	7,00,000	3,99,000	3,01,000		7,00,000	3,99,000	3,01,000

Unrealised Profits

	Profit ₹	Opening Reserve ₹	Closing Reserve ₹	Difference ₹	Actual profits ₹
Process I	36,000	—	—	—	36,000
Process II	60,000	4,000	2,000	2,000	62,000
Process III	1,20,000	4,000	2,000	2,000	1,22,000
Finished Stock	70,000	22,000	11,000	11,000	81,000
					3,01,000

OPERATION COSTING

It is a variation of Process Costing. A manufacturing process may sometimes be sub-divided into a number of parts, each of which is known as operation. Thus a process is a large sphere of activity which may consist of several operations, each showing all characteristics of a process. For a greater accuracy of product costs and more detailed control, costs may be determined by operations, the cost of the process being the total of the costs of the constituent operation.

The procedure for costing of operations is broadly the same as for process costing. Materials, labour and expenses are recorded against each operation and transfer of cost is made from one operation to another as in the case of process costing. When the number of operations is not large, there may be control account in the cost ledger for each operation and where their number is large, there may be control account for each large process.

Illustration 25: An article undergoes three successive operations from raw materials to finished product stage. The following information is available from the production records of a month.

Operation No.	*No. of Pieces Input*	*No. of Pieces Rejected*	*No. of Pieces Output*
1	12,000	4,000	8,000
2	13,200	1,200	12,000
3	9,600	1,600	8,000

Find out what should be the input in the first operation in number of pieces to obtain a finished product of 100 pieces after last operation.

Calculate the cost of raw material required to produce one piece of finished product from following particulars.

Weight of Finished Piece	100 gm per piece
Price of Raw Material	₹. 10 per kg

Solution:

Percentage of Rejection on output

Operation 1 (4000/8000) × 100 = 50%
2 (1200/12000) × 100 = 10%
3 (1600/8000) × 100 = 20%

On the basis of above, taking output of 100 pieces in the third operation, the input in the first process will be ascertained as shown in the following table.

Operation	*Input Pieces*	*Rejection %*	*Rejection Pieces*	*Output Pieces*
1	198	50%	66	132
2	132	10%	12	120
3	120	20%	20	100

Thus when 198 pieces are input of the first operation, 100 units will be the output of the third operation.

Quantity of Raw Materials for 100 units = 198 × 100 gms = 19,800 gm

Cost of Raw Material $19{,}800 \times \frac{10}{1000}$ = ₹. 198

Cost of Raw Material per unit = 198/100 = ₹. 1.98

TYPICAL ILLUSTRATIONS

Illustration 26: **A product which uses 100 tons as input per month passes through two processes. The details of cost in Process 1 for the month of April are.**

Process I	Cost per ton ₹.
Direct Material Cost	26,100
Direct Labour Cost	7,800
Overhead	13,500

The total loss in Process I is 2% of input and the scrap is 8% of input with a value of ₹. 12,000 per ton.

The material to Process II is transferred at cost. The process direct labour cost at Process II is ₹. 9,000 per ton of input. The overhead is 60% of direct labour cost. The scrap at Process II is 20% of input with a value of ₹. 12,000 per ton. Draw up a Cost Sheet to present the manufacturing scrap and waste at each stage of manufacturing.

Solution:

Process Cost Sheet of Process I

	Tons	*Cost per ton* ₹.	*Total* ₹.
1. Input			
Direct Material	100	26,100	26,10,000
Direct Labour		7,800	7,80,000
Overhead		13,500	13,50,000
Total	100	47,400	47,40,000
2. Wastages			
Loss	2		
Scrap	8	12,000	96,000
3. Output (Input – Wastage)	90	51,600	46,44,000

Note: Cost per ton shown above (₹. 51,600) has been calculated on the basis of total i.e. ₹. 46,44,000/90 = ₹. 51,600.

Process Cost Sheet of Process II

	Tons	*Cost per ton* ₹.	*Total* ₹.
1. Input			
Transfer from Process I	90	51,600	46,44,000
Direct Labour		9,000	8,10,000
Overhead (60% of Direct Labour)		5,400	4,86,000
	90	66,000	59,40,000
2. Scrap (20% of inputs)	18	12,000	2,16,000
3. Output (Input-scrap)	72	79,500	57,24,000

Note: Cost per tons of output is ₹. 57,24,000/72 = ₹. 79,500

Illustration 27: A product passes through three process : *A*, *B* and *C*. 10,000 units at a cost of ₹. 1.10 were issued to Process A. The other direct expenses were as follows:

	Process A	*Process B*	*Process C*
	₹.	₹.	₹.
Sundry Materials	1500	1,500	1,500
Direct Labour	4,500	8,000	6,500
Direct Exps.	1,000	1,000	1,503

The wastage of process *A* was 5% and in Process *B* 4%. The wastage of process *A* was sold at ₹ 0.25 per unit and that of *B* of Re 0.50 per unit and that of *C* of ₹. 1.00 per unit. The overhead charges were 160% of direct labour. The final product was sold at ₹. 10 per unit fetching a profit of 20% on sales. Prepare Process Accounts and also find out percentage of wastage in Process *C*.

Solution:

Process A Account

	Units	*Amount* ₹		*Units*	*Amount* ₹
To Units Introduced @ ₹. 1.10	10,000	11,000	By Wastage (5% of input @ ₹. 0.25)	500	125
To Sundry Materials		1,500			
To Direct Labour		4,500	By Process *B* A/c		
To Direct Exps.		1,000	(Transfer @ 25075/9500 = 2.639)	9,500	25,075
To Overheads (160% of Direct labour)		7,200			
	10,000	25,200		10,000	25,200

Process B Account

	Units	Amount		Units	Amount
To Process A Account (Transfer)	9,500	25,075	By Wastage (4% of 9,500 @ ₹. 0.50)	380	190
To Sundry Material		1,500			
To Direct Labour		8,000	By Process *C* A/c		
To Direct Exps.		1,000	(Transfer @ 48,185/9,120 = ₹. 5.283)	9,120	48,185
To Overhead (160% of Direct Labour)		12,800			
	9,500	48,375		9,500	48,375

Process C Account

	Units	*Amount* ₹		*Units*	*Amount* ₹
To Process B A/c (Transfer)	9,120	48,185	By Wastage (see note below) @ ₹. 1	696	696
To Sundry Materials		1,500	By Finished Stock		
To Direct Labour		6,500	A/c @ ₹. 8	8,424	67,392
To Direct Expenses		1,503			
To Overhead (160% of Direct labour)		10,400			
	9,120	68,088		9,120	68,088

Calculation of Wastage in Process

1. Normal Cost per unit in C ₹. 10 – 20% profit ₹. 2 = ₹. 8
2. Assume wastage in $C = x$ units
   Output of C = 9,120 – x units
   Normal Cost (Total) = 68,088 – x @ ₹ 1 = ₹. (68,088 – x)
   Normal Cost per unit = Total Normal Cost/Output unit

$$\text{Hence} \quad \frac{68088 - x}{9120 - x} = 8$$

$$\text{or} \quad 68{,}088 - x = 72{,}960 - 8x$$

$$\text{or} \quad 7x = 72{,}960 - 68{,}088 = 4872$$

$$\text{or} \quad 7x = 4{,}872$$

$$\text{or} \quad x = 696$$

3. Output of Process C 9,120 – 696 = 4,824 units

Illustration 28: In a manufacturing unit, raw materials passes through four Process I, II, III and IV and the output of each process is the input of the subsequent processes. The loss in the four processes I, II, III and IV are respectively 25%, 20%, 20% and 16-2/3% of the input. If the end product at the end of Process IV is 40,000 kg, what is the quantity of raw material required to be fed at the begining of Process I and the cost of same at ₹. 5 per kg. Also find out the effect of increase or decrease in the material cost of the end product for variation of every rupee in the end-product for variation of every repee in the cost of raw material. ***[CA Inter]***

Solution: Suppose the quantity of raw material put in Process I is 100 kg, the output and input in the four processes will be following:

	Process I	*Process II*	*Process II*	*Process IV*
Input (kg)	100	75	60	48
Loss (kg)	25	15	12	8
Output	75	60	48	40

Thus end output is 40% of the input in Process I. If output of process IV is 40,000 kg the input in Process *I* will be 40,000 × 100/40 = 1,00,000 kg or for 1 kg of output 2.5 kg of materials is required. If cost of material increases or decreases by ₹. 1, the effect on output would decrease or increase by ₹. 2.50 per kg.

Illustration 29: An article passes through three successive operations from the raw material to the finished product stage. The following data are available from the production records of a particular month.

Operation No.	*No. of pieces input*	*No. of Pieces rejected*	*No. of pieces output*
1	60,000	20,000	40,000
2	66,000	6,000	60,000
3	48,000	8,000	40,000

(*i*) Calculate the input required to be introduced in the first operation in number of pieces in order to obtain finished output of 100 pieces after last operations.

(*ii*) Calculate the cost of raw material required to produce one piece of finished product, given the following:

Weight of the finished piece is 0.10 kg and the price of raw material is ₹. 20 per kg.

Solution: **(A) Input Rejections and Ouput:**

	Operation I (Pieces)	*Operation II (Pieces)*	*Operation III (Pieces)*
1. Input	60,000	66,000	48,000
2. Rejections	20,000	6,000	8,000
3. Output	40,000	60,000	40,000
4. Rejection as a percentage of output	50%	10%	20%

(B) Input required in Process I to obtain Output of 1000 Pieces:

	Pieces
Finished output after Operation III	100
Rejection in Operation III 20%	20
Input in Operation III	120
Rejection in Operation II 10%	12
Input in Operation II	132
Rejection in Operation I 50%	66
Input in Operation I	198

(C) Cost of Raw Materials:

Weight of 198 pieces of raw material required for an output of 100 pieces

198 × 0.10 kg = 19.80 kg

Cost of Raw Material 19.8 kg × ₹. 20 = ₹. 396

Cost of Raw Material for one piece of finished produce = ₹. 396/100 = ₹. 3.96.

Illustration 30: A certain chemical process yields 75% of material introduced as main product 20% as by product and 5% being lost. In the process one unit of main product requires double the material required for a unit of by-product. Further one unit of main product need 1-1/2 times, the time needed for one unit of by-product. Overheads are absorbed in the ratio of 3 : 1.

During a week 1,000 units of Raw Material at a cost of ₹. 17,000 were introduced. Labour totalled ₹. 5,300. Overheads came to ₹. 2,700. Wastage realised ₹. 300. Ascertain the cost of two products.

Solution: Break-up of the total unit in respect of Main product, By product and Loss is as below.

Main Product	75% of 1,000 = 750
By-product	20% of 1,000 = 200
Loss	5% of 1,000 = 50

Statement of Cost

	Total	*Ratio*	*Main Product (750 units)*		*By Product (200 units)*	
			Total cost ₹	*Cost per unit* (₹)	*Total cost* (₹)	*Cost per unit* (₹)
Material	17,000	15 : 2	15,000	20.00	2,000	10.00
Labour	5,300	45 : 8	4,500	6.00	800	4.00
Overheads	2,400	3 : 1	1,800	2.40	600	3.00
	24,700	—	21,300	28.40	3,400	17.00

Note : 1. ₹. 300 realised from scrap has been deducted from overheads.

2. Material ratio is calculated as below (750 × 2) : (200 × 1) = 15 : 2

3. Labour ratio is calculated as below (750 × 3) : (200 × 2) = 45 : 8

Illustration 31: A product is finished in three stages I, II, III. At the first stage a quantity of 72,000 kg was delivered at a cost of ₹. 2.50 per kg. The entire material was consumed.

The production particulars along with the allocated expenses were as indicated in the table below:

Stage	*Input*	*Output*	*Direct Wages*	*Fixed Overhead*	*Varying Overhead*
	kg	kg	₹.	%	%
I	72,000	67,680	7,500	150	200
II	65,000	60,125	12,000	125	150
III	55,600	50,000	14,500	200	250
				(On Direct Wages)	

The producer, as was his practice assessed his cost at ₹. 6.77 per kg based on his input expenditure and the finished output. With a selling price of ₹. 7.50 per kg he estimated his profit at ₹. 36,500. If you do not approve of his assessment of the end results of the operation, convince him of the real end results in a tabular form. You should assume the normal wastages as only 5% on input at each stage and any excess wastages should not be allowed to inflate the cost of the end product. **[*ICWA Inter*]**

Solution:

The producer's assessment :

			₹.
Material (72,000 kg. at ₹. 2.50)			1,80,000
Stage I :	Direct wages	7,500	
	Fixed overhead	11,250	
	Varying overhead	15,000	33,750
Stage II:	Direct wages	12,000	
	Fixed overhead	15,000	
	Varying overhead	18,000	45,000
Stage III :	Direct wages	14,500	
	Fixed overhead	29,000	
	Varying overhead	36,250	79,750
Total Expenditure			3,38,500
Cost per kg $\frac{3,38,500}{50,000}$ =			6.77
Selling price per kg			7.50
Profit per kg		0.73	
	Total Profit (50,000 × 0.73)		36,500

But this assessment cannot be approved. Following may be the proper calculation. It should be worked out at follows:

Stage I. Account

	Kg	Rate	Amount		Kg	Rate	Amount
To Material	72,000	2.50	1,80,000	By Normal wastage 5% of 72,000	3,600	—	—
To Direct Wages			7,500	By Abnormal loss (72,000 – 3,600 = (68,400) – 67,680	720	3.125	2,250
To Fixed Overhead (150% of 7,500)			11,250	By Output tr. to Stage II	65,000	3.125	2,03,125
To Varying Overhead (200% of 7,500)			15,000	By Closing stock (67,680—65,000)	2,680	3.125	8,375
	72,000		2,13,750		72,000		2,13,750

$$\text{Cost per Kg} = \frac{\text{Total Cost} - \text{Value of normal wastage/scrap}}{\text{Input Qnty.} - \text{Normal wastage Qnty.}}$$

$$= \frac{2,13,750 - \text{Nil}}{72,000 - 3,600} = \frac{2,13,750}{68,400} = ₹.\ 3.125$$

By this rate Abnormal loss and Closing stock will be valued

Stage II Account

	Kg	Kg	Amount (₹)		Kg	Kg	Amount ₹
To Input from I	65,000	3.125	2,03,125	By Normal wastage 5% of 65,000	3,250	—	—
To Direct Wages			12,000	By Abnormal loss (65,000 – 3,250 = 61,750) – 60,125	1625	4.0182	6,530
To Fixed Overhead 125% of 12,000			15,000	By Output tr. to Stage III	55,600	4.0182	2,23,413
To Varying Overhead (150% of 12,000)			18,000	By Closing stock (60125 – 55,600)	4,525	4.0182	18,182
	65,000		2,48,125		65,000		2,48,125

$$\text{Cost per kg.} = \frac{2,48,125 - \text{Nil}}{65,000 - 3,250} = \frac{2,48,125}{61,750} = ₹.\ 4.0182 \text{ per kg}$$

Stage III Account

	Kg	Rate	Amt. ₹		Kg	Rate	Amt. ₹
To Input from II	55,600	4.0182	2,23,413	By Normal wastage 5% of 55,600)	2,780	—	—
To Direct Wages			14,500	By Abnormal loss	2,820	5.7395	16,186
To Fixed Overhead 200% of 14,500			29,000	By Output	50,000	5.7395	2,86,977
To Varying Overhead 250% of 14,500			36,250				
	55,600		3,03,163		55,600		3,03,163

$$\text{Cost per kg} = \frac{3,03,163 - \text{Nil}}{55,600 - 2,780} = \frac{3,03,163}{52,820} = ₹.\ 5.7395 \text{ per kg.}$$

		₹.
Sales 50,000 × 7.50		3,75,000
Cost of finished output *i.e.* cost of goods sold		2,86,977
Gross profit		88,023
Less : Abnormal loss:		
Stage I	2,250	
Stage II	6,530	
Stage III	16,186	24,966
Net profit		63,057

Reconciliation:

Estimated profit as per producer		36,500
Add: Cost of Closing stock:		
Stage I	8,375	
Stage II	18,182	26,557
Net profit		63,057

Illustration 32: A company is manufacturing building bricks and fire bricks. Two processes—brick forming and heat treating are required for completion of both the products.

Time required (in Hours)

	Building Bricks	*Fire Bricks*
Brick forming per 100 bricks	3	2
Heat treating per 100 bricks	2	5

Total costs of the two process departments in a particular month were :

Bricks Forming : ₹ 21,200

Heat Treating : ₹ 48,800

Production during that month was :

Building Bricks : 1,30,000 pieces

Fire Brick : 70,000 pieces

Prepare a statement of manufacturing costs for the two varieties of bricks.

[*ICWA (Inter)*]

Solution:

Working Notes

Statement of Apportionment of Cost on the Basis of Hours

	Hours
Time required for Brick Forming:	
Building Bricks (1,30,000 × 3/100)	3,900
Fire Bricks (70,000 × 2/100)	1,400
Total time required	5,300
Cost per hour of brick forming = $\frac{21,200}{5,300}$ = ₹ 4.00 per hour	₹ 21,200
Time required for Heat Treating	Hours
Building Bricks (1,30,000 × 2/100)	2,600
Fire Bricks (70,000 × 5/100)	3,500
Total time required	6,100
Cost per hour of heat treating = $\frac{48,800}{6,100}$ = ₹ 8.00 per hour	₹ 48,800

Statement of Manufacturing Costs

Particulars	*Building Bricks*	*Fire Bricks*	*Total* ₹
Brick Forming	3,900 × 4 = 15,600	1,400 × 4 = 5,600	21,200
Heat Treating	2,600 × 8 = 20,800	3,500 × 8 = 28,000	48,800
Total Mfg. Costs	36,400	33,600	70,000
Mfg. Cost per brick	$\frac{36,400}{1,30,000}$ = 0.28	$\frac{33,600}{70,000}$ = 0.48	
Mfg. Cost per 100 bricks	₹ 28	₹ 48	

Normal Loss/Abnormal Loss

Illustration 33: Product ZENU is made by three sequential Process, *I*, *II* and *III*. In process *III* a by-product arises and after further processing in Process *XY*, at a cost of ₹ 2 per unit, by-product '*XYZ*' is produced. Selling and distribution expenses of ₹ 1 per unit are incurred in marketing '*XYZ*' at a selling price of ₹ 9 per unit.

	Process I	Process II	Process III
Standards provided for :			
Normal loss in process of input,	10%	5%	10%
Loss in process, having a scrap value, per unit	₹ 1	₹ 3	₹ 5

For the month of April 2004 the following data are given:

	Process I	Process II	Process III	Process XY
Output, in units	8,800	8,400	7,000 of ZENU	420 of XYZ
Costs	₹.	₹.	₹.	Total ₹.
Direct Materials—introduced (10,000 units)	20,000			20,000
Direct materials added	6,000	12,640	23,200	41,840
Direct wages	5,000	6,000	10,000	21,000
Direct Expenses	4,000	6,200	4,080	14,280

Budgeted production overhead for the month was ₹. 84,000.

Absorption is based on a percentage of direct wages.

There are no stocks at the beginning or end of the month.

You are required, using the information given, to prepare accounts for : (*a*) Each Process *I, II* and *III*; (*b*) Process *XY*.

Solution: *Working Note*: Production overhead is ₹. 84,000, while wages are ₹. 21,000. Thus absorption rate is 400% of wages.

(*a*) Process I Account

	Units	Rate	Amt. ₹		Unit	Rate	Amt. ₹
To Direct Materials	10,000	2	20,000	By Normal loss (10%)	1,000	1	1,000
To Direct Wages			6,000	By Abnormal loss	200	6	1,200
To Direct Exp.			5,000	By Output tr. to Process II	8,800	6	52,800
To Production Over head (400% of wages)			4,000 20,000				
	10,000		55,000		10,000		55,000

$$\text{Cost per unit} = \frac{\text{Total Cost} - \text{Value of Normal Loss}}{\text{Input Qty.} - \text{Normal Loss Qty.}}$$

$$= \frac{55,000 - 1,000}{10,000 - 1,000} = \frac{54,000}{9,000} = ₹.\ 6 \text{ per units}$$

Process II Account

	Units	Rate	Amt. ₹		Unit	Rate	Amt. ₹
To Output from P. I	8,800	6	52,800	By Normal Loss 5% of 8,800	440	3	1,320
To Direct Materials			12,640	By Output tr. to Process III	8,400	12	1,00,800
To Direct Wages			6,000				
To Direct Exp.			6,200				
To Production Overheads			24,000				
	8,800		1,01,640				
To Abnormal Gain	40	12	480				
	8,840		1,02,120		8,840		1,02,120

$$\text{Cost per unit} = \frac{1,01,640 - 1,320}{8,800 - 440} = \frac{1,00,320}{8,360} = ₹.\ 12$$

Process III Account

	Units	Rate	Amt. ₹		Unit	Rate	Amt. ₹
To Output from P. II	8,400	12	1,00,800	By Normal Loss			
To Direct Materials			23,200	10% of 8,400	840	5	4,200
To Direct Wages			10,000	By Abnormal Loss	140	24	3,360
To Direct Exp.			4,080	By Product to XY			
To Production			40,000	(Note 1)	420	6	2,520
Overheads				By Finished Stock			
				of ZENU	7,000	24	1,68,000
	8,400		1,78,080		8,400		1,78,080

Note: 1. Process *III* will be credited for By-products as follows:

		₹.
Sales 420 × 9		3,780
Less : Further processing (420 × 2)	840	
S & D Exp. (420 × 1)	420	1,260
Net amount		2,520

The rate will be 2520/420 = ₹. 6

$$\text{Cost per unit} = \frac{1,78,080 - 4,200 - 2,520}{8,400 - 840 - 420} = \frac{1,71,360}{7,140} = ₹.\ 24 \text{ per unit}$$

(*b*) Process XY Account

	Units	Rate	Amt. ₹		Unit	Rate	Amt. ₹
To Output				By Output of			
from III	420	6	2,520	*XYZ*	420	8	3,360
To Further processing							
(420 × 2)			840				
	420		3,360		420		3,360

Note: 2.

Cost of production of *XYZ*		3,360
S & D expenses 420 × 1		420
		3,780
Sales of 420 units of *XYZ* at ₹. 9 per unit	=	3,780

Illustration 34: A product passes through three processes A, B and C. The details of expenses incurred on the three processes during the year 2002 were as under :

Process:	*A*	*B*	*C*
		₹.	₹.
Unit issued/introduced (Cost per unit ₹. 100)	10,000		
Sundry Materials	₹. 10,000	15,000	5,000
Labour	30,000	80,000	65,000
Direct Expenses	6,000	18,150	27,200
Selling price per unit of output	120	165	250

Management expenses during the year were ₹. 80,000 and selling expenses were ₹. 50,000. These are not allocable to the processes.

Actual output of the three processes was:

A—9,300 units, *B*—5,400 units and *C*—2,100 units. Two-thirds of the output of Process *A* and one half of the output of Process *B* was passed on to the next process and the balance was sold. The entire output of Process *C* was sold.

The normal loss of the three processes, calculated on the input of every process was:

Process *A*—5% *B*—15% and *C*—20%

The loss of Process *A* was sold at ₹. 2 per unit, that of *B* at ₹. 5 per unit and of Process *C* at ₹. 10 per unit.

Prepare the three Processes Accounts and the Profit and Loss Account.

[*CS (Inter)*]

Solution:

Process A Account

Particulars	*Units*	*Rate*	*Amt.* ₹	*Particulars*	*Unit*	*Rate*	*Amt.* ₹
To Units introduced	10,000	100	10,00,000	By Normal loss (5% of 10,000 units)	500	2	1,000
To Sundry Materials			10,000	By Abnormal loss	200	110	22,000
To Labour			30,000	By Output transferred to Process '*B*' A/c	6,200	110	6,82,000
To Direct Expenses			6,000	By P & L A/c (Sale)	3,100	110	3,41,000
	10,000		10,46,000		10,000		10,46,000

$$\text{Cost per unit} = \frac{\text{Total cost} - \text{Value of normal loss}}{\text{Input quantity} - \text{Normal loss quantity}}$$

$$= \frac{10,46,000 - 1000}{10,000 - 500} = ₹.\ 110$$

Process B Account

Particulars	*Units*	*Rate*	*Amount*	*Particulars*	*Unit*	*Rate*	*Amount*
To Output from A's A/c	6,200	110	6,82,000	By Normal Loss (15% of 6,200 units)	930	5	4.650
To Sundry Material			15,000	By Output Transferred to Process "C" A/c	2,700	150	4,05,000
To Labour			80,000	By P & L A/c (Sale)	2,700	150	4,05,000
To Direct Expenses			18,150				
	6,200		7,95,150				
To Abnormal Gain	130	150	19,500				
	6,330		8,14,650		6,330		8,14,650

$$\text{Cost per unit} = \frac{7,95,150 - 4,650}{6,200 - 930} = ₹.\ 150$$

Process C Account

Particulars	*Units*	*Rate*	*Amt.* ₹	*Particulars*	*Unit*	*Rate*	*Amt.* ₹
To Output from B	2,700	150	4,05,000	By Normal Loss (20% of 2,700)	540	10	5,400
To Sundry Materials			5,000	By Abnormal Loss	60	230	13,800
To Labour			65,000	By P & L Account	2,100	230	4,83,000
To Direct Expenses			27,200				
	2,700		5,02,200		2,700		5,02,200

$$\text{Cost per unit} = \frac{5,02,200 - 5,400}{2,700 - 540} = \frac{4,96,800}{2,160} = ₹.\ 230$$

Profit & Loss Account

Particulars	Units	Rate	Amt. ₹	Particulars	Unit	Rate	Amt. ₹
To Process *A*	3,100	110	3,41,000	By Sales:			
To Process *B*	2,700	150	4,05,000	Process A	3,100	120	3,72,000
To Process C	2,100	230	4,83,000	Process B	2,700	165	4,45,500
To Management expenses			80,000	Process C	2,100	250	5,25,000
To Selling Expenses			50,000	By Abnormal Gain			18,850
To Abnormal Loss			34,800	By Net loss			32,450
	7,900		13,93,800		7,900		13,93,800

Abnormal Loss Account

Particulars	Units	Rate	Amt. ₹	Particulars	Unit	Rate	Amt. ₹
To Process *A*	200	110	22,000	By Sales	200	2	400
To Process *C*	60	230	13,800	By Sales	60	10	600
				By P & L A/c			34,800
	260		35,800		260		35,800

Abnormal Gain Account

Particulars	Units	Rate	Amt. ₹	Particulars	Unit	Rate	Amt. ₹
To Normal Loss A/c	130	5	650	By Process *B*	130	150	19,500
To P & L A/c			18,850				
	130		19,500		130		19,500

Illustration 35: The input to a purifying process was 16,000 kg of basic material purchased @ ₹. 1.20 per kg. Process wages amounted to ₹. 720 and overhead was applied @ 240% of the labour cost. Indirect materials of negligible weight were introduced into the process at a cost of ₹. 336. The actual output from the process weighed 15,000 kg. The normal yield of the process is 92%. Any difference in weight between the input of basic material and output of purified material (product) is sold @ ₹. 0.50 per kg.

The process is operated under a licence which provides for the payment of royalty @ ₹. 0.15 per kg. of the purified material produced.

Prepare : (*i*) Purifying Process Account (*ii*) Normal Wastage Account (*iii*) Abnormal Wastage/Yield Account (*iv*) Royalty Payable Account. **[*CA (Inter)*]**

Solution:

Purifying Process Account

	Kg	Rate	Amt. (₹)		Kg.	Rate	Amt. (₹)
To Basic Material	16,000	1.20	19,200	By Normal Wastage			
To Process Wages			720	(8% of 16,000)	1,280	0.50	640
To Overheads (240% of labour cost)			1,728	By Output tr. to Prodn. A/c	15,000	1.45	21,750
To Indirect Materials			336				
	16,000		21,984				
To Abnormal Yield	280	1.45	406				
	16,280		22,390		16,280		22,390

Working Note:

(1) Cost per unit $= \dfrac{\text{Total cost} - \text{Value of normal wastage}}{\text{Input Quantity} - \text{Normal Loss Quantity}}$

$$= \frac{21984 - 640}{16{,}000 - 1{,}280} = ₹.\ 1.45 \text{ per kg.}$$

(2) Abnormal yield is calculated as below:

Input	16,000 kg
Normal loss 8%	1280
Normal output	14,720
Actual output	15,000
Abnormal yield	280 kg

Normal Wastage Account

	Kg.	Rate	Amt. ₹		Kg.	Rate	Amt. ₹
To Purifying Process A/c	1,280	0.50	640	By Debtors/cash (Sale)	1000	0.50	500
				By Abnormal Yield A/c (Note 3)	280	0.50	140
	1,280		640		1,280		640

Abnormal Yield Account

	Kg.	Rate	Amt. ₹		Kg.	Rate	Amt. ₹
To Normal Wastage	280	0.50	140	By Purifying Process A/c	280	1.45	406
To Costing P & L A/c (Abnormal profit)			266				
	280		460		280		406

Royalty Payable Account

	₹		₹
To Cash	2,250	By Production A/c (15,000 × 0.15) (Note 4)	2,250

Production Account

	Kg.	Rate	Amt. (₹)		Kg.	Rate	Amt. (₹)
To Purifying Process	15,000	1.45	21,750	By Finished Stock A/c (1.45 + 0.15) = 1.60 per kg)	15,000	1.60	24,000
To Royalty Payable A/c (15,000 × 0.15)			2,250				
	15,000		24,000		15,000		24,000

Equivalent Units of Production

Illustration 36: The following data pertains to Process *I* for March of Beta Limited:

		₹.
Opening Work-in-Progress	1.500 units valued at	15,000
Degree of completion: Materials 100%; Labour and Overheads $33\frac{1}{3}$%		
Input of Materials	18,500 units at	52,000
Direct Labour		14,000
Overheads		28,000
Closing Work-in-Progress	5,000 units	
Degree of completion : Materials 90% and Labour and Overheads 30%		

Normal Process Loss is 10% of total Input (opening work-in-progress units + units put in)

Scrap value ₹. 2.00 per unit

Units transferred to the next process 15,000 units

You are required to:

(*a*) Compute equivalent units of production.

(*b*) Compute cost per equivalent unit for each cost element *i.e.* material, labour and overheads.

(*c*) Compute the cost of finished output and closing work-in-Progress.

(*d*) Prepare the process and other accounts.

Assume: (*i*) FIFO Method is used by the Company. (*ii*) The cost of opening Work in Progress is fully transferred to the next process.

Solution:

Statement of Equivalent Units of Production

Input Units	*Particulars*	*Output*	*Equivalent units*					
			Materials		*Labour*		*Overheads*	
			%	*Units*	%	*Units*	%	*Units*
1,500	Op. WIP	1,500	—	—	$66\frac{2}{3}$	1,000	$66\frac{2}{3}$	1000
18,500	Introduced units							
	Introduced & Completed in the period.	13,500	100	13,500	100	13,500	100	13,500
	Transferred to next Process.	15,000						
	Normal Loss 10% of (1,500 + 18,500)	2,000	—	—	—	—	—	—
	Closing WIP	5,000	90	4,500	30	1,500	30	1,500
		22,000		18,000		16,000		16,000
	Abnormal Gain	(–) 2,000	100	2,000	100	2,000	100	2,000
20,000	Total	20,000		16,000		14,000		14,000

(b) Statement of Cost per unit

	Material	*Labour*	*Overhead*
Materials:	52,000		
Less: Scrap Value			
2,000 × 2 =	4,000		
	48,000	14,000	28,000
Cost per Unit	16,000	14,000	14,000
Total Cost per Unit ₹. 6	= ₹. 3	= ₹. 1	= ₹. 2

(c) Statement of Cost of Finished Output & Closing WIP

			Cost per unit	*Cost* ₹	*Total* ₹
Op. WIP	Materials	—	—		
(for completion)	Labour	1,000	1	1,000	
Introduced &	Overheads	1,000	2	2,000	3,000
Completed					
during period	Total Cost	13,500	6		81,000
Closing WIP	Materials	4,500	3	13,500	
	Labour	1,500	1	1,500	
	Overheads	1,500	2	3,000	18,000
Abnormal gain	Total Cost	2,000	6		12,000

Cost of Finished Output	*Units*	*Cost (₹.)*
Op. WIP	1,500	15,000
Op. WIP for Completion		3,000
	1,500	18,000
Introduced & Completed during period	13,500	81,000
Finished Output tr. to Next Process	15,000	99,000

(d) Process I Account

	Units	*Amount* ₹		*Units*	*Amounts* ₹
To Opening WIP	1,500	15,000	By Normal Loss	2,000	4,000
To Materials	18,500	52,000	By Output tr. to		
To Direct Labour		14,000	Process II	15,000	99,000
To Overheads		28,000	By Closing		
	20,000	1,09,000	WIP.	5,000	18,000
To Abnormal Gain	2,000	12,000			
	22,000	1,21,000		22,000	1,21,000

Abnormal Gain Account

	Units	*Amount*		*Units*	*Amounts*
To Normal Loss A/c	2,000	4,000	By Process I A/c	2,000	12,000
To Costing P & L A/c		8,000			
	2,000	12,000		2,000	12,000

Normal Loss Account

	Units	Amount ₹.		Units	Amounts ₹.
To Process I	2,000	4,000	By Abnormal Gain A/c	2,000	4,000

	Units
Op. WIP	1,500
Introduced	18,500
	20,000
Transferred to Next Process	15,000
Closing WIP	5,000

Illustrator 37: R.P. Ltd. furnishes you the following information relating to Process B for the month of October 2004 :

(*i*) Opening work-in-process — Nil

(*ii*) Units introduced — 10,000 units @ ₹. 3 per unit

(*iii*) Expenses debited to the process :

		₹.
Direct Materials	—	14,650
Labour	—	21,148
Overheads	—	42,000

(*iv*) Normal loss in process—one per cent of input.

(*v*) Closing work-in-progress—350 units—Degree of Completion:

Material — 100%

Labour and Overheads — 50%

(*vi*) Finished Output—9,500 units.

(*vii*) Degree of completion of Abnormal Loss:

Material—100%

Labour and Overheads—80%

(*viii*) Units scrapped as normal loss were sold at ₹. 1 per unit.

(*ix*) All the units of abnormal loss were sold at ₹. 2.50 per unit

Prepare: 1. Statement of Equivalent production: 2. Statement of cost of Finished goods, Abnormal loss and Closing Work-in-Progress. 3. Process B account.

Solution:

Statement of Equivalent Production

Particulars	*Output*	*Equivalent units*					
		Materials		*Labour*		*Overheads*	
		Units	*%*	*Units*	*%*	*Units*	*%*
Finished output	9,500	9,500	100	9,500	100	9,500	100
Normal loss 1% of 10,000	100	—	—	—	—	—	—
Abnormal loss (balancing figure)	50	50	100	40	80	40	80
Closing WIP	350	350	100	175	50	175	50
Total	10,000	9,900		9,715		9,715	

Statement of Cost per unit

	Material	*Labour*	*Overheads*
	₹.	₹.	₹.
Unit introduced 10,000 × 3 =	30,000		
Direct Materials	14650		
Less: Value of normal loss	100		
	44,550	21,148	42,000
Cost per unit of EQP	44550/9900	21148/9715	42,000/9,715
Total ₹. 11.00 per unit	4.50	2.1768	4.3232

2. Statement of Cost

			₹.
Finished Goods 9,500 × 11			1,04,500
Abnormal loss:	Materials 50 × 4.50	225	
	Labour 40 × 2.1768	87	
	Overheads 40 × 4.3232	173	485
Closing work-in-progress :			
	Materials 350 × 4.50	1575	
	Labour 175 × 2.1768	381	
	Overheads 175 × 4.3232	757	2,713

3. Process B Account

	Units	₹		*Units*	₹
To Opening WIP	—	—	By Normal loss	100	100
To Units introduced	10,000	30,000	By Abnormal loss	50	485
To Direct Materials		14,650	By Finished output	9,500	1,04,500
To Labour		21,148	By Closing WIP	350	2,713
To Overheads		42,000			
	10,000	1,07,798		10,000	1,07,798

Abnormal Loss Account

	Units	₹		*Units*	₹
To Process B A/c	50	485	By Cash (sold @ ₹. 2.50	50	125
			By Costing P & L A/c (loss)		360
	50	485		50	485

Illustrator 38: **M/s AB Co. Ltd., is engaged in process in Engineering Industry. During the month of April, 2,000 units were introduced in Process '*X*'. The normal loss was estimated at 5% of input. At the end of the month, 1,400 units have been produced and transferred to Process '*Y*'; 460 units were incomplete; and 140 units, after passing through the process fully, had to be scrapped in full. The incomplete units had reached the following stage of completion.**

Material	**75% complete**
Labour and Overhead	**50% complete**

Following further information is available relating to the Process '*X*'.

	₹.
Cost of 2,000 units	58,000
Additional direct materials	14,400
Direct Labour	33,500
Production Overhead	16,700

Units scrapped realised ₹. 10 each. Prepare Statement of equivalent production, Statement of cost, Statement of evaluation and Process '*X*' Account.

Solution:

Statement of Equivalent Production

Input Units	*Output*	*Units*	*Equivalent Production (Units)*					
			Materials		*Labour*		*Overheads*	
			Qnty.	*%*	*Qnty.*	*%*	*Qnty.*	*%*
	Opening work-in-Progress	—	—	—	—	—	—	—
2000	Introduced during the month	—	—	—	—	—	—	—
	Completed Units	1,400	1,400	100	1,400	100	1,400	100
	Normal Loss (5% of 2000)	100	—	—	—	—	—	—
	Abnormal Loss (Bal. figure)	40	40	100	40	100	40	100
	Closing Work-in-Progress	460	345	75	230	50	230	50
2000	Total	2000	1785		1670		1670	

Statement of Cost per unit

	Cost ₹.	Equivalent Units	Cost per Equivalent Unit ₹.
Materials			
2000 Units introduced	58,000		
Additional Direct Material	14,400		
	72,400		
Less: Scrap value of normal loss (100 × ₹. 10)	1,000		
	71,400	1785	40.00
Direct Labour	33,500	1670	20.06
Overhead	16,700	1670	10.00
Total	1,21,600		70.06

Statement of Cost

		Equivalent Units	*Cost per Eq. Unit*	*Cost*	*Total Cost ₹.*
Units Completed	Total Cost	1,400	70.06		98.084
Abnormal Loss	Total Cost	40	70.06		2,802
Closing WIP	Material	345	40.00	13,800	
	Labour	230	20.06	4,614	
	Overhead	230	10.00	2,300	20,714
					1,21,600

Process 'X' Account

Particulars	*Units*	*Amount ₹.*	*Particulars*	*Units*	*Amount ₹.*
To Units introduced	2,000	58,000	By Normal Loss (100 × 10)	100	1,000
To Materials		14,400	By Abnormal Loss Account	40	2,802
To Labour		33,500	By Units completed and transferred to Process 'Y'	1,400	98,084
To Overheads		16,700	By Closing Work-in-Progress c/d	460	20,714
	2,000	1,22,600		2,000	1,22,600

Illustration 39: The following data are available in respect of Process *I* for the month of February 2005:

(1) Opening Stock of work-in-process: 800 units at a total cost of ₹. 4,000.

(2) Degree of completion of opening work-in-process:

Materials	100%
Labour	60%
Overheads	60%

(3) Input of materials at a total cost of ₹. 36,800 for 9,200 Units.

(4) Direct wages ₹. 16,740.

(5) Production overhead ₹. 8,370.

(6) Units scrapped 1,200 units. The stage of completion of these units was:

Materials	100%
Labour	80%
Overheads	80%

(7) Closing work-in-process: 900 units. The stage of completion of these units was:

Materials	100%
Labour	70%
Overheads	70%

(8) 7,900 units were completed and transferred to the next process.

(9) Normal loss is 8% of the total input (opening stock plus units put in)

(10) Scrap value is ₹. 4 per unit.

You are required to :

(*a*) Compute equivalent production.

(*b*) Calculate the cost per equivalent unit for each element.

(*c*) Calculate the cost of abnormal loss (or gain), closing work-in-process and the units transferred to the next process using the FIFO Method.

(*d*) Show the Process Account for February 2005. **[*C.A. Inter*]**

Solution:

Statement of Equivalent Production

Particulars	*Output*	*Equivalent units*					
		Materials		*Labour*		*Overheads*	
		%	*Units*	%	*Units*	%	*Units*
Op. WIP (for completion)	800	—	—	40	320	40	320
Introduced & completed	7,100	100	7,100	100	7,100	100	7,100
Tr. to next process	7,900						
Normal loss 8% of (800 + 9,200)	800	—	—	—	—	—	—
Abnormal loss 1,200 – 800	400	100	400	80	320	80	320
Closing WIP	900	100	900	70	630	70	630
Total	10,000		8,400		8,370		8,370

Statement of Cost Per Unit

	Material	*Labour*	*Overheads*
(*b*) Current Cost:	36,800	16,740	8,370
Less: Scrap value 800 × 4	3,200	—	—
	33,600	16,740	8,370
Cost per unit	33,600/8400 = 4.00	16740/8370 = 2.00	8370/8370 = 1.00
Total cost per unit ₹. 7.00			

(*c*) Statement of Cost

Particulars	*Elements*	*Units*	*Cost per unit*	*Cost*	*Total*
Op. WIP (for completion	Material	—	—	—	
	Labour	320	2	640	
	Overhead	320	1	320	960
Introduced & completed	Total cost	7,100	7		49,700
Abnormal loss	Materials	400	4	1,600	
	Labour	320	2	640	
	Overhead	320	1	320	2,560
Closing WIP	Materials	900	4	3,600	
	Labour	630	2	1,260	
	Overhead	630	1	630	5,490

Transferred to Next Process (FIFO Method)

	Units	*Cost (₹.)*
Opening WIP	800	4,000
" " (for completion)		960
Introduced & Completed	7,100	49,700
Transferred to next process	7,900	54,660

Process Account

	Units	Amount ₹		Units	Amount ₹
To Opening WIP	800	4,000	By Normal loss	800	3,200
To Materials	9,200	36,800	By Abnormal loss	400	2,560
To Direct wages		16,740	By Completed & transferred to next process	7,900	54,660
To Prodn. Overheads		8,370	By Closing WIP	900	5,490
	10,000	65,910		10,000	65,910

Illustration 40: A company manufactures a product which involves two consecutive processes, viz., Pressing and Polishing. For the month of October, 2004, the following information is available:

	Pressing	Polishing
Opening stock	—	—
Input of units in process	1,200	1,000
Units completed	1,000	500
Units under process	200	500
Materials Cost	₹. 96,000	₹. 8,000
Conversion Cost	₹. 3,36,000	₹. 54,000

For incomplete units in process, charge materials cost at 100 per cent and conversion cost at 60 per cent in the Pressing Process and 50 per cent in Polishing Process. Prepare a statement of cost and calculate the selling price per unit which will result in 25 per cent profit on sale price. **[*CA (Inter)*]**

Solution:

Statement of Equivalent Production of Pressing Process

Input Units	*Output*	*Units*	*Equivalent Production*			
			Materials		*Conversion cost*	
			(Units)	*%*	*(Units)*	*%*
1,200	Completed	1,000	1,000	100	1,000	100
	Work-in-process	200	200	100	120	60
1,200		1,200	1,200		1,120	

Statement of Equivalent Production of Polishing Process

Input Units	*Output*	*Units*	*Equivalent Productions*			
			Materials		*Conversion cost*	
			(Units)	*%*	*(Units)*	*%*
1,000	Completed	500	500	100	500	100
	Work-in-process	500	500	100	250	50
1,000		1,000	1,000		750	

Statement of Cost

Pressing Process: Elements of Cost	*Cost* ₹	*Equivalent units*	*Cost per units*
Materials Cost	96,000	1,200	80
Conversion Cost	3,36,000	1,120	300
Total	4,32,000		380

Cost of unit completed = 1,000 units at ₹. 380 = 3,80,000

Pressing Process: Elements of Cost	*Cost (₹)*	*Equivalent units*	*Cost per unit (₹)*
Input Cost	3,80,000	1,000	380
Materials Cost	8,000	1,000	8
Conversion Cost	54,000	750	72
Total	4,42,000		460

Cost of Units Completed = 500 units at ₹. 460 = ₹. 2,30,000

Selling price per unit:

	₹.
Cost per unit	460.00
Profit at 25% on Sale Price *i.e.*, 33-1/3% on Cost	153.33
Selling Price per unit	613.33

Total Cost of Process

Pressing Process		₹.
Materials	200 units at ₹. 80	16,000
Conversion Cost	120 units at ₹. 300	36,000
Cost of W.I.P.		52,000
Cost of completed units		3,80,000
Total Cost of Process		4,32,000
Polishing process		₹.
Materials	500 units at ₹. 388 (380 + 8)	1,94,000
Conversion Cost	250 units at ₹. 72	18,000
Cost of W.I.P.		2,12,000
Cost of completed units		2,30,000
Total Cost of process		4,42,000

Illustration 41: The following information is given in respect of Process No. 3 for the month of January, 2001.

Opening stock–2,000 units made-up of:

Direct Materials-I	₹. 12,350
Direct Material-II	13,200
Direct Labour	17,500
Overheads	11,000

Transferred from Process No. 2: 20,000 units @ ₹. 6.00 per unit.

Transferred to Process No. 4: 17,000 units

Expenditure incurred in Process No. 3:

Direct Mateials	₹. 30,000
Direct Labour	60,000
Ovhverheads	60,000

Scrap: 1,000 units – Direct materials 100%, Direct Labour 60%, Overheads, 40%.

Normal Loss 10% of production

Scrapped units realised ₹. 4 per unit

Closing Stock: 4,000 units – Degree of completion: Direct Materials 80%, Direct Labour 60% and Overheads 40%.

Prepare Process No. 3 Account using *average price method*, alongwith necessary supporting statements. **[*CS (Inter)*]**

Statements:

Process 3
(Average Method)
Statement of Equivalent Production

Period January, 2001
Output: 17,000 units

Input		*Output*		*Equivalent Production*							
Particulars	*Units*	*Particulars*	*Units*	*Material—I*		*Material—II*		*Labour*		*Overheads*	
				Units	*%*	*Units*	*%*	*Units*	*%*	*Units*	*%*
Op. Stock	2,000	Normal Loss*	1,800	—		—		—		—	
New units introduced	20,000	Units completed & transferred to Process 4	17,000	17,000	100	17,000	100	17,000	100	17,000	100
		C/stock	4,000	4,000	100	3,200	80	2,400	60	1,600	40
			22,800	21,000		20,200		19,400		18,600	
		Abnormal gain	800	800	100	800	100	800	100	800	100
	22,000		22,000	20,200		19,400		18,600		17,800	

* 10% of production or 10% of {2,000 + 20,000 – 4,000} = 1,800 units.

Statement of cost for each element

Elements of Cost	*Cost of opening WIP* ₹	*Cost in Process* ₹	*Total cost* ₹	*Equivalent production (units)*	*Cost per unit* ₹
Material-I	12,350				
Cost transferred from Process No. 2					
20,000 × ₹. 6		1,20,000			
Less: Scrap realised 1,800 × ₹. 4		(7,200)			
	12,350	1,12,800	1,25,150	20,200	6.1955
Material II	13,200	30,000	43,200	19,400	2.2268
Direct Labour	17,500	60,000	77,500	18,600	4.1667
Overhead	11,000	60,000	71,000	17,800	3.9888
Total	54,050	2,62,800	3,16,850		16.5778

Statement of apportionment of cost

Items	*Elements*	*Equivalent Production (units)*	*Cost per unit* ₹	*Cost* ₹	*Total cost* ₹
Units introduced and completed during the period	Material-I	17,000	6.1955	1,05,324	
	Material-II	17,000	2.2268	37,856	
	Labour	17,000	4.1667	70,833	
	Overhead	17,000	3.9888	67,809	2,81,822
Closing Stock	Material-I	4,000	6.1955	24,782	
	Material-II	3,200	2.2268	7,126	
	Labour	2,400	4.1667	10,000	
	Overhead	1,600	3.9888	6,382	48,290
Abnormal Gain	Material-I	800	6.1955	4,956	
	Material-II	800	2.2268	1,782	
	Labour	800	4.1667	3,333	
	Overhead	800	3,9888	3,191	–13,262
Total cost (Total cost less cost of abnormal gain)					3,16,850

Process No. 3 Account

Particulars	Units	Amount ₹.	Particulars	Units	Amount ₹.
To Opening stock	2,000	54,050	By Normal loss	1,800	7,200
To Units introduced	20,000	1,20,000	By Process 4	17,000	2,81,822
To Material-II		30,000	By Closing Stock	4,000	48,290
To Labour A/c		60,000			
To Overhead		60,000			
To Abnormal gain A/c	800	13,262			
	22,800	3,37,312		22,800	3,37,312

Working Note.

Normal loss is 10% of production *i.e.,* opening stock plus receipts minus closing stock

Production = 2,000 units + 20,000 units – 4,000 units = 18,000 units.

Normal Loss = 10 % of 18,000 = 18,000 units.

Illustration 42: Following data are available for a product for the month of July,

	Process I	Process II
Opening work-in-Progress	Nil	Nil
Costs incurred during the month		
Direct Materials	₹. 60,000	
Labour	₹. 12,000	16,000
Factory overheads	₹. 24,000	20,000
Units of Production		
Received in Process	40,000	36,000
Completed and Transferred	36,000	32,000
Closing Work-in-Progress	2,000	?
Normal Loss in Process	2,000	1,500
Production remaining in Process has to be valued as follows:		
Materials	100%	
Labour	50%	
Overheads	50%	

There has been no abnormal loss in Process II.

Prepare Process Accounts after working out the missing figures and with detailed workings.

Solution:

Process I
Statement of Equivalent Production

	Units	Equivalent Production					
		Materials		Labour		Fy. Overheads	
		%	Units	%	Units	%	Units
Completed & transferred	36,000	100	36,000	100	36,000	100	36,000
Normal loss in process	2,000	—	—	—	—	—	—
Closing WIP	2,000	100	2,000	50	1,000	50	1,000
Total	40,000		38,000		37,000		37,000
Costs incurred (₹.)	96,000		60,000		12,000		24,000
Cost per unit			60,000 / 38,000		12,000 / 37,000		24,000 / 37,000
	2.5519		= 1.5789		= 0.3243		= 0.6487

Statement of Cost

			₹.
Completed & transferred (36,000 × 2.5519)			91,869
Closing WIP:			
Materials	(2,000 × 1.5789)	3,158	
Labour	(1,000 × 0.3243)	324	
Overheads	(1,000 × 0.6487)	649	4,131
			96,000

Process I Account

	Units	₹.		Units	₹.
To Direct Materials	40,000	60,000	By Normal loss	2,000	—
To Labour		12,000	By Closing WIP	2,000	4,131
To Fy. Overheads		24,000	By Output tr. to Process II	36,000	91,869
	40,000	96,000		40,000	96,000

Process II
Statement of Equivalent Production

	Units	Equivalent units					
		Materials		Labour		Fy. Overheads	
		%	Units	%	Units	%	Units
Completed & transferred	32,000	100	32,000	100	32,000	100	32,000
Normal loss in process	1,500	—	—	—	—	—	—
Closing WIP (Balancing Figure)	2,500	100	2,500	50	1,250	50	1,250
	36,000		34,500		33,250		33,250
Costs incurred (₹.)	1,27,869		91,869		16,000		20,000
Cost per unit			91,869 / 34,500		16,000 / 33,250		20,000 / 33,200
Total ₹. 3.74557			= 2.66287		= 0.4812		= 0.6015

Statement of Cost

			₹.
Completed & transferred (32,000 × 3.74557)			1,19,858
Closing WIP			
Materials	(2,500 × 2.66287)	6,657	
Labour	(1,250 × 0.4812)	602	
Overheads	(1,250 × 0.6015)	752	8,011
			1,27,869

Process II Account

	Units	₹		Units	₹
To Output from Process I	36,000	91,869	By Normal loss	1,500	—
To Labour		16,000	By Closing WIP	2,500	8,011
To Factory Overheads		20,000	By Output completed	32,000	1,19,858
Total	36,000	1,27,869		36,000	1,27,869

Illustration 43: Prepare a Statement of Equivalent Production, Cost Statement, Statement of Valuation and Process Account from the following particulars using FIFO method :

(*a*) Opening Work-in-Progress – 900 units at ₹. 4,500
Degree of completion:
Material – 100 %
Labour and Overheads – 60%

(*b*) Input of materials – 9100 units at ₹. 27,300
Expenses :
Labour – ₹. 12,300
Overheads – ₹. 8,200.

(*c*) Units scrapped – 1,200 units
Degree of completion :
Material – 100%
Labour and Overheads – 70%

(*d*) Closing Work-in-Progress – 1000 units
Degree of Completion :
Material – 100%
Labour and Overheads – 80%

(*e*) Finished units transferred to next process – 7800

(*f*) Normal Scrap – 10% of input; scrap realisation @ ₹. 3 per unit.

If the above statements are prepared under average cost method, do you need any more details?

Solution:

Statement of Equivalent Production (Under FIFO Method)

Input units	Details	Output Units	Equivalent Units			
			Materials		Labour & Overheads	
			%	Units	%	Units
900	Opening WIP					
9,100	Units introduced					
	Worked on WIP & Completed	900	—	—	40	360
	Units Worked & Completed	6,900	100	6,900	100	6,900
	Units completed & transferred to next process	7,800				
	Normal loss (10%)	1,000	—	—	—	—
	Abnormal loss	200	100	200	70	140
	Closing WIP	1,000	100	1,000	80	800
1,000		10,000		8,100		8,200

Statement of Cost per units

	Amount ₹	Equivalent units	Cost per Equivalent unit ₹
Materials:	27,300		
Less: Realisation			
form normal Scrap 1000 × 3 =	3,000		
	24,300	8,100	3.00
Labour	12,300	8,200	1.50
Overheads	8,200	8,200	1.00
Total	44,800		5.50

Statement of Cost

Item	*Elements*	*Equivalent units*	*Cost per Eq. units*		*Total Cost* ₹
(*i*) Opening WIP completed	Labour	360	1.50	540	
	Overheads	360	1.00	360	900
(*ii*) Units introduced & completed	Total	6,900	5.50	—	37,950
(*iii*) Abnormal Loss	Material	200	3.00	600	
	Labour	140	1.50	210	
	Overhead	140	1.00	140	950
(*iv*) Closing WIP	Material	1,000	3.00	3,000	
	Labour	800	1.50	1,200	
	Overhead	800	1.00	800	5,000
					44,800

Process Account

	Units	Amount ₹		Units	Amount ₹
To Opening WIP	900	4,500	By Transfer to next process	7,800	43,350
To Materials	9,100	27,300	By Normal Loss – realisation	1000	3,000
To Labour		12,300	By Abnormal loss	200	950
To Overheads		8,200	By Closing WIP	1,000	5,000
	10,000	52,300		10,000	52,300

Working Notes:

(*i*) Transfer to next process has been calculated as below

	₹.
Value of opening WIP (900 units)	4,500
Cost incurred for completing opening work-in-progress	900
Units introduced & completed (6900 units)	37,950
Cost of transfer to next process (7,800 units)	43,350

(*ii*) *Average Cost Method* - Under average cost method element-wise cost in respect of opening WIP will be taken up. The average cost is past cost + current cost in respect of materials, labour and overheads separately.

For preparing the above statements under *average cost method*, we require the element-wise cost particulars in respect of opening WIP. In the question, the cost of opening WIP has been given as ₹. 4,500. Break-up of ₹. 4,500 is required *i.e.* how much material cost, labour cost and overheads separately required in order to work out the average cost (*i.e.* past cost + current cost) in respect of materials labour and overheads separately.

Inter-Process Profit

Illustration 44: Product A passes through three processes, before it is transferred to the finished stock. The following information is obtained for the month of July.

	Process I	Process II	Process III	Finished Stock
	₹.	₹.	₹.	₹.
Opening stock	5,000	8,000	10,000	20,000
Direct materials	40,000	12,000	15,000	—
Direct wages	35,000	40,000	35,000	—
Manufacturing overheads	20,000	24,000	20,000	—
Closing stock	10,000	4,000	15,000	30,000
Profit percentage on transfer to next process	25%	20%	10%	—
Inter-process profit for opening stock	—	1,395	2,690	6,534

Stock in process is valued at prime cost and finished stock has been valued at the price at which it is received from Process III. Sales during the period were ₹. 4,00,000. Prepare Process Cost accounts.

Solution:

Process 1 Account

	Total ₹	Cost ₹	Profit ₹		Total ₹	Cost ₹	Profit ₹
To Stock b/d	5,000	5,000	—	By Process 2 (Transfer)	1,20,000	90,000	30,000
To Direct Material	40,000	40,000	—				
To Direct Labour	35,000	35,000	—				
	80,000	80,000					
Less: Stock c/d	10,000	10,000					
Prime Cost	70,000	70,000					
To Prod. Overhead	20,000	20,000					
Process Cost	90,000	90,000	—				
To Profit (25% on transfer Price or 33-1/3% on Cost)	30,000	—	30,000				
	1,20,000	90,000	30,000		1,20,000	90,000	30,000

Process 2 Account

	Total ₹	Cost ₹	Profit ₹		Total ₹	Cost ₹	Profit ₹
To Stock	8,000	6,605	1,395	By Process A/c (Transfer)	2,50,000	1,69,303	80,697
To Process I (Transfer)	1,20,000	90,000	30,000				
To Direct Materials	12,000	12,000	—				
To Direct Labour	40,000	40,000	—				
	1,80,000	1,48,605	31,395				
Less: Stock	4,000	3,302	698				
Prime Cost	1,76,000	1,45,303	30,697				
To Prod. Overhead	24,000	24,000	—				
Process Cost	2,00,000	1,69,303	30,697				
To Profit (25% on Transfer Price or 25% on Cost)	50,000	—	50,000				
	2,50,000	1,69,303	80,697		2,50,000	1,69,303	80,697

Note: Proportionate profit earned by previous process included in closing stock 4,000 × 31,395/1,80,000 = ₹. 696.

Process 3 Account

	Total ₹	Cost ₹	Profit ₹		Total ₹	Cost ₹	Profit ₹
To Stock	10,000	7,310	2,690	By Finished stock A/c	3,50,000	2,35,648	1,14,352
To Process 2 A/c (Transfer)	2,50,000	1,69,303	80,697				
To Direct Materials	15,000	15,000	—				
To Direct Labour	35,000	35,000	—				
	3,10,000	2,26,613	83,387				
Less: Stock	15,000	10,965	4,035				
Prime Cost	2,95,000	2,15,648	79,352				
To Prod. Overhead	20,000	20,000	—				
Process Cost	3,15,000	2,35,648	79,352				
To Profit (10% on Transfer Price 1/9 on Cost)	35,000	—	35,000				
	3,50,000	2,35,648	1,14,352		3,50,000	2,35,648	1,14,352

Note: Proportionate profit earned by earlier processes included on closing stock = 15,000 × 83,307/3,10,000 = ₹. 4,035.

Finished Stock Account

	Total ₹	Cost ₹	Profit ₹		Total ₹	Cost ₹	Profit ₹
To Stock	20,000	13,466	6,534	By Sales	4,00,000	2,28,916	1,71,084
To Process 3 A/c (Transfer)	3,50,000	2,35,648	1,14,352				
	3,70,000	2,49,114	1,20,886				
Less: Stock	30,000	20,198	9,802				
	3,40,000	2,28,916	1,11,084				
To Profit	60,000		60,000				
	4,00,000	2,28,916	1,71,084		4,00,000	2,28,916	1,71,084

Note: Proportionate profit earned by earlier processes included in the closing stock = 30,000 × 1,14,352/3,50,000 = ₹. 9,802.

Actual Realised Profit	₹.	₹.
Process 1		30,000
Process 2	50,000	
Add: Opening Provision	1,395	
	51,395	
Less: Closing Provision	698	50,697
Process 3	35,000	
Add: Opening Provision	2,690	
Less: Closing Provision	37,690	
	4,035	33,655
Finished Stock	60,000	
Add: Opening Provision	6,534	
Less: Closing Provision	66,534	
	9,802	56,732
	Total	1,71,084

QUESTIONS

OBJECTIVE QUESTIONS

I. *State whether the following statements are true or false* :

(*i*) Equivalent production means the production in terms of completed units.
(*ii*) Process costing is suitable for garment industry.
(*iii*) Direct and indirect materials are not ordinarily distinguished in porcess costing.
(*iv*) Process costing and job costing cannot be applied in the same industry simultaneously.
(*v*) Abnormal process loss is absorbed in goods units of production.
(*vi*) Output of one process may be transferred to the subsequent process at market proce or at cost.
(*vii*) There is no difference between operation costing and operating costing.
(*viii*) The main product of one industry may be the by-product of another.
(*ix*) The management may treat a joint product as a by-product.
(*x*) Waste has no realisable market value.
(*xi*) Spoiled work can be rectified while a defective work cannot be rectified.
(*xii*) There is no difference between 'joint cost' and 'common cost'.

[**Ans.** True (*i*), (*iii*), (*vi*), (*viii*), (*ix*), (*x*);
False, (*ii*), (*iv*), (*v*), (*vii*), (*xi*), (*xii*)]

II. *Fill in the blanks*:

(*i*) The excess of anticipated loss over actual loss in a process is called............ ....
(*ii*) Two main methods for computing equivalent production are.............. and .... methods.
(*iii*) In inter-process profits, the output of one process is transferred to the subsequent process at............ .... but not at............. ....
(*iv*) The cost of.............process.......... is abosrbed in the cost of production of good units produced.
(*v*) The stage of production where separate products are identified is called........... ....
(*vi*) The distinction between scrap, by-products is made from the .... of the product.
(*vii*) Costs incurred upto the point where individual products can be identified are called........... costs.

[**Ans.** (*i*) abnormal, gain ; (*ii*) FIFO, Average cost; (*iii*) market price, actual cost ; (iv) normal, loss; (*v*) Split off point ; (*vi*) relative sales value; (*vii*) joint]

III. ***Tick the correct answer:***

(*i*) A process loss which does not affect the cost per unit is :

(a) normal loss ; (b) abnormal loss ; (c) seasonal loss ; (d) standard loss.

(*ii*) In process costing, cost per unit increases due to :

(a) abnormal loss; (b) abnormal gain ; (c) normal loss ; (d) normal gain.

(*iii*) Which method of costing is suitable in chemical industries:

(a) job costing; (b) contract costing; (c) batch costing ; (d) process costing.

(*iv*) Individual products, each of a significant sales value, produced simultaneously from the identical raw material, are called :.

(a) joint products ; (b) common-products ; (c) by-products ; (d) main products.

(*v*) Trimmings in timber industry are treated as :

(a) waste ; (b) by-product ; (c) joint products ; (d) scrap.

[**Ans.** (*i*) (*b*) ; (*ii*) (*c*) ; (*iii*) (*d*) ; (*iv*) (*a*) ; (*v*) (*a*)]

IV. ***Examine correctness of following statements.***

1. Process costing is applied in textile industry.
2. Process costing is used in chemical industry.
3. Normal loss does not increase per unit cost of actual output.
4. Abnormal loss does not increase per unit cost of actual output.
5. Abnormal gain after deducting nomral loss therefrom, balance is transferred to P/L A/c
6. Equivalent product is represented by completed units of products.
7. There is clear difference between main product and by products.
8. By-products can be sold at their original form.

[**Ans.** - False (1), (3) and remaining are correct]

V. ***Indicate whether each of the following statement is 'True or False' Give reason in brief.***

1. In industries using process costing, production is mostly on a continuous basis for stock, and not against customer orders.
2. In process costing cost per unit is calculated separately for each process.
3. Process costing precedure and Job costing procedure is quite similar.
4. Abnormal process loss does not affect cost per unit.
5. In process cost procedure finished product of one process is treated as raw material for the next process.
6. A process cost system is applicable to paper mills, chemical works, textile, mills etc.
7. Process costing is ordinarily applied where all the operations are performed in one department.
8. In process industries, unlike job order industries, all units receive identical attention in each production department or operation.
9. In process costing ordinarily no distinction is made between direct and indirect materials.
10. The cost of abnormal loss is not included in the cost.
11. The output of one process may be transferred to the next process at cost or at market price.
12. Abnormal gain is credited in the process account.

[**Ans.** False are (1) (3) (6) (7), (12) Remaining are true]

VI. ***Fill in the gaps***

1. When actual wastage is more than estimated wastage, the difference is known as...............
2. When in a process 1,000 units are 60% complete then these will be equivalent to............ completed units.
3. .... proces loss is transferred to Costing P/L Account.
4. .... process loss is absorbed to cost-of produced units.

5. Upto seperation point all costs are known as..............cost.
6. That point of production where different products are identified is called.............. .

[**Ans.** (1) Abnormal loss; (2) 600; (3) Abnormal; (4) Normal; (5) Joint; (6) Seperation point]

THEORETICAL QUESTIONS

1. Define Process Costing and explain its working. For which kinds of business is process costing suitable?
2. What is by-product? How should it be treated in the ascertainment of the cost of main product.
3. How would you account for wastage in the cost of production? Define normal wastage and abnormal effective and distinguish between them.
4. Write short notes on :

   (*i*) Scrap and wastage (*ii*) Inter-Process Profit (*iii*) Joint Expenses and separate expenses (*iv*) Equivalent Production.
5. Distinguish between Job Costing and Process Costing. ***[B.Com.(H) Delhi, CA Inter.]***
6. Write short notes on Abnormal Gain in Process Costing.
7. 'The vlaue of scrap generated in a Process should be credited to the Process Account'. Do you agree with this statement? Give reasons.
8. Write short notes on 'Process Costing'.
9. What do you understand by 'Equivalent Production'?
10. Write a note on 'Accounting for by-product.
11. How Equivalent Production is calculated?
12. Distinguish between Process Loss and Scrap.
13. Explain how would you treat the following items in the account of a process costing system : (*i*) waste (*ii*) scrap.
14. Explain the term 'Waste', 'Scrap', 'Spoilage' and 'Defectives'. Enumerate the steps for control and the principles of accounting of such losses to be followed in manufacturing concern.
15. Write notes on accounting for scrap.
16. What are equivalent units of production? State the two principal methods of calculating equivalent units.
17. (*a*) What is by-product and how is it different from joint product? Give a few examples of by-product.

    (*b*) What are various methods of accounting for by-products? Briefly explain each of the methods.

SHORT-ANSWER QUESTIONS

1. Write a short definition of Process Costing.
2. Write two main characteristics of Process Costing.
3. What do you mean by loss in weight ?
4. What is meant by 'By-product' ?
5. How sale of scrap is adjusted in the Process Costing.
6. What do you understand by normal wastage and abnormal wastage ?
7. How cost of abnormal wastage is calculated ?
8. How abnormal gain is calculated ?
9. What are usual items shown in the credit side of the Crushing Process ?
10. What do you understand by Joint Cost and Subsequent Cost ?
11. How joint cost is divided ?
12. What do you understand by valuation of equivalent production ?
13. What is meant by 'Inter-process-profit' ?

SHORT-ANSWER NUMERICAL QUESTIONS

14. From the following prepare Process Account-2.

	₹
Transfer from Process - 1	40,000
Materials	10,000
Wages	20,000
Overheads	10,000
Sale of By-product	10,000

[*Ans. Transfer to Process 3 ₹. 70,000*]

15. From the following prepare Process Account - 2

Cost per unit of Process - 1	₹. 2.00
Units transferred to Process - 2	5,000 units
Opening units in Process - 2	500 units
Opening units on Process - 2	1,000 units
Cost incurred in Process - 2 .	₹. 20,000

Units transferred from Process - 2 to 3: 4000 units

[*Ans. Process 2 total cost ₹. 29,000 per units ₹. 7.25*]

16. Prepare Process Account-I from the following:

Material consumed	1000 tons @ ₹. 200 per ton
Wages and Overheads	₹. 26,000
Loss in Weight	2% of total weight put in
Sale or Scrap	5% of total weight put in @ ₹. 100 per ton.

[*Ans. Transfer to Process- 2: 930 tons at a cost of ₹. 2,21,000*]

17. From the following divide joint cost between product A and B

Total Joint Cost	₹. 19,500
Separate Cost of Product A	₹. 12,500
Separate Cost of Product B	₹. 3,100
Sales of Product B	₹. 6,000

Profit on above 30% of selling price

[*Ans. Joint cost of A ₹. 18,400, B ₹. 1,100*]

18. Divide joint cost to among products. A, B and C from the following:

Total Joint Cost	₹. 2,400
Separate cost	A ₹. 800; B ₹. 325; C ₹. 372
Sales	A ₹,. 3,000; B ₹. 1,000 C ₹. 800
Profit percentage on sales	A 20%; B 17.5% C 16%

[*Ans. Share in Joint Cost A ₹. 1,600, B ₹. 500, C ₹. 300*]

19. Prepare Product A Account on the basis of previous question

[*Ans. Cost of production ₹. 2,400, Profit ₹. 600*]

20. Prepare Process Account from the following :

Raw Material	1,000 kg @ ₹. 1.50 per kg
Direct labour	200 men @ 2.50 per man
Works Overhead	50% of Direct labour
Sale of By-product	400 kg @ ₹. 1 per kg

[*Ans. Cost of Production 600kg, ₹. 1,850 i.e. ₹. 3.08 per kg.*]

21. Prepare Process Account from the following:

Transfer from previous process	600 kg. ₹. 1,850
Direct Labour	300 men @ ₹. 1.50 per man
Works Overhead	50% of Direct labour
Sale of By-product	100kg @ 25 paise per kg

[**Ans.** *Cost of Production 500 kg. ₹. 2,500 i.e. ₹. 5 per kg*]

22. Prepare Process Account from the following :

Materials	2,000 tons at ₹.50 per ton
Wages	60,000
Factory Overheads	50% wages
Wastage	100 tons
Sale of By-product	200 tons sold at cost plus 20%

[***Ans.** Sale of By product ₹. 24,000, Production transferred to next processes 1700 tons ₹. 1,70,000*]

NUMERICAL QUESTIONS

Simple Process Accounts

1. An article has to undergo three different processes before it becomes ready for sale. From the following information, find out the cost of production of that article, if 200 articles were manufactured upto 31st December, 2003.

Expenses of 200 articles :

	Mfg. Process ₹.	*Refining Process* ₹.	*Finishing Process* ₹.
Materials	2,000	1,000	750
Labour	1,500	2,500	1,000
Direct Expenses	400	200	300

The indirect expenses for the period amount to ₹. 6,000 in the factory out of which ₹. 2,000 is attributable to this product. There was no stock at the end in any process. The indirect expenses should be allocated to each process on the basis of direct labour.

[**Ans.** *Mfg. Process : Total Cost ₹. 4,500 Cost per unit ₹. 22.50; Ref. Process : Total Cost ₹. 9,200 Cost per unit ₹. 46.00; Fin. Process : Total Cost ₹. 11,650 Cost per unit ₹. 58.25*]

2. A particular brand phenyl passes through three consecutive processes, *viz. A, B* and *C*. During the week ended 15th March, 2003, 500 grosses of bottles were produced. The cost books reveal the following information:

	Process A ₹.	*Process B* ₹.	*Process C* ₹.
Materials	4,000	1,500	1,000
Labour	2,500	2,000	2,000
Direct Expenses	500	300	400
Cost of Bottles	—	3,000	—
Cost of Corks	—	—	1,300

The indirect expenses for the period amounted to ₹. 1,300. The by-products were sold for ₹. 250 (Process B) and the residue sold for ₹. 150 (Process A).

Prepare the accounts in respect of each of the process showing its cost and cost of production of the finished product per gross of bottle.

[**Ans.** *Process A Total Cost ₹. 7,350, Cost per gross ₹. 14.70. Process B Total Cost ₹. 14,300 Cost per gross ₹. 28.60. Process C Total ₹. 18,400; Cost per gross ₹. 36.80*]

Valuation of Stock Units

3. In a factory the output passes through three processes to completion. The production of each process is passed on to the next process immediately on completion.

	Process A	Process B	Process C
	₹.	₹.	₹.
Materials and Wages	18,000	12,000	10,000
Manufacturing expenses	12,000	6,000	4,000
Output in units	10,000	12,000	15,000
Opening Stock in units	—	5,000	8,000
Closing Stock in units	—	1,000	3,000

[**Ans.** *A. Total Cost ₹ 30,000 : per unit ₹ 3.00 B. Total Cost ₹ 60,000; per unit ₹ 5.00. C. Total Cost ₹ 99,000 : per unit ₹ 6.60*]

Wastage and Sale of By-product and Transfer of a Part of Product for Sales

4. In a factory the output passes through A and B processes. In both processes 5% of the total weight is lost and 10% scrap which realises from process *A* and *B* ₹. 30 and 50 per ton respectively.

	A	B
Materials used (in tons)	10,000	1,200
Cost of materials per ton	₹. 25	50
Wages	₹. 35,000	10,000
Manufacturing Expenses	₹. 15,000	6,000

[**Ans.** *Process A Cost of output ₹ 2,70,000 Cost per ton ₹ 31.76. Process B Cost of output ₹ 2,97,500 Cost per ton ₹ 36.08*]

5. The Products Ltd., manufactures and sells their chemicals produced by consecutive processes. The products of these processes are dealt with as under :

	Process 1	Process 2	Process 3
Transferred to next process	66-2/3%	60%	—
Transferred to warehouse for sale	33-1/3%	40%	100%

In each process 4% of the weight put is lost and 6% is scrap, which from process (1) realises at ₹. 3 per ton; from processes (2) and (3) at ₹. 5 and ₹. 6 per ton respectively. The following particulars relate to October, 2004.

	Process 1	Process 2	Process 3
Raw Materials used	1,400 Tons	160 tons	1,260 Tons
Rate per ton	₹. 10	₹. 16	₹. 7
Wages and other Expenses	₹. 5,152	3,140	2,898

Prepare Process Accounts showing cost per ton of each product.

[**Ans.** *Cost per ton: Process I ₹ 15, Process II ₹ 20; Process III ₹ 13.50.*]

6. A firm has three workshops and a wholesale warehouse. The following details were extracted from its books for the year ended 31st December 2004:

	Workshop A	Workshop B	Workshop C
Raw Materials used: Tones	250	152	145
Cost per tonne	₹. 120	₹. 80	₹. 50
Direct Wages	₹. 85,800	₹. 20,250	₹. 10,560
Direct Expenses	₹. 13,800	₹. 13,870	₹. 2,250
Loss of tonnage due to processing	4%	5%	2-1/2%
Proportion of production transferred :			
To Workshop *B* at cost	20%		
To Workshop *C* at cost		50%	

Proportion of production transferred to wholesale ware-house	80%	50%	100%
Wholesale Warehouse :			
Stock on 1-1-2004 at cost ex-workshop	₹. 2,500	₹. 2,000	₹. 4,000
Stock on 31-12-2004 ex-workshops in tonnes	10	20	40

Sales of Products ₹. 4,00,000

Salaries ₹. 40,000

Administrative Expenses ₹. 20,000

The closing stocks in the wholesale warehouse are to be valued at the prime cost per tonne during the year.

You are required (*a*) to prepare cost accounts for the year in respect of each workshop, (*b*) to calculate the prime cost per tonne of each process, and (*c*) to prepare an account showing the net profit of the business for the year 2004.

[**Ans.** *Prime cost per ton A ₹. 540; B ₹. 380; C ₹. 240 Net Profit ₹. 1,58,160*]

Abnormal Wastage and Gains

7. A product passes through two processes. The output of Process I becomes the input of Process II and the output of Process II is transferred to warehouse. The quantity of raw materials introduced into Process I is 20,000 kgs. at ₹. 10 per kg. The cost and output data for the month under review are as under:

	Process I	*Process II*
Direct Mateials	₹. 60,000	₹. 40,000
Direct labour	₹. 40,000	₹. 30,000
Production Overheads	₹. 39,000	₹. 40,250
Normal loss	8%	5%
Output	18,000	17,400
Loss realisation ₹./Unit	2.00	3.00

The company's policy is to fix the selling price of the end product in such a way as to yield a profit of 20% on selling price.

Required:

(*i*) Prepare the Process Accounts.

(*ii*) Determine the selling price per unit of the end product. *[CA PE II Nov. 2002]*

[**Ans.** *Process I Abnormal loss 400 kgs, ₹. 7300, Transfer to Process II 18,000 kgs ₹. 3,28,500, Process II A/c Abnormal Gain 300 kgs ₹. 7,650, Transfer to warehouse 17,400 kgs ₹. 443,700.*]

8. A product passes through two distinct processes *A* and *B* and to finished stock. From the following information prepare the Process Accounts.

	Process A	*Process B*
Materials consumed	₹. 12,000	₹. 6,000
Direct Labour	₹. 14,000	₹. 8,000
Manufacturing Exps.	4,000	₹. 4,000
Input in Process *A* (units)	10,000 units	
Input in Process *A* (value)	₹. 10,000	
Output (units)	9,400	8,300
Normal Wastage (% of input)	5%	10%
Value of Normal Wastage (Per 100 units)	₹. 8	₹. 10

No opening or closing stock is held in process.

[**Ans.** *Process A—Abnormal wastage 100 units ₹. 421;Ttransfer to Process B—9,400 units ₹. 39,539, Process B. Abnormal wastage 160 units ₹. 1086; Transferred to finished product 8300 units ₹. 56,359*]

9. 600 kg. of a material was charged to Process *I* at the rate of ₹. 4 per kg. The direct labour accounted for ₹. 200 and other departmental expenses amounted to ₹. 760. The normal loss is 10% of input and the net production was 500 kg. Assuming that process scrap is saleable at ₹. 2 per kg. Prepare a ledger account of Process *I* clearly showing the values of normal a abnormal loss.

[**Ans.** *Abnormal wastage 40 kg, ₹. 240; Output 500 kg ₹. 3,000*]

10. Product '*X*' is obtained after it passes through three distinct processes. The following information is obtained through the accounts for the month ending 31st December, 1993.

Item	Total	Processes *I*	*II*	*III*
	₹.	₹.	₹.	₹.
Direct Materials	7,542	2,600	1,980	2,962
Direct Wages	9,000	2,000	3,000	4,000
Production Overheads	9,000			

1,000 units at ₹. 3 each introduced to Process *I*. There was no stock of materials or work-in-progress at the beginning or end of the period. The output of each process passes direct to the next process and finally to finished stores. Production overhead is recovered on 100 per cent of direct wages. The following additional data are obtained:

Process	*Output during the month (units)*	*Percentage of normal loss to input*	*Value of scrap per unit* ₹
Process I	950	5%	2
Process II	840	10%	4
Process III	750	15%	5

Prepare Process Accounts and Abnormal Gain or Loss Accounts. [*B. Com (H) Delhi*]

[**Ans.** *Process I Neither Abnormal Loss nor Abnormal gain. Transferred to Process II 950 units ₹. 9,500; Process II Abnormal Loss 15 units ₹. 300; Transferred to Process III 840 units ₹. 16,800; Process III Effectives 3 units ₹. 1,368; Transferred to finished stock 750 units ₹. 28,500.*]

11. Product X in a manufacturing unit passes through three processes — *A*, *B* and *C*. The expenses incurred in the three processes during the year 2001 were as under:

	Process A	*Process B*	*Process C*
Unit of input issued	9,000		
Cost per unit	₹. 150		
Sundry Materials	23,500	₹. 25,000	₹. 15,000
Direct Labour	80,000	2,07,200	26,110
Direct Expenses	2,250	7,200	8,100
Selling price per unit of output	200	280	600

The actual outputs obtained *vis-a-vis* normal process losses from the processes were:

	Output (units)	Process loss (%)
Process *A*	8,400	5
B	5,700	10
C	3,660	3

During the year, three-fourth of the output of process *A* and two-third of the output of process *B* were transferred to the next process and the balances were sold outside. The entire output of process *C* was, however, sold outside. The losses of the three processes were sold at ₹. 5 per unit for process *A*, ₹. 10 per unit for process *B* and ₹. 15 per unit for process *C*.

Prepare the three process accounts and a statement of income considering a total selling and distribution expenses of ₹. 45,000 which is not allocated to processes. **[*ICWA – Inter June 2002*]**

[**Ans.** *Process A: Abnormal Loss 150 units ₹. 25,500, Transfer to Process B 6,300 units ₹. 10,71,000.*

Process B: Abnormal Gain 30 units ₹. 6,900, Transfer to Process C 3,800 units ₹. 8,74,000.

Process C: Abnormal Loss 26 units ₹. 6,500, Transfer for sale 3,660 units ₹. 9,15,000. Net Profit on sale (after adjusting Abnormal Gain ₹. 6,600 and Abnormal Loss ₹. 30,860) ₹. 13,69,740.]

Crushing, Refining and Finishing Process

12. Copra Product Ltd. is a manufacturing concern, the main product of which passes through three process, namely. Crushing, Refining and Finishing. The following figures were extracted from the books for the four-weeks period ended 28th June, 2003:

	Crushing	*Refining*	*Finishing*
	₹.	₹.	₹.
Wages	10,000	4,000	6,000
Power	2,400	1,440	960
Steam	2,400	1,800	1,800
Other Material	400	8,000	—
Plant Repairs	1,120	1,320	560
Sundry Expenses	5,280	2,640	900

2,000 tons of copra were consumed at ₹. 400 a ton, the output being 1,200 tons of crude oil, 850 tons of oil (refind) and 840 tons oil (casked) ready for delivery.

The difference in tonnage in respect of crude oil is not all loss, 240 tons of crude oil being sold as crude oil at cost plus 20 per cent.

Copra is delivered to the factory baled in heavy sacks, and the sacks were sold for ₹. 1,500.

600 tons of copra residue were sold for ₹. 35,000. 80 tons of waste from the refining process were sold for ₹. 9,500. The cost of casks used in finishing process was ₹. 24,000. Casked oil was sold for ₹. 1,000 a ton.

You are required to prepare cost accounts showing (*a*) the cost per ton of output of each stage of manufacture and (*b*) the total profit for the period.

[**Ans.** *Crushing Process: Cost per ton ₹. 654.25; Profit on crude oil sold ₹. 31,404; 960 tons crude oil transferred at a cost of ₹. 6,28,080.*

Refining Process: Cost per ton ₹. 750.33 per ton; 850 tons of Refined oil transferred at a cost of ₹. 6,37,780.

Finishing Process: Cost per ton ₹. 771.42; 840 tons of finished oil total cost ₹. 6,48,000. Cost of casked oil ₹. 800 per ton. Total cost, ₹. 6,72,000, profit ₹ 1,68,000]

13. The following details are extracted from the costing records of an Oil Mill for the three months-ended 31st March, 2003:

Purchase of 500 tons of Copra ₹. 2,00,000

	Crushing	Refining	Finishing
	₹.	₹.	₹.
Cost of Labour	2,500	1,000	1,500
Electric Power	600	360	240
Sundry Materials	100	2,000	—
Repairs to Machinery	280	330	140
Steam	600	450	450
Factory Expenses	1,320	660	220
Cost of Casks	—	—	7,500

300 tons Crude Oil were produced.

250 tons of Oil were produced by the Refining Process.

248 tons of Refined Oil were finished for delivery.

Copra sacks sold for ₹ 400.

175 tons of copra residue sold for ₹ 11,000.

Loss in weight in Crushing 25 tons.

45 tons of by products obtained from Refining Process valued at ₹ 6,750.

You are required to show the accounts in respect of each of the following stages of manufacture for the purpose of arriving at the cost per ton of each process and the total cost per ton of Finished Oil: (*a*) Copra Crushing Process, (*b*) Refining Process, (*c*) Finishing Process (including casking).

[**Ans.** *Cost of crude oil 300 tons ₹ 1,94,000 (per ton ₹ 646,67); Refined oil 250 tons ₹ 1,92,050 (per ton ₹ 768.2); Finished oil 248 ton ₹ 1,94,600. (per ton ₹ 784.68) Casked oil 248 tons ₹ 2,02,100 (per ton ₹ 814.92).*]

Sale of By-Product at Profit

14. A work order passes through two distinct processes. The product of the first process, less wastage and by-product becomes the raw materials for the second process. All by-products are sold off direct from the factory. The following information is obtained from the factory records:

	First Process	*Second Process*
Raw Materials	1,000 tons at ₹ 30 a ton	
Wages	₹ 25,000	₹ 20,000
Factory Overheads	80% of wages	75% of wages
Wastages	10 tons	15 tons
Sale of by-products	190 tons at cost plus 20%	85 tons at cost plus 25%

Give the ledger accounts for the first and second processes, showing at each stage the cost of production and the profit on the sale of by-products.

[**Ans.** *Process 1—Cost of output ₹ 60,606. Profit on sale By-product ₹ 2879. (Selling price ₹ 17,273). Process 2–Cost of Finished product ₹ 85,254; Profit on sale of By-product ₹ 2,588 (Selling Price ₹ 12,940)*]

15. The following details are available from the books of a factory in which two processes are employed. Prepare necessary ledger accounts.

	Process A	*Process B*
Materials	1,000 tons @ ₹ 50 per ton	—
Wages	₹ 30,000	₹ 20,000
Factory Overhead	50% of wages	30% of wages
Wastage	100 tons	200 tons
By-products	100 tons sold at cost plus 20%	200 tons sold at cost plus 25%

[**Ans.** *Profit on sale of by-products A ₹ 2,111 and B ₹ 9,204*]

16. A certain purifying process yields 80% of the inputs as the main product and 15% as by-product and there is process loss of 5%. The input cost is ₹ 2 per litre and a plant charge of 1,000 litres costs ₹ 1,500 in labour, steam, other indirect materials and overheads. Ascertain the cost of the by-product, having regard for the fact that the steam (which costs ₹ 400) is chargeable to by product and main product in the ratio 2 : 1.

[**Ans.** *Total cost main product ₹ 2743.53 and by product ₹ 756.47*]

[**Hints** Material, will be devided in 80:15 Labour etc ₹ 1100 in 80:15]

Equivalent Units of Production

17. 10,000 units of Raw Materials are introduced into a process at a cost of ₹. 17,000; wages and overheads for the process are ₹. 5,100 and ₹. 3,400 respectively. 7,500 units were completed, of the remaining 2,500 units on an average 40% work has been done. Ascertain the cost of one complete unit. **[*CA Inter June 2003*]**

[Ans. *₹ 3.00***]**

18. In process A of a manufacturing concern 10,000 units are introduced during May 2003. The normal loss is estimated to be 4% of the input. At the end of the month 1,200 units were lying as incomplete. The stagewise completion of the inventory was given as under:

Material: 80%; Labour 60%, Overheads 50%.

You are required to prepare a statement of equivalent production assuming that 8,300 units were transferred to finished stock. **[*CS Inter Dec. 2003*]**

[Ans. *Equivalent units: Material 9,360 units, Labour 9,120 units, Overheads 9,000 units.***]**

19. The finished product of a factory passes through two processes. The materials are added at the beginning of the First Process. From the following details, work out the value of closing inventory and the value of materials transferred to the Second Process :

Process I	₹.
Opening inventory	50,000
Materials	1,37,500
Labour	2,50,000
Overheads	2,00,000
	Units.
Opening inventory (25% Complete)	20,000
Put in process	60,000
Transferred to Process *II*	50,000
Closing inventory (20% Complete)	25,000
Spoilage in process	5,000

[Ans. *Effective Units 50,000; Work-in-Progress ₹ 58,750; 50,000 units valued ₹ 5,78,750 transferred to Process II.***]**

20. From the following information for the month of October 2003, prepare Process III Cost Account:

Opening WIP in Process III	1,800 units at ₹. 27,000
Transfer from Process II	47,700 units at ₹. 5,36,625
Transferred to Warehouse	43,200 units
Closing WIP of Process III	4,500 units
Units scrapped	1,800 units
Direct Material added in Process III	₹. 1,77,840
Direct Wages	₹. 87,840
Production Overheads	₹. 43,920

Degree of completion:

	Opening Stock	*Closing Stock*	*Scrap*
Material	80%	70%	100%
Labour	60%	50%	70%
Overheads	60%	50%	70%

The normal loss in the process was 5% of the production and scrap was sold @ ₹. 6.75 per unit. **[*CA PE II Nov. 2003*]**

[**Ans.** *Process III: Normal Loss (2250 units) ₹ 15,187, Abnormal Gain 450 units ₹ 8,313 Closing WIP ₹ 4,500 units ₹ 70,978, Finished Goods Stock 43200 units ₹ 7,95,373.*]

[**Hints.** Equivalent units Material *A* 45450 units, Material *B* 44,460 units Labour and Overheads 43,920 units.]

21. Following are the details pertaining to process B for the month of March, 2003.

	₹
Opening Stock 1,000 units at	2,790
Transferred from Process *A* 10,600 units at	10,600
Materials added	3,960
Direct Labour	11,520
Production Overheads	8,640
Transfer to process *C*	9,600 units
Units Scrapped	400 units
Closing Stock	1,600 units
Normal loss on production	5%

Degree of completion as regards:

	Materials	*Labour*	*Overheads*
Opening Stock	80%	70%	70%
Units Scrapped	100%	80%	80%
Closing Stock	75%	50%	50%

Prepare Process *B* Account for March, 2003 assuming that the scrap realises ₹ 1 for each unit.

[**Ans.** *Effective unit : for Material (i) 10,100; for Materials (ii) 9,900; Labour and Overheads 9,600; Cost per completed unit : ₹ 1 for Materials (i); ₹ 0.40 for Material (ii); 1.20 for labour, ₹ 0.90 for overheads.*]

22. The following data pertain to Process *I* of Beta Ltd., for April 2005

Opening work-in-progress 1,500 units	₹ 15,000
Degree of Completion : Materials 100%, Labour and Overhead 33-1/3%	
Input of Materials 18,500 units	₹ 52,000
Direct Labour	₹ 14,000
Overheads	₹ 28,000

Closing Work-in-Progress 5,000 units

Degree of completion : Materials 90% and Labour and Overheads 30%

Normal loss is 10% of the total input (opening Work-in-Progress + Units put in)

Scrap value ₹ 2.00 per unit.

Units transferred to the next process 15,000 units. You are required to (*a*) Compute the equivalent units of production (*b*) Compute the cost per equivalent unit (*c*) Compute cost of finished output and closing Work-in-Progress (*d*) Prepare the Process and Other Accounts. Assume that FIFO method is used.

[**Ans.** *(a) Equivalent units Materials 16,000, Labour and Overheads 14,000; (b) Cost per unit Materials ₹ 3, Labour ₹ 1 and Overheads ₹ 2; (c) Cost of finished output ₹ 99,000 Work-in-Progress (5,000 units) ₹ 18,000*. Abnormal Gain 2000 units ₹ 12,000]

23. From the following particulars pertaining to Process *B* for month of March, 2003, prepare Process Account.

Opening stock 600 units	
(Completed 80% as regards Materials, 60% for Labour and Overheads)	₹ 1,050
Transfer from process A 11,000 units at	₹ 5,500

Transfer to Process C 8,800 units	
Direct Materials added	₹. 2,410
Direct Wages	₹. 7,155
Production Overheads	₹. 9,540
Closing Stock (Completed 70% as regards Materials and 60% for labour and overheads)	units 1,600
Wastage (completed 100% as regards Materials and 70% for labour and overheads)	units 1,200
Normal loss on production	10%
Scrap value of wastage per unit	₹. 0.50

[**Ans.** *Effective units : Material (i) 10,000 : Material (ii) 9,640; Labour and overheads 9,540; Work-in-Progress at end valued at ₹ 2,760. Cost per unit as regards Material (i) ₹ 0.50; Material (ii) ₹ 0.25; Labour ₹. 0.75; Overhead ₹. 1 : 8,800 units transferred to Process C at cost of ₹ 22,000.*]

24. From the following information relating to Process I of a factory for the month of April, 2003, **prepare** the statement of equivalent production, statement of cost, statement of evaluation and Process Account, using average cost method:

(*i*) Opening Work in Progress : 500 units

Materials	₹. 27,000
Labour	₹. 8,000
Overheads	₹. 12,500
	₹. 47,500

(*ii*) Cost incurred during April 2003

Input of materials: 14,000 units	₹. 5,74,750
Labour	₹. 1,19,300
Overheads	₹. 1,78,450

(*iii*) Process loss :

Normal loss : 10%

Value of scrapped unit : ₹. 10 each

Actual loss during April 2003 : 1,500 units

Degree of completion : Materials 100%, Labour and Overheads 60%

(*iv*) Closing Work-in-Progress : 1,000 units

Degree of completion : Materials 100%, Labour and Overheads 70%

(*v*) Processed units transferred to Process II : 12,000 units during April 2003.

[*ICWA – Inter June 2003*]

[**Ans.** *Value of closing WIP 1,000 units ₹ 62,500, Transfer to Process II 12,000 units ₹ 8,40,000.* **Hints.** Equivalent units: Material 13,050, Labour and Overheads 12,730; Abnormal Loss ₹. 3,000.]

Inter-Process Profits

25. A product passes through three processes to completion. These processes are known as *A*, *B* and *C*. The output of each process is charged to next process at a price calculated to give a profit of 20 per cent on the transfer price. The output of Process *C* is charged to Finished Stock on a similar basis. There was no partly finished work in any process at 31st December on which date the following information was obtained:

	Process A ₹.	*Process B* ₹.	*Process C* ₹
Materials consumed	2,000	3,000	1,000
Labour	3,000	2,000	4,000

Stock on 31st December	1,000	2,000	3,000

Stock in each process have been valued at prime cost to the process. There were no stocks in hand at 1st January and the absorption overheads has been ignored. Of the goods passed into Finished Stock, ₹. 2,000 worth remained in hand at 31st December and the balance was sold for ₹. 18,000. Prepare Process Cost Accounts, Finished Stock Account and Profit and Loss Account.

[**Ans.** *Reserved for unrealised profit; Process A Nil; Process B ₹. 200; Process C ₹. 560; Finished stock ₹. 699; Total being ₹. 1459. Total Profit ₹. 11,000, Actual Profit ₹. 9,541*]

26. The Rajasthan Manufacturing Co. Ltd. is engaged in the production of certain article which passes through two distinct processes to completion. During the six months ended 31st December, 2003, sale of the product amounted to ₹. 4,00,000 and the following information is obtained from the costing records for the same period:

	Process I ₹.	*Process II* ₹.
Raw Materials drawn from stores	1,00,000	26,000
Labour, as extracted from time cards	50,000	60,000

In the Process Cost Accounts, the on cost for indirect expenses is charged at 20 per cent of labour, and it is the practice to transfer goods from Process I to Process II at a price which is includes a profit of 25 per cent on the transfer price, and from Process II to Finished Goods Account at a price which includes a profit of 20 per cent on the transfer price.

Stocks valued as indicated below, were :

	1st July 2003 ₹.	*31st Dec. 2003* ₹.
Raw Materials in Factory		
used in Process *I* (at cost)	20,000	30,000
used in Process *II* (at cost)	2,000	—
Goods at completion of Process *I* situated in the department, where Process *II* is carried out (at transfer price)	50,000	70,000
Finished goods (at transfer price)	40,000	50,000

Prepare the Process Cost Accounts for the period. Assuming that the indirect expenses were subsequently found amounting to ₹. 24,590, calculate the actual net profit of the business for the period. The provision for unrealised profit included in stocks on 1st July, 2003 amounted to ₹. 16,519.

[**Ans.**	*Process I*	*Process II*	*Finished Goods*	*Actual Net Profit*
Profit (₹)	*50,000*	*70,000*	*60,000*	*1,60,000*

Provision for unrealised profit ₹. 33,929. Additional provision ₹. 17,410].

27. Cheap Products Ltd. divides its manufacture into two processes *A* and *B*. After leaving Process *B*, the product is passed into Finished Stock. The output of Process *A* is transferred to Process *B* at a price which gives Process *A* profit of 25 per cent thereon, and the output of Process *B* is transferred to Finished stock at a price which gives Process *B* a profit of 20 per cent thereon.

The following information is provided in respect of the year ending 31st December, 2003.

	Process A ₹.	*Process B* ₹.
Stock on 1st January, 2003	3,200	2,000
Materials used	6,400	2,700
Direct Labour	12,500	8,500
Overheads	2,500	1,700
Stock on 31st December, 2003	2,100	900

Process stocks consist of products which passed through the process completely and are valued at prime cost to the process concerned. Finished goods were in stock on 1st January, 2003 to the value of ₹. 10,200 and 31st December, 2003 to the value of ₹. 6,200. Both the opening and closing stocks were valued at the price at which they were transferred from Process *B*. Sales amounting to ₹. 68,400 were effected during the year and included all the goods in stock at the beginning of the year.

The reserve on 1st January, 2003 for unrealised profit included in stock valuations were : Process *B*—₹. 350 and Finished Goods ₹. 3,430. Prepare the Process Accounts, Finished Goods Account, and Profit and Loss Account for the year ended on 31st December, 2003 showing adjustment for stock reserves.

[Ans. *Unrealised profit included in the closing stock-Process B ₹. 164, Finished Goods ₹. 2,103. Total Trading Profit ₹. 29,413***]**

Joint Product and By-Product Costing

Joint products and by-products arise in situations where the production of one product makes envitable the production of other products. When a group of individual products is simultaneously produced, and each product has a significant relative sales value, the outputs are usually called '*Joint Products*'.

Those products that are part of the simultaneous production process and have a minor sales value when compared with the joint products are called '*By Products*'. These result incidentally from the main joint products.

Thus Joint products "represent two or more products separated in the course of the same processing operations, usually requiring further processing, each product being in such proportion that no single product can be designated as a major product." By-products have been defined as "any saleable or usual value incidentally produced in addition to the main product." Thus the main difference between by-products and joint product is that in case of the former, generally no extra expense is to be incurred, whereas in the case of the latter additional expenditure will be necessary before the products can be sold.

Another point of distinction is regarding importance. If the various products are of substantial importance, they are termed as joint products.

For example, in the case of a refinery, diesel oil is a joint product when petrol is produced. If the various products differ greatly in importance, the relatively unimportant articles will be by-products such as molasses and bagasse in a sugar factory..

The distinguishing feature of the production of joint and by-products is that the products are not identifiable as different individual products until a specific point in the production process is reached, known as the split-off-point. Before the split-off-point, costs cannot be traced to particular products. After the split-off-point, joint products may be sold or subjected to further processing. If latter is the case, any further processing costs can easily be traced to the specific products involved.

Methods of Apportioning Joint Costs to Products

The methods used to apportion joint cost are based on physical volume and sales value of products.

(1) **Physical Volume Method:** Method assumes to measure benefits received from the joint product costs by the individual products based on *physical measure* such as weights, volume etc.

(2) **Market Value of Products Method.**

(*a*) ***Where by-products are of small value*** the effort to calculate their costs is not warranted. Hence either :

(*i*) the amount realised (or realisable) may be treated as pure profit and credited to the Costing Profit or Loss A/c; or

(*ii*) the amount realised (or realisable) may be credited to the cost of the main product, thus reducing the cost. This method is preferable.

Both the methods are defective because the true cost of the main product cannot be ascertained. In any case the quantity of the by-product must be put on the credit side of the Process Account, so that the total quantity is accounted for.

(*b*) ***Where by-products are of considerable value***, an attempt to find out the cost of each product will be necessary and justified. The total must be apportioned between all products (main and by-products). This will require technical knowledge. Merely to divide the total cost by the number of units of all products will be defective.

Illustration 1: A chemical process yields 70 per cent of the materials introduced as main product and 20 per cent as a by-product, 10 per cent being lost. Technical information reveals that of the materials 75 per cent is absorbed by the main product and 25% by the by-product. One unit of main product needs double the time needed for one unit of by-product and overheads are absorbed in the ratio of 3 : 1.

During a week, 1,000 units of raw materials at a cost of ₹. 5,000 were introduced. Labour totalled ₹. 3,200 and overheads came to ₹. 2,000. Wastage realised ₹. 200.

Ascertain the cost of the two products.

Solution:

Total number of units produced:

		Units
Main product	70%	700
By-product	20%	200
Wastage	10%	100
Materials introduced		1,000

Cost Sheet

	Basic of Allocation	Main Product (700) Total ₹.	Main Product (700) Per unit ₹.	By Product (200) Total ₹.	By Product (200) Per unit ₹.
Materials	75 : 25	3,750	5.36	1,250	6.25
Labour	14 : 2	2,800	4.00	400	2.00
Overheads (₹. 2000 less ₹. 200)	3 : 1	1,350	1.93	450	2.25
Total		7,900	11.29	2,100	10.50

Note : Labour is allocated in the ratio of 14:2 because the main product needs double the wages of that required for the by-product. Hence for purpose of allocation of labour, 700 units of the main product are equivalent to 1,400 units of by-products.

(*c*) ***Where the joint products require further expenditure***, such additional expenditure should be added after apportioning joint expenses as explained in (*b*) above.

(*d*) An alternative to (c) is to ***apportion the common expenses in the ratio of the market value of the various product at the point of separation***. For instance, if *X* and *Y* are two products jointly produced and if *X* sells at ₹. 10 and *Y* at ₹. 8 per unit, the total expenses can be apportioned between *X* and *Y* in the ratio of 10 : 8. If the number of units produced are different, the total sale proceeds of each product should be the basis of allocation. This is to say the selling price per unit should be multiplied by the number of units produced.

This method is useful where the subsequent expenditure (*i.e.*, after separation) is disproportionate. Generally, this method will give good results and, therefore, it should be adopted as a rule unless circumstances suggest otherwise.

(*e*) Another alternative is to apportion the total ***common expenditure in the ratio of the market value of the various products when finally ready for sale***. If the expenditure after separation is disproportionate for each product, this method will not give good results. It is therefore, not recommended.

(*f*) Another method is to deduct from the market value of the by product: (*i*) the reasonable margin of profit and (*ii*) the expenditure after separation and then to treat the balance as a reduction of the cost of the main product. Suppose by-product *Y* realises ₹. 2,000 after a special or seperate expense on it of ₹. 400 and suppose a profit of 25 per cent on selling price is reasonable in case of this product, then ₹. 1100 will be credited to the cost of the main product, thus:

	₹.
Amount realised by sale of *Y*	2,000
Less: 25% Profit	500
	1,500
Less: Special or separate expenditure	400
Share out of common costs	1,100

Illustration 2: (*Joint and Separate Exps.*) A By-product 'Beta' is derived in the course of manufacturing a product 'Alpha'. The by-product is further processed for sale. From the following data available from records, prepare accounting showing the cost per kg of the product 'Alpha' and 'Beta'.

	Joint Exps.	*Separate Expenses*	
		'Alpha'	*'Beta'*
	₹	₹	₹
Materials	10,000	6,000	500
Labour	7,000	5,000	2,000
Overheads	2,500	1,500	600

The quantities produced during the period under consideration were : Alpha, 100 kg; and Beta, 50 kg. The selling price of Beta was ₹. 120 kg, on which the profit earned was estimated at 30% of selling price.

Solution: The share of joint expenses attributable to the by-product `*Beta*' may be calculated as below:

		₹.
Selling Price of Beta : 50 kg @ ₹. 120 per kg (50 × 120)		6,000
Less: Profit 30% of selling price		1,800
Total Cost of Production		4,200
Less: Cost incurred on further processing or separate expenses of *Beta*—		
Materials	500	
Labour	2,000	
Overheads	600	3,100
Share of Joint Expenses for Beta		1,100

Product 'Alpha' Account
(Output : 100 kg)

	₹		₹
To Joint Expenses:		By Cost of By-product	
Materials	10,000	(Beta) transferred to Beta	
Labour	7,000	A/c (Joint Exps.)	1,100
Overheads	2,500	By Cost of Production of	
To Materials	6,000	Alpha (Cost per kg ₹. 309)	30,900
To Labour	5,000		
To Overheads	1,500		
	32,000		32,000

By-product Beta Account
(Output : 50 kg)

	₹.		₹.
To Joint Expenses transferred from Process I (Alpha A/c)	1,100	By Cost of Producing 'Beta' c/d (cost per kg ₹. 84)	4,200
To Materials	500		
To Labour	2,000		
To Overheads	600		
	4,200		4,200
To Cost of Production b/d	4,200	By Sales (50 kg @ ₹. 120 per kg)	6,000
To Profit	1,800		
	6,000		6,000

Illustration 3: (*Joint and Separate Exps*). Two by-products *X* and *Y* are produced in the course of manufacture of Product *A*. Their expenses are as follows:

	Joint Expenses ₹.	*Subsequent or Separate Exps.*		
		A ₹.	*X* ₹.	*Y* ₹.
Materials	800	200	100	80
Labour	1,000	300	125	100
On cost	600	300	100	192
	2,400	800	325	372

Selling Prices are : *A*—₹. 3,000; *X*—₹. 1,000; and *Y*—₹. 800. The estimated profits are 20%, 17.5% and 16% respectively on the turnover. Prepare separate accounts showing the cost of each product.

Solution: **Apportionment of Joint Expenses over *A*, *X* and *Y***

	A	*X*	*Y*
Selling Price	₹. 3,000	₹. 1,000	₹. 800
Less: Profit on Selling Price	600 [20%]	175 [17.5%]	128 [16%]
Total Cost	2,400	825	672
Less: Seperate Expenses	800	325	372
Share in Joint Expenses	1,600	500	300

A (Main Product) Account

	₹.		₹.
To Joint Expenses		By *X* By-product A/c (Share in Joint Exps.)	500
Materials	800		
Labour	1,000	By *Y* By-product A/c (Share in Joint Exps.)	300
On cost	600		
To Material	200	By Cost of Production of A (Main Product) c/d	2,400
To Labour	300		
To On cost 300			
	3,200		3,200
To Cost of Production b/d	2,400	By Sales	3,000
To Profit (20% on Sales)	600		
	3,000		3,000

X (By-Product) Account

		₹		₹
To Joint Expenses transferred from *A* (Main Product A/c)		500	By Cost of Production of *X* (By-Product) c/d	825
To Material		100		
To Labour		125		
To On cost	100			
		825		825
To Cost of Production b/d		825	By Sales	1,000
To Profit (17.5% on Sales)		175		
		1,000		1,000

Y (By-Product) Account

		₹		₹
To Joint Expenses transferred from *A* (Main Product A/c)		300	By Cost of Production of *Y* (By-Product) c/d	672
To Material		80		
To Labour		100		
To On cost	192			
		672		672
To Cost of Production b/d		672	By Sales	800
To Profit (16% on Sales)		128		
		800		800

Alternative Method: There may be an altenative method. *A* Joint Exps. Account is prepared as below:

Joint Expenses Account

		₹		₹
To Materials		800	By *A*	1,600
To Labour		1,000	By *X*	500
To On cost	600	By *Y*	300	
		2,400		2,400

A, *X* and *Y* Accounts will be prepared accordingly. Allocated joint expenses of each will be debited to these accounts.

Illustration 4: A Company producing an article P also produces by-products Q and R. The cost of manufacture are given below:

	Joint Expenses	*Separate Expenses*		
		P	*Q*	*R*
Materials	10,000	1,100	1,300	1,000
Labour	12,000	200	150	100
Overheads	8,000	800	550	400
	₹. 30,000	2,100	2,000	1,500
Sales value		28,000	24,000	20,000
Estimated profit on selling price		30%	25%	20%

Show how would you propose to apportion joint expenses of manufacture and prepare necessary accounts relating to *P*, *Q* and *R*.

Solution:

	P	*Q*	*R*	Total
Sales	28,000	24,000	20,000	72,000
Less: Profit	8,400	6,000	4,000	18,400
Total Cost	19,600	18,000	16,000	53,600
Less: Separate Expenses	2,100	2,000	1,500	5,600
Share in Joint Exp.	17,500	16,000	14,500	48,000

Since the above shares in Joint Exps. are ₹. 48,000, while given Joint Expenses are ₹. 30,000, hence the difference *i.e.* ₹. 18,000 will be taken as selling overheads which will be allocated among products in their sales ratio *i.e.* 28 : 24 : 20 or 7 : 6 : 5.

	P	*Q*	*R*	Total
Share in Joint Exp. allocated	17,500	16,000	14,500	48,000
Less: Selling Overheads	7,000	6,000	5,000	18,000
Share in Joint Exp. (given)	10,500	10,000	9,500	30,000

Main Product (P) Account

	₹.		₹.
To Joint Exps:			
Materials	10,000	By By-product *Q*	10,000
Labour	12,000	By By-product *R*	9,500
Overhead	8,000	By Cost of Production c/d	19,600
To Separate Exps.			
Materials	1,100		
Labour	200		
Overhead	800		
To Selling Overheads	7,000		
	39,100		39,100
To Cost of Production b/d	19,600	By Sales	28,000
To Profit	8,400		
	28,000		28,000

By-Product (Q) Account

	₹.		₹.
To Main Product			
P Account	10,000	By Cost of Production c/d	18,000
To Separte Exps.			
Materials	1,300		
Labour	150		
Overhead	550		
To Selling Overheads	6,000		
	18,000		18,000
To Cost of Production b/d	18,000	By Sales	24,000
To Profit	6,000		
	24,000		24,000

By-Product (R) Account

	₹		₹
To Main Product P Account	9,500	By Cost of Production c/d	16,000
To Separate Exps.			
Materials	1,000		
Labour	100		
Overhead	400		
To Selling Overheads	5,000		
	16,000		16,000
To Cost of Production b/d	16,000	By Sales	20,000
To Profit	4,000		
	20,000		20,000

Illustration 5: In manufacturing the main product *A*, a company processes the resulting waste material into two by-products M_1 and M_2. You are required to apportion total cost up to separation point among : *A*, M_1 and M_2 from the following data. Total cost up to separation point was ₹. 1,36,000.

	A	M_1	M_2
(*i*) Sales	3,28,000	32,000	48,000
(*ii*) Cost after separation		9,600	14,400
(*iii*) Percentage of net profit to sales		20%	30%
(*iv*) Percentage of selling expenses to sales	20%	20%	20%

Solution:

Cost Charged to By-Product

		M_1 ₹.		M_2 ₹.
Sale		32,000		48,000
Less: Profit	6,400		14,400	
Selling Exps.	6,400	12,800	9,600	24,000
Cost of Production		19,200		24,000
Less: Cost after separation		9,600		14,400
		9,600		9,600

Statement Showing Cost and Profit

	A	M_1	M_2
Joint Cost	1,36,000		
Less: Charged to M_1 a M_2 (as per above statement)	19,200	9,600	9,600
	1,16,800	9,600	9,600
Cost after separation		9,600	14,400
Cost of Production	1,16,800	19,200	24,000
Selling Exps. (20% of Sales)	65,600	6,400	9,600
Total Cost	1,82,400	25,600	33,600
Profit	1,45,600	6,400	14,400
Sales ₹.	3,28,000	32,000	48,000

Illustration 6: The yield of a certain process is 80% as to the main product, 15% as to the by-product and 5% as to the process loss. The material put in process (5,000 units) cost ₹. 23.75 per unit and all other charges are ₹. 14,250, of which power cost accounted for $33\frac{1}{3}\%$. It is ascertained that power is chargeable as to the main product and by-product in the ratio of 10:9. Draw up a statement showing the cost of the by-product.

Solution:

Working Notes :

Material put in process	5,000 units at ₹. 23.75
	₹. 1,18,750
Power ($33\frac{1}{3}\%$ of 14,250)	₹. 4,750
Other charges (14,250 – 4,750)	₹. 9,500
Joint Cost	₹. 1,33,000
Main product 80% of 5,000	4,000 Units
By-product 15% of 5,000	750 Units
Process loss 5% of 5,000	250 Units

Statement Showing the Cost of the By-product

Particulars	*Total*	*Main Product*	*By-product*
Production-Units		4,000	750
	₹.	₹.	₹.
Materials (4,000 : 750 units)	1,18,750	1,00,000	18,750
Power (10 : 9 ratio)	4,750	2,500	2,250
Other charges (4,000 : 750)	9,500	8,000	1,500
Total cost	1,33,000	1,10,500	22,500

Illustration 7: JB Limited produces four joint products. *A*, *B*, *C* and *D*, all of which emerge from the processing of one raw material. The following are the relevant data:

Production for the period:

Joint-product	*Number of units*	*Selling price per unit*
		₹.
A	500	18.00
B	900	8.00
C	400	4.00
D	200	11.00

The company budgets for a profit of 10% of sales value. The other estimated costs are:

	₹.
Carriage inwards	1,000
Direct wages	3,000
Manufacturing Overhead	2,000
Administration Overhead	10% of sales value.

You are required to:

(*a*) Calculate the maximum price that may be paid for the raw material.

(*b*) Prepare a comprehensive cost statement for each of the products allocating the materials and other costs based upon:

(*i*) number of units (*ii*) sales value.

Solution:

(a) Joint Product Cost

Joint-product		*No. of units*	*S.P. per units*	*Sales value* ₹
A		500	18	9,000
B		900	8	7,200
C		400	4	1,600
D		200	11	2,200
	Total Sales Value			20,000
Less :	Budget profit 10% of sales value.			2,000
	Joint product cost			18,000
Less:	Other costs:			
	Carriage inwards	1,000		
	Direct wages	3,000		
	Mfg. overhead	2,000		
	Admn. overhead 10% of sales value	2,000		8,000
	Raw Material			10,000

Thus maximum price that may be paid for raw material is ₹. 10,000.

(b) (i) Statement of Cost
(Based upon number of units)

Joint-Products	A	B	C	D	Total
No. of units	500	900	400	200	
	₹.	₹.	₹.	₹.	₹.
Raw material	2,500	4,500	2,000	1,000	10,000
Carriage Inwards	250	450	200	100	1,000
Direct Wages	750	1,350	600	300	3,000
Mfg. Overhead	500	900	400	200	2,000
Admn. Overhead	500	900	400	200	2,000
Total Costs	4,500	8,100	3,600	1,800	18,000

(b) (ii) Statement of Cost
(Based upon Sales Value)

Joint Products	A	B	C	D	Total
Sales Value	₹. 9,000	7,200	1,600	2,200	20,000
Raw material	4,500	3,600	800	1,100	10,000
Carriage Inwards	450	360	80	110	1,000
Direct Wages	1,350	1,080	240	330	3,000
Mfg. Overhead	900	720	160	220	2,000
Admn. Overhead	900	720	160	220	2,000
Total Costs	₹. 8,100	6,480	1,440	1,980	18,000

Illsuration 8: In a concern engaged in process industry four products emerge from a particular process of operation. The total cost of input for the period ended 30th September 2004 is ₹. 2,53,500. The details of output, additional cost after "split-off point" and sales value of the product are appended below:

Products	*Output*	*Additional processing cost after split-off point*	*Sales value*
	Kgs.	₹.	₹.
A	8,000	60,000	1,68,000
B	5,000	10,000	1,10,000
C	3,000	—	60,000
D	4,000	20,000	90,000

If the products are sold at "the split-off point" without further processing, the sales value would have been

	₹.
A	1,15,000
B	90,000
C	55,000
D	80,000

You are required to prepare a statement of profitability based on the products being sold: (*i*) After further processing (*ii*) At the split-off point.

Solution:

Statement Showing Profitability at the Split-off Point

Products	*Sales value at the split-off point (₹.)*	*Joint costs apportioned (₹.)*	*Profit (₹.)*
A	1,15,000	85,743	29,257
B	90,000	67,103	22,897
C	55,000	41,007	13,993
D	80,000	59,647	20,353
Total	3,40,000	2,53,500	86,500

Note: Joint Cost is apportioned in the ratio of sales because joint cost has been incurred upto the split-off point.

$A = 2{,}53{,}500 \times \frac{1{,}15{,}000}{3{,}40{,}000} = 85{,}743$ and so on for *B*, *C* and *D*.

Statement Showing Profitability after Further Processing

Product	*Sales value after further processing (₹.)*	*Additional processing cost (₹.)*	*Net Sales value (₹.)*	*Joint cost (₹.)*	*Profit (₹.)*
A	1,68,000	60,000	1,08,000	85,743	22,257
B	1,10,000	10,000	1,00,000	67,103	32,897
C	60,000	—	60,000	41,007	18,993
D	90,000	20,000	70,000	59,647	10,353
Total	4,28,000	90,000	3,38,000	2,53,500	84,500

Product	*Additional processing cost*	*Incremental Revenue (₹.)*
A	60,000	1,68,000 – 1,15,000 = 53,000
B	10,000	1,10,000 – 90,000 = 20,000
C	—	60,000 – 55,000 = 5,000
D	20,000	90,000 – 80,000 = 10,000

Incremental revenue is greater than additional processing cost in case of *B* and *C*. These may be sold after further processing. *A* and *D* may be sold at the split-off point. Thus profit may be improved.

Product	*Profit (₹.)*	
A	29,257	To be sold at split-off point
D	20,353	To be sold at split-off point
B	32,897	To be sold after additional processing
C	18,993	To be sold after additional processing
Total	1,01,500	Maximum profit

Illustration 9: In a chemical manufacturing company, three products *A*, *B* and *C* emerge at a single split off stage in department *P*. Product *A* is further processed in department *Q*, product *B* in department *R* and product *C* in department *S*. There is no loss in further processing of any of the three products. The cost data for a month are as under:

Cost of raw materials introduced in department *P*	₹. 12,68,800
Direct Wages in Departments	
P	₹. 3,84,000
Q	96,000
R	64,000
S	36,000

Factory overheads of ₹. 4,64,000 are to be apportioned to the departments on direct wages basis.

During the month under reference, the company sold all three products after processing them further as under:

Products	*A*	*B*	*C*
Output sold (kg.)	44,000	40,000	20,000
Selling Price per kg. (₹.)	32	24	16

There are no Opening or Closing Stocks. If these products were sold at the split off stage, that is, without further processing, the selling prices would have been ₹. 20, ₹. 22 and ₹. 10 each per kg respectively for *A*, *B* and *C*.

Required :

(*i*) Prepare a statement showing the apportionment of joint costs to joint products.

(*ii*) Present a statement showing product-wise and total profit for the month under reference as per the company's current processing policy.

(*iii*) What processing decision should have been taken to improve the profitability of the company.

(*iv*) Calculate the productwise and total profit arising from your recommendation in (*iii*) above.

[*CA – Inter May 2002*]

***Solution:* (*i*)** **Statement Showing the Apportionment of Joint Costs.**

Particulars	*Products* A	B	C	*Total*
Output sold (kg.)	44,000	40,000	20,000	
S.P. per kg. at split-off stage (₹.)	20	22	10	
Sales value at split-off stage (₹.)	8,80,000	8,80,000	2,00,000	19,60,000
Joint costs incurred in Deptt. P (₹.) (Apportioned on sales value basis at the split-off point – Ratio 22 : 22 : 5)	8,80,000	8,80,000	2,00,000	19,60,000

Note: Total joint cost of Deptt. P ₹. 19,60,000 (See Working Note)

(*ii*) Statement Showing Product-wise and Total Profit for the Month (Current Position)

Particulars	*Products* A	B	C	*Total*
Output sold (kg.)	44,000	40,000	20,000	
S.P. per kg. after further processing (₹.)	32	24	16	
(*a*) Sales value after further processing (₹.)	14,08,000	9,60,000	3,20,000	26,88,000
Joint costs at split-off (₹.)	8,80,000	8,80,000	2,00,000	19,60,000
Further process costs (See working note)	1,72,800	1,15,200	64,800	3,52,800
(*b*) Total Costs (₹.)	10,52,800	9,95,200	2,64,800	23,12,800
Profit/Loss (*a*) – (*b*)	(₹.) 3,55,200	(35,200)	55,200	3,75,200

(*iii*) Processing decision to improve the profitability of the company

Products *A* and *C* should be sold after further processing as both the products are yielding profit after further processing. However, product *B*, should be sold at split-off point as further processing cost of this product is more than its sales value and it is yielding loss.

(*iv*) Product-wise and total profit arising from the recommendation at (*iii*) above

Profit after further processing:

Product A	₹. 3,55,200
Product C	55,200
Total profit after further processing	4,10,400

Working Note:

Statement Showing Department-wise Costs

Particulars	*Departments* P	Q	R	S
Raw materials (₹.)	12,68,800			
Wages (given) (₹.)	3,84,000	96,000	64,000	36,000
Overheads apportioned (₹.) (96 : 24 : 16 : 9)	3,07,200	76,800	51,200	28,800
Total costs	19,60,000	1,72,800	1,15,200	64,800

It is noted from the above statement that costs incurred in Deptt. *P* are the joint cots at split-off of products *A*, *B* and *C*. The joint costs at split-off point are ₹. 19,60,000. However, costs incurred in Deptt. *Q*, *R* and *S* are further processing costs of products *A*, *B* and *C*. Further processing costs of products *A*, *B* and *C* are ₹. 1,72,800, ₹. 1,15,200 and ₹. 64,800 respectively.

Illustration 10: Tee Pee Ltd. in the course of refining crude oil obtains four joint products. *A, B, C* and *D*. The total cost till the split-off point was ₹. 97,600. The output and sales in the year 2004, were as follows:

Product	*Output (Gallons)*	*Sales (₹.)*	*Separate costs (₹.)*
A	5,00,000	1,15,000	30,000
B	10,000	10,000	6,000
C	5,000	4,000	—
D	9,000	30,000	1,000

You are required to:

(*i*) Calculate the net income for each of the products if the joint costs are apportioned on the basis of sales value of the different products.

(*ii*) What would be the net income of the company from each product if it decides to sell the products at the split-off point itself @ *A* 15 paise; *B* 50 paise; *C* 80 paise and *D* ₹. 3 per gallon?

(*iii*) In case the company expects to operate at the same level of production and sales in the year 2005, could the company increase the net income by altering its processing decisions? If so, what would be the expected overall net income? Which products should be processed further and which should be sold at split-off? Assume that all costs incurred after the split-off are variable.

Solution: **(*i*) Statement of Net Income for Each of the Products**

Product	*Sales Value* ₹.	*Joint Cost* ₹.	*Separate Cost* ₹.	*Total Cost* ₹.	*Sales Value* ₹.	*Profit* ₹.
A	1,15,000	70,592	30,000	1,00,592	1,15,000	14,408
B	10,000	6,138	6,000	12,138	10,000	(–)2,138
C	4,000	2,455	—	2,455	4,000	1,545
D	30,000	18,415	1,000	19,415	30,000	10,585
Total	1,59,000	97,600	37,000	1,34,600	1,59,000	24400

Note: 1 Joint cost has been apportioned to product on the basis of Sales Values

i.e. $\frac{97,600 \times 1,15,000}{1,59,000}$ = 70,592 will be of *A*. For *B, C & D,* similar calculations may be made.

(*ii*) Statement of the Net Income

Product	*Sales Value at Split-off Point* ₹.	*Joint Cost* ₹.	*Profit* ₹.
A	5,00,000 × 0.15 = 75,000	70,592	4,408
B	10,000 × 0.50 = 5,000	6,138	(–) 1,138
C	5000 × 0.80 = 4,000	2,455	1,545
D	9,000 × 3.00 = 27,000	18,415	8,585
Total	1,11,000	97,600	13,400

In case of A and D there is incremental gain after further processing.

		A	*D*
Incremental Sales Value	=	40,000	3,000
Separate Costs		30,000	1,000
Incremental gains		10,000	2000

Hence A & D should be processed further.

Note: Incremental Sales Value Product A ₹. 115000 – 75000 = 40,000 and Product D 30,000 – 27,000 = 3,000.

Statement Showing Overall Income

Product	*Sales value*	*Joint Cost*	*Separate Cost*	*Total Cost*	*Profit*
A	1,15,000	70,592	30,000	1,00,592	14,408
B	5,000	6,138	—	6,138	(–) 1,138
C	4,000	2,455	—	2,455	1,545
D	30,000	18,415	1,000	19,415	10,585
Total	1,54,000	97,600	31,000	1,28,600	25,400

By altering the processing decisions, the overall net income would be ₹. 25,400.

Illustration 11: Three joint products are produced by passing chemicals through two processes. Output from process 1 is transferred to process 2 from which the three joint products are produced and immediately sold. The data regarding the processes for April, 2000 is given below:

	Process 1	*Process 2*
Direct Material 2500 kgs at ₹. 4 per kg	₹. 10,000	—
Direct Labour	₹. 6,250	₹. 6,900
Overheads	₹. 4,500	₹. 6,900
Normal loss	10% of input	Nil
Scrap value of loss	₹. 2 per kgs	—
Output	2300 kilo	Joint products *A* — 900 kgs *B* — 800 kgs *C* — 600 kgs

There were no opening or closing stocks in either process and the selling prices of the output from Process 2 were:

Joint Product *A*	₹. 24 per kg
Joint Product *B*	₹. 18 per kg
Joint Product *C*	₹. 12 per kg

Required:

(*a*) Prepare an account for Process 1 together with any Loss or Gain Account you consider necessary to record the month's activities.

(*b*) Calculate the profit attributable to each of the joint products by apportioning the total costs from Process 2: (*i*) According to weight of output. (*ii*) By the market value of production.

Solution:

Process 1 Account

	Kg.	*Rate*	*Amt.* (₹)		*Kg*	*Rate*	*Amt.* (₹)
To Direct Material	2500	4	10,000	By Normal Loss			
To Direct Labour			6250	(10% of 2,500)	250	2	500
To Overheads			4,500	By Output to			
				Process 2	2,300	9	20,700
	2500		20750				
To Abnormal Gain	50	9	450				
	2,550		21,200		2,550		21,200

$$\text{Cost per unit} = \frac{\text{Total cost} - \text{Value of normal scrap}}{\text{Input} - \text{Normal loss}} = \frac{20,750 - 500}{2,500 - 250}$$

$$= \frac{20,250}{2,250} = ₹.\ 9 \text{ per unit}$$

Abnormal Gain Account

	Kg.	Rate	Amt. (₹.)		Kg	Rate	Amt. (₹.)
To Normal Loss	50	2	100	By Process I.	50	9	450
To Costing P & L			350				
	50		450		50		450

Normal Loss Account

	Kg.	Rate	Amt. (₹.)		Kg	Rate	Amt. (₹.)
To Process I	250	2	500	By Debtors/Cash (Sale of actual scrap)	200	2	400
				By Abnormal Gain	50	2	100
	250		500		250		500

(*b*) Joint Cost of Products

	₹.
Cost of output from Process I (2300 Kg. @ ₹. 9)	20,700
Direct Labour in Process 2.	6,900
Overheads in Process 2.	6,900
Joint Costs of Products	34,500

Output – Joint Products (Kg.)

A	900
B	800
C	600
	2300

(*i*) Apportionment of Joint Costs According to Weight and Calculation of Profit

Joint	*Output Kg.*	*Apportionment Joint Cost (₹.)*	*Sales Value (₹.)*	*Profit or (loss) ₹.*
A	900	13,500	900 × 24 = 21,600	8,100
B	800	12,000	800 × 18 = 14,400	2,400
C	600	9,000	600 × 12 = 7,200	(–) 1,800
Total	2300	34,500	43,200	8,700

Calculations :

$$A = \frac{900 \times 34,500}{2,300} = 13,500$$

$$B = \frac{800 \times 34,500}{2,300} = 12,000$$

$$C = \frac{600 \times 34,500}{2.300} = 9,000$$

(ii) Apportionment of Joint Costs by Marked Value and Calculation of Profit

Joint Product	*Sales Value (₹.)*	*Apportionment Joint Costs (₹.)*	*Profit (₹.)*
A	21,600	17,250	4,350
B	14,400	11,500	2,900
C	7,200	5,750	1,450
Total	43,200	34,500	8,700

Calculations:

$$A = \frac{21,600 \times 34,500}{43,200} = ₹.\ 17,250$$

$$B = \frac{14,400 \times 34,500}{43,200} = ₹.\ 11,500$$

$$C = \frac{7,200 \times 34,500}{43,200} = ₹.\ 5,750$$

Illustration 12: A company's plant processes 1,50,000 kgs of raw material in a month to produce two products, viz. '*P*' and '*Q*'. The cost of raw meterial is ₹. 12 per kg. The process costs per month are:

	₹.
Direct Materials	90,000
Direct Wages	1,20,000
Variable Overheads	1,00,000
Fixed Overheads	1,00,000

The loss in process is 5% of input and the output ratio of *P* and *Q* which emerge simultaneously is 1 : 2. The selling prices of the two products at the point of split off are : *P* ₹. 12 per kg. and *Q* ₹. 20 per kg. A proposal is available to process *P* further by mixing it with other purchased materials. The entire current output of the plant can be so processed further to obtain a new product '*S*'. The price per kg of *S* is ₹. 15 and each kg. of output of *S* will require one kilogram of input *P*. The cost of processing of *P* into *S* (including other materials) is ₹. 1,85,000 per month.

You are required to prepare a statement showing the monthly profitability based both on the existing manufacturing operations and on further processing.

Will you recommend further processing?

Solution:

Working notes:

	Kg.
1. *Input*	1,50,000
Less: Loss in process 5%	7,500
Total output	1,42,500
P = 1/3 of 1,42,500	47,500
Q = 2/3 of 1,42,500	95,000

2. *Joint costs:*	₹.
Raw materials 1,50,000 × 12	18,00,000
Direct Materials	90,000
Direct wages	1,20,000
Variable overheads	1,00,000
Fixed overheads	1,00,000
	22,10,000

3. *Sales:*

$P = 47{,}500 \times 12$	5,70,000
$Q = 95{,}000 \times 20$	19,00,000
Total	24,70,000

Ratio of sales = 57 : 190 *i.e.* 3 : 10

4. *Joint Cost in Sales Ratio*

$P = 22{,}10{,}000 \times 3/13 =$ ₹. 5,10,000

$Q = 22{,}10{,}000 \times 10/13 =$ ₹. 17,00,000

Statement Showing the Monthly Profitability

	Based on existing manufacturing operation products			*Based on further processing of P into S Product*		
	P	*Q*	*Total*	*S*	*Q*	*Total*
Sales quantity (kg.)	47,500	95,000	1,42,500	47,500	95,000	1,42,500
	₹.	₹.	₹.	₹.	₹.	₹.
Sales Revenue	5,70,000	19,00,000	24,70,000	7,12,500	19,00,000	26,12,500
Less: Joint Costs	5,10,000	17,00,000	22,10,000	6,95,000	17,00,000	23,95,000
Profit	60,000	2,00,000	2,60,000	17,500	2,00,000	2,17,500

5,10,000 + 1,85,000 further processing = ₹. 6,95,000

Recommendation : Further processing of P is not recommended as it results in a lower profit of P by ₹. 42,500:

Additional Sales Revenue 47,500 × 3 =	1,42,500	
Further Processing		1,85,000
Loss on processing of *P* into *S* =		(–) 42,500

Illustration 13: Bright Chemicals Ltd. electrolyses common salt to obtain 3 joint products Caustic Soda, Chlorine and Hydrogen. During a costing period, the expenditure relating to the inputs for the common process amounted to ₹. 3,50,000. After separation, expenses amounting to ₹. 1,60,000 ₹. 75,000 and ₹. 10,000 were incurred for caustic soda, chlorine and hydrogen respectively. The entire production was sold and ₹. 3,75,000, ₹. 2,50,000 and ₹. 60,000 were realised for caustic soda, chlorine and hydrogen respectively. The selling expenses were estimated at 5% of realisations from sale. The management expected profits at 15%, 10% and 5% of realisations from sale of caustic soda, chlorine and hydrogen respectively.

Draw a columnar statement showing the apportionment of Joint. Costs and the profitability of each product.

Statement Showing the Apportionment of Joint Costs and the Profitability of Each Product (₹.)

Particulars	*Caustic Soda*	*Chlorine*	*Hydrogen*	*Total*
	₹.	₹.	₹.	₹.
Sales Realisation	3,75,000	2,50,000	60,000	6,85,000
Less : Expected Profit (15%, 10% and 5%)	– 56,250	– 25,000	– 3,000	– 84,250
Less : Selling Expenses at 5% on sales	– 18,750	– 12,500	– 3,000	– 34,250
Estimated Cost of Production	3,00,000	2,12,500	54,000	5,66,500
Less : After Separation Exp.	– 1,60,000	– 75,000	– 10,000	– 2,45,000
Estimated Joint Costs	1,40,000	1,37,500	44,000	3,21,500

Particulars	*Caustic Soda*	*Chlorine*	*Hydrogen*	*Total*
Percentage of Joint Costs	43.546%	42.768%	13.686%	100%
Apportionment of Joint Costs of 3,50,000 on the basis of above percentage	1,52,411	1,49,688	47,901	3,50,000
Add : After Separation Exp.	1,60,000	75,000	10,000	2,45,000
Actual Cost of Production	3,12,411	2,24,688	57,901	5,95,000
Add: Selling expenses at @ 5% on sales	18,750	12,500	3,000	34,250
Total Cost	3,31,161	2,37,188	60,901	6,29,250
Sales	3,75,000	2,50,000	60,000	6,85,000
Profit (Loss)	43,839	12,812	(901)	55,750

Illustration 14: In a manufacturing Company 10,000 kilolitres of '*A*' is processed to produce 6,000 kilolitres of `B' and 4,000 kilolitres of '*C*'. The joint cost before separation point came to an amount of ₹. 24,000. From the following particulars, calculate the apportionment of joint cost and the profit of each product under (*a*) physical measurement, (*b*) market value at separation point, and (*c*) market value after further processing.

	B ₹.	C ₹.
Unit selling price at separation point	5.00	3.75
Unit selling price after further processing	7.00	7.50
Further processing costs after separation	5,000	7,500

Solution:

(*a*) Apportionment of Joint Cost and Profit under Physical Measurement

Total quantity *A* 10,000 *kl* is processed to produce *B* 6,000 *kl* & C 4000 *kl*.

Ratio of *A* in *B* & *C* = 3 : 2

	B ₹.	*C* ₹.	*Total* ₹.
Allocation of Joint Cost of ₹. 24,000 in the ratio of 3 : 2	14,400	9,600	24,000
Selling price @ ₹. 5.00 × 6,000 =	30,000		30,000
@ ₹. 3.75 × 4000 =		15,000	15,000
Profit	15,600	5,400	21,000

(*b*) Apportionment of Joint Cost and Profit Under Market Value at Separation Point

	B ₹.	*C* ₹.	*Total* ₹.
Market value @ ₹. 5.00 × 6,000	30,000		30,000
@ 3.75 × 4,000		15,000	15,000
Allocation of joint cost of ₹. 24,000	30,000	15,000	45,000
in the ratio of sales *i.e.* 30:15	16,000	8,000	24,000
Profit	14,000	7,000	21,000

(c) Apportionment of Joint Cost and Profit Under Market Value after Further Processing

	B ₹	*C* ₹	*Total* ₹
Market value @ 7.00 × 6,000	42,000		42,000
@ 7.50 × 4,000		30,000	30,000
	42,000	30,000	72,000
Allocation of joint cost of ₹. 24,000 in ratio market value	14,000	10,000	24,000
Add: Further processing cost	5,000	7,500	12,500
Total cost	19,000	17,500	36,500
Profit	23,000	12,500	35,500

Illustration 15: *ABC* Ltd. operates a simple chemical process to convert a single material into three separate items, referred to here as *X*, *Y* and *Z*. All the three end-products are separated simultaneously at a single split-point.

Products *X* and *Y* are ready for sale immediately upon split off without further processing or any other additional costs. Product *Z*, however, is processed further before being sold. There is no available market price for *Z* at the split-off point.

The selling prices quoted here are expected to remain the same in the coming year. During 2002-03, the selling prices of the items and the total amounts sold were.

X – 186 tons sold for ₹. 1,500 per ton

Y – 527 tons sold for ₹. 1,125 per ton

Z – 736 tons sold for ₹. 750 per ton

The total joint manufacturing costs for the year were ₹. 6,25,000. An additional ₹. 3,10,000 was spent to finish product Z.

There were no opening inventories of *X*, *Y* or *Z*. At the end of the year, the following inventories of complete units were on hand:

X 180 tons: *Y* 60 tons; *Z* 25 tons;

There was no opening or closing work-in-progress.

Required:

(*i*) Compute the cost of inventories of *X*, *Y* and *Z* for Balance Sheet purposes and cost of goods sold for income statement purpose as on March 31, 2003, using:

(*a*) Net realizable value (NRV) method of joint cost allocation.

(*b*) Constant gross-margin percentage NRV method of joint-cost allocation.

(*ii*) Compare the gross-margin percentages for *X*, *Y* and *Z* using two methods given in requirement (*i*). **[*CA – PE II May 2003*]**

Solution:

(*i*) (*a*) Statement of Joint Cost Allocation of Inventories of *X*, *Y* and *Z* for Balance Sheet Purpose (By Using Net Realizable Value Method)

	Products			
	X ₹	*Y* ₹	*Z* ₹	*Total* ₹
Final sales value of total production	5,49,000	6,60,375	5,70,750	17,80,125
Less: Additional cost	—	—	3,10,000	3,10,000
Net realizable value at split off	5,49,000	6,60,375	2,60,750	14,70,152
Joint cost allocated in proportion of NRV at split-off	2,33,398	2,80,748	1,10,854	6,25,000

Cost of Goods Sold for Income Statement Purposes as on March 31, 2003
(By Using Net Realizable Value Method)

	Products			Total
	X	Y	Z	
	₹	₹	₹	₹
Allocated Joint Cost	2,33,398	2,80,748	1,10,854	6,25,000
Additional Cost	—	—	3,10,000	3,10,000
	2,33,398	2,80,748	4,20,854	9,35,000
Less: Cost of year end inventory (*Note* 1 *X* 49.18%; *Y* 10.22%; *Z* 3.29%)	1,14,785	28,692	13,846	1,57,323
Cost of Goods sold	1,18,613	2,52,056	4,07,008	7,77,677

Income Statement
(Showing Gross Margin and Gross Margin Percentage)
(By Using Net Realizable Value Method)

	Products			Total
	X	Y	Z	
	₹	₹	₹	₹
Sales Revenue	2,79,000	5,92,875	5,52,000	14,23,875
Less: Cost of Goods Sold	1,18,613	2,52,056	4,07,008	7,77,697
Gross Margin	1,60,387	3,40,819	1,44,992	6,46,178
Gross Margin %	57.49%	57.49%	26.27%	

(*b*) Statement of Joint Cost Allocation of Inventories of *X*, *Y* and *Z* for Balance Sheet Purpose
(By Using Constant Gross Margin Percentage NRV Method)

	Products			Total
	X	Y	Z	
	₹	₹	₹	₹
Final sales value of total production	5,49,000	6,60,375	5,70,750	17,80,125
Less: Gross Margin (*Note* 2) 47.4756%	2,60,641	3,13,517	2,70,967	8,45,125
	2,88,359	3,46,858	2,99,783	9,35,000
Less: Additional Cost	—	—	3,10,000	3,10,000
Joint Cost Allocated	2,88,359	3,46,858	(10,217)	6,25,000

Note. The negative joint cost allocation to product *Z* is peculiar feature of Constant Gross Margin NRV Method.

Cost of Goods Sold for Income Statement Purposess
(By Using Constant Gross Margin Percentage NRV Method)

	Products			
	X ₹.	Y ₹.	Z ₹.	Total ₹.
Allocated Joint Cost	2,88,359	3,46,858	(10,217)	6,25,000
Additional Cost	—	—	3,10,000	3,10,000
Cost Goods available for sale	2,88,359	3,46,858	2,99,783	9,35,000
Less: Cost of year-end inventory (*Note I*) *X* 49.18%; *Y* 10.22%; Z 3.29%	1,41,815	35,449	9,863	1,87,127
Cost of Goods Sold	1,46,544	3,11,409	2,89,920	7,47,873

Income Statement
(Showing Gross Margin and Gross Percentage by Using Constant Gross Margin Percentage NRV Method)

	Products			
	X ₹.	Y ₹.	Z ₹.	Total ₹.
Sales Revenue (₹.)	2,79,000	5,92,875	5,52,000	14,23,875
Less: Cost of Goods Sold	1,46,544	3,11,409	2,89,920	7,47,873
Gross Margin	1,32,456	2,81,466	2,62,080	6,76,002
Gross Margin %	47.475%	47.475%	47.478%	47.476%

(*ii*) Comparative Statement of Gross Margin Percentage for *X*, *Y* and *Z*
(Using Net Realizable Value and Constant Gross Margin Percentage NRV Methods)

	Products Gross Margin Percentages		
	X	Y	Z
Net Realizable Value Method	57.49%	57.49%	26.27%
Constant Gross Margin NRV Method	47.48%	47.48%	47.48%

Working Notes:

1. Total production of three products for the year 2002-03.

Items/ Products (1)	*Quantity sold in tons* (2)	*Quantity of year-end inventory in tons* (3)	*Total Production* (4) = (2) + (3)	*Percentage by year-end inventory to total production* (5) = (3)/(4) × 100
X	186	180	366	49.18
Y	527	60	587	10.22
Z	736	25	761	3.29

2. Gross Margin Percentage:

Final Sales Value of Total Production	₹. 17,80,125
Less: Joint Cost and Additional Cost (₹. 6,25,000 + ₹. 3,10,000)	9,35,000
Gross Margin	8,45,125

Gross Margin Percentage (8,45,125/17,80,125) × 100 = 47.4756%.

Illustration 16: **If the products are truly joint products, the cost of the process can be applied to these products:**

(*i*) On the basis of weight or other physical quantity of each product;

(*ii*) In respect of marginal cost of the process on the basis of physical quantities of various products and in respect of fixed costs of the process on the basis of contributions made by various products:

(*iii*) On the basis of sale values of the different products.

Illustrate the above statement by using the following figures in respect of joint production of A and B for a month:

	₹.
Direct Materials	**5,000**
Direct Labour	**3,000**
Variable Overheads	**2,000**
Fixed Overheads	**2,000**

Sales

A—100 quintals @ ₹. 80 per quintal

B—150 quintals @ ₹. 40 per quintal

(*iv*) Also compute the profit/loss per product under each of these methods.

Solution:

Working Notes:

		₹.
1. Sales	*A*: 100 quintals @ ₹. 80	8,000
	B: 150 quintals @ ₹. 40	6,000
	Total Sales Value	14,000
	Marginal cost (5,000 + 3000 + 2000)	10,000
	Contribution	4,000
	Less : Fixed Overheads	2,000
	Profit	2,000

Joint costs of *A* & *B* = Marginal Cost + Fixed Overheads

= 10,000 + 2,000 = 12,000

Apportionment of Joint Costs: ₹.

(*i*) *On the basis of weight i.e. 100 : 150 quintals.*

$A : 12{,}000 \times \dfrac{100}{250}$	4,800
$B : 12{,}000 \times \dfrac{150}{250}$	7,200
	12,000

(*ii*) *Marginal cost on the basis of weight and fixed cost on the basis of contribution:*

A : Marginal Cost $\left(10{,}000 \times \dfrac{100}{250}\right)$	4,000
Fixed Cost	2,000
	6,000
B: Marginal Cost $\left(10{,}000 \times \dfrac{150}{250}\right)$	6,000
Fixed Costs	nil
	6,000

Note :	Total	*A*	*B*
Sales Value	14,000	8,000	6,000
Marginal Cost	10,000	4,000	6,000
Contribution	4,000	4,000	nil

(iii) On the basis of Sales Values:

$$A : 12,000 \times \frac{8,000}{14,000} = 6,857$$

$$B : 12,000 \times \frac{6,000}{14,000} = 5,143$$

12,000

(iv) ***Statement of Profits Under Each of These Methods (₹.)***

Mathod	*i*		*ii*		*iii*	
Product	*A*	*B*	*A*	*B*	*A*	*B*
Sales Value	8,000	6,000	8,000	6,000	8,000	6,000
Total Cost	4,800	7,200	6,000	6,000	6,857	5,143
Profit	3,200	(–) 1,200	2,000	—	1,143	857
Total Profit of *A* + *B*	2,000		2,000		2,000	

Illustration 17: Pokemon Chocolates manufactures and distributes chocolate products. It purchases Cocoa beans and processes them into two intermediate products:

- Chocolate powder liquor base
- Milk-chocolate liquor base.

These two intermediate products become separately identifiable at a single split off point. Every 500 pounds of cocoa beans yields 20 gallons of chocolate-powder liquor base and 30 gallons of milk-chocolate liquor base.

The chocolate powder liquor base is further processed into chocolate powder. Every 20 gallons of chocolate-powder liquor base yields 200 pounds of chocolate powder. The milk-chocolate liquor base is further processed into milk-chocolate. Every 30 gallons of milk-chocolate liquor base yields 340 pounds of milk chocolate.

Production and sales data for October, 2004 are :

- Cocoa beans processed — 7,500 pounds
- Costs of processing Cocoa beans to split off point (including purchase of beans) — ₹. 7,12,500

	Production	Sales	Selling Price
Chocolate Powder	3,000 pounds	3,000 pounds	₹. 190 per pound
Milk Chocolate	5,100 pounds	5,100 pounds	₹. 237.50 per pounds

The October, 2004 separable costs of processing chocolate-powder liquor into chocolate powder are ₹. 3,02,812.50. The October, 2004 separable costs of processing milk-chocolate liquor base into milk-chocolate are ₹. 6,23,437.50.

Pokemon fully processes both of its intermediate products into chocolate powder or milk-chocolate. There is an active market for these intermediate products. In October, 2004, Pokemon could have sold the chocolate powder liquor base for ₹. 997.50 a gallon and the milk-chocolate liquor base for ₹. 1,235 a gallon.

Required :

(i) Calculate how the joint cost of ₹. 7,12,500 would be allocated between the chocolate powder and milk-chocolate liquor bases under the following methods:

(a) Sales value at split off point

(b) Physical measure (gallons)

(c) Estimated net realisable value, (NRV) and

(d) Constant gross-margin percentage NRV.

(ii) What is the gross-margin percentage of the chocolate powder and milk-chocolate liquor bases under each of the methods in requirement (i) ?

(iii) Could Pokemon have increased its operating income by a change in its decision to fully process both of its intermediate products ? Show your computations. ***[CA PE II May 2004]***

1. Comparison of Alternative Joint Allocation Methods

(a) Joint cost allocation on the bases of sales value of split-off point

Sales value of chocolate powder liqour base

$$3000 \text{ Pounds} = 3000 \times \frac{20}{200} = 300 \text{ gallons}$$

Sales value of 300 gallons @ ₹. 997.5 = ₹. 2,99,250

Sales value of milk chocolate liquor base

$$5100 \text{ pounds} = 5100 \times \frac{30}{340} = 450 \text{ gallons}$$

Sales value of 450 gallons @ ₹. 1235 = ₹. 5,55,750

Ratio of Sales Value 2,99,250 : 5,55,750 = 35 : 65

Joint Cost Allocation (₹.)

$$\text{Chocolate powder } 7{,}12{,}500 \times \frac{35}{100} = ₹.\ 2{,}49{,}375$$

$$\text{Milk chocolate } 7{,}12{,}500 \times \frac{65}{100} = ₹.\ 4{,}63{,}125$$

(b) Physical Measure Method (gallons)

Chocolate powder : 300 gallons

Milk chocolate 450 gallons

Ratio of gallons = 300/750 : 450/750

2 : 3

Joint Cost Allocation

$$\text{Chocolate powder} : 7{,}12{,}500 \times \frac{2}{5} = ₹.\ 2{,}85{,}000$$

$$\text{Milk chocolate} : 7{,}12{,}500 \times \frac{3}{5} = ₹.\ 4{,}27{,}500$$

(c) Net Realisable Value Method

	Chocolate powder	*Milk chocolate*
Final Sales	3000 × 190	5100 × 237.5
	5,70,000.00	12,11,250.00
Deduct Separable Cost	3,02,812.50	6,23,437.50
Net realisable value at split off	2,67,187.50	5,87,812.50
Ratio	0.3125	0.6875
Joint cost allocation	7,12,500 × .3125	7,12,500 × .6875
On the bases of above ratio	= 2,22,656.25	= 4,89,843.75

(d) Constant Gross Margin Percentage Method

Final sale value of total production	
(5,70,000 + 12,11,250)	₹. 17,81,250
Deduct total joint and separate cost	
(7,12,500 + 9,26,250)	16,38,750
Gross Margin	1,42,500

Gross Margin Percentage (1,42,500/17,81,500) × 100 = 8%

	Chocolate powder liquor base (₹.)	*Milk chocolate liquor base (₹.)*	*Total (₹.)*
Final sales value	57,000	12,11,250	17,81,250
Less Gross margin @ 8%	45,600	96,900	1,42,500
Cost of goods available for sale	5,24,400	11,14,350	16,38,750
Deduct separable cost	3,02,812.50	6,23,437.50	9,26,250
Joint Cost Allocated	2,21,587.5	4,90,912.50	7,12,500

(*ii*) Gross Margin Percentages

	Chocolate powder liquor base (₹.)	*Milk chocolate liquor base (₹.)*	*Total (₹.)*
Sales value at split off point	3.125%	10.294%	8%
Physical measure method	(3.125%)	13.235%	8%
NRV method	7.812%	8.088%	8%
Constant gross margin % NRV method	8%	8%	8%

1. (*iii*) Further processing of chocolate powder liquor base into chocolate powder-

Incremental revenue-₹. 5,70,000-(997.5 × 300)	= ₹. 2,70,750.00
Incremental Cost	302812.50
Incremental Operating Income	(32112.50)

Since incremental operating income is negative after further processing it should not be processed further but sold only at split off point

Further processing of Milk chocolate liquor base into milk chocolate

Incremental revenue ₹. 1211250-₹. 555750	= ₹. 6,55,500.00
Incremental Cost	6,23,437.50
Incremental Operating Income	3,20,62.50

Pokemon chocolates could increase operating income by ₹. 32,062.50 if chocolate liquor base is sold at split off point and milk chocolate liquor base is further processed into milk chocolate.

Illustration 18: Sellwell Ltd. operates a chemical process which produces four products A, B, C and D from a basic raw material. The company's budget for a month is as under:

	₹.
Raw materials consumption	17,520
Initial processing wages	16,240
Initial processing overheads	16,240

Product	*Production*	*Sales*	*Additional Processing cost after split-off*
	(Kgs.)	(₹.)	(₹.)
A	16,000	1,09,600	28,800
B	200	5,600	—
C	2,000	30,000	16,000
D	360	21,600	6,600

The company presently intends to sell products *B* at the point of split-off without further processing. The remaining products *A, C* and *D* are to be further processed and sold. However, the management has been advised that it would be possible to sell all the four products at the split-off point without further processing and if this course was adopted, the selling prices would be as under:

Product	*A*	*B*	*C*	*D*
Selling Price per kg. (₹.)	4.00	28.00	8.00	40.00

The joint costs are to be apportioned on the basis of the sales value realisation at the point of split-off.

You are required to :

(*a*) Prepare a statement showing the apportionment of joint costs.

(*b*) Prepare a statement showing the productwise and total budgeted profit or loss based on the proposal to sell product *B* at the split-off point and products *A, C* and *D* after further processing.

(*c*) Prepare a statement to show the productwise and total profit or loss if the alternative strategy to sell all the products at split-off stage was adopted.

(*d*) Recommend any other alternative which, in your opinion, can increase the total profit further. Calculate the total profit as also the productwise profit or loss, based on your recommendation.

Solution:

(*a*) Statement Showing the Apportionment of Joint Costs

Total Joint Costs 17,520 + 16,240 + 16,240 = ₹. 50,000

Product	*Sales Value at split-off point*	*Joint Costs Apportioned in the ratio of sales*
A	16,000 × 4 = 64,000	32,000
B	200 × 28 = 5,600	2,800
C	2,000 × 8 = 16,000	8,000
D	360 × 40 = 14,400	7,200
Total	₹. 1,00,000	₹. 50,000

(*b*) Statement Showing Budgeted Profit or Loss (₹.)

Product	*Joint cost* ₹	*Additional Processing cost*	*Total cost* ₹	*Sales value* ₹	*Profit* ₹
A	32,000	28,800	60,800	1,09,600	48,800
B	2,800	—	2,800	5,600	2,800
C	8,000	16,000	24,000	30,000	6,000
D	7,200	6,600	13,800	21,600	7,800
Total	50,000	51,400	1,01,400	1,66,800	65,400

(c) Statement of Profit or Loss at Split-off Point (₹.)

Product	*Joint Cost*	*Sales Value*	*Profit*
A	32,000	64,000	32,000
B	2,800	5,600	2,800
C	8,000	16,000	8,000
D	7,200	14,400	7,200
Total	50,000	1,00,000	50,000

(*d*) Product *B* requires no further processing. In case of Product *C*, if further processed, the incremental sales value will be ₹. 14,000 *i.e.* ₹. 30,000 – 16,000. Thus *C* should not be processed. In case of Product *A* and *D*, the position will be as below.

	A	*D*
Incremental Sales Value	45,600	7,200
Additional Processing Costs	28,800	6,600
Incremental Gain	16,800	600

Hence, *A* & *D* should be processed further, *B* & *C* should be sold at split-off point.

Statement Showing Profit

Product	*Sales Value*	*Total Cost*	*Profit*
A	1,09,600	60,800	48,800
B	5,600	2,800	2,800
C	16,000	8,000	8,000
D	21,600	13,800	7,800
Total	1,52,800	85,400	67,400

Illustration 19: *JKL* Limited produces two products – *J* and *K* together with a by-product *L* from a single main process (Process *I*). Product *J* is sold at the point of separation for ₹. 55 per kg, whereas product *K* is sold for ₹. 77 per kg, after further processing into product *K*2. By product *L* is sold without further processing for ₹. 19.25 per kg.

Process *I* is closely monitored by a team of chemists, who planned the output per 1,000 kg of input materials to be as follows:

Product *J*	500 kg
Product *K*	350 kg
Product *L*	100 kg
Toxic waste	50 kg

The toxic waste is disposed at a cost of ₹. 16.50 per kg, and arises at the end of processing.

Process *II* which is used for further processing of product *K* into product *K*2, has the following cost structure:

Fixed costs	₹. 2,64,000 per week
Variable cost	₹. 16.50 per kg processed

The following actual data relate to the first week of the month:

Process I

Opening Work-in-Progress	Nil
Material input	40,000 kg costing ₹. 6,60,000
Direct labour	₹. 4,40,000
Variable Overheads	₹. 1,76,000
Fixed Overheads	₹. 2,64,000

Output:

Product *J*	19,200 kg
Product *K*	14,400 kg
Product *L*	4,000 kg
Toxic waste	2,400 kg
Closing Work-in-Progress	Nil
Process II	
Opening Work-in-Progress	Nil
Input of product *K*	14,400 kg
Output of product *K*2	13,200 kg
Closing Work-in-Progress (50% converted and conversion Costs were incurred in accordance with the planned Cost structure)	1,200 kg

Required:

(*i*) Prepare Process *I* account for the first week of the month using the final sales value method of attribute the pre-separation costs to joint products.

(*ii*) Prepare the Toxic Waste Account and Process II account for the first week of the month.

(*iii*) Comment on the method used by the *JKL* Limited to attribute the pre-separation costs to joint products.

(*iv*) Advise the management of *JKL* Limited whether or not, on purely financial grounds, it should continue to process product K into product K2:

(*a*) If product *K* could be sold at the point of separation for ₹. 47.30 per kg; and

(*b*) If the 60% of the weekly fixed costs of Process II were avoided by not processing product *K* further. [*CA PE II May 2004*]

Solution:

Process I Account

Particulars	*Qty in kg*	*Rate per kg ₹*	*Amount ₹*	*Particulars*	*Qty in kg*	*Rate per kg ₹*	*Amount ₹*
To Material input	40,000	16.50	6,60,000	By Product L sales	4,000	19.25	77,000
To Direct labour			4,40,000	By Toxic waste (Normal loss)	2,000	16.50	–33,000*
To Variable Overheads			1,76,000	By Abnormal loss	400	44	17,600
To Fixed Overheads			2,64,000	By Joint Product J (Refer to Working Note 2)	19,200		7,21,171
				By Joint product K (Refer to Working Note 2)	14,400		7,57,229
	40,000		15,40,000		40,000		15,40,000

Valuation of abnormal loss per kg (*Using physical measure method*) $= \dfrac{₹.15,40,000 - ₹.77,000 + ₹.33,000}{40,000 \text{ Kgs.} \times 0.85}$

= ₹. 14,96,000/34,000 kgs.

= ₹. 44 per kg.

***Note.** Toxic Waste is not sold. It is disposed off by increasing expenses @ ₹ 16.50 per kg. The amount is shown as minus figure in the credit side (may be debited).

(ii) Toxic Waste Account (Normal Loss)

Particulars	*Qty in kg*	*Rate /kg ₹*	*Amount ₹*	*Particulars*	*Qty in kg*	*Rate/ kg ₹*	*Amount ₹*
To Process *I* A/c	2,000	16.50	(–)33,000	By Balance		16.50	(–)33,000

Process II Account

Particulars	*Qty in kg*	*Rate /kg ₹*	*Amount ₹*	*Particulars*	*Qty in kg*	*Rate/ kg ₹*	*Amount ₹*
To Process *I* A/c (Product *K*)	14,400	52.585	7,57,236	By Product *K*2 account	13,200		11,73,924
To Variable Overheads		16.50	2,37,600	By Closing WIP (Refer to Working Note 3)	1,200		84,912
To Fixed Overheads			2,64,000				
			12,58,836				12,58,836

Working notes:

1. Calculation of joint cost of the output:

= ₹. 15,40,000 – ₹. 77,000 – ₹. (–) 33,000 – ₹. 17,600

= ₹. 14,78,400

2. Allocation of joint cost over joint products J & K

(By using final sales value method)

Products	*Quantity (Kgs)*	*Sales value ₹*	*Joint cost ₹*
J	19,200	10,56,000 (19,200 kgs × ₹. 55)	7,21,171
K	14,400	11,08,800 (14,400 kgs × ₹. 77)	7,57,229
Total		21,64,800	14,78,400

3. Valuation of 1200 Kgs. of Closing WIP :

		₹.
Material I	100% complete (1200 kgs × ₹. 52.5858)	63,103
Fixed & variable overheads	$\left(\frac{₹. 5,01,600}{13,800 \text{ units}}\right) \times 600$ units	21,809
Total valuation of 1,200 kgs of closing WIP		84,912

(iii) Comment on the method used by the JKL Ltd :

(*To attribute the pre-separation costs to joint products*)

For attributing the joint costs over joint products *J* and *K*, *JKLF* Ltd., used the basis of final sales value. This is one of the popular method used in the industry.

Other methods can also be used for the purpose.

(*i*) Physical Measure Method (if both the products are equally complex).

(*ii*) Constant Gross Margin Percentage Method.

(*iii*) Net Realizable Value Method.

(*iv*) Advice to the Management of JKL Ltd.:

	₹.
Incremental sales revenue per kg. from further processing	29.70
Less: Incremental variable cost per kg. of further processing	16.50
Incremental contribution per kg from further processing	13.20
At an output of 14,400 kgs the incremental contribution will be:	1,90,080
Less: Avoidable fixed cost	
(60% × ₹. 2,64,000)	1,58,400
Net benefit (₹.)	31,680

$$\text{Break-even point} = \frac{\text{Avoidable fixed costs}}{\text{Incremental contribution per kg.}} = \frac{₹.1,58,400}{₹.13.20}$$

$$= 12,000 \text{ kgs.}$$

Hence further processing should be undertaken if output is expected to exceed 12,000 kgs. per week.

QUESTIONS

1. **Explain the methods to be adopted in the treatment of joint products and by products.**

[*Delhi B.Com*]

2. **How would you deal with by products in costing : (*a*) where they are of small value (*b*) where they are of considerable value (*c*) where they require further processing.**
3. **Distinguish between joint products and by-products and explain various methods of accounting for then.**
4. **Define joint products and by-products. Give examples of each. Explain the various ways apportioning of joint costs to joint products.**

NUMERICAL QUESTIONS

1. **Work out the estimated pre-separation cost per tonne of by-products *Y* and *Z* from the following data :**

Costs of manufacture before separation : ₹. 25,60,000

Main Product is X

There are two by-products *Y* and *Z* whose normal selling prices are as under :

Sales price of Y : ₹. 500 per tonne

Sales price of Z : ₹. 800 per tonne

Selling and distribution expenses have been estimated to be 25% of selling price and the net profit is expected to be 10% of selling price. Costs to manufacture each tonne after separation from the main products are :

₹. 95 for By-product *Y*

₹. 145 for By-product *Z*

Assume equal weight for *Y* and *Z*.

[**Ans.** *Pre-separation cost per tonne Y ₹. 230 Z ₹. 375*]

2. In a manufacturing process, in the course of manufacture of the product *X*, the by-products *P* and *Q* also emerge. The pre-separation expenses amount to ₹. 1,19,550. All the three products are processed further and sold in the market (details given below).

	Main product	*By-products*	
	X	*P*	*Q*
Sales value (₹.)	90,000	60,000	40,000
Post-separation costs (₹.)	6,000	5,000	4,000
Profit as a percentage of sales	25	20	15

Total fixed selling and distribution expenses are 10% of the total cost of sales and are apportioned to the three products in the ratio of 20:40:40.

(*i*) Prepare a statement showing the apportionment of pre-separation costs to the main product and the two by-products.

(*ii*) If the by-product *P* is not processed further and can be sold just, after separation at ₹. 58,500 without incurring any selling and distribution expenses, would you advise its disposal at that stage?

[**Ans.** (*i*) *Pre-separation cost; Main Product x ₹. 58,510 By Product P ₹. 37,020, Q ₹. 24,020. (ii) Profit without further processing P ₹. 21,480. Profit after further processing 20% of sales ₹. 12,000 then further processing cost ₹. 9,480*]

3. A factory is engaged in the production of a chemical Bomex and in the course of its manufacture, a by-product Brucil is produced, which after further processing has a commercial value. For the month of April, the following are the summarised cost data:

	Joint Expenses	*Separate Expenses*	
		Bomex	*Brucil*
	₹.	₹.	₹.
Materials	90,000	6,000	4,000
Labour	50,000	20,000	18,000
Overheads	30,000	10,000	6,000
Selling price per unit		98	34
Estimated profit per unit on sale of Brucil			4
No. of Units Produced		2,000 Units	2,000 Units

The factory uses reverse cost method of accounting for by-products whereby the sales value of by-products after deduction for the estimated profit, post separation costs and selling and distribution expenses relating to the by-products is credited to the joint process cost account.

You are required to prepare statements showing:

(*i*) The joint cost allocable to Bomex.

(*ii*) The product-wise and over all profitability of the factory for the month of April.

[**Ans.** *(i) ₹. 1,48,000 (ii) Bomex ₹. 1,20,00 + Brucil ₹. 8,000 = ₹. 20,000*]

4. In a process line of *XY* Company three joint products are produced. For the month of May the following data were available.

Product	*L* ₹.	*M* ₹.	*N* ₹.
Sales price per kg	5	10	20
Post-separation point costs	10,000	5,000	15,000
Output in kg	2,500	1,000	1,500
Pre-separation point costs amounted to ₹. 20000			

The joint products are manufactured in one common process, after which they are separated and may undergo further individual processing. The pre-separation point costs are apportioned to joint products according to weight. You are required to prepare a statement showing the estimated profit or loss for each product and in total.

[Ans. *L Loss ₹. 7500, M Profit ₹. 1000, N Profit ₹. 9000. Total Profit ₹. 2,500, Joint Cost L ₹. 10,000 M ₹. 4000, N ₹. 6,000.*]

5. In an Oil Mill four products emerge from a refining process. The total cost of input during the quarter ending March 2010 is ₹. 1,48,000. The output, sales and additional processing costs are as under :

Product	*Output in Litres*	*Additional processing cost after split off point*	*Sales value*
AOXE	8,000	₹. 43,000	₹. 1,72,500
BOXE	4,000	9,000	15,000
COXE	2,000	—	6,000
DOXE	4,000	1,500	45,000

In case these products were disposed off at the split off point that is before further processing the selling price would have been :

AOXE	*BOXE*	*COXE*	*DOXE*
₹. 15.00	₹. 6.00	₹. 3.00	₹. 7.50

Prepare a statement of profitability based on :

(1) If the products are sold after further processing is carried out in the mill.

(2) If they are sold at the split off point. **[*CA Inter*]**

[Ans. *Profits after further processing AOXE ₹. 30,833, BOXE Loss ₹. 13,733, COXE Profit ₹. 1,067, DOXE Profit ₹. 18,333, Total ₹. 37,000, Profit at split off point AOXE ₹. 21,333, BOXE ₹. 4267, COXE ₹. 1067, DOXE ₹. 5333 Total ₹. 32000.*]

6. A company processes a raw material in its Depratment 1 to produce three products, *viz.*, *A*, *B* and *X* at the same split-off stage. During a period 1,80,000 kg., of raw materials were processed in Department 1 at a total cost of ₹. 12,88,000 and the resultant output of *A*, *B* and *X* were 18,000 kg. 10,000 kg and 54,000 kg. respectively. *A* and *B* were further processed in Department 2 at a cost of ₹. 1,80,000 and ₹. 1,50,000 respectively.

X was further processed in Department 3 at a cost of ₹. 1,08,000. There is no waste in further processing. The details of sales effected during the period were as under :

	A	*B*	*X*
Quantity Sold (kg.)	17,000	5,000	44,000
Sales Value (₹.)	12,24,000	2,50,000	7,92,000

There were no opening stock. If these products were sold at split-off stage, the selling proces of *A*, *B* and *X* would have been ₹. 50 ₹. 40 and ₹. 10 per kg respectively :

Required :

(*i*) Prepare a statement showing the apportionment of joint costs to *A*, *B* and *X*.

(*ii*) Present a statement showing the cost per kg of each product indicating joint cost, further processing cost and total cost separately.

(*iii*) Prepare a statement showing the productwise and total profit for the period.

(*iv*) State with supporting calculations as to whether any or all the products should be further processed or not.

[Ans. *(i) Joint Cost A ₹. 630000, B ₹. ₹. 280,000, X ₹. 3,78,000. (ii) A per kg cost ₹. 45, B ₹. 43 X ₹. 9; (iii) Total Profit A ₹. 459,000, B ₹. 35000, X ₹. 3,96,000 (iv) B should not be further processed because then it will be at loss. After processing per unit profit A ₹. 12, X ₹. 6 Loss per Kg B ₹. 5.*]

Activity Based Costing

Activity Based Costing Method is a new concept of overhead absorption. In tradtional method, overheads are absorbed on volume related measures like number of units produced or amount of material consumed or amount of direct labour cost or machine hours or direct labour hours. But there are many activities which are not related to physical volume. Under Activity Based Costing overheads are related to different activities and activity based overheads incurred are absorbed in product cost on the basis of activities related to products.

Tradionally overheads have been allocated to products by using three steps (*i*) From ledger accounts to production and service departments (*ii*) From service departments to production departments and (*iii*) From production departments to end products by using an appropriate basis related to volume of material, direct labour, machine hours etc.

In the late 1980s *Cooper and Kaplan* drew attention to the limitations of traditional product costing system. Their criticisms were related to the method of allocating overheads to products. Tradtional costing system always use volume related measures such as direct labour hours or machine hours to allocate overheads to products. Such volume related costs are materials, direct labour, energy and machine related costs. But there are a number of cost-items which are not related to physical volume. For example activities like material handling, material procurement, performing set-up, production scheduling, inspection activities are not related to physical volume. But under traditional system, it is assumed that all items of cost are consumed by products in proportion to their production volumes.

In 1988 *Cooper and Kaplan* developed a refined approach for assigning overheads to products. The approach is known as Activity Based Costing (*ABC*).

ABC has been increasingly accepted as a better approach. Traditional product costing systems were designed decades ago when most companies manufactured a narrow range of products and direct labour and materials were the dominant factory costs. Overhead costs were relatively small. Today companies produce a wide range of products, direct labour and material represent only a small fraction of total cost and overhead costs are of considerable importance. Simplistic overhead allocation based on direct labour or machine hours cannot be now justified.

Definition

ABC has been defined by *CIMA* as 'cost attribution to cost units on the basis of benefit received from indirect activities *e.g.* ordering setting up, assuring quality'.

According to *Horngren, Foster and Datar* '*ABC* is not an alternative costing system to job costing or process costing. Rather *ABC* is an approach to developing the cost numbers used in job costing or process costing systems. The distinctive feature of *ABC* is its facus on activities as the fundamental cost objects. In contrast most traditional approaches used in job and process costing systems rely on general purpose accounting systems, not tailored to the activities found in individual organisations. The ABC approach has the potential to provide managers with information they find more useful for costing purposes'.

Activity Based Costing is based on the belief that in production process there are various activities which give rise to costs. *ABC* creates a link between activities and products by assigning a cost of activities to products based on an individual product.

According to *Dansby and Lawrence* 'In *ABC* costs are not initially traced to departments. Instead, costs are first traced to activities and then to products : Acititivites causing overheads (or cost drivers) are identified. These activities are later used as a bases for allocating overhead costs to products.

A Comparison of ABC and Traditional Product Cost

ABC and Traditional Overhead Absroption methods both trace overhead costs to product using the two stage allocation process. In the first stage, costs are assigned to cost centres. Under traditional costing system overheads are traced to production and service departments and then service department overheads are reallocated to production departments. Overheads are normally allocated to products using two volume-based allocation rates: direct labour rates and machine hour rates.

With the *ABC* system, separate cost centres are created for each major activity, for example machine related activities, set-up activities and purchasing activities. (In practice there may be approximately twenty to thirty activities). These activities are known as activity drivers and each activity cost is allocated to products on the basis of benefits derived by each product. The benefit derived may be called cost drivers.

Thus *ABC* system assigns overheads to each major activity (rather than department). With *ABC* systems many activity-based cost pools (cost centres) are established, whereas with traditional system overheads tend to be pooled by departments. This can result in extensive reapportionments of service departments costs to ensure that all overheads are allocated to production departments. Therefore traditional system use fewer cost pools. *ABC* systems establish separate cost pools for support (service) activities such as materials handling and maintenance. The costs of these activities are assigned directly to products through cost driver-rates. Thus reapportionment of service department costs is avoided.

INTRODUCTION OF ABC SYSTEM

ABC system assume that activities cause costs and also that products create demands for activities. The system recognises that businesses must understand the factors that drive each major activity, the cost activities and how activities relate to products. The design of *ABC* system involves following stages.

(1) *Identifying activities i.e.* identifying major activities that take place in an organisation.

(2) *Assigning costs to activity cost centres i.e.* assigning costs to cost pools or cost centres for each activity.

(3) *Selecting appropriate cost drivers i.e.* identifying the factors that influence the costs of a particular activities.

(4) *Assigning the cost of activities to products i.e.* assigning such cost according to each products demand for activities.

These stages may be considered in detail.

1. Identifying Activities

The first stage is to identify the functional areas or major activities involved in the production. Examples of activities include machine related activities, divert labour related activities and various support activities like ordering, receiving, material handlinng, packing, despatching. Various activities are identified by carrying out activity analysis. The activities may be basically fall into four categories as suggested by *Cooper and Kaplan*[1].

(*a*) *Unit Level Activities or Primary Activities.* The cost of primary activities (like use of indirect materials and consumables, testing of every item produced) may be correlated to number of units produced (i.e. on volume-basis).

(*b*) *Batch Level Activities.* These are manufactuing support activities (like material ordering, machine set-up costs, inspection of products etc). The cost of such activities are driven by number of batches of units produced.

(*c*) *Product Level Activities.* Activities like designing of the product, keeping technical drawings of product, activities upto date, advertising of a specific product are called product level. The cost of these activities are driven by the creation of a new product line and its maintenance.

(*d*) *Facility Level Activities.* Certain activities cannot be related to a particular product, instead may be related to certain facilities like maintaining the building, security of plant, salaries of production manager, advertisement to promote organisation.

It may be noted that unit level activities and facility level activities are the same as those in traditional absorption costing which will be allocated on physical volume basis, *ABC* will be more useful if there is significant size of batch level and product level activities.

2. Assigning Costs to Activity Cost Centres

The second stage requires that a cost centre (also called a cost pool) be created for each activity. After the activities have been identified the cost of resources consumed over a specified period must be assigned to each activity. These costs will have to be apportioned on some suitable basis. For example the total costs of all set ups might constitute one cost centre for all setup related costs.

3. Selecting Appropriate Cost Drivers

The third stage of designing *ABC* system is to identify the factors that influence the cost of a particular activity. The term cost–driver is used to describe the significant determinant of the cost of the activity. The most suitable cost driver in each activity under functional areas should be identified. A cost driver is any factor that influences costs.

The main functional areas are (*i*) Material Management (*ii*) Stores Management (*iii*) Production Management (*iv*) Quantity Control Management (*v*) Personnel Management (*vi*) Sales Management (*vii*) Repairs and Maintenace (*viii*) Administration and (*ix*) Public Relations.

Following are some activities and their suitable cost drivers.

Functional Areas	*Activities*	*Suitable Cost Drivers*
Material Management	Issue of purchase orders	No. of purchase orders
	Inspection of materials	No. of purchase order
Stores Management	Storing of materials	Value of materials stored
	Servicing of requisitions	No. of requisitions
	Inspection and verification	No. of times inspected
	Stock taking	Value of stock

1. *Cooper and Kaplan.* 'The Design of Cost Management Systems' – Prentice Hall (1991).

Quality Control	Testing of samples	No. of batches produced
Personnel Management	Recruitment of employees	No. of employees recruited
	Maintenance of leave records and attendence	No. of employees
Marketing	Dimand creation	Increase in sales
	Advertising	Increase in sales
	Dispatches	No. of orders
Research and Development	Research	No. of research projects
Machining	Set-up cost	No. of production runs
	Power cost	Machine hours

4. Assigning the Cost of the Activities to Products

The final stage is to trace the cost of the activities to products according to each product's demand for these activities using cost drivers as a measure of demand. A product's demand for the activities is measured by the number of transactions it generates for the cost driver. The cost driver should be measurable in a way that enables it to be identified with individual products.

PURPOSES AND BENEFITS OF *ABC*

As compared to traditional overhead costing, Activity Based Costing provides more accurate cost information for products. *ABC* provides a very different perspective of the cost structure. The managers of production are guided to adjust their pricing policies as they identify that high volume products had been overcosted and low volume products under costed.

ABC has been accepted as very useful for product costing where production overheads are high in relation to direct cost, where there is diversity in the product range, where products consume different amount of overhead and where consumption of overhead is not basically driven by their volume.

In brief following are main benefits of using *ABC* technique.

1. *ABC* helps to reduce costs by providing meaningful information for cost-management. It helps in making the right decision.
2. *ABC* technique provides due importance to non-manufacturing cost which constitute a substantial portion of total cost. For example, in case of a number of products marketing and advertising costs constitute a big portion of cost. These overheads can be allocated easily using *ABC* because the relationship between such costs and their causes can be indentified easily. Traditionally such non-manufacturing costs have been allocated under volume basis and thus high volume products have been overvalued.
3. *ABC* technique provides accurate and reliable cost information. These cost information are essential for recent approaches in productivity imporvement like Total Quality Management (*TQM*) and Business Process Reengineering.
4. *ABC* enables the management in formulating an effective pricing policy while fixing prices.
5. Cost of each activity is determined with the help of *ABC*. There is accuracy in indirect cost-allocation to products. This technique is helpful in make or buy decisions and transfer pricing.

Thus *ABC* has attracted a considerable amount of interest because it provides not only a basis for calculating more accurate product cost but also a mechanism for managing overhead costs. By collecting and reporting on the significant activities in which a business engages, it is possible to understand and manage costs more effectively. It is the area of cost-management rather than product costing, where activity-based systems may have their greatest potential.

Illustration 1: A company manufacturing two products furnishes the following data for a year:

Product	*Annual output (Units)*	*Total machine hours*	*Total number of purchase orders*	*Total number of set-ups*
A	5,000	20,000	160	20
B	60,000	1,20,000	384	44
	65,000	1,40,000	544	64

The annual overheads are as under:

Volume related activity costs	₹. 5,50,000
Set up related costs	₹. 8,20,000
Purchase related costs	₹. 6,18,000
Total	19,88,000

You are required to calculate the cost per unit of each product A and B based on:

(*a*) Traditional method of charging overheads.

(*b*) Activity based costing method. **[*CA – PE II Nov. 2002*]**

Solution:

Working Notes:

1. Machine hour rate = Total annual overheads ÷ Total machine hrs
   = ₹. 19,88,000 ÷ 1,40,000 hrs
   = ₹. 14.20 per hr.

2. Machine hour rate = Total annual overhead cost for volume related activities ÷ Total machine hours
   = ₹. 5,50,000 ÷ 1,40,000 hrs
   = ₹. 3.93

3. Cost of one set-up = Total set-up related cost ÷ Total number of set-ups
   = ₹. 8,20,000 ÷ 64
   = ₹. 12,812.50

4. Cost of a purchase order = Total purchase related cost ÷ Total no. of purchase orders
   = ₹. 6,18,000 ÷ 544 orders
   = ₹. 1,136.03

Statement Showing Overhead Cost
[*Based on Traditional Method of Charging Overheads*]

		A	*B*
A 20,000 MH @ 14.20		2,84,000	
B 1,20,000 MH @ 14.20			17,04,000
	₹.	2,84,000	17,04,000
No. of units		5,000	60,000
Per Unit Overhead Cost		₹. 56.80	₹. 28.40

Statement Showing Overhead Cost
[Based on Activity Based Costing]

	A ₹.	B ₹.
Volume Related Activity Cost		
A 20,000 hrs @ 3.93	78,600	—
B 4,20,000 hrs @ 3.93	—	4 ,71,600
Set-up Related Cost		
A 20 set up @ 12812.5	2,56,250	—
B 44 set up @ 12812.5		5,63,750
Purchase Related Cost		
A 160 orders @ 1136.03	1,81,765	—
B 384 orders @ 1136.03	—	4,36,235
Total	5,16,615	14,71,585
No of units	÷ 5,000	÷ 60,000
Cost per unit	103.32	24.53

Illustration 2: MST Limited has collected the following data for its two activities. It calculates activity cost rates based on cost driver capacity.

Activity	*Cost Driver*	*Capacity*	*Cost*
Power	Kilowatt hours	50,000 kilowatt hours	₹. 2,00,000
Quality Inspections	Number of Inspections	10,000 Inspections	₹. 3,00,000

The company makes three products, *M, S* and *T*. For the year ended March 31,2004, the following consumption of cost drivers was reported:

Product	*Kilowatt Hours*	*Quality Inspections*
M	10,000	3,500
S	20,000	2,500
T	15,000	3,000

Required:

(*i*) Compute the costs allocated to each product from each activity.

(*ii*) Calculate the cost of unused capacity for each activity. **[*CAPE II May 2004*]**

Solution:

Statement of Cost Allocation to Each Product From Each Activity

	Products			
	M ₹.	*S* ₹.	*T* ₹.	*Total* ₹.
Power (See working note)	40,000 (10,000 kwh × ₹. 4)	80,000 (20,000 kwh × ₹. 4)	60,000 (15,000 kwh × ₹. 4)	1,80,000
Quality inspections (See working note)	1,05,000 (3,500 inspections × ₹. 30)	75,000 (2,500 inspections × ₹. 30)	90,000 (3,000 inspections × ₹. 30)	2,70,000

Working note:

(*i*) Rate per unit of cost driver:

Power : ₹. 2,00,000/50,000 kwh = ₹. 4/kwh

Quality inspection : ₹. 3,00,000/10,000 inspections = ₹. 30 per inspection

(*ii*) Computation of cost of unused capacity for each activity:

	₹.
Power (₹. 2,00,000 – ₹. 1,80,000)	20,000
Quality inspections (₹. 3,00,000 – ₹. 2,70,000)	30,000
Total cost of unused capacity	50,000

Illustration 3: Company *A* produces two products *H* and *L*. Both are produced on the same equipment and use similar processes. The products differ by volume. Product *H* is a high volume product while *L* is a low volume product. Details of product inputs, output and the cost of activities are as follows:

	Machine Hour per unit	*Direct Labour Hour per unit*	*Annual Output (units)*	*Total Machine Hours*	*Total Direct Labour Hours*	*No. of Purchase orders*	*No. of Setups*
Product *L*	2	4	1000	2000	4000	80	40
Product *H*	2	4	10,000	20,000	40,000	160	60
			11,000	22,000	44,000	240	100

The cost centres costs (overheads) are ₹. 4,40,000 but have been further analysed as follows:

	₹.
Volume related	1,10,000
Purchasing related	1,20,000
Setup related	2,10,000
	4,40,000

Calculate overhead cost under (*i*) Traditional volume based costing system.
(*ii*) *ABC* system

Solution:

(*i*) *Traditional System*

Cost centre allocated cost (overheads) ₹. 4,40,000

Overhead rate per machine how (MHR) 440,000/22000 = ₹. 20

Overhead rate per DLH 4,40,000/44000 = ₹. 10

Overhead cost per unit → *L* 2 hours @ 20 (MHR) = ₹. 40

or 4 hours @ 10 (DLH) = ₹. 40

H 2 hours @ 20 (MHR) = ₹. 40

or 4 hours @ ₹. 10 (DLH) = ₹. 40

Overheads Allocated to Products

L	1000 units @ 40 = ₹. 40,000	per unit ₹. 40
H	10,000 units @ 40 = ₹. 400,000	per unit ₹. 40

(*ii*) *ABC System*

Activities

	Volume Related	*Purchasing Related*	*Set-up Related*	
Overhead	₹. 1,10,000	₹. 1,20,000	₹. 2,10,000	
Consumption of Activities	22000 MH	240 Purchase orders	100 setup	
Per unit activity cost	₹. 5 per MH	₹. 500 per order	₹. 2100 per set up	
Cost to Products —				
L	2000 × 5 = ₹. 10,000	80 × 500 = ₹. 40,000	40 × 2100 = ₹. 8400	= 1,34,000
H	20,000 × 5 = 1,00,000	160 × 500 = ₹. 80,000	60 × 2100 = ₹. 126,000	= 3,06,000
				4,40,000

Per unit overhead cost *L* 134000/1000 = ₹. 134
H 3,06,000/10,000 = ₹. 30.60

Illustration 4: A company produces three products A, B and C. Their per unit cost-data are as below:

	A	*B*	*C*	*Total*
Units produced	10000	20000	30000	
Direct Material	₹. 50	₹. 40	₹. 30	
Direct Labour	₹. 30	₹. 40	₹. 50	
Labour Hours	3	4	5	
Machine Hours	4	4	7	
No. of Purchase Requisitions	1,200	1800	2000	5000
No. of Set-ups	240	260	300	800

Production Overheads ₹. 26,00,000 split in two Deptts

Deptt. 1 : ₹. 11,00,000

Deptt. 2 : ₹. 15,00,000

Deptt. 1 is labour intensive and Deptt. 2 is machine intensive.

Total Labour Hours in Deptt. 1 = 1,83,333

Total Machine Hours in Deptt. 2 = 5,00,000

Production overheads ₹. 26,00,000 split by activity —

Receiving and inspecting ₹. 14,00,000

Production schedule and machine setup ₹. 12,00,000.

You are required to prepare product cost statement under. (*i*) Tradition Absorption costing and (*ii*) *ABC* methods.

Solution:

Traditional Absorption Costing

Absorption Rate – Deptt. 1. $\frac{11,00,000}{1,83,333 \text{ LH}}$ = ₹. 6 per LH

Deptt. 2 $\frac{15,00,000}{5,00,000 \text{ MH}}$ = ₹. 3 per MH

Statement of Cost

	A ₹	B ₹	C ₹
Direct Materials	50	40	30
Direct Labour	30	40	50
Overheads – Dept. 1 (LH × Rate)	18	24	30
– Dept. 2 (MH × Rate)	12	12	21
	110	116	131

Activity Based Costing

Cost Drivers Rates

$$\text{Receiving and Inspecting} = \frac{14,00,000}{5000 \text{ No. of batches or requisition}}$$

$$= \textbf{₹. 280 per requisition}$$

$$\text{Scheduling and set up} = \frac{12,00,000}{800 \text{ (set ups)}}$$

$$= \textbf{₹. 1500 per set up}$$

Product Cost Statement

	A ₹	B ₹	C ₹
Direct Material	50	40	30
Direct Labour	30	40	50
Overheads			
Receiving and Inspecting A $\frac{280 \times 1200}{10,000}$	34	25	19
Prod. Scheduling & Setup A $\frac{1500 \times 240}{10,000}$	36	20	15
	150	125	114

Illustration 5: Family Store wants information about the profitability of individual product lines: Soft drinks, Fresh produce and Packaged food. Family Store provides the following data for the year 2002-03 for each product line.

	Soft drinks	*Fresh produce*	*Pakaged food*
Revenues	₹. 7,93,500	₹. 21,00,600	₹. 12,09,900
Cost of goods sold	₹. 6,00,000	₹. 15,00,000	₹. 9,00,000
Cost of bottles returned	₹. 12,000	₹. 0	₹. 0
Number of purchase orders placed	360	840	360
Number of deliveries received	300	2,190	660
Hours of shelf-stocking time	540	5,400	2,700
Items sold	1,26,000	11,04,000	3,06,000

Family Store also provides the following information for the year 2002-03:

Activity	*Description of activity*	*Total cost*	*Cost-allocation base*
		₹.	
Bottles returns	Returning of empty bottles	12,000	Direct tracing to softdrink line
Ordering	Placing of orders for purchases	1,56,000	1,560 purchase orders
Delivery	Physical delivery and receipt of goods	2,52,000	3,150 deliveries
Shelf stocking	Stocking of goods on store shelves and on-going restocking	1,72,800	8,640 hours of shelf-stocking time
Customer support	Assistance provided to customers including check-out	3,07,200	15,36,000 items sold

Required:

(*i*) Family Store currently allocates support cost (all costs other than cost of goods sold) to product lines on the basis of cost of goods sold of each product line. Calculate the operating income and operating income as a percentage of revenues for each product line.

(*ii*) If Family Store allocates support costs (all costs other than cost of goods sold) to product lines using an activity-based costing system, calculate the operating income and operating income as a percentage of revenues for each product line.

(*iii*) Comment on your answers in requirements (*i*) and (*ii*). **[*CA PE II – May 2003*]**

Solution:

(*i*) Statement of Operating Income and Operating Income as a Percentage of Revenues for Each Product Line (when support costs are allocated to product lines on the basis of cost of goods sold of each product)

		Soft Drinks	*Fresh Produce*	*Packaged Goods*	*Total*
		₹.	₹.	₹.	₹.
Revenues	(*A*)	7,93,500	21,00,600	12,09,900	41,04,000
Cost of Goods Sold	(*B*)	6,00,000	15,00,000	9,00,000	30,00,000
Support Cost (30% of *B*) [Working Notes 1 and 2]	(*C*)	1,80,000	4,50,000	2,70,000	9,00,000
Total Cost	(*D*) = (*B*) + (*C*)	7,80,000	19,50,000	11,70,000	39,00,000
Operating Income	*E* = (*A*) – (*D*)	13,500	1,50,600	39,900	2,04,000
Operating Income as Percentage of Revenue (*E*/*A*) × 100		1.70%	7.17%	3.30%	4.97%

(*ii*) Statement of Operating Income and Operating Income as a Percentage of Revenue for Each Product Line (when support costs are allocated to product line using an activity-based costing system)

		Soft Drinks	*Fresh Produce*	*Packaged Foods*	*Total*
		₹.	₹.	₹.	₹.
Revenues	(*A*)	7,93,500	21,00,600	12,09,900	41,04,000
Cost of Goods Sold		6,00,000	15,00,000	9,00,000	30,00,000
Bottles Returns		12,000	—	—	12,000
Ordering Cost @ ₹. 100 per order		36,000	84,000	36,000	1,56,000
Delivery Cost @ ₹. 80 per delivery		24,000	1,75,200	52,800	2,52,000

Shelf-Stocking @ ₹. 20 per Shelf-Stocking hours	10,800	1,08,000	54,000	1,72,800
Customer Support Cost @ ₹. 0.20 per item sold	25,200	2,20,800	61,200	3,07,200
Total Cost (*B*)	7,08,000	20,88,000	11,04,000	39,00,000
Operating Income $C = (A) - (B)$	85,500	12,600	1,05,900	2,04,000
Operating Income as Percentage of Revenue	10.78%	0.60%	8.75%	4.97%

(*iii*) Activity based costing system of distribution of support-cost is more reliable than the traditional costing system. It shows cost precisely on how individual product-lines use the resources.

Working Notes:

1. *Total Support Cost :*

	₹.
Bottles Returns	12,000
Ordering	1,56,000
Delivery	2,52,000
Shelf-Stocking	1,72,800
Customer Support	3,07,200
Total Support Cost	9,00,000

2. *Percentage of Support Cost to Cost of Goods Sold :*

$$= \frac{\text{Total support cost}}{\text{Total cost of goods sold}} \times 100 = \frac{9,00,000}{30,00,000} \times 100 = 30\%$$

3. *Cost for Each Activity Cost Driver :*

Activity (*1*)	*Total cost (₹.)* (*2*)	*Cost allocation base* (*3*)	*Cost-driver rate* (*4*) = (*2*) + (*3*)
Ordering	1,56,000	1,560 Purchase orders	₹. 100 per order
Delivery	2,52,000	3,150 Deliveries	₹. 80 per delivery
Shelf-Stocking	1,72,800	8,640 Stock hours	₹. 20 per stocking hour
Customer support	3,07,200	15,36,000 Items sold	₹. 0.20 per item sold

Illustration 6: A Co. assembles two products *A* and *B*. Details of their manufacture are given below :

	A	*B*
Output in units	10,000	15,000
Components used (Numbers)	8	4
Components cost (per unit in ₹.)	4.50	3.60
Number of production runs	200	50
Machine Hours per 100 units	2.6	5.3
No. of items packed in a carton	10 units	50 units

Overhead cost are budgeted as below :

	₹.
1. Components purchasing and handling cost	14,000
2. Production control cost	18,000
3. Machine-set-ups cost	25,000
4. Machine running costs	64,355
5. Packing cost	31,200

You are required to calculate :

(*a*) Overhead recovery rates using activity based costing.

(*b*) Cost of production per unit of the two components.

Solution:

Calculation of OH recovery rates under *ABC*

(*i*) Component purchasing and handling cost (cost-drivers are component numbers)

$$= \frac{\text{Purchasing cost}}{\text{Component numbers}} = \frac{14,000}{(8 \times 10,000) + (4 \times 15,000)}$$

$$= \frac{14,000}{1,40,000} = ₹.\ 0.10 \text{ per component}$$

(*ii*) Production control cost (cost-drivers are prod. runs)

$$= \frac{\text{Production Control Overheads}}{\text{Number of Production Runs}} = \frac{18,000}{200 + 50}$$

$$= \frac{18,000}{250} = ₹.\ 72 \text{ per Production run}$$

(*iii*) Machine setup cost (cost-drivers are Prod. runs)

$$= \frac{\text{Machine setup cost}}{\text{Number of production runs}} = \frac{25,000}{200 + 50}$$

$$= \frac{25,000}{250} = ₹.\ 100 \text{ per Production runs}$$

(*iv*) Machine running cost (cost-drivers are machine hours)

$$= \frac{\text{Machine running cost}}{\text{Machine hours}} = \frac{64,355}{(2.6 \times 100) + (5.3 \times 150)}$$

$$= \frac{64,355}{260 + 795} = ₹.\ 61 \text{ per machine hours}$$

(*v*) Packing cost (cost-drivers are no. of cartons used)

$$= \frac{\text{Packing cost}}{\text{No. of cortons packed}} = \frac{31,200}{(10,000/10) + (15000/50)}$$

$$= \frac{31,200}{1000 + 300} = ₹.\ 24 \text{ per carton.}$$

Statement showing cost of production
per unit of the *A* and *B* products

		A	*B*
Direct Materials		4.50	3.60
Purchasing and Handling			
A	0.10 × 8	0.80	—
B	0.10 × 4	—	0.40
Production Control Cost			
A	Production runs		
	10,000/200 = 50		
	₹. 72/50	1.44	
B	15000/50 = 300		
	₹. 72/300	—	0.24

Machine Set-up Cost			
A	₹. 100/50	2.00	—
B	₹. 100/300		0.33
Machine Running Cost			
A	(2.6/100) × 61	1.59	—
B	(5.3/100) × 61	—	3.23
Packing Cost			
A	24/10	2.40	—
B	24/50	—	0.48
	Total	12.73	8.28

Illustration 7: Following are data related to three products manufactured by a company.

	Product X	*Product Y*	*Product Z*	*Total*
Production and sales (Units)	30,000	20,000	8,000	58,000
Raw Material used (units)	5	5	11	
Direct Material cost per unit	₹. 25	₹. 20	₹. 11	₹. 12,38,000
Direct Labour Hours	$1\frac{1}{3}$	2	1	88,000
Machine Hours	$1\frac{1}{3}$	1	2	76,000
Direct Labour Cost Per Unit	₹. 8	₹. 12	₹. 6	₹. 5,28,000
Number of Production Runs	3	7	20	30
Number of Deliveries	9	3	20	32
Number of Receipts	15	35	220	270
Number of Production Orders	15	10	25	50
Overhead Cost :				₹.
Set up				30,000
Machines				7,60,000
Receiving				4,35,000
Packing				2,50,000
Engineering				3,73,000
				₹. 18,48,000

From the above information you are required to (*a*) compute the product-costs using traditional costing system recovering overheads on the bases of direct labour hours (*b*) compute product cost using activity based costing (*ABC*) system.

Solution:

(*a*) Direct Labour Overhead Rate $= \dfrac{\text{Total Overheads}}{\text{Total Labour Hours}} = \dfrac{18,48,000}{88,000}$ = ₹. 21 per labour hour

Product Cost	*X* (₹.)	*Y* (₹.)	*Z* (₹.)
Direct Material (per unit)	25	20	11
Direct Labour (per unit)	08	12	06
Overheads (DLH basis)	28 $(21 \times 1\frac{1}{3})$	42 (21×2)	21 (21×1)
	61	**74**	**38**

(*b*) *The Cost per Transaction or Activity for Each of the Cost Centres is as follows:*

(*i*) Set up cost Cost per set up = $\frac{\text{Set up cost ₹. 30,000}}{\text{No of production runs 30}}$ = ₹. 1000

(*ii*) Receiving Cost per receiving order = $\frac{\text{Receiving cost ₹. 435000}}{\text{No of orders 270}}$ = ₹. 1,611

(*iii*) Packing Cost per packing = $\frac{\text{Packing cost ₹. 2,50,000}}{\text{No of delivers 32}}$ = ₹. 7,812.5

(*iv*) Engineering Cost per production order = $\frac{\text{Eng. cost ₹. 3,73,000}}{\text{No of Prod. order 50}}$ = ₹. 7,460

(*c*) Machining cost will be charged on the basis of machine hours *i.e.* ₹. 7,60,000/76000 hours = ₹. 10 per machine hour.

Cost for Products (per unit) using ABC System

	X ₹.	*Y* ₹.	*Z* ₹.
Direct Material	25.00	20.00	11.00
Direct Labour	8.00	12.00	6.00
Machine Overheads @ ₹. 10 per MH	13.33	10.00	20.00
Set up cost @ ₹. 1000 per prod. runs ÷ No. of units of product (*X*) 3000/30,000, 7000/20,000 (*Z*) 20,000/8000	0.10	0.35	2.50
Receiving Cost *X* : (1611 × 15)/30,000 ; *Y* : (1611 × 35)/20,000; *Z* : (1611 × 220)/8000	0.81	2.82	44.30
Packing *X* : 7812.5 × 9/30,000; *Y* : 7812.5 × 3/20,000; *Z* : 7812.5 × 20/18000	2.34	1.17	19.53
Engineering X : 7460 × 15/30,000; *Y* : 7460 × 10/20,000; *Z* : 7460 × 25/8000	3.73	3.73	23.31
	53.31	50.07	126.64

Thus traditional product costing system assumes that products consume resources in relation to volume measures such as direct labour, direct materials or machine hours. The *ABC* system recognises that some overheads are not related to production volume and uses activities or cost drivers.

Illustration 7: Alpha Limited has decided to analyse the profitability of its five new customers. It buys bottled water at ₹. 90 per case and sells to retail customers at a list price of ₹. 108 per case. The data pertaining to five customers are:

	Customers				
	A	*B*	*C*	*D*	*E*
Cases sold	4,680	19,688	1,36,800	71,550	8,775
List Selling Price	₹. 108	₹. 108	₹. 108	₹. 108	₹. 108
Actual Selling Price	₹. 108	₹. 106.20	₹. 99	₹. 104.40	₹. 97.20
Number of Purchase Orders	15	25	30	25	30
Number of Customer Visits	2	3	6	2	3
Number of Deliveries	10	30	60	40	20
Kilometers travelled per delivery	20	6	5	10	30
Number of expedited deliveries	0	0	0	0	1

Its five activities and their cost drivers are:

Activity	*Cost Driver Rate*
Order taking	₹. 750 per purchase order
Customer visits	₹. 600 per customer visit
Deliveries	₹. 5.75 per delivery km travelled
Product handling	₹. 3.75 per case sold
Expedited deliveries	₹. 2,250 per expedited delivery

Required:

(*i*) Compute the customer-level operating income of each of five retail customers now being examined (A, B, C, D and E). Comment on the results.

(*ii*) What insights are gained by reporting both the list selling price and the actual selling price for each customer?

(*iii*) What factors Alpha Limited should consider in deciding whether to drop one or more of five customers? **[*CA PE II Nov. 2003*]**

Working Notes:

Computation of Revenues (at listed price), Discount, Cost of Goods Sold and Customer Level Operating Activities Costs:

	Customers				
	A	*B*	*C*	*D*	*E*
Cases sold : (*a*)	4,680	19,688	1,36,800	71,550	8,775
Revenues (at listed price) (₹.): (*b*) {(*a*) × ₹. 108)}	5,05,440	21,26,304	1,47,74,400	77,27,400	9,47,700
Discount (₹.): (*c*) {(*a*) × Discount per case}		35,438 (19,688 cases × ₹. 1.80)	12,31,200 (1,36,800 cases × ₹. 9)	2,57,580 (71,550 cases × ₹. 3.60)	94,770 (8,775 cases × ₹. 10.80)
Cost of goods sold (₹.): (*d*) {(*a*) × ₹. 90)}	4,21,200	17,71,920	1,23,12,000	64,39,500	7,89,750
Customer Level Operating Activities Costs					
Order taking costs (₹.): (No. of purchase orders × ₹. 750)	11,250	18,750	22,500	18,750	22,500
Customer visits costs (₹.) (No. of customer visits × ₹. 600)	1,200	1,800	3,600	1,200	1,800
Delivery vehicles travel costs (₹.) (Kms travelled by delivery vehicles × ₹. 5.75 per km.)	1,150	1,035	1,725	2,300	3,450
Product handling costs (₹.) {(*a*) × ₹. 3.75)	17,550	73,830	5,13,000	2,68,313	32,906
Cost of deliveries (₹.) {No. of expedited deliveries × ₹. 2,250}	—	—	—	—	2,250
Total Cost of Customer Level Operating Activities (₹.): (*e*)	31,150	95,415	5,40,825	2,90,563	62,906

(i) Computation of Customer level Operating Income

	Customers				
	A ₹	B ₹	C ₹	D ₹	E ₹
Revenues (*At list price*) (Refer to working note)	5,05,440	21,26,304	1,47,74,400	77,27,400	9,47,700
Less: Discount (Refer to working note)	—	35,438	12,31,200	2,57,580	94,770
Revenue (At actual price)	5,05,440	20,90,866	1,35,43,200	74,69,820	8,52,930
Less: Cost of goods sold (Refer to working note)	4,21,200	17,71,920	1,23,12,000	64,39,500	7,89,750
Gross margin	84,240	3,18,946	12,31,200	10,30,320	63,180
Less: Customer level operating activities costs (Refer to working note)	31,150	95,415	5,40,825	2,90,563	62,906
Customer Level Operating Income	53,090	2,23,531	6,90,375	7,39,757	274

(*i*) **Comment on the results:**

Customer D is the most profitable customer, despite having only 52.30% of the unit volume of *Customer C*. The main reason is that *C* receives a ₹. 9 per case discount while *customer D* receives only a ₹. 3.60 discount per case.

Customer E is less profitable, in comparison with the small customer *A* being profitable. Customer *E* received a discount of ₹. 10.80 per case, makes more frequent orders, requires more customer visits and requires more delivery kms. in comparison with customer A.

(*ii*) **Insight gained by reporting both the list selling price and the actual selling price for each customer:**

Separate reporting of both–the listed and actual selling prices enables Alpha Ltd. to examine which customer has received what discount per case, whether the discount received has any relationship with the sales volume. The data given below provides us with the following information:

Sales volume	*Discount per case (₹.)*
C (1,36,800 cases)	9.00
D (71,550 cases)	3.60
B (19,688 cases)	1.80
E (8,775 cases)	10.80
A (4,680 cases)	0

The above data clearly shows that the discount given to customers per case has a direct relationship with sales volume, except in the case of customer *E*. The reasons for ₹. 10.80 discount per case for customer *E* should be explored.

(*iii*) **Factors to be considered for dropping one or more customers:**

Dropping customers should be the last resort to be taken by Alpha Ltd. Factors to be considered should include:

(*a*) What is the expected future profitablity of each customer? Are the currently least profitable (E) or low profitable (A) customers are likely to be highly profitable in the future?

(*b*) What costs are avoidable if one or more customers are dropped?

(*c*) Can the relationship with the "less profilable" customers be restructured so that there they may become profitable customers?

Illustration 8: *RST* Limited specializes in the distribution of pharmaceutical products. It buys from the pharmaceutical companies and resells to each of the three different markets:

(*i*) General Supermarket Chains

(*ii*) Drugstore Chains

(*iii*) Chemist Shops.

The following data for the month of April, 2004 in respect of RST Limited has been reported:

	General Supermarket Chains	*Drugstore Chains*	*Chemist Shops*
Average revenue per delivery	₹. 84,975	₹. 28,875	₹. 5,445
Average cost of goods sold per delivery	₹. 82,500	₹. 27,500	₹. 4,950
Number of deliveries	330	825	2,750

In the past, *RST* Limited has used gross margin percentage to evaluate the relative profitability of its distribution channels.

The company plans to use activity-based costing for analysing the profitability of its distribution channels.

The Activity Analysis of *RST* Limited is as under:

Activity Area	*Cost Driver*
Customer Purchase Order Processing	Purchase orders by customers
Line-item ordering	Line-items per purchase order
Store Delivery	Store deliveries
Cartons Dispatched to Stores	Cartons despatched to a store per delivery
Shelf-stocking at Customer Store	Hours of shelf-stocking

The April, 2004 operating costs (other than cost of goods sold) of *RST* Limited are ₹. 8,27,970. These operating costs are assigned to five activity areas. The cost in each area and the quantity of the cost allocation basis used in that area for April, 2004 are as follows:

Activity Area	*Total Cost in April, 2004* ₹	*Total Units of Cost Allocation Base used in April, 2004*
Customer purchase order processing	2,20,000	5,500 orders
Line-item ordering	1,75,560	58,520 line items
Store delivery	1,95,250	3,905 store deliveries
Cartons dispatched to stores	2,09,000	2,09,000 cartons
Shelf-stocking at customer store	28,160	1,760 hours

Other data for April, 2004 include the following:

	General Supermarket Chains	*Drugstore Chains*	*Chemist Shops*
Total number of orders	385	990	4,125
Average number of a line items per order	14	12	10
Total number of store deliveries	330	825	2,750
Average number of cartons shipped per store delivery	300	80	16
Average number of hours of shelf-stocking per store delivery	3	0.6	0.1

Required:

(a) (i) Compute for April, 2004 gross-margin percentage for each of its three distribution channels and compute *RST* Limited's operating income.

(ii) Compute the April, 2004 rate per unit of the cost-allocation base for each of the five activity areas.

(iii) Compute the operating income of each distribution channel in April, 2004 using the activity-based costing information. Comment on the results. What new insights are available with the activity-based cost information?

(iv) Describe four challenges one would face in assigning the total April, 2004 operating costs of ₹. 8,27,970 to five activity areas. **[CA PE II May 2004]**

(i) **RST Limited's**

Statement of Operating Income and Gross Margin Percentage for each of its three distributin channel

	General Super Market chains	*Drugstore Chains*	*Chemist Shops*	*Total*
Revenues: (₹.)	2,80,41,750 (330 × ₹. 84,975)	2,38,21,875 (825 × ₹. 28,875)	1,49,73,750 (2,750 × ₹. 5,445)	6,68,37,375
Less: Cost of goods sold: (₹.)	2,72,25,000 (330 × ₹. 82,500)	2,26,87,500 (825 × ₹. 27,500)	1,36,12,500 (2,750 × ₹. 4,950)	6,35,25,000
Gross margin: (₹.)	8,16,750	11,34,375	13,61,250	33,12,375
Less: Other operating costs: (₹.)				8,27,970
Operating income: (₹.)				24,84,405
Gross margin %	2.91%	4.76%	9.09%	4.96%
Operating income %				3.72%

(ii) Computation of rate per unit of the cost allocation base for each of the five activity areas for April 2004

Customer purchase order processing (₹. 2,20,000/5,500 orders)	₹. 40 per order
Line item ordering (₹. 1,75,560/58,520 line items)	₹. 3 per line item order
Store delivery (1,95,250/3905 store deliveries)	₹. 50 per delivery
Cartons dispatched (₹. 2,09,000/2,09,000 dispatches)	₹. 1 per dispatch
Shelf-stocking at customer store (₹.) (₹. 28,160/1,760 hours)	₹. 16 per hour

(iii) Operating Income Statement of Each Distribution Channel in April 2004 (Using the Activity Based Costing Information)

	General Supermarket Chains	*Drugstore Chains*	*Chemist Shops*
Gross margin (₹.): (*A*) (*Refer to (i) part of the answer*)	8,16,750	11,34,375	13,61,250
Operating cost (₹.): (*B*) (*Refer to working note*)	1,62,910	1,90,410	4,74,650
Operating income (₹.): (*A–B*)	6,53,840	9,43,965	8,86,600
Operating income (in %) (*Operating income/Revenue*) × 100	2.33%	3.96%	5.92%

Comments and New Insights: The activity-based cost information highlights, how the 'Chemist Shops' uses a larger amount of *RST* Ltd's resources per revenue than do the other two distribution channels. Ratio of operating costs to revenues, across these markets is:

General supermarket chains	
(₹. 1,62,910/₹. 2,80,00,750) × 100	0.58%
Drug store chains	
(₹. 1,90,410/₹. 2,38,21,875) × 100	0.80%
Chemist shops	
(₹. 4,74,650/₹. 1,49,73,750) × 100	3.17%

Working Notes:

Computation of operating cost of each distribution channel:

	General Super Market chains ₹	*Drugstore Chains* ₹	*Chemist Shops* ₹
Customer Purchase order processing	15,400 (₹. 40 × 385 orders)	39,600 (₹. 40 × 990 orders)	1,65,000 (₹. 40 × 4125 orders)
Line item ordering	16,170 (₹. 3 × 14 × 385 orders)	35,640 (₹. 3 × 12 × 990 orders)	1,23,750 (₹. 3 × 10 × 4125 orders)
Store delivery	16,500 (₹. 50 × 330 deliveries)	41,250 (₹. 50 × 825 deliveries)	1,37,500 (₹. 50 × 2750 deliveries)
Cartons dispatched	99,000 (₹. 1 × 300 cartons × 330 deliveries)	66,000 (₹. 1 × 80 cartons × 825 deliveries)	44,000 (₹. 1 × 16 cartons × 2,750 deliveries)
Shelf stocking	15,840 (₹. 16 × 330 deliveries × 3 Av. hrs.)	7,920 (₹. 16 × 825 deliveries × 0.6 Av. hrs)	4,400 (₹. 16 × 2,750 deliveries × 0.1 Av. hrs)
Operating Cost	1,62,910	1,90,410	4,74,650

(*iv*) Challenges faced in assigning total operating cost of ₹. 8,27,970:

(*a*) Choosing an appropriate cost driver for activity area.

(*b*) Developing a reliable data base for the chosen cost driver.

(*c*) Deciding, how to handle costs that may be common across several activities.

(*d*) Choice of the time period to compute cost rates per cost driver.

(*e*) Behavioural factors.

QUESTIONS

1. What do you understand by Activity Based Costing System (*ABC*). Explain main characteristics of this system.
2. 'Activity based costing has been developed because traditional product costing has certain limitation's. Discuss.
3. Discuss various stages related to designing of *ABC* System.

NUMERICAL QUESTIONS

1. Paras Company manufactures two products *X* and *Y*, which involve the following overhead activities: power, factory supervision and maintenance. The expected costs for these activities are as follows.

	₹.
Power	1,81,000
Factory supervision	1,25,000
Maintenance	90,000
	₹. 3,96,000

Activity drivers for each product.

Cost	*Activity Driver*
Power	Kilowatt hours
Factory Supervision	Number of employees
Maintenance	Area occupied

Amounts of activity drivers for each product.

Product	*Killowatt Hours*	*No. of Employees*	*Area Occupied Square meters*
X	81,450	32	800
Y	99,550	68	1,200
	1,81,000	100	2,000

Allocate the overhead costs to each product.

[**Ans.** *Overhead rates: Power ₹. 1 per kwh, Factory Supervision ₹. 1250 per employee and Maintenance ₹. 45 per sq. meter. Overhead Cost X ₹. 1,57,450, Y ₹. 2,38,550*]

2. Palash and Co. manufacture two products *X*–1 and *X*–2. The following overhead activities are involved: power, maintenance, factory supervision and quality inspections. The expected costs for these activities are follows:

	₹.
Power	2,20,000
Maintenance	2,00,000
Factory Supervision	1,56,000
Quality Inspections	90,000
	₹. 6,66,000

The activity drivers for each product are follows:

Overhead Cost	*Activity Driver*
Power	Killowatt Hours
Maintenance	Area Occupied
Factory Supervision	Number of Employees
Quality Inspections	Number of Inspections

The amounts of activity drivers for each product are given below:

Product	*Kw hours*	*Area (Sq. meter)*	*No. of Employees*	*No. of Inspection*
X–1	4,00,000	875	48	144
Y–2	6,00,000	1,625	72	216
Total	10,00,000	2,500	120	360

Compute an overhead application rate for each activity and allocate the overhead costs to each product.

[**Ans.** *Rates: Power ₹. 0.22 per kwh; Maintenance ₹. 80 per Sq. meter of area; Factory supervision ₹. 1300 per employee and Quality inspection ₹. 250 per inspection. Overhead cost X–1 ₹. 2,56,400, X–2 ₹. 4,09,600.*]

3. A Company currently made and sold four products. Details of the four products and relevant information are given below for a period.

Product	*A*	*B*	*C*	*D*
Output in units	120	100	80	120
Cost per unit	₹.	₹.	₹.	₹.
Direct Material	40	50	30	60
Direct Labour	28	21	14	21
Machine Hours (per unit)	4	3	2	3

The four products are similar and are usually produced in production runs of 20 units and sold in the batches of 10 units.

The production overheads are currently absorbed by using machine-hour rate and the total of the production overheads for the period has been analysed as follows:

	₹.
(*i*) Machine department cost (rent, rates, depreciation and supervision)	10,430
(*ii*) Set-up costs	5,250
(*iii*) Stores Receiving	3,600
(*iv*) Inspection and Quality Control	2100
(*v*) Material handling and despatch	4620
Total	26,000

You have ascertained that the cost drivers to be used are as listed below for the overhead costs shown:

Cost	*Cost-Driver*
Set-up costs	No. of production runs
Stores receiving	Requisitions raised
Inspection/Quality Control	No. of production runs
Material handling and despatch	Orders executed

The number of requisitions raised on the stores was 20 for each product and the number of orders executed was 42, each order being for a batch of 10 units of a product.

You are required to (*a*) Calculate the total costs for each product if overhead costs are absorbed on a machine hour basis. (*b*) Calculate the total cost of each product using *ABC*.

[Ans & Hints.

(*a*) *MHR ₹ 20 per hour*

Cost (₹) A 17,760; B ₹ 13100; C 6720 D ₹ 16920

(*b*) *Cost (₹) A 16331; B ₹ 13257; C 7984; D ₹ 16928*

Hints

***ABC* Rates:** Machine Deptt. cost per MH 10430/1300 = 8.023, Set-up cost 5250/21 = ₹. 250 per production run; Stores Receiving 3,600/80 = 45 per requisetion; Inspection etc. 2100/21 = ₹. 100 per production runs; Materials handling etc. 4620/42 = ₹. 110 per order executed.

Total Cost	*A* ₹	*B* ₹	*C* ₹	*D* ₹	*Total* ₹
Direct Material	4800	5000	2400	7200	19400
Direct Labour	3360	2100	1120	2520	9100
Overheads					
Machine Deptt. Cost @ ₹. 8.023 per MH	3,851	2,407	1,284	2,888	10430
Set-up Cost @ ₹. 250 per prod. rum	1500	1250	1000	1500	5250

Stores Receiving @ ₹. 45 per requ.	900	900	900	900	3600
Inspection @ ₹. 100 per prod. run	600	500	400	600	2100
Material Handling @ 110 per order	1320	1100	880	1320	4620
Total	16331	13257	7984	16928	54500

4. *MP Ltd.* produces two products, *A* and *B*. Each has two components specified as sequentially numbered part *i.e.* Product *A* (parts 1 and 2) and Product *B* (parts 3 and 4). Two production departments (machinery and fitting) are supported by service activities. Product *A* is uniform product manufactured each year in 12 monthly high volume production runs. Product *B* is manufactured in low volume batches involving 25 separate production runs each month (300 run p.a.). Additional information is as follows:

	Product A	*Product B*
Components	Part 1 and 2	Part 3 and 4
Annual Production	3,00,000 units	3,00,000 units
Annual Direct Labour Hours		
– Machinery Deptt.	5,00,000	6,00,000
– Fitting Deptt.	1,50,000	2,00,000

Cost-Driver Analysis

Cost-Driver	*Annual Cost-Driver Volume per Component*			
	Part 1	*Part 2*	*Part 3*	*Part 4*
Material Movement	180	160	1,000	1,200
Number of Orders	200	300	2,000	4,000
Number of Set-ups	12	12	300	300
Maintenance Hours	7,000	5,000	10,000	8,000
Number of Insepctions	360	360	2,400	1,000
Direct Labour Hours (Machining)	1,50,000	3,50,000	2,00,000	4,00,000
Direct Labour Hours (Fittings)	50,000	1,00,000	60,000	1,40,000

Overhead Cost Analysis

	₹.
Material Handling	15,00000
Material Procurement	20,00000
Set-up	15,00000
Maintenance	25,00000
Quality Control	30,00000
Machinery (machinery power, depreciation etc.)	25,00000
Fitting (Machine, depreciation etc.)	20,00000
	₹. 150,00,000

You are required to compute the cost of overheads of different units using Activity Based Costing System.

[**Ans.** *ABC Rates Materials handling @ ₹. 590.55 per material movement, Material procurement ₹. 307.69 per order, Set-up ₹. 2403.85 per Set-up, Maintenance ₹. 83.33 per maintenance hours,*

Quality control ₹. 728.155 per inspection, Machining ₹. 2.27 per labour hours, Fitting ₹. 5.71 per labour hours per unit cost, Product A I ₹. 5.562, II ₹. 7.504 Product B I ₹. 17.685 II ₹. 19.215]

5. Mansarover Ltd. makes three main products, using broadly the same production methods and equipment for each. A conventional product costing system is used at present although an activity based costing (*ABC*) system is being considered Details of the three products for a period are:

Products	*Hours per unit*		*Materials per unit* ₹.	*Volumes (units)*
	Labour Hours	*Machine Hours*		
Product *X*	0.5	1.5	20	750
Product *Y*	1.5	1.0	12	1250
Product *Z*	1.0	3.0	25	7000

Direct labour costs ₹. 6 per hour and production overheads are absorbed on a machine hour basis. The rate for the period is ₹. 28 per machine hour.

You are required to calculate the cost per unit for each product using conventional methods.

Further analysis shows the total of overheads can be divided as follows:

	%
Costs relating to set-ups	35
Costs relating to machinery	20
Cost relating to material handling	15
Cost relating to inspection	30
Total production overhead	100

The following activity volumes are associated with the product line for the period as a whole. Total activities for the period.

Product	*Number of Set-ups*	*Number of Movements of materials*	*Number of Inspection*
Product *X*	75	12	150
Product *Y*	115	21	180
Product *Z*	480	87	670
	670	120	1000

You are required to calculate the cost per unit for each product using *ABC* principle.

6. The following is budgeted information related to Mansarover Products Co. for the forth coming period.

	XY	*YZ*	*AB*
Sales and production (units)	50,000	40,000	30,000
	₹.	₹.	₹.
Selling price (per units)	45	95	73
Prime cost (per unit)	32	84	65
	Hours	*Hours*	*Hours*
Machining Department Material (Machine hour per unit)	2	5	4
Assembly Department (Direct Labour hour per unit)	7	3	2

Overheads allocated and apportioned to production departments (including service cost centre costs) were to be recovered in product costs as follows:

(*i*) Machines department at ₹. 1.20 per machine hour.

(*ii*) Assembly department at ₹. 0.82453 per direct Labour hour.

You ascertain that the above overheads could be re-analysed into 'cost-pools' as follows:

Cost-pool	₹.	*Cost Driver*	*Quantity for the period*
Machining services	3,57,000	Machine hours	4,20,000
Assembly services	3,18,000	Direct Labour hours	5,30,000
Set-up costs	26,000	Set-ups	520
Order processing	1,56,000	Customers orders	32,000
Purchasing	84,000	Suppliers orders	11,200
	9,41,000		

You have also been provided with the following for the period.

	Products		
	XY	*YZ*	*AB*
Number of set-ups	120	200	200
Customer orders	8,000	8,000	16,000
Suppliers' orders	3,000	4,000	4200

You are required to prepare and present profit statements using (*i*) Conventional absorption costing and (*ii*) Activity Based Costing.

[**Ans.** *Absorption Method Profits XY ₹. 240414*
YZ ₹. 101056, AB ₹. 46,528, ABC Method
XY ₹. 287,500 YZ ₹. 1,19,000, AB ₹. 17,500 (Loss)]

Operating Costing

Operating cost is the name given to the system of cost used in the concern which renders services rather than produces an article. *CIMA* defines the method `Operating costing applies where standardised services are provided by an undertaking'. Such undertakings are: transport concern (shipping, air, railways and motor transport *etc.*), catering establishments (hotels, hostel, canteen *etc.*) and public utility undertakings like gas, electricity, steam generating, hospitals, theatres, schools, laundries *etc.* In many factories utility services like motor transport, power house, hospital and canteen are departmentally run divisions which provide services to the producing departments of the factory.

Operating costing is used by concern running diverse nature of activities, the cost system is obviously different from that for manufacturing concerns. In this system a suitable cost-unit is adopted, which is not a job or process but is related to service rendered *e.g.* ton-kilometer, passenger-kilometer of transport services, unit of electricity or kilowatt hour, cubic meter of gas *etc.*

Unit of Cost

It is quite important to find out a proper unit of cost in case of operating cost so that the cost per unit can be ascertained. In certain cases the unit is obvious. For example in case of hospital it will be bed, in case of water works it will be 1000 litres, in case of electricity it will be a unit or kwh. and in case of a retail store it will be the sale per ₹ 100 In case of transport concerns, however, the unit is likely to be composite. It may be a passenger-km. or ton-km signifying the effort which is made in carrying a passenger one kilometre or a ton of goods one km. Following are composite units based on two or more factors.

Services	*Composite units*
Transport – goods	Per ton km or per quintal – km.
Transport – passengers	Per passenger – km.
Hospital	Per patient – day or per bed – day
Hotel – lodging	Per Room – day or per service day
Canteen	Per meal or per plate
Boiler House	Per 1000 lbs. of Steam
Electricity	Per kilowatt – hours
Water supply	Per thousand litres
Educational Institution	Per student tution fees.

Classification of Cost

Operating costs are classified and accumulated under the following three heads:

(*a*) ***Fixed or Standing Charges***: These are expenses which are more or less fixed in nature. For example in case transport service garage charges, insurance, taxes, licence and depreciation are standing cost. In case of Hospital the depreciation pertaining to the cost of building, equipment, beds, beds insurance etc. are fixed charges. These expenses are constant and are incurred irrespective of the extent of service.

(*b*) ***Maintenance Charges***: These are costs of semi-variable nature and include expenditure on repairs, maintenance, tyres, tubes, accessories and spares.

(*c*) ***Running or Operating Charges***: These are variable cost. For example in case of hospital, the cost of medicine, diet, laundry *etc.* will represent the running charges. In case of transport service petrol or diesel, lubricating oil, wages of driver or cleaner are operating or running charges.

TRANSPORT SERVICES

Costing in a motor transport undertaking consists of determining the operating cost of each vehicle and applying this cost to find out cost per unit of service rendered by a vehicle. The cost-unit is selected with proper care keeping in view the needs of each concern. It may be cost per kilometer, cost per trip, cost per ton kilometer or cost per passenger per trip or per passenger kilometer. The ton-km or passenger km is actually two units combined in one and is based upon the contention that in operation of a transport both the weight or number of passengers and distance covered during the period should be taken into account.

Suppose the following information is given:

Number of Trucks	30 of 3 tons each
Number of km run per day	100 km
Effective days in a month	20
Wastage on loading capacity	10%
Percentage of Trucks laid for repairs etc.	5%

Now, number of km run by this concern will be 30 × 3 × 100 × 20 × 90/100 × 95/100 = 1,53,900.

If the total cost of running these 30 trucks in month comes to ₹ 8,00,000, the cost of carrying one-ton goods for one km, will come to ₹ 8,00,000/1,53,900 *i.e.* ₹ 5.198.

Composite units *i.e.*, tonnes kms., quintal kms. etc. may be computed in two ways :

(*i*) Absolute (weighted average) tonnes-kms., quintal kms. etc.

(*ii*) Commercial (simple average) tonnes-kms., quintal kms. etc.

(*i*) Absolute (weighted average) tonnes-kms : Absolute tonnes-kms. are the sum total of tonnes-kms., arrived at by multiplying various distances by respective load quantities carried.

(*ii*) Commercial (Simple average) tonnes-kms : Commercial tonnes-kms. are arrived at by multiplying total distance kms., by average load quantity.

Note. To udernstand the concept of abolute tonnes-kms., and commercial tonnes-kms., students should refer to the following example.

Example: A lorry starts with a load of 20 tonnes of goods from station A. It unloads 8 tonnes at station B and rest of goods at station C. It reaches back directly to station A after getting reloaded with 16 tonnes of goods at station C. The distance between A and B, B and C and then from C to A are 80 kms., 120 kms., and 160 kms., respectively. Compute 'Absolute tonnes-kms.,' and ' Commercial tonnes-kms'.

Solution :

Absolute tonnes-kms. = 20 tonnes × 80 kms + 12 tonnes × 120 kms + 16 tonnes × 160 kms.
= 5,600 tonnes-kms.

Commercial tonnes-kms. = Average load × total kilometres travelled

$$= \left(\frac{20+12+16}{3}\right) \text{tonnes} \times 360 \text{ km.} = 5{,}760 \text{ tonnes-kms.}$$

Classification of Cost: Costs are classified and accumulated under three heads as explained earlier. The main item under each head may be:

(*a*) *Standing or Fixed charges*: Salary of manager and supervisor, insurance, license fees, vehicles tax, general supervision, interest on capital, garage rent etc.

(*b*) *Maintenance Expenses*: Tyre and tubes, repairs and painting, servicing and cleaning, spare-parts and components, terminal office expenses.

(*c*) *Operating Charges*: Petrol, oil, wages and salaries of driver, conductor, attendant, cleaners *etc.* if payment is related to time or distance of trip, commission, depreciation, Insurance of transit–goods.

But the above classification is not as a matter of rule. For example, drivers engaged on fixed salary may be treated as standing charges. The classification is guided by the nature of expenditure.

Illustration 1: From the following particulars, find out total passenger kilometer per day and per month.

Distance : 50 kilometers

A Vehicle makes three trips round daily carrying 40 passengers and working everyday.

Solution: Total km per day = No. of Vehicle × No. of Days × Trips × 2 (Round) × Km in a trip.

Total km per day = 1 × 1 × 3 × 2 × 50 = 300

Total Passengers km per day = 300 × 40 = 12,000

Total Passengers km per month = 12,000 × 30 = 3,60,000

Illustration 2: Asha Transport Company maintains a fleet of vehicles for carrying goods between two places. The capacity of the vehicles are:

	No. of vehicles	*Capacity (in tons each)*
	10	2
	5	6
	20	5
Total	35	

Each vehicle makes 5 trips a day covering a distance of 20 km in each trip. On average, 10% of the vahicles are held up for repairs daily and 80% of the capacity of each vehicle is actually used. If the Company operates its fleet for 25 days in a month, find out total ton kilometers carried by the Company per month.

Solution:

Total ton-kilometers = (Total capacity) × (average km) × (No. of trip) × (days of the month) × (% of vehicles run on an average) × (% of capacity used).

$$= 150 \times 20 \times 5 \times 25 \times \frac{90}{100} \times \frac{80}{100} = 2{,}70{,}000 \text{ ton-kms}$$

Note: Total capacity has been calculated as under :

Total capacity = (No. of vehicles used) × (tonnes carried)

10 vehicles @ 2 ton each	=	20 tons.
5 vehicles @ 6 " "	=	30 "
20 vehicles @ 5 " "	=	100 "
		150

Illustration 3 : From the following information, calculate total km and passenger km:

No. of Buses 5; Days operated in the month 30; Trips made by each bus – 3 round trips; Distance of route 20 km (one side); Capacity of Bus – 60 Passengers, but it runs at 90 percent capacity.

Solution:

Total km	=	No. of Buses × Days × Trips × 2 × (Distance of the single trip)
Total km	=	5 × 30 × 3 × 2 × 20 = 18,000 km
Total Passengers km	=	(Total km) × Passengers × (Capacity used)
Total Passengers km	=	18,000 × 60 × 90/100
	=	9,72,000 Passengers-km.

Log Book

A log book is maintained for each vehicle to record details of a trips made by a vehicle during a specified period of time, usually on daily basis. Following is a specimen.

Daily Log Sheet

Vehicle No.	Date ....
Licence No.	Time of:
Registration No	Departure ....
Route No.	Arrival ....

Details of Trip

Trip No.	*Station*		*Goods/Packages*		*Km*	*Time*		*Remarks*
	From	*To*	*Out to*	*Collected en route*		*Out*	*In*	

Supplies	**Time of Workers**	**Analysis of Lost time**
Petrol	Driver	Traffic delays ....
Oil	Conductor	Loading ....
Grease	Cleaner	Unloading ....
	Machanics	Accidents ....
		Others ....

The details shown in the log book enable the management to make suitable allocation of vehicle, to avoid unnecessary or duplicate trips and to avoid waste or idle running capacity. The record also provide data for proper allocation of costs and in this respect they may be compared with the production details available in a manufacturing concern.

Statement of Operating Cost

The cost of each vehicles, suitably analysed under the three heads are compiled periodically in a cost sheet or statement of cost. The specimen follows:

Name of the Concern ....
Statement of Operating Cost for....

Expenses	*Vehicle No.* / *Capacity*				*Total*
A. Operating Cost:		—	—	—	—
Petrol		—	—	—	—
Engine oil		—	—	—	—
Lubricating oil, greases		—	—	—	—
Wages of operators		—	—	—	—
Depreciation		—	—	—	—
Insurance on transit goods		—	—	—	—
	Total				
B. Maintenance Cost:		—	—	—	—
Tyres and tubes		—	—	—	—
Repairs		—	—	—	—
Servicing and Cleaning		—	—	—	—
Paintings	—	—	—	—	
Spare Parts and Components		—	—	—	—
Terminal Office Exps.		—	—	—	—
	Total				
C. Standing Charges:		—	—	—	—
Garage Rent		—	—	—	—
Insurance	—	—	—	—	
Vehicle Tax		—	—	—	—
Licence Fees		—	—	—	—
General Supervision		—	—	—	—
Interest on Capital		—	—	—	—
	Total				
D. Total Operating Cost:					—
(*A* + *B* + *C*)					—
Cost per ton-km. (or per					
quintal-km)					—
Operating					—
Maintenance					—
Fixed					—
	Total				

Purposes of Determining Operating Cost

Determining of operating costs for each vehicle serves the following purposes.

(*i*) Control of running or operating cost

(*ii*) Avoidance of waste of fuel and other consumable material.

(*iii*) Cost of running own vehicle may be compared with hired or other forms of transport.

(*iv*) Operating cost facilitates quotation of hiring rates to outside parties.

(*v*) Running cost of different vehicles may be compared.

(*vi*) If transportation is a service department, its costing and allocation among production departments become easier.

Illustration 4: Bhargav Transport Co. owns a fleet of 10 trucks each costing ₹. 90,000. The company has employed one manager, who is paid ₹. 900 p.m., an accountant, who gets ₹. 500 p.m. and a peon who gets ₹. 100 p.m. The trucks are insured @ 2% p.a. The annual total tax is ₹. 1,800 per truck. The other expenses are as follows:

Driver's salary	₹. 150 p.m.
Cleaner's salary	₹. 60 p.m.
Mechanic's salary	₹. 200 p.m.
Repairs and Maintenance	₹. 1,800 per year for one truck
Diesel Consumption	3 kms. per litre @ ₹. 0.90 per litre.

The estimated life of the truck is 5 yrs.

Other information

(*i*) Distance travelled by each truck per day:	200 km
(*ii*) Normal loading capacity	100 quintals
Wastage in loading capacity	10%
(*iii*) Percentage of truck held up for repairs	5%
(*iv*) Effective days in a month	25

Calculate (*a*) Cost per quintal km (*b*) Cost per km.

Solution:

Total km = (Percentage of trucks run on an average) × (Effective days in the month) × (Distance travelled by each truck per day)

$$= \frac{95}{100} \times 25 \times 200 = 4{,}750 \text{ km}$$

Total Quintal km = (Total km) × (Capacity) × (% of Capacity used)

$$= 4{,}750 \times 100 \times \frac{90}{100} = 4{,}27{,}500.$$

Bhargav Transport Company
(Statement of Operating Cost)

	₹	₹
(A) Operating Costs:		
Depreciation [90,000/(5 × 12)]		1,500
Driver's salary		150
Cleaner's salary		60
Diesel (5, 000 × .90/3)		1,500
		3,210
(B) Maintenance Cost:		
Repairs and Maintenance (1800/12)		150
		150
(C) Standing Charges:		
Managers salary	900	
Accountant's salary	500	
Peon's salary	100	
Mechanic's salary	200	
Total for 10 trucks	1,700	
Slanding charges for one truck (1,700/10)		170
Insurance [90,000 × 2/(100 × 12)]		150
Annual Tax (1,800/12)		150
		470
Total (*A* + *B* + *C*)		3,830
(*a*) Cost per quintal km (3,830 ÷ 4,27,500)		.009
(*b*) Cost per km (3,830 ÷ 4,750)		.806

Illustration 5: The following particulars are available in respect of a 8 ton truck maintained by Kanpur Transport Co:

Cost of the truck	₹. 1,20,000
Estimated life	10 years
Petrol, oil, grease etc.	₹. 28 per single trip
Driver's Wages	₹. 300 p.m.
Assistant's Wages	₹. 175 p.m.
Repairs and Maintenance	₹. 250 p.m.
Insurance	₹. 3,600 p.a.
Tax	₹. 1,200 p.a.
General Supervision	₹. 2,400 p.a.

The truck carries goods to and from a town covering a distance of 50 kilometers. On the return journey, freight is available only up to 25% of capacity. Assuming that the truck runs on an average 25 days in a month, find out: (*a*) Operating cost per ton-kilometer (*b*) Rate per ton per trip which the company should charge, if it wants to make a profit of 20% on freight.

Solution: Total ton km = Months × days × trips × distance × capacity

Total ton-kilometers = 1 × 25 × 1 × 50 × 10 = 12,500

Note: Capacity utilisation = Onward 8 tons + Return 25% *i.e.* 2 tons = 10 tons

Kanpur Transport Co.

(*a*) Statement of Operating Cost

		Total	*Cost per ton km.*
Total ton kilometers		12,500	
(A) Operating Costs:			
Petrol oil grease *etc.* (50 × 28)		1,400	
Depreciation (1,20,000) ÷ (10 × 12)		1,000	
Driver's Wages		300	
Assistant's Wages		175	
	Total	2,875	0.230
(B) Maintenance Charges:			
Repairs and Maintenance		250	
	Total	250	0.020
(C) Standing Charges:			
Insurance		300	
Tax		100	
Supervision		200	
	Total	600	0.048
	Total *A* + *B* + *C*	3,725	0.298

(*b*) Rate per ton per trip, if 20% of freight is profit.

Total Operating Costs		₹. 3,725
Profit (25% on cost or 20% of freight)		931
		4,656
Total tons carried per trip		
(Total per trip × No. of days) 10 × 25	= 250 tons	
Rate per ton trip = 4656/250	= ₹. 18.624	
Alternatively, it may be calculated as under:		
Cost per ton kilometer	= 0.2980	
Add: Profit (25% of Cost)	= 0.0745	
	= 0.3725	
Rate per ton per trip	= 0.3725 × 50 km	
	= ₹. 18.625	

Illustration 6: From the following data relating to two different vehicles; compute the cost per running kilometer:

	Vehicle EB–6	*Vehicle WB–10*
Annual kilometers run	15,000	6,000
Cost of vehicles	₹. 25,000	15,000
Annual Licence fee	₹. 750	₹. 75
Insurance p.a.	₹. 700	₹. 400
Garage Rent p.a.	₹. 600	₹. 500
Supervision Charges p.a.	₹. 1,200	₹. 1,200
Driver's wages per hour	₹. 3	₹. 3
Cost of Petrol per litre	₹. 3	₹. 3
Kilometers run per litre	20 kms.	15 kms.
Repairs and Maintenance per km	₹. 1.65	₹. 2.00
Tyre allocation per kilometer	₹. 0.80	₹. 0.60
Life of Vehicles	1,00,000 kms.	75,000 kms.

You may charge interest on cost of vehicles @ 5% p.a. The vehicles run 20 kilometers per hour on average.

Solution:

Statement of Operating Cost

	EB-6		*WB-10*	
Annual kilometers	*15,000*		*6,000*	
	Total (₹)	*Cost per per* (₹)	*Total* (₹)	*Cost per km.* (₹)
(A) Operating Charges:				
Driver's wages	2,250	0.15	900	0.15
Petrol etc.	2,250	0.15	1,200	0.20
Depreciation	3,750	0.25	1,200	0.20
Total	8.250	0.55	3,300	0.55
(B) Maintenance Charges:				
Repairs etc.	24,750	1.65	12,000	2.00
Tyre-allocation	12,000	0.80	3,600	0.60
Total	36,750	2.45	15,600	2.60
(C) Standing Charges				
Licence fee	750	0.050	750	0.125
Insurance	700	0.047	400	0.067
Garage Rent	600	0.040	500	0.083
Supervision	1,200	0.080	1,200	0.200
Interest on capital	1,250	0.083	750	0.125
Total	4,500	0.300	3,600	0.600
Total $A + B + C$	49,500	3,300	22,500	3,750

Illustration 7: Ascertain the cost per quintal-km. from the following data:

Total quintals carried in a week	60
Total km carried in a week	1,200 km

The above has been ascertained on the basis of the following details:

Days	*Km*	*Quintals*
Monday	240	12
Tuesday	250	10
Wednesday	220	8
Thursday	200	11
Friday	160	9
Saturday	130	10
	1,200	60

Expenses for the week have been as under:

Driver's salary	₹. 400 p.m.
Cleaner's salary	₹. 200 p.m.
Petrol, oil, grease	₹. 0.30 per km
Repairs and Maintenance	₹. 600 p.m.
Depreciation	₹. 9,600 p.a.
Other expenses	₹. 400 p.m.

Assume four week in a month.

Solution : Total quintal km being ascertained as under:

	km × quintals	= Total quintal-kms
Monday	240 × 12	= 2,880
Tuesday	250 × 10	= 2,500
Wednesday	220 × 8	= 1,760
Thursday	200 × 11	= 2,200
Friday	160 × 9	= 1,440
Saturday	130 × 10	= 1,300
		12,080

Statement of Operating Costs

Total quintals km	*Total* 12,080	*Cost per quintal km.*
(A) Operating Charges:		
Driver's salary per week	100	
Cleaner's salary per week	50	
Petrol, oil, grease *etc.*	360	
Depreciation $\frac{9,600 \times 1}{12 \times 4}$	200	
Total	710	.059
(B) Maintenance Charges:		
Repairs *etc.*	150	.012
(C) Fixed Charges		
Other exps.	100	.008
Total *A* + *B* + *C*	960	.079

Illustration 8: From the following details, calculate the cost per km run in respect or each vehicle separately :

Particulars	*Shere Punjab*	*Shame Avadh*
1. Driver's salaries p.a.	₹. 4,000	₹. 5,000
2. Salaries of conductors p.a.	₹. 5,000	₹. 6,000
3. Petrol cost per litre	₹. 3	₹. 3
4. Km run per litre of petrol	10 km	12 km.
5. Cost of the vehicle	₹. 1,00,000	₹. 1,30,000
6. Interest on loan taken for the purchase of the vehicle	12% p.a.	12% p.a.
7. Estimated life of the vehicle	10 years	18 years
8. Tyre allocation per km run	12 paise	8 paise
9. Taxes Insurance etc. p.a.	₹. 2,500	₹. 3,000
10. Repairs, Renewals etc. p.a.	₹. 4,500	₹. 3,500
11. Residual value at the end of the life of the vehicle	Nil	Nil
12. Estimated km run p.a.	10,000	10,000

Solution:

Statement of Operating Cost

	Shere Punjab		*Shame Avadh*	
	Total	*Cost per km.*	*Total*	*Cost per km.*
(A) Operating Charges:				
Driver's salary	4,000	0.400	5,000	0.500
Conductor's salary	5,000	0.500	6,000	0.600
Petrol	3,000	0.300	2,500	0.250
Depreciation	10,000	1,000	7,222	0.722
Total (*A*)	22,000	2.200	20,722	2.072
(B) Maintenance Charges:				
Tyre Allocation	1,200	0.120	800	0.080
Repairs Renewals etc.	4,500	0.450	3,500	0.350
Total (*B*)	5,700	0.570	4,300	0.430
(C) Standing Charges:				
Tax Insurance etc.	2,500	0.250	3,000	0.300
Interest on capital	12,000	1,200	15,600	1.560
Total (*C*)	14,500	1.450	18,600	1,860
Total (A) + (B) + (C) (Total cost for 10,000 km)	42,200	4.220	43,622	4,362

POWER, ELECTRICITY AND GAS SUPPLY SERVICES

In these services – concerns, generation of power or electricity or gas is carried on and these are made available to outsiders or to own production departments. A cost statement is prepared to find out cost per unit. The unit may be per kwt (kilowatt) or kWH (kilo-watt Hours). The costs are normally classified as below.

(a) *Fixed Charges*: Depreciation, Supervision, Administrative overheads, Interest on capital.

(b) *Maintenance Charges:* Repairs and Maintenance.

(c) *Variable Charges:* Cost of Steam Used, Coal, Lubricants and supplies, Wages of operators etc.

Following are a specimens of statement of cost.

Specimen 1

Statement of Electricity Generation Cost
Or
Cost Sheet of Generating Electricity

	Total Cost
(A) Variable Expenses:	
Cost of steam used	—
Coal	—
Lubricants and Supplies	—
Wages of operators	—
Total	—
(B) Maintenance Charges:	
Repairs and Maintenance	—
Total	—
(C) Fixed Charges:	
Depreciation	—
Supervision	—
Adm. overheads	—
Interest on capital	—
Total	—
Total $A + B + C$	—

Cost per Unit = $\frac{\text{Total Cost}}{\text{No. of Units}}$; or Cost per kW = $\frac{\text{Total Cost}}{\text{kW}}$; or

Cost per kWH = $\frac{\text{Total Cost}}{\text{kWH}}$

Specimen 2

Statement of Operating Cost of Steam or Steam Cost Sheet

Period

Steam Production ....
Less: Biolar House Use ....
Less: Main Loss ....
Total consumption ....

	Total	*Cost per 1,000 lbs.*
1. Fuel (Coal or Fuel-oil)	—	
2. Labour (Coal-handlers, strokers etc.)	—	
3. Water	—	
4. Indirect Materials	—	

5. Indirect Labour		—
6. *Maintenance*		—
Fixed Plant	—	—
Boilers	—	
Meters	—	
Coal-bunkers	—	
Furanace	—	—
7. *Fixed Overheads*		
Depreciation		—
Interest on Capital		—
General Factory Overheads		—
	Total	

Illustration 9: You are requested to prepare a Cost Sheet showing the cost of generation of power per kilo Watt-Hours (kWH).

Total Units Generated	15,00,000 kilo-Watt-Hours (kWH) per annum
	₹.
Operating Labour	16,500 p.a.
Plant Supervision	5,250 p.a.
Lubricant and Supplies	10,500 p.a.
Repairs and Maintenance	21,000 p.a.
Adm. Overheads	9,000 p.a.
Capital Cost	1,50,000

Coal consumed per kWH is 1.5 lbs and cost of coal delivered to the power station is ₹. 33.06 per metric ton. Depreciation rate chargeable is 4% p.a. and interest on capital is to be taken @ 7%. Take one metric ton = 2205 lbs.

Solution:

Operating Cost Sheet

(Power : Generated : 15,00,000 kWHs for the year)

	₹.
(A) Variable Charges:	
Operating labour	16,500
Lubricants and Supplies	10,500
Coal $\left(\dfrac{15,00,000 \times 1.5 \times 33.06}{2,205}\right)$	33,735
Total	60,735
(B) Maintenance Charges:	
Repairs *etc.*	21,000
Total	21,000
(C) Standing Charges:	
Depreciation (1,50,000 × 4/100)	6,000
Plant Supervision	5,250
Adm. Overheads	9,000
Interest on Capital (1,50,000 × 7/100)	10,500
Total	30,750
Total *A* + *B* + *C*	1,12,485
	0.075
Cost per kWH = $\dfrac{1,12,485}{15,00,000}$ = ₹. 0.7499 or say ₹. 0.075.	

Illustration 10: Misco Ltd. generates its own electricity for the purpose of using the same for running the factory, gives the following information for the month of April, 2004:

1. Fuel—2,000 quintals ₹. 6 per quintal is the quantity of coal consumed during the month of April.
2. Oil—20 Quintals @ ₹. 750 per quintal.
3. Water—1,00,000 litres @ ₹. 2 per 1,000 litres.
4. Cost of Steam Boiler ₹. 50,000, which has the residual value of ₹. 2,000. The life of Boiler is 10 years.
5. Salaries and wages for the Boiler House: 30 men @ ₹ 100 p.m. and 60 women @ ₹ 40 p.m.
6. Share of Administration charges ₹. 1,050 p.m.
7. Sale of Ash ₹. 300.
8. Generating Plant Cost ₹. 1,50,000, Depreciation @ 10%
9. Repairs and maintenance of steam boiler ₹. 1,000.
10. Salaries and wages for generating plant:
    15 Skilled workers @ ₹. 200 p.m.
    25 Unskilled workers @ 60 p.m.
11. No. of units generated 2,00,000.
12. 10% of units generated were used by generating deptt. itself.

Calculate cost per unit of electricity generated.

Solution:

Statement of Cost Per Unit of Electricity

Total units generated	2,00,000
Less: Electricity units used by the Deptt.	20,000
Total units used	1,80,000

		₹.
Steam Production Costs:		
Coal—2,000 Qtls. @ ₹. 6 per Qtl.		12,000
Oil—20 Qtl. @ 750 per Qtl.		15,000
Water—1,00,000 litres @ ₹. 2 per 1,000 litres.		200
Wages and Salaries		
30 men @ ₹. 100 p.m.	3,000	
60 women @ ₹. 40 p.m.	2,400	5,400
Depreciation on steam boiler $\frac{(50,000-2,000)\times 1}{10\times 12}$		400
Repairs and maintenance		1,000
		34,000
Less: Sale of Ash		300
Cost of Steam production		33,700
Cost of Electricity Generated:		
Cost of steam production		33,700
Wages and Salaries		
15 skilled workers @ ₹. 200 p.m. = 3,000		
25 unskilled workers @ ₹. 60 p.m. = 1,500		4,500
Administrative Charges		1,050
Dep. on generating plant $\frac{1,50,000\times 10\times 1}{100\times 12}$		1,250
		40,500
Add: Cost of Electricity used in generation (10% of units generated or 1/9 of the cost before this item)		4,500
	Total Cost	45,000

Total units consumed by Misco Ltd. = 2,00,000 – 20,000 = 1,80,000

Cost per unit = 45,000/2,00,000 = ₹. 0.225 or 40,500/1,80,000 = ₹. 0.225

CANTEEN SERVICES

Following is an specimen of canteen services cost sheet to find out cost per meal or per plate.

Canteen Cost Sheet

No. of Meals ....

	Total	*Cost per Meal*
1. Wages Salaries:		
Canteen Manager		—
Supervisor	—	—
Cooks	—	—
Counter-Helpers	—	—
2. Provisions:		
Meat	—	—
Fish	—	—
Egg	—	—
Vegetables	—	—
Fruits	—	—
Bread, Cakes, Biscuits, Coffee, Tea, Milk, Cold Drinks	—	—
3. Consumable Stores (Details should be given)	—	—
4. Services (Details should be given)	—	—
5. Miscellaneous Exps.	—	—
Total Cost	—	—

Illustration 11: From the following data for the month of April 2005, calculate cost per meal for the canteen run by joint councils of workers and management of Ratex Ltd.:

1. Purchases for the month of April
   Meat 50 kgs @ ₹. 15 per kg
   Eggs. 36 dozens @ ₹. 5 per dozen
   Vegetables ₹. 300
   Bread etc. ₹. 400
   Rice ₹. 600
2. Wages and Salaries:
   2 Cooks @ ₹. 400 p.m. each
   1 Counter clerk @ ₹. 250 p.m.
   5 Helpers @ ₹. 100 p.m. each
   1 Manager who is paid ₹. 50 p.m.as allowance (because he is already an employee)
3. Consumable stores ₹. 5,000 p.a.
4. Gas and Electricity ₹. 200 p.m.
5. Overheads allocated to the canteen ₹. 1,200 p.a.
6. Company subsidy ₹. 2,000 p.a.
7. No. of meals served in the month of April: 2,000.

Solution :

Canteen Cost Sheet

		₹.
1. Wages and Salaries:		
Cooks		800
Counter clerk		250
Helpers		500
Manager's allowance		50
	Total (1)	1,600
2. Provisions:		
Meat		750
Eggs		180
Vegetables		300
Bread *etc.*		400
Rice		600
	Total of (2)	2,230
3. Consumable Stores (5,000 ÷ 12)		417
4. Services—gas, electricity etc.		200
5. Overheads—allocated (1,200 ÷ 12)		100
	Total (3)	717
	Total (1) + (2) + (3)	4,547
Less: Company Subsidy (2,000 ÷ 12)		167
Cost per Meal = $\frac{4,380}{2,000}$ = ₹. 2.19	Net Total Cost	4,380

HOSPITAL SERVICES

Hospital is also a service-concern. Hospitals provide services through three different departments like (*i*) Out Patient Department, (*ii*) Wards (*iii*) Medical Services Department like pathalogy and X-ray etc. (*iv*) General Service Department like Boiler House, Power, Lighting, Catering, Laundry etc. (*v*) Other Departments like—Medical stores, Dispensary, Transportation etc.

Illustration 12: A public health centre runs an intensive medical care unit. For this purpose, it has hired a building at a rent of ₹. 5,250 p.m. with the understanding that it would bear the repairs and maintenance charges also.

The unit consists of 25 beds but 5 more beds can be comfortably accommodated when the occasion demands. The permanent staff attached to the unit is as follows:

2 supervisors, each at a salary of ₹. 2,500 p.m.

4 nurses, each at salary of ₹. 1,500 per month.

2 ward boys, each at a salary of ₹. 750 p.m.

Though the unit remains open for the patients all the 365 days in a year, it has full capacity of 25 patients per day only for 120 days. For 245 days it has on average 20 beds occupied per day. But there are occasions when the beds are full and extra beds are hired from outside at a charge of ₹. 10 per bed per day. However, this does not come to more than 5 extra beds above the normal capacity on any one day. The total hire charges for the extra beds incurred for the whole year amount to ₹. 5,000.

The unit has engaged expert doctors from outside to attend on the patients. The fees are paid on the basis of the number of patients attended and time spent by them. On an average it works out to ₹. 22,500 p.m.

The other expenses for the year are as under :

	₹.
Repairs and maintenance	7,200
Food supplied to patients	88,000
Janitor and other services for them	25,000
Laundry charges for their bed linen	28,000
Medicines supplied	64,000
Cost of oxygen, X-rays etc., other than those directly borne by patients	1,08,000
General administration charges allocated to the unit	99,000
Total	4,19,200

Required:

(*i*) If the unit recovered an over-all average amount of ₹. 150 per patient per day, what is the profit made by the unit (in nearest rupee)?

(*ii*) The unit wants to work on a budget for the next year, but the number of patients requiring intensive medical care is a very uncertain factor.

Assuming that the same revenue and expenses will prevail next year also, workout the number of patient-days required by the unit of break even.

Solution:

(*i*) Public Health Care Centre–intensive Medical Care Unit
Operating Cost Statement for the Year to Calculate
Profit per Patient-day

Note: No. of patient-days:	120 × 25 =	3,000
	245 × 20 =	4,900
Extra beds (₹. 5,000 ÷ 10)	=	500
Total patient-days		8,400

	₹.	₹.
Fixed Costs:		
Rent (₹. 5,250 × 12)	63,000	
Salaries:		
Supervisor (2 × ₹. 2,500 × 12)	60,000	
Nurses (4 × ₹. 1,500 × 12)	72,000	
Ward boys (2 × ₹. 750 × 12)	18,000	
Repairs and maintenance	7,200	
General administration charges	99,000	
Total Fixed Costs		3,19,200
Variable Costs:		
Fees paid to expert doctors	2,70,000	
Hire charges of extra beds	5,000	
Food supplied to patients	88,000	
Janitor and other services	25,000	
Laundry charges	28,000	
Medicines supplied	64,000	
Cost of X-rays, etc.	1,08,000	
Total Variable Costs		5,88,000
	Total Costs	9,07,200
Average charges per patient per day		150
Less: Cost per patient-day (₹. 9,07,200/8,400)		108
Profit per patient day		42

(ii) Computation of the Number of Patient-days to Break even

Contribution per patient-day:	₹.
Charges per patient-day	150
Less: Variable cost per patient-day (₹. 5,88,000/8,400)	70
Contribution (Charges per patient–Variable cost per patient)	80

$$\text{Number of patient-days to break even} = \frac{\text{Fixed Costs}}{\text{Contribution per patient - day}} = \frac{₹.3,19,200}{₹.80}$$

$$= 3,990$$

HOTEL SERVICES

Hotel services include boarding and lodging. Hotels providing food have to calculate their servicing cost on the lines of canteen services. For providing rooms and accomodations, hotels have to calculate cost per room per day.

Illustration 13: Grand Hotel, Kanpur presents the following information:

1. Staff salaries ₹. 60,000 p.a.
2. Room attendants salary—One attendant for one room. The salary is paid on daily basis @ ₹. 3 per day. Services of room attendants are needed only when a room is occupied.
3. Lighting—₹. 60 per month of a room if the room is occupied for the whole month.
4. Heating and Power — only in winter and normal charge per month, if occupied, for a room is ₹. 15.
5. Linen etc. ₹. 4,800 p.a.
6. Repairs to Building ₹. 12,000 p.a.
7. Sundries ₹. 7,200 p.a.
8. Interior Decoration ₹. 8,000 p.a.
9. Cost of Building ₹. 6,00,000; rate of depreciation 4%
10. Other Equipments ₹. 1,00,000; rate of depreciation 8%
11. Interest on capital invested may be charged @ 5% p.a.

There are 60 rooms in the hotel and 90% of the rooms are normally occupied in summer and 40% of the rooms are engaged in winter. The following assumption may be made:

(*a*) The period of summer and winter is six month each.

(*b*) Normal days in a month are 30.

(*c*) Hotel manager is wishing to earn a profit of 25% on cost other than interest.

Find out the rent per room-per day which should be charged from the customers.

Solution:

Calculation of Room-days

Room days = No. of Rooms × Days in the Month × No. of Month × % of the rooms occupied

Summer—60 × 30 × 6 × 90/100	=	9,720
Winter—60 × 30 × 6 × 40/100	=	4,320
		14,040

Statement of Operating Cost

			₹.
1. Staff salaries			60,000
2. Room attendent's salaries			
		Summer 9,720 × 3 = 29,160	
		Winter 4,320 × 3 = 12,960	42,120
3. Lighting, Heating and Power	*Lighting*	Summer 54 rooms for 6 month @ ₹. 60 p.m. = 19,440	
		Winter 24 rooms for six month @ ₹. 60 p.m. = 8,640	
	Heating and Power	24 rooms for six month @ ₹. 15 p.m. = 2,160	30,240
4. Linen *etc.*			4,800
5. Repairs to Building			12,000
6. Sundries			7,200
7. Interior decoration			8,000
8. Depreciation:	on Building	24,000	
	on equipment	8,000	32,000
9. Int. on Capital Investment (5% of ₹. 7,00,000)			35,000
		Total Cost	2,31,360
Add: Profit (25% of cost excluding Interest) *i.e.* 25% of 2,31,360 – 35,000)			49,090
		Total Cost	2,80,450

$$\text{Rent per Room-day} = \frac{2,80,450}{14,040} = ₹.\ 19.975 \text{ or } ₹.\ 20$$

Illustration 14: Oberai Anand, a hotel owned by Mr. H.K Anand, has the following types of suites for its customers:

	Numbers
Single Suite	100
Double Suite	30
Three Room Suite	20

From the particulars mentioned below, compute by preparing a statement the amount of rent which should be charged for each type of suite:

(*i*) *The percentage of rooms, which are occupied in different seasons are :*

	Summer	*Winter*
Single Suite	90%	50%
Double Suite	80%	20%
Three Room Suite	60%	20%

(*ii*) *Annual Expenses are as unders:*

Staff Salaries	₹. 2,20,000
Repairs	₹. 42,000
Interior Decoration	₹. 50,000
Linen etc.	₹. 45,000
Sundries	₹. 31,550

(*iii*) *Capital Investment and Depreciation*

Building ₹. 14,00,000; Dep. Rate 5%

Fixtures ₹. 1,00,000; Dep. Rate 10%

Air Conditioners ₹. 2,00,000; Dep. Rate 10%

(*iv*) *Other Expenses:*

(*a*) Lighting: (*i*) ₹. 40 for single suite per month if occupied for full month for both summer and winter. (*ii*) ₹. 60 for double suite per month if occupied for full month for both summer and winter. (*iii*) ₹. 80 for three rooms suite per month, if occupied for full month for both summer and winter.

(*b*) Power:

Single Suite	₹. 20	Per month if occupied for full month for both summer and winter
Double Suite	₹. 30	
Three Rooms Suite	₹. 40	

(*c*) Room Attendant's Salaries:

	Summer	*Winter*
Per Single Suite	₹. 2 daily	₹. 3 daily
Per Double Suite	₹. 3 "	₹. 4.50 "
Per Three Rooms Suite	₹. 4 "	₹. 6.00 "

Additional Information:

(*i*) Summer may be assumed for 7 months and winter for 5 month in a year. Normal days in month may be taken as 30.

(*ii*) Profit on cost may be taken at 25%. Ignore interest on capital investment.

(*iii*) The rent of double suite is to be fixed at 1-1/2 times of the single suite and that of three rooms. suite at twice of the single suite.

Solution: First of all Room days will be calculated Double suites and three room-suites will be converted into single rooms.

Calculation of Room-days

	Single Suite		*Double Suite*		*Three Room Suite*	
(*i*) Summer	$100 \times 30 \times 7 \times \frac{90}{100} =$	18,900	$30 \times 30 \times 7 \times \frac{80}{100} =$	5,040	$20 \times 30 \times 7 \times \frac{60}{100} =$	2,520
(*ii*) Winter	$100 \times 30 \times 5 \times \frac{50}{100} =$	7,500	$30 \times 30 \times 5 \times \frac{20}{100} =$	900	$20 \times 30 \times 5 \times \frac{20}{100} =$	600
Total Room days		26,400		5,940		3,120
Double and three room suite being converted into single room		26,400	$5{,}940 \times \frac{3}{2}$	= 8,910	$3{,}120 \times 2$	= 6,240

Total room-days in terms of single suite = 41,550

(*b*) **Calculation of Expenses on lighting for summer and winter:**

Single suite (26,400 × 40) / 30	= ₹.	35,200
Double Suite (5,940 × 60) / 30	= ₹.	11,880
Three room Suite (3,120 × 80)/30	= ₹.	8,320
	Total	55,400

(c) Calculation of Power etc. for summer and winter:

Single suite (26,400 × 20)/30	= ₹.	17,600
Double suite (5,940 × 30)/30	= ₹.	5,940
Three room suite (3120 × 40)/30	= ₹.	4,160
	Total ₹.	27,700

(d) Room Attendant's Salaries

	Summer	Winter	Total
	₹.	₹.	₹.
Single suite	18,900 × 2 = 37,800	7,500 × 3 = 22,500	60,300
Double suite	5,040 × 3 = 15,120	900 × 4.50 = 4,050	19,170
Three-room suite	2,520 × 4 = 10,080	600 × 6 = 3,600	13,680
			Total 93,150

Statement of Operating Cost

	₹.	₹.
Staff salaries		2,20,000
Room attendants' salaries		93,150
Lighting		55,400
Power *etc.*		27,700
Repairs		42,000
Interior Decoration		50,000
Linen *etc.*		45,000
Sundries		31,550
Depreciation on:		
Building	70,000	
Fixtures	10,000	
Air conditioner	20,000	1,00,000
Total Cost		6,64,800
Add: Profit (25% on cost)		1,66,200
Total		8,31,000

Rent for room-day = 8,31,000/41,550 = ₹. 20

Thus rent for double room-suite = 20 × 3/2 = ₹. 30

and rent for three room-suite = 20 × 2 = ₹. 40.

Illustration 15: From the following information, you are required to advise the hotel management what room rent per day in the nearest 50 paise should be charged from the customer to able to earn 25% profit on cost other than interest.

1. Staff salaries ₹. 4,00,000 per annum.
2. Room attendants wages ₹. 10 per day. The wages are paid on daily basis and services of room attendants are needed only when the room is occupied. There is one room attendant for one room.
3. Lighting, heating and power: The normal lighting expenses for a room if it is occupied for the whole month are ₹. 250 per room. Power is used only in winter and normal charges per month if occupied for a room are ₹. 100.
4. Repairs to buildings ₹. 50,000 per annum

5. Linen, *etc.* ₹. 24,000 per annum
6. Sundries ₹. 33,000 per annum
7. Interior decoration and furnishing ₹. 50,000 per annum.
8. Cost of Building ₹. 20,00,000. Rate of depreciation 5%
9. Other Equipment ₹. 5,00,000. Rate of depreciation 10%.
10. Interest @ 10% may be charged on the investment of ₹. 25,00,000 in the building and equipment.
11. There are 100 rooms in the hotel and 80% of the rooms are normally occupied in summer and 30% of the rooms are busy in winter. You may assume that period of summer and winter is six months each. Normal days in a month may be assumed to be 30.

Solution:

Cost Sheet of a Hotel for determining room rent per day

	₹.	₹.	₹.
Variable Costs:			
Room attandents wages : (19800 × ₹. 10)		1,98,000	
Lighting heating and power:			
Lighting:			
Summer : 100 rooms × 80% × 6 months × ₹. 250	1,20,000		
Winter : 100 rooms × 30% × 6 months × ₹. 250	45,000		
	1,65,000		
Power : 100 rooms × 30% × 6 months × ₹. 100	18,000	1,83,000	
Total Variable Costs			3,81,000
Fixed costs:			
Staff salaries		4,00,000	
Repairs to buildings		50,000	
Linen, *etc.*		24,000	
Sundries		33,000	
Interior decoration and furnishing		50,000	
Depreciation: Buildings (5% of ₹. 20,00,000)			
Equipments (10% of ₹. 5,00,000)	1,00,000		
	50,000	1,50,000	
Interest (10% on ₹. 25,00,000)		2,50,000	
Total Fixed Cost (*B*)			9,57,000
Total Cost (A + B)			
Add: Profit 25% on ₹. 10,88,000			13,38,000
Total annual revenue required from the rooms			2,72,000
Room rent per day : ₹. 16,10,000/19,800 = ₹. 81.31			16,10,000
Room rent to be charged per day ₹. 81.50.			

Note: Total of room–days in the year:

Summer : 100 rooms × 80% × 6 months × 30 days	=	14,400
Winter : 100 rooms × 30% × 6 months × 30 days	=	5,400
Total		19,800

TYPICAL ILLUSTRATIONS

Illustration 16: Prakash Operators Ltd. has been given a 20 km. long route to run a bus. The cost of the bus is ₹. 50,000 and has been insured @ 6% p.a., while annual taxes amount to ₹. 2,000. Garage rent is ₹. 100 p.m. Yearly repairs will be ₹. 2,000 and the bus is likely to last for 5 years.

The driver's salary will be ₹. 3,000 p.a. and that of conductor's ₹. 1,800 p.a. in addition to 10% of the taking as commission (to be shared by driver and conductor equally). The cost of stationery will be ₹. 600 p.a. Manager's salary is ₹. 400 p.m. who also looks after accounts:

Petrol and oil will be ₹. 25 per 100 km. The bus will make 3 round trips carrying on the average 40 passengers on each trip. Assuming 25% profit on taking, calculate the bus fare to be charged from each passenger. The bus runs on an average 25 days in a month. **[*CA Inter*]**

Solution :

Statement of Operating Cost

	₹.
(A) Operating Charges:	
Driver's salary p.m.	250
Conductor's salary p.m.	150
Commission (See Working Note)	479 .50
Petrol and oil $\left(\frac{25 \times 3,000}{100}\right)$	750
Depreciation $\left(\frac{50,000}{5 \times 12}\right)$	833
Total	2,462 .50
(B) Maintenance Charges:	
Repairs *etc.*	167
Total	167
(C) Standing Charges:	
Insurance $\left(\frac{50,000 \times 6}{100 \times 12}\right)$	250
Taxes	167
Garage Rent	100
Cost of Stationery	50
Manager's Salary	400
Total	967
Total *A* + *B* + *C*	3,596 .50
Add: Profit (25% on taking or 1/3 of cost)	1,198 .83
Taking	4,795 .33

Note: (1) Total km = No. of Return Trips × Days × km of a return trip

Total km = 3 × 25 × 40 = 3,000

(2) Total Passenger km = Total km × Capacity of carrying passengers.

Total Passenger km = 3,000 × 40 = 1,20,000

(3) Calculation of Commission on Taking

It is presumed that taking is *x*

$$\text{Commission} = \frac{x \times 10}{100} = \frac{x}{10} \qquad \text{Profit} = \frac{x \times 25}{100} = \frac{x}{4}$$

Total cost before commission = 1,983 + 167 + 967 = 3,117

$$\therefore \quad x = 3,117 + \frac{x}{10} + \frac{x}{4}$$

$$\text{or} \quad 20x = 62,340 + 2x + 5x$$

$$\text{or} \quad 20x - 7x = 62,340$$

$$\text{or} \quad 13x = 62,340$$

$$\therefore \quad x = 4,795$$

$$\text{Commission} = \frac{4,795 \times 10}{100} = 479.50$$

(4) Bus fare (Per Passenger km) $= \dfrac{4,795.33}{1,20,000} = 0.3996$ approx or 4 Paise.

Illustration 17: A factory which uses a large amount of coal is situated between two collieries 'X' and 'Y', the former being 5 kms. and the later 10 km from the factory. A fleet of lorries of 5 ton carrying capacity is used for the collection of coal from the pitheads. The lorries average a speed of 20 kms. per hour when running and regularly take 10 minutes in the factory premises to unload. At colliery 'X' the loading time averages 30 minutes per load, and at colliery 'Y' 20 minutes per load.

Driver's wages, licences, insurance, depreciation, garage and similar charge are noticed to cost ₹. 12 per hour operated. Fuel oil, tyres, repairs and similar charges are noticed to cost ₹. 1.20 per km run.

Draw a statement showing the cost per ton km of carrying coal from each colliery. If the coal is of equal quality and price at pithead, from which colliery should the purchases be made?

Solution:

Working notes:

	Colliery 'X'	*Colliery 'Y'*
(1) *Total time taken per trip:*		
Running time to and fro	30 minutes	60 minutes
Unloading time	10 munutes	10 minutes
Loading time	30 minutes	20 minutes
Total time	70 minutes or 1 hr. 10 mts.	90 minutes or 1 hr. 30 mits.
(2) Ton-km	5 × 5 = 25	5 × 10 = 50

Statement Showing Cost per ton-km of carrying coal from each colliery

	Colliery 'X' ₹.	*Colliery 'Y'* ₹.
Running and Maintenance Cost (fuel, oil, tyres, repairs *etc.*) per trip:		
X : 10 km @ 1.20 per km	12.00	
Y : 20 km @ ₹. 1.20 per km		24.00
Fixed Cost per trip:		
X : 1 hr. 10 mts. @ ₹. 12 per hr.	14.00	
Y : 1 hr. 30 mts. @ ₹. 12 per hr.		18.00
Total Cost per trip:	26.00	42.00
Cost per ton-km		
X : ₹. 26/25	1.04	
Y : ₹. 42/50		0.84
Cost per ton:		
X : ₹. 26/5	5.20	
Y : ₹. 42/5		8.40

The cost per ton-km is lower in case of colliery Y. But because it is located at a much greater distance, the decision should be based on expenditure per trip or rate per ton. Hence in the present case, it is advantageous to purchase coal from colliery X.

Illustration 18: A practising chartered accountant now spends on an average ₹. 2.50 per km on taxi fare for his client's work. He is considering two alternatives, the purchase of a new small car or an old bigger car. The estimated cost figures are :

Item	*New Small Car* ₹.	*Old Bigger Car* ₹.
Purchase price	84,000	40,000
Sale price, after 5 years	34,000	8,000
Repairs and servicing per annum	1,800	2,400
T: es and insurance per annum	3,400	1,600
Petrol consumption, per litre	15 km	8 km
Petrol price, per litre, including mobile oil	8.50	8.50

He estimates that he does 12,000 km annually. Which of the three alternative will be cheaper? If his practice expands and he has to do 19,000 km per annum, what should be his decision?

Solution:

Statement Showing Comparative Costs of Alternative Mode of Conveyance

Items	*New Small Car* ₹.	*Old Bigger Car* ₹.	*Taxi* ₹.
Fixed Costs per annum:			
Depreciation	10,000	6,400	
Repairs and maintenance	1,800	2,400	
Taxes and insurance	3,400	1,600	
Fixed costs per annum (*A*)	15,200	10,400	
Running cost per annum:			
(*a*) Petrol for 12,000 km (*B*)	6,800	12,750	
(*b*) Petrol for 19,000 km (*C*)	10,767	20,188	
Total cost per annum:			
(*a*) For 12,000 km (*A* + *B*)	22,000	23,150	30,000
(*b*) For 19,000 km (*A* + *C*)	25,967	30,588	47,500

Conclusion: Alternative of *purchasing a new car* is cheaper in both cases *i.e.*, for 12,000 km or 19,000 km.

Working notes:

1. Depreciation per annum on:

New small car : $\dfrac{₹.84,000 - ₹.34,000}{5} = ₹.10,000$

Old bigger car: $\dfrac{₹.40,000 - ₹.8,000}{5} = ₹.\ 6,400$

2. Cost of petrol per annum for new small car : $\dfrac{₹.12,000}{15} \times ₹.8.50 = ₹.\ 6,800$ and

$\dfrac{₹.19,000}{15} \times 8.50 = ₹.\ 10,767$

3. Cost of petrol per annum for old bigger car : $\frac{₹.12,000}{8} \times ₹.\ 8.50 = ₹.\ 12,750$ and

$\frac{₹.19,000}{8} \times ₹.\ 8.50 = ₹.\ 20,188.$

Illustration 19: SMC, a public school, has five buses each plying in different directions for the transport of its school students. In view of a large number of students availing of the bus service, the buses work two shifts daily both in the morning and in the afternoon. The buses are garaged in the school. The work-load of the students has been so arranged that in the morning the first trip picks up senior students and the second trip plying an hour later picks up the junior students. Similarly, in the afternoon the first trip drops the junior students and an hour later the second trip takes the senior students home.

The distance travelled by each bus one way is 8 km. The school works 25 days in a month and remains closed for vacations in May, June and December. Bus fee, however, is payable by the students for all the 12 months in a year. The details of expenses for a year are as under:

Driver's salary	₹. 1,350 per month per driver
Cleaner's salary (Salary payable for all 12 months)	₹. 1087.50 per month per cleaner
Licence fee, taxes, etc.	₹. 1,200 per bus per annum
Insurance	₹. 6,750 per bus per annum
Repairs and maintenance	₹. 7,200 per bus per annum
Purchase price of the bus (Life 12 years)	₹. 2,25,000 each
Scrap value	₹. 45,000
Diesel cost	₹. 3.50 per litre

Each bus gives an average mileage of 4 kms per litre of diesel. Seating capacity of each bus: 50 students.

The seating capacity is fully occupied during the whole year. Students picked up and dropped within a range upto 4 kms. of distance from the school are charged half and fifty per cent of the students travelling in each trip are in this category Ignore interest. Since the charges are to be based on average cost you are required to :

(*i*) Prepare a statement showing the expenses of operating a single bus and the fleet of five buses for a year.

(*ii*) Work out the average cost per student per month in respect of:

(*a*) Student coming from a distance of up to 4 km from the school and

(*b*) Students coming from a distance beyond 4 km from the school.

Solution:

S.M.C. Public School

Statement Showing the Expenses of Operating a Single Bus and the Fleet of 5 Buses for a Year

	Per bus per annum ₹.	*Fleet of 5 buses per annum* ₹.
A. *Running Costs:*		
Diesel (See working note)	12,600	63,000
B. *Repairs and Maintenance Costs*	7,200	36,000
C. *Fixed Charges:*		
Driver's salary	16,200	81,000
Cleaner's salary	13,050	65,250
Licence fee, taxes, *etc.*	1,200	6,000
	6,750	33,750
Depreciation $\frac{(₹.\ 2,25,000 - 45,000)}{12}$	15,000	75,000
Total Fixed Charges	52,200	2,61,000
Total Expenses (A + B + C)	72,000	3,60,000

Working note:

Calculation of diesel cost per bus :

Number of trips each day : 4

Distance travelled in one trip both ways : 8 × 2 = 16 km

Distance travelled per day by a bus : 16 × 4 = 64 km

Distance travelled during a month : 64 × 25 = 1,600 km

Distance travelled per year (1,600 × 9 months) = 14,400 km

(May, June and December being vacations)

Mileage 4 km per litre

Diesel required per year 14,400/4 = 3,600 litres.

Cost of diesel per year : (3,600 × ₹. 3.50) = ₹. 12,600 per bus.

(*ii*) (*a*) Average cost per student per month in respect of students coming from a distance of upto 4 km:

Cost per month per bus (₹. 72,000/12)	₹. 6,000
No. of students to pay half fee (see working note)	150
Cost per student per month	40

(*b*) Average cost per student per month in respect of students coming from a distance beyond 4 km:

They will pay full fee. Hence, cost per student per month in this category will be:

₹. 40 × 2 = ₹. 80

Working note:

Calculation of number of students per bus:

Bus capacity 50 students

Half fare : 50% *i.e.*	25 students
Full fare : 50% *i.e.*	25 students
Full fare students as equivalent to half fare student : *i.e.*	50 students
Total number of half fare students per trip: 75 students	
Total number of half fare students in two trips:	150 students
On full fare basis, number of students in two trips	75 students

Illustration 20: Indicate the fallacy in the undermentioned cases:

(*i*) In a hospital, the number of patients in a year totalled 10,000. The cost of running the hospital was ₹. 50,00,000. The accountant proposes to charge ₹. 500 from each patient.

(*ii*) A truck operator spends on the average ₹. 20,000 in a month; he carries 1,000 tons in a month, the distance involved being different from customer to customer. The accountant proposes to charge ₹. 25 (₹. 5 to cover profit) per ton.

(*iii*) A power house consumes 30,000 tonnes of coal every month @ ₹. 500 per ton. Coal ash of 1,500 tons is produced every month. The accountant says the cost of coal used is 28,500 tons @ ₹. 500 or ₹. 14,25,000.

(*iv*) In a motor repair works, the cost for a job is worked out by adding the cost of parts used and the wages paid to the worker involved.

Solution:

(*i*) Fallacy: The cost unit is not correct. It should be charged on the basis of days spent by the patients. The total cost should be divided by total patient days (i.e. no. of patient × days spent) to arrive at the cost per patient-day.

(*ii*) The cost unit is not correct. Cost per ton-km is to be worked out and profit should be added there on. Then it will be the rate to be charged.

(*iii*) The cost of coal and coal ash will not be the same. The sale value of coal ash should be deducted from the cost of coal.

Cost of Coal 30,000 × 50		15,00,000
Less: Sale value of Coal Ash (1,500 tonnes).	—	
Net Cost		÷ 28,500 tons.
		= cost per ton

(*iv*) It should be worked out as below:

	₹.
Cost of parts used	
Wages paid to the worker involved	
Overheads incurred	
Overheads apportioned	
Total Cost	
Add : Profit	
Amount to be charged	

Illustration 21: Indicate the fallacy in the undermentioned cases:

(*a*) The cost of running a hospital is ₹. 50 lakhs and the patients in a year total, 20,000. The accountant propose to charge ₹. 250 from each patient.

(*b*) In a motor repair garage, the cost for a job is worked out by adding the cost of parts used and the wages paid to the worker involved.

(*c*) 60,000 tonnes of coal is consumed at NTPC thermal power plant @ ₹. 600 per tonne every month. About 3,000 tonnes of coal ash is produced after burning of the coal. The accountant says that the coal used is 57,000 tonnes @ ₹. 600 or ₹. 342 lakhs.

(*d*) A Telco-truck operator spends ₹. 10,000 in a month and hauls 500 tonnes, the distance involved being different from customer to customer. The accountant proposes to charge ₹. 25 (₹. 5 to cover profit) per tonne.

Solution:

(*a*) ***Fallacy***. The cost unit is not correct. Days spent by patients should also be considered. The unit should be patient-days and not only number of patients.

(*b*) *Fallacy*. Overheads and profit should have been taken into account.

	₹.
Cost of parts used	—
Wages paid to the worker involved —	
Overheads incurred	—
Overheads apportioned	—
Total cost	—
Add: Profit	—
Amount to be charged	—

(*c*) The cost of coal and coal ash will not be the same. The sale value of coal ash should be deducted from the cost of coal.

	₹. in lakhs
Cost of coal 60,000 × 600 =	360.00
Less: Sale value of coal ash 1,000 tonnes at ₹. 100 (assumed)	1.00
Net cost [₹. 359 lakhs/59,000 tons = ₹. 608.471]	359.00

(*d*) *Fallacy*. The cost unit is not correct. Cost per ton km should be worked out and profit should be added thereto. It will be the rate per ton-km.

Illustration 22: A company is considering three alternative proposals for conveyance facilities for its sales personnel who have to do considerable travelling, approximately 20,000 kilometres every year.

The proposals are as follows:

(*i*) Purchase and maintain its own fleet of car. The average cost of a car is ₹. 1,00,000.

(*ii*) Allow the executive use his own car and reimburse expenses at the rate of ₹. 1.60 per kilometre and also bear insurance costs.

(*iii*) Hire cars from an agency at ₹. 20,000 per year per car. The company will have to bear costs of petrol, taxes and tyres.

The following further details are available:

Petrol ₹. 0.60 per km.

Repairs and Maintenance ₹. 0.20 per km

Tyre ₹. 0.12 p per km

Insurance ₹. 1,200 per car per annum

Taxes ₹. 800 per car per annum.

Life of the car: 5 years with annual mileage of 20,000 km

Resale value: ₹. 20,000 at the end of the fifth year.

Work out the relative costs of three proposals and rank them.

Solution:

Statement of Relative Costs of 3 Proposals (₹. per Km)

Alternatives	*Use of Co's car* ₹	*Use of own car* ₹	*Use of hired car* ₹
A. Fixed Costs per annum			
Depreciation $\frac{1,00,000 - 20,000}{5}$ = 16,000			
Insurance = 1,200			
Taxes = 800			
18,000			
Per km 18,000/20,000	0.90		
B. Running & Maintenance Costs			
Petrol	0.60		
R & M	0.20		
Tyers	0.12		
C. Reimbursement	–	1.60	
Insurance 1200/20,000		0.06	
D. Hire charges 20,000/20,000	–	–	1.00
Petrol	–	–	0.60
Taxes 800/20,000 =	–	–	0.04
Tyres	–	–	0.12
Total cost per km	1.82	1.66	1.76
Cost for 20,000 km in a year	₹. 36,400	₹. 33,200	₹. 35,200
Ranking	*III*	*I*	*II*

Thus *use of his own car* by executives will be the most economical out of three proposals.

Illustration 23: Mr. *X* owns a bus which runs according to the following schedule:

(*i*) Delhi to Chandigarh and back, the same day.
Distance covered : 150 km one way.
Number of days run each month : 8
Seating capacity occupied 90%.

(*ii*) Delhi to Agra and back, the same day.
Distance covered : 120 km one way.
Number of days run each month: 10
Seating capacity occupied 85%

(*iii*) Delhi to Jaipur and back, the same day.
Distance covered : 270 km one way.
Number of days run each month : 6
Seating capacity occupied 100%

(*v*) Following are the other details :

Cost of the bus	₹. 6,00,000
Salary of the driver	₹. 2,800 p.m.
Salary of the conductor	₹. 2,200 p.m.
Salary of the part-time accountant	₹. 200 p.m.
Insurance of the bus	₹. 4,800 p.a.
Diesel consumption 4 km per litre at	₹. 6 per litre
Road tax	₹. 1,500 p.a.
Lubricant oil	₹. 10 per 100 km
Permit fee	₹. 1000 p.m.
Repairs and maintenance	₹. 315 p.m.
Depreciation of the bus	@ 20% p.a.
Seating capacity of the bus	50 persons.

Passenger tax is 20% of the total takings. Calculate the bus fare to be charged from each passenger to earn a profit of 30% on total takings. The fares are to be indicated per passenger for the journeys: (*i*) Delhi to Chandigarh (*ii*) Delhi to Agra (*iii*) Delhi to Jaipur.

Solution: Workings

1. Calculation of Total Running km per month

	Distance (Km)	*Trips per day*	*Days per month*	*Km per month*
Delhi to Chandigarh	150	2	8	2,400
Delhi to Agra	120	2	10	2,400
Delhi to Jaipur	270	2	6	3,240
				8,040

2. Calculation of Passenger km per month

Delhi to Chandigarh & back	50 seats × 90% × 2,400	1,08,000
Delhi to Agra & back	50 × 85% × 2,400	1,02,000
Delhi to Jaipur & back	50 × 100% × 3,240	1,62,000
		3,72,000

Statement of Monthly Operation Cost

	Basis of Apportionment	₹	Amount (₹)
A. Fixed Costs:			
Salary of driver		2,800	
Salary of conductor		2,200	
Salary of Part-time Accountant		200	
Insurance	4,800 / 12 months	400	
Road Tax	1,500 / 12	125	
Permit Fee		315	
Repairs & Maintenance		1,000	
Depreciation	$\frac{6,00,000 \times 20}{100} \times \frac{1}{12}$	10,000	
	Total (*A*)		17,040
B. Variable Costs:			
Diesel	$\frac{8,040 \times 6}{4}$	12,060	
Lubricant Oil	$\frac{8,040 \times 10}{100}$	804	
	Total (*B*)		12,864
Total Cost Per Month	(*A*) + (*B*)		29,904
Add: Passenger tax	20% of total takings		
Profit	30% of total takings		
	50% of total takings		
	i.e. 100% of total cost		29,904
Total takings			59,808

Rate per passanger km = $\frac{₹. 59,808}{3,72,000 \text{ Passenger km}}$ = 0.1607741. *i.e.* ₹ 0.161

Fare to be charged per passenger:

(*i*) Delhi to Chandigarh 150 × 0.161 ₹. 24.15

(*ii*) Delhi to Agra 120 × 0.161 ₹. 19.32

(*iii*) Delhi to Jaipur 270 × 0.161 ₹. 43.47

Illustration 24. A transport company has a fleet of three trucks of 10 tonnes capacity each plying in different directions for transport of customers' goods. The trucks run loaded with goods and return empty. The distance travelled, number of trips made and the load carried per day by each truck are as under:

Truck No.	*One way Distance Km.*	*No. of trips per day*	*Load carried per trip/day tonnes*
1	16	4	6
2	40	2	9
3	30	3	8

The analysis of maintenance cost and the total distance travelled during the last two is as under:

Year	*Total distance travelled*	*Maintenance Cost* ₹
1	1,60,200	46,050
2	1,56,700	45,175

The following are the details of expenses for the year under review:

Diesel	:	₹. 10 per litre. Each litre gives 4 km per litre of diesel on an average.
Drivers' salary	:	₹. 2,000 per month.
Licence and taxes	:	₹. 5,000 per annum per truck.
Insurance	:	₹. 5,000 per annum for all the three vehicles.
Purchase price per truck	:	₹. 3,00,000. Life 10 years. Scrap value at the end of life is ₹. 10,000.
Oil and sundries	:	₹. 25 per 100 km run.
General overhead	:	₹. 11,084 per annum.

The vehicles operate 24 days per month on an average.

Required

(*i*) Prepare an Annual Cost Statement covering the fleet of three vehicles.

(*ii*) Calculate the cost per km run.

(*iii*) Determine the freight rate per tonne-km to yield a profit of 10% on freight.

Solution:

1. Maintenance cost

Maintenance cost is semi-variable in nature. By using the high-low method, the variable and fixed cost will work out as under:

Year	*Distance travelled*	*Maintenance cost*
1	1,60,200	₹. 46,050
2	1,56,700	45,175
	3,500	875

Variable cost per km = ₹. 0.25

Total variable maintenance cost (year)=1,60,200 × 0.25

= ₹. 40,050

Total fixed maintenance cost = ₹. 46,050 – 40,050

= ₹. 6,000.

2. Vehicle data

Truck No.	*One way distance (km)*	*No. of rips*	*Total distance (1) covered per day (km) (1)*	*Load carried per trip/day(tonne)*	*Total effective tonne km (2)*
1	16	4	128	6	384
2	40	2	160	9	720
3	30	3	180	8	720
			468		1,824

Note: 1. (one-way distance × 2) × No. of trips

2. (one-way distance × No. of trips × Load carried) : return journey empty

Total km travelled by three trucks in one year

(468 km × 24 days × 12 months) = 1,34,784

Total effective tonne-km of load carried by three trucks in one year

(1,824 tonne-km × 24 days × 12 months = 5,25,312

(i) Statement Showing Annual Cost of Three Vehicles

Total km. travelled 1,34,784	*Total effective tonne-km 5,25,312*
Diesel (*For total km. travelled, see Note 2*) (1,34,784 km. × ₹. 10)/4	₹. 3,36,960
Oil and Sundries (1,34,784 km × ₹. 25)/100	33,696
Maintenance (Working 1) – Total variable + Fixed (₹. 1,34,784 × 0.25) + ₹. 6,000	39,696
Drivers' Salary (₹. 2,000 × 12) × 3 trucks 72,000	
Licence and Taxes (₹. 5,000 × 3)	15,000
Insurance	5,000
Depreciation [₹. 3,00,000 – ₹. 10,000)/10] × 3	87,000
General Overheads	11,084
Total Annual Cost	6,00,436
(*ii*) Cost per km. run (₹. 6,00,436 ÷ 1,34,784)	₹. 4.4548
(*iii*) Freight rate per tonne-km to yield a 10% profit on freight	
Freight without profit ₹. 6,00,436 ÷ 5,25,312 tonne-km =	₹. 1.143
Profit (1.143 × 10/90)	0.127
Freight including profit	1.270

Illustration 25. *EPS* is a Public Shool having 25 buses each plying in different directions for the transport of its school students. In view of large number of students availing of the bus service, the buses work two shifts daily both in the morning and in the afternoon. The buses are garaged in the school. The workload of the students has been so arranged that in the morning, the first trip picks up senior students and the second trip playing an hour later picks up junior students. Similarly, in the affternoon, the first trip takes the junior students and an hour later the second trip takes the senior students home.

The distance travelled by each bus, one way is 16 kms. the school works 24 days in a month and remains closed for vacation in May and June. The bus fee, however, is payable by the students for all the 12 months in a year.

The details of expenses for the year 2003–2004 are as under:

Driver's salary–payable for all the 12 months	₹. 5,000 per month per driver
Cleaner's salary payable for all the 12 months (one cleaner has been employed for every five buses)	₹. 3,000 per month per cleaner
Licene Fees, Taxes *etc.*	₹. 2,300 per bus per annum
Insurance Premium	₹. 15,600 per bus per annum
Repairs and Maintenance	₹. 16,400 per bus per annum
Purchase price of the bus	₹. 16,50,000 each
Life of the bus	16 years
Scrap value	₹. 1,50,000
Diesel Cost	₹. 18.50 per litre

Each bus gives an average of 10 kms per litre of diesel. the seating capacity of each bus is 60 students. The seating capacity is fully occupied during the whole year.

The school follows differential bus fees based on distance travelled as under:

Students picked up and dropped within the range of distance from the school	*Bus fee*	*Percentage of students availing this facility*
4 kms	25% of Full	15%
8 kms	50% of Full	30%
16 kms	Full	55%

Ignore interest, Since the bus fees has to be based on average cost, you are required to:

(*i*) Prepare a statement showing the expenses of operating a single bus and the fleet of 25 buses for a year.

(*ii*) Work out averager cost per student per month in respect of:

(*a*) Students coming from a distance of upto 4 kms from the school;

(*b*) Students coming from a distance of upto 8 kms from the school; and

(*c*) Students coming from a distance of upto 16 kms from the school.

[*C.A. PE II May 2004*]

Solution:

(*i*)

EPS Public School
Statement Showing the Expenses of Operating a Single Bus and the Fleet of 25 Buses for a Year

Particulars	*Per bus per annum (₹)*	*Fleet of 25 buses per annum (₹)*
Running Costs: (*A*)		
Diesel	56,832	14,20,800
(*See working note 1*)		
Repairs & Maintenance Costs : (*B*)	16,400	4,10,000
Fixed charges:		
Driver's salary	60,000	15,00,000
Cleaners salary	7,200	1,80,000
Licence fee, taxes etc.	2,300	57,500
Insurance	15,600	3,90,000
Depreciation	93,750	23,43,750
Total Fixed Charges : (*C*)	1,78,850	44,71,250
Total Expenses: (*A* + *B* + *C*)	2,52,082	63,02,050

(*ii*) *Average cost per student per month in respect of students coming from a distance of:*

(*a*) 4 kms. from the school
(₹. 2,52,082 / 354 students × 12 months)
(Refer to working note 2) ₹. 59.34

(*b*) 8 kms from the school
(₹. 59.34 × 2) ₹. 118.68

(*c*) 16 kms from the school
(₹. 59.34 × 4) ₹. 237.36

Working notes:

1. Calculation of diesel cost per bus:

No. of trips made by a bus each day	:	4
Distance travelled in one trip both ways (16 kms × 2 trips)	:	32 kms
Distance travelled per day by a bus (32 kms × 4 shifts)	:	128 kms
Distance travelled during a month (128 kms × 24 days)	:	3,072 kms

Distance travelled per year (3072 kms × 10 months)	:	30,720 litres
No. of litres of diesel required per bus per year (30,720 kms / 10 km)	:	3,072 litres
Cost of diesel per bus per year (3,072 litres × ₹. 18.50)	:	₹. 56,832

2. Calcualtion of number of students per bus:

Bus capacity of 2 trips	:	120 students
1/4th fare students (15% × 120 students)	:	18 students
½fare 30% students (equivalent to 1/4th fare students)	:	72 students
Full fare 55% students (equivalent to 1/4th fare students)	:	264 students
Total 1/4th fare students	:	354 students

Illustration 26. Carryall Enterprise has been permited to run a minibus on a route covering 20 kms. The minibus has been purchased at a cost of ₹. 1 lakh, part of which was financed through bank loan and balance by loan from other sources.

The annual charges for the minibus are insurance ₹. 4,000, road tax ₹. 2,000 and garage rent ₹. 1,200. Cost of repairs and maintenance is estimated at ₹. 6,000 per annum while replacement of tyre and tube will cost ₹. 480 per month. Office expenses are estimated at ₹. 600 per month. Petrol and oil will cost @ 45 paise per km.

Two drivers and two conductors are engaged at a monthly salary of ₹. 500 and ₹. 350 respectively. In addition drivers and conductors are entitled to 5% of the sale of tickets.

The effective life of the vehicle is estimated at 5 years at the end of which the vehicle will have scrap value of ₹. 10,000.

The minibus is 24-seater and is expected to run 6 two-way trips during the day for 25 days in a month.

You are required to submit passenger fare structure for approval by the transport authority which allows 20% profit on net sales. Interest on loang is allowed as cost, if instalments are paid regularly, assume the amount of interest to be ₹. 6,720 p.a.

Solution:

Statement Showing Fare Structure of Minibus

	Cost per annum ₹.	Cost per month ₹.
(*a*) *Standing Charges:*		
Insurance	4,000	
Road tax	2,000	
Garage rent	1,200	
Office expense (₹. 600 × 12)	7,200	
Depreciation (Note 1)	18,000	
Repairs and maintenance	6,000	
Drivers' and conductors' salary (₹. 850 × 2 × 12)	20,400	
Interest on loar	6,720	
Total (*a*)	65,520	5,460
(*b*) *Operating Charges:*		
Petrol and oil (25 days × 6 × 2 trips × 20 km. × 0.45)		2,700
Tyres and tubes		480
Commission 5% on ticket sales (Note 2)		576
Total (*b*)		3,756

Total Cost (*a*) + (*b*)	9,216
Profit (20% on ticket sales – Note 2)	2,304
	11,520

Total km. covered (25 days × 6 × 2 trips × 20 km.)	6,000
Total passenger-km (6,000 × 24 seats)	1,44,000
Rate per passenger km. (₹. 11,520 ÷ 1,44,000)	₹. 0.08

Note 1.

Depreciation = (₹. 1,00,000 – 10,000) / 5 = ₹. 18,000

Note 2.

Let sales be x

Total cost before charging commission (5,460 + 2,700 + 480) = ₹. 8,640

Commission = 5% of x or $x/20$

Profit = 20% of x or $x/5$

Therefore, x = ₹. 8,640 + $x/20$ + $x/5$

Or $x - x/20 - x/5$ = ₹. 8,640 or x = 11,520

Commission = 5% of ₹. 11,520 = ₹. 576

Profit = 20% of ₹. 11,520 = ₹. 2,304.

Illustration 27: A truck starts with a load of 10 tonnes of goods from station *P*. It unloads 4 tonnes at station *Q* and rest of the goods at station *R*. It reaches back directly to station *P* after getting reloaded with 8 tonnes of goods at station *R*. The distances between *P* to *Q*, *Q* to *R* and then from *R* to *P* are 40 km, 60 km and 80 km respectively. Compute '*Absolute Tonne km*' and 'Commercial Tonne-km'.

Solution:

Absolute Tonne-km :

P to Q = 10 tonnes × 40 km	=	400
Q to R = 6 tonnes × 60 km	=	360
R to P = 8 tonnes × 80 km	=	640
		1,400

Commercial Tonne-km:

In case of commercial tonne-km, the trip will be considered as a whole.

$$\text{Average load} = \frac{10+6+8}{3} = 8 \text{ tonnes}$$

Commerical tonne-km = Total Distance × Average load *i.e.*, 180 × 8 = 1,440 tonne-km.

Illustration 28: A lodging home is being run in a small hill station with 50 single rooms. The home offers concessional rates during six off-season months in a year. During this period, half of the full-room rent is charged. The management's profit margin is targeted at 20% of the room rent. The following are the cost estimates and other details for the year ending 31st March, 2000 (assume a month to be of 30 days);

(*a*) Occupancy during the season is 80%, while in the off-season is 40% only:

(*b*) Expenses:

	₹.
(*i*) Staff salary (excluding room attendants)	2,75,000
(*ii*) Repairs to buildings	1,30,500
(*iii*) Laundry & linen	40,000
(*iv*) Interior and tapestry	87,500
(*v*) Sundry expenses	95,400

(*c*) Annual depreciation is to be provided, for buildings at 5% and on furniture and equipments at 15%, on straight line basis:

(*d*) Room attendants are paid ₹ 5 per room-day on the basis of occupancy of the rooms in a month:

(*e*) Monthly lighting charges are ₹ 120 per room except in four months of winter when it is ₹ 30 per room and this cost is on the basis of full occupancy for a month: and

(*f*) Total investments in the home is ₹ 100 lakhs of which ₹ 80 lakhs relate to buildings and balance for furniture and equipments.

You are required to work out the room rent chargeable per day both during the season and the off-season months, on the basis of the foregoing information. **[*CWA (Inter)*]**

Solution:

Occupancy in room days

Season 50 rooms × 80% × 6 months × 30 days =	7,200
Off-season : 50 rooms × 40% × 6 months × 30 days =	3,600
Total room days	10,800

Room Rent

		₹
Full room rent during season : 7,200 × 1		7,200
Half of full room rent during off season: 3,600 × 0.5		1,800
		₹ 9,000
Expenses		₹
Staff Salaries		2,75,000
Repairs to Buildings		1,30,500
Laundry & Linen		40,000
Interior & Tapestry		87,500
Sundry Expenses		95,400
Depreciation		
Buildings 5% of 80 lakhs		4,00,000
Furniture 15% of 20 lakhs		3,00,000
Payment to room attendants : 10,800 × 5 54,000		
Lighting charges for 12 months:		
120 × 6 months × 50 rooms × 80%	28,800	
120 × 2 months × 50 rooms × 40%	4,800	
30 × 4 months × 50 rooms × 40%	2,400	36,000
Total Cost		14,18,400
Add: Profit margin at 20% of room rent i.e. 25% of total cost		3,54,600
Total Room Rent		17,73,000

Room rent per day 17,73,000 7 9,000 = ₹ 197 per day during the season and ₹ 98.50 per day during the off season (*i.e.* 1/2 of rent during season).

Thus total room rent on the basis of these rates:

During season: 7,200 × 197 =	14,18,400
Off season: 3,600 × 98.50	3,54,600
Total room rent	₹ 17,73,000

Illustration 29: A manufacturing firm facing shortage of electric power supply from the State Electricity Board has set up its own power generation plant for efficient running of its production units in the factory. The following information has been taken from the records in connection with the generation of power for a month:

(1) Number of units generated was 10,00,000 for the month of which 10% was utilised by the generator department.

(2) Consumption data of materials, etc. for the month:

(*a*) Coal consumed	300 MTs @ ₹. 3,600 per MT
(*b*) Oil consumed	4.5 MTs @ ₹. 40,000 per MT
(*c*) Cost of water extraction & treatment	For 6 lakhs litres @ 1.25 per litre

(3) Steam boiler cost ₹. 20 lakhs with a residual value of ₹. 2 lakhs after a life of 10 years.

(4) Salaries and wages per month:

(*a*) For staff of generating plant:

(*i*) 100 skilled workers @ ₹. 3,000 p.m.

(*ii*) 150 helpers @ ₹. 1,500 p.m.

(*b*) For staff of boiler house:

(*i*) 60 category A workers @ ₹. 1,500 p.m.

(*ii*) 100 category B workers @ ₹. 1,000 p.m.

(5) Cost of generating plant: ₹. 36 lakhs with no residual value.

Depreciation @ 10% on straight line basis is to be charged.

(6) Repairs and maintenance of generating plant and boiler ₹. 50,000 p.m.

(7) Share of administrative charges ₹. 40,000 p.m.

(8) Sales value of ashes disposed off ₹. 15,000 p.m.

Calculate the per unit cost of electricity generated using a cost sheet format.

Solution:

Cost Sheet of Power House
(No. of Units Generated : 10,00,000)

Month ....

	Total Cost of the Month (₹.)	*Cost per unit or KWH (₹)*
1. Consumption of materials		
(*a*) Coal consumed (300 × 3600)	10,80,000	
(*b*) Oil consumed (4.5 × 40,000)	1,80,000	
(*c*) Cost of water 6,00,000 × 1.25)	7,50,000	
	20,10,000	2.010
2. Salaries & Wages		
(*a*) For staff of generating plant		
100 × 3,000	3,00,000	
150 × 1,500	2,25,000	
(*b*) For staff of boiler house		
60 × 1,500	90,000	
100 × 1,000	1,00,000	
	7,15,000	0.715
3. Depreciation		
(*a*) Steam boiler $\frac{20-2}{10 \times 12}$ lakhs	15,000	
(*b*) Generating plant 10% of 36/12 lakhs	30,000	
	45,000	0.045

4. Repairs & Maintenance	50,000	0.050
Total [1 + 2 + 3 + 4]	28,20,000	2.820
Less: Sale value of ash disposed off	15,000	0.015
Works Cost	28,05,000	2.805
Add: Share of Administrative Charges	40,000	0.040
Cost of electricity generated	28,45,000	2.845

Working Note: Cost of units utilised by generator department : 10% *i.e.* 1,00,000 units @ ₹. 2.845 per unit = ₹. 2,84,500. It should be debited to generator department

QUESTIONS

OBJECTIVE QUESTIONS

I. *State whether following statements are true or false.*

1. There is no difference between operating costing and process costing.
2. Operating costing method can be used in canteens.
3. Operating costing unit is not a simple unit.
4. Cost related to passenger buses is calculated with reference to cost per passenger per kelometer.
5. Operating costing is also used in calculating cost per unit in hospitals.

[**Ans.** False (*I*)]

THEORETICAL QUESTIONS

1. What is meant by 'Operating Costing'? To what industries is this applicable?
2. What is 'composite unit'? What are its advantages? Give six examples of composite unit.
3. Draw up a proforma cost statement for a canteen serviing 1,000 workers in a factory.
4. What are the principal departments of a hospital and what units can be used in respect of these departments?
5. Distinguish between operating costing and operation costing.
6. 'The more kilometres you travel with your own vehicle, the cheaper it becomes'. Comment briefly on this statement.
7. Write short note on 'operating costing'.
8. What do you understand by composite unit in service costing?

SHORT ANSWER QUESTIONS

1. Define Operating Cost.
2. In which services operating cost accounting is used ?
3. Classify Operating cost ?
4. What is meant by unit of operating cost ?
5. Give examples of expenses related to transport services.
6. How total Passenger-kilometer is calculated ?
7. From the following calculate 'Total passenger kilometer per month'.

   Distance (one side) 50 kms

   Passenger 40

   Vehicle makes three round trips daily during 30 days in a month.

   [*Ans. 3,60,000*]
8. From the following information, calculate 'total passenger kms.'

No. of buses 5 making 3 round trips daily during a month of 30 days.

Distance 20 Kms. (one side)

Capacity of Bus : 60 Passenger

Normally Travelling at 90% capacity

[**Ans.** *9,72,000*]

9. From the following calculate cost per passenger kilometer

Total passenger kilometer during month 6,76,000

Per month cost :

(a) Operating charges	₹ 10,400
(b) Maintenance charges	₹ 1,000
(c) Standing charges	₹ 5,500
	₹ 16,900

[**Ans.** .. *0.025*]

10. A bus plies between two points at a distance of 15 km. It is not on the road for 5 days a month on an average. It runs 5 upward and 5 downward journey per day. Its capacity is 50 passenger and an average 80% is full. The expenses of the month on bus are ₹ 7,500. Calculate cost per passenger km.

[**Ans.** *Passenger km. 1,50,000, Cost per Passenger km. ₹ 0.05*]

NUMERICAL QUESTIONS

1. Gwalior Transport Company is running a bus between two places which are 40 km apart. The carrying capacity of the bus is 50 passenger. On an average, 90% of the capacity is utilised. The bus run on all the day of the months and makes two round trips per day. From the following information, calculate the fare to be charged to passengers for travelling 5 km, if the company desires to earn a profit of 20% on the fare.

Cost of the bus ₹ 1,35,000

Estimated life 90,000 kms.

Wages of drivers, conductors etc. p.m. ₹ 1,080

Tax Licence fees etc. p.a ₹ 3,240

Repairs and maintenance p.a. ₹ 4,320

Diesel and other oil: ₹ 5 per litre

The bus runs 10 km per litre.

Insurance charges p.m. ₹ 540

Interest and other charges p.a. ₹ 1,620

[**Ans.** *Cost per passenger km ₹ 0.055 and cost per km ₹ 2.497; Fare for 5 km ₹ 15.60625 or say ₹ 15.61. Fare for per passenger kilometers ₹ 0.069.*

[**Hint:** Total kms = 1 × 30 × 4 × 40 = 4,800 km

Total passenger km = 4,800 × 50 × 90% = 2,16,000; Total cost ₹ 11,985.]

2. From the following data relating to two different vehicles A and B, compute the cost per running kilometer.

	A	*B*
Km run (annual)	20,000	9,000
Km run per gallon	25	18
Estimated life of vehicles in km	1,20,000	81,000
	₹	₹
Cost of vehicles	30,000	18,000
Road licence (annual)	1,000	1,000

Insurance (annual)	800	500
Garage rent (annual)	500	400
Supervision (annual)	1,500	1,500
Drivers wages per hour	5	5
Cost of petrol per gallon	2	2
Repairs and maintenance per km	1.50	2.00
Tyre allocation per km	0.75	0.50

You are to charge interest on the cost of vehicles at 5% p.a. The vehicles run 25 km per hour on an average.

[**Ans.** *Cost per km A ₹ 3.045; B ₹ 3.511*]

3. Mr. Kapadia runs a tempo service in the town and has two vehicles. He has submitted the following particulars and asks you to find out cost per running kilometer:

	Vehicle UXN-I	*Vehicle UXN-II*
Cost of the vehicle	₹ 25,000	₹ 15,000
Licence fee p.a.	₹ 750	₹ 750
Supervision p.a.	₹ 1,800	₹ 1,200
Driver's wages per hour	₹ 4	₹ 4
Petrol per litre	₹ 1.50	₹ 1.50
Repairs and maintenance per km	₹ 1.00	₹ 0.80
Tyre cost per km	₹ 1.50	₹ 2.00
Garage rent p.a.	₹ 1,600	₹ 550
Insurance p.a.	₹ 850	₹ 500
Km run per litre	6	5
Km run during the year	15,000	6,000
Estimated life of the vehicle	1,00,000 km	75,000 km

Interest @ 10% p.a. is to be charged on the cost of the vehicle in each case. The vehicles run 20 km per hour on an average.

[**Ans.** *Cost per km UXN-I ₹ 3.70 and UXN-II . 4.25*]

4. M/s Balwant Motors Ltd. charges ₹ 30 per quintal for 5 quintal load lorry from Patna to Banaras. The charge for return trip is ₹ 28 per quintal. In the month of Sept. 2004, his truck has made 10 outward journeys with full load out of which 3 quintal were unloaded at Ghazipur twice in a month. It returned without any load once only from Ghazipur. The expenses are as under:

Annual standing charges ₹ 9,600

Annual maintenance charges ₹ 4,800

Monthly running charges ₹ 601

You are asked to find out the cost per quintal-km (absolute) and also the profit for the month in question, assuming that no concession is made for delivery at the intermediate stages. Additional data available are :

Distance of Ghazipur from Patna 120 km.

Distance of Banaras from Patna 210 km.

The vehicle carried a load of 8 quintals 5 times in the month while returning from Banaras but once was caught by the police and fined ₹ 500.

[**Ans.** *Total quintal km 9,960 per outward journey and 13,050 per return journey, in all 23,010. Total operating cost including the fine ₹ 2,301; Cost per quintal-km 0.10; Total profit ₹ 1,019.*]

[**Hints.** P to B 8 × 210 × 5 = 8400, P to G 2 × 120 × 5 = 1200, G to B 2 × 90 × 2 = 360, Total 9960. quintal km outward. Inword B to G 1 × 90 × 5 = 450, G to P 1 × 120 × 0 = 0, B to P 5 × 210 × 8 = 8400, B to P 4 × 210 × 5 = 4200 Total 13050 quintal km]

5. Prakash Automobiles distributes its goods to a regional dealer using a single lorry. The dealer's premises are 40 kilometres away by road. The lorry has capacity of 10 tonnes and makes the journey twice a day fully loaded on the outward journeys and empty on return journeys. The following information is available for a four weekly period during the year 2004.

Petrol consumption	8 kilometres per litre
Petrol cost	₹. 13 per litre
Oil	₹. 100 per week
Driver's wages	₹. 400 per week
Repairs	₹. 100 per week
Garage rent	₹. 150 per week
Cost of lorry (excluding tyres)	₹. 4,50,000
Life of lorry	80,000 kilometres
Insurance	₹. 6,500 per annum
Cost of tyres	₹. 6,250
Life of tyres	25,000 kilometres
Estimated sale value of lorry at the end of its life	₹. 50,000
Vehicle licence cost	₹. 1,300 per annum
Other overhead cost	₹. 41,600 per annum

The lorry operates on a five-day week.

Required : (*a*) A statement to show the total cost of operating the vehicle for the four weekly period analysed into running costs and fixed costs.

(*b*) Calculate vehicle cost per kilometre and per tonne kilometre.

[Ans. *(a) Total Cost ₹. 28,800 (b) ₹. 1.80] Hints. Total kms. 3,200, ton–kms 16,000*]

6. Union Transport Company supplies the following details in respect of a truck of 5 tonnes capacity:

	₹.
Cost of truck	90,000
Estimated life	10 years
Diesel, oil, grease	15 per trip each way
Repairs and maintenance	500 per month
Driver's wage	500 per month
Cleaner's wage	250 per month
Insurance	4,800 per year
Tax	2,400 per year
General supervision charges	4,800 per year

The truck carries goods to and from the city covering a distance of 50 km each way. On outward trip freight is available to the extent of full capacity and on return 20% of capacity.

Assuming that the truck runs on an average 25 days a month, work out:

(*a*) Operating cost per tonne-km.

(*b*) Rate per tonne per trip that the company should charge if a profit of 50% on freight is to be earned.

[Ans. *Tonne-km 7,500 (a) Cost per tonne-km ₹ 0.50 (b) ₹. 50*]

7. From the following information calculate the cost of generating electricity per unit:

1. Coal used 1,200 tonnes @ ₹. 10 per tonne.
2. Freight and handling charges : 10% of value of the coal used.
3. Oil : 10 tonnes @ ₹. 250 per tonne.
4. Water : 50,000 litres @ ₹. 0.25 per 100 litres.
5. Depreciation of steam boiler ₹. 250.
6. Salaries and wages of the boiler house:
   10 men @ ₹. 100 each
   40 coolies @ ₹. 20 each
7. Recovery on account of sale of ashes : 100 tonnes @ ₹. 1 per tonne.
8. Salaries and wages of generating station:
   50 men @ ₹. 100 each
   20 coolies @ ₹. 20 each
9. Repairs and maintenance of generating equipment ₹. 260

10. Depreciation of generating equipment ₹. 2,500
11. Share of administrative charges : ₹. 1,750
12. Total number of units generated : 1,46,000.
13. Normal loss in the process : 2,000 units generated.

[**Ans.** *19 paise per unit*]

8. From the following particulars calculate cost per unit of electricity generated for the month of April.

Cost of steam used : 32,000 therms @ 87.37 paise per therm.

Wages and salaries; 10 men @ ₹. 300 p.m.

Repairs and maintenance ₹. 3,000 p.m.

Supervison and administration ₹. 1,000 p.m.

Stores ₹. 500 p.m.

Cost of generating plant ₹. 1,00,000.

Residual value ₹. 4,000.

Estimated life 10 years.

Units of electricity generated in the month, 3,00,000.

[**Ans.** *Cost per unit 12.086 paise*]

9. 'Sawant' a hotel has 10 three-room suites, 40 double room suits and 60 single room suites. Normally 90% of single room suites, 80% of double room suites and 60% of three-room suites are occupied in summer which lasts for 7 months in a year. In winter covering rest 5 months of the year, 50% of the single room suites, 25% of double room suites and 20% of three-room suites are occupied. Find out total room-days for each type of suite. Assume month of 30 days.

[**Ans.** *Single room suite 15,840 room days; double room suites 8,220 room-days and three-room suites 1560 room-days.*]

10. Following are information given by the owner of a hotel. You are requested to advise him what rent should be charged by him from his customers per day so that he is able to earn 20% on cost other than interest.

1. There are 100 rooms in the hotel and 90% of the rooms are generally occupied in the year. Normal days in a month may be taken to be 30.
2. Room attendants' salaries ₹. 36,000 p.a.
3. Staff salaries ₹. 60,000 p.a.
4. Lighting, heating and power ₹. 30,000 p.a.
5. Repairs to building ₹. 10,000 p.a.
6. Linen etc. ₹. 5,000 p.a.
7. Interior decoration ₹. 12,000 annually.
8. Cost of building ₹. 5,00,000; rate of depreciation 4%.
9. Other equipments ₹. 2,00,000; rate of depreciation 5%.
10. Interest on capital investment in building and equipments may be charged @ 5% p.a.

[**Ans.** *Total room-days 32,400; Total cost before interest on capital ₹ 1,83,000; Profit ₹ 36,600; Total taking ₹ 2,54,600, Rent room-day ₹ 7.86 or ₹ 8*]

Chapter 13 Cost Control Accounts

When Cost Accounting was evolved, the necessary data for cost ascertainment were collected from documents which were entirely independent of documents used by financial accounts. Normally at that time two sets of primary documents and accounting books were used.

With the growth of Cost Accounting System, the fixation of selling price before actual production and control over cost became important, two independent sets of books (in Cost and Financial Accounting) are kept and both used the same primary documents. The profits shown by these two sets are periodically reconciled through a reconciliation statement in the pattern of bank reconciliation. Since the same set of primary documents are used, certain control accounts are opened in cost and financial books. These control accounts are called Cost Ledger Adjustment or Control Account in the financial books and General Ledger Adjustment or Control Account in the cost books.

COST LEDGER

In cost books two kinds of ledgers are kept (*i*) Principal ledger or cost ledger and (*ii*) Subsidiery ledger.

In the principal ledger all impersonal accounts are kept. These are (*a*) General Ledger Adjustment Account and (*b*) Control Accounts for subsidiery ledger.

In subsidiery ledger the accounts kept are (*a*) Stores ledger in which separate accounts are opened for each item of stores (*b*) Work-in-progress ledger which accounts of each job or batch or process and (*c*) Finished goods ledger which has accounts of finished goods.

It is to be noted that following Control Accounts are opened for each subsidiary ledger in the cost ledger along with General Ledger Adjustment or Control Account:

(1) Stores Ledger Control Account

(2) Work-in-Progress Ledger Control Account

(3) Finished Goods Control Account

Besides above, there are certain other control accounts related to impersonal account.

(4) Wages Control Account

(5) Factory Overhead Control Account

(6) Office Overhead Control Account

(7) Selling and Distribution Overhead Control Account

(8) Cost of Sales Account

(9) Costing Profit and Loss Account

(10) Overhead Suspenses Account

GENERAL LEDGER ADJUSTMENT OR CONTROL ACCOUNT
[Cost Ledger Control Account]

No personal accounts are kept in the cost books but as the cost books are maintained on the principle of double entry, all transactions which arise in the financial accounts are debited or credited to General Ledger Control Account maintained for this purpose. This account makes the cost ledger self balancing. Basically, this account represents personal or cash or Bank

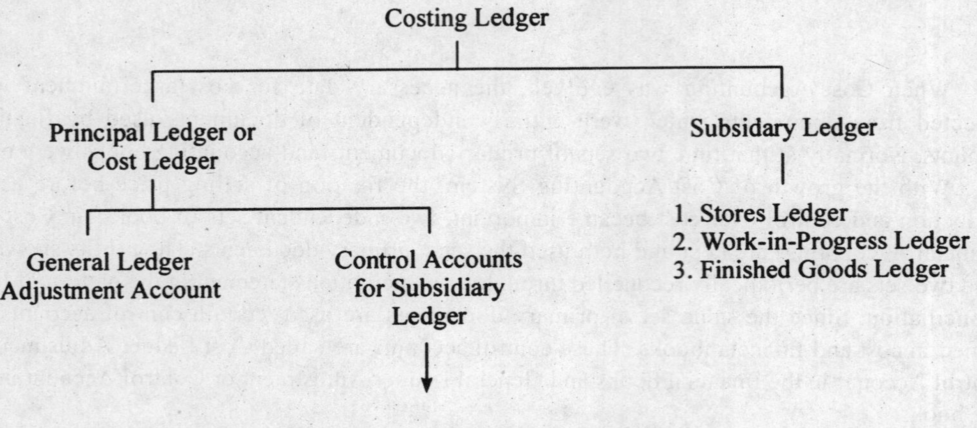

(1) Stores ledger Control Account
(2) Work-in-Progress Ledger Control Account
(3) Finished Goods Control Account
(4) Wages Control Account
(5) Factory Overhead Control Account
(6) Office Overhead Control Account
(7) Selling and Distribution Overhead Control Account
(8) Cost of Sales Account
(9) Costing Profit and Loss Account
(10) Overhead Suspenses Account

Accounts in the financial books. For example, materials purchased against cash is debited to Stores Ledger Control Account and credited to General Ledger Control Account.

Stores Ledger Control Account: It deals with transactions of materials. All receipts are debited and issues are credited, the balance shows the stock of raw materials.

Work-in-Progress Ledger Control Account: This account is debited with the opening balance of work-in-progress, materials, labour and factory overhead costs (recovered) and is credited with the cost of finished goods. Balance will be closing work-in-progress.

Finished Goods Control Account: This account is debited with the opening balance of finished goods, the cost of finished goods for the period transferred from the Work-in-Progress Control Account and the amount of administrative overhead recovered. The goods sold are credited from Finished Goods Control Account to Cost of Sales Account. The closing balance will show unsold stock carried over.

Wages Control Account: It records labour transactions. The account is debited with the gross wages and is credited by the transfer of direct labour to work-in-progress and indirect labour to Factory. Administration and Selling and Distribution Overhead Control Account.

Factory Overhead Control Account: It deals with manufacturing overhead expenses. It is debited by the amount of indirect material, indirect labour and indirect expenses incurred. This account is credited by the amount of overhead recovered.

Office Overhead or Administration Overhead Control Account: Administrative overhead cost is debited to this account, the amount of overhead recovered in the finished goods sold is credited to this account. It may be, alternatively, transferred to Costing Profit and Loss Account if it is not charged to Cost of Goods Sold.

Selling and Distribution Overhead Account: In this account selling and distribution costs are debited and it is credited by transfer to Cost of Sales Account by recovered selling and distribution overheads.

Cost of Sales Account: This account is debited with the cost of goods sold and selling and distribution overhead recovered and is closed by transfer to Costing Profit and Loss Account.

Costing Profit and Loss Account: This account records the transfer of amounts of under and over absorbed overheads, the sale value of goods sold, and the balance from the Cost of Sales Account. Abnormal losses or gains are debited and credited to this account. The closing balance of this account represents the costing profit or loss. The costing profit and loss is reconciled with the profit or loss shown by the financial profit or loss.

Overhead Suspense or Adjustment Account: In this account under or over absorbed overheads (of factory, administration and selling and distribution) are debited or credited. The balance of this account, if carried to next period will be shown as balance, if not carried to next period will be transferred to Costing Profit and Loss Account, if charged as subsidiary rate to production transferred to Cost of Sales Account (on units sold), Work-in-Progress (on units incomplete) and to Finished Goods sold (on units not sold) Sometimes this account is not maintained and the amount of under or over absorbed overheads is transferred direct to Costing Profit and Loss Account.

Entries in Control Accounts

Following are the Journal entries in brief which will explain the accounting in the Control Accounts.

	Transations	*Entry in Cost Ledger*
	Materials	
(*i*)	Receipts of materials into stores.	Debits Stores Ledger Control Accounts Credit Cost Ledger Control Account or Gen. Ledger Control Account.
(*ii*)	Return of materials to suppliers	Reverse of the above entry.
(*iii*)	Receipt of materials for direct issue.	Debit Work-in-Progress Control Account. Credit Cost Ledger Control Account.
(*iv*)	Issue of materials and stores for production (as per requisition slips in Materials Abstract)	Debit Work-in-Progress Control Account Credit Stores Ledger Control A/c.
(*v*)	Issue of material as indirect material.	Debit Factory Overhead Control Credit Stores Ledger Control A/c.
(*vi*)	Return of material form Job to stores.	Revere of (*iv*) entry.
(*vii*)	Transfer from one job to another job.	Debit Trnsferee Job A/c Credit Transferor Job A/c.

Transaction	Entry
Labour:	
(*i*) Payment of Wages/Outstanding wages	Debit Wages Control Accounts. Credit Gen. Ledger Control Account
(*ii*) Allocation of wages to production (as per Wages Abstract).	Debit Work-in-Progress Control Account Credit Wages Control Account.
(*iii*) Absorption of indirect labour (works overhead)	Debit Works Overhead Control Account Credit Wages Control Account.
Direct Exps:	
(*i*) Charging Direct Exps.	Debit Work-in-Progress Control Account Credit Gen. Ledger Control Account.
Works Overheads:	
(*i*) Works overhead paid or outstanding	Debit Works Overhead Control Account. Credit Gen. Ledger Control Account
(*ii*) Works overhead recovered	Debit Work-in-Progress Control Account. Credit Works Overhead Control Account.
(*iii*) Under absorption of works overhead	Debit Overhead Suspense Account. or Debit Costing P & L Account Credit Works Overhead Control Account
(*iv*) Over absorption of work overhead	Reverse to above entry.
Administration Overheads	
(*i*) Office and Administrative Overhead paid or outstanding	Debit Office and Adm. Overhead Control Account Credit Gen. Ledger Control A/c.
(*ii*) Office and Admn. overhead recovered	Finished Stock Ledger Control A/c. Credit Office and Adm. OH Control Account
(*iii*) Office and Admn. Overhead under recovered	Debit Overhead Suspense Account. or Debit Costing Profit and Loss Account Credit Office and Admn. Overhead Control Account.
(*iv*) Over absorption overheads	Reverse to above entry.
Selling and Destribution Overheads	
(*i*) Overhead paid or outstanding	Debit Selling and Distr. OH Control A/c Credit Gen. Ledger Control Account
(*ii*) Overhead recovered	Debit Cost of Sales Account Credit Selling and Distr. OH Control A/c
(*iii*) Under absorption of overhead	Debit Overhead Suspense Account or Debit Costing Profit & Loss Account Credit Selling & Distr. OH Control A/c
(*iv*) Over absorpton of selling and disribution overheads.	Reverse to above entry.
Normal and Abnormal Wastage:	
(*i*) Normal wastage of stores and normal idle time.	Debit Works Overhead Control Account Credit Stores Ledger Control Account. Credit Wages Control Account.
(*ii*) Abnormal wastage of stores and abnormal idle time.	Debit Costing Profit and Loss Account. Credit Stores Ledger Control Account. Credit Wages Control Account.

Finished Stock, Sale and Profit

(*i*) Cost of production of finished goods.	Debit Finished Stock Ledger Control A/c Credit Works-in-Progress Control Account
(*ii*) Cost of goods sold.	Debit Cost of Sales Account. Credit Finished Stock Ledger Control A/c
(*iii*) Sales	Debit Cost Ledger Control Account Credit Cost of Sales Account
(*iv*) Profit (or Loss) on sales (as per Cost of Sales Account).	Debit Cost of Sales Account Credit Costing Profit and Loss Account.
(*iv*) Final Profit as per Costing P & L Account	Debit Costing of Profit and Loss Account. Credit Gen. Ledger Control Account.

Debit and Credit to Various Control Accounts

On the basis of above entries following are in brief debits and credits of various control accounts.

Name of Account	*Debit side*	*Credit side*
Stores Ledger Control A/c.	(*i*) Materials purchased (as per stores receipt notes). (*ii*) Materials returned (as per stores returned notes).	(*i*) Materials charged to costs (as per stores requisition slips). (*ii*) Materials returned to suppliers (as per purchase return statements).
Wages Control A/c.	(*i*) Gross wages paid or o/s (as per pay roll).	(*i*) Wages charged to costs (as per wages abstract).
Works Overhead Control A/c	(*i*) Works overhead expenses incurred (as per financial books and charged through General Ledger Control A/c.) (*ii*) Indirect materials and indirect labour charged to production.	(*i*) Works overhead expenses charged to costs (WIP) (at pre-determined rates.)
Administration Overhead Control A/c.	(*i*) Administration overhead expenses incurred (as per financial books and charged through General Ledger Control A/c.) (*ii*) Administration department's wages.	(*i*) Administration overhead expenses charged to costs (at predetermined rates.) Through finished stock ledger control A/c.
Distribution Overhead Control A/c.	(*i*) Distribution overhead expenses incurred (as per financial books and charged through General Ledger Control A/c.) (*ii*) Distribution Department's wages.	(*i*) Distribution overhead expenses charged to costs (at pre-determined rates). Through Finished Stock Ledger Control or cost of sales A/c.
Selling Overhead Control A/c	(*i*) Sellng overhead expenses incurred (as per financial books and charged through General Ledger Control A/c.) (*ii*) Selling Department's wages.	(*i*) Selling overhead expenses charged to costs (at pre-determined rates). Through Cost of Sales A/c.

Work-in-progress Ledger Control A/c	(*i*) Amounts credited to stores, wages, and works overhead. (*ii*) Direct expenses charged through General Ledger Control A/c.	(*i*) Transfers to Finished Goods Ledger Control A/c. (as per Finished Production Transferred to finished stock).
Finished Stock Ledger Control A/c.	(*i*) Amount credited to Work-in-progress Control A/c. (*ii*) Administration overhead charged to costs.	(*i*) Transfer to Costs of Sales A/c as per quantities of finished products sold.
Cost of Sales A/c.	(*i*) Amount credited to Finished Goods Ledger Control A/c. (*ii*) Selling and Distribution Overhead charged to costs.	(*i*) Sales value of the finished products sold as per sales register.
Costing Profit and Loss A/c	(*i*) Overhead Control Account under absorption or recovery. (*ii*) Balance transferred to Gen. Ledger Controls A/c.	(*i*) Profit transferred from Cost of Sales Account. (*ii*) Overhead Control Account if over recovery is transferred to Costing P & L A/c.
General Ledger Control or Adjustment Account	(*i*) Selling Price of Finished Goods (*ii*) Balance (closing)	(*i*) Opening balance (*ii*) Stores Ledger Control A/c (Purchase of Materials) (*iii*) Wages Control A/c (Wages paid or outstanding) (*iv*) Works Overhead Control Account (Paid) (*v*) Office and Admn. Overhead Control A/c. (Paid) (*vi*) Selling and Distribution Overhead Control A/c (Paid) (*vii*) Costing P & L A/c (Profit on sales)

Illustration 1: [*Accounting for Materials*]

During the month of January, following transactions regarding materials took place in Hind Co.

	₹.
1. Material Purchased:	
(a) Credit purchases	18,000
(b) Credit purchases for a special job	800
(c) Cash purchases	2,000
2. Returns to suppliers	1,000
3. Direct materials issued to production	12,000
4. Indirect materials issued	1,200
5. Material returned from production to stores	200
6. Material transferred (from Job. No. 1 to Job No. 2)	400

You are required to enter these transactions in the cost books (under cost control accounting system)

Solution:

Cost Books

			₹.	₹.
1.	(*a*) Stores Ledger Control A/c To General Ledger Adjustment A/c (Being Credit Purchases)	Dr.	18,000	18,000
	(*b*) Work-in-Progress Ledger Control A/c To General Ledger Adjustment A/c (Being credit purchases for a special job)	Dr.	800	800
	(*c*) Stores Ledger Control A/c To General ledger Adjustment A/c (Being Cash Purchases)	Dr.	2,000	2,000
2.	General Ledger Adjustment A/c To Stores Ledger Control A/c (Being return of materials to supplier)	Dr.	1,000	1,000
3.	Work-in-progress Ledger Cöntrol A/c To Stores Ledger Control A/c (Being direct material issued to production)	Dr.	12,000	12,000
4.	Works-overhead Control A/c To Stores Ledger Control A/c (Being issue of indirect materials)		1,200	1,200
5.	Stores Ledger Control A/c To Work-in-Progress Ledger Control A/c (Being materials returned from production)	Dr.	200	200
6.	Job No.2 A/c To Job No 1 A/c (Being transfer of materials from Job 1 to Job 2)	Dr.	400	400

Illustration 2 : [*Accounting for Wages*]
Enter the following transactions in cost books (under Cost Control Accounting System):

	₹.
Wages paid to direct labour	4,000
Salaries paid to production staff	525
Salaries paid to administration staff	400
Salaries paid to selling and distribution staff	600
	₹. 5,525

Solution:

Cost Books

		₹.	₹.
Wages Control A/c To General Ledger Control A/c (Being the amount of total wages)	Dr.	5,525	5,525
Work-in-Progress Ledger Control A/c To Wages Control A/c (Being the amount of direct wages)	Dr.	4,000	4,000
Works Overhead Control A/c	Dr.	525	
Administration Overhead Control A/c	Dr.	400	
Selling and Distribution Overhead Control A/c To Wages Control A/c (Being transfer of indirect wages)	Dr.	600	1,525

Illustration 3: [*Accounting for Direct Expenses and Overhead*]
Enter the following transactions in the cost books.

	₹.
1. Direct Expenses	500
2. Analysis of overheads (services by creditors)	
Works Overhead	2,000
Administration Overhead	1,000
Selling and Distribution Overhead	2,000
3. Analysis of petty cash reveals:	
Works Overhead	120
Administration Overhead	10
Selling and Distribution Overhead	70
4. Overhead is absorbed as under:	
Works overhead	1,900
Administration Overhead	1,050
Selling and Distribution Overhead	2,000

Solution:

Cost Books

			₹.	₹.
1.	Works-in-progress Ledger Control A/c	Dr.	500	
	To General Ledger Adjustment A/c			500
	(Being amount of direct expenses)			
2.	Works Overhead Control A/c	Dr.	2,000	
	Administrative Overhead Control A/c	Dr.	1,000	
	Selling and Distribution Overhead Control A/c	Dr.	2,000	
	To General Ledger Adjustment A/c			5,000
	(Being amount of overhead)			
3.	Works Overhead Control A/c	Dr.	120	
	Administrative Overhead Control A/c	Dr.	10	
	Selling and Distribution Overhead Control A/c	Dr.	70	
	To General Ledger Adjustment A/c			200
	(Being amount of overhead as per petty cash)			
4.	Work-in-progress Ledger Control A/c	Dr.	1,900	
	To Works Overhead Control A/c			1,900
	(Being absorption of overhead by production)			
	Finished Goods Ledger Control A/c	Dr.	1,050	
	To Administration Overhead Control A/c			1,050
	(Being administration overhead recovered by finished goods)			
	Cost of Sales A/c	Dr.	2,000	
	To Selling and Distribution Overhead Control A/c			2,000
	(Being selling and distribution overhead recovered)			

Costing Profit and Loss A/c	Dr.	290	
To Works Overhead Control A/c			220
To Selling and Distribution Overhead Control A/c			70
(Being the amount of under absorption transferred to Costing P&L A/c.			
Administrative Overhead Control A/c	Dr.	40	
To Costing Profit & Loss A/c			40
(Being the amount of over absorption transferred to Costing P&L A/c)			

From the above, it will be observed that works overhead and selling and distribution overhead are under recovered and administration overhead is over recovered.

	Overhead incurred	*Overhead absorbed*	*Under Recovery*	*Over Recovery*
Works Overhead	2120	1900	220	—
Administration Overhead	1010	1050	—	40
Selling and Dist. Overhead	2070	2000	70	—

Note: Over recovery or under recovery may be put as balances of Overhead Control Accounts i.e. not transferred to Costing P/L A/c.

Illustration 4: From the following figures, ascertained from Costing Records and Financial Books of a factory, you are required to pass necessary entries in the cost journal (assume that a system of maintaining control accounts prevails in the organisation).

	₹.
Purchases	3,90,000
Carriage Inward	5,850
Stores issued	3,58,800
Productive wages	3,46,320
Unproductive labour	1,21,680
Works on cost	3,48,400
Materials used in repairs	3,120
Cost of completed jobs	12,80,630

Solution:

Cost Journal

		₹.	₹.
Stores Ledger Control A/c	Dr.	3,90,000	
To General Ledger Control A/c			3,90,000
(Being the total amount of purchases as appeared in financial books)			
Stores Ledger Control A/c	Dr.	5,850	
To General Ledger Control A/c			5,850
(Being the amount of carriage inwards as per financial books)			
Work-in-Progress Ledger Control A/c	Dr.	3,58,800	
To Stores Ledger Control A/c			3,58,800
(Being the amount of stores issued as per materials abstract)			
Wages Control A/c	Dr.	4,68,000	
To General Ledger Control A/c			4,68,000
(Being the amount of direct and indirect wages expended)			

		Dr. ₹	Cr. ₹
Work-in-Progress A/c	Dr.	3,46,320	
To Wages Control A/c			3,46,320
(Being the amount of direct wages)			
Works Overheads A/c	Dr.	1,21,680	
To Wages Control A/c			1,21,680
(Being the amount of indirect wages allocated to works overhead)			
Works Overheads A/c	Dr.	3,48,400	
To General Ledger Control A/c			3,48,400
(Being the amount works expenses other than indirect wages as per Financial Books)			
Works Overheads A/c	Dr.	3,120	
To Stores Ledger Control A/c			3,120
(Being the cost of materials used in repairs)			
Finished Goods Ledger Control A/c	Dr.	12,80,630	
To Work-in-Progress Ledger Control A/c			12,80,630
(Being the cost of completed jobs transferred from Work-in-Progress A/c)			

Illustration 5: The balances in Cost Ledger of a manufacturing company on January 1, 2002 were :

	₹.
Stores Ledger Control Account	7,000
Work-in-Progress Ledger Control Account	12,800
Finished Stock Ledger Control Account	2,000
Cost Ledger Control Account[1]	21,800

You are given the following information for the year

Purchases of materials	40,000
Direct factory wages	60,000
Manufacturing expenses	34,600
Selling and distribution expenses	5,400
Materials issued to production	37,200
Manufacturing expenses recovered	34,440
Selling and distribution expenses recovered	5,320
Sales	1,50,000
Stock of material at December 31, 2002	9,800
Stock of finished goods at December 31, 2002	4,700
Work-in-progress at December 31, 2002	14,700

You are required to show the accounts in the Cost Ledger for the year 2002, to prepare the Costing Profit and Loss Account for the year and extract a trial balance.

Solution:

Stores Ledger Control Account

	₹		₹
To Balance b/d	7,000	By Work-in-Progress Ledger Control A/c (issues)	37,200
To Cost Ledger Control A/c (purchases)	40,000	By Balance c/d	9,800
	47,000		47,000

[1]Cost Ledger Control A/c means General Ledger Adjustment or Control A/c.

Manufacturing (Works) Overhead Control Account

	₹		₹
To Cost Ledger Control A/c	34,600	By Work-in-Progress Ledger Control A/c	34,440
		By Balance c/d	160
	34,600		34,600

Work-in-Progress Ledger Control Account

	₹		₹
To Balance b/d	12,800	By Finished Stock Ledger Control A/c	1,29,740
To Cost Ledger Control A/c (wages)	60,000	By Balance c/d	14,700
To Stores Ledger Control A/c (material)	37,200		
To Manufacturing Overhead Control A/c (mfg. exps)	34,440		
	1,44,440		1,44,440

Selling and Distribution Overhead Control Account

	₹		₹
To Cost Ledger Control A/c	5,400	By Cost of Sales A/c	5,320
		By Balance c/d	80
	5,400		5,400

Finished Stock Ledger Control Account

	₹		₹
To Balance b/d	2,000	By Cost of Sales A/c	1,27,040
To Work-in-Progress Ledger Control A/c	1,29,740	By Balance c/d	4,700
	1,31,740		1,31,740

Cost of Sales Account

	₹		₹
To Finished Stock Ledger Control A/c	1,27,040	By Cost Ledger Control A/c (Sales)	1,50,000
To Selling and Distribution Overhead Control A/c	5,320		
To Costing and P&L A/c	17,640		
	1,50,000		1,50,000

Costing Profit and Loss Account

	₹		₹
To Cost Ledger Control A/c	17,640	By Cost of Sales	17,640

Cost Ledger Control Account

	₹		₹
To Cost of Sales A/c	1,50,000	By Balance b/d	21,800
To Balance c/d	29,440	By Stores Ledger Control A/c	40,000
		By Mfg. Overheads Control A/c	34,600
		By Work-in-Progress Ledger Control A/c	60,000
		By Selling and Distribution Overheads Control A/c	5,400
		By Costing Profit and Loss A/c	17,640
	1,79,440		1,79,440

Trial Balance

	Dr. ₹.	Cr. ₹.
Stores Ledger Control A/c	9,800	
Manufacturing Overhead Control A/c	160	
Selling and Distribution Overheads Control A/c	80	
Work-in-Progress Ledger Control A/c	14,700	
Finished Stock Ledger Control Ac/	4,700	
Cost Ledger Control A/c		29,440
	29,440	29,440

Note: (*i*) Cost Ledger Control A/c = General Ledger Adjustment A/c

(*ii*) Balances of Overhead Controls Accounts will be their over or under absorption, these can be transferred to Costing P&L Account.

Illustration 6: The cost ledger of a company showed the following balances as at 1st January 2003.

	₹.	₹.
Stores Ledger Control A/c	1,05,000	
Work-in-progress Account	78,400	
Finished Goods Account	55,800	
Works on Cost Account		1,000
Administration on Cost	600	
Cost Ledger Control Account or General Ledger Adjustment A/c		2,38,800
	2,39,800	2,39,800

Further balances resulting from the operations for the year ended 31st December 2003 were:

	₹.
Stores Purchases	3,60,000
Stores Issued to Production Order	3,93,000
Stores Issued to Works and Repair Order15,000	
Wages	6,15,000
Production Labour	5,90,000
Unproductive Labour	25,000
Carriage Inwards	6,000
Works on Cost Allocated to Production Order	1,79,000
Works Expenses	1,40,000
Administration Expenses	18,000
Administration on Cost Allocation to Production Order	18,400
Goods Finished During the Year	11,72,000

Finished Goods Sold (Cost)	12,00,000
Sales Expenses	13,400

Prepare the necessary accounts in the cost ledger schedule of balances for the year ended 31st December, 2003.

Solution:

Note: It may be noted that

1. Stores Ledger A/c = Stores Ledger Control A/c
2. Work-in-Progress A/c = Work-in-Progress Ledger Control A/c.
3. Finished Goods A/c = Finished Goods Ledger Control A/c.
4. Work on Cost A/c = Works overhead Control A/c.
5. Administration on Cost A/c = Administration Overhead Control A/c
6. Cost Ledger Control A/c = General Ledger Adjustment A/c.
7. Wages A/c = Wages Control A/c.

Stores Ledger Account

	₹		₹
To Balance b/d	1,05,000	By Work-in-Progress A/c	3,93,000
To Cost Ledger Control Accounts (purchases)	3,60,000	By Work on Cost: (Stores issued to works and repair order)	15,000
To Cost Ledger Control A/c (Carriage inwards)	6,000	By Balance c/d	63,000
	4,71,000		4,71,000

Work-in-Progress Accounts

	₹		₹
To Balance b/d	78,400	By Finished Goods A/c	11,53,600
To Store Ledger Account	3,93,000	BY Balance c/d	86,800
To Wages A/c	5,90,000		
To Works on cost A/c	1,79,000		
	12,40,400		12,40,400

Finished Goods Account

	₹		₹
To Balance b/d	55,800	By Cost of Sales A/c	12,000,000
To Work-in-Progress A/c	11,53,600	By Balance c/d	27,800
To Administration on cost A/c	18,400		
	12,27,800		12,27,800

Works on Cost Account

	₹		₹
To Stores Ledger A/c	15,000		
To Wages A/c	25,000	By Work-in-Progress A/c	1,79,000
To Cost Ledger Control Account (expenses)	1,40,000	By Balance b/d	1,000
	1,80,000		1,80,000

Administration on Cost Account

	₹		₹
To Balance b/d	600	By Finished Goods A/c	18,400
To Cost Ledger Control Account (expenses)	18,000	By Balance c/d	200
	18,600		18,600

Wages Account

	₹		₹
To Cost Ledger Control Account	6,15,000	By Work-in-Progress A/c	5,90,000
		By Work on Cost A/c	25,000
	6,15,000		6,15,000

Cost of Sales Account

	₹		₹
To Finished Goods Account	12,00,000	By Cost Ledger Control A/c	12,13,400
To Cost Ledger Control Account (expenses)	13,400		
	12,13,400		12,13,400

Cost Ledger Control Account

	₹		₹
To Cost of Sales A/c	12,13,400	By Balance b/d	2,38,800
To Balance c/d	1,77,800	By Stores A/c (purchases)	3,60,000
		By Wages A/c	6,15,000
		By Stores A/c (Carriage inwards)	6,000
		By Works Expenses A/c	1,40,000
		By Administration Expanses A/c	18,000
		By Sales Expenses A/c	13,400
	13,91,200		13,91,200

Trial Balance as at 31st December, 2002

	₹.	₹.
Stores Ledger Account	63,000	
Work-in-Progress Account	86,800	
Finished Goods Account	27,800	
Administration on Cost Account	200	
Cost Ledger Control Account		1,77,800
	1,77,800	1,77,800

Illustration 7: The Rajasthan Manufacturing Company, commenced operations on 1st April, 2002 and completed the following transactions during the year ended 31st March, 2003.

(*i*) Purchased materials for ₹. 10,40,000.

(*ii*) Requisitioned direct materials totalling ₹. 6,00,000 for job orders.

(*iii*) Requisitioned indirect materials worth ₹. 60,000.

(*iv*) Returned materials worth ₹. 20,000 to the vendors.

(*v*) Returned materials to the stores room: from job orders ₹. 24,000, from indirect materials issued– ₹. 10,000.

(*vi*) Paid for wages ₹. 13,00,000.

(*vii*) Distributed wages as follows: direct labour ₹. 12,84,000; indirect ₹. 16,000.

(*viii*) Recorded additional actual overhead costs of ₹. 5,80,000.

(*xi*) Applied overhead to production at 50% of direct labour cost.

(*x*) Completed jobs during the year costing ₹. 23,00,000.

(*xi*) Sold finished goods as follows: selling price ₹. 37,00,000 cost of finished goods sold ₹. 22,20,000.

(*xii*) Allowed credit for finished goods returned by customers ₹. 30,000. These finished goods cost ₹. 18,000.

(*xiii*) Carried forward to next year the over or under-absorbed overhead.

Show how these transactions will be recorded in the Cost Ledger of the company for the year 2002-03. Also record only transaction (XI) and (XII) in the Cost Journal of the Company.

Solution:

Stores Ledger Control Account

	₹.		₹.
To General Ledger Adjustment A/c	10,40,000	BY Work-in-Progress Ledger Control A/c	6,00,000
To Work-in-Progress Ledger Control A/c	24,000	By Works Overheads Control A/c	60,000
To Works Overheads Control A/c	10,000	By General Ledger Adjustment A/c	20,000
		By Balance c/d	3,94,000
	10,74,000		10,74,000

Wages Control Account

	₹.		₹.
To General Ledger Adjustment A/c	13,00,000	By Work-in-Progress Ledger Control A/c	12,84,000
		By Works Overhead Control A/c	16,000
	13,00,000		13,00,000

Works Overheads Control Account

	₹.		₹.
To Stored Ledger Control A/c	60,000	By Stores Ledger Control A/c	10,000
To General Ledger Adjustment A/c	5,80,000	By Work-in-Progress Ledger Control A/c	6,42,000
To Wages Control A/c	16,000	By Balance c/d	4,000
	6,56,000		6,56,000

Work-in-Progress Ledger Control Account

	₹		₹
To Stores Ledger Control A/c	6,00,000	By Stores Ledger Control A/c	24,000
To Wages Control A/c	12,84,000	By Finished Goods Ledger Control A/c	23,00,000
To Works Overhead Control A/c	6,42,000	By Balance c/d	2,02,000
	25,26,000		25,26,000

Finished Goods Ledger Control Account

	₹		₹
To Work-in-Progress Ledger Control A/c	23,00,000	By Cost of Sales A/c	22,20,000
To Cost of Sales A/c	18,000	By Balance c/d	98,000
	23,18,000		23,18,000

Cost of Sales Account

	₹		₹
To Finished Ledger Control A/c	22,20,000	By General Ledger Adjustment A/c	37,00,000
To General Ledger Adjustment A/c	30,000	By Finished Goods Control A/c	18,000
To Costing Profit and Loss A/c	14,68,000		
	37,18,000		37,18,000

Costing Profit and Loss Account

	₹		₹
To General Ledger Adjustment A/c	14,68,000	By Cost of Sales A/c	14,68,000

General Ledger Adjustment Account

	₹		₹
To Cost of Sales A/c	37,00,000	By Stores Ledger Control A/c	10,40,000
To Stores Ledger Control A/c	20,000	By Wages Control A/c	13,00,000
To Balance c/d	6,98,000	By Works Overheads Control A/c	5,80,000
		By Cost of Sales A/c	30,000
		By Costing Profit and Loss A/c	14,68,000
	44,18,000		44,18,000

Trial Balance
(As at 31st March, 2003)

	Dr. ₹.	*Cr.* ₹.
Stores Ledger Control A/c	3,94,000	
Work-in-Progress Ledger Control A/c	2,02,000	
Finished Goods Ledger Control A/c	98,000	
Works Overhead Control A/c	4,000	
General Ledger Adjustment A/c		6,98,000
	6,98,000	6,98,000

Entries in Cost Journal
(For transactions XI and XII)

		₹.	₹.
General Ledger Adjustment A/c To Cost of Sales A/c (Being amount of sales)	Dr.	37,00,000	37,00,000
Cost of Sales A/c To Finished Goods Ledger Control A/c (Being cost of finished goods sold transferred)	Dr.	22,20,000	22,20,000
Cost of Sales A/c To General Ledger Adjustment A/c (Being cost of returns from customers)	Dr.	30,000	30,000
Finished Goods Ledger Control A/c To Cost of Sales A/c (Being cost of returned goods, transferred)	Dr.	18,000	18,000

Illustration 8: M/s Beta Ltd. uses the perpetual inventory procedure for all inventory accounting. Total debits and credits in certain of their accounts on 31st March, 2004 are given below:

	Total Debits	*Total Credits*
Raw materials	₹. 5,60,000	₹. 4,80,000
Work-in-Progress	16,96,000	14,80,000
Direct labour	6,72,000	6,72,000
Manufacturing Overhead	3,04,000	–
Finished goods	18,72,000	14,56,000
Cost of goods sold	14,56,000	–
Manufacturing Overheads applied	–	3,36,000

The accounts given above did not include the following costs that should be recognised.

Direct labour	₹. 32,000
Indirect labour	2,400
Other manufacturing Overheads	2,880

Raw materials purchased during the year amounted to ₹. 5,20,000. Manufacturing overheads is applied as a percentage of direct labour.

Prepare all the control accounts showing the opening and closing inventories of raw materials, work-in-progress and finished goods, all adjusting and closing entries and appropriating over/under applied overhead among work-in-progress, finished goods and cost of goods sold.

Solution:

Stores Ledger Control Account

2003, April 1		₹	2004		₹
	To Balance c/d (Balancing figure)	40,000	March 31	By Work-in-Progress Ledger Control A/c	4,80,000
	To General Ledger Adjustment A/c (purchases)	5,20,000		By Balance c/d	80,000
		5,60,000			5,60,000

Work-in-progress Ledger Control Account

	₹		₹
2003, April 1		2004, March 31	
To Balance b/d (see Note)	2,08,000	By Finished Goods Ledger Control A/c	14,80,000
To Stores Ledger Control A/c	4,80,000	By Balance c/d	
To Wages Control A/c (672000 + 32000)	7,04,000	(Cost of Work-in-Progress at the end)	2,64,000
To Manufacturing Overheads Control A/c (50% of 7,04,000)	3,52,000		
	17,44,000		17,44,000
2004, March 31	₹	2004, March 31	₹
To Balance c/d	2,64,000	By Overhead Control A/c (See working note 2)	6,467
		By Balance c/d	2,57,533
	2,64,000		2,64,000

Manufacturing Overheads Control Account

	₹		₹
2004, April 1		2004, March 31	
To General Ledger Adjustment A/c	3,04,000	By Work-in-Progress Control A/c	3,52,000
March 31			
To General Ledger Adjustment A/c	5,280		
To Work-in-Progress (2400 + 2880) Control A/c (Working note 3)	6,467		
To Finished Goods Control A/c (Working note 3)	10,190		
To Cost of Goods Sold A/c (See note No. 3)	26,063		
	3,52,000		3,52,000

Finished Goods Ledger Control Account

	₹		₹
2003, April 1		2004, March 31	
To Balance b/d (Balancing figure)	3,92,000	By Cost of Goods Sold	14,56,000
To WIP Ledger Control A/c	14,80,000	By Balance c/d (Stock-in-hand)	4,16,000
	18,72,000		18,72,000
March 31, 2004		2004 March 31	
To Balance b/d	4,16,000	By Manufacturing Overhead A/c (See Note 3)	10,190
		By Balance c/d	4,05,810
	4,16,000		4,16,000

Cost of Goods Sold Account

2004, March	₹.	2004, March 31	₹.
To Finished Goods Ledger Control A/c	14,56,000	By Manufacturing Overheads Control A/c	26,063
		By Costing Profit and Loss A/c	14,29,937
	14,56,000		14,56,000

Note: (1) Total debits in the Work-in-Progress Ledger Control Account are ₹. 16,96,000, without considering the debits arising out of the wages outstanding, the other debits are:

Materials	₹. 4,80,000
Labour	6,72,000
Overheads	3,36,000
	14,88,000

The balance, *i.e.* ₹. 2,08,000 must be the opening balance.

(2) Total wages are ₹. 7,04,000 including ₹. 32,000 outstanding. Manufacturing overhead applied is ₹. 3,36,000 based presumably on ₹. 6,72,000 which works out @ 50%. On this basis the total overhead to be debited to the Work-in-progress Control Account is ₹. 3,52,000, *i.e.* 50% of ₹. 7,04,000.

(3) There is an over-recovery of ₹. 42,720 in case of manufacturing overheads. This is to be apportioned over Work-in-progress, Finished Goods Stock and Cost of Goods Sold. The ratio of these items is as follows:

Work-in-progress	₹. 2,64,000
Finished goods stock	₹, 4,16,000
Cost of goods sold	₹. 10,64,000

(*i.e.* total goods sold ₹. 14,56,000—₹. 3,92,000 opening stock presuming that the goods are sold on FIFO basis).

The amounts are respectively ₹. 6,467; ₹. 10,190 and ₹. 26,063.

TYPICAL ILLUSTRATIONS

Illustration 9: On 31st March, the following balances were extracted from the books of the Supreme Manufacturing Company:

	Dr. ₹.	*Cr.* ₹.
Stores Ledger Control A/c	35,000	
Work-in-Progress Control A/c	38,000	
Finished Goods Control A/c	25,000	
Cost Ledger Control A/c		98,000
	98,000	98,000

The following transactions took place in April:	₹.
Raw Materials:	
Purchased	95,000
Returned to Suppliers	3,000
Issued to Production	98,000
Returned to Stores	3,000
Productive Wages	40,000
Indirect Labour	25,000
Factory Overhead Expenses Incurred	50,000
Selling and Administrative Expenses	40,000
Cost of Finished Goods Transferred to Warehouse	2,13,000
Cost of Goods Sold	2,10,000

Sales 3,00,000

Factory overheads are applied to production at 150% of direct wages, any under/over absorbed overhead being carried forward for adjustment in the subsequent months. All administrative and selling expenses are treated as period costs and charged off to the Profit and Loss Account of the month in which they are incurred.

Show the following Accounts: (*a*) Cost Ledger Control A/c; (*b*) Stores Ledger Control A/c; (*c*) Work in Progress Control A/c; (*d*) Finished Goods Stock Control A/c; (*e*) Factory Overhead Control A/c; (*f*) Costing Profit and Loss A/c; (*g*) Trial Balance as at 30th April.

Solution :

(*a*) Cost Ledger Control A/c

	₹		₹
To Costing Profit & Loss A/c (Sales)	3,00,000	By Balance b/d	98,000
" Stores Ledger Control A/c	3,000	" Stores Ledger Control A/c	95,000
" Balance c/d	95,000	" Wage Control A/c (Productive Wages + Indirect labour)	65,000
		" Factory Overhead Control A/c	50,000
		" Selling & Admn. Overhead Expenses A/c	40,000
		" Costing Profit & Loss A/c	50,000
	3,98,000		3,98,000

(*b*) Stores Ledger Control A/c

	₹		₹
To Balance b/d	35,000	By Cost Ledger Control A/c	3,000
" Cost Ledgey Control A/c	95,000	" Work-in-Progress Control A/c	98,000
" Work-in-Progress Control A/c	3,000	" Balance c/d	32,000
	1,33,000		1,33,000

(*c*) Work-in-Progress Control A/c

	₹		₹
To Balance b/d	38,000	By Stores Ledger Control A/c	3,000
" Stores Ledger Control A/c	98,000	" Finished Goods Control A/c	2,13,000
" Wages Control A/c	40,000	" Balance c/d	20,000
" Factory Overhead Control A/c (15% of Direct Wages)	60,000		
	2,36,000		2,36,000

(*d*) Finished Goods Control A/c

	₹		₹
To Balance b/d	25,000	By Cost of Goods Sold A/c	2,10,000
" Work-in-Progress	2,13,000	By Balance c/d	28,000
	2,38,000		2,38,000

(e) Factory Overhead Control A/c

	₹		₹
To Wages Control A/c (Indirect Labour)	25,000	By Work-in-Progress Control A/c	60,000
" Cost Ledger Control A/c	50,000	" Balance c/d	15,000
	75,000		75,000

(f) Costing Profit and Loss A/c/Cost of Sales A/c

	₹		₹
To Cost of Goods Sold A/c	2,10,000	By Cost Ledger Control A/c (Sales)	3,00,000
" Selling and Admn. Overhead A/c	40,000		
" Cost Ledger Control A/c (Costing profit)	50,000		
	3,00,000		3,00,000

Trial Balance

	Dr. ₹	Cr. ₹
Stores Ledger Control A/c	32,000	
Work-in-Progress Control A/c	20,000	
Finished Goods Control A/c	28,000	
Factory Overhead Control A/c	15,000	
Cost Ledger Control A/c	–	95,000
	95,000	95,000

Working Notes:

(1) Wage Control A/c

	₹		₹
To Cost Ledger Control A/c	65,000	By Work-in-Progress Control A/c	40,000
		" Factory Overhead Control A/c	25,000
	65,000		65,000

Dr. **Cost of Goods Sold A/c**

	₹		₹
To Finished Goods Control A/c	2,10,000	By Costing Profit & Loss A/c	2,10,000
	2,10,000		2,10,000

Dr. **Selling & Administrative Expenses A/c**

	₹		₹
To Cost Ledger Control A/c	40,000	By Costing Profit & Loss A/c	40,000
	40,000		40,000

Illustration 10: A company operates on historic job cost accounting system, which is not integrated with the financial accounts. At the beginning of a month, the opening balances in cost ledger were:

	₹. (in lakhs)
Stores Ledger Control Account	80
Work-in-Progress Control Account	20
Finished Goods Control Account	430
Building Construction Account	10
Cost-Ledger Control Account	540

During the month, the following transactions took place:

Materials	Purchased	40
	Issued to production	50
	Issued to general maintenance	6
	Issued to building construction	4
Wages	Gross wages paid	150
	Indirect wages	40
	For building construction	10
Works Overheads	Actual amount incurred (excluding items shown above)	160
	Absorbed in building construction	20
	Under absorbed	8
Royalty paid		5
Selling, distribution and administration Overheads		25
Sales		450

At the end of the month, the stock of raw material and work-in-progress was ₹. 55 lakhs and ₹. 25 lakhs respectively. The loss arising in the raw material account is treated as factory overheads. The building under construction was completed during the month. Company's gross profit margin is 20% on sales.

Prepare the relevant control accounts to record the above transactions in the cost ledger of the company.

Solution:

Stores Ledger Control Account (SLC)

	₹. (in laksh)		₹. (in laksh)
To Balance b/d	80	By WIP A/c	50
To CLC A/c (purchases)	40	By Admn. Overhead (General Maintenance) A/c	6
		By Building A/c	4
		By Factory Overhead (B/F)	5
		By Balance c/d	55
	120		120

Work-in-Progress Control A/c (WIP)

To Balance b/d	20	By FGC (B/F)	327
To SLC A/c	50	By Balance c/d	25
To Wages Control	100		
To Works Overhead A/c	177		
To CLC A/c (Royalty)	5		
	352		352

Finished Goods Control A/c (FGC)

Particulars	Amount	Particulars	Amount
To Balance b/d	430	By Cost of Sales	360
To WIP (finished goods produced in the month)	327	By Balance c/d	397
	757		757

Building Construction A/c

Particulars	Amount	Particulars	Amount
To Balance b/d	10	By CLC A/c	44
To SLC A/c		4 (Capitalised as Building)	
To Wages Control A/c	10		
To Works Overheads A/c	20		
	44		44

Cost Ledger Control A/c (CLC)

Particulars	Amount	Particulars	Amount
To Building Costn. A/c	44	By Balance b/d	540
To Costing P & L A/c	450	By SLC A/c	40
To Balance c/d	477	By Wages Control A/c	150
		By Work Overhead A/c	160
		By WIP (Royalty) A/c	5
		By SDA Overheads A/c	25
		By Costing P&L A/c (NP)	51
	971		971

Works Overhead A/c

Particulars	Amount	Particulars	Amount
To SLC A/c	5	By Building Construction A/c	20
To Wages Control	40	By WIP (B/F)	177
To CLC A/c	160	By P & L A/c Under Absorption	8
	205		205

Wages Control A/c

Particulars	Amount	Particulars	Amount
To CLC A/c (gross wages)	150	By WIP A/c (Direct wages)	100
		By Factory Overheads A/c (Indirect wages)	40
		By Building Consts A/c	10
	150		150

S & D Admn. Overheads Control A/c (SDA Overheads)

Particulars	Amount	Particulars	Amount
To CLC A/c	25	By Cost of Sales A/c	31
To SLC A/c	6		
	31		31

Cost of Sales A/c

Particulars	Amount	Particulars	Amount
To FGC A/c	360	By CLC A/c - Sales A/c	450
To SDA Overheads A/c	31		
To Costing P/L A/c	59		
	450		450

Costing of P&L A/c

To Works Overhead A/c	8	By Cost of Sales A/c	59
To CLC A/c—Net Profit	51		
	59		59

Trial Balance at the end of the month

	Dr.	Cr.
Stores Ledger Control A/c	55	
Work-in Progress Control A/c	25	
Finished Goods Control A/c	397	
Cost Ledger Control A/c		477
	477	477

Note:

1. Works overhead is underabsorbed by ₹. 8 lakh, since it is a negligible amount, therefore it has been transferred to Costing P&L A/c.
2. Royalty paid on production is transferred to WIP Control A/c (as a direct expenses).
3. Cost of Sales = Sales – GP

   i.e. ₹. 450 – 90 = ₹. 360 lakhs.

QUESTIONS

OBJECTIVE QUESTIONS

I. *True or False Statement. Give reason in brief.*

1. The purpose of cost control accounts is not to control the cost of production.
2. Cost Ledger Control Accounts is a system of integrating cost and financial accounts.
3. Cost control accounts are prepared on the fundamental principles of double entry book keeping.
4. Cost Ledger Adjustment Account represent *inter alia* personal accounts shown in financial books.
5. The balance of Stores Ledger Control Account does not represent the total balance of stock of all items of material.
6. Selling and distribution costs incurred are credited to selling and distribution overhead account.
7. The closing balance of costing Profit and Loss Account represents under or over-absorption of overheads.
8. Overhead Adjustment Account always has debit balance.
9. Cost Ledger Control Accounts always show a credit balance.
10. Cost Ledger Control Account is maintained to make the cost ledger self balancing.
11. Under-absorbed Overhead are always credited to Costing P & L A/c.

    [*Ans.* *False (1) (2) (5) (6) (7) (8) (11) other True*]

II. ***State whether following statements are True or False.***

1. Purpose of cost control is to control production cost.
2. Posting in Wages Control Accounts is done from wages analysis table.
3. Balance of Stores Ledger Control Account show total balance of each type of stock.
4. General Ledger Adjustment account is personal account as shown in the general ledger.
5. Control accounts are complete accounts kept in the costing ledger.

   [**False** *(1) others are correct*]

III. *Fill in the gaps*

1. ....Account makes the cost ledger self balancing.
2. Closing balance of Costing Profit and Loss A/c shows................ .
3. .... is credited from Work-in-progress Account.
4. Purchase for specific jobs are directly debited to .... account.
5. When stores is issued for production,..................Control Account is debited .... Control Account is credited.

[***Ans.*** *(1) General Ledger Adjustment (2) Profit or loss (3) Cost of finished goods (4) Work-in-progress Control (5) Work-in-progress, Stores*]

THEORETICAL QUESTIONS

1. What are `Control Account'? Mention the main control accounts and explain their utility.
2. What are principal and subsidiary books that are kept in costing system under double entry basis? Mention their importance and explain how the subsidiary books are written?
3. What is the purpose of preparing General Ledger Adjustment Account or Cost Ledger Control Account? How are entries recorded in this account?
4. Write short note on `Cost-Ledger Control Account'.
5. `Non-integrated Accounting is one of the system of Cost Control Accounting to keep cost books'. Explain.
6. (*a*) Define the term `Non-Integrated Accounting'

   (*b*) Explain the system of non-integrated accounting and state the principal ledgers that are to be maintained (briefly mention about the contents) and the principal accounts that are to be maintained.

SHORT ANSWER QUESTIONS

1. What do you understand by Cost Control Account?
2. Write names of Control Accounts kept in Cost Ledger.
3. Give an outline of Work-in-progress Ledger Control Account.
4. Write journal entries of following under Cost Control System.

   (*a*) Raw material purchased on credit

   (*b*) Material issued for production (direct)

   (*c*) Material return to supplier.
5. What is purpose of preparing Cost Ledger Control Account?
6. What are advantages of Cost Control Accounts?

NUMERICAL QUESTIONS

1. The following transactions took place for the month of April 2005 in A & Co. Enter the transactions in the cost books pertaining to material.

   (1) Materials Purchase: (*a*) Credit purchases ₹. 3,000, (*b*) Cash purchases ₹. 1,000 (*c*) Credit purchases for a special job ₹. 1,000.

   (2) Returned to suppliers ₹. 250.

   (3) Direct materials issued to jobs ₹. 2,000.

   (4) Indirect materials issued to jobs ₹. 500.

   (5) Materials returned from jobs to stock ₹. 200.

   (6) Materials transferred from Job No. 101 to Job No. 102 ₹. 75.
2. Enter the following transactions of a company for the month of April 2005 pertaining to labour.

	₹.	₹.
(*a*) Wages		12,000
Less: Deduction:		

Employees Provident Fund	800	
State Insurance Premium	400	
Income Tax	240	1,440
Net wages to be paid in cash		10,560

Employers contribution are: Provident Fund ₹ 800 and State Insurance ₹ 200

From the wages analysis books, we found the following details of total wages:

1. Direct labour	8,000	
2. Indirect labour	2,000	
3. Salaries to administrative staff	2,000	
4. Salaries to selling and distribution staff	1,000	
		13,000
(*b*) Direct expenses		4,000

3. Pass journal entries in the financial and cost books from the following information regarding overheads. Prepare statement of recovery of overhead and pass suitable entries for under/over recovery.

			₹
(*i*) (*a*) Outstanding Expenses			6,000
(*b*) Cash expenses			500
Analysis of above	*Outstanding Exps.*	*Cash Exps.*	*Total*
	₹	₹	₹
Factory Overhead	3,000	300	3,300
Admn. Overhead	2,000	100	2,100
Selling and Distribution Overhead	1,000	100	1,100
	6,000	500	6,500

(*ii*) Absorption of Overheads is as under:

(*a*) Factory Overheads	2,800
(*b*) Adm. Overheads	2,000
(*c*) Selling and Distribution Overheads	1,300
	6,100

4. From the following details show the necessary accounts in the cost ledger.

	Opening Balance	Closing Balance
	₹	₹
Materials	8,000	11,000
Work-in-Progress	5,000	9,000
Finished Goods	10,000	12,000
Transaction during the period		
Materials purchased		25,000
Wages paid (including ₹ ,000 indirect wages)		10,000
Overhead incurred (Overhead recovered ₹ 9,000)		8,000
Sales		50,000

[**Ans.** *Direct Materials issued to Production ₹ 22,000; Cost of Completed Work ₹ 35,000; Cost of Goods Sold ₹ 33,000; Profit ₹ 16,000;-Overhead under-recovered ₹ 1000 TR to P/L*]

[**Hints** : *Opening balance of GL Adj A/c. ₹ 23,000, closing balance of GL Adj A/c ₹ 32000. Tatal closing T/B ₹ 32,000*]

5. From the following figures ascertained from the records of a company for the year ended 30th June, 2004 you are required to pass necessary entries and to prepare the Ledger Accounts and the Trial Balance.

	30th June 2003	*30th June 2004*
General Ledger Adj. A/c	3,60,950	—
Work-in-Progress Accounts-balance	1,40,000	89,100
Stock of Finished Goods-balance	1,36,750	1,41,750
Stores on hand balance	84,200	1,31,400
Purchases		4,50,000
Carriage inwards		6,300
Stores issued		4,05,000
Productive wages		3,70,200
Unproductive wages		1,21,600
Works on cost		3,68,400
Material used in repair		4,100
Cost of completed jobs		13,90,000
Cost of finished goods sold		13,85,000
Selling expenses		28,000
Office administration		70,000
Works on cost allocated to Work-in-Progress		4,95,000
Office on cost allocated to Work-in-Progress		68,900

[**Ans.** *Trial Balance Total ₹. 3,63,350; Balances: General Ledger Adj. A/c ₹. 3,62,450 (Cr.); Work-in-Progress ₹. 89,100 (Dr.) Stock of Finished goods ₹. 1,41,750 (Dr.) Stores 1,31,400 (Dr.); Works on cost ₹. 900 (Cr.); Office on cost 1,100 (Dr.)*]

Integrated or Integral Accounts

Integrated (or Integral Accounts) is the name given to a system whereby cost and financial accounts are kept in the same set of books. Obviously then there will be no separate set of books for costing and financial purposes. According to *CIMA*, `It is a system in which the financial and cost accounts are interlocked to ensure that all relevant expenditure is absorbed into the Cost Accounts'. Integrated Accounts will have to afford full information required for costing as well as for financial accounts. In other words, information and data should be recorded in such a way as to enable the firm to ascertain the cost (together with the necessary analysis) of each product, job, process, operation or any other identifiable activity. It should be possible to ascertain marginal cost, variances, abnormal losses and gains; in fact, all information that management requires from a system of costing for doing its work properly. It should also be possible to have accounts to see that the firm maintains full control over its assets and liabilities and to enable the firm to prepare the Profit and Loss Account and the Balance Sheet as required by law or for income-tax purposes at the end of each year.

Usually, financial accounts require expenditure and revenue to be recorded according to its nature rather than the benefit derived from it. Thus all salaries paid are recorded together. But for costing purposes, there must be detailed analysis *functionally*, that is, according to the identifiable unit of cost classification of expenses. Integrated Accounts record transactions so as to be able to collect and analyse information both ways.

While preparing financial accounts, the following points will have to be noted:

(*i*) Items of financial nature, not included in costs, will have to be taken into account for preparing the Profit and Loss Account and the Balance Sheet. Such expenses should, therefore, be recorded separately.

(*ii*) Items which are considered for costing purposes but ignored in financial accounts (e.g., rent for firm's own premises) will have to be similarly recorded separately and not debited to the Profit and Loss Account.

(*iii*) Similar treatment is necessary for abnormal losses and gains—there is no special treatment in the Profit and Loss Account which records actual expenses or losses.

(*iv*) Valuation of both the closing stock of finished goods and work-in-progress usually is different in financial accounts as compared to cost accounts. In costing, finished stock may be valued at full cost of production, that is, including office and administration expenses and work-in-progress is usually valued at works cost. But in financial accounts, finished stock may be valued at works cost and work-in-progress at prime cost. This will have to be considered while preparing the Profit and Loss Account and the Balance Sheet.

Scheme of Making Entries

Since the cost and financial books are not separate, there will be no need for a Cost Ledger Control Account. Entries will be made in the usual way. If the concern is big, a system of self-balancing ledgers should be adopted. In other words, there should be a number of subsidiary ledgers to record information of a particular type. There will then be control accounts in the main ledger. The following are the various subsidiary ledgers and control accounts that may be required:

Subsidiary Ledger	*Control Account*
1. Sales Ledger (for accounts of customers).	Sales Ledger Control Account or Total Debtors Account.
2. Bought Ledger (for accounts of suppliers)	Bought Ledger Control Account or Total Creditors Account.
3. Store Ledger (for accounts relating to individual itmes of materials and stores kept in stock).	Stores Ledger Control Account.
4. Stock Ledger (for accounts relating to individual items of finished goods in stock).	Stock Ledger Control Account.
5. Job Ledger (containing accounts of individual jobs on hand).	Work-in-Progress Account.
6. Expenses Ledger (containing accounts of expenses, kept separately for factory, office and selling expenses)	(*a*) Works Expenses Account (*b*) Office Expenses Account. (*c*) Selling Expenses Account.

Some of the entries to be made in control accounts, if costing and financial books are separate and if they are integrated, are given on next page for illustration.

Third Entry Method

Third entry is a variant of integrated accounts. In this case, in the financial books as ordinarily maintained, an account called Cost Ledger Control Account is debited whenever any expenditure relating to costs is incurred. This debit is in addition to the ordinary and usual accounts to be debited. In respect of Cost Ledger Control Account there will be no double entry. For instance, when wages are paid, the entry will be :

		₹.	₹.
Wages Account	*Dr.*	15,800 (say)	
Cost Ledger Control A/c	*Dr.*	15,800	
To Bank			15,800

Similarly, for depreciation say, ₹. 11,000 of machinery:

		₹.	₹.
Depreciation Account	*Dr.*	11,000	
Cost Ledger Control A/c	*Dr.*	11,000	
To Machinery Account			11,000

Complete analysis is made in a separate ledger, which is called Cost Ledger, of all debits placed to the Cost Ledger Control Account and accounts are constructed in the ledger to show cost of production of various jobs, products, *etc*., but without double entry.

In the financial ledger, the Cost Ledger Control Account is closed by being credited when the various expenses accounts are transferred to the Profit and Loss Account at the end of the year.

Journal Entries For Integrated Accounts

In the following *Table* entries under Cost Control System and Integral System both have been given for comparative study.

Journal Entries

Transaction	*Non-Integral System (Cost Control)*		*Integral System (Inter-locking)*
	Financial Books	*Cost Book*	
1. Credit purchase of materials	Purchases (or stores) A/c ... *Dr.* To Sundry Creditors A/c (or Account payable)	Stores (or materials) Control or Stores Ledger Control A/c ... *Dr.* To Cost Ledger Control or General Ledger Adjustment A/c	Stores (or materials) Control A/c ... *Dr.* To Creditors A/c or Bought Ledger Control A/c
2. Cash purchase of materials	Purchases A/c ... *Dr.* To Cash	–do–	Stores Ledger Control A/c ... *Dr.* To Cash
3. Purchase of material for a specified job	Purchase A/c ... *Dr.* To Sundry Creditors or Cash	Work-in-Progress Ledger Control A/c ... *Dr.* To Cost Ledger Control or General Ledger Adjustment A/c	Work-in-Progress Ledger Control A/c ... *Dr.* To Creditors or Cash
4. Materials purchased for repairs	–do–	Works Overhead Control A/c ... *Dr.* To Cost Ledger or Gen. Ledger Adjustment A/c	Work Overhead Control A/c ... *Dr.* To Creditors or Cash
5. Materials returned to suppliers	Sundry Creditors A/c ... *Dr.* To Purchases	Cost Ledger or Gen. Ledger Adjustment A/c ... *Dr.* To Stores Control A/c	Sundry Creditors A/c ... *Dr.* To Stores Ledger Control A/c
6. Payment to creditors	Sundry Creditors A/c ... *Dr.* To Cash	No entry	Creditors A/c ... *Dr.* To Cash
7. Issue of direct material for production	No entry	Work-in-Progress Ledger Control A/c To Stores Ledger Control A/c	Work-in-Progress Ledger Control A/c ... *Dr.* To Stores Ledger Control A/c
8. Issue of indirect material	No entry	Work Overhead Control A/c ... *Dr.* To Stores Ledger Control A/c	Works Overhead Control ... *Dr.* To Stores Ledger Control A/c
9. Return of direct material to stores	No entry	Stores Ledger Control A/c ... *Dr.* To Work-in-Progress Ledger Control A/c	Stores Ledger Control A/c. ... *Dr.* To Work-in-Progress Ledger Control A/c
10. Return of indirect material to stores	No entry	Stores Ledger Control A/c ... *Dr.* To Works Overhead Control A/c	Stores Ledger Control A/c ... *Dr.* To Works Overhead Control A/c

11. Payment of wages	Wage/Payroll A/c To Tax To Provident Fund To Wages payable (for unpaid wages) To Cash	Wages Control A/c To Cost Ledger Control or Gen. Ledger Adjustment A/c	Wages Control A/c ... *Dr*. To Insurance To Provident Fund To Wages Payable (for unpaid wages) To Tax To Cash
12. Allocation and distribution of wages	No entry	Work-in-Progress Ledger Control (for direct labour) A/c ... *Dr*. Works Overhead Control (for indirect labour) A/c ... *Dr*. Administration Overhead Control (for office salary) A/c ... *Dr*. Selling & Distribution Overhead Control (for sales staff salaries) A/c ... *Dr*. To Wages Control A/c	Work-in-Progress Ledger Control A/c ... *Dr*. Works Overhead Control A/c ... *Dr*. Administration Overhead Control A/c ... *Dr*. Selling & Distribution Overhead Control A/c ...*Dr*. To Wages Control A/c
13. Payment of expenses like rent, fuel, repairs	Expenses A/c ... Dr. To Sundry Creditors To Cash	Works Overhead Control ... *Dr*. Administration Overhead Control A/c ... *Dr*. Selling and Distribution Overhead Control A/c. ... *Dr*. To Cost Ledger Control A/c or Gen. Ledger Adj. A/c	Overhead Control (Factory, Administration or Selling and Distribution) A/c ... *Dr*. To Creditors To Cash
14. Depreciation charged	Depreciation A/c ... Dr. To Capital Assets	Works Overhead Control A/c ... *Dr*. Administration Overhead Control A/c ... *Dr*. Selling and Distribution Overhead Control A/c ... *Dr*. To Cost Ledger Control A/c or Gen. Ledger Adj. A/c	Works Overhead Control A/c ... *Dr*. Administration Overhead Control A/c Selling and Distribution Overhead Control A/c ... *Dr*. To Capital Assets.
15. Recovery of works overhead predetermined rate	No entry	Work-in-Progress Control A/c ... *Dr*. To Works Overhead Control (departmentwise) A/c	Work-in-Progress Ledger Control A/c ... *Dr*. To Factory Overhead Control A/c
16. Finishing goods transferred from Work-in-Progress A/c	No entry	Finished Goods Control or Finished Goods Ledger Control A/c *Dr*. To Work in Progress Ledger Control A/c	Finished Goods Control A/c *Dr*. To Work in-Progress Ledger Control A/c

17. Cost of Goods sold	No entry	Cost of Sales (or Cost of Goods sold) A/c ... *Dr.* To Finished Goods (at cost) Costing Profit and Loss A/c ... Dr. To Cost of Sales (at cost)	Cost of Sales A/c ... *Dr.* To Finished Goods (at cost) A/c Profit and Loss A/c ... *Dr.* To Cost of Sales A/c
18. Sales	Debtors (or Cash for Cash Sales, or Accounts Receivable) A/c ... *Dr* To Sales	Cost Ledger Control or Gen. Ledger Adj. A/c ...*Dr.* To Cost of Good Sold A/c (Sales price)	Debtors or Cash (Sales Price) A/c ... *Dr.* To Sales (Sales Price)
19. Allocation of administration overhead	No entry	Finished Goods Control A/c ... *Dr.* To Administration Overhead Control A/c	Finished Goods Control A/c ... *Dr.* To Administration Overhead Control A/c
20. Allocation of selling and distribution Overheads	No entry	Cost of sales A/c ... *Dr.* To Selling and Distribution Overhead Control A/c	Cost of sales A/c ... *Dr.* To Selling and Distribution Overhead Control A/c

Illustration 1: Journalise the following transactions assuming that cost and financial accounts are integrated:

	₹.
Raw materials purchased	1,50,000
Direct materials issued to production	1,12,500
Wages paid (30% Indirect)	90,000
Wages charged to production	75,000
Manufacturing expenses incurred	63,000
Manufacturing overhead charged to production	69,000
Selling and Distributive costs	15,000
Finished Product at cost	1,50,000
Sales	2,25,000
Receipts from customers	52,500
Paid to creditors	82,500
Closing Stock	Nil

Solution:

Journal Entries

		₹.	₹.
Stores Ledger Control A/c	...Dr.	1,50,000	
To Creditors A/c			1,50,000
(Being raw materials bought)			
Work-in-Progress Ledger Control A/c	...Dr.	1,12,500	
To Stores Ledger Control A/c			1,12,500
(Being materials issued for production)			
Wages Control A/c	... Dr.	63,000	
Factory Overhead Control A/c	... Dr.	27,000	
To Bank A/c			90,000
(Being wages paid)			

Particulars		Dr.	Cr.
Work-in-Progress Ledger Control A/c	... Dr.	75,000	
To Wages Control A/c			52,500
To Factory Overhead Control A/c			22,500
(Being the allocation of wages to production)			
Factory Overhead Control A/c	... Dr.	63,000	
To Bank A/c			63,000
(Being the manufacturing expenses incurred)			
Work-in-Progress Ledger Control A/c	... Dr.	69,000	
To Factory Overhead Control A/c			69,000
(Being overheads charged to production)			
Selling and Distributive Overhead Control A/c	... Dr.	15,000	
To Bank A/c			15,000
(Being selling and distributive cost incurred)			
Finished Stocks Control A/c	... Dr.	1,50,000	
To Work-in-Progress Ledger Control A/c			1,50,000
(Being cost of production of completed jobs)			
Cost of Sales A/c	... Dr.	1,65,000	
To Finished Stock Ledger Control A/c			1,50,000
To Selling and Distributive Overhead Control A/c			15,000
(Being the cost of products sold)			
Sales Ledger Control A/c / Debtors A/c	... Dr.	2,25,000	
To Sales			2,25,000
(Being the amount of sales)			
Bank A/c	... Dr.	52,500	
To Sales Ledger Control A/c / Debtors A/c			52,500
(Being amount received from customers)			
Creditors A/c	... Dr.	82,500	
To Bank A/c			82,500
(Being amount paid to creditors)			

Illustration 2: Messers. Essbee Ltd., maintain integrated accounts of cost and financial accounts. From the following details write up control accounts in the general ledger of the factory and prepare a trial balance.

	₹.
Share Capital	3,00,000
Reserve	2,00,000
Sundry Creditors	5,00,000
Plant and Machinery	5,75,000
Sundry Debtors	2,00,000
Closing stock (Raw Material)	1,50,000
Bank and cash balance	75,000
Transactions during the year were as follows:	
Stores purchased	10,00,000
Stores issued to production	10,50,000
Stores in hand	95,000
Direct wages incurred	6,50,000
Direct wages charged to production	6,00,000

Manufacturing expenses incurred	3,00,000
Manufacturing expenses charged to production	2,75,000
Selling and distribution expenses	1,00,000
Finished stock production (at cost)	18,00,000
Sales at selling price	22,00,000
Closing stock	95,000
Payments to creditors	11,00,000
Receipts from debtors	21,00,000

Solution:

General Ledger of M/s Essbee Ltd.

Share Capital A/c

	₹		₹
To Balance c/d	3,00,000	By Balance b/d	3,00,000

Reserve A/c

	₹		₹
To Balance c/d	2,00,000	By Balance b/d	2,00,000

Sundry Creditors A/c

	₹		₹
To Bank A/c	11,00,000	By Balace b/d	5,00,000
To Balance c/d	4,00,000	By Stores Ledger Control A/c	10,00,000
	15,00,000		15,00,000

Plant & Machinery A/c

	₹		₹
To Balance b/d	5,75,000	By Balance c/d	5,75,000

Sundry Debtors A/c

	₹		₹
To Bank b/d	2,00,000	By Bank A/c	21,00,000
To Sales A/c	22,00,000	By Balance c/d	3,00,000
	24,00,000		24,00,000

Bank and Cash A/c

	₹		₹
To Balance b/d	75,000	By Wages Control	6,50,000
To Sundry Debtors A/c	21,00,000	By Manufacturing Overhead Control A/c	3,00,000
		By Selling and Distribution Overhead Control A/c	1,00,000
		By Sundry Creditors	11,00,000
		By Balance c/d	25,000
	21,75,000		21,75,000

Stores Ledger Control A/c

	₹		₹
To Balance b/d	1,50,000	By Work-in-Progress A/c	10,50,000
To Sundry Creditors	10,00,000	By Inventory Adjustment A/c	5,000
		By Balance c/d	95,000
	11,50,000		11,50,000

Wages Control A/c

	₹		₹
To Bank A/c	6,50,000	By Work-in-Progress A/c	6,00,000
		By Balance c/d (Advance wages)	50,000
	6,50,000		6,50,000

Manufacturing Overhead Control A/c

	₹		₹
To Bank A/c	3,00,000	By Work-in-Progress A/c	2,75,000
		By Balance c/d	25,000
	3,00,000		3,00,000

Work-in-Progress A/c

	₹		₹
To Stores ledger control A/c	10,50,000	By Finished Stock Control A/c	18,00,000
To Wages Control A/c	6,00,000	By Balance c/d	1,25,000
To Manufacturing Overhead Control A/c	2,75,000		
	19,25,000		19,25,000

Selling and Distribution Overhead Control A/c

	₹		₹
To Bank A/c	1,00,000	By Cost of Sales A/c	1,00,000
	1,00,000		1,00,000

Finished Stock Control A/c

	₹		₹
To Work-in-Progress A/c	18,00,000	By Cost of Sales A/c	18,00,000

Cost of Sales A/c

	₹		₹
To Finished Stock Control A/c	18,00,000	By Sales A/c	22,00,000
To Selling & Distribution Overhead Control A/c	1,00,000		
To Costing P/L A/c	3,00,000		
	22,00,000		22,00,000

Sales A/c

	₹		₹
To Cost of Sales A/c	22,00,000	By Sundry Debtors A/c	22,00,000
	22,00,000		22,00,000

Inventory Adjustment A/c

	₹		₹
To Stores ledger control A/c	5,000	By P/L A/c	5,000
	5,000		5,000

Trial Balance

	Dr. ₹	Cr. ₹
Share Capital A/c		3,00,000
Reserve A/c		2,00,000
Sundry Creditors A/c		4,00,000
Plant and Machinery A/c	5,75,000	
Suntry Debtors A/c	3,00,000	
Bank and Cash a/c	25,000	
Stores Ledger Control A/c	95,000	
Wages Control A/c (Advance wages)	50,000	
Manufacturing Overhead Control A/c	25,000	
Work-in-Progress A/c	1,25,000	
Costing P/L A/c		2,95,000
Total	11,95,000	11,95,000

Illustration 3: BPR Limited keeps books on integrated accounting system. The following balance appear in the books as on April 1, 2002:

	Dr. ₹	Cr. ₹
Stores Ledger Control A/c	40,950	–
Work-in-Progress A/c	38,675	–
Finished Goods A/c	52,325	–
Bank A/c	–	22,750
Creditors A/c	–	18,200
Fixed Assets A/c	1,47,875	–
Debtors A/c	27,300	–
Share Capital A/c	–	1,82,000
Provision for Depreciation A/c	–	11,375
Provision for Doubtful Debts A/c	–	3,725
Factory Overheads Outstanding A/c	–	6,250
Pre-Paid Administration Overheads A/c	9,975	–
Profit & Loss A/c	–	72,800
	3,17,100	3,17,100

The transactions for the year ended March 31, 2003, were as given below:

	₹.	₹.
Direct Wages	1,97,925	
Indirect Wages	11,375	2,09,300
Purchase of materials (on credit)		2,27,500
Materials issued to production		2,50,250
Materials issued for repairs		4,550
Goods finished during the year (at cost)		4,89,125
Credit Sales		6,82,500
Cost of Goods sold		5,00,500
Production Overheads absorbed		1,09,200
Production Overheads paid during the year		91,000
Production Overheads outstanding at the end of year		7,775
Administration Overheads paid during the year		27,300
Selling Overheads incurred		31,850
Payment to Creditors		2,29,775
Payment received from Debtors		6,59,750
Depreciation of Machinery		14,789
Administration Overheads outstanding at the end of year		2,225
Provision for doubtful debts at the end of the year		4,590

Required:

Write up accounts in the integrated ledger of BPR Limited and prepare a Trial balance.

[*C.A PE II Nov. 2003*]

Solution:

Stores Control A/c

Dr.	₹		Cr. ₹
To Balance b/d	40,950	By WIP A/c	2,50,250
To Creditors A/c	2,27,500	By Production Overheads A/c	4,550
		By Balance c/d	13,650
	2,68,450		2,68,450

Wages Control A/c

Dr.	₹		Cr. ₹
To Bank	1,97,925	By Work-in-Progress A/c	1,97,925
To Bank	11,375	By Production Overheads A/c	11,375
	2,09,300		2,09,300

Work-in-Progress A/c

Dr.	₹		Cr. ₹
To Balance b/d	38,675	By Finished Goods A/c	4,89,125
To Wages Control A/c	1,97,925	By Balance c/d	1,06,925
To Stores Control A/c	2,50,250		
To Production Overheads A/c	1,09,200		
	5,96,050		5,96,050

Production Overheads A/c

Dr.	₹	Cr.	₹
To Wages Control A/c	11,375	By WIP A/c	1,09,200
To Stores Control A/c	4,550	By Profit & Loss A/c	
To Bank (91,000 – 6,250)	84,750	(Under-absorbed overheads written off)	14,039
To Production Overheads outstanding	7,775		
To Provision for depreciation	14,789		
	1,23,239		1,23,239

Finished Goods A/c

Dr.	₹	Cr.	₹
To Balance b/d	52,325	By Cost of sales A/c	5,00,500
To Work-in-Progress A/c	4,89,125	By Balance c/d	80,450
To Admn. Overheads A/c	39,500		
	5,80,950		5,80,950

Administration Overheads A/c

Dr.	₹	Cr.	₹
To Pre-paid Admn. Overheads A/c	9,975	By Finished Goods A/c	39,500
To Bank	27,300		
To Admn. Overheads Outstanding	2,225		
	39,500		39,500

Cost of Sales A/c

Dr.	₹	Cr.	₹
To Finished Goods A/c	5,00,500	By Sales A/c	5,32,350
To Selling Overheads	31,850		
	5,32,350		5,32,350

Sales A/c

Dr.	₹	Cr.	₹
To Cost of Sales A/c	5,32,350	By Debtors A/c	6,82,500
To Profit & Loss A/c	1,50,150		
	6,82,500		6,82,500

Factory Overheads / Production Overheads Oustanding A/c

Dr.	₹	Cr.	₹
To Bank	6,250	By Balance b/d	6,250
To Balance c/d	7,775	By Production Overheads	7,775
	14,025		14,025

Prepaid Administration Overhead A/c

Dr.	₹	Cr.	₹
To Balance	9,975	By Admn. Overheads A/c	9,975
	9,975		9,975

Provision for Depreciation A/c

Dr.	₹		Cr. ₹
To Balance c/d	26,164	By Balance b/d	11,375
		By Production Overheads A/c	14,789
	26,164		26,164

Provision for Doubtful Debts A/c

Dr.	₹		Cr. ₹
To Balance c/d	4,590	By Balance b/d	3,725
		By Profit & Loss A/c	865
	4,590		4,590

Profit & Loss A/c

Dr.	₹		Cr. ₹
To Provison for doubtful debts	865	By Balance b/d	72,800
To Production Overheads	14,039	By Sales A/c	1,50,150
To Balance c/d	2,08,046		
	2,22,950		2,22,950

Debtors A/c

Dr.	₹		Cr. ₹
To Balance b/d	27,300	By Bank A/c	6,59,750
To Sales A/c	6,82,500	By Balance c/d	50,050
	7,09,800		7,09,800

Creditors A/c

Dr.	₹		Cr. ₹
To Bank	2,29,775	By Balance b/d	18,200
To Balance c/d	15,925	By Stores Control A/c	2,27,500
	2,45,700		2,45,700

Fixed Assets A/c

Dr.	₹		Cr. ₹
To Balance b/d	1,47,875	By Balance c/d	1,47,875
	1,47,875		1,47,875

Bank A/c

Dr.	₹		Cr. ₹
To Debtors A/c	6,59,750	By Balance b/d	22,750
		By Direct Wages	1,97,925
		By Indirect Wages	11,375
		By Production Overheads (₹. 84,750 + ₹. 6,250)	91,000
		By Admn. Overheads A/c	27,300
		By Selling Overheads A/c	31,850
		By Creditors A/c	2,29,775
		By Balance c/d	47,775
	6,59,750		6,59,750

Trial Balance As on March 31, 2003

	Dr. ₹.	Cr. ₹.
Stores Control A/c	13,650	–
Work in Progress A/c	1,06,925	–
Finished goods A/c	80,450	
Bank A/c	47,775	
Creditors A/c		15,925
Fixed Assets A/c	1,47,875	
Debtors A/c	50,050	
Share Capital A/c		1,82,000
Provision for Depreciation A/c		26,164
Profit & Loss A/c		2,08,046
Production Overheads Outstanding A/c		7,775
Outstanding Administrative Overheads A/c		2,225
Provision for Doubtful Debts A/c		4,590
	4,46,725	4,46,725

Illustration 4: In the absence of the Chief Accountant, you have been asked to prepare a month's cost accounts for a company which operates a batch costing system fully integrated with the financial accounts. The following relevant information is provided to you :

	₹.	₹.
Balance at the beginning of the month:		
Stores Ledger Control Account		25,000
Work-in-Progress Control Account		20,000
Finished Good Control Account		35,000
Prepaid Production Overheads brought forward from previous month		3,000
Materials Purchased		75,000
Materials Issued:		
To Production	30,000	
To Factory Maintenance	4,000	34,000
Materials transferred between batches		5,000
Total wages paid		
To Direct workers	25,000	
To Indirect workers	5,000	30,000
Direct wages charged to batches		20,000
Recorded non-productive time of direct workers		5,000
Selling and Distribution Overheads Incurred		6,000
Other Production Overhead Incurred		12,000
Sales		1,00,000
Cost of Finished goods sold		80,000
Cost of Goods completed and transferred into fiished goods during the month		65,000
Physical value of work-in-progress at the end of the month		40,000

The production overhead absorption rate is 150% of direct wages charged to work-in-progress.

Required: Prepare the following accounts for the month: (*a*) Stores Ledger Control Account. (*b*) Work-in-Progress Control Account (*c*) Finished Goods Control Account. (*d*) Production Overhead Control Account (*e*) Profit and Loss Account.

Solution:

(*a*) Stores Ledger Control (SLC) Account

	₹		₹
To Balance b/d	25,000	By WIP A/c	30,000
To Bank/Creditors (purchases)	75,000	" POH A/c	4,000
		" Balance c/d	66,000
	1,00,000		1,00,000

(*b*) Work-in-Progress (WIP) Control A/c

	₹		₹
To Balance b/d	20,000	By FGC A/c	
65,000			
" SLC A/c	30,000	" Balance c/d	40,000
" P&L A/c (excess physical value)	5,000		
" Wages control A/c	20,000		
" POH. A/c	30,000		
	1,05,000		1,05,000

(*c*) Finished Goods Control (FGC) Account

	₹		₹
To Balance c/d	35,000	By COS A/c	
80,000			
W. I. P. A/c	65,000	" Balance c/d	20,000
	1,00,000		1,00,000

(*d*) Production Overheads Control (POH) Account

	₹		₹
To Balance b/d (Prepaid)	3,000	By WIP A/c	
" SLC	4,000	150% of Direct wages	30,000
" Wages Control A/c (5,000 + 5,000)	10,000		
" Bank A/c	12,000		
" P & L A/c (Over absorption)	1,000		
	30,000		30,000

Cost of Sales (COS) Account

	₹		₹
To FGC A/c	80,000	By P & L A/c	86,000
" S&D Overheads	6,000		
	86,000		86,000

(*e*) P & L Account

	₹		₹
To COS. A/c	86,000	By Sales	1,00,000
" Profit c/d to B/S	20,000	" POH. A/c (Overhead absorption)	1,000
		" WIP A/c	5,000
	1,06,000		1,06,000

Wages Control Account

	₹.		₹.
To Bank	30,000	By WIP A/c (Direct wages)	20,000
		" POH A/c (non-productive time)	5,000
		" POH A/c (indirect workers)	5,000
	30,000		30,000

S & D Overhead Account

	₹.		₹.
To Bank A/c	6,000	By COS A/c	6,000

Illustration 5: Dutta Enterprises operates an integral system of accounting. You are required to pass the Journal Entries for the following transactions that took place for the year ended 30-6-2004. (Narrations are not required)

	₹.
Raw Materials Purchased (50% on credit)	6,00,000
Materials Issued to Production	4,00,000
Wages Paid (50% Direct)	2,00,000
Wages Charged to Production	1,00,000
Factory Overheads Incurred	80,000
Factory Overheads Charged to Production	1,00,000
Selling and Distribution Overheads Incurred	40,000
Finished Goods at Cost	5,00,000
Sales (50% Credit)	7,50,000
Closing Stock	Nil
Receipts from Debtors	2,00,000
Payment to Creditors	2,00,000

Solution:

Journal Entries

		₹.	₹.
1. (*a*) Stores Ledger Control A/c	*Dr*	6,00,000	
To Sundry Creditors A/c			3,00,000
To Cash or Bank A/c			3,00,000
(*b*) WIP Control A/c	*Dr.*	4,00,000	
To Stores Ledger Control A/c			4,00,000
2. (*a*) Wages Control A/c	*Dr.*	2,00,000	
To Cash or Bank A/c			2,00,000
(*b*) WIP Contol A/c	*Dr.*	1,00,000	
Factory Overhead Control A/c	*Dr.*	1,00,000	
To Wages Control A/c			2,00,000
3.(*a*) Factory Overheads Control A/c	*Dr.*	80,000	
To Cash or Bank A/c			80,000
(*b*) WIP Control A/c	*Dr.*	1,00,000	
To Factory Overhead Control A/c			1,00,000
4.(*a*) S. & D Overheads Control A/c	*Dr.*	40,000	
To Cash or Bank A/c			40,000

5.(a)	Finished Goods Control A/c	Dr.	5,00,000	
	To WIP Control A/c			5,00,000
(b)	Cost of Sales A/c	Dr.	5,40,000	
	To Finished Goods Control A/c			5,00,000
	To S & D Overheads Control A/c			40,000
6.	Sundry Debtors A/c	Dr.	3,75,000	
	Cash or Bank A/c	Dr.	3,75,000	
	To Sales A/c			7,50,000
7.	Cash or Bank A/c	Dr.	2,00,000	
	To Sundry Debtors A/c			2,00,000
8.	Sundry Creditors A/c	Dr.	2,00,000	
	To Cash or Bank A/c			2,00,000

Illustration 6: The following incomplete accounts are furnished to you for the month ended 31st October 2004.

Stores Control Account

1.10.04 To Balance	54,000		

Work-in-Progress Control Account

1.10.04 To Balance	6,000		

Finished Goods Control Account

1.10.04 To Balance	75,000		

Factory Overheads Control Account

1.10.04 To Total debits for October	45,000		

Factory Overheads Applied Account

Cost of Goods Sold Account

Creditors for Purchases Account

		1.10.04 To Balance	30,000

Additional information

(*i*) The factory overheads are applied by using a budgeted rate based on Direct Labour Hours. The budget for overheads for 2004 is ₹. 6,75,000 and the budget of direct labour hours is 4,50,000.

(*ii*) The balance in the account of creditors for purchases on 31.10.04 is ₹. 15,000 and the payments made to creditors in October, 2004 amount to ₹. 1,05,000.

(*iii*) The finished goods inventory as on 31st October, 2004 is ₹. 66,000.

(*iv*) The cost of goods sold during the month was ₹. 1,95,000.

(*v*) On 31st October, 2004, there was only one unfinished job in the factory. The cost records show that ₹. 3,000 (1,200 direct labour hours) of Direct Labour Cost and ₹. 6,000 of Direct Material Cost had been charged.

(*vi*) A total of 28,200 direct labour hours were worked in October, 2004. All factory workers earn same rate of pay.

(*vii*) All actual factory overheads incurred in October, 2004 have been posted.

You are required to find:

(*a*) Materials purchased during October, 2004.

(*b*) Cost of goods completed in October, 2004.

(*c*) Overheads applied to production in October, 2004.

(*d*) Balance of work-in-progress on 31st October, 2004.

(*e*) Direct materials consumed during October, 2004.

(*f*) Balance of Stores Control Account on 31st October, 2004.

(*g*) Overabsorbed or underabsorbed overheads for October, 2004. **[*C.A. Inter*]**

Solution: *Working Notes*:

(*i*) **Overhead Recovery Rate per Direct Labour Hour**

Budgeted factory overheads ₹. 6,75,000

Budgeted direct labour hours ₹. 4,50,000

$$\text{Overhead recovery rate} = \frac{\text{Budgeted factory overheads}}{\text{Budgeted direct labour hours}}$$

$$= ₹.\frac{6,75,000}{4,50,000} = ₹.1.50 \text{ per DLH}$$

(*ii*) **Direct Wage Rate Per Hour**

Direct Labour Cost WIP (on 31st October) ₹. 3,000

Direct labour hours of WIP 1200 hours

$$\text{Direct Wage rate per hour} = \frac{\text{Direct Labour Cost on WIP}}{\text{Direct Labour hours on WIP}}$$

$$= \frac{3,000}{1,200} = ₹.2.50$$

(*iii*) **Total Direct Wages Charged to Production**

Total direct labour hours spent on production × Direct wages rate per hour

= 28,200 hours × ₹. 2.50 = ₹. 70,500.

	₹.
(*a*) *Payment made to creditors*	1,05,000
Add: Closing balance in the account of Creditors for purchase (on 31.10.2004)	15,000
	1,20,000
Less: Opening balance (on 1.10.2004)	30,000
Material purchased during Oct. 2004	90,000
(*b*) *The cost of goods sold during the month*	1,95,000
Add: Closing finished goods inventory	66,000
	2,61,000
Less: Opening finished goods inventory	75,000
Cost of goods completed in Oct. 04	1,86,000

(*c*) *Overhead applied to production in* October, 2004

= 28,200 hours × ₹. 1.50 = ₹. 42,300

(*d*) Balance of Work-in-progress on 31st October, 2004

	₹.
Direct material cost	6,000
Direct labour cost	3,000
Overhead (1200 hours × ₹. 1.50)	1,800
	10,800

(e) Work-in-progress Control A/c

	₹		₹
To Opening Balance	6,000	By Finished goods	1,86,000
To Direct Wages	70,500	By Balance of WIP	10,800
To Factory Overheads	42,300		
To Material consumed (Balancing figure)	78,000		
	1,96,800		1,96,800

(f) Stores Control Account

	₹		₹
To Balance	54,000	By W.I.P. Control A/c	78,000
To Creditors A/c for materials purchased	90,000	By Balance c/d	66,000
	1,44,000		1,44,000

(g) Factory Overhead Account

	₹		₹
To General Ledger Adj. A/c (Total debits for Oct. 1994)	45,000	By Factory Overhead applied	42,300
		By Balance (Under-absorbed)	2,700
	45,000		45,000

QUESTIONS

OBJECTIVE QUESTIONS

I. *State whether following statements are True or False.*

1. Cost and financial books need not be reconciled under system of non-integral account.
2. Cost and financial accounts can be integrated by third Entry method.
3. Integral accounts eliminate the necessity of operating cost ledger accounts.
4. In integrated accounts no entry is passed for using material to production by stores department.
5. Under integral system no accounts are opened for debtors and creditors.
6. Integration of cost and financial accounts avoid duplication of accounting work.

II. *State whether following statements are True or False.*

1. There is no need of General Ledger Control Account in integrated accounting.
2. There are no debtors and creditors accounts in the integral accounting.
3. Profit or loss on sale of asset is not included in integral accounting.
4. There is only one amount of profit in integral accounting.
5. There is no need of reconcilliation of profit in integral accounting.

[**Ans.** *False (2) (3) other are true*]

SHORT ANSWER QUESTIONS

1. What do you understand by integrated accounts' ?
2. What are advantages of integral account system ?
3. What control accounts are opened in integrated general ledger under integrated accounting system.
4. Write entries of following under integral accounts.
   (*i*) Materials purchased on credit (*ii*) Material purchased for a specific job.
   (*iii*) Materials returned to suppliars.

THEORETICAL QUESTIONS

1. What do you understand by `Integrated Accounts' and what are the principles involved? State the advantages of integrated accounts.

2. What is Integrated Accounting. State its advantages.
3. List down any four advantages of Integral System of Accounts.
4. Write short notes on `Integrated Accounting'.
5. State the essential pre-requisites of Integrated Accounting System.
6. Define Integrated Accounting System and briefly explain the same highlighting the advantages of the system.

NUMERICAL QUESTIONS

1. Journalise the following transactions assuming Cost and Financial Accounts are integrated.

	₹.
Wages paid (30% indirect)	12,000
Raw Materials purchased	20,000
Direct Materials issued to production	15,000
Wages charged to production	9,500

2. From the following information you are requested to pass journal entries and prepare necessary accounts under the system of integrated accounts.

	₹.
Materials purchased on credit	1,48,000
Wages paid	1,68,000
Wages productive	1,48,000
Wages unproductive	20,000
Finished Goods at cost (during the period)	2,56,500
Materials issued to production	1,28,000
Works exps: incurred	65,000
Works exps. charged to production	66,000
Office and administration exps. paid	44,000
Office and administration exps. charged to production	43,500
Selling overhead paid	45,000
Selling overhead charged to sales	45,000
Sales (Credit)	3,90,000

[**Ans.** *Balances: Stores Ledger Control A/c ₹. 20,000; Works Overhead Control A/c ₹. 1,000; Office and Admn. Overhead Control A/c ₹. 500; Works-in-Progress Ledger Control A/c ₹. 1,05,500; Profit 45,000.*]

3. The following are the extracts of balance of Mehta & Co. in its integrated Ledgers on 31st March 2003

	Dr. (₹.)	*Cr.* (₹.)
Stores Control A/c	3,600	
Finished Goods A/c	2,600	
Work-in-Progress A/c	3,400	
Creditors Control A/c		1,600
Cash at Bank	2,000	
Debtors Control A/c	2,400	
Fixed Assets A/c	11,000	
Profit and Loss A/c		6,400
Depreciation Provision A/c		1,000
Share Capital A/c		16,000
	25,000	25,000

Transactions for the year ending 31st March 2004 were as under:

	₹.
Wages — Indirect	1,000
— Direct	17,400
Stores purchased on credit	20,000
Stores issued to production	22,000
Stores issued to repair order	400
Goods Finished during period at cost	43,000

Goods Sold at cost	44,000
Goods Sold at sales value (On credit)	60,000
Production overhead recovered	9,600
Production overhead paid for by cheque	8,000
Administration overhead paid for by cheque	2,400
Selling and distribution overhead paid for by cheque	2,800
Depreciation (works)	260
Payments from customers	58,000
Payment to suppliers	20,200
Purchases of fixed assets in cash	400
Fines paid	100
Income Tax	4,000
Charitable Donations	200
Rates prepared included in production overhead incurred	60
Interest on bank loan	20

You are required to write up the accounts in Integral Ledger and take out a Trial balance. The Administration Overhead is written off to Profit and Loss A/c.

[Ans. *Total of the Trial Balance ₹ 31,540; Balance of Accounts: Stores Control A/c ₹ 1,200; Work-in-Progress A/c ₹ 9,400; Profit to P/L A/c from Costing P/L A/c ₹ 10,800; Net Profit ₹ 12,880, Balance of Bank A/c ₹ 3,480.*]

4. Record the following transactions in the ledger under integral system and prepare a trial balance.

Trial Balance at the beginning.

	Dr. (₹.)	Cr. (₹.)
Bank Balance	3.000	
Stock: Finished Goods	4.000	
Work-in-Progress	6.500	
Raw Materials	6.000	
Creditors		2.000
Debtors	1.000	
Fixed Assets	1.02,000	
Depreciation Provision		2,500
Capital Account		1,10,000
P & L A/c		8,000
	1.22,500	1.22,500

		₹.
Materials pruchased on credit		10,000
Materials issued to production		
Direct	7,000	
Indirect	1,000	8,000
Payment to Creditors		6,000
Wages Paid : Direct	10,000	
" Indirect	2,000	12,000
Finished Goods produced		30,000
Cost of Finished Goods Sold		32,000
Sales Value		40,000
Receipts from Debtors		35,000
Overhead incurred : Factory	6,000	
Office	1,000	
Selling and Distribution	1,000	8,000
Depreciation (in addition to overhead)		500

[Ans. *Balance : Bank ₹ 12,000; Finished Goods Ledger Control A/c ₹ 3,000; Stores Ledger Control A/c ₹ 8,000; Creditors A/c ₹ 6,000; Debtors ₹ 6,000; Profit from Cost of Sales A/c ₹ 8,000; Net Profit from P & L A/c ₹ 7,000. Total of the Trial Balance ₹ 1,34,000.*]

Reconciliation of Cost and Financial Accounts

In case information regarding costs is derived from the financial books themselves, for example, in the case of a contractor, there will not be much difficulty in reconciling the profit disclosed by costing and financial record. But if a large number of jobs is undertaken or a large number of products are produced, separate books will be required for costing and financial purposes. To check the accuracy of both, reconciliation of results obtained from each set of books is essential. Reconciliation is mostly done with regard to the profits disclosed. The financial books generally, however, required some remodelling for this purpose. This is discussed below.

Remodelling of Financial Books

(1) *Materials:* There will be no difference for materials used; in the cost books as well as financial books exact and correct figures are used. But to avoid all possibilities of differences, the financial books should not maintain the usual "opening stock", "purchases" accounts, etc., but should make a distinction between direct and indirect materials and also between normal and abnormal losses.

Carriage inwards should be treated in the same way as in Cost Accounts–that is, if the practice there is to include it in the value of materials purchased, in the financial books also it should be debited to the Stores Ledger Control Account. If the practice in Cost Accounts is to include it in works or factory expenses, in the financial books it should be recorded in a separate account. Also similarity of treatment is needed in case of consumption and loss or wastage of materials. The total of the requisition slips representing the value of materials should then be debited to "Materials Consumed Account" to the credit of the Stores Ledger Control Account. (This account has already been discussed in *Chapter II*). Materials purchased not for store but for direct issue to jobs should also be debited to the "Materials Consumed Accounts"; but the accounts should be so ruled as to give separate figures for materials issued out of stores and materials directly bought for jobs.

(2) *Wages:* Usually, the financial books contain one Wages Account comprising both direct and indirect wages. This will render reconciliation very difficult. It would be better if two accounts, `Direct Wages Account' and `Indirect Wages Account', are maintained. As regards the allocation of the total wage bill in the two, the Wages Abstract should be the guide. The Wages Abstract shows the total wages directly charged to jobs or products.

(3) *Direct Expenses and Indirect Expenses or Overheads:* Similarly, the same distinction should be observed between direct and indirect expenses as is observed by the Costing Office. In fact, there would be no harm if a separate account, "Direct Charges Account", is opened in financial books also, the costing office keeping the main Accounts Office informed as to which expenses should be so treated. In the absence of such an account, a complete record of such expenses should be maintained by the Costing Office, so that later items can be checked.

In the Cost Ledger, indirect expenses will be recorded under three heads: Works or Factory Expenses, Office and Administrative Expenses and Selling and Distributive Expenses, and an expense is included in one or the other according to its functions. In the financial books usually this is not done. For example, Stationery and Printing or Telephone Expenses may record the total expenditure under that head without being analysed for expenditure in the factory, general office or sales office. It is desirable that financial books should so record the indirect expenses that they can be categories into the three main types maintained by the Costing Office.

RECONCILIATION OF PROFITS

Reconciliation will be with regard to profits disclosed by the two sets of books and will depend on the explanation of the discrepancy between the actual overheads as recorded in the financial books and the estimates for such expenses included in costing books. But there are certain expenses which are not included in cost books at all and certain other expenses which are not included in financial books but are included in costing books. Apart from the appropriation of profits such as provision for income tax or dividends paid, certain expenses will not be found in costing books.

Expenses Not Included in Cost Accounts:

(*a*) Excess depreciation on plant, buildings, *etc.*, (with a view to creating secret reserves).
(*b*) Provision for bad and doubtful debts.
(*c*) Amounts written off intangible assets like goodwill or expenses of capital nature like preliminary expenses, underwriting commission, *etc*.
(*d*) Capital expenditure written off.
(*e*) Interest paid (if the concern decides to include interest in the cost accounts, there will still be a difference; financial books will show only the actual interest paid whereas cost books may show interest on the entire capital employed).
(*f*) Losses on the sale of investment or fixed assets.
(*g*) Expenditure on the share transfer office of the company.
(*h*) Damages payable through courts (except liability for workmen's compensation).
(*i*) Penalities for late execution of contracts.
(*j*) Abnormal losses of materials, abnormal idle time, scrapping of machinery before its estimated life is over.
(*k*) Remuneration payable to the proprietor in excess of the reasonable limit.

***Incomes Not Included in Cost Books*:**

The following items found on the credit side of the Company's Profit and Loss Account will not be considered in cost books:

(*a*) Interest, dividends, rents, *etc*., received by the company.
(*b*) Profit on sale of investments or fixed assets
(*c*) Transfer fees received on share transfers.
(*d*) Damages received by the company from others.

***Expenses included only in Cost Books*:**

If the company owns the premises, it will not pay rent and it will not, therefore, appear on the debit side of the Profit and Loss Account but, as has been pointed out in the Chapter on Indirect Expenses, a reasonable amount by way of rent will be included, all the same, in the indirect expenses by the Costing office.

Valuation of Stock: Difference in the two sets of books arises also because the valuation of the closing stock is done on different basis. The practice in case of costing may be to value the stocks at the office cost, *i.e.*, materials, wages, works overheads and office overheads. In case of work-in-progress, the equitable share of works overheads and office overheads is placed to suspense accounts. In case of financial accounts, practice varies. The closing stock is usually valued at works cost and work-in-progress at prime cost; of course, if market price is lower than the cost, market price will be the basis for finished stock valuation. Thus a difference between results shown by cost accounts and that by financial accounts is bound to emerge.

Method of Reconciliation

Reconciliation is effected at the end of a period by preparing a Reconciliation Statement. We may start either with profit as per Cost Accounts or with profit as per Financial Account (or Profit and Loss Account) and modify it in the light of discrepancies or items of difference, the adjusted profit should then be equal to the profit disclosed by the other set of account *i.e.* Financial Account or Cost Accounts respectively. It is usual however to start with the Profit as disclosed by Cost Accounts.

Items to be added to Profit as per Cost Account

If certain items of expenses have been overcharged in Cost Accounts or if certain receipts or items of profit have accrued but not have been included in Cost Accounts should be added to profit as per Cost Accounts with a view to make it agree with the profit as per Financial Accounts. Examples of such items are:

(*i*) Overcharge in Factory on cost, office on cost and selling on cost in cost books (or under charge in financial books).

(*ii*) Incomes shown only in financial books

(*iii*) Opening stock overvalued in cost books and closing stock undervalued in cost books.

(*iv*) Depreciation overcharged in Cost Accounts etc.

Items to be Deducted from Profit as per Cost Accounts

From the profit as revealed by Cost Accounts expenses not included in Cost Accounts or under absorption of indirect expenses will have to be deducted. Examples of such items are:

(*i*) Under allocation or undercharge of overheads in Cost Accounts (or overcharge in financial books.)

(*ii*) Expenses incurred and included in Financial Accounts, but not shown in Cost Accounts

(*iii*) Undervaluation of opening stock and overvaluations of closing stock in the Cost Accounts.

(*iv*) Depreciation undercharged in Cost Accounts.

Following is specimen format of Reconciliation statement:

Reconciliation Statement

		₹.
Profit as per Cost Books:		
Add:	1. Overheads and expenses overcharged in cost books (or undercharged in financial books).	
	2. Incomes shown only in financial books.	
	3. Opening stock over-valued in cost books.	
	4. Closing stock under-valued in cost books.	
	5. Depreciation overcharged in cost books.	
Less:	1. Expenses undercharged in cost books.	
	2. Expenses shown in financial books only.	
	3. Undervaluation of opening stock in cost books.	
	4. Overvaluation of closing stock in cost books.	
	5. Depreciation undercharged in cost books.	
Profit as per Financial Books.		

The reconciliation can also be shown by preparing a Memorandum Reconciliation Account. An outlay of this account is given ahead:

Memorandum Reconciliation Account

To Overhead undercharged in cost books	By *Profit as per cost books*
" Exps. shown in financial books only	" Overheads overcharged in cost books
" Undervaluation of opening stock in cost in cost books	" Income shown only in Financial books
" Overvaluation of opening stock in cost books	" Opening stock over valued in cost
" Dep. undercharged in cost books	" Closing stock under valued in cost
" *Profit as per financial books.*	" Dep. overcharged in cost

Illustration 1: From the following particulars prepare: (1) A Statement of cost of manufacturing for the year 2003. (2) A statement of profit as per Cost Account. (3) Profit and Loss Account in the financial books and (4) A Statement Reconciling the profits shown by above (2) and (3).

	₹.
Opening Stock of Raw Materials	1,40,000
Opening Stock of Finished Articles	2,80,000
Purchase of Raw Materials	8,50,000
Stock of Raw Materials at end	2,00,000
Stock of finished Articles at end	50,000
Wages	3,50,000

Calculate Factory on cost at 20% on Wages and Office on cost at 75% on Factory on cost. Actual Factory expenses amounted to ₹. 72,000 and actual Office Expenses amounted to ₹. 50,000. The Selling Price was fixed at 20% above Cost Price.

Solution:

(1) Statement of Cost

	Dr. ₹	*Cr.* ₹
Raw Materials Consumed:		
Opening Stock of Raw Materials	1,40,000	
Add: Purchases of Raw Materials	8,50,000	
	9,90,000	
Less: Closing Stock of Raw Materials	2,20,000	
		7,90,000
Wages		3,50,000
Prime Cost		11,40,000
Factory On Cost (20% of Wages)		70,000
Factory Cost		12,10,000
Office On Cost (75% of Factory on cost)		52,500
Total Cost		12,62,500

(2) Statement of Profit as per Cost Accounts

	₹
Total Cost	12,62,500
Add: Opening Stock of Finished articles	2,80,000
	15,42,500
Less: Closing Stock of Finished articles	50,000
Cost of Articles Sold	14,92,500
Profit: 20% of Cost	2,98,500
Selling Price	17,91,000

(3) Profit Loss Account

	₹		₹
To Opening Stock:		By Sales	17,91,000
Raw Materials	1,40,000	" Closing Stocks:	
Finsihed Articles	2,80,000	Raw Materials	2,00,000
" Purchases	8,50,000	Finished Articles	50,000
" Wages	3,50,000		
" Factory Expenses	72,000		
" Office Expenses	50,000		
" Profit	2,99,000		
	20,41,000		20,41,000

Analysis: The difference between the two profits is due to (1) an undercharge in Cost Account of ₹. 2,000 in respect of Factory on cost and (2) an overcharge in Cost Account of ₹. 2,500 in respect of Office on cost.

Reconciliation Statement

	₹
Profit as per Cost Account	2,98,500
Less: Factory on cost undercharged (72,000 – 70,000)	2,000
	2,96,500
Add: Office on cost overcharged (52,500 – 50,000)	2,500
Profit as per P & L: A/c	2,99,000

Illustration 2: The Profit and Loss Account of a company for the year ended 31st Dec., 2000 is as follows:

	₹		₹
To Materials Consumed	60,000	By Sales	1,50,000
" Carriage Inwards	1,000		
" Direct Wages	40,000		
" Works Expenses	10,000		
" Administration Exps.	5,000		
" Selling and Distribution Exps.	6,000		
" Debenture Interest	2,000		
" Profit	26,000		
	1,50,000		1,50,000

The profit shown by the Cost Accounts for the year is ₹. 28,600; upon a detailed comparison of the two sets of accounts, it is found that:

(*a*) The amount charged in the Cost Accounts in respect of overhead charges are as follows:

Works overhead charges	₹. 9,500
Office overhead charges	₹. 5,100
Selling and Distributing Exps.	₹. 5,800

(*b*) No charge has been made in the Cost Accounts in respect of debenture interest.

You are required to reconcile the profits shown by the two sets accounts.

Solution:

Reconciliation Statement

	₹.
Profit as per Cost Account	28,600
Less: Works overhead charges undercharged in Cost Accounts (10,000 – 9,500)	500
	28,100
Add: Office overheads overcharged in Cost Account (5,100 – 5,000)	100
	28,200
Less: Selling and Distributing Exps. undercharged in Cost Accounts (6,000 – 5,800)	200
	28,000
Less: Debenture interest not charged in Cost Accounts	2,000
Profit as per Profit Loss Account	26,000

Illustration 3: A cycle manufacturing company manufactures three types of cycles namely, Model *A*, Model *B*, and Model *C*. The practice followed by the company is to charge material and wages at actual cost works overhead at 75%, 80% and 90% of wages cost of Models *A*, *B* and *C* respectively and office on cost is charged at 20%, 25% and 30% of the works cost of these respective models. The company's accounts provide you with the following information:

	Model A ₹.	*Model B* ₹.	*Model C* ₹.
Materials per unit	300	410	600
Wages per unit	200	350	300
Selling price per unit	800	1,350	1,550

You are further provided an information that there is no cycle in the stock and number of cycles manufactured were of Model *A* 200, Model *B* 300 and Model *C* 100.

Prepare the relevant statement showing the profit per units, if actual works on cost happened to be ₹. 1,50,000 (on *A* ₹. 36,000, on *B* ₹. 90,000 on *C* ₹. 24,000) and office overheads ₹. 1,42,000 (on *A* ₹. 30,000, on *B* ₹. 70,000 and *C* ₹. 42,000).

Solution:

Cost Sheet Showing Cost and Profit

	Model A (200 units)		*Model B (300 units)*		*Model C (100 units)*		*Total*
	Per unit ₹.	*Total* ₹.	*Per unit* ₹.	*Total* ₹.	*Per unit* ₹.	*Total* ₹.	₹.
Materials	300	60,000	410	1,23,000	600	60,000	2,43,000
Wages	200	40,000	350	1,05,000	300	30,000	1,75,000
Prime Cost	500	1,00,000	760	2,28,000	900	90,000	4,18,000
Works on Cost as directed (75%, 80%, 90% of wages)	150	30,000	280	84,000	270	27,000	1,41,000
Works Cost	650	1,30,000	1,040	3,12,000	1,170	1,17,000	5,59,000
Office overhead as given (20%, 25% and 30% of works cost)	130	26,000	260	78,000	351	35,100	1,39,100
Total Cost	780	1,56.000	1,300	3,90,000	1,521	1,52,100	6,98,100
Profit	20	4,000	50	15,000	29	2,900	21,900
Selling Price	800	1,60,000	1,350	4,05,000	1,550	1,55,000	7,20,000

Trading and Profit and Loss Account

	₹.		₹.
To Materials	2,43,000	By Sales	7,20,000
To Wages	1,75,000		
To Work Exps.[1]	1,50,000		
To Office Exps.[2]	1,42,000		
To Net Profit	10,000		
	7,20,000		7,20,000

1. Given in the question (36,000 + 90,000 + 24,000)
2. Given in the question (30,000 + 70,000 + 42,000)

Reconciliation Statement

				₹.
Profits as per Cost Accounts				21,900
Add: Works on Cost over-recovered		27,000		
on model '*C*'		24,000	3,000	
" Office on cost over-recovered		78,000		
on model '*B*'		70,000	8,000	11,000
				32,900
Less: Works overheads under-recovered on				
Models *A*	*B*			
30,000	90,000			
30,000	84,000		12,000	
6,000	6,000			
Less: Office overheads under-recovered on				
Models *A*	*B*			
30,000	42,000			
26,000	35,100		10,900	22,900
4,000	6,900			
Profit as per Profit and Loss A/c				10,000

Illustration 4: The net profit of the Kamta Manufacturing Co. Ltd. appeared at ₹. 64,377 as per the financial records for the year ended 31st March, 2003. The Cost Books, however, showed a net profit of ₹. 86,200 for the same period. A scrutiny of the figures from both the sets of accounts revealed the following facts:

	₹.
Works Overheads under-recovered in Costs	1,560
Administrative overheads recovered excess in Costs	850
Depreciation charged in Financial Accounts	5,600
Depreciation recovered in Costs	6,250
Interest on investments not included in cost	4,000
Loss due to obsolescence charged in Financial A/cs	2,850
Income-tax provided in Financial Accounts	20,150
Bank interest and transfer fee in Financial Books	375
Stores Adjustment credited in Financial Books	237
Loss due to depreciation in stock charged in Financial Account	3,375

Prepare a statement showing the reconciliation of profit between Cost Accounts and Financial Account.

Solution:

Statement Reconciling the Figures of Profits

	₹.	₹.
Profit as per Cost Books		86,200
Add: Administrative Overhead recovered excess in cost	850	
Depreciation recovered excess in costs	650	
Interest on investments not included in costs	4,000	
Bank Interest and Transfer Fees	375	
Stores Adjustment not credited in costs	237	6,112
		92,312
Less: Work Overheads under-recovered in cost	1,560	
Depreciation in stock not charged in Cost Accounts	3,375	
Loss due to obsolescence	2,850	
Income-tax	20,150	27,935
Profit as per Financial Accounts		64,377

Illustration 5: Shobha Co. maintains separate Cost Books which disclosed a profit of ₹. 60,228 for the year ended March 31, 2010. The net profits disclosed by financial accounts amounted to ₹. 39,520. Upon enquiry, following information were obtained:

(*a*) The company made a provision of ₹. 1,200 for bad debts;

(*b*) Overheads charged to production in Cost Books were ₹. 15,000 whereas actual overhead expenses amounted to ₹. 13,864;

(*c*) Directors were paid fees amounting to ₹. 1,500;

(*d*) Installation of a new plant involved an expenditure of ₹. 24,000 but it had not gone into production as yet; Depreciation @ 5% was provided on the cost of plant;

(*e*) The company received interest on bank deposit amounting to ₹. 56; and

(*f*) It paid Income-tax ₹. 18,000.

Prepare a Reconciliation Statement explaining the difference between the profits revealed by the Cost and Financial Books

Solution:

Reconciliation Statement

	₹.	₹.
Profit as per Cost Books		60,228
Less: Expenses included in Financial Accounts only		
Provision for bad debts	1,200	
Directors Fees	1,500	
Depreciation of new plant	1,200	
Income tax paid (appropriation of profits)	18,000	21,900
		38,328
Add: Interest of Bank deposits included in Financial A/c only.		56
		38,384
Add: Overhead charges overcharged in Cost A/c (15,000 – 13,864)		1,136
Profit as per Financial Accounts		39,520

Illustration 6: The profit as per Cost Accounts is ₹. 82,650. The following points are found out on comparison between Cost Accounts and Financial Accounts:

	Cost Accounts ₹.	*Financial Accounts* ₹.
(1) Opening Stock:		
Materials	16,300	16,500
Work-in-Progress	10,000	10,500
(2) Closing Stocks:		
Materials	18,000	17,200
Work-in-Progress	8,000	7,600

(3) Dividend and interest received ₹. 400
(4) Loss on sale of Motor Car ₹. 500.
(5) ₹. 3,000 interest charged, not considered in financial accounts.
(6) Goodwill ₹. 6,000 has been written off during the year.
(7) Overheads incurred ₹. 60,600; but overheads recovered amounted to ₹. 63,000.

Find out profit as per Financial Accounts through (*a*) Memorandum Reconciliation Account and (*b*) Reconciliation Statement.

Solution:

(*a*) Memorandum Reconciliation Account

		₹.		₹.
To Diffence in opening Stocks of Materials and W.I.P.			By Profit as per Cost Accounts	82,650
Financial	27,000		" Dividend and Interest	400
Costing	26,300	700	" Interest charged but not considered in Financial Accounts	3,000
" Difference in Closing Stock of Materials W.I.P. Costing	26,000		" Over-recovery of Overheads in Cost Accounts (₹. 63,000 – 60,600)	2,400
Financial	24,800	1,200		
" Loss on Sale of Motor Car		500		
" Goodwill written off		6,000		
" Profit as per Financial Accounts		80,050		
		88,450		88,450

Statement of Reconciliation

	₹.	₹.
Profit as per Cost Accounts		82,650
Add: Dividend and Interest credited in Financial Accounts	400	
" Interest charged in Cost Accounts (63,000 – 60,600)	3,000	
" Over-recovery of Overheads in Cost Accounts (63,000 – 60,600)	2,400	5,800
		88,450
Less: Under-valuation of Opening Stock of materials and Work-in-Progres in Cost Account (₹. 27,000 – 26,300)	700	
" Over valuation of Closing Stock of materials and Work-in-Progress in Cost Account (₹. 26,000 – 24,800)	1,200	
" Loss on sales of motor-car charged in Financial Accounts but not in Cost Accounts	500	
" Goodwill written off in Financial Accounts but ignored in Cost Accounts	6,000	8,400
Profit as per Financial Accounts		80,050

Illustration 7: Given following is the summarised Trading and Profit and Loss Account of M/s Zivago Manufacturing Co. Ltd., for the year ended 31st Dec. 2009.

Trading and Profit and Loss Account
(For the year ending 31st Dec. 2009)

	₹.			₹.
To Wages	75,500	By Sales (6,000 units)		3,00,000
" Materials used	1,37,000	" Finished stock (200 units)		8,000
" Factory expenses	41,500	" Work-in-Progress:		
" Expenses on administration	19,120	Materials	3,200	
" Selling expenses	22,500	Wages	1,800	
" Goodwill written off	1,000	Other Exps.		
" Preliminary-exps. written off	2,000	in factory	1,000	6,000
" Net Profit	16,280	" Dividends received.		900
	3,14,900			3,14,900

In the Cost Accounts:

(1) Factory expenses have been allocated to the production at 20% on prime cost.

(2) Expenses of administration at ₹. 3 per unit produced.

(3) ₹. 4 per unit sold for selling expenses.

Prepare Costing Profit and Loss Accounts of the Co. and reconcile the profits disclosed by Cost Account and those shown by Financial Account.

Solution:

Statement Showing Cost and Profit

	₹.	₹.
Materials	1,37,000	
Less: Work-in-Progress	3,200	1,33,800
Labour	75,500	
Less: Work-in-Progress	1,800	73,700
Prime Cost		2,07,500
Factory Expenses (20% of Prime Cost)		41,500
Factory Cost		2,49,000
Administrative Exps. @ ₹. 3 per unit (6,200 × 3)		18,600
Cost of Production		2,67,600
Less: Closing Stock 200 units valued at Cost of Production		8,632
Cost of Goods Sold		2,58,968
Selling Expenses @ ₹. 4 : (6,000 × 4)		24,000
Cost of Sales		2,82,968
Profit		17,032
Sales		3,00,000

Note: Closing stock is valued at cost of production

i.e., ₹. 2,67,600 × 200/6,200 = ₹. 8,632 (approx.)

Reconciliation Statement

	₹.	₹.
Profit as per costing books		17,032
Add		
Over recovery of selling exps. (24,000 – 22,500)		1,500
Over recovery of factory exps. (41,500 – 40,500)		1,000
Dividend received recorded in financial books		900
		20,432
Less:		
Under-recovery of adm. (19,120 – 18,600)	520	
Preliminary exps. written off in financial books	2,000	
Goodwill written off	1,000	
Closing stock adjustment (8,632 – 8,000)	632	4,152
Profit as per financial accounts		16,280

Illustration 8: A manufacturer produces patent fire extinguishers of a standard type. The following is the Trading and Profit and Loss Account for the year ended 31st December, 2004.

Trading and Profit and Loss Account
(For the year ended 31st Dec., 2004)

	₹.			₹
To Materials used	29,150.00	By Sales		75,000.00
" Productive Wages	18,610.00	" Stock of Finished goods		1,812.50
" Factory Expenses	14,055.00	" Work-in-Progress:		
" Gross Profit c/d	20,527.50	Materials	2,800	
		Wages	1,560	
		Factory Expenses	1,170	5,530.00
	82,342.50			82,342.50
To Admin. Expenses	13,650.00	By Gross Profit b/d		20,527.50
" Net Profit c/d	6,877.50			
	20,527.50			20,527.50

1,550 Extinguishers were manufactured during the year and 1,500 were sold during the same period.

The cost records showed that factory expenses worked out at ₹. 8.25 and administrative expenses at ₹. 9.0625 per article produced. The Cost Accounts was showing an estimated total profit of ₹. 7,031.25 for the year. From the given information, you are required to prepare (*a*) Factory On cost Account (*b*) Administration On cost Account and (*c*) An account showing the reconciliation between the total net profit as per the Cost Account and the figure of net profit shown in the Financial Books.

Solution:

(*a*) Factory on Cost Account

	₹.		₹.
To Factory Expenses	14,055.00	By Finished Articles (1550 @ ₹. 8.25)	12,787.50
		By Work-in-Progress	1,170.00
		" Under-recovery	97.50
	14.055.00		14.055.00

(b) Administration Overheads Account

	₹		₹
To Administration Expenses	13,650.00	By Finished Articles	
" Over-recovery	396.87	(1550 @ ₹. 9.0625)	14,046.87
	14,046.87		14,046.87

(c) Reconcilliation Account

	₹		₹
To Under-recovery of		By Profit as per Cost Account	7,031.25
Factory overheads	97.50	" Over-recovery of	
" Administration		Administration overhead	396,87
Expenses on sold stock			
(50 @ ₹. 9.0625)	453.12		
" Profit as per Profit			
and Loss A/c	6,877.50		
	7.428.12		7,428.12

Illustration 9: The net profit shown by financial accounts of X Ltd. amounted to ₹. 37,100, while the profit disclosed by Cost Accounts were ₹. 57,320. On reconciliation of the figures, the following differences were noted:

(*i*) Director's fees not charged in Cost Account ₹. 1,300.

(*ii*) A provision for bad and doubtful debts not charged in Cost Accounts ₹. 1,140.

(*iii*) Income Tax paid shown only in Financial Accounts ₹. 16,600.

(*iv*) Overheads in Cost Accounts were estimated at ₹. 17,000. The charge shown by Financial books was ₹. 16,640.

(*v*) Work was started during the year on a new factory and expenditure of ₹. 16,000 was incurred. Depreciation of 10% was provided in Financial Accounts.

(*vi*) Bank interest received ₹. 60

Prepare Reconciliation Statement.

Solution:

Reconciliation Statement

	₹.	₹.
Profit as per Cost Account		57,320
Add:		
Overheads overcharged in Cost Accounts	360	
Bank Interest not shown in Cost Accounts	60	420
Less: (*i*) Income Tax not charged to Cost A/c	16,600	57,740
(*ii*) Directors fees not charged to Cost A/c	1,300	
(*iii*) Provision for b/d not charged	1,140	
(*iv*) Depreciation on new factory not charged	1,600	20,640
Profit as per P/L A/c		37,100

Illustration 10: The financial records of Modern Manufacturing reveal the following for the year ended ....

		₹ *in Thousands*
Sales (20,000 units)		4,000
Materials		1,600
Wages		800
Factory Overheads		720
Office and Administrative Overheads		416
Selling and Distribution Overheads		288
Finished goods (1,230 units)		240
Work-in-Progress		
Materials	48	
Labour	32	
Factory Overheads	32	112
Goodwill written off		320
Interest on Capital		32

In costing records, factory overhead is charged at 100% of wages, administrative overhead 10% of factory cost and selling and distribution overhead at the rate of ₹. 16 per unit sold.

Prepare a statement reconciling the profit as per cost records with the profit as per financial records of the company.

Solution:

Modern Manufactures Profit and Loss Account

(For the year ended ....) (₹ *in thousands*)

	₹		₹
To Materials	1,600	By Sales (20,000 units)	4,000
" Wages	800	" Costing Stock:	
" Factory Overheads	720	Finished Goods	
" Office and Admn. overheads	416	(1230 units)	240
" Selling and Distribution Overheads	288	Work-in-progress	112
" Goodwill written off	320		
" Interest on capital	32		
" Net profit	176		
	4,352		4,352

Statement of Cost (*In thousand rupees*)

	₹
Materials	1,600.00
Wages	800.00
Prime Cost	2,400.00
Factory Overhead (100% of Wages)	800.00
Gross Factory Cost	3,200.00
Less: Closing work-in-progress	112.00
Factory Cost (21,230 units)	3,088.00
Administrative Overhead (10% of factory Cost)	308.80
Cost of Production (21,230 units)	3,396.80
Less: Closing Stock (1,230 units) (3396.80 × 1,230/21,230)	196,80
Cost of Goods Sold (20,000 units)	3,200.00
Selling and Distribution Overheads (@ ₹. 16 per unit)	320.00
Cost of Sales	3,520.00
Profit	480.00
Sales (20,000 units)	4,000.00

Reconciliation Statement *(In Thousand Rupees)*

	₹.	₹.
Profit as per Cost Accounts		480.00
Add: Factory Overheads over recovered (800 – 720)		80.00
Selling and Distribution Overhead		
Over absorbed (320–288)		32.00
Closing stock over valued in financial accounts (240 – 196.8)		43.20
		635.20
Less: Administrative Overhead under absorbed (416 – 308.80)	107.20	
Goodwill written off in financial accounts only	320.00	
Int. on capital charged in financial accounts only	32.00	459.20
Profit as per Financial Accounts		176.00

Illustration 11: From the following expenses given below, prepare (*a*) a statement showing costing profit and loss and (*b*) another statement reconciling the costing profits with those shown by financial accounts.

Trading and Profit and Loss Account

	₹.		₹.
Materials consumed	1,50,000	Sales (1,50,000 units)	3,00,000
Direct Wages	75,000		
Indirect Factory Exps.	45,000		
Office Expenses	13,500		
Selling and Distribution exps.	9,000		
Net Profit	7,500		
	3,00,000		3,00,000

The normal output of the factory is 2,25,000 units. Factory expenses of a fixed nature are ₹. 27,000. Office expenses are for all practical purposes constant. Selling and distribution expenses are constant to the extent of ₹. 3,000 and the balance varies with sales.

Solution:

Statement of Profit as per Cost Accounts
(Units : 1,50,000)

		₹.
Materials Consumed		1,50,000
Direct Wages		75,000
Prime Cost		2,25,000
Works Overheads		
Variable (45,000 – 27,000)	18,000	
Fixed (27,000 × 1,50,000 / 2,25,000)	18,000	36,000
Works Cost		2,61,000
Office Overhead (13,500 × 1,50.000 / 2,25,000)		9,000
Cost of Production		2,70,000
Selling and Distribution Overhead		
Variable (9,000 – 3,000)	6,000	
Fixed (3,000 × 1,50,000 / 2,25,000)	2,000	8,000
		2,78,000
Profit		22,000
Sales (1,50,000 units)		3,00,000

Note: It has been assumed that fixed overhead must have been determined on the basis of normal output *i.e.* 2,25,000 units. Fixed Overheads recovered in cost would be:

Amount of fixed overhead × 1,50,000/2,25,000.

Reconciliation Statement

	₹.
Profit as per Financial Accounts	7,500
Add: Under recovery of Works Overhead in Cost Accounts (₹. 45,000 – 36,000)	9,000
Add: Under recovery of Office Overheads in Cost Accounts (₹. 13,500 – 9,000)	4,500
Add: Under recovery of Selling and Distribution Overheads in Cost Accounts (₹. 9,000 – 8,000)	1,000
Profit as per Cost Accounts	22,000

TYPICAL ILLUSTRATIONS

Illustration 12: The profit and loss account of Oil India (Pvt.) Ltd. for the year ended 31st March, 2004 is as follows:

	₹.			₹.
To Materials	4,80,000	By Sales		9,60,000
" Wages	3,60,000	" Closing Stock		1,80,000
" Direct Expenses	2,40,000	" Work-in-Progress:		
" Gross Profit	1,20,000	Materials	30,000	
		Wages	18,000	
		Direct Expenses	12,000	60,000
	12,00,000			12,00,000
To Administrative Expenses	60,000	By Gross Profit		1,20,000
" Net Profit	60,000			
	1,20,000			1,20,000

As per the records, the direct expenses have been estimated at a cost of ₹. 30 per kg and administrative expenses at ₹. 15 per kg. The profit as per the costing records are ₹. 1,10,400. During the year 6,000 kg were manufactured and 4,800 kg were sold.

Prepare a statement of costing profit and loss account and reconcile the profit with financial records.

Solution:

Statement of Costing Profit and Loss Account

	₹.	₹.
Materials	4,80,000	
Less: Work-in-Progress	30,000	4,50,000
Wages	3,60,000	
Less: Work-in-Progress	18,000	3,42,000
		7,92,000
Direct Expenses @ ₹. 30 per kg (6,000 × 30)		1,80,000
		9,72,000
Administrative Expenses @ ₹. 15 per kg on 6,000 kg		90,000
Cost of Production [6,000 kg (₹. 177 per kg)]		10,62,000
Less: Closing Stock [1,200 units @ ₹. 177 per kg]		2,12,400
Cost of Goods Sold 4,800 units		8,49,600
Sales (4,800 × 200)		9,60,000
Profit as per Cost Records		1,10,400

Reconciliation Statement

		₹.	₹.
Profit as per Cost records			1,10,400
Add : Admn. Exp. Overabsorbed in Cost A/cs			30,000
			1,40,400
Less: Closing stock overvalued in Cost A/cs.		32,400	
Direct Expenses under-absorbed in Cost Account			
Financial A/c. (2,40,000 – 12,000)	2,28,000		
Cost A/cs	1,80,000	48,000	80,400
Profit as per Financial Account			60,000

Illustration 13: M/s. Rana Traders have furnished the following information from financial books for the year ended 31st March, 2010.

Trading and Profit and Loss A/c for the year ended 31st March, 2010

	₹		₹
To Opening Stock		By Sales (10,250 units)	7,17,500
(500 units at ₹. 35 each)	17,500	" Closing Stock	
" Materials consumed	2,60,000	(250 units at ₹. 50 each)	12,500
" Wages	1,50,000		
" Gross Profit	3,02,500		
	7,30,000		7,30,000
To Factory Overheads	94,700	By Gross profit	3,02,500
" Office Overheads	1,06,000	" Interest	250
" Selling Expenses	55,000	" Rent	10,000
" Bad debts	4,000		
" Goodwill written off	5,000		
" Net Profit	48,050		
	3,12,750		3,12,750

The cost sheet shows the following:

(*a*) Cost of materials at ₹. 26 per unit and labour cost ₹. 15 per unit produced.

(*b*) Factory overheads are absorbed at 60% of labour cost.

(*c*) Office overheads are absorbed at 20% of factory cost.

(*d*) Selling expenses are charged at ₹. 6 per unit.

(*e*) Opening stock of finished goods is valued at ₹. 45 per unit and closing stock as valued in financial books.

You are required to prepare (*i*) a Statement showing cost and profit as per cost accounts for the year ended 31st March, 2010 and (*ii*) Statement showing the reconciliation of profit disclosed in cost accounts with the profits shown in financial accounts.

Solution:

Statement Showing Cost and Profit for the year ended 30.3.2010

	₹.
Materials consumed [10,000 units @ ₹. 26]	2,60,000
Labour Cost (10,000 units @ ₹. 15)	1,50,000
Direct Expenses	Nil
Prime Cost	4,10,000
Factory Overheads @ 60% of labour cost	90,000
Factory Cost	5,00,000
Office Overheads @ 20% of factory cost	1,00,000
Cost of Production (10,000 units)	6,00,000
Add: Opening Stock 500 units at ₹. 45	(+) 22,500
Less: Closing Stock 250 units at ₹. 50	(–) 12,500
Cost of Goods Sold (10,250 units)	6,10,000
Selling Expenses (10,250 @ ₹. 6)	61,500
Cost of Sales (10,250 units)	6,71,500
Sales (10,250 units @ ₹. 70)	7,17,500
Profit (10,250 units)	46,000

Note: Units Purchases = Sales + Closing Stock – Opening Stock units
= 10,250 + 250 – 500 = 10,000 units

(*ii*) Reconciliation Statement

	₹.	₹.
Profit as per Cost Accounts		46,000
Add : Opening Stock overvalued in Cost A/cs (22,500 – 17,500)	5,000	
Selling Exp. over absorbed in Cost A/cs (61,500 – 55,000)	6,500	
Interest and rent not charged in Cost A/cs (250 + 10,000)	10,250	21,750
		67,750
Less : Overheads under-absorbed in Cost A/cs:		
Factory Overheads (94,700 – 90,000)	4,700	
Office Overheads (1,06,000 – 1,00,000)	6,000	
Bad debts and goodwill written off (4,000 + 5,000)	9,000	19,700
Profit and per Financial A/cs		48,050

Illustration 14: The following figures have been extracted from the financial accounts of a manufacturing firm for the first year of its operation.

	₹.
Direct material consumption	50,00,000
Direct wages	30,00,000
Factory overheads	16,00,000
Administrative overheads	7,00,000
Selling & distribution overheads	9,60,000
Bad Debts	80,000
Preliminary expenses written off	40,000
Legal charges	10,000
Dividends received	1,00,000
Interest on deposit received	20,000
Sales – 1,20,000 units	1,20,00,000
Closing Stock :	
Finished stock – 4,000 units	3,20,000
Work-in-Progress	2,40,000

The Cost Accounts for the same period reveal that the Direct material consumption was ₹. 56,00,000; Factory overhead is recovered at 20% on Prime cost; Admn. overhead is recovered @ ₹. 6 per unit of production; and selling and distribution overheads are recovered at ₹. 8.00 per unit sold.

You are required to prepare Costing and Financial Profit & Loss Accounts and reconcile the difference in the profits as arrived at in the two sets of accounts.

Solution:

Costing Profit & Loss Account

	₹.		₹.
To Direct Materials consumed	56,00,000	By Sales (1,20,000 units	
To Direct Wages	30,00,000	@ ₹. 100 per unit)	1,20,00,000
Prime Cost	86,00,000		
To Factor overheads (20% of prime cost)	17,20,000		
Factory Cost	1,03,20,000		
Less: Closing WIP	2,40,000		
Factory Cost of 1,24,000 units	1,00,80,000		
To Admn. overheads of 1,24,000 units at ₹. 6	7,44,000		
Cost of Prodn. of 1,24,000 units (₹. 87.2903 per unit)	1,08,24,000		
Less: Closing finished stock 4,000 × ₹. 87.2903	3,49,161		
Cost of Goods Sold (1,20,000 units)	1,04,74,839		
To S&D Overheads (1,20,000 × 8)	9,60,000		
Cost of Sales (1,20,000 units)	1,14,34,839		
To Profit on 120,000 units	5,65,161		
	1,20,00,000		1,20,00,000

Financial Profit & Loss Account

	₹.		₹.
To Direct Materials	50,00,000	By Sales	1,20,00,000
" Direct Wages	30,00,000	By Closing Stock:	
" Factory Overheads	16,00,000	Finished Stock	3,20,000
" Gross Profit c/d	29,60,000	WIP	2,40,000
	1,25,60,000		1,25,60,000
To Admn. Overheads	7,00,000	By Gross Profit b/d	29,60,000
" S & D Overheads	9,60,000	" Dividends recd.	1,00,000
" Bad Debts	80,000	" Int. on deposits received	20,000
" Preliminary exp.	40,000		
" Legal Charges	10,000		
" Net profit	12,90,000		
	30,80,000		30,80,000

Reconciliation Statement

	₹.	₹.
Profit as per Cost Accounts		5,65,161
Add: Dividends received (in Financial A/cs only)	1,00,000	
Ind. on deposit received	20,000	
Direct materials consumed excess in Cost A/cs	6,00,000	
Factory overhead overabsorbed in Cost A/cs	1,20,000	
Admn. overhead overabsorbed in Cost A/cs	44,000	8,84,000
		14,49,161
Less: Bad debts (in Financial A/cs only)	80,000	
Preliminary exp. (–do–)	40,000	
Legal Charges (–do–)	10,000	
Difference in Valuation of Closing Finished Stock (3,49,161 – 3,20,000)	29,161	1,59,161
Profit as per Financial Accounts:		12,90,000

Illustration 15: The financial books of a company reveal the following data for the year ended 31st March, 2010:

	₹.
Opening Stock:	
Finished goods 875 units	74,375
Work-in-process	32,000
1.4.09 to 31.3.10	
Raw materials consumed	7,80,000
Direct labour	4,50,000
Factory overheads	3,00,000
Goodwill	1,00,000
Administration overheads	2,95,000
Dividend paid	85,000
Bad Debts	12,000
Selling and Distribution overheads 61,000	
Interest received	45,000
Rent received	18,000
Sales 14,500 units	20,80,000
Closing Stock: Finished Goods 375 units	41,250
Work-in-process	38,667

The cost records provide as under:

- Factory overheads are absorbed at 60% of direct wages
- Administration overheads are recovered at 20% of factory cost.
- Selling and distribution overheads are charged at ₹. 4 per unit sold.
- Opening Stock of finished goods is valued at ₹. 104 per unit.
- The company values work-in-process at factory cost for both Financial and Cost Profit Reporting.

Required :

(*i*) Prepare statements for the year ended 31st March, 2010 to show:

– the profit as per financial records

– the profit as per costing records.

(*ii*) Present a statement reconciling the profit as per Costing Records with the profit as per Financial Records.

Solution:

Statement of Profit as per Financial Records
or
Profit and Loss Account of the company for the year ended 31st March, 2010

Particulars	₹.	*Particulars*	₹.
To Opening stock of finished goods	74,375	By Sales	20,80,000
To Work-in-process	32,000	By Interest received	45,000
To Raw material consumed	7,80,000	By Rent received	18,000
To Direct labour	4,50,000	By Finished stock	41,250
To Factory Overhead	3,00,000	By Work-in-process	38,667
To Goodwill	1,00,000		
To Adm. Overheads	2,95,000		
To Selling and distribution ovhds.	61,000		
To Dividend paid	85,000		
To Bad debts	12,000		
To Profit	33,542		
	22,22,917		22,22,917

Statement of Profit as per Costing records for the year ended 31st March, 2010

	₹.
Sales revenue (14,500 units) (*A*)	20,80,000
Cost of Sales	
Opening stock (875 × ₹ 104*)	91,000
Add: Cost of production of 14,000 units	17,92,000
Less: Closing stock (₹. 17,92,000 ÷ 14,000) × 375	48,000
	18,35,000
Selling and distribution overheads: 14,500 units × ₹. 4	58,000
Cost of sales (*B*)	18,93,000
Profit (*A*) – (*B*)	1,87,000

(*ii*) Statement of Reconciliation between Profit as per Costing Records with Profits as per Financial Records

	₹.	₹.
Profit as per Cost Accounts		1,87,000
Add: Adm. overhead overcharged (₹. 2,98,667 – 2,95,000)	3,667	
Opening stock overvalued (₹. 91,000 – 74,375)	16,625	
Interest received	45,000	
Rent received	18,000	83,292
		2,70,292
Less: Factory overheads undercharged (3,00,000 – 2,70,000)	30,000	
Selling and distribution overheads undercharged (61,000 – 58,000)	3,000	
Closing stock overvalued (48,000 – 41,250)	6,750	
Goodwill	1,00,000	
Dividend	85,000	
Bad Debts	12,000	2,36,750
Profit as per Financial Accounts		33,542

Working Notes:

1. *Number of units produced*

	Units
Sales	14,500
Add: Closing stock of finished goods	375
	14,875
Less: Opening stock of finished goods	875
Number of units produced	14,000

2. *Cost Sheet*

	₹
Raw material consumed	7,80,000
Direct labour	4,50,000
Prime Cost	12,30,000
Factory overheads (60% of wages)	2,70,000
Factory Cost	15,00,000
Add: Opening work-in-progress	32,000
Less: Closing work-in-progress	(38,667)
Factory Ccost of Goods Produced	14,93,333
Administration overheads 20% of factory cost or ₹. 14,93,333	2,98,667
Cost of production of 14,000 units	17,92,000

3. *Cost of Production per unit*

$$= \frac{\text{Total cost of production}}{\text{No. of units produced}} = \frac{₹.17,92,000}{14,000} = ₹.128$$

Illustration 16: The summarised P & L A/c of a company for the year ended 31.3.2010 is given below:

Particulars	₹	*Particulars*		₹
Material consumed	44,00,000	Sales (2,00,000 units)		1,00,00,000
Wages	24,00,000	Finished Goods Stock C.B.		
Factory Overheads	14,00,000	(12,000 units)		5,00,000
Admn. Overheads	5,20,000	Work in progress: C.B.		
Selling and disribution Overheads	4,80,000	Materials	1,20,000	
Bad debts written off	40,000	Labour	80,000	
Preliminary Expenses written off	60,000	Factory overheads	40,000	2,40,000
Net profit	16,00,000	Agricultural income		32,000
		Miscellaneous receipts		1,28,000
	1,09,00,000			1,09,00,000

The following additional information is also furnished:

(*i*) In cost accounts, factory overheads have been absorbed at 22% of prime cost.

(*ii*) In cost accounts, admn. overheads have been absorbed at a flat rate of ₹. 3 per unit.

(*iii*) In cost accounts, selling and distribution overheads have been absorbed at ₹. 2.50 per unit.

(*iv*) Closing W.I.P. valued by the cost department has been incorporated in financial accounts.

(*v*) Valuation of finished goods (C.B.) has been independently made by the financial accounts branch.

You are required to prepare the Cost Profit and Loss Account and reconcile the profit as per cost profit and Loss Account with the Profit as per Financial Account.

Solution:

Costing Profit and Loss Account for the year ended 31st March 2010

Dr. *Cr.*

Particulars	₹.	*Particulars*	₹.
To Materials	44,00,000	By Sales (2,00,000 units)	1,00,00,000
To Wages	24,00,000	By Closing Stock	
To Factory Overheads (*Note 1*)	14,96,000	Finished Goods	4,92,000
To Admn. Overhead (*Note 1*)	6,36,000	Work-in-progress	2,40,000
To Selling and Distribution Overhead (2,00,000 × ₹. 2.50)	5,00,000		
To Profit (net)	13,00,000		
	1,07,32,000		1,07,32,000

Reconciliation Statement

	₹.	₹.
Profit as per Costing Profit and Loss Account		13,00,000
Add: Items overabsorbed in Cost Accounts		
Factory Overheads, (₹. 14,96,000 – 14,00,000)	96,000	
Adm. Overhead (₹. 6,36,000 – 5,20,000)	1,16,000	
Selling and Distribution Overhead (₹. 5,00,000 – 4,80,000)	20,000	2,32,000
		15,32,000
Add: Finished stock overvalued in Financial Accounts (₹. 5,00,000 – 4,92,000)		8,000
		15,40,000
Add: Items not included in Cost Profit and Loss A/c		
Agricultural Income	32,000	
Miscellaneous receipts	1,28,000	1,60,000
		17,00,000
Less: Expenses not included in Cost P & L A/c		
Bad debts	40,000	
Preliminary Expenses	60,000	1,00,000
Profit as per Financial Accounts		16,00,000

Working Notes :

1. **Cost Sheet**

		₹.
Material consumed		44,00,000
Wages		24,00,000
Prime Cost		68,00,000
Factory overheads (₹. 68,00,000 × 22%)		14,96,000
Works Cost		82,96,000
Less: Cost of WIP (given)		2,40,000
		80,56,000
Add: Administration Overheads (2,00,000 + 12,000) × ₹. 3		6,36,000
Cost of production		86,92,000
Cost per unit ₹. (86,92,000 ÷ 2,12,000) = ₹. 41 per unit		

2. Value of finished goods = 12,000 × ₹. 41 = ₹. 492,000.

Illustration 17: M/s Sellwell Ltd. has furnished you the following information from the financial books for the year ended 31st March, 2003.

Profit and Loss Account
for the year ended 31st March, 2003

	₹.		₹.
Opening stock of finished goods:		Sales 10,250 units	3,58,750
500 units @ ₹. 17.50 each	8,750	Closing stock of finished goods:	
Materials consumed	1,30,000	(250 units @ ₹. 25 each)	6,250
Wages	75,000		
Gross Profit c/d	1,51,250		
	3,65,000		3,65,000
Factory Overheads	47,375	Gross Profit c/d	1,51,250
Administration Overheads	53,000	Interest	125
Selling Expenses	27,500	Rent received	5,000
Bad Debts	2,000		
Preliminary Expenses	2,500		
Net Profit	24,000		
	1,56,375		1,56,375

The cost sheet shows: (*i*) the cost of materials at ₹. 13 per unit; (*ii*) the labour cost at ₹. 7.50 per unit; (*iii*) the factory overheads are absorbed at 60% of labour cost; (*iv*) the administration overheads are absorbed at 20% of factory cost; (*v*) selling expenses are charged at ₹. 3 per unit; (*vi*) the opening stock of finished goods is valued at ₹. 22.50 per unit.

You are required to prepare:

(*i*) The cost sheet showing the number of units produced and the cost of production, by elements of costs, per unit and in total.

(*ii*) The statement of profit or loss as per Cost Accounts for the year ended 31st March, 2003.

(*iii*) The Statement Showing the Reconciliation of Profit or loss as shown by the Cost Accounts with the profit as shown by the Financial Accounts.

Solution:

(*i*) Cost Sheet for 10,000 units

	Cost per unit ₹.	Total Cost ₹.
Material	13.00	1,30,000
Labour	7.50	75,000
Factory Overheads (60% of Labour Cost)	4.50	45,000
Factory Cost	25.00	2,50,000
Administrative Overheads (20% of Factory Cost)	5.00	50,000
Total Cost of Production	30.00	3,00,000

(*ii*) Statement of Profit or Loss as per Cost Accounts

	No. of Units	*Amount* (₹.)
Opening Stock of finished goods:		
(500 × ₹. 22.50)	500	11,250
Add: Cost of Production at ₹. 30 per unit	10,000	3,00,000
Total	10,500	3,11,250

Less: Closing Stock of finished goods @ ₹. 30 per unit	250	7,500
Cost of goods sold	10,250	3,03,750
Selling Expenses @ ₹. 3 per unit	10,250	30,750
Cost of Sales	10,250	3,34,500
Sales revenue	10,250	3,58,750
Profit	10,250	24,250

(*iii*) Statement showing the Reconciliation

	₹.	₹.
Profit as per Cost Accounts	—	24,250
Add: Selling Expenses over-absorbed in Cost Accounts (₹. 30,750 – ₹. 27,500)	3,250	
Over-valuation of opening stock in Cost Account: (₹. 11,250 – ₹. 8,750)	2,500	
Income excluded from Cost Accounts:		
Interest	125	
Rent	5,000	10,875
		35,125
Less: Factory Overheads under-absorbed in Cost Accounts: (47,375 – 45,000)	2,375	
Admn. overheads under-absorbed in Cost Accounts (53,000 – 50,000)	3,000	
Closing Stock of finished goods over valued in Cost Accounts (7,500 – 6,250)	1,250	
Bad debts accounts in Financial Accounts only	2,000	
Preliminary Expenses written off in Financial Accounts	2,500	11,125
Profit as per Financial Accounts		24,000

Illustration 18. The following information is available from the financial books of a company having a normal production capacity of 60,000 units for the year ended 31st March, 2010:

(*i*) Sales ₹. 10,00,000 (50,000 units)

(*ii*) There was no opening and closing stock of finished units.

(*iii*) Direct material and direct wages cost were ₹. 5,00,000 and ₹. 2,50,000 respectively.

(*iv*) Actual factory expenses were ₹. 1,50,000 of which 60% are fixed.

(*v*) Actual administrative expenses were ₹. 45,000 which are completely fixed.

(*vi*) Actual selling and distribution expenses were ₹. 30,000 of which 40% are fixed.

(*vii*) Interest and dividends received ₹. 15,000.

You are required to:

(*a*) Find out profit as per financial books for the year ended 31st March, 2010;

(*b*) Prepare the cost sheet and ascertain the profit as per cost accounts for the year ended 31st March, 2010 assuming that the indirect expenses are absorbed on the basis of normal production capacity; and

(*c*) Prepare a statement reconciling profits shown by financial and cost books.

Solution:

(a) Profit & Loss Account

	₹		₹
To Direct Material	5,00,000	By Sales	10,00,000
To Direct Wages	2,50,000	50,000 units	
To Actual factory expenses	1,50,000	By Interest and dividends	15,000
To Actual administrative expenses	45,000		
To Actual selling and distribution expenses	30,000		
To Profit	40,000		
	10,15,000		10,15,000

Cost Sheet
(For the year ended 31st March, 2010)

		₹.
Direct Materials		5,00,000
Direct Wages		2,50,000
Prime Cost		7,50,000
Factory Expenses:		
Variable : (40% of 1,50,000)	60,000	
Fixed : ₹. 90,000 × 50,000 / 60,000 units	75,000	1,35,000
Works Cost		8,85,000
Administrative Expenses : ₹. 45,000 × 5/6		37,500
Cost of Production		9,22,500
Selling & Distribution expenses:		
Variable : ₹. 18,000		
Fixed : ₹. 12,000 × 5/6 = 10,000		28,000
Cost of Sales		9,50,500
Profit		49,500
Sales Revenue		10,00,000

(c) Statement of Reconciliation

	₹.	₹.
Profit as per Cost Account	49,500	—
Add: Income from interest and dividends	15,000	64,500
Less: Factory Expenses undercharged in Cost Accounts (₹. 1,50,000 – ₹. 1,35,000)	15,000	
Administrative Expenses undercharged in Cost Accounts (₹. 45,000 – ₹. 37,500)	7,500	
Selling & distribution Expenses under-charged in Cost Accounts (₹. 30,000 – ₹. 28,000)	2,000	24,500
Profit as per Financial Accounts		40,000

QUESTIONS

OBJECTIVE QUESTIONS

I. *Examine the truth in following statements.*

1. Reconciliation of cost and financial accounts is prepared in non-integral accounting.
2. While calculating costing profit or loss, all those financial items are included which are not included in cost determination.
3. Income tax not recorded in cost accounts.
4. In reconciliation statement, dividend received is added to profit as per cost accounts.
5. If businessmen is owner of the premises, rent is not included in cost of products.

[*Ans.* False (2) and (5)]

THEORETICAL QUESTIONS

1. What do you know about Reconciliation Statement in Cost Accounts? Explain fully.
2. What is a Profit and Loss Reconciliation Statement? How is it prepared? Taking imaginary figures, you are required to prepare a statement.
3. Why is it necessary to work out from time to time reconciliation between Cost and Financial Accounts?
4. What value do you attach to the reconciliation of Cost Account and Financial Accounts? Explain the main sources of difference which might entĕr into such a reconciliation.
5. Why it is necessary to reconcile the profits between cost Accounting and Financial Accounting.
6. State the reasons for the difference between the profits shown in the cost accounts and those shown in the financial accounts of an industrial organisation.
7. Why should cost and financial accounts be reconciled? What are the reason for the difference between the two sets of accounts that needs to be reconciled?
8. Why is it necessary to reconcile the profits as shown by the cost and the financial accounts? State the various causes for such differences.
9. State the need for reconcilliation of cost and financial accounts.
10. `Reconciliation of cost and financial accounts in the modern computer age is reductant, 'Comment'.
11. `There is generally a divergence between financial profit and cost profit'. Explain this statement and give reason for such divergence.

SHORT ANSWER QUESTIONS

1. Write three main causes which create difference between profits as per cost accounts and financial accounts.
2. Mention those items of expenses and losses which are generally shown only in the financial accounts.
3. Mention those items of gains which are disclosed only in the financial accounts.
4. How the difference in the valuation of stock in Cost and Financial Accounts create difference in the profits disclosed by these two?
5. Correct the following statement if it has mistaken and prepare corrected Statement of Reconciliation of Profit.

   Profit as per cost Accounts

   Add Overhead and expenses overcharged in cost accounts.

   Add Expenses undercharged in cost account.

   Add Expenses shown in financial books only

   Less Closing stock under valued in cost account.

Less Depreciation undercharged in cost books.

Profit as per Financial Accounts

[*Hints*: Items 2, 3, 4 are wrong]

6. From the following prepare Profits Reconciliation Statement :

Profit as per cost account	₹. 2,98,500
Factory on Cost undercharged in Cost Accounts	₹. 2,000
Office on cost overcharged in Cost Accounts	₹. 2,500
Interest on capital debited in Profit and Loss Account	₹. 9000

[*Ans.* Profit as per P & L A/c ₹. 2,90,000]

7. From the following prepare Profits Reconciliation Statement:

Net Profit as per Cost Accounts	₹. 60,228
Overhead overcharged in Cost Accounts	₹. 1,136
Items included in financial Accounts only	
Provision for bad Debts	₹. 1,200
Directors Fees	₹. 1,500
Depreciation on new plant	₹. 18,000
Income tax paid	₹. 190
Interest on Bank deposit (Cr)	₹. 56

[*Ans.* Profit as per Financial Accounts ₹. 40,530]

8. From the following particulars, calculate profit as per financial accounts :

Profit as per Cost books	₹. 1,72,400
Works overhead under recovered in cost	₹. 3,120
Administrative overhead recovered in excess in cost	₹. 1,700
Depreciation overcharged in Cost Accounts	₹. 1,300
Interest on investment not included in costs	₹. 8,000

[*Ans.* ₹. 1,80,280]

NUMERICAL QUESTIONS

1. From the following particulars prepare : (*a*) A Profit and Loss Account, (*b*) A Statement showing the cost of manufacture and the percentage of each item of cost to total cost, calculating Factory on cost at 25% on Prime cost, and Office on cost at 75% on Factory on cost: (*c*) A Statement reconciling the profit shown by the Cost Account with that shown by the Profit and Loss Account. The selling price is fixed at cost plus 25%.

	₹.
Stock last January, 2003	
Raw Materials	4,000
Finished articles	8,000
Stock 31st December, 2003	
Raw Materials	6,000
Finished articles	2,000
Purchased of Raw Materials	24,000
Wages	10,000
Sales	65,000
Works Expenses	7,750
Office Expenses	6,100

[**Ans.** *(a) Profit as per P and L A/c 13,150 (b) Cost of Manufacture ₹. 46,000. Percentages: Materials 47.83; Wages 21.74; Factory on cost 17.39. Office on cost 13.04 Profit as per Cost A/c ₹. 13,000*]

2. From the following particulars, prepare a statement showing the cost per fan sold. The fans manufactured are classed into 'Royal' and 'Popular'. There is no opening or closing stock of fans.

	Royal ₹.	Popular ₹.
Materials	1,200	1,616
Labour	2,280	2,828

Works on cost to be 100% on Labour, and Office on cost to be 25% on works cost. One hundred and twenty 'Royal' fans were sold during the year at ₹. 75 each, whereas the price per 'Popular' fan was ₹. 55 and the number sold was 202. What is the total profit for the year in the financial books of the company, the following being additional particulars given:

Works Expenses ₹. 4,960 and Office Expenses ₹. 3,380.

How would you account for the difference between the two figures of profits.

[**Ans.** *Profit as per Cost Accounts ₹. 3,820. Profit as per Profit and Loss A/c ₹. 3,846*]

3. The net profit shown by financial accounts of a company amounted to ₹. 18,550 whilst the profits disclosed by company's cost accounts for that period were ₹. 28,660. On reconciling the figures, the following differences were noted:

		₹.
(*i*)	Director's fees not charged in cost accounts	650
(*ii*)	A provision for bad and doubtful debts	570
(*iii*)	Bank interest credited in P and L A/c	30
(*iv*)	Income–tax	8,300
(*v*)	Overheads in the cost accounts were estimated at 8,500 The charge shown by the financial books was 8,320	
(*vi*)	Works was started during the year on a new factory and a capital expenditure ₹. 16,000 was incurred thereon. Depreciation of 5% on it was provided in financial account.	

Prepare a statement reconciling the figures shown by the cost and financial accounts.

4. A manufacturing company disclosed a net loss of ₹. 3,47,000 as per their cost accounts for the year ended March 31, 2003. The financial accounts however disclosed a net loss of ₹. 5,10,000 for the same period. The following information was revealed as a result of scrutiny of the figures of both the sets of accounts :

		₹.
(*i*)	Factory overheads under-absorbed	40,000
(*ii*)	Administration overheads over-absorbed	60,000
(*iii*)	Depreciation charged in Financial Accounts	3,25,000
(*iv*)	Depreciation charged in Cost Accounts	2,75,000
(*v*)	Interest on investments not included in Cost Accounts	96,000
(*vi*)	Income-tax provided	54,000
(*vii*)	Interest on loan funds in Financial Accounts	2,45,000
(*viii*)	Transfer fees (credit in financial books)	24,000
(*ix*)	Stores adjustment (credit in financial books)	14,000
(*x*)	Dividend received	32,000

Prepare Memorandum Reconciliation Account.

[**Ans.** *Total of Memorandum Reconciliation Account*]

5. The costing department of SMG Ltd. absorbs Factory overheads @ 60% of Labour and Office overheads @ 20% of Factory Cost. The total expenditure for the factory is as under:

	₹.
Materials	4,00,000

Labour	–	3,00,000	
Factory Expenses	–	1,96,000	
Office Expenses	–	1,70,000	Total ₹. 10,66,000.

10% of the output is in Stock, Sales amounted to ₹. 10,20,000, Stock has been valued at Total cost in both accounts. Prepare a Statement of Cost and a Reconciliation Statement.

[**Ans.** *P/L Profit ₹. 59,600; Costing Profit ₹. 69,600, Overcharge in Office Overhead ₹. 6,000; Undercharge in Factory Overhead ₹. 16,000, Closing stock 1,05,600*]

6. Calculate the amount of profit as per Profit and Loss Account on the basis of the following informations:

(*a*) The Profit as per Cost Accounts was ₹. 1,50,300;

(*b*) Works overheads were under-recorded in Cost Accounts by ₹. 4,000.

(*c*) Administrative expenses were under recorded in Financial Accounts by ₹. 1,500;

(*d*) Depreciation charges were over-recovered in Cost Accounts by ₹. 950;

(*e*) Interest received on investments during the year amounting to ₹. 495;

(*f*) Transfer fees amounting to ₹. 120 were received during the year in connection with registration of transfer of shares;

(*g*) Provisions for Income-tax made in Financial Accounts was ₹. 48,500.

[**Ans.** *Profits as per P/L A/c ₹. 1,00,865.*]

7. The following is a summary of the Trading and Profit and Loss Account of M/s Alpha Manufacturing Company Ltd., for the year ended on 31st March, 2003.

	₹.			₹.
To Materials Consumed	27,40,000	By Sales (1,20,000 units)		60,00,000
" Wages	15,10,000	By Finished Stock (4,000 units)		1,60,000
" Factory Expenses	8,30,000	" Work-in-Progress		
" Administration Exps.	3,81,400		₹.	
" Selling and Distribution Expenses	4,50,000	Materials	64,000	
		Wages	36,000	
" Preliminary Exps. (written off)	40,000	Factory Exps.	20,000	
" Goodwill (written off)	20,000			1,20,000
" Net Profit	3,26,600	" Dividend Received		18,000
	62,98,000			62,98,000

The company manufactures a standard unit. In the Cost Accounts:

(1) Factory expenses have been allocated to the production at 20 per cent on Prime Cost;

(2) Administration expenses at ₹. 3.00 per unit on units produced;

(3) Selling and distribution expenses at ₹. 4.00 per unit on units sold.

You are required to prepare a Costing Profit and Loss Account of the company and to reconcile it from the profit disclosed in the financial Accounts.

[**Ans.** *Profit as per Costing P/L A/c. ₹. 3,40,645.*]

Cost Audit and Cost Accounting (Record) Rules

Cost Audit is a critical review undertaken to verify the correctness of Cost Accounts and to check that cost accounting principles and planning have been efficiently followed. It is noteworthy that India is the only country which has introduced statutory cost audit to regulate about 45 vital industries of the country.

Cost Audit has been defined by the Chartered Institute of Management Accountants (CIMA) of Landon as "the verification of cost accounts and a check on the adherence to the cost accounting plan." This definition implies the following :

(*i*) The objects of cost accounting with reference to which the cost accounting plan must have been drawn up have to be kept in mind to see whether or not the plan itself and the figures collected will lead to the achievement of the goal or objective set. For instance, if the objective is to achieve maximum efficiency, the plan and the analysis of data will be different from the case where the only objective is to fix prices.

(*ii*) It has to be examined whether the methods laid down for ascertaining costs and other relevant decisions are being implemented. Treatment and determination of abnormal losses of gains or treatment of certain expenses as direct or indirect are cases in point.

(*iii*) The correctness of the figures has to be vouched.

'**Statutory Cost Audit** is a system of audit introduced by the Government of India for the review examination and appraisal of the cost accounting record and added information required to be maintained by specified industries' (*ICWA of India*).

The concept of cost audit has been elaborated by *ICWA* as 'an audit of efficiency of minute details of expenditure, while the work is in progress and not a post mortem examination. Financial audit is a '*fait accompli*', cost audit is mainly a preventive measure, a guide for management policy and decision in addition, to being a barometer of performance'.

Cost Audit can be called efficiency audit. It is evidenced by amendment in section 209 which reads. 'The object of the amendment of the section is to ensure specified company proper records relating to utilisation of material labour are available which would make efficiency audit (cost-audit) possible'.

Management Auditing is the process of "auditing the quality of managers through appraising them as individual managers and appraising the quality of the total system of managing in an enterprise." Thus management audit aims at assessing how managers perform different functions of management, *e.g.*, planning, coordinating, motivating, etc.

ADVANTAGES OF COST AUDIT

The chief advantage of a cost audit will be that management will be sure to get reliable data for its objectives — price fixing, decision-making, control, etc. Existence of such a system of audit will also be of great use for maintaining internal check and control and will be of great help to even financial audit. But it must be understood that the aims of financial and cost audit are different. The former aims at prevention of frauds and errors and with presentation of Profit and Loss Account and Balance Sheet which exhibit a true and fair view of the state of affairs (of profit earned during the year and of financial position at the end of the year). It is concerned with totality of expenditure and revenue rather than its functional analysis. Cost Audit will establish the accuracy of cost of each product, job, activity, etc., and is concerned with proper analysis of information and its estimation so that management gets the necessary information promptly. Apart from reliability of data, cost audit should afford certain incidental advantages. Rather, it should be said that cost audit will help consolidate and realise advantages expected from a system of costing. Following statement of the HR Gokhale Ex-minister of Law, Justice and Company Affairs emphasises the social advantage of cost audit.

'The objective of this measure (cost audit) is to protect consumers from unwarranted increase in prices. Reasonableness of the prices charged can only be ensured by correct determination of costs and the margin charged by producers and their retailers. Another object underlying this step is to make the industries covered by such rules alert and efficient and also to make them know their rational cost with a view to reducing it to the extent possible. Thus by resorting to this method, the interest of consumer is safeguarded and it is definite step towards removal of social injustice'.

The *advantages*, briefly, are as follows :

(*i*) A close check will be maintained on all wastages—materials in store, labour, etc.—and they will be promptly located and reported.

(*ii*) Inefficiencies in production (or efficiencies) will be located and converted into monetary terms.

(*iii*) Through fixation of individual responsibility, management by exception will be possible.

(*iv*) The system of budgetary control and standard costing will be greatly facilitated with cost audit at the hands of a qualified cost accountant.

(*v*) Records will be up-to-date and information for various purposes will be available.

(*vi*) Cost audit may unearth a number of errors and frauds which may not be revealed otherwise. This is because a cost auditor examines expenditure minutely and compares it with standards and ascertains exact reasons for discrepancy.

Cost audit offers many advantages to management, cost accountant, shareholders, statutory auditor, consumers and the government. These advantages are summarised below.

Advantages to Management

(*i*) Errors in following *costing principles and techniques* are detected. Inconsistencies and frauds can also be detected. This keeps everyone alert and promotes efficiency.

(*ii*) Cost audit can serve to *measure performance of managers* and better performance can be rewarded.

(*iii*) It helps to prepare accurate cost reports and this business planning can be more accurate.

(*iv*) Inter-firm comparisons can be made with ease and this might be a very useful proposition if industrial intelligence is good.

(*v*) Cost audit can give an idea about *the comparative operational efficiency* of each department of division; and may thus pin-point deficiencies and also encourage to operate in a competitive spirit.

Advantages to Management/Cost Accountant

Important advantages are :

(*i*) His task is facilitated since errors, deficiencies, etc., are pointed out. Costing plans can be prepared to take care of these things.

(*ii*) Cost audit may help in easier reconciliation of cost and financial accounts.

(*iii*) If the cost auditor is an outsider and is an expert, he can certainly give some practical and sound advice to streamline costing systems and organisation.

(*iv*) Cost audit helps to focus attention of management on the problems faced by the cost accountant. This helps him to realise his goals and objectives with ease.

Advantages to Statutory Auditor

Important advantages are :

(*i*) Audited cost data helps him to determine the value of stocks, remuneration of managerial personnel, etc., with ease and accuracy.

(*ii*) Data and statements of cost audit help him to prepare his audit programme and plan so that he concentrates more on those aspects which have not been adequately covered by cost audit.

Advantages to Consumers

(*i*) The direct benefit accrues where a statutory cost audit has been done to fix a reasonable price for the consumers.

(*ii*) Since cost audit aims at ensuring efficiency in the organisation, this may also get reflected in reduced prices to the consumers.

Advantages to Labour

(*i*) If cost audit is done thoroughly labour also stands to gain through increased profitability in the shape of bonus and other benefits.

(*ii*) Also it brings into focus the role of labour in improving efficiency in term of increased productivity.

Advantages to Shareholders

(*i*) There is correct valuation of all kinds of inventories. This may project a true picture of the organisation before shareholders and other investors and help them to assess its performance.

(*ii*) External cost audit highlights efficiency or inefficiency, utilisation of manpower and other resources, adequacy of return, etc.

Advantages to Government and Economy

(*i*) It helps the government to settle accounts where *cost-plus* contracts have been made.

(*ii*) The government can intervene to protect the interests of the consumers, labour, shareholders and investors from exploitage or inefficient managements.

(*iii*) At the national level, cost audit promotes cost consciousness and overall efficiency. This means that every rupee invested produces the maximum quantity of goods and services.

TYPES OF COST AUDIT

The main types of Cost audit are the following :

(*i*) *Cost Audit as an Aid to Management.* The aim is to see that all information placed before management is relevant, reliable and prompt so that management can discharge its duties well. It must also be seen that no relevant or pertinent information is suppressed.

(*ii*) *Cost Audit on Behalf of a Customer.* Often contracts are placed on "Cost Plus" basis. In other words, the customer will determine the final price to be paid on the basis of exact cost plus an agreed margin of profit. The customer, in such a case, usually gets cost accounts of the product concerned audited to establish correct cost and, therefore, price.

(*iii*) *Cost Audit on Behalf of Government.* Sometimes the Government is approached with request for financial help or protection. Before taking a decision on the request, the Government may choose to get cost accounts of the applicant audited to establish whether the need for help is genuine or is a result of mere inefficiency.

(*iv*) *Cost Audit under Statute.* The Amendment Act of 1965 has inserted a new section, 233B, in the Companies Act, 1956 whereby the Central Government may order that certain classes of companies will get their cost accounts audited by a member of the Institute of Cost and Works Accounts of India. Only such companies as are required to maintain proper records regarding materials consumed, labour and other expenses under Section 209 (as amended to date) and may be required to get their cost accounts audited. The powers and duties and manner of appointment of the cost auditor are the same as that of external financial auditor and the same disqualifications will apply. The cost auditor will submit his report to the Company Law Board with a copy to the company. The right to investigate all aspects of cost accounts is presumably granted to the cost auditor. The aim of cost audit under statute seems to be that the Government wishes to know, as an instrument of control, the costs of various goods. Government has the power to prescribe the forms in which cost audit reports are to be made out. These are designed not only to verify information, but also to convey good deal of infomation to Government.

(*v*) *Cost Audit on Behalf of the Trade Association.* Sometimes trade associations seek to maintain prices at a certain level. For this purpose, the accuracy of costing information submitted by various concerns has to be checked. The trade associations may seek to have full information about production capacity and the relative efficiency of productive processes.

COST AUDIT IN INDIA

Cost audit in India is conducted in accordance with section 233-B read with sub-secton 1 (*d*) of section 209 of the Companies Act 1956. Till now the Govt. of India has issued Cost Accounts. (Record) Rules for 44 industries. But the scope may widen if the Central Government prescribes Cost Accounting Record Rules for more number of industries.

The cost audit should be done by Cost Accountant within the meaning of the Cost and Works Accountant Act 1959. However if sufficient number of cost accountants are not available, Govt. may notify that Chartered Accountants may do cost audit for a specified period.

Role of Cost Audit

Given below is a tabulation of the *role of cost audit* as compared to that the financial audit. This has been taken from a booklet named "*Cost Audit, Its Significance*" issued by the Institute of Cost and Works Accountants of India.

PRODUCTION

(i) Inventory

Cost Audit

The Cost Auditor will examine the following :

(a) Is the size of the inventory adequate or excess compared with the production programme ?

(b) Is the provisioning drill most economical ?

(c) Does it ensure optimum order size ?

(d) Does it take into account the storage cost on the one hand, and carrying cost on the other hand

(e) Does it take note of lead time of the various items or groups of itmes?

(f) Does the receipt and issue system cause any bottleneck in production ?

(g) Does it involve too many forms and too much paper work ?

(h) Is there any room for reduction of inventory cost consistent with production needs ?

(i) Is the inventory as per the priced store ledger and as certified by the Management physically correct ?

(j) Is the same amount of attention and care given to monies translated into material things like raw materials, stores and supplies or kind as is given to liquid cash ?

(k) Does the issue of raw materials make the production in accordance with the standard or schedule or otherwise, or covered by authorised schedule ?

(l) Is the expenditure of consumbale stores within the standard ? If not, why not ?

Financial Audit

The Financial Auditor has to see the following :

(a) That in the company's Balance Sheet the inventory and its valuation has been duly certified by the management.

(b) that all entries in the ledger—receipts and issues—are properly authorised and authenticated.

(c) that all entries in the ledger—receipts and issues—are supported by appropriate vouchers.

(d) that the ledger entries and costing are arithmetically correct.

(ii) Opening and Closing Stocks

(1) The Cost Auditor will see the following :

(a) that the opening stock is not unduly large compard with the volume of production during the year;

(b) that the opening stock against various jobs does really represent the actual physical stock in the production shop–and is not merely an accounting figure;

(1) The Financial Auditor will see the following :

(a) that the total stock in hand, as per financial ledger as certified by the management is correctly reflected in the Balance Sheet and Store Accounts.

(c) that the responsibility of the Shop Foreman in charge of the stock held in the production shop is clear and properly documented; that he maintains proper record of actual consumption vis-a-vis the actual withdrawal from the stock.

(2) Valuation and correct indication of closing stock in the Trading and Profit and Loss Account and in Balance Sheet is important. The Cost Auditor will examine and certify :

(a) that the physical verification is correctly carried out;

(b) that the valuation is correct with reference to the actual cost of production and recognised policy for valuation;

(c) that the volume of closing stock in commensurate with the volume of production and that it does not reflect any failure or bottleneck in sales budget or production budget;

(d) that the volume of unmoved stores is not abnormal in comparison with normal rate of yearly consumption. The Cost Auditor will recommend disposal of such unmoved stores with consequent release of capital unneccessarily locked upto the advantage of the financial resources of the concern.

(2) The Financial Auditor will normally accept the closing stock as certified by the management—as regards volume and value; he has no further responsibility in the matter.

(*Author's note:* This position is fast changing and no auditor remains unconcerned with correctness of stock).

(iii) Stores Issue Procedure in Shops

(1) The cost Auditor will see :

(a) that withdrawal of materials from stores to production shop is scientific or covered by authorised schedule and permits receipts to be located;

(b) that surplus materials and scraps arising in production shops are returned to store correctly and without delay for which necessary credit is given to unit cost of production. If transferred to other jobs, proper transfer voucher has been prepared and copies sent to the accounts, stores, etc.

(1) The Financial Auditor has no particular responsibility to watch this aspect, except that vouchers, receipts and issue notes are properly authenticated.

(iv) Inventory

Cost Audit

(1) The Cost Auditor will see the following :

(a) that the work-in-progress has been physically verified and that it agrees

Financial Audit

(1) The Financial Auditor will not exercise any independent check on work-in-progress. He will accept valuation from the management

with the balance in the incomplete cost cards :

(*b*) that the valuation of the work-in-progress is correct with reference to the stage of completion of each job or process and the value job cost cards or process cost sheet;

(*c*) that there is no over-valuation or under-valuation of opening work-in-progress, or closing work-in-progress thereby artificially pushing up or down net profit or net assets as the case may be;

(*d*) that the volume and value of work-in-progress is not disproportionate compared with the finished out-turn.

for the prupose of Profit and Loss Accounts and Balance Sheet.

(*Author's note :* Same as given earlier)

(v) Labour

(1) Proper utilisation of labour and increase in productivity are now receiving attention. Several Productivity Teams have emphasised importance of higher productivity. It is, therefore, essential to assess the performance efficiency of the labour and compare it with the standard performance, so that labour utilisation could be progressively improved. The labour force in Indian industries is generally very high compared to similar type of industries in other developed countries. Our aim should be to reach that level, though not immediately but over some time. A study of this nature would give an idea where the inefficiency lies so that timely and adequate steps should be taken to ensure maximum utilisation of labour and to reduce the labour cost.

(2) Cost of labour is allocated to different jobs with reference to time or job cards.

(1) The Financial Auditor is more interested in the total expenditure on labour rather than on the allocation between Direct and Indirect. He will check only the total payments authorised and included in the accounts.

(*vi*) Capacity Utilisation

(1) The Cost Auditor will see :

(*a*) that the idle capacity in any production shop or of transport facilities for distribution is not excessive;

(*b*) that production volume and overall machine time utilised are commensurate. In other words, the machine hours utilised have given the optimum out-turn.

(1) The Financial Auditor has no duty or responsibility in the matter.

(*vii*) Overheads and Indirect Expenditure

(1) The Cost Auditor will see and certify :

(*a*) that allocation of indirect expenditure over production, sales and distribution is logical and correct;

(1) The Financial Auditor will only see :

(*a*) that expenses are properly vouched for and supported in cash memos, acquittance, appropriate receipts, etc.

(*b*) that compared with the volume of production in a production shop, the overhead charges are not excessive;

(*c*) that the actual indirect expenditure does not exceed budgets or standard expenditure significantly and that any variations are satisfactorily explained and accounted for;

(*d*) that the relation of indirect expenditure in keeping with the load on individual production shop is appropriate;

(*e*) correctness of appropriate allocation of overhead expenditure (both production and sales) will be certified by the Cost Auditor:

(*f*) that allocation of overheads between finished products and unfinished products is in accordance with correct principles.

THE BASIC APPROACH FOR COST AUDITORS

The cost auditor's main task is to establish the accuracy of costing information. This will differ from concern to concern, specially from the point of view of the objectives to be achieved. For instance, if the objective is merely to quote a price, all expenses and costs will be added up. But if the objective is measurement of efficiency, good deal of analysis is necessary so that the effect of each cause or factor is separately known. Basically, however, a cost auditor will do well to keep the following in mind:

(*i*) The effect of all abnormal factors should be separated. This will necessitate the determination of normal losses so that a comparison of actuals with expected figures will reveal abnormal losses or gains. Quantitative figures multiplied by standard rates will reveal the amount of abnormal loss or gain.

(*ii*) Costing 'rates' should be checked to see that expenses that are meant to be directly recovered are so recovered. For instance, wage rates for costing purposes may also include a suitable amount for provident fund contribution, bonus etc.

It should be seen that items that are excluded from the calculation of "costing rates" are included in overheads.

(*iii*) Complete quantitative reconciliation should be obtained. For instance, total hours paid for should be tallied with hours embodied in actual production (at standard) and idle time because of various reasons. In the same way, actual materials consumed should be reconciled not only for opening and closing stocks.

(*iv*) The accuracy of stores records should be checked by seeing whether or not there is an efficient system of continuous stock checking.

(*v*) For overheads, the cost auditor should see that they are classified properly and that overhead recovery rates are properly calculated. This should be done department by department.

(*vi*) The items to be excluded from costs and notional costs to be included in them should be checked.

(*vii*) The reasons for under or over absorption of overheads should be ascertained. This will help checking the accuracy of both collection of overheads, their recovery rates and the method of absorption.

(*viii*) Cost for various activities should be compared against standards and against costs relating to previous periods.

(*ix*) The profit revealed by absorption costing should be reconciled with that revealed on the basis of marginal costing.

(*x*) Profit as per cost records should be reconciled with that as per financial accounts.

(*xi*) The actual effect upon profit of the various decisions taken by the management during the year should be compared with that anticipated before the decision was taken. In case there is a material difference between the actual and the anticipated figure, the reasons therefore should be examined. This should involve an examination of

(1) the basis of the decision including relevant factors that might have been ignored;

(2) the figures taken into consideration; and

(3) changes that might have taken place subsequent to the decision having been taken.

On the whole, the cost auditor must examine whether the management is being supplied with information needed for its purposes and whether cost accounting is fulfilling the objectives for which it was established. Detailed checking is important but the accuracy of the results, as a whole, must be established—the reasonableness of cost of work done or goods produced the profits earned must be checked by comparing the figures with standards and those for previous years.

Industries Covered by Cost Accounting (Record) Rules:

As stated earlier Government can order cost audit of a company for a year or year if it is required to maintain cost records. Maintenance of cost records has been ordered for the specified industries which are about 44 at present.

1. Cement
2. Cycles
3. Tyres and Tubes
4. Caustic soda
5. Room air conditioners
6. Batteries other than dry cell batteries
7. Refrigerators
8. Electric lamps
9. Electric fans
10. Electric motors
11. Motor Vehicles
12. Dyes
13. Rayon
14. Soda Ash
15. Nylon
16. Polyster
17. Textiles
18. Drycell batteries
19. Sulphuric Acid
20. Steel Tube and Pipes
21. Engineering
22. Electrical cables and conductors
23. Mining and Machinery
24. Aluminium
25. Vanaspati
26. Bulk Drugs
27. Sugar
28. Infant milk foods
29. Jute goods
30. Industrial Alcohol
31. Paper
32. Bearings
33. Milk Food
34. Chemicals
35. Formulations (Drugs)
36. Steel Plant
37. Insecticide
38. Fertilizer Industry
39. Soaps and Detergent
40. Cosmetics and Toiletories
41. Footwear
42. Chemicals
43. Shaving System
44. Industril Gases

Separate Cost Accounting (Record) Rules have been prescribed for each industry. However, most requirements are similar. The following requirements in respeci of various elements of cost and items may therefore be treated a representative.

1. *Raw materials and components purchased :*

   (*a*) Adequate records should be kept showing the receipts, issues and balances, both in quantities and values, of raw materials and components required for the manufacture of the product.

   (*b*) The basis on which the value of purchases and issues have been calculated should be indicated in the records and the basis adopted should be followed consistently throughout the relevant period.

   (*c*) The value should include all direct charges such as freight, insurance, etc., and also the wastage, whether in storage, transit or for other reasons.

   (*d*) If the consumption value is determined on any basis other than actual, the method adopted should be explained and a reconciliation with actuals and the treatment of variations should be dealt with in the records.

2. *Manufactured components :*

Detailed records showing the cost of manufactured components should be maintained in the form prescribed in the rules. The records should also indicate quantities, values and wastage as in the case of purchased components. Quantities manufactured, rejected with accepted together with the losses on account of rejection should also be mentioned in the records.

3. *Stores and spare parts :*

   (*a*) Adequate records should be kept showing the receipts, issues and balances, both in quantities and value, of various items of stores and spares required for repairs, maintenance or manufacture. The value should include all direct charges upto the works such as freight, insurance, etc.

   (*b*) The value of issues and balances may be recorded monthly or at such shorter intervals as may be decided by the company or may be kept in the form of control accounts, the balances being reconciled atleast once a year with the values of the quantity shown by the quantity accounts for each item of stores.

   (*c*) The value of stores consumed should be charged to relevant heads like manufacturing, repairs to plant and machinery, repairs to buildings, township, maintenance of vehicles, capital items, etc.

   (*d*) The value of stores charged to manufacture should further be allocated to the different departments or manufacturing units or cost centres and products, if any manufactured therein.

   (*e*) Stores issued for capital works like additions to plant and machinery and other assets should be shown separately under the capital heads.

   (*f*) Any wastage, whether in stores or in transit or for other causes, should be recorded separately and their treatment explained.

   (*g*) Stores should be valued consistently during the relevant period on a reasonable basis and the method adopted should be recorded.

4. *Labour :*

With regard to labour, proper and systematic accounts should be maintained in respect of:

(*i*) attendance of workers and other staff;

(*ii*) all payments made for overtime work;

(*iii*) cost of wages and salaries relating to various manufacturing departments or units in the factory being the amounts payable and allocated to the different departments or units;

(*iv*) idle time, giving reasons for such idle time and the method of its treatment in calculating cost of products;

(*v*) the extent of wages and salaries capitalised as additions to plant and machinery and other assets; and

(*vi*) where piece rate payment system is applicable, the records should be so maintained as to enable department of wages payable to such workers.

5. *Overheads* :

(*a*) The overhead expenses should be classified as works overhead, administration overhead and selling and distribution overhead.

(*b*) Adequate records should be kept showing the accounts comprising the overhead expenses and the details of apportionment of overhead expenses to the various departments, manufacturing units and cost centres. The details of such expenses should be collected from the financial accounts.

(*c*) Capital jobs carried out during the year should bear their appropriate share of overhead expenses. The basis of allocation of such expenses should be indicated in the relevant records.

(*d*) The works overheads should include, among other items, indirect wages and salaries relating to works, indirect materials consumed, staff and labour welfare expenses and expenditure on repairs and maintenance.

(*e*) The method of apportioning overheads to various departments or manufacturing units or cost centres should be followed consistently and explained in the records.

(*f*) If overheads are recovered on a basis other than actual, the method of reconciliation with actuals and treatment of variances should be disclosed in the cost records.

(*g*) The shares of selling and distribution expenses, if any, applicable to products sold should be shown separately in the cost records stating clearly the basis of apportionment.

6. *Services* :

(*a*) Proper records should be maintained so that the cost of services such as power, water, electricity and steam produced and utilised in manufacturing operations can be ascertained.

(*b*) The power cost should include cost of units consumed, fixed charges and duties.

(*c*) If power, water or steam is generated by the company, the records maintained should show the different items making up the cost of such power, water or steam produced and consumed.

(*d*) The allocation of the consumption of services by different departments or manufacturing units should be shown in the records. If actual allocation is no possible, the basis of allocation should be indicated in the cost records.

7. *Depreciation* :

(*a*) Adequate records should be maintained in respect of fixed assets showing (*i*) the cost of each item of asset, (*ii*) date of acquisition. (*iii*) rate of depreciation, and (*iv*) the amount of depreciation provided.

(*b*) Depreciation chargeable to the different departments of cost should be less then the amount chargeable under section 205(2) of the Companies Act, 1956 and should relate to the plant and machinery and other assets utilised in the department or cost centre. The method of depreciation, once adopted, should be applied consistently.

8. *Production and Sales*

(*a*) Adequate records should be maintained in respect of production, showing the receipts, issues and balances of the goods produced by the company. The value should be based on the cost of production of the items concerned. The value of the issues and balances may be recorded monthly or at such shorter intervals as may be decided.

9. *Inventories*

(*a*) Inventories may be classified as (*i*) raw materials (*ii*) stores and spare parts, (*iii*) work-in- progress, and (*iv*) finished goods. The records required for raw materials, stores and spares and finished goods production have already been dealt with.

(*b*) Proper records should be maintained to show the quantities and value of work-in-progress at the end of the period for which the costs are made up. It should represent the cost incurred upto the relevant stage of manufacture.

(*c*) Stock verification records should be maintained in respect of all raw materials, components, stores, and spares including tools, etc. The method of dealing with the discrepancies arising out of such verification should be indicated in the records.

Sachar Committee stressed the importance of *CARR* as below.

"We are of the opinion that maintenance of the cost accounting records in certain types of industries and their continuous audit by an appropriate Cost Auditor will not only be a step in the direction of consumer protection but also will be of an advantages to the company itself.... We must add here that management of progressive companies have as a matter of prudence instituted cost accounting system and have also authorised *cost audits even when not so ordered by any appropriate order*."

Cost and Management Accountants in Practice Bombay have pronounced following guidelines regarding the books of accounts required to be maintained to comply with the requirements of Cost Accounting Records Rules :

1. A crucial question which arises is what are cost records? Sub-section (3) of section 209 only states that `proper books of account' shall be deemed to have been kept with respect to the matters specified in sub-sections (1) and (2), if there are kept such books as are necessary to give a true and fair view of the state of affairs of the company or branch office, as the case may be and to explain its transactions.
2. Books of account will also include vouchers which should be made available for inspection and investigation and should be preserved for a period of 8 years. Accordingly, the necessary amendments were made in Section 209(1) by the addition of sub-section (4-A), as stated therein.
3. As vouchers are treated as a part and parcel of financial books of account, it should be considered whether in relation to cost accounting records, they would include the statements received by the costing department from the production and service departments, stores, time office, sales and accounts departments etc., of a company or also the subsidiary records maintained by those departments, *e.g.*, log books, stores requisition slips, attendance cards of workers etc. Say, in a composite cotton textile mill, there may be over 40 cost centres. Each centre might be producing several kilos of records every year."

Following are essential cost records and subsidiary records :

1. Preservation of books of account and records by company for a certain number of years is a statutory requirement under Section 209 of the Companies Act, 1956. Since cost accounting records are also a part of accounting records and are governed by the

provisions of Section 209, these records would also have to be preserved for the statutory period as per that section.

2. However, it is necessary to determine as to what records relating to the cost accounting are essential records and are required to be preserved for the statutory period. This question assumes importance because a large number of subsidiary and supporting records/papers come into existence, which may not strictly be termed as accounting records, to enable and facilitate construction of cost accounting data and cost accounting records. Hence, it is necessary to identify and specify such records which are essential records and upon which the authenticity of such essential records depends and to distinguish the same from the remaining records which may have helped at sometime in building up and construction of cost accounting data but may not be quite important after their purpose is over the therefore need not be preserved for a longer period. It would have, therefore, to be examined as to what type of subsidiary records may be eliminated as soon as their purpose is over.
3. As in case of financial accounting records, vouchers are also required to be maintained, it would have to be ascertained for the purpose of cost accounting records as to what would be interpreted to mean vouchers. And therefore, what will qualify for being preserved. The prevailing practices of various companies in preserving several subsidiary records such as stores requisition slips, workmens' attendance cards, allocation of direct and indirect overheads etc., would have to be studied.
4. Since it is not only impracticable but also costly to preserve of a large bulk of records for want of space and administrative cost involved, all non-essential records which lose significance after the audit or internal certification of certain registers and statement prepared on the basis of such records, is over, could be done away with much before the statutory period applicable to the records.
5. Once a particular statement relating to various cost centres and various items of costs has been prepared, audited and/or certified by a competent authority, that statement should be taken to form basic record and should therefore be required to be preserved for the statutory period. Whether this is in the form of a statement or in the form of a book or register is a matter of internal convenience. But the requisition slips and/or other notes on the basis of which such a record is compiled, need not be preserved any longer. These papers should not be deemed to form part of vouchers as mentioned under the said sub-section (4-A), because these are purely internal memos for facilitating recording of entries under different cost centres or items of cost, and are not required for substantiating any activity or supporting any payment item.
6. For example, in the case of cash book, the cash vouchers including the supporting documents like bills and receipts, on the basis of which entries are made in the cash book, are of great importance and must be preserved because these are the documents on which the authenticity as also the legality of the entries in the cash book are based. Again since it is not practicable to incorporate all the details of such vouchers in the cash book, the supporting vouchers and documents are necessary to be preserved as to give complete explanation of the related transactions. But in the case of cost statements, internal memos need not be preserved after the basic records have been created and certified. Moreover, since such cost statements/records will contain all the necessary particulars which are included in the memos, there will be no need for the memos to be preserved for a longer time.
7. The practices of various companies with regard to the maintenance of such records would have to be studied in depth and the material would have to be made use of for identifying what can be eliminated and what must be preserved for statutory period.

Also, it would have to be borne in mind that if certain records already form part of financial records, a duplicate thereof need not be separately prepared and preserved for the purpose of cost accounting records although at the time of internal transfer or building up of cost accounting records, a duplicate might have had to be prepared to facilitate maintenance of cost records for variety of reasons, for example, for inter-unit transfers or inter-region transfers."

The records contemplated under *Section 209(1) (d) of the Companies Act, 1956* would include all the accounting records maintained by the Company and made available for audit by the financial auditor. In addition, the following records would also have to be maintained;

1. Production
   — Raw material consumption register/report;
   — Production report;
   — Rejections/wastages/scrap report;
   — Report on stoppage of machines with reasons;
   — Idle time report with reasons;
   — Machine utilisation report
2. Work-in-progress and finished goods
   — Process stock register — cost centrewise and productwise;
   — Finished goods stock register — Productwise.
3. Repairs and maintenance
   — Works order register/card showing material and spares consumed and labour utilised;
   — In case of workshop, additional records as described under 1(1) above.
4. Utilities (steam, power, water)
   — Record of inputs and outputs;
   — Record of cost centrewise allocation of outputs.
5. Raw materials and stores
   — Goods received register;
   — Bin cards;
   — Materials/Stores ledgers.
6. Wages and salaries
   — Attendance registers/sheets;
   — Wages/salary sheets;
   — Leave and gratuity payments.
7. Overheads

Details such as production hours, labour hours, machine hours to facilitable distribution to production.

8. Cost Accounts
   — Overheads analysis register;
   — Cost centrewise assets register;
   — Product ledger;
   — Annexures and proforma as per the rules;
   — Reconciliation of profit/loss as per cost records and financial records.
9. Sales : Sales Analysis by products."

COST AUDIT (REPORT) RULES

The following are the salient features of the Cost Audit (Report) Rules, 2001, applicable to every company in respect of which an audit of the cost accounting records has been ordered by the Central Government.

1. The cost audit report prepared by the cost auditor must be sent to the Company Law Board in the form and in accordance with the procedure laid down in the Schedule annexed to the Cost Audit (Report) Rules. A copy of the report must be forwarded to the company as well.
2. The report must be sent within 120 days for the end of the company's financial years.
3. The company and every officer thereof must make available to the cost auditor within 90 days from the end of the financial year, necessary cost accounting records, cost statements and other books and papers required for conducting the cost audit.
4. If default is made by the cost auditor in the submission of cost audit report and by the company in making available the necessary cost records within the prescribed time limit, they will be punishable with fine which may extend to ₹. 500.

Under the Cost Audit (Report) Rules, 1968 an Annexure has been provided to be filled by the cost auditor and annexed to the report that the cost auditor makes. The *Annexure* to the Cost Audit (Report) Rules is reproduced below :

1. *General*

(*i*) Name and address of the registered office of the company whose accounts are audited.

(*ii*) Name and address of cost auditor.

(*iii*) Reference No. and date of Government Order under which the audit is conducted.

(*iv*) Date of the Board meeting of the company in which the auditor under Section 233–B has been appointed.

(*v*) The company's financial year, for which the audit report is rendered.

(*vi*) Date of incorporation of the company and its status' (*i.e.*, whether it is a public company / private company which is a subsidiary of a public company, etc.).

(*vii*) Location where accounts are maintained.

(*viii*) Location of factory/factories.

(*ix*) If there is any foreign technical collaboration for the product under reference, attach a copy of the collaboration agreement. If this is not possible, prepare a brief note indicating:

(*a*) Name and address of the foreign collaborators.

(*b*) Main terms of the agreement.

(*c*) Amount of Royalty/technical aid fee payable and the basis of calculating the same.

(*d*) Whether the technical collaborator has contributed to the share capital. If so, the paid-up value of share so held.

(*x*) Licensed, installed and utilised capacities of the factories for the product under reference.

(*xi*) Date of first commencement of commercial production of the product under reference (if more than one factory under the some company produces the product under reference, particulars in respect of each may be given).

(*xii*) If the company is engaged in other activities besides the manufacture of the product under reference, give a brief note of such other activities.

2. *Cost Accounting System*

Briefly comment on the Cost Accounting system and its adequacy or otherwise to determine correctly the cost of the product under reference.

3. [1]*Financial Position*

"(Relating to the product under reference if possible, otherwise for the company as a whole. Indicate the particulars of the amounts included in items (1), (2), (3), below, duly reconciled with the financial accounts of the company for the relevant period)."

(1) *Capital employed.* Capital employed, defined as total assets at book value (excluding investments outside the business) minus corrent liabilites.

(2) *Net worth.* Net worth, *i.e.*, Capital plus Reserves or Capital less losses as the case may be. If there is any change in the composition of the net worth during the year, special mention may be made.

(3) *Profit before tax.* Profit after providing for depreciation and all other expenditure except interest on borrowing and debentures but before providing for tax on income.

(4) (*i*) *Expenses to be specified.* The amount in respect of the following:

(*a*) Annual bonus to employees.

(*b*) Interest on borrowing and debentures, etc.

(*c*) Bad debts.

(*d*) Donations of all kinds.

(*e*) Retrenchment or other compensation to employees excluding premia on account of workmen's compensation insurance.

(*f*) Lay-off wages.

(*g*) Expenditure on special exhibitions, etc., other than normal trade advertisements.

(*h*) Commission based on profit to managerial personnel.

(*i*) Income-tax and Sur-tax.

(*j*) Any other item of expenditure the incidence of which is neither normal nor of a recurring nature.

(*ii*) Income to be specified.

(*a*) Interest received on investments outside the business.

(*b*) Capital gains.

(*c*) Any other income which is neither normal of a recurring nature.

5. *Ratios.*

(*a*) Profit arrived at as per 3 (1) above expressed as a percentage of :

(*i*) capital employed as per 8(1) above.

(*ii*) net sales.

(*b*) (*i*) Current assets expressed as a percentage of current liabilities.

(*ii*) Net worth expressed as a percentage of long-term borrowing and liabilities.

(*iii*) Net worth expressed as a percentage of capital employed as per (3) (1) above.

(*c*) Cost of production as a percentage of :

(*i*) Capital employed as per 3(1) above.

(*ii*) Working capital (*i.e.*, current assets less current liabilities).

4. *Production*

(This information is to be given for each type of product under reference).

(1) Production in quantities.

(2) Indicate percentage of production of the product under reference in relation to installed capacity. If there is any shortfall in production as compared to the installed capacity, comment briefly as to the reasons for the shortfall.

(3) If there is any addition to the production capacity during the year under review or in the immediately preceding two years, this may also be mentioned.

5. *Process of Manufacture*

A brief note regarding the process of manufacture of the product under reference may be given.

6. *Raw materials*

(1) Show the cost of major raw materials consumed both in terms of quality and value. Where the cost of transport, etc., of raw materials is significant, specify the same separately.

(2) (*a*) Consumption of major raw materials per unit of production compared with the standard requirements, if any.

(*b*) Explanations for variations, if any, in the consumption of major raw materials per unit of production as compared to the preceding two years.

(3) Briefly comment on the method of accounting followed for recording the quantities and value of receipts, issues and balances of all materials directly used in production.

7. *Power and Fuel*

Quantity, rate per unit and total cost separately for each major form of power and fuel used in production, *e.g.*, coal, furnace oil, electricity, etc. Compare the actual consumption per unit of production with standards, if any. Special features, if any, may also indicated.

8. **Wages and Salaries*

(1) Total wages and salaries paid for all categories of employees. separately in respect of the following :

(*a*) Direct labour cost on production.

(*b*) Indirect employee costs on production.

(*c*) Employee costs on administration.

(*d*) Employee costs on selling and distribution.

(*e*) Other employee costs, if any (specifying purpose).

(*f*) Total employee costs [Total of items (*a*) to (*c*) above].

(2) Total man days of direct labour available and actually worked for the year.

(3) Average number of workers employed for the year.

(4) Direct Labour cost per unit of output of the product under reference (if more than one type of product is produced, give information in respect of each).

(5) Brief explanations for variations in (4) above, if any, as compared to the previous two years.

(6) Comments on the incentive schemes, if any, with particular reference to its contributions towards increasing productivity and, its effect on cost of production.

9. *Stores and Spare Parts*

(1) The expenditure per unit of output on stores, etc.

(2) Discuss the system of stores accounting for recording receipts, issues and balance, both in quantities and values.

(3) Indicate, if practicable, the proportion of closing inventory of stores representing items which have not moved for over 24 months.

10. *Depreciation*

(1) State the method of depreciation adopted by the company e.g., straight line or diminishing balance, etc. State whether the depreciation provided by the company is more or less than the amount of depreciation worked out in accordance with provisions of Sub-section (2) of Section 205 of the Companies Act, 1956.

(2) State the basis of allocation of depreciation on common assets to the different departments.

(3) Indicate the basis of charging depreciation to the cost products.

11. *Overheads*

(1) Give separately the amounts of the following overheads and a breakup of items (*a*) (*b*) and (*c*) below.

(*a*) Factory overheads.
(*b*) Administration overheads.
(*c*) Selling and distribution overheads.
(*d*) Interest.
(*e*) Bonus to employees.
(*f*) Commission to managerial personnel.

State whether any amounts in respect of items (*d*), (*e*) or (*f*) have been included in the total amount of items (*a*), (*b*) or (*c*) and give the amounts so included, if any.

(2) Indicate reasons for any significant variations in the expenditure incurred against the items, included in overheads as compared with the previous two years.

(3) State the basis of allocation of overheads to cost centres and of absorption to products. Give brief comments, if any, on the basis of allocation adopted by the company.

(4) Cost of packing, if any, of the products under reference to be shown separately with details to the extent possible.

12. *Royalty/Technical Aid Payments*

State the total amount of Royalty/Technical Aid Fees payable for the year and the amounts, chargeable per unit of the product.

13. *Sales*

(1) Indicate sales in quantities and net sales realisation of the products under reference showing the average sales realisation per unit. (if more than one type of product is sold, information is to be given in respect of each).

(2) If product under reference is exported, indicate quantity exported, net realization per unit, countries to which exported—details may be given. Indicate the profit/loss incurred in exports.

14. *Abnormal Non-Recurring Costs*

If there were any abnormal features affecting production during the year *e.g.*, strikes, lock outs, major breakdowns in the plant, substantial power cuts, serious accidents, etc., they should wherever practicable, be briefly mentioned indicating their effect on the cost of production.

15. *Other items*

If there are any special expenses which have been directly allocated to products under reference, the total amount as also the unit incidence shall be shown.

16. *Auditor's Observations and Conclusions*

(*i*) The cost auditor may here report on :

(*a*) matters which appear to him to be clearly wrong in principle or apparently unjustifiable;

(*b*) cases where the company's funds have been used in a negligent or inefficient manner;

(*c*) factors which could have been controlled, but have not been, resulting in increase in the cost of production.

(*d*) contracts or aggrements, if any between the company and other parties relating to selling, purchasing etc.;

(*e*) (*i*) the adequacy or otherwise of budgetary control system, if any, in vouge in the company;

(*ii*) the scope and performance of internal audit, if any;

(*f*) suggestions for improvements in performance, if any, *e.g.*, by :

(1) rectification of general imbalance in production facilities;

(2) full utilisation of installed capacity;

(3) concentration on areas offering scope for :

(*i*) cost reduction

(*ii*) increased productivity,

(*iii*) key limiting factors causing production "bottlenecks";

(4) improved inventory policies.

The opinions expressed shall be based on verified data, reference to which shall be made here and shall, wherever practicable, be included after the company has been afforded an opportunity to comment on them.

(*ii*) Copies of the statements in respect of completed products as given in Schedule II of the relevant notification issued under clause (*d*) of Sub-section I of Section 209 of the Companies Act, 1956 duly completed and audited shall be appended to the report.

If, as a result of the examination of the books of account, the auditor desires to give a qualified report, he shall indicate the extent to which he has to qualify the report and the reasons therefore.

Cost Audit Report Rules, 2001
Ministry of Law, Justice and Company Affairs
(Department of Company Affairs)
Notification

New Delhi, the 27th December, 2001

G.S.R. 924(E). In exercise of the powers conferred by sub-section (4) of 'section 233B, read with sub-section (1) of section 227 and clause (*b*) of sub-section (1) of section 642, of the Companies Act, 1956 (1 of 1956), and in suppression of the Cost Audit (Report) Rules, 1996, except as respect things done or omitted to be done, before such suppression, the Central Government hereby makes the following rules, namely:

1. Short title and commencement.

(1) These rules may be called the Cost Audit Report Rules, 2001.

(2) They shall come into force on the date of their publication in the Official Gazette.

2. Definitions. In these rules, unless the context otherwise requires,

(*a*) "Act" means the Companies Act, 1956 (1 of 1956);

(*b*) "Cost Auditor" means an auditor directed to conduct an audit under sub-section (1) of section 233B of the Act;

(*c*) "Form" means the Form the Cost Audit Report and includes auditor's observations and suggestions, Annexure and Proforma to the Cost Audit Report;

(*d*) "Report means Cost Audit Report duly audited and signed by the Cost Auditor in the prescribed form of Cost Audit Report;

(*e*) "Product under reference" means the **product or activity** to which the Report relates;

(*f*) All other words and expressions used in these rules but not defined, and defined in the Act and rules made under clause (*d*) of sub-section (1) of section 209 of the Act shall have the same meaning as assigned to them in the Act or rules, as the case may be.

3. Application. These rules shall apply to every company in respect of which an audit of the cost accounting records has been ordered by the Central Government under sub-section (1) of section 233 B of the Act. The Cost Audit Report submitted on or after 1st October, 2002, irrespective of the financial year of the company to which it relates, shall be in the form prescribed under these rules.

4. Form of the Report. (1) Every Cost Auditor, who conducts an audit of the cost acounting records of the company shall submit the report (a hard copy and a soft copy) along with auditor's observations and suggestions. Annexure and Proforma to the Central Government in the prescribed form and at the same time forward a copy of the report to the company.

(2) Every Cost Auditor, who submits a report under sub-rule (1), shall also give clarifications, if any, required by the Central Government on the Cost Audit Report submitted by him, within thirty days of the receipt of the communication addressed to him calling for such clarifications.

5. Time limit for submission of Report. The Cost Auditor shall forward his report referred to in sub-rule (1) of rule 4 to the Central Government and to the concerned company within one hundred and eighty days from the close of the company's financial year to which the report relates.

6. Cost Auditor to be furnished with the cost accounting records etc. Without prejudice to the powers and duties to the Cost Auditor shall have under sub-section (4) of section 233B of the Act, the company and every officer thereof, including the persons referred to in sub-section (6) of section 290 of the Act, shall make available to the Cost Auditor to in sub-section (6) of section 209 of the Act, shall make available to the Cost Auditor within one hundred and thirty five days from the close of financial year of the company, such cost accounting records, cost statements, other books and documents, Annexure and Proforma to the Report, duly completed, as would be required for conducting the cost audit, and shall render necessary assistance to the Cost Auditor so as to enable him to complete the cost audit and submit his report within the time limit specified in rule 5.

7. Authentication of Annexure to the Cost Audit Report. The Annexure and Proforma prescribed with the Cost Audit Report shall be approved by the Board of Directors before submitting the same to the Central Government by the Cost Auditor. The Annexure and Proforma, duly audited by the Cost Auditor, shall also be signed by the Company Secretary and at least one Director on behalf of the company. In the absence of Company Secretary in the company, the same shall be signed by at least two Directors.

8. Penalties. (1) If default is made by the Cost Auditor in complying with the provisions of rule 4 or rule 5, he shall be punishable with fine, which may extend to five thousand rupees.

(2) If the company contravenes the provisions of rule 6 or rule 7, the company and every officer thereof who is in default, including the persons referred to in sub-rule (6) of section 209 of the Act, shall, subject to the provisions of section 233B of the Act, be punishable with fine which may extend to five thousand rupees and where the contravention is a continuning one, with a further fine which may extend to five hundred rupees for every day after the first day during which such contravention continues.

Saving of action taken or that may be taken for contravention of Cost Audit (Report) Rules, 1996

It is hereby clarified that the suppressin of the Cost Auudit (Report) Rules, 1996, shall not in any way affect:

(*i*) any right, obligation or liability acquired, accrued or incurred thereunder :

(*ii*) any penalty, forfeiture or punishment incurred in respect of any contravention committed thereunder;

(*iii*) any investigation, legal proceeding or remedy in respect of any such right, privilege, obligation, liability, penalty, forfeiture, or punishment as aforesaid, and; any such investigation, legal proceeding or remedy may be instituted, continued or enforced and any such penalty, forfeiture or punishment may be imposed as if those rules had not been superseded.

Forms of the cost audit report

[See rule 2 (c) and rule 4]

I/We, ... having been appointed as Cost Auditor(s). Under Section 233B of the Companies Act, 1956 (1 of 1956) of .... (mention name of the company) having its registered office at....... (mention registered office address of the company) (hereinafter referred to as the company), have examined the books of account prescribed under clause (d) of sub-section (1) of section 209 of the said Act, and other relevant records in respect of the unit... (mention name and location of the unit) for the period/year ....(mention the financial year) relating to....... (mention name of the product or activity) maintained by the company and report, in addition to my/our comments in para 3 relating to auditor's observations and suggestions, that

1. (*i*) I/We have/have not obtained all the information and explanations, which to the best of my/our knowledge and belief were necessary for the purpose of this audit;

(*ii*) proper cost accounting records: as prescribed under clause (d) sub-section (1) of section 209 of the Companies Act. 1956, have/have not been kept by the company;

(*iii*) proper returns adequate for the purpose of my/our Cost Audit have/have not been received from the branches not visited by me/us;

(*iv*) the said books and records give/do not give the information required by the Companies Act, 1956 in the manner so required;

(*v*) the cost statements in respect of product or activity under reference as specified in the Annexures/Proforma of Schedules I, Schedule II or Schedule III of the concerned Cost Accounting Records (**............) Rules duly audited by me/us are kept in the company.

2. In my/our opinion, the company's cost accounting records have/have not been properly kept so as to give a true and fair view of the cost of production, cost of sales and margin of the product under reference as prescribed under the rules.

3. Based on my/our examination of the records of the company subject to aforesaid qualifications, if any, I/We give my/our **observations and suggestions** on the following

(*a*) the adequacy or otherwise of the cost accounting system including inventory valuation in vogue in the company and suggestions for the improvement thereof. The Cost Auditor shall also indicate the persistent deficiencies in the system, pointed out in earlier reports but not rectified;

(*b*) the adequacy or otherwise of the budgetary control system, if any, in vogue in the company;

(*c*) matters which appear to him to be clearly wrong in principle or apparently unjustifiable;

(*d*) cases, where price charged for related party transactions as defined in the respective Cost Accounting Records Rules is different from normal price, impact of such lower/higher price on margin of the product under reference shall be specified;

(*e*) areas where the company is incurring losses or where there is considerable decline in profitability, the cost auditor should comment on the reasons thereof including indicative break-even point. The cost auditor shall also comment on the default, if any on the payments due to the Government, financial institutions and banks, penal interest levied thereon and its impact on the cost of the sales and profitability;

(*f*) steps required to strengthen the company under the competitive environment especially with regard to need for protection from cheaper imports, if any;

(*g*) export commitments of the company profitability and princing policy of the company for domestic and export sales. Give impact of exports benefits/incentives offered by the Government on export profitability;

(*h*) the scope and performance of internal audit of cost records, if any, and comment on its adequacy or otherwise.

4. The Cost Auditor shall suggest measures for making further improvements in the performance in respect of cost control and cost reduction.

5. The Cost Auditor may also give his other observations and suggestions, if any, relevant to the cost audit.

Dated : this——date of——200——at——(mention name of place of signing this report).

Signatures & seal of the Cost Auditor(s)
Membership Number

Notes:

(1) Delete words not applicable.

(2) ***Specify the title of the concerned Cost Accounting Records Rules made under clause (d) of sub-section (1) of section 209 of the Companies Act, 1956 which are applicable to the product or activity of the company.

(3) If as a result of the examination of the books of account, the Cost Auditor desires to point out any material deficiency or give a qualified report, he shall indicate the same against the relevant para (*i*) to (*vi*) only in the prescribed form of the Cost Audit Report giving details of discrepancies he has come across.

(4) The report, suggestions, observations and conclusions given by the Cost Auditor under this paragraph shall be based on verified data, reference to which shall be made here and shall, wherever practicable, be included after the company has been afforded an opportunity to comment on them.

QUESTIONS

1. Define Cost Audit and state the various types of cost audit.
2. How will you check the accuracy of materials and labour charged to a job ?
3. The Government seeks your advice in checking the accuracy of the price under a "cost plus" contract. State how the checking should be done.
4. Compare cost and financial audit, both internal and external.
5. "The work of the cost audit depends upon the objectives of the concern." Explain.
6. Define Cost Audit. How is it useful (*i*) to the management (*ii*) to the society (*iii*) to the shareholders and (iv) to the Government.
7. Write explanatory note on Cost Audit.

8. (*a*) Define Cost Audit. Indicate the circumstances under which a cost-audit is ordered.

(*b*) Mention any eight areas of maintenance of Cost Accounting Record.

9. What as a cost account? Would you verify in the area of work-in progress?

10. Distinguish between cost audit and statutory Audit.

11. Distinguish between Efficiency Audit and Proprietary Audit.

12. What are purposes of cost Audit.

13. How is cost audit useful to management Society, shareholders and Government.

Uniform Costing and Interfirm Comparison

UNIFORM COSTING

Concept and Objectives

Uniform costing is not a particular method of costing. It is adoption of common accounting principles and in some cases common methods by member companies in the same industry so that their cost figures may be comparable. Uniform costing can be defined as the `use by several undertakings of the same costing principle and practices'. In other words, it is a technique or method of costing by which different firms of a field or industry apply similar costing system so as to produce cost data which have maximum comparability. Standard costs may be developed and cost-control is secured in firm through mutual comparison. Relative efficiency and inefficiencies in production may be identified and suitable steps may be suggested to control and reduce the cost.

The objectives of uniform costing is to standardise accounting methods and to assist in determining suitable prices of products of firms which adopt this method. Thus objects of an uniform costing system are :

(*a*) It provides reliable data for making inter-unit comparisons of cost performances.

(*b*) It helps to arrive at the cost of production for the industry as a whole on a common basis acceptable to all individual units or firm of the industry.

(*c*) It provides data to compare the cost of production and the production efficiencies between one firm and others.

(*d*) It ensures that the product prices are based on authentic costing data.

Application of Uniform Costing (Scope)

Uniform costing may be applied in two different situations.

(*a*) **Common Control and Management :** Uniform costing may be applied when number of units or firm producing similar goods and services are under a common control or controlled by the same group of management.

(*b*) **Trade Associations :** Uniform costing may be adopted by firms or units which are related to a trade association. Different firm may form an association through which they may adopt common costing method and practice.

Requisites of Uniform Costing

Uniform costing can be adopted if certain pre-conditions exists. The success of an uniform costing system depends primarily on the cooperation extended by different units or firm towards the working of the system. Every unit should agree to supply required accounting and costing information without reservation to a central body formed by them for implementation of the uniform costing scheme. This body has to correlate, analyse and consolidate the information received from the different units. Following are pre-requisites of uniform costing.

(*a*) Firms or units adopting uniform costing must be ready to provide and share accounting and costing information freely.

(*b*) They should adopt a common system of costing regarding classification, distribution and absorption of costs. They must agree on a common technique of costing *e.g.*, absorption costing, standard costing or marginal costing.

(*c*) The firms must use a common terminology and procedure for cost ascertainment and cost control.

(*d*) There should not be any restriction from the Government in adopting uniform costing.

(*e*) A central body or proper organisation must be set up for preparing comparative statistics for the use of member units participating in the uniform costing.

(*f*) Above all, the most important is that units or firms must have mutual trust, confidence and cooperation.

Key Factors : The success of uniform costing depends on certain key factors which would be peculiar to each unit. These factors are uniformity in method of production, the size of organisation and accounting method.

The *Method of Production* of units should be uniform. Besides similarity in output, the types of machinery used should be identical. The difference in the type of machinery used will create variation in the efficiency and therefore in costs. There may be some other varying factors in produciton. Unless these factors are levelled out by giving weightage on an equitable basis the object of uniform costing will not by served.

The *Size of Organisation* of participating units should not be different. If production capacities of units are widely different, they cannot follow the same principles and practices.

The *Accounting Method* of different member units should be identical. If the accounting method are different, the information needed for uniform costing may not be available within reasonable time and frequency without unnecessary delay.

Standardisation: The essential feature of Uniform Costing is adoption of standardised principles and methods of cost accounting by different units introducing the method. The standardisation may extend to following :

1. Method of Cost Accounting *e.g.*, job costing, process costing or a variation of one or both of these.
2. Accounting classification including coding.
3. Content of each account.
4. Methods of defining costs : (*a*) direct material (*b*) direct labour (*c*) direct expenses (*d*) overhead costs regarding factory, selling, distribution, administration, research and development.
5. Methods of recovering depreciation.
6. Methods of allocating and/or apportioning overheads costs to cost centres and jobs or products
7. Material control including the pricing of issue and valuation of stocks.
8. Methods of recording accounting data e.g., integrated accounting system.
9. Reports and statements for planning and control.
10. System of remunerating labour e.g., time rate or piece rates.
11. A Central Body should be established for carrying out the work of uniform costing.

The standardisation should be achieved by developing a '*Uniform Costing Manual*'

Practical Difficulties in Introduction of Uniform Costing or Problems of Application

The introduction of Uniform Costing system faces a number of difficulties since the cost structure of participating units or firm may vary due to following factors.

1. **Difference in size of the firm and the organisation structure :** The difference in the size of firms will result in difference in the division of work and process of output. Larger firms may have more division of work than that of smaller firms in the same process. The number of departments and supporting services will be more in a large firm than the smaller ones and this will result in higher overhead cost. Moreover, a large size firm can achieve economies of bulk purchase which will not be available to the small firm.
2. **Difference in technology :** There may be difference in the technology used by member firms. Firms using more sophisticated plant may lead to greater division of work into process. Their nature and sequence of work will also differ from firms adopting less sophisticated technology.
3. **Difference in range of products :** A firm may produce only a few variety of products whereas the other may produce large number of varieties of products. The firm producing large variety will be in advantageous position with regard to distribution of overheads.
4. **Diffenence is the level of productivity and efficiency:** Levels of efficiency and productivity may vary from firm to firm depending upon skilled and experienced personnel, their tracing, supervison, motivation and cooperation of trade union.
5. **Difference in managerial planning and growth rates :** There may be different growth rates of the member firms. With the result, the planning of each firm may be different in terms of costing and pricing while uniform costing requires common pricing system.
6. **Difference in costing methods and principles :** There may be difference in costing principle and procedure adopted by member firms. For example, a firm may recover overheads on the basis of direct wages whereas another may recover overheads on labour hour rate or machine hour rate which may result dissimilarity in costs of the same type of product. Uniform costing depends upon elimination of such differences. These differences can be eliminated by application of common principles and procedure by member firms.
7. **Difference in geographical situation :** In a big country regional difference create difference in cost structure of different firms. There may be availability of cheap labour, nearness to raw material, advantage of market and favourable climate to some firms. Many states may offer concessions in power rates, interest rates, tax rates. All these factors will create difference in the cost structure. These require reconciliation before implementation of costing structure.

Installation of Uniform Costing System

As explained earlier, there should be standardisation in the adoption of principles and methods of cost accounting by member firms who intend to unstall uniform costing. Moreover their should be mutual trust, confidence and an exhaustive spirit of cooperation among participating firms or units. Every unit should agree to supply required accounting and costing information without reservation to a central body formed to coordinate the system.

Before installaton of uniform costing system, it is desirable to carry out certain **preparatory work** as outlined below :

1. The central body or association of firms seeking uniform costing should convey the objective of the system to the member firms. It will be better to obtain the opinions of member firms so that the method may become cohesive and acceptable to all.
2. A careful study of condition in the industry and units should be carried out to ensure that their various operations are comparable.
3. It is desirable to establish a standard procedure for the analysis of costs of member firms. For example, the overhead recovery method should be same in all units. Thus standardisation of costing procedure and principles must be incorporated in member firms.

Proper Planning: After the above noted preparatory steps taken up, there should be proper planning of uniform costing system. Planning require careful attention to the following points :

1. Planning should be made regarding system of costing to be adopted by firm. It should be decided that whether they should adopt job costing or process costing.
2. It should be decided whether firms will use the technique of actual costing or standard costing or marginal costing.
3. Every firm should adopt an uniform or common method of classfying accounts and forms of various statements.
4. The unit of cost of firms should be carefully defined. Each firm should adopt same unit of cost.
5. There should be a proper and common method of segregation of direct and indirect material and labour.
6. There should be a proper and common method of classification of production and service departments.
7. There should be a common principle of classification of overheads.
8. The method of pricing of issue of material should be common and uniform.
9. The method of valuing stock, work-in-progress should be common.
10. The method of remunerating labour should be uniform or common in all firms.
11. There should be a common approach regarding inclusion or non-inclusion of interest on capital in the cost.
12. There should be a common method adopted for charging depreciation on plant, machinery and other equipments.
13. The method and principle of allocation, appointment and absorption of overhead should be uniform in the all member firms.

Only planning and implementation of uniform costing method may not be fruitful unless the system is properly controlled and followed up. It must be observed that a common costing technique is adopted and implemented by all member units. Moreover a uniform costing committee or a central body should be formed consisting representative of different firm which may coordinate and look after the proper functioning of the system. This representative body should ensure a better cordination among member firms. It should ensure a better monitoring service for exchange of information among member. Moreover this committee should also prepare a costing manual which should contain information and instruction regarding different aspects of uniform costing technique.

Working of the System

The full benefits arising out of an uniform costing system may be derived if it is decided before hand the statements to be prepared under the system and the form in which they will be prepared. These periodical statements should be regularly sent to the central body. The central body will collate and study the results of each member unit and will finally prepare a comparative statements. These comparative statements will be useful in showing cost per unit and their relative efficiencies. It is also useful to appoint a coordinating committee to supervise and review the working of the uniform costing system.

Uniform Costing Manual

Uniform costing manual is a written record of information and instruction regarding policies, regulations, functions, system, procedures and methods framed with a view to guide the efforts of employees in the organisation under the uniform costing system. It is a manual which contains exhaustive guidelines for the effective performance of the functions of cost ascertainment and cost control. It provides a guideline of the costing plan so that member firms arrange their accounting system and procedure on an uniform basis. An uniform costing manual generally contains following.

(*i*) A brief introduction covering objectives, purpose and scope of the uniform system.

(*ii*) Advantages which are expected.

(*iii*) Extent of the cooperation needed for the successful implementation of the system.

(*iv*) Accounting system to be followed by participating firms.

(*v*) Methods of costing to be used, method of cost collection, method of ascertainment of cost, uniform terminology and concepts.

(*vi*) Method of inventory control and pricing of issue of material.

(*vii*) Essential details regarding control of labour and overheads. Methods related overhead collection, distribution and absorption.

(*viii*) Treatment of depreciation and interest on capital.

(*ix*) Disposal of over and under recovery of overheads, wastage, scraps and by-products

(*x*) Forms and contents of statements for submission of information to the management.

(*xi*) Analysis of statements and computation of various ratios for the purpose of evaluation of performance and efficiency etc.

The size, form and contents of a cost manual may vary depending upon the nature and extent of the uniform costing plan and the method of presentation of data.

Advantages of Uniform Costing

In brief, the advantage of uniform costing system are achievement of greater operating efficiency through common understanding of cost and a competitive spirit introduced by comparison of cost, adoption of realistic pricing policies and establishment of the best methods and principles of costing. The following are various advantages of uniform cost accounting system.

1. Uniform costing helps member firms to adopt one of the best method of cost accounting system known to the industry. This eliminates unsound methods and also saves cost required in perfecting systems through expensive trial and error or experimentation.
2. Uniform costing tends to convince the member firms for adoption of method used by the competitors.
3. Uniform costing develops better informed and healthy competition within the industry which result in control and reduction of cost.
4. Uniform costing provides the members with all benefits of sound costing system. On the basis of available reliable cost information, product pricing is taken up on sound basis.

It checks unhealthy competition and price-cutting below costs. Moreover report are provided for comparison of major cost items with predetermined standard costs. It helps in controlling costs and increasing operating efficiency. The system also provides information which guide to the performance and efficiency of labour, machine and methods.

5. Uniform costing system reveals unprofitable products or product lines and provide valuable information to strengthen them.
6. Uniform costing also creates confidence in the customers that prices have been fixed with reliable data of costs.
7. Uniform costing enables regulatory bodies and government to collect required data relating to the industry.

Thus uniform costing is a useful tool for managerial control, performance appraisal and standardisation of operation in the industry. It avoids cut-throat competition. Weaker member units can avail advantage of the efficient methods of production, cost control and the research and development in the field.

Limitations and Disadvantages of Uniform Costing

Uniform costing is sometimes opposed due to a number of problems and difficulties. Standardisation of definition and method is the key factor of uniform costing but it is difficult to accomplish. Moreover if standardisation is achieved, there is great difficulty in fitting the method into the framework of each individual business because many differences exist such as age of plant, geographical location, availability of labour etc. How can a firm working with manual labour be compared with a highly mechanised firm? Following points may be noted as limitations of the method :

(1) The arguments generally advanced against the use of a uniform costing system are :

(*a*) Sharing of confidential data with other competitors in the industry; (*b*) Accounting inconveniences arising out of each individual unit having own principle and practice which may be different (C). The limited advantages which an unit can derive from the scheme.

(2) From the standpoint of the society, the disadvantage of uniform costing is formation of trade association by firms just to restraining trade and impending competition.

(3) Uniform costing generally creates conditions which develop monopolistic tendencies under trade association. These association may raise prices arbitrarily.

INTERFIRM COMPARISON (*IFC*)

Interfirm comparison is a natural outcome of uniform costing system. Uniform costing is the foundation stone over which the structure of *IFC* is developed and adopted in a large scale.

Interfirm comparison can be defined as the technique of evaluating the relative performance, efficiency, costs and profits of firms in a given industry'. The meaning of *IFC* can be easily explained by considering the main object of the system. In other words *IFC* consists of following procedure.[1]

(*a*) Data are collected from participating organisation or firm by their trade organisation or centre of interfirm comparison.

(*b*) The management of an organisation are provided with information which will allow them to determine the efficiency being achieved, measured by comparing the performances of other business.

1. *J. Battey* 'Management Accountancy'.

(*c*) An attempt is made to show why results vary from one business to another, i.e., any weakness is highlighted.

(*d*) Extensive use is made of financial and cost ratios.

Objects of Inter Firm Comparison

The main purpose of *IFC* is improvement of efficiency by showing the management of participating firm its present achievements and possible weaknesses. These firms have to contribute their data to the central body which acts as a neutral body. This central body ensures confidence and it gives report regarding comparisons only to participants.

Following are important objectives of interfirm comparison :

(*a*) *IFC* analyses costs of different firms with a view to spot out relative efficiency.

(*b*) *IFC* provides aid to management in enforcing and reviewing budgetary control and standard costing. These techniques enforced in one firm are compared with those in other firms making more efficient use of the same. Inadequacies of standard costing and budgetary control are located by making interfirm comparisons and remedial measures are introduced.

(*c*) *IFC* helps to prepare a comprehensive and detailed plan for firms or units to obtain optimum use of human and material resources.

The main objection of *IFC* is the improvement of efficiency and identification of weak points. *IFC* is a scheme consisting of exchange of information with regard to cost, profit, productivity and efficiency between the participating firms through a central organisation. *IFC* focuses the remedial measure of a number of problems related to profit, sales and production. In interfirm comparison coordinated and monitored through an apex body or central organisation, attention is usually concentrated on the following major important are :

(*i*) Is profit adequate ?

(*ii*) How efficient is selling ?

(*iii*) How efficient is production ?

Organisation of *IFC*

The organisational set up for inter firm comparison may be in the form of either a trade association or a Government department or centre for interfirm comparison.

There may be a trade association of participating firms. Firms submit their required information to the association. Trade association analyses the information collected from firm and presents report to each member firm.

The job of coordinating and analysing of data provided by firms of an industry may be entrusted to a Government Department. The main objective of such organisation structure of *IFC* is to exercise price control and regulation of firms.

In UK, the British Institute of Managment had set up centre for Inter-firm comparison in association with British Productivity council. The centre was established just to meet the demands of trade and industry for an expert body for inter firm comparison. Such a type of organisation has to prepare schemes for inter firm comparison. In India also there is need of such centre.

Thus there should be a central body to coordinate and monitor interfirm comparison.

Method or Approach for Interfirm Comparison

Firms wishing to obtain the benefits of interfirm comparison have to approach the central body or apex body constituted for *IFC*. A fee may be charged for carrying out comparisons.

The method of approach adopted by the central body will be governed by the type of industry or trade and the problems and circumstances present. The possible procedure may be as below.[1]

1. Firms which are to participate in an interfirm comparison have to submit their data to the central body. These figures are compiled on the basis of uniform definitions of terms, procedures, methods and accounting periods.
2. After all necessary steps have been taken to ensure that the participating firms can benefit from the comparison, a number of *ratios* are compiled. These ratios are shown in a summary form distinguishing.
   (*a*) Ratios for the group of firm participating in the interfirm comparison.
   (*b*) Ratios for a single firm.

Each firm is given a report compiled along these lines.

3. The ratios for the group and the ratios for the single firm are compared one by one.
4. Once any significant deviation from the norm (average return on capital employed) is established, the possible reasons for this deviation may be located by examining other ratios.

Ratios of Inter firm comparison

Ratios used in the interfirm comparison are of four types :

(*i*) Primary Ratios
(*ii*) Supporting Ratios
(*iii*) General Explanatory Ratios
(*iv*) Specific Explanatory Ratios

All the ratios can be taken together to form a pyramid as given below :

Ratio Pyramid of a Manufacturing Industry

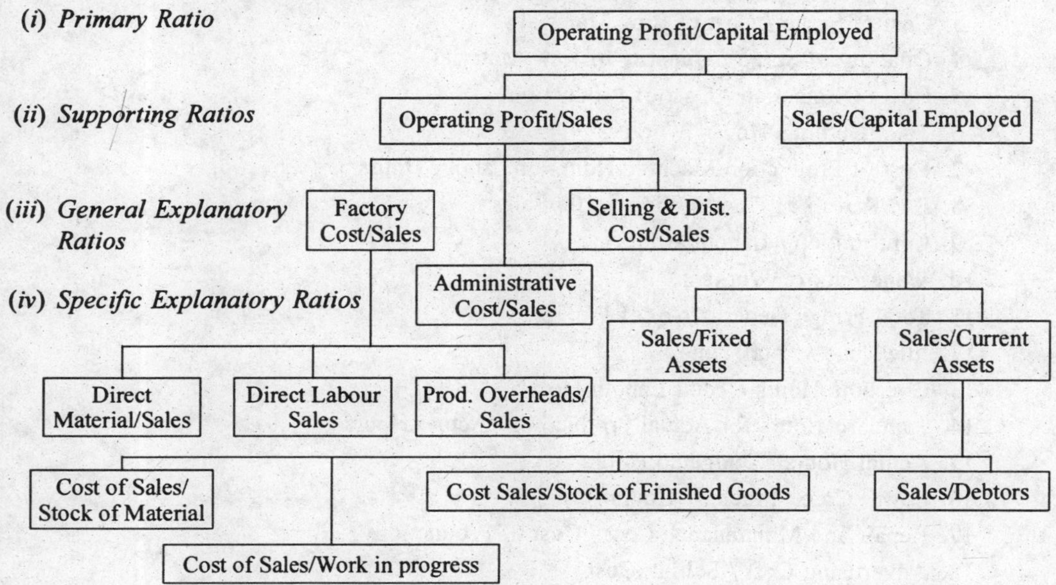

1. *J. Battey* 'Management Accountancy'

Pyramid Ratio of a Distributive Trade

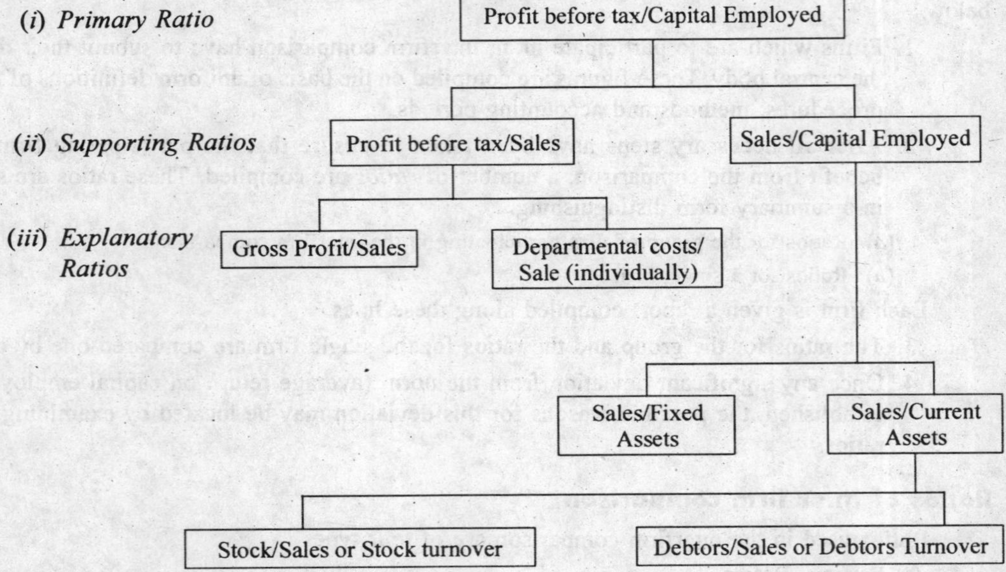

In addition to above ratios, some other ratios may be used for the purpose of systematic analysis of operational results. These cover all aspects of business activities and are meant for measurement of effectiveness of the resources. These additional ratios are briefly explained below.

(A) Ratios of Performance Measurement :

1. Value of Direct Material/Value of Production
2. Cost of Materials/Quantity Produced
3. Cost of Scrap / Cost of Raw Material
4. Quantity of Scrap / Quantity of Raw Material
5. Cost of Rejection / Cost of Production
6. Total Output / No. of Workers
7. Cost of Production/Machine Hours or Labour Hours
8. P.V. Ratio *i.e.*, Contribution × 100/Sales
9. Contribution / Labour Hours
10. Wages/No. of Workers
11. Total Fringe Benefits/No. of Workers
12. Idle Time / Total Time
13. Overtime Hours / Total Labour Hours
14. Standard Hours for Actual Production / Actual Hours
15. Actual Hours / Budgeted Hours
16. Power Cost / Machine Hours
17. Repair and Maintanance Cost / Cost of Production
18. Advertising Cost / Selling Cost

(B) Ratios to Judge Profitability :

These ratios show how profitable are company's operations.

1. Gross Profit Ratio *i.e.*, (GP/Sales) × 100

2. Net Profit Ratio *i.e.*, (NP / Sales) × 100

GP ratio indicates manufacturing or trading efficiency while NP ratio shows overall profitability

3. Return on capital employed *i.e.*, Profit / Capital employed

ROLE indicates overall performance from the stand point of profitability. It is primary ratio in the pyramid of ratios

(C) Ratios related to Turnover :

Turnover Ratio show how efficiently company is managing current assets.

1. Stock turnover ratio *i.e.*, cost of sales/Average stock

This ratio shows the efficiency of inventory management. Average stock is average of opening and closing stock

2. Debtors Turnover Ratio *i.e.*, Debtors × Days or Months in a year / Annual Credit Sales

Debtors turnover measures the efficiency in collection of debts

3. Creditors Turnover Ratio *i.e.*, (Creditors × No. of days of months in a year)/Annual Credit Purchases.

This ratio measures the efficiency of purchase department in realising credit facilities

(D) Liquidity Ratios :

These ratios show the liquidity position of the company to meet its day to day needs of working capital

1. Current Ratio *i.e.*, Current Assets/Current Liabilities

Current Ratio shows the ability of the company to meet its maturing current liabilities. An ideal ratio is 2:1 but it may differ due to nature of business.

2. Quick Ratio or Acid Test Ratio *i.e.*, Quick Assets *i.e.*, Current Assets excluding inventory/ Current Liabilities

Quick Ratio indicate ability of the company to meet its immediate current liabilities out of readily realisable current assets.

Reporting

The central body collects and analysis the data supplied by participating firm, calculates relevant ratios and prepares report to be sent to individual member firm. Normally code numbers are used in place of names of the firms so that information may remain confidential. The results and interpretators are presented in the report in such a way that individual firm data could not be identified.

On receipt of the comparative data and report of interfirm comparison, it is the job of the management of the firm to compare operating and other results and the corresponding ratios with ratio furnished by the central body of *IFC*.

Advantages of Interfirm Comparison

1. Under *IFC* the weakness of participating firms are revealed and the management will be guided to remedial actions.

2. The firm will come to know the trend of sales, profit and cost of an industry or trade as shown by different ratios. If all firms are suffering from falling sales, it will be indicated by sales

to capital or asset employed ratio. When an individual firm compares its own ratio with the ratio of the group, it will see that there is general reduction sales.

3. Management of participating firm are provided with most significant facts on the basis of ratios carefully selected by the central body. The firm will have to do only the study of the ratios and the necessary action.

4. Whether firm is doing better or worse than other firms is made known through the ratios. The firm can take positive steps to improve efficiency.

5. The experience of the central body is at the disposal of participating firms. This knowledge can be very valuable in the analysis of performance and profitability of the firm.

6. Participating firm provide information willingly knowing that this remains confidential.

7. *IFC* develops cost consciousness among participating firm.

8. *IFC* leads to avoidance of unfair competition. It guides in the direction of proper and positive efforts towards improvement of performances.

9. Interfirm comparisons and related data help in representing the problem of the industry to regulating authorities and the Government in an effective and convincing matter. Information regarding entire industry can be presented before the Government and not the isolated problem of individual firm.

10. Collective information provided under *IFC* can help the industry in its negotiations with trade unions.

Limitations of *IFC*

It is obvious that interfirm comparison is useful in improving productivity, efficiency and profitability. But benefits are obtained only when ratios are properly calculated and impartially used. The limitations of ratio analysis should be taken into consideration. It should be noted that a single ratio is of a limited value and their trend is most important. Moreover the limitation of uniform costing should also be taken into consideration because uniform costing provides the very basis of interfirm comparison.

It should also not be ignored that certain extraneous factors such as prolonged strike, power shortage may also adversely affect the performance of the industry in a particular period.

Limitations and short comings of annual returns and data may also affect the realibility of conclusions.

It can also be pointed out that there are practical limitation in the formation and maintenance of an independent central agency for interfirm camparisons. The cost of introducing uniform costing may make the management of firm reluctant to participate in a scheme of interfirm comparison.

QUESTIONS

1. What do you understand by uniform costing ? Outline the factors that led to its introduction.

2. Define uniform costing and discuss fundamental costing principles involved in the uniform costing.

3. What is uniform costing? Outline the procedure for the introduction of uniform costing.

4. What are the purposes of interfirm comparisons ? What procedure is followed for this?

5. What are essential requisites of interfirm comparison ? *[CA PE II May 2002, Nov. 2001]*

6. Explain what do you understand by uniform costing? Discuss the points in respect of which uniformity is required to be established before introduction of uniform costing in an industry.

7. Write short notes on

(i) Uniform Costing

(*ii*) Uniform Cost Manual

(*iii*) Interfirm Comparison

8. A firm printers is of contemplating joining the uniform costing system being operated by its Trade Association but the Managing Director is doubtful about the advantages of becoming involved in the scheme. Prepare a report to the M.D. describing the advantages that firm is likely to gain.

9. What are the requisites for the installation of the uniform costing system?

10. Write four limitations of inter firm comparisons.

11. Discuss the limitations of uniform costing.

12. What is meant by 'Inter firm comparison ? Describe the requisites to be considered while installing a system of inter-firm comparison.

Cost Control, Cost Reduction, Control Systems and Reporting

PRODUCTIVITY

It goes without saying that all industrial concerns, in fact all organisations, which work using resources, normally expressed in terms of money, must try to reduce costs on a continuous basis. It is quite correct to say that normally no element of cost is in such a condition that its cost cannot be reduced further. Factors of production can always be made to yield more and should be made to do so. In other words, productivity should be increased. But, first let us understand some of the basic terms.

Productivity denotes greater yield from the same given resources, like a worker producing more goods per day or less materials being used for producing goods of the same quantity and quality as previously. Productivity should be distinguished form more production; greater production may be obtained by, say, employing more workers or installing more machines. But productivity will indicate either increasing production without increasing the number of workers employed or installing more machines or it may mean producing the same quantity of goods as previously by using lesser resources, say, a lesser number of hours of work, or resources costing less like materials of a different quality. Greater productivity will lead to lower cost per unit; it may also lead to greater production. But greater production may be achieved at the cost of lower productivity; in other words, with increase in production it is possible that there may also be an increase in the cost per unit. Productivity and efficiency can be used as synonyms.

The input-output ratio, *i.e*,

$$\frac{\text{Output}}{\text{Input}}\ e.g., \left(\frac{\text{Total production in terms of standard hours}}{\text{Actual time spent}}\right)$$

indicates movement in productivity.

Cost Control means the procedures and measures by which the cost of carrying out an activity is kept under check. In this case, the aim is to see that costs do not go beyond a certain level.

Cost reduction is a further step after cost control; it involves such measures and procedures by which the cost per unit of the goods produced will be lower than previously. Ultimately the aim of cost control must be cost reduction. But it is possible to separate the two, at least conceptually.

Permanent Constraints

There are certain factors which have a binding and permanent influence on the cost of activities of an industrial concern. These factors are the location of the factory, its layout, size, the character of the product, etc.

The proper location of a factory should be where the total transport costs, both of finished goods and of raw materials, should be the minimum. This further involves the character of the raw materials used. If the raw material is of a weight-losing character, *i.e.*, if the quantity of material embodied in the finished product is much less than the quantity of the material used, the location should be near the source of raw materials. If more than one material is used, the location should be near that material which losses more of its weight during the process of manufacture, of course, keeping in mind the total quantities used. A steel mill, for instance, will be located near coal mines and not near iron ore mines since the quantity of coal used is very large and the whole of the weight of coal is lost. If the material is non-weight losing, the factory should be located near the market. Cotton, after ginning, is non-weight losing since the quantity of cloth obtained is only slightly less than the quantity of cotton used. It is, therefore, natural to find cotton textile mills near the markets.

If this basic principle is lost sight of and the factory is located at the wrong point, extra transport cost will have to be incurred as long as the factory remains and will have an adverse influence on the cost of production. However, it is possible that another place may offer to many advantages that it may be cheaper to incur extra transport cost to some extent.

Availability of labour possessing right skills is an important factor. This is one of the reason why new industries are often set up in a place like Bombay, where othewise it is quite costly. In Bombay, skilled labour of all types is available and even if the skill required is new, the labour will very quickly pick it up. A place where already there is good deal of industrialisation will also offer many advantages since it may mean *availability of repairs and maintenance facilities, banking facilities*. etc., A big city by itself also offers a *big market*. However, sometimes big cities become prohibitively costly; that is why there are a number of factories which are established away from big cities because of low land costs, low cost of water, lack of trade union organisation amongst workers, etc. The chief point is that the location of the factory should be very carefully decided upon as, otherwise, the company's products may permanently have high costs.

Apart from location, another factor which will have a lasting influence on costs is the *layout*. Different departments of the factory should be so laid out that work should move in its natural direction without going backwards and forwards. The aim here also is to see that internal transport and handling is as little as possible. Again, there can be exceptions. There can be specialised departments where work may be brought and the special operations performed and then the work may be taken back. There is extra handling but the location of the specialised operations under one roof may be much more economical than the extra handling cost. Such specialisation may permit the use of machines, the employment of highly skilled people and the number of men employed may even be less than if the operations were to be performed in all the departments separately. Layout also should be decided upon from the point of view of effective use of space, effective supervision and separation of noise-making departments from those departments which require absence of noise for effective work.

Another important factor is the *size of the factory*. It is well known that there is a certain optimum technical size since machines come in certain sizes only. A size which is too small or too big will mean extra costs. It is usually better to buy machines which are readily available in the market rather than order specially big or small machines. It is also important that there should be a proper balance of machinery used at various points. If there is no balance, there will be a bottleneck at some point where work will accumulate leading to idleness of machines before that point. Though a number of individual machines are employed, the factory as a whole works as one machine.

In India, there is another point to take note of. This is the *degree of mechanisation*. It is well known that labour in India does not take kindly to efforts at machinsation or automation, even though there is assurance that the workers will not lose their jobs. There have been cases when a company, in its anxiety to introduce new and up-to-date machines in place of labour, has been forced to keep the labour on its rolls. It would be extremely costly to have both.

The question of mechanisation surely is decided with reference to the cost of work done with the aid of human labour and without such labour *i.e.*, with the help of machines. Of course, in case of machines the interest involved on the investment should also be reckoned. But one should remember that if a machine is installed, the cost will be pegged at a certain level for as long as the machine works, whereas in case of labour, there is no surety that the costs will remain what they are at present. Labour costs are going up with increasing demands from trade unions. Against this it should also remembered that installation of machinery means incurring a fixed expenses burden which will be extremely costly if the machines remain idle. Mechanisation, therefore, is a question which has to be decided by reference not only to present- day costs but also by reference to the possible fluctuations in production in future. If it is thought that the demand will be maintained at a fairly high level, it would be better to introduce as high a degree of mechanisation in the very beginning as possible and to employ as few workers as possible. The effect of this will be that the number of workers will be smaller than otherwise; smaller number of workers can be looked after better by the firm and there can be greater satisfaction amongst the labour force. Attempts at mechanisation at a later stage are likely to meet stiff resistance and may not be successful.

Character of Product. In the cost of production, the *nature and character of the product* also plays a very important role. The fundamental point to remember is that the cost of production will depend upon the scale of production, not of the product as a whole but of each variety, For example, if a fountain pen is produced in 50 different varieties and the total output is 1,00,000 pens, one cannot think of the cost of production having regard to 1,00,000 units but only with regard to 2,000 units on the average. If the number of varieties is reduced to 10, the scale of production will immediately increase to 10,000 on the average and this will immediately bring down the cost of production. This process is known as *standardisation*. As far as possible the number of varieties should be small.

However, it is not always safe to concentrate one's attention only on standardisation, to the neglect of the wishes of the customers. It is a common practice with new firms, and those firms which wish to expand their market, to introduce new varieties of the same product so that customers, who always want something new, buy the newer varieties. Of course, when the customer is not willing to pay a high price, he is satisfied with a smaller number of varieties; but when he is affluent and can afford to pay a good price, he is always on the look of a newer variety. It is always a question of compromise between the marketing people and the production people as to how many varieties of the product will be produced and put on the market.

A connected question is that of *simplification*. There may be only one variety on the market but it may have a number of unneccessary details or decoration or, as it is said, frills. Instead of straight corners, these may be rounded. A chair may have straight legs of so many different shapes. Simplification of a product is again a very important factor for reducing the cost of production. Here again, however, the question is as to what the market really demands and this question, again, has to be decided between the Production Manager and the Sales Manager to arrive at a solution whereby simplification to the utmost possible extent, having regard to the wishes of the customers and to the cost of production as also the selling price, is achieved.

Decision regarding the character of the products, of course, can be changed from time to time. But very often a decision taken will be enforced for quite some time, since there is a natural inertia for changing such important decisions — one certainly would like to see the results of a decision in the matter before a change is affected. A decision to change the character of the product may mean a change in moulds and dyes, etc., and those are both time and money consuming. As long as certain decisions about standardisation and simplification of the product are in force, the cost would be at a certain level and would not permit reduction.

We have discussed above some of the important factors which operate as a constraint on cost reduction. Apart from this, however, there is a wide field in which it is possible to exercise cost control and cost reduction and it is generally this field which engages the attention of the cost accountant and industrial engineers from day-to-day.

The Role of Cost Accountant in Cost Control

At the outset it should be understood that a cost accountant can at best only suggest areas which promise to be fruitful for the purpose of cost reduction. It may be possible for him to locate wastage. But the most important work in this respect is done by the production people, including the industrial engineer. It is they who fix the right quantities of materials and the right amount of time for producing a product. For example, for determining standard time for completing an operation or a job, time and motion study is required. This is carried out not by the cost accountant but by the industrial engineer. Reduction in time or even any reduction in use of materials may involve a changed process of manufacture; that again is a field for the production people. Substitution of material is another matter where production will have the final say. For distribution of goods, it is the sales people who would be able to suggest proper location of godowns to effect economy in transport, or will help greatly in this regard. Basically, therefore, it is the people who actually carry out operations that have the responsibility and the opportunity for effecting economy.

This does not mean that the cost accountant has no role to play. The cost accountant has past figures with him and, if no standards are developed, he can easily compare present performance with the past performance, both for quantities and amounts and locate wastages and losses. His awareness that standards can be developed may force the production people to adopt standards. His analysis of cost into variable and fixed categories helps to determine the proper level of cost to be incurred for any level of output and, of course, if standards are developed, comparison of actuals with the standards enables him to prepare a detailed statements, showing how exactly discrepancies have arisen. This shows areas where management action may lead to stoppage of wastages and losses. One can say, therefore, that in the field of cost control and cost reduction, both the production people and the cost accountant have to work together; the former have greater responsibility for cost reduction and the latter has greater responsibility for cost control by reporting deviations from accepted standards and targets.

VALUE ANALYSIS

In the business and commercial world, the object of all activities is to earn a profit. Profit results when the selling price exceeds the cost. In normal times, the selling price would depend upon the eagerness of the customers to buy the product or the service. In other words, it depends on the benefit which the customers expect to derive from the use of the product or service. This is translated into the amount of money which the customer is willing to pay; this is the value which the customer places on the article which he is purchasing. It depends entirely on the wishes of the body of customers, that is to say, on the market. The amount of money spent on producing the article or the service usually is irrelevant, at least when there is a free market and a free competition.[1]

If costs were relevant for determining value and, therefore, the price, there would not be any case of failure of busienss. The very fact that a number of business houses have to close down, within a short time, shows that the cost of production of an article is not considered by the market when determining prices in the short period; the market only considers the value which is placed upon it by the users, as expressed through the demand curves. Also, there are instances where the price paid by the customers is very high even though the cost of production is small. The reason

1. In case the price of an article is controlled by the government or is regulated by the trade association, the price will depend upon the cost. Such a condition, however, normally does not prevail unless there are great shortages in the country concerned.

for this is that the customer is most anxious to buy the product and is, therefore, willing to pay a high price for it; to him the fact that it costs only a little to the producer is, at that moment, not important.

The above discussion would indicate the necessity on the part of the producer of goods and services to always remember that incurring of costs is no guarantee of earning a profit. He must incur costs in such a manner as to evoke a good response from the customers. He must always be careful to see that when money is being spent by him to produce the article or the service, it will be appreciated by the customers through payment of a remunerative price. Producers of goods and services, except the traditional Indian farmer, have always tried to produce that article which customers would like to have and for which they would be willing to pay a good price. At least this is the hope with which businessmen men work. But what is required is a more systematic effort to find out whether the costs which are being incurred are really resulting in any value. When such a systematic effort is made, the process would be known as *value analysis*.

The process would consist of the following :

(*a*) Noting different distinguishable features of the product or the service and ascertaining the price which is obtained for each feature individually. This is easily done when there are separable accessories; for example, the wringer can be separately quoted to the customer when he is wanting to buy a washing machine. However, the article may have a number of features, without which it will not be sold. It is here that a careful attempt is to be made as to the utility which customers place on each feature—for example, the additional price that the customer will pay for thermostatic control in an electric iron or in a water heater. It may be noted here that the additional benefit from an additional feature may not only be in the form of a higher price which is available but also in the form of a larger volume of sale, leading to a lower cost per unit.

(*b*) Whether a component should be made or bought ? This is one of the most familiar problems in an industrial concern and the basic factors governing this have been stated in the Chapter on Marginal Costing.

(*c*) Whether a component should made or brought? This is one has been stated above that cost of production depends on the volume of production which depends on the number of varieties of the products. But a related question is the volume of sales which will be obtained by increasing the number of varieties or reducing them.

(*d*) Whether the product should be further simplified or not ? Here also simplification of the production will lead to lower cost of production but this has to be set against possible loss of sales.

(*e*) Whether materials which are being used at present should be substituted by lower priced materials ? Materials of a cerain quality will give rise to product of a certain quality. If materials of slightly lower quality are used, it may lead to lowering of the quality of the finished product. The important question is : if this happens, what will be the reaction of the customers? If the reaction is going to be adverse, such a change should not be made. But if the customers do not mind the change, considering their requirements, there is no reason why the change should not be made. For example, when exercise books are prepared for rough work, one may even use odd sheets of paper which would otherwise go waste. Of course, if by using lower quality materials, the quality of the final product is not affected, the change should be made.

(*f*) Whether for production of the article or the service, workers with lesser skill can be employed? In this case also the question will turn on the quality of the final product and also the reaction of the customers. But it may be noted that by simplification of the process of manufacture, it may be possible to utilize the services of workers with lesser skills and lower wage rates without adversely affecting the quality of the final product.

The up shot of the discussion above is that the management must continuously watch costs and must try to reduce them having regard to the market for the product, the image of the product in the eyes of the customers, the price which they are willing to pay, etc. The approach is not only negative. It has a positive side also. If, for example, by adding a new feature, and thus incurring additional costs, the image of product can be improved substantially so that it begins to sell more or fetch higher price, the feature should be added. An example is the package of breakfast food (cornflakes) in small-size cartoons which can be slit in the middle and opened. The package is such that milk can be poured into it and the cornflakes can be eaten out of it, avoiding use of a plate. An other example is the introduction of tea bags (with a string attached) where each tea bag contains enough tea for one person; the packet is put into the tea pot with boiling water and tea is ready; then the bag is pulled back and thrown in the waste paper basket. This would be an example of positive approach to value analysis since the extra cost of packing would lead to a better response from customers, leading to higher sales and better prices.

COST CONTROL

The Chartered Institute of Management Accountants of defines cost control as "The regulation by executive action of the costs of operating an undertaking, particularly where such action is guided by cost accounting." The terms `regulation' and `executive action' would indicate a conscious attempt on the basis of predetermined ideas about what the cost should be; even if there is just an idea of unnecessary wastage, it would be based on some idea of what the permissible wastage is. In fact distinction between normal and abnormal wastage is of the greatest importance. The cost accountant can also play his proper role only when he is given a firm idea of what the target costs are beyond which they would be regarded as excessive. Of course, the cost accountant can always base upon costs actually incurred in the past–the time spent or materials used per unit of output. However, it is only when costs are predetermined, in other words, when a system of standard costing is in operation, that cost control measures can be fully effective. The systems of standard costing and budgetary control have cost control as one of their chief objectives; the whole objective of variance analysis is also that.

Cost Control works best when the following measures are adopted :

(*i*) Targets for performance of work as well as the costs to be incurred for the purpose are laid down by each area of responsibility as far as practicable. It should be possible to locate the exact person responsible for a given state of affairs. Everyone should have his power, responsibilities and obligations defined. When conditions change, the targets should be revised.

(*ii*) Costs should be collected by each area of responsibility and reports should be drawn up similarly. The reports should clearly bring out in monetary terms the effect of efficiency or inefficiency displayed by each section or department.

(*iii*) The reports should be prompt and regular and should reach the persons concerned (the line officer concerned and his boss) before it is too late for taking action. Reports must of course be accurate but fastidious accuracy causing delay is not desirable. The degree of accuracy required for each report should therefore be determined.

(*iv*) The factors leading to exceptionally good or bad performance should be enquired into and appropriate remedial action should be taken. The aim should be to locate and remove the factors leading to wastage and losses rather than to punish people. If the emphasis is on punishment, it is possible that figures will be cooked and the truth hidden.

(*v*) The reports should be used with care for making a judgement about the efficiency or inefficiency of people; a single report is liable to be misleading sometimes; hence a number of reports should be considered together.

(*iv*) Good performance should attack immediate reward and consistent bad performance should attract the necessary disincentive. This should also cover those whose task is to prepare reports.

COST REDUCTION

Whereas cost control seeks adherence to standards, cost reduction is a challenge to the standards themselves. In other words, the aim of cost reduction is to see whether there is any possibility in bringing about a saving in the costs incurred–materials, labour, overheads, etc., Costs may come down if prices of inputs, such as materials, come down. But usually, in such a case, sooner or later the price of the finished product also has to be reduced and, therefore, such cost reduction does not benefit the producer much—a reduction in the price of groundnut seeds will mean a reduction in the price of groundnut oil.

Real cost reduction comes through greater productivity which may be through the following:

(*i*) Obtaining a large quantity of production from the same facilities, *i.e.*, without increasing investment in fixed assets; this can generally be obtained by proper production planning and control. Even installation of some extra equipment may help in reducing idleness; for example, if taxis have wireless equipment, they can be directed to proceed to a fare without their coming to the stand first.

(*ii*) Using materials of lower or different quality and price, without however sacrificing the quality of the finished product. This is known as the process of substitution.

(*iii*) Breaking up and simplifying the process of manufacture so as to be able to use labour of lower skill without, again, sacrificing the quality of the finished product.

(*iv*) Making a judicious choice between parts to be made and those to be bought from the market.

(*v*) Changing features of the product suitably, so as to reduce costs, without affecting the volume of sales.

(*vi*) Changing the method of distribution of the goods, say, from retailers directly to wholesales.

(*vii*) Determining the points at which finished goods godowns will be located and the quantities that will be stored there at different points of time. This will mean transport in bulk, leading to transport economies, as also prompt compliance with customer's order or prompt despatch of goods to the prices where they are required.

Value analysis gives valuable guidance about the areas where cost education efforts are necessary and may prove fruitful. Such an analysis may show up the following :

(*a*) Redundant features of the product, which may have been useful once or which may easily be dispensed with.

(*b*) Simplification and/or standardisation of the production.

(*c*) Substitution of high cost materials by low cost ones.

(*d*) Purchase from outside of something being made in the factory or vice versa.

It may be noted that cost reduction which is obtained by increasing production without increasing investment in machinery, etc., is doubly useful since this means a large flow of goods augmenting the national income as also larger profits to the manufacturer; such profits are not at the cost of anyone. A developing country which suffers from scarce resources can develop faster if full attention is paid to productivity and cost reduction.

CONTROL SYSTEMS

Control means ensuring that the costs to be incurred on the total activity and various parts of it are kept under check and also that the quantum and quality of activity are up to the mark. As is well known, there are two types of costs — variable and fixed. These are also known as controllable and uncontrollable. As far as variable costs are concerned, the amount spent always depends on the quantum of activity or rather the effort made in respect of the work to be done. If, for example, workers are engaged on doing some work, the variable expenses, connected with workers or the work, will be incurred even if later it is found that the work was spoiled. One may, however, broadly accept that there is a close relationship between the variable expenses and the quantum of work. Therefore, if the quantum of work is less than it should be, there would not be much loss as far as variable expenses are concerned.

Fixed expenses represent permanent facilities in the shape of production equipment, including buildings and machinery and also staff which is employed on a permanent basis. There cannot be any substantial saving in such expenses since the amount is committed for a period and must be paid. It is in this sense that fixed expenses are called uncontrollable. However, one must remember that these facilities are meant for doing work and the incidence of fixed expenses per unit of work will always depend on the quantity of work done. One can always reduce the incidence by increasing the quantity. We have already seen, while discussing standard costing, how idle time leads to non-recovery of fixed overhead-that is a measure of cost of idle facility. This must always be minimised. Control in respect of fixed expenses, therefore, means using the facilities represented by fixed expenses to the best possible advantage. This can be done by increasing the production by adding new lines of production, etc. Usually, the additional expenses to be incurred on introducing a new line will not be as much as the revenues that may be produced by the new products. For example, if a company has built up a marketing organisation, it will be easy for that organisation to handle the sales of a new product without much extra cost. This also goes for general administration costs as well as the cost incurred in connection with the administration of the factory.

One can, therefore, say that, broadly, control should mean that as far as the variable expenses are concerned, the amount to be spent should always be strictly in proportion to the quantity produced and, as far as fixed expenses are concerned, with the quantum of work is minimised. This does not mean that there should be no attempt of cost reduction. Cost control will be meaningless unless constant attempts are made for reducing the cost. This has already been seen in the previous chapter.

Broader Perspective. One can think of control also in a broad perspective—that the total return from the facilities which are at the disposal of an undertaking should be the best possible, taking the long-term point of view. In other words, it means that the profitability of the concern over the long period should be as high a possible. The long-term period is important since it is always possible to increase profits immediately or in the short period, say, by not spending much on research or training of staff and workers or even by cutting down expenditure on sales promotion or postponing over-hauling of machines. Such steps, however, are always at the cost of future profits. Another example would be reducing the quality of the product. This will also increase the profits immediately, but will turn the customers away from the product every soon, leading to very low profit or losses in the future.

This aspect of control really sums up the aspects in respect of fixed and variable expenses, but also takes into account a number of other measures which. strictly, will not be considered if attention is paid only to fixed and variable expenses. For example, the very question of committing of funds for a new product or a new project must be always considered; strategy as regards competitors and also financial policy as regards raising of resources are other aspects of this aspect of control.

An organisation works at two important levels. One is the level of management at the top. Such management usually is not considered with day-to-day operations though it will be keeping track of the broad results achieved both as regards production and sales. At this level, management is really concerned with how people work and with the climate in which the company is working—the general state of affairs of the industry and the attitudes and behaviour of competitors which give rise to the particular shape of demand and the prices that are obtained or that have to be paid for raw materials, etc. At this level, the work assumes the character of a rather strategic character where planning on a broader canvas assumes a great importance. The plan has to be of course implemented but it can never be a rigid plan and it must always be adapted to the changing conditions. The decisions made at this level are generally qualitative rather than quantitative. In other words, the management personnel will have to exercise great deal of judgement. Of course, it is likely that some time things will go wrong and that has to be accepted. Another important characteristic is that the results of the decision made will be apparent not immediately, but cover a period of time. If, for instance, a manager has initiated research and development programmes, it would be idle to accept that the expenses incurred will result in new product or products quickly. In the same way, measures for increasing the productivity of labour will take time to bear fruit.

The control system at this level of management usually consists of laying down a target of rate of return and measuring against it the actual rate of return which is obtained. The target may be determined every year or for a period of years, but, for best results, it is necessary to take into consideration the budgets and estimates prepared by the manager himself. Normally, the rate of return should be based on profits which are under the control of the manager himself; it would be better to exclude expenses that are apportioned to him but are incurred by some one else and also to exclude income-tax and non-operating expenses like interest. Depreciation is also better excluded for this purpose. In other words, it should be strictly operating profit before depreciation. Depreciation should be excluded because it is always possible to change the method of depreciation and thus change the amount of depreciation and the profit.

It is also necessary to exactly define what investment will mean—whether it will be total of all assets, *i.e.*, fixed as well as current or whether it will be fixed assets plus net working capital, *i.e.*, current assets minus-current liabilities. It is also necessary to define whether fixed assets will be at their gross value or at their net value, *i.e.*, after deducting depreciation.

The second method of exercising control is the residual income method. In this case, the target for the management is laid down as such and such percentage of the capital placed at its disposal plus a certain amount in rupees as profit. The percentage usually depends on the cost of capital, which is normally a weighted average of the interest which has to be paid on loans and debentures and the profit which has to be earned in a year to maintain the market prices of shares.

The main point to remember about these two systems is that both are rather quantitative whereas the decisions made by management are qualitative. It is always dangerous to judge qualitative decisions on the basis of quantitative information, at least for the short period. As has been pointed out above, it is always possible to increase profits in the short run at the cost of profits in future. If managers are rigidly judged on the basis of their quantitative performance, *i.e.*, their rate of return or the amount of profit, they will tend to do such things as will increase profits in the short run and will not care much for the future. This will be dangerous, because this will jeopardise the future of the company itself. Therefore, the judgement should be on the basis of the manner in which the manger tackled the problems and took decisions, rather than on just the rate of return or the residual value. Of course, if a manager has not been able to meet his target in respect of profit or rate of return over a very long period, a deep investigation must be made to find out the factors.

Control over Divisions or Department. The system described above can also be used for control of managements of autonomous departments of divisions. But, for the system to work, it is essential that profitabilty of each department or division should be established separately. It is also neccessary that the department or the division concerned should be autonomous in respect of the essential operations of production and sales and allied activities. Normally, in companies which have autonomous divisions, finance, capital budgeting decisions and research and development are all centralised. Apart from these, all the other functions or activities are decentralised. The department is then controlled on the basis of a pre-determined target of rate of return or the amount of profit to be produced by it.

It should be noted that it is not essential that the department or divisions should be physically separated. What is essential in autonomy as regards decision-making and determination of profits of different departments. The degree of autonomy usually enjoyed is such that, if the goods or services produced by one department are required by another department belonging to the same company, the producing department will adopt the same attitude towards the buying department as it adopts for an outside customer. In the same way the purchasing department will consider the sister selling department as if it is an outside supplier. Prices will be negotiated at, what is known as, arm's length—as if the two departments are owned by different concerns. The purchasing department should be free to purchase its requirements from the outside market and, similarly, the selling department should be free to refuse to sell to its sister divisions and sell its product in the market. Normally, however, the divisions do transfer the goods and services mutually. This raises the question of the price which should be put on the transfer from one department to another. Without having a proper transfer price, also, the main requirement of determining the profitability of each department will not be met. The question of transfer price, therefore, is important.

Transfer Price. The prices of goods or services transferred from one department to another may be according to the following methods :

(*i*) *At Cost.* In such method, as the name implies, the transferring department will not make any profit; it is only the ultimate selling department which will show the whole profit. In this case both the efficiencies and inefficiencies of a department are passed on to the next department. It is obvious that in such cases the profit of no department can be measured separately. This method of transfer price, therefore, is defective. The only advantage would be that the stock which are lying ultimately unsold will have been valued at cost and will not include any measure of unrealised profit. This, however, is a small advantage compared to the fact that exercise of control over departments through measurement of profits will not be possible.

(*ii*) *Cost plus profit.* In this method a margin of profit at a predetermined rate is added to the cost and the transfer of goods or services to the next department is made at such a price. In this manner, the total profit earned by the company will be shown as earned separately by various departments. However, this method is as defective as the first one; in fact it may lead to the undesirable practice of not exercising any control over cost since higher the cost, higher would be profit added to it. The receiving department will be burdened with the inefficiencies of the previous department; also, it may receive the benefit of efficiency shown in the previous department. In many cases, where prices cannot be otherwise determined this method may, however, prove useful provided there is a system by which no department is encouraged to be wasteful. The incentive system should be followed whereby, if cost rises above a certain level, part of the cost must be borne by the producing department itself.

(*iii*) *Market Price.* This is the best method of transfer price since the produce of one department will be transferred to the next department at a prevailing market price. The selling department will not receive anything more than what it could by selling the production in the market; similarly, the receiving department will not pay more than what it would have paid to purchase the goods from the market. The transfer price will represent in case of the producing department, the sale value of its produce; the comparison with its cost will automatically reveal profit. This profit can be the basis of control of the management concerned.

An important question may arise, however, in this respect. Suppose department 'A' has produced goods the cost of which is higher than the prevailing market price. Department 'B' which uses the product naturally will object to pay anything more than the prevailing market price and will insist on buying from the market. If it actually buys the requirements from the market, the company will suffer a big loss since department `A' will be saddled with unsold goods and therefore, unrealised cost. To avoid such a case, it is necessary that the transfer may be made at the marginal cost of production of goods rather than at the full cost. This will ensure that the goods produced anywhere in the company are disposed off. However, if the prevailing market price is lower even than the marginal cost, obviously it would be proper to stop production. On the whole, transfer of goods and services to the next department at the marginal cost is a good idea since it would encourage each department to maximise its production.

Control over Lower Levels. What we have discussed so far relates to management at rather the top either of the company or the individual departments. It is obvious that top management cannot do its work properly unless the shop floor operations are also performed in the most efficient manner. One aspect of control is rigid control over cost. At the shop floor level, almost all the activities can be strictly planned or engineered. Also, it is possible to foresee and plan and fix standards of costs. There is not much reason why ordinary actual costs should exceed the plan or the targeted costs. Standard Costing and Budgetory Control methods are absolutely essential for controlling costs at stop floor levels. The total control system will comprise budgetary control and standard costing for the shop floor level and the control of management through proper evaluation of profits and the decision-making process at the top level.

CONTROL REPORTS

In exercise of control, reports play a very important role since it is only through reports that information reaches the various levels of authority concerned with dicision-making and control. In order to be useful, the reports should be drawn up on the principles and lines stated below.

Preparation of regular reports to help management is the most important function of the cost accountant. The aim is control of the firm's affairs through preparation and study of the reports. The following principles should be kept in mind while preparing and submitting reports :

(1) The report should be factual and objective; the whims and ideas of the person preparing the report must not be allowed to colour the report.

(2) The report should relate to a definite period and to a definite activity and should be prepared in such a way that the responsibilities of various persons and departments are clearly demarcated. A report about a person or a department should not contain information about activities beyond the control of the person or department. For instance, a foreman may not be able to control overheads; therefore, a report about his work should have no reference to overheads.

(3) The report should be brief and concise but clear. The main report should not exceed a page, although schedules may be appended.

(4) The report should clearly show what is exceptional or extra-ordinary so that management's attention is immediately drawn to it.

(5) Reports which no one uses should be immediately stopped.

(6) A copy of the report should be sent to the person responsible for the activity covered so that he is kept informed about the progress of his work. Report to higher authorities should be summarised but should be accompanied by copies of reports of activities lower down.

(7) Above all, the report must be prompt, even if it contains the permissible degree of inaccuracy.

Below we give some forms of reports which may prove useful to adopt :

(*i*) To measure the effectiveness of management through controlable profit, the statement given below may be prepared quarterly, six monthly or annually :

(*i*) Profit and Loss Statement

		This period ₹	₹	*Previous Period* ₹ *(Same columns)*
Period Ended				
Sales:	To outside customers	...		
	To other division at market value	...		
	Variable charges to other divisions for transfers not priced at market value	...	...	
Less:	Variable cost of goods sold & transferred			
	Variable divisional expense	...	...	
Variable Profit :				
Add :	(deduct) Fixed charges made to (by) other divisions for transfers not placed at market value.			
		...		
Less :	Controllable Divisional Overhead	...		
	Depreciation on controllable fixed assets Property	...		
	taxes & Insurance on controllable fixed assets :			
		...	...	
Controllable Operating Profit :				
Add :	(deduct) Non-operating gains & losses	...		
Less :	Interest on controllable investment	...	...	
	Controllable residual Income before taxes			
Less :	Non-controllable divisional overhead	...	...	
	Increments central expenses chargeable to division			
	Interest on non-controllable Investment	...	...	
	Net residual income before tax	...	...	
	Tax on income	...	...	
		...	...	
	Not residual income after taxes		...	
Total investment				
% of Controllable Operating Profit to Total Investment				

Proposed by ....

Checked by ....

(*ii*) To measure the performance of the Sales Department, the form given below is suggested. (It is better if it is prepared monthly.)

Statement of Sales

	Month								Cumulative Figures							
Products	*Units Sold*		*Amount*		*Price Per unit*		*Variance*		*Units Sold*		*Amount*		*Price Per unit*		*Variance*	
	Budgeted	*Actual*	*Budgeted*	*Actual*	*Budgeted*	*Actual*	*Quantity*	*Selling Price*	*Budgeted*	*Actual*	*Budgeted*	*Actual*	*Budgeted*	*Actual*	*Quantity*	*Selling Price*
			₹.	₹.	₹.	₹.	₹.	₹.			₹.	₹.	₹.	₹.	₹.	₹.
Total																

Date .... Prepared by .... Checked by .... Submitted to ....

(*iii*) A monthly statement of production will also prove useful. The form suggested is given below :

Statement of Production

Month .... Cumulative Figures ....

Department	*Units Produced*			*Hours*			*Units Produced*			*Hours*		
	Budgeted	*Actual*	*Variance*	*Paid for*	*Std. Hrs. for output*	*Idle Time**	*Budgeted*	*Actual*	*Variance*	*Paid for*	*Std. Hrs. for output*	*Idle Time**

*Reasons for Idle Time :

Lack of Materials ....

Breakdown of Power ....

Breakdown of Machine ....

Miscellaneous ....

Prepared by ....

Checked by .... Date .... Submitted to ....

(*iv*) Control over expenses will be assisted by a monthly report in the form given below :

Month .... **Statement of Expenses** *Coumulative figures*

Month ....

Expenses Allocated to output or sales	Works Expenses	Office & Admn. Expenses	Selling & Distribution Expenses	Works Expenses	Office & Adminsis-trative Expenses	Selling & Distribution Express
	₹.	₹.	₹.	₹.	₹.	₹.
Budget : Fixed Variable						
Total Variance : Expenditure Volume Calendar Efficiency Capacity						
Actual						

Prepared by .... Submitted to ....

Checked by ....

Statement (*iii*) and (*iv*) should be prepared for each department.

CAPITAL BUDGETING

Capital Budgeting[1] or investment decisions play a vital role in the future profitability of a concern. The process of decisions to invest a sum of money when the expected results will flow after the lapse of a period of more than one year is called Capital Budgeting. It also includes the process of decision regarding disinvestment. *i.e.*, a decision to sell off an undertaking or a part of it. Normally, however, specially in these days, it is the former type of decision which predominates. It is a most important decision to make since afterwards, after money has been irrevocably committed, it may not be possible to do much in improving results. If, for example, it is found that a factory has been put up to produce something for which there is not enough demand, nothing that can be done to avoid heavy losses. It is for this reason that the decision to invest has to be taken with very great care. There are various methods by which a proposed investment is evaluated. Before the methods are discussed, it would be proper to note that all method involve great deal of careful estimates being made for the future — the likely demand for the goods or services to be produced over a number of years, the likely selling price, the likely costs of materials, wage rate and, therefore, the likely profit. It is a difficult exercise and involves great deal of analysis and weighing the evidence regarding the future course of economic events, effecting the economy as a whole or the industry. Unless such estimates are prepared, it would be risky to make an investment decision.

1. It is an important and very significent topic of Financial Management. For detail see a text book on Financial Management.

Methods of Capital Budgeting

(i) Pay-back Period (PBP)

According to this method, the number of years in which the amount to be invested will be received back by the firm through operations is calculated. One should note that the amount of money which a firm receives back every year is the amount of profit after income-tax plus the amount of depreciation. If a firm earns a profit of ₹. 4,00,000 before writing off depreciation of ₹. 1,00,000 and the rate of income-tax is 50%, the amount left with the company after paying the tax will be ₹. 2,50,000 as shown below :

Profit	₹. 4,00,000
Less Depreciation	₹. 1,00,000
	₹. 3,00,000
Income-tax @50%	₹. 1,50,000
Profit after tax	₹. 1,50,000

Thus, out of ₹. 4,00,000 of profit earned ₹. 1,50,000 has been paid as income-tax, leaving ₹. 2,50,000. This sum could also be arrived at by adding the profit after tax and depreciation. The pay back period will be calculated as shown below :

$$\frac{\text{The investment on the Project}}{\text{The annual cash flow operations}}$$

If, in the above example, the investment is ₹. 10,00,000, they pay-back period will be four years. A project is accepted or rejected by comparing the pay-back period with the standard figure which the firm may have in mind. Normally, a pay-back period of 2 or 3 years is considered proper.

This method is rather crude since it ignores the vital question of interest, i.e., it equates money at present with money in future. Also it does not take into account the fact that often profits are very low in the beginning and then they rise and, after a period, they will again begin to fall. There may also be fluctuations from year to year.

However, this method is quite popular because :

(a) It is simple to calculate.

(b) It brings out a very important fact that unless the project is able to function for a number of years equal to the pay-back period at least, there will be no profit on the projects. Profit can arise only if the project runs for a period longer than the pay-back period.

(c) This method is useful for those concerns which suffer from rather a shortage of funds so that they want to use the same funds for many projects. They would like to invest the funds with short pay-back period so that, when they receive the funds back, they use it for the next project.

(d) A new concern will know from the pay back period the initial period during which it should absolutely refuse to pay dividends even though the Profit and Loss Account will be prepared every year and even though that may reveal profit.

(e) It is very useful for industries where the technological development, and therefore obsolescence, is very fast.

(ii) The Accounting Rate of Return (ARR)

The rate of return is calculated as follows :

$$\frac{\text{Profit after tax}}{\text{Investment}} \times 100$$

In the above example, the profit after tax is ₹. 1,50,000 and the investment is ₹. 10,00,000; therefore the rate of return will be 15%. It is for every firm to decide as to what rate of return is adequate for its purpose. By comparing the expected rate of return against the standard figure, the firm will be able to decide whether a particular investment shall be made or not.

This method is also quite simple and is quite popular. This is chiefly because this conforms with the popular ideas of profitability. However, this method also suffers from certain grave defects. These are as follows :

(*a*) This method ignores the fact of fluctuations in profits and also the fact that in case of a new venture, the profits will be low in the beginning and then high and then again low. It uses only a rather crude average of profits which may not be really borne out by actual experience.

(*b*) This method also treats money at present and money in future at par; in other words, it ignores the question of interest.

(*c*) The rate of return may also become the target figure for those who are incharge of the venture. If later, actually, the venture produces less than the estimated rate of return, the management may be treated as insufficient. However, the original rate of return is likely to be not arrived at on a scientific basis and, therefore, this may lead to wrong judgement of the people concerned.

(*d*) This method really does not take into account scientifically the life of the venture. The real assumptions is that the venture will be perpetual whereas it is never so.

(*iii*) Net Present Value (*NPV*)

According to this method, the firm determines, beforehand, the proper rate of return for its ventures, say, 10%. Then it will discount all future cash flows from the project at this rate of return and compare it with the amount to be invested. For example, suppose a project will render service only over two years, and at the end suppose a project will render service only over two years, and at the end of the first year. it will produce cash equal to ₹. 1,00,000 and at the end of the second year equal to ₹. 1,50,000. If the rate of interest is 10%, present values of these two flows will be ₹. 2,14,800. The present value of one rupee at 10% is 0.909, if the rupee is after one year and 0.826 if it is received after two year. Therefore, the present value of receivable after two years is ₹. 1,23,900–the total of the two is ₹. 2,14,800. (Table are available which show readily the present value of a rupee with respect to various rates of interests and also for various periods). The toal present value of expected cash flows from the project can be compared with the investment; if it exceeds the investment, there will be net present value (*NPV*) (the difference between the two figures) and the projects may be accepted. If, however, this is less than the investment, it will show that the project will not earn the required rate of return and, therefore, should be rejected.

This method works on the very important assumption that funds that will be generated by the project will again be invested at the required rate of return immediately. If this cannot be so, the results will be misleading.

The method has the most important advantage of equating like with like. The investment to be made is in present-day rupees and the discounted value of future cash flows is also in terms of present-day rupees. Therefore, both can be compared. It has also the additional advantage; fluctuations over the life of the project can be easily taken into account; it is not at all necessary to strike averages.

Other Considerations. The methods of capital budgeting stated above are obviously applicable when the firm has a choice to invest or not to invest. However, when the firm has no choice, the investment must be made; the only thing that the firm can do is to see that the cost of the investment is as low as possible. For example, if in a factory the Government orders fencing of the machines, there is no option but to provide the fencing, whatever the cost.

The following further points may also be noted :

(*i*) If the firm has plenty of funds for almost all the projects that are being considered, the only way to judge them would be to see whether or not the income will exceed the target figure. If, however, the funds that are available are limited, all the projects should be taken up which produce the highest rate of return.

(*ii*) Certain projects are complimentary and have to be taken together. In such a case, the project should be considered as one whole. For example, if a computer is to be installed, the cost of air-conditioning the premises, in which it is to be installed, must be treated as part of the project itself.

QUESTIONS

1. "Cost control and cost reduction are thoroughly inter-related." Discuss the truth or otherwise of this statement.
2. A manufacturing concern is operating without a system of standard costing. State in what manner cost control may be exercised there.
3. "Value analysis is nothing but a new fangled phrase to describe the old fashioned device of cost reduction." State with arguments whether you agree with this statement.
4. A concern employing 1,000 workers produces 20,000 units in a year; another concern in the same industry employing 1,200 workers produces 25,000 units. How much is the latter concern more efficient that the former? Do you wish to qualify your answer?
5. B. Ltd. employs 1,500 workers; who work normally 200 hours per month. It produces three products A, B, and C; the standard time required respectively is 20 hours, 25 hours and 35 hours. The production in a particular month was; A 6,000 units; B 5,000 units and C 2,000 units. Ascertain the productivity of labour.
6. Explain the importance of productivity for an individual concern and for the economy as a whole.
7. State the difference in the nature of the control system at various levels.
8. Bring out the use of "Rate of Return" as a tool of control.
9. What is the role of rate of return in capital budgeting decisions ?
10. Distinguish present value from net present value. An investment of ₹. 5,50,000 immediately will generate cash flows as follows :

Year 1	₹. 1,00,000
Year 2	₹. 2,50,000
Year 3	₹. 3,00,000

    The firm insists on earning 10%. At this rate of present values of a rupee received at the end of year 1, 2 and 3 are respectively 0.909, 0.826 and 0.751.

    Is the investment acceptable ?

    [Hint: No]
11. Explain the importance of control reports and state how they should be drawn up.
12. Distinguish between Cost Control and Cost Reduction.

Marginal Costing, Cost-Volume-Profit Analysis and Decision Making

MARGINAL COSTING

It is clear that, broadly speaking, the total cost of an article is made up of (*i*) the variable expenses which are incurred per unit of output, and (*ii*) its share of the fixed or constant expenses-factory, office and selling. If, from cost per unit, the record of fixed or constant expenses were excluded and if, therefore, *only variable expenses were recorded*, the system would be known as "*Marginal Costing*". The cost sheet would look like this:

	Cost per Unit
	₹.
Materials	7.00
Labour	3.50
Variable Factory Overheads	3.00
Variable Selling Overheads	2.00
Marginal Cost	15.50

Under this method fixed costs are not allotted to cost units but are written off against "margin" in the period in which they arise. The word "margin" is not really proper since what it meant is the difference between the selling price and variable costs–the term should be *contribution*. Thus:

Selling Price – (Variable Costs + Fixed Costs) = Profit;

Selling Price – Variable Costs = Contribution; and

Contribution – Fixed Costs = Profit.

Marginal cost shows the additional amount to be spent if one more unit is produced. In the above example, the total variable expenditure will be ₹. 15,500 if 1,000 units are produced, and ₹. 17,050 if 1,100 units are produced.

The difference between the price obtained and the marginal cost is known as the '*contribution*'; it will first go to meet fixed expenses and then to earn a profit. The number of units sold multiplied by the margin or contribution per unit will get the amount recovered against fixed expenses. Suppose the selling price of an article is ₹. 25 and its variable or marginal cost is ₹. 20 per unit. In that case the margin or contribution is ₹. 5. If 30,000 units are sold, a total contribution of ₹. 1,50,000, *i.e.*, 30,000 × 5 will be recovered. If the fixed expenses total ₹. 1,10,000, there will be a net profit of ₹. 40,000, *i.e.*, ₹. 1,50,000 minus ₹. 1,10,000. If the fixed expenses amount to ₹. 1,70,000, there will be a loss of ₹. 20,000. The truth of this is brought out if the following example is studied.

Example: On the basis of normal capacity of 10,000 units, the cost sheet showing per unit figures was as follows:

	₹.
Materials	11.00
Labour	8.00
Overhead – Variable	3.00
– Fixed	6.00
	28.00
Profit	2.00
Selling Price	30.00

If production (and sales) is 10,000 units, the profit will be ₹. 20,000, *i.e.*, 10,000 × ₹. 2. But if the output and sales are 8,000 units, the profit will not be ₹. 16,000, *i.e.* 8,000 × 2; it will be ₹. 4,000, (as shown below because total fixed overheads were 10,000 × 6 = ₹. 60,000 :)

		₹.
Materials	(8,000 × 11)	88,000
Labour	(8,000 × 8)	64,000
Overheads:		
Variable	(8,000 × 3)	24,000
Fixed	(Total)	60,000
		2,36,000
Profit		4,000
Sales	(8,000 × 30)	2,40,000

It can also be presented in the following manner:

(output and sales 8000 units)

		Per Unit ₹.	₹.	*Total* ₹.
Sales		30.00		2,40,000
Less: Variable Costs				
Materials	11.00		88,000	
Labour	8.00		64,000	
Variable Overhead	3.00	22.00	24.000	1,76,000
Contribution		8.00		64,000
Fixed Overheads				60,000
Profit				4,000

Thus, the contribution approach, resulting from the marginal cost system, enables one to calculate the profit at various levels of activity accurately. The figures will not be readily available if cost, including fixed expenses, is compared with selling price.

Thus the technique of marginal costing involves two principal steps:

(*a*) Determination of Marginal Cost

(*b*) Arrangement of these costs in the most suitable manner for showing the state of profitability and enabling management to reach conclusions.

The marginal costing system should be distinguished from the one, usually followed, under which fixed overheads are also allotted to cost units. The name given to this system is Absorption Costing which means:

"The practice of charging all costs, both variable and fixed, to operations, processes or products."

There are a number of terms which more or less describe the system of marginal costing but before we discuss them we should be clear about the meaning of marginal cost and marginal costing. The *Chartered Institute of Management Accountants* (*CIMA*) England has adopted the undermentioned definitions:

1. *Marginal Cost:* 'The amount at any given volume of output by which aggregate costs are charged if the volume of output is increased or decreased by one unit. In practice this is measured by the total variable cost attributable to one unit.'

Note: In this context a unit may be a single article, a batch of articles, an order, a stage of production capacity, a process or a department. It relates to the change in output in the particular circumstances under consideration."

In other words, marginal cost means the amounts by which total costs incurred will change for a given change, say, increase or decrease in output, adopting one process as against another, producing one product as against another, etc. In other words, the marginal cost is the additional expenditure caused by an increase in output, or the saving resulting from a decrease in output

2. *Marginal Costing:* "The ascertainment of marginal costs and of the effect on profit of changes in volume or type of output by differentiating between fixed costs and variable costs.

Note: In this method of costing only variable costs are charged to operations, processes or products while fixed costs are written off against profits in the period in which they arise."

It would seem to be the idea that in some cases fixed expenses which are direct to a product may be added to the marginal cost. For instance, all expenses of a department, variable and fixed may be added up to ascertain the cost of articles produced there but no allotment of other fixed overhead should be made. This naturally will be different from the marginal cost (which excludes all fixed overheads) and will be, according to the Chartered Institute of Management Accountants (*CIMA*) in England, the system of Direct Costing. However, *it should be noted that most often Marginal Costing and Direct Costing are treated as synonyms, the latter term being more popular in the U.S.A.*

There are some other terms which one may come across, specially "Incremental Cost" and "Differential Cost". The definition of marginal cost as given above by the *CIMA* wide enough to cover these terms. If a distinction has to be made, incremental cost will mean the difference made to total cost when the change in output is of a sizeable character, say, 1,000 units whereas marginal cost means the change in costs because of increase or decrease in output by a single unit. If the "unit" means the regular lot of articles by which change in output will be effected, marginal cost and incremental cost will be the same thing. *Differential cost* will mean the change in total cost because of a change of fundamental nature like closing down a department, replacing one process or product by another etc. To repeat, the idea behind all the terms is the same–the measurement of change in total costs because of any change in the production department or the distribution process.

The following *other definitions* should be noted:

Fixed Cost: "A cost which tends to be unaffected by variations in volume of output. Fixed costs depend mainly on the effluxion of time and do not vary directly with volume or rate of output. Fixed costs are sometimes referred to as period costs in systems of direct costing.

Note: There may be different levels of fixed costs at different levels of output; for example, where extra output is only obtainable by extra capital equipment or extra services. At the other extreme, when a whole department may be shut down, many of these costs will, in fact, disappear."

Variable Cost: "A cost which tends to vary directly with volume of output. Variable costs are sometimes referred to as direct costs in systems of direct costing".

Semi-fixed or Semi-variable Cost: "A cost which is partly fixed and partly variable."

Main Features of Marginal Costing

It may be noted that Marginal Costing is not a distinct method of ascertainment of cost such as job costing or process costing. It is a technique of applying the existing method to bring out the relationship between profit and volume of output which may be used in all types of costing like job and process.

The main features, in brief, of marginal costing may be narrated as below:

(*i*) The usefulness of this technique depends upon identification of costs with changes in output. The costs are divided into fixed and variable element. In case of semi-variable cost, it should also be seggregated into fixed and variable.

(*ii*) In computing production cost only variable or marginal costs are taken into account.

(*iii*) The values of stocks of finished products and work-in-progress are also calculated only on variable costs.

(*iv*) Fixed costs are absorbed or written off during the period they are incurred and therefore they are not included in product cost or in cost of stocks or inventories.

(*v*) Profitability of departments or products is determined in the terms of *contribution i.e.* sales *less* marginal cost.

Importance of Marginal Costs to Management

Following are in brief points of importance to the management:

1. To aid the decision on whether additional sales at a price below full cost should be made, and generally to aid in the formulation of pricing policy.
2. To choose between different methods of manufacturing or operating.
3. To decide whether parts and components should be made within the business, bought outside or sub-contracted.
4. To asses the economics of proposed capital investment e.g. plant and machinery.
5. To assess whether to initiate or proceed with a development project.
6. To calculate the level of sales required to break-even or to achieve a given profit, or the profit likely to result from a given level of sales, or the most economic mix of products for sale.

Shortcomings or Limitations of Marginal Costing

The system of marginal costing is of great use in times of depression and otherwise as has been shown. But in normal times it is better to find out the total cost (variable and constant or fixed)–if it is ascertained on the basis of normal capacity, the danger of misleading fluctuations in the cost of production (which is the case when costs are calculated on the basis of actual output) is avoided. The following short comings can be noticed in marginal costing:

(1) If costs are to be used for fixing normal selling prices, obviously marginal costing is of little value. Constant as well as variable costs should be included in the total cost of production for determining prices in the ordinary times.

(2) Marginal costing ignores the time factor entirely (only constant expenses reflect cost being connected with time). Profitability of two jobs cannot be compared suitably unless constant expenses are included.

(3) Sometimes a specially low price is quoted to a new customer. The price is based on the argument that if marginal costs are met, it will be profitable. This may, however, lead to a general lowering of price and thus to losses.

(4) By ignoring the fixed expenses, orders may be accepted which do not permit acceptance of other but more profitable jobs. By allocating fixed expenses total capacity can be easily kept in mind.

(5) A big danger is that in one's anxiety to maximise production by accepting orders at concessional prices the output may overstep present limits of capacity. This will mean a big increase in fixed expenses also and this may result in a loss on additional orders. This danger should be guarded against.

DIFFERENCE BETWEEN ABSORPTION COSTING AND MARGINAL COSTING

Under *absorption costing*, fixed factory overheads (and may be office and administrative expenses also if the firm treats them as part of production costs) are added to the cost of production and the value of closing stock is determined accordingly. But if *marginal costing* is adopted, the value of closing stock will consist only of variable expenses and no part of fixed expenses will be included. There will be no effect on profits if the whole of the output is sold but if part of it remains unsold, profit under marginal costing will be lower than under absorption costing–the reverse will be the case if opening stock exceeds closing stock.

The difference between Marginal Costing and Absorption Costing can be narrated as below:

1. *Calculation of Manufacturing Overhead Rates.* In Absorption Costing absorption rate include both fixed and variable manufacturing overhead. In Marginal Costing rates includes only variable manufacturing overhead.
2. *Valuation of Inventory.* In Absorption Costing valuation is on Product Cost *i.e.* Prime cost + applied fixed and variable manufacturing overheads. In Marginal costing it will be at Prime cost + applied variable manufacturing overhead.
3. *Classification of Overhead.* In absorption costing the overhead may be classified as factory, administrative, selling and distribution. But in Marginal costing overheads are classified as variable and fixed.
4. *Operating Profit.* Under Absorption Costing Gross Profit = Net Sales – Manufacturing Cost of goods sold. Manufacturing Costs = Prime Cost + Fixed and variable manufacturing overheads. But in Marginal costing, Marginal income or Contribution = Net sales – Variable manufacturing cost of goods sold – variable administrative, selling and distribution overheads.
5. *Net Operating Profit.* Under Absorption Costing, Net Operating Profit = Gross Profit – Administrative selling and distribution overheads (fixed and variable combined). Under marginal costing Net Operating Profit = Marginal income or Contribution – Fixed manufacturing overhead – fixed administrative overhead – fixed selling and distribution overhead.
6. *Difference of Profit.* When production volume exceeds sales volume the net profit under absorption costing will exceed marginal costing net profit. The Net profit will be equal wnen production volume is equal to sales volume. When production volume is less than sales volume, absorption costing net profit will be less than marginal costing net profit.
7. *Reconciliation of Net Profit.* Net operating profit under Marginal Costing = Net Operating Profit – Fixed Overhead cost in closing inventory under absorption costing + Fixed Overhead cost in opening inventory under absorption costing.

Illustration 1. The undermentioned costs are incurred in each of the three years, 2000, 2001, 2002, when output annually is 10,000 units.

	₹.
Materials	6,00,000
Labour	3,50,000
Variable Factory Overheads	1,50,000
Fixed Factory Overheads	2,00,000
Total	13,00,000

In 2000 only 8,000 units were sold; in 2001 sale was 10,500 units and in 2002, 11,500 units. The selling price is uniform at ₹. 150 per unit.

Solution: The closing stocks are 2,000 units at the end of 2000, 1,500 units at the end of 2001 and nil at the end of 2002. The statements showing profits or losses for the three years under the two systems will be as follows:

Statement of Profit or Loss Under Absorption Costing

	2000 ₹.	*2001* ₹.	*2002* ₹.
Opening Stock	—	2,60,000	1,95,000
Cost of goods produced	13,00,000	13,00,000	13,00,000
	13,00,000	15,60,000	14,95,000
Less Closing Stock	2,60,000	1,95,000	—
Cost of Goods Sold	10,40,000	13,65,000	14,95,000
Profit	1,60,000	2,10,000	2,30,000
Sales	12,00,000	15,75,000	17,25,000

(Stocks valued at ₹. 130 per unit)

Statement of Profit or Loss Under Marginal Cost

	2000 ₹.	*2001* ₹.	*2002* ₹.
Opening Stock	—	2,20,000	1,65,000
Cost of goods produced (variable)	11,00,000	11,00,000	11,00,000
	11,00,000	13,20,000	12,65,000
Less Closing Stock	2,20,000	1,65,000	—
	8,80,000	11,55,000	12,65,000
Add Fixed Factory Overheads	2,00,000	2,00,000	2,00,000
Total	10,80,000	13,55,000	14,65,000
Profit	1,20,000	2,20,000	2,60,000
Sales	12,00,000	15,75,000	17,25,000

Taking the three years period, there being no opening and closing stocks, the total profit under the two systems is the same, *viz.*, ₹. 6,00,000.

Illustration 2: Your company has production capacity of 2,00,000 units per year. Normal capacity utilisation is reckoned as 90%, Standard variable production costs are ₹. 11 per unit. The fixed costs are ₹. 3,60,000 per year, Variable selling costs are ₹. 3 per unit and fixed selling costs are ₹. 2,70,000 per year. The unit selling price is ₹. 20. In the year just ended on 30th June, the production was 1,60,000 units and sales were 1,50,000 units. The closing inventory was 20,000 units. The actual variable production costs for the year were ₹. 35,000 higher than standard.

Calculate the profit for the year (*a*) by the Absortpon Costing Method and (*b*) by the Marginal Costing Method. Also explain the difference in the profit.

Solution:

Statement of Cost and Profit Under Absorption Costing

	₹.	₹.
Sales (1,50,000 × ₹. 20)		30,00,000
Cost of Production		
Variable Cost (1,60,000 × ₹. 11)	17,60,000	
Increase in Variable cost	35,000	
Fixed Cost	3,60,000	
	21,55,000	
Add Opening Stock (10,000 × ₹. 13)	1,30,000	
	22,85,000	
Less Closing Stock (20,000 units)	2,69,375	20,15,625
Gross Profit		9,84,375
Less Selling Expenses		
Variable	4,50,000	
Fixed	2,70,000	7,20,000
Net Profit		2,64,375

Working Notes. (1) Opening stock is valued at variable cost per unit (₹. 11) plus fixed cost per unit at normal capacity *i.e.* ₹. 3,60,000/1,80,000 = ₹. 2 per unit (₹. 11 + 2 = ₹. 13 per unit) (2) closing stock has been valued on the basis of total cost of 1,60,000 units *i.e.* ₹. 21,55,000

$$\frac{₹.\ 21{,}55000 \times 20{,}000 \text{ units}}{1{,}60{,}000 \text{ unit}} = ₹.\ 2{,}69{,}375$$

It is to be noted that the above valuation is based upon *FIFO* approach presuming that closing stock will be out of current production. It may be valued at average cost approach, then current cost plus cost of opening stock would have been the basis of valuation.

Statement of Cost and Profit Under Marginal Costing

	₹.	₹.
Sales (1,50,000 × ₹. 20)		30,00,000
Variable Cost of Production (1,60,000 × ₹. 11)	17,60,000	
Additional Variable Cost	35,000	
Opening Stock at Variable Cost (10,000 × 11)	1,10,000	
	19,05,000	
Less Closing Stock (20,000 units) (17,95,000/1,60,000) × 20,000	2,24,375	
	16,80,625	
Variable Selling Cost (1,50,000 × ₹. 3)	4,50,000	21,30,625
Contribution (Sales – Variable cost)		8,69,375
Less Fixed cost	3,60,000	
Fixed Selling Cost	2,70,000	6,30,000
Net Profit		2,39,375

The profit as per Absorption Costing ₹. 2,64,375 and as per Marginal Costing ₹. 2,39,375. The difference of ₹. 25,000 is due to element of fixed cost included in the valuation of opening and closing stock under Absorption Costing Method.

Reconciliation of Profits	₹.
Profit under Absorption Costing	2,64,375
Add Opening stock under valued in Marginal Costing	20,000
	2,84,375
Less Closing stock under valued in Marginal Costing	45,000
Profit under Marginal Costing	239,375

SEGREGATION OF SEMI-VARIABLE OVERHEADS

Semi variable cost is a cost which is partly fixed and partly variable. These overheads may be segregated into fixed and variable by any of the following methods

a. Level of Activity Method
b. Range Method
c. Degree of Variability Method
d. Scattergraph Method
e. Least Square Method

(a) Level of Activity Method.

Under level of activity method the outputs of two different levels are compared. Fixed expenses remain fixed or constant, the remaining part being variable overheads are calculated by the ratio of change in expenses to change in output *i.e.*

$$\frac{\text{Change in amount of expense}}{\text{Change in activity or quantity}}$$

Illustration 3: From the following information, find out the amount of fixed and variable overheads

Months	*Production units*	*Semi Variable Overheads* ₹
January	60	130
February	40	110
March	70	150
April	120	210

Solution: From the above information, two levels of activity say, January and February may be taken to find out ratio of change

	Units	*Semi-variable (₹.)*
January	60	130
February	40	110
Difference	20	20

$$\text{Variable Expenses per unit} = \frac{\text{Charge in expense}}{\text{Charge in output}} = \frac{₹.\ 20}{20 \text{ units}} = ₹.\ 1$$

Thus in January variable expense will be 60 × 1 = ₹. 60 and fixed expense will be ₹. 130 – 60 = ₹. 70

In February variable expense will be 40 × 1 = ₹. 40 and fixed expense will be ₹. 110 – 40 = ₹. 70

(b) Range Method of Segregation of Variable Overheads

Range method is quite similar to Level of Activity Method, but in Range Method the highest and lowest activity levels are taken into consideration to calculate the ratio.

Illustration 4: From the information given in the previous illustration, calculate fixed and variable overheads on the basis of Range Method.

Solution:

Months	*Units*	*Semi-variable Expanses (₹.)*
February (Lowest)	40	110
April (Highest)	120	210
Difference	80	100

Variable Expenses per unit $\frac{₹.100}{80} = 1.25$

Fixed Overheads for February = ₹. 110 – (40 × 1.25) = 110 – 50 = ₹. 60

Fixed Overheads for April = ₹. 210 – (120 × 1.25) = 210 – 150 = ₹. 60

Illustration 5: The following are the maintenance cost incurred in a machine shop for - six months with corresponding machine hours

Months	*Machine Hours*	*Maintenance Cost* ₹.	*Months*	*Machine Hour*	*Maintenance Cost* ₹.
January	2000	300	April	2400	340
February	2200	320	May	1800	280
March	1700	270	June	1900	290
				12,000	1800

Analyse the maintenance cost which is semi-variable into fixed and variable element

[*CA – Inter*]

Solution: By using Range Method:

	Machine Hours	*Maintenance Cost (₹)*
Highest Point : April	2400	340
Lowest Point : March	1700	270
	700	70

$$\text{Variable cost per hour} = \frac{\text{Change in cost}}{\text{Change in hours}}$$

= 70/700 = ₹. 0.10

Fixed cost for 2400 hours = ₹. 340 – (2400 × .10)

= 340 – 240 = 100

(c) Degree of Variability Method

Under the Degree of Variability Method, the degree of variability is noted or identified for each item of semi-variable expense. It may be noted, while analysing, an expense that degree of variability is 60% and then variable expenses will be 60%. But this identification is not easy. Degree of variability is very difficult to be noted. Thus the method is not practicable.

For example, in the figures of preceeding Illustration No. 4, it may be assumed that degree of variability is 60% of the total expenses taking the month of April as a basis, the segregation will be as below

Variable Exps (April) ₹. 210 × 60% = 126

Per unit Variable Expense ₹. 120 units or 120/120

Fixed Expenses = ₹. 210 – 126 = 84

(d) Scattergraph Method

Under this method, the semi-variable expenses at a number of levels of output are plotted in a graph. The x axis (horizontal axis) represents volume of output and y axis (vertical axis) represents the amount of expenditure. A straight line, known as line of best fit is drawn through the points plotted for output and expenditure. This line is drawn in such a manner that there are normally equal number of points on both sides of the line but points falling far beyond the line are not considered.

The line of best fit is total cost line. The point where this line intersects the vertical axis is taken to be the amount of fixed cost. A parallel line is drawn from this point to the horizontal axis representing fixed cost. The variable cost at any level of output may be ascertained by taking the difference between fixed cost line and total cost line.

Illustration 6. Following figures have been extracted from the books of a manufacturing company. Plot suitable scatter points to ascertain fixed overheads.

Months	*Output units (in thousands)*	*Semi-variable Overheads (₹. in thousands)*
January	40	25
February	50	35
March	45	30
April	60	40
May	65	45
June	70	55

Solution :

The line of best fit shows degree of variability and the point where it cuts overhead cost line denotes the amount of fixed cost *i.e.* ₹. 16000.

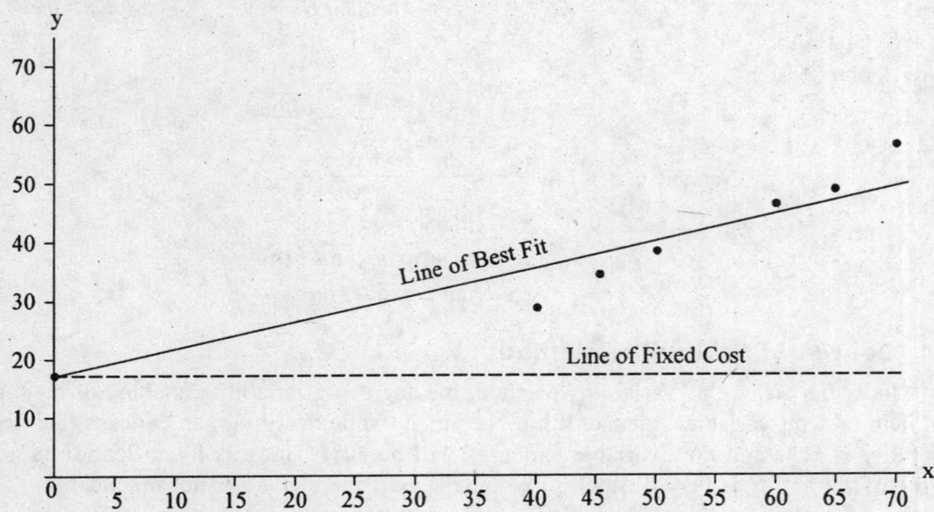

(e) Least Square Method

There is another method of seggregating semi-variable cost. In this method the technique used is explained in following example.

In the following table number of units and semi variable cost of 6 months have been given. We have to calculate fixed cost included in semi-variable cost.

Months	Units	Semi Variable Overheads ₹.	Deviations of units from its average (x)	Deviation of Overheads from its average (y)	x^2	xy
January	1500	2500	– 400	– 400	1,60,000	1,60,000
February	1700	2700	– 200	– 200	40,000	40,000
March	1600	2600	– 300	– 300	90,000	90,000
April	2100	3100	200	200	40,000	40,000
May	2300	3300	400	400	1,60,000	1,60,000
June	2200	3200	300	300	90,000	90,000
Total	11,400	17,400	0	0	5,80,000	5,80,000
Average	1,900	2,900			$= \Sigma x^2$	$= \Sigma xy$

Average of units and semi-variable overheads are 1900 units and ₹. 2,900. Deviations have been calculated from averages known as x and y. Thereafter x^2 and xy are calculated.

$$\text{The variable component per unit} = \frac{\Sigma xy}{\Sigma x^2} = \frac{5,80,000}{5,80,000} = ₹\ 1$$

$$\text{Fixed cost} = \text{Average cost} - (\text{Variable cost per unit} \times \text{Average number of units})$$
$$= ₹.\ 2,900 - (1 \times 1,900) = ₹.\ 1,000$$

There is an alternative method[1] of segregating semi-variable expenses under Least Square Method. It is a mathematical technique of fitting an equation by 'Line of Best Fit' with a number of observations. The linear equation is

$$y = a + bx$$

Its sub equations may be

$$\Sigma y = na + b\ \Sigma\ x$$
$$\Sigma xy = a\ \Sigma\ x + b\ \Sigma\ x^2$$

A second order equation *i.e.* a curvi–linear equation can be drawn as follows

$$Y = a + bx + ex^2$$
$$\Sigma y = na + b\Sigma x + c\Sigma x^2$$
$$\Sigma xy = a\ \Sigma x + b\Sigma x^2 + c\Sigma x^3$$
$$\Sigma x^2 y = a\ \Sigma x^2 + b\Sigma x^3 + c\ \Sigma x^4$$

It is illustrated in following example.

Illustration 7. From the following information find out the amount of fixed and variable expenses out of semi variable expenses:

Months	*Production units*	*Semi-variable Expenses (₹)*
January	60	130
February	40	110
March	70	150
April	120	210
May	90	170
June	130	245
	510	1,015

1. Please study 'Time Series Technique' by a text book of Statistics for clear understanding of linear equations.

Solution. Presuming production units as x and semi-variable expenses *y*; *a* as fixed cost and *b* as variable cost per unit, the equations will be

$$\Sigma y = na + b\Sigma x$$
$$\Sigma xy = a\Sigma x + b\Sigma x^2$$

Following will be the required calculations

Months	*Production Units*	*Semi Variable Exps (₹.)*	*Square of x*	*Product of x and y*
	x	y	x^2	xy
January	60	130	3,600	7,800
February	40	110	1,600	4,400
March	70	150	4,900	10,500
April	120	210	14,400	25,200
May	90	170	8,100	15,300
June	130	245	16,900	31,850
	$\Sigma x = 510$	$\Sigma y = 1{,}015$	$\Sigma x^2 = 49{,}500$	$\Sigma xy = 95{,}050$

By putting the values in the equations

$$\Sigma y = na + b\Sigma x = 1{,}015 = 6a + 510b$$
$$\Sigma xy = a\Sigma x + b\,\Sigma\,x^2 = 95{,}050 = 510\,a + 49{,}500\,b$$

or $\quad 6a + 510\,b = 1{,}015$

$510\,a + 49{,}050\,b = 95{,}050$

By solving above $a = 47.617$ (fixed cost) and

$b = 1.43$ (per unit variable cost)

We can find out total semi-variable cost at any level of production (*y* being total semi variable) cost and *x* being number of units)

$$y = 47.62 + 1.43\,x$$

CONTRIBUTION

As mentioned in the beginning, in the marginal costing concept, the difference between aggregate sales value and the marginal cost or variable cost of sales provides a fund known as contribution towards meeting the fixed cost and also generating surplus in the form of profit. Thus difference between selling price and marginal cost is contribution. Contribution minus fixed cost is profit, but where fixed cost is more than contribution, the difference is loss.

Selling Price – Variable cost = Contribution

Contribution – Fixed cost = Profit

Profit = Selling price – Variable cost – Fixed cost

The character of contribution may be as below:

(*a*) If selling price contains profit : Contribution = Fixed cost + Profit

(*b*) If selling price is at cost : Contribution = Fixed cost

(*c*) If selling price is at loss : Contribution = Fixed Cost – Loss

Contribution may be calculated per unit (per unit selling price – per unit variable cost) or on total sales. By using contribution per unit; we can calculate profit or loss at different volume of production.

Suppose per unit selling price and variable cost of a product were ₹. 20 and ₹. 16 respectively. The fixed cost of the factory was ₹. 10,000. Find out profit or loss on sales of 1000 units, 4,000 units and 10,000 units.

Contribution per unit ₹. 20 – ₹. 16 = ₹. 4

Sales (units)	1000	4000	10,000
Contribution @ ₹. 4 per unit (₹)	4000	16,000	40,000
Less Fixed Cost	10,000	10,000	10,000
Loss (–) or Profit (+)	(–) 6,000	+ 6,000	+ 30,000

Under Marginal Costing the term 'profit' is not given much importance but 'contribution' is given more weightage. The analysis of contribution is helpful in various decisions of maximising profit and spreading of the fixed cost over larger volume of sales. Contribution is a very useful guide towards profitability in business. It is useful in deciding a number of issues like choosing a profitable product mix, accepting or rejecting an offer, identifying optimal capacity points, optimal use of resources, make or buy decision, profit planning, continuing or discontinuing a product selling etc. These points of the use of contribution will be discussed in detail later on in this chapter.

BREAK EVEN POINT (*BEP*)

A particular advantage of marginal costing is that the margin between the price available and the marginal cost being known, it would immediately show up the quantity of output needed to reach the break even point, viz., the quantity of output where there would be neither loss nor profit.

Suppose (*i*) the marginal cost is ₹. 15.50 per unit, (*ii*) the total of all constant or fixed expenses amounts to ₹. 2,00,000, and (*iii*) the price at which the article is sold in the market is ₹. 25.50. The margin between the price available and the cost of producing each unit would be ₹. 10, i.e., ₹. 25.50 minus ₹. 15.50; this ₹. 10.00 would be available to meet fixed expenses. For every unit sold, ₹. 10.00 will be recovered and hence the break even point will be reached when 20,000 units are sold. Every unit sold over (or under) 20,000 will bring a net profit (or net loss) of ₹. 10.00. The knowledge of the output needed to make a certain amount of profit is of great value to the manufacturer.

We may say that the break even point is calculated by the formula:

$$\text{Break Even Point (volume)} = \frac{\text{Total Fixed Expenses}}{\text{Selling price per unit minus marginal or variable cost per unit i.e., Contribution per unit.}}$$

or

$$\frac{\text{Fixed cost}}{\text{(Total sales – Total variable cost)/Volume units}}$$

or

$$\frac{\text{Fixed cost}}{\left(1-\dfrac{\text{Total variable cost}}{\text{Total sales}}\right)\times \text{Selling Price Per Unit}}$$

From the above formulae, we can calculate number of units sold at break even *i.e.* where there is no profit no loss. If break even is to be calculated in term of sales amount (total sales), then the number of units at break even derived from above formula should be multiplied by selling price per unit.

$$\text{Break even point (Amt. of Sales)} = \frac{\text{Total Fixed cost}}{\text{Contribution per units}} \times \text{Selling price per unit}$$

or

$$\frac{\text{Fixed cost}}{1-\dfrac{\text{Total variable cost}}{\text{Total sales}}}$$

Break even technique can also be used to find out units or amount of sales to earn a desired amount of profit.

Sales (volume or units) at a desired profit

$$= \frac{\text{Fixed cost} + \text{Desired Profit}}{\text{Contribution per unit}}$$

$$\text{or } \frac{\text{Fixed cost} + \text{Desired Profit}}{\left(1 - \dfrac{\text{Total variable cost}}{\text{Total sales}}\right) \times \text{Selling price per unit}}$$

Sales (in amount) at desired profit

$$= \left(\frac{\text{Fixed cost} + \text{Desired Profit}}{\text{Contribution per unit}}\right) \times \text{Selling price per unit}$$

$$\text{or } \left(\frac{\text{Fixed cost} + \text{Desired Profit}}{1 - \dfrac{\text{Total variable cost}}{\text{Total sales}}}\right)$$

Illustration 8. From the following data, calculate (*i*) Break-even point expressed in amount of sales in rupees (*ii*) Number of units that must be sold to earn a profit of ₹. 1,00,000 per year

Sales price	₹. 20 per unit
Variable manufacturing cost	₹. 12 per unit
Variable selling cost	₹. 2 per unit
Fixed overheads	₹. 7,92,000 per year

Solution.

(*i*) Break Even point $= \dfrac{\text{Total Fixed cost}}{\text{Contribution per unit}}$

$= \dfrac{7,92,000}{20-14} = \dfrac{7,92,000}{6} = = 1,32,000$ units

Break Even Sales = Break Even units × Selling price per unit

= 1,32,000 units × ₹. 20

= ₹. 26,40,000

(*ii*) Sales units at desired profit

$= \dfrac{\text{Fixed cost} + \text{Desired profit}}{\text{Contribution per unit}}$

$= \dfrac{7,92,000 + 1,00,000}{6} = \dfrac{8,92,000}{6}$

= 1,48,667 units

Illustration 9. From the following information relating to Quick Standard Ltd. you are required to find out (*a*) Contribution (*b*) Break Even point in units (*c*) Profit.

Total fixed cost	₹. 4,500
Total variable cost	₹. 7,500
Total sales	₹. 15000
Units sold	5,000 units

Also calculate the volume of sales to earn a profit of ₹. 6,000.

Solution. (1) Sales per unit = ₹. 15,000/5,000 = ₹. 3

Variable cost per unit = ₹. 7,500/5,000 = ₹. 1.5

Contribution per unit = Sales – Variable cost

= 3 – 1.5 = ₹. 1.5

Total Contribution = 1,5000 – 7,500 = ₹. 7,500

$$\text{Break Even point (units)} = \frac{\text{Total Fixed Cost}}{\text{Contribution per unit}}$$

$$= \frac{4,500}{1.5} = 3,000 \text{ units}$$

Profit = Sales – Variable cost – Fixed cost

= 15,000 – 7,500 – 4,500 = ₹. 3,000

or Contribution – Fixed cost = 7,500 – 4,500 = ₹. 3,000

Volume of Sales to earn a profit of ₹. 6,000

$$= \frac{\text{Total Fixed Cost + Desired Profit}}{\text{Contribution per unit}}$$

$$= \frac{4,500 + 6,000}{1.5} = 7,000 \text{ units}$$

Illustration 10. From the following data, calculate

(*i*) Break Even point expressed in amount of sales in rupees

(*ii*) Number of units that must be sold to earn a profit of ₹. 60,000 per year.

(*iii*) How many units must be sold to earn a net profit of 10% of sales.

Sales price	₹. 20 per unit
Fixed Factory Overheads	₹. 5,40,000 per year
Fixed Selling costs	₹. 2,52,000 per year
Variable Manufacturing costs	₹. 11 per unit
Variable Selling costs	₹. 3 per unit

Solution.

$$(i) \text{ Break-even Point} = \frac{\text{Fixed cost} \times \text{Selling price per unit}}{\text{Contribution per unit}}$$

$$= \frac{7,92,000}{20-11-3} \times 20 = \frac{7,92,000 \times 20}{6}$$

= ₹. 26,40,000

(*ii*) Units to be sold to earn a profit of ₹, 60,000

$$= \frac{\text{Fixed cost + Desired profit}}{\text{Contribution per unit}} = \frac{7,92,000 + 60,000}{6}$$

= 1,42,000 units

(*iii*) Presume that x units are to be sold

Total Sales = 20 x; Desired profit 10% sales = $2x$

Total Sales = Total Fixed Cost + Total Variable Cost + Profit

$20x = 7,92,000 + 14x + 2x$

$20x - 16x = 7,92,000$

$4x = 7,92,000$ or $x = 1,98,000$

Thus number of units = 1,98,000 units

Illustration 11. Indian Plastics make plastic buckets. An analysis of their accounting reveals.

Variable cost per bucket	₹. 20
Fixed cost	₹. 50,000 for the year
Capacity	2,000 buckets per year
Selling price per bucket	₹. 70

Required: (*i*) Find the break-even-Point (*ii*) Find the number of buckets to be sold to get a profit of ₹. 30,000. (*iii*) If the company can manufacture 600 buckets more per year with an additional fixed cost of ₹. 2,000, what would be the selling price to maintain the profit per bucket as at (*ii*) above.

Solution:

(*i*) Break-even Point $= \dfrac{\text{Fixed Cost}}{\text{Contribution per unit}} = \dfrac{50{,}000}{50}$

$= 1000$ buckets

(*ii*) Buckets to be sold for desired profit of ₹. 30,000

$$= \frac{\text{Fixed Cost + Desired Profit}}{\text{Contribution per unit}} = \frac{50{,}000 + 30{,}000}{50}$$

$$= \frac{80{,}000}{50} = 1600 \text{ units}$$

Profit per bucket $= \dfrac{\text{Profit}}{\text{No. of units}} = \dfrac{30{,}000}{1{,}600} =$ ₹. 18.75

(*iii*) Total sales at profit of ₹. 30,000 = 1600 units

Increase in sales 600 units

2,200

Total desired profit = 2,200 × 18.75 = ₹. 41,250

Pressume that selling price is ₹. x

Total sales = Total Fixed Cost + Total Variable Cost + Profit

$2{,}200\,x = 52{,}000 + (2{,}200 \times 20) + 41250 = 1{,}37{,}250$

$x = 62.39$

Thus selling price per unit ₹. 62.39.

Illustration 12. Cadbury Ltd., a British Chocolate and Soft Drink Company is planning to establish a subsidiary company in India to produce Mineral Water.

Based on the estimated annual sales of 40,000 bottles of mineral water, cost studies produced the following estimates for the Indian subsidiary.

	Total Annual Cost	*Percentage of Total Annual Cost*
	₹	₹
Material	1,93,600	100
Labour	90,000	70
Overhead	80,000	64
Administration	30,000	30

The Indian production will be sold by manufacturer's representatives who will receive a commission of 8 percent of the sale price. No portion of the British office expenses is to be allocated to the Indian subsidiary.

It is required to (*i*) compute the sale price per bottle to enable management to realise an estimated 10 per cent profit on sale proceeds in India and (*ii*) calculate the break even point in rupee sales for the Indian subsidiary on the assumption that the sale price is ₹. 11 per bottle.

Solution.

(*i*) Presume that selling price per unit is ₹. x

Total sales = Total cost + Commission + Profit

$$40000\,x = 1,93,600 + 90,000 + 80,000 + 30,000 + 8\% \text{ of } 40,000\,x + 10\% \text{ of } 40,000\,x$$
$$= 3,93,600 + 3,200\,x + 4,000\,x$$
$$= 3,93,600 + 7,200\,x$$
$$40,000\,x - 7,200\,x = 3,93,600$$
$$32,800\,x = 3,93,600 \text{ or } x = 3,93,600/32,800$$
$$x = 12. \text{ Thus selling price per bottle ₹. } 12$$

(*ii*) Calculation of Variable and Fixed Cost

		Variable Cost	*Balance being Fixed Cost*
		₹.	₹.
Material 100%		1,93,600	
Labour 70%	90,000 × 70/100	63,000	27,000
Overhead 64%	80,000 × 64/100	51,200	28,800
Administration 30%	30,000 × 30/100	9,000	21,000
Selling Commision 8%	4,40,000 × 8/100	35,200	
		₹. 3,52,000	76,800

Total Contributions = Total Sales – Total variable cost

= 4,40,000 – 3,52,000 = ₹. 88,000

$$\text{Breake-even Sales} = \frac{\text{Total Fixed Cost}}{\text{Total Contribution}} \times \text{Total Sales}$$

$$= \frac{76,800}{88,000} \times 4,40,000 = ₹.\ 3,84,000$$

Illustration 13. Modern Sports Ltd has for the past several years produced boxing gloves which are sold at ₹. 28 per pair. Higher cost in recent years have made the management to consider about the adequacy of this selling price.

The labour rate was increased from ₹. 1.75 per hour to ₹. 2.25 per hour and the cost of leather has gone up from ₹. 1.10 to ₹. 2.15 per square foot during the last 5 years. Fixed expenses have increased by 25% from the level of ₹. 18,000 five years ago. Over the same period variable overhead has increased 30% or ₹. 3 per pair of gloves. Each glove requires 1.5 sq. ft. of leather and one hour of direct labour.

Calculate the selling price that the company has to charge under the new cost structure to break-even at the same number of units as five years ago. **[*B.Com (H) Delhi*]**

Solution. Selling price of a pair of gloves is ₹. 28. A pair of gloves will require 3 sq. ft. of leather and 2 hours of direct labour.

		Old Cost		*New Cost*
		₹.		₹.
Leather	1.10 × 3 =	3.30	2.15 × 3 =	6.45
Labour	1.75 × 2 =	3.50	2.25 × 2 =	4.50
Variable Overhead (Note 1)		10.00		13.00
Marginal cost		16.80		23.95
Contribution (Note 2)		11.20		14.00
Selling Price		28.00		37.95

Note 1. Variable Overhead: 30% increase is ₹. 3, therefore old cost will be 10 and new cost ₹. 13.

2. In above old cost contribution per unit was ₹. 11.20. The number of units sold at BEP were total fixed cost/per unit contribution i.e. ₹. 18,000/11.20 = 1,607 unit (approx). The present fixed overhead are 25% more *i.e.* ₹. 18,000 + 25% = 22,500. Per unit fixed overheads on same units of production will be ₹. 22,500/1,607 = 14.

Illustration 14. A factory engaged in manufacturing of plastic buckets is working at 40% capacity and produced 10,000 buckets per annum. The present cost break-up for one bucket is as under

Materials	₹. 10
Labour	₹. 3
Overheads	₹. 5 (60% Fixed)
Selling price	₹. 20

If it is decided to work the factory at 50% capacity, the selling price falls by 3%, At 90% capacity, the selling price falls by 5% accompanied by a similar fall in the prices of material. You are required to calculate the profit at 50% and 90% capacities and also calculate break-even point for the same capacity productions.

Solution.

Statement of Marginal Cost and Profit

	At 50% capacity 12,500 units		*At 90% capacity 22,500 units*	
	Per unit ₹.	*Total* ₹.	*Per unit* ₹.	*Total* ₹.
Sales (S)	19.40	2,42,500	19.00	4,27,500
Variable Cost (VC)				
Material	10.00	1,25,000	9.50	2,13,750
Wages	3.00	37,500	3.00	67,500
Overheads	2.00	25,000	2.00	45,000
	15.00	1,87,500	14.50	3,26,250
Contribution (S – VC)	4.40	55,000	4.50	1,01,250
Less: Fixed Cost	—	30,000	—	30,000
Profit		25,000		71,250

Break-even Point		At 50% capacity	At 90% capacity
$\frac{\text{Fixed Cost}}{\text{Contribution per unit}}$	=	$\frac{30,000}{4.40}$	$\frac{30,000}{4.50}$
	=	6818 units	6667 units
Break-even Point in sales value	=	6818 × 19.40	6667 × 19
		₹. 1,32,270	₹. 1,26,673

Illustration 15. From the following figures find the break-even volume:

Selling Price per ton	₹. 69.50
Variable cost per ton	₹. 35.50
Total Fixed Exps.	₹. 18.02 lakhs

If his volume represents 40% capacity, what is the additional profit for an added production of 40% capacity, the selling price of which is 10% lower for 20% capacity production and 15% lower than the existing price, for the other 20% capacity.

Solution:

$$\text{Break-even Point} = \frac{\text{Fixed Cost}}{\text{Contribution per ton}} = \frac{18.02 \text{ lakh}}{34}$$

$$= 53,000 \text{ tons}$$

Present break-even level of 53,000 tons is for 40% capacity. For another 40% capacity the production will be further 53,000 tons.

Selling price per ton for additional 20% capacity (*i.e.* 26500 units)	
[69.50 – 10% of it]	₹. 62.55
Less variable cost	35.50
Profit per ton **[See Note]**	27.05
Totoal Profit 26,500 × 27.05	₹. 7,16,825
Selling Price per ton for next 20% capacity	
[69.50 – 15%]	₹. 59.075
Less variable cost	35.500
Profit per ton [See Note]	23.575
Total Profit 26,500 × 23.575	₹. 6,24,737

Thus total additional profit for additional 40% capacity ₹. 7,16,825 + 6,24,737 = ₹ 13,41,562.

Note. Selling Price – Variable cost = Profit, because fixed cost have already been absorbed in the production of initial 40% capacity.

Illustration 16. Frazer Ltd. Manufactures and sells a product, the selling price and raw material cost of which have remained unchanged during the past two years. The following are the relevant data.

	Year 1	*Year 2*
Quantity sold (kgs)	100	150
	₹.	₹.
Sales Value	20,000	?
Raw Materials	10,000	?
Direct Wages	3,000	?
Factory Overheads	5,000	5,700
Profit	2,000	2,550

During year 2 direct wages rates increased by 50% but there was a saving of ₹. 300 in fixed factory overheads.

Required: What quantity (in kgs) the company should have produced and sold in year 2 in order to maintain the same amount of net profit per kg as it earns during year 1.

Solution.

Statement of Marginal Cost

		₹.
Selling Price per kg (20,000/100)		200
Variable Cost per kg		
Raw Material (10,000/100)	100	
Direct Wages (3,000/100) + 50%	45	
Factory Overhead (Note 1)	20	165
Contribution per kg		35
Less Profit required per kg (2,000/100)		20
Fixed Cost per kg		15

Fixed Factory Overhead in	Year 1	Year 2
Total Factory Overhead	5,000	5,700
Less Variable Overhead	2,000	3,000
Fixed Overhead	3,000	2,700

Thus quantity to be produced and sold

Fixed overhead/Fixed cost per unit

2700/15 = 180 kg

Note. Variable Factory Overhead has been calculated as below

	Total Factory Overhead in Year 2	₹. 5,700
	Add Savings	300
		6,000
Less	Total Factory Overhead in Year 1	5,000
	Increase in factory overhead for 50 kg	1,000
	Per kg 1000/50 = ₹. 20	

Factors Which Can Change Break Even Point (*BEP*)

Break-even point will change due to change in following

(*i*) Change in the Fixed Cost

(*ii*) Change in Variable Cost

(*iii*) Change in Selling Price Per Unit

(*iv*) Change in Production Quantity Beyond Present Capacity Limits.

(1) **Change in the Fixed Cost.** If other factors do not change, an increase in the fixed cost will lead the BEP to go up and vice-versa because BEP is calculated on the basis of fixed cost (BEP = Total Fixed cost ÷ Contribution per unit). It is to be noted that only significant change in the fixed cost will result in a significant change in the BEP.

(2) **Change in the Variable Cost.** Change in the variable cost results in change in the BEP more effectively. Even a little change in the variable cost will bring about significant change in the BEP because BEP is based upon contribution per unit and contribution is selling price less variable cost.

(3) **Change in the Selling Price Per Unit.** Change in the selling price per unit will change contribution per unit which will ultimately affect BEP.

(4) **Change in Production Quantity Beyond Capacity.** If there is change in the output quantity in excess of the capacity limit, the fixed cost will increase, which will ultimately affect the BEP.

Calculation of Break Even Point from Total Sales

We have discussed above calculation of Break Even Point in case of individual products. Some firms sell a large number of products and, therefore, it may be necessary to ascertain what sales volume is necessary to meet fixed expenses. In this case the variable expenses should be worked out as a percentage of sales. Suppose total sales are ₹. 10,00,000 and variable expenses are ₹. 6,00,000. Then variable expenses form 60% of sales. This means that if a sale of ₹. 100 takes place, ₹. 60 is spent to make the goods ready for sale and that ₹. 40 will be left to meet fixed expenses. If the fixed expenses are ₹. 3,00,000, a sale of ₹. 7,50,000 will be required to recover the fixed expenses fully, *i.e.*, $\frac{3,00,000}{40} \times 100 = 7,50,000$. This figure of sale is the Break Even Point.

Illustration 17. From the following figures relating to A Ltd., calculate the Break Even Point:

	₹.
Total Sales	20,00,000
Variable Expenses	11,00,000
Net Profit	2,25,000

Solution. Fixed Expenses are ₹. 6,75,000, *i.e.*, ₹. 20,00,000 less ₹. 11,00,000 (variable expenses) and ₹. 2,25,000 (net profit).

Variable Expenses to sales are 55%, *i.e.*, $\frac{11,00,000}{20,00,000} \times 100$ leaving ₹. 45 out of sale of every ₹. 100 of sale to meet fixed expenses.

Break Even Point is ₹. 15,00,000 *i.e.*, $\frac{6,75,000}{45} \times 100.$

In above illustration the ratio of variable expenses to sales is 55% and the ratio of contribution to sales is 45%. The ratio of contribution to sales is also known as ***Profit Volume Ratio*** which indicates the difference made to total profit by a given change in sales. Profit volume ratio or P/V ratio has been discussed below in detail.

PROFIT-VOLUME RATIO (*P/V RATIO*)

There is another method to determine relationship between cost volume and profit. It is a ratio between marginal contribution and sales known as Profit-Volume Ratio or P/V Ratio. This ratio is also known as contribution to sales ratio or variable profit ratio or marginal income ratio. P/V Ratio (normally a percentage) is the rate at which contribution or profit increases with volume

$$\text{P/V Ratio} = \frac{\text{Contribution} \times 100}{\text{Sales}}$$

(Here either total contribution and total sales or per unit contribution and per unit sales may be considered. P/V Ratio is constant for a single unit of product or a number of units. It remains constant over substantial changes of volume).

$$\text{P/V Ratio} = \left(\frac{\text{Sales} - \text{Variable Cost}}{\text{Sales}}\right) \times 100$$

or $$= \left(1 - \frac{\text{Variable Cost}}{\text{Sales}}\right) \times 100$$

or $$= \frac{(\text{Fixed Cost} + \text{Profit})}{\text{Sales}} \times 100$$

The variable cost and Break-even Point can be calculated with the help of P/V Ratio.

$$\text{Variable Cost} = (1 - \text{P/V}) \times \text{Sales}$$

$$\text{BEP (Sales value)} = \frac{\text{Fixed Cost}}{\text{P/V Ratio}}$$

P/V Ratio can also be calculated by determining the amount of change in profit and change in the total sales between two periods

$$\text{PV Ratio} = \frac{\text{Change in Profit (of two periods)} \times 100}{\text{Change in Sales (of two periods)}}$$

By the use of P/V Ratio the management can determine the profit changed with result from change in volume

$$\text{Total Contribution} = \text{Sales} \times \text{P/V Ratio}$$

$$\text{Total Profit} = (\text{Sales} \times \text{P/V Ratio}) - \text{Fixed Cost}$$

The P/V Ratio may be used for determining the volume of sales at a desired profit

$$\text{Sales at desired profit} = \frac{\text{Fixed Cost} + \text{Desired Profit}}{\text{P/V Ratio}}$$

A high P/V Ratio indicates that a slight increase in volume without any increase in fixed cost would give higher profit. A product with low P/V Ratio indicates low profitability so that management's efforts may be made to improve P/V Ratio by raising selling price of the product or by reducing variable cost or marginal cost of the product.

P/V Ratio also indicates that profitability may also be improved if the management concentrate on the manufacture of only those products which show a high P/V Ratio.

It is to be noted that this ratio is not affected by any change in the fixed overhead, although the change in fixed overhead will affect the total profit.

P/V Ratio is a very useful index in a number of management decisions. The profitability of product–lines, sales areas, sales men, methods of sales and classes of customers may be compared and analysed with the help of this ratio. It is one of important ratios used in interfirm comparison. A high P/V Ratio suggests that a small increase in sales will earn higher profit if fixed costs remain constant. P/V Ratio can be used for ascertaining desired sales at a desired profit. In case of a product mix, we can study profit margin on the various products without taking cost and prices of each product separately. Low P/V Ratio of a product shows less productivity.

Illustration 18. From the following particulars calculate P/V Ratio and also sales required to earn a profit of ₹. 1,20,000.

Sales	₹. 6,00,000;	Variable cost ₹. 3,75,000
Fixed cost	₹. 1,80,000.	

Solution.

$$\text{P/V Ratio} = \frac{\text{Contribution}}{\text{Sales}} \times 100 = \frac{2,25,000}{6,00,000} \times 100 = 37.5\%$$

[Contribution = Sales – Variable Cost = 6,00,000 – 3,75,000 = 2,25,000]

$$\text{Sales for a Desired Profit} = \frac{\text{Fixed Cost + Desired Profit}}{\text{P/V Ratio}}$$

$$= \frac{1,80,000 + 1,20,000}{37.5\%}$$

$$= \frac{3,00,000 \times 100}{37.5} = ₹.\ 8,00,000$$

Illustration 19. Sale of a product amounts to 200 units per month at ₹. 10 per unit. Fixed overhead is ₹. 400 per month and variable cost ₹. 6 per unit. There is a proposal to reduce prices by 10% per unit. Calculate the present and future P/V Ratio. How many units must be sold to maintain total profit?

Solution.

$$\text{Present P/V Ratio} = \frac{\text{(Selling Price – Variable Cost)}}{\text{Selling Price}} \times 100$$

$$= \frac{(10-6)}{10} \times 100 = \mathbf{40\%}$$

$$\text{Future P/V Ratio} = \frac{(9-6)}{9} \times 100 = \mathbf{33\frac{1}{3}\%}$$

Present Profit = (Sales × P/V Ratio) – Fixed Cost

= (2,000 × 40/100) – 400

or Contribution – Fixed cost = 800 – 400 = **₹. 400**

Units to be sold in future to earn profit of ₹. 400

$$= \frac{\text{Fixed Cost + Desired Profit}}{\text{Contribution Per Unit}}$$

$$= \frac{400 + 400}{3} = \textbf{267 units} \text{ (Approx)}$$

[Contribution Per Unit = Selling price Per Unit – Variable Cost Per Unit = 9 – 6 = 3]

Illustration 20. The following data are obtained from the records of a company

	First Years (₹.)	Second Year (₹)
Sales	80,000	90,000
Profit	10,000	14,000

Calculate P/V Ratio, Fixed cost and Break Even sales.

Solution.

$$\text{P/V Ratio} = \frac{\text{Change in Profit}}{\text{Change in Sales}} \times 100$$

$$= \frac{4{,}000}{10{,}000} \times 100 = \textbf{40\%}$$

Contribution = Sales × P/V Ratio

= 80,000 × 40/100 = ₹. 32,000

Fixed Cost = Contribution – Profit

= 32,000 – 10,000 = 22,000

$$\text{Break Even Sales} = \frac{\text{Fixed Cost}}{\text{P/V Ratio}}$$

$$= \frac{22{,}000}{40\%} = \frac{22{,}000 \times 100}{40} = \textbf{₹. 55,000}$$

Illustration 21. A company sells its product at ₹. 15 per unit. In a period, if it produces and sells 8,000 units, it incurred a loss of ₹. 5 per unit. If the volume is raised to 20,000 units, it earns a profit of ₹. 4 per unit. Calculate P/V Ratio, BEP in units and Rupees.

Solution. Selling price per unit is given. To calculate P/V Ratio, we have to ascertain variable cost per unit.

$$\text{Variable cost per unit} = \frac{\text{Change in the total cost}}{\text{Change in the volume of product}}$$

Total cost at 8,000 units = (SP + Loss per unit) × 8,000

= (15 + 5) 8,000 = ₹. 1,60,000

Total Cost at 20,000 units = (SP – Profit per unit) × 20,000

= (15 – 4) 20,000 = ₹. 2,20,000

$$\text{Variable cost per unit} = \frac{₹.\ 2{,}20{,}000 - 1{,}60{,}000}{20{,}000 - 8{,}000 \text{ units}}$$

$$= \frac{60{,}000}{12{,}000} = ₹.\ 5$$

Contribution per unit = SP per unit – VC per units

= 15 – 5 = 10

$$\text{P/V Ratio} = \frac{\text{Contribution per unit} \times 100}{\text{SP per unit}}$$

$$= \frac{10}{15} \times 100 = 66\frac{2}{3}\%$$

Fixed Cost = Total Cost of 8,000 units – Variable Cost of 8,000 units

= 1,60,000 – (8,000 × 5)

= 1,60,000 – 40,000 =1,20,000

$$\text{BEP in units} = \frac{\text{Total Fixed Cost}}{\text{Contribution per unit}} = \frac{1,20,000}{10} = 12,000 \text{ units}$$

$$\text{BEP in Rupees} = \frac{\text{Total Fixed Cost}}{\text{P/V Ratio}} = \frac{1,20,000}{66\frac{2}{3}\%} = 1,80,000$$

Illustration 22. Examine whether the following equations are correct

(*a*) $\text{Sales} = \frac{\text{Contribution}}{\text{P/V Ratio}}$,

(*b*) $\text{Contribution} = \frac{\text{P/V Ratio}}{\text{Sales}}$.

Solution. (*a*) P/V Ratio is ratio between contribution and sales

$$\text{P/V Ratio} = \frac{\text{Contribution}}{\text{Sales}}$$

or

$$\text{Sales} \times \text{P/V Ratio} = \text{Contribution}$$

or

$$\text{Sales} = \frac{\text{Contribution}}{\text{P/V Ratio}}$$

Thus equation (*a*) is correct.

(*b*)

$$\text{P/V Ratio} = \frac{\text{Contribution}}{\text{Sales}}$$

$$\text{Contribution} = \text{Sales} \times \text{P/V Ratio}$$

Thus equation (*b*) is not correct.

Illustration 23. A company sold in two successive periods 7,000 and 9,000 units respectively and incurred a loss of ₹. 10,000 and earned a profit of ₹. 10,000 in the two periods respectively. Calculate:

(*i*) the amount of fixed expenses,

(*ii*) the number of units to break even, and

(*iii*) the number of units to earn a profit of ₹. 40,000.

The selling price of the article is ₹. 100 per unit.

Solution.

(*i*) *Fixed Expenses:*

	Sales units	*Profit ₹.*
I Period	7,000	– 10,000
II Period	9,000	10,000
Difference	2,000	20,000

Since 2,000 units yield a contribution of ₹. 20,000, the contribution per unit is ₹. 10. Therefore the variable cost is ₹. 90, *i.e.*, ₹. 100 less ₹. 10.

	₹.
Sales Value of 7,000 units @ ₹. 100	7,00,000
Less Total Variable Cost @ ₹. 90	6,30,000
Total Contribution	70,000
Loss during the period	10,000
Total Fixed Expenses	80,000

(*ii*) *Break Even Point:*

	₹.
Fixed Expenses	80,000
Contribution per unit	10

No. of units required to meet fixed expenses 80,000 ÷ 10 or FC/C or 8,000 units.

(*iii*) *Units Required for a Profit of ₹. 40,000*

Total contribution required (Fixed Expenses plus desired profit) 1,20,000

No. of units required to produce the contribution : FC + P/C 1,20,000 ÷ 10 or 12,000

MARGIN OF SAFETY (*M/S*)

Any sales in excess of break-even volume represents margin of safety. It is sales beyond break-even volume which brings in profit.

Margin of Safety (*M/S*) =Actual Sales – Sales at *BEP*

M/S is normally expressed in percentage

$$i.e.\ M/S\ (\%) = \frac{(\text{Actual Sales} - \text{Sales at } BEP)}{\text{Sales}} \times 100$$

When BEP of sales is constant, the M/S increases with increase in sales. The profitability of a business may be measured by the size of margin of safety A high margin of safety makes a business less vulnerable to a decline in sales because in such a case the BEP will be much below the actual sales and in case there is fall in sales, there will still be a profit. On the other hand if there is low margin of safety, it indicates a difficult position.

If there is low margin of safety along with high fixed cost, it is desirable that efforts should be made to reduce fixed cost or increase sales volume. Where margin of safety and contribution margin ratio (*i.e.* P/V Ratio) both are low, the efforts should be made to reduce variable cost or to increase the selling price.

With the help of margin of safety some other calculation can be made.

$$\text{Profit} = \text{Margin of Safety} \times \text{PV Ratio}$$

$$\text{Margin of Safety} = \frac{\text{Profit}}{\text{PV Ratio}}$$

$$\text{Margin of Safety (Units)} = \text{Profit/Contribution per unit}$$

$$\text{P/V Ratio} = \frac{\text{Profit} \times 100}{\text{Margin of safety}}$$

It should be noted that above relationships show that once break even sales amount is achieved contribution from additional sales (margin of safety) generates profit only.

Improvement of margin of safety is very important for a business. It can be improved by taking certain steps (*i*) lowering fixed cost, (*ii*) lowering variable cost (*iii*) Increasing volume of sales if there is capacity (*iv*) Increasing selling price if the market permits (*v*) Changing the product mix so as to increase total contribution.

Illustration 24: Given the following find of Margin of Safety Sales — (*i*) Profit earned ₹. 24,000 (*ii*) Selling price per unit ₹. 10, (*iv*) Marginal cost per unit ₹. 7.

Solution. Contribution per unit ₹. 3

$$\text{Margin of safety sales (units)} = \frac{\text{Profit}}{\text{Contribution per unit}}$$

$$= \frac{24{,}000}{3} = 8{,}000 \text{ units}$$

$$\text{Margin of Safety Sales in value} = 8{,}000 \times 10 = ₹.\ 80{,}000$$

Illustration 25. Raj Co. Ltd. has prepared following budget estimates for the year 2004–05.

Sales Units	15,000	Sales Value	₹. 1,50,000
Fixed Expenses	₹.34,000	Variable Costs	₹. 6 per unit

You are required to (*i*) Find out P/V Ratio, Break Even Point and Margin of Safety (*ii*) Calculate the revised P/V Ratio, BEP and Margin of Safety in each of the following cases:

(*a*) Decrease of 10% in selling price

(*b*) Increase of 10% in variable cost

(*c*) Increase of sales volume by 2,000 units

(*d*) Increase of 6,000 in fixed cost.

Solution.

	P/V Ratio $= \frac{C}{SP} \times 100$ $C = SP - VC$	*BEP (₹.)* $= \frac{FC}{PV\ Ratio}$	*Margin of Safety (₹.)* *= Actual Sales – BEP Sales*
(*i*) Original data	$\frac{10-6}{10} \times 100 = 40\%$	$\frac{34{,}000}{40\%} = 85{,}000$	1,50,000 – 85,000 = 65,000
(*ii*) (*a*) Decrease of 10% in SP	$\frac{9-6}{9} \times 100 = 33\frac{1}{3}\%$	$\frac{34{,}000}{33\frac{1}{3}\%} = 1{,}02{,}000$	1,35,000 – 1,02,000 = 33,000
(*b*) Increase of 10% in VC	$\frac{10-6.6}{10} \times 100 = 34\%$	$\frac{34{,}000}{34\%} = 1{,}00{,}000$	1,50,000 – 1,00,000 = 50,000
(*c*) Increase of Sales volume by 2,000 units	$\frac{10-6}{10} \times 100 = 40\%$	$\frac{34{,}000}{40\%} = 85{,}000$	1,70,000 – 85,000 = 85,000
(*d*) Increase of ₹. 6,000 in fixed cost	$\frac{10-6}{10} \times 100 = 40\%$	$\frac{40{,}000}{40\%} = 1{,}00{,}000$	1,50,000 – 1,00,000 = 50,000

Illustration 26. S. Ltd furnishes you the following information relating to half year ending 30th June 2004.

Fixed Expenses	₹. 50,000
Sales	₹. 2,00,000
Profit	₹. 50,000

During the second half of the same year, the company has projected a loss of ₹. 10,000. Calculate (*i*) P/V Ratio, BEP and Margin of Safety for six months ending June 2004; (*ii*) Expected sales volume for second half of the year assuming that selling price and fixed expenses remain unchanged in the second half year also; (*iii*) The Break Even Point and Margin of Safety for the whole year 1990.

Solution.

(*i*) **Contribution** = Fixed Cost + Profit = 50,000 + 50,000 = ₹. 1,00,000

$$\text{P/V Ratio} = \frac{\text{Contribution}}{\text{Sales}} \times 100 = \frac{1,00,000}{2,00,000} \times 100 = 50\%$$

$$\text{BEP} = \frac{\text{Fixed Cost} \times 100}{\text{P/V Ratio}} = \frac{50,000}{50\%} = ₹.\ 1,00,000$$

Margin of Safety = Actual Sales – BEP Sales = 2,00,000 – 1,00,000 =₹. 1,00,000

$$\text{or} \quad = \frac{\text{Profit}}{\text{P/V Ratio}} = \frac{50,000}{50\%} = ₹.\ 1,00,000$$

(*ii*) **Second half year**

Contribution = Fixed Cost – Loss = 50,000 – 10,000 = 40,000

$$\text{P/V Ratio} = \frac{\text{Contribution}}{\text{Sales}} = 50\% \text{ as it was in the first half year}$$

$$\text{Sales} = \frac{\text{Contribution}}{\text{P/V Ratio}} = \frac{40,000}{50\%} = ₹.\ 80,000$$

(*iii*) **For the whole year**

P/V Ratio will be same because selling price and variable expenses per unit have not changed

P/V Ratio = 50%; Fixed Expenses for full year ₹, 1,00,000

$$\text{BEP Sales} = \frac{\text{Fixed Cost}}{\text{P/V Ratio}} = \frac{1,00,000}{50\%} = ₹.\ 2,00,000$$

Margin of Safety = Actual Sales – BEP Sales

= (2,00,000 + 80,000) – 2,00,000 = ₹. 80,000

BREAK-EVEN BY GRAPH

The break even point can also be calculated by means of a chart, or graph. On the X-axis is plotted the output (or volume of sales if quantity of output is not available). On the Y-axis the amount of expenses in total is shown. Fixed Costs will be shown by a line parallel to the X-axis. Then a line is drawn to show for various levels of output, the total costs, *i.e.*, variable expenditure plus the fixed costs. Altèrnatively, a variable cost line and a total cost line may be drawn. A line is also drawn to indicate sale proceeds at various levels of output. A perpendicular on the X-axis from the point where the total cost line and sales line intersect will give the break even point. (See the explanation to the following illustration).

Illustration 27. Draw the chart to show break even point from the following information.

	₹.
Variable Cost per unit	15
Selling Price per unit	25
Total Fixed Expenses	1,80,000

Solution: The following points (showing total expenditure and sale) should be plotted in the graph.

Output (Units)	*Fixed Expenses* ₹	*Variable Cost* ₹	*Total Expenditure* ₹	*Sales Proceeds* ₹
0	1,80,000	...	1,80,000	0
10,000	1,80,000	1,50,000	3,30,000	2,50,000
20,000	1,80,000	3,00,000	4,80,000	5,00,000

(The levels of output have been chosen at random: any other levels will also do).

The chart appears below.

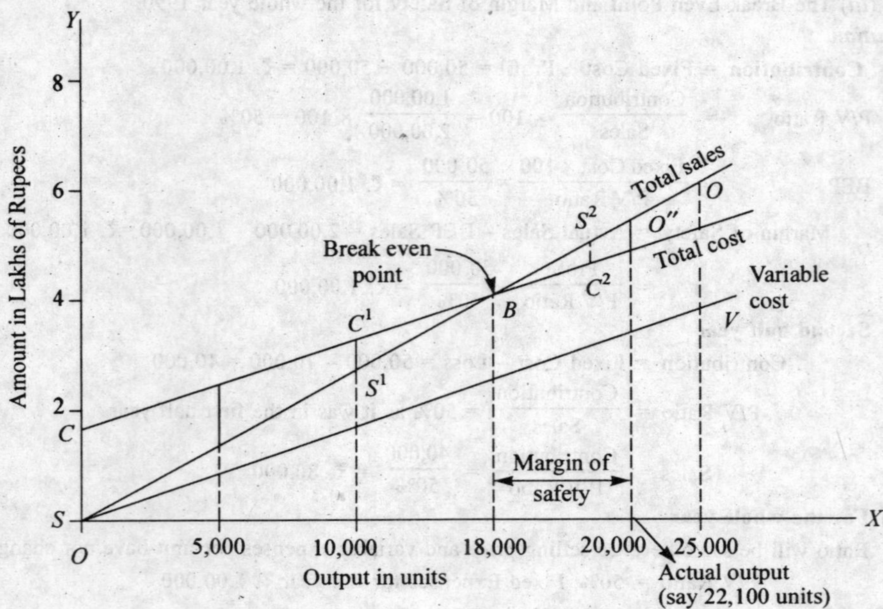

Explanation: First plot the points to show cost. Point C shows total cost when output is zero. C^1 shows total cost when output is 10,000 units and C^2 indicates the total cost when the output is 20,000 units. The line joining these points is the line showing total cost at various levels. Then plot the points to show Sales. S is the point showing sales when output is zero. S^1 indicates sales at the output of 10,000 units and S^2 is the point to show sales at the output of 20,000 units. The line joining these points is the line for total sales. The point where the two lines intersect, B, indicates the Break Even Point. To the left of this point there is loss and to the right of it there is profit.

The line OV represents variable cost and runs parallel to the total cost line.

The chart can give (1) Profit or loss at any level of output and (2) The output required to give a given profit. For instance, if the output is 22,500 units, the profit will be ₹. 75,000 – the distance between the sales line and the cost line against the output of 22,500 units. If the profit desired is ₹. 1,00,000 one will have to see where the distance between the two lines equals ₹. 1,00,000. The distance O^1 and O^2 equals ₹. 1,00,000. A perpendicular on the X-axis will indicate the output required. It is 25,000 units.

Break Even Chart can also be prepared on the basis of Total Sales. One should plot total expenditure at various levels of sale. See following *Example*

Total Sales Volumes ₹.	Fixed Expenses ₹.	Variable Expenses ₹.	Total ₹.
0	6,75,000	...	6,75,000
10,00,000	6,75,000	5,50,000	12,25,000
20,00,000	6,75,000	11,00,000	17,75,000

The *X*-axis of the chart will measure sales valume in amount and the Y-axis will measure total expenses as well as sales volume. (If the same scale is used on the X-axis and Y-axis, the line to represent sales volume can be drawn at 45° to the X-axis). The chart is given below:

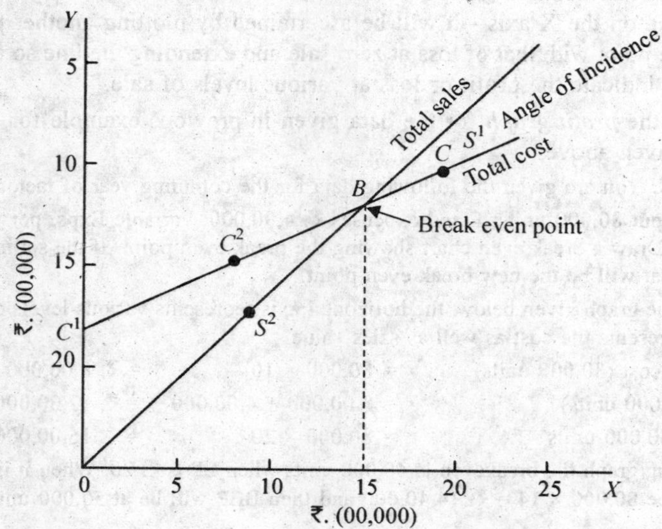

Point C^1 represents total cost at zero sale, C^2 at a sale of ₹. 10,00,000 and C^3 at a sale of ₹. 20,00,000. The line joining these points represents total cost. The line joining points S^1, S^2 and S^3 represents sale. The two lines meet at point B; a perpendicular from B will show the break even sales at ₹. 15,00,000.

Angle of Incidence: This is the angle at which the sales line intersect the total cost line. If angle of incidence is large it shows a high rate of profit. A narrow angle indicates that fixed overheads are absorbed, the profit accross at relatively low rate. In this case the variable costs form a large part of cost of sales.

Profit Graph: *Another way* of drawing up the break-even chart is to show the profit or loss at various levels of sale. The Y-axis shows the profit (above the X-axis) or loss (below the X-axis),

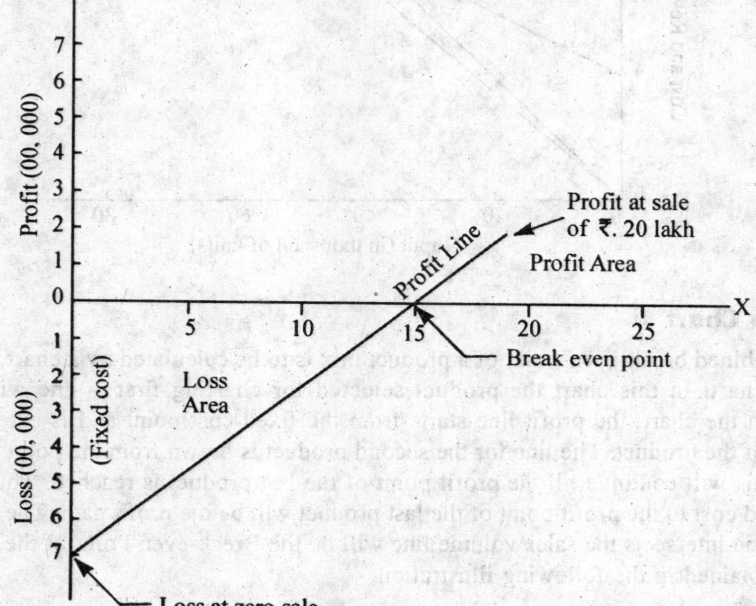

the X-axis shows the sale. At zero sale the loss will be equal to the fixed expenses; the break even point of sale will lie on the X axis—it will be ascertained by plotting another point of profit or loss and joining the point with that of loss at zero sale and extending the line so as to cross the X-axis. This line will indicate the profit or loss at various levels of sale.

Following is the *profit graph* for the data given in previous example for which one graph has already been given above.

Illustration 28: You are given the following data for the comming year of factory.

Budgeted out put 80,000 units; Fixed expenses ₹. 4,00,000; variable Exps. per unit ₹. 10; Selling price per unit ₹. 20. Draw a break even chart showing the break even point. If the selling price is reduced to ₹. 18 per unit, what will be the new break even point.

Solution: In the graph given below, the horizontal axis represents various levels of budgeted output and vertical axis represents the cost as well as sales value

Total variable cost (80,000 units)	= 80,000 × 10	= ₹. 8,00,000
Total cost (80,000 units)	= 8,00,000 + 4,00,000	= ₹. 12,00,000
Sales for 80,000 units	= 80,000 × 20	= ₹. 16,00,000

In the following graph the breakeven is 40,000 units when SP is ₹. 20. When it is reduced to ₹. 18, the sales value will be 80,000 × 14 = ₹. 14,40,000 and then BEP will be at 50,000 units.

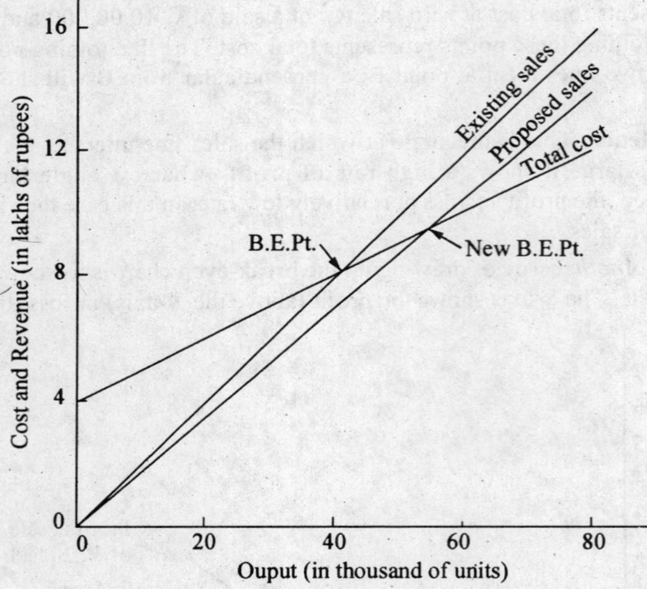

Profit Path Chart

If combined break-even-point of a product mix is to be calculated by a chart, it is known as profit path chart. In this chart the product selected for charting first is one with the highest P/V Ratio. In the chart, the profit line starts from the fixed cost point and is extended upto the profit point of the product. The line for the second product is drawn from the point where the first line ends. This will continue till the profit point of the last product is reached. Thus line starting from the fixed cost to the profit point of the last product will be the profit path. The point at which total profit line intersects the sales volume line will be the Break-even Point of the entire product mix. It is explained in the following illustration.

Illustration 29. The following figures supply to a manufacturing company producing a wide, angle of products which may be classified into three main groups

Product Mix	*Annual Sales (₹.)*	*Variable cost (₹.)*
A	30,00,000	10,00,000
B	30,00,000	20,00,000
C	35,00,000	30,00,000

The fixed costs were ₹. 25,00,000. Plot on a graph a marginal income slopes (*Profit Path*) for the total output.

Solution: For plotting *Profit Path* we have to ascertain progressive or cumulative net profit as below.

[*Figures in Lakhs Rupees*]

Product	Annual Sales	Progressive Sales [*x*]	Variable Cost	Contribution	Progressive Contribution	Fixed Cost	Progressive Net Profit [*y*]
A	30	30	10	20	20	25	– 5
B	30	60	20	10	30	25	5
C	35	95	30	5	35	25	10

In the graph data *x* (progressive annual sales) and *y* (progressive net profit) will be plotted in X axis and Y axis. The line connecting fixed cost point and last point of profit of C product will be called average marginal income slope. This line is intersecting the sales line at a point, which is BEP sales.

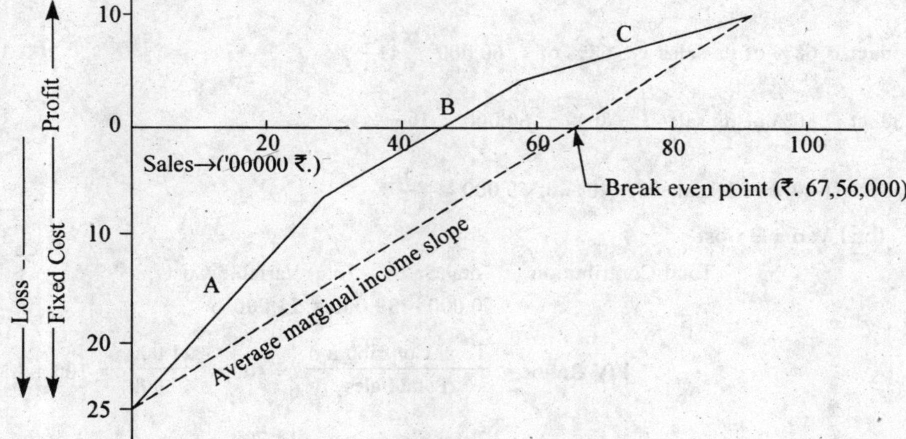

Cash Break-Even-Point (Units). In the computation of Cash BEP only cash fixed costs are consideration. Cash fixed costs exclude depreciation and other non-cash fixed expenses. By Cash BEP we can ascertain that level of output or sales at which the sales revenue will be equal to net cash inflow

$$\text{Cash BEP} = \frac{\text{Cash Fixed cost}}{\text{Contribution per unit}}$$

Composite Break Even Point (Sales). Composite BEP is calculated taking into consideration the data related to all products together where more than one product are manufactured by a firm. For this calculation total fixed cost is divided by Composite P/V Ratio. Composite profit volume ratio is calculated by dividing total contribution (of all products) by total sales (of all products) and multiplied by hundred.

$$\text{Composite P/V Ratio} = \frac{\text{Total contribution} \times 100}{\text{Total Sales}}$$

$$\text{Composite Break Even Sales} = \frac{\text{Total Fixed Cost}}{\text{Composite P/V Ratio}}$$

$$\text{Composite Break even (units)} = \frac{\text{Total Fixed Cost}}{\text{Composite contribution per unit}}$$

Composite contribution per unit can be calculated by adding contribution from various products in the proportion of their product mix.

Illustration 30. A Co. manufactures and sells four products – A, B, C and D. The Sale Mix in value comprises $33\frac{1}{3}$%, $41\frac{2}{3}$% $16\frac{2}{3}$% and $8\frac{1}{3}$% of A, B, C and D respectively. The total budgeted sales (100%) are ₹. 60,000 per month. Operating or variable costs are as below:

Product A	60% of Sales	Product C	80% of Sales
Product B	68% of Sales	Product D	40% of Sales

Total fixed cost are ₹. 14,700 per month. Calculate break even point for the enterprise as a whole.

[*B Com.(H) Delhi*]

Solution:

Calculation of Variable Cost

	₹.
Product A 60% of its sales (*i.e.* 60% of ₹. 60,000 × $33\frac{1}{3}$%) *i.e.* 60% of 20,000	12,000
Product B 68% of its sales *i.e.* 68% of ₹. 60,000 × $41\frac{2}{3}$ %	17,000
Product C 80% of its sales *i.e.* 80% of 60,000 × $16\frac{2}{3}$%	8,000
Product D 40% of its sales *i.e.* 40% of 60,000 × $8\frac{1}{3}$ %	2,000
Total Variable Cost	39,000

Total Contribution = Total Sales – Total Variable Cost
= 60,000 – 39,000 = 21,000

$$\text{P/V Ratio} = \frac{\text{Total Contribution}}{\text{Total Sales}} \times 100 = \frac{21{,}000}{60{,}000} \times 100 = 35\%$$

$$\text{Composite BEP Sales} = \frac{\text{Total Fixed Cost}}{\text{P/V Ratio}} = \frac{14{,}700}{35\%} = ₹.\ 42{,}000$$

Thus ₹. 42,000 is Composite BE Sales. In case of each product, the BEP sales will be allocated in their 'sales mix'.

Cost Break Even Point

Cost BEP is that level of activity at which the cost (operating) in two alternative plants are equal. Normally two plants producing similar product may have different fixed and variable costs per unit. It is desired to determine that point at which total cost (fixed + variable) of operating both the plants are equal. This point is known as 'Cost Break Even Point'. It is usually calculated as below:

$$\text{Cost BEP} = \frac{\text{Difference in Fixed Cost}}{\text{Difference in Variable Cost per unit}}$$

It is to be noted that cost BEP is useful to identify which plant is more profitable for a given level of output (according to high and low demand). In other words, both plants will be equal at the cost break-even but if activity level goes up, that plant will be more profitable which has lower variable cost per unit or higher contribution per unit. It will also be observed that if activity level is less than cost break even level, that plant which has lower fixed costs will be more profitable.

Illustration 31. There were two plants *A* and *B* operating in a firm. Their fixed cost were *A* ₹. 3,00,000 and *B* ₹. 4,50,000. The variable cost per unit of plant *A* was ₹. 6 and that of plant *B* ₹. 5. you are required (*i*) to find out BEP for plant *A* and *B* (*ii*) to indicate the level where operation of a particular plant was more profitable and (*iii*) to show the financial implication when demand is 1,00,000 units and 2,00,000 units.

Solution.

(*i*) Cost break even for plant *A* and *B*

$$= \frac{\text{Difference in Fixed Cost}}{\text{Difference in Variable Cost per unit}}$$

$$= \frac{4,50,000 - 3,00,000}{6-5} = \frac{1,50,000}{1} = 1,50,000 \text{ units}$$

(*ii*) Thus at production level of 1,50,000 units both plants will be at equal total cost. At this level, the firm will be indifferent in respect of the use of these two plants. But if output goes up or down to this level (1,50,000 units) the profit will change. In this case, if output is less than 1,50,000 units plant A will be more profitable and if output is more than 1,50,000 units, plant *B* will be more profitable (It is proved by following calculation).

(*iii*) The financial implication of operating the two plants at given level will be as below:

(*a*) If demand is 1,00,000 units		*Plant A*	*Plant B*
		₹.	₹.
Fixed Cost		3,00,000	4,50,000
Variable Cost @ ₹. 6 and ₹. 5 per unit		6,00,000	5,00,000
	Total Cost	9,00,000	9,50,000

[When demand is less than 1,50,000 units plant A is more profitable because its total cost is less]

(*b*) If demand is 2,00,000 units			
Fixed Cost		3,00,000	4,50,000
Variable Cost @ ₹. 6 and ₹. 5 per unit		12,00,000	10,00,000
	Total Cost	15,00,000	14,50,000

[When demand is more than 1,50,000 units Plant B is more profitable because its total cost is less]

Breakeven of Merged Plants

When two or more plant of a firm are merged, there is need of calculating break even point of the merged plant. The BEP of merged plants will be calculated on the basis of sales and cost figures of different plants at their 100 per cent capacity level. Thus sales and cost data of all plants will be calculated at 100% capacity level thereafter BEP will be ascertained on the basis of totals of sales and costs of all plants taken together.

Illustration 32. *A*, *B* and *C* are three similar plants under the same management which wants to merge for better operation. The results are as under:

Plant	*A*	*B*	*C*
Capacity Operated	100%	70%	50%
Turnover (₹ in lakhs)	300	280	150
Variable Cost (₹ in lakhs)	200	210	75
Fixed Cost (₹ in lakhs)	70	50	62

Find out (*i*) the capacity of the merged plant at break even (*ii*) the profit at 75% capacity of the merged plant (*iii*) the turnover from the merged plant to give a profit of ₹. 28 lakhs. **[*CA–Inter*]**

Solution:

Statement showing turnover and cost of plants before and after merger [₹. in lakhs]

	Before Merger			After Merger
	A	B	C	
Capacity	100%	100%	100%	100%
Turnover (₹. in Lakhs)	300	400	300	1,000
Variable Cost	200	300	150	650
Contribution	100	100	150	350
Fixed Cost	70	50	62	182

(*i*) P/V Ratio of Merged Plant = (Contribution × 100)/Sales

= (350 × 100)/1,000 = 35%

$$\text{BEP of Merged Plant} = \frac{\text{Fixed Cost}}{\text{P/V Ratio}} = \frac{182}{35\%} = ₹.\ 520 \text{ lakhs}$$

$$\text{Capacity of Merged Plant at BEP} = \frac{\text{BEP Turnover} \times 100}{\text{Total Turnover}} = \frac{520}{1,000} \times 100 = 52\%$$

(*ii*) Profit at 75% Capacity of the Merged Plant

	₹. in lakhs
Turnover at 75% Capacity 1,000 × 75%	750.00
Contribution = Turnover × PV Ratio = 750 × 35%	262.5
Fixed Cost	182.0
Profit	80.5

(*iii*) Turnover of the merged plant to earn profit of ₹. 28 lakhs

$$= \frac{\text{Fixed Cost + Desired Profit}}{\text{P/V Ratio}} = \frac{182 + 28}{35\%} = \textbf{₹. 600 lakhs}$$

KEY FACTOR OR LIMITING FACTOR

Under the marginal costing, profitability is ascertained as aggregate of contributions from all products sold. With an objective to maximise profit, those products which yield highest contribution are sold in maximum quantities. It is generally assumed that there will be no limitation which may create restriction in increasing quantities of one or more products. But in practice there may be a number of factors which may create limitations. These may be shortage of material, labour, plant capacity or sales. These are called key factors or limiting factors.

If materials are available in limited quantity, the selection of profitable product will be on the basis of contribution per unit of material. This will also be in the case of other factors. Thus

$$\text{Contribution per unit} = \frac{\text{Contribution}}{\text{Key factor}}$$

But when sales is the key factor, the profitability of a product is measured by P/V Ratio.

Thus where a business produces a variety of products, the objective should be to produce and sell a mix of products which gives the greatest contribution per unit of the limiting factor or key factor. For the purpose of maximising profits the products should be listed in order of their respective contributions per unit of the limited factor. With the priorities thus established, the resources should first be applied to producing and selling the utmost volume of products with the highest unit contribution, then to the product with the next highest contribution and so on until the capacity of plant is exhausted.

Illustration 33. The following particulars are extracted from the record of a company.

	Per unit	
	Product A	*Product B*
Sales	₹. 100	₹. 120
Consumption of materials	2 kg	3 kg
Materials Cost	₹. 10	₹. 15
Direct Wages Cost	₹. 15	₹. 10
Direct Expenses	₹. 5	₹. 6
Machine hours used	3 hours	2 hours
Overhead Expenses		
Fixed	₹. 5	₹. 10
Variable	₹. 15	₹. 20

Direct wages per hour is ₹. 5. Comment on profitability of each product (both use the same raw material) when:

(*i*) Total sales potential in units is limited.

(*ii*) Total sales potential in value is limited

(*iii*) Raw material is in short supply

(*iv*) Production capacity (in term of machine hours) is the limiting factor.

Solution.

Statement Showing Contribution and P/V Ratio

	Per unit	
	Product A ₹.	*Product B* ₹.
Sales (*a*)	100	₹. 120
Materials	10	15
Direct Wages	15	10
Direct Expenses	5	6
Variable Overhead	15	20
Total Marginal Cost (*b*)	45	51
Contribution per unit (*a*) – (*b*)	55	69
Contribution per kg of Material (Contribution ÷ kg)	27.5	23
Contribution per machine hour (Contribution ÷ hours)	18.33	34.50
P/V Ratio [(C × 100)/S]	55%	57.5%

On the basis of key factor technique, profitability of each product will be determined on the basis of per unit limiting factor. If contribution per unit of limiting factor is higher; the product is more profitable.

When material is key factor, contribution per kg raw material is more in A product (₹. 55 ÷ 2 kg). Similarly when machine hour is key factor per hour contribution is more in product B (₹. 69 ÷ 2 hours).

If Sale potential is limited, the more profitable product is that whose per unit contribution is more *i.e.* product B. But when total Sales value is a key factor the profitable product will be that which shows higher P/V Ratio *i.e.* product B.

Limiting Factor	*Ranking a product*		*Ranking based on*
	First	*Second*	
(*i*) Sales	*B*	*A*	Per unit contribution
(*ii*) Sales Value	*B*	*A*	P/V Ratio
(*iii*) Raw Material	*A*	*B*	Contribution per kg of material
(*iv*) Production Capacity	*B*	*A*	Contribution per machine hour

MARGINAL COST AND DECISION MAKING

Marginal cost helps management to make decision involving consideration of cost and revenue. Basically, marginal costing furnishes information regarding additional costs to be incurred if an additional activity is to be taken up or the saving in costs which may be expected if an activity is given up. This can be compared with the benefit expected from the proposed course of action and thus the management will be able to take the appropriate decision. Below we discuss the important decisions which can be taken with the help of marginal costing.

1. FIXATION OF PRICES

Usually it is estimated that price charged from customers must cover costs fully. This is quite true in normal times and normal cases as otherwise a profit cannot be earned. But in special circumstances price may be below the total cost and yet bring advantage to the producer. These special circumstances are a recession when sales are difficult to make, sale to a special customer who buys an additional quantity but is not willing to pay a price covering total cost and sales in special markets where prices do not cover the full cost.

(*i*) Pricing in Recessions or Depressions

During depression the problem is to reduce prices, which may have to be reduced even below the total cost. It is quite a mistake to believe that unless the total costs are realised, it is not worthwhile to do any business. (Of course the business should be given up if it is thought prices will never again be remunerative). It is obvious that fixed expenses will have to be incurred even if no goods are produced or sold, in which case the business will suffer a net loss equal to fixed cost.

(*a*) Let us suppose that goods are sold at ₹. 19.00 per unit and that only 30,000 units are sold. The summarised position are given in the following Trading & P/L Account.

Trading and Profit and Loss Account

	₹.		₹.
To Materials (30,000 × 7)	2,10,000	By Sales (30,000 ×@₹. 19)	5,70,000
To Labour (30,000 × ₹. 3.50)	1,05,000	By Loss	95,000
To Variable Factory Exps. (30,000 × ₹. 3)	90,000		
To Variable Selling Exps. (30,000 × ₹. 3)	60,000		
To Fixed Expenses	2,00,000		
	6,65,000		6,65,000

At the output of 30,000 units total cost would have been ₹. 22.17 (₹. 15.50 variable cost plus fixed expenses which are ₹. 2,00,000, i.e., ₹. 6.67 per unit); but by selling at ₹. 19.00 per unit, the loss is only ₹. 95,000 as against ₹. 2,00,000 which would have been the case if no goods had been produced.

(*b*) Suppose only 10,000 units are sold and that too @ ₹. 16.00 per unit. The Trading and Profit and Loss Account will be:

Trading and Profit and Loss Account

	₹.		₹.
To Materials (10,000 × ₹. 7)	70,000	By Sales (10,000 × ₹. 16)	1,60,000
To Labour	35,000	By Loss	1,95,000
To Variable Factory Expenses	30,000		
To Variable Selling Expenses	20,000		
To Fixed Expenses	2,00,000		
	3,55,000		3,55,000

Even at such a low output as 10,000 units and even at such a low price as ₹. 16.00 per unit (only fifty paise above the marginal cost of ₹. 15.50 per unit) the loss has been reduced from ₹. 2,00,000 (had there been no output) to ₹. 1,95,000.

(*c*) If 40,000 units are sold at ₹. 15.00 per unit, the position will be as follows:

Trading and Profit and Loss Account

	₹		₹
To Materials (40,000 × ₹. 7)	2,80,000	By Sales (40,000 × ₹. 15)	6,00,000
To Labour	1,40,000	By Loss	2,20,000
To Variable Factory Expenses	1,20,000		
To Variable Selling Expenses	80,000		
To Fixed Expenses	2,00,000		
	8,20,000		8,20,000

At comparatively higher output of 40,000 units, the loss has been increased from ₹. 2,00,000 (at no output level) to ₹. 2,20,000. This is because the price is only ₹. 15.00 and it costs ₹. 15.50 to produce and sell each additional unit. The extra loss of 20,000 is 50 paise per unit on 40,000 units.

The moral of the different situations discussed above is that as long as (but only so long as) price available is higher than the total variable cost, it will do to produce and sell as large a quantity as possible even if the price is below the total cost; it will reduce the loss which will result if there is no output. But if the price is below the marginal cost, any production and sales will increase the loss. During depressions, therefore, price reductions can safely be made as long as the price is sufficient to cover the marginal cost.

Price below the Marginal Cost

In the following circumstances production may be continued even if the price obtainable is below the marginal cost:

(*a*) If the firm has already bought large quantities of raw materials and if the attempt to sell the raw materials will result in heavy loss or if continued storage will result in deterioration in quality, this giving rise to an extraordinary loss, it may be better to turn the raw materials into finished goods and sell these. Total loss may be reduced somewhat; but even if it is not so, there will be the advantages of continuity of business as discussed below.

(*b*) Closure of business temporarily will mean severance of connection with customers (unless large stocks are built up). The connection will be re-established at heavy expenses in advertising and sales promotion and the success is likely to be partial. This will be so because other firms will take advantage of the particular firm's closure and seek the custom of the clients.

(*c*) Closure of business temporarily will also mean discharge of old employees and workers who will be experienced and skilled. Those workers who have worked in the firm for long understand the atmosphere of the firm well. The experience of workers is valuable, especially when a firm tries to cater to the individual taste of the customers. If business is closed and reopened later, the services of these workers may not be available necessitating recruitment of fresh hands and entailing all the expenditure on training, etc.

(*d*) There are certain expenses of closing and reopening. At the time of closing the works machinery has to be dismantled and greased up. At the time of reopening machinery will have to be assembled again and overhauled thoroughly. These expenses can be avoided if production is continued.

Apart from depressions, sometimes prices below cost are charged. This will be the case when in the event of a keen competition, losses may be deliberately incurred to defeat and eliminate competitors. Also when a new line of goods is introduced to the public, losses may be incurred to make the goods popular. In the latter case the hope is that the quantity of sales will go up, thus automatically reducing the cost and bringing it in line with the price.

(*ii*) Sale in a Special Market

When a firm is earning a profit already, it can increase the profit by selling an additional quantity even below the total cost as long as the price available is above the marginal cost. This is because the additional quantity can be produced without increase in fixed expenses and only the variable cost will be incurred. The price available being higher than this, an additional profit will emerge. A firm cannot normally sell additional quantities at concessional prices in its normal markets since it will lead to lowering of prices all round. Therefore, additional sales should be made only in special markets or untapped markets. Also, only if there is idle capacity.

(*iii*) Sale to Special Customers

The argument given above also applies to sale to special customers like the Government who can be offered price concessions without there being a demand for similar concessions from other customers. The concessional price below the total cost, but above the marginal cost, will bring additional profits if additional sales are made. Magazines and journals work on the same principle when they offer specially low subscription rates to new customers (for a limited period generally) or to students. Here also, the condition is that there should be idle capacity to be utilised.

Illustration 34. Indian Plastics produces a bucket which is sold for ₹. 16; the output and sale is 60,000 pieces (60% of the capacity), the profit per bucket is ₹. 1.25. The costs *inter alia*, are per bucket:

	₹.
Materials	5.00
Wages	1.60
Works Overhead	5.00 (50% fixed)
Sales Overhead	2.40 (40% fixed)

During the coming year, it is anticipated that all fixed expenses will increase by 10% whereas per unit costs of materials and wages will increase by 4% and 5% respectively. The number of units to be sold will remain unaffected. However, a public sector unit is interested in buying the buckets—the order is expected to absorb 20% of the capacity.

What should be the minimum price to be quoted for the additional order so as to produce a total profit of ₹. 1,00,000? **[*C.A.*]**

Solution:

Cost Sheet of Indian Plastics for the year ended..................
[Production: 60,000 units (60% of capacity)]

	Per Units ₹.	*Total* ₹.
Materials	5.00	3,00,000
Wages	1.60	96,000
Works Overhead:		
Variable (50%)	2.50	1,50,000
Fixed (50%)	2.50	1,50,000

Works Cost	11.60	6,96,000
Administrative Expenses	0.75*	45,000*
Sales Overhead		
Variable (60%)	1.44	86,400
Fixed (40%)	0.96	57,600
	14.75	8,85,000
Profit	1.25	75,000
Sales	16.00	9,60,000

Variable Cost Per Unit

	Current Year	Next Year	Remarks
	₹.	₹.	
Materials	5.00	5.20	4% increase
Wages	1.60	1.68	5% increase
Variable Works Overhead	2.50	2.50	
Variable Selling Overhead	1.44	1.44	
	10.54	10.82	

*Balancing figure—this item appears to have been omitted from the information given in the question; without this, the profit per unit would not be ₹. 1.25.

Fixed Cost (Total)	₹.	₹.	
Fixed Works Overhead	1,50,000	1,65,000	10% increase
Administrative Expenses	45,000	49,500	"
Fixed Selling Overhead	57,600	63,360	"
	2,52,600	2,77,860	

Total Contribution Required:

Fixed Costs	2,77,860
Profit	1,00,000
	3,77,860

Contribution produced by existing sales:

	₹.
Sales price per unit	16.00
Variable Costs per unit	10.82
Contribution per unit	5.18
Total Contribution on 60,000 units	3,10,800
Balance of Contribution required on additional 20,000 units	67,060
Total Required Contribution (as above)	3,77,860
Contribution required per unit of additional sale	
67,060 ÷ 20,000	3.353

Minimum price to be quoted: for additional sale

Variable Cost per unit	10.82
Contribution required	3.353
Price	14.173

Illustration 35. The following data relate to a manufacturing company.

Plant Capacity: 4,00,000 units per annum. Present utilisation 40%.

Actuals for the year were: Selling price ₹. 50 per unit; Material cost ₹. 20 per unit; Variable manufacturing cost ₹. 15 per unit; Fixed cost ₹. 27,00,000.

In order to improve capacity utilisation the following proposals are considered:

1. Reduce selling price by 10%
2. Spend additionally ₹. 3,00,000 on sales promotion.

How many units should be sold to earn a profit of ₹. 5,00,000 per year. ***[CA–Inter]***

Solution:

Proposale 1: Reduction of selling price by 10%.

	Selling Price (₹. 50 less 10%) per unit		₹. 45
Less	Variable Cost per unit		
	Material	₹. 20	
	Variable Manufacturing Cost	₹. 15	35
	Contribution per unit		10

No. of units to be sold to earn a profit of ₹. 5,00,000

$$= \frac{\text{Fixed Cost} + \text{Desired Profit}}{\text{Contribution per unit}} = \frac{27,00,000 + 5,00,000}{10}$$

$$= \frac{32,00,000}{10} = 3,20,000 \text{ units}$$

Proposal 2: Sales Promotion expenditures ₹. 5,00,000

Selling Price Per unit	₹. 50
Less Variable cost (20 + 15)	35
Contrubution per unit	15

No of units to be sold

$$= \frac{\text{Fixed Cost} + \text{Additional Cost} + \text{Desired Profit}}{\text{Contribution per unit}}$$

$$= \frac{27,00,000 + 3,00,000 + 5,00,000}{15} = \frac{35,00,000}{15} = 2,33,334$$

Illustration 36: A toy manufacturer earns an average net profit of ₹. 3 per piece in a selling price of ₹. 15 by producing and selling 60,000 pieces at 60% of the potential capacity. Composition of his cost of sales is :

Direct Material	₹. 4	Works Overhead	₹. 6 (50% fixed)
Direct Wages	₹. 1	Sales Overhead	₹. 1 (25% variable)

During the current year, he intends to produce the same number but anticipates that

(*a*) his fixeds charges will go up by 10%

(*b*) rates of direct labour will increase by 20%

(*c*) rates of direct material will increase by 5%

(*d*) Selling price cannot be increased.

Under these circumstances, he obtains on order for a further 20% of his capacity. What minimum price will you recommend for accepting the order to ensure the manufacturer an overall profit of ₹. 1,80,500. ***[B Com (H) Delhi]***

Solution:

Statement Showing Marginal Cost for the Current Year

		₹.
Direct Material (₹. 4 + 5%)		4.20
Direct Wages (₹. 1 + 20%)		1.20
Variable Overheads		
Works Overheads		3.00
Sales Overhead		.25
	Total Marginal Cost	8.65
	Contribution per unit	6.35
	Selling Price	15.00

Statement Showing Profit on Sales of 60,000 Units

		₹.
Sale (60,000 × 15)		9,00,000
Less Variable Cost (60,000 × 8.65)		5,19,000
Contribution		3,81,000
Less Fixed Cost –		
Works Overhead (1,80,000 + 18,000)	1,98,000	
Sales Overhead (45,000 + 4,500)	49,500	2,47,500
Profit		1,33,500
Desired Profit	1,80,500	
Less Profit on 60,000 units	1,33,500	
Profit to be earned on 20,000 units	47,000	

Minimum Selling Price per unit of an order of 20,000 units	₹.
Variable Cost (20,000 × 8.65)	1,73,000
Profit to be earned	47,000
	2,20,000

Selling Price Per Unit 2,20,000/20,000 = ₹. 11

2. MAKE OR BUY

It may be necessary to decide whether a part already being made should be bought from outside. This decision can be arrived at only by comparing the price asked by the outside supplier with the marginal cost. Suppose the total cost of making a part comes to ₹. 15 consisting of ₹. 11 variable cost and ₹. 4 fixed expenses. Suppose further an outside firm is willing to supply the same part (equal in all respects) at ₹. 13. The offer should be rejected because the acceptance will mean that the total cost of the bought part will come to ₹. 17, *i.e.* ₹. 13 plus ₹. 4, the fixed expenses (which cannot be saved if the output is given up). The proper figure to compare with the price asked for is the marginal cost–the amount which can be saved if the production of the part in question is stopped. If the supplier offers it at ₹. 10, the offer should be accepted but only if adequate and regular supplies are assured. This argument will not apply if the production facilities released by stoppage of production can be used for other purposes. However, in case the part is being bought at present and the decision to be taken is whether it should be made, the present price being paid should be compared with the total cost of making it–including even such costs as will become fixed later.

It must be remembered that what is to be compared is the present price and the costs to be incurred if purchase from outside is stopped. For instance, if at present 20,000 units are being purchased at ₹. 4 per unit, then, if there is a proposal to make the part in the factory itself, ₹. 80,000 must be compared with the amount to be spent on producing 20,000 units and this amount should include not only the materials and labour required but also the salaries of additional staff, repairs and depreciation of additional machinery and interest on the capital outlay. Salaries of staff and depreciation, etc. will later become fixed (once staff is engaged and machinery installed); but at the moment they are not being incurred and will be incurred only if the production of the part is undertaken. Hence they must be considered.

Illustration 37: Auto Parts Ltd has an annual production of 90,000 units for a motor component. The components' cost structure is as given below:

Materials		₹. 270 per unit
Labour (25% fixed)		180 per unit
Expenses:	Variable	90 per unit
	Fixed	135 per unit
		675 per unit

(*a*) The purchase manager has an offer from a supplier who is willing to supply the component at ₹. 540. Should the component be purchased and production stopped?

(*b*) Assume the resources now used for this components manufacturing are to be used to produce another new product for which the selling price is ₹. 485.

In the latter case material price will be ₹. 200 per unit, 90,000 units of this product can be produced, at the same cost basis as above for labour and expenses. Discuss whether it would be advisable to divert the resources to manufacture that new product, on the footing that the component presently being produced would, instead of being produced, be purchased from the market.

Solution:

(*a*) Statement of Cost

	Per Unit ₹.	For 90,000 Units ₹.
Variable Cost:		
Materials	270	2,43,00,000
Labour	135	1,21,50,000
Expenses	90	81,00,000
	495	4,45,50,000
Cost of purchase from a supplier	540	4,86,00,000
Excess purchase price over variable cost	45	40,50,000

From the above, it is clear that the company will have to pay ₹. 45 per unit more if purchased from the market. The excess amount for 90,000 units will be ₹. 40,50,000. It is, therefore, advisable that the company should not stop its production.

(*b*) Statement of Cost on Production of Another Product

	₹.	Per unit ₹.
Selling price of new product		485
Less Variable Cost:		
Material	200	
Labour (Variable)	135	
Expenses (Variable)	90	425
Contribution per unit		60
Loss per unit cost if present component is purchased from a supplier (as above)		45
New Savings		15

Thus if another product is produced, there will be saving of ₹. 15 per unit. The savings on 90,000 units will be ₹. 13,50,000. It is advisable that the company should manufacture new product and the old product may be purchased from the market.

3. FIXING PRIORITY AMONG PRODUCTS

Sometimes due to limited capacity, the production of one of the articles may have to be curtailed. The decision regarding the choice of the article whose production is to be increased, reduced or given up will be made on the basis of the contribution to the overheads and profits. The article which makes the least contribution should have the lowest priority. (It should be noted that contribution means the difference between the selling price and the marginal cost). Choice merely on the basis of the price obtained or "net profit" will be wrong. Consider the following figures:

	Article A ₹.	*Article B* ₹.
Direct Materials	5.00	8.50
Direct Labour	4.00	3.00
Variable Expenses	3.00	4.00
Fixed Expenses	3.50	2.00
Total Cost	15.50	17.50
Profit	1.50	2.00
Price	17.00	19.50

Even though Article B sells for more amount and even shows higher profit than Article *A*, its contribution is ₹. 4 whereas the contribution in case of Article A is ₹. 5 Article A should be encouraged against Article B. (The student can verify this himself by assuming that the units sold are 10,000 in number for each article.)

The important point, however, is to work out the contribution per unit of "scarce" (key or limiting) factor of production. Suppose the contribution in case of article X is ₹. 10 and in case of article Y it is ₹. 12, the same imported material being used for the production of both. Two units of raw materials are required for producing X and three for Y. In that case the contribution per unit of raw materials is ₹. 5 in case of X and ₹. 4 in case of Y. If supplies of the material are limited, the available quantity should first be used for producing X (up to the limit of demand for it) and then only for Y; profits will be maximised in this fashion.

Illustration 38. A farmer owns an orchard having an area of 300 acres on which he wants to grow apples, apricots, cherries and plums. 200 acres are unsuitable for apples or plums; on the remaining 100 acres any of the four fruits can be grown. Marketing considerations require that all fruits must be grown so as to produce at least 6,000 boxes in a season per fruit.

The following details are available:

	Apples ₹.	*Apricots* ₹.	*Cherries* ₹.	*Plums* ₹.
Selling price per box	10	10	20	30
Seasonal yield (boxes per acre)	500	150	100	200
Weight per box (kgs.)	30	30	40	20
Cost	₹.	₹.	₹.	₹.
Materials per acre	180	70	60	100
Labour	200	150	100	130
Harvesting & Packing per box	1	1	2	3
Transport per box	2	2	1	3

Fixed Overheads per season	₹.
Cultivation and tending trees	1,28,000
Harvesting	21,000
Transport	5,000
Administration	42,000
Land Revenue	9,000

Advise the farmer as to how much area he should allot to each fruit. Work to the nearest acre and show the estimated profit.

Solution:

Statement Showing Contribution per Acre

	Apples	*Apricots*	*Cherries*	*Plums*
Output per acre (boxes)	500	150	100	200
	₹.	₹.	₹.	₹.
Sales Revenue (*i*)	5,000	1,500	2,000	6,000
Variable Cost: Materials	180	70	60	100
Labour	200	150	100	130
Harvesting and Packing	500	150	200	600
Transport	1000	300	100	600
Total Variable Cost (*ii*)	1,880	670	460	1,430
Contribution per acre [(*i*) – (*ii*)]	3,120	830	1,540	4,570

Ranking: (on the basis of contribution per acre)

First	Plums
Second	Apples
Third	Cherries
Fourth	Apricots

Minimum area to be allotted to produce 6,000 boxes.

Plums	6,000 ÷ 200	30 acres
Apples	6,000 ÷ 500	12 acres
Cherries	6,000 ÷ 100	60 acres
Apricots	6,000 ÷ 150	40 acres

Since 200 acres are suitable only for cherries and apricots, the allotment should be as follows:

Cherries, Minimum 60 plus 100 surplus out of 200 acres	160 acres
Apricots (Minimum required)	40 "
Apples (Minimum required)	12 "
Plums (Balance)	88 "
Total	300 "

Estimated profit :

Contribution from :			₹.
Cherries	:	160 acres @ ₹. 1,540 per acre	2,46,400
Apricots	:	40 acres @ ₹. 830 per acre	33,200
Apples	:	12 acres @ ₹. 3,120 per acre	37,440
Plums	:	88 acres @ ₹. 4,570 per acre	402,160
Total contribution			7,19,200

	₹.	
Less: Fixed Costs:		
Cultivation and tending trees	1,28,000	
Harvesting	21,000	
Transport	5,000	
Administration	42,000	
Land Revenue	9,000	2,05,000
Net Profit		5,14,200

4. Optimising Product Mix

The contribution per unit of each product should be considered to identify optimum product mix. The product yielding highest contribution should be given highest priority and the least priority should be given to the product whose contribution is the least. If any product gives negative contribution it should be discontinued.

Illustration 39: Given following information you are required to (*a*). Calculate and present the marginal product cost and contribution per unit, (*b*) State which of the alternative sales mix you would recommend to the management, and why

	Per unit
Selling price	X ₹. 25; Y ₹. 20
Direct Materials	X ₹. 8; Y ₹. 6
Direct Wages	X 24 hrs at ₹ 0.25 per hour Y 16 hurs at ₹ 0.25 per hour
Fixed Overhead	₹. 750
Variable Overhead	150% of direct wages

Alternative Sales mix

(*i*) 250 units of X and 250 unit of Y

(*ii*) Nil unit of X and 400 units of Y

(*iii*) 400 units of X and 100 units of Y

Solution:

Statement Showing Contribution

	Product X ₹.	*Product Y* ₹.
Sales	25	20
Variable Cost :		
Direct Material	8	6
Direct Wages	6	4
Variable Overhead	9	6
	23	16
Contribution (S – VC)	2	4
P/V Ratio (C × 100/S)	8%	20%

Comparison of Alternatives

	Alternative I	*Alternative II*	*Alternative III*
Total Contribution	(250 × 2) + (250 × 4) = 1,500	(400 × 4) = 1,600	(400 × 2) + (100 × 4) = 1,200
Less Fixed Overhead	750	750	750
Profit	750	850	450

Thus, alternative II is more profitable because it gives highest contribution and profit.

5. DISCONTINUANCE OF A PRODUCT LINE

Unprofitable or less profitable product line should be discontinued. To identify such product line, the contribution of different products should be calculated. Fixed cost should be apportioned over different products on some logical basis. Thus we can identify less profitable product. Moreover capacity utilisation by the firm should also be seen. If there is idle capacity, the production of a product showing better contribution may be increased so that it may recover fixed cost. Other factors which may simultaneously be considered are availability of product to replace the discontinued product, the long term prospects of the product in the market and effect on total sale of products.

Illustration 40: The Novelties Ltd is not keen on making special efforts to push the sales of product B, one of three main products it deals in, since product B is not considered to be as profitable as the other two. The selling prices and cost of the three products are :

Product	*Selling Price*	*Direct Material*	*Direct Labour*		
			Dept X	*Dept Y*	*Dept. Z*
	₹	₹	₹	₹	₹
A	340	50	40	10	10
B	290	30	10	40	10
C	320	40	10	10	40

Overhead rates for each department per rupee of direct labour are as follows:

	Dept X	*Dept Y*	*Dept Z*
	₹.	₹.	₹.
Variable Overhead	1.20	0.40	1.00
Fixed Overhead	1.20	2.00	1.40
	2.40	2.40	2.40

What will be your advice about the profitability of Product B? Give reasons.

Solution:

Statement of Cost

	Product A	*Product B*	*Product C*
	₹	₹	₹
Direct Material	50	30	40
Direct Labour	60	60	60
Variable Overhead (As calculated below)	62	38	56
	172	128	156
Selling Price	340	290	320
Contribution	168	162	164
Less Fixed Overheads (As calculated below)	82	106	88
Profit	86	56	76
P/V Ratio	49.4%	55.9%	51.3%

From the above statement it is clear that contribution per unit of B is not very less. It is slightly less to that of C. Moreover P/V ratio of B is the highest. The per unit profit of B may be less due to unequitable apportionment of fixed overhead. As long as B gives good contribution its production should be encouraged.

Calculation of Variable and Fixed Overheads

		Dept X. ₹	Dept Y ₹	Dept Z ₹	Total ₹
Variable Overhead:					
Product	A	40 × 1.20	10 × 0.40	10 × 1.00	62.00
	B	10 × 1.20	40 × 0.40	10 × 1.00	38.00
	C	10 × 1.20	10 × 0.40	40 × 1.00	56.00
Fixed Overheads:					
Product	A	40 × 1.20	10 × 2.00	10 × 1.40	82.00
	B	10 × 1.20	40 × 2.00	10 × 1.40	106.00
	C	10 × 1.20	10 × 2.00	40 × 1.40	88.00

TYPICAL ILLUSTRATIONS

Absorption Costing and Marginal Costing

Illustration 41. The data below relates to a company which makes and sells computers.

	March Units	*April Units*
Sales	5,000	10,000
Production	10,000	5,000
	₹.	₹.
Selling price/unit	100	100
Variable Production Cost/unit.	50	50
Fixed Production Overhead Incurred	1,00,000	1,00,000
Fixed Production Overhead Cost, per unit, being the predetermined overhead absorption rate	10	10
Selling distribution and administration cost (all fixed)	50,000	50,000

You are required to present comparative profit statements for each month using. (*i*) Absorption costing; (*ii*) Marginal costing.

Solution:

(*i*) Absorption Costing

	March ₹.		*April* ₹.
Opening Stock	Nil	Opening Stock	3,00,000
Production Cost:		Production Cost:	
Variable (10,000 × 50)	5,00,000	Variable (5,000 × 50)	2,50,000
Fixed (10,000 × 10)	1,00,000	Fixed (5,000 × 10)	50,000
	6,00,000		6,00,000
Less: Closing stock		*Less:* Closing Stock	Nill
$6,00,000 \times \frac{5,000}{10,000} =$	3,00,000		6,00,000
	3,00,000		
Add: Under-absorption of Overhead	—	*Add:* Under-absorption of Overhead (1,00,000 – 50,000)	50,000
Production Cost	3,00,000	Production Cost	6,50,000
Sales (5,000 × 100)	5,00,000	Sales (10,000 × 100)	10,00,000
Gross Profit	2,00,000	Gross Profit	3,50,000
Less: Selling and Distribution and Admn. Cost (all fixed)	50,000	*Less:* Selling and Distribution and Admn.Cost (all fixed)	50,000
Net Profit	1,50,000	Net Profit	3,000.00

Working Notes:

	March (Units)	April (Units)
Opening Stock	Nil	5,000
Production	10,000	5,000
	10,000	10,000
Sales	5,000	10,000
Closing Stock	5,000	Nil

(ii) Marginal Costing

	March ₹.		April ₹.
Opening Stock	Nil	Opening Stock	2,50,000
Variable Production Cost (10,000 × 50)	5,00,000	Variable Production Cost (5,000 × 50)	2,50,000
Closing Stock (5,000 × 50)	(–)2,50,000	Closing stock	Nil
Cost of Sales	2,50,000	Cost of Sales	5,00,000
Fixed Production Overhead	1,00,000	Fixed Production overhead	1,00,000
	3,50,000		6,00,000
Sales	5,00,000	Sales	10,00,000
Gross Profit	1,50,000	Gross Profit	4,00,000
Selling and Distribution and Admn. Cost (all fixed)	50,000	Selling and Distribution and Admn. Cost (all fixed)	50,000
Net Profit	1,00,000	Net Profit	3,50,000

Cost, Profit, Volume Analysis (BEP, P/V Ratio And M.S. Etc)

Illustration 42. The Asian Industries specialise in the manufacture of small capacity motors . The cost structure of a motor is as under :

Material	₹. 50
Labour	₹. 80
Variable Overheads	75% of labour cost.

Fixed overheads of the Company amount to ₹. 2.40 lakhs per annum. Sale price of the motor is ₹. 230 each.

(*a*) Determine the number of motors that have to be manufactured and sold in a year in order to break-even.

(*b*) How many motors have to be made and sold to make a profit of ₹. 1 lakh per year?

(*c*) If the sale price is reduced by ₹. 15 each, how many motors have to be sold to break-even?

Solution:

Calculation of Contribution

Sale Price per motor		₹. 230
Less: Marginal Cost per motor:		
Material	₹. 50	
Labour	₹. 80	
Variable Overheads (75% of ₹. 80)	₹. 60	190
Contribution per unit		₹. 40

Fixed Overheads per year = ₹. 2,40,000

$$\text{B.E.P. (Units)} = \frac{\text{Fixed Cost}}{\text{Contribution Per Unit}}$$

$$= \frac{2,40,000}{40} = 6,000 \text{ Motors}$$

(*b*) $\text{Sales (Units)} = \frac{\text{Fixed cost + Profit}}{\text{Contribution Per Unit}} = 8,500 \text{ Motors.}$

(*c*) Revised Selling Price = (230 – 15)	215
Marginal Cost	190
Revised Contribution per motor	25

$$\text{BEP (Units)} = \frac{2,40,000}{25} = 9,600 \text{ Motors}$$

Illustration 43. **The following figures are extracted from the books of a manufacturing concern for the year 1990–91.**

	₹.
Direct Materials	2,05,000
Direct Labour	75,000
Fixed Overheads	60,000
Variable Overheads	1,00,000
Sales	5,00,000

Calculate the break-even point (B.E.P.). What will be the effect on B.E.P. of an increase of 10% in: (*i*) Fixed Expenses; and (*ii*) Variable Expenses?

Solution:

Calculation of P/V Ratio	₹.
Direct Materials	2,05,000
Direct Labour	75,000
Variable Overheads	1,00,000
Variable Expenses or Cost	3,80,000
Sales	5,00,000
Contribution	1,20,000

$$\text{P/V Ratio} = \frac{\text{Contribution} \times 100}{\text{Sales}} = \frac{1,20,000}{5,00,000} \times 100 = 24\%$$

$$\text{BEP (Value)} = \frac{\text{Fixed Cost}}{\text{P/V Ratio}} = \frac{64,000}{24\%} = ₹.\ 2,50,000$$

Effect on BEP:

(*i*) If fixed expenses increase by 10% *i.e.* 60,000 + 10% = ₹. 66,000

$$\text{BEP} = \frac{66,000}{24\%} = ₹.\ 2,75,000.$$

(*ii*) If variable expenses increase by 10% *i.e.*

3,800,000 + 10%	=	4,18,000
Sales		5,00,000
Contribution ₹.	=	82,000

$$\text{Revised P/V Ratio} = \frac{82,000}{5,00,000} \times 100 = 16.4\%$$

$$\text{BEP} = \frac{60,000}{16.4\%} = ₹.\ 3,65,854$$

Illustration 44. Find the profit from the following data:

	₹.
Sales	80,000
Marginal Cost	60,000
Break-even point	60,000 (sales)

Solution.

$$\text{P/V Ratio} = \frac{\text{Sales} - \text{Variable Cost}}{\text{Sales}} \times 100 = \frac{80,000 - 60,000}{80,000} \times 100 = 25\%$$

$$\text{B.E.P.} = \frac{\text{Fixed Cost}}{\text{P/V Ratio}}$$

$$60,000 = \frac{\text{Fixed Cost}}{25\%}$$

$$\text{Fixed Cost} = 60,000 \times 25\% = ₹.\ 15,000$$

$$\text{Profit} = (\text{Sales} \times \text{P/V Ratio}) - \text{Fixed Cost}$$

$$= (80,000 \times 25\%) - 15,000 = 20,000 - 15,000 = ₹.\ 5,000$$

Illustration 45: **A company earned a profit of ₹. 30,000 during the year. If the marginal cost and selling price of a product are ₹. 8 and ₹. 10 per unit respectively, find out the amount of 'Margin of Safety'.**

Solution:

$$\text{Contribution per unit} = \text{Selling Price} - \text{Marginal Cost}$$

$$= 10 - 8 = 2$$

$$\text{P/V Ratio} = \frac{\text{Contribution}}{\text{Sales}} \times 100 = \frac{2}{10} \times 100 = 20\%$$

$$\text{Margin of Safety} = \frac{\text{Profit}}{\text{P/V Ratio}} = \frac{₹.30,000}{20\%} = ₹.\ 1,50,000$$

It may be noted that :

$$\text{M/S} = \text{Sales} - \text{BEP}$$

$$\text{Sales} = \text{BEP} + \text{M/S}$$

$$\frac{F + P}{P/V} = \frac{F}{P/V} + \frac{P}{P/V}$$

Illustration 46. Discuss the Influence of Fixed Cost, Variable Cost and Selling Price on P/V Ratio, BEP and Profit.

Solution: The influence of fixed cost, variable cost and selling price on P/V Ratio, BEP and Profit may be given as below:

	Effect on		
Change	*P/V Ratio*	*BEP*	*Profit*
1. Increase in Fixed Cost	No effect	Higher	Lower
2. Decrease in Fixed Cost	No effect	Lower	Higher
3. Increase in Variable Cost	Decrease	Higher	Lower
4. Decrease in Variable Cost	Improve	Lower	Higher
5. Increase in Selling Price	Improve	Lower	Higher
6. Decrease in Selling Price	Decrease	Higher	Lower
7. Increase in Sales Volume	No effect	No effect	Higher
8. Decrease in Sales Volume	No effect	No effect	Lower

Illustration 47: By noting P/V will increase or P/V will decrease or P/V will not change, as the case may be, state how the following independent situations will affect the P/V Ratio:

(*i*) An increase in the physical sales volume;
(*ii*) An increase in the fixed cost;
(*iii*) A decrease in the variable cost per unit;
(*iv*) A decrease in the contribution margin;
(*v*) An increase in the selling price per unit;
(*vi*) A decrease in the fixed cost;
(*vii*) A 10% increase in both selling price and variable cost per unit;
(*viii*) A 10% increase in the selling price per unit and 10% decrease in the physical sales volume:
(*ix*) A 50% increase in the variable cost per unit and 50% decrease in the fixed cost.
(*x*) An increase in the angle of incidence.

Solution: P/V Ratio is relationship between contribution and sales. P/V ratio will change only when there is change in contribution and sales. In the following table various items of the question are explained.

Item No.	*P/V Ratio*	*Reason*
(*i*)	Will not change	No change in contribution and sales per unit
(*ii*)	Will not change	No change in contribution and sales per unit
(*iii*)	Will increase	Contribution per unit will increase
(*iv*)	Will decrease	Contribution will decrease
(*v*)	Will increase	Contribution per unit will increase
(*vi*)	Will not change	Contribution per unit and sales per unit will not change
(*vii*)	Will not change	Contribution and selling price per unit both will change proportionately.
(*viii*)	Will increase	Contribution per unit will increase
(*ix*)	Will decrease	Contribution per unit will decrease
(*x*)	Will increase	When the angle increases, profit will be at higher rate

Items no VII, VIII, IX and X are further explained as below:

(*vii*) A 10% increase in both selling price and variable cost per unit.

Assumptions: (*a*) Variable cost is less than selling price.

(*b*) Selling price ₹. 100 variable cost ₹. 90 per unit

(*c*) P/V Ratio – $\frac{100-90}{100}$ = 10%

10% increase in S.P. = ₹. 110

10% increase in variable cost = ₹. 99

$$\text{P/V Ratio} = \frac{110-99}{100} = 10\%$$ *i.e.* P/V Ratio will not change

(*viii*) Increase or decrease in physical sales **volume** will not change P/V ratio. But 10% increase in selling price per unit will increase contribution per unit and therefore P/V ratio will increase.

(*ix*) Increase or decrease in fixed cost does not change P/V ratio because contribution and sales per unit will not change. But 50% increase in the variable cost per unit will decrease P/V ratio because contribution per unit will increase.

(*x*) Angle of incidence is the angle at which sales line intersects the total cost line. If this angle is large, it indicates that the profits are being earned at higher rate. Hence increase in the angle of incidence will increase the P/V ratio.

Illustration 48. (*a*) From the following data, find out (*i*) sales; and (*ii*) new break-even sales, if selling price is reduced by 10%:

Fixed Cost	₹. 4,000
Break-even sales	₹. 20,000
Profit	₹. 1,000
Selling price per unit	₹. 20

(*b*) From the following data, compute break-even sales and margin of safety:

Sales	₹. 10,00,000
Fixed Cost	₹. 3,00,000
Profit	₹. 2,00,000

(*c*) From the following data, calculate break-even point (BEP) :

Selling Price per unit	₹. 20
Variable Cost per unti	₹. 15
Fixed Overheads	₹. 20,000

If sales are 20% above BEP, determine the net profit.

Solution:

(*a*) Contribution at BEP = Fixed Cost = ₹. 4,000

$$\text{P/V Ratio} = \frac{\text{Contribution}}{\text{Sales}} \times 100 = \frac{4{,}000}{20{,}000} \times 100 = 20\%$$

Percentage of Variable Cost = (100% – P/V Ratio) of Sales
= 100% – 20% = 80% of sales

i.e. 80% of 20 = ₹. 16 per unit

(*i*) Sales required to earn a profit of ₹. 1,000

$$= \frac{\text{Fixed Cost + Profit}}{\text{P/V Ratio}} = \frac{4{,}000 + 1{,}000}{20\%} = ₹.\ 25{,}000$$

(*ii*) New BEP, if selling price is reduced by 10%

New selling price = 20 – 10% of 20 = 20 – 2 = ₹. 18 per unit
Variable cost = ₹ 16 per unit
New contribution ₹. 2 per unit

$$\text{New P/V Ratio} = \frac{2}{18} \times 100 = 11\frac{1}{9}\%$$

$$\text{New BEP (Units)} = \frac{\text{Fixed Cost}}{\text{Contribution per unit}} = \frac{4{,}000}{2} = 2{,}000 \text{ units}$$

$$\text{New BEP (Value)} = \frac{\text{Fixed Cost}}{\text{P/V Ratio}} = \frac{4{,}000}{11\frac{1}{9}\%} = ₹.\ 36{,}000$$

(*b*) Variable Cost will be calculated as below:

Sales – Variable Cost = Fixed Cost + Profit

10,00,000 – V = 3,00,000 + 2,00,000

V = 10,00,000 – 3,00,000 – 2,00,000 = 5,00,000

$$\text{P/V Ratio} = \frac{\text{Sales – Variable Cost}}{\text{Sales}} \times 100 = \frac{(10{,}00{,}000 - 5{,}00{,}000)}{10{,}00{,}000} \times 100 = 50\%$$

$$\text{BEP} = \frac{\text{Fixed Cost}}{\text{P/V Ratio}} = \frac{3{,}00{,}000}{50\%} = ₹.\ 6{,}00{,}000$$

Margin of Safety = Sales – BEP = 10,00,000 – 6,00,000 = ₹. 4,00,000.

(*c*) (*i*) Selling Price 20

Variable Cost 15

Contribution per unit ₹. 5

$$\text{BEP (Units)} = \frac{\text{Fixed Cost}}{\text{Contribution per unit}} = \frac{20,000}{5} = 4,000 \text{ units}$$

(*ii*) When sales are 20% above BEP:

Sales 4,000 + 20% = 4,800 units @ ₹. 20 = ₹. 96,000

$$\text{P/V Ratio} = \frac{\text{Contribution}}{\text{Sales}} \times 100 = \frac{5}{20} \times 100 = ₹.25\%$$

Profit = (Sales × P/V Ratio) – Fixed Cost

= (96,000 × 25%) – 20,000

= 24,000 – 20,000 = ₹. 4,000.

Illustration 49. A company producing a single product sells it at ₹. 50 per unit. Unit variable cost is ₹. 35 and fixed cost amounts to ₹. 12 lakhs per annum. With this data you are required to calculate the following, treating each independent of the other:

(*a*) P/V ratio and Break-even sales.

(*b*) New Break-even sales if variables cost increases by ₹. 3 per unit, without increase in selling price.

(*c*) Increase in sales required if profits are to be increased by ₹. 2.4 lakhs.

(*d*) Percentage increase/decrease in sales volume units to off-set.

(*i*) an increase of ₹. 3 in the variable cost per unit.

(*ii*) a 10 per cent increase in selling price without affecting existing profits quantum.

(*e*) Quantum of advertisement expenditure permissible to increase sales by ₹. 1.2 lakhs, without affecting existing profits quantum.

Solution:

(*a*) Contribution = Selling Price – Variable Cost

= 50 – 35 = ₹. 15 per unit

$$\text{P/V Ratio} = \frac{\text{Contribution}}{\text{Sales}} \times 100$$

$$= \frac{15}{50} \times 100 = 30\%$$

$$\text{Break-even sales} = \frac{\text{Fixed Cost}}{\text{P/V Ratio}}$$

$$= \frac{₹.\ 12 \text{ lakhs}}{30\%} = ₹.\ 40 \text{ lakhs}$$

or ₹. 40 lakhs/₹. 50 = 80,000 units.

(*b*) Revised contribution = Selling Price – Revised Variable Cost

= 50 – 38 = 12 per unit

$$\text{P/V Ratio} = \frac{\text{Contribution}}{\text{Sales}} \times 100 = \frac{12}{50} \times 100 = 24\%$$

$$\text{New Break-even sales} = \frac{\text{Fixed Cost}}{\text{P/V Ratio}} = \frac{₹.12,00,000}{24\%} = ₹.\ 50 \text{ lakhs}$$

or ₹. 50 lakhs/₹. 50 = 1,00,000 units.

(*c*) Increase in sales = $\frac{\text{Profit}}{\text{P/V Ratio}} = \frac{₹.\ 2.4 \text{ lakh}}{30\%}$ = ₹. 8 lakhs

Thus increase in sales amounting to ₹. 8 lakhs will be required to increase the profits by ₹. 2.4 lakhs.

(*d*) (*i*) At variable cost of ₹. 35 per unit, BEP sales ₹. 40 lakhs.

At variable cost of ₹. 38 per unit, BEP sales ₹. 50 lakhs.

Thus, for an increase of ₹. 3 in the variable cost per unit, increase of sales by ₹. 10 lakhs is required. The percentage increase will be

$$\frac{10}{40} \times 100 = 25\%$$

Thus 25 per cent increase in sales volume is required to off set an increase of ₹. 3 in the variable cost per unit.

(*ii*) Revised contribution = Revised Selling Price – Variable Cost

= 55 – 35 = ₹. 20 per unit

$$\text{BEP (Units)} = \frac{\text{Fixed Cost}}{\text{Contribution per unit}} = \frac{₹.\ 12 \text{ lakhs}}{₹.\ 20} = 60{,}000 \text{ units}$$

Thus units will be decreased by 20,000. The percentage decrease will be:

$$\frac{20{,}000 \times 100}{80{,}000} = 25\%$$

(*e*) When sales is increased by ₹. 1,20 lakhs then Sales × P/V ratio will be Contribution. Thus 30 per cent of ₹. 1.20 lakhs = ₹. 36,000 will be additional contribution. Hence, ₹. 36,000 can be spent on advertisement without affecting existing amount of profit.

Illustation 50.

	Sales ₹.	Profit ₹.
Period 1	10,000	2,000
Period 2	15,000	4,000

You are required to calculate:

(*i*) P/V Ratio; (*ii*) Fixed Cost; (*iii*) Break-even sales volume; (*iv*) Sales to earn a profit of ₹. 3,000: and (*v*) Profit when sales are ₹. 8,000.

Solution: (*i*)

Period	Sales	Profit
2	15,000	4,000
1	10,000	2,000
Difference	5,000	2,000

$$\text{P/V Ratio} = \frac{\text{Change in Profit}}{\text{Change in Sales}} \times 100$$

$$= \frac{2{,}000}{5{,}000} \times 100 = 40\%$$

Variable Cost = 100 – 40 *i.e.* 60% of Sales

(*ii*) Sales – Variable Cost = Fixed Cost + Profit

100,000 – (60% of 10,000) = Fixed Cost + 2,000

4,000 = Fixed Cost + 2,000

Fixed Cost = ₹. 2,000

Or

$$15{,}000 - (60\% \text{ of } 15{,}000) = \text{Fixed Cost} + 4{,}000$$
$$6{,}000 = \text{Fixed Cost} + 4{,}000$$
$$\text{Fixed Cost} = 2000$$

(*iii*) Break-even sales $= \dfrac{\text{Fixed Cost}}{\text{P/V Ratio}} = \dfrac{2{,}000}{40\%} =$ ₹. 5,000

(*iv*) Sales to earn a profit of ₹. 3,000:

Sales $= \dfrac{\text{Fixed Cost} + \text{Profit}}{\text{P/V Ratio}} = \dfrac{2{,}000 + 3{,}000}{40\%} =$ ₹. 12,500 sales

(*v*) Profit when sales are ₹. 8,000 :

Profit = (Sales × P/V Ratio) – Fixed Cost
= (8,000 × 40%) – 2,000
= 3,200 – 2,000
= ₹. 1,200 Profit.

Illustration 51: Following is the data taken from the records of a concern manufacturing a special part ZED.

	₹.
Selling price per unit	20
Direct material cost per unit	5
Direct labour cost per unit	3
Variable overhead cost per unit	2
Budgeted level of output and sales	80,000 units
Budgeted recovery rate of fixed overheads cost per unit	₹. 5

You are required to :

(*a*) Draw a break-even chart showing the break even point.

(*b*) In the same chart show the impact of break even point:

1. If selling price per unit is increased by 30% and
2. If selling price per unit is decreased by 10%.

Solution:

Rupees in lakhs

Units	20,000	40,000	60,000	80,000
Fixed Cost (80,000 × 5)	₹. 4.00	₹. 4.00	₹. 4.00	₹. 4.00
Variable Cost at ₹. 10 per unit	2.00	4.00	6.00	8.00
Total Cost	6.00	8.00	10.00	12.00
Sales Revenue at ₹. 20 per unit	4.00	8.00	12.00	16.00
Sales Revenue at ₹. 26 per unit (₹. 20 + 30%)	5.20	10.40	15.60	20.80
Sales Revenue at ₹. 18 per unit (₹. 20 less 10%)	3.60	7.20	10.80	14.40

(*a*) BEP when selling price at ₹. 20 per unit = 40,000 units

(*b*) (*i*) BEP when selling price at ₹. 26 per unit = 25,000 units

(*ii*) BEP when selling price at ₹. 18 per unit = 50,000 units

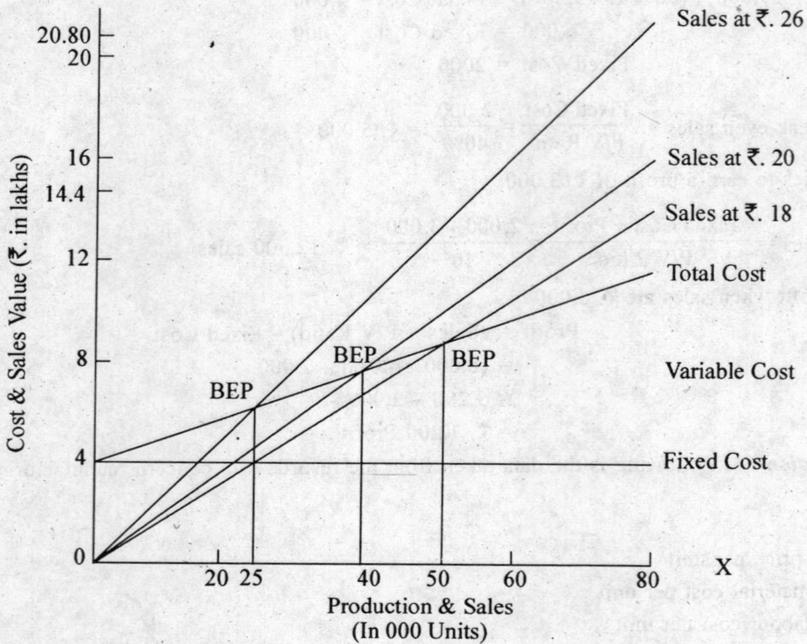

Key Factor

Illustration 52. The following particulars are extracted from the records of a Company.

	Product A Per Units	*Product B* Per Unit
Sales	₹. 100	₹. 120
Consumption of Material	2 Kg.	3 Kg.
Material Cost	₹. 10	₹. 15
Direct Wages Cost	₹. 15	₹. 10
Direct Expenses	₹. 5	₹. 6
Machine hours used	3	2
Overhead Expenses:		
Fixed	₹. 5	₹. 10
Variable	₹. 15	₹. 20

Direct wages per hour is ₹. 5. Comment on profitability of each product (both use the same raw material) when

(*i*) Total sales potential is limited:

(*ii*) Raw Material is in short supply;

(*iii*) Production capacity (in terms of machine hours) is the limiting factor.

(b) Assuming raw material as the key factor, availability of which is 10,000 Kg. and maximum sales potential of each product being 3,500 units, find out the product mix which will yield the maximum profits.

Solution:

Statement Showing Contribution

	Product A ₹	*Product B* ₹
Materials Cost	10	15
Direct Wages	15	10
Direct Exp.	5	6
Variable Overhead	15	20
Marginal Cost	45	51
Sales	100	120
Contribution per Unit	55	69
Contribution per kg. of Material	$\frac{55}{2} = 27.50$	$\frac{69}{3} = 23.00$
Contribution per machine hour	$\frac{55}{3} = 18.33$	$\frac{69}{2} = 34.50$
P/V Ratio = $\frac{\text{Contribution}}{\text{Sales}} \times 100$	55%	57.5%

(*i*) When total sales potentiality is limited, Product *B* should be given preference because its contribution per unit and P/V ratio are higher.

(*ii*) When raw material is key factor *i.e.* in short supply, Product A should be given preference, as its Contribution per kg of material is higher.

(*iii*) When Production Capacity is the limiting factor or key factor, Product B is to be given preference, as its contribution per machine hour is higher.

(*b*) There are two Key factors or limiting factor in this case.

Raw Material is available 10,000 kg.

Maximum Sales potential of each Product = 3,500 Units.

When raw material is in short supply, Product A is to be given preference *i.e.*, Product A should be produced and sold to the maximum extent *i.e.* 3,500 Units. Balance of raw material should be used for Product of B, then the profit will be maximum.

Thus Product A would consume 7,000 kg of raw material. Remaining 3,000 kg of raw material will be used in Product B (which will produce 1,000 units)

Product	*No. of Units*	*Material (Kg)*	*Contribution per Unit (₹)*	*Total Contribution (₹)*
A	3,500	3,500 × 2 = 7,000	55	3,500 × 55 = 1,92,500
B	$\frac{3,000}{2} = 1,000$	3,000	69	1000 × 69 = 69,000
Total		10,000		2,61,500
Less: Fixed Overheads A 3,500 × 5 = 17,500 B 1,000 × 10 = 10,000				27,500
Profit (Maximum)				2,34,000

Thus product Mix A 3,500 units and B 1,000 units will yield maximum profit.

Illustration 53. A company manufactures and markets three products X, Y and Z. All the three products are made from the same set of machines. Production is limited by machine capacity. From the data given below, indicate priorities for products X, Y and Z with a view to maximising profits:

	Products		
	X	*Y*	*Z*
Raw material cost per unit (₹.)	11.25	16.25	21.25
Direct labour cost per unit (₹.)	2.50	2.50	2.50
Other variable cost per unit (₹.)	1.50	2.25	3.55
Selling price per unit (₹.)	25.00	30.00	35.00
Standard Machine time required per unit in minutes	39	20	28

Solution:

Statement Showing Contribution & Priority

Product	*X (₹.)*	*Y (₹.)*	*Z (₹.)*
Raw material cost per unit	11.25	16.25	21.25
Direct labour cost per unit	2.50	2.50	2.50
Other variable cost per unit	1.50	2.25	3.55
Total variable cost per unit	15.25	21.00	27.30
Selling price per unit	25.00	30.00	35.00
Contribution per unit	9.75	9.00	7.70
Standard machine time required per unit in minutes	39	20	28
Contribution per Machine Hour $= \frac{\text{Contribution per unit}}{\text{Machine Hour}}$	$\frac{9.75}{39} \times 60$ = ₹. 15.00	$\frac{9}{20} \times 60$ = ₹. 27.00	$\frac{7.70}{28} \times 60$ = ₹. 16.50
Priority	III	I	II

Production is limited by machine capacity and therefore, machine hour is the limiting factor or key factor. On the basis of contribution per machine hour, the priority for product will be : Product Y Ist priority; Product Z 2nd priority, Product X 3rd priority. This, will maximise the profits.

Decision Making by Marginal Costing

Illustration 54: Two firms A & Co. and B & Co sell the same type of product in the same market. Their budgeted Profit & Loss Account for the year ending 31st March, ... are as follows:

	₹.	*A & Co.* ₹.	₹.	*B & Co.* ₹.
Sales		5,00,000		6,00,000
Variables Costs	4,00,000		4,00,000	
Fixed Costs	30,000	4,30,000	70,000	4,70,000
Net Profit		70,000		1,30,000

Required: 1. Calculate at which sales volume both the firms will earn equal profit. 2. State which firm is likely to earn greater profits in condition of (*i*) heavy demand for the product. (*ii*) low demand for the product. Give reasons:

[*CS Inter Dec.*]

Solution.

Calculation P/V Ratios

	A & Co.	*B & Co.*
Sales	5,00,000	6,00,000
Variable Cost	4,00,000	4,00,000
Contribution	1,00,000	2,00,000
P/V Ratio = $\frac{\text{Contribution}}{\text{Sales}} \times 100$	$\frac{1,00,000}{5,00,000} \times 100$ = 20%	$\frac{2,00,000}{6,00,000} \times 100$ $33\frac{1}{3}\%$

Profit = (Sales × P/V Ratio) – Fixed Cost

A & Co. Profit = (Sales × 1/5) – 30,000 ... (1)

B & Co Profit = (Sales × 1/3) – 70,000 ... (2)

By equating equations 1 & 2, we get

1/5 S – 30,000 = 1/3 S – 70,000

1/3 S – 1/5 S = 70,000 – 30,000

2/15 S = 40,000

$S = 40,000 \times \frac{15}{2}$ = ₹. 3,00,000

At the sale values of ₹. 3,00,000, both the firms will be earning equal profit. It can be proved as below

A & Co. : P = (3,00,000 × 20%) – 30,000 = ₹. 30,000

B & Co. : P = $(3,00,000 \times 33\frac{1}{3}\%)$ – 70,000 = ₹. 30,000

Calculation of BEP

	A & Co.	*B & Co.*
BEP = $\frac{\text{Fixed Cost}}{\text{P/V Ratio}}$	$\frac{30,000}{20\%}$ = 1,50,000	$\frac{70,000}{33\frac{1}{3}\%}$ = 2,10,000

2 (*i*) In the condition of heavy demand for the product, B & Co. will be more profitable because its P/V ratio is higher. After meeting its fixed cost of ₹. 70,000, the profit in B & Co. will be $33\frac{1}{3}\%$ of sales, whereas in case of A & Co. it will be 20% of sales after meeting its fixed cost of ₹. 30,000.

(*ii*) In the condition of low demand for the product, A & Co. will be profitable as its fixed cost and BEP are very low. After meeting its fixed cost of ₹. 30,000 it will earn profit.

Illustration 55: A company, seeking to improve the competitive position, has launched a cost reduction programme in its existing plants, apart from trying to increase output.

The present profit-before-tax comes to 15% of turnover and 30% of capital employed. Other relevant working ratios are:

Gross Margin	35%
Margin of Safety	43%
Capital Turnover Ratio	2

The operating figures for the last year were as follows:

	₹.
Total sales Value	12,00,000
Variable Costs	7,80,000
Fixed Costs	2,40,000
Capital employed	6,00,000
Break-even sales	6,84,000

It has been proposed to reduce the sale price by 10% and increase the output by 20%. No change in fixed costs is expected. The estimated cost reduction amount to ₹. 42,000.

You are required to work out the relevant figures and ratios based on the proposal and present those along with the existing ones in a meaningful manner and offer your comments.

Statement Showing Comparative Profitability and Ratios

Particulars	*Existing (₹.)*	*Proposed (₹.)*	*Remarks*
Sales Value (S)	12,00,000	12,00,000	
		(–) 1,20,000 (10%)	Price reduction by 10%
		10,80,000	
		(+) 2,16,000 (20%)	Increase in output by 20%
		12,96,000	
Variable Costs (V)	7,80,000	7,80,000	
		(+) 1,56,000 (20%)	Increase in output by 20%
		9,36,000	
		(–) 42,000	Cost reduction (given)
		8,94,000	
Contributions (S–V)	4,20,000	4,02,000	
Less Fixed Costs	2,40,000	2,40,000	
Profits	1,80,000	1,62,000	

Solution:

Calculation of Ratios

		Existing	*Proposed*
1.	P/V Ratio = $\frac{\text{Contribution}}{\text{Sales}} \times 100$	$\frac{4,20,000}{12,00,000} \times 100$ = 35%	$\frac{4,02,000}{12,96,000} \times 100$ = 31.02%
2.	BEP = $\frac{\text{Fixed cost}}{\text{P/V Ratio}}$	$\frac{2,40,000}{35\%}$ = ₹. 6,85,715	$\left(\frac{2,40,000}{31.02\%}\right)$ = ₹. 7,73,695
3.	Profit-before-tax to sales = $\frac{\text{Profit before tax}}{\text{Sales}} \times 100$	$\frac{1,80,000}{12,00,000} \times 100$ = 15%	$\frac{1,62,000}{12,96,000} \times 100$ = 12.5%
4.	Profit on Capital Employed = $\frac{\text{Profit}}{\text{Capital employed}} \times 100$	$\frac{1,80,000}{6,00,000} \times 100$ = 30%	$\frac{1,62,000}{6,00,000} \times 100$ = 27%

		Existing	Proposed
5.	Margin of Safety		
	$= \dfrac{\text{Total Sales} - \text{BEP Sales}}{\text{Total Sales}} \times 100$	$\dfrac{12,00,000 - 6,85,715}{12,00,000} \times 100$	$\dfrac{12,96,000 - 7,73,695}{12,96,000} \times 100$
		= 42.86%	= 40.3%
6.	Capital Turnover Ratio		
	$= \dfrac{\text{Sales}}{\text{Capital employed}}$	$\dfrac{12,00,000}{6,00,000}$	$\dfrac{12,96,000}{6,00,000}$
		= 2	= 2.16

If the proposal is implemented, P/V Ratio, Profit before tax to Sales Ratio, Profit on capital employed and Margin of Safety will go down and BEP will also be achieved at higher level. Hence new proposal should not be recommended.

Illustration 56. **S. Ltd. manufactures and markets a single product. The following information is available :**

	₹. per Unit
Materials	8.00
Conversion Costs (variable)	6.00
Dealer's Margin	2.00
Selling price	20.00

Fixed Cost : ₹. 2,50,000

Present Sales : 80,000 units

Capacity Utilisation : 60%

There is acute competition. Extra efforts are necessary to sell. Suggestions have been made for increasing sales : (*i*) by reducing sales price by 5%; and (*ii*) by increasing dealer's margin by 25% over the existing rate. Which of the two suggestions would you recommend if the company desires to maintain the present profit? Give reasons.

Solution:

Calculation of Present Profit

	₹.
Materials	8
Conversion Cost (variable)	6
Dealer's margin	2
Variable Cost	16
Selling Price	20
Contribution per unit	4
Total Contribution : (4 × 80,000)	3,20,000
Less : Fixed Cost	2,50,000
Profit	70,000

Suggestion (i) Increasing sales by reducing sales price by 5%	₹.
Revised selling price (20 – 5%)	19
Variable Cost	16
Contribution per unit	3

$$\text{Sales} = \frac{\text{Fixed Cost + Profit}}{\text{Contribution per unit}} = \frac{(2,50,000 + 70,000)}{3}$$

$$= \frac{3,20,000}{3}$$ = 1,06,667 units should be sold to maintain the present profit of ₹. 70,000.

Present sales of 80,000 units is 60% capacity utilisation

1,06,667 units will be at 80% capacity utilisation:

$$\frac{1,06,667}{80,000} \times 60\% = 80\% \text{ capacity utilisation}$$

Suggestion (ii) Increasing sales by increasing dealer's margin by 25%

	₹.
Materials	8
Conversion Cost	6
Dealer's margin = (2 + 25%)	2.50
Variable Cost	16.50
Selling Price	20.00
Contribution per unit	₹. 3.50

$$\text{Sales} = \frac{\text{Fixed Cost + Profit}}{\text{Contribution on per unit}} = \frac{2,50,000 + 70,000}{3.50}$$

$$= \frac{3,20,000}{3.50}$$ = **91,429 units are to be sold to maintain the present profit of ₹. 70,000.**

80,000 units are at 60% capacity utilisation

91,429 units will be at 68.57 capacity utilisation

$$\frac{91,429}{80,000} \times 60\% = 68.57\% \text{ capacity utilisation}$$

Illustration 57. A firm can produce three different products from the same raw material using the same production facilities. The requisite labour is available in plenty at ₹. 8 per hour for all products. The supply of raw material which is imported at ₹. 8 per kg., is limited to 10,400 kgs. for the budget period. The variable overheads are ₹. 5.60 per hour. The fixed overheads are ₹. 50.000. The selling commission is 10 per cent on sales.

(*a*) From the following information, you are required to suggest the most suitable sales mix, which will maximise the firm's profits. Also determine the profit that will be earned at that level.

Product	*Market demand (units)*	*Selling price per unit*	*Labour hours required per unit*	*Raw material required per unit kgs.*
X	8,000	30	1	0.7
Y	6,000	40	2	0.4
Z	5,000	50	1.5	1.5

(*b*) Assume, in above situation, if additional 4,500 kgs. of raw material is made available for production, should the firm go in for further production, if it will result in additional fixed overheads of ₹. 20,000 and 25 per cent increase in the rates per hour for labour and variable overheads.

Solution:

Statement Showing Contribution and Ranking

Products per unit	*X* ₹.	*Y* ₹.	*Z* ₹.
Direct Material	5.60 (0.7 kg. × ₹. 8)	3.20 (0.4 kg. × ₹. 8)	12.00 (1.5 × ₹. 8)
Direct Labour	8.00 (1 hr. × ₹. 8)	16.00 (2 hrs. × 8)	12.00 (1.5 hr. × 8)
Variable Overhead	5.60 (1hr. × ₹. 5.60)	11.20 (2 hrs. × ₹. 5.60)	8.40 (1.5 hrs. × ₹. 5.60)
Selling Commission (10% on sales)	3.00	4.00	5.00
Total Variable Cost	22.20	34.40	37.40
Selling Price	30.00	40.00	50.00
Contribution per unit	7.80	5.60	12.60
Contribution per kg. of raw material	11.14 (₹. 7.80/0.7 kg.)	14.00 (₹. 5.60/0.4 kg.)	8.4 (₹. 12.60/1.5 kg.)
Ranking	II	I	III

Note: There are two limiting factors–market demand and raw material. Raw material is available 10,400 kgs only. Therefore ranking will be on the basis of contribution per kg of raw material.

Statement Showing the Most Suitable Sales Mix and Profitability

Product	*Priority*	*Market demand (units)*	*Raw material consumed (kg.)*	*Contribution per kg.*	*Total contribution (₹.)*
Y	I	6,000	6,000 × 0.40 = 2,400	14.00	33,600
X	II	8,000	8,000 × 0.7 = 5,600	11.14	62,384
Z	III	1,600	Balance 2,400	8.40	20,160
		(2,400/1.5 kg)	10,400		
Total Contribution					1,16,144
Less: Fixed Overheads					50,000
Profit (Maximum)					66,144

(*b*) When 4,500 kg additional raw material is further available, only Product Z will be made because market demand for Product X and Z has been fully met.

		₹.
Production of Z (4,500/1.5 kgs.)	3000 units	
Contribution on the above production 3,000 units at ₹. 12.60		37,800
Less: Increase in Labour cost (3,000 × 12 × 25%)	9,000	
Increase in Variable Overheads (3,000 × 8.40 × 25%)	6,300	15,300
Net Contribution		22,500
Less: Additional Fixed Overheads		20,000
Additional profit		2,500

For earning additional profit of ₹. 2,500, the firm should produce 3000 units of Z.

***Illustration* 58.** A company presents the following cost estimates for three prospective plants A, B & C.

	Plant A	*Plant B*	*Plant C*
Annual Fixed Cost (₹.)	60,000	1,08,000	1,20,000
Variable Cost per unit (₹.)	2.50	2.20	2.10
Annual Capacity (units)	75,000	1,20,000	1,50,000

(*i*) Calculate the range of output over which each of the plants would be most economical.

(*ii*) If sales are ready at 1,00,000 units per year and the unit selling price is ₹. 4 per unit, what will be the profits earned with each of the plants? Assume that Plant A can be worked double shift with an additional expense of 10% in fixed costs and 5% in variable costs of all units.

Solution:

(*i*) Statement of Economic Range of Output

	Plants A	*Plants B*	*Plants C*
	₹.	₹.	₹.
Selling price per unit	4.00	4.00	4.00
Less Marginal cost per unit	2.50	2.20	2.10
Contribution per unit	1.50	1.80	1.90
Annual Fixed Costs	60,000	1,08,000	1,20,000
BEP (Units)	60,000/1.50 = 40.000	1,08,000/1.80 = 60,000	1,20,000/1.90 = 63,158
Annual Capacity—Units	75,000	1,20,000	1,50,000
Economical range of output *i.e.* beyond BEP	40,001 to 75,000	60,001 to 1,20,000	63,159 to 1,50,000

(*ii*) Statement of Profits on the Sale of 1,00,000 units

	A	*B*	*C*
	₹.	₹.	₹.
Contribution per unit (See Note for A)	1.375	1.80	1.90
Total Contribution on 1,00,000 units	1,37,500	1,80,000	1,90,000
Less: Fixed Cost	(–) 66,000	(–) 1,08,000	(–) 1,20,000
Profit	71,500	72,000	70,000

Note: Annual capacity of Plant A is 75,000 units, if required Sales are 1,00,000 units, balance 25,000 units can be produced in Plant A by working double shift with an additional expense of 10% in fixed costs and 5% in variable costs of all units:

Annual Fixed Costs 60,000 + 10% = ₹. 66,000

Variable Cost = 2.50 + 5% = ₹. 2,625 per unit

Contribution = 4.00 – 2.625 = ₹. 1.375 per unit

***Illustration* 59:** A Multi Product Company has the following costs and output data for the last year:

	Products		
	X	*Y*	*Z*
Sales Mix	40%	35%	25%
	₹.	₹.	₹.
Selling Price	20	25	30
Variable Cost Per unit	10	15	18
Total Sales			₹. 1,50,000
Total Sales			₹. 500,000

The company proposes to replace Product S by Product *S*. Estimated Cost and output data are:

	X	*Y*	*S*
	50%	30%	20%
	₹.	₹.	₹.
Selling Price	20	25	28
Variable Cost/unit	10	15	18
Total Fixed Cost			₹. 1,50,000
Total Sales			₹. 5,00,000

Analyse the proposed change and suggest what decision the company should take.

Solution:

Present Profitability:

	X	*Y*	*Z*	*Total (₹.)*
Selling Price	20	25	30	
Less: Variable Cost	10	15	18	
Contribution Per unit (₹.)	10	10	12	
P/V Ratio = (Contribution/Sales) × 100	50%	40%	40%	
Sales (40%, 35% and 25% of sales)	2,00,000	1,25,000	1,25,00	5,00,000
Contribution = Sales × P/V Ratio	1,00,000	70,000	50,000	2,20,000
Less: Fixed Cost				1,50,000
Profit				70,000
Over all P/V Ratio				$\frac{2,20,000}{5,00,000} \times 100 = 44\%$
BEP = (Fixed Cost/P.V. Ratio)				$\frac{1,50,000}{44\%}$ = ₹. 3,40,909
Proposed Profitability:	*X*	*Y*	*S*	
Selling Price	20	25	28	
Variable Cost	10	15	14	
Contribution Per unit (₹.)	10	10	14	
P/V Ratio	50%	40%	50%	
Sales (50%, 30% and 20% of sales)	2,50,000	1,50,000	1,00,000	5,00,000
Contribution : (Sales × P/V Ratio)	1,25,000	60,000	50,000	2,35,000
Less: Fixed Costs				1,50,000
Profit				85,000
Overall P/V Ratio				$\frac{2,35,000}{5,00,000} \times 100 = 47\%$
BEP				$\frac{1,50,000}{47\%}$ = ₹. 3,19,149

Following suggestions may be given:

1. Proposed change of Z to S will increase profit from ₹. 70,000 to ₹. 85,000.
2. BEP will come down.
3. Contribution from X will increase from 1,00,000 to ₹. 1,25,000.

Hence it is advised that the Company should replace Z by S.

Illustration 60: Taurus Ltd. produces three product A, B and C from the same manufacturing facilities. The cost and other details of the three products are as follows:

	A	*B*	*C*
Selling Price per unit (₹.)	200	160	100
Variable Cost per unit (₹.)	120	120	40
Fixed Expenses per month ₹. 2,76,000			
Maximum Production per month (units)	5,000	8,000	6,000
Total hours available for the month 200 hours			
Maximum demand per month (units)	2,000	4,000	2,400

The processing hours cannot be increased beyond 200 hours per month.

You are required to:

(*a*) Compute the most profitable product-mix;

(*b*) Compute the overall break-even sales of the company for the month based on the mix calculated in (*a*) above.

Solution:

Statement Showing Contribution and Priority

	A	*B*	*C*
Maximum production per month–Units	5,000	8,000	6,000
Maximum production per hour-Units	5,000/200 = 25	8,000/200 = 40	6,000/200 = 30
Hours required for Maximum demand	2,000/25 = 80	4,000/40 = 100	2,400/30 = 80
	₹.	₹.	₹.
Selling price per unit	200	160	100
Less: Variable cost per unit	120	120	40
Contribution per unit	80	40	60
Contribution per hour (key factor)	80 × 25 = 2,000	40 × 40 = 1,600	60 × 30 = 1,800
Priority (On the basis of contribution)	I	III	II

(*a*) Statement Showing Profitable Product-mix.

Products	Units	Hours
A	Maximum Demand 2,000 units	$\frac{2,000}{25} = 80$
C	Maximum Demand 2,400 units	$\frac{2,400}{30} = 80$
B	Balance (For 40 hours) 1,600 units	$\frac{1,600}{40} = 40$
Total		200

Statement Showing Profit of Products

(₹ in lakhs)

	A	B	C	Total
Sales Value	4.00	2.56	2.40	8.96
Less: Variable Cost	2.40	1.92	0.96	5.28
Contribution	1.60	0.64	1.44	3.68
Less : Fixed Expenses				2.76
Profit				0.92

(*b*) P/V Ratio $= \frac{\text{Contribution}}{\text{Sales}} \times 100 = \frac{3,68,000}{8,96,000} \times 100 = 41.0714\%$

Overall Break-even Sales of the Company:

$= \frac{\text{Fixed Cost}}{\text{P/V Ratio}} = \frac{2,76,000}{41.0714\%} =$ ₹. 6,72,000

Illustration 61: M/s PL Agro Ltd., engaged in agricultural activities has 500 hectares of virgin land, which can be used for growing jointly or individually tea, coffee and cardamom. The yield per hectare of the different crops and selling prices per kg. are as under :

	Yield (Kgs)	Selling Price (₹. per kg)
Tea	2,500	25
Coffee	625	50
Cardamon	125	300

The relevant cost data are given below:

(*a*) *Variable Cost per Kg.*

	Tea (₹.)	*Coffee* (₹.)	*Cardamom* (₹.)
Labour Charges	10.00	12.50	150.00
Packing Material	2.50	2.50	12.50
Other Costs	5.00	1.25	25.00
	17.50	16.25	187.50

(*b*) *Fixed Cost per Annum*

	₹.
Cultivation and Growing Cost	16,00,000
Administrative Cost	4,50,000
Land Revenue	2,75,000
Repairs and maintenance	5,00,000
Other Costs	6,75,000
	35,00,000

The policy of the company is to produce and sell all the three kinds of products and the maximum and minimum area to be cultivated per product is as follows:

	Maximum Area Hectares	*Minimum Area Hectares*
Tea	320	240
Coffee	100	60
Cardamom	60	20

Calculate the priority of production, the most profitable product mix and the maximum profit which can be achieved. **[*C.S. (Inter) June, 1994*]**

Solution:

Statement Showing Contribution of Products & their Priority

	Tea ₹.	*Coffee* ₹.	*Cardamom* ₹.
Selling Price per kg.	25.00	50.00	300.00
Less: Variable Cost per kg.	17.50	16.25	187.50
Contribution per kg.	7.50	33.75	112.50
Yield per Hectare (₹.)	2,500	625	125
Contribution per (Yield × Contribution)	18,750	21,093.75	14,062.50
Priority (on the basis of contribution)	II	I	III

Note: There is no constraint so far as the land is concerned because land available is sufficient.

Statement Showing Most Profitable Product Mix & Maximum Profit

Crop	*Priority*	*Policy*	*No. of Hectares*	*Contribution per Hectares* ₹.	*Total Amt.* ₹.
Coffee	I	Maximum	100	21093.75	21,09,375
Tea	II	Maximum	320	18750.00	60,00,000
Cardamom	III	Maximum	60	14,062.50	8,43,750
Total			480		89,53,125
Less: Fixed Cost per annum					35,00,000
Profit (Maximum)					54,53,125

Note: Balance 20 hectares land available can be used for any other purpose.

Illustration 62: Expansion Ltd. manufactures automobile accessories and parts. The following are the total costs of processing 1,00,000 units.

Direct Material Cost	₹. 5 lakhs
Direct Labour Cost	₹. 8 lakhs
Variable Factory Overhead	₹. 6 lakhs
Fixed Factory Overhead	₹. 5 lakhs

The purchase price of the component is ₹. 22. The fixed overhead would continue to be incurred even when the component is bought from outside, although there would have been reduction to the extent of ₹. 2,00,000.

Required:

(*a*) Should the part be made or bought considering that the present facility when released following a buying decision would remain idle?

(b) In case the released capacity can be rented out to another manufacturer for ₹. 1,50,000 having good demand, what should be the decision?

Solution:

(*a*) Statement Showing Comparative Cost **(₹. in lakhs)**

	Make	*Buy*
Marginal Cost or Total Variable Cost	19	—
Purchase Cost	—	22
Fixed Factory Overhead	5	3
Total Cost	24	25

The part should be made because the fixed overhead would continue to be incurred to the extent of ₹. 3 lakhs (5 – 2 lakhs) even if the component is bought from outside.

(b) Statement Showing Comparative Cost **(₹. in lakhs)**

	Make	Buy
Total Cost (as worked out above)	24.00	25.00
Less: Rented out for	—	1.50
Net Cost	24.00	23.50

The part should be bought because its net cost is less.

Illustration 63: A company annually manufactures 10,000 units of a product at a cost of ₹. 4 per unit and there is home market for consuming the entire volume of production at the sale price of ₹. 4.25 per unit in the year, there is a fall in the demand for home market which can consume 10,000 units only at a sale price of ₹. 3.72 per unit. The analysis of the cost per 10,000 units is:

	₹.
Material	15,000
Wages	11,000
Fixed Overheads	8,000
Variable Overheads	6,000

The foreign market is explored and it is found that this market can consume 20,000 units of the product if offered at a sale price of ₹. 3.55 per unit. It is also discovered that for additional 10,000 units of the product (over initial 10,000 units) the fixed overheads will increase by 10%. Is it worthwhile to try to capture the foreign market?

Solution:

Statement Showing Comparative Profitability

Particulars	*Present*	*Next year*		
	Home Market	*Home Home*	*Foreign Market*	*Total*
Sales Units	10,000	10,000	20,000	30,000
	₹.	₹.	₹.	₹.
Materials	15,000	15,000	30,000	45,000
Wages	11,000	11,000	22,000	33,000
Variable Overheads	6,000	6,000	12,000	18,000
Variable Cost	32,000	32,000	64,000	96,000
Fixed Overheads	8,000	8,000	1,600 (20% of 8,000)	9,600
Total cost	40,000	40,000	65,600	1,05,600
Sales	42,500 (10,000 × 4.25)	37,200 (10,000 × 3.72)	71,000 (20,000 × 3.55)	1,08,200
Profit (Loss)	2,500	(2,800)	5,400	2,600

In the current year there is profit. But in the next year, sale in the home market @ ₹. 3.72 per unit will result in a loss of ₹. 2,800. If foreign market is captured @ ₹. 3.55 per unit, there will be profit of ₹. 2,600. It is advisable that company should try to capture the foreign market.

Illustration 64: The following extracts are taken from the sales budget of a company for the current year:

		(Rupees in 000)
Sales: 40,000 units @ ₹. 25 per unit		1,000
Selling Costs:		
Advertising	100	
Salesman's Salaries	80	
Travelling Expenses	50	
Rent of sales office	10	
Others	10	250

The management is considering a proposal to establish a new market in the eastern region in the next year. It is proposed to increase the advertising expenditure by 25% and appoint an additional sales supervisor at a salary of ₹. 30,000 per year to establish a market. This will involve additional travelling and travelling expense shall increase by 10%.

Target annual sales volume at the existing selling price for the new market is 10,000 units. The estimated variable cost of production is ₹. 12 per unit.

Should the company try to establish the new market?

Solution:

		(₹. '000)
Incremental Sales Revenue :		
New Market 10,000 units @ ₹. 25		250
Less: Differential Cost:		
Variable Cost of production		
10,000 units at ₹. 12 =	120	
Increase in advertising exp.		
25% of ₹, 1,00,000	25	
Additional sales supervisor		
Salary of ₹. 30,000 per year	30	
Additional travelling exp.		
10% of ₹. 50,000	5	180
Incremental profit		70

It may be advised that in view of the additional profit (incremental profit) of ₹. 70,000, the company should try to establish the new market.

Illustration 65: A company produced a single product which is sold by it presently in the domestic market at ₹. 75 per unit. The present production and sales is 40,000 units per month representing 50% of the capacity available. The cost data of the product are as under :

Variable costs per unit ₹. 50

Fixed costs per months ₹. 10 lakhs

To improve the profitability, the management has 3 proposals on hand as under :

(*a*) to accept an export supply order for 30,000 units per month at a reduced price of ₹. 60 per unit, incurring additional variable cost of ₹. 5 per unit towards export packing, duties etc:

(*b*) to increase the domestic market sales by selling to a domestic chain stores: 30,000 units at ₹. 55 per unit, retaining the existing sales at the existing price;

(*c*) to reduce the selling price for the increased domestic sales as advised by the sales department as under :

Reducing selling price per unit by	Increase in sales expected (in units)
(*i*) ₹. 5	10,000
(*ii*) ₹. 8	30,000
(*iii*) ₹. 11	35,000

Prepare a table to present the results of the above proposals and give your comments and advice on the proposals. **[*ICWA (Inter)*]**

Solution:

1. Calculation of Present profitability

	₹.	₹.
Selling Price	75	
Less : Variable Cost	50	
Contribution per unit	25	
Total Contribution in a month (40,000 units at ₹. 25)		10,00,000
Less: Fixed Costs per month		10,00,000
Profit		Nil

Note: The present production and sales is 40,000 units per month representing 50% of the capacity available.

Statement showing Result of the Proposals

Proposal	(*a*)	(*b*)	c(*i*)	c(*ii*)	c(*iii*)
Selling price per unit (₹.)	60	55	70	67	64
Variable cost per unit (₹.)	55	50	50	50	50
Contribution per unit (₹.)	5	5	20	17	14
Sales (in units)	30,000	30,000	50,000	70,000	75,000
Total Contribution (₹. lakhs)	1.50	1.50	10.00	11.90	10.50
Less: Fixed Costs (₹. lakhs)	—	—	10.00	10.00	10.00
Profit per month (₹. lakhs)	1.50	1.50	Nil	1.90	0.50

30,000 units of sales under proposals (*a*) & (*b*) are sales in addition to present sales.

The total sales (in units) under proposal (*c*).

(*i*) 10,000 + 40,000 = 50,000 (*ii*) 30,000 + 40,000 = 70,000

(*iii*) 35,000 + 40,000 = 75,000

The proposal at *c* (*ii*) is more profitable i.e. sale of 70,000 units at a price of ₹. 67 (75 – 8) because it yields profit of ₹. 1.90 lakhs.

QUESTIONS

OBJECTIVE QUESTIONS

I. *State whether the following statements are True or False* :

(*i*) Contribution is the difference between the sales and the total cost of sales.

(*ii*) At break-even point the company earns only a marginal profit.

(*iii*) Contribution is also known as Gross Margin.

(*iv*) P/V ratio can be improved by increasing the selling price.

(*v*) P/V ratio can be improved by reducing the fixed costs.

(*vi*) Margin of safety = $\frac{\text{Fixed Expenses}}{\text{P/V ratio}}$.

(*vii*) Margin of safety can be improved by reducing the fixed cost.

(*viii*) Break-even analysis is fundamentally a static analysis.

[**Ans.** (*i*) False ; (ii) False; (*iii*) True; (*iv*) True; (v) False; (vi) False; (vii) True; (*viii*) False

II. *Whether the following statements are true or false*?

1. Break-even Poing is that where a firm neither earns profit nor loss.
2. At B.E.P. the firm earns no profit.
3. Profit = P/V Ratio × Margin of Safety.
4. Margin of Safety = Sales – Sales of BEP
5. Contribution = Sales – Variable Cost
6. Profit volume Ratio = $\frac{\text{Contribution}}{\text{Sales}} \times 100$
7. B.E.P. = $\frac{\text{Fixed Cost}}{\text{P/V Ratio}}$
8. Contribution is the difference between the sales and the total cost of sales.
9. Contribution is also known normal cost.
10. P/V Ratio can be improved by decreasing the selling price.
11. Break-even analysis is not a static analysis.
12. Margin of safety can be improved by reducing fixed cost.
13. P/V Ratio can be improved by increasing the fixed costs.
14. Sales = Variable cost + Profit.
15. Break-even Charts depict cost volume profit relationship.

[**Ans.** 1. True, 2. True, 3. True, 4. True, 5. True, 6. True, 7. True, 8. False, 9. False, 10. False, 11. False, 12. True, 13. False, 14. False, 15. True.]

III. *Fill in the blanks* :

1. Contribution is the difference between sales and ....
2. Break-even point is a point of ....
3. In a profit volume graph, Break-even Point takes place where .... intersect each other.
4. P/V Ratio shows the relationship between ....
5. The difference between actual sales and Break even sales is called ....

[***Ans.** 1. Variable Cost, 2. No Profit no Loss, 3. Profit and Sales Lines, 4. Contribution and Sales, 5. Margin of Safety*]

THEORETICAL QUESTIONS

1. What is Marginal Costing? `The technique of marginal costs can be valuable aid to the management', Discuss.
2. Distinguish between Marginal Costing and Absorption Costing.
3. Write short notes on
   (*i*) Contribution
   (*ii*) P/V Ratio
   (*iii*) Break-even-point
4. Define Break-even-point. What are underlying assumptions in break-even analysis?
5. Distinguish between Marginal Costing and Differential Costing. ***[B Com (H) Delhi]***

6. Point out elearly the relationship between sales mix and break-even analysis. *[B Com. (H) Delhi]*
7. What are the various metnods by which you split semi-variable costs into its fixed and variable elements?
8. `The effect of a price reduction is always to reduce the P/V ratio to raise the break-even-point and to shorten the margin of safety'. Explain with a suitable illustration.
9. Discuss the importance of key factor or limiting factor in an organisation.
10. Explain briefly three specific decision-making areas where the principle of marginal costing could be applied.

SHORT ANSWER QUESTIONS

1. What are the limitation of a break even chart?
2. Distinguish between Marginal Costing and Defferential Costing.
3. Write a note on value analysis.
4. Write a note on 'Key Factor'.
5. Write Short notes on
   (*i*) Break even point
   (*ii*) Break even analysis
   (*iii*) Marginal cost
6. Distinguish between
   (*i*) Contribution and Profit
   (*ii*) Break-even analysis and profit planning
   (*iii*) Marginal Costing and Defferential Costing

NUMERICAL QUESTIONS

Marginal Cost Statement

1. From the following details prepare Marginal Cost Statement:

	Products (₹.)		
	A	B	C
Direct Material	2,500	10,000	1,000
Direct Labour	3,000	3,000	500
Factory Overhead			
Fixed	1,000	500	500
Variable	1,300	3,000	1,500
Selling Overhead			
Fixed	500	300	200
Variable	700	2,000	1,000
Sales	10,000	20,000	5,000

Also prepare a cost statement under absorption costing and comment on the comparative results.
[**Ans.** *Marginal cost A ₹. 7,500, B ₹. 18,000 C ₹. 4,000; Contribution A ₹. 2,500, B ₹. 2,000 C ₹. 1,000; Net Profit ₹. 2,500 Under Absorption Method Total Cost A 9,000, B ₹. 18,800 C ₹. 4,700; Net Profit ₹. 2,500. Net Profit is same because there are no opening and closing stocks*]

2. The following data are given to you:
Selling price per ton ₹. 5; Variable cost per ton ₹. 3; Fixed cost per ton ₹ 1 (for normal output of 39,000 tons) per month; Total fixed cost per month ₹. 39,000.
The production and stock figure are as follows

	January (Tons)	February (Tons)	March (Tons)
Opening stock	—	9,000	3,000
Closing stock	9,000	3,000	—
Production	45,000	36,000	45,000
Sales	36,000	42,000	48,000

You are required to (a) Prepare a marginal cost statement (b) Prepare a cost statement under absorption costing (c) Comment on the comparative profit figures.

[**Ans.** *(a) Contribution Jan. ₹. 72,000, Feb. 84,000, March ₹. 96,000, Profit Jan ₹. 33,000, Feb. ₹. 45,000, March ₹. 57,000; (b) Profit Jan 42,000, Feb. ₹. 39,000, March ₹. 54,000*]

3. Production costs of Oriental Enterprises Limited are as follows:

	Level of Activity		
	60%	70%	80%
Output (in units)	1,200	1,400	1,600
Cost (in ₹.)			
Direct Materials	24,000	28,000	32,000
Direct Labour	7,200	8,400	9,600
Factory Overheads	12,800	13,600	14,400
Works Cost	44,000	50,000	56,000

A proposal to increase production to 90% level of activity is under consideration of management. The proposal is not expected to involve any increase in fixed factory overheads.

Prepare a statement showing the Prime Cost, Total Marginal Cost and Total Factory Cost at 90% level of activity. **[*B. Com. (Hons.), Delhi*]**

[**Ans.** *Variable factory Overhead per unit ₹. 4; Fixed Factory Overhead ₹. 8,000. Prime Cost ₹. 46,800; Marginal Cost ₹. 54,000; Works Cost ₹. 62,000*]

4. Ambitious Enterprises is currently working at 50% capacity and produces 10,000 units.

At 60% working, raw material cost increases by 2% and selling price falls by 2 per cent. At 80 per cent working raw material cost increases by 5 per cent and selling price falls by 5 per cent.

At 50% capacity working, the products costs ₹. 180 per unit and is sold at ₹. 200 per unit.

The unit cost of ₹. 180 is made up as follows:

Material	₹. 100	
Wages	30	
Factory Overheads	30	(40% fixed)
Administration Overheads	20	(50% fixed)

Prepare a Marginal Cost Statement showing estimated profit of the business when operated at 60% and 80% capacity. **[*B.Com. (Hons), Delh*]**

[**Ans.** *Profit on 60% capacity ₹. 2,12,000 or ₹. 17.67 per unit; Profit on 80% Capacity ₹. 2,12,000 or ₹. 13.25 per unit*]

Break-even Point etc.

5. From the following particulars, calculate the break-even point

Variable cost per unit ₹. 12   Fixed Expenses ₹. 60,000

Selling Price per unit ₹. 18

[**Ans.** *10,000 units*]

6. From the following particulars, find out the selling price per unit if Break-even-point is to be brought down to 9,000 units

Variable cost per unit ₹. 75   Fixed Expenses ₹. 2,70,000

Selling Price per unit ₹. 100

[**Ans.** *₹. 105 per unit*]

7. The following information relating to a company is given to you

Sales	₹. 4,00,000	Fixed cost ₹. 1,80,000
Variable cost	₹. 2,50,000	

Ascertain how much the value of sales must be increased for the company to breakeven.

[Ans. *₹ 80,000***]**

8. From the following data find out how many units should be sold to earn a net profit of 10% on sales

Selling price per unit	₹. 20	Variable cost per unit ₹. 14
Fixed cost (total)	₹. 7,92,000	

[Ans. *1,98,000 units***]**

9. You are given the following data of a firm for the year 2004

	₹.	Percentage
Variable cost	6,00,000	60
Fixed cost	3,00,000	30
Net Profit	1,00,000	10
Sales	10,00,000	100

Find out break-even-point, P/V ratio and margin of safety.

[Ans. *(i) BEP ₹ 7,50,000 i.e. 75% of sales, (ii) P/V ratio 40%, (iii) M.S. ₹ 2,50,000***]**

10. A plant produces a product which costs ₹. 3 per unit when produced in quantities of 10,000 units and ₹. 2.50 per unit when produced in quantities of 20,000 units. You are asked to estimate total fixed costs.

[Ans. *₹ 10,000***]**

11. From the following data, calculate (*i*) P/V Ratio; (*ii*) Profit when sales are ₹. 20,000; (*iii*) New break-even-point if selling price is reduced by 20%.

Fixed Expenses	₹.	4,000
Break-even Point	₹.	10,000

[Ans. *(i) 40%; (ii) ₹ 4,000; (iii) ₹ 16,000***]**

12. From the following information calculate the Break-even Point and turnover required to earn a Profit of ₹. 36,000.

Fixed Overheads ₹. 1,80,000	Selling Price per unit ₹. 20
Variable Cost per unit ₹. 2	

If the company is earning a profit of ₹. 36,000, express the margin of safety available to it.

[Ans. *M.S. ₹ 40,000, BEP ₹ 2,00,000; Required Sales ₹ 2,40,000***]**

13. The Price structure of a chair made by a Co. is as follows:

	Per Chair (₹.)
Materials	60
Labour	20
Variable Overheads	20
	100
Fixed Overheads	50
Profit	50
Selling Price	200

This is based on the manufacture of one lakh chairs per annum. Calculate how many chairs will be made to get the same amount of profit if (*a*) the selling price is reduced by 10% (*b*) the selling price is reduced by 20%.

[Ans. *(a) 1,25,000 chair (b) 1,66,667 chair***]**

14. An analysis of a company led to the following information:

	Variable Cost (% of sales)	*Fixed Cost (₹)*
Direct Material	32.8	
Direct Labour	28.4	
Factory Overheads	12.6	1,89,900
Distribution Overheads	4.1	58,400
General Admn. Overheads	1.1	66,700

Budgeted sales are ₹. 18,50,000 you are required to determine (*i*) the breakeven sales volume; (*ii*) the profit at the budgeted sales volume; (*iii*) the profit if actual sales (*a*) drop by 10% (*b*) increase by 5% from budgeted sales.

[Ans. *(i) ₹. 15,00,000; (ii) ₹. 73,500; (iii) (a) ₹. 34,650; (b) ₹. 92,925*]

15. Company A and Company B both under the same management make and sell the same type of product. Their budgeted Profit & Loss Account for January-June 2004 are as under.

	Company A ₹.	₹.	*Company B* ₹.	₹.
Sales		3,00,000		3,00,000
Less: Variable Cost	2,40,000		2,00,000	
Fixed Costs	30,000	2,70,000	70,000	2,70,000
		30,000		30,000

You are required to (*i*) calculate break-even-point for each company; (*ii*) calculate the sale volume of which each of the two companies will make a profit of ₹. 10,000 (*iii*) Assess how their profitability will change with decrease or increase in volume.

[Ans. *(i) A 20%, B 33 1/3% ; A ₹ 1,50,000, B ₹ 2,10,000 (ii) A ₹. 2,00,000, B ₹. 2,40,000; (iii) Change in profitability with change in volume can be assessed by their P/V Ratio*]

16. A company has a P/V Ratio of 40 per cent. By what percentage must sales be increased to offset:

(*i*) 10% reduction in selling price and

(*ii*) 20% reduction in selling price

[Ans. *(i) 33 1/3% ; (ii) 100%*]

17. The output of a firm when sold, would receive ₹.70,000. The variable cost for this production would be ₹. 30,000. The fixed costs are ₹. 20,000. Determine the following; (*i*) The break-even point of the company, (*ii*) The profit or loss to the company on sales of ₹. 49,000 and ₹. 28,000 (*iii*) The amount of sales that will enable the company to earn a net profit of ₹. 28,000.

[*B. Com (H) Delhi*]

[Ans. *(i) PV Ratio 57.143%; BEP sales ₹. 35,000; (ii) Profit ₹. 8,000, Loss ₹. 4,000; (iii) ₹. 84,000*]

18. A company budgets for a production of 1,50,000 units. The variable cost per unit is ₹. 14 and fixed cost is ₹. 2 per unit. The company fixes its selling price to fetch a profit of 15% on cost

(*a*) What is the break-even-point; (*b*) What is profit volume ratio; (*c*) If it reduces its selling price by 5%, how the revised selling price affect the break-even point and profit volume ratio?; (*d*) If a profit increase of 10% is desired more than the budget, what should be the sales at reduced price.

[*B.Com (H) Delhi*]

[Ans. *(a) ₹. 12,54,545, (b) 23.91%, ₹. 15,70,318 (c) BEP 86,207 units; ₹ 15,70,358 PV Ratio 19.90%, (d) ₹. 34,96,000*]

19. The following are the cost and the sales data of a manufacturer selling three products X, Y, and Z.

Product	*Selling Price Per Unit (₹.)*	*Variable Cost per unit (₹.)*	*Sales Volume Ratio*
X	4	3	20
Y	5	4	40
Z	8	6	40

Capacity of the manufacture is ₹. 15,00,000 as total sales volume, Annual Fixed Cost ₹. 2,30,000 (*a*) Find the break-even point in rupees (*b*) Calculate his profit or loss at 80% of capacity. **[*CA*]**
[Ans. *(a) PV Ratio 23%, BEP ₹. 10,00,000; (b) ₹. 46,000*]

20. The following data are obtained from the records of a factory

	₹.	₹.
Sales 4,000 units @ ₹. 25 each		1,00,000
Material Consumed	40,000	
Variable Overheads	10,000	
Labour Charges	20,000	
Fixed. Overheads	18,000	
		88,000
Net Profit		12,000

Calculate (*i*) the number of units by selling which the company will neither lose nor gain anything; (*ii*) the sales needed to earn a profit of 20% on sales; (*iii*) the extra units to be sold to obtain the present profit if it is proposed to reduce the selling price by 20% and 25% (*iv*) the selling price to be fixed to bring down its BEP to 500 units under present conditions.
[Ans. *(i) 2,400 units; (ii) ₹. 1,80,000; (iii) 8,000 units and 20,000 units; (iv) ₹. 53.50 per unit*]

21. From the following data, you are required to calculate the break-even-point and sales value at this point

			₹.
Selling Price per unit	₹. 25		
Direct Material cost per unit	₹. 8	Fixed Overheads	24,000
Direct Labour cost per unit	₹. 5	Variable Overheads @ 60% on direct labour	
		Trade Discount	4%

If sales are 15% and 20% above the break-even volume, determine the net profits.
[Ans. *P/V Ratio 32% BEP 3,000 units; BE Sales ₹. 75,000; If sales is 15% above BEP, profit ₹. 3,600; If sales is 20% above BEP, Profit ₹. 4,800*] **Hint :** Trade discount is variable cost

22. The following figures are available for the records of Venus Enterprises as at 31st March.

	2003 (*₹. Lakhs*)	*2004* (*₹. Lakhs*)
Sales	150	200
Profit	30	50

Calculate:
(*a*) the P/V ratio and total fixed expenses; (*b*) the break-even level of sales; (*c*) Sales required to earn a profit of ₹. 90 lakhs; (*d*) Profit or loss that would arise if the sales were ₹. 280 lakhs.
[Ans. *(a) P/V ratio 40%, Fixed cost ₹ 30 lakhs (b) ₹. 75 lakhs (c) ₹. 300 lakhs (d) ₹. 82 lakhs*]

23. Kalyan University conducts a special course on computer application for a month during summer. For this purpos, it invites applications from graduates. An entrance test is given to the candidate and based on the same, a final selection of a hundred candidates is made. The entrance test consists of four objective type examinations and is spread over four days, one examination per day. Each candidate is charged fee of ₹. 50 for taking up the entrance test. The following data was gathered for the past two years.

Statement of Net Revenue from the Entrance Test

	2003 ₹.	2004 ₹.
Gross Revenue (fees collected)	1,00,000	1,50,000
Cost : Valuation	40,000	60,000
Question Booklets	20,000	30,000

Hall Rent @ ₹. 2,000 per day	8,000	8,000
Honourarian to Chief Administrator	6,000	6,000
Supervision charges (one supervisor) for every 100 candidates @ ₹. 50 per day	4,000	6,000
General Admin. Overheads	6,000	6,000
Total Cost	84,000	1,16,000
Net Revenue	16,000	34,000

You are required to compute:

(*a*) The budgeted net revenue of 4,000 candidate take up the entrance test in 2005.

(*b*) The break-even number of candidates.

(*c*) The number of candidates to be enrolled if the net revenue ₹. 20,000 is desired.

[*CA Inter*]

[**Ans.** *(a) ₹ 52,000 (b) 1,120 candidates (c) 2230 candidates*]

24. Two manufacturing companies which have the following operating details decided to merge.

	Company No. 1	*Company No.2*
Capacity utilisation percentage	90	60
Sales (₹. lakhs)	540	300
Variable Cost (₹. lakhs)	396	225
Fixed Costs (₹. lakhs)	80	50

Assuming that the proposal is implemented, calculate

(*i*) Break-even sales of the merged plant and the capacity utilisation at that stage.

(*ii*) Profitability of the merged plant at 80% capacity utilisation.

(*iii*) Sales turnover of the merged plant to earn a profit of ₹. 75 lakhs.

(*v*) When the merged plant is working at a capacity to earn a profit of ₹. 75 lakhs, what percentage increase in selling price is required to sustain an increase of 5% in fixed overheads. **[*ICWA–Inter*]**

[**Ans.** *(i) BEP of merged plant ₹. 501.76 lakh, Capacity utilisation 45.61%, (ii) Profit ₹. 98 lakh (iii) ₹. 791.23 lakhs (iv) Percentage increase in selling price 0.8215%*]

Key Factor

25. From the following data, which product would you recommend to be manufactured in a factory, time being the key factor?

	Per unit of Product 'A'	*Per unit of Product 'B'*
Direct Material	₹. 24	₹. 14
Direct Labour at ₹. 1 per hour	2	3
Variable Overhead at ₹. 2 per hour	4	6
Selling Price	100	110
Standing time to produce	2 hours	3 hours

[**Ans.** *Contribution per hour A ₹. 35 B ₹. 29, A is recommended*]

26. From the following data, recommend the most profitable product mix, presuming that direct labour hours available are only 700.

	Products	
	A	*B*
Contribution per unit	₹. 30	₹. 20
Direct Labour per unit	10 hrs.	5 hrs.

The maximum production possible for each of the products *A* and *B* is 100 units.

The Fixed Overheads are ₹. 1,000.

[*An Contribution per labour hour A ₹. 3, B ₹. 4; B is more profitable, Profitable mix B 100 units A 20 units; Profit ₹. 1,600*]

27. Mansarovar Auto Products produces and sells two small components *P* and *Q*, used in automobiles. The details regarding unit income and costs of these components are as under:

	Products P (₹)	Q (₹)
Selling Price	12	20
Direct Materials	2	4
Direct labour	2	1
Variable Factory Overheads	2	4
Fixed Factory Overhead	2	4
Total Cost of goods sold	8	13
Gross Profit per unit	4	7

Factory Overheads, both fixed and variable, have been accounted for on a machine hour basis. As far as can be determined, the sales outlook is such that the plant could operate at full capacity on either or both products. Both *P* and *Q* are processed through the same cost centres. Selling costs are all fixed.

Which product should be preferred? Give a brief explanation in support of your answer.

[*B. Com. (Hons) Delhi*]

[**Ans.** *Contribution per machine hour P ₹. 6, Q ₹. 5.50. P is more profitable*]

28. Vinak Ltd. operating at 75% level of activity produces and sells two products *A* and *B*. The cost sheets of these two products are as under:

	Product A	*Product B*
Unit produced and sold	600	400
Direct Materials	₹. 2.00	₹. 4.00
Direct Labour	4.00	4.00
Factory Overheads (40% fixed)	5.00	3.00
Selling and Administration Overheads (60% fixed)	8.00	5.00
Total Cost per unit	19.00	16.00
Selling Price per unit	23.00	19.00

Factory Overheads are absorbed on the basis of machine hour which is the limiting (key) factor. The machine hour rate is ₹. 2 per hour.

The company receives an offer from Canada for the purchase of product A at a price of ₹. 17.50 per unit.

Alternatively, the company has another offer from the Middle East for the purchase of product B at a price of ₹. 15.50 per unit.

In both the cases, a special packing charge of fifty paise per unit has to be borne by the company. The company can accept either of the two export orders and in either case the company can supply such quantities as may be possible to produce by utilising the balance of 25% of its capacity.

You are required to prepare:

(*i*) A statement showing the economics of the two export proposals giving your recommendations as to which proposal should be accepted, and

(*ii*) A statement showing the overall profitability of the company after incorporating the export proposal recommended by you. **[*CA Inter*]**

[**Ans.** *Contribution per unit of Product A ₹. 4.80, Product B ₹. 3.20; Contribution per machine hour A ₹. 1.92, B ₹. 2.13. The order of Product B from the Middle East should be preferred, (ii) [600 (23–19) = 2400] + [400 (19 – 16) = 1200] + [320 × 133 = 425.6] D = ₹ 4025.6*

Decisions Involving Alternative Choice

(a) Sales Decision

29. With a view to increase the volume of sales, Ambitious Enterprises has in mind a proposal to reduce the price of its product by 20%. No change in total fixed costs or variable costs per unit is estimated. The directors, however, desire the present level of profit to be maintained.

The following information has been provided:

Sales 50,000 units	₹. 5,00,000
Variable Costs	₹. 5 per unit
Fixed costs	₹. 50,000

Advise management on the basis of the various calculations made from the data given.

[**Ans.** *Present P/V Ratio 50%, Future P/V Ratio on reduction of selling price by 20% = 37.5%, Sales to maintain present profit ₹. 6,66,667 or 83,333 units (Fixed cost + desired profit/PVR). The price may be reduced if sales volume can be pushed up to 83,333 units*]

30. Quality Product Ltd., manufactures and markets a single product. The following data are available:

	Per Unit		Per Unit
Materials	₹. 16	Dealer's Margin	₹. 4
Conversion Costs (variable)	12	Selling Price	40

Fixed Cost ₹. 5 lakhs

Present Sales: 90,000 units

Capacity utilisation: 60 per cent

There is acute competition. Extra efforts are necessary to sell. Suggestions have been made for increasing sales:

(*a*) By reducing selling price by 4.5 per cent.

(*b*) By increasing dealer's margin by 25 per cent over the existing rate.

Which of these two suggestions you would recommend, if the company desires to maintain the present profit? Give reasons. **[*CA*]**

[**Ans.** *Contribution per unit ₹. 8, Profit ₹. 2,20,000. Total contribution required for each case = fixed cost + profit = ₹. 7,20,000. (a) When SP is reduced by 4.5% contribution per unit ₹. 6.20, Sales required 7,20,000 ÷ 6.20 = 1,16,129 units (b) when dealer's margin is increased contribution per unit ₹. 7, sales of 1,02,857 units. Second proposal may be recommended*]

31. Vinak Ltd. which produces three product furnishes you the following data for 2003–04

	Products		
	A	*B*	*C*
Selling Price per unit (₹.)	100	75	50
Profit/Volume Ratio (%)	10	20	40
Maximum Sales Potential (Units)	40,000	25,000	10,000
Raw material content as percentage of variable costs (%)	50	50	50

The Fixed Expenses are estimated at ₹. 6,80,000. The company uses a single raw material in all the three products. Raw material is in short supply and the company has quota for the supply of raw materials of the value of ₹. 18,00,000 for the year 2003-04 for the manufacture of its products to meet its sales demand.

You are required to

(*i*) Set a product mix which will give the maximum overall profit keeping the short supply of raw material in view.

(*ii*) Compute the amount of maximum profit **[*C.A. Inter*]**

[**Ans.** *Contribution as a percentage of raw material cost A 22.22%, B 50%, C 133.33%, the priority should be C, B and A respectively. Profit ₹. 95,000*]

Exploration of New Markets

32. A company annually manufactures 10,000 units of a product at a cost of ₹ 4 per unit and there is home market for consuming the entire volume of production at the sale price of ₹. 4.25 per unit. In the year 2004, there is a fall in the demand for home market which can consume 10,000 units only at the sale price of ₹ 3.72 per unit. The analysis of the cost per 10,000 units is as follows:

	₹		₹
Materials	15,000	Fixed Overheads	8,000
Wages	11,000	Variable Overheads	6,000

The foreign market is explored and it is found that this market can consume 20,000 units of the product if offered at a sale price of ₹ 3.55 per unit. It is also discovered that for additional 10,000 units of the product (over initial 10,000 units), the fixed overheads will increase by 10 per cent. Is it worth while to try to capture the foreign market?

[**Ans.** *Home market loss ₹ 2,800, Foreign market profit ₹ 5,400. It is advisable to sell goods in foreign market which will compensate domestic loss*]

33. A factory produces 24,000 units. The cost sheet gives the following information:

	₹
Direct Material	1,20,000
Direct Wages	84,000
Variable Overheads	48,000
Semi-variable Overheads	28,000
Fixed Overheads	80,000
Total Cost	3,60,000

The product is sold at ₹ 20 per unit.

The management proposes to increase the production by 3,000 units for sales in the foreign market. It is estimated that the semi-variable overheads will increase by ₹ 1,000. But the product will be sold at ₹ 14 per unit in the foreign market. However, no additional capital expenditure will be incurred. The management seeks your advice as a cost accountant. What will you advise them?

[**Ans.** *Contribution per unit ₹ 9.50. If aditional 3,000 units sold in foreign market at ₹ 14, there is net addition to profit ₹ 9,500*]

Hint. *when 3,000 unit are increases the same variable cost increases by ₹ 1000, thus there is variable incrase per unit 1/3 i.e., 0.33*

Discontinuance of Product Line

34. A manufacturer is thinking whether he should drop one item from his product line and replace it with another. Below are given his present cost and output data;

Product	*Price*	*Variable costs per unit*	*Percentage of sales*
Book-shelfs	₹ 60	₹ 40	30%
Tables	100	60	20%
Beds	200	120	50%
Total Fixed Costs per year		₹ 7,50,000	
Sales of last year		₹ 25,00,000	

The change under consideration consists in dropping the line of tables in favour of cabinets. If this drop and change is made, the manufacturer forecasts the following cost and output data:

Product	*Price*	*Variable cost per unit unit*	*Percentage of sales*
Book-self	60	40	50%
Cabinets	160	60	10%
Beds	200	120	40%
Total fixed costs per year		₹ 7,50,000	
Sales this year		₹ 26,00,000	

[**Ans.** *Profit in existing situation ₹. 2,00,000; Profit in proposed situation (dropping tables in preference to cabinets) ₹. 2,61,833. The proposal should be accepted if demand for cabinets is of a permanent nature*]

35. A Limited manufactures three different products and the following information has been collected from the books of accounts:

		Products		
		S	*T*	*Y*
Sales Mix		35%	35%	30%
Selling Price		₹. 30	40	20
Variable Cost		₹. 15	20	12
Total Fixed Costs	₹. 1,80,000			
Total Sales	₹. 6,00,000			

The company has currently under discussion, a proposal to discontinue the manufacture of product Y and replace it with product M, when the following results are anticipated:

		Products		
		S	*T*	*M*
Sales Mix		50%	25%	25%
Selling Price		₹. 30	40	30
Variable Cost		₹. 15	20	15
Total Fixed Costs	₹. 1,80,000			
Total Sales	₹. 6,40,000			

Will you advise the company to changeover to production of M? Given reasons for your answer.

[**Ans.** *Present profit ₹. 1,02,000. Profit on proposed production ₹. 1,40,000, Present BEP ₹. 3,83,000 Proposed BEP ₹. 3,60,000. New proposal may be accepted as its BEP is lower and profit is more*]

Make or Buy Decisions

36. A radio manufacturing company finds that while it costs ₹. 6.25 each to make component No. X 273, the same is available in the market at ₹. 5.75 each, with an assurance of continued supply. The break-up of cost is:

Materials	₹. 2.75 each	Other Variable Costs	₹. 0.50 each
Labour	1.75 each	Depreciation and other Fixed Cost	1.25 each
		Total Cost	6.25 each

(*a*) Show whether you make or buy?

(*b*) What would be your decision if the supplier offered the component at ₹. 4.85 each?

[**Ans.** *(a) Since the market price ₹. 5.75 is more than the variable cost by ₹. 0.75, it is not profitable to procure from outside because in any case the fixed costs will have to be incurred. But if surplus capacity may be put to a more profitable product, then it may be better to buy from outside. (b) If supply from outside is available at ₹. 4.85, it will result in saving of 15 paise in variable cost then it may be profitable to procure from outside and surplus capacity may be used in some other profitable use*]

Standard Costing and Variance Analysis

STANDARD COSTING AND STANDARD COST

Standard costing is a system which seeks to control the cost of each unit or batch through determination beforehand *what should be the cost* and then its comparison with actual cost. The standard cost is what the cost of an operation or service ought to be under given conditions and subject to given conventions of costing.

Standard costing is defined by *CIMA* London as `the preparation and use of standard costs, their comparison with actual cost and the analysis of variances to their causes and points of incidence'.

Wheldon defines standard costing as 'a method of ascertaining the cost whereby statistics are prepared to show (*a*) standard cost (*b*) the actual cost and (*c*) the difference between these costs which is termed the variance'.

According to *WW Bigg* "Standard costing discloses the cost deviations from standard cost and classifies these as to their causes, so that managements is immediately informed of the spheres of operations in which remedial action is necessary".

Thus standard costing is preparation and uses of standard costs. According to *CIMA London*, standard cost is a pre-determined cost which is calculated from the managements standard of efficient operation and the relevant necessary expenditure. According to *Blocker and Weltmer*, Standard cost of a product is 'pre-determined costs, based upon engineering specifications and representing highly efficient production for quantity standards and forecasts of future market trends for the price, standards with fixed amount expressed in rupees for materials, labour and overheads for an estimated quantity of production'. Another author '*Gillespi* define standard cost' as usually employed are pre-determined operation costs computed to reflect specified quantities, prices and level of operations.

Standards may be fixed on an idealistic basis assuming everyone will perform at utmost efficiency. Since this may be rather unrealistic and therefore standards may be fixed on the basis of past average performance. But this will serve no purpose unless past performance was excellent or upto the level. As a general rule standards should be attainable with some effort-these should not be such as to be unattainable or such as to be attained without any effort.

Thus standard costs are fixed for each product or job. Last experience and experiments are the basis to proceed upon. Standard cost are pre-determined for each element namely material, labour and overhead. These represent attainable targets and helps to frame budgets, measure performance and obtain product costs. As the work is done and actual costs are obtained, these are compared with standard cost to find out variances. These variances are analysed further with a view to control the cost and to discover better ways of achieving standards or to revise standards to accomplish the objective.

It may be noted from the aforesaid discussion that the *standard costing involves following process* :

(*i*) Establishment of standard cost

(*ii*) Ascertainment of actual cost

(*iii*) Comparison of the above two and measurement of variances.

(*iv*) Analysis of variances.

(*v*) Reporting to responsibility centres to take appropriate and necessary remedial actions.

Development of Standard Costing

Historical cost or actual cost alone gives no indication as to whether the cost is an economic cost. Basically historical cost is merely a record of what has happened. Actual cost may be inflated due to inefficiences and wastages of materials and time. But to stand in the competition, cost must be rational and economic, or in other words controlled cost. Due to shortcomings of historical costing, standard costing came to be developed as a systematic method of comparing actual cost with the predetermined standard cost. It is a technique of locating inefficiencies and shortcomings at the source by setting up standards as a basis of evaluating actual performance.

Standard Cost and Estimated Cost

In standard cost system the *Standard Costs* recorded in accounts are based upon standard rate that are very carefully developed and set as scientifically as possible while in an *estimated cost* system, the estimated cost are not standards based upon a predetermination of what the production should be but are only expression of opinion based mainly upon past experience. There are some significant *differences* between the two :

(*i*) Estimated cost is basically reasonable approximations of what a cost *will be*, whereas standard cost is a specification of what a cost *should be.*

(*ii*) Usually estimated cost are based on average of past actual costs which have been adjusted for anticipated changes in future, whereas standard costs are fixed after scientific analysis of the relevant factors deciding costs.

(*iii*) Estimated costs are used as a guide line for price fixation and these are not concerned with cost control whereas the cost control is the main purpose of standard costing. Thus standard costs serve as an effective tool for cost control.

(*iv*) The estimated costs are used as figures or statistical data for future costs whereas standard costs are used as a regular system from which variances are calculated (between standard cost and actual cost) and causes of variances are analysed in detail.

Standard Costing and Budgetary Control[1]

Budgeting is for the entire activity. Budgetary control means laying down in monetary and quantitative terms what exactly has to be done and how exactly it has to be done over a coming period and then to ensure that actual results do not diverge from the planned course more than necessary.

Standard costing is a system which seeks to control the cost of each unit or batch through determination before hand of what should be the cost and then its comparison with actual cost. Thus standard cost is pre-determined or budgeted cost of a unit of a product or job.

In both systems there are some common basic principles :

(*i*) In both systems the performance target or standard is predetermined.

(*ii*) The actual performance is ascertained and both have appraisal of the actual performance.

1. Budgetary Control is discussed in detail in a seperate chapter.

(*iii*) In both systems there is comparison of actual performance and costs against budget or standard. There is computation and analysis of variances between the actual cost and budgeted or standard cost.

(*iv*) Both need revision of standard or budget whenever necessary in the light of attainment.

Yet both have some *specific differences as narrated below :*

1. Budgetary control deals with the operation of a department or the business as a whole in the terms of revenue and expenditure. Standard costing is used in manufacturing or producing of a product or in rendering a service. Hence budgetary control is more extensive because it is concerned with entire organisation while standard costing is related to product and its cost and therefore more intensive.

2. Budgetary control seeks to keep in focus the total amount involved and total activity to be carried on. Standard costing provides control to be exercised in the cost of production.

3. Budgets prepared under budgetary control system are for specific periods and are based on totals of amounts while in standard costing, the standard costs are worked out generally per unit of production or service.

4. Basically a budget under budgetary control is a projection of financial accounts while standard cost is merely a projection of cost accounts.

5. Budgetary control is generally applicable to all business establishments, while standard costing can be usefully applied in manufacturing concerns producing standard products and services.

6. Budgetary control is an effective tool in the control of all types of expense while standard costing is a very effective tool in the matter of control of elements of costs like direct costs (direct material, direct labour etc.) and overheads.

7. Budgetory control is an effective tool to plan and exercise control over capital expenditure, finance and cash forecast etc., where standard costing can offer no help.

8. Budgets provide ceiling or limits of expenses beyond which the actual expenditure should not normally go up otherwise the planned profit will be reduced. On the other hand standard costs are usually minimum targets which are to be achieved by the actual performance. Thus the former puts more emphasis on revenue and expenditure not crossing the budget, while the standard costing lays importance to costs approaching the standard cost.

9. Budgets are prepared for all the activities and functions of an establishment such as purchasing, production, research and development, capital and financing, selling and distribution etc., whereas standard costing relates only to production and its manufacturing cost.

10. Variance analysis is more intensive and searching in case of standard costing in comparison to budgetory system. In standard costing, if even standards are achieved, further analysis is carried on to achieve further efficiency. If expenditure exceed the budget it simply shows that situation is unsatisfactory but if actual cost of production exceeds standard cost, the variances are analysed in detail to search out possible improvements.

Considering the basic principles and approach, standard costing and budgetary control are somewhat inter-related, but basically these two are independent. A system of budgetory control may be efficiently and effectively operated even if there is no standard costing system in use in a concern. Standard costing may also be operated without budgetory control, but introduction of standard costing will be more facilitated if budgetary system is in operation. Budgetary control will provide basic frame work required in the fixation of realistic standards. If both techniques are adopted simultaneously, there will be very effective cost control machinery. Thus budgetary control and standard costing are essentially complimentary to each other. Both provide cost control and improve efficiency.

Advantages of Standard Costing

1. *Exact degree of efficiency in various operations can be ascertained through comparison of actual and standard cost.* The variances between acutal and standard costs reveal the weaknesses and inefficiencies. This enables management to remove causes of inefficiency.

2. *Management by exception is possible,* since it is possible to separate the efficient from inefficient operations. Variance analysis helps management to concentrate on those areas where corrective measures are to be taken in time. They do not go to the masses of details. They are attracted towards faults which should not be overlooked.

3. *Efficiency* is consolidated and if necessary, the standards are revised after identifying exact causes of deviations of actual costs from standard costs.

4. T*here can be effective delegation of authority* since the people concerned are told what they have to achieve and by what they will be judged. Control itself becomes effective.

5. *The effect of idle capacity or fluctuations in output or sales is also, highlighted.* Variances due to idle capacity and fluctuations in sales are ascertained in the standard costing system which provide very useful information to the management.

6. *The whole firm is imbued with a dynamic forward looking mentality.* Standard costing provides in attainable costing targets. The entire management is guided by a progressive outlook.

7. *Standard costing is of immense benefit for cost audit* since if variances are satisfactorily explained, the accuracy of costing can be safety assumed.

8. *The cost of accounting itself is reduced* since all rates are fixed and do not have to be calculated again and again. Also, automatically the effect of efficiency or inefficiency is revealed.

9. *Standard costing can be used in formulating production and price policies in advance.* Standard costs are the best basis for establishing policies in as much as such standards which usually eliminate the effect of fluctuating volume and again avoid any cost-increase due to waste or inefficiency.

10. *Standard costs provide basis of incentive schemes to workers and supervisors.* The system determines standard labour costs of a product and with help of these, incentive schemes are formulated.

11. *Standard costing provides faster reporting of operating data.* It is important due to the fact that the value of any information declines as it relates to a period farther and farther in the past.

12. *Standard costing provides a common denominator for comparison* between one period to another.

13. Standard costing, due to the stress of the standard cost and variance analysis, makes the whole organisation cost conscious; foremen and workers are encouraged to realise the importance of efficient operations.

14. *Standard costing provides a stable product cost per unit.* The actual cost of a product may vary from period to period due to many reason. It cannot be used as a basis of fixation of selling price of a product since selling price should not be frequently adjusted to suit the change in the actual cost. It is, therefore desired that selling price be based on a fixed cost structure relating to normal standard of efficiency. The standard costing provide such a desired structure. The actual cost is normally exepcted to be at close as possible to the standard cost. Therefore selling price based on standard cost will be more reliable and representative and will remain fixed for a long time. Moreover, on the assumption that variances could be eliminated, the standard cost provide a sound and consistent basis for price-determination, especially on competitive markets.

15. *Standard costing helps to pinpoint the responsibility* of variation in the cost and thereby it facilitates prompt communication to individuals concerned. The system also identifies the specific reason therefor so that prompt remedial action could be taken.

16. *Standard costing simplifies the cost control procedure* as the figures for control purposes are easily and directly obtained. Thus there is saving in the accounting computation. Moreover the standard cost rates of materials, labour and overheads are available which make accounting calculation more easier.

17. *Standard costing helps in business planning, budgeting and marginal costing.* Standard costs are pre-determined costs and are therefore very useful in planning and budgeting. Standard costing can be very easily and suitably used for budgetory planning. These help in estimating the effect in cost-price-volume relationship.

18. *Standard costs are used for inventory valuation.* Once the standards have been set, it is the standard costs, not the `actual' or `historical' costs, which are entered in the accounts for the purpose of valuing material-stock, work-in-progress and finished goods consequently the cost of goods sold in the trading account because the standard cost and the gross profit is 'at standard'.

Limitations of Standard Costing

Standard costing may not prove a success in certain organisation due to difficulty in fixing up reliable and workable standards. If standards are not correctly established, the cost control and variance analysis will not be effective. Conclusions drawn on such variances will be doubtful and it will be detrimental to the system and it will be worse than having no standard at all.

Thus the basic limitation is that fixation of standard cost is somewhat difficult in practice. Moreover, the stanards fixed may become rigid in course of time or even in short period. Standards cannot be revised at every frequent change in the manufacturing condition.

Some worth mentioning points of limitations of standard costing are narrated below.

1. *It is expensive technique* because it requires technically skilled staff. Small concerns may not find standards easy to establish due to their limited resources. But, it must be noted that once the standard are established, the advantages achieved will be far more than cost involved in the beginning.

2. Business conditions are rapidly changing and therefore standard costs once fixed may not be reliable even for a short period. Standards are to be *revised frequently* so as to make these comparable with actuals. But the revision will create the problem of inventory adjustment.

3. In small concerns, where production is not carefully scheduled, standard costing may not be suitable. The system is also not very useful in industries dealing with non-standardised products. For example, it cannot be successfully used in repairs jobs which are carried on according to customers' requirement. In those contracts and jobs also, standard costing is not suitable, where the work is carried on for more than one accounting year.

Preliminaries to the Establishment of Standard Cost

Standards may be fixed on an idealistic basis assuming everyone will perform at utmost efficiency. This is rather unrealistic. Or, standards may be fixed on the basis of past average performance. This will serve no purpose, unless past performance was excellent. As a general rule, standards should be attainable with some effort—they should not be such as to be unattainable or such as to be attained without any effort. In the former case, they will not interest anybody and, in the letter case, they are meaningless.

Standard Costs are fixed for each product or job in detail. Past experience and experiments is the basis to proceed upon. For instance, in case labour, time and motion study will determine how much time is to be allowed. In the same way it should be found out by experiments how many units of raw materials will suffice to make a unit of finished product. The experiments will also disclose whether any change in operations or in the materials to be ordered is called for. To take a simple example, if stationary is ordered all pre-punched, much clerical labour will be saved at the time of filing.

As far as possible standards should also be fixed for indirect expenses in quantitative terms—petrol consumed per 100 km, and lublicating oil per hour of machine working are instances. Having fixed the standard in terms of quantity, they should be converted into money at the prices expected to prevail.

While setting up a standard costing system in a concern, the following *preliminary steps* should be carefully considered on the basis of technical and operational aspects of the concern, manufacturing process and organisation etc.

(*i*) Cost centres should be set up.

(*ii*) Classification and coding of accounts should be done.

(*iii*) Type of standard cost should be decided.

(*iv*) Setting of standard costs should be carried out.

(*i*) **Establishment of cost centres.** Cost centre has been defined as '*a location, person or item of equipment* (*i.e., department or operator or machine etc.*) *or group of these for which cost may be ascertained and used for the purpose of cost control*'. The concern or the organisation should be divided into cost centres so that responsibilities may be fixed and line of authority may be defined. An officer acting as incharge of a cost centre should be conversant with his responsibility and the cost to be controlled by him.

(*ii*) **Classification of accounts.** Accounts are classified to meet the needed purpose of collection and analysis. The classification may be on the basis of functions, revenue items or assets and liability items etc. Codes and symbols may be assigned to each account to facilitate speedy collection and analysis of accounts. Direct materials, indirect materials, direct wages, indirect wages and other expenses etc. should be given different codes or symbols.

(*iii*) **Types of standard cost**. There are various types of standards in use. Out of these, the suitable standard should be selected for effective cost control. The selected standard should be measuring rod to compare all actual figures. Following are main types of standards.

(*a*) Current standard based upon Ideal standard or Expected standard

(*b*) Basic Standard

(*c*) Normal Standard

(*d*) Historical Standard

(*a*) **Current Standard.** Current standards show what should be the performance under current conditions. Current conditions are conditions during the period the concern will be using standards. These standard are for use over a short period of time and therefore, these are subject to be adjusted according to changes in the conditions. Thus current standards require periodical revision.

Normally current standards are based upon *Ideal standard* or *Expected standard. Ideal standard* is that which can be attained under ideal conditions like most favourable prices of materials and labour, maximum utilisation of resources and capacity and maximum production and sales. Expected standard is that which is expected to be achieved during a future specified budget period. *Expected standards* are set up by taking into consideration the circumstances prevailing within a particular industry. These standards are supposed to be more realistic and helpful to identify inefficiencies at all levels.

(*b*) ***Basic Standards.*** Basic standards are those which remain constant or unaltered over a long period. These are set on long term basis by taking a base year, just like index numbers are calculated. Basic standards are more suitable to small manufactures having a limited range of products and long term production. But these are quite unsuitable for cost control and cost ascertainment.

(*c*) ***Normal standard.*** Normal standards are average standards. These are suitable for a long period covering one trade cycle. These standards do not require revision or adjustment when used in a long term planning and decision making. Normal standards are theoretically sound but cannot be used in forecast with reasonable degree of accuracy.

(*d*) ***Historical Standard.*** Historical standards are the average standards set on the basic of average cost incurred during several past years. These are not of much use in future in setting up standard. These may be of some use to those who are starting the setting up of a standard cost system.

Setting up of Standards

In a big establishment, generally a *standard cost committee* is set-up which is entrusted the work of setting up standard costs. This committee is normally consists of Production Manager, Purchases Manager, Sales Manager and Cost Accountants etc. Out of these executives, the function of the Cost Accountant is of great importance because he alone can provide all necessary data relating to cost and he has to coordinate the activities of the standard cost-cost committee.

Standard cost is divided into three main heads: 1. Direct Materials, 2. Direct Labour. 3. Direct and Indirect Overhead Expenditure. Standards for each of these elements of cost are set.

1. Direct Material Cost Standard. This standard consist of two basic elements. Standard material quantity or usage and standard material rate or price.

(*a*) ***Material Quantity or Usage Standard.*** The standard quantities of direct materials, which are required to manufacture a product, are normally decided or fixed by Production Manager and engineers. For this purpose material specification, standard ratio of their mix (when more than one direct materials are needed), product design and quality should be kept in consideration. Moreover normal wastage or scrap should also be kept in a view while deciding quantity or usage of direct material.

(*b*) ***Material Price Standard.*** For determining material standard consumed, the cost accountant will have to decide standard price in consulation with the Purchase Manager. The standard price may be based on past average prices of raw material or on current prices or on expected future prices. It is desirable that prevailing current prices should be adjusted to suit future price-variations. While determining expected prices following points should be taken into consideration.

(*i*) Prices of opening stock in hand

(*ii*) Prices for which contracts have been undertaken to obtain material

(*iii*) Expected price-changes

(*iv*) Price-rebate and discounts which can be availed.

2. Direct Labour Cost Standards. There are two elements of standard direct labour—(*a*) standard labour time, and (*b*) standard labour rate.

(*a*) ***Standard Labour Time.*** Standard labour time is to be set for each grade of labours and also for each operation involved in the production. It is set with the help and advice of the work-study engineers. With the technique of motion and time study, the standard time for performance of labour is fixed. Due allowance should be made for fatigue, tool setting and other normal delays.

(*b*) ***Standard Labour Rate.*** Rate of wages to be paid to workers should be very properly decided. Wage paid to efficient and skilled workers having technical knowledge may be higher than those for unskilled and non-technical workers. There may be workers under a contract, then rate approved by the contract may usually become the standard.

The standard labour hours multiplied by standard labour rate become standard labour cost.

3. Overhead Costs Standard. Overheads may be classified into Indirect Material, Indirect Labour, Fixed Overheads and other variable overheads. Indirect material cost is determined per machine or production hour. Indirect labour cost is determined per machine or production hour or percentage of direct labour. Fixed expenses are total amount for the period of budgeted production hours. Variable overhead cost is determined on the basis of cost per unit of output or cost per production hour.

The total fixed overhead cost remains fixed and remain unchanged by changes in the volume of production. For this purpose, it is necessary to ascertain budgeted fixed overheads for the period and the budgeted units or standard hours for the period.

Standard cost for variable overheads, once calculated, remains the same per unit or per hour irrespective of volume of production because standard for variable cost tends to vary directly with the volume of production. While calculating its standard unit cost, due consideration should be given to past records and future trend of prices.

It is to be noted that standards fixed should be comprehensive and realistic. They should be related to the specific period and to the stipulated working conditions. The standard need not be `ideal' but should be easily attainable. The attainable standard is a normal standard fixed on the basis of average efficiency of men, machine and material. It provides reasonable allowances for wastage of material and idle time. On the other hand an ideal standard is based on minimum prices of material and maximum efficiency of men and machinery. It may be said that an ideal standard is most favourable but can rarely be achieved in practice.

It is necessary that the standard cost should be related to a common measurement unit. This common unit is normally a time unit and is called standard hour. It is the quantity of production units which can be completed in one hour. After fixing standards hour for each product, the standard for the different items of cost of production are related to standard hour. Thus standard hour may be defined as 'a hypothetical hour representing the amount of work which should be performed on an hour under standard conditions'.

On the basis of standard hour, we can calculate `Efficiency Ratio' and `Activity Ratio' of the organisation.

Efficiency Ratio and Activity Ratios

There are a number of ratios which are used for reprorting to the management related to the effective use of material, labour and other resources of an undertaking. Some of these are given below :

1. Efficiency Ratio. It is the 'standard hours equivalent to the work produced expressed as a percentage of the actual hours spent in producing that work'.

$$\textit{Efficiency Ratio} = \frac{\text{Standard hours for actual production}}{\text{Actual hours for budgeted production}} \times 100$$

2. Activity Ratio. It is the number of standard hours equivalent to the work produced, expressed in a percentage of the budgeted standard hours.

$$\textit{Activity Ratio} = \frac{\text{Standard hours for actual production}}{\text{Standard hours for budgeted production}} \times 100$$

The Activity Ratio measures the effectiveness of sales campaign in achieving the budgeted production while the efficiency ratio measures the production efficiency.

3. Capacity Uses Ratio. It is the relationship between the budgeted number of working hours and the maximum possible number of working hours in a budget period.

$$\textit{Capacity Usage Ratio} = \frac{\text{Budgeted hours}}{\text{Maximum possible hours in budget period}} \times 100$$

4. Capacity Utilisation Ratio. It is the relationship between actual hours in a budget period and the budgeted working hours in the period.

$$\textit{Capacity Utilisation Ratio} = \frac{\text{Actual hours}}{\text{Budgeted hours}} \times 100$$

5. Calender Ratio. It is the relationship between the number of working days in a period and the number of working days in the relative budget period.

$$\textit{Calender Ratio} = \frac{\text{Available working days}}{\text{Budgeted working days}} \times 100$$

Illustration 1: Calculate different ratios used in standard costing regarding efficiency, activity and capacity from the following figures for a four-week period. In this period there was a special one-day holiday due to national event

Standard working : 8 hours per day, 5 days per week
Maximum Capacity : 50 employees
Actual Working : 40 employees
Actual hour expected to be worked per 4 weeks: 6400 hours
Standard hours expected to be earned per 4 weeks : 8000 hours
Actual hours worked in the four week period: 6000 hours
Standard hours earned in the four-week period: 7000 hours

Solution:

1. Efficiency Ratio $= \dfrac{\text{Standard hours for actual production}}{\text{Actual hours for budgeted production}} \times 100$

$= \dfrac{7000 \times 100}{6000} = 117\%$

2. Activity Ratio $= \dfrac{\text{Standard hours for actual production}}{\text{Standard hours for budgeted production}} \times 100$

$= \dfrac{7000 \times 100}{6400} = 109\%$

3. Capacity Usage Ratio $= \dfrac{\text{Budget hours}}{\text{Maximum possible hours in budgeted period}} \times 100$

$= \dfrac{6400 \times 100}{8000} = 80\%$

4. Capacity Utilisation Ratio $= \dfrac{\text{Actual hours}}{\text{Budgeted hours}} \times 100$

$= \dfrac{6000}{6400} \times 100 = 94\%$

5. Calender Ratio $= \dfrac{\text{Available working hours}}{\text{Budgeted working hours}} \times 100$

$= \dfrac{[(5 \times 4) - 1]}{5 \times 4} \times 100 = \dfrac{19 \times 100}{20} = 95\%$

ANALYSIS OF VARIANCES

'Cost variance is the difference between a standard cost and the comparable actual cost incurred during a given period'.

— *CIMA London*

'Variance analysis is the analysis of the cost variances into its component parts and the explanation of the variances'.

— *CIMA London*

The cost variances are normally calculated in respect of three main elements of cost *viz.* material, labour and overhead. These are based on comparison of actuals and standard cost.

Care to be taken while comparing actuals and standard costs

Standard should be frequently reviewed and changed because working and market conditions are always changing. Standard costs which are carefully determined and regularly reviewed will give a valid basis for comparison with actual performance but some points must be kept in mind while making a judgement. These are :

(*a*) Conditions might have changed, thus rendering the standard costs unrealistic—for instance the quality of available materials may be low.

(*b*) Standards fixed upon on too idealistic a basis will remain unattainable.

(*c*) The service rendered by service departments may not be up to the mark so that, for example, time is lost due to a machine working slow.

(*d*) In certain activities, fixation of standard is either not possible or not desirable. Goods requiring artistic work of high qualtity cannot be and should not be subject to quantitative standards. In certain cases work cannot be properly measured. Standards in these cases will be useless.

Variances

The deviations of the actual cost from the standard cost is known as "variance". There are a number of causes which lead to a differnece between the actual and standard costs. All the causes are weighed and the amount connected with each is ascertained and described in a way to indicate the cause leading to the variance. For instance, the variance caused by a change in prices of materials will be described as "Materials Price Variance". A variance which increases profit is called favourable or just "Cr" or (F); the variance which reduces profit is unfavourable and is described as "Dr." or (A). *i.e.*, adverse. Variance are of various kinds. Chiefly, however, they may be grouped under two broad categories. These are :

(*i*) Variance indicating efficiency or inefficiency, for example, saving in materials consumed or wastage of time, and

(*ii*) Variances that result from a change in prices, say, wage rates or prices at which materials have been purchased.

Broadly, vaiances which show efficiency or inefficiency will be calculated as :

Standard rate × Difference between standard and actual quantities (*e.g.*, materials consumed or hours spent).

Variances which show up the effect of price changes are calculated as.

Actual quantity × Difference between standard price and actual price (*e.g.*, wage rates).

Variance analysis is a part of process of control and involves calculation of variances and interpretation of results so as to localise the various factors that are responsible for the variance. Variances analysis leads to ascertain the magnitude of each of the variances and causes thereof so that corrective measures may be taken.

The variances may be *broadly classified under heads* displayed in following chart.

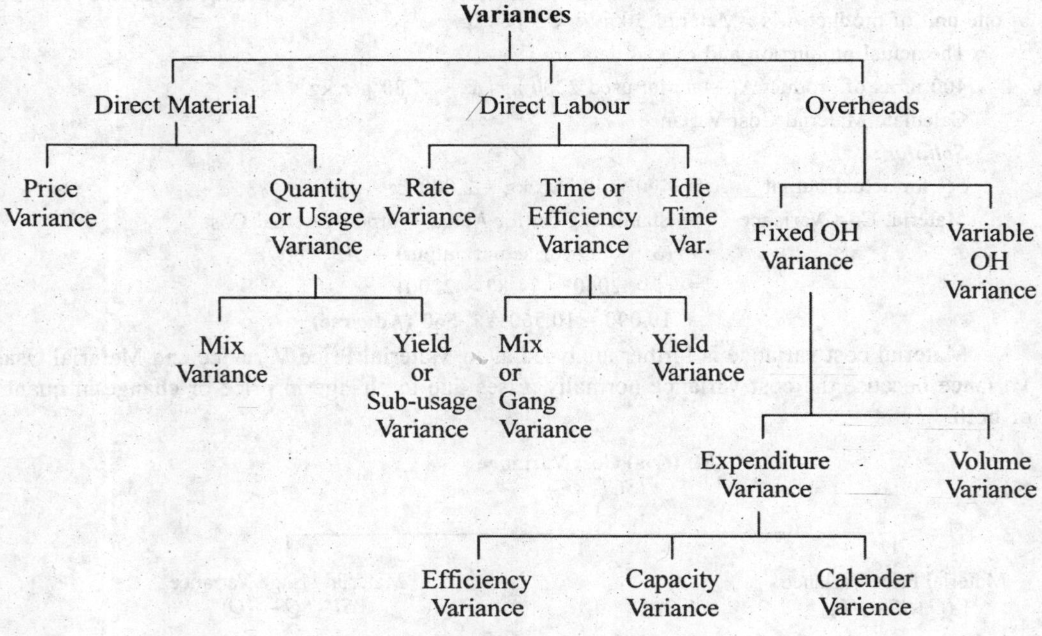

DIRECT MATERIAL VARIANCES

Direct Materials Cost Variance (DMCV)

It is the difference between the standard cost of standard quantity of material for actual output and acutal cost of material consumed. *CIMA* London has defined *DMCV* as 'difference between standard cost of material specified and the actual cost of material used'.

Standard Cost of Direct Material = Standard Price Per Unit × Standard Quantity for Actual Output

Actual Cost of Diret Material = Actual Price per Unit × Actual Quantity Consumed

Standard Quantity means the Quantity of material which ought to have been consumed according to standard usage rate for producing the actual output. Thus

Direct Material Cost Variance (DMCV) = Standard cost for actual output – Actual cost

or (Standard Price × Standard Quantity for actual output) – (Actual Price × Actual Quantity)

or $(SP \times SQ) - (AP \times AQ)$ *i.e.*, $S\dot{C} - AC$

When the actual cost is more than standard cost, there will be adverse or unfavourable variance and *vice-versa.*

Illustration 2: Product A requires 10 kgs of material at the rate of ₹ 4 per kg. The actual consumption of material for the manufacturing of Product A came to 12 kgs of material at the rate of ₹. 4.50 per kg. Calculate material cost variance.

Solution:

Material Cost Variance = Standard Cost for Actual Output – Actual Cost

= $(SP \times SQ) - (AP \times AQ)$

= (4 × 10) – (4.50 × 12)

= 40 – 54 = **₹. 14** (Unfavourable or Adverse)

Illustration 3: The standard material and standard cost per kg of material required for the production of one unit of product A is : Meterial 5 kg @ ₹ 5 per kg.

The actual production and related data are :

400 units of product A, Material used 2200 kgs @ ₹. 4.80 per kg.

Calculate Material Cost Variance.

Solution:

SQ for actual output	=	400 units × 5 kg = 2,000 kg
Material Cost Variance	=	Standard Cost for Actual Output – Actual Cost.
	=	(*SP* × *SQ* for actual output) – (*AP* × *AQ*)
	=	(5 × 2000) – (4.80 × 2200)
	=	10,000 – 10,560 = **₹ 560 (Adverse)**

Material cost variance is further analysed as to Material Price Variance and Material Usage Variance because the cost variance normally arises due to change in price or change in quantity or both.

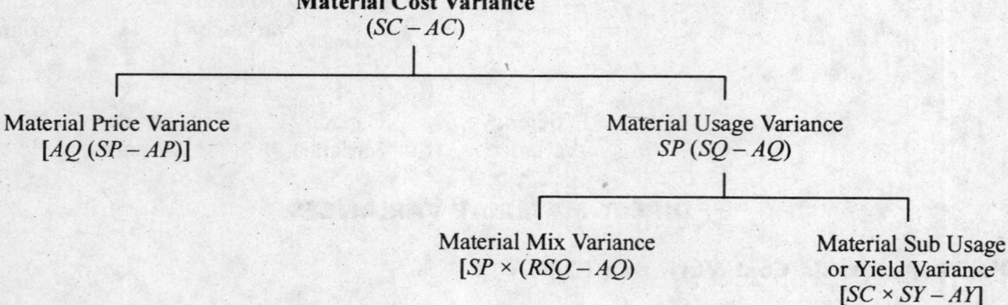

(a) Direct Material Price Variance

It is that `portion of material cost variance which is due to the difference between the standard price specified and actual price paid[1].

Direct Material Price Variance (*DMPV*) = Actual Quantity × (Standard Price – Actual Price)

***i.e., AQ* × (*SP* – *AP*)**

If actual price is more than standard price, there will be adverse or unfavourable variance and when actual price is less than standard price, the variance will be favourable.

Illustration 4: Calculate Material Price Variance from the data given in the Illustration No. 3.

Solution: Material Price Variance = *AQ* (*SP* – *AP*)

= 2200 (5 – 4.80) = 440 (Favourable)

(*b*) Direct Material Usage or Quantity Variance

It indicates the deviation caused from the standard due to difference in quantities used. It is that 'portion of material cost variance which is due to the difference between the standard quantity specified and the actual quantity used[1]'. It is calculated by multiplying the standard price with the difference between the actual and standard quantities.

Direct Material Usage Variance (*DMUV*) = Standard Price × (Standard Quantity for actual output × Actual Quantity)

= *SP* × (*SQ* for Actual output – *AQ*)

1. *CIMA* London.

It is to be noted that if standard output differ from actual output, the standard quantity in the above calculation will be standard quantity for actual output as it is used in the Direct Material cost variance.

If Actual Quantity is less than Standard Quantity there will be favourable variance and vice versa.

Check. These two variances when added will be equal to Material Cost Variance

Direct Material Price Variance + Direct Material Usage Variance = Direct Material Cost Variance

Illustration 5: The standard cost of material for manufacturing a unit of a particular product PEE is estimated as follows : 16 kg of raw material @ ₹. 1 per kg.

On completion of the unit, it was found that 20 kg, of raw material costing ₹. 1.50 per kg has been consumed. Compute material variances.

Solution:

Direct Material Price Variance (*DMPV*) = Actual Qty. × (Std. rate – Actual rate)
= 20 × (1 – 1.50) = ₹. 10 (Adverse)

Direct Material Usage Variance (*DMUV*) = Std. rate × (Std. qty. for actual output – Actual qty.)
= 1 × (16 – 20) = ₹ 4 (Adverse)

Direct Material Cost Variance (*DMCV*) = Std. cost for Actual output – Actual cost
= (16 × 1) – (20 × 1.50)
= 16 × 30 = ₹. 14 (Adverse)

Thus, *DMCV* = *DMPV* + *DMUV*
= 10 (A) + 4 (A) = **14 (Adverse)**

Illustration 6: From the following particulars compute (a) Material cost variance, (*b*) Material price variance, and (*c*) Material usage variance:

Quantity of materials purchased	3,000 units
Value of materials purchased	₹. 9,000
Standard quantity of materials required per tonne of output	30 units
Standard rate of material	₹. 2.50 per unit
Opening stock of materials	Nil
Closing stock of materials	500 units
Output during the period	80 tonnes

[*B. Com., Hons., Delhi*]

Solution :

Materials consumed = 3,000 – 500 = 2,500 units

Actual rate of material = ₹. 9,000/3,000 = ₹. 3 per unit

Standard quantity for actual output = 30 × 80 = 2,400 units

Material Cost Variance (*MCV*) = Standard cost – Actual cost

$$= \left(\begin{matrix}\text{Standard} \\ \text{price}\end{matrix} \times \begin{matrix}\text{Standard} \\ \text{Quantity}\end{matrix}\right) - \left(\begin{matrix}\text{Actual} \\ \text{price}\end{matrix} \times \begin{matrix}\text{Acutal} \\ \text{Quantity}\end{matrix}\right)$$

= (₹. 2.50 × 2,400) – (₹. 3 × 2,500) = ₹. 1,500 (A) (Adverse)

Material Price Variance (*MPV*) = Acutal quanity × (Standard price – Actual price)
2,500 × (₹. 2.50 – ₹. 3) = ₹. 1,250 (Adverse)

Material Usage Variance (*MUV*) = Standard price × (Standard quanity – Actual quantity
= ₹. 2.50 × (2,400 – 2,500) = **₹. 250 (Adverse)**

Thus, $MCV = MPV + MUV$

1500 (A) = 1250 (A) + 250 (A)

Illustration 7: Standard set for material consumption was 100 kg @ ₹. 2.25 per kg

In a cost period : Opening stock was 100 kg @ 2.25 per kg

Purchases made 500 kg @ ₹ 2.15 per kg

Consumption 110 kg

Calculate :

(*a*) Usage variance:

(*b*) Price variance : (*i*) When variance is calculated at point of purchase; (*ii*) when variance is calculated at point of issue on FIFO basis; (*iii*) when variance is calculated at point of issue on LIFO basis;

(*c*) What is the effect on closing stock valuation when materials are charged out to cost on basis (*ii*) and (*iii*) above?

Solution:

(*a*) (*i*) Usage variance = Std. price × (Std. qty. – Actual qty.)

= 2.25 × (100 – 110) = ₹. 22.50 (A)

(*b*) Price variance = Actual qty. × (Std. price – Actual price)

(*i*) Price variance at the point of purchase

= 500 × (2.25 – 2.15) = ₹. 50 (F)

(*ii*) Price variance at the point of issue under FIFO Method

= 100 × (2.25 – 2.25) + 10 × (2.25 – 2.15)

= 0 + 10 × (.10) = ₹. 1 (F)

(*iii*) Price variance at the point of issue under LIFO Method

= 110 × (2.25 – 2.15) = ₹. 11 (F)

(*c*) Effect on closing stock valuation when materials are charged on FIFO bases: Closing stock: 490 units @ 2.15 = ₹. 1053.50 while if valued at standard cost: 490 @ 2.25 ₹. = 1102.50. Thus it will be valued ₹ 49 less than the standard price.

If LIFO is used for issues, the closing stock will 100 units @ 2.25 per unit + 390 @ 2.15 per unit. Thus it will be valued at ₹ 39 less than the standard price.

(x) Material Mix Variance

When more than one type of materials are used for production, the usage variance may be subdivided into (*x*) Material Mix Variance and (*y*) Material Yield Variance or Material Revised Usage Variance (Sub Usage Variance).

Material Mix Variable is defined as that portion of the Direct Material Usage Variance which is due to difference betwen the standard and actual composition of a mixture of material.[1]

One of the reasons of material usage variance is the change in the composition of the material mixture when more than one type of materials are used. Normally such a situation arises in the chemical, textile, rubber and similar other industries where different raw materials are used in a definite proportion. When there is change in the standard proportion or mix, this variance is separately analysed. It may be due to shortage of a particular material. If there is increase in the proportion of a costly material in the mix, it will result in an unfavourable variance and vice versa.

Direct Material Mix Variance (*DMMV*) = Standard Price (Revised Standard Quantity – Actual Quantity)

= *SP* (*RSQ* – *AQ*)

1. *CIMA* London.

It may be noted that this variance is calculated separately for each material used in a mix. Moreover Revised Standard Quantity will be calculated where there is *variation in the total of composition of standard material quantity* and the composition of actual material quantity, in other words when there is variation in total of input quantities in the standard mix and actual mix.

Revised Standard Quantity or *RSQ*

$$= \frac{\textbf{Total Weight or Quantity of Actual Mix}}{\textbf{Total Weight or Quantity of Standard Mix}} \times \textbf{Standard Quantity of the material.}$$

Illustration 8: Calculate the Materials Mix Variance from the following :

Material	*Standard*	*Actual*
A	90 Units at ₹. 12	100 Units at ₹ 12
B	60 Units at ₹ 15	50 Units at ₹ 16
	150	150

Solution:

Materials	*Standard*			*Actual*		
	Quantity (kg)	*Rate per kg (₹)*	*Amount (₹)*	*Quantity (kg)*	*Rate per kg (₹)*	*Amount (₹)*
A	90	12	1,080	100	12	1,200
B	60	15	900	50	16	800
	150		1,980	150		2,000

$$\text{Direct Material Mix Variance} = \text{Standard Price or Rate} \begin{pmatrix}\text{Revised Std.}\\\text{Quantity}\end{pmatrix} - \begin{pmatrix}\text{Actual}\\\text{Quantity}\end{pmatrix}$$

But in this problem total standard mix and actual mix are same *i.e.* 150 units, hence Revised Standard Quantity and Standard Quantity will be same.

$$A = ₹\ 12 \times (90 - 100)$$
$$= ₹\ 12 \times 10 = ₹.\ 120 \text{ (Adverse)}$$
$$B = ₹\ 15 \times (60 - 50)$$
$$= ₹\ 15 \times 10 = ₹\ 150 \text{ (Favourable)}$$
$$\text{Total} = ₹\ 30 \text{ (Favourable)}$$

Illustration 9: The standard material cost to produce a tonne of chemical *X* is:

300 kg of material *A* @ ₹ 10 per kg

400 kg of material *B* @ ₹ 5 per kg

500 kg of material *C* @ ₹ 6 per kg.

During a period, 100 tonnes of mixture X were produced from the usage of:

35 tonnes of material *A* at a cost of ₹ 9,000 per tonne

42 tonnes of material *B* at a cost of ₹ 6,000 per tonne

53 tonnes of material *C* at a cost of ₹ 7,000 per tonne.

Calculate material price, usage and mix variances. **[*B. Com.,* (*Hons.*), *Delhi*]**

Solution:

Materials	*Standard*			*Actual*		
	Quantity	*Rate*	*Amount (₹)*	*Quantity*	*Rate*	*Amount (₹)*
A	30,000	10	3,00,000	35,000	9	3,15,000
B	40,000	5	2,00,000	42,000	6	2,52,000
C	50,000	6	3,00,000	53,000	7	3,71,000
	1,20,000		8,00,000	1,30,000		9,38,000

Direct Material Cost Variance (*DMCV*) = Std. cost for actual output – Actual cost
= ₹ 8,00,000 – ₹ 9,38,000
= ₹ 1,38,000 (Adverse)

Direct Material Price Variance (*DMPV*) = Actual quantity × (Std. Rate – Actual Rate)

A	= 35,000 × (10 – 9) =	₹. 35,000 (F)
B	= 42,000 × (5 – 6) =	42,000 (A)
C	= 53,000 × (6 – 7) =	53,000 (A)
	Total	₹. 60,000 (A)

Direct Material Usage Variance (*DMUV*) =Std. Rate × (Std. Qty. for actual output – Actual Qty.)

A	= 10 × (30,000 – 35,000) =	₹. 50,000 (A)
B	= 5 ×(40,000 – 42,000) =	₹. 10,000 (A)
C	= 6 × (50,000 – 53,000) =	₹. 18,000 (A)
	Total	₹. 78,000 (A)

Direct Material Mix Variance (*DMMV*) = Std. Rate × (Revised Std. Qty. – Acutal Qty.)

A = ₹. 10 × (32,500 – 35,000)
= 10 × 2,500 = ₹. 25,000 (A)

B $= 5 \times \left(\frac{1,30,000}{3} - 42,000\right)$

$= 5 \times \frac{4,000}{3}$ = ₹. 6,667 (F)

C $= 6 \times \left(\frac{1,62,500}{3} - 53,000\right)$

$= 6 \times \frac{3,500}{3}$ = ₹. 7,000 (F)

Total 11,333 (A)

Working:

1. Revised Standard Quantity $= \frac{\text{Total actual weight of mix.}}{\text{Total standard weight of mix}} \times \text{Standard Quantity}$

A $= \frac{1,30,000}{1,20,000} \times 30,000 = 32,500 \text{ kg}$

B $= \frac{1,30,000}{1,20,000} \times 40,000 = \frac{1,30,000}{3} \text{ kg.}$

C $= \frac{1,30,000}{1,20,000} \times 50,000 = \frac{1,62,500}{3} \text{ kg.}$

(y) Direct Material Revised Usage Variance (DMRUV) or Sub Usage Variance (DMSUV)

If there is difference between standard quantity for actual output (as used in Usage Variance) and Revised Standard Quantity (as used in Mix Variance), their variance will be known as Revised Usage Variance. This variance arises when standard output and actual output shows no difference. (where there is difference between standard output and actual output, then there will be material yield variance and there will be no need of calculating Revised Usage Variance. Yield Variance has been explained below).

It is clear that if there is no difference between standard quantity (as used in Usage Variance) and Revised Standard Quantity (as used in Mix. Variance) there will be no Revised Usage Variance. Then Usage Variance will be equal to Mix Variance.

Revised Usage Variance = Standard Price × (Standard Quantity for Actual Output – Revised Standard Quantity)

or

$$= SP \times (SQ - RSQ)$$

Revised Usage Variance will be calculated for each item of material used in the mix separately.

Thus total Mix variance and total Revised Usage Variance will be equal to the Total Usage Variance. (DMMV + DMRUV = DMUV)

Illustration 10: From the following information compute material (*a*) Mix variance (*b*) Price Variance (*c*) Usage Variance (*d*) Sub-usage Variance, and (*e*) Cost Variance.

Materials	*Standard*			*Actual*		
	Quantity	*Rate*	*Amount (₹.)*	*Quantity*	*Rate*	*Amount (₹.)*
A	10	2	20	5	3	15
B	20	3	60	10	6	60
C	20	6	120	15	5	75
Total	50	4	200	30	5	150

Solution:

(1) Material Cost Variance = Standard Cost – Actual Cost
= 200 – 150 = ₹. 50 (Favourable)

(2) Material Price Variance = Actual Quantity × (Standard Price – Actual Price)
or $AQ \times (SP \times AP)$ ₹.

Material			
Material *A*	5 × (2 – 3)	5	(Adverse)
B	10 × (3 – 6)	30	(Adverse)
C	15 × (6 – 5)	15	(Favourable)
		20	(Adverse)

(3) Material Usage Variance = St. Price × (St. Quantity for Actual Output – Actual Quantity)

i.e., $SP \times (SQ - AQ)$ ₹.

Material			
Material *A*	2 × (10 – 5)	=	10 (Farourable)
B	3 × (20 – 10)	=	30 (Favourable)
C	6 × (20 – 15)	=	30 (Favourable)
	Total		70 (Favourable)

(4) *Material Mix Variance*

For the calculation of Material Mix Variance, Revised Standard Quantity (*RSQ*) will have to be calculated

$$RSQ = \frac{\text{Actual Mix} \times \text{Standard Quantity}}{\text{Standard Mix}}$$

$$\text{Material } A = \frac{30}{50} \times 10 = 6 \text{ kg}$$

$$\text{Material } B = \frac{30}{50} \times 20 = 12 \text{ kg}$$

$$\text{Material } C = \frac{30}{50} \times 20 = 12 \text{ kg}$$

Mix Variance = St. Price × (*RSQ* – *AQ*)

Material *A*	2 × (6 – 5)	= ₹. 2 (Favourable)
Material *B*	3 × (12 – 10)	6 (Favourable)
Material *C*	6 × (12 – 15)	18 (Adverse)
	Total	10 (Adverse)

(5) Material Subusage Variance = St. Price (Standard Quantity – Revised Standard Quantity) or *SP* × (SQ – *RSQ*)

			₹.
Material	*A*	2 × (10 – 6)	8 (Favourable)
	B	3 × (20 – 12)	24 (Favourable)
	C	6 × (20 – 12)	48 (Favourable)
		Total	80 (Favourable)

Verification

Material Usage Variance = Mix Variance + Sub-usage Variance
70 (F) = 10 (A) + 80 (F)

Material Cost Variance = Material Price Variable + Material Usage Variance
50 (F) = 20 (A) + 70 (F)

(y) Direct Material Yield Variance

As said earlier there may be either Revised Usage Variance (when there is no change in standard and actual output) or yield variance (when there is difference in standard output and actual output).

Direct Material yield variance is defined as 'that portion of material Usage Variance which is due to difference between the standard yield (output) specified and actual yield (output) obtained'[1]. It may be noted that yield variance is based on output while all other variances are based on input.

Direct Material Yield Variance (*DMYV*) = Standard Cost Per Unit × (Standard yield or output for actual input – Actual yield or output)

= *SC* × (*SY* – *AY*)

Standard yield is the production which should result in by the input of actual quantity of materials.

$$\text{Standard Yield (SY)} = \frac{\text{Standard Production} \times \text{Total Actual Quantity of Input}}{\text{Total Standard Quantity of Input}}$$

$$\text{Standard Cost per Unit} = \frac{\text{Total cost of standard mix of material}}{\text{Net standard output quanity}}$$

If standard yield, or production is more than actual yield or production the variance will be unfavourable or adverse and vice-versa. (Thus in this variance negative figure of variance will be favourable).

It may be noted that *where several types of raw material are used Revised Usage Variance and Yield Variance imply the same thing.* Revised usage variance is based on input where there is no difference in standard output and actual output, while yield variance is based on output where

1. *CIMA* London

there is difference between standard output for actual input and actual output. It may be again repeated that total of Mix Variance and Revised Usage Variance or Yield Variance (as the case may be) will be equal to Material Usage Variance.

Illustration 11: The standard cost of a certain chemical mixture is:

35% Material A at ₹ 25 per kg

65% Material B at ₹ 36 per kg

A standard loss of 5% is expected in production.

During a period there is used:

125 kg of Material A at ₹ 27 per kg and

275 kg of Material B at ₹ 34 per kg.

The actual output was 365 kgs.

Calculate:

(*a*) Material Cost Variance

(*b*) Material Price Variance

(*c*) Material Mix Variance

(*d*) Material Yield Variance

[*B. Com. Hons. Delhi*]

Solution:

Materials	*Standard*			*Actual*		
	Kg.	*Rate*	*Amt*	*Kg.*	*Rate*	*Amt.*
A	140	25	3,500	125	27	3,375
B	260	36	9,360	275	34	9,350
	400		12,860	400		12,725
Standard Loss 5%	20					
Standard Output	380					

Standard output : 400 – 20 = 380 kg.

Actual output (given) = 365 kg.

Standard Cost per kg = Total Standard Cost/Standard Output = 12,860/380 = ₹. 33.84

Calculation of Variances :

(*a*) *DMCV* = Standard Cost for Actual Output – Actual Cost

= 365 × 33.84 – 12,725

= 12,352 – 12,725 = ₹ 373 (Adverse)

(*b*) *DMPV* = Actual Quantity × (Standard Rate – Actual Rate)

A = 125 × (25 – 27) = 250 (A)

B = 275 × (36 – 34) = 550 (F)

₹. 300 (Favourable)

(*c*) *DMMV* = Standard Rate × (Revised Standard Quantity – Actual Quantity)

[Note. Since Standard Mix and Actual Mix are the same, the Revised Standard Quantity and Standard quantity will also be the same.]

Material *A* = 25 × (140 – 125) = 375 (F)

Material *B* = 36 × (260 – 275) = 540 (A)

165 (Adverse)

(*d*) *DMYV* = Standard Cost per kg. × (Standard Output of Actual Mix – Actual Output)

= 33.84 × (380 – 365) = ₹ 508 (Adverse)

Verification:

DMCV = *DMPV* + *DMMV* + *DMYV*

₹. 373 (A) = 300 (F) + 165 (A) + 508 (A)

Illustration 12: The standard material cost for 100 kg. of Chemical D is made up of:

Chemical A – 30 kgs @ ₹. 4.00 per kg

Chemical B – 40 kgs @ ₹ 5.00 per kg

Chemical C – 80 kgs @ ₹. 6.00 per kg

In a batch, 500 kg of Chemical D were produced from a mix of :

Chemical A – 140 kgs at a cost of ₹ 588

Chemical B – 220 kgs at a cost of ₹ 1,056

Chemical C – 440 kgs at a cost of ₹ 2,860

How do the yield, mix and the price factors contribute to the variance in the actual cost per 100 kgs. of chemical D over the standard cost?

Solution:

Chemicals	*Standard for 100 kg of Chemical D*			*Actual for 100 kg of Chemical D*		
	Quantity Kgs.	*Rate Per kg.*	*Amount (₹)*	*Quantity Kg.*	*Rate Per kg.*	*Amount (₹)*
A	30	4	120	28	4.2	117.6
B	40	5	200	44	4.8	211.2
C	80	6	480	88	6.5	572.0
	150		800	160		900.8
Output	100			100		

Actual quantity has been taken for 100 kg of Chemical *D* as required.

Material price variance = Actual quantity × (Standard price – Actual price)

Chemical *A* = 28 × (4 – 4.20) = ₹.5.60 (A)

B = 44 × (5 – 4.80) = 8.80 (F)

C = 88 × (6 – 6.50) = 44.00 (A)

40.80 (A)

Material usage variance = Standard price × (Standard quantity – Actual quantity)

Chemical *A* = ₹. 4 × (30 – 28) = ₹. 8 (F)

Chemical *B* = 5 × (40 – 44) = 20 (A)

Chemical *C* = 6 × (80 – 88) = 48 (A)

60 (A)

$$\text{Revised standard qty.} = \frac{\text{Total weight of acutal mix}}{\text{Total weight of std. mix}} \times \text{Standard qty.}$$

$$\text{Chemical } A = \frac{160}{150} \times 30 = 32 \text{ kg}$$

$$\text{Chemical } B = \frac{160}{150} \times 40 = \frac{640}{15} \text{ or } 42\frac{2}{3}$$

$$\text{Chemical } C = \frac{160}{150} \times 80 = \frac{1280}{15} \text{kg. or } 85\frac{1}{3}$$

Material Mix Variance: Standard Rate × (*RSQ* – *AQ*)

Chemical *A* = ₹. 4 × (32 – 28) = ₹. 16 (F)

Chemical *B* = $5 \times \left(42\frac{2}{3} - 44\right)$ = 6.67 (A)

Chemical C = $6 \times \left(85\frac{1}{3} - 88\right)$ = 16 (A)

Total Mix Variance 6.67 (A)

Yield Variance = Standard cost per unit × (Standard output for actual mix – Actual output)

Standard cost per kg of chemical *D*:

= Standard Cost/Standard Output

= ₹. 800/100 = ₹. 8

Standard output for actual mix = $\frac{100}{150} \times 160 = 106\frac{2}{3}$ kg.

Yield variance = ₹. 8 $\left(106\frac{2}{3} - 100\right)$ = ₹. 53.33 (A)

Illustration 14: S.V. Ltd. manufactures *BXE* by mixing three raw materials. For every batch of 100 kgs of *BXE,* 125 kgs of raw materials are used. In Februrary, 60 batches were prepared to produce an output of 5,600 kg of BXE. The standard and actual particulars for February are as under:

Raw Material	*Standard*		*Actual*		
	Mix %	*Price Per kg.* ₹.	*Mix %*	*Price per kg* ₹.	*Quantity of Raw Material Purchased* kg
A	50	20	60	21	5,000
B	30	10	20	8	2,000
C	20	5	20	6	1,200

Calcualte:

(*i*) Material Cost Variance (*ii*) Material Price Variance

(*iii*) Material Mix Variance (*iv*) Material Yield Variance.

[*B. Com. Hons. Delhi*]

Solution:

Raw Material	*Standard*			*Actual*		
	Kg.	*Rate*	*Amount* (₹)	*Kg.*	*Rate*	*Amount* (₹.)
A	3,750	20	75,000	4,500	21	94,500
B	2,250	10	22,500	1,500	8	12,000
C	1,500	5	7,500	1,500	6	9,000
	7,500		1,05,000	7,500		1,15,500
Output	6,000			5,600		

Direct Material Cost Variance (*DMCV*)

= Standard Cost for Actual Output – Actual Cost

$= \frac{1,05,000}{6,000} \times 5,600 - 1,15,500$

= 98,000 – 1,15,500 = 17,500 (A)

Direct Material Price Variance (*DMPC*)

= Actual qty. × (*SR* – *AR*)

A = 4,500 × (20 – 21) = 4,500 (A)

B = 1,500 × (10 – 8) = 3,000 (F)

C = 1,500 × (5 – 6) = 1,500 (A)

3,000 (A)

Direct Material Usage Variance (*DMUV*)

= Standard Rate × (Std. qty. for actual output – Actual qty.)

$$A = 20 \times \left(\frac{3,750}{6,000} \times 5,600 - 4,500\right)$$

= 20 × (3,500 – 4,500) = 20,000 (A)

$$B = 10 \times \left(\frac{2,250}{6,000} \times 5,600 - 1,500\right)$$

= 10 × (2,100 – 1,500) = 6,000 (F)

$$C = 5 \times \left(\frac{1,500}{6,000} \times 5,600 - 1,500\right)$$

= 5 × (1,400 – 1,500) = 500 (A)

₹. 14,500 (A)

Direct Material Mix Variance (*DMMV*) = Standard Rate × (Revised Std. Qty. – Actual Qty.)

A = 20 × (3,750 – 4,500) = 15,000 (A)

B = 10 × (2,250 – 1,500) = 7,500 (F)

C = 5 × (1,500 – 1,500) = —

7,500 (A)

[**Note.** Since the Standard Mix and Actual Mix are the same, the Standard Quantity and Revised Standard Quantity will also be the same.]

Direct Material Yield Variance (*DMYV*)

= Std. cost per unit × (Std. output for actual mix – Actual output)

$$= \frac{1,05,000}{6,000} (6,000 - 5,600) = 17.5 \times 400 = ₹.\ 7,000\ (A)$$

The Direct Material Yield Variance is equal to Direct Material Revised Usage Variance calculated as follows :

DMRUV = *SR* × (Standard Qty. for actual output – Revised Std. Qty.)

A = 20 × (3,500 – 3,750) = 5,000 (A)

B = 10 × (2,100 – 2,250) = 1,500 (A)

C = 5 × (1,400 – 1,500) = 500 (A)

₹ 7,000 (A)

Illustration 14A: Common brass is an alloy consisting of 70% copper and 30% zinc. In melting and processing it is expected that a 4% loss of metal will occur. Standard prices are ₹ 40 per kg for copper and ₹ 15 per kg for zinc. Using suitable figures for the purpose of illustration, show clearly how you would record (*a*) Material Price Variance, (*b*) Material Usage Variance, (*c*) Material Mix Variance and (*d*) Material Yield Variance. **[*Delhi, B.Com. (H)*]**

Solution: It is *assumed* that following figures will be for standard and actual material based on the information given:

Materials	*Standard*		*Actual*	
	Quantity kg	*Rate* ₹	*Quantity* kg	*Rate* ₹
Copper	700	40.00	600	50.00
Zinc	300	15.00	600	10.00
	1000		1200	
Less Standard Loss 4%	40	*Less* loss	144	
Output	960		1056	

Material Cost Variance (*MCV*) = Standard Cost for actual Output – Actual Cost
= (Standard Rate × Standard Quantity of actual output) – (Actual Rate × Actual Quantity)

[Here, Standard Quantity for Actual Output = Actual output × Standard Quanity/ Standard Output

For Copper = 1056 × 700/960 = 770 kg

For Zinc = 1056 × 300/960 = 330 kg]

MCV For Copper = (40 × 770) – (50 × 600) = 30,800 – 30,000 = 800 (F)

MCV For Zinc = (15 × 330) – (10 × 600) = 4950 – 6000 = 1,050 (A)

Total 250 (A)

Material Price Variance (*MPV*) = Actual Quantity × (Standard Rate – Actual Rate)

MPV for Copper = 600 × (40 – 50) = 6000 (A)

MPV for Zinc = 600 × (15 – 10) = 3000 (F)

Total 3000 (A)

Material Usage Variance (*MUV*) = Standard Rate × (Standard Quantity for Actual Output – Actual Quantity).

MUV for Copper = 40 × (770 – 600) = 6800 (F)

MUV for Zinc = 15 × (330 – 600) = 4050 (A)

Total 2750 (F)

Verification :

Material Cost Variance = Material Price Variance + Material Usage Variance
= 3000 (A) + 2750 (F) =250 (A)

Material Mix Variance (*MMV*)= Standard Rate per unit × (Revised Standard Quantity – Actual Quantity)

[Here, Revised Standard Quantity = $\frac{\text{Total Weight of Actual Mix} \times \text{Standard Quantity}}{\text{Total Weight of Std. Mix.}}$

RSQ for Copper = 1200 × 700/1000 = 840 kg

RSQ for Zinc = 1200 × 300/1000 = 360 kg]

MMV for Copper = 40 × (840 – 600) = 9,600(F)

MMV for Zinc = 15 × (360 – 600) = 3,600 (A)

Total 6,000 (F)

Material Yield Variance (*MYV*)=Standard Cost Per Unit ×(Standard yield for actual input – Actual yield)

[Here, St. Cost per unit = $\frac{(700 \times 40) + (300 \times 15)}{960 \text{ kg}} = \frac{32500}{960} = 33.85$

Standard yield = 1200 kg – 4% *i.e.*, 48 = 1152 kg]

MYV = 33.85 × (1152 – 1056) = 3,250 (A)

Verification :

Material Usage Variance = Material Mix Variance + Material Yield Variance

= 6000 (F) + 3250 (A) = 2750 (F)

Illustration 15: Vinak Ltd. produces an article by blending two basic raw materials. It operates a standard costing system and the following standards have been set for raw materials:

Material	*Standard Mix*	*Standard Price per kg*
A	40%	₹ 4.00
B	60%	3.00

The standard loss in processing is 15%.

During April, 1990, the company produced 1,700 kg of finished output.

The position of stock and purchases for the month of April, 1990 is under:

Material	*Stock on 1-4-90*	*Stock on 30-4-90*	*Purchased during April, 1990*	
	kg.	kg.	kg.	Cost (₹.)
A	35	5	800	3,400
B	40	50	1,200	3,000

Calculate the following variances:

(*i*) Material Price Variance.

(*ii*) Material Usage Variance.

(*iii*) Material Yield Variance.

(*iv*) Material Mix Variance.

(*v*) Total Material Cost Variance.

[B.Com Hons., Delhi]

Solution:

Type of Material	*Standard*			*Actual*		
	Quantity Kg.	*Rate ₹*	*Amount (₹)*	*Quanity Kg.*	*Rate ₹*	*Amount (₹)*
A	800	4	3,200	35	4	140.00
				795	4.25	3,378.75
				40	3.00	120.00
B	1,200	3	3,600	1,150	2.50	2,875.00
Total	2,000		6,800	2,020		6513.75
Less	300			320		
	1,700			1700		

Calculation :

1. The standard loss is 15% of the input. Thus to produce 1,700 kg. of the article, standard quantity of material required is

$$\frac{100}{85} \times 1{,}700 = 2{,}000 \text{ kg}$$

Out of the 2,000 kg. of material used, 40% is of type A and 60% is of type B, *i.e.*, 800 kg of *A* and 1200 kg of *B*.

2. *Standard cost per unit* $= \frac{\text{Total standard cost}}{\text{Total standard output}} = \frac{₹.\,6{,}800}{1{,}700} = ₹.\,4$ per kg.

1. *Material Price Variance* = Actual Quantity × (Standard Rate – Actual Rate)

Material A: Since the actual price and standard price in respect of 35 kg. of raw materials are the same, price variance will be in respect of 795 kg:

$$= 795 \times (4.0 - 4.25) = ₹.\ 198.75 \text{ (Adverse)}$$

Material B: In respect of Material B also, price variance will be only in respect of 1,150 kg.

$$1{,}150 \text{ kg} \times (3 - 2.50) = ₹\ 575 \text{ (Favourable)}$$

Total Material Price Variance

of *A* and *B* = ₹. 198.75 (A) + 575 (F) = ₹. 376.25 (Favourable)

2\. *Material Usage Variance* = Std. Rate × (Std. Qty. for actual output – Actual Qty.)

A = 4 × (800 – 830)	=	₹. 120 (A)
B = 3 × (1,200 – 1,190)	=	₹. 30 (F)
Total		₹. 90 (Advese)

3\. *Material Yield Variance* = Std. cost per unit × (St. output for actual mix – Actual output)

$$= 4 \times \left(\frac{1{,}700}{2{,}000} \times 2{,}020 - 1{,}700\right)$$

$$= 4 \times (1{,}717 - 1{,}700) = ₹.\ 68 \text{ (Adverse)}$$

4\. *Material Mix Variance* = Std. Rate per kg × (Revised Std. Qty. – Actual Qty.)

Revised Std. Qty.:

$$A = \frac{2{,}020}{2{,}000} \times 800 = 808$$

$$B = \frac{2{,}020}{2{,}000} \times 1{,}200 = 1{,}212$$

Variance:

A = 4 × (808 – 830)	=	₹. 88 (A)
B = 3 × (1212 – 1190)		₹. 66 (F)
Total		₹. 22 (Adverse)

5\. Material Cost Variance = Standard cost for actual output – Actual cost
= 6,800 – 6,513.75 = ₹. 286.25 (Favourable)

Verification:

Material Cost Variance = Material Price Variance + Material Usage Variance.
= 376.25 (F) + ₹ 90 (A) = ₹ 286.25 (Favourable)

Material Usage Variance = Material Mix Variance + Material Yield Variance
= 22 (A) + 68 (A) = ₹ 90 (Adverse)

Illustration 16: Modern Tiles Limited makes plastic tiles of standard size of 6″ × 6″ × 1/8″. From the following information, you are required to calculate for direct materials:

(*i*) the cost variance in total

(*ii*) the cost variance sub-divided into: (*a*) Price, (*b*) Usage

(*iii*) the usage variance analysed to show: (*a*) mixture, (*b*) yield.

A standard mix of the compound required to produce an output of 20,000 square feet of tiles 1/8″ thick is as follows:

Direct Materials			*Quantity*	*Price per kg*
A	...	...	600 kg	₹ 0.90
B	...	...	400	0.65
C	...	...	500	0.40

During the month of December, 8 mixes were processed and actual materials consumed were:

Direct Materials			*Quantity*	*Price per kg*
A	...	...	5,000 kg	₹ 0.85
B	...	...	2,900	0.60
C	...	...	4,400	0.45

Actual production for December was 6,20,000 tiles. **[*C.A., (Inter)*]**

Solution:

Material	*Standard (for 6,20,000 tiles)*			*Actual (for 6,20,000 tiles)*		
	Qty. (*kg*)	*Rate per kg* (₹)	*Amt.* (₹)	*Qty.* (*kg.*)	*Rate per kg* (₹)	*Amt.* (₹)
A	4,650	0.90	4,185	5,000	0.85	4,250
B	3,100	0.65	2,015	2,900	0.60	1,740
C	3,875	0.40	1,550	4,400	0.45	1,980
	11,625		7,750	12,300		7,970

(*i*) Material Cost Variance (*DMCV*) = Standard Cost – Actual Cost
= ₹. 7,750 – ₹. 7,970 = ₹. 220 (A)

(*ii*) (*a*) Material Price Variance (*DMPV*) = Actual Quantity × (Standard Rate – Actual Rate)

A = 5,000 × (.90 – .85) = ₹. 250 (F)
B = 2,900 × (.65 – .60) = 145 (F)
C = 4,400 × (.40 – .45) = 220 (A)
175 (F)

(*b*) Material Usage Variance (*DMUV*) = Standard Price × (Standard Qty. – Actual Qty.)

A = .90 × (4,650 – 5,000) = ₹. 315 (A)
B = .65 × (3,100 – 2,900) = 130 (F)
C = .40 × (3,875 – 4,400) = 210 (A)
395 (A)

(*iii*) (*a*) Material Mix Variance (*DMMV*)

= Standard Rate × (Revised Standard Quantity – Actual Quantity)
A = .90 × (4,920 – 5,000) = ₹ 72 (A)
B = .65 × (3,280 – 2,900) = 247 (F)
C =. 40 × (4,100 – 4,400) = 120 (A)
55 (F)

Revised Standard Quantity (*RSQ*)

$$= \frac{\text{Actual Mix}}{\text{Standard Mix}} \times \text{Standard Quantity}$$

$$A = \frac{12,300}{11,625} \times 4,650 = 4,920$$

$$B = \frac{12,300}{11,625} \times 3,100 = 3,280$$

$$C = \frac{12,300}{11,625} \times 3,875 = 4,100$$

(*b*) Material Yield Variance (*DMYV*)

= Std. Cost per Unit × (Std. Output for Actual Mix – Actual Output)

= 0.0125 × (6,56,000 – 6,20,000) = ₹ 450 (Adverse)

Calculations

(*i*) Std. Cost per unit of tile $= \frac{\text{Total Std. Cost}}{\text{No. of Tiles}} = \frac{7,750}{6,20,000}$ = ₹. .0125

(*ii*) Std. Output for Actual Mix $= \frac{6,20,000}{11,625} \times 12,300 = 6,56,000$ tiles

(*iii*) Output of tiles:

One Mix produces 20,000 square feet of tiles. Each tile requires 36 square inches of 1/8″ thickness

∴ Total output of one mix $= \frac{20,000 \times 144}{36} = 80,000$ tiles

(*iv*) Standard quantity for actual output:

Material *A* $= \frac{600 \times 6,20,000}{80,000} = 4,650$ kg

Material *B* $= \frac{400 \times 6,20,000}{80,000} = 3,100$ kg

Material *C* $= \frac{500 \times 6,20,000}{80,000} = 3,875$ kg.

Illustration 17: One kilogram of Product K requires two chemicals A and B. The following were the details of product K for the month of June :

(*a*) Standard mix Chemical *A* 50% and Chemical *B* 50%.

(*b*) Standard price per kilogram of Chemical *A* ₹ 12, Chemical *B* ₹ 15.

(*c*) Actual input of Chemical *B* 70 kilograms.

(*d*) Actual price per kilogram of Chemical *A* ₹ 15.

(*e*) Standard normal loss 10% of total input.

(*f*) Materials cost variance total ₹ 650 adverse.

(*g*) Materials yield variance total ₹ 135 adverse.

You are required to calculate:

(1) Materials mix variance total.
(2) Materials usage variance total.
(3) Materials price variance
(4) Actual loss of actual Input
(5) Actual input of Chemical A.
(6) Actual price per kilogram of Chemical *B*.

Solution:

Calculations:

(*i*) Since actual output has not been given, it has been presumed to be 90 kg.

(*ii*) The standard input for actual output :

Total Mix = 90 × 100/90 = 100 kg.

The standard input of material A and B will be 50 kg. each because their input proportion is 50% each.

(*iii*) Material Cost Variance total is ₹ 650 (A).

Therefore, the acutal cost of material is ₹ 2,000 [*i.e.*, (50 × 12 + 50 × 15) + 650)] and standard cost is ₹. 1350.

(*iv*) Material yield variance is ₹ 135 (A). The standard output for actual mix is presumed to be x in following calculations.

Material Yield Variance = Std. cost per unit × (Std. output for actual mix – Actual output)

$$135\ (A) = \frac{1{,}350}{90} \times (x - 90)$$

or $$135\ (A) = 15 \times (x - 90)$$

or $$135\ (A) = 15x - 1{,}350 \text{ or } x = 99$$

The standard output for actual mix is 99 kg. Therefore, the actual input should be:

$$99 \times 100/90 = 110 \text{ kg.}$$

(*v*) Total actual mix is 110 kg. out of which 70 kg. is that of material B. Thus, input of material A 40 kg.

(*vi*) The total actual cost of material *A* is ₹ 600 (*i.e.*, 40 × 15). The total actual cost of material *B* will be total actual cost – Cost of *A i.e.*, ₹ 1,400 (*i.e.*, 2,000 – 600). The rate per kg. of material *B* ₹. 20 per kg. *i.e.*, 1400 ÷ 70 = 20.

Cost-Table of *A* and *B*

Chemical	*Standard*			*Actual*		
	Qty. (kg)	*Rate (₹)*	*Amount (₹)*	*Qty. (kg.)*	*Rate (₹)*	*Amount (₹)*
A	50	12	600	40	15	600
B	50	15	750	70	20	1,400
	100		1,350	110		2,000

Standard output for actual mix 99 kg.

Actual output for actual mix. 90 kg.

(1) **Material Mix Variance Total** = Standard Rate × (Revised Std. Qty. – Actual Qty.)

$$A = 12 \times \left(\frac{50}{100} \times 110 - 40\right) = 12 \times (55 - 40) = 180\ (F)$$

$$B = 15 \times \left(\frac{50}{100} \times 110 - 70\right) = 15 \times (15 - 70) = 225\ (A)$$

Total ₹. 45 (A)

(2) **Material Usage Variance** = Std. Rate × (Std. Qty. for actual output – Actual Qty.)

$A = 12 \times (50 - 40) =$ 120 (F)

$B = 15 \times (50 - 70) =$ 300 (A)

Total ₹. 180 (A)

(3) **Material Price Variance** = Actual Qty. × (Std. Rate – Actual Rate)

$A = 40 \times (12 - 15) =$ 120 (A)

$B = 70 \times (15 - 20) =$ 350 (A)

Total 470 (A)

(4) Actual Loss of Actual Input :

Actual Input	110
Actual Output	90
Loss	20

(5) Actual Input of Chemical *A* : 40 kg

(6) Actual price per kg. of Chemical *B*: ₹. 20.

Causes of Direct Material Variances

Direct material cost variances arise due to variations in the material prices and usage or quantity of material.

Material Price Variance. It arises normally due to following possible causes. The related responsible person is also mentioned along with.

Possible Causes of Material Price Variance	*Person Responsible*
(*i*) Inefficient buying	Purchasing Management
(*ii*) Change in the market price.	Uncontrollable
(*iii*) Rush order to meet shortage of supply or emergency purchase	Purchase Manager
(*iv*) Purchase in bulk quantity or in uneconomic quantity.	Purchase Manager
(*v*) Failure to avail advantage of off-season price or failure to purchase when price were low	Purchase Manager
(*vi*) Failure to avail trade discount	Purchase Manager
(*vii*) Payment to avail cash discount	Accounts Officer
(*viii*) Payment of excess or less frieght	Purchase Manager
(*ix*) Non-availability of standard quality	Uncontrollable
(*x*) Change in the material purchase, upkeep and store keeping cost	Purchase Manager and Store Keeper
(*xi*) Change in the taxes and duties	Uncontrolable
(*xii*) Use of substitute materials at different prices	Production Manager
(*xiii*) Change in the quality and specification of material purchased	Production Manager

It may be noted that the above list is not comprehensive but suggestive. There may be other simillar reasons of material price variance.

For material price variances mainly the Purchase Department and its manager is repossible. But certain causes may be uncontrollable and for which the Purchase Manager will not be held responsible. Moreover where purchases have been intentionally made in uneconomic quantities due to lack of working capital, the General Manager and the Administration will be responsible.

Price variances provide useful information for taking remedial actions, such as increase in production prices if variance is uncontrollable or adoption of cost reduction method and improvement in the efficiency of the Purchase Department.

Material Usage Variance. It arises normally due to following possible causes. The person responsible is also mentioned.

Possible Causes of Material Usage Variance	*Person Responsible*
(*i*) Poor quality of direct material	Purchase Manager
(*ii*) Variation in usage of material due to inefficient or uneconomic use	Production Manager or Foreman
(*iii*) Inefficient workmanship	Production Manager or Foreman
(*iv*) Defective Machinery	Production Manager or Foreman
(*v*) Use of substitute materials	Production Manager or Foreman
(*vi*) Defective machines, tools and equipment	Production Manager or Foreman
(*vii*) Less or more yield	Production Manager or Foreman
(*viii*) Accounting error	Accounting Officer
(*ix*) Change in the composition of mixture	Production Manager

For Material Usage Variances, the production department, its manager and foreman should be held responsible.

Usage variance may be divided into mix variance and yield variance. Mix variance may arise due to change in the composition of material mix, which may be due to the non-availability of specified material for the mix and the use of substitute material. Increase in the propotion of expensive material in the mix will show unfavourable variance. If cheaper substitutes are used, it may result in favourable mix variance.

DIRECT LABOUR VARIANCES

1. Direct Labour Cost Variance

Like material cost variance, direct labour cost variance is the difference between the standard direct labour cost for actual output and actual cost of labour paid. It is defined as the difference between direct wages specified for the activity achieved and the actual direct wages paid'.[1]

Direct Labour Cost Variance = Standard Labour Cost for Actual Output – Actual Labour Cost

Calculation:

Standard Labour Cost for Actual Output = Standard Time for Actual Output × Standard Rate

Actual Cost = Actual Time × Actual Rate

$$\text{Standard Time for Actual Output} = \frac{\text{Standard Time}}{\text{Standard Output}} \times \text{Actual Output}$$

When the Actual Labour Cost is more than standard cost, there will be adverse variance and *vice-versa*.

Direct labour cost variance may be further analysed as Direct Labour Rate Variance and Direct Labour Time or Efficiency Variance because the Labour Cost Variance normally arises due to change in labour rate or change in time or both.

(a) Direct Labour Rate Variance (Wage Rate Variance)

It is the difference between the standard labour rate specified and the actual labour rate paid. In other words `it is that portion of direct labour (wages) variance which is due to the difference between stanard rate of pay specified and actual rate paid.[2]

Direct Labour Rate Variance = Actual Time × (Standard Wage Rate – Actual Wage Rate).

or

$$= AT \times (SR - AR)$$

It may be seen that Wage Rate Variance is comparable with Material Price Variance and it is calculated in a similar manner.

If actual wage rate is more than standard wage rate, there will be adverse variance and when actual wage rate is less than standard wage rate, the variance will be favourable.

Illustration 18: The standard time and rate for unit component A are given below:

Standard hours 15; Stanard rate ₹. 4 per hour

The actual data and related information are as under –

Actual Production 1000 units; Actual hours 15300 hours, Actual Rate ₹. 3.90 per hour.

Calculate Labour Rate Variance

1. *CIMA* London

2. *CIMA* London

Solution:

Labour Rate Variance = Actual hours × (Standard Wage Rate – Actual Wage Rate)

= 15,300 × (4 – 3.9) = ₹ 1,530 (Favourable)

(b) Direct Labour Efficiency Variance or Labour Time Variance

It is 'that portion of labour cost variance which is due to the difference between labour hours specified for the activity achieved and the actual labour hour expended'[3]. This variance can be compared with Direct Material Usage Variance and is calculated likewise.

Labour Efficiency Variance or time variance is the result of taking more or less time than the standard time specified for the performance of a work.

Direct Labour Efficiency or Time Variance = Standard wage rate × (Standard Hours for Actual Output – Actual hours) or

= *SR* × (*SH* – *AH*)

It is to be noted that if standard output differ from actual output, the standard hours in the above calculation will be standard hours for actual output as it is used in the Direct Labour Cost Variance.

If actual hours are less than standard hours there will be favourable variance and *vice-versa*.

It may be verified that:

Direct Labour Rate Variance + Direct Labour Efficiency or Time Variance

= Direct Labour Cost Variance.

Illustration 19: From the data of previous illustration, calculate labour efficiency variance.

Solution:

Labour Efficiency Variance = Standard Wage Rate × (Standard hours – Actual hours)

= 4 × (15300 – 15000)

= 1200 (Adverse)

Illustration 20: From the following data calculate (*i*) Labour Cost Variance (*ii*) Labour Efficiency Variance, and (*iii*) Labour Rate Variance.

Workmen	*Standard*			*Actual (for 6,20,000 tiles)*		
	Hours	*Rate per hour* (₹)	*Total* (₹) (₹)	*Hours*	*Rate per hour* (₹)	*Total* (₹)
Workman *A*	20 hrs.	3.00	60.00	30 hrs.	3.00	90.00
Workman *B*	25 hrs.	4.00	100.00	15 hrs.	4.50	67.50
			160.00			157,50

Solution:

(*i*) Labour Cost Variance = Standard Labour Cost – Actual Labour Cost

= 160 – 157.50 = ₹. 2.50 (Favourable)

(*ii*) Labour Efficiency Variance = Standard Wage Rate × (Standard hours – Actual hours)

A = 3 × (20 – 30) = 30 (Adverse)

B = 4 × (25 – 15) = 40 (Favourable)

Total 10 (Favourable)

1. *CIMA* London.

(*iii*) Labour Rate Variance = Actual Time × (Standard Wage Rate – Actual Wage Rate

A = 30 × (3 – 3) = Nil

B = 15 × (4 – 4.50) = 7.50 (Adverse)

Total 7.50 (Adverse)

Verification

Labour Cost Variance = Labour Efficiency Variance + Labour Rate Variance

= 10 (F) + 7.50 (A) = 2.50 (F)

Illustration 21: From the data given below, calculate labour variance for the two deparments:

	Deptt. A	*Deptt. B*
Actual Gross Wages (direct)	₹. 2,000	₹. 1,800
Standard Hours	8,000	6,000
Standard Rate per Hour	30 paise	35 paise
Actual Hours Worked	8,200	5,800

Solution:

		Deptt. A	*Deptt. B*
Labour Cost Variance	=	(Standard Cost for Actual Output – Actual Cost)	
		(8,000 × .30) – ₹. 2,000	(6,000 × .35) – ₹. 1,800
	=	₹, 2,400 – ₹. 2,000	= ₹. 2,100 – ₹. 1,800
	=	₹. 400 (Favourable)	= ₹. 300 (Favourable)
Labour Rate Variance	=	Actual Time × (Std. Rate – Actual Rate)	
		or Std. Wages for Actual Time – Actual Wages	
		8,200 × .30 – ₹. 2,000	5,800 × .35 – ₹.1,800
	=	₹. 2,460 – ₹. 2,000	= ₹. 2,030 – ₹. 1,800
	=	₹. 460 (Favourable)	= ₹. 230 (Favourable)
Labour Efficiency Variance	=	Std. Rate × (Std. Time for Actual Output – Actual Time)	
		.30 × (8,000 – 8,200)	.35 × (6,000 – 5,800)
	=	₹. 60 (Adverse)	= 2,100 – 2,030 = ₹. 70 (Fav.)

Verification:

Labour Cost Variance	=	Labour Rate Variance + Labour Efficiency Variance	
		₹. 460 (F) + ₹. 60 (A)	₹. 230 (F) + ₹. 70 (F)
	=	₹. 400 (F)	= ₹. 300 (F)

Illustration 22: Stanard hours for manufacturing two products *M* and *N* are 15 hours per unit and 20 hours per unit respectively. Both products require identical kind of labour and the standard wage rate per hours is ₹. 5. In the year 2004, 10,000 units of *M* and 15,000 units of *N* were manufactured. The total of labour hours actually worked were 4,50,500 and the actual wage bill came to ₹. 23,00,000. This included 12,000 hours paid for @ ₹ 7 per hour and 9,400 hours paid for @ ₹. 7.50 per hour, the balance having been paid at ₹. 5 per hour. You are required to compute the labour variances.

Solution:

Labour Cost Variance = Standard Cost of Actual Output – Actual Cost

Standard Cost

For Product *M*	=	10,000 × 15 × 5 =	7,50,000
For Product N	=	15,000 × 20 × 5 =	15,00,000
Total Standard Cost			₹. 22,50,000

Total Actual Cost = ₹ 23,00,000

Labour Cost Variance = ₹. 22,50,000 – ₹. 23,00,000

= ₹. 50,000 (Adverse)

Labour Rate Variance = Actual Hours × (Std. Rate – Actual Rate)

12,000 × (₹. 5 – ₹. 7)	=	₹. 24,000 (A)
9,400 × (₹. 5 – ₹. 7.50)	=	₹. 23,500 (A)
4,29,100 × (₹. 5 – ₹. 5)	=	—
Total		47,500 (A)

Labour Efficiency Variance = Std. Rate × (Std. Time – Actual Time)

= ₹. 5 × (4,50,000 – 4,50,500) = ₹. 2,500 (Adverse)

[**Note.** Standard Time = (10,000 × 15) + (15,000 × 20) = 4,50,000]

Verification:

Labour Cost Variance = Labour Rate Variance + Labour Efficiency Variance

= ₹. 47,500 (A) + ₹. 2,500 (A) = ₹. 50,000 (Adverse)

CLASSIFICATION OF TOTAL EFFICIENCY VARIANCE : This variance may be further analysed as below:

(1) When abnormal idle time occurs, total efficiency variance will have two sub-variances

(*x*) Idle Time Variance

(*y*) Revised Efficiency Variance or Labour Yield Variance

(2) When there is composition of different types of workers or gang and where the composition of standard gang and actual gang differs and abnormal idle has been paid for, the efficiency variance may have three sub-variances.

(*x*) Idle Time Variance

(*y*) Mix Variance or Gang Composition Variance

(*z*) Revised Efficiency Variance or Labour Yield Variance

(x) Idle Time Varianice

It is a sub-variance of Wage Efficiency or Time Variance. The standard cost of actual hours of any employee may remain idle due to abnormal circumstances like strikes, lock outs, power failure etc. Standard cost of such idle time is called Idle Time Variance. This variance is always adverse or unfavourable. It requires investigation to discover the cause of abnormal Idle hours. This variance is a part of Efficiency Variance.

Idle Time Variance = Idle Hours × Standard Rate Per Hour

Note: If there are idle hours, actual horus used in mixed variance and yield variance will be reduced by idle hours. Revised standard hours will also be calculated on adjusted actual hours. Standard yield for actual hours will also be on adjusted actual hours. But in the calculation of Efficiency and Rate variance, total actual hours will be taken.

If there is idle variance but no mix or yield variance, actual hours in efficiency variance will be reduced by idle hours.

(y) Direct Labour Mix Variance or Gang Composition Variance

Some time when more than one grades of workers are required in a specified proportion, their composition is called gang. The composition of actual gang of labour may differ from composition of standard gang due to shortage of a particular grade of workers or some other reason. Labour mix variance is calculated to show how much of the total efficiency variance is due to the change in the composition of labour force. This variance is like material mix variance. It is separately calculated for each grade of worker.

Direct Labour Mix Variance is defined as `that part of the wages variance which is due to the difference between standard labour grades specified and the actual labour grades utilised'.

Direct Labour Mix Variance or Gang Composition Variance

= Standard Wage Rate × (Revised Standard labour hours – Actual labour hours)

or

= *SR* × (*RSH* – *AH*)

Revised standard labour hours will be calculated where there is variation in the total composition of standard labour hours and in the composition of actual labour hours, *i.e.*, when there is variation in total of input hours in the standard mix or actual mix.

Revised Standard Hours (*RSH*) of each grade

$$= \frac{\text{Total hours of actual mix or gang}}{\text{Total hours of standard mix or gang}} \times \text{Standard hours of the grade}$$

Note: It is calculated for each grade of worker separately.

(Za) Revised Efficiency Variance

This variance is on the pattern of Revised Direct Material Usage Variance.

If there is difference between standard time for actual output (as used in Labour Efficiency or Time Variance) and Revised Standard Time (as used in Labour Mix Variance), the variance is known as Revised Efficiency Variance. Moreover the variance arises when standard output and actual output shows no difference (where there is difference when there is difference between standard output and actual output, then there will be Labour Yield Variance and no Revised Efficiency Variance.

Revised Efficiency Variance = (Standard Labour Hours for Actual Output – Revised Standard Hours) × Standard Labour Rate

or

= (*SH* – *RSH*) × *SR*

Revised Efficiency Variance will be calculated for each grade of workers separately.

(Zb) Direct Labour Yield Variance

Just like Material Yield Variance, Direct Labour Yield Variance can also be ascertained. It is calculated when there is difference between standard output and actual output. But if there is no such difference, then Revised Efficiency Variance is calculated as explained earlier.

Direct Labour Yield Variance may be defined as that portion of Labour Efficiency Variance which is due to the difference between the standard yield (output) specified and actual yield (output) obtained'.

It may be noted that yield variance is based on output while all other variance are based on input.

***Direct Labour Yield Variance* = Standard labour cost per unit of output × (Standard yield or output for actual mix or gang hours – Actual output)**

Standard yield is the output which should result on input of actual hours mix

$$\text{Standard labour cost per unit of output} = \frac{\text{Total labour cost of standard mix}}{\text{Net standard output}}$$

If standard yield or output is more than actual yield or output, the variance will be unfavourable or adverse and vice-versa. (Thus in this variance negative figure of variance will be favourable).

Illustration 23: The details regarding the composition and the weekly wage rates of labour force engaged on a job scheduled to be completed in 30 weeks are as follows :

Workers	*Standard*		*Actual*	
	No. of Labourers	*Weekly Wage Rate per Labourer*	*No. of Labourers*	*Weekly Wage Rate per Labour* ₹.
Skilled	75	60	70	70
Semi-skilled	45	40	30	50
Unskilled	60	30	80	20

The work is actually completed in 32 weeks. Calculate the various labour variances.

[B. Com. (H) Delhi]

Solution:

Labour Cost Variance = (Standard Cost of Labour – Actual Cost of Labour)

[Standard Cost of Labour = Standard No. of Workers × Standard Weekly Wage Rate × Standard No of Weeks

		₹.
Skilled	= 75 × 60 × 30	= 1,35,000
Semi-skilled	= 45 × 40 × 30	= 54,000
Unskilled	= 60 × 30 × 30	= 54,000
Standard Cost of Labour		= 2,43,000

Actual Cost of Labour = Actual No. of Workes × Actual Weekly Wage Rate × Actual No. of Weeks

		₹.
Skilled	= 70 × 70 × 32	= 1,56,800
Semi-skilled	= 30 × 50 × 32	= 48,000
Unskilled	= 80 × 20 × 32	= 51,200
Actual Cost of Labour		= 2,56,000
Total Labour Cost of Variance		= 2,43,000 – 2,56,000
		= 13,000 (A)

Labour Rate Variance = Actual Weeks × (Standard Wage Rate – Actual Wage Rate)

Skilled	= (70 × 32) × (60 – 70)	= 22,400 (A)
Semi-skilled	= (30 × 32) × (40 – 50)	= 9,600 (A)
Unskilled	= (80 × 32) × (30 – 20)	= 25,600 (F)
	Total	₹. 6,400 (A)

Labour Efficiency Variance = Standard Wage Rate × (Standard Weeks – Actual Weeks)

Skilled	= 60 × [(75 × 30) – (70 × 32)	= 600 (F)
Semi-skilled	= 40 × [(45 × 30) – (30 × 32)]	= 15,600 (F)
Unskilled	= 30 × [(60 × 30) – (80 × 32)]	= 22,800 (A)
	Total	6,600 (A)

Verification

Labour Cost Variance = Labour Rate Variance + Labour Efficiency Variance

= 6400 (A) + 6600 (A) = 13,000 (A)

Labour Mix Variance

Calculation of Revised Standard Time = $\frac{\text{Actual Mix of Time} \times \text{Std. Time}}{\text{Standard Mix of Time}}$

Skilled = 5760 × 2250/5400 = 2400

Semi-skilled = 5760 × 1350/5400 = 1440

Unskilled = 5760 × 1800/5400 =1920

Calculation of Actual Hours = No. of Labours × Actual Week

Skilled = 70 × 32 = 2240

Semi-skilled = 30 × 32 = 960

Unskilled = 80 × 32 = 2560

5760

Labour Mix Variance = Standard Wage Rate × (Revised Standard Time – Actual Time)

Skilled = 60 × (2400 – 2240) = ₹. 9,600 (F)

Semi-skilled = 40 × (1440 – 960) = 19,200 (F)

Unskilled = 30 × (1920 – 2560) = 19,200 (A)

Total 9,600 (F)

Revised Efficiency Variance

= Standard Wage Rate × (Standard Time – Revised Standard Time)

Skilled = 60 × (2250 – 2400) = 9000

Semi-skilled = 40 × (1350 – 1440) = 3600

Unskilled = 30 × (1800 – 1920) = 3600

= 16200 (A)

Illustration 24: A gang of workers usually consists of 10 men, 5 women and 5 boys in a factory. They are paid at standard hourly rates of ₹ 1.25, ₹. .80 and ₹. .70 respectively. In a normal week of 40 hours the gang is expected to produce 1000 units of output.

In certain week, the gang was consisted of 13 men, 4 women and 3 boys. Actual wages were paid at the rates of ₹ 1.20, Re. 85 and Re. 65 respectively. Two hours were lost due to abnormal idle time and 960 units of output were produced.

Calculate various labour variances. **[*B.Com. (H) Delhi*]**

Solution:

Workers	*Standard*			*Actual*		
	Hours (Workers × Week)	*Rate (₹)*	*Amount (₹)*	*Hours (Workers) × Week)*	*Rate (₹)*	*Amount (₹)*
Men	400	1.25	500	520	1.20	624
Women	200	0.80	160	160	0.85	136
Boys	200	0.70	140	120	0.65	78
	800		800	800		838

1. **Direct Labour Cost Variance** (*DLCV*)

= Standard Cost for Actual Output – Actual Cost

Standard Cost for Actual Output = Standard Cost per Unit × Acutal output

$= \frac{₹.\ 800}{1000 \text{ units}} \times 960 \text{ units} = ₹.\ 768$

DLCV = 768 – 838 = ₹. 70 (A)

Direct Labour Rate Variance (*DLRV*) = Actual Hours (Standard Wage Rate – Actual Wage Rate)

Men	= 520 × (1.25 – 1.20) =	₹. 26 (F)
Women	= 160 × (0.80 – 0.85) =	8 (A)
Boys	= 120 × (0.70 – 0.65) =	6 (F)
Total		₹. 24 (F)

Direct Labour Efficiency Variance (*DLEV*) = Standard Wage Rate × (Standard Time for Actual Output – Actual Time paid for]

[Here Standard Time for Actual Output $= \text{Standard Hours} \times \dfrac{\text{Actual Output}}{\text{Standard Output}}$

Men $= 400 \times \dfrac{960}{1000} = 384$ hours

Women $= 200 \times \dfrac{960}{1000} = 192$ hours

Boys $= 200 \times \dfrac{960}{1000} = 192$ hours]

DLEV for Men	= 1.25 × (384 – 520) =	₹. 170 (A)
Women	= 0.80 × (192 – 160) =	25.60 (F)
Boys	= 0.70 × (192 – 120) =	50.40 (F)
	Total	94.00 (A)

Idle Time Variance (*ITV*) = Idle hours × Standard Wage Rate
= (Workers × hours) × Standard Wage Rate

Men	= (13 × 2) × 1.25	=	₹. 32.50 (A)
Women	= (4 × 2) × 0.80	=	6.40 A)
Boys	= (3 × 2) × 0.70	=	4.20 (A)
	Total		43.10 (A)

Direct Labour Mix Variance = Standard Wage Rate × (Revised Standard Time – Actual Time taken)

[Here Revised Standard Time $= \dfrac{\text{Total Actual Time}}{\text{Total Standard Time}} \times \text{Standard Time}$

Total Actual Time will be 800 – 40 Idle hours = 760

Men = 760 × 400/800 = 380

Women = 760 × 200/800 = 190

Boys = 760 × 200/800 = 190]

DLMV for Men	= 1.25 × (380 – 494)	=	142.50 (A)
Women	= 0.80 × (190 – 152)	=	30.40 (F)
Boys	= 0.70 × (190 – 114)	=	53.20 (F)
	Total		58.90 (A)

Direct Labour Yield Variance (DLYV) = Standard Cost per unit × (Standard Output for Actual Time – Actual output)
= ₹ 0.80 × (950 – 960) = ₹. 8 (F)

[Here standard output for actual time will be $\dfrac{\text{1000 units}}{\text{800 hrs}}$ × Actual hours 760 = 950 units]

Verification

Labour Cost Variance = Labour Rate Variance + Labour Efficiency Variance
= ₹. 24 (F) + 94 (A)
= ₹. 70 (A)

Labour Efficiency Variance = Direct Labour Mix Variance + Idle Time Variance + Direct Labour Yield Variance
= ₹. 58.90 (A) + 43.10 (A) + 8 (F)
= 94 (A)

Illustration 25: The standard labour component and the actual labour component engaged in a week for a job are as under :

		Skilled Workers	*Semi-skilled Workers*	*Unskilled Worked*
(*a*)	Standard Number of Workers in the Gang	32	12	6
(*b*)	Standard Wage Rate per Hours (₹)	3	2	1
(*c*)	Actual Number of workers employed in the Gang during the week	28	18	4
(*d*)	Actual Wage Rate per Hour (₹)	4	3	2

During the 40-hour working week, the gang produced 1,800 standard labour hours of work. Calculate the different labour variances.

***Solution*:**

Caterogy of Workers	*Standard*			*Actual*		
	Hours	*Rate*	*Amount (₹.)*	*Hours*	*Rate*	*Amount (₹.)*
Skilled	1,280	3	3,840	1,120	4	4,480
Semi-skilled	480	2	960	720	3	2,160
Unskilled	240	1	240	160	2	320
	2,000		5,040	2,000		6,960

Direct Labour Cost Variance (*DLCV*) = Standard Cost for Actual Output – Actual Cost
= ₹. 4,536 – ₹ 6,960
= ₹. 2,424 (Adverse)

Direct Labour Rate Variance (*DLRV*) = Actual Time × (Standard Rate – Actual Rate)
Skilled = 1,120 × (3 – 4) = ₹ 1,120 (A)
Semi-skilled = ₹ 720 × (2 – 3) = ₹ 720 (A)
Unskilled = ₹ 160 × (1 – 2) = ₹ 160 (A)
Total = ₹ 2,000 (Adverse)

Direct Labour Efficiency Variance (*DLEV*) = Std. Rate × (Std. Time for Actual Output – Actual Time)
Skilled = 3 × (1,152 – 1,120) = ₹ 96 (F)
Semi-skilled = 2 × (432 – 720) = ₹ 576 (A)
Unskilled = 1 × (216 – 160) = ₹ 56 (F)
Total = ₹ 424 (A)

Direct Labour Mix Variance (*DLMV*) = Standard Rate × (Revised Standard Time – Actual Time)
Skilled = 3 × (1,280 – 1,120) = ₹ 480 (F)
Semi-skilled = 2 × (480 – 720) = ₹ 480 (A)
Unskilled = 1 × (240 – 160) = ₹ 80 (F)
Total = ₹. 80 (Favourable)

Direct Labour Yield Variance (*DLYV*)= Std. Cost per hour of work × (Std. Output for Actual Mix – Actual Output)

= 2.52 × (2,000 – 1,800) = ₹ 504 (Adverse)

Verification:

DLCV = *DLRV* + *DLEV*

= 2,000 (A) + 424 (A) = ₹ 2,424 (Adverse)

DLEV = *DLMV* + *DLYV*

= ₹ 80 (F) + ₹ 504 (A) = ₹ 424 (Adverse)

Calculations:

(1) Standard Cost for Actual Output $= \frac{5,040}{2,000} \times 1,800 =$ ₹, 4,536

(2) Standard Time for Actual Output:

Skilled $= \frac{1,800}{2,000} \times 1,280 = 1,152$ hrs.

Semi-skilled $= \frac{1,800}{2,000} \times 480 = 432$ hrs.

Unskilled $= \frac{1,800}{2,000} \times 240 = 216$ hrs.

(3) Revised Standard Time $= \frac{\text{Actual Mix}}{\text{Standard Mix}} \times \text{Standard Time}$

(4) Since, Standard Mix and Actual Mix are the same, the Standard Time will also be the Revised Standard Time.

(5) Standard Cost per hour of standard work

$= \frac{\text{Total Standard Cost}}{\text{Total Standard Hours of Work}}$

$= \frac{5,040}{2,000} =$ ₹. 2.52

Revision Variance

Sometimes wage rate have to be revised, subsequent to the setting up of the standards, on account of agreement with workers or trade unions or revision of wage rates by the governemnt. If rates are revised and its effects are to be considered, a Wages Revision Variance is calculated.

***Direct Labour Revision Variance (DLRV)* = Standard labour cost of actual production at original standard rate – Standard labour cost of actual products at revised standard rate**

DLRV is usually adverse or unfavourable as revised standard wage rate is ordinarily higher than original standard rate.

Illustration 26: From the following data calculate the Direct Labour Revision Varainces:

Category	*Original Standard*			*Revised Standard*			*Actual*		
	Hrs.	*Rate*	*Amt.*	*Hrs.*	*Rate*	*Amt.*	*Hrs.*	*Rate*	*Amt.*
Skilled	60	3	180	40	3	120	50	4	200
Semi-skilled	40	2	80	60	2	120	50	2	100
Total	100		260	100		240	100		300

Standard Output 100 units ; Actual Output 80 units

Solution:

Direct Labour Revision Variance (*DLRV*) = Original Std. cost for Actual Output – Revised Std. cost for Actual Output

= 80 × 2.60 – 80 × 2.40

= 208 – 192 = ₹ 16 (Favourable)

After calculating the Revision Variance, other variances will be calculated as if the "Revised Standard" is the real standard.

Causes of Labour Variances

There are basically two labour variances : Labour Rate Variance and Labour Efficiency Variance. Labour Rate Variance may arise due to following reasons:

Possible Causes of Labour Rate Variance	*Person Responsible*
1. Employment of wrong grade of workers	Personnel Manager and Foreman
2. Excessive overtime for urgent completion	Production Manager and Sales Manager
3. Permananet revision in labour rate and special increments or allowances	Uncontrollable
4. Amount paid to make up minimum wages	Uncontrollable
5. Special rates for experimental production	Uncontrollable
6. Composition of labour gang different from standard	Production Manager and Foreman

The above list is suggestive only.

Labour Efficiency Variance or Time Variance may arise due to following possible causes

Possible Causes of Labour Efficiency or Time Variance	*Person Responsible*
1. Inefficient workmen	Personnel Manager and Foreman
2. Break-down of machinary	Maintenance Engineer
3. Inefficient supervision	Foreman
4. Poor quanitity of material	Purchase Manager
5. Hours lost in waiting etc.	Maintenance Engineer
6. Bad working condition	General Manager
7. Change in designing and quality of product	Maintenance Engineer

OVERHEAD VARIANCES

Overhead Variance is the difference between the standard overhead specified and the actual overhead incurred.

Overhead variance is segregated into

(*i*) Variable Overhead Variances (*VOV*)

(*ii*) Fixed Overhead Variances (*FOV*)

Variable Overhead Variance

Variable overhead variance represent the difference between standard variable overhead (specified for actual units produced) and the actual variable overhead incurred.

Variable Overhead Cost Variance = **Standard Variable Overhead on actual production – Actual variable overhead**

or

(Actual time or Standard hours for actual production × Standard Variable Overhead Rate) – (Actual Variable Overhead)

Here, Standard Variable Overhead Rate per Unit or per hours = $\dfrac{\text{Budgeted Overhead}}{\text{Budgeted Output or Hours}}$

[**Note:** Budgeted overhead are overheads for budgeted time or budgeted output. On the other hand standard overheads are overhead for actual time or for budgeted output in actual time].

The calculation of variable overhead variance is fairly simple as the standard is specified as a rate per unit. By multiplying standard rate by actual units produced, the standard variable overhead is obtained. This is compared with the actual variable overhead to find out variable overhead variance.

Illustration 27: The following information is available from the books of a manufacturing company regarding variable overheads. Calculate variable overhead cost variance.

Budgeted Production for the year	:	5000 units
Actual Production	:	4600 units
Budgeted Variable Overheads		₹. 1,000,00
Actual Variable Overheads		₹ 93,000

Solution:

Variable Overhead Rate per unit = $\dfrac{\text{Budgeted Overhead}}{\text{Budgeted Production}}$

$= \dfrac{1,00,000}{5,000}$ = ₹. 20.

Standard Variable Overhead on actual Production = Actual Production × Overhead Rate

or

Recovered Variable Overhead = 4,600 × 20 = ₹. 92,000

Variable Overhead Cost Variance = [Standard Variable Overhead on Actual Production – Actual Variable Overhead] or Recovered Variable Overheads – Actual Variable Overheads

= 92,000 – 93,000 = ₹. 1,000 (unfavourable)

Sub-division of Variable Overhead

Normally there is only one variable overhead variance because variable overheads vary according to output and not according to time. However, some cost accountants aruge that certain variable overheads may vary on the basis of time also and therefore there may be two sub divisions of variable overhead variance:

(*i*) **Variable Overhead Expenditure or Budget Variance**

= Standard Variable Overheads for Actual Time – Actual Variable Overheads

[Here, standard variable overheads for Actual Time = Standard Variable Overhead Rate per hour × Actual Hours. It may also be called 'Budgeted Variable Overhead for Actual hours]

(*ii*) **Variable Overhead Efficiency Variance**

= Standard Variable Overheads on Actual Production – Standard Variable Overheads for Actual Time

Calculations

1. Standard or Budgeted Variable Overhead for Actual Time

= Standard Overhead Rate per Hour × Actual hours

2. Standard Variable Overhead on Actual Production

= Standard Variable Overhead per unit × Actual Output

Illustration 28: From following data, calculate (*i*) Variable Overhead Variance, (*ii*) Variable Overhead Expendition or Budget Variance and (*iii*) Variable Overhead Efficiency Variance:

1. Standard hours per unit 3; Variable overhead rate per hour ₹ 2
2. Actual Variable Overhead Incurred ₹. 1,08,000
3. Actual output : 20,000 units
4. Actual hours worked : 56000 hours

Solution:

Calculations :

1. Standard or Budgeted Variable Overhead on Actual Time

= Standard Overhead Rate × Actual hours

= 2 × 56,000 = ₹. 1,12,000

2. Standard Variable Overhead for Actual Output

= Standard Variable Overhead rate per unit × Actual Output

= (3 × 2) × 20,000 = 1,20,000

Variable Overhead Variance = Standard Variable Overhead – Actual Variable Overhead

= 1,20,000 – 1,08,000 = ₹. 12,000 (F)

Variable Overhead Expenditure or Budget Variance

= Budgeted or St. Variable Overhead for actual time – Actual Variable Overhead

= 1,12,000 – 1,08,000 = ₹. 4000 (F)

Variable Overhead Efficiency Variance

= Standard Variable Overhead on Actual Production – Standard Variable Overhead for Actual Time

= 1,20,000 – 1,12,000 = ₹. 8000 (F)

Verification:

Variable Overhead Variance = Variable Overhead Expenditure Variance + Variable Overhead Efficiency Variance

= 4000 (F) + 8000 (F) = ₹. 12,000 (F)

Fixed Overhead Variances

Fixed overhead variance depends upon two factors, which are (*i*) fixed expenses incurred and (*ii*) volume of production obtained. The volume of production depends upon (*a*) capacity at

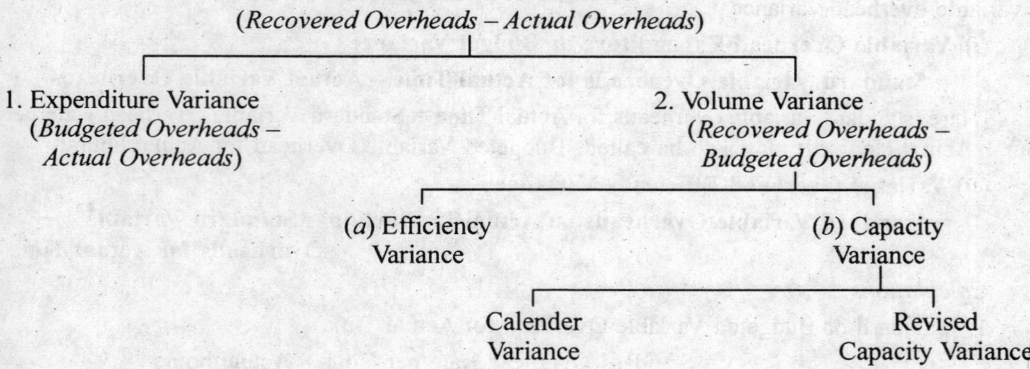

which the factory worked (*b*) number of days factory works and (*c*) efficiency at which factory worked. Thus, while analysing the fixed overhead variance the variance due to each of above factors is independently worked out.

These variances may be briefly defined as below:

1. Fixed Overhead Cost Variance	It is difference between standard fixed overheads a actual output and actual fixed overhead incurred *i.e.*, *Recovered fixed Overhead – Actual fixed overheads.* It is total of fixed Overhead Expenditure Variance and Fixed Overhead Volume Variance
2. Fixed Overhead Expenditure Variance	It is difference between standard expenses specified and the actual expenses incurred *i.e.*, *Budgeted Overheads – Actual Overheads*
3. Fixed Overhead Volume Variance	It is the portion of overhead variance which is due to the difference between budgeted level of output *i.e.*, *Recovered Overheads – Budgeted Overheads.*
Volume variance may be divided into following three varience (a), (b) and (c)	
(*a*) Fixed Overhead Efficiency Variance	It is the that portion of Overhead Volume Variance which is due to the difference between the budgeted efficiency of production and actual efficiency attained *i.e.*, *Recovered Fixed Overheads – Standard Fixed overheads.*
(*b*) Fixed Overheads Capacity Variance	It is variance which is related to the over and under utilisation of plant and equipment *i.e.*, *Standard Fixed Overheads – Budgeted Fixed Overheads.*
(*c*) Fixed Overhead Calender Variance	It is that portion of fixed overhead varience which is due to the difference between the number of working days in the period to which budget is applied *i.e.*, *Possible Fixed Overheads – Budgeted Fixed Overheads.*

Two Variance or Three Variance Methods

Overhead Cost Variance normally arises due to change in expenditure (which is called Overhead Expenditure Variance) and/or change in the volume (which is known as Overhead Volume Variance). If only these two variances are analysed, the method is known is two variance method.

There is three variance method where overhead volume variance is further analysed. Change in volume may be due to change in capacity (Capacity variance), and change in the level of efficiency (Efficiency variance). Thus in three method there will be three variance (*i*) Overhead Expenditure Variance, (*ii*) Overhead Capacity Variance and (*iii*) Overhead Efficiency Variance.

Basic Terms or Calculations – Before calculating Overhead Variances, following terms should be understood.

Standard Overhead Rate per unit or per hour or Budgeted Overhead Rate per unit

$$= \frac{\text{Budgeted Overheads}}{\text{Budgeted Output Units or Budgeted Hours}} \text{ or per hour.}$$

1. Recovered or Absorbed Ovrheads [*i.e.*, Standard Overheads for actual output or actual hours]	= Standard Overheads Rate per unit × Actual Output or Standard Overhead Rate per hour × Standard hours for actual output.
2. Budgeted Overheads (for budgeted hours or budgeted output)	= Standard overhead rate per unit × Budgeted output units or Standard overhead rate per hour × budgeted hours [Note Budgeted Output or hours are equal to Standard Output or Hours]
3. Standard Overheads (For actual time or budgeted output for actual time)	= Standard Overhead Rate Per Unit × Standard Output for actual time or Standard Overhead Rate per hour × Actual hours
4. Actual Overheads	= Actual Overhead Rate per unit × Actual Output or Actual Rate per hours × Actual hours
5. Standard hours for actual output	$= \frac{\text{Budgeted Hours}}{\text{Budgeted Output}} \times \text{Actual Output}$
6. Standard Output for Actual Time	$= \frac{\text{Budgeted Output}}{\text{Budgeted Hours}} \times \text{Actual Hours}$

Fixed Overhead Cost Variance (*FOCV*)

FOCV is the difference between standard overhead recovered or absorbed for actual output and the actual fixed overhead.

$$FOCV = \begin{pmatrix}\textbf{Recovered or Absorbed} \\ \textbf{Fixed Overhead}\end{pmatrix} - \begin{pmatrix}\textbf{Actual Fixed} \\ \textbf{Overhead}\end{pmatrix}$$

or

(Actual Output) × (Standard Overhead Rate) – (Actual Overhead Rate × Actual Output)

FOCV may be analysed into following variances:

(*a*) Fixed Overhead Expenditure Variance (FOEV)

FOEV is the difference between actual expenditure and budgeted expenditure.

***FOEV* = Budgeted Overhead – Actual Overhead**

or

(Standard Overhead Rate × Budgeted Output) – (Actual Overhead Rate × Actual Output)

(*b*) Fixed Overhead Volume Variance (*FOVV*)

FOVV is the difference between fixed overhead recovered on actual output and fixed overhead on budgeted output. It is the result of difference in volume of production multiplied by the standard rate.

***FOVV* = Recovered Fixed Overhead – Budgeted Fixed Overhead**

or

(Standard Overhead Rate × Actual Output) – (Standard Overhead Rate × Budgeted Output)

Seggregation of Fixed Overhead Volume Variance

Fixed Overhead Volume Variance (*FOVV*) can further be analysed as Fixed Overhead Efficiency Variance and Fixed Overhead Capacity Variance.

(*a*) Fixed Overhead Efficiency Variance (*FOEFV*)

It is that portion of volume variance which arises due to difference between budgeted efficiency of production and the actual efficiency attained.

***FOEFV* = Recovered Fixed Overheads – Standard Fixed Overhead**

or

(Standard overhead Rate × Actual Output) – (Standards Overhead Rate × Standard Output for Actual Time)

(*b*) Fixed Overhead Capacity Variance (*FOCPV*)

It is that portion of volume variance which arises due to budgeted capacity specified and the actual capacity attained. It reveals whether the plants are over or under utilised. This variance may arise due to break-down in machinary, idle time, failure of power etc.

***FOCPV* = Standard Fixed Overheads – Budgeted Fixed Overheads**

or

(Standard overhead Rate × Standard Output for Actual Time) – (Standard Overhead Rate × Budgeted Output)

Illustration 29: From the following data, calculate Fixed Overhead Expenditure Variance (*FOEXPV*) and Volume Variances (*FOVV*):

Fixed Overhead Budget for the Month	₹ 1,00,000
Budgeted Production for the Month	50,000 units
Actual Production for the Month	54,000
Actual Fixed Overhead incurred	₹1,20,000

Solution:

Fixed Overhead Exp. Variance (*FOEXPV*) = Budgeted Overheads – Actual Overhead

= ₹ 1,00,000 – ₹ 1,20,000 = ₹ 20,000 (A)

Fixed Overhead Volume Variance (*FOVV*) = Recovered Overheads – Fixed (Budgeted) Overhead

[Recovered Overheads $= \frac{\text{Budgeted Overheads}}{\text{Budgeted Output}} \times \text{Actual Output}$]

$= \frac{1,00,000}{50,000} \times 54,000 =$ ₹. 1,08,000]

= ₹. 1,08,000 – ₹. 1,00,000 = ₹. 8,000 (F)

Overhead Cost Variance (*OCV*) = Recovered Overheads – Actual Overheads

= ₹. 1,08,000 – ₹ 1,20,000 = ₹. 12,000 (A)

Verification :

Overhead Cost Variance = Expenditure Variance + Volume Variance

= ₹ 20,000 (A) + ₹ 8,000 (F) = ₹ 12,000 (A)

Illustration 30: From the following information compute Fixed Overhead Cost, Expenditure and Volume Variances.

Normal capacity is 5,000 hours. Budgeted Fixed Overhead Rate is ₹. 10 per standard hour. Actual level of capacity utilised is 4,400 standard hours. Actual Fixed Overheads ₹. 52,000.

[B.Com. Hons. Delhi]

Solution:

Fixed Overhead Cost Variance (*FOCV*) = Recovered Fixed Overheads – Actual Fixed Overheads

= 44,000 – 52,000 = 8,000 (Adverse)

Fixed Overhead Exp. Variance (*FOEXPV*) = Budgeted Fixed Overheads – Actual Fixed Overheads

= 50,000 – 52,000 = ₹. 2,000 (Adverse)

Fixed Overhead Volume Variance (*FOVV*) = Recovered Fixed Overheads – Budgeted Fixed Overheads

= 44,000 – 50,000 = ₹. 6,000 (Adverse)

Illustration 31: From the following prepare variance analysis of a particular department for a month :

Variable Overhead Items	*Actual (₹)*	*Fixed Overheads Items*	*Actual (₹)*
Materials handling	8,325	Supervision	1,700
Idle time	850	Depreciation—Plant	2,000
Re-work	825	Depreciation—Equipment	5,000
Overtime premium	250	Rates	1,150
Supplies	4,000	Insurance	350
Total	14,250	Total	10,200

Normal capacity 10,000 standard hours, budgeted rate ₹ 1.70 per standard hour for variable overhead and ₹ 1 per standard hour for fixed overhead. Actual level: 8,000 standard hours.

[*ICWA Inter*]

Solution:

Variable Overhead Cost Variance (*VOCV*) = Recovered Variable Overheads – Actual Variable Overheads

= 8,000 × 1.70 – 14,250

= 13,600 – 14,250 = 650 (Adverse)

Fixed Overhead Cost Variance (*FOCV*) = Recovered Fixed Overheads – Actual Fixed Overheads

= 8,000 × 1 – 10,200 = ₹ 2,200 (Adverse)

Fixed Overhead Expenditure Variance (*FOEV*) = Budgeted Fixed Overheads – Actual Fixed Overheads

= 10,000 × 1 – 10,200 = ₹ 200 (Adverse)

Fixed Overhead Volume Variance (*FOVV*) = Recovered Fixed Overheads – Budgeted Fixed Overheads

= 8,000 – 10,000 = ₹. 2,000 (Adverse)

Fixed Overhead Capacity Variance may be further analysed into Fixed Overhead Calender Variance and Fixed Overhead Revised Capacity Variance or Fixed Overhead Yield Variance.

(x) Fixed Overhead Calender Varience (*FOCALV*)

FOCALV is that portion of capacity variance which arises due to difference between the number of working days anticipated in the budget period and the actual working days in the budget period. The number of working days in the budget are arrived at by dividing the number of annual days by twelve. But the actual days of a month may be more or less than the standard days and with the result there may be calender variance.

FOCALV **= Possible Fixed Overheads – Budgeted Fixed Overheads**

or

(Standard Overhead Rate per hour × Possible Hours) – (Standard Rate per hour × Budgeted Hours)

[Here, Possible Hours = Standard working hours per day × Actual number of working days]

(y) Fixed Overhead Revised Capacity Variance (*FORCAPV*)

FORCAPV will be the remaining part of capacity variance as reduced by calender variance.

FORCAPV **= Standard Fixed Overhead – Possible Fixed Overheads**

(z) Fixed Overhead Yield Variance (*FOYV*)

Just like material or labour yield variance, overhead yield variance may be calculated. This variance shows the gain or loss incurred by way of overhead cost incidence on account of loss or wastage in production.

FOYV **= Recovered Fixed Overhead – Expected Fixed Overheads**

[Here; Expected Fixed Overhead = Standard Overhead Rate per Unit × Expected Output]

Note: Expected output means output on actual input after allowing standard loss.

Illustration 31: In a factory the standard units of production of the year were fixed at 1,20,000 units and overhead expenditures were estimated to be:

Fixed	₹. 12,000	Variable	₹. 6,000
Semi-variable	₹. 1,800		

Actual production during the month of April of the year was 8,000 units. Each month has 20 working days.

During the month in question there was one statutory holiday. The actual overheads amounted to:

Fixed	₹. 1,190	Variable	₹. 480
Semi-variable	₹. 192		

Semi-variable charges are considered to include 60 per cent expenses of fixed nature and 40 per cent of variable character.

Find out the Overhead Expenditure, Volume and Calender Variances. **[*C.A. Inter*]**

Solution:

Overhead Cost Variance (*OCV*) = Recovered Overheads – Actual Overheads ₹.

= ₹. 1,320 – 1,862 542.00 (Adverse)

(*a*) *Expenditure Variance*:

Variable Overheads Exp. Variance

= Standard Variable Overhead Absorbed – Actual Variable Overheads

= ₹. 448 – 556.80 108.80 (Adverse)

Fixed Overheads Exp. Variance = Budgeted Fixed Overhead – Actual Fixed Overheads

= ₹. 1,090 – 1,305.20 215.20 (Adverse)

Total Overhead Expenditure Variaince 324.00 (Adverse)

(*b*) *Overhead Volume Variance* :

Fixed Overheads Volume Variance= Recovered Overheads – Budgeted Overheads

= ₹. 872 – 1,090 218.00 (Adverse)

Total 542.00 (Adverse)

(*c*) *Calender Variance*: (included in the volume variance)

Fixed overheads to be absorbed per day

$$= \frac{₹.13,080}{240} = ₹.54.50$$

Loss due to one day (54.50 × 1) ₹. 54.50 (Adverse)

Calculations

1. (*A*)Standard Rate of Overhead absorption per unit :

Fixed Overheads : $\frac{\text{Budgeted Fixed Over Heads}}{\text{Budgeted Output}}$

$= \frac{12,000}{1,20,000}$ ₹. 0.100

Fixed overheads element in semi-variable overheads

i.e., 60% of ₹. 1,800 = $\frac{1080}{1,20,000}$ 0.009

Standard Rate of Absorption of Fixed Overheads per unit ₹. 0.109

Fixed Overheads recovered on 8,000 units, @ ₹. 0.109 ₹. 872

(*B*) *Budgeted Variable Overheads*	₹. 6,000
Add: Variable element in semi-variable overheads 40% of ₹. 1,800	720
Total Budgeted Variable Overheads	6,720

Standard Variable Cost per unit = $\frac{6,720}{1,20,000}$ = ₹. 056

Variable Overheads for 8,000 units @ ₹. 0.056 = ₹. 448

2. Budgeted Annual Fixed Overheads are ₹. 12,000 + 60% of ₹. 1,800 = 12,080

Budgeted Monthly Fixed Overheads are = $\frac{13,080}{12}$ = ₹. 1,090

3. Actual Fixed Overheads are ₹. 1,190 + 60% of ₹. 192 = ₹. 1,305.20
4. Actual Variable Overheads are ₹. 480 + 40% ₹. 192 = ₹. 556.80

Illustration 32 : A Cost Accountant of a company was given the following information regarding the overheads for the month of February,

(*a*) Overheads cost variance : ₹ 1,400 adverse.

(*b*) Overheads volume variance : ₹. 1,000 adverse.

(*c*) Budgeted hours for February : 1,200 hours.

(*d*) Budgeted overheads for February : ₹. 6,000.

(*e*) Actual rate of recovery of overheads : ₹. 8 per hour.

You are required to assist him in computing the following for the month of February,

(1) Overhead expenditure variance.
(2) Actual overhead incurred
(3) Actual hours for actual production
(4) Overheads capacity variance.
(5) Overheads efficiency variance.
(6) Standard hours for actual production.

[*CA Inter*]

Solution:

Variances :

(1) Overheads Expenditure Variance (*OEXPV*)

= Overheads Cost Variance – Overheads Volume Variance

= ₹. 1,400 (A) – ₹. 1,000 (A) = ₹. 400 (A)

(2) Actual Overheads incured

= Budgeted Overheads – Overhead Expenditure Variance

= ₹. 6,000 – ₹. 400 (A) = ₹. 6,400

(3) Actual hours for actual production

$$= \frac{\text{Actual Overheads Incurred}}{\text{Actual Rate of Recovery of Overhead per hour}}$$

= 6400/8 = 800 hours

(4) Overheads Capacity Variance

= Standard Overhead Rate × (Actual Hours – Budgeted Hours)
= 5 × (800 hours – 1,200 Hours) = ₹. 2,000 (A)

$$\left[\text{Standard Overhead Rate} = \frac{\text{Budgeted Overheads}}{\text{Budgeted Hours}} = \frac{₹.\ 6{,}000}{1{,}200}\ ₹.\ 5 \text{ per hour}\right]$$

(5) Overhead Efficiency Variance

= Overheads Volume Variance – Overhead Capacity Variance
= ₹. 1,000 (A) – ₹. 2,000 (A) = ₹. 1,000 (F)

(6) Standard Hours for Actual Production

Volume Variance = Standard Overhead Rate × Std. hours for actual production – Budgeted hours)

Budgeted hours are presumed to be x.

or 1,000 (A) = 5 $(x - 1{,}200)$
or 1,000 (A) = $5x - 6{,}000$
or $-5x = -5{,}000$
or x = 1,000 hours.

Causes of Overhead Variances

Some of possible causes of overhead variances are given below:

Variance	*Possible Causes*	*Person Responsible*
1. Overhead Expenditure Variance	(*i*) Rise in wages	Uncontrollable
	(*ii*) Rise is price level	Uncontrollable
	(*iii*) Lack of effective control	Departmental Manager
	(*iv*) Change in methods of production	Production Manager
	(*v*) Change in the policy of manufacturing	Top Management
2. Overhead Efficiency Variance	(*i*) Inefficient workmen	Foremen
	(*ii*) Break-down of machinery	Production Manager
	(*iii*) Inefficient supervisor	Foremen
	(*iv*) Loss of timeProduction Manager	
	(*v*) Lack of proper planing	Planning Engineer
	(*vi*) Poor efficiency of machinery	Maintenance Engineer
	(*vii*) Old and obsolete machinery	Uncontrollable
3. Overhead Capacity Variance	(*i*) Lack of orders	Sales Manager
	(*ii*) Lock-outs and strikes	Uncontrollable
	(*iii*) Seasonel cuts in production	Uncontrollable
4. Overhead Calender Variance	(*i*) Differences between budgeted days and actual days	Uncontrollable

SALES VARIANCES

The Actual Profit and Standard Profit should also be analysed. Since profit is the difference between sales and cost, the analysis of cost variances would be incomplete if sales variances are not analysed.

Sales variances are the variances which are due to (*i*) difference between standard sale-quantity and actual sale-quantity, and/or (*ii*) difference between standard selling price or profit per unit and actual selling price or profit per unit.

There are two methods of computing sales variances.

(1) Sales Turnover or Value Method

(2) Profit or Sales Margin Method

In the sales value method, the variances are calculated on the basis of sales value. In the second method, sales variances are computed with reference to profit per unit.

Sales Variances with reference to turnover or sales value

Sales value variance is the difference between standard value of sales and the actual value of sales effected during the period. Since change in the sales value may be due to change in selling price/quantity and sales mix etc., this variance may be analysed as below:

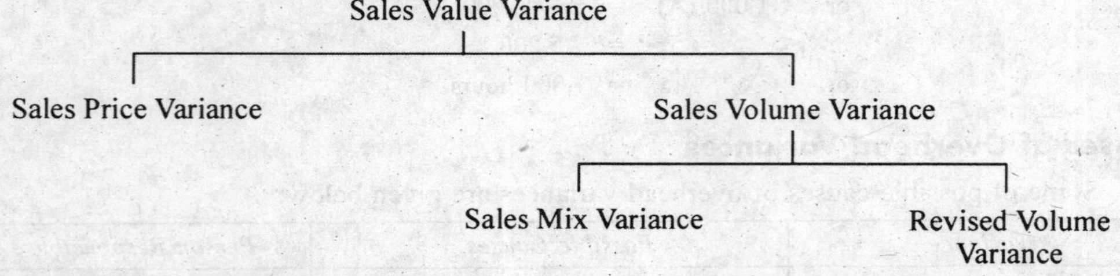

Before calculating various sales variances the following terms should be understood.

Budgeted Sales	= Standard or Budgeted Quantity of Sales × Standard Selling Price
Actual Sales	= Actual Quantity of Sales × Actual Selling Price
Standard Sales	= Actual Quantity of Sales × Standard Selling Price

Sales Value Variance = **Budgeted Sales – Actual Sales**

or

(Standard Selling Price × Standard Quantity) – (Actual Selling Price × Acutal Quantity)

If Actual Sales are more than Budgeted sales, the variance will be favourable and vice-versa. Sales Value Variance may be further analysed as (*i*) Sales Price Variance and (*ii*) Sales Volume Variance.

It may be noted that these variances are calculated just like material variances.

Sales Price Variance

It is that portion of sales value variance which is due to difference between the standard selling price specified and actual selling price charged.

Sales Price Variance = **Standard Sales – Actual Sales**

or

= **Actual Quantity Sold × (Standard Selling Price – Actual Selling Price)**

If the actual prices of sales attained are more than standard prices, there will be favourable variance and *vice-versa*.

Sales Volume Variance

It is the difference between the budgeted sales and the standard sales.

Sales Volume Variance **= Budgeted Sales – Standard Sales**

or

= Standard Selling Price × (Budgeted or Standard Quantity – Actual Quantity)

If the actual sales at standard price *i.e.*, standard sales are more than budgeted sales, there is favourable variance and vice-versa.

Illustration 33: The budgeted and actual sales of a concern manufacturing and marketing a single product are furnished below:

Budgeted Sales	10,000 units at ₹ 4 per unit
Actual Sales	5,000 units at ₹ 3.5 pe unit
	8,000 units at ₹ 4 per unit

Calculate: (*a*) Sales Price Variance (*b*) Sales Volume Variance and (*c*) Sales Value Variance.

Solution:

(*a*) *Sales Price Variance* = *AQ* (*SP* – *AP*)

= 5000 (4 – 3.5) = 2500

(*b*) *Sales Volume Variance* = Budgeted Sales – Standard Sales or St. S.P. (*SQ* – *AQ*)

= ₹. 40,000 – ₹. 52,000

= ₹. 12,000 (Favourable)

(*c*) *Sales Value Variance* = Budgeted Sales – Actual Sales

= ₹. 40,000 – ₹. 49,500

= ₹. 9,500 (Favourable)

Verification

Sales Value Variance = Sales Price Variance + Sales Volume Variance

= 2,500 (A) + 12,000 (F) = 9,500 (F)

Segregation of Sales Volume Variance

Sales volume variance may be further sub-divided into (*a*) Sales Mix Variance, and (*b*) Sales Quantity Variance.

(*a*) **Sales Mix Variance.** It is that portion of sales value variance which is due to the difference between the standard and actual mix of the quantities of each product or product group of which the sales are composed of. It is calculated just like material mix variance. As it is in the material mix variance, the Revised Standard Quantity (or Revised Standard Sales) is calculated:

The standard is revised by two methods: (*i*) based on quantity, and (*ii*) based on value.

Based on Quantity. If products are homogenious (of same kinds) the revised standard quantities will be calculated as these are calculated in Material Mix Variance.

$$\text{Revised Standard Quantity} = \frac{\text{Total Quantity of Actual Mix} \times \text{Standard Quantity}}{\text{Total Quantity of Standard Mix}}$$

Sales Mix Variance **= Standard Selling Price × (Revised Standard Quantity – Actual Quantity)**

If actual quantity is more than the Revised Standard Quantity, there will be favourable variance and *vice-versa.*

Based on Value. If the products are not homogenous (not of same kinds), the actual sales at standard price (*i.e.*, standard sales) are revised in budgeted ratio of sales in order to calculate Revised Standard Sales.

$$\text{Budgeted Ratio of Sales} = \frac{\text{Budgeted Sales of a Product}}{\text{Total Budgeted Sales}}$$

Revised Standard Sales = Budgeted Ratio of Sales × Standard Sales

***Sales Mix Variance* = Revised Standard Sales – Standard Sales**

The mix variance, if standard sales are more than the revised standard sales, will be favourable.

Usually the second method (based on sales value) is considered more reasonable.

(*b*) **Revised Volume Variance.** When there is difference between Revised standard sales and Budgeted sales, it is called Revised Volume Variance. When Revised Standard Sales are more than Budgeted Sales, it is favourable variance and *vice-versa.*

Revised Sales Volume Variance = Budgeted Sales – Revised Standard Sales
or Standard Selling Price × (Budgeted Quantity – Revised Standard Quantity)

It may be noted that total of Sales Mix Variance and Revised Volume Variance is equal to Sales Volume Variance.

Illustration 34: Pioneer Plastics Limited operates a budgetary control and standard costing system. From the following data calculate:

(*i*) Sales Variance
(*ii*) Sales Volume Variance
(*iii*) Sales Price Variance

Product	*Std. cost of sales per unit*	*Std. selling price per unit*	*Budget*		*Actual*	
			Units to be sold	*Sales values*	*Units sold*	*Sales value*
A	₹. 10.00	₹. 12.00	100	₹. 1,200	100	₹. 1,100
B	9.40	12.00	50	600	50	600
C	7.50	9.00	100	900	200	1,700
D	4.00	6.00	75	450	50	300
Total	–	–	325	3,150	400	3,700

[*C.A.*]

Solution:

Sales (Value) Variance = Budgeted Sales – Actual Sales
or Actual Qty. × (Std. Price – Actual Price)

A	= 100 × (12 – 11)	=	₹. 100 (Adverse)
B	= 50 × (12 – 12)	=	Nil
C	= 200 × (9 – 8.50)	=	₹. 100 (Adverse)
D	= 50 × (6 – 6)	=	Nil
		Total	₹. 200 (Adverse)

Sales Volume Variance = Budgeted Sales – Standard Sales
or Std. Price × (Budgeted Qty. – Actual Qty.)

A	= 12 × (100 – 100)	=	Nil
B	= 12 × (50 – 50)	=	Nil
C	= 9 × (100 – 200)	=	900 (Favourable)
D	= 6 × (75 – 50)	=	150 (Adverse)
		Total	₹. 750 (Favourable)

Verification:

Sales Value Variance = Sales Price Variance + Sales Volume Variance
= ₹. 200 (A) + ₹. 750 (F) = ₹ 550 (Favourable)

Sales Margin Variance or Sales Variance with Reference to Profit

While calculating Sales Margin Variance, following terms should be clearly understood.

Budgeted Profit	= Budgeted or Standard Quantity of Sales × Standard Profit per unit
Actual Profit	= Actual Quantity of Sales × Actual Profit per unit
Standard Profit	= Actual Quantity of Sales × Standard Profit per unit
Revised Standard Profit	= Revised Standard Sales × Standard Rate of Profit
Standard Rate of Profit	= Standard Proft per Unit ÷ Standard selling price per unit

Sales Margin Value Variance or Total Sales Margin Variance – It is difference between Budgeted Profit and Actual Profit

Sales Value Variance = Budgeted Profit – Actual Profits

Sales Margin Value Variance may be analysed as (*i*) Sales Margin Price Variance, and (*ii*) Sales Margin Volume Variance.

(*a*) **Sales Margin Price Variance :** It is the difference between Standard Profit and Actual Profit. This variance is calculated just like Material Price Variance.

Sales Margin Price Variance **= Standard Profit on Actual Quantity – Actual Profit on Actual Quantity**

or

Actual Quantity Sold × (Standard Profit per Unit – Actual Profit per Unit)

If Standard Profit is more than Actual Profit, it will be unfavourable variance and *vice-versa.*

(*b*) **Sales Margin Volume Variance** – It is the amount by which standard profit differ from Budgeted Profit.

Sales Margin Volume Variance **= Budgeted Profit – Standard Profit**

or

Standard Rate of Profit per uit × (Budgeted or Standard Quantity – Actual Quantity)

If Standard Profit is more than budgeted profit it will be favourable variance and *vice versa.*

The sales volume variance may be further analysed as (i) Sales Mix Variance, and (ii) Sales Quantity Variance.

(*i*) Sales Margin Mix Variance (Based on Profit)

There may be variance in profit due to change in the composition or mix or various products sold. On change in the mix, revised standard profit will be calculated.

Revised Standard Profit = Revised Standard Sales × Standard Rate of Profit

Standard Rate of Profit $= \dfrac{\text{Standard Profit per Unit}}{\text{Standard Price per Unit}}$

Revised standard sales will be calculated on the basis of Budgeted Ratio of Sales

Budgeted Ratio of Sales $= \dfrac{\text{Budgeted Sale of a Product}}{\text{Total Budgeted Sales}}$

Revised Standard Sales of each product will be Standard Sales × Budgeted Ratio of Sales.

Sales Margin Mix Variance = Revised Standard Profit × Standard Profit

If the standard profit is more than revised standard profit, there will be a favourable variance and *vice-versa*.

(*ii*) Sales Margin Quantity Variance (Based on Profit)

It is that part of volume variance which arises due to difference between budgeted profit and revised standard profit.

Sales Margin Quantity Variance **= Budgeted Profit – Revised Standard Profit**

If Revised Standard Profit is more than Budgeted Profit, there will be favourable variance and *vice-versa.*

Illustration 35: From the following budgeted and actual figures, calculate sales variances on sales margin basis and cost of sales variance.

	₹.
Budgeted	
Sales 2000 units @ ₹ 30 each	60,000
Cost of Sales @ ₹ 24 each	48,000
Profit	12,000
Actual	
Sales 1900 units @ ₹ 28 each	53,200
Cost of Sales @ ₹ 20 each	38,000
Profit	15,200

[*ICWA*]

Solution:

Calculation:

(*i*) Actual Margin or Profit per unit = Actual Selling Price – Budgeted Cost of Sales per Unit
= ₹ 28 – 24 = ₹ 4

(*ii*) Budgeted Margin or Profit per unit = Budgeted Selling Price – Budgeted Cost of Sales per Unit
= ₹ 30 – 24 = ₹ 6

1. Total Sales Margin Variance = Budget Profit – Actual Profit
= 12,000 – 15,200 = ₹ 3,200 (F)

2. Sales Margin Price Variance = Standard Profit on Actual Quantity – Profit on Actual Quantity)
or
Actual Quantity Sold (Standard Profit per Unit – Actual Profit per Unit)
1,900 × (6 – 4) = 3,800 (A)

3. Sales Margin Volume Variance = Budgeted Profit – Standard profit
or
= Standard Profit per Unit × (Budgeted Quantity – Actual Quantity)
= 6 × (2,000 – 1,900) = 600 (A)

4. Cost of Sales Variance = Actual Quantity (Budgeted Cost of Sales per Unit – Actual Cost of Sales per Unit)
= 1900 × (₹ 24 – 20) = 7600 (F)

Verification.

Total Sales Margin Variance = Sales Margin Price Variance + Sales Margin Quantity Variance + Cost of Sales Variance

₹ 3200 (F) = 3800 (A) + 600 (A) + 7600 (F)

Illustration 36: From the following information, calculate sales margin variances.

Product	*Budgeted Sales*			*Actual Sales*	
	Quantity (unit)	*Sales Price per Unit ₹*	*Standard Cost per Unit ₹*	*Quantity (Units)*	*Sales Price per Unit ₹*
X	900	20	15	1,200	24
Y	600	15	10	900	12
	1,500			2,100	

Solution:

1. *Total Sales Margin Variance* = Budgeted Profit or Margin – Actual Profit
= (Standard or Budgeted Quantity × Standard Profit per Unit) – (Actual Quantity × Actual Profit per Unit)
= [(900 × 5) + (600 × 5)] – [(1200 × 9) + (900 × 2)]
= 7500 – 12600 = 5100 (F)

2. *Total Sales Margin Price Variance*
= Standard Profit on Actual Quantity – Profit on Actual Quantity
or
= Actual Quantity Sold × (Standard Profit per unit – Actual Profit per unit

Product *X* = 1200 (₹ 5 – ₹ 9) = 4,800 (F)
Product *Y* = 900 (₹ 5 – ₹ 2) = 2,700 (A)
₹. 2,100 (F)

Total Sales Margin Volume Variance = Budgeted Profit – Standard Profit
or
Standard Profit per unit × (Budgeted Quantity – Actual Quantity)

Product *X* = ₹ 5 × (900 – 1,200) = 1,500 (F)
Product *Y* = ₹ 5 × (600 – 900) = 1,500 (F)
₹ 3,000 (F)

Total Sales Margin Mix Variance = Revised Standard Profit – Standard Profit
or
Standard Profit per unit × (Standard Proportion of Mix – Actual Mix)

Product *X* = ₹ 5 (1,260 – 1,200) = 300 (A)
Product *Y* = 5 (840 – 900) = 300 (F)
Nil

Total Sales Margin Quantity Mix = Budgeted Profit – Revised Standard Profit

or

$= [5 \times (900 + 600)] - 5\ (1260 + 840)]$

$7500 - 10500 = 3000$ (F)

Working: Standard Proportion of Mix

$X \quad 900 \times \dfrac{2100}{1500} = 1260$ units

$Y \quad 600 \times \dfrac{2100}{1500} = 840$ units

PRESENTATION OF STANDARD COST STATEMENT

Standard cost statement is prepared to show reconcilliation between the Standard Profit and the Actual Profit. The statement is a consolidated summary of all variences.

Item	*Standard*	*Variances*		*Actual*
		Favourable	*Adverse*	
Standard Sales Values				
Sales Variances				
Price				
Quantity				
Mix				
Actual Sales Value				
Less Standard Cost of Sales				
Direct Material				
Direct Labour				
Variable Overhead				
Fixed Overhead				
Standard Net Profit				
Cost Variances:				
(*a*) Material:				
Price				
Mix				
Yield				
(*b*) Labour				
Rate				
Efficiency				
Mix				
(*c*) Variable Overhead				
Expenditure				
(*d*) Fixed Overhead				
Expenditure				
Efficiency				
Calender				
Total Cost Variance				
Actual Net Profit				

CONTROL OF VARIANCES

For control purposes, variances should be attributed to the managers normally responsible. Thus the responsible manager in the case of a Material Price Variance is the Purchase Manager and in case of labour inefficiency is the Production Manager. However, business functions are so much inter-related that the variance attributed to a Manager may not be within his control. Thus an adverse Material Price Variance may be due to a reduction in the volume of purchase due to fall in output which in turn may have been caused by a recession in demand, excess tunes in the workshop may be due to faulty material; Overhead variances may be due to restrictions on output. But it can be said that ultimately variance are the combined responsibility of the entire management.

It can be understood that all variances are controllable at some level of management. If various adverse variances are the result of recession and reduction in sale, it is responsibility of top management to apply the resources of business to alternative outlets or there may be a programme of contraction.

But some variances are uncontrollable by the management, particularly where external factors such as government-intervention impose price increases on raw material and other supplies or price reduction on output or increase in administrative costs. Thus it is desirable that variances which are controllable or uncontrollable should be separately considered. If a variance is not controllable at any level of management then the standard should be revised at the next review period. If it is controllable, then the standard should not be revised merely on the grounds that the actual performance does not meet the correctly assessed standard.

The success of a standard costing system depends on the involvement of the managers. It is the managers who should assess and revise the standards and take what action they can take to eliminate the variances.

DISPOSITION OF VARIANCE

The usual practice is to transfer all variances to the Costing Profit and Loss Account. But a question may arise whether inventory valuations as determined according to standard costs, should be adjusted for variances. It would not be proper to do so for variances which have resulted only from inefficiency or extra efficiency. Price variances can be properly adjusted in the valuation placed on inventory. For instance, if Materials Price Variance is unfavourable, inventory values may be suitably increased so that inventory is valued at cost. One must, however, remember that sometimes efficiency and price variance are interlinked. For instance materials usage variance may be adverse because of a decision to use inferior material but this may (and should) result in favourable price variaince. In such a case, the two variances should first be adjusted against one another and then the net amount adjusted in the value placed on the inventory. This also applies to variances connected with labour. Variances connected with overheads should all be transferred to the Costing Profit and Loss Account but if changes in output leading to over or under recovery of overheads are because of unavoidable causes (say, because of restrictions imposed by Government), such variances should be adjusted in inventory values.

In brief following are the various methods which are generally used.

(*i*) Where the cost of variances are considered as a cost of inefficiency and not as a cost of product, they are to be transferred to Profit and Loss Accounts to maintain the same standard in future.

(*ii*) Where the cost of variances are considered as cost of product they are to be allocated to cost of sales, finished stock and work-in-progress.

(*iii*) Controllable variance can be adjusted against income of that period and uncontrollable variances, such as materials price change, wages rate increase due to national awards etc. are to be allocated over cost of sales and closing inventores of work-in-progress and finished goods.

Accounting Procedure

The accounting procedure regarding treatment of variances is based on following principles.

(*i*) Work-in-progress A/c should be debted by standard cost.

(*ii*) All Expenses Control A/c should be credited at their actual cost.

(*iii*) Favourable variances under separate accounts should be credited. Adverse variances should be debited. These accounts should be closed by transferring them to Costing P&L A/c.

On the basis of these principles, the accounting entries will be :

			₹.
1. **Material Cost Variance** [Suppose Mix and Yield Variances are adverse by ₹. 30 and 20. Price variance is favourbale ₹. 18. Material Cost Variance is ₹. 32 (A). Standard Cost ₹. 340 and Actual Cost ₹. 372]	Work-in-Progress A/c Dr. Material Mix Variance A/c Dr. Material Yield Variance A/c Dr. To Material Price Variance " Stores Ledger Control A/c	340 30 20	 18 372
2. **Labour Variance** [Suppose Wage Cost Variance ₹. 500 (A), Wage Rate Variance ₹. 100 (A), Labour Efficiency Variance ₹. 350 (A), Labour Mix Varinace ₹. 50 (A); Standard Wage ₹. 1000. Actual Wageş ₹. 15000].	Work-in-Progress A/c Dr. Wage Rate Variance A/c Dr. Labour Efficiency Variance A/c Labour Mix Variance A/c Dr. To Wages Control A/c	1,000 100 350 50	 1,500
3. **Overhead Variance** [Standard Overhead ₹. 33,000 Expendigure Variance ₹. 1000 (F), Volume Variance ₹. 2000 (F) Efficiency Variance ₹. 2400 (F) Calender Variance ₹. 2000 (A)	Work-in-Progress A/c Dr. Calender Variance A/c Dr. To Expenditure Variance A/c To Efficiency Variance A/c To Capacity Variance A/c To Overhead Control A/c	33,000 2,000	 2,000 2,400 1,600 29,000
4. **Closing Entires**	Finished Stock A/c To Work-in-Progress A/c	34,340	 34,340
	Material Price Variance A/c Dr. Expenditure Variance A/c Dr. Efficiency Variance A/c Dr. Capacity Variance A/c Dr. To Material Mix Variance A/c " Material Yield Variance A/c " Wage Rate Variance A/c " Labour Efficiency Variance A/c " Labour Mix Variance A/c " Claender Variance A/c " Costing P & L A/c	18 2,000 2,400 1,600	 30 20 100 350 50 2,000 3,468

TYPICAL ILLUSTRATIONS

Material Variances

Illustration 37: The standard mix of product A 2 is as follows:

Kgs.	*Material*	*Price per kg. (₹)*
45	X	6.00
25	Y	4.50
30	Z	9.50

The standard loss in production is 10% of input. There is no scrap value. Actual production for a month was 7.425 kgs. of A 2 from 80 mixes. Actual purchases and consumption of material during the month were:

Kgs.	*Material*	*Price per kg. (₹)*
4,200	X	6.50
1,700	Y	4.25
2,600	Z	9.75

You are required to calculate the following variances for presentation to the management :

(*i*) Material cost variance

(*ii*) Material price variance

(*iii*) Material mix variance

(*iv*) Material yield variance

Solution:

Standard Cost				*Actual Cost*			
Material	*Kg*	*Price*	*Amount* ₹	*Material*	*Kg*	*Price*	*Amount* ₹
X	80 × 45 = 3600	6.00	21,600	X	4200	6.50	27,300
Y	80 × 25 = 2000	4.50	9,000	Y	1700	4.25	7,225
Z	80 × 30 = 2400	9.50	22,800	Z	2600	9.75	25,350
Input	8000		53,400	Input	8,500		59,875
Loss 10%	800		—	Loss	1,075		—
Output	7200		53,400	Output	7,425		59,875

Standard Cost per unit = $\frac{53400}{7200}$ = 7.4167 per kg

Standard Cost of Actual Production = 7425 × 7.4167 = 55,069

(*i*) Material Cost Variance (*MCV*) = Standard Cost for Actual Production – Actual Cost

= 55,069 – 59,875 = ₹. 4,806 (A)

(*ii*) Material Price Variance (MPV) = Actual Quantity (Standard Rate – Actual Rate)

X = 4,200 (6,00 – 6.50) = 2,100 (A)

Y = 1,700 (4.50 – 4.25) = 425 (F)

Z = 2,600 (9.50 – 9.75) = 650 (A)

Total ₹. 2,325 (A)

(*iii*) Material Mix Variance (*MMV*) = Standard Rate (Revised St. Quantity – Actual Quantity)

X = 6.00 (3825 – 4200) = 2250 (A)

Y = 4.50 (2125 – 1700) = 1912.50 (F)

Z = 9.50 (2550 – 2600) = 475 (A)

Total 812,50 (A)

(*iv*) Material Yield Variance (*MYV*):

For 8000 Input — Yield 7200

For 8500 " — $\frac{8,500}{8,000} \times 7,200 = 7,650$ kgs

MYV = Standard Cost per kg (Actual yield – Standard yield)

= 7.4167 (7425 – 7650)

= ₹. 1,668.50 (A) (appx.)

Verification

$MCV = MPV + MMV + MYV$

= 2325 (A) + 812.50 (A) + 1668.50 (A) = 4806 (A)

Calculations:

Revised Standard Quantity (*RSQ*)

		Kgs.
$X = 3,600 \times \frac{8,500}{8,000}$	=	3,825
$Y = 2,000 \times \frac{8,500}{8,000}$	=	2,125
$Z = 2,400 \times \frac{8,500}{8,000}$	=	2,550
Total	=	8,500

Illustration 38: Compute the missing data indicated by the Question Marks from the following :

Particulars	*A*	*B*
Standard Price/Unit	₹. 12	₹. 15
Actual Price/Unit	₹. 15	₹. 20
Standard Input (kgs.)	50	?
Actual Input (kgs.)	?	70
Material Price Variance	?	?
Material Usage Variance	?	₹. 300 Adverse
Material Cost Variance	?	?

Material mix variance for both products together was ₹.45 adverse.

Solution:

1. **Standard Input of Product *B*:**

Material Usage Variance = $SR\ (SQ - AQ)$

₹. 300 A = $15\ (SQ - 70)$

– 300 = $15\ SQ - 1050$

$SQ = \frac{1050 - 300}{15}$ = 50 kg. Std. input of *B*

2. **Actual Input of Product *A* :**

This can be ascertained with the help of material mix variance. Let A be the actual input in kgs. for Product *A*.

Material Mix Variance = *AQ* (Std. cost of Std. mix per kg. – Std. cost of actual mix per kg.)

$$-45 = (A + 70 \text{ kg.})(₹.\ 13.50) - \left(\frac{12A + 1050}{A + 70}\right)$$

$$-45 = 13.50\ (A + 70) - (12\ A + 1050)$$

$-45 = 13.5\text{ A} + 945 - 12\text{ A} - 1050$

$-45 = 1.5\text{ A} - 105$

$A = \frac{105 - 45}{1.5}$ 40 kgs. (Actual input of Product A)

3. (*a*) Material Price Variance of *A* = $AQ\ (SR - AR)$
   = 40 kg. (12 – 15) = ₹. 120 (A)

   (*b*) Material Price Variance of *B* = 70 (15 – 20) = ₹. 350 (A)

4. Material Usage Variance of *A* = $SR\ (SQ - AQ)$
   = 12 (50 – 40) = ₹. 120 (F)

5. (*a*) Material Cost Variance of *A* = $SC - AC$
   = 50 kgs at ₹. 12 – 40 kgs. at ₹. 15
   = 600 – 600 = Nil

   (*b*) Material Cost Variance of *B* = (50 kgs. at ₹. 15) – (70 kgs. at ₹. 20)
   = 750 – 1400 = ₹. 650 (A)

Calculations:

1. Std. Cost of Std. mix per kg.:

   A 50 kgs. at ₹.12 = ₹. 600
   B 50 kgs. at ₹. 15 = ₹. 750

   Total 100 kgs. = ₹.1,350

   ₹. 1350/100 = ₹. 13.50

   Standard Cost of Actual Mix of *B*

   ₹. 15 × 70 kgs. = ₹. 1050

2. Standard Cost of Actual Mix:

	SC		*AM*		Amount (₹.)
A	12	×	A	=	12 A
B	15	×	70	=	1050
Total			A + 70		12 A + 1050

Standard Cost of Actual Mix = $\frac{12\text{ A} + 1050}{\text{A} + 70}$

3.

	Standard Cost				Actual Cost		
	Kg.	*Price*	*Amount* (₹.)		*Kg.*	*Price*	*Amount* (₹.)
A	50	12	600	*A*	40	15	600
B	50	15	750	*B*	70	20	1,400
Input	100		1,350	Input	110		2,000

Material Mix Variance = $SR\ (RSQ - AQ)$

A $= 12\left(\frac{110}{100} \times 50 - 40\right)$

$= 12\ (55 - 40) = 180\text{ (F)}$

B $= 15\ (55 - 70) = 225\text{ (A)}$

45 (A)

Illustration 39: The following information has been extracted from the records of a chemical company:

Standard price : Raw material A – ₹. 2 per kg.
Raw material B – ₹. 10 per kg.
Standard mix : A : 75% : B : 25% (by weight)
Standard yield : 90%

In a period, the actual costs, usages and output were as follows :

Used : 2,200 kgs. of A, costing ₹. 4,650
800 kgs. of B, costing ₹. 7,850
Output : 2,850 kgs. of products.

Calculate material cost variances.

Solution:

Calculations

1. Materials used 2,200 + 800 = 3,000 kgs.
2. Standard Cost (*SC*)
3. Actual Cost (*AC*)

Material	*Kg*	*Rate*	*Amt.* (₹)	*Material*	*Kg.*	*Amt.* (₹)
A	75% of 3,000 = 2,250	2	4,500	A	2,200	4,650
B	25% of 3,000 = 750	10	7,500	B	800	7,850
Input	3,000		12,000	Input	3,000	12,500
Loss 10%	300	—		Loss	150	—
Output	2,700		12,000	Output	2,850	12,500

4. Standard yield rate $= \dfrac{12{,}000}{2{,}700}$ = ₹ 4.444 per unit
5. Standard Cost of Actual Production (*SCAP*) = 2,850 × 4.444 = ₹. 12,667
6. Standard Cost for Standad Mix = ₹. 12,000
7. Actual Rate of Material used :

$$A = \frac{4{,}650}{2{,}200} = ₹.\ 2.1135 \text{ per unit}$$

$$B = \frac{7{,}850}{800} = ₹.\ 9.8125 \text{ per unit}$$

8. Standard Cost for Actual Mix

Material	*SC*	*AM*	*Amount* (₹)
A	2	2,200	4,400
B	10	800	8,000
		3,000	12,400

Variances

(*a*) Material Cost Variance (*MCV*) = Standard Cost of Actual Production – Actual Cost
= 12,667 – 12,500 = ₹. 167 (F)

(*b*) Material Price Variance (*MPV*) = Actual Quantity (Standard Rate – Actual Rate)

A = 2,200 (2 – 2.1136) = 250 (A)

B = 800 (10 – 9.8125) = 150 (F)

Total 100 (A)

(*c*) Material Mix Variance (*MMV*) = Std. Rate (*RSQ* – *AQ*)

A = 2 (2250 – 2200) = 100 (F)

B = 10 (750 – 800) = 500 (A)

Total 400 (A)

or

= Total Standard Cost for Standard Mix · Total Standard Cost for Actual Mix

= 12,000 – 12,400 = 400 (A)

(*d*) Material Yield Variance (*MYV*) = *SYR* (*AY* – *SY*)

= 4.4444 (2,850 – 2,700) = ₹. 667 (F)

Verification

MCV = *MPV* + *MMV* + *MYV*

= 100 (A) + 400 (A) + 667 (F) = 167 (F)

Labour Variances

Illustration 40: The standard labour complement and the actual labour complement engaged during the month are given below:

	Skilled	*Semi-skilled*	*Unskilled*
(*a*) Standard number of workers in a group	30	10	10
(*b*) Standard wage rate (Rupees per hour)	5	3	2
(*c*) Actual number of workers employed during the month in the group	24	15	12
(*d*) Actual wage rate per hour (₹.)	6	2.5	2

During the month of 200 working hours, the group produced 9,600 standard hours of work.

Required

Calculations showing Wage rate variance, Labour efficiency variance, Labour mix variance and Total labour cost variance.

Solution :

Calculations :

1. Standard Labour Hour Rate of the Standard Group

Category	*No. of men*	*Hours per month*	*Total hours*	*Standard Rate* ₹	*Standard Labour Cost* ₹.
Skilled	30	200	6,000	5	30,000
Semi-skilled	10	200	2,000	3	6,000
Unskilled	10	200	2,000	2	4,000
			10,000		40,000

Hence, standard rate per hour of the group = 40,000/10,000 = ₹. 4.0

2. Standard Cost for Actual Mix

Category	*No. of men*	*Hours per month*	*Total hours*	*Standard Rate* ₹.	*Standard Labour Cost* ₹.
Skilled	24	200	4,800	5	24,000
Semi-skilled	15	200	3,000	3	9,000
Unskilled	12	200	2,400	2	4,800
			10,200		37,800

3. Actual Labour hour rate of Actual Mix

Category	*No. of men*	*Hours per month*	*Total hours*	*Standard Rate ₹*	*Standard Labour Cost ₹*
Skilled	24	200	4,800	6.00	28,800
Semi-skilled	15	200	3,000	2.50	7,500
Unskilled	12	200	2,400	2.00	4,800
			10,200		41,100

Variances

a. Wages Rate Variance = *AHP (SR – AR)*

Skilled = 4,800 (5 – 6) = 4,800 A

Semi-skilled = 3,000 (3 – 2.50) = 1,500 F

Unskilled = 2,400 (2 – 2) = Nil

Total 3,300 A

b. Labour Efficiency Varinace = SR (SH – AHP)

Skilled = 5 (6,000 – 4,800) = 6,000 F

Semi-skilled = 3 (2,000 – 3,000) = 3,000 A

Unskillec = 2 (2,000 – 2,400) = 800 A

2,200 F

c. Labour Mix Variance = Standard Cost for St. Mix – St. Cost of Actual Mix

= 40,000 – 37,800 = 2200 F

d. Total Labour Cost Variance = SC – AC

= 4,00,000 – 41,100 = ₹. 1,100 A

Note:

e. *Labour yield Variance:*

St. yield is not given in the question. Actual output is 9,600 standard hours of work. Henc. labour yield variance could not be worked out. It has been presumed that standard output and actual output both have been 9600 hours.

Illustration 41: From the particulars given below compute : Material Price Variance, Material Usage Variance, Labour Rate Variance, Idle Time Variance and Labour Efficiency Variance with full working details.

One tonne of material input yields a standard output of 1,00,000 units. The standard price of material is ₹. 20 per kg. Number of employees engaged is 200. The standard wage rate per employee per day is ₹ 6. The standard daily output per employee is 100 units. The actual quantity of material used is 10 tonnes and the actual price paid is ₹. 21 per kg. Actual output obtained is 9,00,000 units. Actual number of days worked is 50 and actual rate of wages paid is ₹.6.50 per day. Idle time paid for and included in above time is 1/2 day.

Solution:

(A) Material Variances :

Standard Cost = 10 tonnes at ₹. 20,000 = ₹. 2,00,000

Actual Cost = 10 tonnes at ₹. 21,000 = ₹. 2,10,000

Standard Cost for Actual Production = $\frac{9,00,000}{1,00,000}$ or 9 tonnes at ₹. 20,000 = ₹. 1,80,000

(*i*) Material Price Variance = *AQ (SR – AR)*

= 10 (20,000 – 21000) = ₹. 10,000 (A)

(*ii*) Material Usage Variance = *SR (SQ for actual output – AQ)*

= 20,000 (9 – 10) = ₹. 20,000 (A)

(*iii*) Material Cost Variance = SCAP – AC
= 180000 – 210000 = ₹. 30000 (A)

Verification

Standard Cost Variance = Price Variance + Usage Variance
= 10,000 (A) + 20,000 (A) = 30,000 (A)

(*B*) Labour Variances

No. of employees : 200. Standard daily output employee = 100 units

One day output for 200 employees = 200 × 100 = 20,000 units

Days required $= \frac{\text{9,00,000 units}}{\text{20,000 units}}$ = 45 days

Standard Cost for Actual Output (*SCAP*) = 45 days × ₹. 6 × 200 employees = ₹. 54,000

Actual Cost = 50 days × ₹. 6.50 × 200 employees = ₹. 65,000

Actual No. of days paid = 50 days × 200 employees = 10,000 man days

Idle time = 200 × 1/2 day = 100 man days

Actual No. of days worked = 9,900 man days

Standard Mandays required $= \frac{\text{9,00,000 units}}{\text{100 units}}$ = 9,000 man days

(i) Labour Rate Variance = Actual days paid (*SR* – *AR*)
= 10,000 (6 – 6.50) = ₹. 5,000 (A)

(*ii*) Idle Time Variance = *SR* × Idle Time
= 6 × 100 man days = ₹. 600 (A)

(*iii*) Labour Efficiency Variance = *SR* (Std. man days – Actual man days worked)
= 6 (9000 – 9900) = ₹. 5400 (A)

(*iv*) Labour Cost Variance = *SCAP* – *AC*
= 54000 – 65000 = ₹. 11,000 (A)

Verification

Labour Cost Variance = Labour Rate Variance + Idle Time Variance + (Revised) Labour Efficiency Variance
= 5000 (A) + 600 (A) + 5400 (A) = 11,000 (A)

Overhead Variances

Illustration 42: The following information is available from the records of a factory

	Budget ₹.	*Actual* ₹.
Fixed Overhead for June	10,000	12,000
Production in June (units)	2,000	2,100
Standard time per unit (hours)	10	—
Actual hours worked in June	—	22,000

Compute :

(*i*) Fixed Overhead Cost Variance (*ii*) Expenditure Variance

(*iii*) Volume Variance (*iv*) Capacity Variance

(*v*) Efficiency Variance **[*C.A. Inter*]**

Solution:

Calculate :

1. Budgeted Quantity (*B.Q.*) = 2,000 Units
2. Actual Quantity (*A.Q.*) = 2,100 Units

3. Standard Quantity $(S.Q.)\ \frac{22{,}000}{10}$ = 2,200 Units (should have been produced)

Standard Rate $(S.R.) = \frac{BFO}{B.Q.} = \frac{₹.\ 10{,}000}{2{,}000 \text{ units}}$ = ₹. 5 per unit.

Budgeted Fixed Overhead $(B.F.O.)$ = ₹. 10,000

5. Actual Fixed Overhead $(A.F.O.)$ = ₹. 12,000

6. Standard Fixed Overhead $(S.F.O.)$ = 2,100 × 5 = ₹. 10,500 (should have been incurred)

Variances :

(*i*) Fixed Overhead Cost Variance = $S.F.O. - A.F.O$
= 10,500 – 12,000 = ₹. 1,500 (A)

(*ii*) Fixed Overhead Expenditure Variance = $B.F.O. - A.F.O.$
= 10,000 – 12,000 = ₹. 2,000 (A)

(*iii*) Fixed Overhead Volume Variance = S.R. $(A.Q. - B.Q.)$
= 5 (2,100 – 2,000) = ₹. 500 (F)

(*iv*) Fixed Overhead Capacity Variance = $S.R. (S.Q. - B.Q.)$
= 5 (2,200 – 2,000) = ₹. 1,000 (F)

(*v*) Fixed Overhead Efficiency Variance = $S.R. (A.Q. - S.Q.)$
= 5 (2,100 – 2,200) = ₹ 500 (A)

Verification :

Fixed Overhead Cost Variance = Fixed Overhead Exp. Variance + Fixed Overhead Volume Variance
= 2000 (A) + 500 (F) = 1500 (A)

Fixed Overhead Volume Variance = Fixed Overhead Capacity Variance + Fixed Overhead Eff. Variance
= 1000 (F) + 500 (A) = 500 (F)

Illustration 43: The following information was obtained from the records of a manufacturing unit using Standard Costing System :

	Standard *4,000 units*	*Actual* *3,800 units*
Working Days	20	21
	₹.	₹.
Fixed Overhead	40,000	39,000
Variable Overhead	12,000	12,000

Your are required to calculate the following overhead variances :

(*a*) Variable Overhead Variance

(*b*) Fixed Overhead Variance

(*i*) Expenditure Variance (*ii*) Volume Variance

(*iii*) Efficiency Variance (*iv*) Calender Variance

(*c*) Also prepare a Reconcilation Statement for the standard fixed expenses worked out at Standard Fixed Overhead and the Actual Overhead.

Solution :

Calculations

Standard Rate $(S.R.) = \frac{₹.\ 12{,}000}{4{,}000 \text{ units}}$ = ₹. 3 per Unit

Standard Variable Overhead $(S.V.O.)$ = 3,800 × 3 = ₹. 11,400

(*a*) **Variable Overhead Variance** = Standard Variable Overhead – Actual Variable Overhead
= (*SVO* – *AVO*)
= 11,400 – 12,000 = ₹. 600 (A)

Basic Data

1. Budgeted Qty. (*B.Q.*) = 4,000 units
2. Actual Qty. (*A.Q.*) = 3,800 units
3. Standard Qty. (*S.Q.*) = $4{,}000 \times \frac{21}{20}$ = 4,200 Units
4. Standard Rate (*S.R.*) = $\frac{₹.\ 40{,}000}{4{,}000 \text{ units}}$ = ₹. 10 per Unit
5. Budgeted Fixed Overhead (*B.F.O.*) = ₹. 40,000
6. Actual Fixed Overhead (*A.F.O*) = ₹. 39,000
7. Standard Fixed Overhead (*S.F.O.*) = 3,800 × 10 = ₹. 38,000
8. Revised Budgeted Qty. (*R.B.Q.*) = $4{,}000 \times \frac{21}{20}$ = 4,200 Units

(*b*) **Fixed Overhead Variance** = (*S.F.O.* – *A.F.O.*)
= 38,000 – 39,000 = ₹. 1,000 (A)

(*i*) Expenditure Variance = (*B.F.O.* – *A.F.O.*)
= 40,000 – 39,000 = ₹. 1,000 (F)

(*ii*) Volume Variance = *S.R.* (*B.Q.* – *A.Q.*) = 10 (4000 – 3,800)
= ₹. 2,000 (A)

(*iii*) Efficiency Variance = *S.R.* (*S.Q.* – *A.Q.*) = 10 (4,200 – 3,800)
= ₹. 4,000 (A)

(*iv*) Calendar Variance = *S.R.* (*B.Q.* – *R.B.Q.*)
= 10 (4,000 – 4,200) = ₹. 2,000 (F)

(*c*) **Reconciliation Statement for Overhead Variances**

	₹.	
Standard Fixed expenses worked out at Standard Fixed Overhead rate (3.800 × 10)	38,000	
Less : Expenditure Variance	1,000	(F)
	37,000	
Add: Efficiency Variance	4,000	(A)
	41,000	
Less: Calender Variance	2,000	(F)
Actual Fixed Overheads	39,000	

Verification :

Volume Variance = Efficiency Variance + Calendar Variaince
= 4,000 (A) + 2,000 (F) = 2000 (A)

Illustration 44: The following data have been collected from the cost records of a unit for computing the various fixed overhead variances for a period :

Number of budgeted working days	25
Budgeted man-hours per day	6,000
Out-put (budgeted), per man-hour (in units)	1
Fixed overhead cost as budgeted	₹. 1,50,000
Actual number of working days	27
Actual man-hours per day	6,300
Actual output per man-hour (in units)	0.9
Actual fixed overhead incurred	₹. 1,56,000

Calculate Fixed Overhead Variances :

(*a*) Expenditure Variance (*b*) Calender Variance,

(*c*) Capacity variance, (*d*) Efficiency Variance,

(*e*) Volume Variance, (*f*) Fixed Cost Variance,

Solution :

Calculations

Budgeted Quantity (BQ) = 25 × 6,000 × 1 = 1,50,000 units

Actual Quantity (AQ) = 27 × 6,300 × 0.9 = 1,53,090 units

Standard Quantity (SQ) = 27 × 6,300 = 1,70,100 × 1 = 1,70,100 units

Budgeted Fixed Overheads (BFO) = ₹. 1,50,000

Actual Fixed Overheads (AFO) = ₹. 1,56,000

$$\text{St. Rate} = \frac{BFO}{BQ} = \frac{1{,}50{,}000}{1{,}50{,}000 \text{ units}} = ₹, 1.00 \text{ per unit}$$

Revised Budgeted Quantity (RBQ) = 27 × 6,000 × 1 = 1,62,000 units

St. Fixed Overheads for Actual product (SFO) = 1,53,090 × 1 = ₹. 1,53,090

(should have been incurred for AQ produced).

Variances :

(*a*) Expenditure Variance = $BFO - AFO$

= 1,50,000 – 1,56,000 = ₹. 6,000 (A)

(*b*) Calendar Variance = $SR\ (RBQ - BQ)$

= 1.00 (1,62,000 – 1,50,000) = ₹. 12,000 (F)

(*c*) Capacity Variance = $SR\ (SQ - RBQ)$

= 1.00 (1,70,100 – 1,62,000) = ₹. 8,100 (F)

(*d*) Efficiency Variance = $SR\ (AQ - SQ)$

= 1.00 (1,53,090 – 1,70,100) = ₹. 17,010 (A)

(*e*) Volume Variance = $SR\ (AQ - BQ)$

= 1.00 (1,53,090 – 1,50,000) = ₹. 3,090 (F)

(*f*) Fixed Cost Variance = $SFO - AFO$

= 1,53,090 – 1,56,000 = 2,910 (A)

Verification :

Fixed Overhead Variance = FO Exp. Varience + FO Volume Variance

= 6000 (A) + 3090 (A)

= 2910 (A)

FO Volume Variance = Effeciency Variance + Cap. V + Calender V.

= 17,010 (A) + 8,100 (F) + 12,000 (F)

= 3090 (F)

Material, Labour & Overhead Variances

Illustration 45: The following information is available from the cost records of a Company for the month of February,

	₹.
Materials purchased : 20,000 pieces	88,000
Materials consumed: 19,000 pieces	
Actual wages paid for 4,950 hours	24,750
Factory overheads incurred	44,000
Factory overheads budgeted	40,000
Units produced 1,800	

Standard Rates and Prices are

Direct material rate ₹. 4 per piece

Standard input 10 pieces per unit

Direct labour rate ₹. 4 per hour

Standard requirement 2.5 hours per unit

Overhead ₹. 8 per labour hour.

Required (*a*) Show the Standard Cost Card; (*b*) Compute all material, labour and overhead variances for the month of February,

Solution:

Calculations

(*a*) *Standard Cost Card*	₹. per unit
Direct Materials 10 pieces at ₹. 4 per piece	40
Direct labour 2.5 hours at ₹. 4 per hour	10
Overheads 2.5 hours at ₹ 8 per hour	20
	₹. 70

(*b*) (*i*) **Material Variance**

Standard Cost (*SC*) = 1,800 units × 10 pieces
= 18,000 pieces at ₹. 4.00 per piece = ₹. 72,000

Actual Rate of purchase = ₹. $\frac{88,000}{20,000}$ = ₹. 4.40 per piece

Actual Cost (AC) = 19,000 pieces consumed at ₹. 4.40 per piece
= ₹. 83,600

1. Material Cost Variance (*MCV*) = *SC* – *AC*
= 72,000 – 83,600 = ₹. 11,600 (A)
2. Material Price Variance (*MPV*) = *AQ* (*SR* – *AR*)
= 19,000 (4.00 – 4.40) = ₹. 7,600 (A)
3. Material Usage Variance (*MUV*) = *SR* (*SQ* – *AQ*)
= 4.00 (18,000 – 19,000) = ₹. 4,000 (A)

Verification

MCV = *MPV* + *MUV*
= 7,600 (A) + 4,000 (A) = 11,600 (A)

(*ii*) **Labour Variances:**

Standard Cost 1,800 × 2.5 *i.e.* 4,500 hours at ₹. 4 per hour = ₹. 18,000

Actual Cost = 4,950 hours amounting to ₹. 24,750 *i.e.*, ₹. 5.00 per hour paid.

1. Labour Cost Variance (*LCV*) = *SC* – *AC*
= 18,000 – 24,750 = ₹. 6,750 (A)
2. Labour Rate Variance (*LRV*) = *AH* (*SR* – *AR*)
= 4,950 (4.00 – 5.00) = ₹. 4,950 (A)
3. Labour Efficiency Variance (*LEV*) = *SR* (*SH* – *AH*)
= 4.00 (4,500 – 4,950) = ₹. 1,800 (A)

Verification :

LCV = *LRV* + *LEV*
= 4,950 (A) + 1,800 (A)
= 6,750 (A)

(*iii*) **Fixed Overhead Variances:** (All overheads are assumed to be fixed)

St. Rate (*SR*) = ₹. 8.00 per hour; Actual Hours (*AH*) = 4,950

Budgeted Fixed Overhead (*BFO*) = ₹. 40,000;

Actual Fixed Overhead (*AFO*) = ₹. 44,000

Budgeted Hours (*BH*) $= \frac{BFO}{SR} =$ ₹. $\frac{40,000}{8.00} = 5,000$ hours

Standard Hous (*SH*) = 1,800 × 2.5 = 4.500

Standard Fixed Overhead (*SFO*) = 1,800 × 2.5 = 4,500 hours at ₹. 8 per hour = ₹. 36,000 or 1,800 units at ₹. 20 per unit = ₹. 36,000.

1. *FOH* Variance = *SFO* – *AFO*
   = 36,000 – 44,000 = ₹. 8,000 (A)
2. Expenditure Variance = *BFO* – *AFO*
   = 40,000 – 44,000 = ₹. 4,000 (A)
3. Efficiency Variance = *SR* (*SH* – *AH*)
   = 8.00 (4,500 – 4,950) = ₹. 3,600 (A)
4. Capacity Variance = *SR* (*AH* – *BH*)
   = 8.00 (4,950 – 5,000) = ₹. 400 (A)

Verification

FOH V. = *EXP. V* + *Effy.V.* + *Capacity V*
= 4,000 A + 3,600 A + 400 A = 8,000 (A)

Illustration 46: S. Ltd. operates a system of standard costing in respect of one of its products which is manufactured within a single cost centre, the following information is available:

For one unit of product the standard material input is 20 litres at a standard price of ₹. 2 per litre. The standard wage rate is ₹. 6 per hour and 5 hours are allowed in which to produce one unit. Fixed production overhead is absorbed at the rate of 100% of direct wages cost.

During the month just ended the following occurred:

Actual price paid for material purchased	₹. 1.95 per litre
Total direct wages cost	₹. 1,56,000
Fixed production overhead incurred	₹. 1,58,000

Variances	*Favourable* (₹.)	*Adverse* (₹.)
Direct material price	8,000	
Direct material usage		5,000
Direct labour rate		5,760
Direct labour efficiency	2,760	
Fixed production overhead expenditure		8,000

Required

Calculate the following for the month:

(*i*) Budgeted output in units, (*ii*) Number of litres purchased, (*iii*) Number of litres used above standard allowed, (*iv*) Actual units produced, (*v*) Actual hours worked, (*vi*) Average actual wage rate per hour.

Solution:

Calculations: Standard labour cost per unit = 5 hours at ₹. 6 per hour = ₹. 30 per unit. Fixed Production overhead is absorbed at the rate of 100% of direct wages cost i.e. ₹. 30 per unit. = Fixed production overhead.

Variances

(*i*) Fixed Production Overhead Expenditure Variance

= Budgetd Fixed Overhead – Actual Fixed Overhead

8000 A = (Budgeted output × ₹. 30) – 1,58,000

Budgeted output $= \dfrac{1,58,000 - 8,000}{30} = 5,000$ units

(*ii*) Material Price Variance = $AQ\ (SR - AR)$

8,000 F = AQ (2,00 – 1,95)

+ 8,000 = 0.05 AQ

$AQ = \dfrac{8,000}{0.05} = 1,60,000$ litres purchased

(*iii*) Actual units produced = 5,100 units

Standard quantity allowed for actual production

= 5,100 × 20 litres = 1.02,000 litres

Material Usage Variance = $SR\ (SQ - AQ)$

5,000 A = 2.00 (1,02,000 – AQ)

– 5,000 = 2,04,000 – 2 AQ

$AQ = \dfrac{2,04,000 + 5,000}{2} = 1,04,500$

AQ consumed = 1,04,500 litres

SQ allowed = 1,02,000 litres

No. of litres used above standard = 2,500 litres

No. of litres purchased = 1,60,000 litres

AQ consumed = 1,04,500 litres

(*iv*)		
Direct Wages Cost (Actual)		₹. 1,56,000
Direct Labour Rate Variance	5,760 (A)	
Direct Labour Efficiency Variance	2,760 (F)	
Direct Labour Cost Variance	3,000 (A)	3,000 (A)
Direct wages Cost (std)		1,53,000
Actual units produced =	$\dfrac{1,53,000}{30}$	5,100 units

Note: Standard wages cost of actual production = 5,100 × 30 = ₹. 1,53,000

Actual wages 1,56,000

Direct labour cost variance 3,000 A

(*v*) Standard hours required for actual production = 5,100 × 5 = 25,500

Labour Efficiency Variance = $SR\ (SH - AHW)$

2760 F = 6.00 (25,500 – AHW)

+ 2,760 = 1,53,000 – 6 AHW

$AHW = \dfrac{1,53,000 - 2,760}{6} = 25,040$

Average actual wage rate per hour $= \dfrac{1,56,000}{25,040} =$ ₹. 6.23

Assumption: Actual hours worked (*AHW*) taken as Actual Hours paid (*AHP*) in the absence of any idle time.

QUESTIONS

OBJECTIVE QUESTIONS

I. ***Choose the correct answer.***

(*A*) *Standard costing involves the* :

(*a*) Fixation of estimated cost (b) Determination of standard cost

(c) Setting of budgeted cost

(*B*) *The difference between actual cost and standard cost is known as* :

(*a*) Variance (*b*) Profit (*c*) Differential cost

(*C*) *Standard costing helps in* :

(*a*) Measuring efficiency (*b*) Reducing losses (*c*) Controlling cost

(*D*) *Standard costing cannot be used* :

(*a*) Where management is inefficient. (*b*) Workers are slow

(*c*) Where non-standard products are manufactured.

(*E*) *Basic standard is established for a* :

(*a*) Short period (*b*) Current period (*c*) Indefinite period

[**Ans.** A (*b*) , B (*a*), C (*a*) D (*c*), E (*c*)]

II. ***Correct the following*** :

(*a*) Material Price Variance = Standard Quantity (Standard Price – Actual Price)

(*b*) Material Mix Variance = Standard cost of standard mix - Actual cost of actual mix

(*c*) Idle Time Variance = Idle Hours × Actual Rate

(*d*) Expenditure Variance = (Budgeted Fixed Overheads – Standard Fixed Overheads)

(*e*) Sales Price variance = Standard Quantity (Actual Price – Standard Price).

[**Ans.** (*a*) Actual quantity, (*b*) – Standard cost of actual mix (*c*) Standard Rate (*d*) – Actual Fixed Overheads (*e*) Actual Quantity.]

III. ***Fill in the blanks***:

(*a*) Three types of standards are ....

(*b*) Idle time variance is....................... .

(*c*) The technique of standard costing may not be applicable in case of.............. .

(*d*) Total labour cost variance ....

(*e*) Material usage variance = material mix variance + ...

[***Ans.*** (*a*) Current standard, basic standard and normal standard (*b*) Idle Time × Standard Rate (*c*) Small concerns (*d*) Rate of Pay Variance + Labour efficiency variance (*e*) Material Yield Variance]

THEORETICAL QUESTIONS

1. Define "Standard Cost" and "Standard Costing". In which type of industries standard costing is employed.
2. What is meant by standard costing? State its main objectives.
3. 'Standard costs today are basis for a proper managerial control of manufacturing operation' Define standard cost and explain the above statement.
4. What are the various circumstances in which material price and usage variances are likely to arise?
5. Define and explain briefly the following terms:

(*a*) Material Price Variance (*b*) Material Usage Variance
(*c*) Material Mix Variance (*d*) Material Yield Variance

6. Indicate briefly, the meaning causes and disposal of the following types of variances:
(*i*) Material Price variance (*ii*) Material Quantity Variance
(*iii*) Wage Rate Variance (*iv*) Labour Efficiency Variance
(*v*) Overhead Budget Variance (*vi*) Overhead Capacity Variance
(*vii*) Overhead Volume Efficiency Variance

7. Explain the possible cause for Material Price Variance and Material Usage Variance in standard cost. What are remedial measures?

8. Compare and contrast the Standard Costing System and Budgetary Control System.

SHORT ANSWER QUESTIONS

1. What is standard costing ?
2. Discuss the objects of standard costing ?
3. Discuss the limitations of standard costing.
4. What is the difference between actual costing method and standard costing method ?
5. What is cost variance analysis ?
6. What is controllable and uncontrollable variance ?
7. Discuss the managerial uses of variance analysis.
8. What is material variance ?
9. What is material yield variance ?
10. What is labour efficiency variance ?
11. What is calender variance ?
12. What is sales variance ?

NUMERICAL QUESTIONS

Material Variances

1. The standard material and standard cost per kg of material required for the production of one unit of Product A is as follows;

Material 5 kg Standard Price ₹. 5 per kg.

The actual production and related material data are as follows:

400 units of Product A

Material used	2,200 kg
Price of Material	₹. 4.80 per kg

Calculate (*i*) Material Cost Variance (*ii*) Material Usage Variance (*iii*) Material Price Variance.

[**Ans.** *(i) ₹. 560 (A), (ii) ₹. 1,000 (A), (iii) ₹. 440 (F)*]

2. A manufacturing concern which has adopted standard costing turnishes the following information:

Standard:

Material (for 70 kg. of finished products)	100 kg
Price of materials	₹ 1 per kg

Actual:

Output	2,10,000 kg
Materials used	2,80,000 kg
Cost of materials	₹. 2,52,000

Calculate :

(*a*) Material Usage Variance

(*b*) Material Price Variance

(*c*) Material Cost Variance. **[*C.A. Inter*]**

[Ans. *(a) ₹ 20,000 (F); (b) ₹ 28,000 (F) (c) ₹ 48,000 (F)* ***Hint*** *Standard Quantity for Actual Output 2,10,000 × 100/70 = 3,00,000 kg; Actual rate per kg 2,52,000/2,80,000 = .90*]

3. Gemini Chemical Industries provide the following information from their records:

For making 10 kg of GEMCO the standard material requirement is:

Material	*Quantity (kg)*	*Rate per kg (₹)*
A	8	6.00
B	4	4.00

During April, 20..., 1,000 kg. of GEMCO were produced. The actual consumption of materials is as under:

Material	*Quantity (Kg)*	*Rate per kg (₹)*
A	750	7.00
B	500	5.00

Calculate:

(*a*) Material Cost Variance;

(*b*) Material Price variance;

(*c*) Material Usage Variance. **[*CA Inter, B.Com (Hons) Delhi*]**

[Ans. *DMCV = ₹ 1,350 (A), DMPV ₹ 1,250 (A), DMUV ₹ 100 (A)*

Hint. *Standard Cost for actual Output ₹ 6,400, Actual Cost ₹ 7,750*]

4. The standard quantity and standard price of raw material required for one unit of product A are given as follows:

	Quantity	Standard Price
Material X	2 kg	₹. 3 per kg
Material Y	4 kg	₹. 2 per kg
	6 kg	

The actual production and relevant data are as follows:

Material	Total Quantity for 500 units	Total Cost ₹.
X	1,100 Kg	3,410
Y	1,800 Kg	3,960

Calculate material variances

[Ans. *Material Cost Variance = 410 (A) + 40 (F) = 370 (A)*

Material Usage Variance = 300 (A) + 400 (F) = 100 (F)

Material Price Variance = 110 (A) + 360 (A) = 470 (A)]

5. From the following information of Production No. 142 calculate (1) Material Cost Variance (2) Material Mix Variance (3) Material Sub-usage Variane (4) Material Price Variance.

Material	*Standard Quantity Kg*	*Standard Price ₹*	*Actual Quantity Kg.*	*Actual Price ₹*
X	10	5	12	4.00
Y	8	4	7	4.50
Z	6	3	5	3.25
	24		24	

[**Ans.** *Material Cost Variance ₹. 2.00 (F) + 0.50 (F) + 1.75 (F) = 4.25 (F)*
Material Price Variance ₹ 12.00 (F) + 3.50 (A) + 1.25 (A) = 7.25 (F)
Material Mix Variance ₹. 10 (A) + 4 (F) + 3 (F) = ₹. 3 (A)
Material Sub usage Variance. Since input and output is same there is no difference in Standard Quantity and RSQ, hence no sub usage variance]

6. From the following figures given to you, calculate material variances.

Production for the period 192 units

	Material X	*Material Y*
Standard price per ton	₹. 240	₹. 320
Actual price per ton	₹. 227.50	₹. 308
Actual weight	16 tons	13 tons

The standard production for the period represented by the above figures is 400 units for which the standard quantity allowance for material are 30 tons of X and 25 tons of Y.

[**Ans.** *Material Cost Variance* = *184 (A) + 164 (A) = ₹. 348 (A)*
Material Price Variance = *200 (F) + 156 (F) = ₹. 356 (F)"*
Material Mix Variance = *43.64 (A) + 58.18 (F) = 14.54 (F)*
Material Sub-usuage Variance = *340.36 (A) + 378.18 (A) = 718.54 (A)*
Material Usage Variance = *704 (A) Mix Variance + Sub-usage Variance*]

7. Given the following information, caluclate material yield variance.

Material	*Standard*			*Actual*		
	Qty kg	*Price per unit ₹.*	*Total ₹.*	*Qty kg*	*Price per unit ₹.*	*Total*
A	200	5	1,000	200	5	1,000
B	500	3	1,500	500	3	1,500
	700		2,500	700		2,500
Less Normal Wastage	75			Actual wastage 100		
Output	625			600		

[**Ans.** *MYV = ₹. 100 (A)*]

8. 80 kgs. of Material A at a standard price of ₹. 2 per kg and 40 kgs of Material B at a standard price of ₹. 5 per kg were to be used to manufacture 100 kgs of a Chemical.

During a month, 70 kgs of Material A priced at ₹. 2.10 per kg and 50 kgs of Material B priced at ₹. 4.50 per kg. were actually used and the output of the Chemical was 102 kgs.

Find out the Material Variances.

[**Ans.** *DMCV ₹ 4.8 (A), DMPV ₹ 18 (F), DMUV ₹ 22.8 (A) DMMV ₹ 30(A) DMYV ₹ 7.20 (F).*]
Hints Standard Output 100 kg, Actual output 102 kg]

9. The Standard Cost of a certain chemical mixture is

40% Material A at ₹. 200 per ton
60% Material B at ₹. 3,00 per ton

A standard loss of 10% is expected in production. During a period there is used.

90 tons Material A at the cost of ₹. 180 per ton
110 tons Material B at the cost of ₹. 340 per ton.

The weight produced is 182 tons of production. Calculate (*a*) Material Price Variance (*b*) Material Usage Variance (*c*) Material Mix Variance (*d*) Material Yield Variance.

[**Ans.** *Material Price Variance ₹. 2,600 (A); Material Usage Variance ₹. 1,577.77 (F), Material Mix Variance ₹. 1,000 (F), Material Yield Variance ₹. 577.77 (F).*]

10. A company manufacturing `distempers' operates a costing system. The standard cost of one of the products of the company shows the following standards:

Materials	*Quantity*	*Standard price per kg*	*Total*
		₹.	₹.
A	40kg	75	3,000
B	10 kg	50	500
C	50 kg	20	1,000
Material cost per unit (Total)			4,500

The standard input of mix is 100 kg. and the standard output of the finished product is 90 kg. The actual results for period are:

A	2,40,000 kg	@ ₹. 80 per kg
B	40,000 kg	@ ₹. 52 per kg
C	2,20,000 kg	@ ₹. 21 per kg

Actual output of the finished product = 4,20,000 kg.

You are required to calculate the material price, mix and yield variances.

[**Ans.** *DMCV ₹. 49,00,000 (A), DMPV ₹. 15,00,000 (A), DMUV ₹. 34,00,000 (A), DMMV ₹. 19,00,000, DMYV ₹. 15,00,000 (A).*

[**Hint:** Standard output 4,50,000 kg, Actual Output 4,20,000 kg, Standard Cost per unit ₹. 50]

11. The standard material cost for a normal mix of one tonne of Chemical X is based on:

Chemical	*Usage* kg	*Price per kg.* ₹.
A	240	6
B	400	12
C	640	10

During a month, 6.25 tonnes of *X* were produced from:

Chemical	*Consumption (Tonnes)*	*Cost (₹.)*
A	1.6	11,200
B	2.4	30,000
C	4.5	47,250
	8.5	88.450

Analyse the variances. **[*CA*]**

[**Ans.** *DMCV ₹. 9450 (A), DMPV ₹. 5050 (A); DMUV ₹. 4400 (A), DMMV ₹. 537.5 (F) DMYV ₹. 4937.5 (A)*

Hint. Standard cost for Actual output ₹. 79,000 Actual Cost ₹. 88,450; st. cost per unit ₹. 12,640]

Labour Variances

12. The following information is gathered from the labour records of Ramkishan & Co.

Payroll allocation for direct labour ₹. 20,000.

Time card analysis show: that 9,000 hours were worked on production lines.

Production reports for the period showed that 4,000 units have been completed, each having standard labour time of 1.5 hours and a standard labour rate of ₹. 2 per hour."

Calculate the labour variances.

[**Ans:** *Labour Rate variance ₹. 2,000 (A); Labour Efficiency Variance ₹. 6,000 (A); Labour Cost Variance ₹. 8,000 (A).*

Hint: Standard Time for one unit : 1.5 hours; For 4,000 Units : 6,000 hours]

13. Using the following information, calculate each of three labour variances for each department.

	Dept X	*Dept Y*
Gross Direct Wages (₹.)	28,080	19,370
Standard hours produced	8,640	6,015
Standard Rate per hour (₹.)	3	3.40
Actual hours worked	8,200	6,345

[**Ans.** *Labour Cost Variance X ₹. 2,160 (A); Y 1,081 (F)*
Labour Rate Variance X ₹. 3,480 (A); Y 2,203 (F)
Labour Efficiency Variance X ₹. 1,320 (F), Y 1,122 (A)]

14. The details regarding composition and the weekly wage rate of labour force engaged on a job scheduled to be completed in 30 weeks are as follows:

	Standard		*Actual*	
Category of Workers	*No. of labourers*	*Weekly wage rate (₹.)*	*No. of labourers*	*Weekly wage rate (₹.)*
Skilled	75	60	70	₹. 70
Semi-skilled	45	40	30	50
Unskilled	60	30	80	20

The work is actually completed in 32 weeks. Calculate the various labour variances.

[*B. Com., (H). Delhi*]

[**Ans.** *DLCV ₹. 13,000 (A) DLRV ₹. 6,400 (A); DLEV ₹. 6,600 (A) DL Mix or Gang V = ₹. 9,600 (F) Revised LEV ₹. 16,200 (A).*]

15. Standard labour hours and rates for production of Article A are given

	Hours	*Rate* ₹.	*Total* ₹.
Skilled Worker	5	1.50 per hour	7.50
Unskilled worker	8	0.50 per hour	4.00
Semi-skilled worker	4	0.75 per hour	3.00
			14.50

Actual data:

Articles Produced (1,000 Units)

Skilled worker	4,500	2.00	9,000
Unskilled worker	10,000	0.45	4,500
Semi-skilled worker	4,200	0.75	3.150
			16,650

Calculate (*a*) Labour Cost Variance (*b*) Labour Rate Variance (*c*) Labour Efficiency Varience (*d*) Labour Mix Variance.

[**Ans.** *Labour Cost Variance ₹. 2,150 (A); Labour Price Variance ₹. 1,750 (A), Labour Mix Variance ₹. 1,050 (F) Labour Efficiency Variance 400 (A), Revised Efficiency Variance ₹. 1,450 (F)*]

Material and Labour Variances

16. The following details relating to the Product *X* during the month of March are available. You are required to compute the material and labour cost variances and also to reconcile the standard and the actual costs with the help of such variances:

Standard Cost per unit:

Materials	50 kg. @ ₹. 40 per kg.
Labour	400 hours @ 1 per hour

Actual Cost for the months:

Material	4,900 kgs. @ ₹. 42 per kg.
Labour	39,600 hours @ ₹. 1.10 per hour.

Actual Production—100 units

[Ans. *Direct Material Cost Variance ₹. 5,800 (A), DMPV ₹. 9,800 (A), DMUV ₹. 4,000 (F) Direct Labour Cost Variance ₹. 3,560 (A), DLRV ₹. 3,960 (A); DLEV ₹. 4,00 (F) Total Standard Cost of 100 units ₹. 2,40,000 Actual cost of 100 unit ₹. 2,49,360.***]**

17. Following data are available :

		Standard	₹.		*Actual*	₹.
Input	500 kg	Material 500 kg @ ₹. 39 per kg	19,500	500 kg	Material @ ₹. 42 per kg	21,000
		Labour 4,000 hours @ ₹. 1.50 per hour	6,000		Labour 4,000 Hours @ ₹. 1.50 per hour	6,000
Normal Loss	20			40		
Output	480	₹.	25,500	460 kg		27,000

Calculate (*i*) Material Cost Variance (*ii*) Material Price Variance (*iii*) Material Yield Variance (*iv*) Labour Cost Variance (*v*) Labour Price Variance (*vi*) Labour Yield Variance.

[Ans. *Standard Quantity for actual production = 500 × 460/480 = 479.16667 kg. Standard labour for actual production = 4,000 × 460/480 = 3833.3333 hrs.*

*Material Cost Variance ₹. 2312.50 (A); Material Price Variance ₹. 1,500 (A) Material Yield Variance ₹. 812.50 (A) Labour Cost Variance ₹. 250 (A), Labour Rate Variance Nil; Labour Yield Variance ₹. 250 (A).***]**

Overhead Variances

18. From the following data, calculate Overhead Cost Variance and Overhead Budget Variance

Budgeted hours for month of March: 180 hours, Actual production for March: 9,200 units; Standard rate of articles propduced per hour: 50 units, Atual hour for production: 175 hrs. Budgeted Fixed Overheads ₹. 2,700, Actual Fixed Overheads: ₹. 2,800.

[Ans. *Overhead Cost Variance ₹. 40 (A); Overhead Budget or Expenditure Variance. ₹. 100 (A)***]**

19. (A) From the data of above Question, Calculate Overhead Volume Variance (*i*) when standard overhead rate per unit is given (*ii*) when standard overhead rate per hour is given.

[Ans. *(i) (9,200 – 9,000) × 0.30 = ₹. 60 (F) (ii), (184 – 180) × 15 = ₹. 60 (F)***]**

(B) From the data given in the above Question calculate Overhead Efficiency Variance and Overhead Capacity Variance.

[Ans. *₹. 135 (F); ₹. 75 (A)***]**

20. (*a*) The Budget for a period indicates:

Works Overhead Fixed	₹. 50,000	Works Overhead Variable	₹. 1,50,000
Normal Activity	100%		

During the period the actual activity was only 70% of the normal load for a total expenditure of ₹. 1,50,000. What are the budget and volume variances?

(*b*) Determine the budget and capacity variances from the following data:

Estimated Factory Overhead	₹. 25,000	Actual Overhead Expenses	₹. 26,500
Estimated Direct labour Hrs.	5,000	Applied Overhead Expense	₹. 22,500

[**Ans.** *(a) Budgeted Works Overhead for Actual Quantity ₹. 1,55,000 Recovered Works Overhead for actual activity ₹. 1,40,000; Overhead Budget Variance ₹. 5,000 (F); Overhead Volume Variance ₹. 15,000 (A).*

(b) Overhead Budget Variance ₹. 1,500 (A); Overhead Capacity Variance ₹. 2,500 (A)]

21. In Department A, the following data is submitted for the week ended 31st October:

Standard Output for 40 hours per week	1,400 units
Standard Fixed Overhead	₹. 1,400
Actual Output	1,200 units
Actual Hours Worked	32 hours
Actual Fixed Overhead	₹. 1,500

Prepare a Statement of Fixed Overhead Variances

[**Ans.** *St. Overhead Rate per unit ₹1, St Fixed Overhead Rate per hour ₹. 35. Standard output per hour 35 units; Fixed Overhead Cost Variance ₹. 300 (A); Fixed Overhead Expenditure Variance ₹. 100 (A); Fixed Overhead Volume Variance ₹. 200 (A); Fixed Overhead Capacity Variance ₹. 80 (F)*]

22. The following information is available from the records of factory:

	Budget	*Actual*
Fixed overhead for June (₹.)	10,000	12,000
Produciton in June (units)	2,000	2,100
Standard time per unit (hours)	10	
Actual hours worked in June	22,000	

Compute :

(*i*) Fixed overhead cost variance (*ii*) Expenditure variance

(*iii*) Volume variance (*iv*) Capacity variance

(*v*) Efficiency variance

[**Ans.** *(i) FOCV ₹. 1,500 (A), (ii) FOEXPV ₹. 2,000 (A) (iii) FOVV ₹. 500 (F) (iv) FOCAPV ₹. 1,000 (F); (v) FOEFV ₹. 500 (A)*]

23. The following information was obtained from the records of a manufacturing unit using Standard Costing System:

	Standard	*Actual*
Production	4,000 units	3,800 units
Working Days	20	21
Fixed Overhead	₹. 40,000	₹. 39,000
Variable Overhead	12,000	12,000

You are required to calculate the following Overhead Variances:

(*a*) Variable Overhead Variances

(*b*) Fixed Overhead Variance

(*i*) Expenditure Variance (*ii*) Volume Variance

(*iii*) Efficiency Variance (*iv*) Calendar Variance

(c) Also prepare a Reconciliation Statement for the standard fixed expenses worked but at Standard Fixed Overhead Rate and the Actual Fixed Overhead.

[**Ans.** *St. Variable overhead rate per unit ₹. 3, St. Production per day 200 units, St fixed overhead per day ₹. 2000. (a) Variable Overhead Variance ₹. 600 (A).*

(b) Fixed Overhead Cost Variance ₹. 1,000 (A); Fixed Overhead Exp. Variance ₹. 1,000 (F); Fixed Overhead Volume Variance ₹. 2,000 (A); Fixed Overhead Efficiency Variance ₹.4,000 (A); Fixed Overhead Calender Variance ₹. 2,000 (F).

(c) Reconcilliation – Standard Fixed Overhead (3800 × 10) = ₹. 38,000

Less [Fixed Overhead Expenditure Variance ₹. 1,000 (F) + Fixed Overhead Calender Variance ₹. 2,000 (F)]

Add Fixed Overhead Efficiency Variance ₹. 4,000 (A) = Actual Fixed Overhead ₹. 39,000]

Sales Variances

24. PH Ltd. furnishes the following information relating to budgeted sales and actual sales for the month of April,

	Product	*Sales Quantity Units*	*Selling Price Per unit.*
Budgeted Sales:			₹.
	A	1,200	15
	B	800	20
	C	2,000	40
Actual Sales:			
	A	880	18
	B	880	20
	C	2,640	38

Calculate the following variances :

(*i*) Sales Quantity or Volume Variance
(*ii*) Sales Mix Variance
(*iii*) Sales Price Variance
(*iv*) Total Sales Variance

[Ans. *(i) ₹. 22,400 (F), (ii) ₹. 11,000 (F), (iii) ₹. 2,640 (A) (iv) ₹. 19,760 (F)***]**

25. From the following information about sales, calculate.

(*a*) Total Sales Variance
(*b*) Sales Price Variance
(*c*) Sales Volume Variance
(*d*) Sales Mix Variance
(*e*) Sales Revised Quantity Variance

Product	*Standard*			*Actual*		
	Nos	*Rate in unit*	*₹.*	*Nos.*	*₹. per unit*	*₹.*
A	5,000	5	25,000	6,000	6	36,000
B	4,000	6	24,000	5,000	5	25,000
C	3,000	7	21,000	4,000	8	32,000
	12,000		70,000	15,000		93,000

[Ans. *(a) Total Sales Variance ₹. 23,000 (F); (b) Sales Price Variance ₹. 5,000 (F); (c) Sales Volume Variance ₹. 18,000 (F); (d) Sales Mix Variance ₹. 500 (F); Sales Quantity Variance ₹. 17,500 (F)***]**

26. From the following data Calculate (1) Sales Value Variance (2) Sales Price Variance (3) Sales Mix Variance (4) Sales Sub-Volume Variance.

Product	*Standard*			*Actual*		
	Qty. (Kg.)	*Sale Price ₹.*	*Total ₹.*	*Qty Kg*	*Sale Price ₹.*	*Total ₹.*
x	500	5	2,500	500	5.00	2,500
y	400	6	2,400	600	6.25	3,750
z	300	7	2,100	400	6.75	2,700
	1,200		7,000	1,500		8,950

[Ans. *Sales Value Variance ₹. 1,950 (F); Sales Price Variance ₹. 50 (F); Sales Mix Variance ₹. 150 (F) Sales Sub-Volume Variance ₹. 1,750 (F).***]**

27. From the following budgeted+ and actual figures, calculate the variance on sales margin basis.

Budget

Sales – 2,000 units @ ₹. 15 each	₹. 30,000
Cost of Sales @ ₹. 12 each	24,000
Profit	6,000

Actual

Sales – 1,900 units @ ₹. 14 each	26,600
Cost of Sales @ ₹. 10 each	19,000
Profit	7,600

[**Ans.** *Sales Margin Quantity Variance ₹ 300 (A), Sales Margin Price Variance ₹ 1900 (F); Total Sales Margin Variance ₹ 1600 (F)*]

Chapter 21 Budgetary Control

The information provided in Cost Accounting is historical. Achievement of maximum efficiency demands more. Briefly, a concern must try to know what objectives it has to achieve in the near future and then to plan for the realisation of the objectives as efficiently as possible. This has two aspects—budgetary control and standard costing. The former is concerned with total activity in a period and the latter deals with expenditure on various units of production and service.

Budgetary Control

According to the Chartered Institute of Management Accountants (*CIMA*), England a *Budget* is :

"a financial and/or quantitative statement, prepared and approved prior to a defined period of time, of the policy to be pursued during that period for the purpose of attaining a given objective. It may include income, expenditure and employment of capital."

The Institute defines *Budgetary Control* as :

"The establishment of budgets relating the responsibilities of executives to the requirements of a policy, and the continuous comparison of actual with budgeted results either to secure by individual action the objectives of that policy or to provide a firm basis for its revision."

In short, budgetary control means laying down in monetary and quantitative terms what exactly has to be done and how exactly it has to be done over a coming period and then to ensure that actual results do not diverge from the planned course more than necessary. The word "necessary" is not to be loosely interpreted. Divergence due to inefficiency is not necessary.

The chief advantage of budgetary control has been very well summarised by *De Paula* :

"The position may be likened to the navigation of a ship across the seas. The log is kept written recording every happening and the position of the ship from hour to hour, and valuable lessons are to be learned by the Captain from a study of the factors that caused by misadventures of the past. But to navigate his ship safely over the seven seas, the captain requires his navigating officer to work out the course ahead and constantly to check his ship's positon against the predetermined one. If the ship is off its course, then the navigating officer must report immediately so that the Captain may take prompt action to regain his correct course.

Exactly so it is with the industrial ship; the past records represent the log and the auditor is responsible for verifying, so far as he can, that those records are correct and reveal a true and fair view of the financial positon of the concern. But what modern management requires, for day-to-day operating purpsoes, is forecasts showing in detail the anticipated course of business for (say) the coming year. During the course of the year management requires immediate reports of any material variance from the predetermined course, together with explanation of the reason for them."

The business budgets represent management's plans for the future. The overall business plan is crystalaized in the form of projected accounts for each year of the budgetary period, including the manufacturing or operating accounts, trading and profit and loss account, a cash forecast and a balance sheet. The projected accounts will therefore cover the whole of the future expected transaction of the business and will include budgets for expenditure on capital equipment, the acquistion and repayment of capital, appropriation to reserves and dividends. They will constitute a Master Budget'.

Budgeting, undertaken as a routine activity, loses much of its value. But as dynamic forward looking exercise, it can be of immense use. The very first requirement in this regard is that all the people should be actively involved. All sections and departments and divisions should try to see what can be achieved given a willing and coordinated effort. Thus the Sales Manager would be thinking how new market may be tapped and how the existing market may be exploited more fully. The production manager would undertaken a serious exercise to see how production can be increased further and how costs may be reduced. When every one is committed to budgeting as a means of achieving set goals and of going from one objective to another, budgeting will be most valuable. The whole idea is to see what can be achieved and then making a determined effort to see that actual performance matches the target.

Zero-based budgeting is a new technique now being talked of. It really means a very close look on all the activities that are proposed to be undertaken, even if they are already there, and on the costs to be incurred.

Objective of Budgetary Control

The general objectives of a budgetary control are :

1. to lay down a plan to implement the policy of the firm;
2. to co-ordinate the activities of the various departments of a business; and
3. to control each function so that the best possible results are achieved.

Thus Budgetary Control provides for *logical forward planning* for the organisation and its subunits. It encourages managers to control the performance for which they are responsible by relating this to budgets.

Advantages of Budgetry Control

The chief advantages of a system of budgetary control are:

1. Wastages and losses of all types are avoided and thus maximum efficiency is achieved.
2. Every one concerned knows what exactly to do.
3. There is no delay since budgets, once adopted, operate as a sanction to proceed.
4. Expenditure beyond what is included in budgets is not incurred without prior sanction; thus an opportunity to scrutinise it before it is incurred there.
5. Budgets serve as targets and, therefore, as a measure of efficiency of departments and people.
6. The employees themselves know what is it exactly that they will be judged by.
7. "Management by exception" is possible since the comparison of actual and budgeted performances will show up which section of activity needs supervison and which activities are being carried out efficiently.
8. Managers will be well motivated to achieve the forward plan.
9. Cost control and control of efficiency are encouraged by the periodic comparison between actual and budgetary performance.

Requisites of Effective Budgetory Control

(*a*) *Determination of the Objective*. To achieve success, the exact goal to be reached must be laid down, otherwise budgeting will be aimless. The goal can be greater profits, greater share of the market or easier financial positon, etc. Objectives for each field of activity should also be determined.

(*b*) *Fixation of the Budget Period.*[1] Usually budgets are drawn up for a year but this will depend upon the nature of business—a seasonal industry will budget for each season (and off season) and an industry requiring long periods to complete its work will budget for 3 or 4 or 5 years. However from the control point of view it is important that budgets should not be for periods longer than necessary.

(*c*) *Locating the Principal Budget or Key Factor*. In every business there is one or more limiting factor. For instance, availability of equipment of skilled labour or raw materials may not permit output to go up beyond a certain limit. Or, the markets may not absorb more than a certain quantity. Such limiting factors are known as key factors. It is no use planning without taking into account the factors that have a vital influence.

(*d*) *Appointment of Budgetary Controller.* Budgetary Controller is an executive equal in rank to other departmental managers. His duties are :

(*i*) to help draw up budget on time and, if necessary, later to change them suitably in view of changed conditions; and

(*ii*) to regularly compare actual performance with the relative budget and to draw the attention of the department concerned to any discrepancy.

Budgetary Controller plays a very important role in the success of the system of budgetary control.

(*e*) *Consent of all Concerned.* Budgets are drawn up for all aspects of activity of a concern. It is necessary that all concerned should have the right to criticise a proposed budget fully and that no budget is laid down unless the person concerned gives his full and free consent. Budgets are drawn up after full and frank-discussion, otherwise co-operation will not be forthcoming.

(*f*) *Flexible Budgets.* Actual business conditions may be different from what were anticipated. Hence, it becomes necessary to scale down the budgets (if sales or output is down) or to scale them up. A system which permits easy adjustment of the budgets according to changed business conditions is necessary and is known as "flexible budgets". The Budgetary Controller is most concerned with it.

Budget Key Factor, Budget Centres, Budget Period

There are three essential factors in preparation of Budget.

(*a*) *Budget Key Factor :* Budget key factor is also called `limiting factor'. Budgets depend upon the level of activity which depends upon production. The production depends in turn on how much the organisation plans to produce. Thus production is the key factor or limiting factor. It has further to be ascertained what are those production factors which limits the production. These may be machine capacity, material availability, labour procurement, restricted working hours or capital resources. Based upon these factors or factor the maximum that can be produced is determined and on this level of activity the budget are based.

Following are the key factors which can probably affect budgeting

(*a*) Sales
- (*i*) Shortage of talented and experienced salesmen
- (*ii*) Weak market demand or consumers' resistance.
- (*iii*) Inadequate advertising due to lack of funds.

(*b*) Materials
- (*i*) Availability of supply
- (*ii*) Contraints due to licences and quotas

1. These are discussed in detail in following pages.

(*c*) Labour	(*i*)	Shortage of labour
	(*ii*)	Shortage in labour related facilities.
(*d*) Plant and Equipment	(*i*)	Limited capacity due to lack of capital.
	(*ii*)	Inadequate capacity due to shortage of simply
	(*iii*)	Inadequate capacity due to shortage of space.
(*e*) Management	(*i*)	Overall inadequancy of capital
	(*ii*)	Limited availability of technical and managerial experts
	(*iii*)	Inadeaquate research efforts and product designing.

(*b*) *Budget Centres :* Budget centre has been defined as a section of the organisation if an undertaking defined for the purpose of budget control'. It is said that two or more cost centre can make up a budget centre. Under cost control responsibilities are decentralised and make one individual responsible for the control of expenses under a specific function, department or process. This will necessitate to decide the process or department, the expenses of which will be under his direct control.

Thus it is necessary that in every organisation the level of responsibility should be clearly laid down and the sphere of control of each individual should be specifically defined. Once the budget centre are decided upon, all budgets should be related to the budget centres.

(*c*) *Budget Period :* A budget period means the period for which a budget is prepared and employed. The period of budget depends upon (*i*) the nature of budget (*ii*) nature of demand and supply of product and (*iii*) extent of control needed.

The nature of budget means the functional aspect of budget. The budget may be Production Budget, Sales Budget, Cash Budget, Capital Expenditure Budget etc., The budget period for each functional budget may be different. But if Master Budget is also prepared, the functional budgets periods should also be adjusted to the budget period of the Master Budget. Most of the manufacturing industries use one year as budget period. But the budget may be of short term.

Budget Committee

In a small size business, one person is appointed as incharge of budgetary arrangement. He is called Budget Officer. In large concerns a Budget Committee is setup to formulate policy for preparing budgets and exercising overall control. Budget committee is an advisary body. The main functions of the budget committe are : (*i*) to lay down general policies of management in relation to the budgetary system (*ii*) to provide necessary information to incharges of various departments to prepare budgets for their department, (*iii*) to make available the advice and guidelines, if needed, for the preparation of budgets (*iv*) to receive and scrutinize budgets (*v*) to evaluate and suggest lines of revisions and amendments where necessary. (*vi*) to formulate master budget after the functional budgets have been cleared (*vii*) to compare the actual results with the budget estimates and to recommend corrective actions to be taken if required (*viii*) to coordinate the budgetary programme.

Thus the entire budgetary organisation plan is as below :

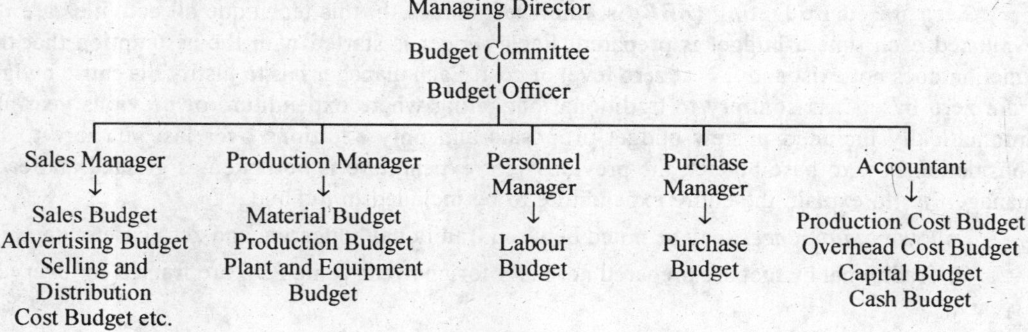

Budget Manual

It is a document which contains all aspects of budgeting and their administration. It is defined as 'A document which sets out inter-alia the responsibilities of persons engaged in the routine of, and the forms and records required for budgetary control'

The budget manual has following main contents (*i*) A statement of objectives and procedures to be followed. (*ii*) A statement defining responsibilities and duties of each functional manager regarding preparation and execution of budgets (*iii*) A statement showing the procedure for budget preparation and control (*iv*) A statement showing time schedules for all stages of budgeting.

Limitations and Problems of Budgetary Control

There are certain limitation of Budgetary control.

(*i*) *Based on Estimates :* Total accuracy is not certain in budgeting because budget are based on estimates.

(*ii*) *Misleading as Standards :* In the business there are inherent uncertainties and the budget assumptions are often falsified by event, unpredictable changes occur in markets, technology, prices, labour rates, economic and social conditons. As a result budgets tend to lose their validity in the course of the time and become misleading as of performances. With the result, managers lose faith in the system.

(*iii*) *Regidity and Overbudgeting :* In budgets even most minor expenses are analysed in detail. Managers are left with a very little freedom in operating the departments. These aspects are called overbudgeting and regidity.

(*iv*) *Hiding of Inefficiency :* Budgets are usually devices of hiding inefficiency. Once a department has spent a given amount, it becomes basis for future budget. Moreover the managers may inflate their demands in the hope that the Budget Committee would cut down their allocation.

(*v*) *Inflexibility :* In budgeting, the managers may have to operate within budget limits even if circumstances require a change. Long-term budgets suffer from inflexibility.

(*vi*) *Complacency :* Managers tend to become complacent if the budgeted performance is easy to achieve.

(*vii*) *Less Effective :* Cost control through budget has limited effectiveness. This is because monthly cost and budget comparisons appear too long after the events.

The above problems are basically related to fixed budgets. These defects can be minimised to some extent by the use of flexible budgeting and frequent revisions and by integration of standard costing with the budgetary system. Some form of *zero-based budgeting* would also help. In the zero based budgeting, assessment of budgets ignores past and present levels of cost and activity. The budget of a department is assessed from a zero base after a detailed study of the performance required from it.

Zero Based Budgeting (*ZBB*) is a new techniques. In this technique all activities are re-evaluated each time a budget is prepared. Each budget is started with the assumption that the function does not exist and it is at zero level of cost. Each manager has to justify his entire budget from zero base. It is contrary to traditional budgeting where expenditure of previous year are automatically included in new budget proposals and only additions over last year are to be considered. In zero base budget, the previous year expenditure is not taken as granted and each manager has to explain the entire expenditure to be included in the budget.

Following *differences* may be noted between traditional budgeting and zero base budgeting.

(*i*) Traditional budget are prepared normally for one year while *ZBB* are framed for every 3-5 years.

(*ii*) Traditional budgets have last year's budget at starting point but *ZBB* have zero as starting point.

(*iii*) In traditional budgets demand is made for inflation and new expenditure or over past year's level but in *ZBB* entire expenditure are analysed.

(*iv*) In tranditions budgeting managers deliberately inflate their budget demand so that after cuts they may get sufficient allocation but in *ZBB* a rational analysis of entire demand is done.

Programme Budgeting or Planning Programming Budgeting Systems or Performance Budgeting

It is a technique used in non-commercial organisation to enable them more informed decision about resource allocation. It is a system devised for effective utilisation of public funds. Its objective is to bring about more effective and efficient use of public funds through improved allocation of resources. This method is useful in hospitals, schools, defence projects etc.

A programme budget provides a closer linkage between planning and action. It also provides a more common basis for review, control and reporting.

CLASSIFICATION OF BUDGETS

Various budgets may be classified on following basis.

(*a*) Classification according to Time Factor

(*b*) Functional Classification

(*c*) Classification according to Flexibility.

(a) Classification According to Time Factor

There may be three types of budgets under this classification.

1. *Long Term Budgets :* When budgets are prepared for a period of 5 to 10 years these are called long-term budget. These budgets are usually in physical quantities for operation covering operations ranging from 5 to 10 years.

2. *Short-term Budgets :* These are budgets for a short period of a year or two. These are prepared in the form of production plan in monetary term.

3. *Current Budgets :* These are very short term budgets covering a period of a month or so. These are prepared considering current conditions or prevailing circumstances.

Industries which require huge capital investment (like shipping, transport services, electric-generation etc) may have long term budgets extending from 5 to 10 years, because there is changes in the equipment and operations very slow. A medium term budgets are prepared by industries producing television, radio, refrigeration and motor vehicles. Short term budgets are used for mass production industries and concerns producing fashionable products. Usually most of the manufacturing industries use one year as budget period.

(b) Functional Classification of Budgets

Budget may be classified on the basis of the processes of other business. Main functional budgets are :

(1) Sales Budgets

(2) Production Budget

(3) Direct Material Usage Budget

(4) Direct Material Purchase Budget

(5) Direct Labour Cost Budgets
(6) Factory Overhead or Production Overhead Budgets
(7) Plant Utilisation Budget
(8) Production Cost Budget
(9) Stock Budget
(10) Cost of Goods Sold Budget
(11) Administration Cost Budget
(12) Selling and Distribution Cost Budgets
(13) Research and Development Cost Budget
(14) Capital Expenditure Budget
(15) Cash Budget
(16) Master Budget

Actually functional classification is based on coverage. On the basis of coverage there are two categories.

(1) Functional Budgets (as above)
(2) Master Budget – It is summary of all functional budgets.

(c) Classification According to Flexibility (Capacity)

(1) *Fixed Budgets :* Fixed budget is a budget for a given capacity or level of activity. It does not provide for any change in expenditure arising out of changes in the level of activity or of capacity of production.

(2) *Flexible Budgets :* Fixed budgets are designed to change with the level of activity attained. For preparing these budgets, expenses are classified as fixed, semi-variable and variable.

All of these kinds of budgets have been explained ahead with examples.

1. SALES BUDGETS

Sales budget is often the starting budget since usually the limiting factor is sales. The sales budget is a forecast of the sales for the year. On the basis of market research, it is possible to make an estimate of sales likely to be effected in the next year or period. This estimate must be prepared both in terms of quantities and amounts and must be analysed for products, territories, types of customers and seasons. Alternate sales budgets may be prepared tentatively out of which one may be adopted. For example, one budget may be based on the sale of 10,000 units of article A and 6,000 units of article B and another on the basis of 8,000 units A and 7,500 units of B.

The Sales Budget shows the total sale proceeds. In addition, it msut be supplemented by an estimate of selling and distribution costs which in turn will be split into two parts, fixed and variable. The following is a rough example :

Sales Budget for Six Months to June 30, 2004

		₹.
Sales :	10,000 units of A @ ₹. 150	15,00,000
	6,000 units of B @ ₹. 200	12,00,000
	Total Gross Sales	27,00,000

		₹.
Selling & Distribution Expenses :		
Fixed—Salaries : Sales Office		35,000
Travellers		20,000
Travellers's Expenses		25,000
Show Rooms		26,000
Godown Rents		8,000
Advertising		76,000
		1,90,000
Variable—Packing:		
A 10,000 units @ ₹. 2	20,000	
B 6,000 units @ ₹. 3	18,000	38,000
Carriage :		
A 10,000 units @ ₹. 1	10,000	
B 6,000 units @ ₹. 2	12,000	22,000
	Total	2,50,000
Net Sale Proceeds (27,00,000 – 2,50,000)		24,50,000

Illustration 1: The Best Writing Ltd. manufactures two brands of pens—one sold under the name 'Bright' and another under the name of 'Hans'. The sales department of the company has three departments in different areas of the country.

The sales budgets for the year ending 31st December 2004 were: Bright—Department I, 3,00,000 : Department II 5,62,500; Department III 1,80,000; and Hans—Department I 4,00,000; Department II 6,00,000 and Department III 20,000. Selling prices are ₹. 3 and ₹. 1.20 in all departments for Bright and Hans.

It is estimated that by forced sales promotion the sale of 'Hans' in Department I will increase by 1,75,000. It is also expected that by increasing production and arranging extensive advertisement Department III will be enabled to increase the sale of 'Hans' by 50,000.

It is recognised that the estimated sales by Department II represent an unsatisfactory target. It is agreed to increase both estimates by 20%.

Prepare a Sales Budget for the year to 31st December, 2005.

Solution:

Sales Budget for 2005

	Bright @ ₹ 3		*Hans* @ ₹. 1.20		*Total*
	Quantity	₹.	Quantity	₹.	₹.
Department I	3,00,000	9,00,000	5,75,000	6,90,000	15,90,000
Department II	6,75,000	20,25,000	7,20,000	8,64,000	28,89,000
Department III	1,80,000	5,40,000	70,000	84,000	6,24,000
Total	11,55,000	34,65,000	13,65,000	16,38,000	51,03,000

Illustration 2 : Beta Manufacturing Ltd., manufactures three products X, Y and Z and sells them through three divisions — North, South and West.

Sales Budgets for the current year based on the estimates of the sales division manager, were: X—North 15,220, South 12,500 and West 17,560; Y—North 18,000, South 7,500 and West 8,000; and Z—North 16,500, South 20,500 and West 6,000. Sales prices are ₹. 12, ₹ 8 and ₹. 10 in all areas.

Acutal sales for the year were X—North 16,200, South 13,800 and West 18,000; Y—North 12,500, South 7,000 and West 6,000 and Z—North 14,000, South 16,500 and West 7,500.

A market research was conducted by the management of company and it was found out that product X has a favour among customers, but is under-priced. It is expected that if the price is increased by ₹. 1, its sale will not be affected. The price of product Y is proposed to be reduced by Re. 1 as it is over-priced. Product Z is properly priced; but extensive advertisement is required to push up its sales.

On the basis of above information and information provided by salesmen, it is estimated by the divisional managers that percentage increase in sales will be: X-North 10%, South 5% and West 5%; Y-North 10%. South 5%, West 10% and Z—North 5%, South 10% and West 15%.

It is also expected that there will be further 'push up' in sales if intensive advertisement is resorted to. The increase will be: X—North 1,500, South 240, West 55, Y—North 600, South 1,000, West 1,050 and Z—North 600, South nil, and West 700.

Prepare a Sales Budget and also show the budgeted actual sales of current year.

Solution:

Division	*Product*	*Budget for future period*			*Budget for current period*			*Actual Sales for current period*		
		Quantity	*Price* ₹	*Amount* ₹	*Quantity*	*Price* ₹	*Amount* ₹	*Quantity*	*Price* ₹	*Amount* ₹
North	X	18,242	13	2,37,146	15,220	12	1,82,640	16,200	12	1,94,400
	Y	20,400	7	1,42,800	18,000	8	1,44,000	12,500	8	1,00,000
	Z	17,925	10	1,79,250	16,500	10	1,65,000	14,000	10	1,40,000
		56,567		5,59,196	49,720		4,91,640	42,700		4,34,400
South	X	13,365	13	1,73,745	12,500	12	1,50,000	13,800	12	1,65,600
	Y	8,875	7	62,125	7,500	8	60,000	7,000	8	56,000
	Z	22,550	10	2,25,500	20,500	10	2,05,000	16,500	10	1,65,000
		44,790		4,61,370	40,500		4,15,000	37,300		3,86,600
West	X	18,493	13	2,40,409	17,560	12	2,10,720	18,000	12	2,16,000
	Y	9,850	7	68,950	8,000	8	64,000	6,000	8	48,000
	Z	7,600	10	76,000	6,000	10	60,000	7,500	10	75,000
		35,943		3,85,359	31,560		3,34,720	31,500		3,39,000

2. PRODUCTION BUDGET

Production Budget is drawn up after taking into account the expected opening stock, the estimated sales and the desired closing stock of each article. Thus, if in the earlier example of sales budget if the opening stock of article A is likely to be 1,000 units and it is desired that a stock of 1,200 limits should be maintained, the production will have to be of the order of 10,200 units, *i.e.*, 10,000 + 1,200 – 1,000. Similarly for B. Of course, productive capacity is of importance but often it can be expanded by giving work out.

Having determined the quantity to be produced, the requirements of raw materials for each article have to be laid down. It should be known what quantity of raw materials is needed for each unit–for instance to produce one tonne of steel nearly 1.5 tonnes of iron ore and 2 tonnes of coal are needed. Thus the total quantity of raw material requirements are determined. Since often a number of materials are required to make a product (*e.g.*, to produce cloth not only raw cotton is needed but also caustic soda, bleaching materials, etc., will be needed), all requirements will be carefully listed. Thus the raw material budget is drawn up after costing the quantities required.

Time and motion study helps to find out how much time is needed of each type of worker to make a product. To make article A, it is possible that one needs 20 hours of one type of worker and 10 hours of another. The total quantity to be produced being known, it is easy to find out how many hours in all will be required to each type of worker. This will enable the labour budget to be drawn up.

Machine requirements are also carefully listed. If one unit of article A require 10 hours at a lathe, one will have to have 10,000 hours on lathes to produce 1,000 units. The number of lathes required can thus be determined.

In addition to budgets for raw materials, labour and machine capacity, a budget for the other expenses required to be incurred will be necessary. Such expenses must be split into fixed and variable portions. The total of all these budgets will show the total amount to be spent on production.

Illustration 3: The Golden Company plans to sell 1,08,000 units of certain product line in the first fiscal quarter, 1,20,000 units in the second quarter, 1,32,000 units in the third quarter and 1,56,000 units in the fourth quarter and 1,38,000 units in the first quarter of the following year. At the beginning of the first quarter of the current year, there are 18,000 units of product in the stock. At the end of each quarter, the company plans to have an inventory equal to one-sixth of the sales for the next fiscal quarter.

How many units must be manufactured in each quarter of the current year?

Solution.

The Golden Company
Production Budget

	First Quarter	Second Quarter	Third Quarter	Fourth Quarter
	Units	Units	Units	Units
Sales Budget	1,08,000	1,20,000	1,32,000	1,56,000
Add Stock required at the end of period	20,000	22,000	26,000	23,000
Total	1,28,000	1,42,000	1,58,000	1,79,000
Less Stock in the begining	18,000	20,000	20,000	26,000
Estimated Production	1,10,000	1,22,000	1,36,000	1,53,000

3. DIRECT MATERIAL USAGE BUDGET

Direct Material Budget deals with direct material. Indirect material and stores are included in the works overhead budgets. Direct Material Budget shows quantities of material required in budgeted production. It also shows the level of material stocks to be maintained at the end of the period

Illustration 4. Draw a material procurement budget (quantitative) from the following information :

Extimated sales duing next year will be 40,000 units. Materials required will be 3 units of A and 5 units of B for each unit of finished product sold.

Estimated opening balances at the commencement of the next year:

Finished product	5,000 units	Materials on order :	
Material A	12,000 units	Material A	7,000 units
Material B	20,000 units	Material B	11,000 units

The desirable closing balances at the end of the next year:

Finished product	7,000 units	Materials on order :	
Material A	15,000 units	Material A	8,000 units
Material B	25,000 units	Material B	10,000 units

Solution:

Materials Procurement Budget (Quantitative)

		A		B	
Units of Material Required			1,26,000		2,10,000
Add:	Closing Stock Required	15,000		25,000	
	Material on order	8,000	23,000	10,000	35,000
			1,49,000		2,45,000
Less:	Opening Stock	12,000		20,000	
	Material on order	7,000	19,000	11,000	31,000
Units to be purchased			1,30,000		2,14,000

Note: The total production required for the year has been calculated as below :

	Units
Estimated sales	40,000
Add: Closing Stock	7,000
	47,000
Less: Opening Stock	5,000
Production in units	42,000

Materials required A 42,000 × 3 = 1,26,000. B 42000 × 5 = 2,10,000.

4. DIRECT MATERIAL PURCHASE BUDGET

The purchase department on the basis of material budget prepares a purchase budget. This budget shows the quantity of raw material which should be available at a particular time and the estimated cost of the material. This budget provide a plan that enables the purchase department to purchase the required material sufficiently in advance so that material may be made available within time. Purchase manager has to formulate purchasing plans in accordance with established inventory procedure and available raw material on hand.

Illustration 5 : It is estimated that on 1st January 2004, the Alpha Manufacturing Co. Ltd., will have the following raw materials inventory.

Type of Material	*Quantity*	*Price* ₹	*Amount* ₹
L	700	3	2,100
M	15 tons	35	525
N	1,500 kg	0.75	1,125
O	800 gallons	1.00	800
P	10,500	0.20	2,100
			6,650

The management summarised the consumption of different types of raw material for various departments in the following manner :

Material	Departments			
	I	II	III	IV
L (units)	4,500	—	3,000	500
M (tons)	11	3	—	4
N (kg)	—	600	700	1,350
O (gallons)	350	700	—	—
P (units)	5,600	6,300	1,500	800

The following inventory at 31st December 2004, is desired:

L	800 units
M	7 tons
N	1,050 kg.
O	750 gallons
P	600 units

Assuming that all prices will remain constant, prepare the Purchase Budget.

Solution:

Purchase Budget

Material	*Units*	*Opening stock*	*Expected consumption*	*Closing stock*	*Requirement*	*Price* ₹	*Budget* ₹
L	units	700	8,000	800	8,100	3.00	24,300
M	tons	15	18	7	10	35.00	350
N	kg	1,500	2,650	1,050	2,200	0.75	1,650
O	gallons	800	1,050	750	1,000	1.00	1,000
P	units	10,500	14,200	600	4,300	0.20	860
							28,160

5. DIRECT LABOUR COST BUDGET

Direct labour budget is also a part of production budget. This budget contains an estimate of all direct labour cost required to produce the budgeted products shown in the production budget. Labour of different grades needed for a product or job or process is ascertained in terms of labour hour, machine hours and wage rate. The total labour cost is ascertained accordingly *i.e.*, budgeted output multiplied by labout cost per unit.

Illustration 6 : P. Ltd. manufacturers two products using one type of material and one grade of labour. Shown below is an extract from the company's working papers for the next period's budget :

	Product A	*Product B*
Budgeted sales (units)	3,600	4,800
Budgeted material consumption, per unit (kg.)	5	3
Budgeted materials cost ₹. 12 per kg.		
Standard hours allowed per unit	5	4
Budgeted wage rate ₹. 8 per hour		

Overtime premium is 50% and is payable, if a worker works for more than 40 hours a week. There are 90 direct workers.

The target productivity ratio (or efficiency ratio) for the productive hours worked by the direct workers in actually manufacturing the products is 80%; in addition the non-productive down-time is budgeted at 20% of the productive hours worked.

There are twelve 5-day weeks in the budget period and it is anticipated that sales and production will occur evenly throughout the whole period.

It is anticipated that stock at the beginning of the period will be Product A 1,020 units; Product B 2,400 units; Raw material 4,300 kgs.

The target closing stock, expressed in terms of anticipated activity during the budgeted period are; Product A 15 days sales; Product B 20 days sales; Raw material 10 days consumption.

Required

Prepare the material purchase budget and the wages budget for the direct workers, showing the quantities and values, for the next period.

Solution:

Production Budget (In Units)

	Product A Units	Product B Units
Budgeted Sales	3,600	4,800
Add: Closing Stock (see note)	900	1,600
	4,500	6,400
Less: Anticipated Opening Stock	1,020	2,400
Budgeted Production	3,480	4,000

Note: There are 12 × 5 *i.e.*, 60 days in the budget period. Closing stock for A and B are for 15 and 20 days sales.

Hence budgeted closing stock : A: $\frac{3600}{60} \times 15 = 900$ units

B: $\frac{4800}{60} \times 20 = 1{,}600$ units

Material Purchases Budget

	Product A	Product B	Total
Material requirements for production (Kgs.)	17,400 (3,480 × 5)	12,000 (4,000 × 3)	29,400
Add: Closing stock of materials (Kgs.) (see note)			4,900
			34,300
Less: Opening stock of materials (Kgs.)			4,300
Total materials to be purchased (Kgs.)			30,000
Budgeted materials cost per kg. (₹.)			12
Total value of materials to be purchased			₹. 3,60,000

Note. Closing stock of materials : 10 days consumption

i.e. $\frac{29{,}400}{60} \times 10 = 4{,}900$ kgs.

Wages Budget (For Next Period)

	Product A	Product B	Total
Budgeted production (Units)	3,480	4,000	
Standard hours per unit	5	4	
Standard hours for budgeted production	17,400	16,000	33,400
Budgeted productive input hours (Productive hours worked)			
At 80% efficency $\left(\frac{100}{80} \times 33{,}400\right)$			41,750
Add: Budgeted non-productive down time (20% of 41,750)			8,350
Budgeted attendance hours required			50,100
Budgeted wages :			
Normal hours: 90 workers × 40 hours × 12 weeks = 43,200			₹.
Wages for normal hours (43,200 × ₹. 8)			3,45,600
Overtime hours: 50,100 – 43,200 = 6,900 hour			
Overtime wages: 6,900 × ₹. 8 × 1.5			82,800
Total Budgeted Wages			4,28,400

6. FACTORY OVERHEAD OR PRODUCTION OVERHEAD BUDGETS

Factory Overhead Budget shows the forecast of all production overheads. Production overheads are divided between fixed factory overhead, variable factory overhead and semi-variable express. Fixed overheads normally remain fixed but it may increase when there is necessity to increase capacity or size of the factory. Variable and semi-variable expenses change with the level of activity. Factory overheads are distributed among produciton and service departments and thereafter service department overheads are re-allocated to production department as it has been explained in the Chapter of 'Overheads' distribution.

Budget for factory overhead is based on level of activity to be attained. Variable and semi-variable overhead can be forecasted accurately on the basis of level of activity.

Budget Allowance

Budget allowance is the amount of overhead which a budget centre or department is expected to incurr during a given period of time. It is different to overhead absorption which is the process of recovery of overheads from production at a pre-determined rate.

Illustration 7: The budget manager of Alankar Cosmetics Limited is preparing budget for the accounting year starting from 1st April, 2004.

As part of the budget operations, some items of factory overhead costs have been estimated by him under specified conditions of volume as follows :

Volume of Production (in units)	1,20,000	1,50,000
Expenses:		
Indirect Materials	₹. 2,64,000	₹. 3,30,000
Indirect Labour	1,50,000	1,87,500
Maintenance	84,000	1,02,000
Supervision	1,98,000	2,34,000
Engineering Services	94,000	94,000

Calculate the cost of factory overhead items given above at 1,40,000 units of production.

[B. Com. (Hons.), Delhi]

Solution:

Factory Overhead Budget
(Production 1,40,000 Units)

		₹.	₹.
Indirect Material (Variable @ ₹. 2.20 per unit)			3,08,000
Indirect Labour (Variable @ ₹. 1.25 per unit))			1,75,000
Maintenance :	Fixed	12,000	
	Variable @ ₹. 0.60 per unit	84,000	96,000
Supervision :	Fixed	54,000	
	Variable @ ₹. 1.20 per unit	1,68,000	2,22,000
Engineering Service (Fixed)			94,000
			8,95,000

Note : Fixed and variable elements in the items of factory overhead has been calculated on the basis of change in expenses and change in output.

$$\text{Variable cost per unit} = \frac{\text{Change in Expenses}}{\text{Change in Output}}$$

If there is no change in expenses, it will be a fixed overhead.

7. PLANT UTILISATION BUDGET

Plant utilisation budget represents the plant and machinery requirements to meet the production budget. Such a budget will show the load on machine in each department and shows the extent of under and over loading on plant and machinery. Plant utilisation budget is of much use because it shows machine load in every production department, over loading or under loading identified and corrective measures may be taken in time.

Illustration 8 : Three articles X, Y & Z are produced in a factory. They pass through two cost centres A and B. From the data furnished compile a statement for budgeted machine utilisation in both centres.

(*a*) Sale budget for the year.

Product	*Annual Budgeted Sales (units)*	*Opening stock of finished product (units)*	*Closing stock*
X	4,800	600	Equivalent to two month sales
Y	2,400	300	Equivalent to two month sales
Z	2,400	800	Equivalent to two month sales

(*b*) Machine hours per unit of production

	Cost Centre A	Cost Centre B
Product X	30	70
Y	200	100
Z	30	20

(*c*) Total number of machines

Cost centre A	284
Cost centre B	256
Total	540

(*d*) Total working hours during the year : Estimated 2,500 hours per machine

Solution.

Production Budget

Product	*Sales (units)*	*Closing stock (units)*	*Opening stock (units)*	*Production Budget: Sales + Closing Stock – Opening Stock*
X	4800	800	600	5000
Y	2400	400	300	2500
Z	2400	400	800	2000

Machine Utilisation Budget

Product	*Units of Production*	*Cost centre A*			*Cost centre B*		
		Hours per units	*Total Machine Hours*	*No. of Machine required*	*Hours per unit*	*Total Machine hours*	*No. of Machine required*
X	5000	30	1,50,000	60	70	3,50,000	140
Y	2500	200	5,00,000	200	100	2,50,000	100
Z	2000	30	60,000	24	20	40,000	16
			7,10,000	284		6,40,000	256
Number of Machine × Hours			284 × 2500 = 7,10,000			256 × 2500 = 6,40,000	

8. PRODUCTION COST BUDGET

Production cost budget is combination of three budgets viz., Material Purchase Budget, Labour Budget and Factory Overhead Budget.

Illustration 9 : Prepare a production budget for each month and a summarised. Production Cost Budget for the six months period ending 31st December, 2003 from the following data for Product X.

(*i*) The units to be sold for different months are as follows :

July 2003	1,100
August	1,100
September	1,700
October	1,900
November	2,500
December 2003	2,300
January 2004	2,000

(*ii*) There will be no work in progress at the end of any month.

(*iii*) Finished units in stock will be equal, at the end of each month, of half the sales for the following month.

(*iv*) Budgeted Production and Production Cost for the year ending 31st December, 2003 are follows:

Production (units)		22,000
Direct materials per units	₹.	10.00
Direct wages per unit	₹.	4.00
Total factory overhead apportioned to product :		
Variable per unit	₹.	1.50
Fixed per unit	₹.	2.50

Solution:

Production Budget for Product X–6 months ending Dec. 31, 2003

(*figures in units*)

	July	Aug.	Sept.	Oct.	Nov.	Dec.	Total
Estimated Sales	1,100	1,100	1,700	1,900	2,500	2,300	10,600
Add: Desired closing stock	550	850	950	1,250	1,150	1,000	1,000
	1,650	1,950	2,650	3,150	3,650	3,300	11,600
Less: Likely Opening Stock	550	550	850	950	1,250	1,150	550
	1,100	1,400	1,800	2,200	2,400	2,150	11,050

Production Cost Budget

	Rate per unit ₹.	Total ₹.
Direct Material	10.00	1,10,500
Direct Wages	4.00	44,200
Variable Overheads	1.50	16,575
Fixed Overheads $\left(\dfrac{22,000 \times 2.50}{2}\right)$		27,500
Total		1,98,775

Illustration 10 **:** The following are the details of the budgeted and the actual cost in a factory for six months from January to June, 2000. From the figures given below, you are required to prepare the production cost budget for the period from January to June, 2001:

	January-June 2000	
	Budget	*Actual*
Production (units)	20,000	18,000
Material cost	₹. 40,00,000	39,90,000
	(2,000 MT @ ₹. 2,000)	(1,900 MT @ 2,100)
Labour cost	₹. 8,00,000	₹. 7,99,920
	(@ ₹. 20 per hour)	(₹. 22 per hour)
Variable overheads	₹. 2,40,000	₹. 2,16,000
Fixed overheads	₹. 4,00,000	₹. 4,20,000

In the first half of 2001, production is budgeted for 25,000 units. Material cost per tonne will increase from last year's actual by ₹. 100 but is proposed to maintain the consumption efficiency of 2000 as budgeted.

Labour efficiency will be lower by another 1% and labour rates will be ₹. 22 per hour.

Variable and fixed overheads will go up by 20% over 2000 actual.

You are required to prepare the production cost budget for the period January-June, 2001 giving all the workings.

Solution:

Production Cost Budget

for the months ending 31th June, 2001

Production	25,000 units	
	Total Cost	Unit Cost
Material Cost	₹. 55,00,000	₹. 220.00
Labour Cost	11,22,000	44.88
Variable Overheads	3,60,000	14.40
Fixed Overheads	5,04,000	20.16
Total	74,86,000	299.44

Working Notes: Calculation of above costs have been as below:

(1) *Material cost*		
Consumption per unit	2,000/20,000	0.10 *MT*
Consumption for	25,000 Units	2,500 *MT*
Cost of 2,500 *MT* @ ₹. 2,200 per *MT*		₹. 55,00,000
(2) *Labour cost*		Hrs.
2000: Total budgeted labour hours	8,00,000/20	40,000
Labour hour budget for each unit	40,000/20,000	2
Actual time paid for	7,99,920/22	36,600
Less: Standard labour hours for 18,000 units ₹ 2 per hours.		36,000
Extra-time taken (*i.e.*, 1% extra)		360
2001		Hrs.
Time required for 25,000 Units @ ₹ 2 per hour		50,000
Add: 2% for lower efficiency		1,000
		51,000
51,000 Hrs. at ₹. 22 per hour		₹. 11,22,000

(3) *Variable Overheads :*

Actual Rate per unit in 2000	2,16,000/18,000 = ₹. 12	
Cost for 25,000 @ ₹. 12		3,00,000
Add 20%		60,000
		3,60,000

(4) *Fixed Overheads*

Actual in 2000	4,20,000
Add 20%	84,000
	5,04,000

9. STOCK BUDGETS

Stock budget is prepared in respect of stocks of raw material, work-in-progress and finished goods. Closing stocks are shown in this budget in terms of quantity as well as money. Finished stock is based on per unit cost of production.

10. COST OF GOODS SOLD BUDGET

Cost of Goods Sold Budget is prepared to depict budgeted cost of goods meant for sales. This budget is prepared by adjusting cost of production by opening or closing stocks of finished goods. This budget may also be prepared product wise.

11. ADMINISTRATION COST BUDGET

Administration Cost Budget shows estimated expenditure of administration, offices and management remunerations during the budget period. There may be several departments or budget centres which are responsible for the preparation of its own budgets. These petty budgets are incorporated in the Administration Cost Budget. In this budget also expenditure may be classified into fixed and variable overheads which are estimated on the basis of past records and future plans.

12. SELLING AND DISTRIBUTION COST BUDGET

Selling and Distribution Cost Budget is the forecast of all expenses incurred in selling and distribution function during the budget-period. This budget is closely connected with Sales Budget because it is based on the volume of sales projected for the budget-period. But there may be certain expenses which may cover future budget period, for example an advertising campaign may be launched in the year may have influence our sales in forthcoming year or years.

This budget is normally prepared by the sales manager and selling office manager, distribution manager and advertising or publicity manager. Advertising is now a days a costly item in the selling and distribution cost budgets.

Illustration 11: You are requested to prepare a Sales Overhead Budget from the estimates given below:

Advertising	₹. 2,500	Expenses of sales department	₹. 1,500
Salaries of the sales department	5,000	Counter salesmen's salaries and dearness allowances	6,000

Commission to counter salesmen at 1% on their sales.

Travelling salesmen's commission at 10% on their sales and expenses at 5% on their sales.

The sales during the period were estimated as following :

	Counter Sales (₹.)	Travelling Salesmen's Sales (₹.)
Period I	80,000	10,000

Period II 1,20,000	15,000
Period III 1,40,000	20,000

Solution:

Sales Overhead Budget

Estimated Sales	₹. 90,000	₹. 1,35,000	₹. 1,60,000
Fixed Overheads:			
Advertising	2,500	2,500	2,500
Salaries of sales department	5,000	5,000	5,000
Expenses of sales department	1,500	1,500	1,500
Counter salesmen's salaries and D.A.	6,000	6,000	6,000
	15,000	15,000	15,000
Variable Overheads :			
Counter salesmen's commission @ 1% on sales	800	1,200	1,400
Travelling salesmen's commission @ 10%	1,000	1,500	2,000
Expenses 5%	500	750	1,000
	2,300	3,450	4,400
Total Sales Overheads	17,300	18,450	19,400

13. RESEARCH AND DEVELOPMENT BUDGET

Research to find new products and to find new ways of old products is a vital function. For this an adhoc allocation out of revenues is made. The budget is naturally drawn up taking into account the research projects in hand and the new projects to be taken up. This budget will also necessitate the analysis of expenses into fixed and variable categories. This budget is not a part of production budget.

R&D Budget is normally a long term budget. It is prepared for each project separately and should be sub-divided into short-term budgets on annual basis.

The R&D Budget provide information regarding control of research and development cost.

14. CAPITAL EXPENDITURE BUDGET

It is closely connected with the production budget which will show how much machine capacity is needed and when. This enable one to determine what new machines have to be installed and at what time. This also goes for buildings and other assets of fixed nature. Of course, much of the capital expenditure may be avoided by getting some work done by outsiders. For instance, the whole work of packing can be contracted out. Such giving out of contracts in fact has an effect upon the whole of the production budget.

Capital Expenditure Budget may be short term or long term budgets. In this budget the availability of capital fund is a limiting factor. It is desirable that capital expenditure budget must be coordinated with each budget because in the cash budget, provision for cash required for capital expenditure has to be made. In the factory overhead budget also, there should be provision for repairs maintenance, insurance and depreciation on new capital asset.

15. CASH OR FINANCIAL BUDGET

Cash Budget is another important budget. Its object is to indicate the flow of funds and their requirements. It takes into account the amount received from sales—cash sales and payments made by credit customers and the expenditure to be incurred in cash—both capital and revenue. The budget shows up whether and when arrangements should be made for overdraft, loans etc.

Cash Budget is the budget of anticipated receipts and payment of cash during the budget period and this budget is considered as a *nerve centre of the entire budgetary control system*. It is to be noted that most of the necessary details of this budgets are available from sales budget, production budget, overhead budgets and capital expenditure budgets.

There are three methods of preparing a cash budget :

(*i*) Receipt and Payment Method

(*ii*) Adjusted Profit and Loss Method

(*iii*) Balance Sheet Method

Receipt and Payment Method of Cash Budget

It is similar to Receipt and Payment Account but for future period or budget period.

The detail of cash receipts from sales debtors, B/R, income from investment, sale of assets and investment, probable borrowings will have to be anticipated for the budget period taking into consideration the delay in cash receipts. These details of cash receipts are put at one side of the budget. On the other side anticipated cash requirements during budget period are to be shown. Cash expenditure required in purchase of materials payment of wages and salaries, payment of various overhead expenditure and miscellaneous expenditure, payment for purchase of asset are shown. In this connection lags or delay in payment have to be carefully considered. It is to be noted that adjustments and accurals are excluded in the preparation of cash budget.

The closing balance of cash in hand for the budget period is found out by adding opening cash balance and expected cash receipt and deducting there from the total of the anticipated cash payments during the budget period.

Illustration 12: AB Co. wished to arrange overdraft facilities with its bankers during the period April to June 2010 when it will be manufacturing mostly for stock. Prepare a Cash Budget for the above period from the following data, indicating the extent of the bank facilities the company will require at the end of each month :

(*a*)	Sales	Purchases	Wages
February	₹. 1,80,000	₹. 1,24,800	₹. 12,000
March	1,92,000	1,44,000	14,000
April	1,08,000	2,43,000	11,000
May	1,74,000	2,46,000	10,000
June	1,26,000	2,68,000	15,000

(*b*) 50 per cent of the credit sales are realised in the month following the sales and the remaining 50 per cent in the second month following. Creditors are paid in the month following the month of purchase.

(*c*) Cash at Bank on 1.4.10 (estimated) is ₹. 25,000.

Solution:

ABC Co.

Cash Budget (For April to June 2010)

	April	*May*	*June*
Cash Balance (Overdraft)	₹. 25,000	₹. 56,000	₹. (47,000)
Receipts:			
Collections from Debtors	1,86,000	1,50,000	1,41,000
	2,11,000	2,06,000	94,000
Payments to Creditors	1,44,000	2,43,000	2,46,000
Wages	11,000	10,000	15,000
Cash Balance (Overdraft)	56,000	47,000	94,000

ABC Co. will be in need of overdraft.

(*i*) In May ₹. 47,000

(*ii*) In June 1,67,000

Collections From Debtors have been calculated as below:

		₹.
April		
Sales for February	1,80,000 × 1/2	90,000
Sales for March	1,92,000 × 1/2	96,000
		1,86,000
May		
Sales for March	1,92,000 × 1/2	96,000
Sales for April	1,08,000 × 1/2	54,000
		1,50,000
June		
Sales for April	1,08,000 × 1/2	54,000
Sales for May	1,74,000 × 1/2	87,000
		1,41,000

Illustration 13: A firm expects to have ₹. 25,000 in bank on 1st May, 2010 and requires you to prepare an estimate of cash position during the three months, May–July, 2010. The following information is supplied to you :

	Sales	*Purchases*	*Wages*	*Factory Expenses*	*Office Expenses*	*Selling Expenses*
	₹.	₹.	₹.	₹.	₹.	₹.
March	50,000	30,000	6,000	5,000	4,000	3,000
April	56,000	32,000	6,500	5,500	4,000	3,000
May	60,000	35,000	7,000	6,000	4,000	3,500
June	80,000	40,000	9,000	7,500	4,000	4,500
July	90,000	40,000	9,500	8,000	4,000	4,500

Other Information:

(*i*) 20 p.c. of sales is for cash; remaining amount is collected in the month following that of sale.

(*ii*) Suppliers supply goods at 2 months' credit.

(*iii*) All expenses are paid in the month following the one in which they are incurred.

(*iv*) The company pays devidends to shareholders and bonus to workers of ₹. 10,000 and ₹. 15,000 respectively in the month of May.

(*v*) Plant has been ordered and is expected to be received in June; it will cost ₹. 80,000.

(*vi*) Income tax, ₹. 25,000, is payable in July.

Solution:

Cash Budget

	May ₹.	*June* ₹.	*July* ₹.
Opening Balance	25,000	7,800	– (60,700)
Receipts :			
Cash Sales (20% of current month)	12,000	16,000	18,000
Credit Sales (80% of Previous month)	44,800	48,000	64,000
Total	81,800	71,800	21,300

Payments:			
Purchases	30,000	32,000	35,000
Wages	6,500	7,000	9,000
Factory Expenses	5,500	6,000	7,500
Office Expenses 4,000	4,000	4,000	
Selling Expenses	3,000	3,500	4,500
Dividend to Shareholders	10,000	—	—
Bonus to workers	15,000	—	—
Plant	—	80,000	—
Income Tax	—	—	25,000
Total	74,000	1,32,500	85,000
Closing Balance	7,800	– (60,700)	– (63,700)

The firm will require overdraft facilities in June and July to the extent of ₹. 60,700 and ₹. 63,700 respectively.

Illustration 14: From the information given below, prepare a cash budget of the Jaipur Refrigators(P) Ltd., for the quarter January-March 2010.

	Dec '09	*Jan. '10*	*Feb. '10*	*March '10*	*April '10*
(*a*) Sales Budget units	60	60	65	75	80
(*b*) Selling price per units	₹. 1,000	1,000	1,000	1,000	1,000
(*c*) Off-season discount	20%	20%	10%	—	—
(*d*) End of month inventory units	10	12	15	25	25

(*e*) Half the sales proceeds are collected in the month of sale and the other half in the month following.

(*f*) Materials amounting to ₹. 300 per unit manufactured are purchased one month in advance of manufacture and paid for in cash, earning 5% cash discount on half of the material purchased.

(*g*) Direct labour budget was ₹. 50 per unit and variable overheads ₹. 100 per unit.

(*h*) Indirect labour budget was ₹. 6,000 per month.

(*i*) Depreciation was provided uniformly at ₹. 3,000 per month.

(*j*) The fixed overhead budget was ₹. 6,000 per month during off season and ₹. 7,000 during the season. Out of this the quarterly premium for fire insurance amounting to ₹. 600 was payable in the first month of each quarter.

(*k*) Dividends for the year 2003, amounting to ₹. 20,000 were expected to be declared in March 2010 and payments were to be spread between March and April.

(*l*) A machine was sold for ₹. 10,000 in December 2009 on 3 months' cerdit.

(*m*) The company had overdraft arrangements with the State Bank of Jaipur and Bikaner upto ₹. 50,000.

Solution:

Cash Budget

	January 10 ₹.	*February 10* ₹.	*March 10* ₹.
Opening Balance	—	6,410	12,797.50
Estimated Cash Receipts:			
Sales	48,000	53,250	66,750.00
Sales of machine	—	—	10,000.00
Total	48,000	59,660	89,547.50

Estimated Cash Payments:			
Materials	19,890	24,862.5	23,400
Labour @ ₹. 50 per unit	3,100	3,400	4,250
Variable overhead @ ₹. 100 per unit	6,200	6,800	8,500
Indirect labour	6,000	6,000	6,000
Fixed overhead	6,400	5,800	5,800
Dividend	—	—	10,000
Total	41,590	46,862.5	58,950
Closing Balance	6,410	12,797.5	30,597.5

1. *Calculation of Sales*

For December 2009 (60 × 1,000)		₹. 60,000
Less: 20% discount		12,000
		48,000
For January 2010 (60 × 1,000)	60,000	
Less: 20% discount		12,000
		48,000
		65,000
For February 2010		
Less: 10%		6,500
		58,500
For March 2010 (75 × 1,000)		75,000

2. *Receipt on Account of Sales:*

In January,	₹. 24,000	
	24,000	48,000
In February,	24,000	
	29,250	53,250
In March,	29,250	
	37,500	66,750

3. *Calculation of Payment for Material*

Unit manufactured in February: (65 + 15 – 12) = 68	
Payment in January (68 × 300)	₹. 20,400
Less : 5% cash discount on ₹. 10,200	510
Net payment	19,890
Units manufacturede in March (75 + 25 – 15) = 85	
Payment in February (85 × 300)	₹. 25,500
Less: 5% cash discount on ₹. 12,750	637.50
Net payment	24,862.50
Units manufactured in April (80 + 25 – 25) = 80	
Payment in March (80 × 300)	₹. 24,000
Less: 5% cash discount on ₹. 12,000	600
Net payment	23,400

4. *Payment of Labour and Variable overheads:* For units manufactured in January (60 + 12 – 10) = 62, in February: 68, and in March: 85@ ₹. 50 for labour and @ ₹. 100 for overhead per unit.

5. Payment of Fixed Overhead : ₹. 6,000 paid in January, of which ₹. 200 included in every month's budget.

Budget for February = ₹. 6,000 – ₹. 200 (paid in January)
= ₹. 5,800

Budget for March = ₹. 7,000 – ₹. 200 (paid in January)
= ₹. 6,800

6. Depreciation would not affect cash budget.
7. Overdraft arrangements may be availed, if needed.

Illustration 15: XYZ Company Ltd., has given the following particulars. You are required to prepare a cash budget for the three months ending 31st December, 2004.

(i)

Months	*Sales* ₹.	*Materials* ₹.	*Wages* ₹.	*Overheads* ₹.
August	40,000	20,400	7,600	3,800
September	42,000	20,000	7,600	4,200
October	46,000	19,600	8,000	4,600
November	50,000	20,000	8,400	4,800
December	60,000	21,600	9,000	5,000

(ii) Credit terms are –

Sales/debtors – 10% sales are on cash basis; 50% of the credit sales are collected next month and the balance in the following month :

Creditors — Materials 2 months.
— Wages 1/5 month.
— Overheads 1/2 month.

(iii) Cash balance on 1st October, is expected to be ₹. 8,000

(iv) A machinery will be installed in August, at a cost of ₹. 1,00,000. The monthly instalment of ₹. 5,000 is payable from October onwards.

(v) Dividend at 10% on Preference Share Capital of ₹. 3,00,000 will be paid on 1st December.

(vi) Advance to be received for sale of vehicle ₹. 20,000 in December.

(vii) Income-tax (advance) to be paid in December ₹. 5,000.

Solution:

Calculation of Cash from Sales

Month	*Credit Sales* (₹.)		*Realisation from Debtors* (₹.)
August	40,000 × 90% *i.e.*, 36,000	50%	18,000
September	42,000 × 90% *i.e.*, 37,800	50%	18,900
	Realised in October		36,900
September			18,900
October	46,000 × 90% *i.e.*, 41,400	50%	20,700
	Realised in November		39,600
October			20,700
November	50,000 × 90% *i.e.*, 45,000	50%	22,500
	Realised in Dec.		43,200

Cash Budget
for 3 months ending 31-12-2004

	Oct. 04 (₹)	Nov. 04 (₹)	Dec. 04 (₹)
Cash Balance	8,000	11,780	18,360
Receipts:			
Cash Sales	4,600	5,000	6,000
Debtors	36,900	39,600	43,200
Advances	—	—	20,000
Total	49,500	56,380	87,560
Payment : Creditors	20,400	20,000	19,600
Wages 1/5 of last month	1,520	1,600	1,680
4/5 of current month	6,400	6,720	7,200
Overheads 1/2 of last month	2,100	2,300	2,400
1/2 of current month	2,300	2,400	2,500
Machinery instalment	5,000	5,000	5,000
Preference Dividend	—	—	30,000
Income-tax (advance tax)	—	—	5,000
Total	37,720	38,020	73,380
Closing Balance	11,780	18,360	14,180

Adjusted Profit and Loss Method of Cash Budget (Cash Flow Statement Basis)

There is another method of preparing Cash Budget. It is Adjusted Profit and Loss Method. Under this method a cash forecast is prepared starting with the Net Profit or Net Loss and by eliminating from this figure all non-cash items of income and expenses and making adjustments for changes in the cash position as a result of forecasted changes in the Balance Sheet. The principle is that the adjustment of the forecasted profit or loss figure relating to a period provides the net increase or decrease in cash for the same period.

This method is based on the assumption that cash is available due to profit. The method is more useful in long term forecasting. The method is quite similar to cash flow statement.

Following is a form of cash forecast under this method.

Cash Budget / Forecast

Cash Balance (opening)

Additions

Budgeted Net Profit
Depreciation
Provisions and losses written off
Accrued or Outstanding Expenses
Capital Receipts/Sale of Assets
Reduction in Debtors and B/R
Reduction in Stock and other Current Assets Except Cash
Increase in Creditors & B/P
Increase in other liabilities
Issue of Capital or Increase in Capital
Issue of Debentures

Deductions

Prepaid Expenses
Dividends Paid
Taxes Paid
Capital Payments/Purchase of Assets
Increase in Debtors and B/R
Increase in Stocks and other Current Assets except cash
Decrease in Creditors & B/P
Decrease in Other Liabilities
Redemption of Shares and Debentures
Total
Balance (Being Closing Cash Balance)

Illustration 16: The Board of Directors of Punjab Cable Factory Ltd., have arranged for repayment of loan to a financial institution. You have been asked to prepare a projected Profits and Loss account for 2011 on the basis of the figure available for 2009 and 2010 and to submit the net cash flow. If 75% of the net cash flow is estimated as the fair amount for repayment of loan, ascertain the sum that may be borrowed.

Profit and Loss Account

	2009 ₹.	*2010* ₹.
To Cpening Stock	80,000	1,00,000
To Raw Material	3,00,000	4,00,000
To Stores	1,00,000	1,50,000
To Manufacturing Exps.	1,00,000	1,20,000
To Other Expenses	1,00,000	1,30,000
To Depreciation	1,00,000	1,00,000
To Net Profit	1,30,000	1,60,000
	9,10,000	11,60,000
By Sales	8,00,000	10,00,000
By Closing Stock	1,00,000	1,50,000
By Misc. Income	10,000	10,000
	9,10,000	11,60,000

Sales are expected to increase to ₹. 12,00,000 along with which raw materials, stores and manufacturing expenses are expected to rise by the same amount as they rise between 2009 and 2010. Other expenses will increase by ₹. 50,000. Depreciation will remain constant. Assume sales and purchases in cash terms and the closing stock is expected to go up by the same amount as between 2009 and 2010. You may assume that no dividend is being paid.

Solution:

Projected Profit and Loss Account for the year ending 2011

	₹.		₹.
To Opening Stock	1,50,000	By Sales	12,00,000
To Raw Material	5,00,000	By Closing Stock	2,00,000
To Stores	2,00,000	By Misc. Income	10,000
To Mfg Expenses	1,40,000		
To Other Expenses	1,80,000		
To Depreciation	1,00,000		
To Net Profit	1,40,000		
	14,10,000		14,10,000

Cash Flow Statement

	₹.
Net Profit	1,40,000
Non cash charges item: Depreciation	1,00,000
Cash in flow	2,40,000

As 75% of the net cash flow is estimated as the fair amount for repayment of loan the amount of loan will be 75% of ₹. 2,40,000 *i.e.*, ₹. 1,80,000, if the loan is to be repaid within one year.

Balance Sheet Method of Cash Budget or Cash Forecast

This method is used in long term forecasting – normally for a year or for a long period. The method is somewhat similar to Profit & Loss Method. Under this method a Budgeted Balance Sheet is prepared showing all items of assets and liabilities at the end of the budgeted period. The balancing figure on the asset side is taken as cash balance at the end of that period. If there is excess of asset side, the balance will be bank overdraft.

Illustration 17: From the following information, prepare a cash budget showing cash at bank on 31.12.2004 under the balance sheet method.

Balance Sheet as at 1-1-2004

Liabilities	₹.	*Assets*	₹.
Share Capital	2,50,000	Land and Buildings	1,50,000
Capital Reserve	25,000	Plant and Machinery	1,00,000
Profit & Loss Account	45,000	Furniture	25,000
Debentures	50,000	Closing Stock	20,000
Creditors	1,44,000	Debtors	1,30,000
Accrued Expenses	1,000	Bank	90,000
	5,15,000		5,15,000

Trading and Profit and Loss Account for the year ending 31-12-2004

		₹.		₹.
To Opening Stock		20,000	By Sales	4,00,000
To Purchased		3,00,000	By Closing stock	50,000
To Gross Profit c/d		1,30,000		
		4,50,000		4,50,000
To Salary and				
Wages	12,500		By Gross Profit	1,30,000
Outstanding	2,500	15,000	By Interest recd.	500
To Depreciation				
Plant & Machinery	10,000			
Furniture & Fixture	5,000	15,000		
To Administrative expenses		17,500		
To Selling expenses		12,500		
To Net profit c/d		70,500		
		1,30,500		1,30,500
To Dividend paid		50,000	By Balance	45,000
To Balance c/d to Balance Sheet		65,000	By Net Profit b/d	70,500
		1,15,500		1,15,500

The following are the additional information for the year 2004 :

Share Capital issued ₹. 50,000

Debenture issued ₹. 10,000

On 31st December 2004, the accrued expenses were ₹. 2,500. Debtors ₹. 1,00,000, Creditors ₹. 1,50,000 and Land and buildings ₹. 2,00,000.

Solution:

Forecasted Balance Sheet as at 31.12.2004

Liabilities	₹	*Assets*	₹
Share Capital	3,00,000	Land and Buildings	2,00,000
Capital Reserve	25,000	Plant and Machinery	90,000
Profit & Loss Account	65,500	Furniture & Fixture	20,000
Debentures	60,000	Closing Stock	50,000
Creditors	1,50,000	Debtors	1,00,000
Accrued Expenses	2,500	Bank Balance (Balancing figure)	1,43,000
	6,03,000		6,03,000

The balancing figure on the asset side of ₹. 1,43,000 represents cash at bank on 21.12.2004. This is arrived at by taking the difference of assets and liabilities side.

Master Budget

Master Budget is the `summary budget, incorporating its component functional budgets, which is finally approved, adopted and employed'. Master budget gathers together all the budgets of various departments and makes a summary of them.

Master budget is prepared in two parts; Forecast Income Statement and Forecast Balance Sheet. In the former part, the principal items of revenue, expenses, losses and profits are shown. In the Forecast Balance Sheet the items of balance sheet *i.e.*, fixed assets, current assets, total capital employed and liabilities are shown.

Master Budget is an outlay showing the proposed activity and the anticipated financial results during the coming year or budgeted year. It is presented before the Board of Directors for adoption and approval. After approval of the Master Budget, various functional budgets are sent to the concerned departments, so that, they can plan their working according to their budgets.

Illustration 18: A Glass Manufacturing Company requires you to calculate and present the budget for the next year from the following information:

Sales:	
Toughened Glass	₹. 3,00,000
Bent-toughened Glass	₹. 5,00,000
Direct Material Cost	60% of sales
Direct Wages	20 workers @ ₹. 150 per month
Factory Overheads:	
Indirect Labour:	
Works Manager	500 per month
Foreman	400 per month
Stores and Spares	2½% on sales
Depreciation on Machinery	₹. 12,600
Light and Power	5,000
Repairs and Maintenance	8,000
Other Sundries	10% on Direct Wages

Administration, Selling and Distribution Expenses : ₹ 14,000 per year.

Solution:

Master Budget (For the period ending on......)

			₹.
Sales (as per Sales Budget):			
Toughened glass ... units @ ₹. ...			3,00,000
Bent toughened glass ... units @ ₹. ...			5,00,000
			8,00,000
Less: Cost of Production (as per Cost of Production Budget)			
Direct Material (... units @ ₹. ...)		₹. 4,80,000	
Direct Wages		36,000	
Prime Cost		5,16,000	
Factory Overheads:			
Variable:	₹.		
Stores and Spares (2½% of sales)	20,000		
Light and Power	5,000		
Repairs and Maintenance	8,000	33,000	
Fixed:			
Works Manager's Salary	6,000		
Foremen's Salary	4,800		
Depreciation	12,600		
Sundries	3,600	27,000	
Works Cost			5,76,000
Gross Profit			2,24,000
Less: Administration, Selling and Distribution Overheads			14,000
Net Profit			2,10,000

FIXED BUDGET

As mentioned earlier, Fixed Budget is budget for a given capacity or level of activity. Fixed Budget does not make provision for any change in the expenditure arising due to change in the level of activity or capacity of production. Thus a fixed budget remains unchanged irrespective of change in volume of output or level of activity. It is based on the assumption that the forecast of a business activity and level of production will prove correct. For example if a fixed labour budget is prepared for a period, it will show estimated labour requirement and cost and no provision will be made in the budget for any change in the labour requirement and cost.

But fixed budgeting is not suitable for long period because of its regidity. It is not suitable where labour cost, materials costs and other factors are constantly changing. Thus fixed budgets can be used in a limited way.

FLEXIBLE BUDGET

Flexible budget is a budget which is designed to change with the level of activity attained. Its preparation requires an intelligent classification of all expenses between fixed, semi-fixed or semi-variable and variable. On the basis of this classification budget is prepared for different level of activity and capacity.

In certain industries level of activity during the year varies from period to period due to change in demand or due to seasonal nature of the industry. In such industries fixed budget is not suitable. Flexible budget is needed because it shows the budget at every level of change.

But the usefulness of the flexible budget depends very much on the accuracy of classification of exepnses under fixed, semi-fixed and variable. It is to be noted that fixed expenses remain fixed at all level of activity, semi-fixed vary with the different level of activity and variable expenses vary with every unit of producton[2]. Thus a detailed anlysis is called for to determine how each item of expenditure will be affected if the total output changes.

Illustration 19. ABC Ltd., has prepared a budget for the produciton of one lakh units of the only commodity manufactured by them for a costing period as under :

	₹.	
Raw material	2.52	per unit
Direct labour	0.75	per unit
Direct expenses	0.10	per unit
Works overheads (60% fixed)	2.50	per unit
Administration overheads (80% fixed)	0.40	per unit
Selling overheads (50% fixed)	0.20	per unit

The actual production during the period was only 60,000 units. Calculate the revised budgeted cost per unit.

Solution:

Revised (Flexible) Budget

	Original Budget (output 1,00,000 units)		*Revised Budget (output 60,000 units)*		*Nature of Cost*
	Per unit ₹.	Amount ₹.	Per unit ₹.	Amount ₹.	
Raw material	2.52	2,52,000	2.52	1,51,200	Variable
Direct labour	0.75	75,000	0.75	45,000	"
Direct expenses	0.10	10,000	0.10	6,000	"
Prime cost	3.37	3,37,000	3.37	2,02,200	
Works overheads	2.50	2,50,000	3.50	2,10,000	60% fixed
Cost of Production	5.87	5,87,000	6.87	4,12,200	
Administration overheads	0.40	40,000	0.61	36,800	80% fixed
Selling overheads	0.20	20,000	0.27	16,000	50% fixed
Cost of sales	6.47	6,47,000	7.75	4,65,000	

Notes. 1. 60% of works overheads (*i.e.*, ₹. 1,50,000) are fixed. Therefore, remaining 40% of ₹. 2,50,000 (*i.e.*, ₹. 1,00,000) is a variable cost.

Therefore the works overheads for actual output of 60,000 units will be

$$= 1{,}50{,}000 + 1{,}00{,}000 \times \frac{60{,}000}{1{,}00{,}000} = ₹.\ 2{,}10{,}000.$$

2. 80% of ₹. 40,000 of administrative expenses is fixed.

Therefore, the administrative expenses for the actual output of 60,000 units will be

$$= 32{,}000 + 8{,}000 \times \frac{60{,}000}{1{,}00{,}000} = ₹.\ 36{,}800$$

3. Selling overheads are fixed to the extent of 50%.

Therefore, selling overheads for the actual output of 60,000 units will be

$$= 10{,}000 + 10{,}000 \times \frac{60{,}000}{1{,}00{,}000} = ₹.\ 16{,}000.$$

2. See Chapter 'Overheads'.

Illustration 20: The cost of an article at capacity level of 5,000 units is given under A below. For a variation of 20% in capacity above or below this level, the individual expenses vary as indicated under B below :

	A (₹)	B
Material cost	25,000	(100% varying)
Labour cost	15,000	(100% ")
Power	1,250	(80% ")
Repairs and maintenance	2,000	(75% ")
Stores	1,000	(100% ")
Inspection	500	(20% ")
Depreciation	10,000	(100% fixed)
Administration overheads	5,000	(25% varying)
Selling overheads	3,000	(50% ")
	62,750	
Cost per unit	12.55	

Find the unit cost of the product under each individual expense at production levels of 4,000 units and 6,000 units.

Solution:

Flexible Budgets

	4,000 units		5,000 units		6,000 units		Nature
	Per unit ₹.	Amt. ₹.	Per unit ₹.	Amt. ₹.	Per unit ₹.	Amt. ₹.	of cost ₹.
Material	5.00	20,000	5.00	25,000	5.00	30,000	Variable
Labour	3.00	12,000	3.00	15,000	3.00	18,000	Variable
Prime cost	8.00	32,000	8.00	40,000	8.00	48,000	
Power	0.26	1,050	0.25	1,250	0.24	1,450	Semi-V.
Repairs and maintenance	0.43	1,700	0.40	2,000	0.38	2,300	Semi-V.
Stores	0.20	800	0.20	1,000	0.20	1,200	Variable
Inspection	0.12	480	0.10	500	0.09	520	Semi-V.
Depreciation	2.50	10,000	2.00	10,000	1.67	10,000	Fixed
Cost of Production	11.51	46,030	10.95	54.750	10.58	63,470	
Admn. overheads	1.19	4,750	1.00	5,000	0.87	5,250	Semi-V
Selling overheads	0.67	2,700	0.60	3,000	0.55	3,300	Semi-V
Total Cost	13.37	53,480	12.55	62,750	12.00	72,020	

Variability of an item of expense will be found out as follows :

$$\text{Fixed portion} + \text{Variable portion} \times \frac{4{,}000 \text{ (or 6000)}}{5{,}000}$$

For example 80% of Power is variable and 20% fixed. The power expense for 4,000 units will be calculated as :

$$= 250 + 1{,}000 \times \frac{4{,}000}{5{,}000}$$

$$= 250 + 800 = ₹.\ 1{,}050$$

Illustration 21: Draw up a flexible budget for overhead expenses on the basis of the following data and determine the overhead rates at 70%, 80% and 90% plant capacity.

	Capacity levels 70%	80%	90%
Variable Overheads:	₹.	₹.	₹.
Indirect labour	—	12,000	—
Stores including spares	—	4,000	—
Semi-variable Overheads:			
Power (30% fixed, 70% variable)	—	20,000	—
Repairs and maintenance (60% fixed, 40% variable)	—	2,000	—
Fixed Overheads:			
Depreciation	—	11,000	—
Insurance	—	3,000	—
Salaries	—	10,000	—
Total Overheads	—	62,000	—
Estimated direct labour hours	—	1,24,000 hrs	—

Solution:

Flexible Budget

Capacity	70%	80%	90%
Variable Overheads:			
Indirect labour	₹. 10,500	12,000	13,500
Stores including spares	3,500	4,000	4,500
Semi-variable Overheads:			
Power: Fixed	6,000	6,000	6,000
Variable	12,250	14,000	15,750
Repairs and Maintenance:			
Fixed	1,200	1,200	1,200
Variable	700	800	900
Fixed Overheads:			
Depreciation	11,000	11,000	11,000
Insurance	3,000	3,000	3,000
Salaries	10,000	10,000	10,000
Total Overheads:	58,150	62,000	65,850
Estimated direct labour hours	1,08,500	1,24,000	1,39,500
Direct labour hour rate (Overhead ÷ Labour hours)	₹ 0.536	0.500	0.472

Illustration 22: For production of 10,000 Electrical Automatic Irons the following are budgeted expenses:

	Per unit (₹.)
Direct materials	60
Direct labour	30
Variable overheads	25
Fixed overheads (₹. 1,50,000)	15
Variable expenses (direct)	5
Selling expenses (10% fixed)	15
Administrative expenses (₹. 50,000 fixed for all levels of production)	5
Distribution expenses (20% fixed)	5
Total cost of sale per unit	160

Prepare a budget for production of 6,000, 7,000 and 8,000 Irons showing distinctly Marginal cost and Total cost.

Solution:

Flexible Budget of Electrical Automatic Irons

Production Elements of Cost	*6,000 units*		*7,000 units*		*8,000 units*	
	Total ₹	*Per unit* ₹	*Total* ₹	*Per unit* ₹	*Total* ₹	*Per unit* ₹
Direct Materials	3,60,000	60.00	4,20,000	60.00	4,80,000	60.00
Direct labour	1,80,000	30.00	2,10,000	30.00	2,40,000	30.00
Direct variable expenses	30,000	5.00	35,000	5.00	40,000	5.00
Variable overheads:						
Production	1,50,000	25.00	1,75,000	25.00	2,00,000	25.00
Selling	81,000	13.50	94,500	13.50	1,08,000	13.50
Distribution	24,000	4.00	28,000	4.00	32,000	4.00
Marginal cost	8,25,000	137.50	9,62,500	137.50	11,00,000	137.50
Fixed production overheads	1,50,000	25.00	1,50,000	21.43	1,50,000	18.75
Administration overheads (Fixed)	50,000	8.33	50,000	7.14	50,000	6.25
Selling overheads (Fixed)	15,000	2.50	15,000	2.14	15,000	1.88
Distribution overheads (Fixed)	10,000	1.67	10,000	1.43	10,000	1.25
Fixed cost	2,25,000	37.50	2,25,000	32.14	2,25,000	28.13
Total cost (Marginal cost plus fixed cost)	10,50,000	175.00	11,87,500	169.64	13,25,000	165.63

Working Notes:

	Selling Expenses ₹	*Distribution Expenses* ₹
Total for 10,000 units	1,50,000	50,000
Less: Fixed expenses 10% and 20% of total respectively	15,000	10,000
Variable exps	1,35,000	40,000
Per Unit variable exps	13.50	4.00

The Concept of Standard Hour

This concept is useful for measuring output specially when the output comprises two or more products. The concept involves computing the time which the production of one unit of an article ought to take; it ignores, in a way, the actual time taken. Suppose the time allowed for one unit is 2 hours and in a day, from 8 a.m. to 6 p.m. with one hour for lunch, the production is 5 units. The actual time taken is 9 hours but the work done is equal to 10 hours, *i.e.*, 5 × 2. The standard hours produced will thus be 10; it would have been only 8 if only 4 units had been produced.

Example: In factory three products are made – X, Y and Z; the time allowed or the standard time for one unit respectively is 3 hours, 4.5 hours and 4 hours. In a month the production was : X 2,000 units; Y 1,000 units and Z 1,600 units. The standard hours produced are 17,200 hours –

X	2,000 units	@ 3 hours	6,000	
Y	1,000 "	@ 4 "	4,000	
Z	1,600 "	@ 4.5 "	7,200	17,200

CAPACITY AND ACTIVITY RATIOS

These two ratios are worked out to show the ratio of the actual capacity and actual work done and the level of efficiency attained.

The *Capacity Ratio* is worked out as follows:

(*i*) $\frac{\text{Machine Hours Recorded}}{\text{Budgeted Machine Hours}} \times 100.$

Or (*ii*) $\frac{\text{Direct Labour Hours Recorded}}{\text{Budgeted Direct Labour Hours}} \times 100.$

Efficiency Ratio can be worked out as:

$$\frac{\text{Standard Hours Actually Produced}}{\text{Actual Direct Labour Hours}} \times 100.$$

The level of *Activity Ratio* is worked out as:

$$\frac{\text{Standard Hours Actually Produced}}{\text{Budgeted Standard Hours}} \times 100.$$

One can see that

Capacity Ratio × Efficiency Ratio = Level of Activity Ratio.

Illustration 23: Calculate:

(*a*) Efficiency Ratio; (*b*) Activity Ratio; (*c*) Capacity Ratio from the following figures:

Budgeted production	88 units	Actual production	75 units
Standard hours per unit	10	Actual working hours	600

Solution:

(*a*) Efficiency Ratio $= \frac{\text{Standard hours for actual production}}{\text{Actual hours worked}} \times 100$

Standard hrs. for actual production = Standard hours per unit × Actual production

= 10 × 75 units = 750

∴ Efficiency Ratio = 100 × 750/600 = 125%

(*b*) Activity Ratio $= \frac{\text{Standard hours for actual production}}{\text{Budgeted hours}} \times 100$

Budgeted hours = Standard hours per unit × Budgeted production

= 10 × 88 = 880 hours

∴ Activity Ratio = 100 × 750/880 = 85.23%

(*c*) Capacity Utilisation ratio $= \frac{\text{Actual hours worked}}{\text{Budgeted hours}} \times 100$

= 100 × 600/880 = 68.18%

Illustration 24: Narang Ltd., produces two commodities, Good and Better, in one of its department. Each unit takes 5 hrs. and 10 hrs. as production time, respectively. 1,000 units of Good and 600 units of Better were produced during March 1992. Actual man-hours spent on this production were 10,000. Yearly budgeted hours are 96,000.

Compute the various Control Ratios. ***[B.Com.Hons., Delhi]***

Solution:

Budgeted hours per month = 96,000/12 = 8,000 hrs

Actual hours worked = 10,000

(1) Capacity Ratio $= \frac{\text{Actual hours worked}}{\text{Budgeted hours}} \times 100$

$= \frac{10{,}000 \times 100}{8.000} = 125\%$ or $\frac{10{,}000}{8.000} = 1.25.$

(2) Efficiency Ratio $= \dfrac{\text{Standard hours for actual production}}{\text{Actual hours worked}} \times 100$

$= \dfrac{11{,}000 \times 100}{10{,}000} = 110\%$ or $\dfrac{11{,}000}{10{,}000} \times 1.10$

(3) Activity Ratio $= \dfrac{\text{Standard hours for actual production}}{\text{Budgeted hours}} \times 100$

$= \dfrac{11{,}000 \times 100}{8{,}000} = 137.5\%$ or $\dfrac{11{,}000}{8{,}000} = 1.375$

Or Activity Ratio = Capacity Ratio × Efficiency Ratio

= 1.25 × 1.10 = 1.375 or 137.5%

Budget Report

Budget reports are reports submitted by the Budgetary Controller or Budget Officer to various functionaries and departments setting out their budget (revised if necessary) for the period concerned and the actual performance together with reasons for any difference between the actual and budgeted performance. It is on the basis of these reports that every one is kept informed about his own performance and that of his subordinates and that remedial measures are taken. The essential features of a good budget report are the following:

(*i*) The report is factual–opinions and facts are separated and separately stated.

(*ii*) The report must be prompt, that is, it should be prepared and submitted soon after the period concerned is over.

(*iii*) It should be as accurate as possible but a degree of inaccuracy is permissible for promptness.

(*iv*) It should be drawn up for each area of responsibility separately so that individual responsibility may be fixed.

(*v*) It should set out the standards and actuals in a way to afford ready comparison.

(*vi*) Departure from what was expected or from the ordinary course should be prominently set out to permit and help management by exception.

(*vii*) Controllable and uncontrollable items should be separately stated.

(*viii*) It should be brief; if long, it should be summarised on one page and accompanied by supporting schedules.

(*ix*) The heading should convey the purpose of the report.

(*x*) It should be dated.

(*xi*) It must state who has prepared it and to whom it is being forwarded.

TYPICAL ILLUSTRATIONS

Production Cost Budgets

Illustration 25: The following budget of PQ Company Limited, a manufacturing organisation, has been prepared for the current year

	(*% of Sales Value*)
Raw materials	40
Direct wages	25
Factory overheads (variable)	10
Factory overheads (fixed)	5

Administration and Selling & Distribution overheads (variable)	6
Administration and Selling & Distribution overheads (fixed)	12
Profit	2
Sales value	100

After considering the quarterly performance, it is felt that the budgeted volume of sales would not be achieved. But the company expects to achieve 80% of the budgeted sales (equivalent to a sales value of ₹. 1,60,00,000). At this stage, the company has received an export order for its usual line of products. The estimated prime cost and special export expenses for fulfilling the export order are ₹. 13,00,000 and ₹. 40,000 respectively.

You are required to

(*i*) present the original budget and the revised budget based on 80% achievement of the target sales, showing the quantum of profit (loss) for both:

(*ii*) prepare a statement of budgeted costs for working out the overhead recovery rates (in percentage);

(*iii*) work out the lowest quotation for the export order.

Solution:

Statement Showing Original Budget and Revised Budget

Particulars	%	*Original budget (₹. in lakhs)*	%	*Revised budget (₹. in lakhs)*
Sales	100	200.00	80	160.0
Raw materials	40	80.00	40	64.00
Direct wages	25	50.00	25	40.00
Factory overheads (variables)	10	20.00	10	16.00
Administration and Selling & Distribution Overheads (variable)	6	12.00	6	9.60
Total Variable costs	81	162.00	81	129.60
Contribution	19	38.00	19	30.40
Factory overheads (Fixed)	5	10.00		10.00
Administration and Selling & Distribution overheads (fixed)	12	24.00		24.00
Fixed Costs	17	34.00		34.00
Profit (Loss)	2	4.00	Loss	(3.60)

(*ii*) Statement Showing Budgeted Costs Overhead Recovery Rates (Based on Original Budget)

(*a*) Factory overheads (variable)

(based on direct wages) $= \dfrac{20,00,000}{50,00,000} \times 100 = 40\%$ of direct wages

(*b*) Factory overheads (fixed)

(based on direct wages) $= \dfrac{10,00,000}{50,00,000} \times 100 = 20\%$ of direct wages

(*c*) Administration and Selling &

Distribution overheads (variable) $= \dfrac{12,00,000}{1,60,00,000} \times 100 = 7.5\%$ of works cost

(based on works cost) (Note: 1)

(*d*) Administration and Selling & Distribution overheads (fixed) (based on works cost) $= \frac{24,00,000}{1,60,00,000} \times 100 = 15\%$ of works cost

(*iii*) Statement Showing Quotation of the Export Order

	₹. *in lakhs*
Raw Materials $\left(\frac{40}{65} \times 13\right)$	8.00
Direct Wages $\left(\frac{25}{65} \times 13\right)$	5.00
Prime cost	
(Prime cost 65% = raw materials 40% + Direct wages 25%)	13.00
Factory overheads (variable) (40% of direct wages)	2.00
Works cost	15.00
Administration and selling & Distribution overheads (7.5% of works cost)	1.125
Special export expenses	0.400
Total Cost for export order 16.525	

The lowest quotation for export order is ₹. 16,52,500. Any price above ₹. 16,52,500 may be quoted for the export order.

Cash Budget

Illustration 26: Based on the following information, prepare a Cash Budget for ABC Ltd.

	Ist quarter ₹.	*2nd quarter* ₹.	*3rd quarter* ₹.	*4th quarter* ₹.
Opening Cash balance	10,000			
Collection from customers	1,25,000	1,50,000	1,60,000	2,21,000
Payments:				
Purchase of materials	20,000	35,000	35,000	54,200
Other expenses	25,000	20,000	20,000	17,000
Salary and wages	90,000	95,000	95,000	1,09,200
Income Tax	5,000	—	—	—
Purchase of machinery	—	—	—	20,000

The company desires to maintain a cash balance of ₹. 15,000 at the end of each quarter. Cash can be borrowed or repaid in multiples of ₹. 500 at an interest of 10% per annum. Management does not want to borrow cash more than what is necessary and wants to repay as early as possible. In any event, loans cannot be extended beyond 4 quarters. Interest is computed and paid when the principal is repaid. Assume that borrowings take place at the beginning and repayments are made at the end of the quarters.

Solution:

Cash Budget ABC Ltd.

Particulars	*Ist quarter*	*2nd quarter*	*3rd quarter*	*4th quarter*
Opening Cash Balance	10,000	15,000	15,000	15,325
Collection from customers	1,25,000	1,50,000	1,60,000	2,21,000
Total Receipts	1,35,000	1,65,000	1,75,000	2,36325

Payments:				
Purchase of materials	20,000	35,000	35,000	54,200
Other expenses	25,000	20,000	20,000	17,000
Salary & Wages	90,000	95,000	95,000	1,09,200
Income Tax	5,000	—	—	—
Purchase of Machinery	—	—	—	20,000
Total Payments	1,40,000	1,50,000	1,50,000	2,00,400
Minimum Cash Balance	15,000	15,000	15,000	15,000
Total Cash required	1,55,000	1,65,000	1,65,000	2,15,400
Excess/(Deficit)	(20,000)	NIl	10,000	20,925
Borrowing	20,000	—	—	—
Repayment	—	—	9,000	11,000
Interest Payment	—	—	675	1,100
Total	—	—	9,675	12,100
Closing Cash Balance:	15,000	15,000	15,325	23,825

Calculation of Interest:

1. Interest is computed and paid when the principal is repaid. Interest on 9,000 for 3 quarters at 10% is:

$$9{,}000 \times \frac{9}{12} \times \frac{10}{100} = ₹.675$$

2. ₹. 11,000 repaid at the end of 4th quarter interest on ₹. 11,000 for 4 quarters at 10% will be ₹. 1,000.

Flexible Budgets

Illustration 27: The monthly budgets for manufacturing overhead of a concern for two levels of activity were as follows:

Capacity	60%	100%
Budgets production (units)	600	1,000
	₹.	₹.
Wages	1,200	2,000
Consumable stores	900	1,500
Maintenance	1,100	1,500
Power & fuel	1,600	2,000
Depreciation	4,000	4,000
Insurance	1,000	1,000
	9,800	12,000

You are required to:

(*i*) Indicate which of the items are fixed, variable and semi-variable.

(*ii*) Prepare a budget for 80% capacity; and

(*iii*) Find the total cost, both fixed and variable, per unit of output at 60%, 80% and 100% capacity.

Solution:

(*i*) *Fixed costs* : Depreciation ₹. 4,000

Insurance ₹. 1,000

Variable costs: Wages $= \frac{₹.1{,}200}{600 \text{ units}}$ or $\frac{₹.2{,}000}{1{,}000 \text{ units}}$ = ₹. 2.00 per unit

Consumable stores = $\frac{₹.900}{600 \text{ units}}$ or $\frac{₹.1,500}{1,000 \text{ units}}$ = ₹. 1.50 per unit

Semi-variable costs:

(a) Maintenance = 1,000 units ₹. 1,500

600 units ₹.1,100

Difference = 400 units ₹.400

Variable = $\frac{₹.400}{400 \text{ units}}$ = ₹. 1.00 per unit

Fixed = Total – Variable

= 1,500 – (1,000 × 1.00) = ₹. 500

(*b*) Power & Fuel: 1,000 units ₹. 2,000

600 units ₹. 1,600

400 units ₹. 400

Variable = $\frac{₹.400}{400 \text{ units}}$ = ₹. 1.00 per unit

Fixed = Total – Variable.

= 1,600 – (600 × 1) = ₹. 1,000 fixed.

(*ii*) Budget for 80% capacity. (Output 800 units)

	₹.
Wages: 800 × 2.00	1,600
Consumable stores : 800 × 1.50	1,200
Maintenance: 500 + (800 × 1)	1,300
Power & Fuel : 1,000 + (800 × 1)	1,800
Depreciation: Fixed	4,000
Insurance: Fixed	1,000
Total Cost	10,900

(*iii*) Flexible Budget

Capacity	60%	80%	100%
Units	600	800	1,000
	₹.	₹.	₹.
A. Fixed Cost			
Depreciation	4,000	4,000	4,000
Insurance	1,000	1,000	1,000
Maintenance	500	500	500
Power & Fuel	1,000	1,000	1,000
Total	6,500	6,500	6,500
B. Variable Cost			
Wages at ₹. 2.00 per unit	1,200	1,600	2,000
Consumable stores at ₹. 150 per unit	900	1,200	1,500
Maintenance at ₹. 1.00 per unit	600	800	1,000
Power & Fuel at ₹. 1.00 per unit	600	800	1,000
Total	3,300	4,400	5,500
Total Cost (A + B)	9,800	10,900	12,000
Fixed cost per unit	10.833	8.125	6.50
Variable Cost per unit	5.50	5.50	5.50
Total cost per unit	16,333	13.625	12.00

Illustration 28: A factory is currently running at 50% capacity and produces 5,000 units at a cost of ₹. 90 per unit as per details below:

	₹.
Material	50
Labour	15
Factory overheads	15 (₹. 6 fixed)
Administrative overheads	10 (₹. 5 fixed)

The current selling price is ₹. 100 per unit. At 60% working, material cost per unit increases by 2% and selling price per unit falls by 2%.

At 80% working, material cost per unit increases by 5% and selling price per unit falls by 5%.

Estimate profits of the factory at 60% and 80% working and offer your comments.

Solution:

Statement of Comparative Profitability

Capacity		50%	60%	80%
Production and Sales (Units)		5,000	6,000	8,000
		₹.	₹.	₹.
Material		50	51	52.50
Labour		15	15	15.00
Variable Factory overhead		9	9	9.00
Variable Admn. overhead		5	5	5.00
Marginal cost per unit		79	80	81.50
Selling price per unit		100	98	95.00
Contribution per unit		21	18	13.50
Total Contribution		1,05,000	1,08,000	1,08,000
Fixed overheads:				
Factory	5,000 × 6 = 30,000			
Administration	5,000 × 5 = 25,000	55,000	55,000	55,000
Profit		50,000	53,000	53,000

Note: Total cost per unit at 50% capacity is ₹. 90 as below :

Marginal cost per unit	₹. 79
Fixed Factory overhead per unit	6
Fixed Admn. overhead per unit	5
Total cost per unit	₹ 90

Comment: Profit at 60% and 80% capacity is equal i.e. ₹. 53,000. It may be recommended that factory should work at 60% capacity.

Illustration 29: The following data are available for a manufacturing company for a yearly period:

	₹ *(in lakhs)*
Fixed Expenses:	
Wages and salaries	9.5
Rent, Rates and Taxes	6.6
Depreciation	7.4
Sundry administrative expenses	6.5

Semi-variable Expenses (at 50% of capacity):	
Maintenance and repairs	3.5
Indirect labour	7.9
Sales department's salaries etc.	3.8
Sundry administrative expenses	2.8
Variable expenses (at 50% of capacity):	
Materials	21.7
Labour	20.4
Other expenses	7.9
Total Cost	98.0

Assume that fixed expenses remain constant at all levels of production; semi-variable expenses remain constant between 45% and 65% of capacity, increasing by 10% between 65% and 80% capacity and by 20% between 80% and 100% capacity.

Sales at various levels are:

	₹ (*in lakhs*)
50% capacity	100
60% capacity	120
75% capacity	150
90% capacity	180
100% capacity	200

Prepare a flexible budget for the year at 60% and 90% capacities and estimate the profit at these levels of output.

Solution:

Flexible Budget (₹ *in lakhs*)

Capacity	*60%*	*90%*
A. Fixed Expenses		
Wages & Salaries	9.50	9.50
Rent, Rates & Salaries	6.60	6.60
Depreciation	7.40	7.40
Sundry Admn. exp.	6.50	6.50
Total	30.00	30.00
B. Semi-Variable Exp.		
Maintenance & Repairs	3.50	3.50 + 20% = 4.20
Indirect Labour	7.90	7.90 + 20% = 9.48
Sales Dept. Salaries	3.80	3.80 + 20% = 4.56
Sundry Admn. exp.	2.80	2.80 + 20% = 3.36
Total	18.00	21.60
C. Variable Exp.		
Materials	$21.7 \times \frac{60\%}{50\%} = 26.04$	$21.7 \times \frac{90\%}{50\%} = 39.06$
Labour	$20.4 \times \frac{60\%}{50\%} = 24.48$	$20.4 \times \frac{90\%}{50\%} = 36.72$
Other exp.	$7.9 \times \frac{60\%}{50\%} = 9.48$	$7.9 \times \frac{90\%}{50\%} = 14.22$
Total	60.00	90.00
Total Cost (*A* + *B* + *C*)	108.00	141.60
Sales	120.00	180.00
Profit	12.00	38.40

QUESTIONS

OBJECTIVE QUESTIONS

I. *Fill up the blanks* :

(*a*) Budgetary control is a system of controlling.................... .

(*b*) A Budget manual spells out................of various executives concerned with budgets.

(*c*) A factor which influences all other budgets is called.................factor.

(*d*) Master budget incorporates all................budgets.

(*e*) Zero-Base Budgeting was first used by....................

[Ans. (*a*) costs (*b*) duties and responsibilities (*c*) key (d) functional (e) Jimmy Carter.

II. *State whether these statements are true or false* :

(*a*) Efficiency ratio determines the capacity used by the factory.

(*b*) Calendar ratio calculates the ratio between Actual and Budgeted days.

(*c*) Zero base budgeting will be appropriate in areas where output is not related to production.

(*d*) Flexible budgets change with the level of activity.

(*e*) Budgeting may be said to be an act of determining costing standards.

[***Ans.*** True —(*b*), (*c*), (*d*) ; False—(*a*), (*e*)]

III. ***(a)*** *The basic difference between a fixed budget and flexible budget is that a fixed budget* :

(*i*) is concerned with fixed expenses whereas flexible budget deals with variable expenses.

(*ii*) cannot be changed whereas flexible budget can be easily changed.

(*iii*) is a budget for single measure of activity whereas flexible budget is on different activity levels.

(b) *A flexible budget requires careful study and classification of expenses into* :

(*i*) Past and current expenses.

(*ii*) Fixed, semi-variable and variable expenses

(*iii*) Administrative, selling and factory expenses.

[Ans. (*a*) (*iii*) ; (*b*) (*ii*)**]**

IV. *State whether the following statements are 'True' or 'False'*:

1. The budget is an estimate prepared in advance for future specific period.
2. Budget is a statement which is expressed in terms of money.
3. Budget is based on plan estimates.
4. Budget is automatic.
5. Zero-based budgeting was first used by Jimmy Carter.
6. Flexible budgets does not change with the level of activity.
7. Budgeting may be said to be an act of determining costing methods.
8. Calander ratio calculates the ratio between actual and standard days.
9. Zero-base budgeting will be appropriate in areas where output is related to production.
10. Efficiency ratio determines the efficiency used by the factory.

[Ans. 1. True, 2. True, 3. True, 4. False, 5. True, 6. False, 7. False, 8. False, 9. False, 10. False.]

V. *Fill in the blanks* :

1. Budget plan is based on................ .
2. Budget is a .... planning.
3. Production budget is governed by ....budget.
4. .... budget is useful where it is difficult to forsee the demand.
5. Budget relating to a key factor should be prepared................. .

[**Ans.** 1. Estimates, 2. Financial 3. Sales, 4. Flexible, 5. First.]

VI. *Select correct option* :

1. Production budget is governed by :
   (*a*) Sales Budget (*b*) Flexible Budget (*c*) Material Budget
2. Where demand forecasting is difficult, Budget is prepared :
   (*a*) Production (*b*) Sales (*c*) Financial (*d*) Flexible
3. Budgetary control is useful for cost control :
   (*a*) Short-term budgets (*b*) Long-term Budgets (*c*) Middle-term Budgets
4. Master budget is :
   (*a*) Expansion of all Budgets
   (*b*) Total of all Budgets
   (*c*) Summary of all Budgets.
5. Budget is prepared –
   (*a*) In advance for a specified Period
   (*b*) After a Specified Period

[***Ans.*** 1. *(a)*, 2. *(d)*, 3. *(a)*, 4. *(c)*, 5. *(a)*]

THEORETICAL QUESTIONS

1. Define `Budget' and `Budgetary control'. What are objectives of Budgetary control?
2. Define `Budget' and Budgetary control. Give description of two important budgets. **[*B. Com. (H) Delhi*]**
3. What is Budgetary control? How is a system of Budgetary Control operates in an undertaking engaged in manufacturing business? **[*B. Com. (H) Delhi*]**
4. Explain the difference between fixed budget and flexible budget. How a flexible budget is drawn?
5. What is production budget? What are the steps involved in the preparation of production budget.
6. Enumerate the various factors which should be considered while preparing the sales budget and the production budget.
7. Write short notes on :
   1. Budget Allowance
   2. Zero-base Budgeting
   3. Cash Budget
   4. Performance Budgeting.

SHORT ANSWER QUESTIONS

1. What do you understand by budget?
2. Discuss the objects of budget.
3. Give the elements of an effective budget.
4. What are the limitations of budgeting?
5. What is budget committee?
6. What is production budget?
7. What is master budget?
8. What do you understand by flexible budget?
9. What is budgetary control?
10. What is budgetary control?
11. Discuss the advantages of budgetary control.
12. Distinguish between budget, budgeting and budgetary control.
13. (*a*) Distinguish between Standard Costing and Budgetary control.
    (*b*) List the various functional budgets prepared by a business.

14. Distinguish between fixed and flexible budget. Briefly state the circumstances in which flexible budgets are used.
15. Define the terms `Budget' and 'Bugetary Control'. List down any five objectives of a Bugetary Control system.
16. Distinguish between Budgetary Control and Standard Costing.
17. Distinguish between flexible budget and fixed budget.
18. What do you understand by master budget?
19. Write short note on Flexible Budget.
20. Write short note on `Zero Base Budgeting'.
21. Distinguish between `Fixed Budget' and `Flexible Budget.
22. Distinguish between `Budgetary Control and `Standard Costing.
23. Enumerate the steps involved in 'Budgetary control.
24. Explain the concept of 'Zero Base Budgeting'.
25. Write short note on performance budgeting.
26. State the importance of 'Budget Key Factor'.
27. State the striking feature of 'Flexible Budget'.
28. Define 'Flexible Budget' and explain its importance as a budgeting technique and tool of control.

NUMERICAL QUESTIONS

1. Chhaju Bros. sells two products which are manufactured in one plant. During the year 2002 it plans to sell the following quantities of each product.

Sales Budget (Units)

	First quarter	*Second quarter*	*Third quarter*	*Fourth quarter*	*Total*
Product 1	90,000	2,30,000	3,00,000	80,000	7,00,000
Product 2	85,000	75,000	55,000	85,000	3,00,000

Each of these two products is sold on a seasonal basis. Product I tends to sell better in summer months, while product 2 sells better during the winter. Chhaju Bros. plan to sell product 1 throughout the year at a price of ₹.10 a unit and product 2 at a price of ₹. 20 a unit.

A study of the past experiences reveals that Chhaju Bros. has lost about 3% of its billed revenue each year because of returns (constituting 2% of loss of revenue) allowances and bad debts (1% loss).

Prepare a budget incorporating the given information.

[Ans. *Net sales I quarter ₹. 25,22,000, II ₹. 36,86,000, III ₹. 39,77,000, IV ₹. 24,25,000. Total ₹. 12,61,000*]

2. The sales director of a manufacturing company reports that next year he expects to sell 54,000 units of a certain product.

The production manager consults the storekeeper and casts his figures as follows:

Two kinds of raw materials. A and B are required for manufacturing the product. Each unit of the product requires 2 units of A and 3 units of B. The estimated opening balances at the commencement of the next year are:

Finished product– 10,000 units, A–12,000 units, B–15,000 units

The desirable closing balances at the end of the next year are:

Finished product–14,000 units, A–13,000 units. B–16,000 units.

Draw up a quantitative chart showing the material purchase budget for the next year.

[Ans. Purchase of material A 1,17,000 units B 1,75,000 units.]

Cash Budget

3. ABC Co. wishes to arrange overdraft facilities with its Bankers during the period April to June. 2004, when it will be manufacturing mostly for stock. Prepare a Cash Budget for the above period from the following data, indicating the extent of the bank facilities the company will require at the end of each month:

(*a*)

	Sales ₹.	*Purchases* ₹.	*Wages* ₹.
February,	1,80,000	1,24,800	12,000
March,	1,92,000	1,44,000	14,000
April,	1,08,000	2,43,000	11,000
May,	1,74,000	2,46,000	10,000
June,	1,26,000	2,68,000	15,000

(*b*) 50 per cent of credit sales are realised in the month following the sales and the remaining 50 per cent in the second month following. Creditors are paid in the month following the month of purchase. Wages are paid in the next month.

(*c*) Cash at bank on 1st April 2004 (estimated) ₹. 25,000.

[**Ans.** *Cash Balances April ₹. 53,000, May Overdraft ₹, 51,000, June Overdraft ₹. 1,66,000*]

4. From the following information and the assumption that the balance in hand on 1st Jan. 2004 is ₹. 72,500 prepare a Cash Budget:

Month	*Sales* ₹.	*Materials* ₹.	*Wages* ₹.	*Selling and Dis. cost* ₹.	*Production cost* ₹.	*Adminis-tration cost* ₹.
Jan.	72,000	25,000	10,000	4,000	6,000	1,500
Feb.	97,000	31,000	12,100	5,000	6,300	1,700
March	86,000	25,500	10,600	5,500	6,000	2,000
April	88,000	30,600	25,000	6,700	6,500	2,200
May	1,02,500	37,000	22,000	8,500	8,000	2,500
June	1,08,700	38,800	23,000	9,000	8,200	2,500

Assume that 50% are cash sales. Assets are to be acquired in the month of February and April. Therefore, provision should be made for the payment of ₹. 8,000 and ₹. 25,000 for the same. An application has been made to the bank for the grant of a loan of ₹. 30,000 and it is hoped that it will be received in the month of May.

It is anticipated that a dividend of ₹. 35,000 will be paid in June. Debtors are allowed one month's credit. Sales commission @ 3% on sales is to be paid. Creditors (for goods or overheads) grant one month's credit.

[**Ans.** *Balances Jan ₹. 96,340, Feb. ₹. 121,330, March 1,55,650; April 1,51,010; May ₹ 2,05,185; June ₹. 1,93,524*].

5. Glass manufacturing company requires you to calculate and present the budget for the next year from the following information:

Sales	
Toughened Glass	₹. 3,00,000
Bent Toughened Glass	₹. 5,00,000
Direct Material cost	60% of sales
Direct Wages	20 workers @ ₹. 150 p.m.

Factory overheads :

Indirect labour :

Works Manager	₹. 500 per month
Foreman	₹. 400 per month
Stores and spares	₹. 2½% on sales
Depreciation on Machinary	₹. 12,600
Light and Power	₹. 5,000
Repairs etc.	₹. 8,000
Other sundries	10% on Direct Wages.

Administration Selling and Distribution expenses ₹. 14,000 per annum.

[**Ans.** *Sales ₹. 8,00,000 Adm. selling and Distr. Exts. 14,000. Prime cost ₹.5,16,000. Variable Factory overhead ₹. 33,000. Fixed factory overhead ₹. 27,000 Works cost ₹. 5,76,000. Profit 2,10,000*].

Flexible Budget

6. Production costs of Oriental Enterprises Limited are as follows:

	Level of Activity		
	60%	70%	80%
Output (in units)	1,200	1,400	1,600
Cost (in ₹.):	₹.	₹.	₹.
Direct Materials	24,000	28,000	32,000
Direct Labour	7,200	8,400	9,600
Factory Overheads	12,800	13,600	14,400
Works Cost	44,000	50,000	56,000

A proposal to increase production to 90% level of activity is under the consideration of the management. The proposal is not expected to involve any increase in fixed factory overheads. Prepare a statement showing the prime cost, total marginal cost and total factory cost at 90% level of activity. ***[B. Com. (Hons.) Delhi]***

[**Ans.** *Prime Cost ₹ 46,800, Marginal Cost ₹. 54,000; Factory Cost ₹. 62,000*

Hint: Fixed overheads ₹. 8000. Variable overheads @ ₹. 4 per units]

7. Gemini Steel Ltd. manufactures a single product for which market demand exists for additional quantity. Present sales of ₹. 60,000 per month utilises only 60% capacity of the plant. Marketing Manager assures that with the reduction of 10% in the price he would be in a position to increase the sale by about 25% to 30%.

The following data are available:

(*i*) Selling price	₹. 10 per unit
(*ii*) Variable cost	₹. 3 per unit
(*iii*) Semi-variable cost	₹ 6,000 fixed + 50 paise per unit
(*iv*) Fixed cost	₹. 20,000 at present level, estimated to be ₹. 24,000 at 80% output.

You are required to prepare the following statements:

(*a*) The operating profits at 60%, 70% and 80% levels at current selling price, and

(*b*) The operating profits at proposed selling price at the above levels.

[B. Com. Hons., Delhi]

[**Ans.** *Profit at 60% ₹ 13,000; at 70% ₹ 19,500 at 80% ₹ 22,000.*

Profit at proposed selling prices in above levels ₹. 7,000, ₹. 12,500, ₹. 14,000].

8. A department of Company X attains sale of ₹. 6,00,000 at 80 per cent on its normal capacity and its expenses are given below:

Administration costs:		**Selling costs:**	
Office salaries	₹. 90,000	Salaries	8% of sales
General expenses	2% of sales	Travelling expenses	2% of sales
Depreciation	₹. 7,500	Sales Office	1% of sales
Rates and taxes	₹. 8,750	General expenses	1% of sales

Distribution costs:

Wages	₹. 15,000
Rent	1% of sales
Other expenses	4% of sales

Draw up flexible administration, selling and distribution costs budget, operating at 90 per cent and 110 per cent of normal capacity.

[**Ans.**	*Adm Cost* ₹	*Selling Cost* ₹	*Distribution Cost* ₹	*Total* ₹
At 80%	*1,18,250*	*72,000*	*45,000*	*2,35,250*
At 90%	*1,19,750*	*81,000*	*48,750*	*2,49,500*
At 100%	*1,21,250*	*90,000*	*52,500*	*2,63,750*
At 110%	*1,22,750*	*99,000*	*56,250*	*2,78,000*]

9. The budgeted cost of a factory specialising in the production of a single product at the optimum capacity of 6,400 units per annum amounts ₹.1,76,048 as detailed below:

	₹.	
Fixed cost		₹. 20,688
Variable costs:		
Power	1,440	
Repairs etc.	1,700	
Miscellaneous	540	
Direct material	49,280	
Direct labour	1,02,400	1,55,360
		1,76,048

Having regard to possible impact on sales turnover by market trends the company decided to have a flexible budget with a production target of 3,200 and 4,800 units (the actual quantity proposed to be produced being left to a later date before commencement of the budget period). Prepare a flexible budget for production levels at 50% and 75% capacity.

Assume selling price per unit is maintained at ₹. 40 as at present, indicate the effect on net profit. Administration, selling and distribution expenses continue at ₹. 3,600.

[**Ans.** *Capacity*	*100%*	*75%*	*50%*
Output (units)	*6400*	*4800*	*3200*
Total factory cost	*1,76,048*	*1,37,208*	*98,368*
Net profit	*76,352*	*51,192*	*26,032*]

Budget Ratios

10. From the following data, calculate 'activity ratio' and 'efficiency ratio'

A factory manufactures two products 'A' and 'B'. Standard time to manufacture product 'A' is 2 hours and product 'B' 10 hours. The budgeted and actual production in December were as follows :

	Budgeted Production	Actual Production
Product 'A'	125 units	100 units
Product 'B'	30 units	24 units

Total actual hours worked were 660.

[**Ans.** *Activity Ratio 80%, Efficiency Ratio 66.67%*]